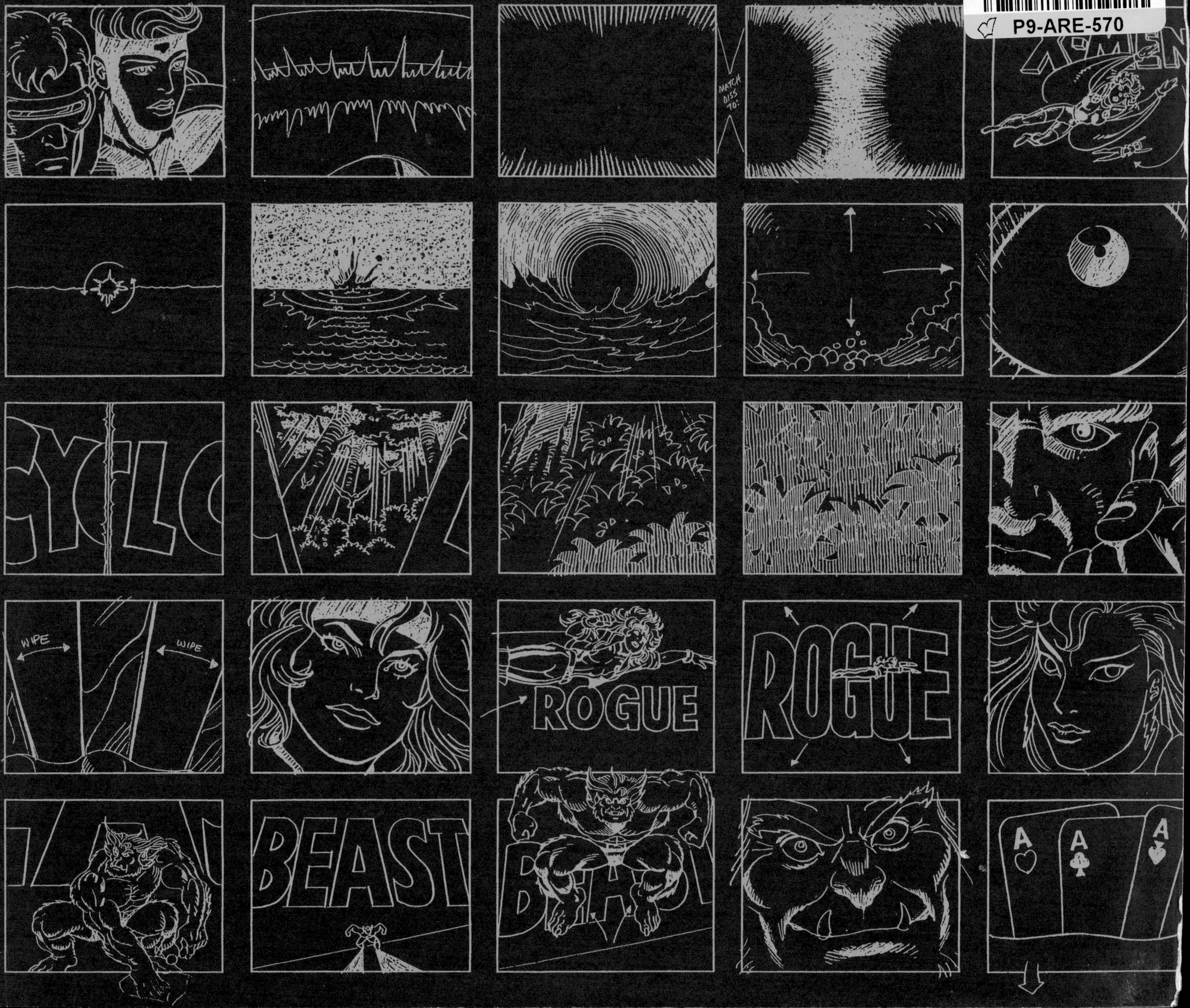
MATCH DISS TO:
X-MEN
WIPE
WIPE
ROGUE
ROGUE
BEAST
A
A
A

ENTERTAINMENT

12509 Oxnard St. Ste. N
No. Hollywood, CA. 91606

RECEIVED
SEP 9 1992
SIDNEY IWANTER

WITHDRAWN

ROUGH STORYBOARD

ISSUED FOR DISTRIBUTION
BY PRODUCTION DEPT.

BY _B.J._ DATE 9/11/__

300-11

"FUTURE PART I"

STORYBOARD

100-29   •   BG 167   —   Bio

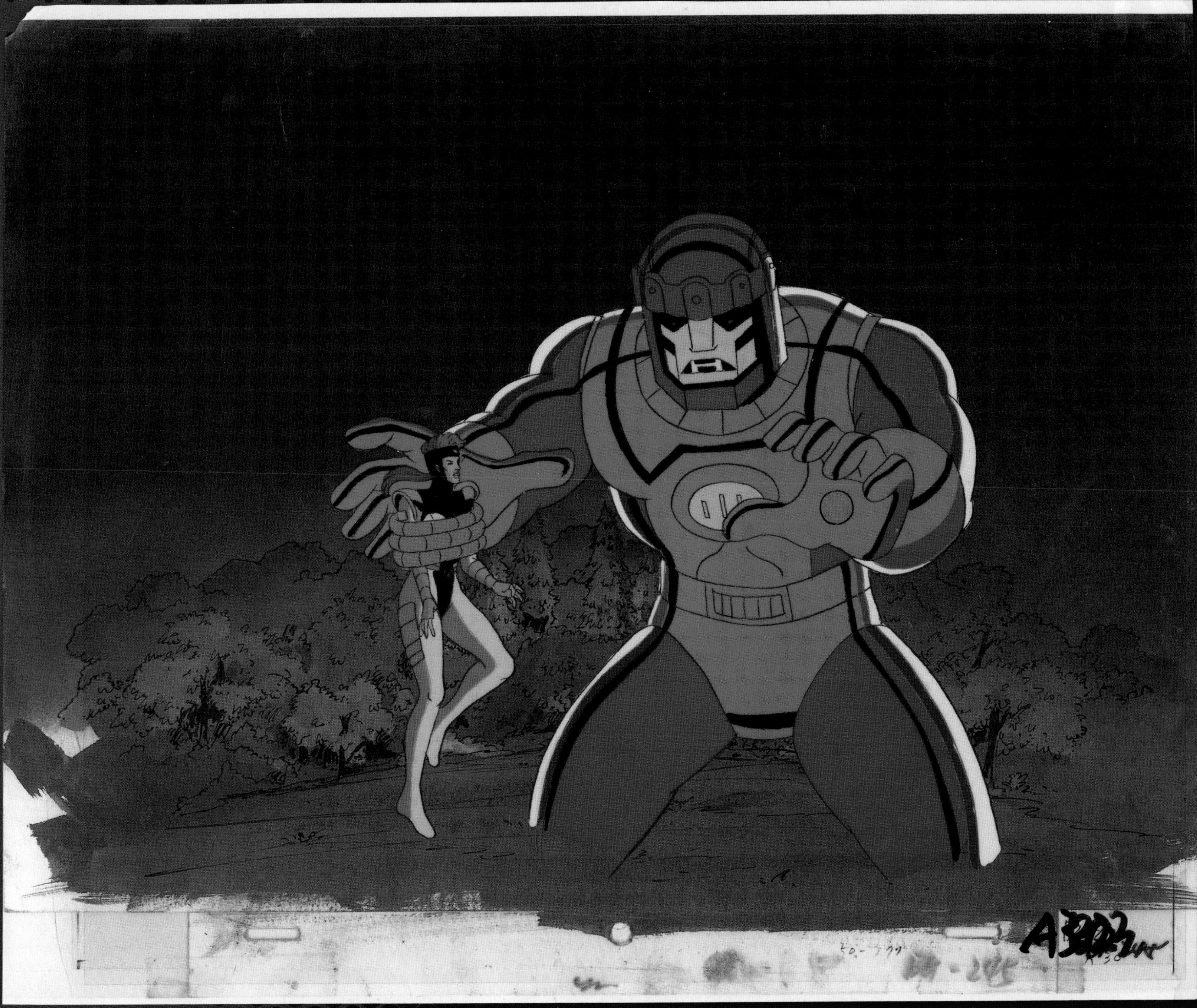

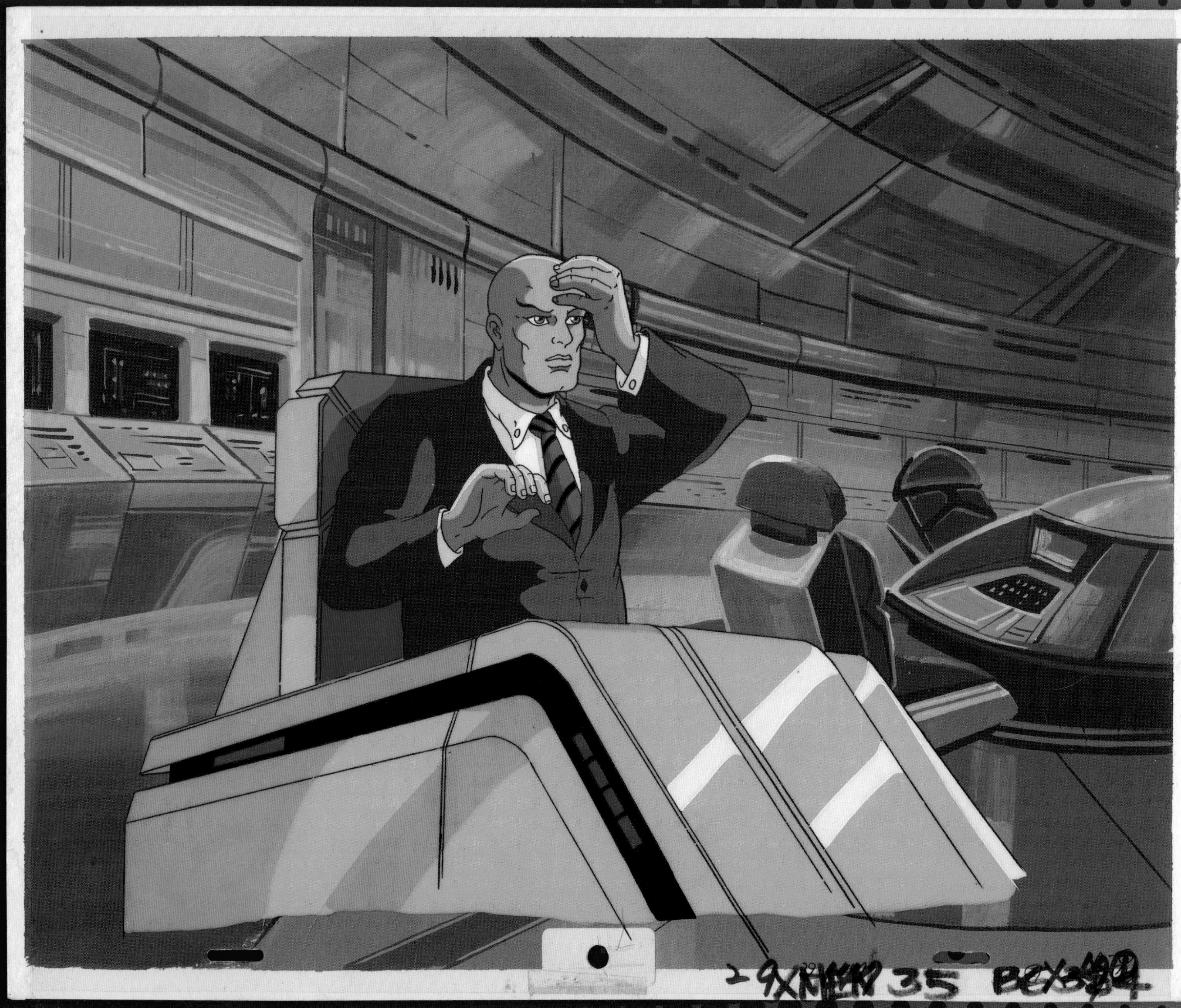

MARVEL

THE ART AND MAKING OF THE ANIMATED SERIES

By Eric Lewald and Julia Lewald

ABRAMS, NEW YORK

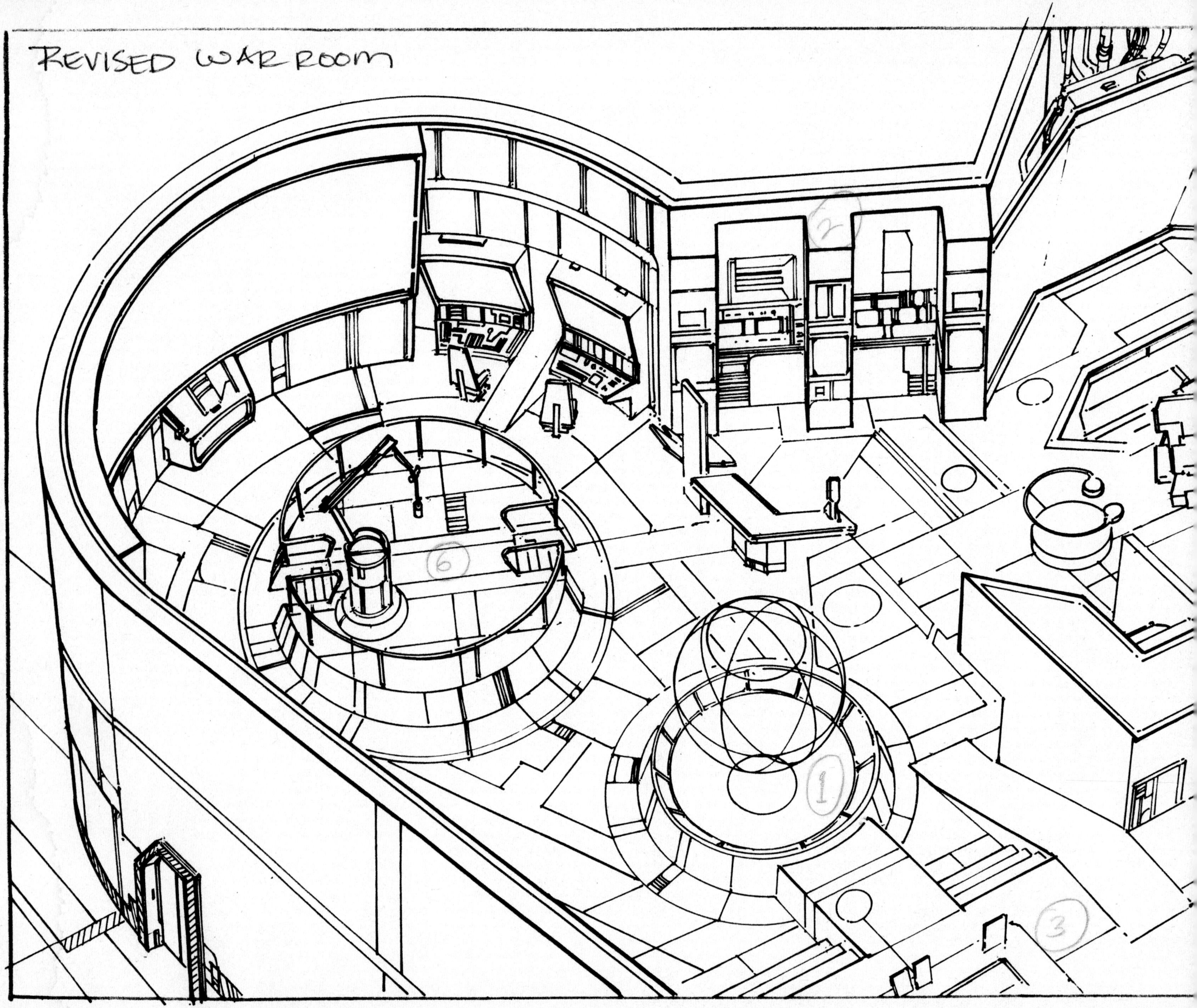

REVISED WAR ROOM
2
6
1
3

① DANGER ROOM MASTER CONTROL
② SHI'AR FAST PROCESSING COMPUTERS
  (FULL SYSTEM ANALYSIS COMPUTER)
③ SPECIALIST DESK
④ DEFENCE COORDINATION POSITION - DCP
⑤ DCO VIEW SCREEN
⑥ COMBAT OPERATIONS CENTER
⑦ CEREBRO

PAGE 1 Cover of the first-draft storyboard for "Days of Future Past, Part 1." Teleplay by Julia Lewald; storyboard by Will Meugniot and Larry Houston; received by Fox TV executive Sidney Iwanter on September 9, 1992. PAGE 2 Production cel of Jubilee and Storm from "Phoenix Saga, Part 1: Sacrifice." PAGE 3 Production cel of Jean Grey and Sentinel, unknown episode. PAGE 4 An early production cel of Charles Xavier, with mismatched background (see page 93), that was cut and replaced when troubled episodes 34 and 35 were re-animated. LEFT Background layout of the X-Men's principal action location, the War Room, lifted directly from X-Men Annual (vol. 2) #1 and re-cleaned by Zhaoping Wei, with notes by producer/director Frank Squillace. This design is from later in the series, since there is a reference to an area (2) that has "Shi'ar fast processing computers" (the Shi'ar were not introduced into X-Men: The Animated Series [TAS] until the third season).

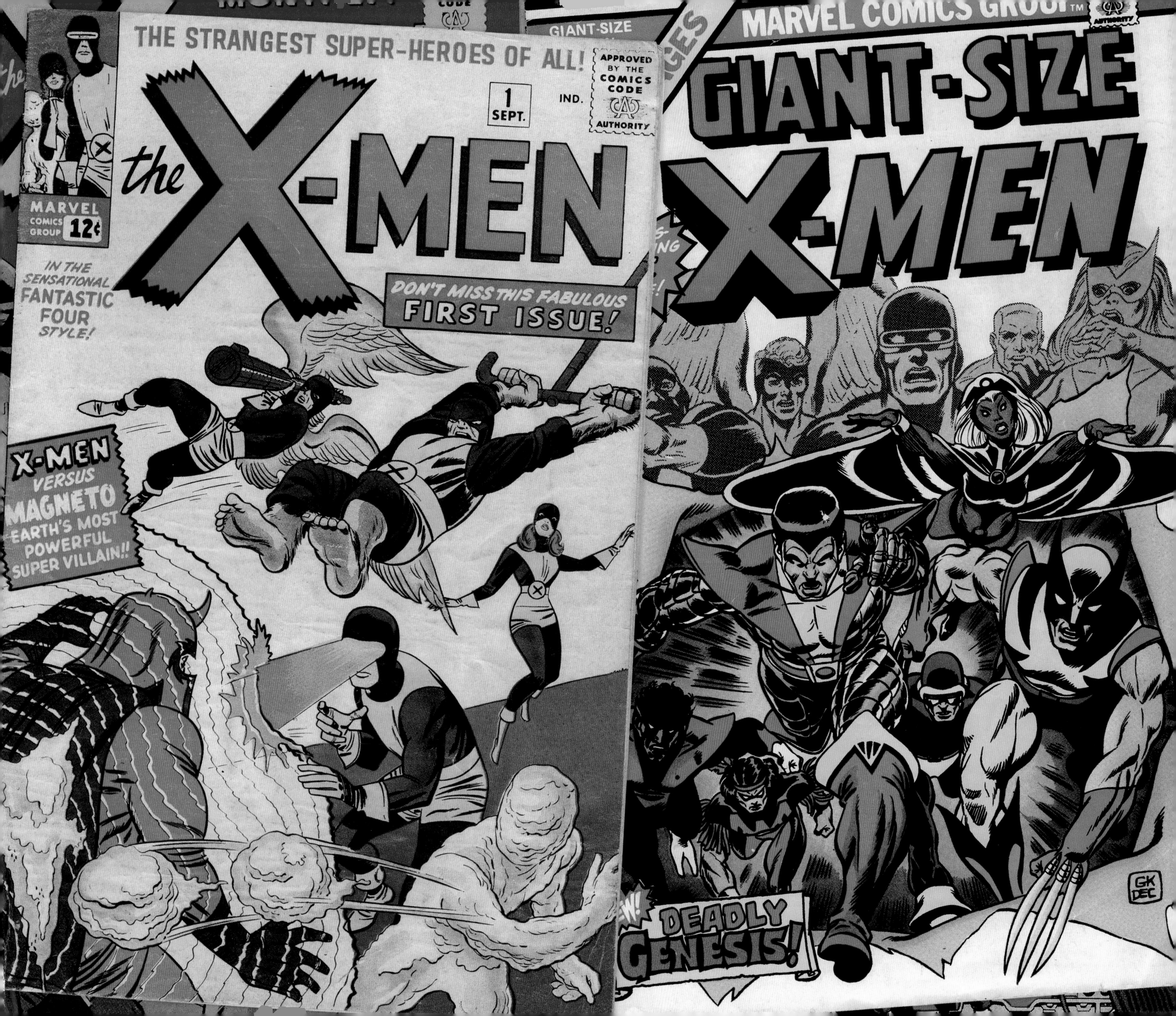
THE STRANGEST SUPER-HEROES OF ALL!
APPROVED BY THE COMICS CODE AUTHORITY
1 SEPT.
IND.
MARVEL COMICS GROUP 12¢
the X-MEN
IN THE SENSATIONAL FANTASTIC FOUR STYLE!
DON'T MISS THIS FABULOUS FIRST ISSUE!
X-MEN VERSUS MAGNETO EARTH'S MOST POWERFUL SUPER VILLAIN!!
MARVEL COMICS GROUP
GIANT-SIZE
GIANT-SIZE X-MEN
GK DEC
DEADLY GENESIS!

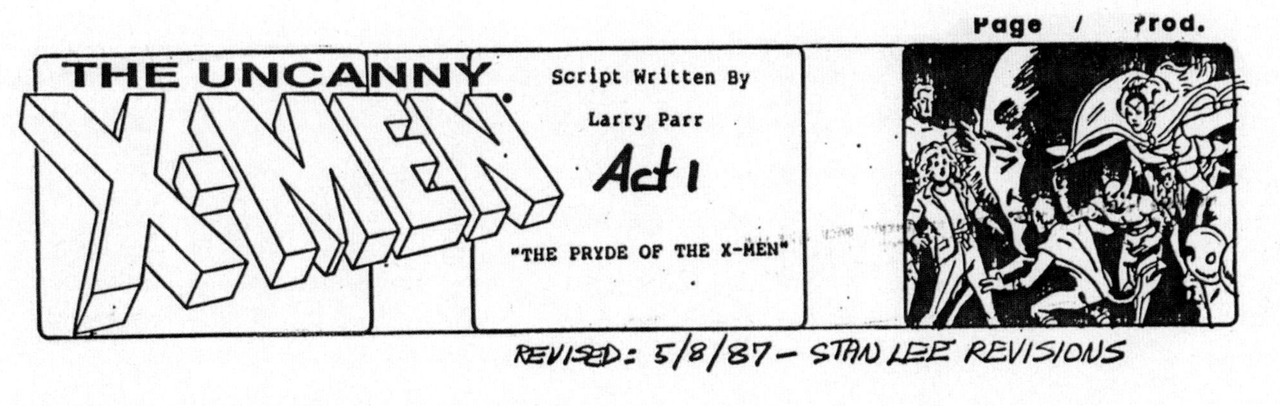
Page / Prod.
THE UNCANNY X-MEN
Script Written By
Larry Parr
Act 1
"THE PRYDE OF THE X-MEN"
REVISED: 5/8/87 – STAN LEE REVISIONS

04

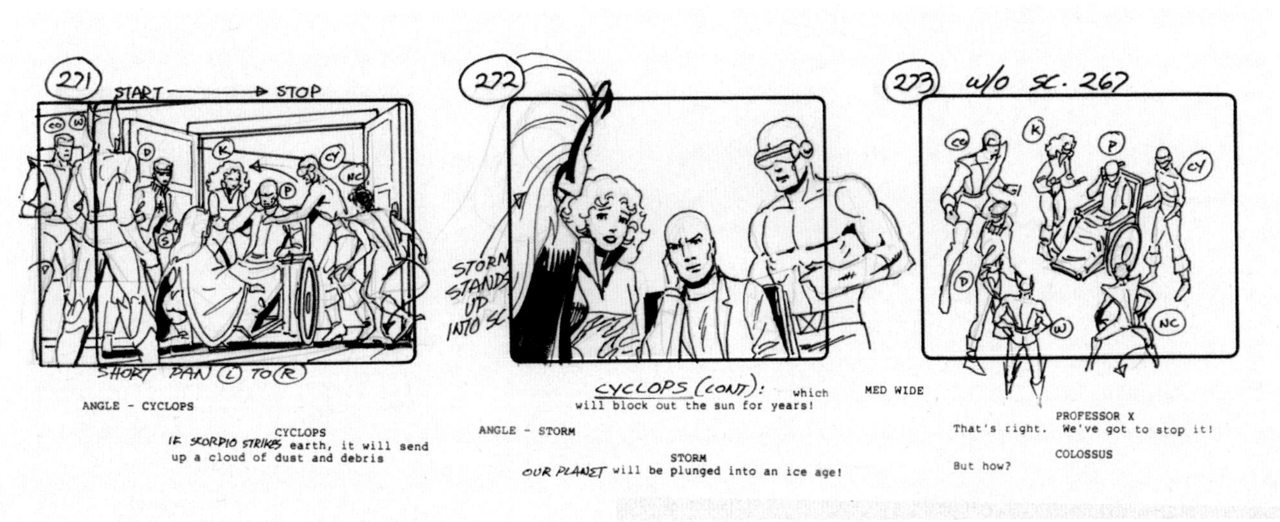
271 START → STOP
SHORT PAN L TO R
272
STORM STANDS UP INTO SC
273 w/o SC. 267
ANGLE - CYCLOPS
CYCLOPS
IF SCORPIO STRIKES earth, it will send up a cloud of dust and debris
CYCLOPS (CONT): which will block out the sun for years!
ANGLE - STORM
STORM
OUR PLANET will be plunged into an ice age!
MED WIDE
PROFESSOR X
That's right. We've got to stop it!
COLOSSUS
But how?

05

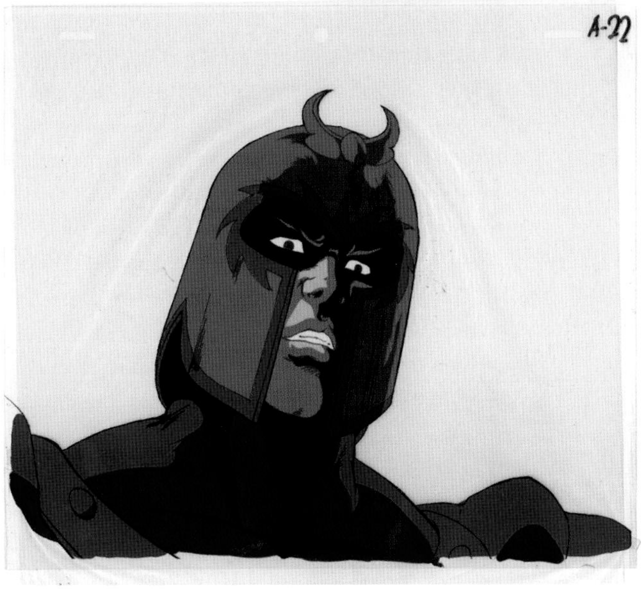
A-22

06

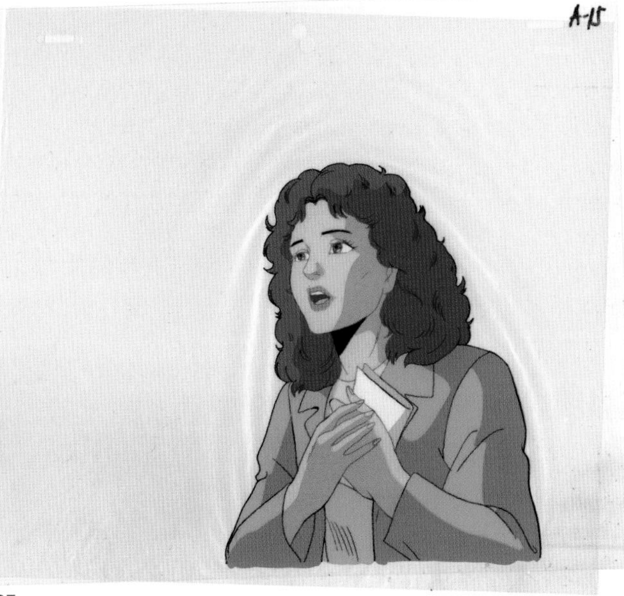
A-15

07

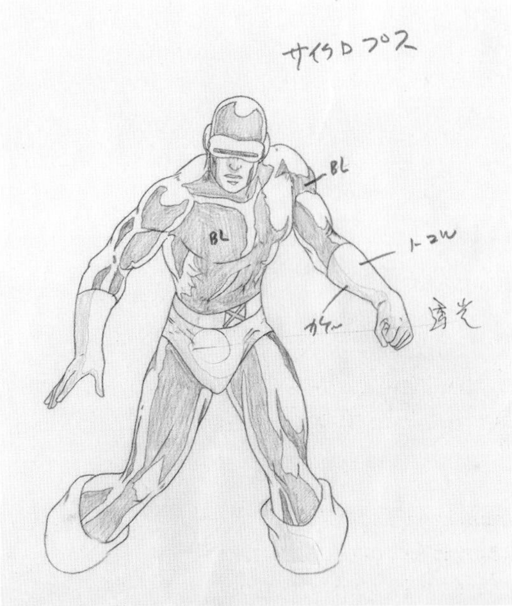
BL
BL

08

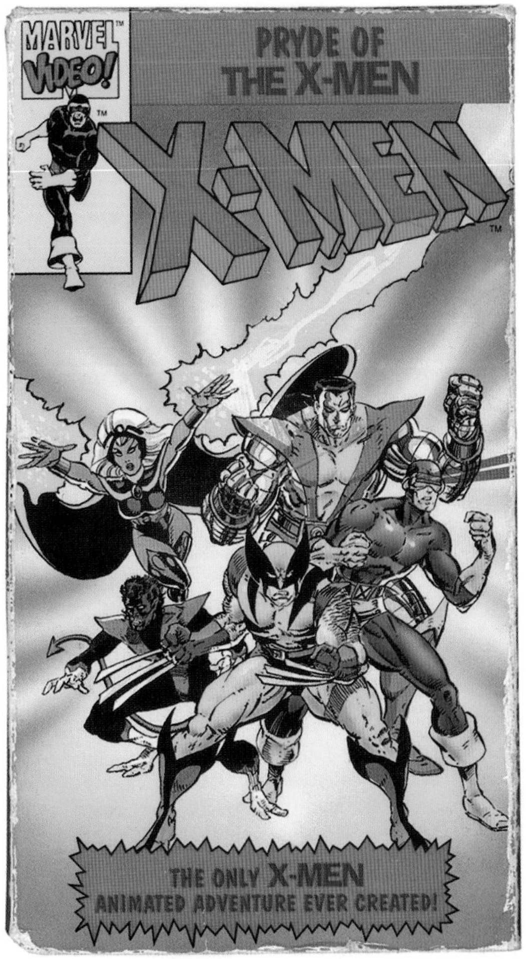
MARVEL VIDEO!
PRYDE OF THE X-MEN
X-MEN
THE ONLY X-MEN ANIMATED ADVENTURE EVER CREATED!

09

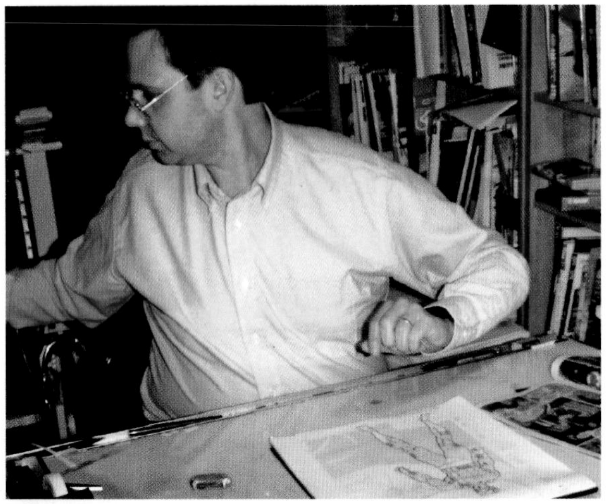

01

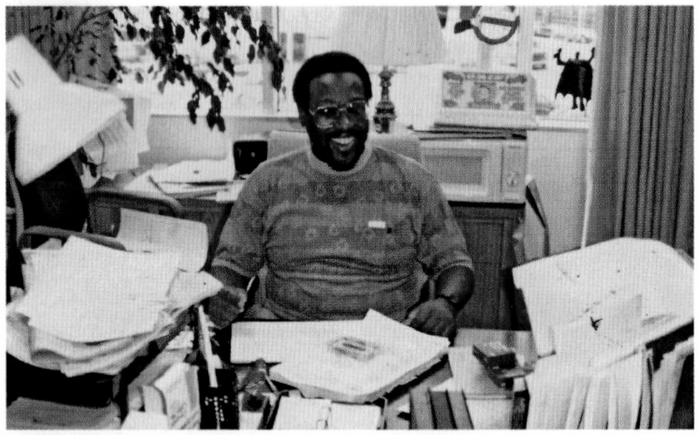

02

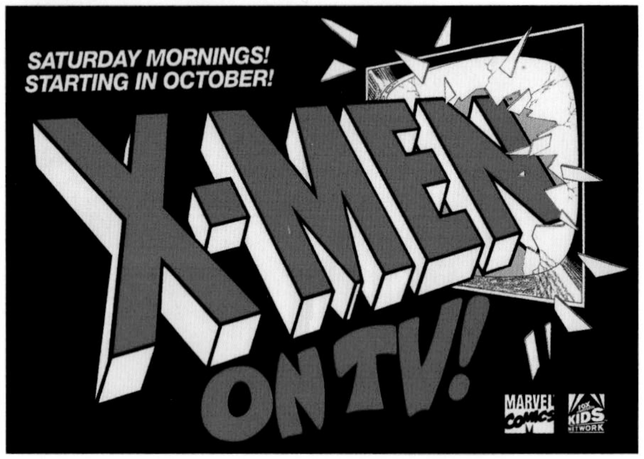
SATURDAY MORNINGS!
STARTING IN OCTOBER!
X-MEN
ON TV!

03

01 *X-Men: TAS* supervising producer and design supervisor Will Meugniot working on a character model for Cyclops. **02** *X-Men: TAS* producer/director Larry Houston digging through a day's work. **03** An overly optimistic ad for the premiere of *X-Men: TAS*. Although the two-part pilot aired as a sneak preview across two nights in the fall of 1992 (October 31 and November 7), our actual Saturday morning premiere, due to production delays, was pushed to January 9, 1993.

So, as the 1980s came to a close, Margaret and her team of Marvel-loving true believers found themselves back at square one—no Marvel shows on TV's big three networks and no prospects for any.

But then a little, new network—a half network, really, patched together from TV stations in smaller markets across the nation—struggled to life. The Fox television network only aired programming for twelve out of twenty-four hours a day, but it had nationwide reach. In 1990, Margaret was asked to come on as president of their new Fox Kids division.

She brought along her right-hand man, program developer Sidney Iwanter, as well as producer Stephanie Graziano from their Marvel Productions days.

Now there was a place to sell TV shows that was friendly to the idea of animated adaptations of comic books.

It takes a while to ramp up a television network. The first season or two, Margaret showed old series, or ones quickly producible, as she prepped her priorities: *X-Men, Batman, Spider-Man, Silver Surfer*. *Batman* had just been a hit movie, so Margaret's bosses immediately okayed developing it as an animated series. Marvel titles were harder. Her boss, Jamie Kellner, looked at the *X-Men* books—too dark, too adult—and just didn't see them as a kids' show. There was little excitement from local Fox affiliate TV stations around the country or from advertisers: Where are the laughs? Other kid shows have a goofy dog: Where's the goofy dog? Kids will never get it.

Margaret kept pushing the show for months. Finally, as she told me: "My boss asked, 'You're not giving up on the X-Men, are you?' 'No, I'm not.' 'Would you bet your job on it? If it fails, you're fired?' 'Yes.'"

So Margaret bet on the X-Men once again—this time with her career on the line. The series was a go. Now to find a TV production company to produce it.

She wanted someone she could trust. Stephanie Graziano had worked for Margaret as a producer at MP and then as a programmer at Fox, but she was far more experienced as a producer. Stephanie had recently quit Fox to form her own studio, Graz Entertainment, with her husband, fellow animation producer Jim Graziano.

Knowing the X-Men project was there to be won, they quickly hired top former Marvel Productions artists Will Meugniot and Larry Houston to show Fox that Graz had the talent in place to make a good show.

As Stephanie told us: "I was at Fox and Jim was still at Marvel Productions when we decided to open our own [pre-production] studio. Sunbow [an established animation studio] helped us get started and gave us our first two series [*Conan the Adventurer* and *My Little Pony*], but running our own place was something we always wanted to do. When we looked at trying to secure Fox's upcoming *X-Men* series, we thought that winning the job would be about the players that we had to offer. So we brought in Will and Larry and all of the creative artists who had been so passionate at MP about Marvel properties and specifically about the X-Men.

"Even though we were putting them on other shows for a while to keep them busy, we knew eventually that as the conversations with Fox deepened around *X-Men*, there was going to be a benefit to having a creative team that was so experienced and so passionate. It gave us great credibility about being able to design and draw *X-Men*. Who else would you go with?"

Haim Saban came in with his larger organization, Saban Entertainment, to supervise the overall project from beginning to end. It took months, but Fox Kids TV finally had a business plan in place for *X-Men*. Luckily for me, I had recently served as a showrunner on the final season of the animated series *Beetlejuice*, at Fox, for Margaret and Sidney, where I used college buddies (and brothers) Mark and Michael Edens as my main writers. Evidently, the folks at Fox thought that we transplanted Tennesseans were the right tools for the *X-Men* job.

So when the green light was given to do *X-Men*, Julia and I got that late-night phone call. Sidney had asked me some days earlier to commit to Fox to do a season of *Attack of the Killer Tomatoes* as a trick to lock me in for the year . . . without mentioning *X-Men*. Margaret was being secretive as they built the *X-Men: The Animated Series* (*TAS*) creative team.

THE NEXT MORNING, February 17, 1992, I entered an expansive conference room on the top floor of the Saban building in Toluca Lake, California. The meeting was hosted by Fox Kids TV's Margaret and Sidney, whom of course I knew, but was full to bursting with perhaps twenty-five people I'd never met, all crowded around a massive, square table that filled the room. There was project partner Saban and his staff. There was the Marvel Comics team from New York: *X-Men* comic-book editor Bob Harras, longtime media executive Joseph Calamari, and creator emeritus Stan Lee. There were folks from the chosen production company, Graz Entertainment (producers Stephanie and Jim Graziano, and artist Will Meugniot). And me.

There was an excitement in the air like I'd never felt in my seven years in the TV business. *X-Men*—it didn't have *The Animated Series* as a subtitle yet—was evidently a big deal for everybody involved.

Marvel, a much smaller company then than today, was pleased that Hollywood was paying for the animated television rights to one of their properties for the first time in a while. But they were also concerned, given Hollywood's lousy track record, that their number-one-selling book at the time might not be done properly. In fact, Saban's first pitch for the series was horrifying. As our supervising producer Will Meugniot remembers: "The Saban people had consulted with Stan [Lee] prior to the meeting and sold Stan on the notion that what we needed to do was a conventional little-kids show about two guys in a van with a dog looking for mutants. The version of the series that they first pitched at the meeting was that Professor X and Cyclops were going to be in a van with Cerebro and an animal sidekick, cruising the country, finding mutants in a mutant-of-the-week show. That was when I thought, 'This is where we gotta draw the line.'" Luckily, cooler heads prevailed.

For Haim, this series was a jump into the big leagues for his company—getting his name on a national television network's pet project. For Graz, *X-Men: TAS* was the way to make their reputation. If they performed well, there would be many more series assignments to come. For lifelong Marvel fan Will Meugniot—onetime Marvel comics penciler, and many-time animated series supervising producer—this was his chance, after the failure of *Pryde*, to get a Marvel series right.

It would not be easy. *X-Men: TAS*, as all network TV shows back then, had a premiere date set in early September. That gave the creative team seven months to develop, write, storyboard, cast, record, hand-paint, animate, and edit thirteen half-hour shows, fixing inevitable first-season problems on the fly. *Batman: The Animated Series*, which had begun development a year earlier at the massive Warner Bros. studio, had been given nineteen months for the same amount of work and was afforded at least double our budget. There were thirty years of *X-Men* comic books to review as we tried to figure out the best storytelling tone and how to make this particular comic-book world work on television; Julia and I and half the writers I picked had no previous familiarity with the material. Mark Edens and I were given two weeks to create the series and lay out the first thirteen stories in their connected arc—a Saturday-morning novelty at the time.

Fox wanted a great, popular show so their network would thrive. Graz wanted the writing done yesterday because they had artists and animators waiting. Marvel wanted us to be faithful to their most prized property, as no one had managed to in the past. And Saban wanted everything done for no money. I just wanted to survive and pay our mortgage—Julia and I had just learned that we had a second child coming. We hit the ground running.

AUTHORS' NOTE

BEFORE WE START, "we" should introduce ourselves.

We, Eric Lewald and Julia Lewald, write for television, primarily for animated series. You have just read how Eric became the showrunner on *X-Men: TAS*. Together or separately, we have showrun fourteen TV series. Combined we have credits on more than seven hundred half-hour televised episodes. It's been fun work, and it's been demanding—and *X-Men: TAS* was the best job we ever had.

We met on staff at Disney Television Animation in 1988, during the time of an explosion of animated TV series collectively called "The Disney Afternoon"—*Chip 'n' Dale Rescue Rangers, DuckTales, TaleSpin, Darkwing Duck, Winnie the Pooh*, etc.—most of which we each wrote for.

Before we left in 1991, we were married and expecting. That old Disney magic.

During the five years of production on *X-Men: TAS* (1992–97), Eric, of course, was living and breathing all things X-Men. Every moment of every story was created, adjusted, or okayed by him. Julia kept her hand in, writing two scripts—"Days of Future Past, Part 1" and "Whatever It Takes"—and coming up with the ideas for others ("Beauty and the Beast") before she had a network show of her own to run, CBS's *Skeleton Warriors*, and an award-winning animated TV movie to write for Fox, Robert Heinlein's *Red Planet*.

Despite these and other commitments, Julia managed to remain a strong voice in the development meetings for each of the five *X-Men* seasons.

But that was the nineties. During the past few years, Julia has led the effort to celebrate *X-Men: TAS*. From running social media platforms—@xmentas on Twitter and Instagram; our Xmentas.com website; or at facebook.com/xmentas—to hosting dozens of panels at comics conventions, innumerable podcasts and video streams, and helping Eric amass the materials for an exhaustive history of the show (*Previously on X-Men*, Jacobs/Brown 2017), Julia is a crucial, committed member of the core *X-Men: TAS* family.

Previously on X-Men was a thorough, dense history of the making of the series, but it lacked any exploration of the show's art and color. This one, streamlined and art-focused, celebrates the visual creativity that made *X-Men: TAS* so memorable.

Together, we, the series architect and its current main proselytizer, would like to tell more tales—and show far more examples—of how the art of *X-Men: TAS* came to be and of the remarkable artists who made it happen.

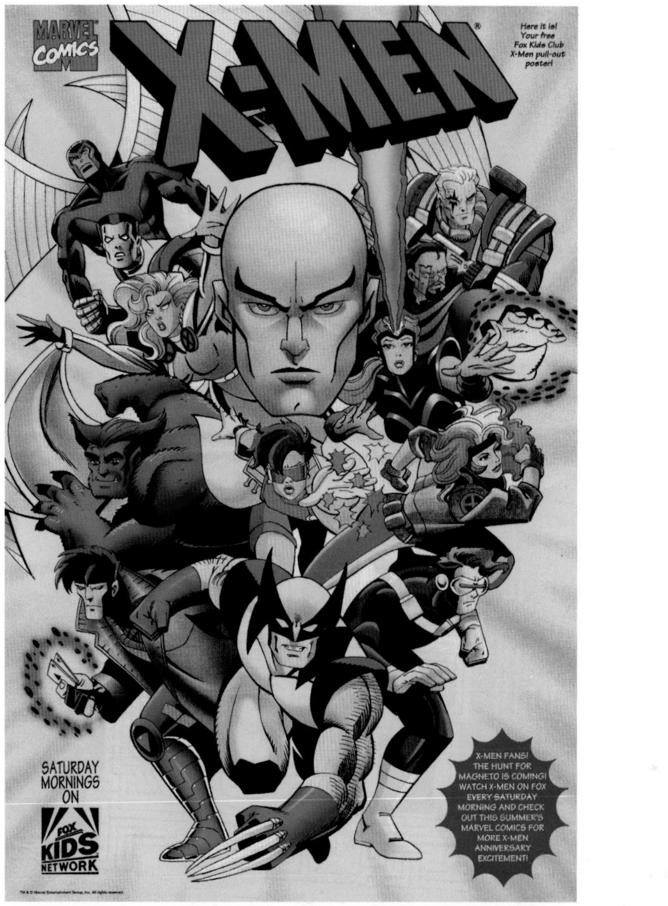

MARVEL COMICS
X-MEN®
Here it is! Your free Fox Kids Club X-Men pull-out poster!
SATURDAY MORNINGS ON
FOX KIDS NETWORK
X-MEN FANS! THE HUNT FOR MAGNETO IS COMING! WATCH X-MEN ON FOX EVERY SATURDAY MORNING AND CHECK OUT THIS SUMMER'S MARVEL COMICS FOR MORE X-MEN ANNIVERSARY EXCITEMENT!

04

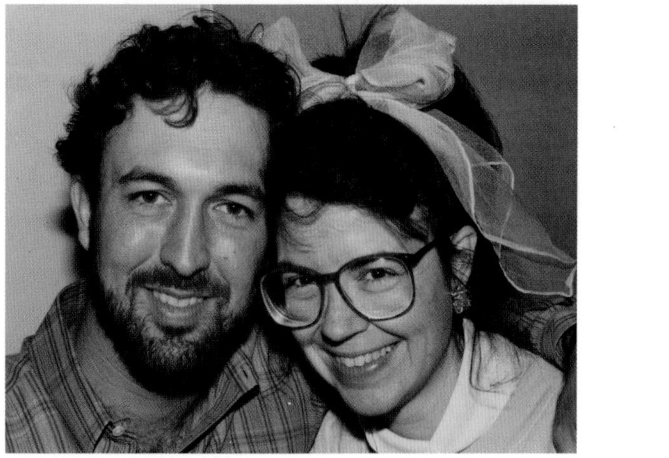

05

04 Fold-out centerpiece poster from the summer 1993 issue of *Totally Kids: The Fox Kids Club Magazine*, a quarterly fan magazine that Fox published from 1991 through 2001 and distributed to members of the Fox Kids Club. **05** The authors while working at Disney TV Animation, shortly before the start of *X-Men: TAS*.

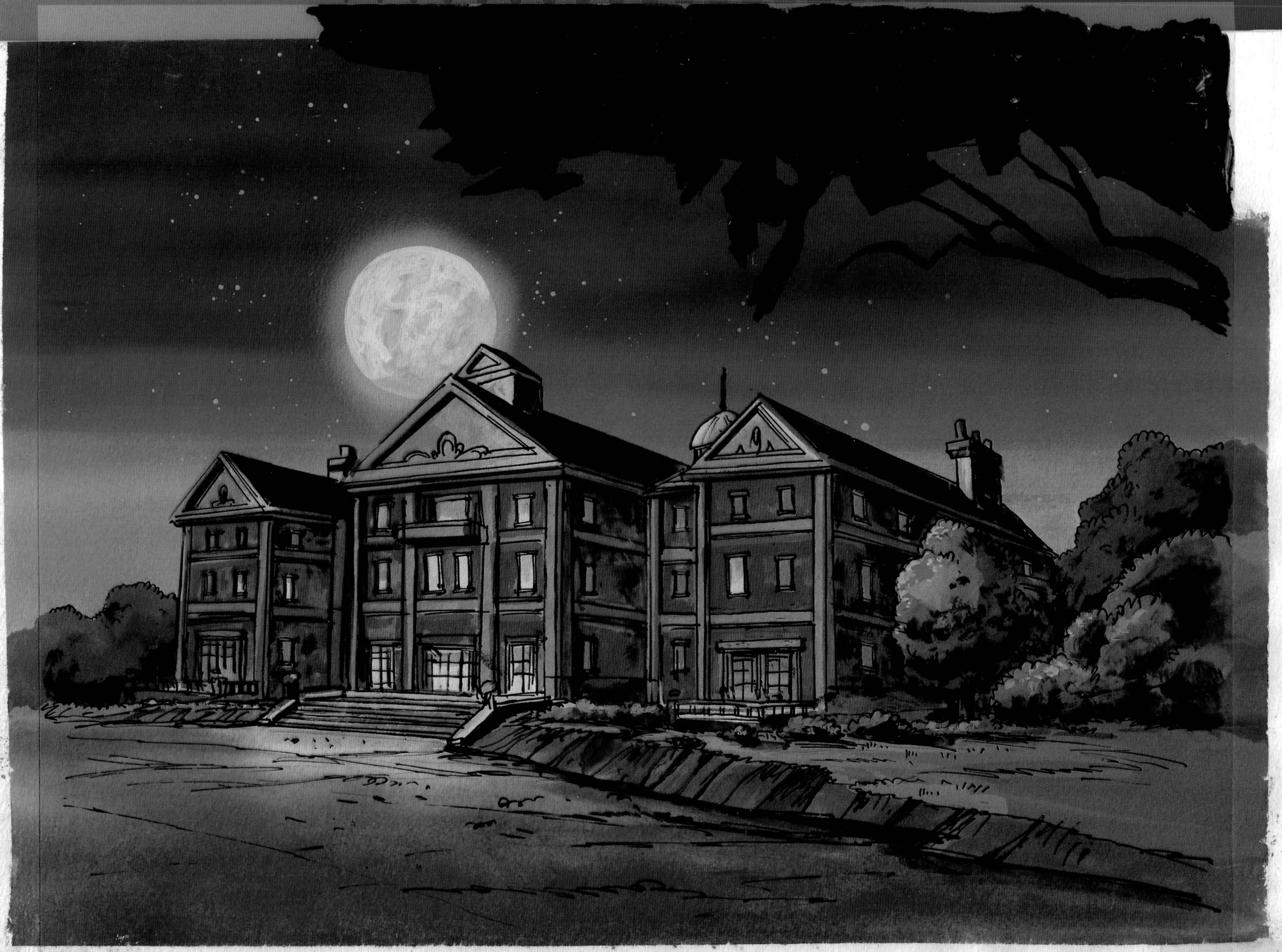

300-07 — BG-84

INTRODUCTION

"ERIC, YOU'RE DOING THE X-MEN."

It's ten fifteen on a February night in 1992, and, over the phone, Fox TV executive Sidney Iwanter sounds, if possible, more intense than usual.

I frown. "That's a comic book, right?"

"Right. Be at Saban's offices at ten."

My wife, Julia, who was feeding our nine-month-old son, Carter, walks in and asks: "Was that about *Attack of the Killer Tomatoes*?"

"No. We're doing *X-Men* instead."

"That's a comic book, right?"

In less than twelve hours, and with no comic-book stores open and no Wikipedia to Google, I needed to "prepare" for a meeting with more than twenty executives, producers, and artists—half a dozen flown in from Marvel Comics in New York, along with Stan Lee himself—where I would smile and nod my head and, with luck, not have to explain my "personal vision" for developing a television world for a bunch of characters that I knew nothing about. Julia tried to be comforting: "Just keep quiet and hope for the best."

JULIA AND I, who write animated cartoons for a living—but not comic books—quickly discovered that *X-Men* was, at the time, the biggest comics title in the world. This had not always been the case. When it debuted in 1963, created by the hall-of-fame team of Jack Kirby and Stan Lee, it struggled. The original X-Men mutant team was younger, looked and sounded nearly identical to one another in their blue, masked uniforms, and, as wisecracking "unusual teenagers," they didn't catch on, drifting into reprints by 1970.

OPPOSITE, LEFT Cover of the first issue of *X-Men* (vol. 1), originally published in September 1963. Art by Jack Kirby and Sol Brodsky. **OPPOSITE, RIGHT** Cover of *Giant-Size X-Men* #1—the team's rebirth in 1975 after five years in reprints. Art by Dave Cockrum, Danny Crespi, and Gil Kane. **01** Ad for the first attempt at animating Marvel characters: *The Marvel Super Heroes* (1966). There was almost no true animation done for the series; most footage was comprised of static or lightly animated shots of comic-book panels drawn by Kirby. **02** The first television appearance of the X-Men characters, on *The Marvel Super Heroes*. **03** The X-Men guest star on *Spider-Man and His Amazing Friends* (1983).

But the *idea* was great: extraordinary people, feared and attacked for their innate differences, who yet struggled to act heroically, often at great personal sacrifice.

That's almost the textbook definition of classical tragedy, and it laid the foundation for the more successful books to come—and, we hoped, for our animated television series.

As legendary comics writer and Wolverine co-creator Len Wein told us in 2015, recalling his days at Marvel Comics: "The idea to resurrect the X-Men [in 1975] came from somebody upstairs—one of the accountants, of all people. The bean counters had noticed that the reprints were selling decently overseas: What if the X-Men were to become more international? Like, um, a Canadian (Wolverine), a Russian (Colossus), a German (Nightcrawler), and a Central African (Storm)?"

Editor in chief Roy Thomas had Len and artist Dave Cockrum build a new team and get the remade series going—and suddenly it was something special. Adult characters with real lives and real crises. Spectacle and drama worthy of the original idea. Writer Chris Claremont and artist John Byrne soon leapt in and took the idea of a struggling family of mutants to unprecedented heights. Others followed.

But how do you translate Marvel comic-book stories into compelling television? Comic books feature static images, seas of internal thought bubbles, splash pages with eleven embattled characters all talking at once. How did Hollywood manage it before this?

Not very successfully, we discovered. From the barely animated *The Marvel Super Heroes* (1966) to the absurdly conceived *Fred and Barney Meet the Thing* (1979), Saturday-morning television in the 1960s and seventies did Marvel characters few favors. And in 1992 there were no successful Marvel movies to look back on.

The 1980s had seemed to be poised for a Marvel television breakout. Marvel Comics set up their own Hollywood-based TV production company, Marvel Productions (MP), bringing in Stan Lee and a respected group of animation writers and artists.

Led by president and animation-industry veteran Margaret Loesch, they all understood Marvel comic books and worked tirelessly to get them on the air.

Sadly, the "air" (national TV networks ABC, CBS, and NBC) didn't want Marvel characters. Margaret and MP were able to

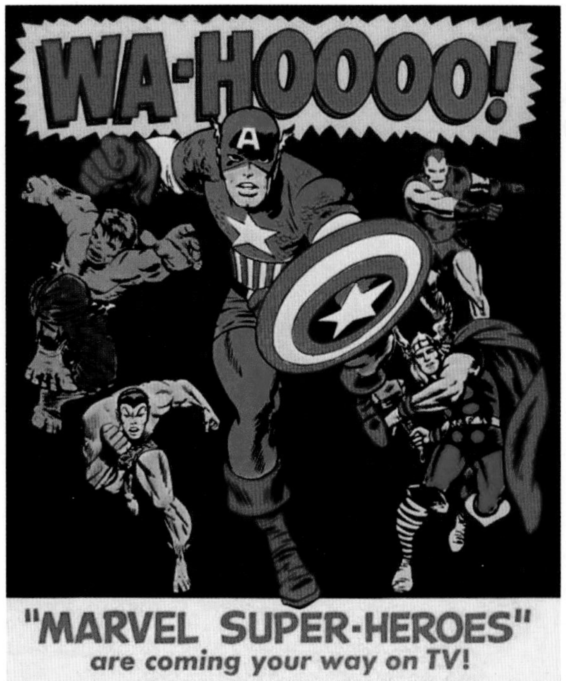
WA-HOOOO!
"MARVEL SUPER-HEROES"
are coming your way on TV!

01

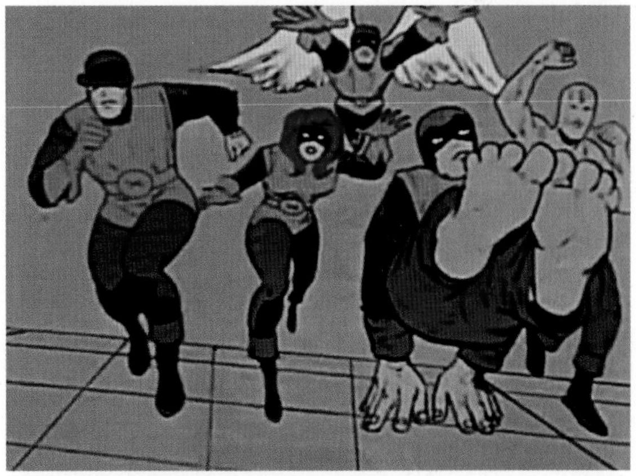

02

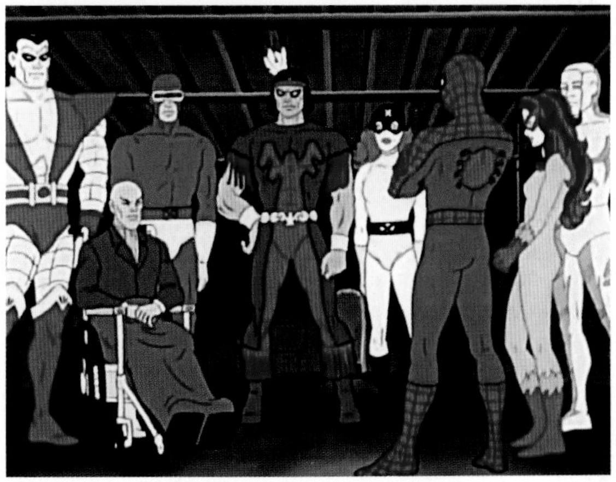

03

MARVEL PRODUCTIONS LTD.
A NEW WORLD COMPANY

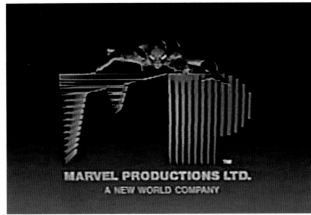

01

place several major hit shows that they produced on television (*Muppet Babies*, *G.I. Joe*, *Transformers*). But their Marvel titles stalled (beyond a couple of brief early attempts at Spider-Man and a Hulk). Loesch recalled: "For years we couldn't give a Marvel property away."

Finally, in 1987, a frustrated president Loesch decided to force the issue. She took the money set aside for an episode of MP's animated *RoboCop* series and made a "sales video," a one-off, half-hour episode of her favorite Marvel property, the X-Men.

She made a $300,000 gamble that when the TV networks saw how great an animated show *X-Men* could be, they'd *have* to order the series. Sadly, the result—*Pryde of the X-Men*—convinced nobody.

As so often happens, a good project got lost in everybody's "great ideas." Creative talent at MP who knew and respected the books—artists Will Meugniot, Larry Houston, and Rick Hoberg—put their best efforts forward on the production side. *Pryde* looked great: faithful character design, sharp animation. It just didn't work as a story or a series showcase. Too many corporate "cooks" with influence ("*Crocodile Dundee* is popular—let's make Wolverine Australian!" "Let's put twenty extra Marvel characters in it so we can sell toys!") insisted on story revisions that the creative staff were powerless to resist.

COLOSSUS
6'10"
STORM
5'9"
PYRO 5'10"
WOLVERINE
KITTY
5'3"
NIGHTCRAWLER
5'2"
TOAD
4'11"

02

JUGGERNAUT
8'
BLOB
7'
MAGNETO
6'10"
CYCLOPS
6'1"
WHITE QUEEN
5'10"
DAZZLER
PROFESSOR X
4'8"
(SITTING)
LOCKHEED 1½"

03

01 Production logo for Marvel Productions (1981–1993). **02–03** Cast model lineup for the "Pryde of the X-Men" pilot (produced 1987–88; first broadcast 1989) by Russ Heath. Will Meugniot, Larry Houston, and Rick Hoberg staffed the show. **04–05** Storyboard panels for "Pryde of the X-Men." Top row drawn in May 1987 by Meugniot; bottom row by Hoberg. **06–07** Production cels of Magneto and Kitty Pryde for "Pryde of the X-Men." **08** Color key art of Cyclops for "Pryde of the X-Men." **09** VHS cover for "Pryde of the X-Men" (tape released July 1, 1992).

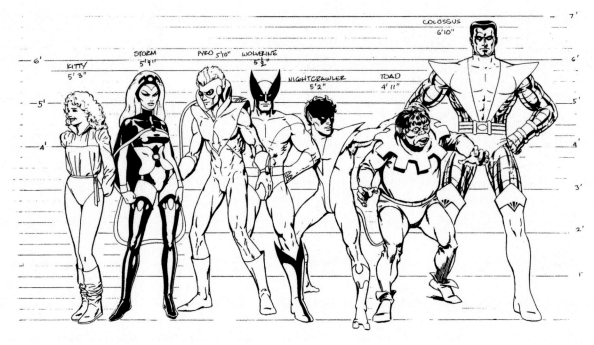

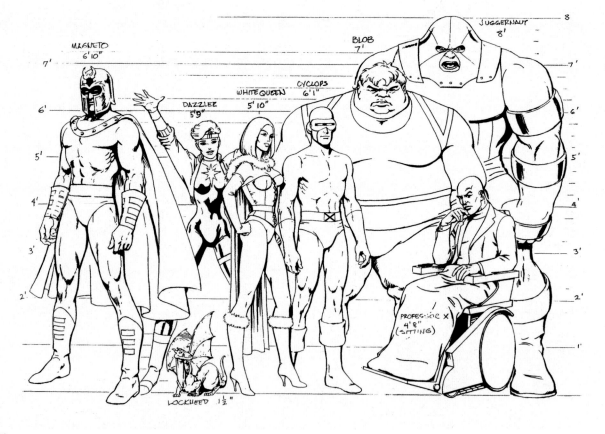

CHAPTER ONE

SEASON ONE, OR JUST ONE SEASON?

SEASON ONE, EPISODES 1–13

THE FIRST SEASON, produced in 1992, was the by far the hardest—the most rushed and most uncertain. And in spite of Margaret's enthusiasm, the assumption was that *X-Men: TAS* would only last one season. We writers and artists had to prove ourselves creatively, usually against serious doubts and pushback. It would be seven long months before the first completed episode could air and we would know if our efforts had succeeded or crashed and burned. This worry was made real by the fact that we all knew we were set to be let go when these thirteen episodes were completed—and in fact we were all let go—with no provision in our contracts to be rehired.

During the first crazed two weeks when *X-Men: TAS* was hammered into being, Eric and head writer Mark Edens spent long days at Eric and Julia's dining-room-table work space, digging through the massive *Official Handbook of the Marvel Universe* series from 1988—a photocopied version, annotated by Larry Houston—for details about these strange X-Men characters, their histories, their relationships, and their world.

We also purchased a "Marvel Super Heroes: The Uncanny X-Men Special Campaign Set" board game because it came with a "Roster Blueprint" poster that laid out each of the nine X-Teams formed up until then—twenty-three different X-Men and that many more mutants in related teams—and had a blueprint of the X-Mansion and Muir Island. With no real Internet in 1992, we grabbed X-Men knowledge where we could.

Eric was in constant contact with Marvel-knowledgeable *X-Men: TAS* designer-producer Will Meugniot and *X-Men* megafan and series producer-director Larry Houston, who were, with their undersize staff, designing the series as fast as they could draw.

Eric had endless questions for *X-Men* comics editor and series consultant Bob Harras, who was busy back in New York, working eighty hours a week running three or four series of the comic books—but who found the time to help. Prospective *X-Men: TAS* animation writers who knew the books (especially Bob Skir) overflowed with advice.

Marvel and Fox had agreed to a core team of six characters out of the couple dozen available in 1992: Wolverine, Cyclops, Storm, Rogue, Gambit, and Jubilee.

This was a great starting point for the writers. These six lead characters were all quite different from one another. They had complementary voices, powers, and personalities.

But as Eric and Mark built the first thirteen connected stories, three team members considered by Marvel to be "secondary"—that we could "use sometimes if we wanted"—kept asserting themselves. Eric and Mark just couldn't make the stories work the way they liked without the major participation of Professor Xavier, the idealistic architect of the X-Men, and Jean Grey, the team's empathic heart and soul. And Beast, Dr. Henry Philip "Hank" McCoy, so thoughtful, so articulate, so steady amid the crazed emotions of the others. They just couldn't keep him out of the stories.

As head writer Mark Edens recalls, "Beast was probably my favorite character to write for. Writers like words, and they like to think they're intelligent, and Beast was a brilliant guy who liked to talk. And he could beat up people. For a writer, he's what the executives in charge of children's programming call 'aspirational.'"

Still the team was not quite complete. As Mark reminded us, "We need an X-Man to kill." Mark and Eric were adamant: During the first story ("Night of the Sentinels"), one of the X-Men would need to die. We were determined to show the audience that there were consequences to being an X-Man. No heroism without heroic sacrifice.

At first, we chose Thunderbird—a major new-generation X-Man who had in fact been killed in the comics while helping the X-Men. In fact, that's why there is a "villain" in the opening credits that looks like Thunderbird: It's his twin brother, Warpath. Thunderbird's animation model had already been designed, so using Warpath for the opening credits saved the design team precious drawing time.

Then, someone in authority decided that killing off the only Native American X-Man on our core team might not be a wise idea. And so the sacrificial team member was changed to the shape-shifter Changeling, who had sacrificed himself for Professor X in the books back in 1968.

But... there was also a DC comics character named Changeling. Even though DC's Changeling was created after Marvel's, lawsuits loomed. And thus, with a simple name change, Morph was born.

We later heard that Morph voice actor Ron Rubin was not happy to discover that his character died early in the second episode. "Everybody else got thirteen paychecks!" he complained. "And I got two!"

Morph's unwanted—at least by us—and unplanned resurrection in season two, as PTSD-suffering "damaged Morph," would help soothe Ron's pain and lead to some strong stories.

OPPOSITE Layered production cels, line and color, of Xavier's mansion at night. This was our standard night background of the school.

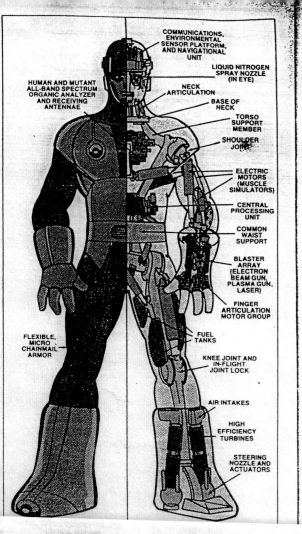

COMMUNICATIONS, ENVIRONMENTAL SENSOR PLATFORM, AND NAVIGATIONAL UNIT

LIQUID NITROGEN SPRAY NOZZLE (IN EYE)

HUMAN AND MUTANT ALL-BAND SPECTRUM ORGANIC ANALYZER AND RECEIVING ANTENNAE

NECK ARTICULATION

BASE OF NECK

TORSO SUPPORT MEMBER

SHOULDER JOINT

ELECTRIC MOTORS (MUSCLE SIMULATORS)

CENTRAL PROCESSING UNIT

COMMON WAIST SUPPORT

BLASTER ARRAY (ELECTRON BEAM GUN, PLASMA GUN, LASER)

FINGER ARTICULATION MOTOR GROUP

FUEL TANKS

FLEXIBLE, MICRO CHAINMAIL ARMOR

KNEE JOINT AND IN-FLIGHT JOINT LOCK

AIR INTAKES

HIGH EFFICIENCY TURBINES

STEERING NOZZLE AND ACTUATORS

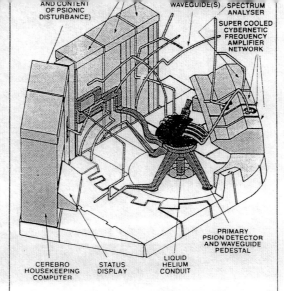

...erebro does so by detecting the unusual ...aves of psionic energy ("brain waves") ...ich superhumanly powerful mutants emit ... reasons and through processes which ...main unknown. The computer system in ...erebro can roughly measure the amount ... superhuman power possessed by the ...utant, determine the mutant's geographi- ... location, and even specify the identity of ... mutant if given sufficient data.

...Although anyone can be taught to use it, ...erebro acts most effectively when it is ...ked to the mind of Professor Xavier or a ...ing with similar telepathic abilities. By ...aring a special headset connected to ...erebro, Xavier is able to use his psionic ...wers to increase Cerebro's ability to de- ...ct psionic waves. Individual members of ...e X-Men have sometimes carried smaller ...rsions of Cerebro colloquially termed ...ortable Cerebros" with them. A "portable ...erebro," in telemetric contact with the main ...mputer console, can detect the presence ... a human mutant at short range.

...Xavier began work on developing Cerebro ...fore he founded the X-Men. He used an ...rly version of the device, which he called ...berno, to locate Scott Summers, who, as ...yclops, became Xavier's first recruit for the ...Men (see Cyclops). Xavier completed ...e first true Cerebro machine shortly after ...e fifth X-Man, Marvel Girl, joined the team ...ee Marvel Girl). He named Cerebro after ...e human cerebrum, the largest section of ...e human brain and the part responsible ... transmitting psionic waves. ■

AND CONTENT OF PSIONIC DISTURBANCE)

WAVEGUIDE(S) SPECTRUM ANALYSER

SUPER COOLED CYBERNETIC FREQUENCY AMPLIFIER NETWORK

PRIMARY PSION DETECTOR AND WAVEGUIDE PEDESTAL

CEREBRO HOUSEKEEPING COMPUTER

STATUS DISPLAY

LIQUID HELIUM CONDUIT

MEN

...X-Men is an organization of superhumanly powerful mutants ...as founded by Professor Charles Xavier for two purposes: ...o train such mutants in the uses of their superhuman powers, ...econd, to serve as a combat team that could defend humanity ...st attacks by superhumanly powerful mutants who use their ...s for criminal ends, as well as against other threats (see ...essor X).

...civilian identities of most of the X-Men are unknown to the ... In their civilian identities the X-Men are officially students at ...mni of Professor Xavier's School for Gifted Youngsters. The ...ol, where the X-Men are based, is housed in Charles Xavier's ...ion at 1407 Graymalkin Lane, Salem Center, Westchester ...ty, New York. The Mansion serves as the X-Men's base of ...tions, training center, and living quarters. Although the true ...ties of two of the X-Men's founding members, the Angel and ...east, have become public knowledge, they have apparently ...ged somehow to conceal the fact that they attended Xavier's ...ol from public awareness.

...ually every member of the X-Men is a superhuman mutant ...have, however, been exceptions, such as the Mimic, who ...d duplicate the superhuman powers of mutants, and Longshot, ...artificially created, genetically engineered humanoid from an ... Deceased: Mimic).

...man mutant who, as a young ... battle various menaces. After ...he alien Lucifer, Xavier led a ...scientific researcher (see Ap- ...to help Jean Grey, who was ...control her newly emerged ...Xavier used his own psychic ...rey's mind to prevent her from ...e was mature enough to deal ...s Xavier worked with Grey to ...s.

...man beings would eventually ...owing number of superhuman ...eports of an adolescent mutant ...mob violence after he publicly ...This mutant was being investi- ...he Federal Bureau of Investiga- ...told him of his intention to find ...rain them in the uses of their ...Duncan and Xavier agreed to ...operation between Xavier and ...several years, but Xavier put an ... government's attitude towards ...g to turn hostile. Xavier and his ...t with computers, have seen to it ...X-Men dating from the years of ...en destroyed. Duncan was once ...be untrue. His current activities,

...educed that the young mutant ...ott Summers) Xavier sought out ...first of his X-Men, Cyclops (see ..."X-Men" because each one had ...ple lacked. (Not so coincidentally ...fter of Xavier's last name, and he ...essor X.")

...vier recruited three more super- ...g them in the use of their powers: ... Iceman, Warren Worthington, the ...career as a costumed crimefighter, ...tudent who became known as the ...n). Xavier then invited Grey, who ...in the use of her powers due to his ...k the code name Marvel Girl (see

...all adolescents when they joined ...ly not opposed to inducting an adult ...red membership in the team to the ...Blob). Afterwards, Xavier seemed ...iting new members for the X-Men. ...ed on joining the group, although he ...other young mutants, Lorna Dane, ...ers' brother Alexander, alias Havok, ...the X-Men, although it is unclear ...k members of Xavier's school (see

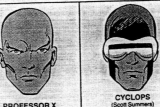

PROFESSOR X
(Charles Xavier)
Founder, leader
Active as of X-MEN #1

CYCLOPS
(Scott Summers)
Former Deputy Leader
Active as of X-MEN #1
Now member of X-Factor

ICEMAN
(Robert "Bobby" Drake)
Active as of X-MEN #1
Now member of X-Factor

ANGEL
(Warren K. Worthington III)
Active as of X-MEN #1
Now member of X-Factor

BEAST
(Henry "Hank" P. McCoy)
Active as of X-MEN #1
Now member of X-Factor

MARVEL GIRL
(Jean Grey)
Joined in X-MEN #1
Now member of X-Factor

MIMIC
(Calvin Rankin, deceased)
Former Deputy Leader
Joined in X-MEN #27
Resigned in X-MEN #29

CHANGELING
(Real name unknown, deceased)
Honorary member
Active as of X-MEN #41
Died in action in X-MEN #42

POLARIS

...be the men- ...tants ...nited States

...deceased), ...Kurt Marko ...arko (step- ...on) ...d mentor of ...now allied

... Xavier's ...em Center, ...currently in ...the Shi'ar

...utant son of ...and his wife ...ent, Xavier ...s to sense ... emotions. ...father was ...est. Shortly ...ue, Dr. Kurt ...Sharon for ...evious mar- ...the Xavier ...ter County, ...to Charles,

...eaten by his ...on Charles ...anguished ...een beaten ...t time that ...ed another ...experienced ...his powes ...the contact ...e to put an ...ded for un- ...ensed that ...d had dis- ...n believed ...ights delib- ...d Charles

...ilized how ..., and her ...ath shortly ...ement with ...explosive ...ngulf his ...ough Kurt ...Cain and ...died from

...ned how to ...As a side ...s powers, ...by the time ...was com- ...College in ...rk at 16 ...achelors de- ...He was ...ent by En- ...he earned ...ics at the ...er met the ...and, a col- ...was also a ...etics (see ...Pending

NO! HE CAN'T WALK! HE IS IN A FLOATING WHEELCHAIR NOW!

...ntinels and the X-Men. ...ft a "mindless vege- ...f his own 30-foot tall ...is destroyed in an en- ...see Hulk) ...were inferior to the

...government, is himself a mutant (see Black King). Shaw Industries, which Shaw owns and heads, has been licensed by the gov- ...ernment under heavy secrecy to construct ...Sentinels for use by Project Wideawake, and ...by the Department of Defense. So far Shaw

...using propulsion units in their feet. Omega Sentinels can fire energy blasts from their palms, and form non-metallic "catchwebs" from their fingers in order to imprison oppo- nents. Omega Sentinels contain self-repair- ...ing systems. Like Mark II Sentinels,

101

X-MEN-CHARACTER/EPISODE		1	2	3	4	5	6	7	8	9	10	11	12	13
"A TEAM"	CYCLOPS	3	3	2	2	4	3	2	4	3	3	3	3	3
	WOLVERINE	3	3	3	3	4	4	2	?	?	?	3	3	3
	STORM	1	1	?	?	3	2	3	2	?	?	2	2	3
	ROGUE	1	1	2	2	?	2	2	2	4	3	2	2	2
	JUBILEE	4	4	1	1	?	2	4	?	?	?	2	2	2
	GAMBIT (a mention)	2	2	?	?	2	2	3	2	?	?	2	2	2
"B TEAM"	COLOSSUS								3					
	BEAST	2	2	2	2	-			1					1
	BISHOP											3	3	
	CABLE (4 intro)							3						
	XAVIER	3	3	4	4	?				3	4	4	4	4
	ARCHANGEL									2	3			
	JEAN GREY	1	1	—	—	4								
	CHANGELING	2	1											
	JUGGERNAUT								3					
	SENTINELS	3	3				1	3						3
	TRASK	2	2				1	3						2
	HODGE			2	2			2						
	PETRIE			1										
	SEN. KELLY	1	1	1	1	1			1			1	1	1
	GYRICH	2	2	1	1		1	2						2
	MAGNETO			4	4									4
	CALLISTO					3								
	SABERTOOTH	—	—	3	3	1	3							
	APOCALYPSE									2	4			
	MYSTIQUE									2	2	2	2	
	CALIBAN					2		2		1	1			
	AVALANCHE											2	2	
	PYRO									1	1	2	2	
	BLOB									1	1			

01

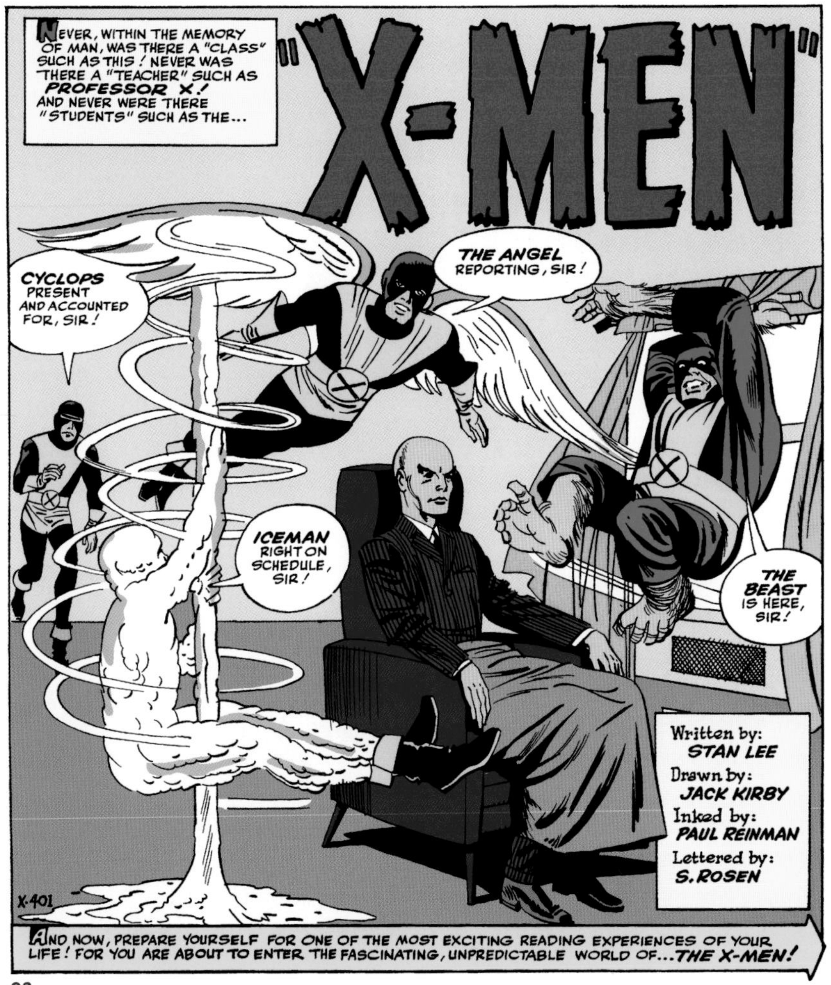
NEVER, WITHIN THE MEMORY OF MAN, WAS THERE A "CLASS" SUCH AS THIS! NEVER WAS THERE A "TEACHER" SUCH AS PROFESSOR X! AND NEVER WERE THERE "STUDENTS" SUCH AS THE...
"X-MEN"
CYCLOPS PRESENT AND ACCOUNTED FOR, SIR!
THE ANGEL REPORTING, SIR!
ICEMAN RIGHT ON SCHEDULE, SIR!
THE BEAST IS HERE, SIR!
Written by: STAN LEE
Drawn by: JACK KIRBY
Inked by: PAUL REINMAN
Lettered by: S. ROSEN
X-401
AND NOW, PREPARE YOURSELF FOR ONE OF THE MOST EXCITING READING EXPERIENCES OF YOUR LIFE! FOR YOU ARE ABOUT TO ENTER THE FASCINATING, UNPREDICTABLE WORLD OF...THE X-MEN!

02

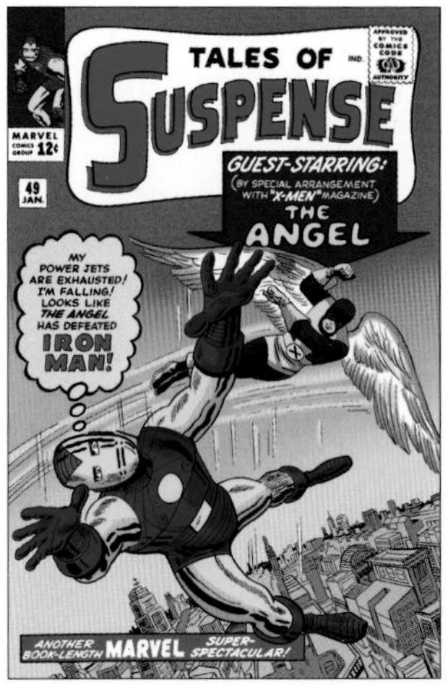
TALES OF SUSPENSE
MARVEL COMICS GROUP 12¢
49 JAN.
GUEST-STARRING: (BY SPECIAL ARRANGEMENT WITH "X-MEN" MAGAZINE) THE ANGEL
MY POWER JETS ARE EXHAUSTED! I'M FALLING! LOOKS LIKE THE ANGEL HAS DEFEATED IRON MAN!
ANOTHER BOOK-LENGTH MARVEL SUPER-SPECTACULAR!

03

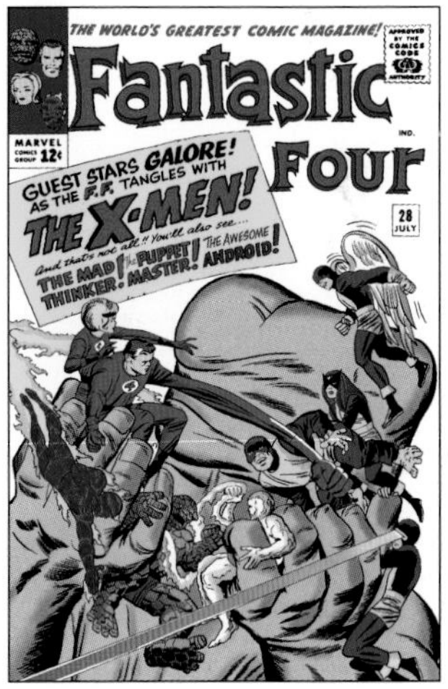
THE WORLD'S GREATEST COMIC MAGAZINE!
Fantastic Four
MARVEL COMICS GROUP 12¢
28 JULY
GUEST STARS GALORE! AS THE F.F. TANGLES WITH THE X-MEN!
And that's not all!! You'll also see...
THE MAD THINKER! The PUPPET MASTER! THE AWESOME ANDROID!

04

NOW THAT THE TEN MEMBERS OF THE TEAM had been established, what would they look like? Over the thirty years of *X-Men* comics, many excellent artists had drawn "their" version of the X-Men. Costumes and attitudes had changed. Will Meugniot, in charge of the series overall design, remembers growing up with these changes.

Will says, "I was with the X-Men from their first issue and actually liked the (yellow-and-blue) school uniforms the team members initially wore. The attention to detail Jack Kirby had put into them appealed to me, particularly the way the Beast was barefoot and the 'cuffs' of his leggings were always drawn as being loose.

"But, despite my continuing patronage of the title, after the first year or so, the book's sales began to slip. I remember Stan mentioning that it was often the poorest seller of the Marvel Superhero books. (A note to younger readers: During the early Silver Age, Marvel published a diversified line of comics, including teen titles like the long-running *Millie the Model*, Western heroes such as the recently re-imagined masked hero version of *The Two-Gun Kid*, and war books with *Sgt. Fury* as their leading title in that category.)

"Stan was pulling out the stops to promote the faltering title: You can tell by the number of times the X-Men, both as individuals and as a team, started showing up in the other, better-selling Marvel comics. 1964 started out with The Angel guest-starring in *Iron Man* in January, followed by Iceman hanging out with the Human Torch in May, and then, in July, the entire team meets up with the Fantastic Four. However, it seems this was no help in raising sales.

"Through this period the only tinkering with the basic costume designs happened with an on-again-off-again change to Marvel Girl's mask and Iceman dumping his cavalier boots and then realizing he could freeze himself 'harder,' changing his form from that of a snowman to the crystalline ice version we know today.

OPPOSITE Photocopies of pages from Larry Houston's reference copy of *The Official Handbook of the Marvel Universe*, used by Eric and his head writer Mark Edens to quickly learn the nature of, history of, and relationships among the X-Men and their friends and adversaries. Note highlighting, underlining, annotations. **01** Eric's early chart of the estimated usage and prominence (color/number) of various characters during the first season, made as he and the writers planned the stories to give Marvel and Fox a sense of how much exposure each character would get. Note that Xavier, Jean, and Beast are not yet listed in the "A Team." **02** Panel from the title page of *X-Men* (vol. 1) #1. Written by Stan Lee; pencils by Jack Kirby; inks by Paul Reinman; lettering by Sam Rosen. **03** Cover of *Tales of Suspense* (vol. 1) #49. Art by Kirby, Steve Ditko, Stan Goldberg, and Artie Simek. **04** Cover of *Fantastic Four* (vol. 1) #28. Art by Kirby, Sol Brodsky, Goldberg, and Rosen.

"Apart from Marvel Girl's mask vacillating between the full hood and peaked design, things stayed pretty static with the team's costumes until December of 1967, when in issue #39, the cover ballyhooed: 'New Costumes!!' 'New Thrills!' From then on the team members each wore a distinctive individual uniform.

"At the time, I liked the concept better than the execution. Marvel Girl's costume was the best to my eyes, but The Angel's new threads didn't make any sense to me. The others were OK, but no great shakes—until Jim Steranko took over the art reins for a few covers and two stories: *X-Men* #49–51. Then they all looked unfathomably cooler! That trend of artistic approach trumping weak design continued when Neal Adams [see page 266] started penciling the book with issue #56.

"During Adams's run on the book, we started seeing hints of the X-Men's future design aesthetic, particularly in his two-stage redesign of the Angel. Suddenly in issue 60, the flying X-Man's costume has a halo as an element; in issue 62, his entire costume gets a sleek new look whose clean lines appear to have been very influential in the series' later revival.

"Despite the improvements, *X-Men* was cancelled with issue #66. But an interesting thing happened. After Neal Adams's work made its mark, despite the book's cancellation, most of the art samples coming to Marvel for consideration featured the uncanny mutants! Stan and Roy Thomas speculated that Marvel's publisher, Martin Goodman, had canceled the comic too soon, before the final sales figures were in. So, for four years the X-Men lived on in reprints, guest-starring appearances, and occasional short filler strips.

"Then in 1975, the team returned in *Giant-Size X-Men* #1, but in a vastly different form, featuring new characters hailing from around the globe. It was part of a larger merchandising initiative to make Marvel's characters more compelling to the international market. On a side note, this initiative also led to Marvel collaborating with Toei in Japan to create an early *Sentai* show, the multi-nationally-themed *Battle Fever J*, which was the predecessor to many series, including *Zyuranger*, revamped as *The Power Rangers* for the US market.

"The art for the new *X-Men* series was handled by Dave Cockrum, one of the first artists to be inspired by Neal Adams and Jim Steranko, and his streamlined costumes reflected and expanded upon Adams's work. He thoughtfully designed uniforms that accented the characters as individuals and reflected the wearer's powers. Colossus with the cut-out areas to showcase his armored form, Storm with her wind-billowed cloak and flowing long hair, and the ill-fated Thunderbird with his unfortunate Native American tropes clearly demonstrate this new approach.

MEANWHILE, IN A DORMITORY ROOM AT THE WORLD'S MOST EXCLUSIVE PRIVATE SCHOOL, JEAN GREY IS ABSORBED WITH HER REFLECTION IN THE FULL-LENGTH MIRROR ... THE REFLECTION WHICH REVEALS THE NEW MARVEL GIRL!
MMM, WHOEVER DESIGNED THIS UNIFORM COULD HAVE GIVEN CHRISTIAN DIOR A RUN FOR HIS MONEY!
WHERE DID THE NEW DOLL GO? OH ... THERE SHE IS!
WOWEE! LOOKS LIKE SHE WAS POURED INTO THAT UNIFORM!
01

NOW, STAND WHERE YOU ARE AND PRACTICE REFINING YOUR ICE CRYSTALS, AS I'VE SUGGESTED!
OKAY, TEACH! --- WATCH THIS!
EXCELLENT! BY INCREASING YOUR DEGREE OF COLD, YOUR BODY BECOMES EVEN MORE ICY, MAKING YOU ALMOST TRANSPARENT!
YOU'RE BECOMING A REGULAR SUE STORM, KIDDO!
AW, SHUDDUP, ANGEL!
2.
02

the X-MEN
MARVEL COMICS GROUP
12¢ IND. 49 OCT
WHO DARES DEFY-- THE DEMI-MEN?
STERANKO
03

X-MEN
MARVEL COMICS GROUP
12¢ IND. 50 NOV
STERANKO
04

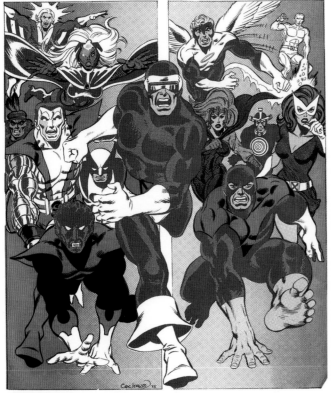

FOOM TEN

05

CHAPTER II "...AND WHEN THERE WAS ONE!"
WESTCHESTER, NEW YORK: THE SCHOOL HAD SEEMED A LATTER-DAY TOWER OF BABEL AT FIRST-- BUT A TELEPATHIC CRASH COURSE IN THE ENGLISH LANGUAGE HAD CLOSED THE COMMUNICATION GAP IN MERE MINUTES.
NOW PROFESSOR CHARLES XAVIER SITS, SOMBERLY STUDYING HIS COLORFULLY-COSTUMED HOUSE-GUESTS--
--AND WHATEVER THOUGHTS HE MIGHT HAVE AT THIS POINT ARE HIS ALONE TO KNOW.
IN ALL MY LIFE, SUCH CLOTHING AS THIS I HAVE NEVER SEEN!
THE COSTUME IS BEAUTIFUL, AND THE FIT--PERFECT! BUT HOW DID YOU...?
THE UNIFORMS ARE CONSTRUCTED FROM UNSTABLE MOLECULES, WHICH ADJUST THEMSELVES WHERE NECESSARY.
I OBTAINED THEM FROM A MAN NAMED REED RICHARDS, AND I'M CERTAIN YOU'LL LEARN MORE OF HIM AND HIS FRIENDS LATER.
BUT RIGHT NOW...

06

HULLO, KITTEN.
MY APOLOGIES FOR BEING LATE.

07

STRANGE TALES
APPROVED BY THE COMICS CODE AUTHORITY
NICK FURY, AGENT OF S.H.I.E.L.D.
MARVEL COMICS GROUP
12¢ IND. 167 APR
STERANKO

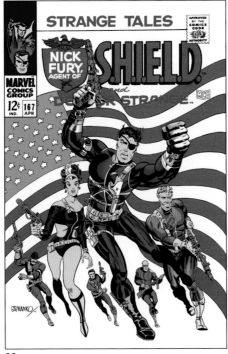

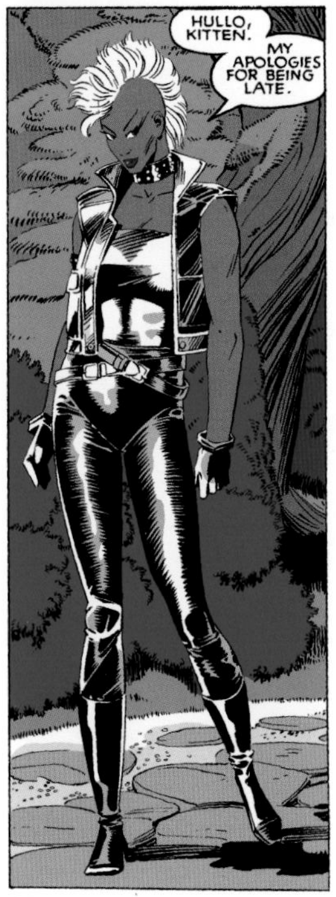

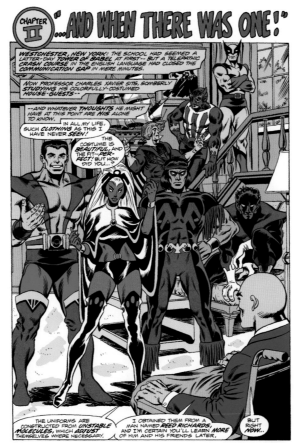

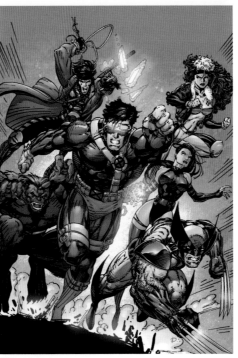

08

09

"After Cockrum left the series, artists John Byrne and Paul Smith continued the '70s streamlining to good effect. But in Smith's issue #173, we start seeing the changes that lead us to the '90s look: Rogue's jacket over tights and Storm's punk fashion. Suddenly, the characters are wearing clothes that reflect more realistic and contemporary fashions.

"If I'm honest, I didn't catch this new design trend until Larry [Houston], Rick [Hoberg], and I were developing the *Pryde of the X-Men* pilot, and the character that caught my eye was Dazzler in her leather jacket ensemble by John Romita Jr.

"The move toward more clothing-like costumes with realistic detailing continued through the late '80s, and when Jim Lee came aboard as the X-Men's main artist, he consolidated the look and added a touch that brought me back to my days as a Silver Age Marvel reader: the Steranko-style belts, packets, and pockets. For the first time in years I was back 'in' as a delighted fan."

Will and director Larry Houston lobbied successfully for using then-current artist Jim Lee's versions of the characters as a base to work from. Our tight animation budget and schedule required a simplicity of line, as well as a varied-but-unified sense of color design. Jim's work had that. Marvel and Fox agreed, and the *X-Men: TAS* team and their signature look were in place. The show's very first design sketches were Will's "roughs" of his favorite X-Men character, Jean Grey (see page 24).

Will explains, "I loved that she was just Jean Grey and didn't have a code name. It just amused me."

We handed out—to all our production colleagues and to prospective writers—a very short, half-complete "show bible," with a page dedicated to each character. Again, X-fan Bob Skir helped us with his take on characters we were just learning.

01 Page 16 from *X-Men* (vol. 1) #1. Written by Stan Lee; pencils by Jack Kirby; inks by Paul Reinman; lettering by Sam Rosen. **02** Page 2 from *X-Men* (vol. 1) #8. Written by Stan Lee; pencils by Kirby; inks by Chic Stone; lettering by Rosen. **03** Cover of *X-Men* (vol. 1) #49. Art by Jim Steranko. **04** Cover of *X-Men* (vol. 1) #50. Art—and a revised X-Men logo design, which debuted with this issue—by Steranko. **05** Cover of *FOOM*—an acronym for "Friends of Ol' Marvel"—(vol. 1) #10. Art by Dave Cockrum. Note that Cockrum picks up Neal Adams's "halo" costume design for Angel at top right. **06** Page 14 (title page for the "Deadly Genesis" story, Chapter 2) from *Giant-Size X-Men* #1. Written by Len Wein; pencils by Cockrum; inks by Cockrum and Peter Iro; colors by Glynis Wein; letters by John Costanza. **07** Panel from page 19 of (by-then-retitled) *Uncanny X-Men* (vol. 1) #173. Written by Chris Claremont; pencils by Paul Smith; inks by Bob Wiacek; colors by Wein; letters by Top Orzechowski. **08** Cover of *Strange Tales* (vol. 1) #167. Art by Steranko. **09** Art by Jim Lee for the cover of *X-Men Annual* (vol. 2) #1. "Remastered" digital colors by Thomas Mason.

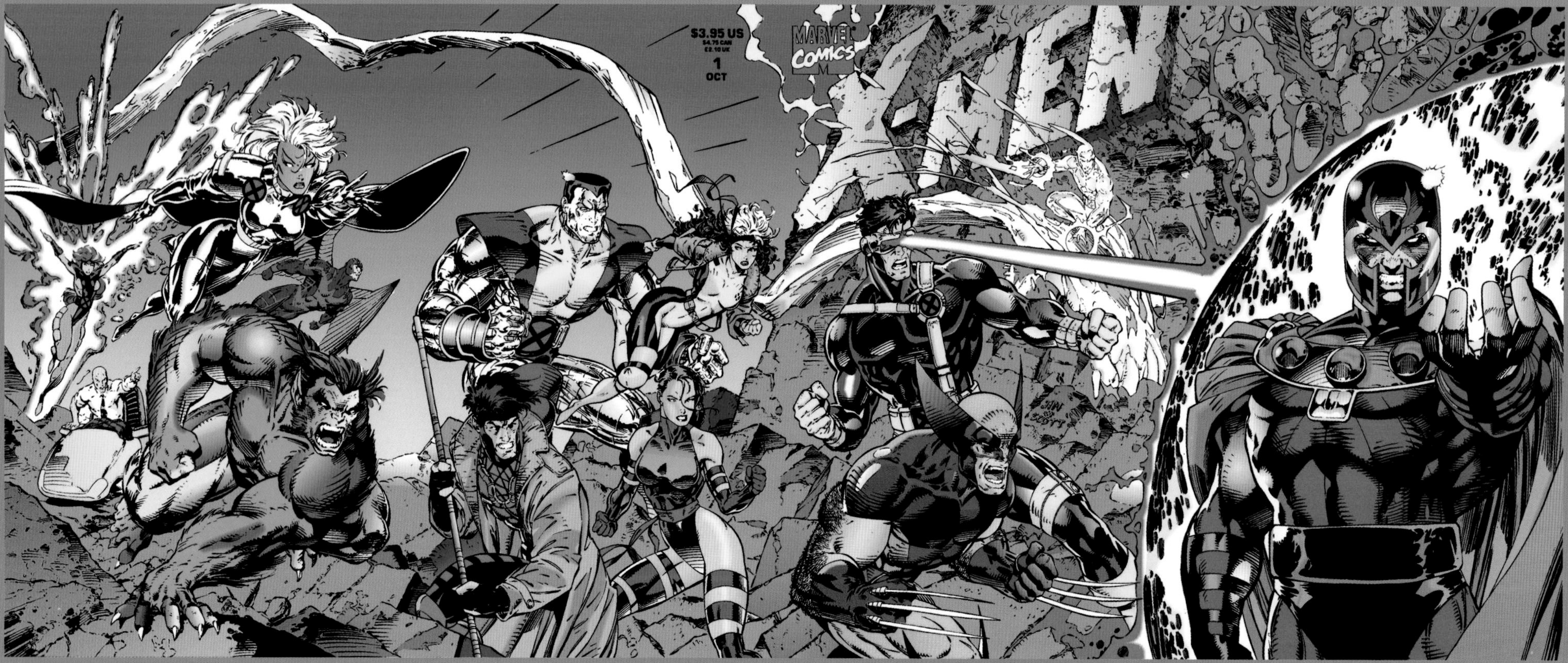
$3.95 US
1
OCT
MARVEL COMICS
X-MEN

01

The Art of Jim Lee

Jim Lee began his professional comics career as a penciler on *Alpha Flight* (vol. 1) #51 (October 1987). Two years later, Lee filled in on *Uncanny X-Men* (vol. 1) #248 for regular series artist Marc Silvestri; Lee then filled in for Silvestri on two other occasions before taking over as the series' ongoing artist with issue #267. Lee's subsequent run of *Uncanny* saw the beginning of his long-running collaboration with inker Scott Williams and also introduced the Lee– and Chris Claremont–created character Gambit.

In 1991, with Claremont and Lee at the reins, Marvel relaunched the X-Men line with *X-Men* vol. 2. Issue #1 was a massive hit and quickly became the best-selling comic book of all time (a record it holds to this day), moving more than eight million copies. For the relaunch, Lee designed new costumes for Cyclops, Jean Grey, Storm, Rogue, and Psylocke, as well as a hoverchair for Professor X. Lee also created the villain Omega Red, who made his first appearance in issue #4. (And while Jubilee was co-created by Claremont and Silvestri, Lee designed her signature *X-Men* vol. 2 and *TAS* look for *Uncanny X-Men* [vol. 1] #257; colorist Glynis Wein later refined Jubilee's costume colors from a red to a pink shirt—and from green to blue shorts, gloves, and boots—for *Uncanny* #271.)

Lee's character designs and overall aesthetic were key inspirations for *X-Men: The Animated Series*, as well as Marvel's X-Men consumer-products style guides from the early to mid-1990s.

01 Gatefold cover ("cover E") of *X-Men* (vol. 2) #1. Art by Jim Lee and Scott Williams. **02** Original art by Lee for the cover of *Advance Comics* #32, the monthly advance-solicitation catalog published by Capital City Distribution. That issue's cover copy encourages readers to "Collect all 5 versions!" of *X-Men* (vol. 2) #1. **03** Cover of *Uncanny X-Men* (vol. 1) #248. Art by Lee (his first *X-Men* issue/cover) and Dan Green. **04** Cover of *X-Men* (vol. 2) #4. Art by Lee and Williams. **05** Cover of *X-Men* (vol. 2) #6. Art by Lee and Art Thibert. **06** Cover of *X-Men* (vol. 2) #8. Art by Lee. **07** Cover of *X-Men* (vol. 2) #11. Art by Lee and Bob Wiacek. Lee departed *X-Men*—and Marvel—with this August 1992 issue, but Lee's five years with the team had already cemented his status as one of the most influential X-Men artists.

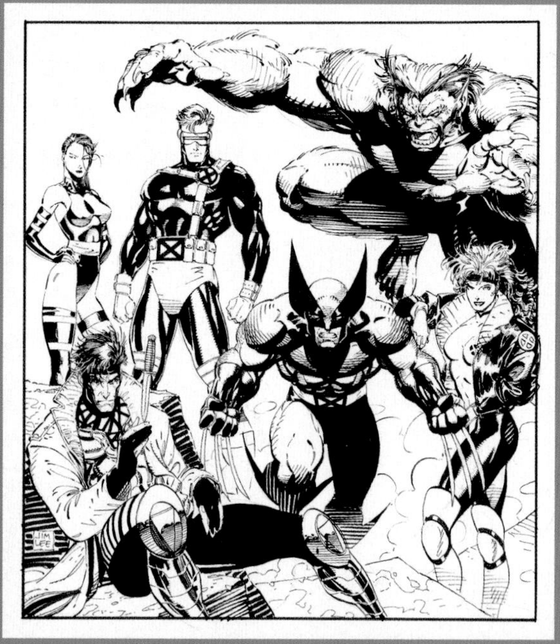

02

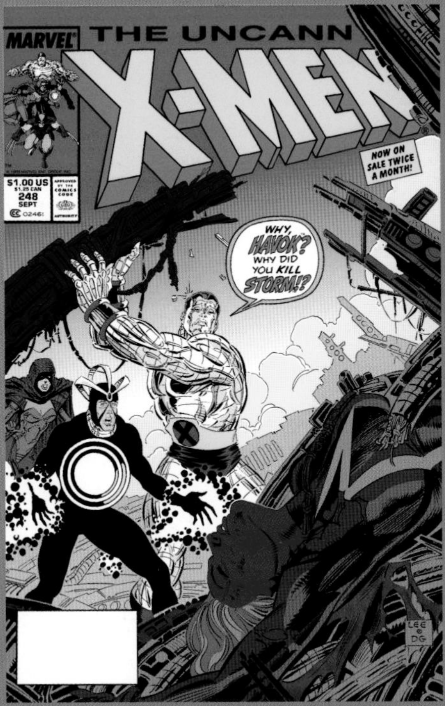
MARVEL
THE UNCANN
X-MEN
$1.00 US
248
SEPT
NOW ON SALE TWICE A MONTH!
WHY, HAVOK? WHY DID YOU KILL STORM!?

03

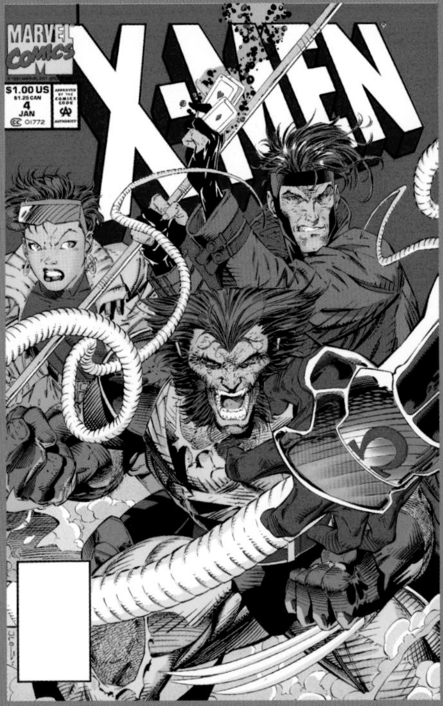
MARVEL COMICS
$1.00 US
4
JAN
X-MEN

04

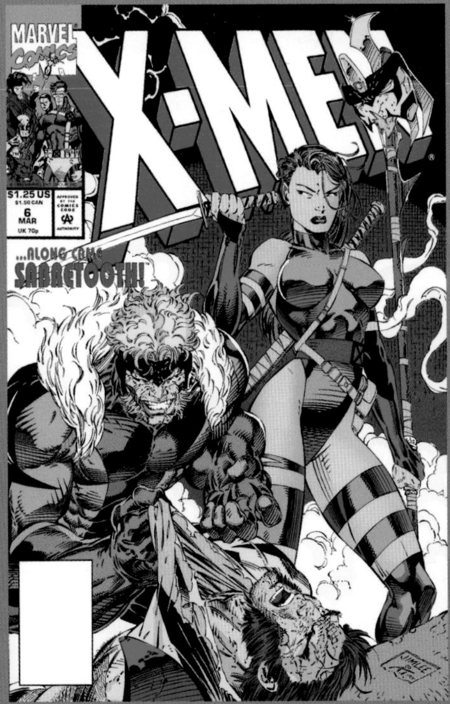
MARVEL COMICS
X-MEN
$1.25 US
6
MAR
SABRETOOTH!

05

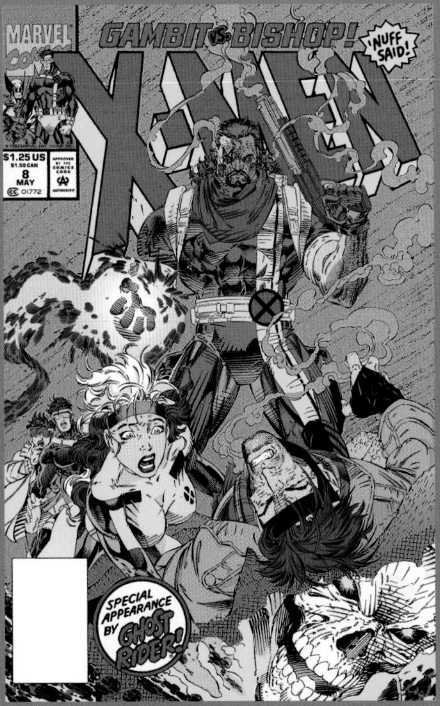
MARVEL COMICS
GAMBIT & BISHOP!
'NUFF SAID!
X-MEN
$1.25 US
8
MAY
SPECIAL APPEARANCE BY GHOST RIDER!

06

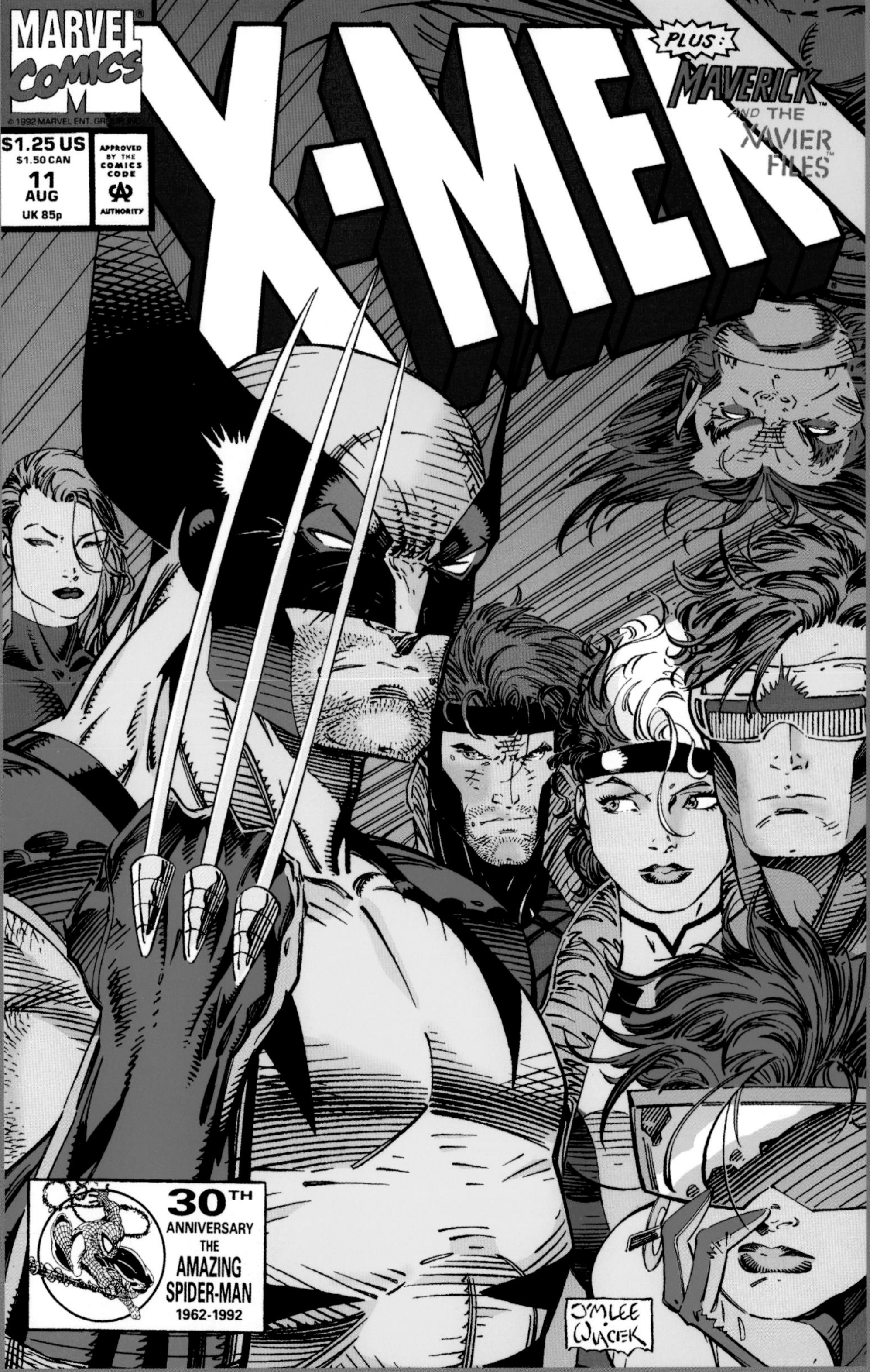
MARVEL COMICS
© 1992 MARVEL ENT. GROUP, INC.
$1.25 US
$1.50 CAN
11
AUG
UK 85p
APPROVED BY THE COMICS CODE AUTHORITY
X-MEN
PLUS:
MAVERICK
AND THE
XAVIER FILES
30TH ANNIVERSARY
THE AMAZING SPIDER-MAN
1962-1992
JIM LEE
WILLIAMS

07

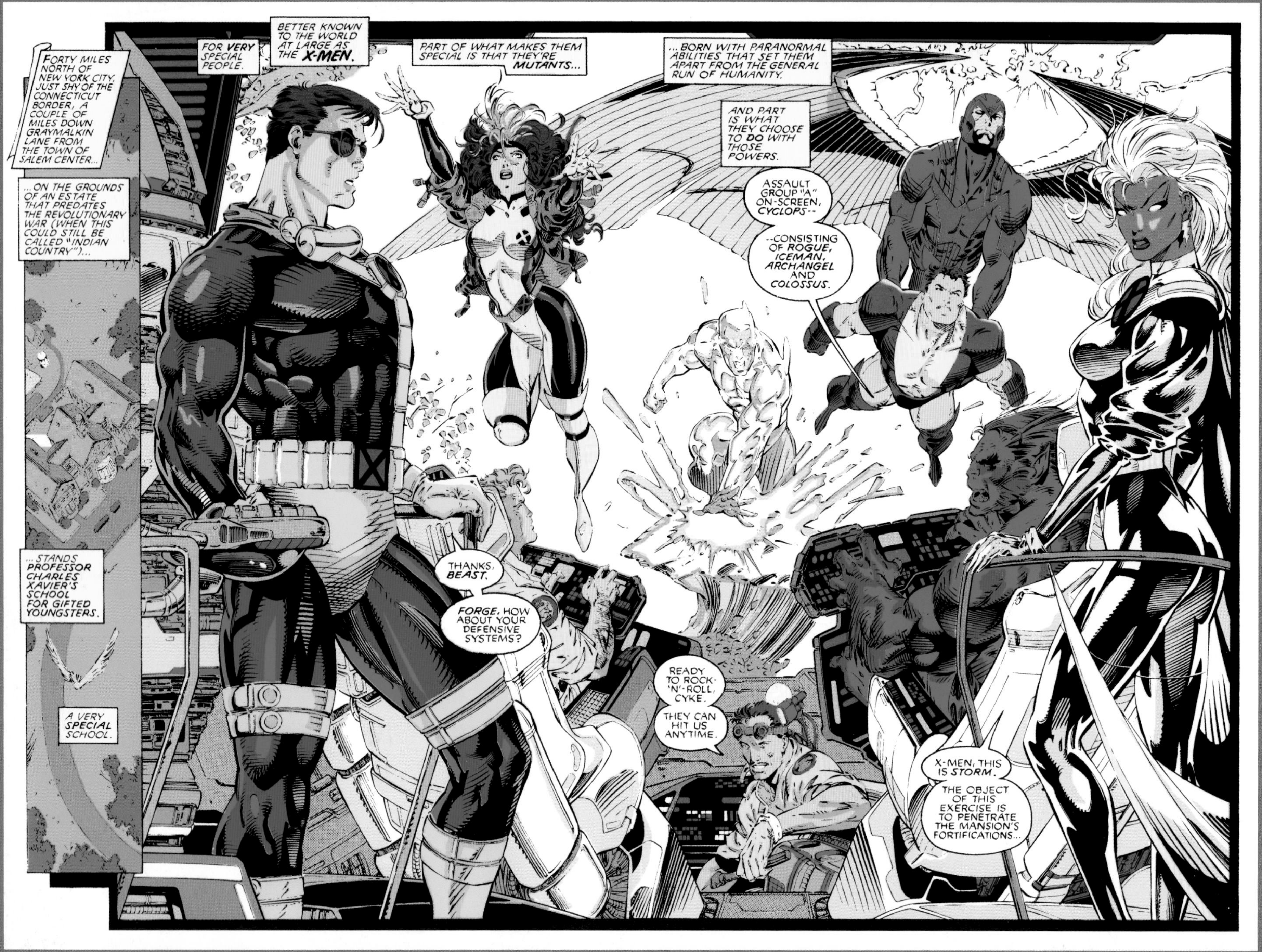
FORTY MILES NORTH OF NEW YORK CITY, JUST SHY OF THE CONNECTICUT BORDER, A COUPLE OF MILES DOWN GRAYMALKIN LANE FROM THE TOWN OF SALEM CENTER...
FOR VERY SPECIAL PEOPLE.
BETTER KNOWN TO THE WORLD AT LARGE AS THE X-MEN.
PART OF WHAT MAKES THEM SPECIAL IS THAT THEY'RE MUTANTS...
...BORN WITH PARANORMAL ABILITIES THAT SET THEM APART FROM THE GENERAL RUN OF HUMANITY.
AND PART IS WHAT THEY CHOOSE TO DO WITH THOSE POWERS.
...ON THE GROUNDS OF AN ESTATE THAT PREDATES THE REVOLUTIONARY WAR (WHEN THIS COULD STILL BE CALLED "INDIAN COUNTRY")...
ASSAULT GROUP "A" ON-SCREEN, CYCLOPS--
--CONSISTING OF ROGUE, ICEMAN, ARCHANGEL AND COLOSSUS.
...STANDS PROFESSOR CHARLES XAVIER'S SCHOOL FOR GIFTED YOUNGSTERS.
THANKS, BEAST.
FORGE, HOW ABOUT YOUR DEFENSIVE SYSTEMS?
READY TO ROCK-'N'-ROLL, CYKE.
THEY CAN HIT US ANYTIME.
A VERY SPECIAL SCHOOL.
X-MEN, THIS IS STORM.
THE OBJECT OF THIS EXERCISE IS TO PENETRATE THE MANSION'S FORTIFICATIONS...

01

01 Pages 6 and 7 from *X-Men* (vol. 2) #1. Co-written by Chris Claremont and Jim Lee; pencils by Jim Lee; inks by Scott Williams; colors by Joe Rosas; letters by Tom Orzechowski. **02** Pages 14 and 15 from *X-Men* (vol. 2) #11. **03** In 1992, Impel Marketing (later renamed SkyBox International before shuttering in 1995) published a series of one hundred Jim Lee–drawn X-Men trading cards. Each card back features a "Cerebro scan" that gives a brief character bio as well as the character's power level. Jean Grey appeared on card #24 in the set; her card back reveals that her "mental powers" power level sits at 6 out of a possible 7.

04 Pages 38 and 39 from *X-Men* (vol. 2) #1. **05** The inside of *X-Men* (vol. 2) #1's gatefold/"E" cover served double duty as a pull-out poster/pin-up. Art by Lee and Williams.

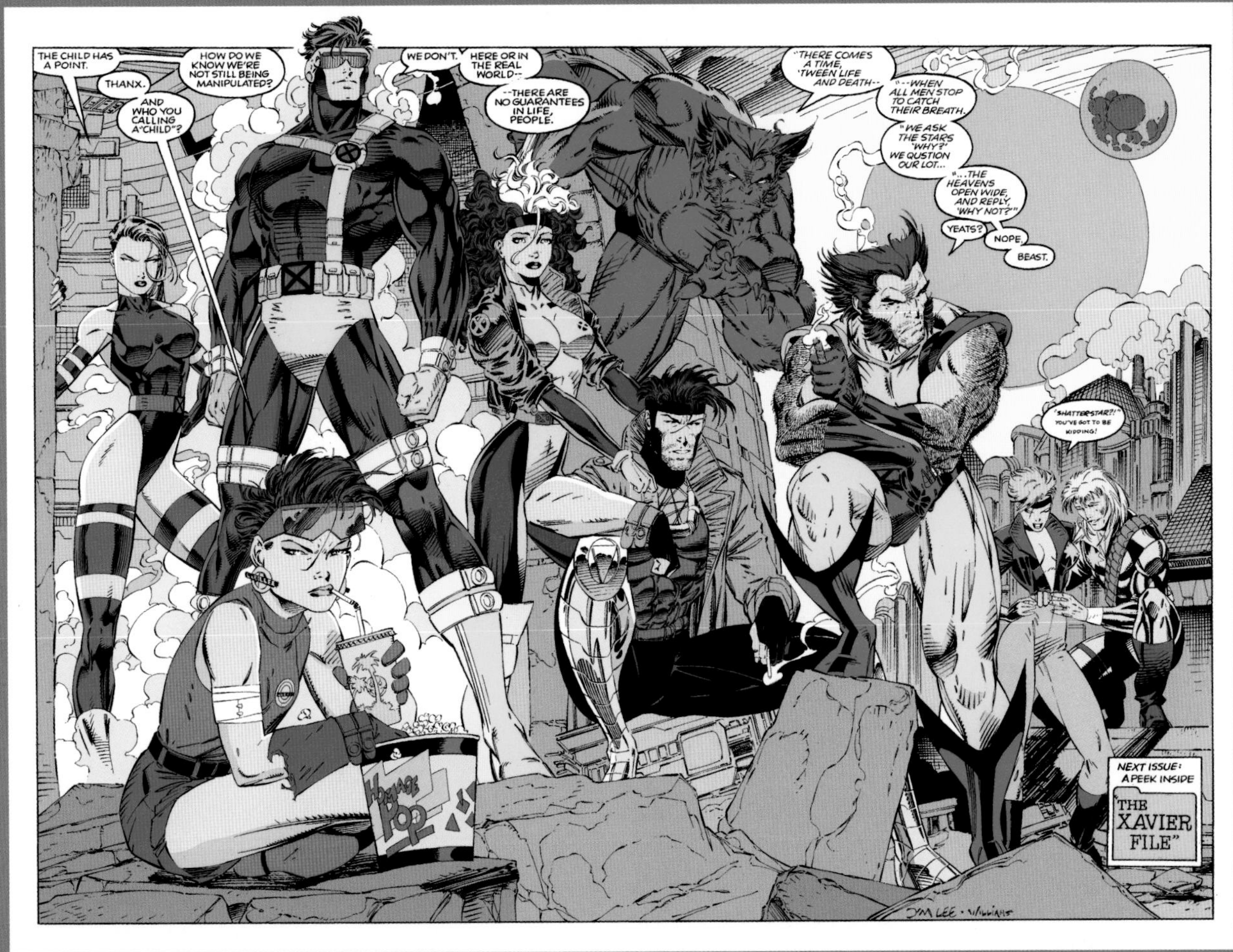
THE CHILD HAS A POINT.
THANX.
AND WHO YOU CALLING A "CHILD"?
HOW DO WE KNOW WE'RE NOT STILL BEING MANIPULATED?
WE DON'T.
HERE OR IN THE REAL WORLD--
--THERE ARE NO GUARANTEES IN LIFE, PEOPLE.
"THERE COMES A TIME, 'TWEEN LIFE AND DEATH--
"--WHEN ALL MEN STOP TO CATCH THEIR BREATH.
"WE ASK THE STARS 'WHY?' WE QUSTION OUR LOT...
"...THE HEAVENS OPEN WIDE, AND REPLY, 'WHY NOT?'"
YEATS?
NOPE,
BEAST.
"SHATTERSTAR?!" YOU'VE GOT TO BE KIDDING!
NEXT ISSUE: A PEEK INSIDE "THE XAVIER FILE"
JIM LEE • WILLIAMS

02

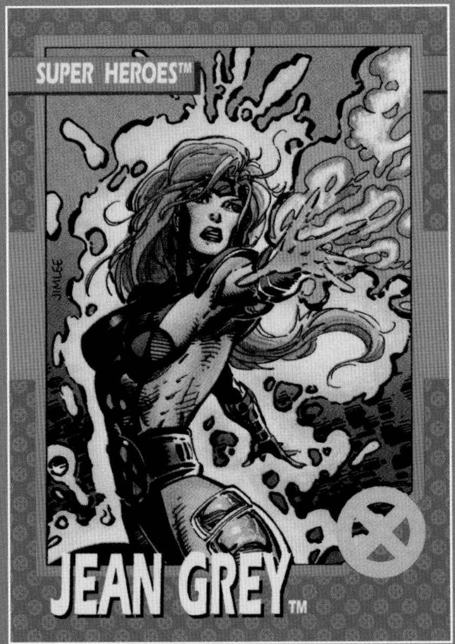
SUPER HEROES™
JIM LEE
JEAN GREY™

03

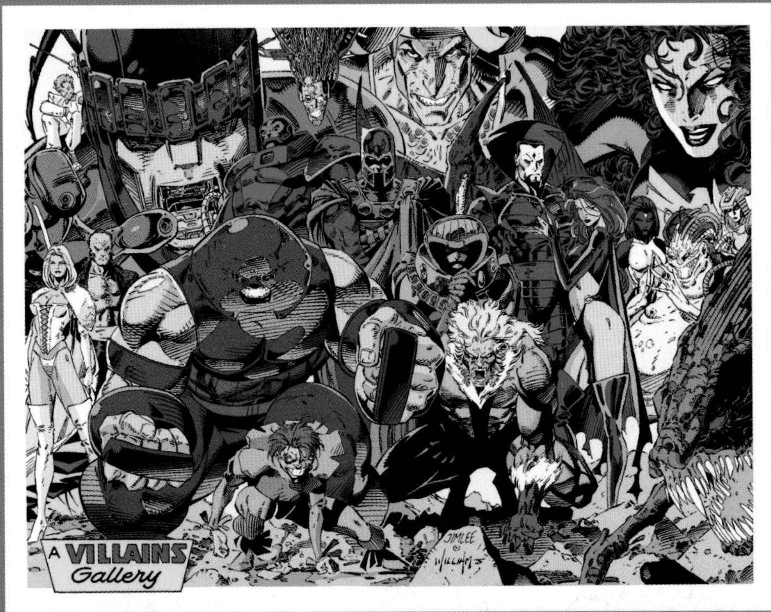
A VILLAINS Gallery
JIM LEE
WILLIAMS

04

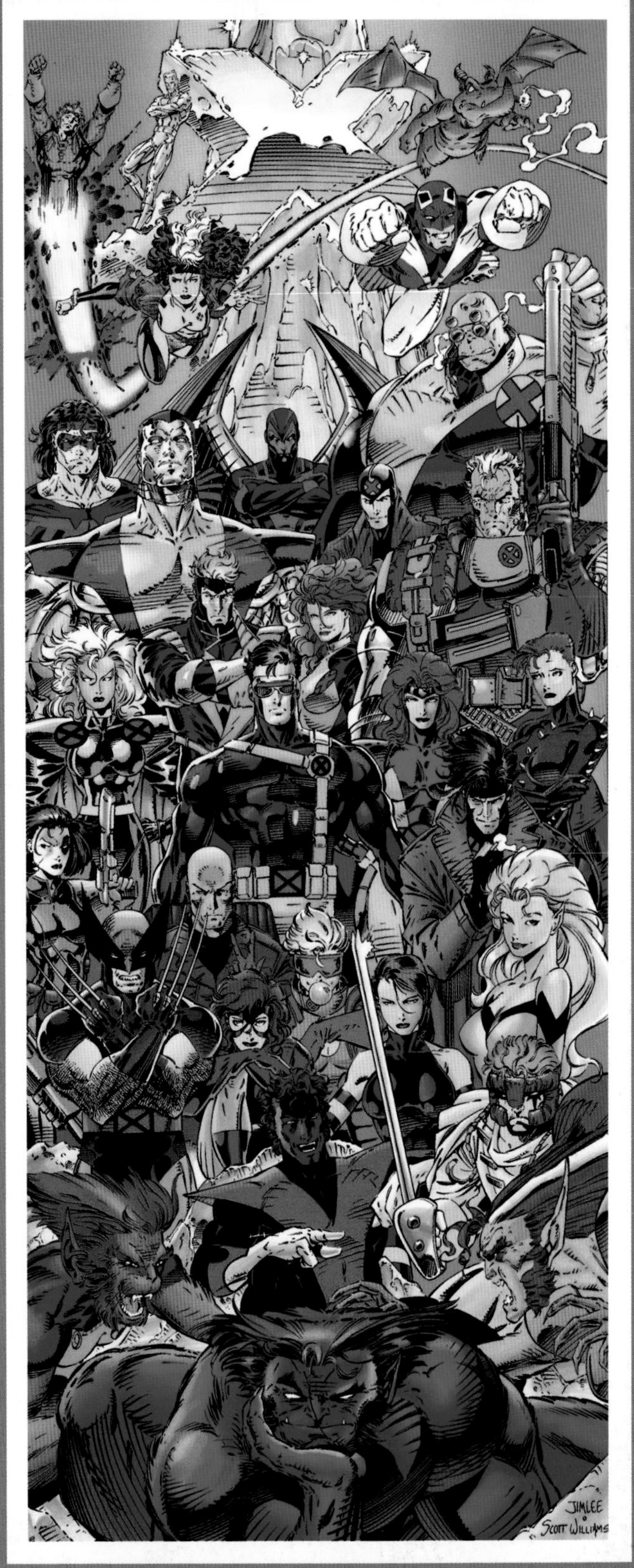
JIM LEE
SCOTT WILLIAMS

05

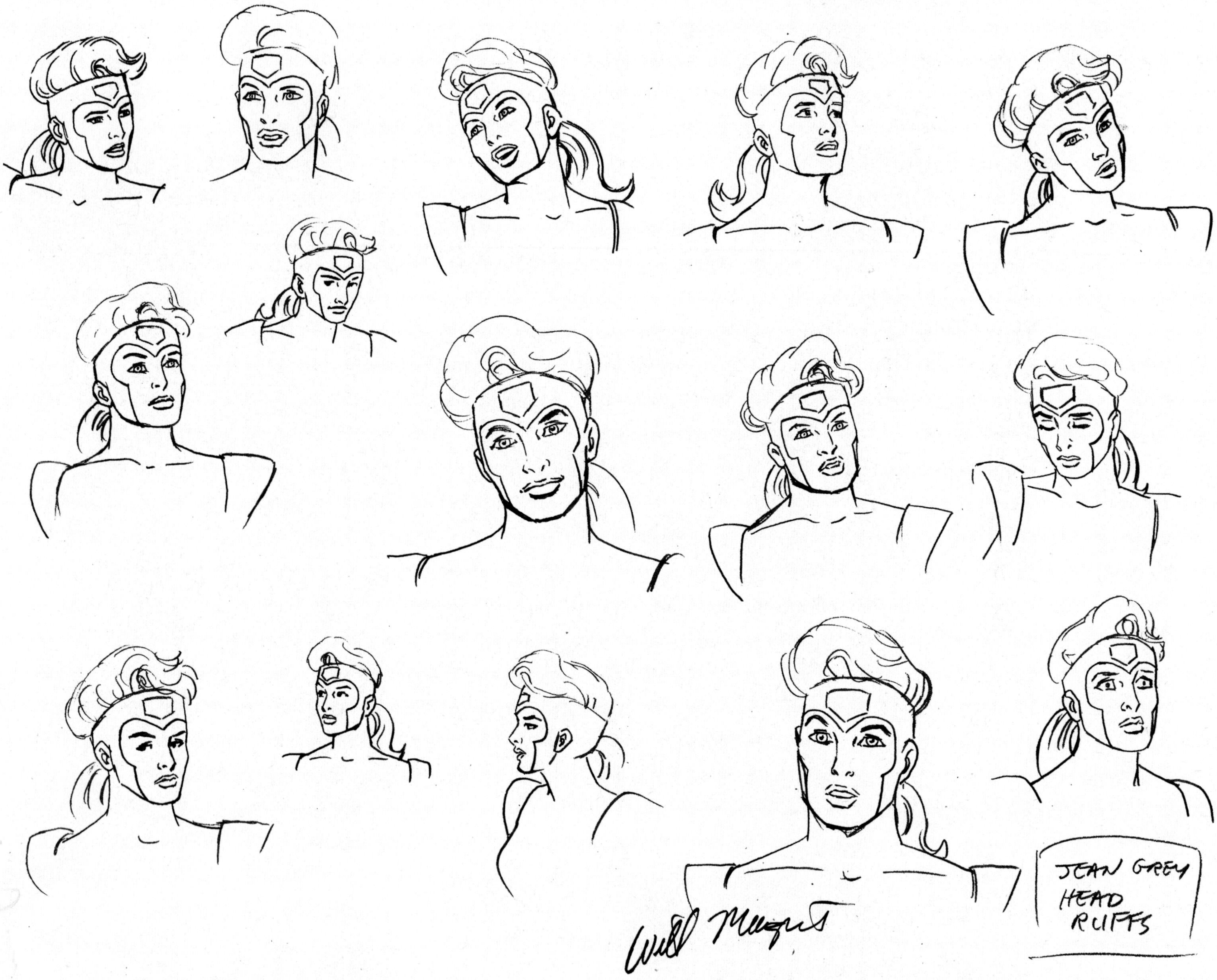
JEAN GREY
HEAD
RUFFS

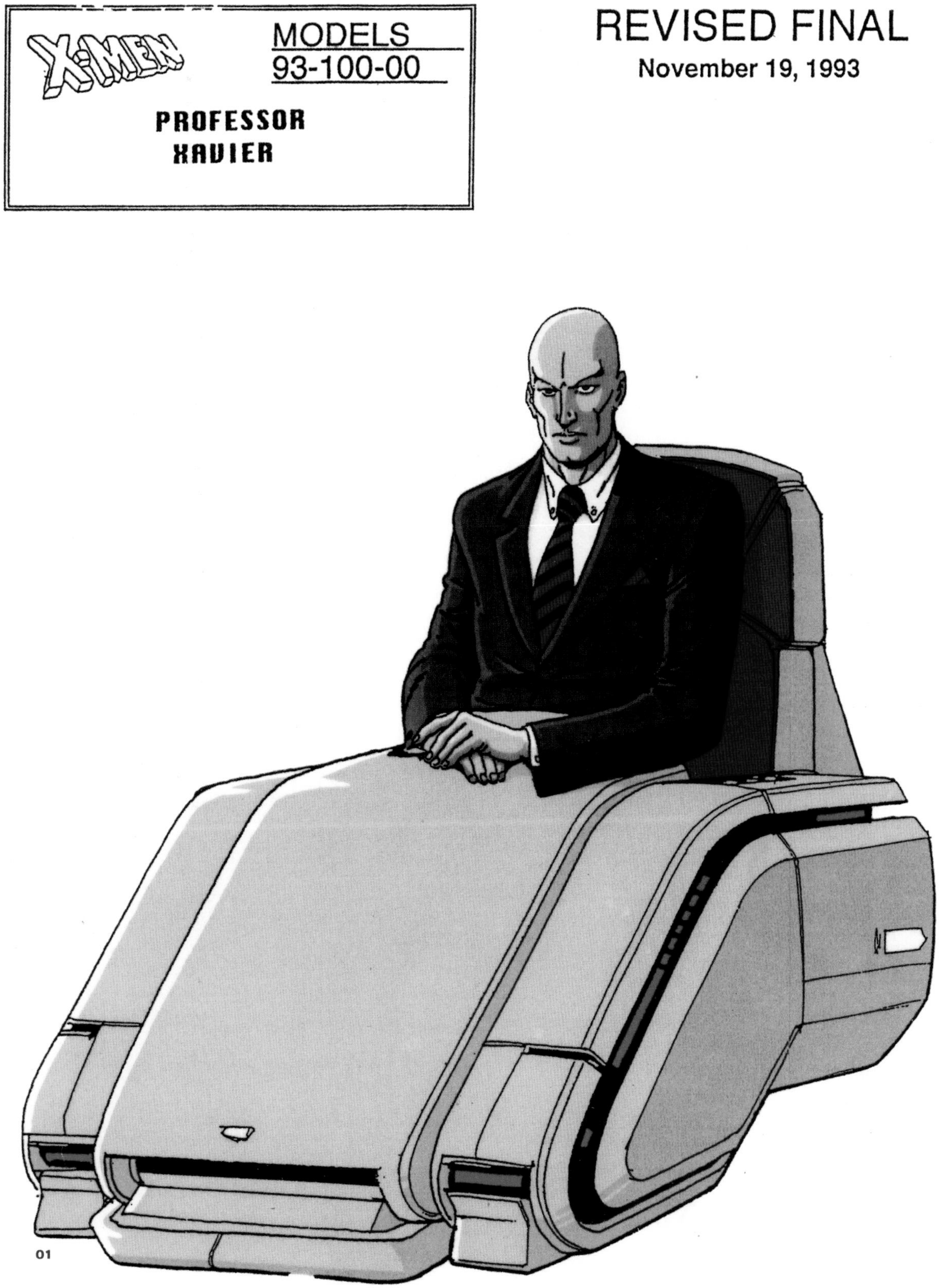
X-MEN
MODELS
93-100-00
PROFESSOR XAVIER
REVISED FINAL
November 19, 1993

01

PROFESSOR CHARLES XAVIER

Professor Xavier is creator of the X-Men team, tactical and moral teacher to its members, and guardian of the vision of Mutant-human harmony that gives the team its reason to exist.

An American in his mid-fifties, Xavier is a brilliant scientist and one of Earth's first known Mutants. His Mutant superpowers are mental. Xavier can probe people's minds and will often communicate to his students, the X-Men, telepathically. He uses his super-computer, CEREBRO, as a mental amplifier and to locate and track other Mutants he can train and add to the X-Men roster.

Wheelchair-bound Xavier is fiercely dedicated to his vision of a tolerant world and to the students he has trained to help achieve it. He can seem like a meddling parent sometimes to many of the young adult superbeings he has trained, but most have come to realize the importance of his continued guidance.

Xavier is often cut off from the X-Men during their great battles. They call for advice, train, and commiserate with Xavier, but in battle, they usually have to fend for themselves. Like a loving, concerned parent, Xavier is torn between wanting to help and protect his "children," and hoping that they can learn to be strong and independent enough to handle the world on their own.

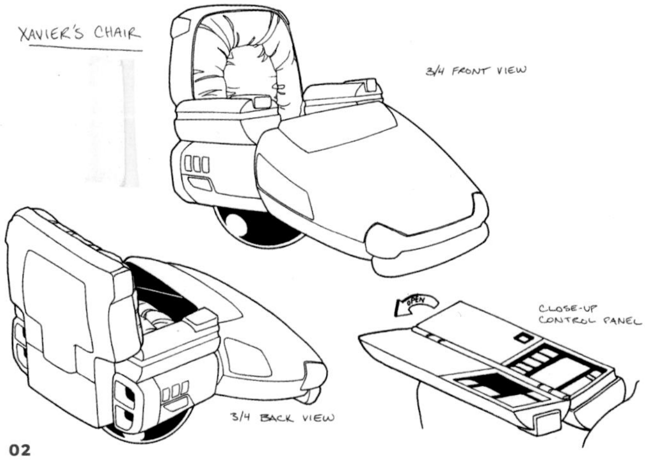
XAVIER'S CHAIR
3/4 FRONT VIEW
CLOSE-UP CONTROL PANEL
3/4 BACK VIEW

02

OPPOSITE Will Meugniot's first designs for *X-Men: TAS*: Jean Grey head poses. **01** Final color character model, first season, for Professor Xavier, drawn by Rick Hoberg. **02** Later prop models of details of Xavier's hoverchair, drawn by Marcos Borregales.

CYCLOPS (SCOTT)

Cyclops was born Scott Summers. He is a 26-year-old American. He was Xavier's first X-Man and is their leader in the field. Unless covered by a visor or glasses, his eyes, when opened will shoot out a horribly destructive "optic energy beam." More than other Mutants, he must work to control his superpower.

Scott is a true rule follower, a lieutenant who goes strictly by the book. For Cyclops there's a right way and a wrong way of doing things. His major fear is letting Xavier down. He was an orphan, and Xavier found and trained him. The burden of command, of having the life and death of Xavier's Dream resting on his shoulders, is a heavy one. He takes his job seriously, perhaps too seriously. Scott's rigidity can get him in trouble, but occasionally he finds a way to transcend it.

Scott knows Jean Grey is in love with him. He loves her, too, but doesn't want his feelings to interfere with his need to be the leader of the X-Men.

Scott resents rebellious Wolverine, the bane of his existence. Wolverine's a loose cannon, one he must live with but cannot control. Scott has no idea that Wolverine secretly respects him; this revelation would probably bowl him over.

Cyclops, more even than Professor X, personifies what this group is all about—community. He is always telling the X-Men to stay in ranks and to work together. The highest compliment you're likely to get from him is, "Good teamwork!"

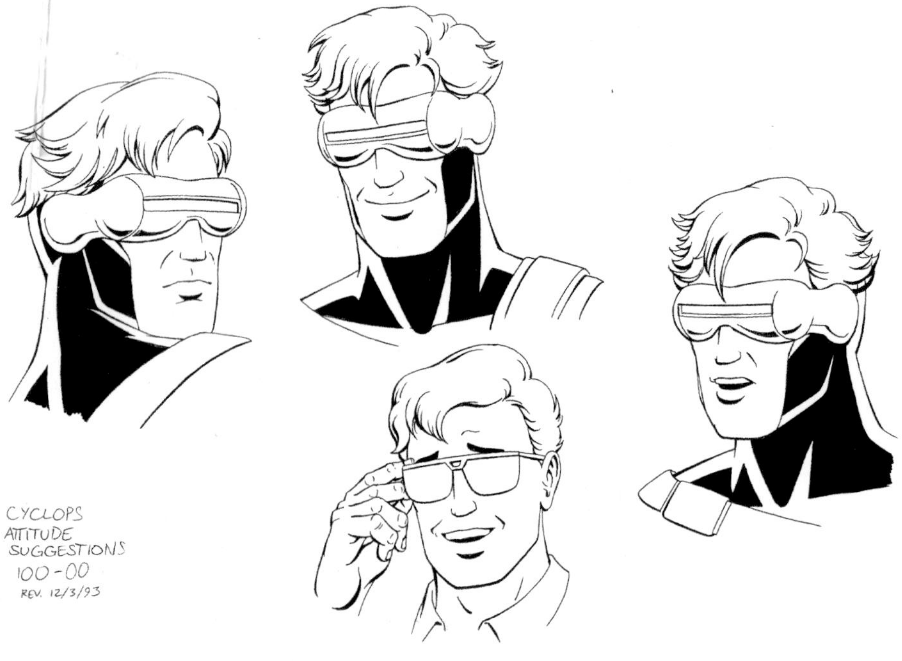
CYCLOPS
ATTITUDE
SUGGESTIONS
100-00
REV. 12/3/93

01

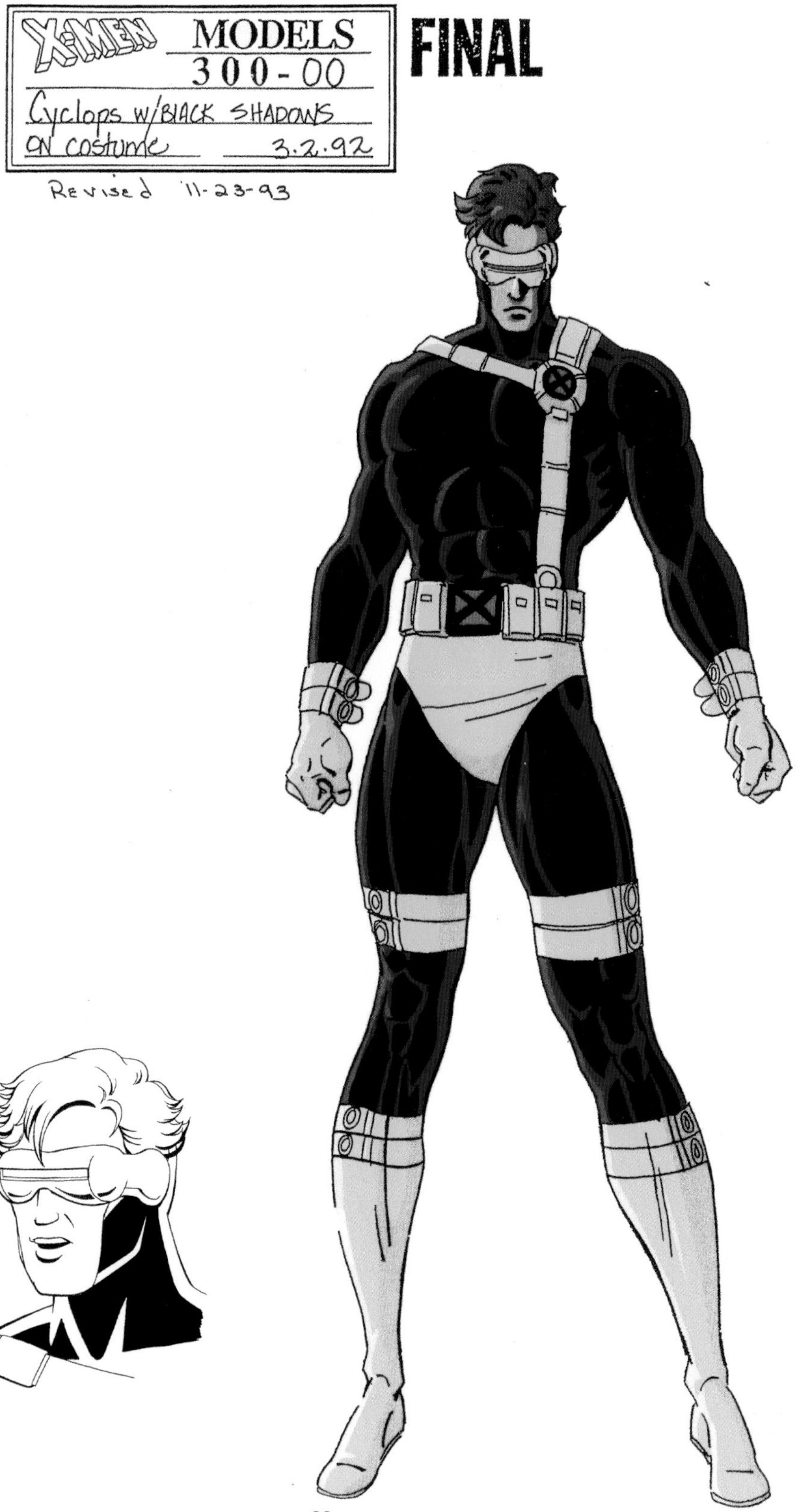
X-MEN
MODELS
300-00
Cyclops w/BLACK SHADOWS
ON costume
3.2.92
Revised 11-23-93
FINAL

02

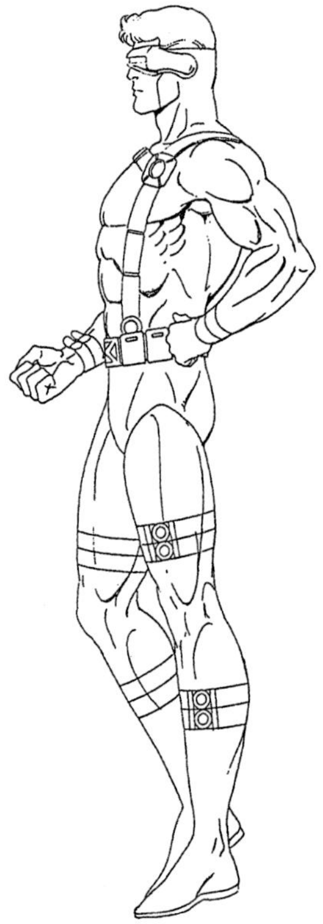

03

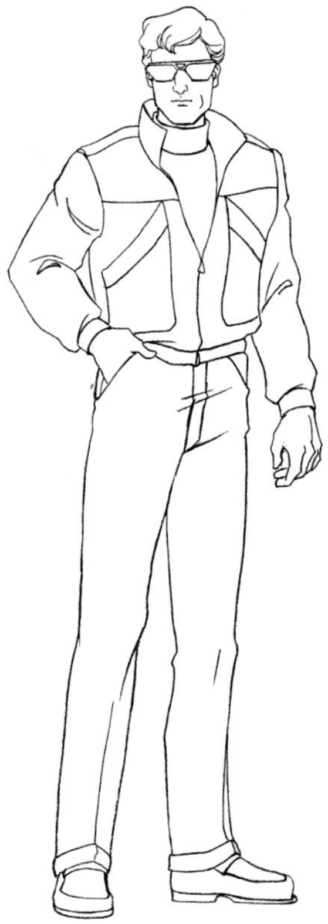

04

X-MEN MODELS
300-00
Wolverine
4.7.92
REV 3/14-3/22
FINAL

05

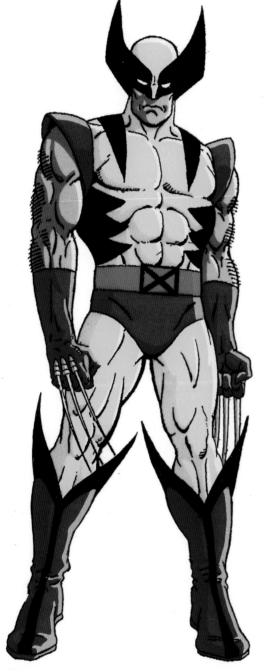

WOLVERINE (LOGAN)

Wolverine is Canadian—down to earth, no nonsense. He looks to be in his thirties, but actually was born in 1900. His incredible Mutant healing powers keep him young and repair him quickly after injury. His senses, especially smell, are hyper-keen. He is gruff, emotional, rebellious, and takes no grief from anybody. He is by far the comic book series's most popular character.

Wolverine's skeleton was replaced by one made of a super strong metal (Adamantium), which helps him withstand punishment. But his most compelling weapons are his massive retractable claws, made of the same material, which "can slice through anything."

Wolverine tends to be a brooding loner who others take to be unreliable, vicious, and primitive, but who is actually thoughtful and fiercely loyal. The model artists and writers have used in the past for Wolverine is the Clint Eastwood of the "Dirty Harry" movies. This is a good reference for the terseness of his dialogue, and his ability to be relentless and merciless. But Wolverine is far more volatile, emotional, and uncontrollable than Dirty Harry.

His real name is Logan. He's traveled the world and seen it all. He has worked for the CIA, the Canadian Special Forces (from which he escaped/went AWOL to join the X-Men). He's fought many battles and has lots of enemies and former lovers.

Wolverine has a terrible temper and is merciless in combat. Forget fair play. He is cunning and violent. But he has a great sense of honor. This means if he owes his life to somebody, he will gladly lay it down for them.

Logan loves to ride Scott/Cyclops simply because Scott's in charge. He respects Scott but would never let him actually know it. He disrespects Scott for not taking more initiative, not breaking more rules, and for taking so many orders from Xavier instead of thinking for himself.

Wolverine respects no one until they have proved themselves in battle. But even a 13-year-old like Jubilee will receive his loyalty once she has earned it. In fact Logan feels older-brother protective toward Jubilee, and genuinely likes her. But if she makes one mistake or steps out of line, he'll certainly let her know!

06

07

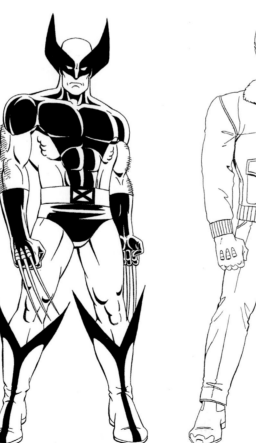

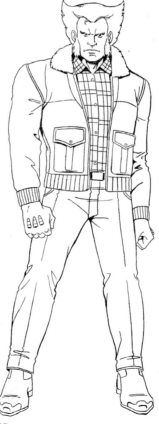

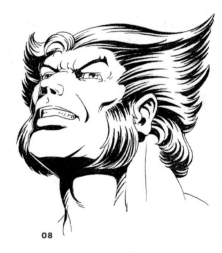

08

01 Cyclops attitude suggestions—four head poses—drawn for the second season by Frank Brunner, inked by Mark Lewis. **02** Revised (11/23/93) Cyclops color character model, in uniform, for the second season. "Black-spotting" added to original design by Lewis. **03-04** Cyclops character model, in uniform, left side view, then in civilian clothes—with required sunglasses—both by Rick Hoberg. **05** Wolverine color character model, in uniform (revised 3/93), by Hoberg. **06** Wolverine early character model, in uniform, by Lewis. **07** Wolverine character model, in civilian clothes (Logan), by Hoberg. **08** Wolverine (Logan) attitude suggestion, second season, by Brunner.

STORM (ORORO)

Storm, known also as Ororo, is African. Her great Mutant power is that she has control over the elements. Like Cyclops, she has a difficult time controlling her power, so she's emotionally restrained. Storm is dignified, elegant, almost regal. She loves nature; her room at the school is an atrium. Alone there, she creates small storms to water the plants and to cut loose (for her it's liberating, like dancing).

When she was a child, her parents were killed in Cairo when a bombed building collapsed around them, leaving her buried in rubble. The incident left her horribly claustrophobic.

Orphaned, she grew up in the streets of northern Africa, where she was an ace pickpocket. This is a portion of her past she's not ashamed of—she did what was necessary to survive.

Storm is everything Wolverine is not—dignified, respectful of life, serene. He thinks she should let the storm inside go free. She thinks he should tame his animal passions.

When the team splits apart, Storm tends to lead the section Cyclops is not in. Don't let her serenity fool you—she's a fierce leader. And when Wolverine's on her team, she won't let him step out of line.

Storm adores Jubilee, her newfound younger sister.

Storm can create any weather system the local environment will permit. She can create a snow-storm if in New York (but not in the Sahara). She "flies" on self-created air currents. In space, she's virtually powerless. She's very strong, and her senses (like her eyesight) are nearly as keen as Wolverine's.

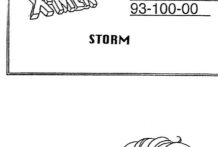

MODELS
93-100-00

STORM

REVISED FINAL
December 3, 1993

THE BLACK AREAS ARE SHADOWS. AS THE LIGHT SOURCE CHANGES, THE SHADOWS SHOULD CHANGE ACCORDINGLY. SHADOWS ARE PROVIDED AS REFERENCE ON SELECTED MODELS; BUT SHADING ON ALL CHARACTERS SHOULD BE CONSISTENT DURING ANIMATION.

03

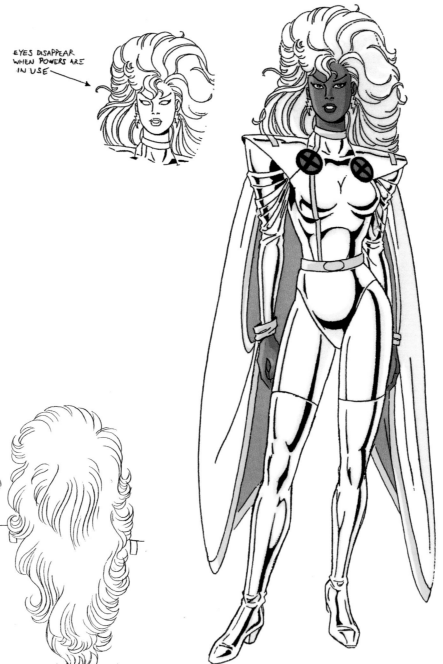

EYES DISAPPEAR WHEN POWERS ARE IN USE

02

04

01

X-MEN

MODELS
93-100-00

ROGUE

REVISED FINAL
December 3, 1993

THE BLACK AREAS ARE <u>SHADOWS</u>. AS THE LIGHT
SOURCE CHANGES, THE SHADOWS SHOULD CHANGE
ACCORDINGLY.   SHADOWS ARE PROVIDED AS
REFERENCE ON SELECTED MODELS; BUT SHADING ON
<u>ALL</u> CHARACTERS SHOULD BE CONSISTENT DURING
ANIMATION.

X-MEN

MODELS
300-00

Gambit

Rev. 4.8.92

3/14 - 3/18

FINAL

ROGUE

Rogue is a good ol' Southern gal in her mid-twenties. Her special Mutant power enables her to
absorb other people's powers just by touching
them. This also renders them unconscious, and
with continued exposure can permanently take
their consciousness away. She is invulnerable and
can fly, both powers she absorbed from others.
The mind/memories of others can occasionally
emerge, running around in her head, co-existing
with her own mind.

Rogue can't turn this power off and on. This
means that, to her great sadness, she cannot
touch other people, lest she steal them away.
Even a kiss is too dangerous to risk.

Rogue was on her own until discovered by the
leader of the New Brotherhood of Evil Mutants,
MYSTIQUE. She raised Rogue like a daughter, and
there is a close bond between them. Rogue left
Mystique as a matter of rebellion, the need to be
her own person and grow away from her surrogate
mother. So she sought out the X-Men, who (mostly
grudgingly) accepted her onto the team. Getting
the full trust of the X-Men, especially Wolverine,
is going to be tough.

GAMBIT

Not much is known about Gambit. He's in his
mid-twenties, Cajun, and he appeared virtually
out of nowhere one day and saved Storm's life.
A thief and a gambler, he keeps his past to
himself.

Gambit is the first X-Man anyone would suspect
of duplicity or shady dealing. He may be corrupt,
loaded with hidden agendas. Also, he's a lady-
killer. Even women who know better seem to be at
his mercy. (It's almost another Mutant power.)

His actual Mutant power is the ability to
charge small objects with kinetic energy until
they explode. Small darts or playing cards thus
become explosive devices in his hands. Who knows
how big an object he can get to blow up? We'll see.

Gambit is a crafty, circumspect loner. No one
on the team is close to him. He seems to come
through when the chips are down, but somehow, no
one is sure about him. . . .

01 Storm head designs—front, left profile, back—by Rick Hoberg and
Will Meugniot. **02** Storm color character model, in uniform (revised
12/3/93), by Larry Houston and Hoberg. **03–04** Storm character
models in civilian clothes by Hoberg. **05** Rogue color character
model, in uniform (revised 12/3/93), by Hoberg. **06** Gambit color
character model, in uniform (revised 3/92), by Hoberg.

05

06

MODELS
93-100-00

BEAST

REVISED FINAL
November 19, 1993

02

01

THE BEAST (DR. HANK MCCOY)

Beast, also known as Henry (Hank) McCoy is an American in his late twenties. Contrary to his furry, animalistic appearance, Beast is the intellectual and scholar of the team. A brilliant scientist (specialty: Chemistry), Beast is literate, urbane, and has a dry, well-developed sense of humor.

Beast speaks fluent Russian—and probably any other language you need him to—and is nonchalant about his intellect. He never condescends to the other X-Men and seems about as well adjusted and wise as a Mutant can be.

Beast is called on to deal with higher technology that might baffle the others. In battle, he has the agility of a jungle cat.

MODELS
93-100-00

JUBILEE

REVISED FINAL
November 19, 1993

MODELS
93-100-00

JEAN GREY

REVISED FINAL
November 19, 1993

EYE DETAIL

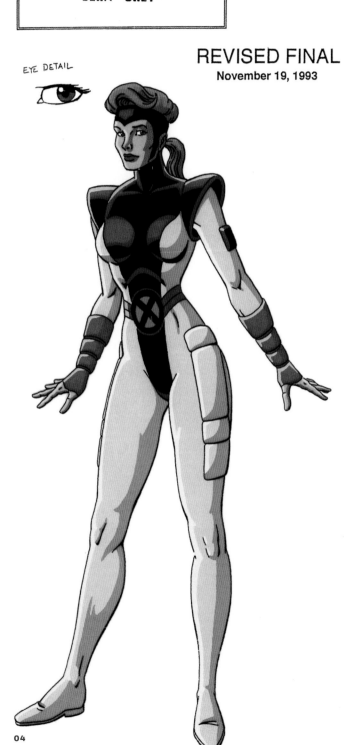

03

04

JUBILEE

Jubilee is 13, a part-Asian California teen and total shopping mall zombie. In the comic books, she was created to be Wolverine's "Robin," a lighthearted, irrepressible, vivacious counterpoint to his dark, angry moods.

She's cocky and has a smart mouth. She wants to be taken seriously, but when you're surrounded by such impressive heroes who've been through so many battles together, it's often hard just to get their attention. But she has self-confidence in spades. She'll show 'em.

New recruit Jubilee's training sessions with Professor Xavier are going to be great. Jubilee knows all the answers. What does she need with authority figures telling her what to do?

Her Mutant power is the ability to create small explosions. The effects are not that different from Gambit, so we will probably avoid using them as a fighting team.

As our token adolescent among seasoned adults, Jubilee may inherit some elements from stories featuring former 13-year-old X-Man Kitty Pryde.

JEAN GREY

Jean is an American in her mid-twenties. A founding member of the group, she has now faded a bit into the background.

She's deeply, truly in love with Scott Summers. He's too wrapped in responsibility to allow such feelings to distract from his leadership responsibilities. He turns these feelings off, much to her anguish.

Her powers were originally telekinetic, allowing her to move objects merely by thinking about it. She is now also telepathic.

Wolverine has a crush on Jean, which she doesn't reciprocate. She has grown to like Wolverine but could never love him.

(Note: Morph was not part of these initial descriptions because he hadn't been chosen yet.)

01 Beast color character model, in uniform (revised 11/19/93), by Will Meugniot and Rick Hoberg. **02** Beast attitude suggestions, four head poses, by Frank Brunner. **03** Jubilee color character model, in uniform (revised 11/19/93), by Meugniot and Hoberg. **04** Jean Grey color character model, in uniform (revised 11/19/93), by Meugniot and Hoberg, revised by Mark Lewis.

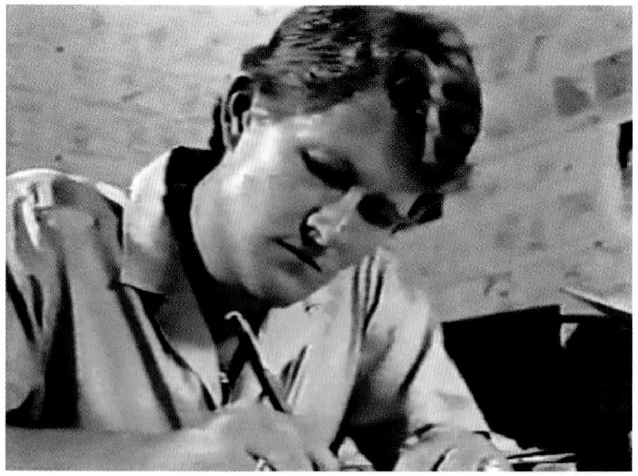

01

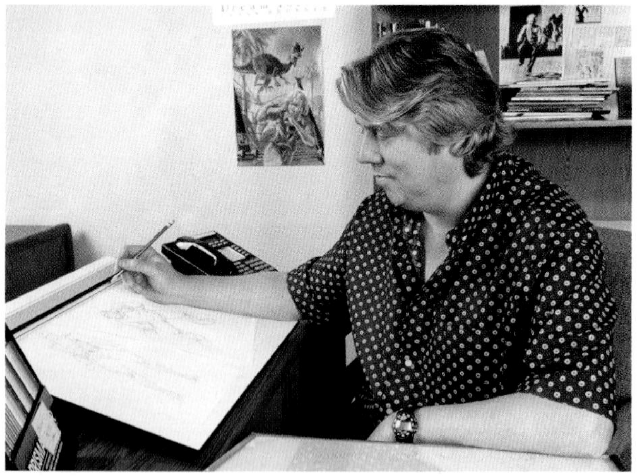

02

FOR HELP WITH THE INITIAL DESIGNS, supervising producer Will Meugniot had many of his favorite artists on board. There was producer/director Larry Houston, of course—who would direct our first sixty-five storyboards—and Rick Hoberg, both of whom had worked with Will on *Pryde of the X-Men*. Will had known them both for most of his career.

Will says, "Rick and I started our careers on the same day at Hanna-Barbera in 1978. We shared an art and comics background and enjoyed a kind of creative shorthand between us."

Animation model designer and comics artist Frank Brunner rounded out a veteran design crew.

Together, these four gave the characters and their world the look we all know and love.

01 Designer Rick Hoberg at work. **02** Designer Frank Brunner at work. **RIGHT** First-season main characters size-comparison lineup. Primarily the work of Hoberg, with supervision by Will Meugniot and work by Larry Houston.

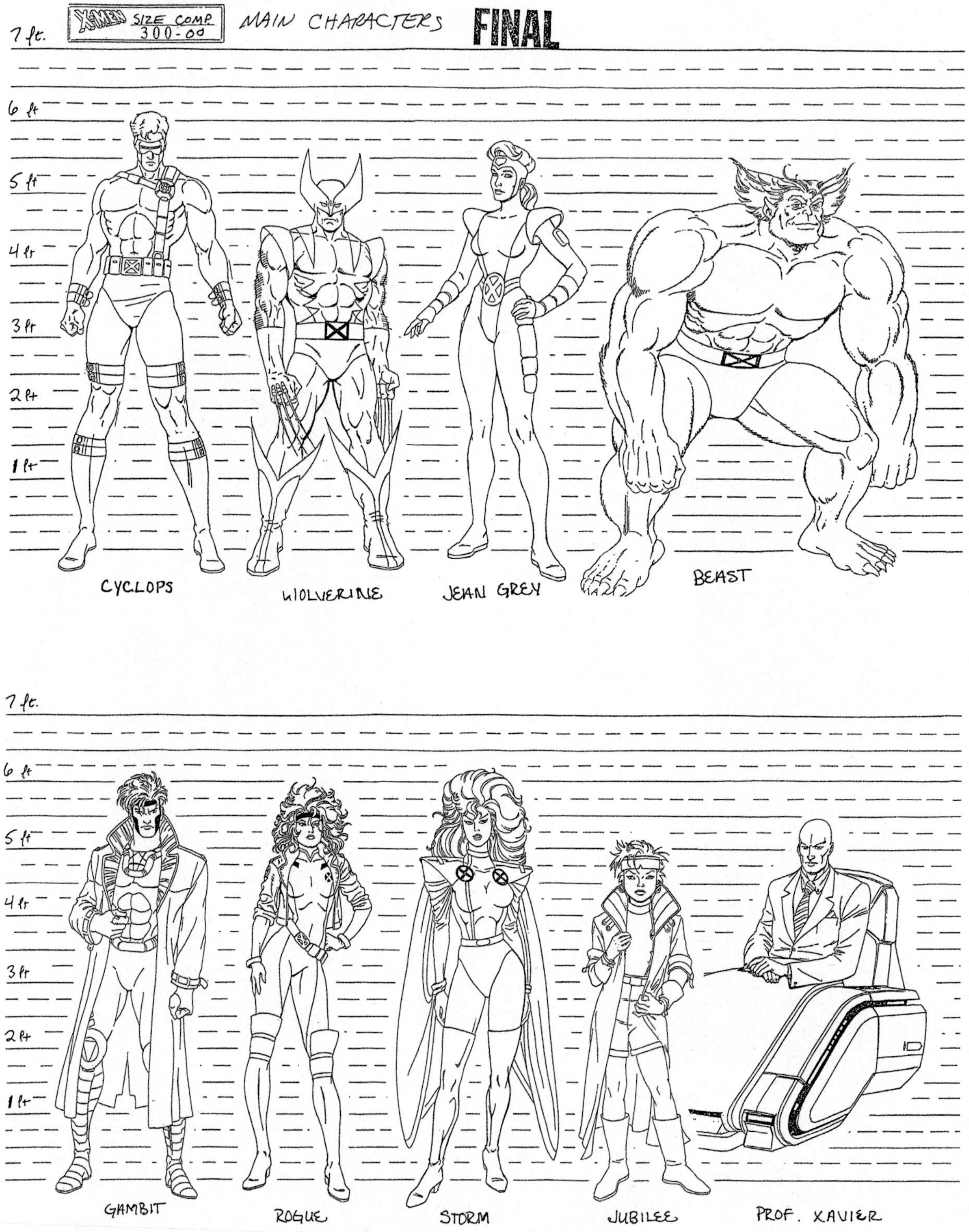
X-MEN SIZE COMP
300-00
MAIN CHARACTERS
FINAL
7 ft.
6 ft
5 ft
4 ft
3 ft
2 ft
1 ft
CYCLOPS
WOLVERINE
JEAN GREY
BEAST
7 ft.
6 ft
5 ft
4 ft
3 ft
2 ft
1 ft
GAMBIT
ROGUE
STORM
JUBILEE
PROF. XAVIER

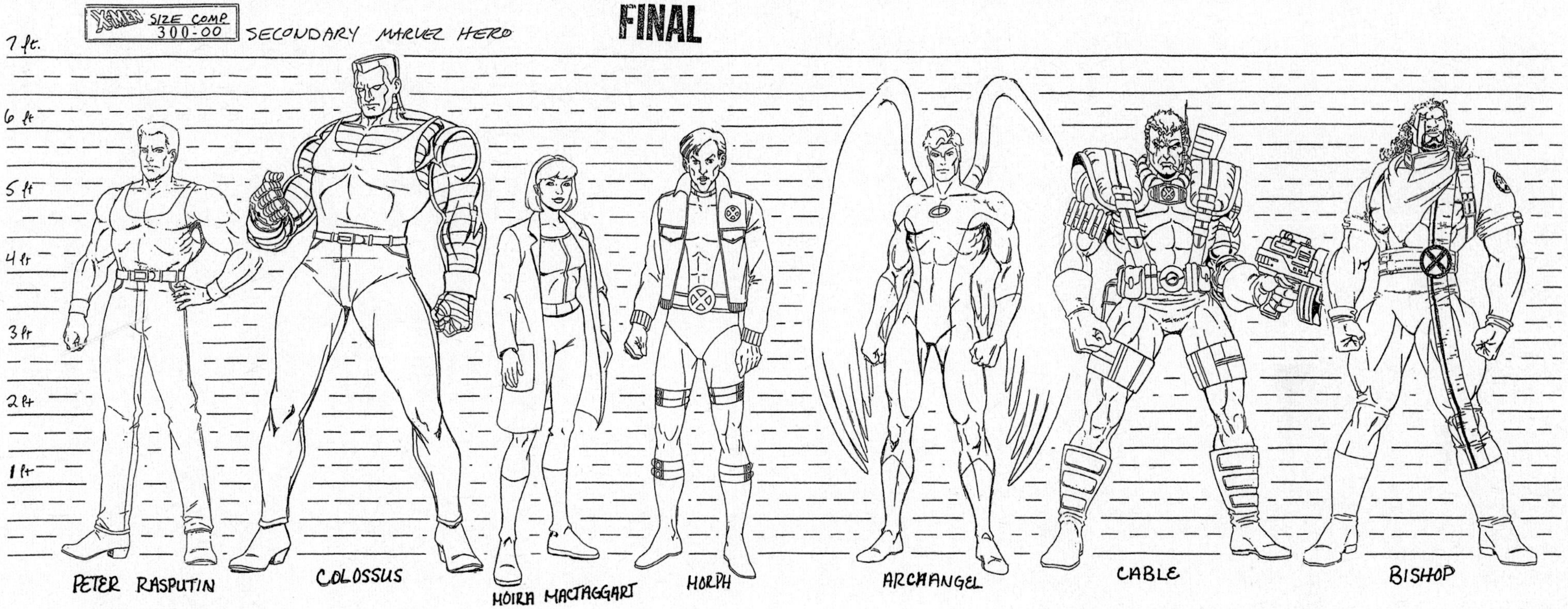

X-MEN SIZE COMP 300-00
SECONDARY MARVEL HERO
FINAL
7 ft.
6 ft
5 ft
4 ft
3 ft
2 ft
1 ft
PETER RASPUTIN
COLOSSUS
MOIRA MACTAGGART
MORPH
ARCHANGEL
CABLE
BISHOP

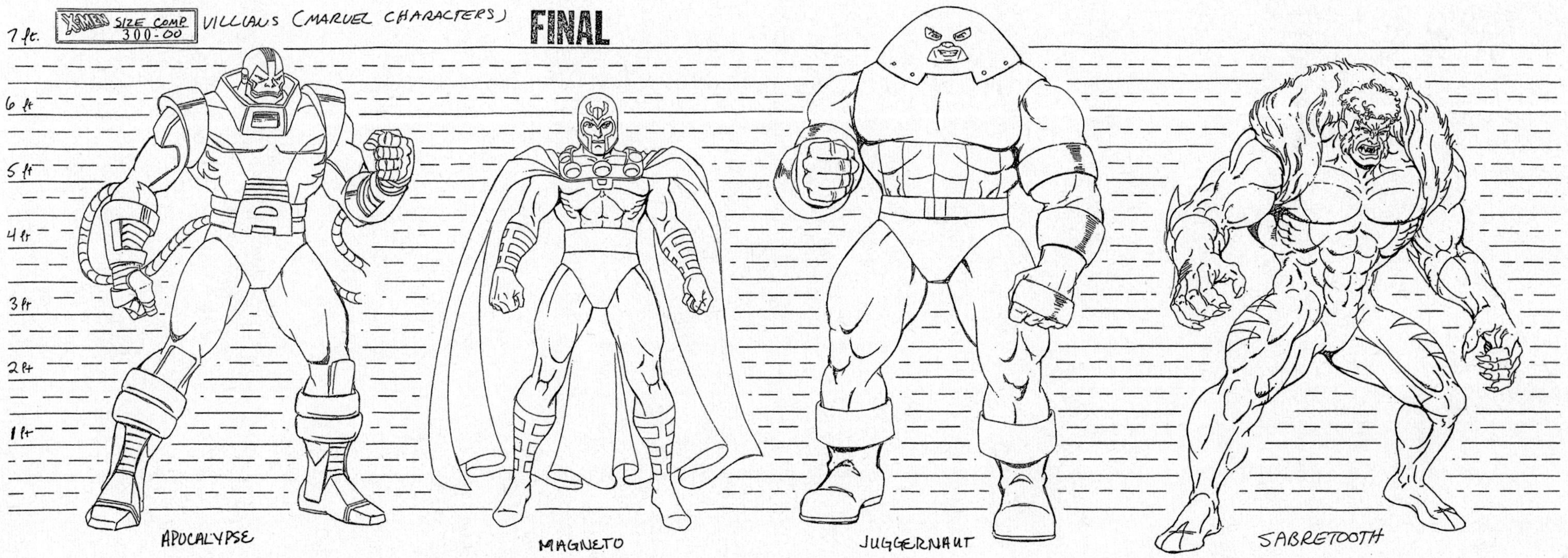

X-MEN SIZE COMP 300-00
VILLIANS (MARVEL CHARACTERS)
FINAL
7 ft.
6 ft
5 ft
4 ft
3 ft
2 ft
1 ft
APOCALYPSE
MAGNETO
JUGGERNAUT
SABRETOOTH

Title Design

In 1992, 90 percent of our television audience didn't know who the X-Men were. It was a popular comic, but comics were just a small part of our popular culture. We were planning to introduce a core cast of ten, plus new guest characters every week. There was widespread concern that "the kids" watching would get confused and turn us off. We had to reach them quickly. The opening titles became a crucial, seventy-five-second introduction to this brave new world.

How to do it? A perky song, like the sixties *Spider-Man* theme? God-like third-person narration? Series advisor Stan Lee pushed hard for narration—with Stan himself as live-action narrator introducing each show in person, then talking over the episode as the story went along. Producer/designer Will Meugniot knew that approach was trouble.

Will Meugniot: "Everybody knew doing it Stan's way wouldn't work on this series. When Stan had been given his head back at Marvel [Productions, in the '80s], we wound up with things like *Pryde of the X-Men* having a questionable theme song with [Stan's] lyrics. On *X-Men: TAS* I'd gotten a call from Margaret that Stan had persuaded her that he should be narrating the episodes, that they should open with Stan at a desk like Walt Disney in the 1960s, explaining what was going to be happening. I had a tough phone call with Margaret because she'd decided to let a very persistent Stan introduce the series, and I had to talk her out of it. I said: 'We're going up against our own sophisticated Fox show, *Batman: TAS*. Even though we're both on the same network, that's our biggest competition. If you start out with this nice old man explaining who the X-Men characters are and what the lesson is, you're going to kill the show.'"

Sidney Iwanter: "Stan in live action. Introducing it, narrating it, and then coming out at the end and saying, 'Wasn't that a great idea, kids?' Trying to tell the audience what they had just seen. Exact opposite of what we needed."

Series artist Rick Hoberg remembered a similar moment with Stan during the creation of *Pryde of the X-Men*.

Rick Hoberg: "When Will, Larry, and I were given the assignment by Margaret to put *Pryde* together [in 1987], the first thing she did was set up a meeting with Stan. We'd all known Stan for years [at Marvel Productions]. Quickly we realized that *he didn't know the characters we were talking about* for the show. He thought we were talking about Marvel Girl and Iceman. We told him, 'No, we're talking about Wolverine and Colossus and Storm, the current team.' He said: "I don't know who that is, so why don't you just go off and do this.'"

Will Meugniot and Larry Houston had worked on other series where Stan had appeared in the introduction, and they knew this "kiddie-show host" direction didn't fit our more adult series. Older fans would know him, but the "new 90 percent" wouldn't. Worse, Stan was fighting to change our work into a much younger show, based on his brief experience with the concept thirty years earlier. As with so many things, the final decision lay with Margaret Loesch, and Stan had her ear. And so Stan was allowed to write a narration.

**OPENING OF EACH X-MEN SHOW
(45 SECONDS)**

Was it caused by atomic testing, by the radiation that has spread around the world?

Or is it nature herself, deciding the time has come to change the human race?

Whatever the answer, a new breed of people now dwell among us! People born with strange and frightening super powers!

Some say they're freaks. Some call them monsters! Some think of them as-- inhuman!

But all over the planet they are known, and feared, as-- MUTANTS!

This is the saga of the X-MEN, a brave band of mutants who want to use their awesome power to benefit mankind-- only to learn that they must battle the very people they're trying to help!

This was not our show. We didn't care so much why mutants existed; we were interested in them as individuals and how they were dealing with their fate. Luckily, Will and Sidney were able to talk Margaret out of using narration, both for the opening titles and for the show itself. But now the pressure was on Larry and Will to come up with a compelling title sequence that did the job.

Larry took the first stab. He admired Doug Wildey's opening to the original *Jonny Quest* series in the midsixties: all fast-paced action and driving music. He drew an exciting, action-packed, mutant-filled opening. Everyone liked it, but for Margaret Loesch, it didn't perform its most crucial task: It didn't introduce the lead X-Men characters, clearly and cleanly, to a new audience. The X-Men in Larry's storyboard were simply nine of twenty-two strange creatures all thrown at the audience at once. Comics fan Larry knew all these mutants, their names, their powers, and their place in X-Men lore, but most of the 1992 audience wouldn't. Our show leads were lost in a crowd.

As Will Meugniot told Eric: "Larry did a brilliant version of the title, but it had everybody in the Marvel Universe pertaining to the X-Men crammed into it. After talking with Sidney, who was distressed, along with Margaret Loesch, that a viewer might come out of the title not knowing who anybody was, Larry and I went back and reworked the first half of the title. That's why the first half has logos, names, and focuses on our lead characters."

And so Will sketched out a revision for the titles' beginning and ending. He retained Larry's best action set pieces in the middle, but he focused the new images on the lead characters, one at a time, featuring each of their faces and having their names streak across the screen as each unleashed his or her powers. At the opening, he showed the X-Men in action as a team before shifting to them as individuals. Will trimmed out the other X-Universe mutants except prime adversary Magneto, then brought the team together at the end. Since some character-specific logos did not exist, Larry designed them. He then polished up Will's changes, and that was it. We now had a slam-bang seventy-five-second opening whose focus was: Meet the X-Men. This is what they're like, and this is how they live and fight. Two drafts drawn over a few days, and one of the most memorable opening titles in TV history was brought to life.

The last crucial element was the music. Saban's music department came up with a number of very wrong, cartoony takes. Then their composer Ron Wasserman hit on the driving rock beat that worked. Will and Sidney wore Ron out, pushing him again and again to add more speed, depth, and drama until the score matched the intensity of the animation they were envisioning. Ron didn't have an orchestra—the dense, driving score that the audience has come to love ("Duh-duh-duh-duh-*duh*-duh-duh...") was Ron alone at the synthesizer.

Ron says, "When that initial bassline came in, I went, 'Here's our foundation.' Almost like a synopsis of a story. That was from Ron Cannon. Once that foundation was there, then it was kind of easy to write the whole basic thing over it. We didn't have a cut of the opening [images] yet, from what I remember, just it's a one-minute theme [75 seconds, actually]. Like everything else I've ever written, it just came to me and it was done. Then everybody's notes started coming in. They just wanted a bigger, fatter sound, and back then it was much harder to do with no money for musicians. Instead we were just stacking [tape] tracks. I remember somebody going, 'The guy's got thirty high-hat tracks!' That's because you can't get that eighth-note or sixteenth-note rhythm to cut through the mix. Erase twenty-nine and find the right high hat, I knew by then. It was miserable, but now I sure am glad we made the effort. I was really floored recently when I saw all the X-Men feature-movie actors singing it online."

So, pressed by practical needs—a complex world of strange new characters, little time to second-guess—three veteran craftsmen threw together a seventy-five-second classic that, to this day, hundreds of millions of viewers still find themselves humming. The rest of the crew had a high standard to match in making the series to come.

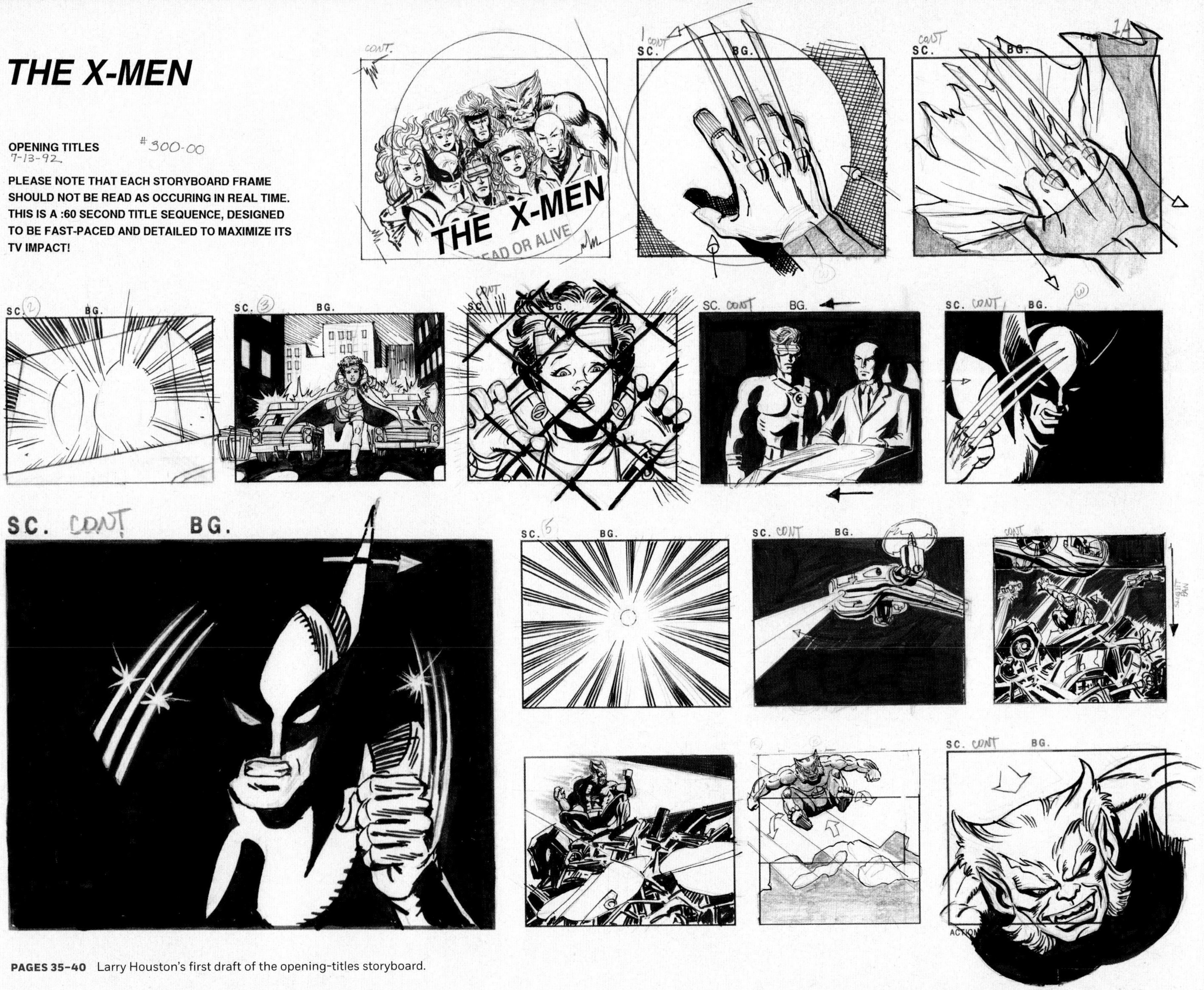
THE X-MEN
OPENING TITLES
#300-00
7-13-92
PLEASE NOTE THAT EACH STORYBOARD FRAME SHOULD NOT BE READ AS OCCURING IN REAL TIME. THIS IS A :60 SECOND TITLE SEQUENCE, DESIGNED TO BE FAST-PACED AND DETAILED TO MAXIMIZE ITS TV IMPACT!
THE X-MEN
SC.
BG.
CONT.
SLIGHT PAN
ACTION

PAGES 35–40 Larry Houston's first draft of the opening-titles storyboard.

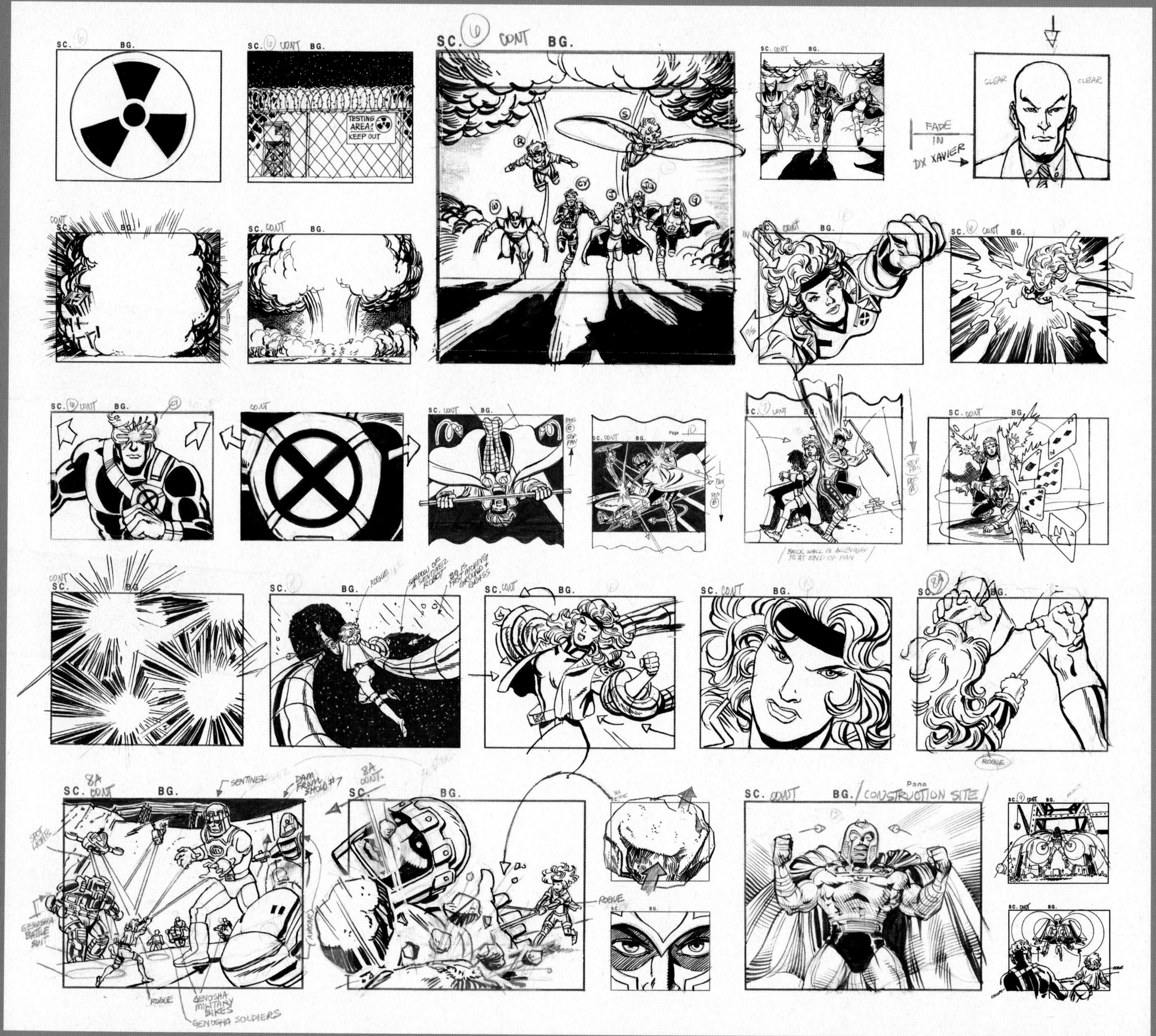
TESTING AREA! KEEP OUT
FADE IN
DX XAVIER
CLEAR
BRICK WALL IN ALLEYWAY IS AT END OF PAN
SHADOW OF A SENTINEL ROBOT
ROGUE
SENTINEL
DAM FROM SHOW #7
GENOSHA BATTLE SUIT
GENOSHA MILITARY BIKES
GENOSHA SOLDIERS
CONSTRUCTION SITE

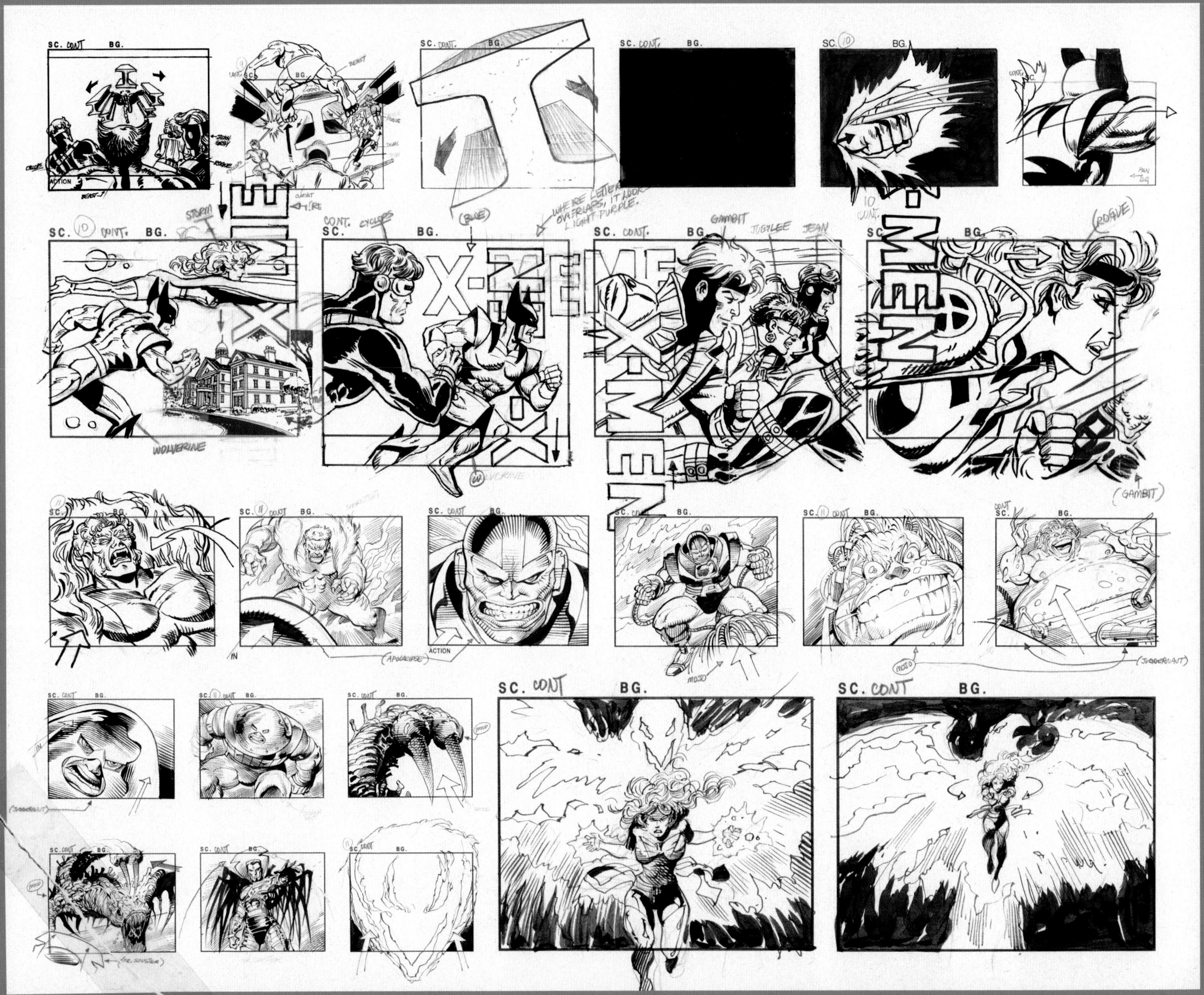
SC. CONT. BG.
ACTION
STORM
WOLVERINE
CYCLOPS
(BLUE)
WHERE LETTERS OVERLAPS, IT LOOKS LIGHT PURPLE.
GAMBIT
JUBILEE
JEAN
(ROGUE)
X-MEN
(GAMBIT)
(APOCALYPSE)
MOJO
(JUGGERNAUT)
(MR. SINISTER)

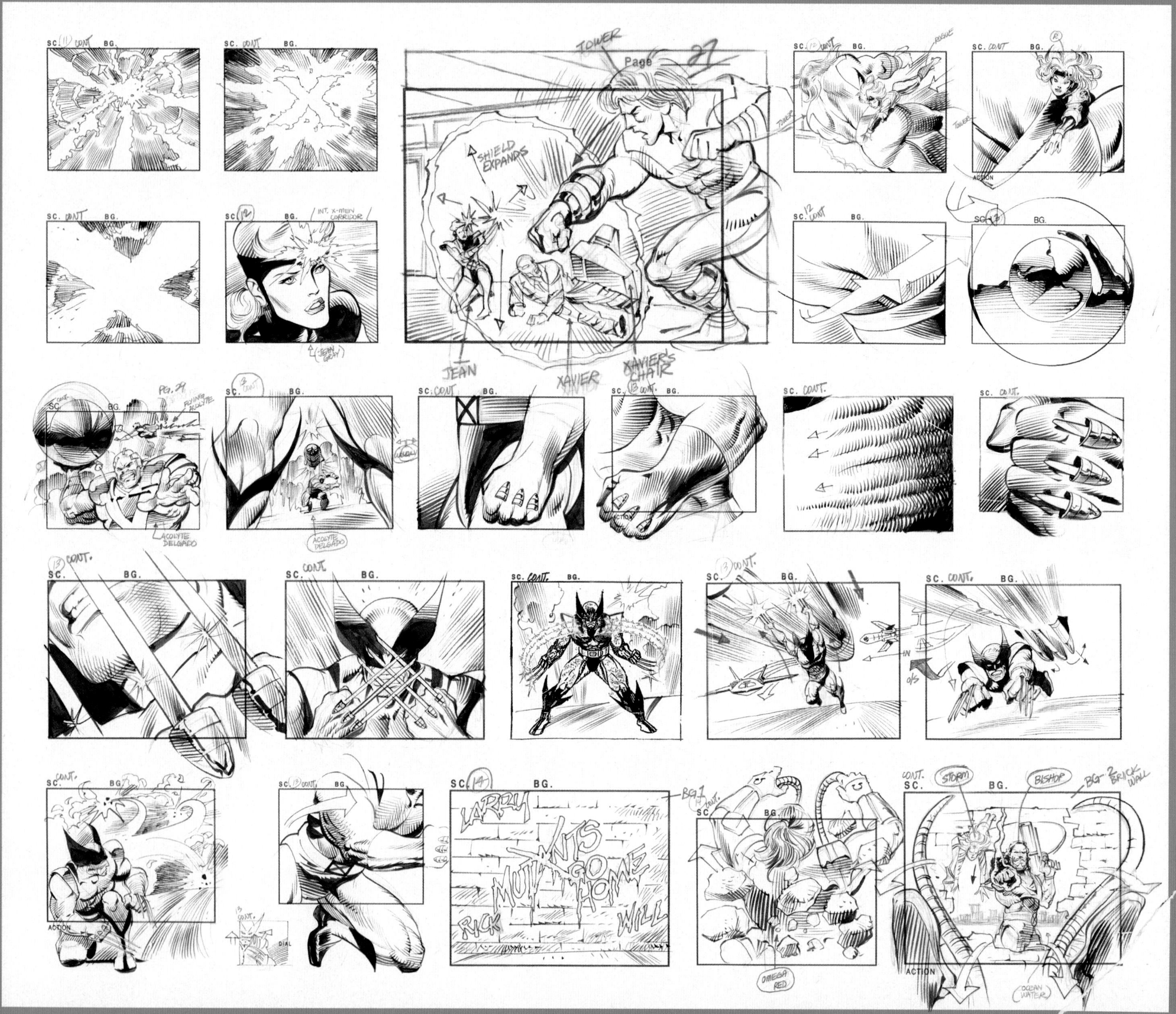
TOWER
Page 27
SHIELD EXPANDS
JEAN
XAVIER
XAVIER'S CHAIR
INT. X-MEN CORRIDOR
JEAN GREY
ROGUE
FLYING ACOLYTE
ACOLYTE DELGADO
LARRY
MUTANTS GO HOME
RICK
WILL
OMEGA RED
STORM
BISHOP
BG-2 BRICK WALL
OCEAN WATER
ACTION

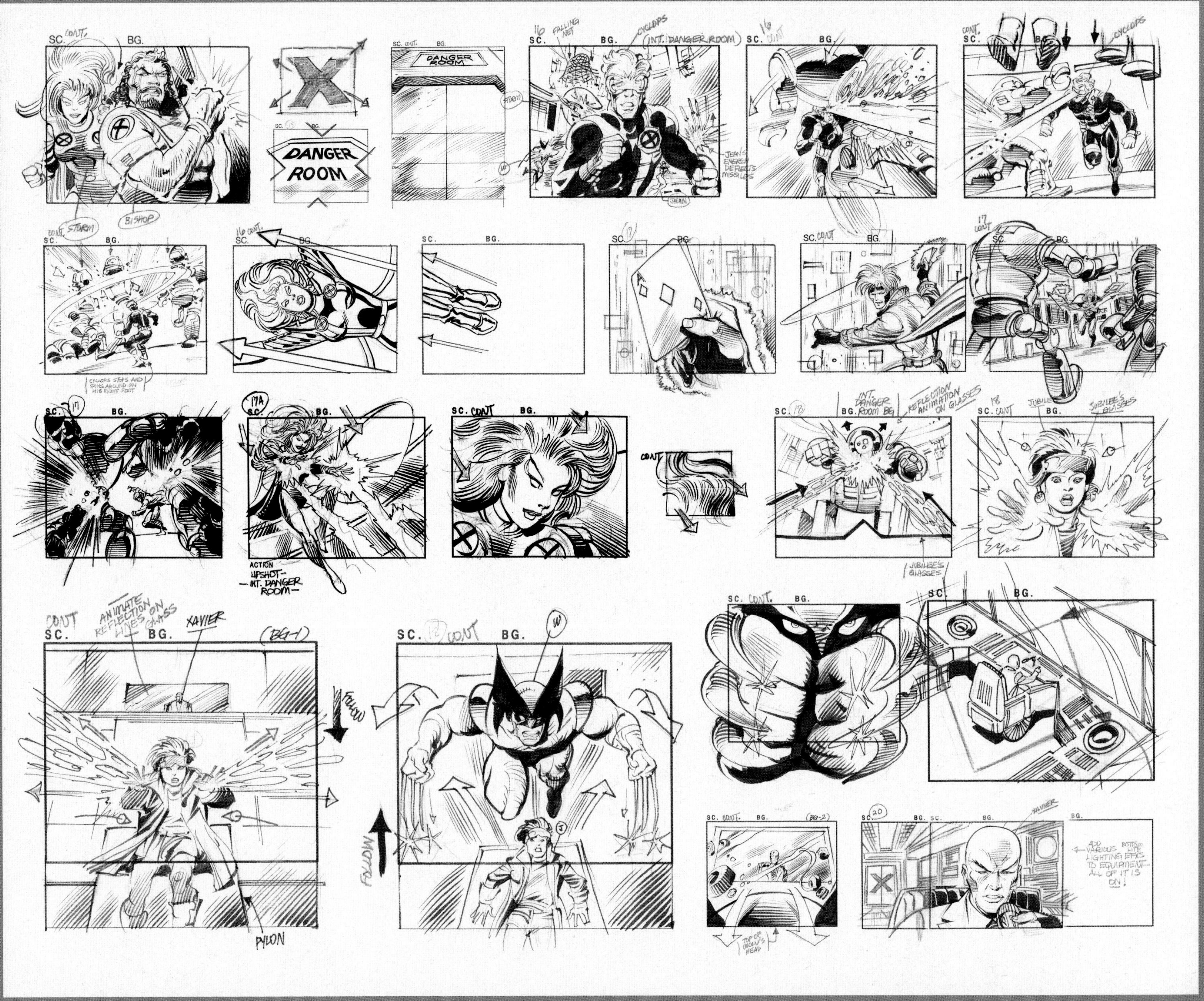

SC. CONT. BG.
STORM
BISHOP
DANGER ROOM
DANGER ROOM
16 FALLING NET
CYCLOPS
(INT. DANGER ROOM)
JEAN'S ENERGY DEFLECTS MISSILES
JEAN
CYCLOPS
CYCLOPS STEPS AND SPINS AROUND ON HIS RIGHT FOOT
17A
ACTION UPSHOT - INT. DANGER ROOM -
INT. DANGER ROOM BG
REFLECTION ANIMATION ON GLASSES
JUBILEE
JUBILEE'S GLASSES
JUBILEE'S GLASSES
ANIMATE REFLECTION LINES ON GLASS
XAVIER
(BG-1)
FOLLOW
FOLLOW
PYLON
(BG-2)
TOP OF WOLV'S HEAD
XAVIER
ADD VARIOUS LITE LIGHTING EFX TO EQUIPMENT. ALL OF IT'S ON!

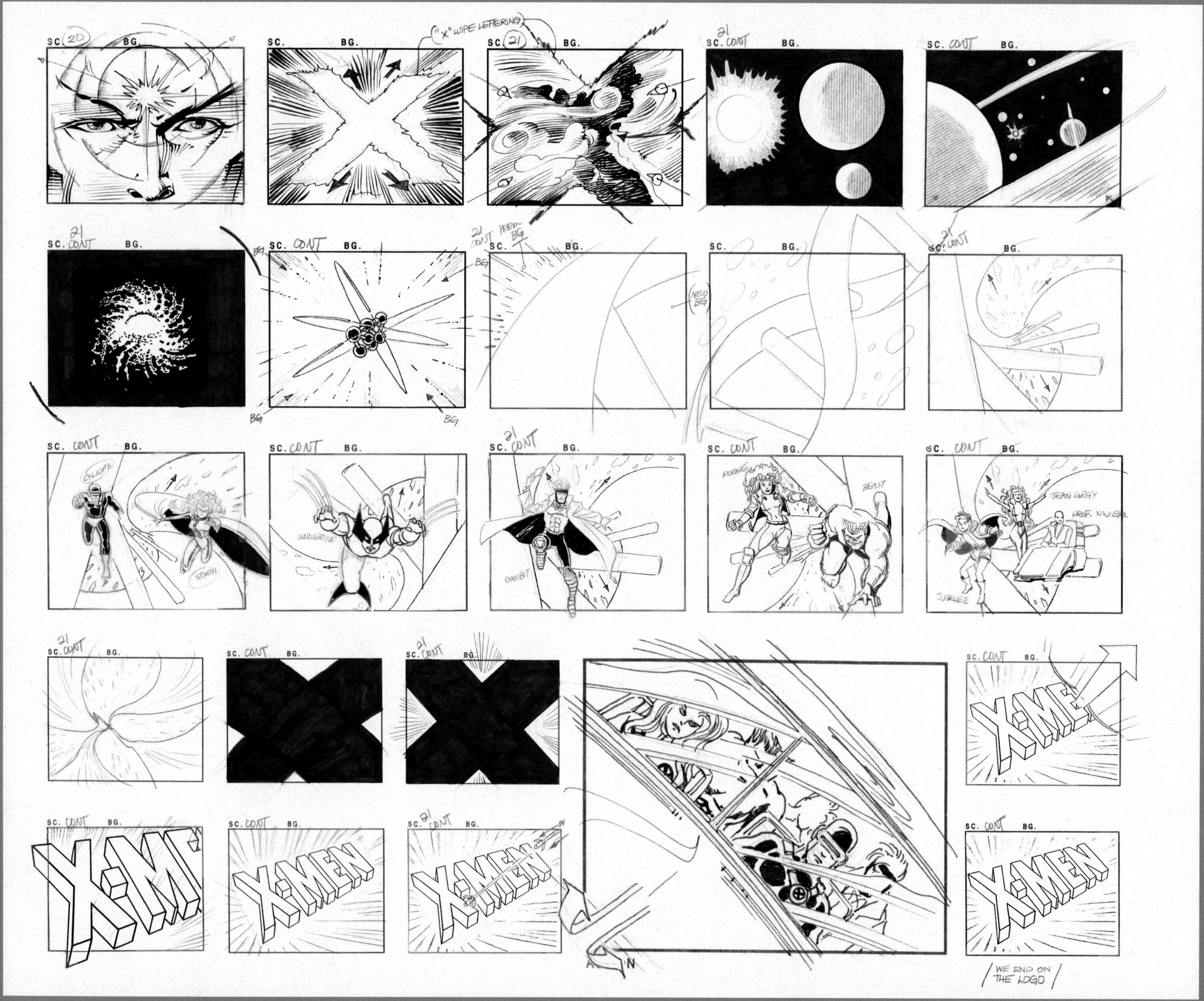
SC. 20 BG.
"X" WIPE LETTERING
SC. 21 BG.
SC. 21 CONT BG.
CYCLOPS
STORM
WOLVERINE
GAMBIT
ROGUE
BEAST
JEAN GREY
PROF. XAVIER
JUBILEE
X-MEN
WE END ON THE LOGO

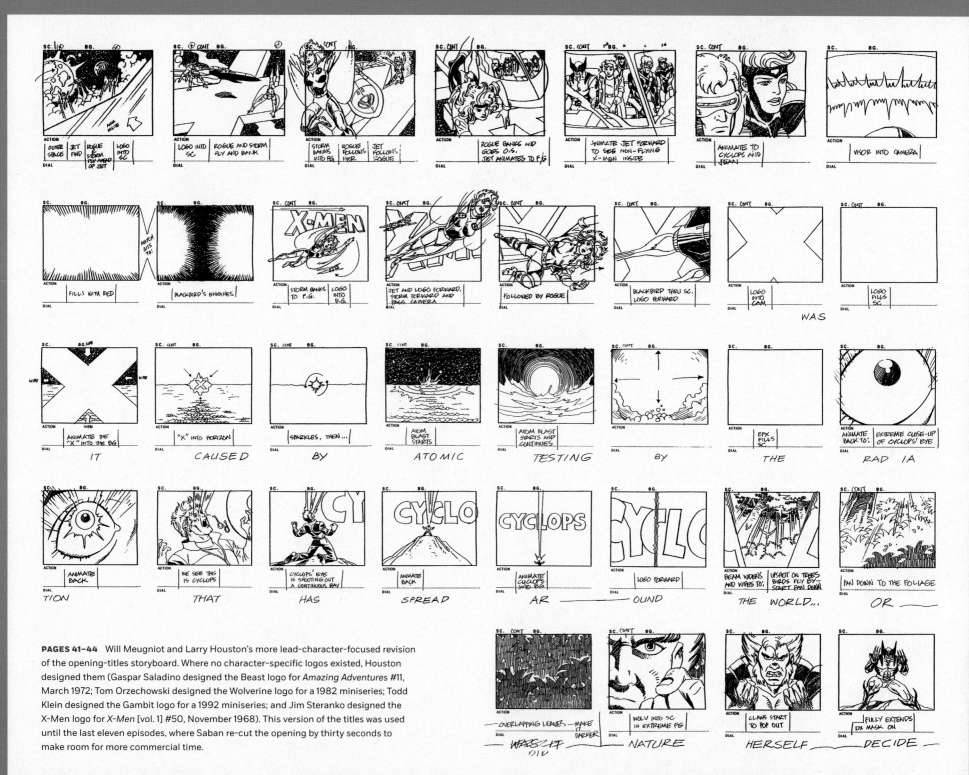

PAGES 41–44 Will Meugniot and Larry Houston's more lead-character-focused revision of the opening-titles storyboard. Where no character-specific logos existed, Houston designed them (Gaspar Saladino designed the Beast logo for *Amazing Adventures* #11, March 1972; Tom Orzechowski designed the Wolverine logo for a 1982 miniseries; Todd Klein designed the Gambit logo for a 1992 miniseries; and Jim Steranko designed the X-Men logo for *X-Men* [vol. 1] #50, November 1968). This version of the titles was used until the last eleven episodes, where Saban re-cut the opening by thirty seconds to make room for more commercial time.

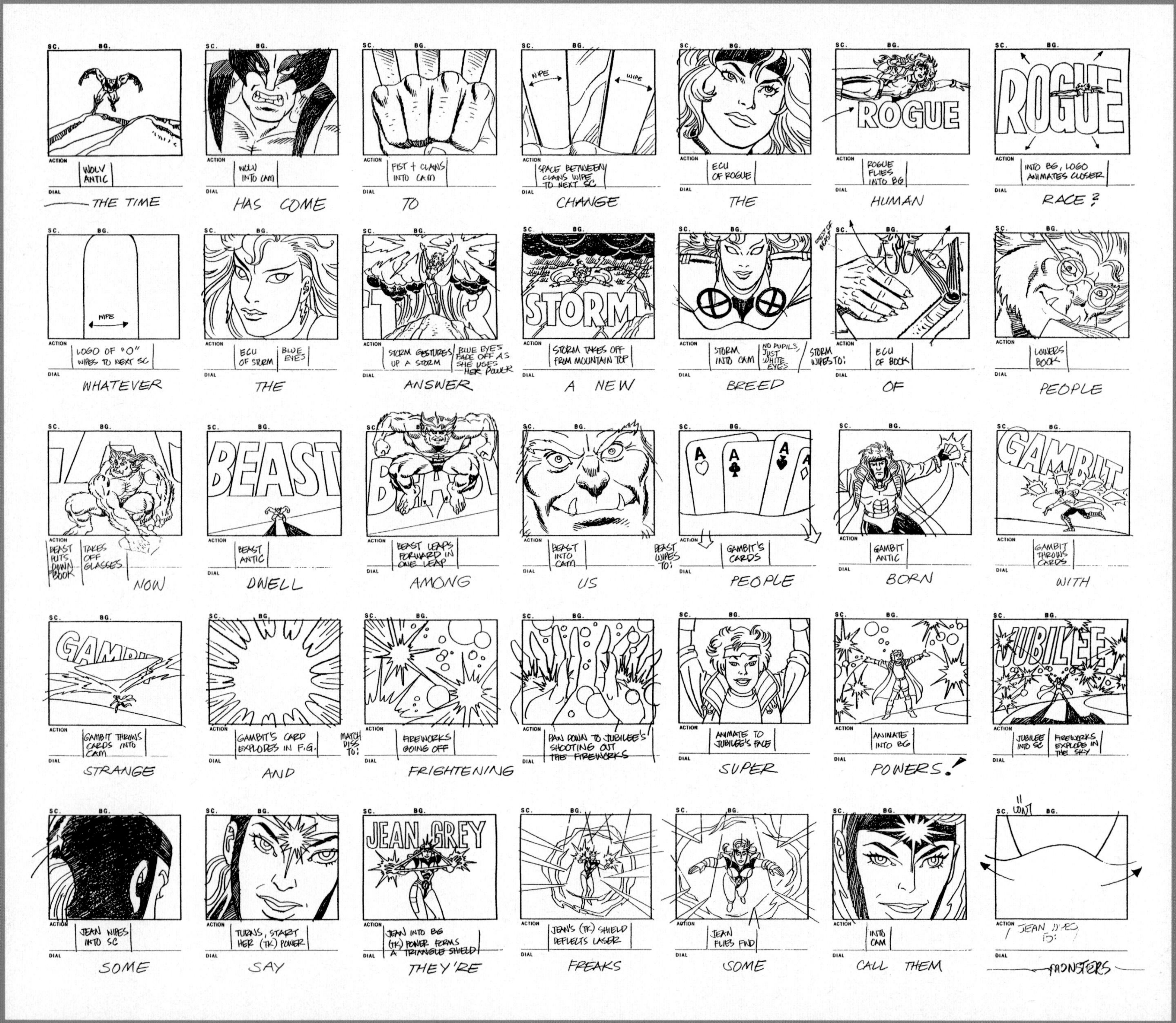
WOLV ANTIC
THE TIME
WOLV INTO CAM
HAS COME
FIST + CLAWS INTO CAM
TO
WIPE
SPACE BETWEEN CLAWS WIPE TO NEXT SC
CHANGE
ECU OF ROGUE
THE
ROGUE
ROGUE FLIES INTO BG
HUMAN
ROGUE
INTO BG, LOGO ANIMATES CLOSER
RACE?
WIPE
LOGO OF "O" WIPES TO NEXT SC
WHATEVER
ECU OF STORM
BLUE EYES
THE
STORM GESTURES UP A STORM
BLUE EYES FADE OFF AS SHE USES HER POWER
ANSWER
STORM
STORM TAKES OFF FROM MOUNTAIN TOP
A NEW
STORM INTO CAM
NO PUPILS, JUST WHITE EYES
BREED
STORM WIPES TO:
ECU OF BOOK
OF
LOWERS BOOK
PEOPLE
BEAST PUTS DOWN BOOK
TAKES OFF GLASSES
NOW
BEAST
BEAST ANTIC
DWELL
BEAST LEAPS FORWARD IN ONE LEAP
AMONG
BEAST INTO CAM
BEAST WIPES TO:
US
GAMBIT'S CARDS
PEOPLE
GAMBIT ANTIC
BORN
GAMBIT
GAMBIT THROWS CARDS
WITH
GAMBIT THROWS CARDS INTO CAM
STRANGE
GAMBIT'S CARD EXPLODES IN F.G.
MATCH DISS TO:
AND
FIREWORKS GOING OFF
FRIGHTENING
PAN DOWN TO JUBILEE'S SHOOTING OUT THE FIREWORKS
ANIMATE TO JUBILEE'S FACE
SUPER
ANIMATE INTO BG
POWERS!
JUBILEE
JUBILEE INTO SC
FIREWORKS EXPLODE IN THE SKY
JEAN WIPES INTO SC
SOME
TURNS, START HER (TK) POWER
SAY
JEAN GREY
JEAN INTO BG (TK) POWER FORMS A TRIANGLE SHIELD
THEY'RE
JEAN'S (TK) SHIELD DEFLECTS LASER
FREAKS
JEAN FLIES FWD
SOME
INTO CAM
CALL THEM
MONSTERS

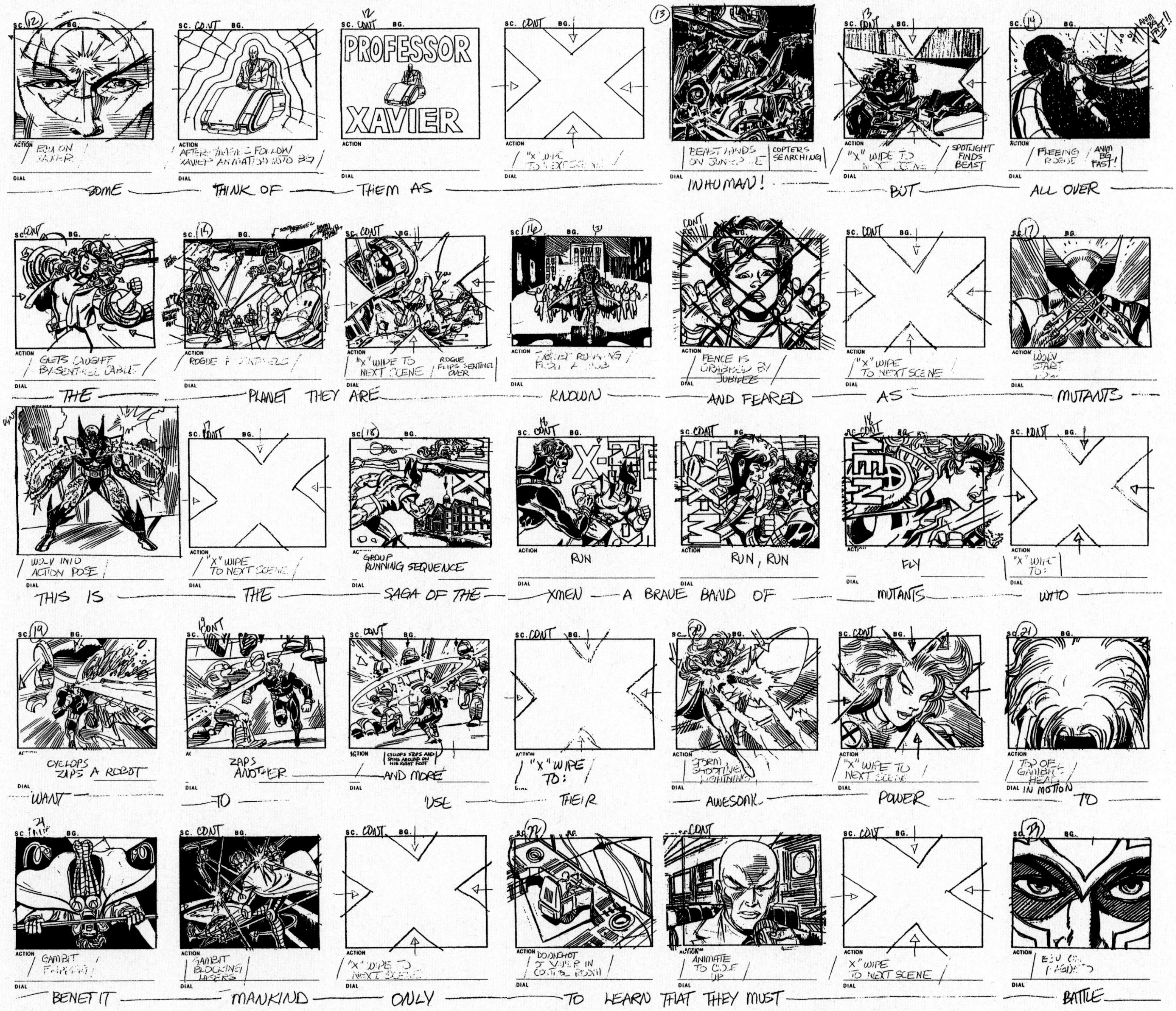
PROFESSOR
XAVIER
SOME THINK OF THEM AS INHUMAN! BUT ALL OVER
"X" WIPE TO NEXT SCENE
THE PLANET THEY ARE KNOWN AND FEARED AS MUTANTS
GROUP RUNNING SEQUENCE
RUN
RUN, RUN
FLY
THIS IS THE SAGA OF THE XMEN A BRAVE BAND OF MUTANTS WHO
CYCLOPS ZAPS A ROBOT
AND MORE
WANT TO USE THEIR AWESOME POWER TO
GAMBIT BLOCKING LASERS
TO NEXT SCENE
BENETIT MANKIND ONLY TO LEARN THAT THEY MUST BATTLE

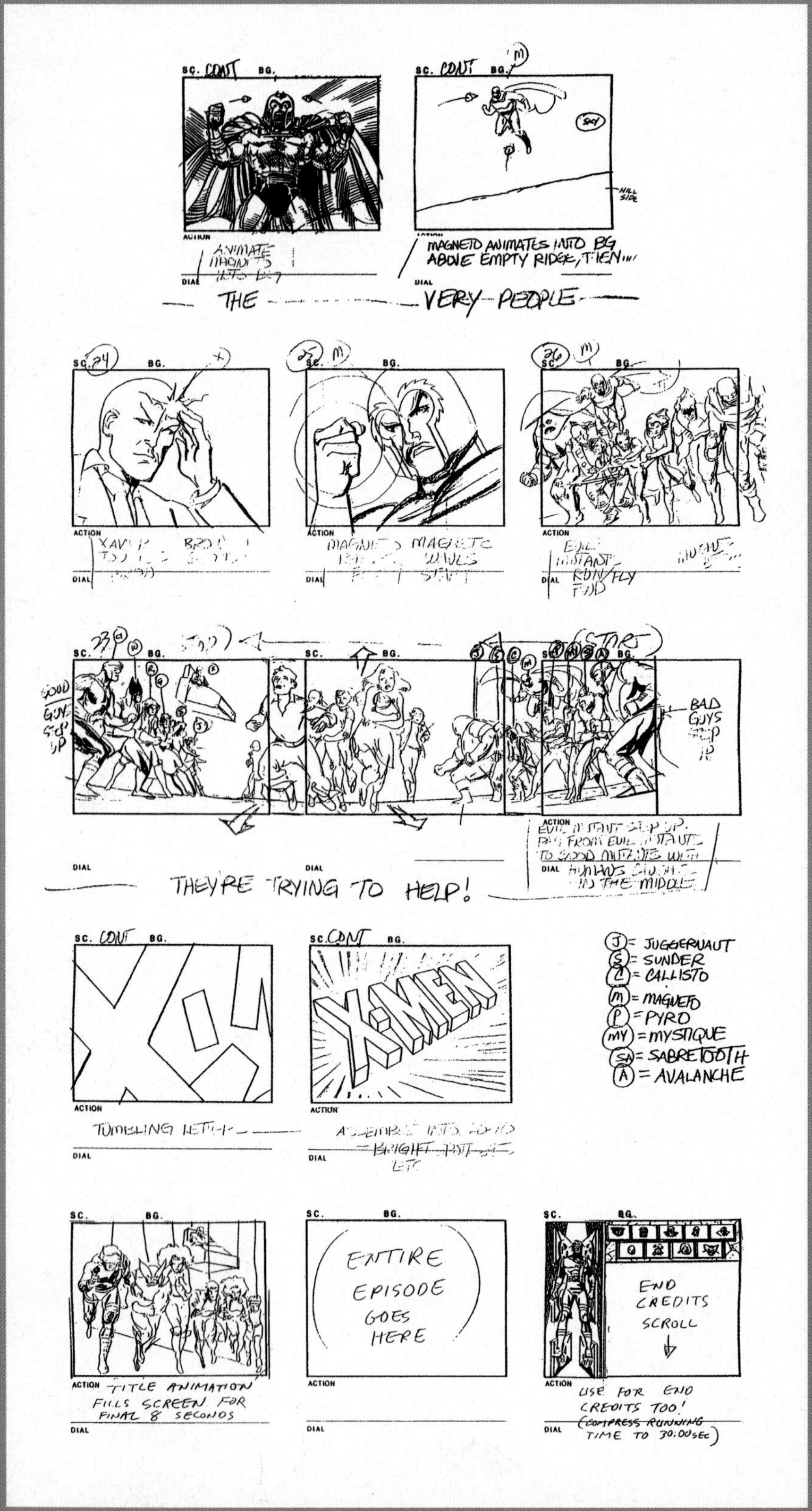
MAGNETO ANIMATES INTO BG ABOVE EMPTY RIDGE, THEN...
THE VERY PEOPLE
BAD GUYS
THEY'RE TRYING TO HELP!
Ⓙ = JUGGERNAUT
Ⓢ = SUNDER
Ⓒ = CALLISTO
Ⓜ = MAGNETO
Ⓟ = PYRO
(MY) = MYSTIQUE
(SB) = SABRETOOTH
Ⓐ = AVALANCHE
TUMBLING LETTERS
TITLE ANIMATION FILLS SCREEN FOR FINAL 8 SECONDS
ENTIRE EPISODE GOES HERE
END CREDITS SCROLL
USE FOR END CREDITS TOO!
(COMPRESS RUNNING TIME TO 30.00SEC)

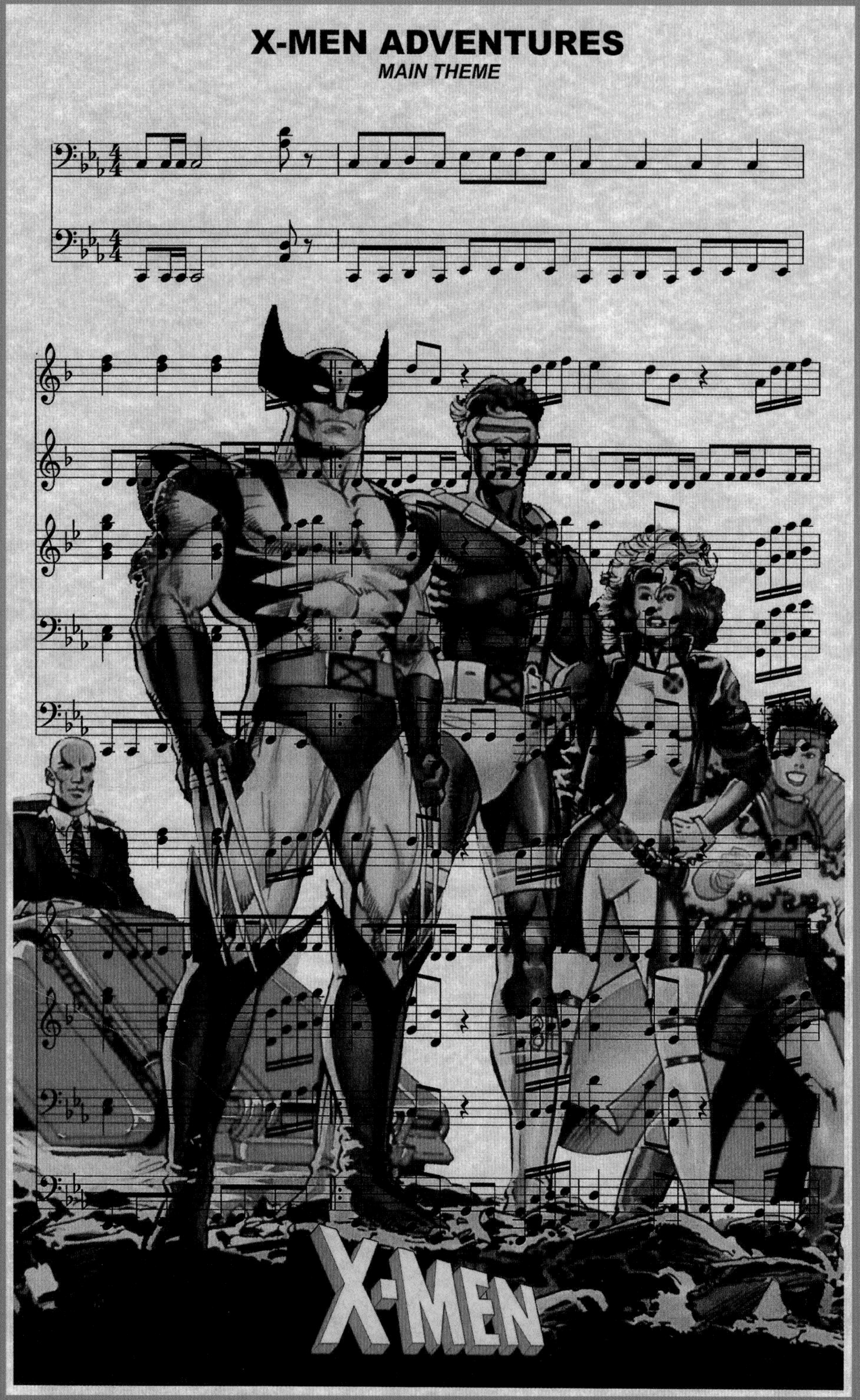
X-MEN ADVENTURES
MAIN THEME
X-MEN

ABOVE Ron Wasserman's opening-titles score. **OPPOSITE** Highlight still-frames from the finished animation of Will Meugniot and Larry Houston's revision of the opening titles.

MEANWHILE, Mark Edens and Eric were still working to construct the season-one story arc. For the one-hour, two-part pilot, Will suggested the bare bones of the story he had wanted to tell in *Pryde*. It focused on a young outsider (then Kitty Pryde, now Jubilee) discovering the X-Men along with the audience. Starting with Jubilee gave the audience fresh eyes and ears with which to learn the X-Men's world.

Will's story idea, importantly, focused on the Sentinels as the threat.

Will says, "'Night of the Sentinels' was the story I'd wanted to do for the *Pryde of the X-Men* pilot—an updating of the story from the first issue of the *X-Men* comic book."

Will's insistence on using the Sentinels was perfect for Mark and Eric—both of whom saw the series primarily as a struggle between mutants and humans instead of the mutant-mutant battles that were the focus of many of the books. The Sentinels are a human-created, towering embodiment of the human need to control or even oppress mutants. Great animation visuals. And as Will knew, "They give Wolverine something to slash." We couldn't have the comic book's favorite character unable to use his signature action move. We all knew the severe limits on battle action in 1990s kids' TV: Violence between living things was barely permitted, but attacks on machines, especially evil ones, were possible.

Mark and Eric were pleased when their first stab at the story—a twenty-page outline as the basis for the eighty-page, two-part script—gained Will's approval.

Since we had committed to a "serialized," comic-book-style, progressing, connected set of stories for these—perhaps the only—thirteen episodes, Mark and Eric figured that the last episode needed to resolve the Sentinel threat in a big, spectacular battle at the Sentinels' home base, the factory where their twisted "mother," super-Sentinel breeder Master Mold, churned them out.

During the ten episodes in between, we got to meet many other significant adversaries and allies of our core team, establishing the X-Men's world. But the Sentinels would always linger in the background.

The structure of season one was:

Episodes 1 and 2: Show Jubilee's background and the Sentinel threat; meet each X-Men team member through her eyes; and establish the nature of mutants, their place in society, and the X-Men's place as well. Let Morph die heroically and allow our newly met X-Men "family" to come together in their grief.

Episodes 3 and 4: Meet top X-Men villain Magneto and establish the contrast between his and his adversary—and closest friend—Xavier's philosophies. Learn more about Wolverine's nemesis, Sabretooth.

Episode 5: Get to know more about Storm—give her a command challenge.

Episode 6: Learn more about Wolverine's internal struggles with his fierce nature.

Episode 7: Take the Sentinel conspiracy to control and destroy mutants to a new level—a slave labor camp. Meet major series guest character Cable.

Episode 8: Meet major X-Men universe characters Colossus and Juggernaut.

Episodes 9 and 10: Learn more about Rogue as we meet and get to know the backstory of major X-Men Universe characters Apocalypse and Archangel.

Episodes 11 and 12: Adapt a fan-favorite Marvel book—"Days of Future Past"—while integrating it into our original story arc, fitting it to our team.

Episode 13: Resolve the Sentinel threat by defeating the conspirators and Master Mold. Welcome Jubilee into the X-Men family.

This was a lot to blend into thirteen twenty-two-minute episodes. But Eric, Mark, Will, Larry, and the other partners felt it came close to doing the comics justice.

The show bible that we sent out about a week in contained the following guidelines about our artistic and storytelling intentions:

> **A FOREWORD TO WRITERS AND ARTISTS**
>
> More than most animated series, "X-MEN" will rely on the creative contributions of writers and artists who have preceded the current development team. While we are responsible for the quality of the television series, we will be using many characters, images, and ideas that have been created by others. We respect their work and are heavily in their debt.
>
> The "X-Men" comic book series is a world-wide phenomenon. It represents a thirty-year tradition of storytelling, begun by creators Stan Lee and Jack Kirby and developed by dozens of writers and artists such as Chris Claremont and John Byrne. Our ambition with this series is to continue that tradition in another medium, not to change it, "update" it, or pretend that we have found a way to improve upon it. If you want to know the essence of this show, read the comics.
>
> We do not intend for this respect of the X-Men legacy to discourage your creativity and invention. We look on the tradition we have inherited as a gold mine of inspiration, not a straitjacket. But please remember that much of our audience

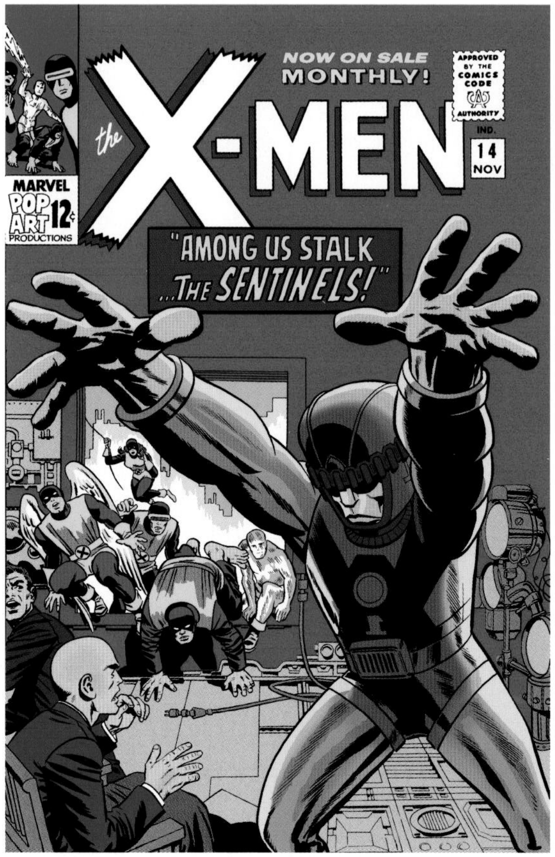
NOW ON SALE MONTHLY!
APPROVED BY THE COMICS CODE AUTHORITY
the X-MEN
IND. 14 NOV
MARVEL POP ART 12¢ PRODUCTIONS
"AMONG US STALK ...THE SENTINELS!"

01

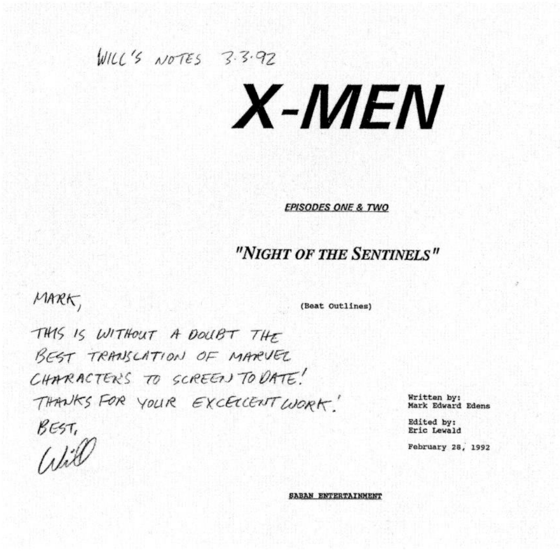

WILL'S NOTES 3.3.92

X-MEN

EPISODES ONE & TWO

"NIGHT OF THE SENTINELS"

MARK,

(Beat Outlines)

THIS IS WITHOUT A DOUBT THE BEST TRANSLATION OF MARVEL CHARACTERS TO SCREEN TO DATE! THANKS FOR YOUR EXCELLENT WORK! BEST, Will

Written by:
Mark Edward Edens

Edited by:
Eric Lewald

February 28, 1992

SABAN ENTERTAINMENT

02

01 Cover of *X-Men* (vol. 1) #14, the debut appearance of the Sentinels—the villains of our pilot episode. Art by Jack Kirby, Wally Wood, and Sam Rosen. **02** Lifelong Marvel fan Will Meugniot's note, reacting to Mark Eden's and Eric Lewald's first stab at an *X-Men: TAS* story.

will know these characters and have definite expectations of the series. Our job, in thirteen short shows, will be to both satisfy and surprise the fans as we introduce the excitement and drama of "X-Men" to a whole new audience.

WHAT IS AN "X-MEN" STORY?

"X-Men" is different from most animated action adventure shows you may have seen or written. It is more about the lives of our characters—heroes and villains alike—than ingenious plots or non-stop, death-defying physical jeopardy. It's not important whether or not a bad guy succeeds in blowing up the Pentagon. What matters is how Wolverine deals with the pain of losing a friend while trying to stop it. Use plot to showcase character, not the other way around.

Which is not to say that "X-Men" will lack action, pace, or intensity. We want these shows to move fast and to be dense with dramatic crises. Action scenes will play like "Terminator 2" on speed. But more often than not the crisis is personal, not physical. Think of the famous "Star Trek" scene where Kirk has to let the woman he loves get killed for the sake of future lives. There was matchless dramatic tension created by a man watching a woman walking slowly across a street. The drama was inside the character.

"X-Men" is a show of gray areas. We understand most of our villains, even sympathize with some. X-Men victories tend to be mixed blessings and are never achieved without a loss of some kind. "Good guys" fight with each other, have bad days, and are capable of being petty and intolerant. One might even leave the X-Men in disgust and join the enemy.

Through it all, however, our X-Men distinguish themselves by maintaining their values of friendship, loyalty, and personal sacrifice. Whatever the cost, they do what must be done.

THE WORLD OF "X-MEN"

The X-Men's world is a difficult world, a combative, contentious world full of anxiety and distrust. It's modern-day Earth, but an Earth seemingly overcome by the darker forces of the 20th Century. Political upheaval isn't confined to a few regions, say, Lebanon, Communist China, Nazi Germany, Northern Ireland, or South Africa. It's worldwide. Passions are erupting over a single problem which threatens the future of the human race.

That problem—and the critical difference between "X-Men" earth and our own—is that human mutations have begun to occur. These Mutant humans have spectacular powers which frighten the normal humans, who reasonably fear for their future. Human distrust and attacks follow, making

the Mutants, mostly innocent and few in number, the world's most ferociously oppressed minority. Not surprisingly, many are fighting back. A handful use their newfound abilities to indulge in the pleasure of criminal power.

No one chooses to be a Mutant. It is a genetic accident of birth that lies dormant until the person reaches puberty. Then the amazing powers emerge, often to the person's horror. Mutants then have three choices: attempt to live quietly with the stigma and harassment that their powers attract; strike out angrily at the world, often as part of rogue Mutant gangs; or work to find a way to try to change the human/Mutant conflict. The third choice is the most difficult since it requires the Mutants to put aside their rage at their ill treatment as they struggle to persuade the humans that hate and fear them.

This third path is the path of the X-Men—and finding a way to deal with its conflicts and contradictions is central to each X-Man's character. Though they are Mutants, the X-Men want to work with humankind, not overwhelm it. Led by visionary teacher Dr. Charles Xavier, they have dedicated themselves to creating a world where Mutant and human can live together in peace. Many Mutants, idealists and criminals alike, oppose the X-Men's integrated vision of the world. Most humans do. The X-Men are caught in the middle of a deadly ongoing conflict, with the future of the world hanging in the balance.

The primary emotional appeal of the X-Men derives from the fact that they are misunderstood by the powers that be, outcasts born with powers that make them different. They don't fit in with their families, their peers, or their communities. But they want to fit in. They want to make the world understand. They've joined with Dr. Xavier in the hope that they can change things before the two forces, fearful humans and persecuted Mutants, destroy each other.

The X-Men stay together and fight on against long odds for two reasons: to help make the human world accept Mutants, and to find a way to cope with the power and stigma of their newfound abilities. Xavier organizes and gives a focus to their personal struggles. In battles with intolerant humans and bitter Mutants, he stresses teamwork, giving the X-Men a sense of community, something larger than self to fight and live for—the very thing that the human community has denied them.

Though the series is set in the present, there will be flash-backs and a major flash-forward. No year will be established.

The action will take place primarily in America, though there will be some globetrotting, especially to established places like Genosha and Muir Island. We don't plan to go into space.

Xavier's "School" in New York will be used, but not overused. It will be treated more as a research center and X-Men headquarters than as a school.

AFTER TWO AND A HALF NONSTOP-WORKING WEEKS, it looked like everything was in place. Half a dozen writers were burning the midnight oil crafting their stories, and twice as many artists were drawing stacks of inspired X-Men images.

Then, late on Friday, March 6, "The Memo" arrived. A senior executive at Marvel Comics in New York—*not* our advisors Bob Harras or Joe Calamari—had written an eight-page memo trashing our story choices, in effect saying we should start over, which would destroy our already tight schedule. Marvel's offices were closed for the weekend. Not many people had cell phones then, and folks didn't have one another's home phone numbers. There was no effective way to reach out to the New York office until it reopened on Monday morning. Waiting to find out how this would resolve—did this guy have the leverage to enforce this?—made for a tense three days.

Luckily, Will Meugniot had a pointed, persuasive answer for every "concern" that the Marvel gentleman had, and on the following Monday, with The Memo dealt with, we were able to proceed. To clear the air, Eric wrote a "Statement of Priorities," a kind of mission statement, and circulated it to everyone involved with the show, including Saban Entertainment's series supervisor Winston Richard.

TO: Sidney Iwanter, Bob Harras, Winston Richard, etc.
FROM: Eric Lewald
RE: Questions of Establishing the Series (Marvel Memo, etc.)
DATE: 3-9-92

STATEMENT OF PRIORITIES

There has been much debate since Friday about the direction taken in the 13-episode story arc—why certain villains and not others, why portrayals of certain U.S. government workers or policies, why this or that order of events. Part of the problem lies in the fact that we are still at premise stage, and much that we intend has yet to be detailed. Some differences, however, are genuine. I need to make it clear that Will, Mark, and I are confident that we know exactly what the basic direction of this series needs to be and why. I want to make our purpose clear so that future suggestions can be better focused and even more helpful.

I might add that we are ANXIOUS for help from those who know the details of this world so well. Every day that we are without every possible resource available from Marvel, for example, is a day that we are delayed or that we are using inferior or incomplete information. It is our biggest problem at the moment. We feel like we are working in the dark. Much more delay will make this help useless.

Our show is about the X-Men. They are our title characters. All other considerations are secondary. When a conflict occurs and we have to slight other characters or groups, we will.

The underlying focus of the show is: "Why do the X-Men exist?" The stories we have chosen to tell—of the hundreds we could have chosen—serve this purpose. An outgrowth of this focus is the continuing question, "And what does their future hold?"

Questions of the X-Men's purpose immediately center on XAVIER'S VISION OF HUMAN-MUTANT HARMONY. Stories and characters were chosen that best focus on the challenges to that harmony—from all sources, mutant and human.

All other concerns, though real, are secondary. Which adversaries we use and how we treat them; how various groups like the government or business or individuals within them appear; and which X-Men we use (given stated priorities) and which sides of their characters we are able to reveal in the short time allotted all are important but will be sacrificed when necessary to maintain the series focus and the strength of the unfolding drama.

An excellent example is the question of the initial use of the Sentinels instead of Magneto in the two-part pilot. It is suggested that Magneto is a bigger, more interesting villain. And how, it is asked, can we use the Sentinels without first seeing a major story of mutant violence that might justify the robots' existence? Doesn't this make the U.S. government look terrible?

Though important—and we are carefully addressing the second question in the script—those are the wrong principal questions to ask. Our purpose in the pilot is to introduce the X-Men and the world which has made their existence necessary. Either we focus on the problem of violent mutants or the problem of repressive humans. It's a chicken-and-egg question. They co-exist. We must make a moral judgment. We have chosen to give a slight emphasis to the problem of human repression over mutant terrorism. To do the reverse would be to establish the X-Men as primarily policemen, prison guards protecting humankind from incorrigible members of their own (mutant) people. It would also lean the show toward a series of fights against "The Bad Mutant of the Week"—the least interesting, easiest, most overdone approach possible.

Nothing better illustrates the primary reason for the existence of the X-Men than a physical manifestation of humans' anxiety over the existence of mutants: the Sentinels. The robots' precise, PUBLICLY STATED, SEEMINGLY BENIGN MISSION—and its evolving perversion at the hands of a SMALL ROGUE GROUP of anti-mutant humans—is open to fine-tuning. Their presence as a dramatic metaphor for human-mutant anxiety and distrust is essential. Five billion humans are not simply background in this world. They are easy to lose track of amidst the battles of super-beings. We must work to keep them involved. Mutant registration and the existence of the Sentinels are the best way I have seen so far of accomplishing this.

In short, do not worry about the overall direction of the series. We won't make the U.S. government look like drooling fascists. Individuals will be extreme, the institution will not. When Jesse Helms speaks, it is not "the policy of the U.S. government" that he espouses, but his own. Oliver North ran an entire war on the sly. No, what we need is help with details—primarily character and power details—so that these stories can be the best they possibly can. I don't want to find out three weeks after we've done recording that Jubilee is Cyclops and Jean Grey's daughter and that Rogue can demagnetize Magneto. While creative suggestions can be helpful, what we really need is raw information. I would appreciate any help you can give me in getting this message across while it still can do some good.

Look for a first draft of the script to Episode #1 on Thursday afternoon. I believe it will answer many of your questions.

ERIC

WITH THE FIRST MAJOR CRISIS of the production behind us, scripts poured forth with storyboards starting up right behind them.

Until the next crisis. Nearly a month in, all of a sudden, we were told that the agreed-upon character designs were all wrong. Quite literally we were told to "go back to the drawing board." Our September airdate now seemed an impossible goal. But why?

Will recalls, "After I had gotten the initial designs of Wolverine, Cyclops, and Jean approved, suddenly I got a note from Marvel saying, 'You have to put away all the Jim Lee references. We can't do a show that looks like his stuff.'

"The problem turned out to be that Jim and a few other major Marvel artists had announced that they were leaving to found Image Comics. I knew that we had to use those costumes, so I thought, 'I'm going to do a model sheet that's so dumb they will be forced into using the right ones.' So I drew and submitted a young/funny—completely wrong—Hanna-Barbera, 1970s version of the X-Men team.

"We had just added artist/designer Rick Hoberg to the mix on the crew. Rick wasn't aware of the politics, and when he got the Hanna-Barbera versions, he about had a heart attack. He was on the phone to Stan [Lee] and others, horrified, saying, 'We can't do this, what is Will thinking?! He's going to ruin the show!' It worked out well that Stan sincerely thought I was being an idiot for doing the wrong designs that upset Rick so much.

"The danger when you play that card, of course, is that there's going to be somebody somewhere who thinks the awful stuff is a good design.

"After that, Marvel realized that they had to do the version that was more like Jim Lee, so we took the Lee costume designs and made them a little bit more animate-able. Then Rick's line work unified it into that cohesive style. That's when I started shifting off character design more to focus on story with you guys [Eric and Mark], and then the day-to-day operation of the show, trying to make sure it didn't go off the tracks. Rick and Larry started taking over the designs, but there were certain characters, like the Beast and Colossus, where nobody was comfortable drawing them as big as they should be, so I wound up doing them because I was the only one who was willing to go to that level of the grotesque, to get the Beast to be as huge as he was in the comics then."

Two crises, two saves by force of Will.

Then, about a month in, the first voice tracks came in.

As the first few scripts were being finished, a voice cast had been assembled in Toronto, Canada. Many modest-budget US animated shows were voice-recorded there—their actors' guild had a less expensive deal that producers like Saban couldn't resist. They also had a large pool of experienced voice-over people, many of whom had done excellent work for Fox TV, most recently on the animated *Beetlejuice* series, which had just won the Emmy Award for best animated show of 1990.

But at first they didn't understand our show. The initial voice recording of "Night of the Sentinels" was so misguided that Sidney Iwanter and Larry Houston had to go to Toronto for two weeks—joined by Bob Harras and Joe Calamari from Marvel Comics—to recast and rerecord.

What we all wanted for *X-Men: TAS* was so different from the animated network series that had come before, veteran actors and voice directors just couldn't imagine it. They had offered us a young, cartoony, *Scooby-Doo*-ish version of the X-Men. It was what they were used to doing.

It was horrifying.

Sidney recalls, "It was one of those situations where the scripts were light-years different from what most producers had seen in the '70s or '80s doing action-adventure shows. Their recording played like *Casper and the Space Angels*. All the voices sounded alike. I said to Margaret, 'If you're going to have dialogue like this, if you're going to have situations like this, there's got to be some gravitas and a distinctiveness to their voices.' So I went up to Toronto and recast with casting director Karen Goora—she was really good.

"We cast a wide net, and we got Cedric Smith for Professor X—Shakespearean trained with a voice like God's—David Hemblen, who was Magneto, same thing. The great thing about Toronto is that they're second only to New York as a North American theater community, so we were picking theater-trained individuals, some of whom had never done animation before. There was a richness. Then we had to tell the voice director that we weren't going to do it the same way as always. We weren't just going to take the first or second read— we were going to get this dramatically correct. Or in the case of characters like Morph or Mojo, comically correct. Because if the writers were building in character traits and personalities, we had to show it.

"We cast a guy named Cathal "Cal" Dodd, who was a jazz singer. Guys like that understand microphones. He's asking us, 'What kind of character is Wolverine?' I remember saying, 'He's got Adamantium claws, he's been screwed around with, he's Canadian, but he's feral, he's one angry guy.' I said feral, and Cal's in front of the microphone and he starts growling, he's playing with his voice, and I said, 'Do that!' *Cal invented the Wolverine growl!*"

Cal says, "I asked: 'Who is this guy, Wolverine? What does he do?' They said: 'He's short.'" In the sample dialogue I was given (aka 'sides'), Logan was confronting someone who had been bullying people: 'You like picking on people smaller than you? Pick on me, *I'm* smaller than you, pal.' I grew up in a small town where that happened a lot, a little place on Lake Erie. There were a lot of fights, so it came naturally to me: 'Pick on me, punk, *I'm* smaller than you.' I read it once, and when I looked through the glass [to the recording booth], they all jumped out of their seats. Literally, because they'd been auditioning for this part for weeks."

Cal remembered feelings he had about working with specific characters. "One of my favorites was Beast. I just loved his character, loved the voice that [George] Buza came up with— because he was very refined, a refined blue beast who hangs upside down from things, with this *wonderful* voice. George

worked at Stratford [Shakespeare] Theater, so when he read any of that poetry it would seem to flow right into whatever he was saying.

"The scenes I didn't really look forward to, although they were fantastic for the kids to watch, but which just tore my throat apart, were with Sabretooth [Don Francks]. The fight scenes went on forever. All that shouting and screaming. I'd hear [from voice director Dan Hennessey]: 'Could you do that one more time, Cal?' 'Well maybe *you* can, Dan. Why don't *you* come in and scream it?'"

Alyson Court, who voiced Jubilee, remembers Cal as a gruff, real-life protector: "It was sort of art imitating life. I grew up in the same neighborhood [in Toronto] that Cal lived in, right around the corner from his house. Whenever there were *X-Men: TAS* crew and cast parties, they would end up back at Cal's house. I think I still have one of his tracksuits after ending up one night unexpectedly in the pool with the rest of the cast. He was very protective, and I was eighteen at the time and the

youngest full-time cast member, so when we were in party situations where adults are going to do adult things, Cal would kind of raise one eyebrow and look at people." Problem solved.

Alyson remembers how hard the cast worked to get the *X-Men: TAS* tone just right: "Well, you know that we recorded that first double episode four times? I cannot imagine how much it cost them for those first few episodes because they would have the entire cast there, and then they would have a bunch of us wait outside—thank goodness the place had a pinball machine. Then they would bring us in, in groups, and they would work their way through the scripts. We were all on the clock, so we were all getting paid for waiting around all this time. In hindsight, they knew what they were doing because they didn't go to air until they had the voices exactly the way that they wanted them, so I respect them for it. But those were

ABOVE Production cel of Wolverine, unknown origin. Background from Irish castle in "The Phoenix Saga, Part 3: The Cry of the Banshee."

some brutal first sessions. You would record one line and then Dan Hennessey, our voice director, would just be like, 'Aaaand hang on.' He'd sit back, and you'd see him waiting as you watched all these men behind him [Sidney, Joe, Larry] arguing, hands flying up in the air, very strident, with hyperbolic conversations going on. As the actor in the recording room, it was fascinating to watch. Initially, it was terrifying because, like, 'What did I say? What did I do that was so horribly wrong that all these people are having this screaming match now?' Often it didn't end up having much to do with the actor: They were trying to get their own personal vision into it so the intonation was exactly as each one of them had heard it in his head. That took a lot of wrestling and trial and error to work its way through."

Norm Spencer, who played straight-arrow Scott Summers/Cyclops, remembers working with the cast and a favorite episode: "We certainly all became the old cliché, like a family, doing this together. One episode I do remember distinctly, and that was when Don Francks played my father, Corsair ["Orphan's End," ep. 44]. What a great guy! That story was fun because it was the two of us doing big scenes together. Any voice session he would do he did in his bare feet. I don't know why, that's just the way he did it. We had a great time, and it was a real dialogue between us. We formed a father-son relationship with the dialogue, and afterward he said, 'It was so rewarding working with you!' I took that as a such huge compliment because he's somewhat of an icon for me—as a performer, not just as an actor, but a writer, a poet."

Lenore Zann, the voice of Rogue, remembers that, at first, she resisted even auditioning for "just a cartoon." Then she discovered who she would be working with. "That serious cast was a new thing for the cartoon world there in Toronto. The actors who joined X-Men: TAS really had talent. We had great respect for each other: We'd seen each other in major plays, we'd seen each other in other television series or movies, and a lot of us had worked together on film or onstage. It was like doing a play with a cast that you were seriously getting to know: We made each other be better.

"It was great when the show got picked up again each time because we got to come back together and hang and create magic, create these incredible stories and bring them to life. When we were in the studio, it felt like we were doing classic radio drama. I seem to remember hanging out a lot with Ron Rubin [Morph] and Norm Spencer [Cyclops] and Cal and Catherine [Disher, who played Jean Grey]. Whenever there were guest stars that were in just a few episodes at a time, we'd hang out together too, so there was a real camaraderie. I think that really helped our performances in the show."

01

Lenore is currently a member of the Canadian Parliament—where her history as Rogue helps her in efforts to pass legislation. When she meets forty-year-old male colleagues, who were fifteen when the show was on, and tells them that she was Rogue, they often go weak in the knees.

Lenore says, "The guys almost faint, it's weird to watch them. Something comes over their faces, and they just start to shiver and shake, and they have trouble breathing."

George Buza, who played Beast, was the one *X-Men: TAS* cast member who ended up in the first X-Men live-action movie some years later (2000).

George: "They found out I was the voice of Beast and gave me that truck-driver role delivering Rogue to the town where she meets Wolverine. It was exciting, very interesting to see that whole project take flight. They told me that if it weren't for our series, that movie never would've been made."

Eric: "Do you remember your first voice direction on Beast?"

George: "Make it natural. They told me: 'Don't come up with a voice that makes them think you're blue.'"

Catherine Disher, who was our Jean Grey, remembers how special the series was at an unusual time in her life: "The thing I remember most that made *X-Men* special—because I do a lot of cartoons—was that the scripts really had very deep emotions to them. There was right and wrong and prejudice and doing the right thing and these beleaguered X-Men doing all they could. It just felt heroic. They're the best scripts I've ever seen for cartoons, and I've been doing cartoons now for over thirty years.

"The X-Men had so much important dialogue between people it made a lot of sense to record together when we could. I got pregnant and had my son in September of '93. I remember having my son and nursing him behind the potted palm in the big lobby of this recording-studio complex. His father, of course, was Professor X. The first guy who was Professor X was another actor, and then they quickly replaced him with Cedric Smith, who is my son's father.

"It wasn't until my son got to school age when he would tell people, 'My mom is Jean Grey,' and they would freak out. He loved to go with me to comic book stores, like when he was ten and I was doing a television series in Halifax, in Nova Scotia. I remember he told these two guys who were looking at the *X-Men* comics, 'Oh yeah, well you know my mom is Jean Grey, and my dad is Professor X.' You should've seen the looks on these two guys' faces—I thought they were going to swallow their tongues! That's when I realized, 'I'm kind of a hero.'

"Because of Jean Grey, I became *proud* of doing cartoons. I used to keep it secret until my son helped me discover that it was a cool thing to do."

Some actors were "utility players," hired to do many different voices. Lawrence Bayne was primarily known as our Cable, but he voiced a dozen more.

Lawrence says, "I've got the baritone that can growl, and I can also high-end it. I was Eric the Red, and then yeah, a whole lot of minions with three lines before they got blown up. I was the go-to guy for that. Sidney trusted how many voices I had, and then later Dan Hennessey, who wanted to rein in the energy, just wanted to see what I could do. Dan stretched me; Sidney just counted on me. I like being the utility guy; it's fun to do. I do my main character and they'll say, "Can you do this other line?" Of course, you're gonna do it, because it's a few more ducats in your envelope, but it's also a fantastic way to demonstrate to them, 'Ya know, maybe next time you don't have to audition me? Maybe you can just call me?'"

Lawrence loved working with Cal Dodd. "Cal and I get along great," he says. "We're just two Toronto tough guys, both of us. I'm street level. Cal's a real 'take no shit' kinda guy, always been a good friend. Cal and I did an episode where he was Wolverine and I was Captain America. Loved it. You know, I auditioned for Wolverine first. But I knew Cal would get it because Cal's a fucking genius."

Another fan of Cal's was Hugh Jackman, who followed Cal in the movie versions of the Wolverine role. When the two met, after the first movie, Hugh famously told Cal: "I am *so* sick of hearing your voice! I can't quite get it, but I know that's what they want." Jackman, like the entire *X-Men* movie crew, went to school on *X-Men: TAS*.

FINALLY, after those four grueling attempts at rerecording the pilot script, over two days, the right tone was achieved. The new cast, and their new attitude, sounded great. The first storyboard was finished, and it looked spectacular.

Over the next three months, eight of the thirteen scripts were finalled, six voice tracks were recorded, and half the storyboards were drawn. The relentless pace of an episode a week schedule was straining but holding.

Finally, in late July, more than five months after *X-Men: TAS* started, just after the last script had been turned in, the first animated footage came back from AKOM, the animation production house in South Korea. With the tight scripts, masterful storyboards, and heartfelt recordings, expectations were high.

DAILY VARIETY
85 CENTS
FRIDAY
FEBRUARY 5, 1993
ANIMATION SPECIAL REPORT
X-PLOSIVE RATINGS!
The #1 Saturday Morning Kids Show
Boys 6-11 10.8
Boys 12-17 10.5
MARVEL COMICS
X-MEN®

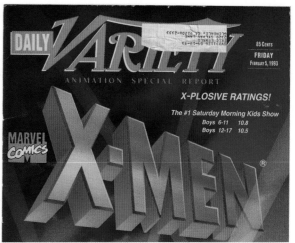

02

But the animated footage was awful. It felt like five months' hard work had been for nothing.

Margaret Loesch said Fox wouldn't accept it; the animation studio had to fix their work or the series wouldn't air.

The animation studio swore they needed more time and money: This was by far the most demanding series they had ever been asked to do. And so Margaret, at a great price, got the Fox network to take the huge risk of putting off the series premiere for four months, from September 1992 to January 1993, to give the animators time to get things right. And Marvel Comics, to their everlasting credit, stepped up with some of the needed extra cash, contributing their licensing fee to help pay to get the footage redone when no one else would.

By the end of July, the writers had finished their work. Six weeks later, so had the artists. All were let go, forced to take other work while everyone waited the four months for the January premiere, hoping for news of good ratings and a possible second season.

There were hints that success was possible. Two sneak previews of the pilot story—pushed through by Margaret, in Fox prime time on Halloween and Thanksgiving—were widely watched and seemed, pre-Internet-feedback, to be well received. The fans were excited, curious.

Then, to the team's great gratification, when the series properly premiered in January, it shot right to number one in the ratings and never looked back.

01 Production cel of Rogue in action, unknown episode. **02** Authors' copy of "the bible of Hollywood," *Daily Variety*, which proclaimed that, after only four weeks on the air, *X-Men: TAS* had rocketed to become the number one Saturday-morning program nationwide.

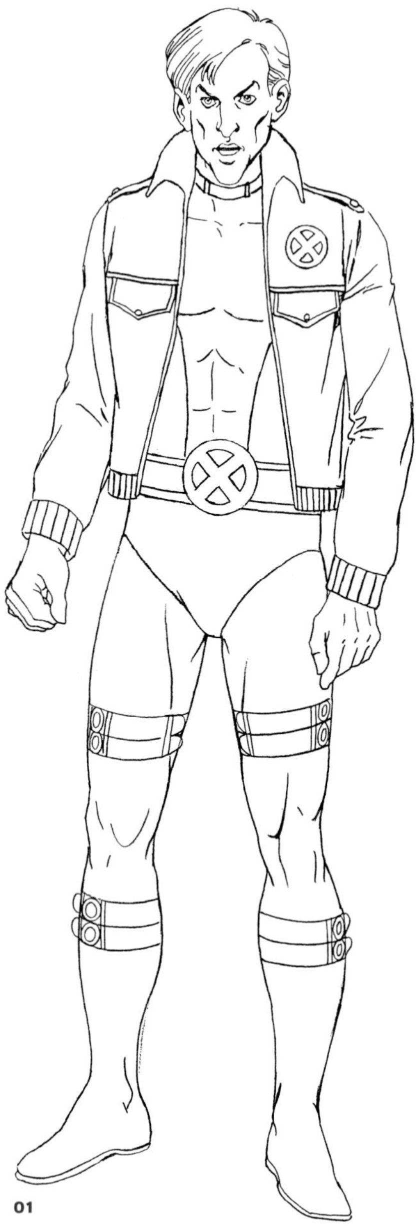

01

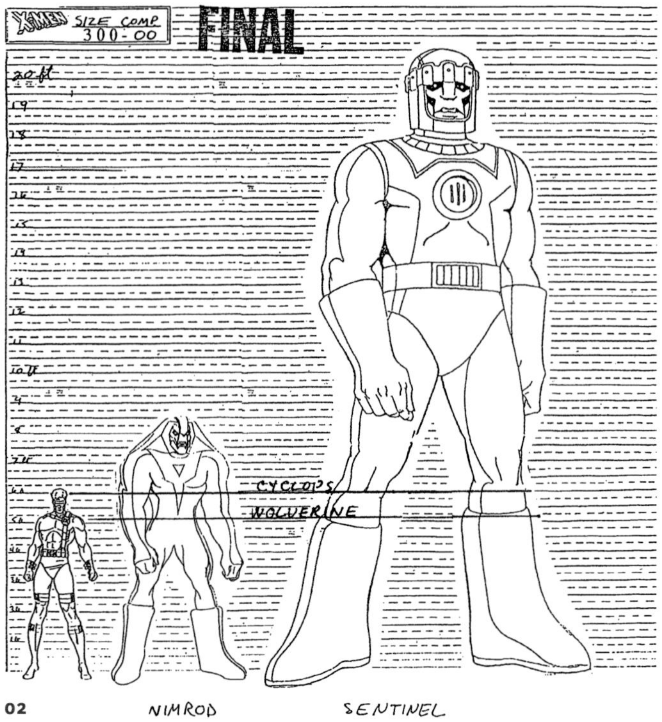

X-MEN SIZE COMP
300-00
FINAL
CYCLOPS
WOLVERINE
NIMROD
SENTINEL

02

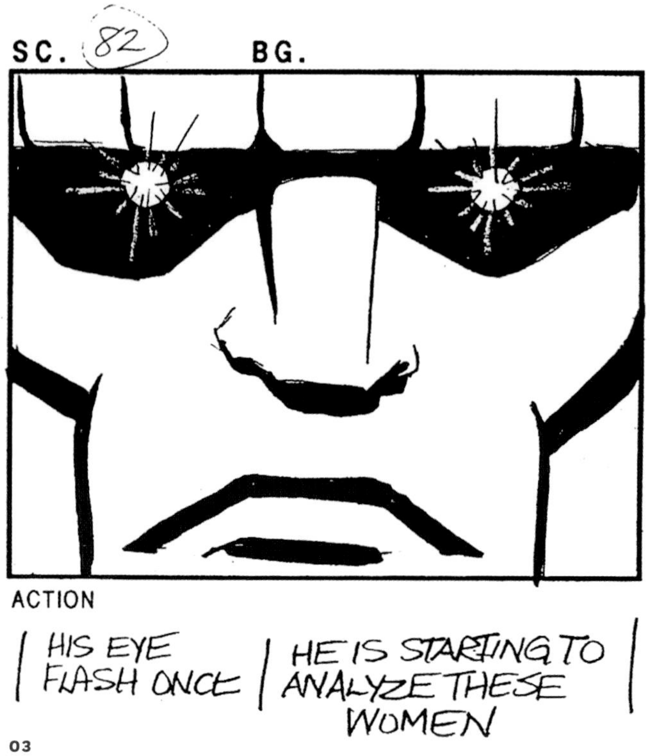

SC. 82
BG.
ACTION
HIS EYE FLASH ONCE
HE IS STARTING TO ANALYZE THESE WOMEN

03

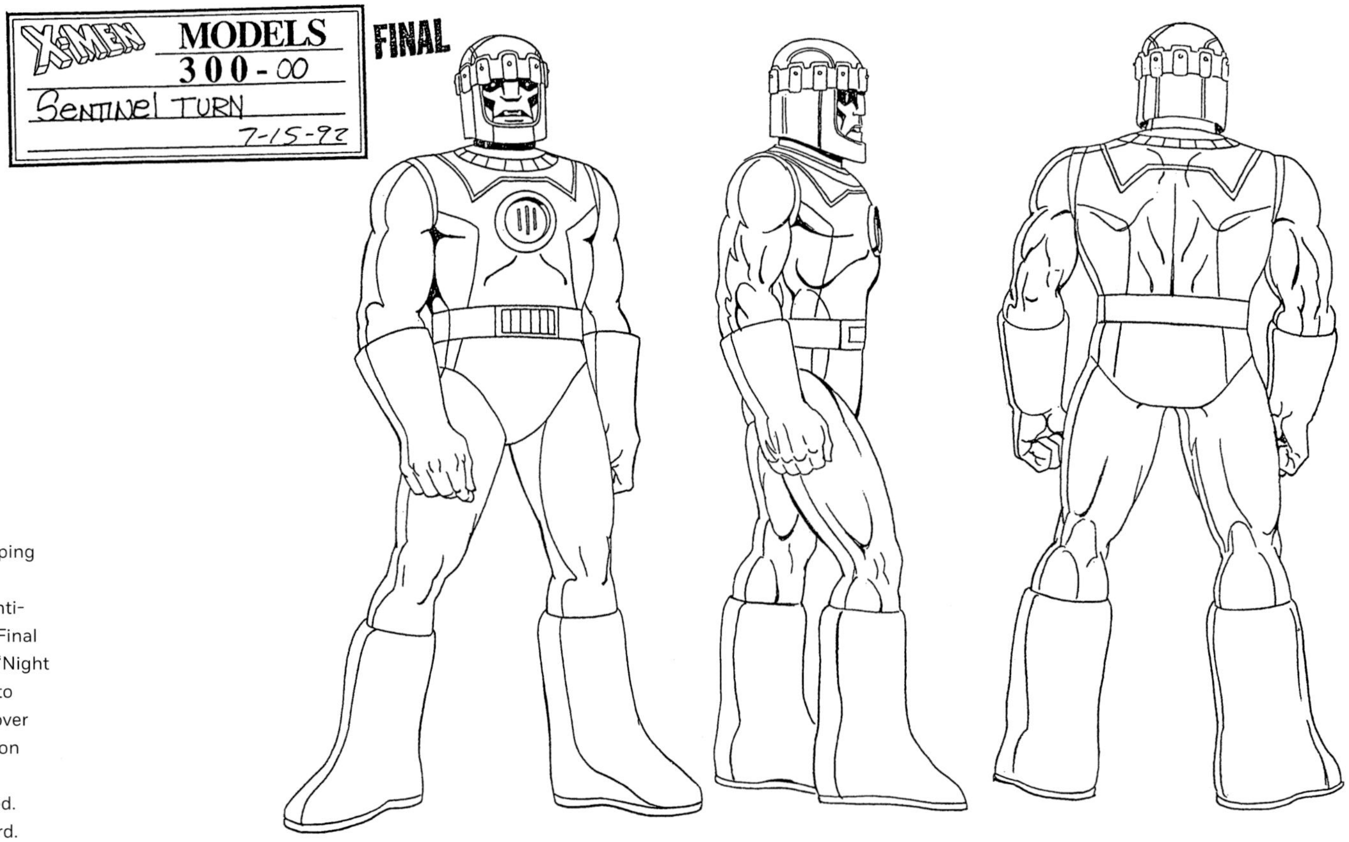

X-MEN
MODELS
300-00
Sentinel TURN
7-15-92
FINAL

04

01 Final character model for Morph, who was to give his life helping the team, by Rick Hoberg. **02** Artists' model lineup to establish Sentinel scale vs. X-Men, by Hoberg. **03** The face of soulless, anti-mutant evil; image from first storyboard by Larry Houston. **04** Final character model for the Sentinels in our two-part pilot episode "Night of the Sentinels," by Hoberg. **05** The one time we were allowed to show one X-Man hitting another, when Wolverine was grieving over the death of his best friend, Morph. **06** Eric's editorial suggestion given to director Larry Houston at storyboard stage—a rare instance where Larry ended up saying no. The moment remained. **07** Dramatic camerawork called out in the "Sentinels" storyboard.

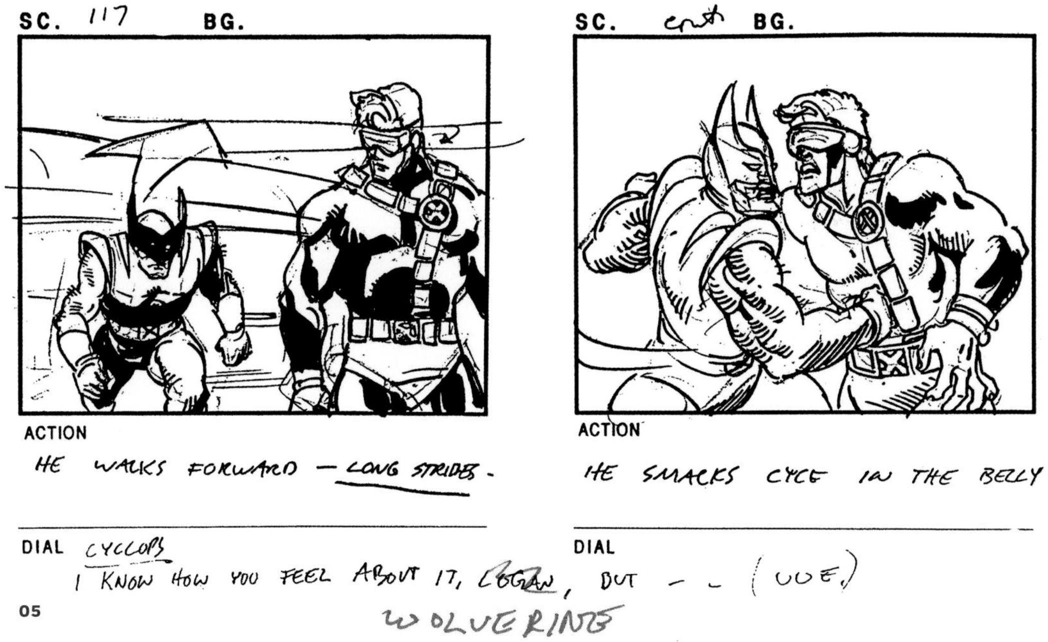
SC. 117 BG.
ACTION
HE WALKS FORWARD — LONG STRIDES -
DIAL CYCLOPS
I KNOW HOW YOU FEEL ABOUT IT, LOGAN, BUT - - (V.O.)
WOLVERINE
SC. BG.
ACTION
HE SMACKS CYCE IN THE BELLY
DIAL

05

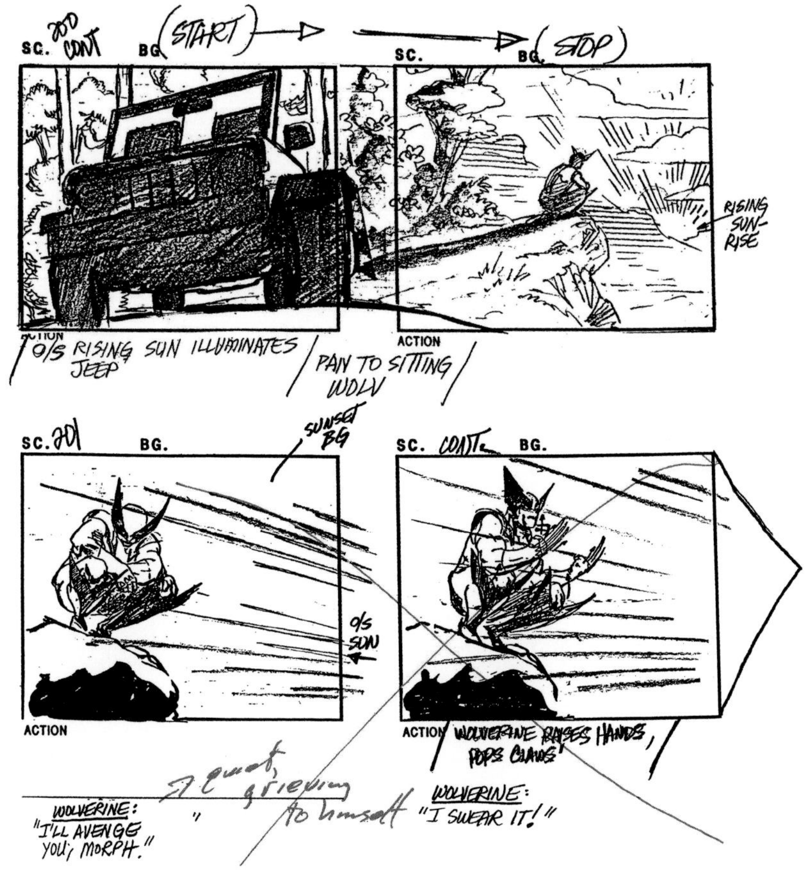
SC. 200 CONT BG. (START)
SC. BG. (STOP)
RISING SUN-RISE
ACTION
O/S RISING SUN ILLUMINATES JEEP
ACTION
PAN TO SITTING WOLV
SC. 201 BG.
SUNSET BG
O/S SUN
ACTION
WOLVERINE: "I'LL AVENGE YOU, MORPH."
SC. CONT BG.
ACTION WOLVERINE RAISES HANDS, POPS CLAWS
WOLVERINE: "I SWEAR IT!"

06

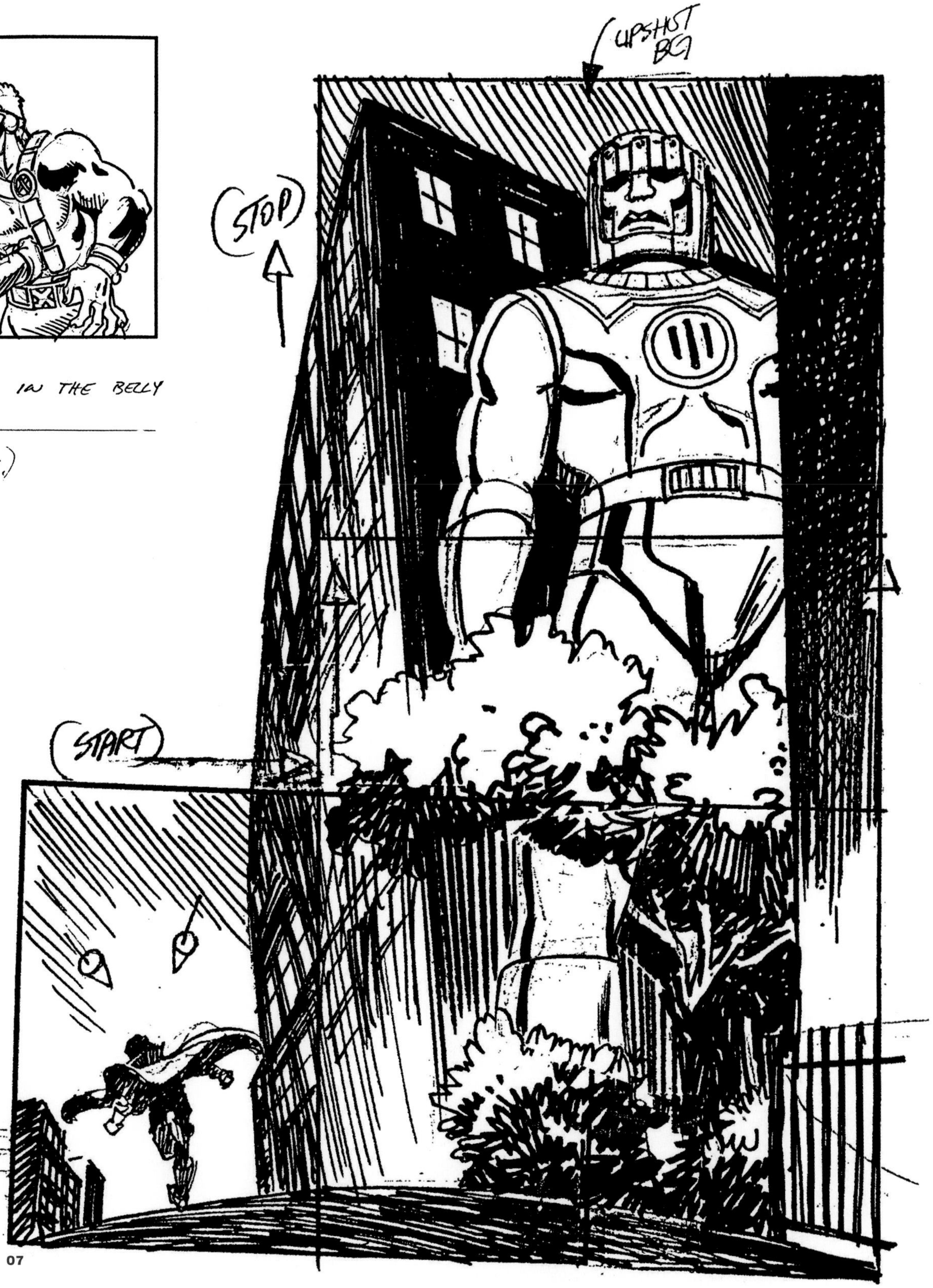
UPSHOT BG
(STOP)
(START)

07

X-MEN	MODELS 300-00	FINAL REVISED
MAGNETO	7-15-92	

01

X-MEN	MODELS 300-00	FINAL
SABERTOOTH - TURNAROUND	8-3-92	

02

X-MEN	MODELS 300-03
YOUNG MAGNETO	REV 5-13-92

5-11-92

03

X-MEN	MODELS 300-03
XAVIER AS YOUNG MAN IN MEDICAL COAT	4-28-92

04

FINAL

JANICE

SHIVA

OMEGA RED

MAVERICK

DEAD POOL

05

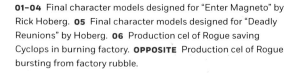

01–04 Final character models designed for "Enter Magneto" by Rick Hoberg. **05** Final character models designed for "Deadly Reunions" by Hoberg. **06** Production cel of Rogue saving Cyclops in burning factory. **OPPOSITE** Production cel of Rogue bursting from factory rubble.

06

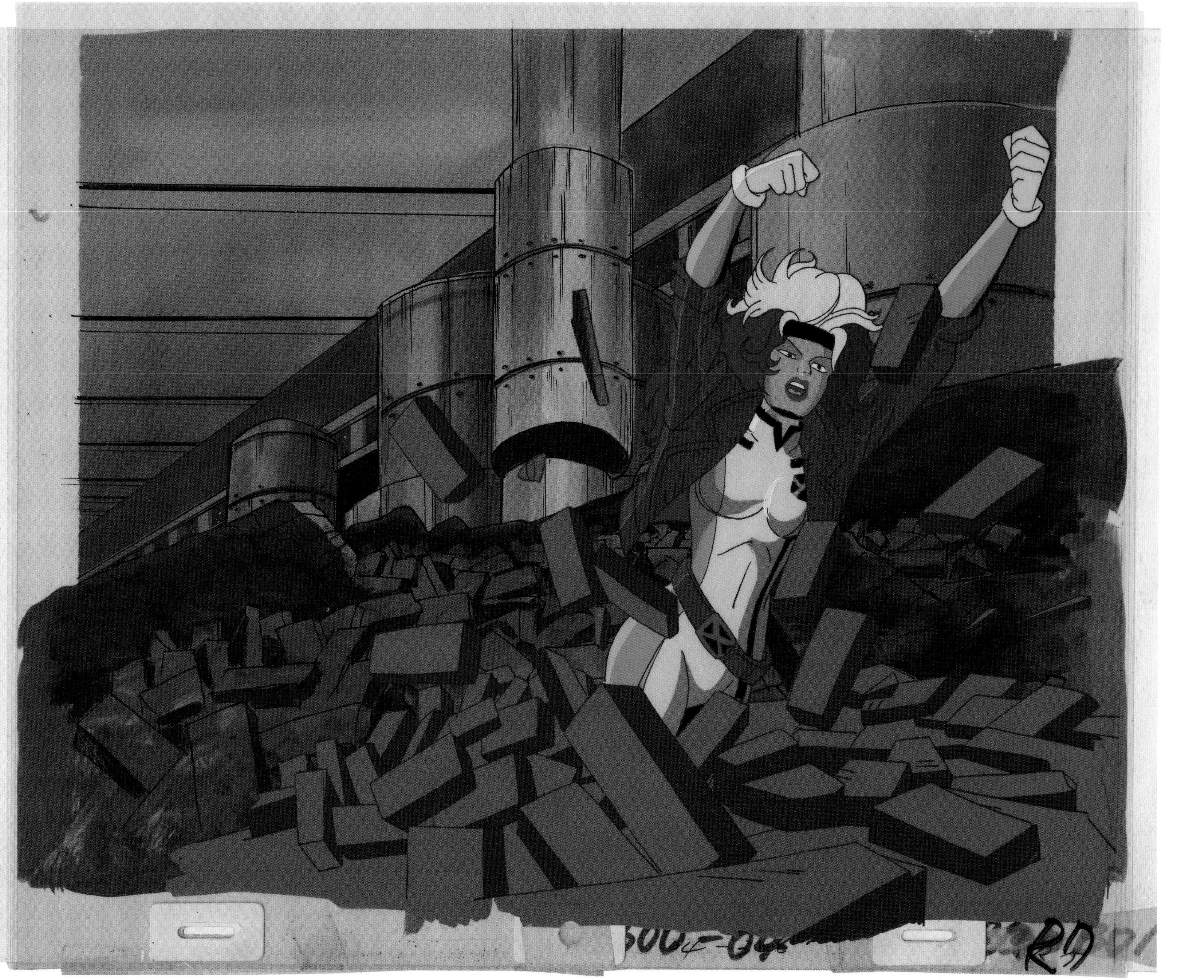

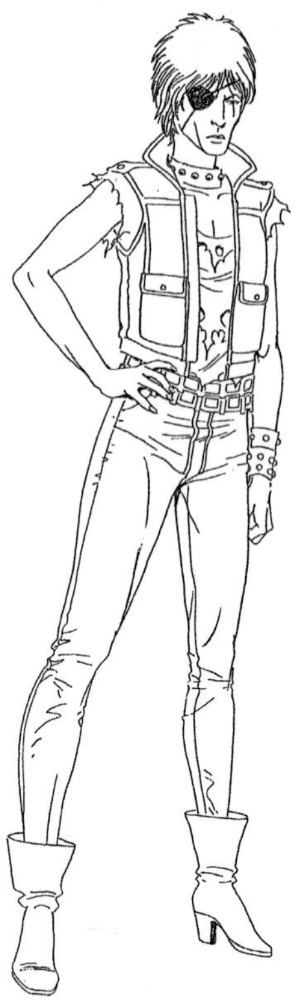

01

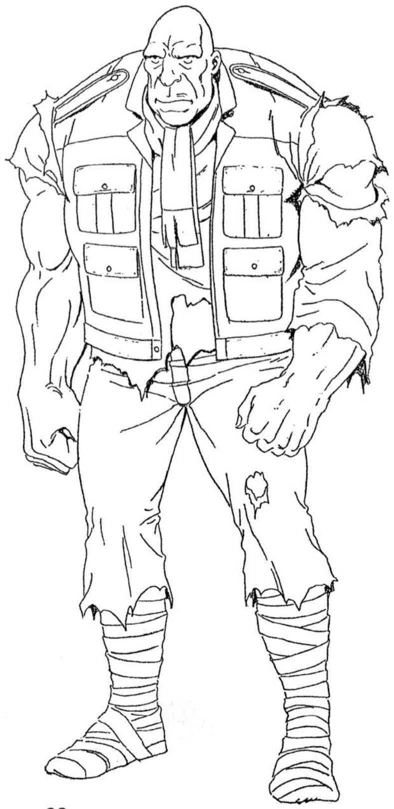

02

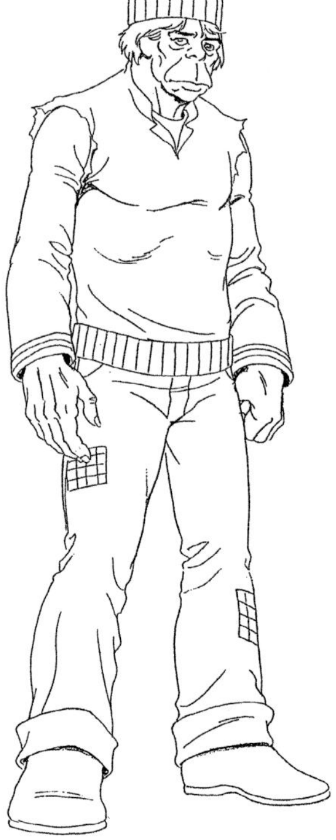

03

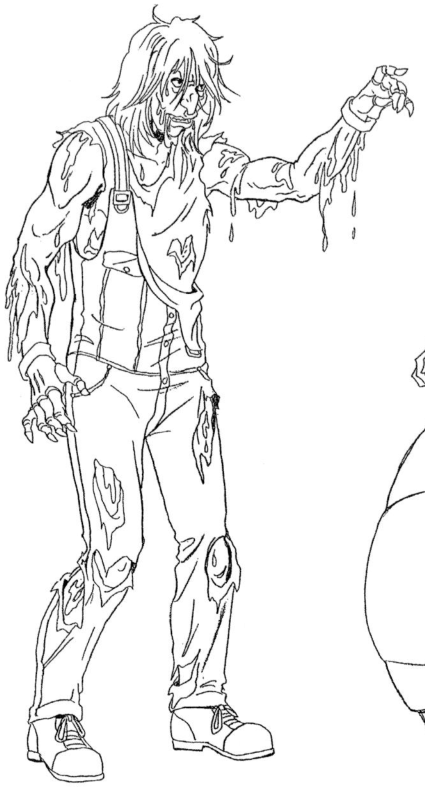

04

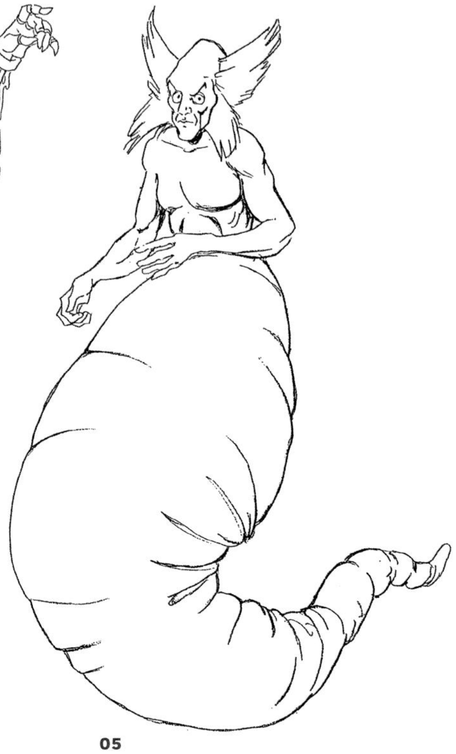

05

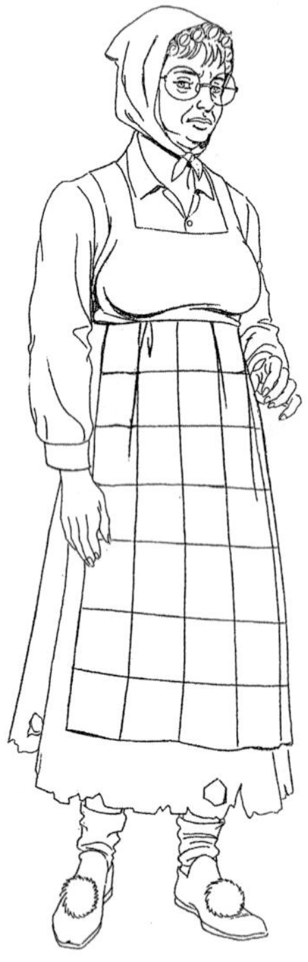

06

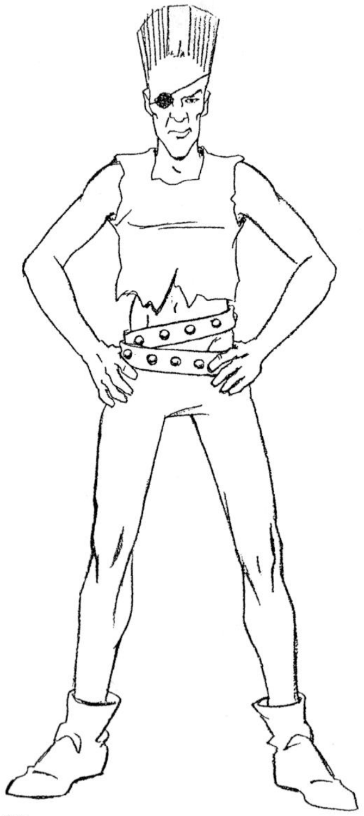

07

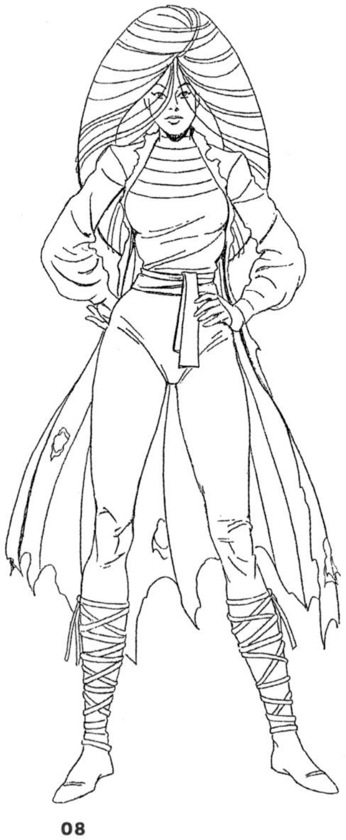

08

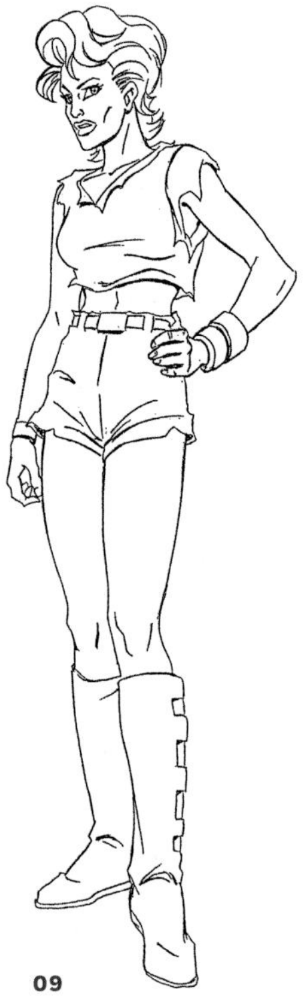

09

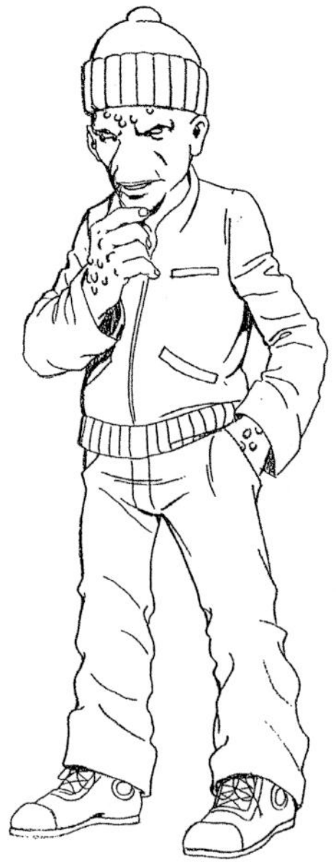

10

01–10 Rough (not final) character models of Morlocks: Callisto, Sunder, Ape, Tar Baby, Glowworm, Annalee, Erg, Tommy, Scaleface, and Leech. Sometimes storyboard artists had to use un-inked, not-final models like these—by Rick Hoberg, with assists from Lewis Williams—if schedules were too tight. **OPPOSITE** Production cel of Sabretooth, as he follows Wolverine to the ends of the Earth (Logan's northern Canada), proving Wolverine can't run away from his problems. Mismatched background, from same episode.

300-06   #0300 3606 S25   BG-36

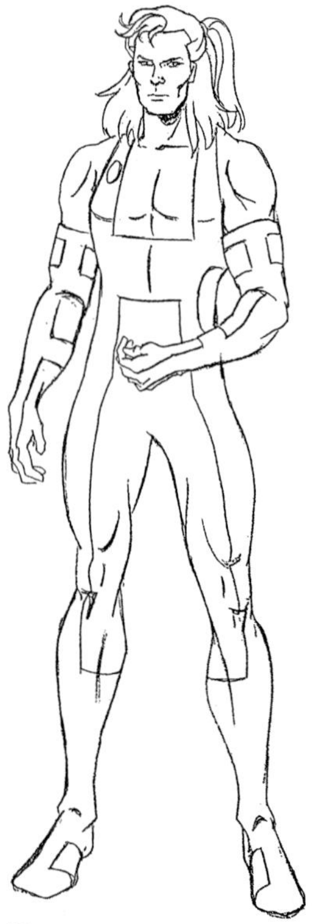

01

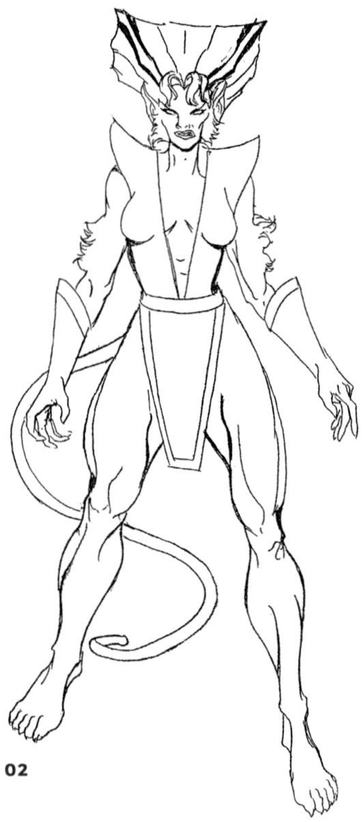

02

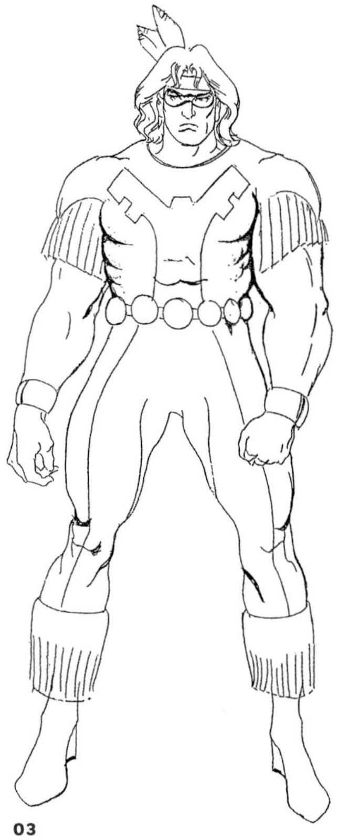

03

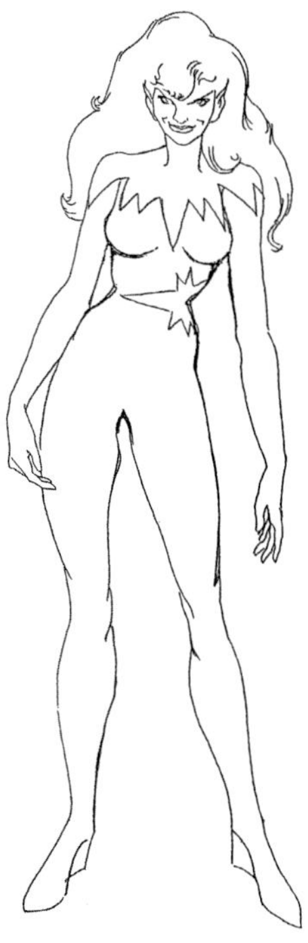

04

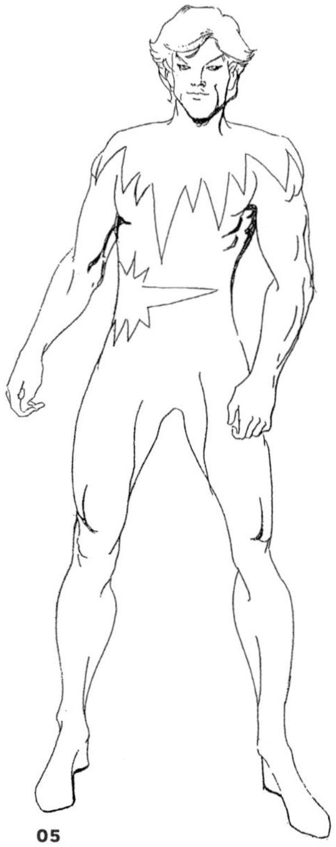

05

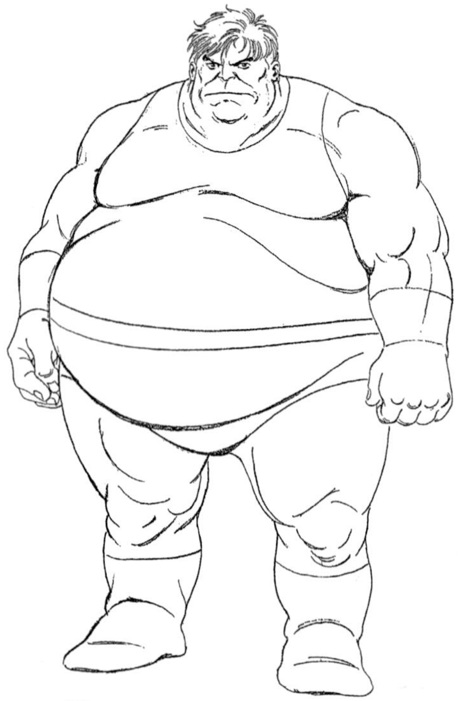

06

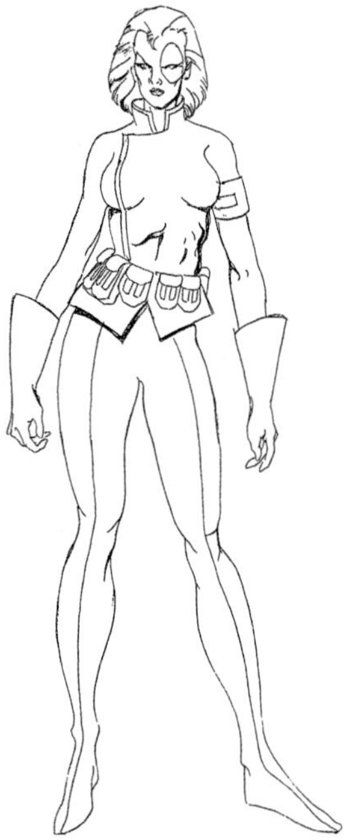

07

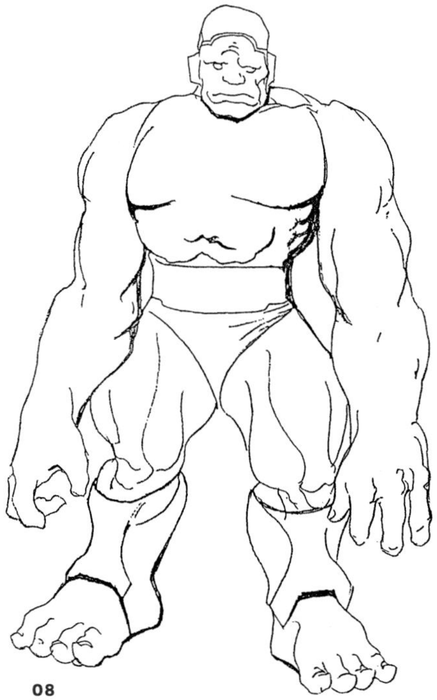

08

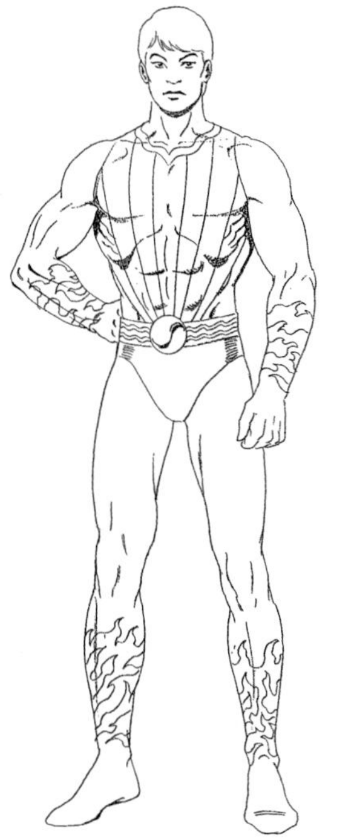

09

01–09 Rough (not final) character models of miscellaneous enslaved mutants among an island full of them. Models by Rick Hoberg, with assists from Lewis Williams. **10** Production cel of three of the enslaved mutants: Feral, Northstar, and Warpath. **11** Bionic eye-action detailed in Cable head mode, by Hoberg. **12** Size comparison design to introduce the “mother” of Sentinels, Master Mold. **13** Storyboard panel introducing Cable in full armor, confronting Gambit.

10

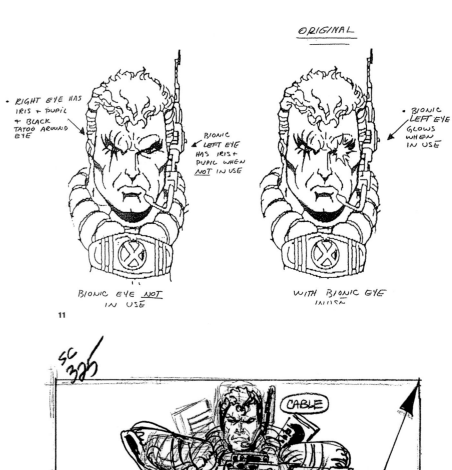

ORIGINAL

• RIGHT EYE HAS
IRIS + PUPIL
+ BLACK
TATOO AROUND
EYE

← BIONIC
LEFT EYE
HAS IRIS +
PUPIL WHEN
NOT IN USE

BIONIC
LEFT EYE
GLOWS
WHEN
IN USE

• BIONIC
LEFT EYE
GLOWS
WHEN
IN USE

BIONIC EYE <u>NOT</u>
IN USE

WITH BIONIC EYE
IN USE

11

✱ THIS IS <u>NOT</u> A SCENE. FOR
ARTIST
REFERENCE
OF
SIZE
ONLY

SIZE
COMPARISON

12

SC
325

CABLE

13

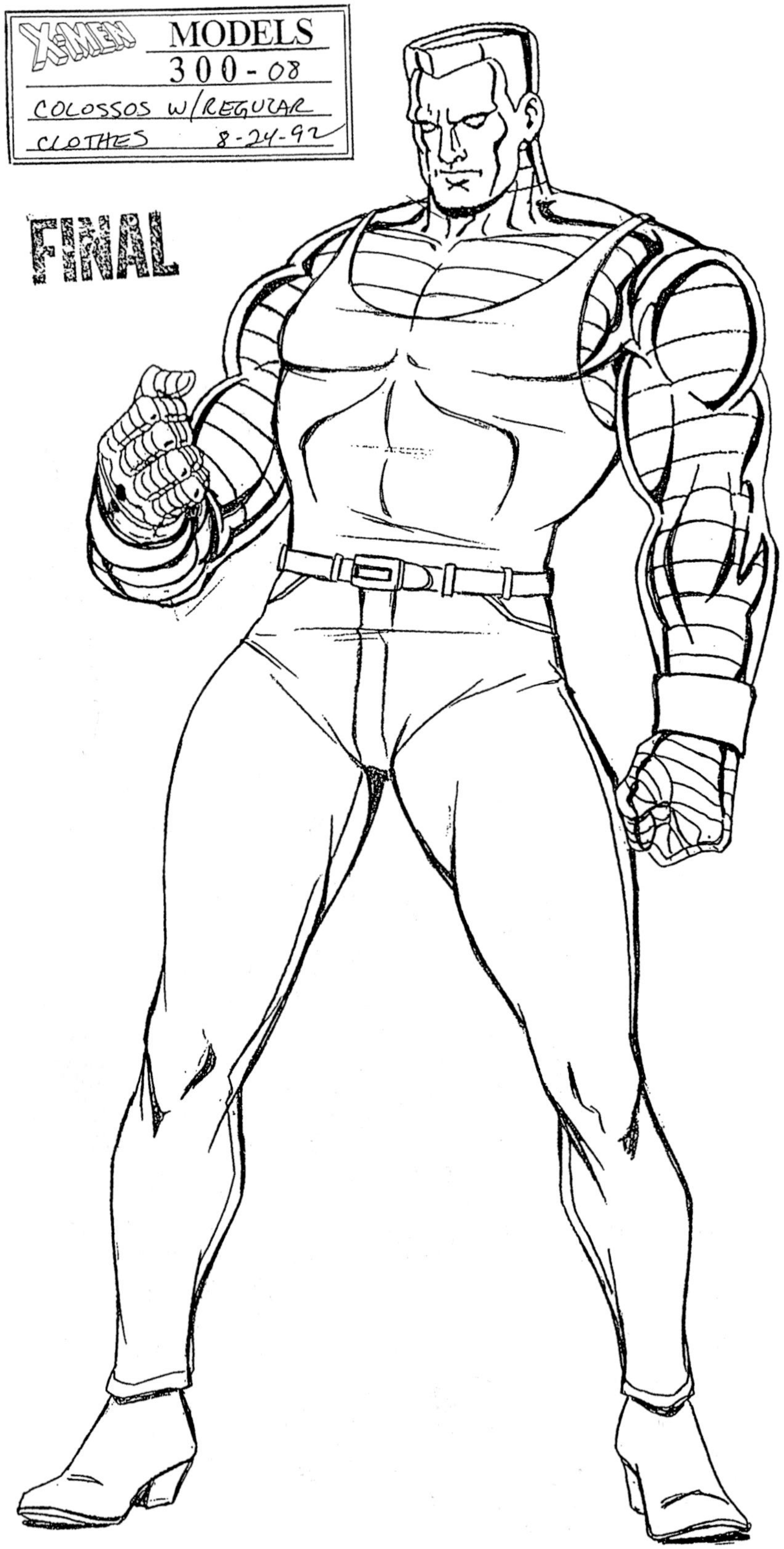
X-MEN MODELS
300-08
COLOSSOS W/REGULAR
CLOTHES 8-24-92
FINAL

01

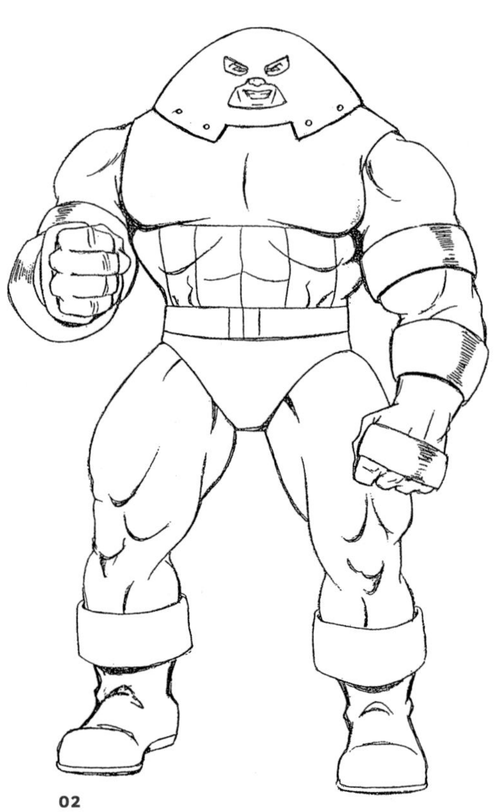

02

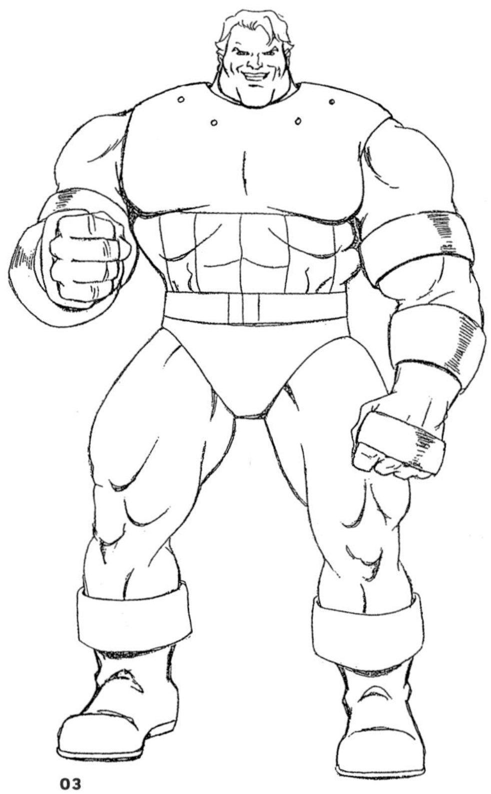

03

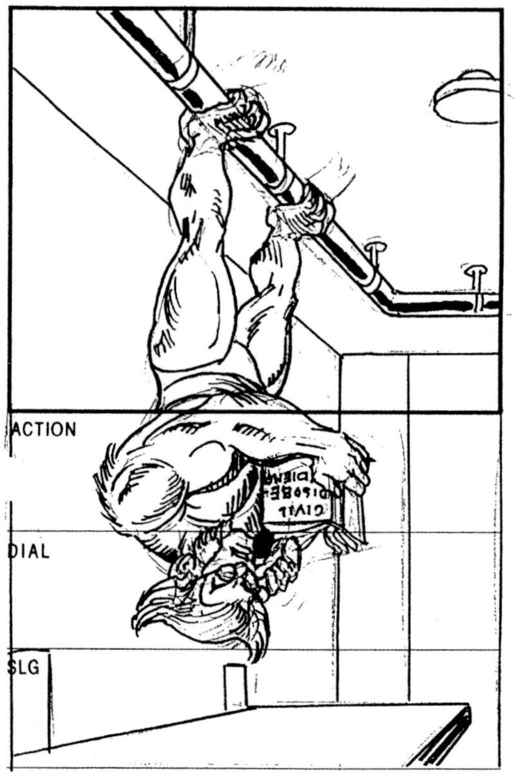
ACTION
DIAL
SLG

04

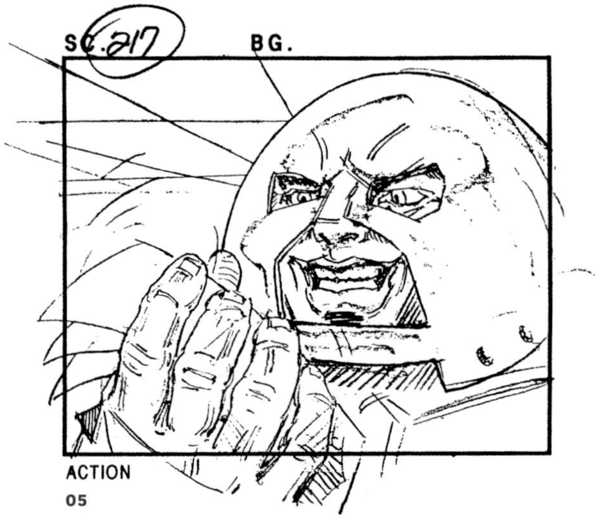
SC 217
BG.
ACTION

05

01 Character model of Colossus in his metallic form, by Rick Hoberg. **02–03** Rough character models of Juggernaut, with and without his helmet, both by Hoberg. **04** Storyboard panel of Beast, reading, patiently awaiting his day in court. **05** Storyboard panel of Juggernaut enjoying the criminal activity that will draw his stepbrother Charles Xavier's team out to confront him. **OPPOSITE** Production cel of Storm in action as the team struggles against Juggernaut.

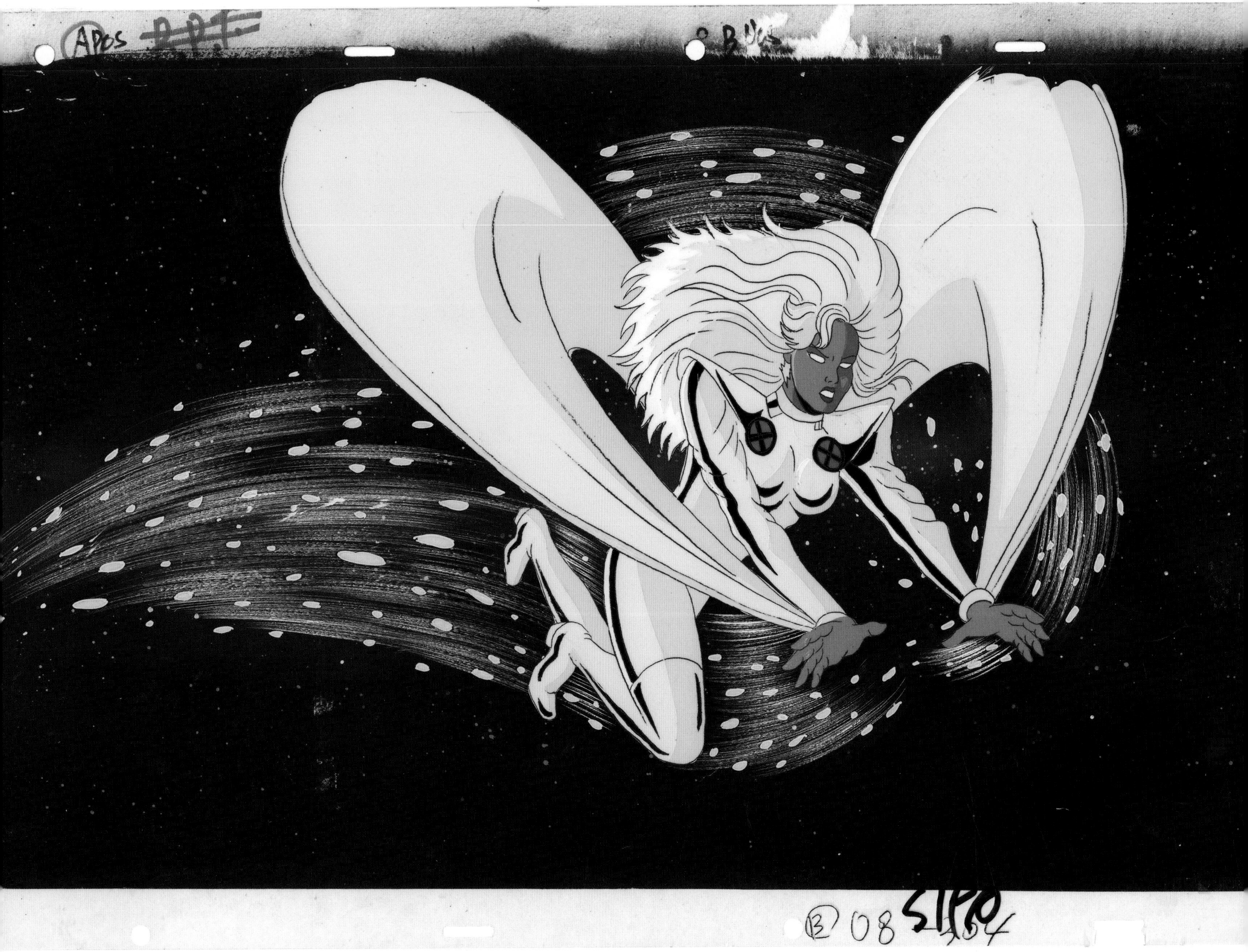

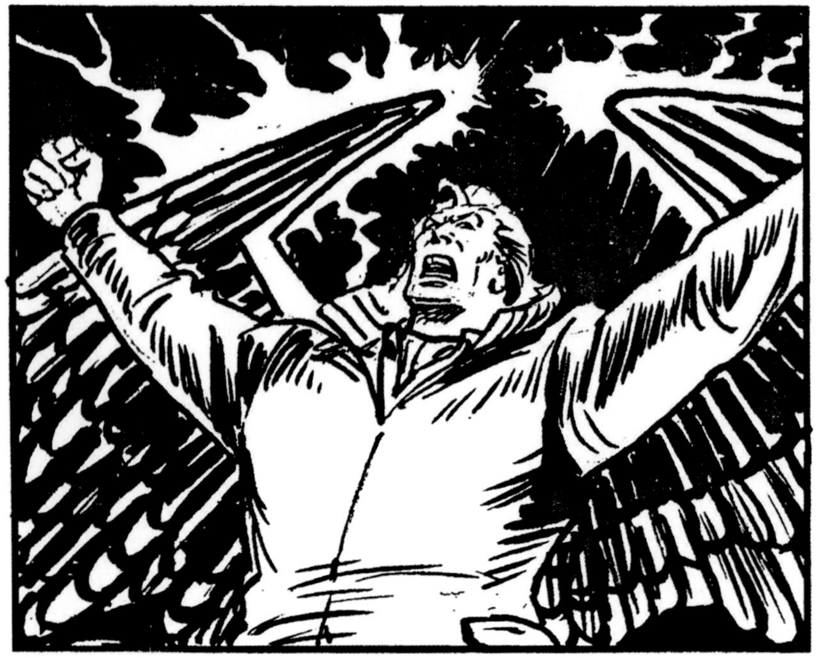
01

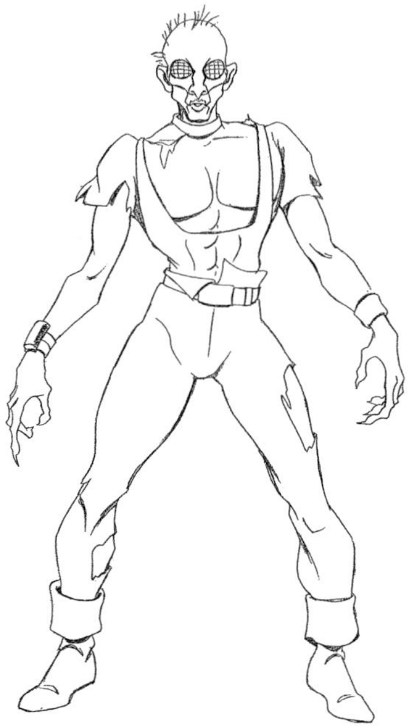
02

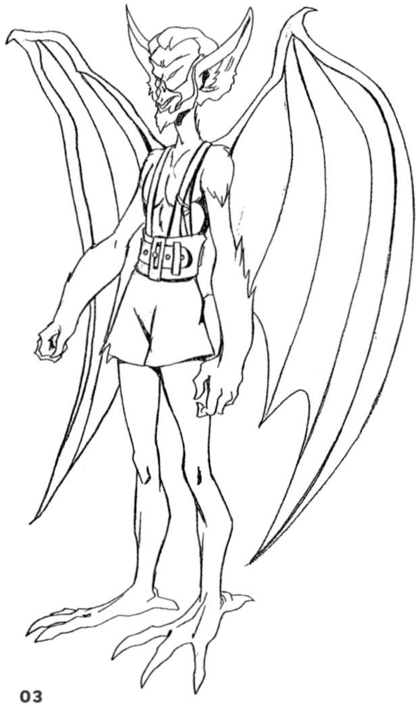
03

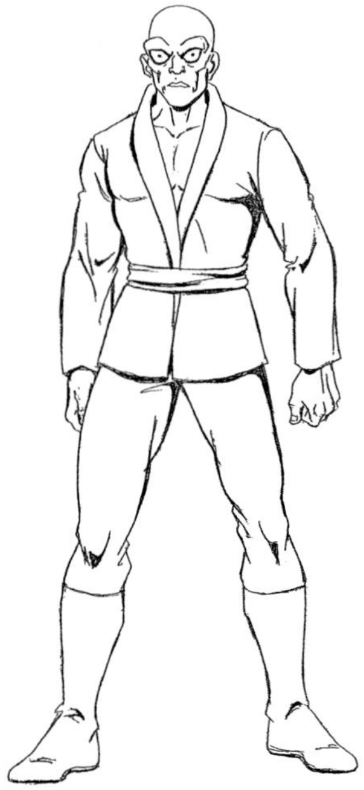
04

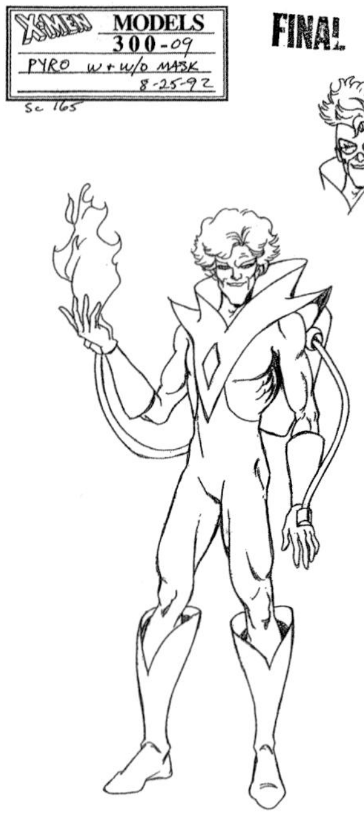
X-MEN MODELS
300-09
PYRO w+w/o MASK
8-25-92
Sc 165
FINAL
05

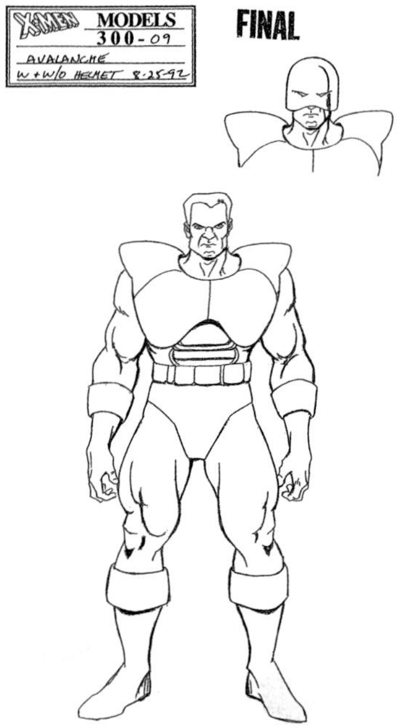
X-MEN MODELS
300-09
AVALANCHE
w+w/o HELMET 8-25-92
FINAL
06

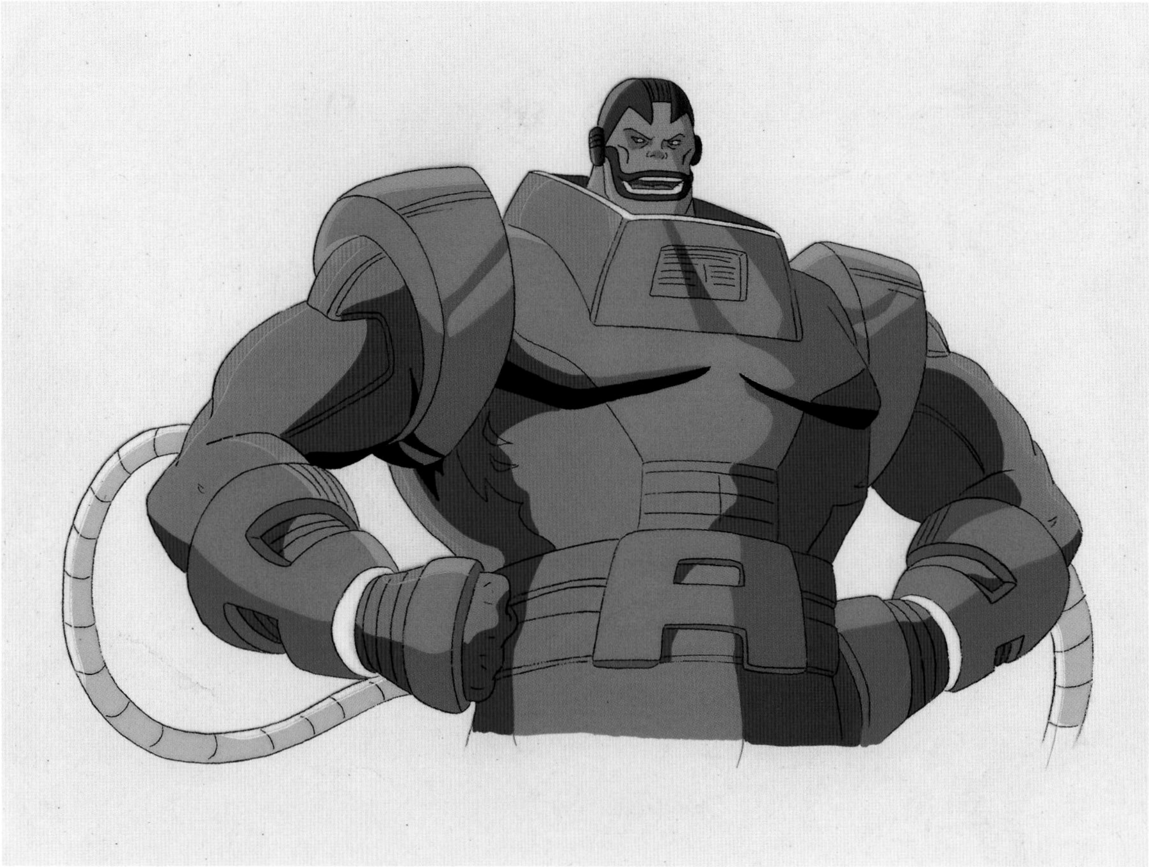
07

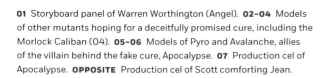

01 Storyboard panel of Warren Worthington (Angel). **02–04** Models of other mutants hoping for a deceitfully promised cure, including the Morlock Caliban (04). **05–06** Models of Pyro and Avalanche, allies of the villain behind the fake cure, Apocalypse. **07** Production cel of Apocalypse. **OPPOSITE** Production cel of Scott comforting Jean.

#09   BG SC 5434   A14

01 Model of one of Apocalypse's four horsemen: War. These and all other models on these two pages by Rick Hoberg. **02** Model of one of Apocalypse's four horsemen: Famine. **03** Background painting of Muir Island lab. **04–05** Warren Worthington (now transformed into Archangel by Apocalypse). **06** Character model of future super-Sentinel Nimrod. **07** Layered production cels of destroyed Sentinel. **08** Character model of Blob, in new clothes. **09** Character model of Pyro, in new clothes. **10** Character model of Avalanche, in new clothes. **11** Final character model of major guest star, the time-traveler Bishop. Hoberg's first-season model, "black-spotted" and revised for season two by Mark Lewis.

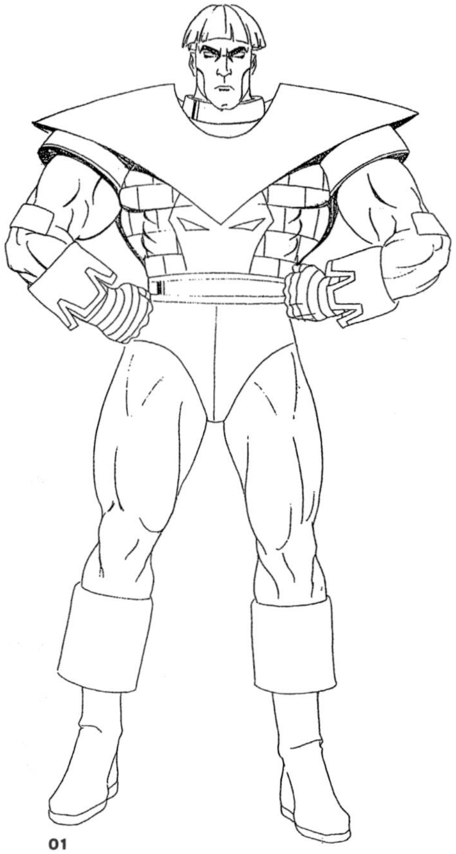

01

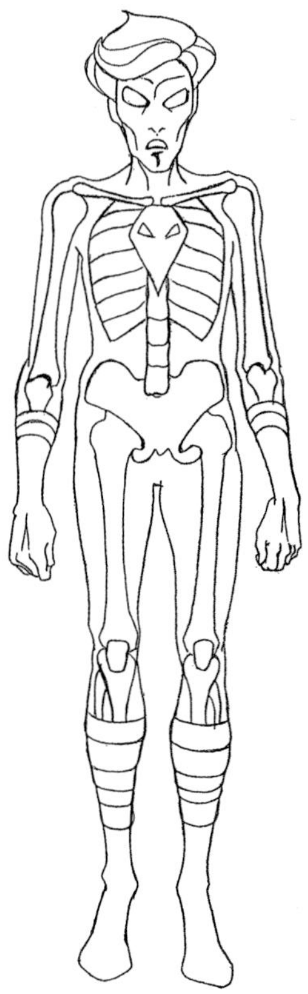

02

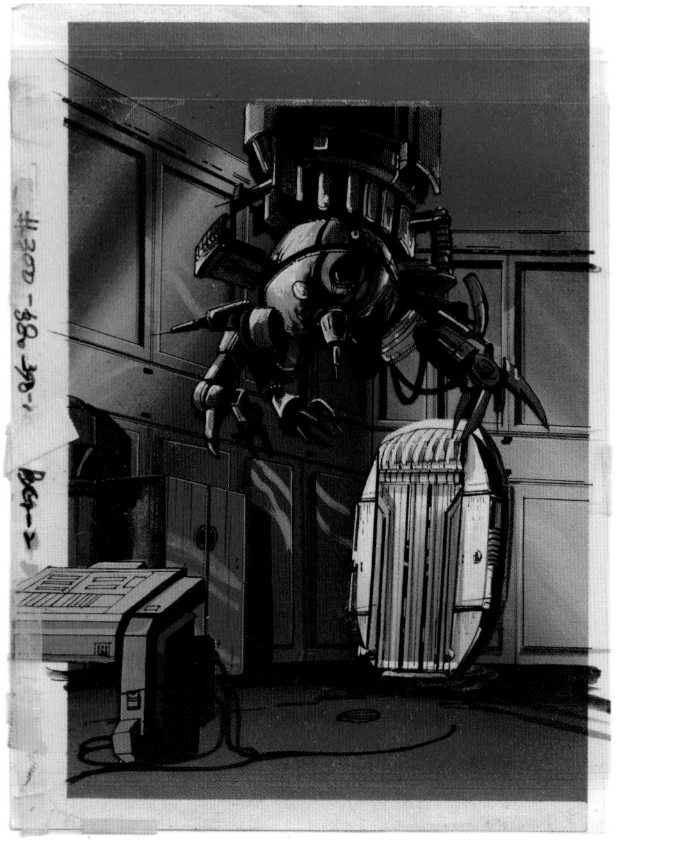

03

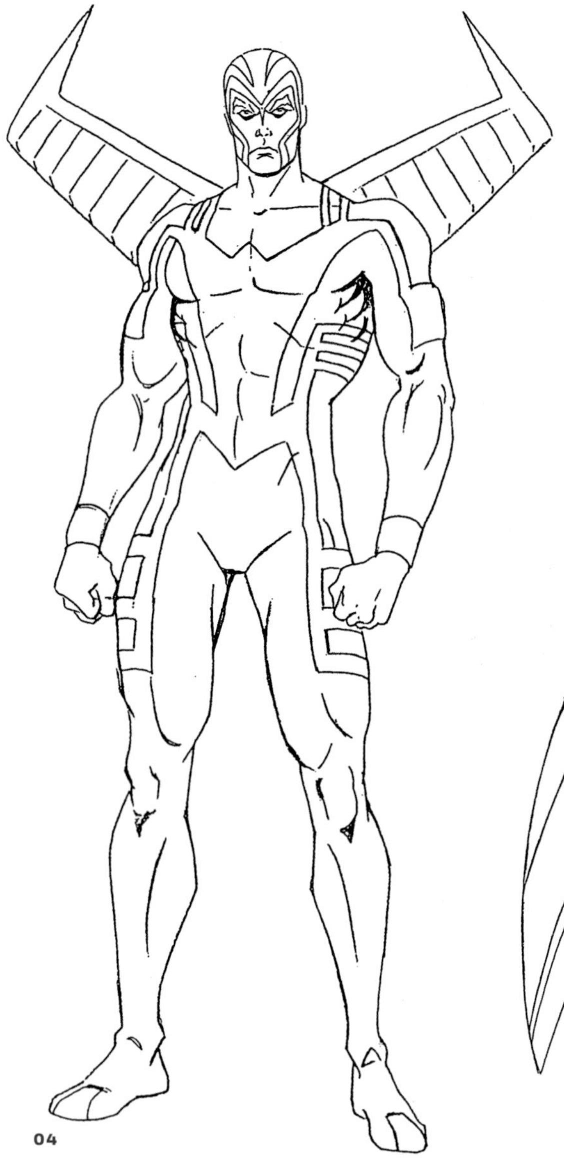

04

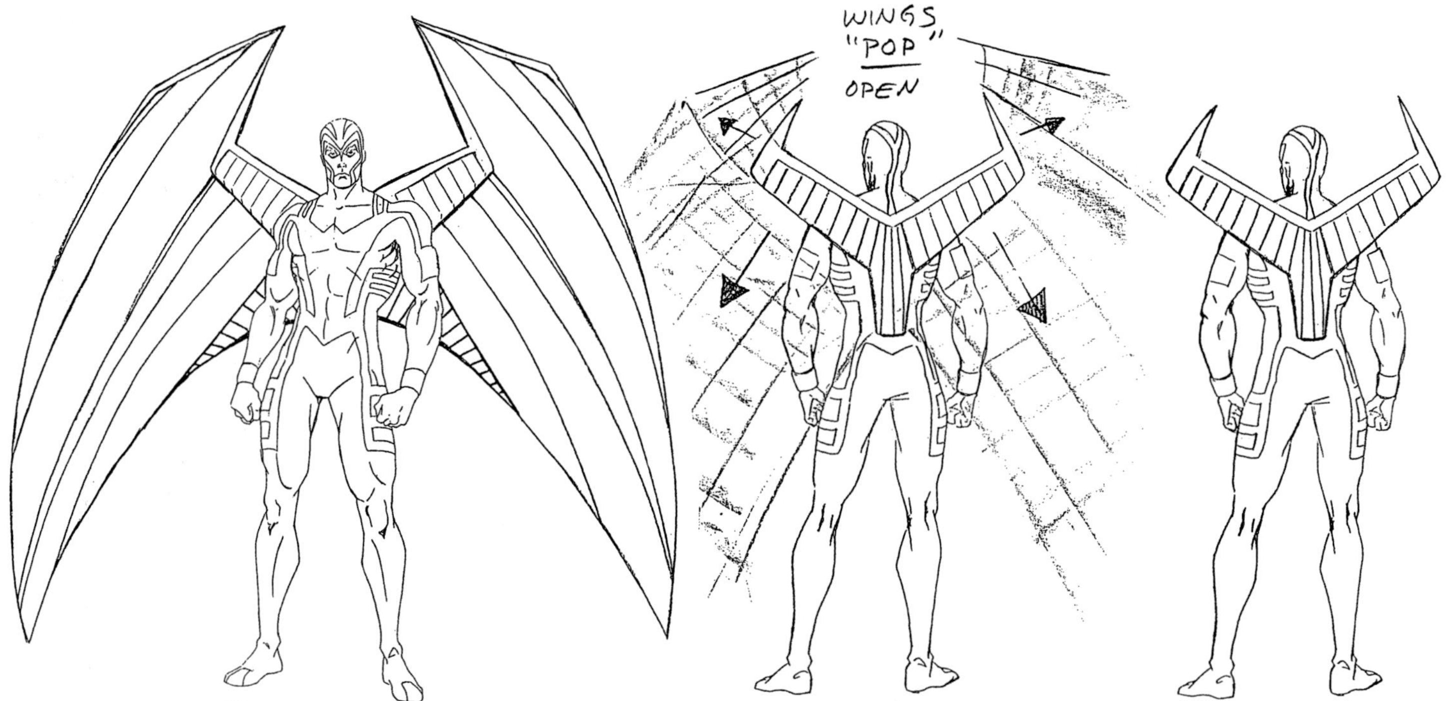
WINGS
"POP"
OPEN

05

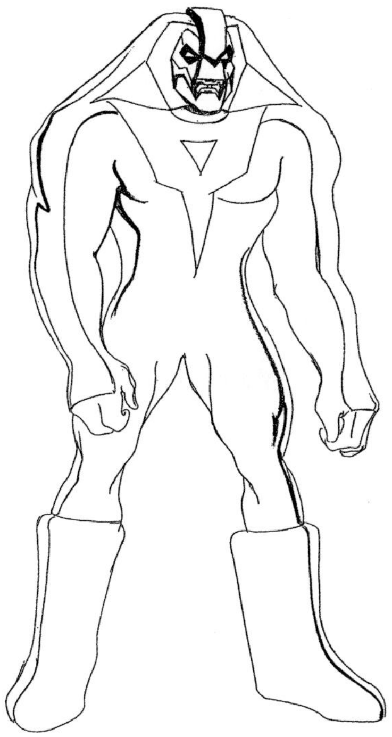

06

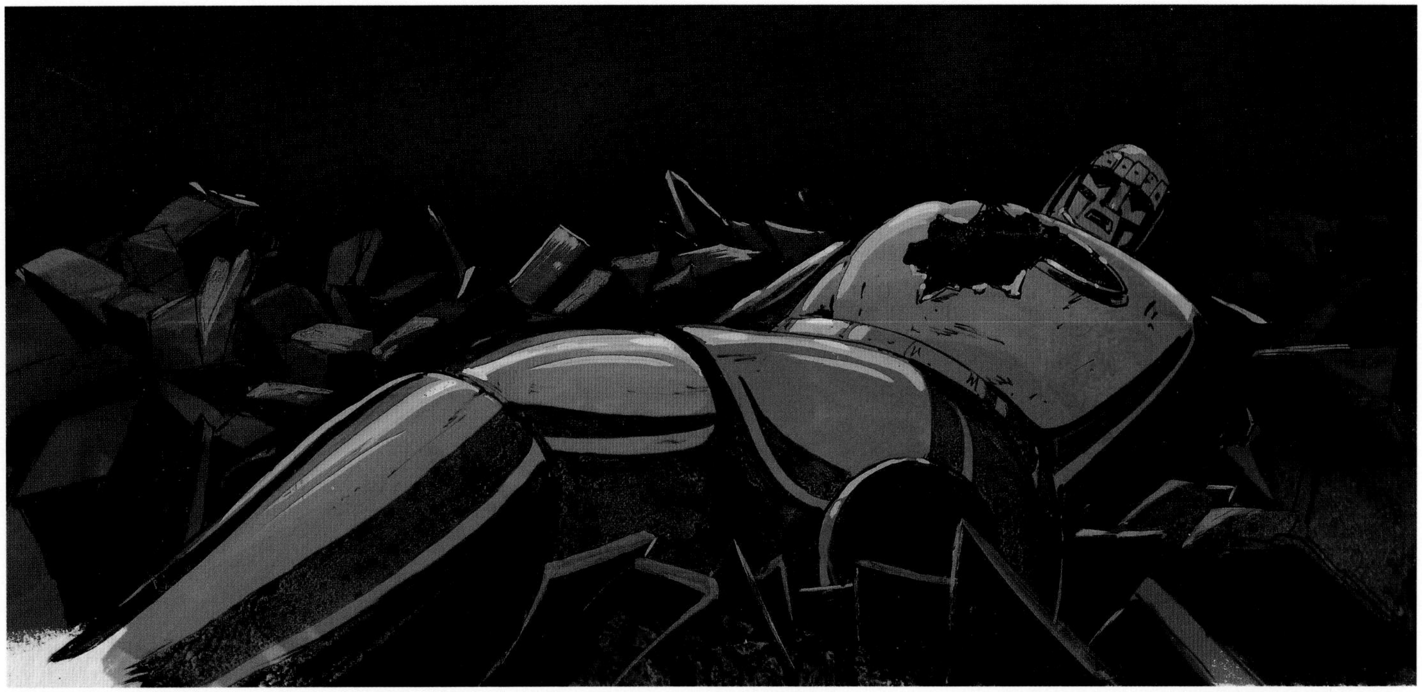

07

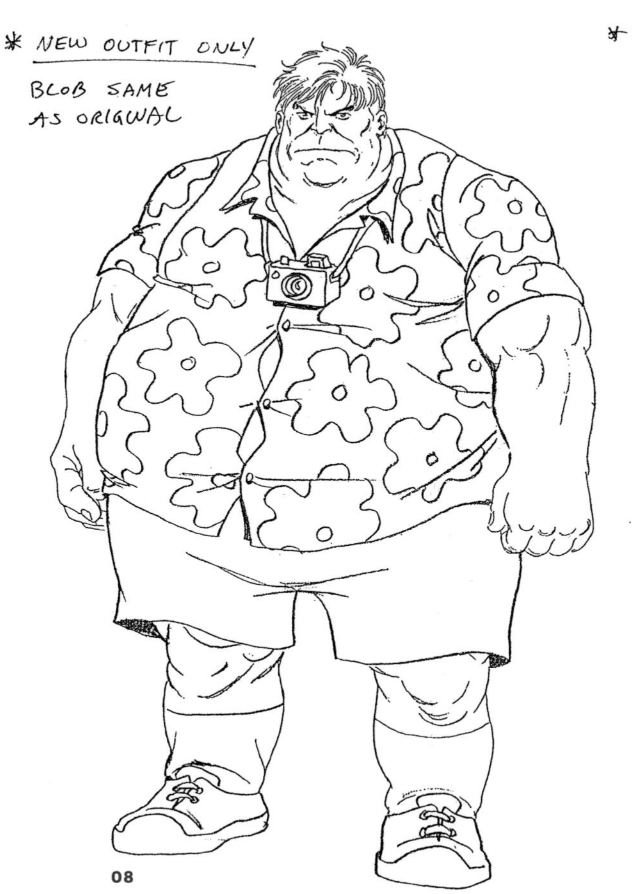
* NEW OUTFIT ONLY
BLOB SAME AS ORIGINAL

08

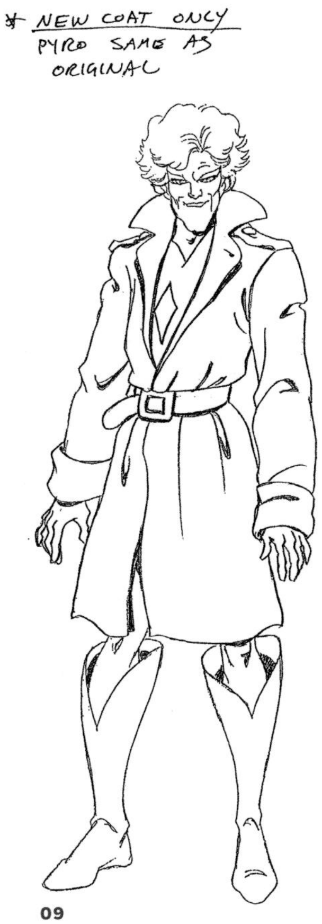
* NEW COAT ONLY
PYRO SAME AS ORIGINAL

09

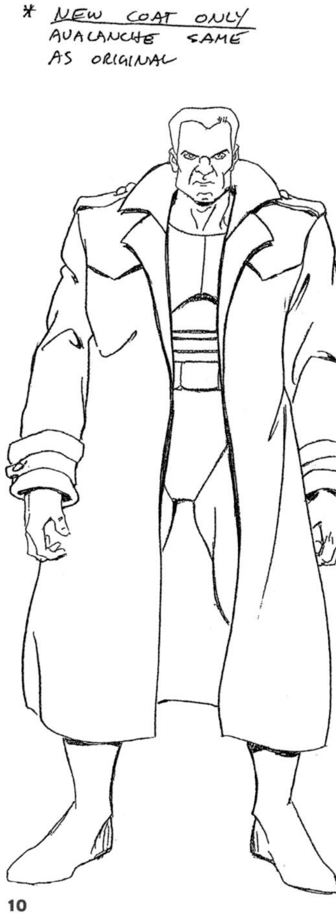
* NEW COAT ONLY
AVALANCHE SAME AS ORIGINAL

10

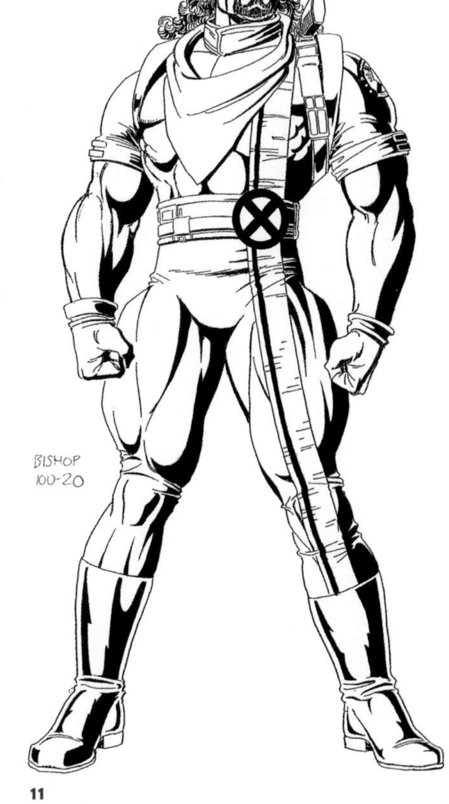
BISHOP
100-20

11

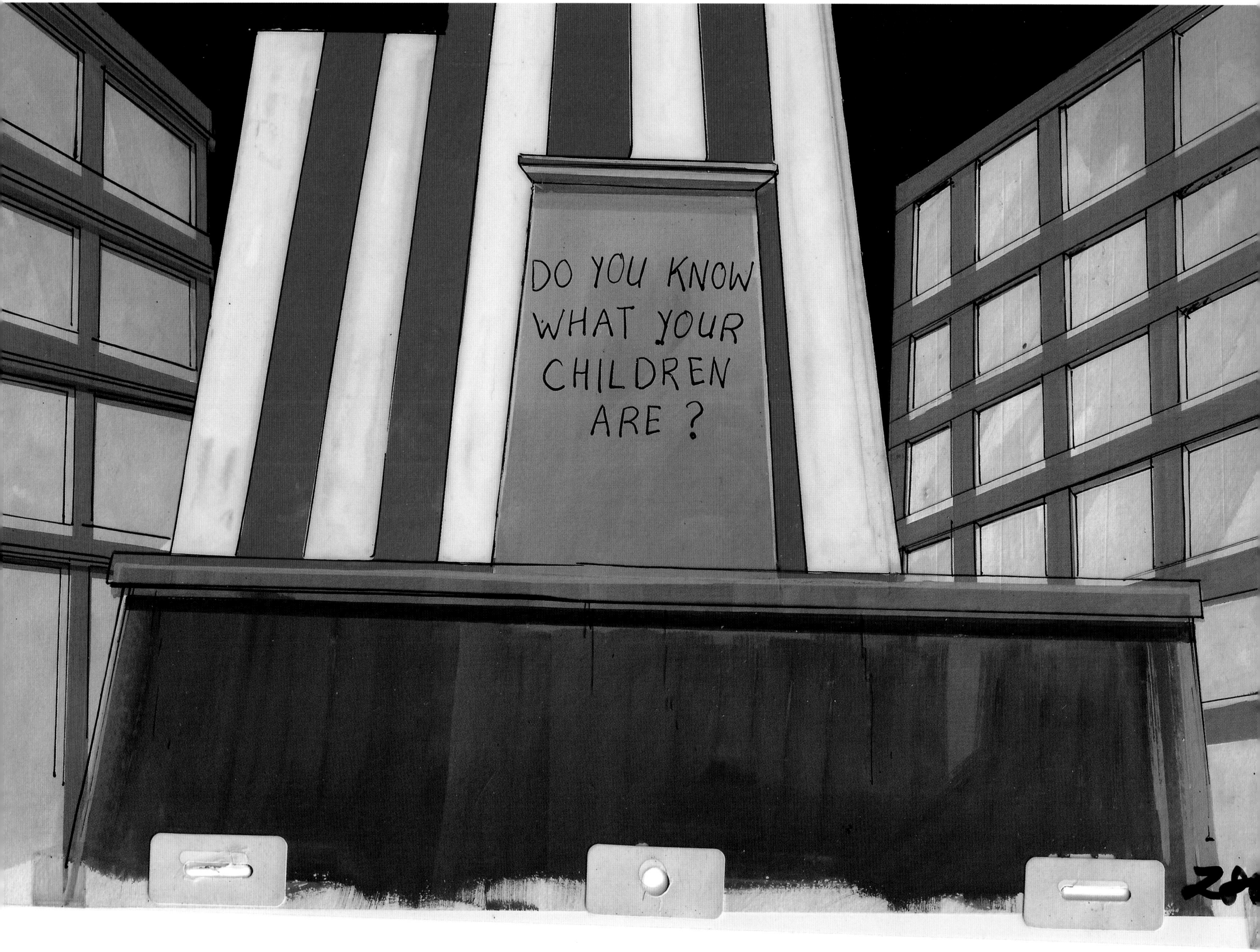
DO YOU KNOW
WHAT YOUR
CHILDREN
ARE ?

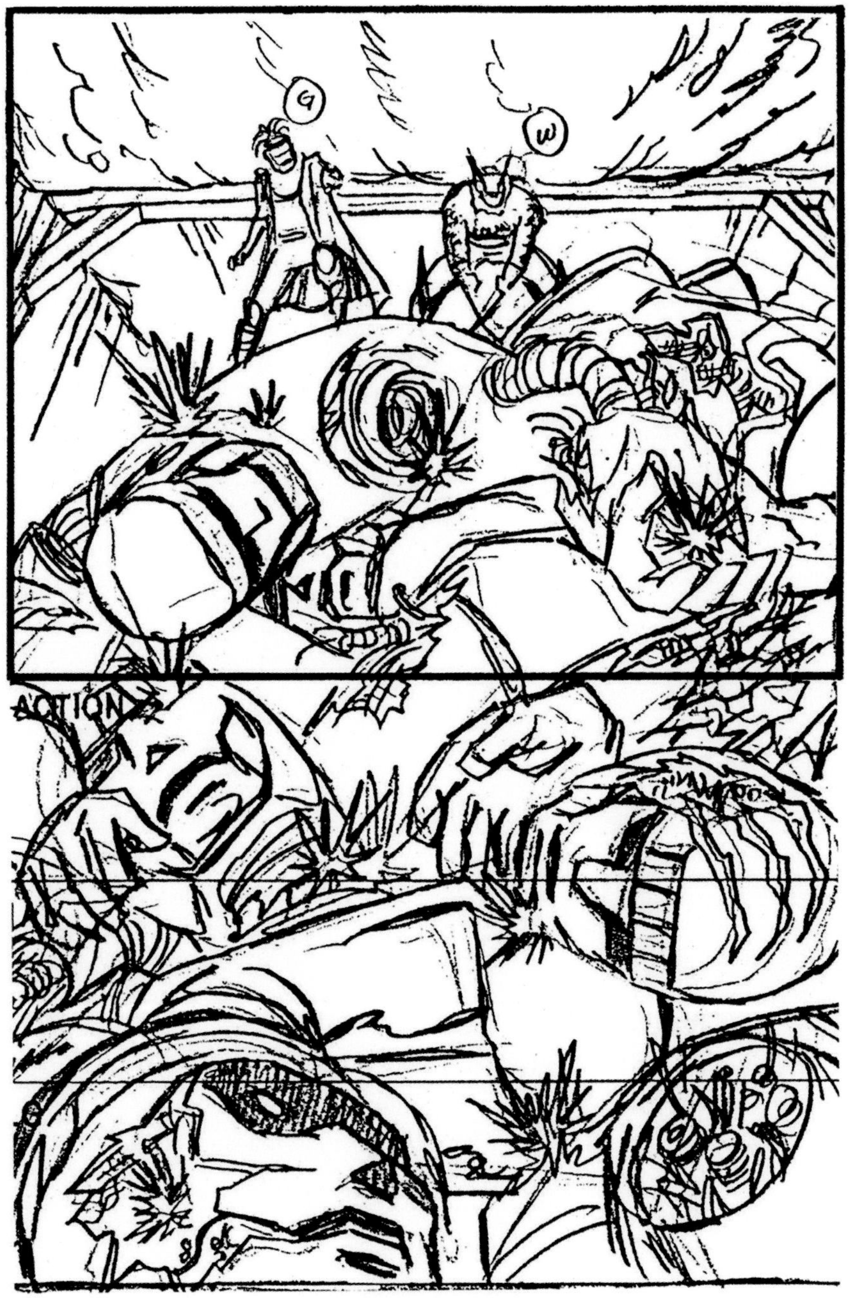
ACTION

01

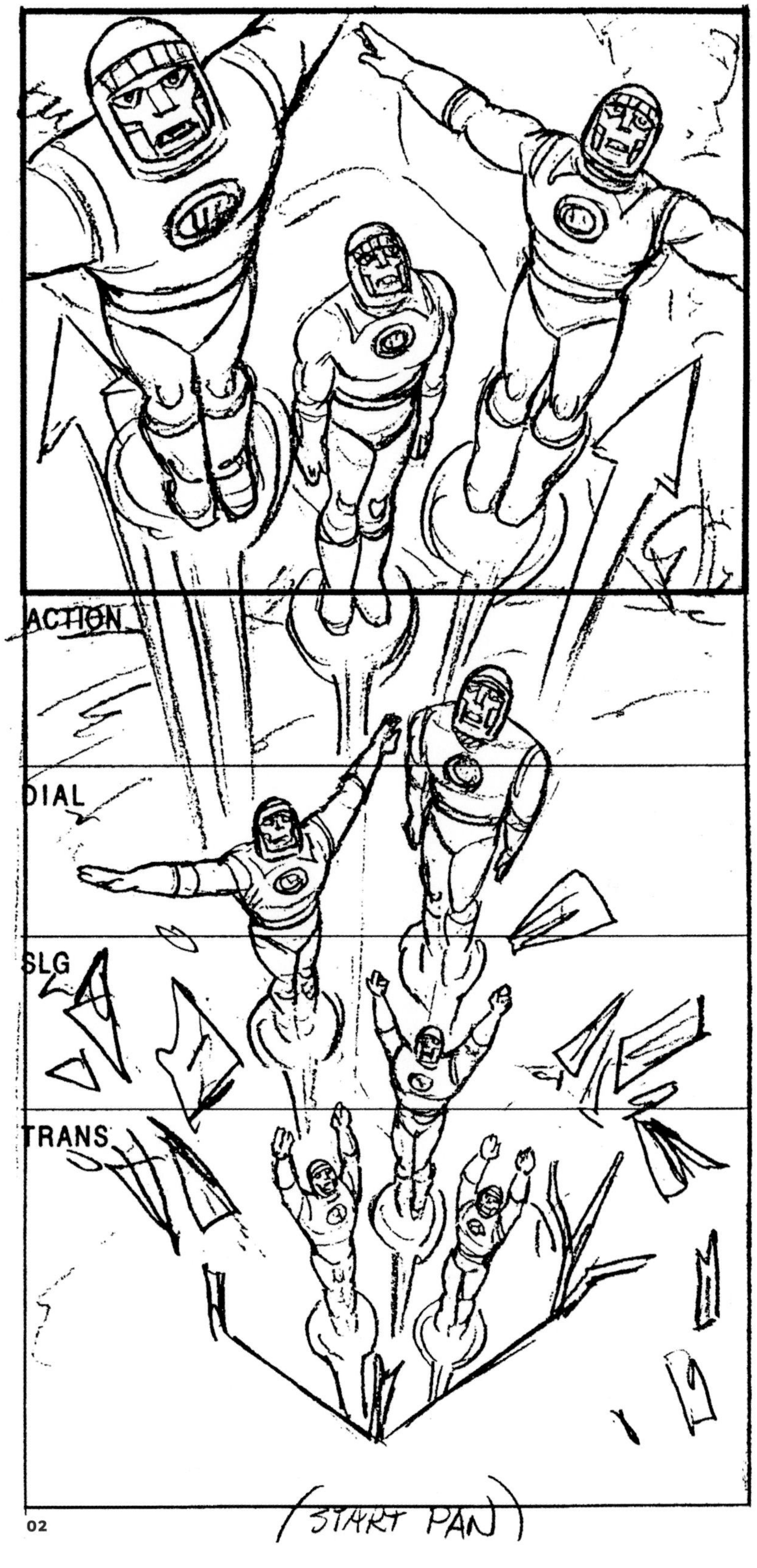
ACTION
DIAL
SLG
TRANS
(START PAN)

02

OPPOSITE Production cel of podium covered with anti-mutant graffiti. **01** Storyboard of Gambit and Wolverine atop a mountain of destroyed Sentinels. **02** Storyboard panel of dozens of Sentinels streaming up out of their factory to attack the X-Men, drawn by Larry Houston.

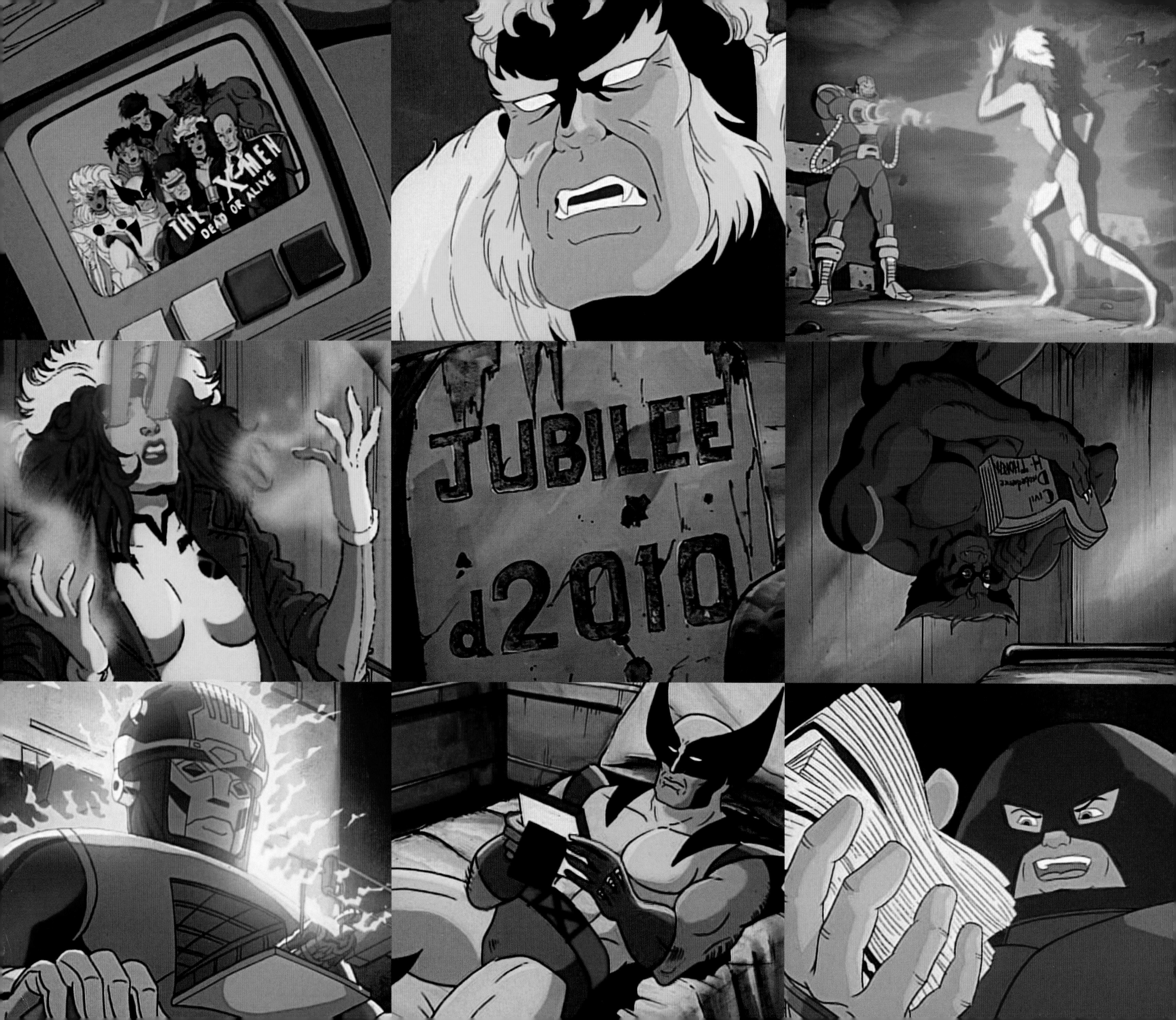
THE X-MEN
DEAD OR ALIVE
JUBILEE
d2010

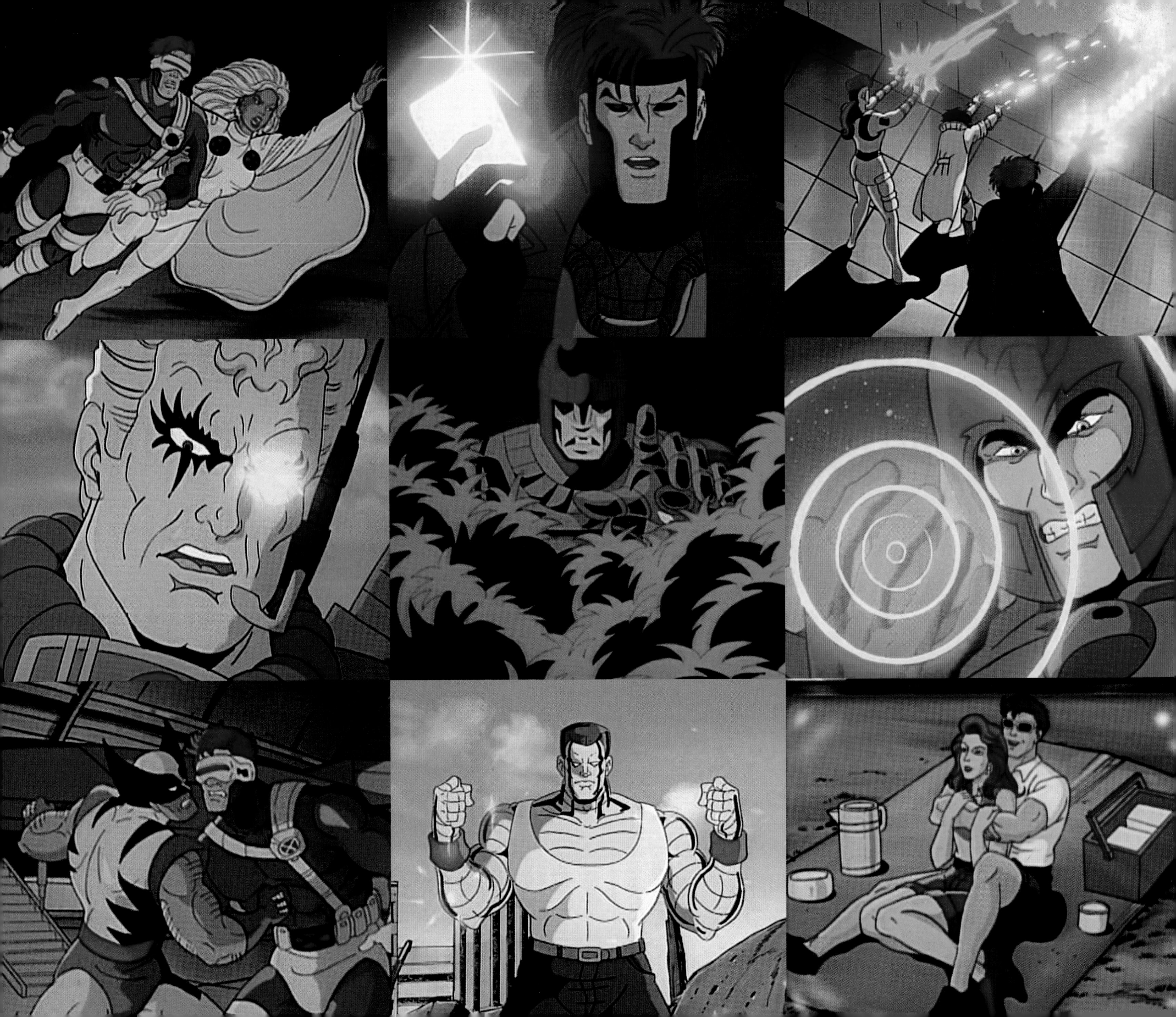

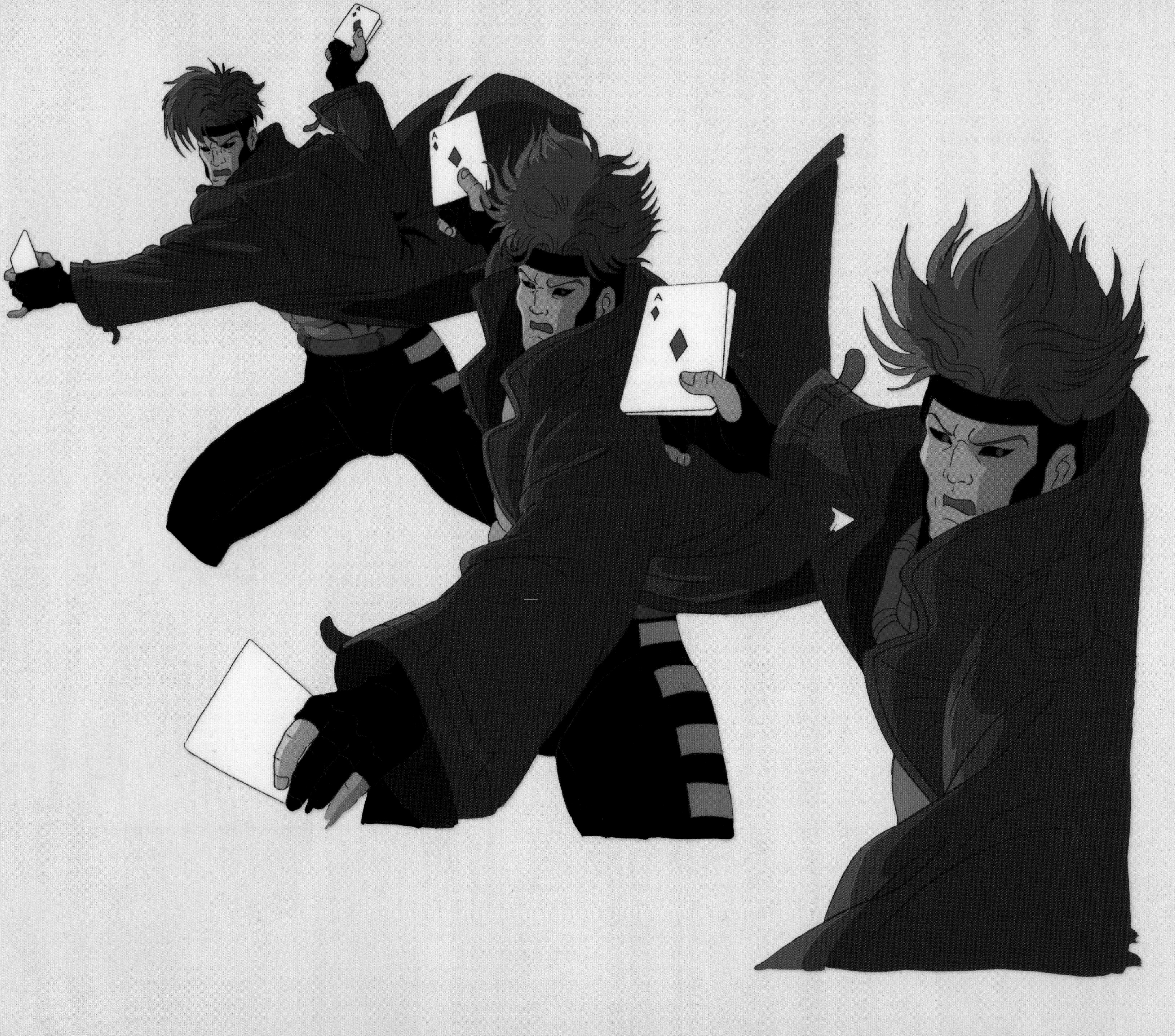

MAKING AN ANIMATED SERIES

IN 1992 the process of producing a series of animated cartoons for television, on a tight network schedule, was vastly different from today.

Now every element of the production—scripts, voice recordings, storyboards, animation art, video files—is stored as computer files and is transferrable, around the world, in seconds. There's software for everything.

On *X-Men: TAS*, every creative element that had to be shared with other craftsmen and -women, for every stage of every episode, needed to be shipped somewhere—voice recordings, on audiocassettes, from Toronto to Los Angeles; stacks of paper scripts, storyboards, location designs, prop designs, character movement, and timing charts from Los Angeles to Asia; then, months later, the roughly animated episodes were sent, on film, back to Los Angeles from South Korea or the Philippines.

PRE-PRODUCTION

THE FIRST STAGE took place in Southern California. Stephanie and Jim Graziano's eponymous GRAZ Entertainment was responsible for generating or amassing all of the show's creative elements, organizing them, and sending them to the AKOM animation studio in South Korea to be hand-painted and animated.

Eric asked Stephanie how Graz and Saban divided up the work on the series.

Stephanie says, "That was a big negotiation. Saban wanted his company to handle the scriptwriting and the

OPPOSITE Three combined production cels, in series, of Gambit in action.

post-production [video editing]. We knew design and production. Margaret told Haim: 'Scripts, post—fine, you know those things. But I want somebody credible in the middle [of design and production] who can deliver.'"

Jim Graziano was Margaret's head of production for four years at Marvel Productions, so there was an earned level of trust.

Stephanie recalls, "Saban had never done production. It was a perfect match. Haim had respect for us; we did the entire series on a handshake. Whenever push came to shove about the quality of the show, he would let us take that side (if we paid for it). He was a great partner.

"Haim used to say, 'I'll never stab you in the back, I'll stab you in the front. You'll see it coming. If I have something to say or do, you'll know it. I'm not going to go behind your back.' We'll play with our cards on the table, and if somebody has to give, then we'll decide who that is."

Producer/designer Will Meugniot had a similar memory of dealing with Saban. "Haim is like the genie from the bottle: He won't lie to you, but you must be very clear about what the deal is. I've never had a bad dealing with Haim, but I knew to be very specific with my language. People always bitch about how cheap Haim is, but if you talk to anybody who was at Fox Kids during the good years, Saban was the best employer that most of us had. Haim was a man of his word; he would honor the deals he made—you just had to be careful about the deal. That said, when Haim suddenly had money from *X-Men: TAS* and *Power Rangers* being such huge hits, he tried upping the production budgets on shows that he owned. Unfortunately, he made a couple of bad calls. He spent *Batman*-level money on *The Silver Surfer* and on *Cyber Six*, and they didn't pay off. On *X-Men: TAS*, I suspect Haim paid what he said was going to pay but perhaps people didn't listen, precisely, to what they were going to get."

Fair or not, Haim had a well-earned penny-pinching reputation. Series writer Steven Melching (nine scripts) talked to Eric about a rare writers' group meeting: "Well, it was the first story meeting that Dave McDermott and I attended [Season Three] after we had written our first script, the 'Longshot' script. Eric invited us to come to a big conference room, and we sat around the huge table in the Saban building in Toluca Lake. There were five or six other writers, and we all just pitched our stories. At one point in the meeting the door opens and in steps Saban himself, our lord and master (he paid us). Haim glances around the room like he's puzzled, like he didn't know what was happening in there. You spoke up and said, 'This is an *X-Men* writers' meeting, Haim!' We expected him to say maybe, 'Hey, great job! Number One animated show on television, thanks for all the great work!' Instead he sees that we're in the middle of eating lunch and frowns and asks, 'Who's paying for the lunch?' You laughed and said, 'I'm paying for it.' He smiled and said, 'Very good,' and then left. That's why he's a billionaire and we're not."

Back to pre-production. Before Graz's artists had something to draw, the stories needed to be chosen and the scripts written. Eric and his writers—all home-based freelancers, no staff writers' room—would pitch story ideas, which were then selected and polished by Eric, usually in batches of about a dozen. Eric would fax his chosen pitches to Fox TV and Marvel Comics. A pitch needed to be more than a simple idea, like, say, "Storm falls for the wrong guy, leaves the X-Men, and her friends have to go to her new planet to stop their wedding," which is a good log line for the two-episode "Storm Front" but not a full story.

Everyone who was to decide on whether a pitch could go forward to become an episode needed a better sense of the story, with a beginning, middle, and an end, a sense of the cast, the action, and a sense of the stakes involved. An example of a thorough pitch is this one for episode twenty-three:

BEAUTY AND THE BEAST

The X-Men are mutant human beings, struggling to do what's right in a world that dislikes and fears them. Many mutants, like the X-Man Dr. Hank McCoy, look so unusual that they have no hope of "passing" in normal society. Some despair of their condition. But scholarly, gentle "Beast" long ago came to terms with his animalistic appearance.

Now, for the first time since Hank's troubled adolescence, anxious feelings about his mutancy have arisen: Beast has fallen in love with a woman who has never seen him. Carly Anne Crocker has been blind since birth. Beast has helped develop the treatment which will give Carly her sight. She has grown to care for him, and Hank fears the day she will first see him.

When that day comes, Beast discovers that his fears were groundless. Carly "wonders why the other doctors don't have his beautiful blue fur." Hank is thrilled and relieved.

But his happiness is short-lived. Bigots crying "no more mutants" firebomb the hospital and kidnap Carly. Though Beast and his X-Men friends are able to save her, Beast sees the danger that their love would bring to Carly. The world is not yet ready to accept them. To protect the woman he loves, Hank says goodbye to her, and walks off, sad and alone.

Executives from Fox TV (Sidney Iwanter) and Marvel Comics (Joe Calamari and Bob Harras) would green-light those of Eric's pitches that they liked—usually three or four out of the dozen. Fox—through Sidney and Broadcast Standards executive Avery Cobern—had the final say.

Sidney says, "We were breaking new ground. Like the change with *Hill Street Blues* in prime-time television in the 1980s. That show was crucial to my understanding of how to tell TV stories. Before it would be single, 'stand-alone' episodes: set up a problem, develop the problem, and then solve the problem. One week didn't have anything to do with the previous week. I said to Margaret [Loesch], 'We ought to do the same kind of stuff that they do on *Hill Street Blues* and *St. Elsewhere*. Interconnecting storylines, multiple arcs.' Margaret worried: 'How is a kid going to remember from one week to the next?' I said, 'Why don't we do "previously on" recaps?' I said, 'Look, within one minute, you can catch up on what's going on.' This is not string theory. The genesis of that was me seeing how storytelling had changed thanks to guys like Steven Bochco. Saturday morning was the same old, same old. *X-Men: TAS* proved that the kids watching on Saturday morning were more sophisticated than the executives at the other networks thought they were.

"So much of kids' TV writing is uninspired. This is because the writers were frustrated by their bosses at the networks, who wouldn't let them challenge the audience. I fear we are sliding back into that. The genius of Marvel was creating the vulnerability of these characters. No matter how powerful Rogue is, she can't touch anybody. Storm's background as an orphan. Wolverine, as tough as he is, can't get Jean Grey because she's in love with somebody else.

"A good deal of the success of *X-Men* and *Batman* involved being able to make creative compromises with Broadcast Standards. No matter how much power a network executive thinks he or she has, the Broadcast Standards people [censors] have the final say. We were lucky to have Avery Cobern, because she understood the changing mores of society. Some kids' TV censors felt like angry teachers."

Eric would assign a writer to the episode—often the creator of the pitch, but not always. A two-page premise would be written, polished, sent around to all concerned—executives, producers, censors—notes made and incorporated by Eric, and then the writer would create a ten-page outline. This in turn would be polished by Eric, sent around, with more notes made and incorporated. Finally, the writer would be allowed to create the first draft of a forty-page script, which would make the same journey until it was declared "final."

The pre-production, production, and post-production processes followed.

Stephanie says, "Once we knew which characters were in the episode [at outline], we made the list of them, then created all the standard turnarounds and poses and expressions and movements for the animators to work from. Characters have attributes that are specific to them. You have to design them all in detail because when the scenes get to the animators, you don't want them making up how people look and move. Our character designers had to ensure this consistency—they literally had to draw every hand movement for each character. How do those claws work? What do they look like when they're only half out? Because we were still using traditional animation, our model designers had to show the board artists and the animators how all those pieces acted. It all had to be designed before we started drawing the storyboards."

Producer/director Larry Houston, who was in charge of the first sixty-five storyboards for his boss Stephanie, seconded her.

01

Larry says, "Once we'd get an outline, I started thinking about how many locations we were going to need, how many characters, so I could schedule the right artists."

Production manager Dana Booton had to make sure that every element that Stephanie and Larry promised the overseas animators was in hand before the package was shipped. Eric asked her about character poses.

Dana Booton: "We'd do, for instance, four or six images of Gambit in different moods. These gave the animators a feel of the character. We drew color models, original development models, painted on clear plastic cels. We would paint a few of them, here, and put them on a painted background to get an idea of what the look would be once it came back from Asia on film."

Stephanie: "All the art departments were in-house at Graz. You needed to be able look in on it during the day. The design artists needed insight from the director, they needed reference to the comic books and to people who knew the characters. From a design standpoint, I'd say six to eight people were working on each episode: key designers, cleanup people, other people who are just working on the minutiae of turnarounds and expressions.

"Once you have a written story outline you can understand most of the main characters you need, and you start drawing. When you get the first draft of the script you know who the

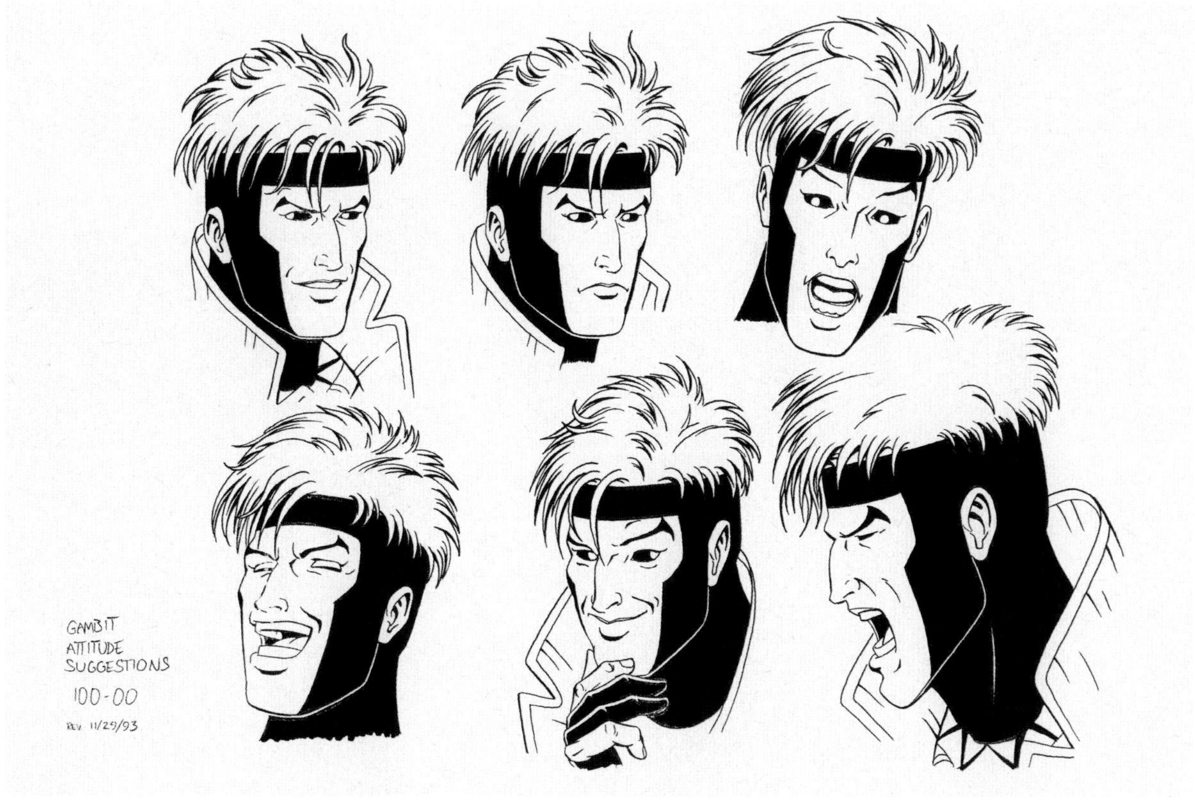
GAMBIT
ATTITUDE
SUGGESTIONS
100-00
REV 11/29/93

02

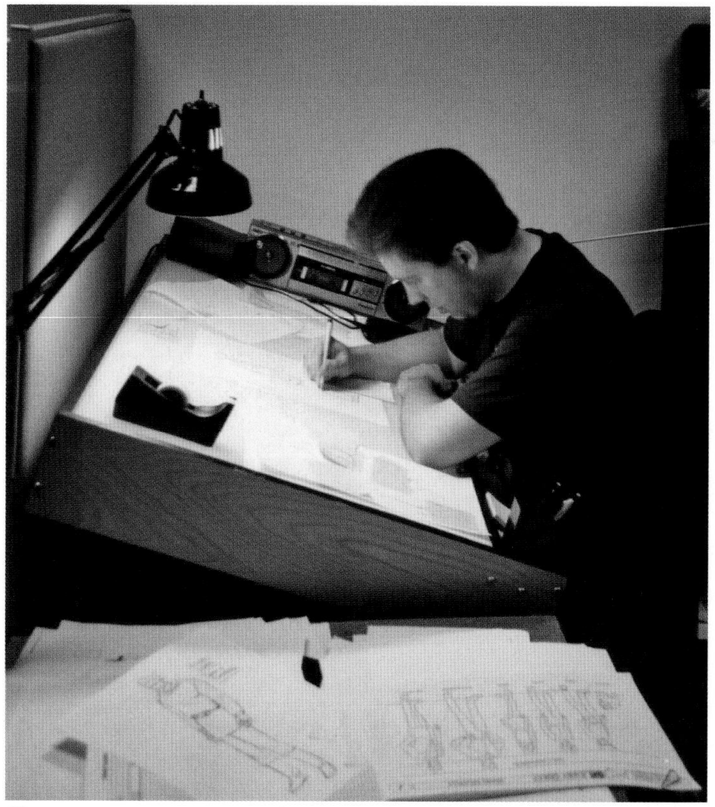

03

secondary characters are going to be. Some of these might get cut at the final script draft, so there were times when we designed characters that didn't actually make it into the episode, but you can't wait. Same thing with props: You had to have them all ready to ship. Characters, props, all of it, and it's all money. It's all time, which equals money.

"There's so much depth to the show, there are so many character details, that if you don't get them right the fan base is going to see through it. You've got artists who think they know how to draw the character when no, there are idiosyncrasies about the thickness of the calf or the point of the black area of the boot. The smallest detail of those characters could make or break the authenticity of the series. We're already starting late (seven months allotted, versus nineteen for *Batman*), but at every stage you're hitting hiccups of a learning curve that this process doesn't allow you to have. You're behind and must decide: Do we air a crappy show that we're only half happy with, or do we pay to fix the stuff?"

Out of the dozen series Graz was to produce in its seven-year run—*The Tick, Street Fighter, Conan the Adventurer*—*X-Men: TAS* proved to be the largest pre-production challenge that Stephanie and her company were ever to face.

Stephanie says, "The tussle was that we had Saban's low budgets and Marvel's expansive universe, and the two are distinctly opposite. So as we got in scripts that made Marvel happy, our Saban budget didn't work. We had to fight to navigate between the two: 'We gotta cut the story in half! What's most important? Can we get more money out of a layout drawing if we use it in three different locations?'"

The vast design process would start with supervising producer Will Meugniot and producer/director Larry Houston and his team.

Larry says, "I would take someone like designer Mark Lewis, and we'd go through the script and break it down. How many locations. How many characters, how many props. The location background art pieces were referred to as layouts.

"Dana Booton would get all the different people to do their jobs. I would start going through it to see if I caught anything we could reuse, to save time and money. For instance, a stage with a podium in episode eleven, 'Days of Future Past, Part 1,' was reused in episode thirteen, 'The Final Decision.'"

Then Larry would assign three artists to start the storyboard—each taking one-third, drawing and choreographing the twenty-two-minute script in eight or nine hundred images.

"Over the years I developed relationships with artists," Larry says. "I hired people that I could depend on, that I could count on their turning a month's worth of work in on time. I also based assignments on their strengths. One guy was really good at drawing action, another really good at people. So when a script would come up, if they were next on rotation, I'd do my best—it wasn't perfect, but I tried—to schedule them for the section of the script that would excite their imagination. You're going to get better work out of them. It was like casting a movie."

As the three artists worked on the storyboard for each script, Larry would have to make sure all three were seeing the action the same way: "Once I got a final script, I would draw a map based on it. I would list the sequence of the locales—they

01 Dana Booton, *X-Men: TAS* production manager, Graz studio, 1990s. **02** Gambit attitiude suggestions. Art by Frank Brunner, cleanup by Mark Lewis. **03** Mark Lewis, *X-Men: TAS* model designer, Graz studio, 1990s.

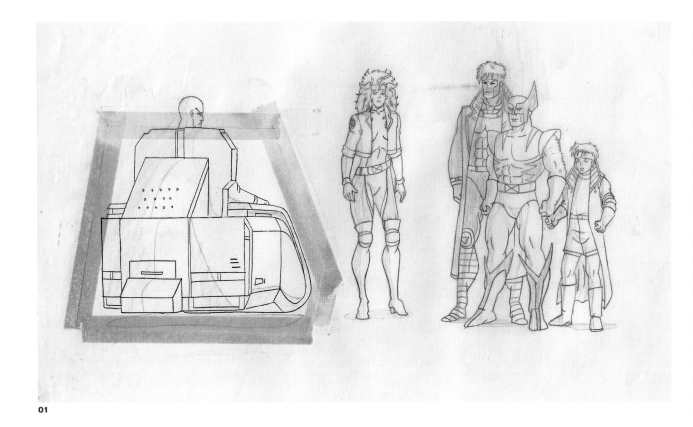

01

go to a factory, then to a beach—and set up a left-to-right map for the storyboard artists. On previous shows, I'd had different artists doing different sections, and it would get messed up because every artist would have their own idea about the flow of action, where to stage the characters. I put the locations on a timeline, writing down where everything was and how people moved. I put an arrow, 'X-Men go this way, the villains go that way,' so all three artists would be on the same page. It'd take about four weeks for the three artists, and then a fifth week for fixes."

Julia Lewald: "Did the storyboard artists ever confer among themselves during those four weeks?"

Larry: "They didn't talk to each other. I was the person they brought questions to."

WILL MEUGNIOT AND LARRY had a challenge. They needed to draw a big show on a small budget and have it turn out in a way that respected the X-Men source material that they so admired. Both had ideas for highlighting the show's strengths while trying to hide its weaknesses.

Larry says, "Will and I and Rick [Hoberg] all started our careers just as untranslated anime [stylized Japanese animation] was becoming available here in the late 1970s—on twelve-inch laser discs! We studied the anime techniques of how to make stuff look really awesome without spending a lot. We'd watch Miyazaki films and collect books of his storyboards. I would redesign the shots that people were drawing in the X-Men boards, knowing that we weren't going to get a lot of smooth animation. We focused on the poses, not the big action that we knew we wouldn't get animated well. I got rid of the walking. That's part of the efficiency. A character says, 'Let's go!' and you're there. Some of that comes from my early years of watching the original Jonny Quest, where stuff didn't move much, but it was great to look at—the layouts look great, like in the anime stuff, so that was always in my subconscious."

Eric says, "In the scripts we called it 'density.' To crank up the pace, we jammed twice the usual lazy-paced story into twenty-two minutes—which is why our scripts were forty pages instead of twenty-five or thirty. No one ever 'quietly exited scene' or 'stepped into the aircraft.' We'd start in the middle of a scene's action and cut to the middle of the next scene's action. No pauses, no transitions, no gradual lead-ins. We'd overlap dialogue over what normally was only visual action—which got us in trouble with the production people, who kept on saying there

was no room, that we were 50 percent over what would fit in twenty-two minutes. But somehow they made room."

Will remembered the same kind of intensifying both in the speed and number of shots called out in the storyboards and in the amount of information crammed into each frame: "I storyboarded, earlier, on Batman, and their goal was to intentionally keep that Batman pacing slow: they wanted between 280 and 300 shots for a show. In X-Men, we were between 400–500 shots, so you get a different pacing just because we were burning through shots so fast. That was to emulate the kinetic energy of the comics.

"X-Men was one of those shows that was made during the transition from editing physical film on a Moviola [editor/projector] to editing digitally. I remember when we were cutting the first episode, we were still doing it on a Moviola, and I noticed a scene of the team sitting around the console in X-Men headquarters. I remember looking around that single frame and seeing all the density of the art, with the multi-colored shadows and blackline on the background. It wasn't great drawing, but when I looked at it, I knew we'd succeeded: That was not a frame that you would've seen on any show before it. We didn't have the elegance of Batman, but we did have something unique. You could stop the Moviola on any X-Men frame and you would know that it was that show" [see page 87].

AS THE THIRTEEN-EPISODE SEASON PROGRESSED, the logjam of pre-production elements built up as different premises, outlines, scripts, layout sets, prop packets, model packets, storyboards, voice recordings, and color keys arrived. Production manager Dana Booton had to keep it all straight.

Dana says, "When we had all the episodes at various stages of completion, it was like herding cats in that office. I'd help Larry cut and paste dialogue and put it onto the storyboards. I'd help with directing: They'd find hookup issues, they'd find continuity issues, and then it would come back to Larry, and then I would make sure that fixes were handled by the storyboard artists, then run it by Larry again. When we had a finished board and every element in hand, we used to ship huge boxes overseas to the animators. The shipment had five hundred exposure [timing] sheets. Copying these was a pain because you couldn't just run them through a copy machine—they were all different sizes, and they were all taped up differently. It was the same with the storyboards because there'd be so many cut-and-paste revisions."

01 Example of cut-and-taped material, causing difficulty in photocopying; see also page 158.

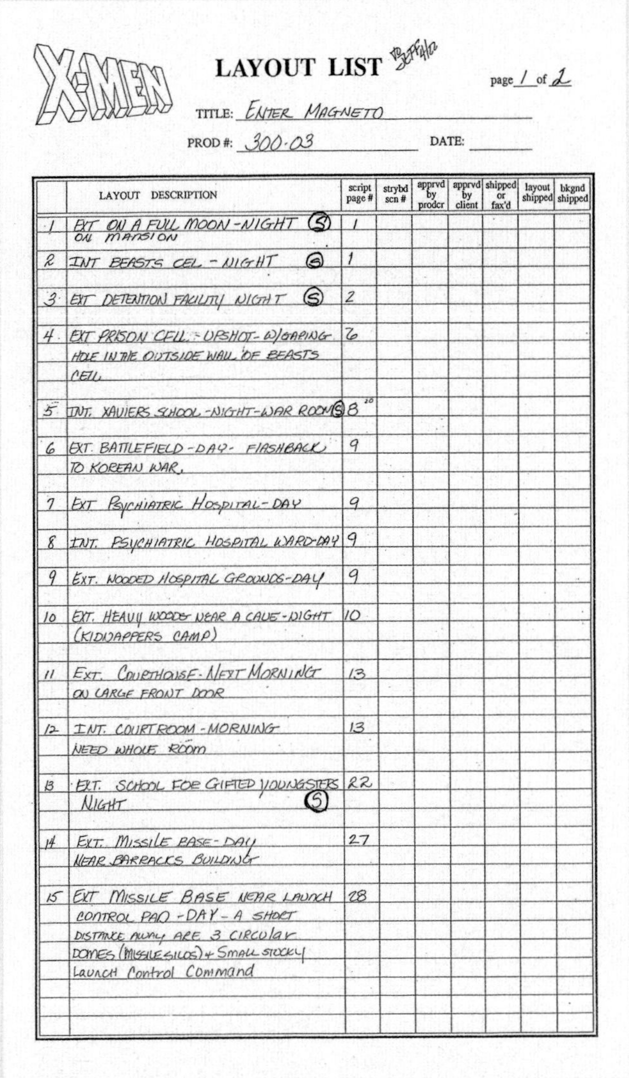

LAYOUT LIST

page 1 of 2

TITLE: _Enter Magneto_

PROD #: _300-03_   DATE: _____

	LAYOUT DESCRIPTION	script page #	strybd scn #	apprvd by prodcr	apprvd by client	shipped or fax'd	layout shipped	bkgnd shipped
1	EXT. ON A FULL MOON - NIGHT ⑤ ON MANSION	1						
2	INT. BEASTS CEL - NIGHT ⑥	1						
3	EXT. DETENTION FACILITY NIGHT ⑤	2						
4	EXT. PRISON CELL - UPSHOT - W/GAPING HOLE IN THE OUTSIDE WALL OF BEASTS CELL	6						
5	INT. XAVIERS SCHOOL - NIGHT - WAR ROOM ⑧ 18							
6	EXT. BATTLEFIELD - DAY - FLASHBACK TO KOREAN WAR	9						
7	EXT. PSYCHIATRIC HOSPITAL - DAY	9						
8	INT. PSYCHIATRIC HOSPITAL WARD - DAY	9						
9	EXT. WOODED HOSPITAL GROUNDS - DAY	9						
10	EXT. HEAVY WOODS NEAR A CAVE - NIGHT (KIDNAPPERS CAMP)	10						
11	EXT. COURTHOUSE - NEXT MORNING ON LARGE FRONT DOOR	13						
12	INT. COURTROOM - MORNING NEED WHOLE ROOM	13						
13	EXT. SCHOOL FOR GIFTED YOUNGSTERS ⑤ NIGHT	22						
14	EXT. MISSILE BASE - DAY NEAR BARRACKS BUILDING	27						
15	EXT. MISSILE BASE NEAR LAUNCH CONTROL PAD - DAY - A SHORT DISTANCE AWAY ARE 3 CIRCULAR DOMES (MISSILE SILOS) + SMALL STOCKY LAUNCH CONTROL COMMAND	28						

X-MEN LAYOUTS 300-03   **FINAL**

EXTERIOR PSYCHIATRIC HOSPITAL W/ WOODED GROUNDS (DAY)

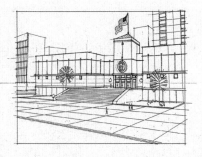
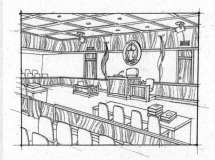

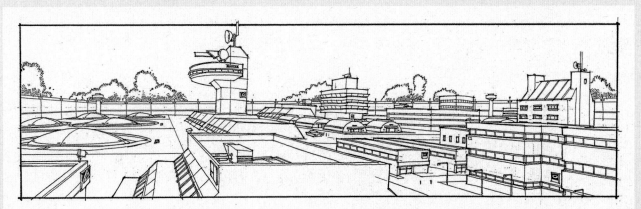

02 Layout list, "Enter Magneto." **03** Final layouts, including Ext. Psychiatric Hospital; Ext. Heavy Woods Near a Cave, Ext. Courthouse, Int. Courtroom Looking Towards Bench, and Ext. Missile Base; layouts by Steve Olds.

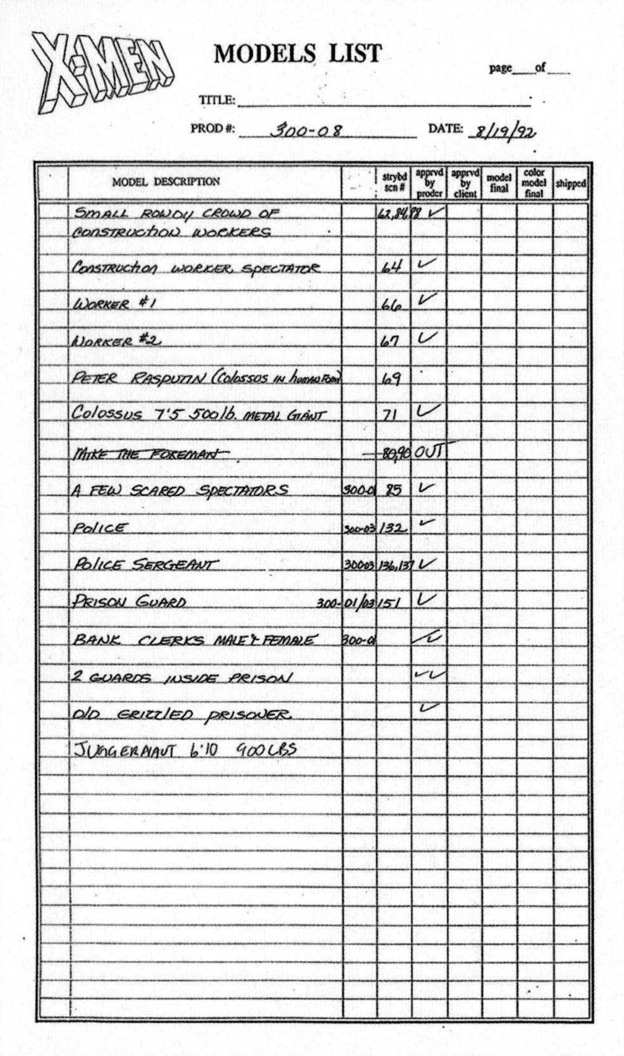

X-MEN **MODELS LIST** page___of___

TITLE: ____________________

PROD #: 300-08 DATE: 8/19/92

	MODEL DESCRIPTION		strybd scn #	apprvd by prodcr	apprvd by client	model final	color model final	shipped
	SMALL ROWDY CROWD OF CONSTRUCTION WORKERS		62,84,88	✓				
	Construction WORKER SPECTATOR		64	✓				
	WORKER #1		66	✓				
	WORKER #2		67	✓				
	PETER RASPUTIN (Colossos in human Form)		69					
	Colossus 7'5 500 lb. METAL GIANT		71	✓				
	~~MIKE THE FOREMAN~~		~~80,90~~	OUT				
	A FEW SCARED SPECTATORS	300-01	85	✓				
	POLICE	300-03	132	✓				
	POLICE SERGEANT	300-03	136,137	✓				
	PRISON GUARD	300-01/03	151	✓				
	BANK CLERKS MALE & FEMALE	300-01		✓				
	2 GUARDS INSIDE PRISON			✓✓				
	Old GRIZZLED PRISONER			✓				
	JUGGERNAUT 6'10 900 LBS							

01

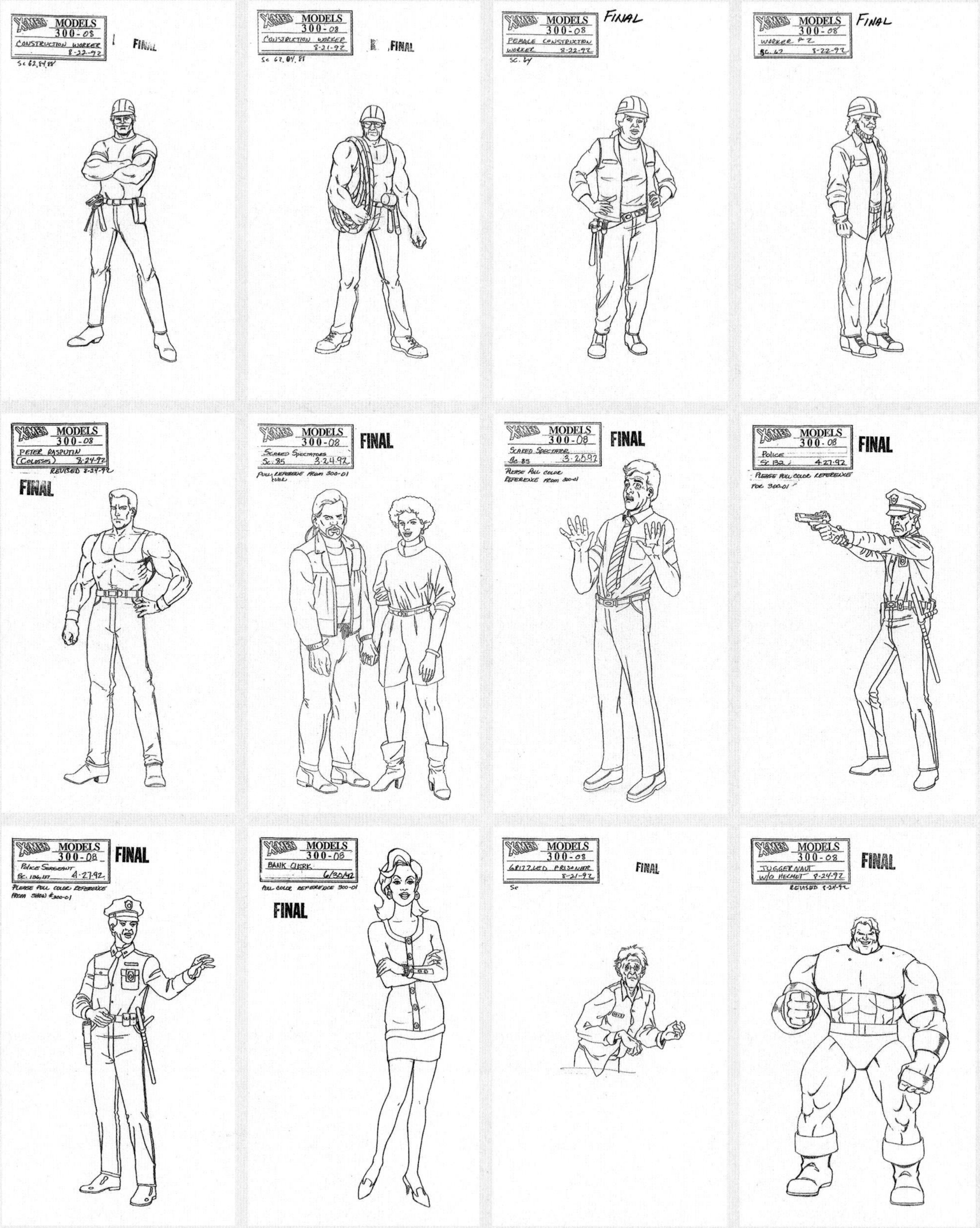

MODELS 300-08
FINAL

02

01 Models list, "The Unstoppable Juggernaut."
02 Character models of Construction Workers 1, 2, 3, and 4 by Peter Rasputin; Scared Spectators 1-2, 3, Police, Police Sergeant, Bank Clerk, Grizzled Prisoner, and Juggernaut, all by Rick Hoberg.

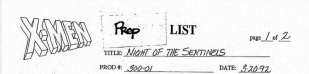

X-MEN Prep LIST

page 1 of 2

TITLE: NIGHT OF THE SENTINELS

PROD #: 300-01 DATE: 3-20-92

	MODEL DESCRIPTION	script page #	strybd scn #	apprvd by prodcr	apprvd by client	model final	color model final	shipped
1	POLICE CAR + PADDY WAGON (PULL FROM #7)		4,5	✓				
2	TWISTED SCORCH REMAINS OF VCR ✓		18	✓				
3	CAR		29B	✓				
4	VIDEO GAME ROBOT		37	✓				
5	XAVIERS CHAIR			✓				
5A	XAVIE							
[illegible]	[illegible] ✓	[illegible]	[illegible]					
6	EVIL LOOKING VIDEO GAME ROBOT ✓	4	37	✓				
7	LARGE ORDER OF CHILI FRIES ✓	4	39	✓				
8	GIANT SLURPEE ✓	4	39	✓				
9	DOZEN DECKS OF PLAYING CARDS ✓	7	93	✓				
10	BELT OF STEPS RIPPED OFF ESCALATOR ✓	9	89	✓				
11	CAR (USE #3 CAR ABOVE) ✓	13	274	✓				
12	CRUSHED CAR (CHECK W/ L.O.) ✓	13	138	✓				
13	REMOTE CONTROL ✓	17	163	✓				
14	MACE LIKE STUDDED STEEL BALL ✓	19	190	✓				

03

PROPS 300-
FINAL
POLICE
PROPS 300-
FINAL
POLICE
300-01 3-30-92
TWISTED SCORCHED REMAINS OF VCR
FINAL
Sc 18
300-01 3-30-92
CAR 6/16/92
FINAL
Sc. 29B, 294, 275
PROPS 300-01
XAVIERS CHAIR W/DRIVE UNITS RETRACTED AND EXTENDED 3/4 REAR
FINAL
Sc 175,176
EXTENDED
AT REST
300-01 3-30-92
Chili Fries Giant Slur-P
FINAL
Sc 39,43
SLUR-P
PROPS 300-01
DECKS OF PLAYING CARDS
FINAL
BACKSIDE
300-01 3-30-92
BELT OF STAIRS RIPPED OFF ESCALATOR
FINAL
Sc 89

04

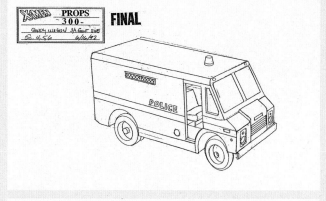

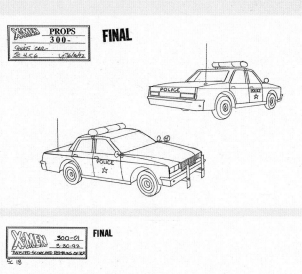

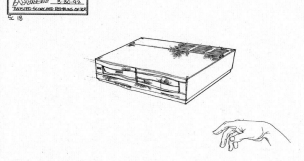

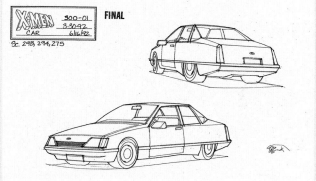

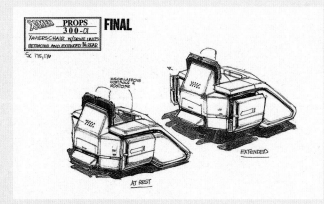

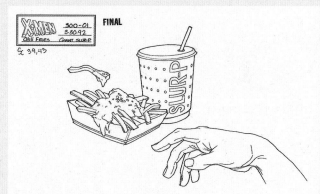

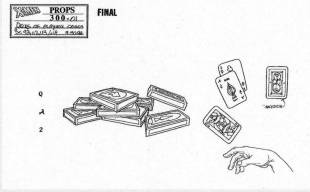

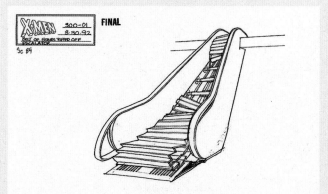

03 Prop list, "Night of the Sentinels." **04** Prop models of Police Squad Car, Police Paddy Wagon, Damaged VCR, Wheelchair, Large Order of Chili Fries and Giant Slur-P (answering Jubilee's rhetorical question "Does a mall babe eat chili fries?"), Decks of Playing Cards, and Belt of Damaged Escalator, all by Steve Olds.

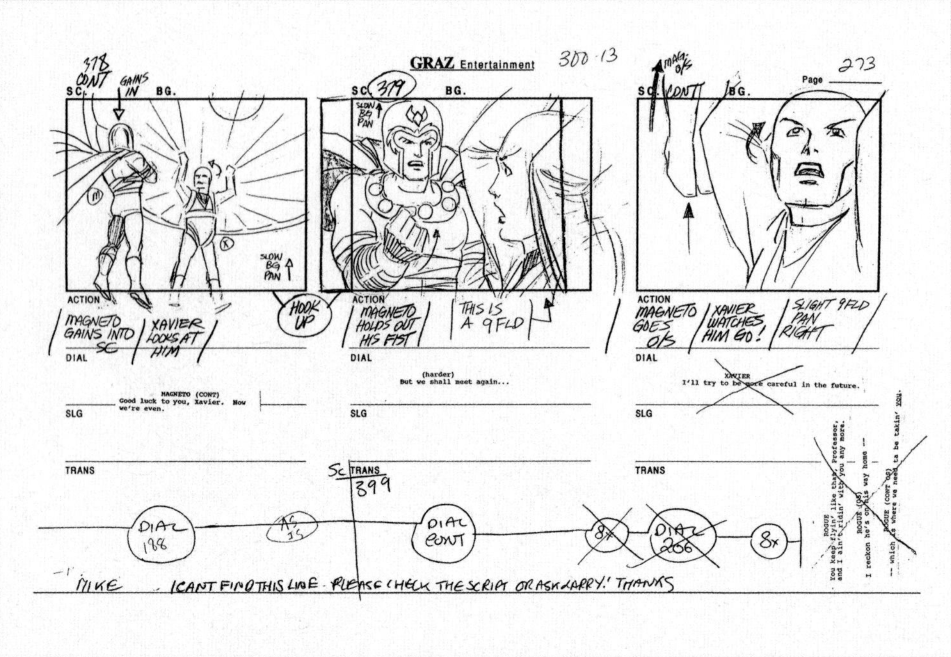
GRAZ Entertainment
300-13
273
MAGNETO GAINS INTO SC
XAVIER LOOKS AT HIM
HOOK UP
MAGNETO HOLDS OUT HIS FIST
THIS IS A 9FLD
MAGNETO GOES O/S
XAVIER WATCHES HIM GO!
SLIGHT 9FLD PAN RIGHT
Good luck to you, Xavier. Now we're even.
But we shall meet again...
I'll try to be more careful in the future.
MIKE - I CANT FIND THIS LINE - PLEASE CHECK THE SCRIPT OR ASK LARRY! THANKS

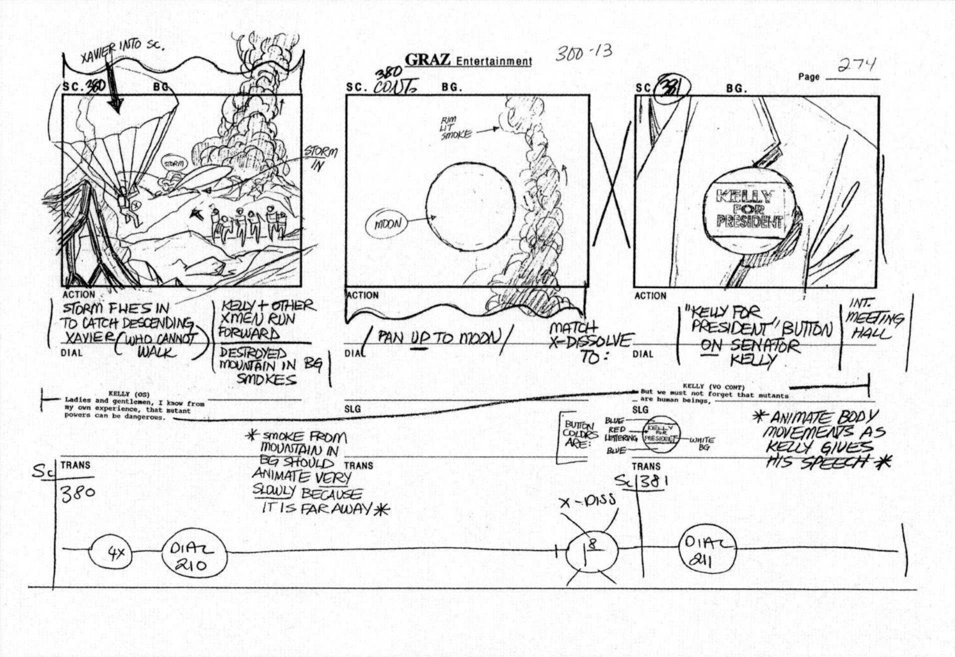
GRAZ Entertainment
300-13
274
XAVIER INTO SC.
STORM IN
MOON
KELLY FOR PRESIDENT
STORM FLIES IN TO CATCH DESCENDING XAVIER (WHO CANNOT WALK)
KELLY + OTHER XMEN RUN FORWARD
DESTROYED MOUNTAIN IN BG SMOKES
PAN UP TO MOON
MATCH X-DISSOLVE TO:
"KELLY FOR PRESIDENT" BUTTON ON SENATOR KELLY
INT. MEETING HALL
Ladies and gentlemen, I know from my own experience, that mutant powers can be dangerous.
But we must not forget that mutants are human beings,
* SMOKE FROM MOUNTAIN IN BG SHOULD ANIMATE VERY SLOWLY BECAUSE IT IS FAR AWAY *
* ANIMATE BODY MOVEMENTS AS KELLY GIVES HIS SPEECH *

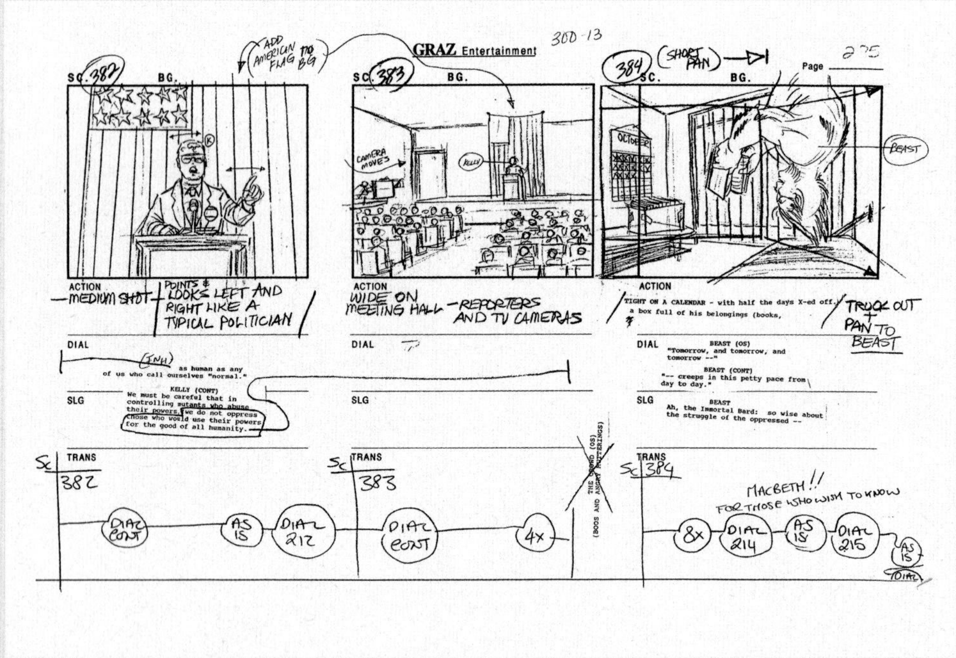
GRAZ Entertainment
300-13
275
ADD AMERICAN FLAG TO BG
SHORT PAN
BEAST
MEDIUM SHOT
POINTS & LOOKS LEFT AND RIGHT LIKE A TYPICAL POLITICIAN
WIDE ON MEETING HALL - REPORTERS AND TV CAMERAS
TIGHT ON A CALENDAR - with half the days X-ed off. a box full of his belongings (books,
TRUCK OUT PAN TO BEAST
as human as any of us who call ourselves "normal."
We must be careful that in controlling mutants who abuse their powers, we do not oppress those who would use their powers for the good of all humanity.
"Tomorrow, and tomorrow, and tomorrow --"
"-- creeps in this petty pace from day to day."
Ah, the Immortal Bard: so wise about the struggle of the oppressed --
MACBETH!! FOR THOSE WHO WISH TO KNOW

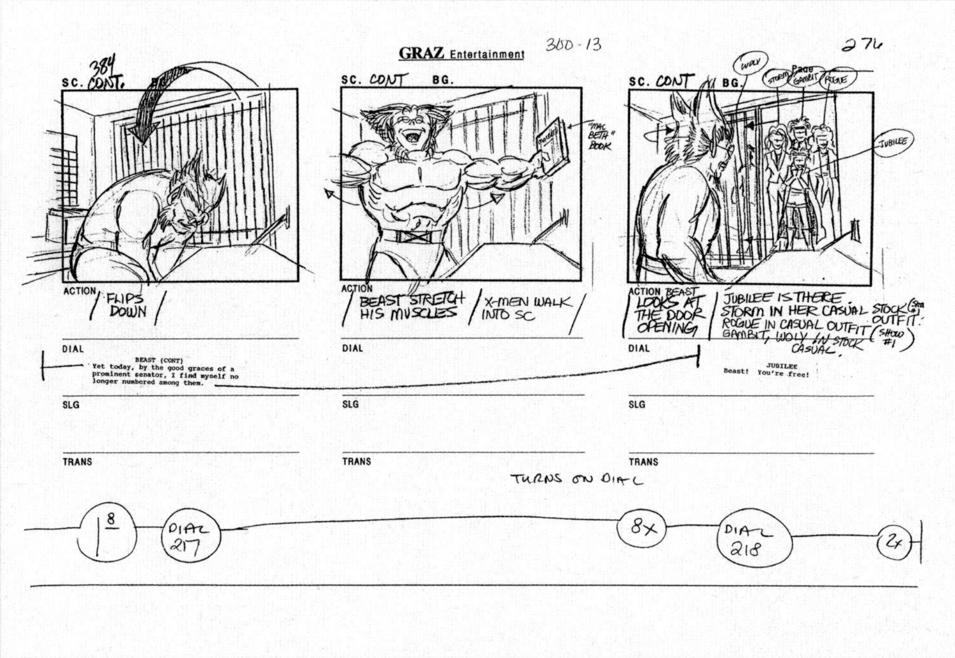
GRAZ Entertainment
300-13
276
FLIPS DOWN
BEAST STRETCH HIS MUSCLES
X-MEN WALK INTO SC
LOOKS AT THE DOOR OPENING
JUBILEE IS THERE. STORM IN HER CASUAL OUTFIT. ROGUE IN CASUAL OUTFIT. GAMBIT, WOLY IN STOCK CASUAL.
Yet today, by the good graces of a prominent senator, I find myself no longer numbered among them.
Beast! You're free!
TURNS ON DIAL

THIS SPREAD Final eight storyboard pages of "The Final Decision," with original ending (no Mister Sinister added), utilizing layouts, models, and props, by Larry Houston.

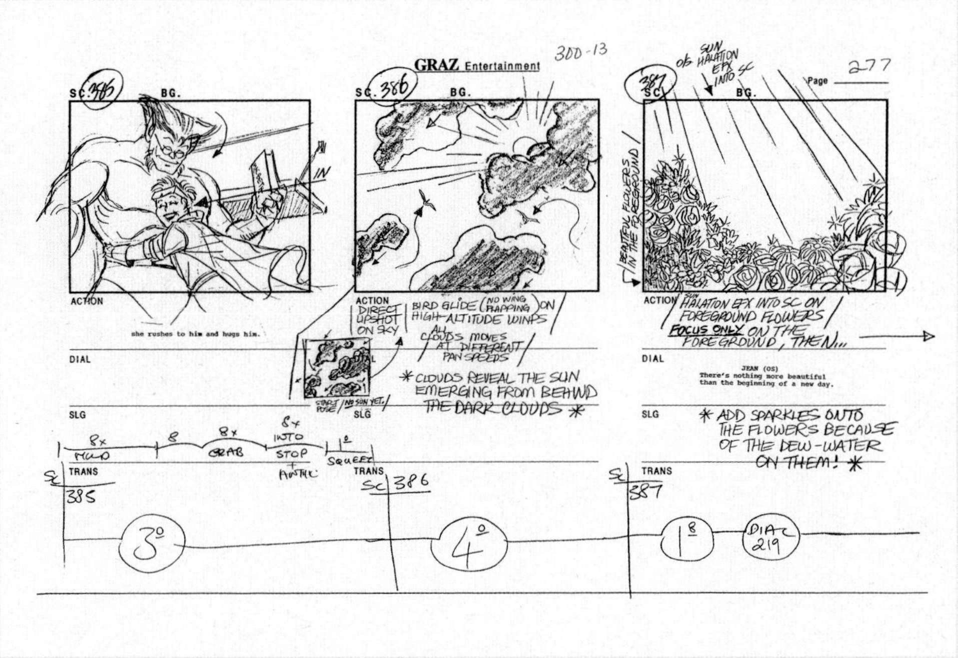
GRAZ Entertainment
300-13
Page 277
SC. 385
she rushes to him and hugs him.
SC. 386
DIRECT UPSHOT ON SKY
BIRD GLIDE (NO WING FLAPPING) ON HIGH-ALTITUDE WINDS
ALL CLOUDS MOVES AT DIFFERENT PAN SPEEDS
START POSE / NO SUN YET.
* CLOUDS REVEAL THE SUN EMERGING FROM BEHIND THE DARK CLOUDS *
O/S SUN HALATION EFX INTO SC
SC. 387
BEAUTIFUL FLOWERS IN THE FOREGROUND
SUN HALATION EFX INTO SC ON FOREGROUND FLOWERS
FOCUS ONLY ON THE FOREGROUND, THEN...
JEAN (OS)
There's nothing more beautiful than the beginning of a new day.
* ADD SPARKLES ONTO THE FLOWERS BECAUSE OF THE DEW-WATER ON THEM! *

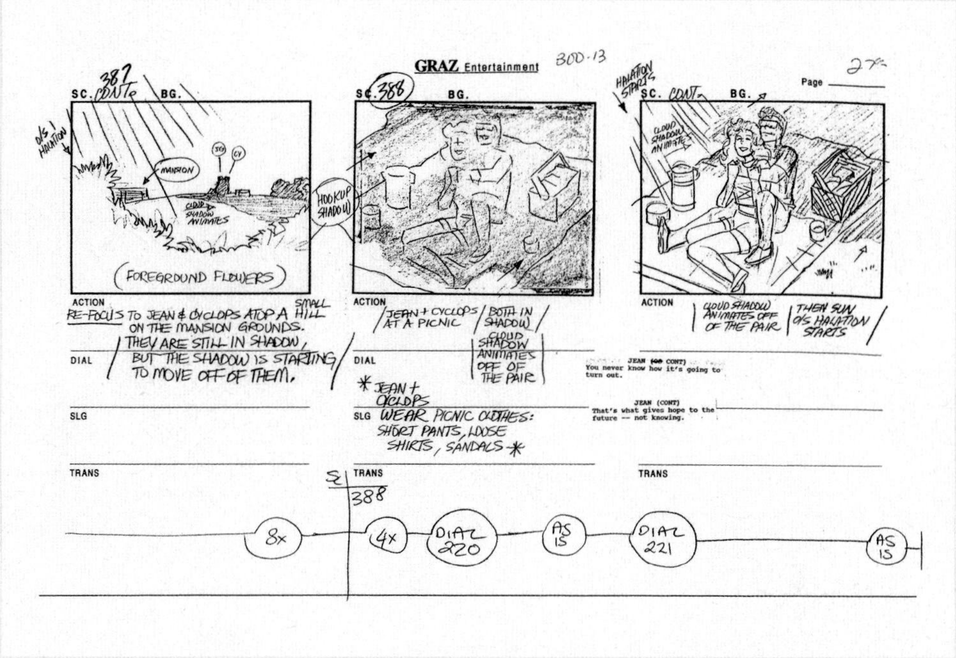
GRAZ Entertainment
300-13
SC. 387 CONT.
O/S HALATION
MANSION
CLOUD SHADOW ANIMATES
(FOREGROUND FLOWERS)
RE-FOCUS TO JEAN & CYCLOPS ATOP A SMALL HILL ON THE MANSION GROUNDS. THEY ARE STILL IN SHADOW, BUT THE SHADOW IS STARTING TO MOVE OFF OF THEM.
HOOKUP SHADOW
SC. 388
JEAN + CYCLOPS AT A PICNIC
BOTH IN SHADOW
CLOUD SHADOW ANIMATES OFF OF THE PAIR
* JEAN + CYCLOPS WEAR PICNIC CLOTHES: SHORT PANTS, LOOSE SHIRTS, SANDALS *
HALATION STARTS
SC. CONT.
CLOUD SHADOW ANIMATES OFF OF THE PAIR
THEN SUN O/S HALATION STARTS
JEAN (CONT)
You never know how it's going to turn out.
JEAN (CONT)
That's what gives hope to the future -- not knowing.

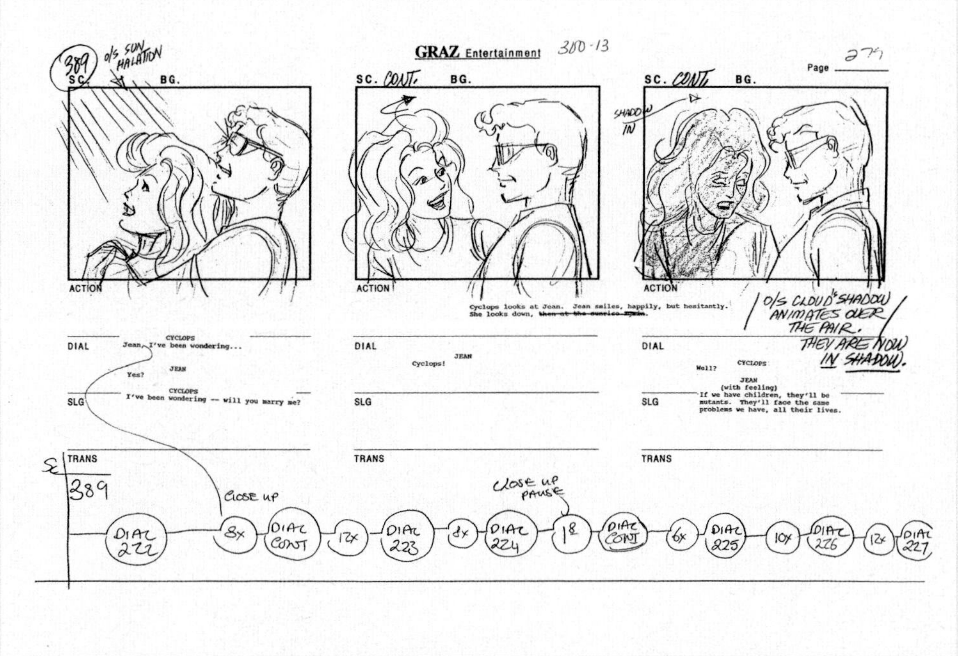
GRAZ Entertainment
300-13
SC. 389
O/S SUN HALATION
CYCLOPS
Jean, I've been wondering...
JEAN
Yes?
CYCLOPS
I've been wondering -- will you marry me?
SC. CONT.
Cyclops looks at Jean. Jean smiles, happily, but hesitantly. She looks down.
JEAN
Cyclops!
SHADOW IN
SC. CONT.
O/S CLOUD'S SHADOW ANIMATES OVER THE PAIR. THEY ARE NOW IN SHADOW.
CYCLOPS
Well?
JEAN
(with feeling)
If we have children, they'll be mutants. They'll face the same problems we have, all their lives.
CLOSE UP
CLOSE UP PAUSE

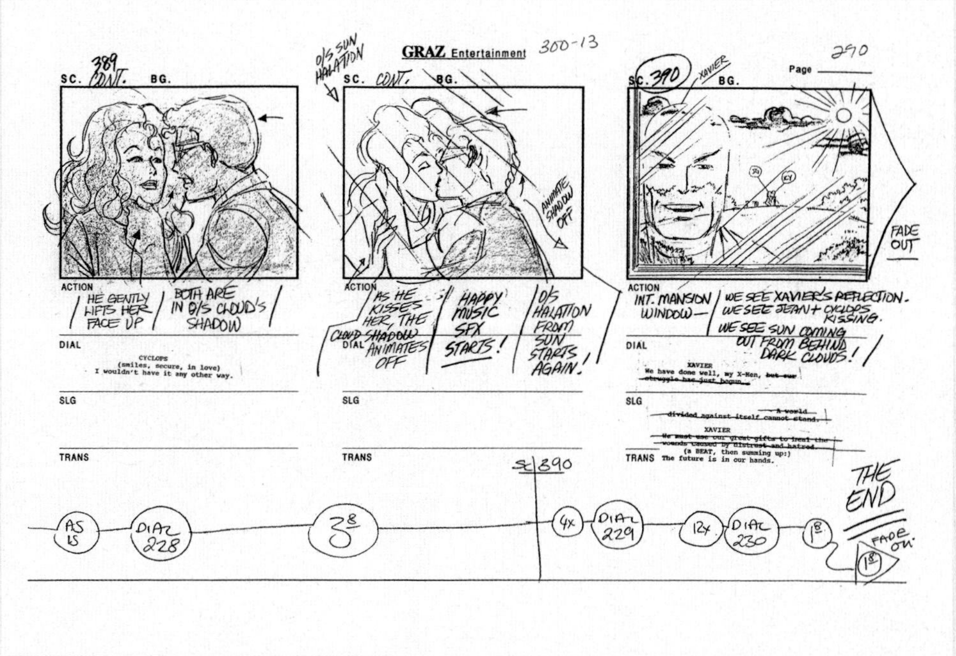
GRAZ Entertainment
300-13
Page 290
SC. 389 CONT.
HE GENTLY LIFTS HER FACE UP
BOTH ARE IN O/S CLOUD'S SHADOW
CYCLOPS
(smiles, secure, in love)
I wouldn't have it any other way.
O/S SUN HALATION
SC. CONT.
ANIMATE SHADOW OFF
AS HE KISSES HER, THE CLOUD SHADOW ANIMATES OFF
HAPPY MUSIC SFX STARTS!
O/S HALATION FROM SUN STARTS AGAIN!
SC. 390
XAVIER
FADE OUT
INT. MANSION WINDOW—
WE SEE XAVIER'S REFLECTION. WE SEE JEAN + CYCLOPS KISSING. WE SEE SUN COMING OUT FROM BEHIND DARK CLOUDS!
XAVIER
We have done well, my X-Men,
(a BEAT, then summing up:)
The future is in our hands.
THE END
FADE ON

DURING THE STORYBOARDING, the voice talent in Toronto would record the script. Graz would receive audiocassettes of the voice recordings and make timing sheets to show the animators how each character's mouth would move to fit the dialogue. They would take the storyboard images, which indicate movement, and time out how many frames of animation each would require for each sound of each word, thus establishing the speed.

Stephanie recalls, "We had to slug [space the dialogue amid the action images] the storyboards, have the timing on the boards get translated into the sheets, have all the dialogue's mouth movements. It had the timing within the storyboard of the walk timing or the arm movements: how many frames for each gesture. Timing directors and storyboard directors, I just think of as gods! They had to visualize every movement in the show. So you would see them at their desk, walking, mumbling, 'That was a good pace. That took me how many seconds? Okay, if I translate it onto the page it means walking a step every half of a second.' And it was crazy because it all needed to be broken down into tiny little pieces of movement. Another challenge was that a lot of the overseas animators didn't speak English. So on the timing sheets, you're doing specific, agreed-to mouth movements to stand in for the words. There's a different mouth movement indicated by 'A' through 'G'—closed, open, half-open, full open, ooh, ah. Amazingly, these seven mouth shapes form every sound we make (at least in English), so they are the only shapes that you need to match the sounds coming from the voice tracks. Anyone who was on camera and you saw their mouth move, it was based on this series of seven letter-named movement references. That was its own special job."

Larry: "The entire storyboard was sent out to have all the sheets exposed—they call it exposure. A director breaks down the action; like if a character is talking, pointing, grabbing a french fry. They time all that stuff, put it on those sheets, and ship it overseas."

Dana: "Exposure sheets tell the animation studio, frame-by-frame, how to move the characters. We assign the mouth charts, and then you have the actual character designs of how they're supposed to move. So it's frame by frame. Karen Peterson was our main timing director. She would have a team of

GRAZ
ENTERTAINMENT, Inc.
PROD. NO.
FOOTAGE
ANIMATOR
SCENE NO.
SHEET NO.
SC.
Cont.
ACTION
DIALOG
EXP
CAMERA NOTES
MARVEL PRODUCTIONS
X-MEN
WALLY BURR RECORDING
5/15/87

01 02

01 Mouth timing SFX sheet for how to do the special Phoenix Effect for the Dark Phoenix saga, provided by production manager Dana Booton. **02** Audio cassette, voice recording, "Pryde of the X-Men," shown as reference for similar *X-Men: TAS* tapes. **03** Mouth timing SFX sheet, Dark Phoenix saga, provided by Dana Booton. **04** Still-frames of Beast showing examples of called-for mouth positions.

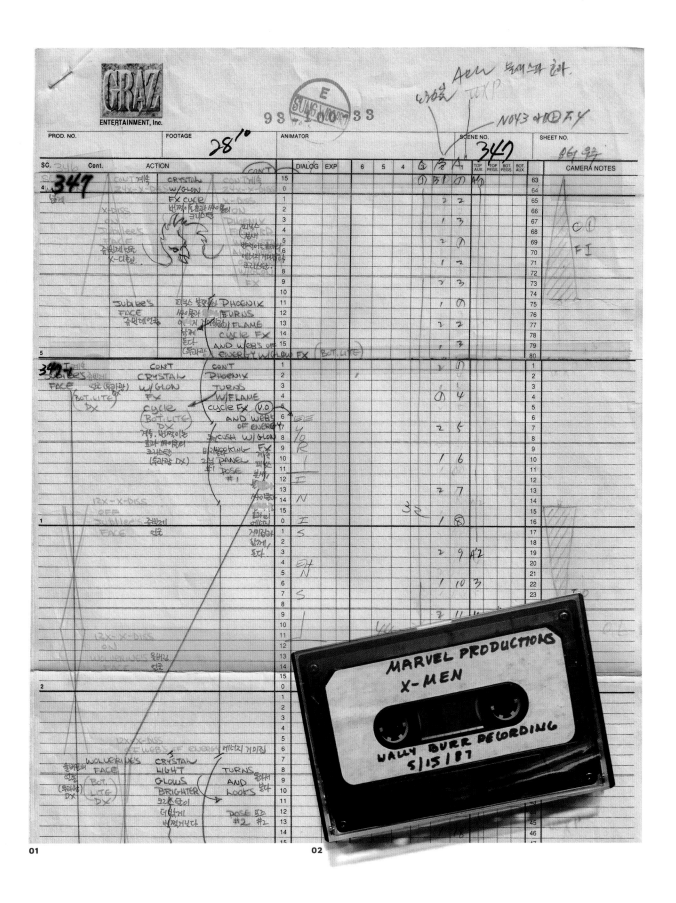

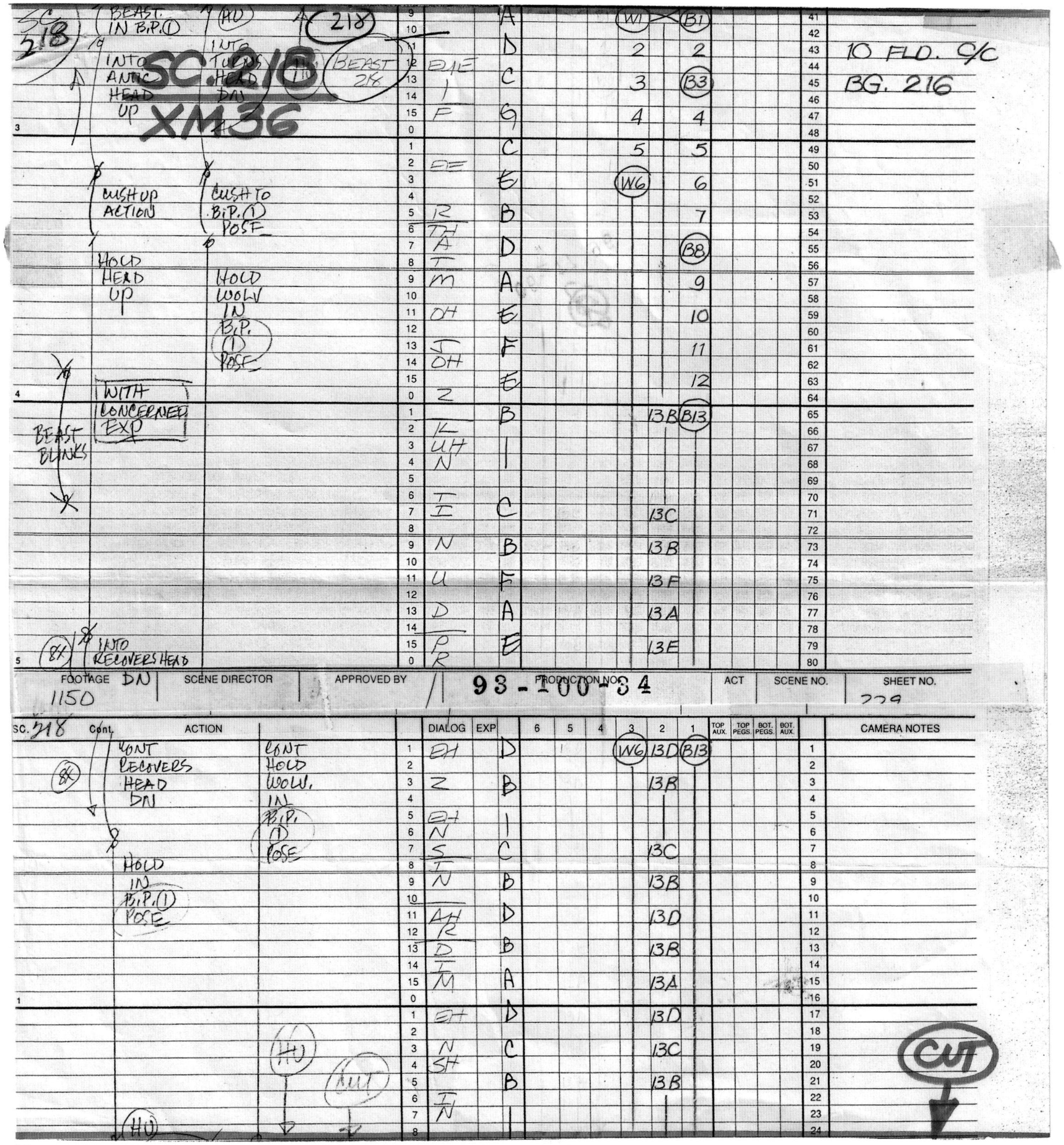
SC. 218
XM36
BEAST 218
10 FLD. C/C
BG. 216
FOOTAGE
SCENE DIRECTOR
APPROVED BY
93-100-34
PRODUCTION NO.
ACT
SCENE NO.
SHEET NO.
ACTION
DIALOG
EXP
CAMERA NOTES
CUT

03

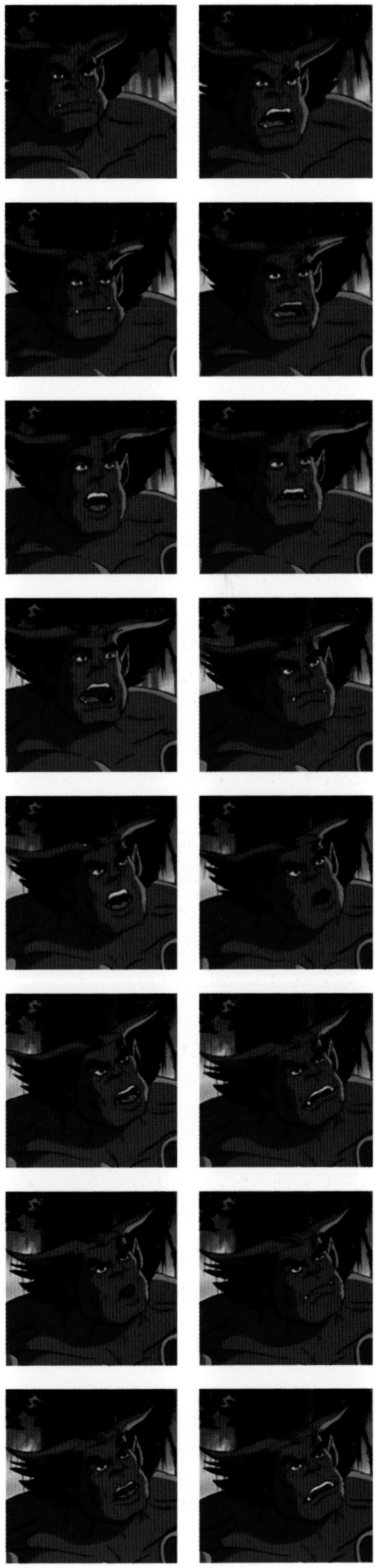

04

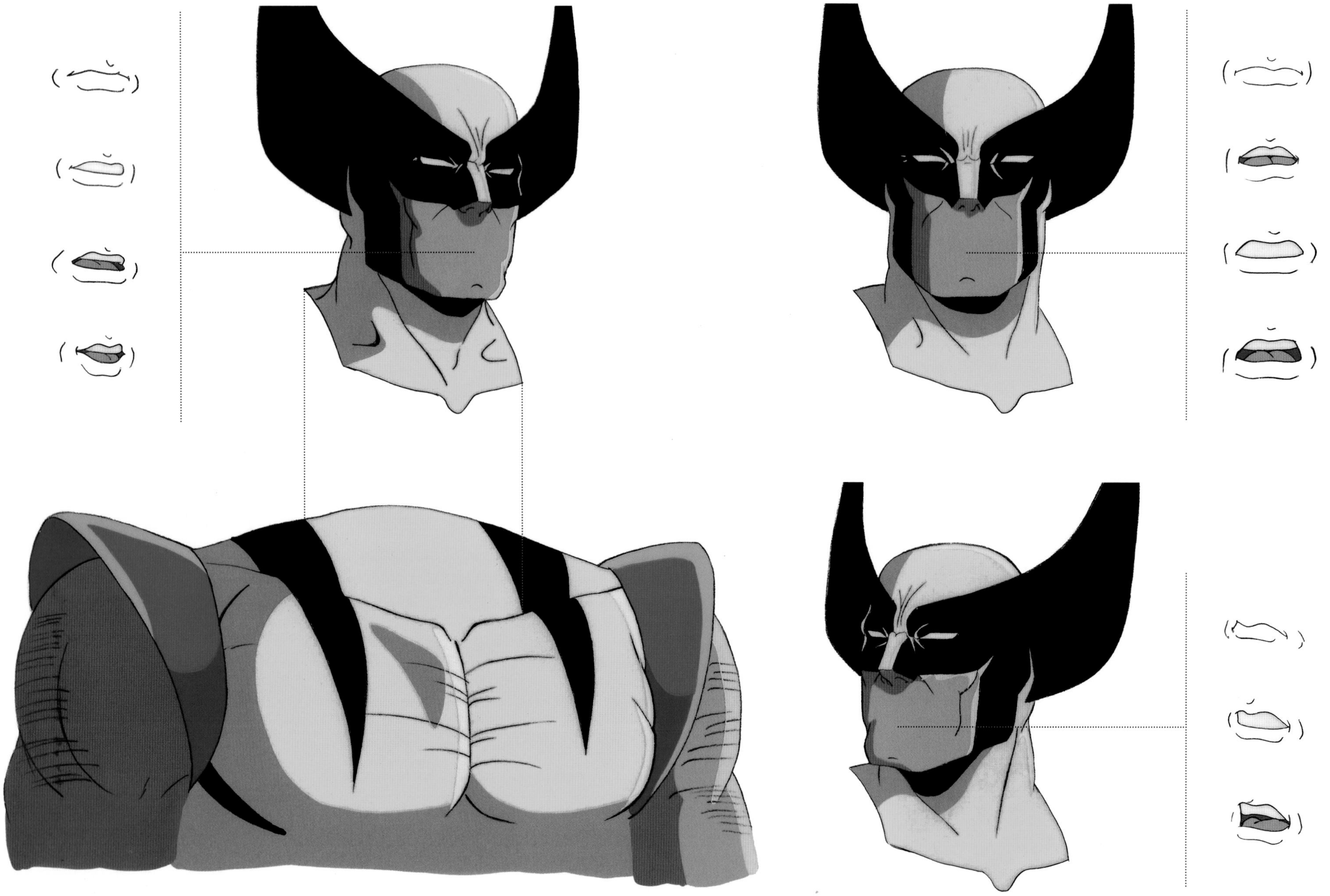

ABOVE Clockwise from upper left: Mouth movements with Wolverine head 1; Wolverine head 2 with mouth movements; Wolverine head 3 with mouth movements; Wolverine shoulders. **OPPOSITE** Turning Wolverine's head, including original drawings, in-between drawings, and cel art—note red outline on top left and bottom right images, indicating the television screen frame.

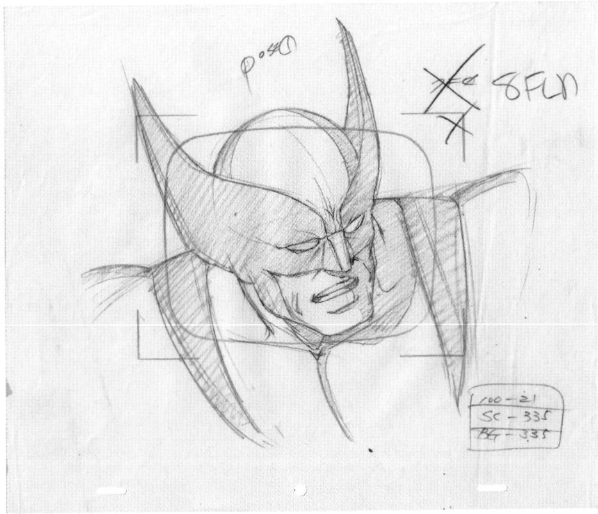
100-21
SC-335
BG-335
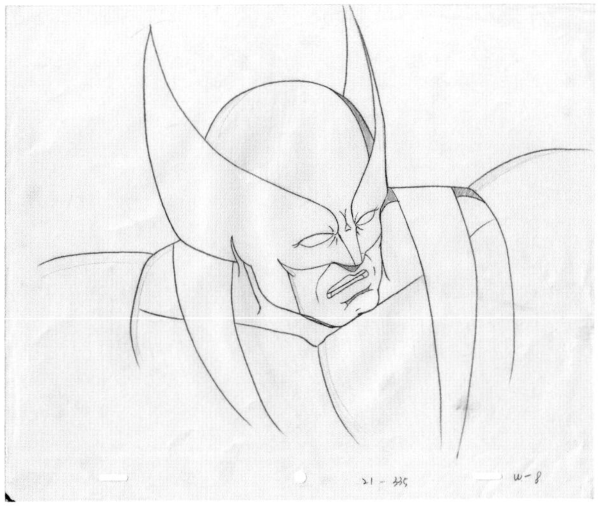
21-335
W-8
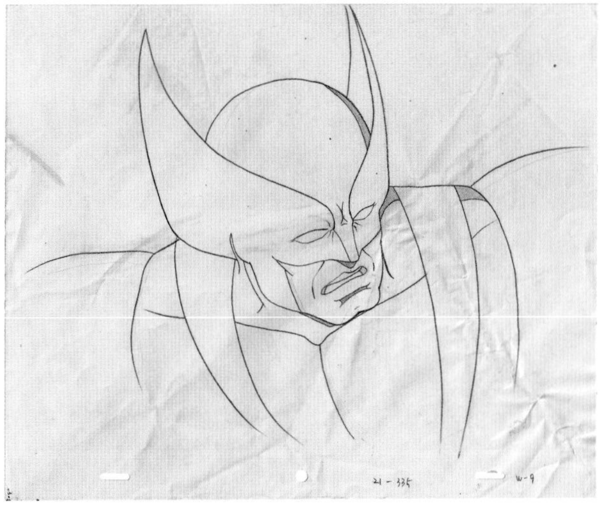
21-335
W-9
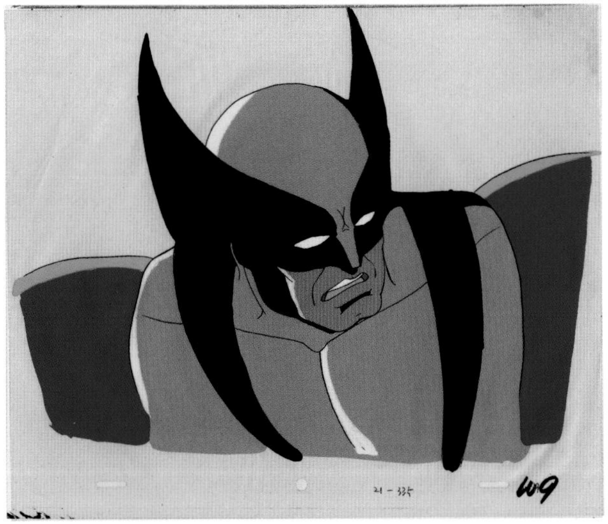
21-335
W9
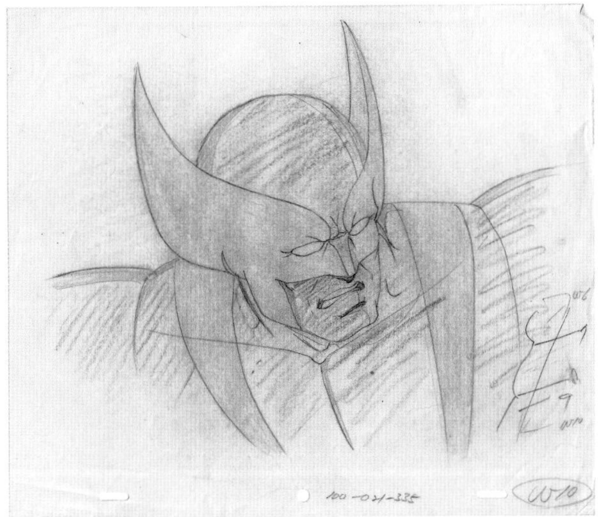
100-021-335
W10
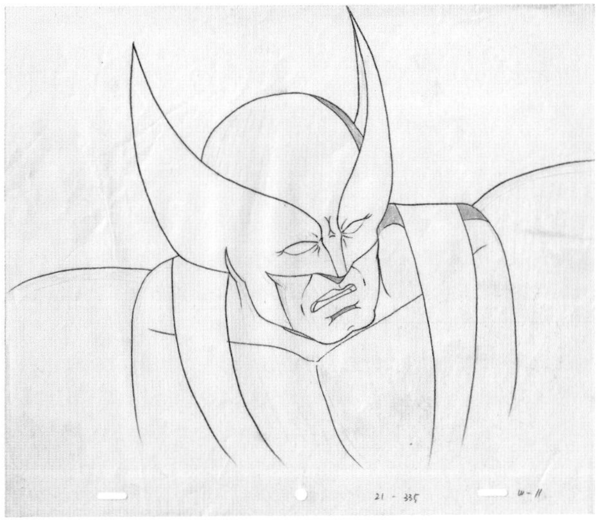
21-335
W-11
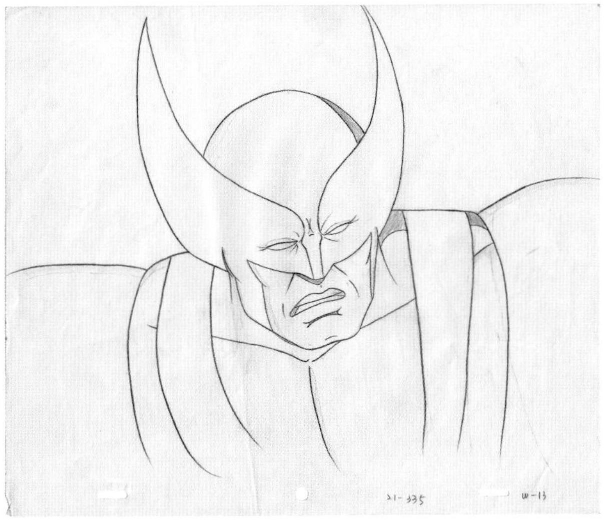
21-335
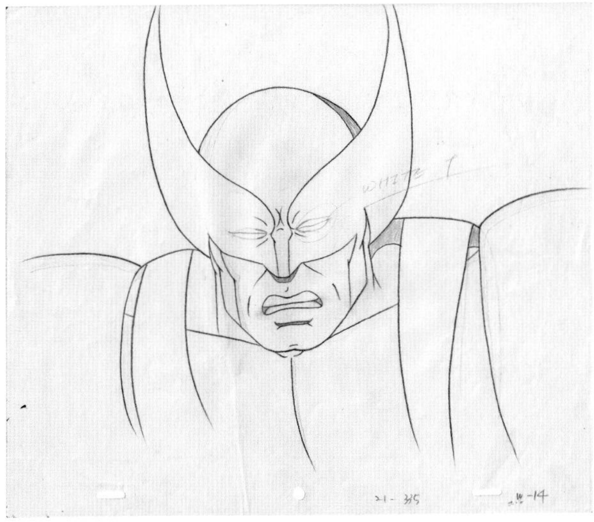
21-335
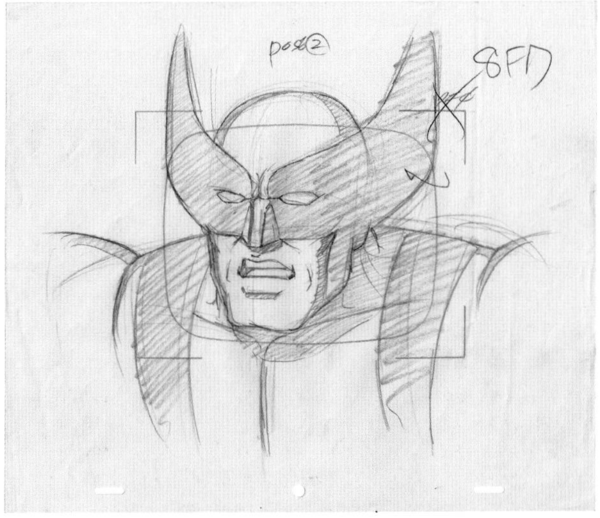

three timers; we'd have a lip-sync person, Erik Peterson, and then we'd probably have anywhere from three to six timers on a show. Once we'd sent it all overseas, we thought of this as the blueprint.

"We'd do all sorts of things to help the overseas artists know our intentions. Say Magneto was in the cast. You'd go through the storyboard and see where he was in each scene, and the character design of him that we would send overseas would have a list on the side here of every scene that he was in.

"Same with the background layouts. You'd go through and mark as many scenes as possible to show them where that layout would be used. We would send maybe fifteen painted backgrounds to indicate the color palette and tone. And because of our modest budget we were always scrambling as far as how many background keys we could send. When we set up the show, we created a paint palette of perhaps two hundred colors, where today you can you use any color. The ink-and-paint person would paint a chip on a piece of cardboard of each of the two hundred colors. Two hundred was a lot for back then."

Graz would make this huge shipment of creative elements and then hope for the best.

Stephanie explains, "We had copies of everything in those boxes: storyboards, characters, props, background layouts, color keys—color comps for characters and props and backgrounds. They weren't full-size, but they were to scale, and they had to be designed and painted per the lighting needs. Today you can relight a scene electronically, adjusting the colors for the light. Then it had to be hand-painted individually so you could know if you were on one corner of the room that the lighting was a specific way and the colors matched it. If the camera came at you from another direction, the lighting was different, requiring a different set of colors. These all had to be in the materials that you sent, along with the voice recordings, and the directed sheets and timing. None of these were small."

Filling the boxes with every element needed to create an *X-Men: TAS* episode was only part of the battle. There was getting it all into a foreign country, quickly and safely.

Stephanie says, "Because of our deadlines, getting all the materials through customs was an art, and so you wanted someone who was your regular carrier who had a relationship where the customs people knew what it was they were moving and allowed it to move quickly."

Then everyone in pre-production jumped onto the elements of the next episode in line as they waited eighteen long, anxious weeks to see how the hand-painted animation turned out when it returned, in its rough cut, on film.

SKIN
TRIM:
★S B40 (H) 230 B
549 A
SKIN:
1129 (H) DO
355 A
CLAWS:
480 B (H) W
210 B
BODYSUIT:
619 (H) 488 B
1160
BOOTS:
★S B40 (H) 230 B
549 A
BODYSUIT:
619 (H) 488 B
1160
BELT:
★S 821 (H) R70
528 A
PANTS & GLOVES:
★S B40 (H) 230 B
549 A
Color Reuse
Wht. of Eye - W
Highlight -
Iris - 810
Teeth - W
Ins. Mouth - RP40M
Tongue - 985
Throat - RP70M
Lips -
SABAN
SHOW # 1499-
CHARACTER
WOLVERINE
PAGE: 2
SCENE: 2

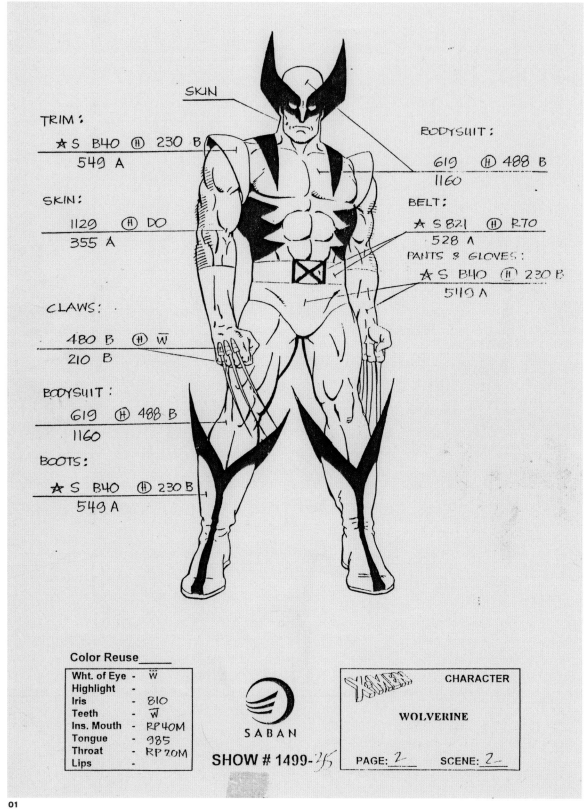

01

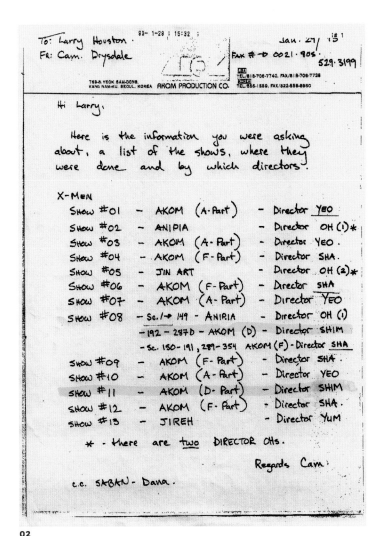

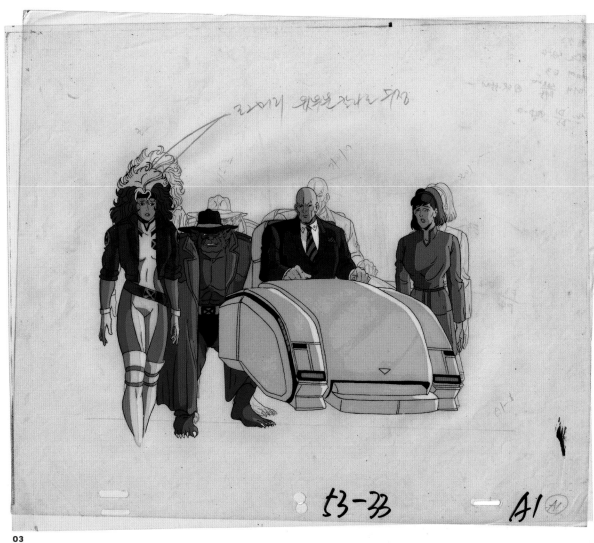

93- 1-29 ; 15:32 ; #1

To: Larry Houston.
Fr: Cam. Drysdale

Jan. 27/ '93
Fax # → 0021·805·529·3199

769-8, YEOK SAM-DONG, KANG NAM-KU, SEOUL, KOREA AKOM PRODUCTION CO.
USA TEL/818-706-7740, FAX/818-706-7738
KOREA TEL/556-1559, FAX/822-558-8960

Hi Larry,

Here is the information you were asking about, a list of the shows, where they were done and by which directors.

X-MEN

Show #01	- AKOM (A-Part)	- Director YEO	
Show #02	- ANIPIA	- Director OH (1)*	
Show #03	- AKOM (A-Part)	- Director YEO.	
Show #04	- AKOM (F-Part)	- Director SHA.	
Show #05	- JIN ART	- Director OH (2)*	
Show #06	- AKOM (F-Part)	- Director SHA	
Show #07	- AKOM (A-Part)	- Director YEO	
Show #08	- Sc. 1 → 149 - ANIPIA	- Director OH (1)	
	-192 - 287D - AKOM (D)	- Director SHIM	
	- Sc. 150-191, 289-354 AKOM (F)	- Director SHA	
Show #09	- AKOM (F-Part)	- Director SHA.	
Show #10	- AKOM (A-Part)	- Director YEO	
Show #11	- AKOM (D-Part)	- Director SHIM	
Show #12	- AKOM (F-Part)	- Director SHA.	
Show #13	- JIREH	- Director YUM	

* - there are two DIRECTOR OHs.

Regards Cam.

c.c. SABAN - Dana.

02

S3-33
A1

03

PRODUCTION

THE LARGE MAJORITY of the series's animation production was done at AKOM studios in South Korea, but work was also subcontracted. The skills of different "teams" of animators at the studio varied. Larry Houston claimed he would always ask for the moon, for extra spectacle and detail, knowing that they would produce perhaps 50 percent of what he asked for.

Dana explains, "Our eighteen weeks overseas was unheard of at our budget level. Every smaller studio was doing shows at twelve or fourteen, but because [of] the extra work that we were looking for with *X-Men,* we needed at least eighteen weeks—and some of the shows actually went to twenty-six. The line detail, the big action scenes, the effects: They were just huge shows."

Luckily, we had an excellent overseas supervisor, Cam Drysdale, who was in constant contact with Dana and Stephanie.

Stephanie says, "We had an animation supervisor from our team who stayed at the overseas studio for as long as it took—in this case, four years. His job was to be the communicator between the animation teams and us. When they open that box of a thousand pre-production elements, if there's anything that they're not sure about, it's his job to connect back with our team and get clarification. Cam would have daily correspondence where he would fax us a list of questions. He was so detailed! The animators would have dozens of questions, and because they were on a deadline, we'd have to get answers to them right away. If they needed new material, we would have to fix or draw and ship it, so it'd be at least two days before they'd get it."

The time difference between Los Angeles and South Korea didn't help.

Stephanie says, "I think six in our evening was their eight o'clock in the morning, so between the time we got off work and the time we went to bed was when we had the most communication with Cam and the animators. Typically the lead directors and I really had to be available at almost any hour."

01 Saban color key for Wolverine, by Rick Hoberg. **02** Memo from overseas production supervisor Cam Drysdale to Larry Houston: a list of studios and directors for each episode of season one. **03** Production cel for "Proteus: Part 2," over drawing, with studio annotations.

B25

01

paint a background, it would be a background—but so many of these backgrounds had, because of the comic book look, this black line [see opposite].

"And so you now are double designing because you're designing the background itself and painting it, and then you're designing this piece that gets laid over the top as accent detail. You look at your sheets and you say, 'For our character, we need the overlay B-12 and then we need the B-25 character.' You shoot it, this comes off, B-26 character goes on, shoot it, comes off, so you've got that pile and then your working pile, so you grab the next one."

Eric: "So the background is static, and the overlay cels are changing in size to indicate movement."

Stephanie: "So the green goo is flying, and as you're animating, you're flipping these drawings, you're looking at the movement of it all. You only have so much time for this scene and this character's movement. So you animate accordingly—which tells you how fast something's moving.

"If this only had five cels and all that green stuff needed to fly off of there, it's flying off fast because it's only five cels. If you had thirty cels for that green stuff to go away, it might be oozing off. Those are the things that, all the way from the original director, they're visualizing, so they can slug [space and time] the storyboard; they tell you about how long in their mind they're giving that piece of that scene. The sheet timers time out all the nuances. The lead animator will probably do the first and last drawing and the assistants do the 'in-betweens,' but the timing chart tells you how many you get to make that motion happen."

Julia: "How many people end up working on an animated episode? Hundreds?"

Stephanie: "Pre-production and production, sure. You don't want to spread it out further than you have to because the communication and the quality control starts to suffer, but you're guided by the amount of time you have. We had the 'luxury' of an eighteen-week overseas schedule. Still, think about all of this having to happen in a matter of weeks—the creation of thousands and thousands of precisely animated paintings."

THE ANIMATORS' WORK WAS GRUELING. There are more than thirty thousand frames in twenty-two minutes of film. Animation was painted by hand, frame by frame. Each frame had four or five layers—background color art, background line design, characters, props, effects—that needed to be photographed, each one leading smoothly into the next. They would start with the animators' sketches.

Stephanie says, "These are the actual animation sheets. This is what gets actually animated. This is the animator's drawing; it gets photocopied onto a clear plastic cel—you see it'll match up perfectly. And then it goes through the ink and paint department, then from there it goes into the camera department and gets married up with the backgrounds. So you've got the exposure sheets hanging up on the camera;

you put the background down first position—'What cels do I need? Those go on there—*click*, take those cels off, change the mouth—*click*.' You had to have rows of shelves with all of these things in the proper order so that you're following the sheets, calling for cel H7 with mouth HA1 when one character's talking versus the next character, over BG layout H.

"Your exposure sheet is going to call for the background, so the first thing you're going to do is put down the background and you're going to know what field you were working in. It's gonna call for an overlay cel."

Julia: "The overlay is the detailed line-drawing outline?"

Stephanie: "Yes. Not all backgrounds have these. This is one of the things that made this series so unique, and when you say 'extra pencil mileage'—because normally you would just

01 Production cel of Beast, from "Proteus: Part 2," with combined "green goo" cel overlay. 02–04 Painted backgrounds, overlay cels, and the two combined. Top to bottom: X-Mansion war room from "Slave Island;" X-Mansion jet hangar and Mister Sinister's lair from "Till Death Us Do Part, Part 2."

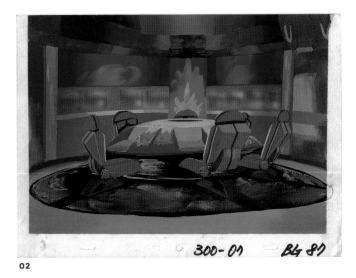

300-01   BG 87

300-01   BG 87

02

100-15   BG 220

15   BG 220

15   100-15   BG 220   BG 220

03

100-15   BG 285

15   BG 285

15   100-15   BG 285   BG 285

04

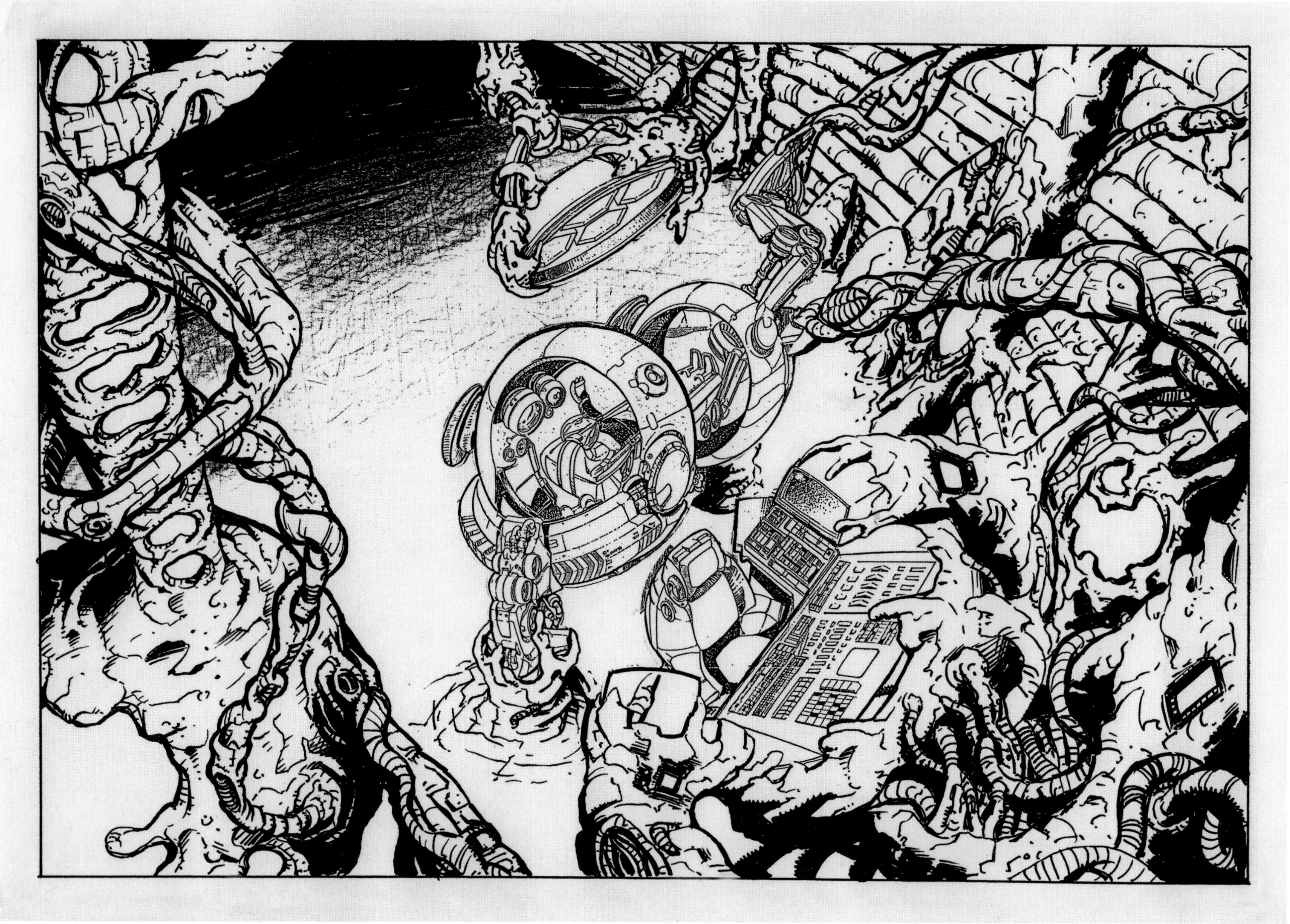

01

01 Detailed background drawing of Mister Sinister's lair for "Till Death Us Do Part, Part 2," by Frank Squillace. (Squillace designed and cleaned the overlay of organic growth on the floor, ceiling, walls, consoles, and devices, but the devices themselves were lifted directly from *X-men Annual* [vol. 2] #1.) **02** Painted production cel background for same location, with background orientation reversed. **03** Overlay production cel for painted cel. **04** Painted foreground cel, to go over both. **05** Overlay production cel, to go over all three. **06** All four elements combined.

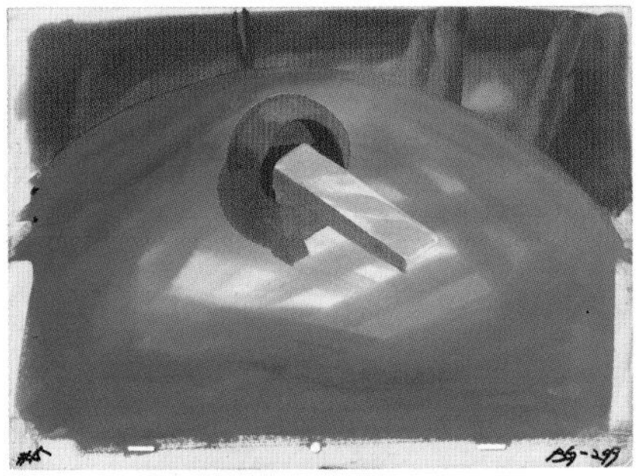

02

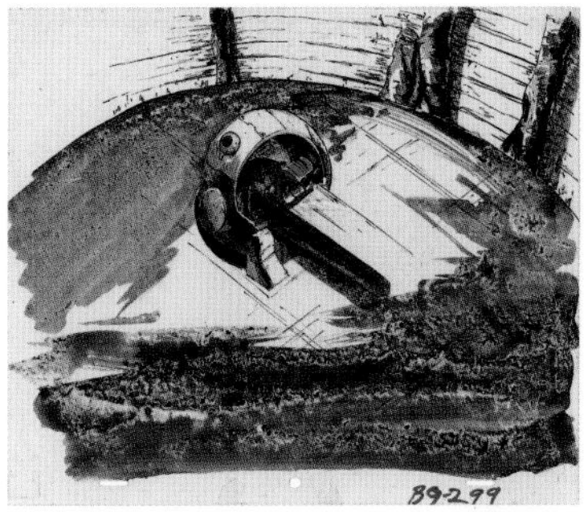

03

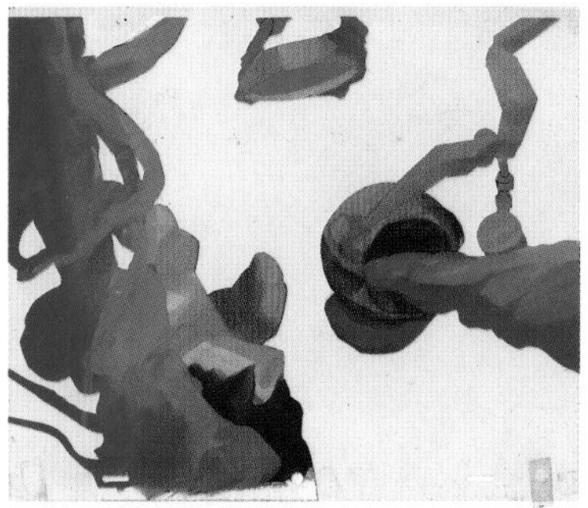

04

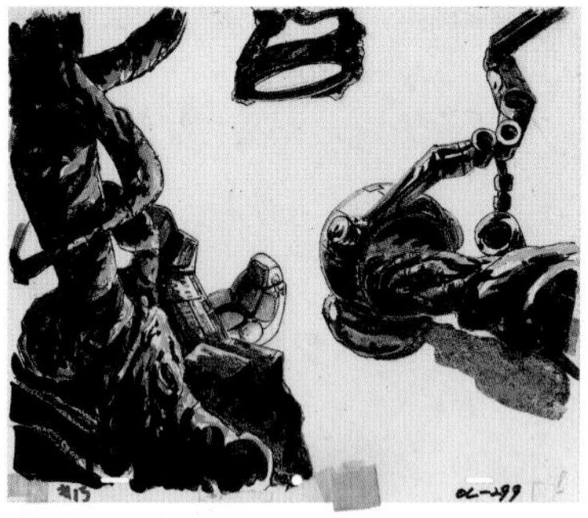

05

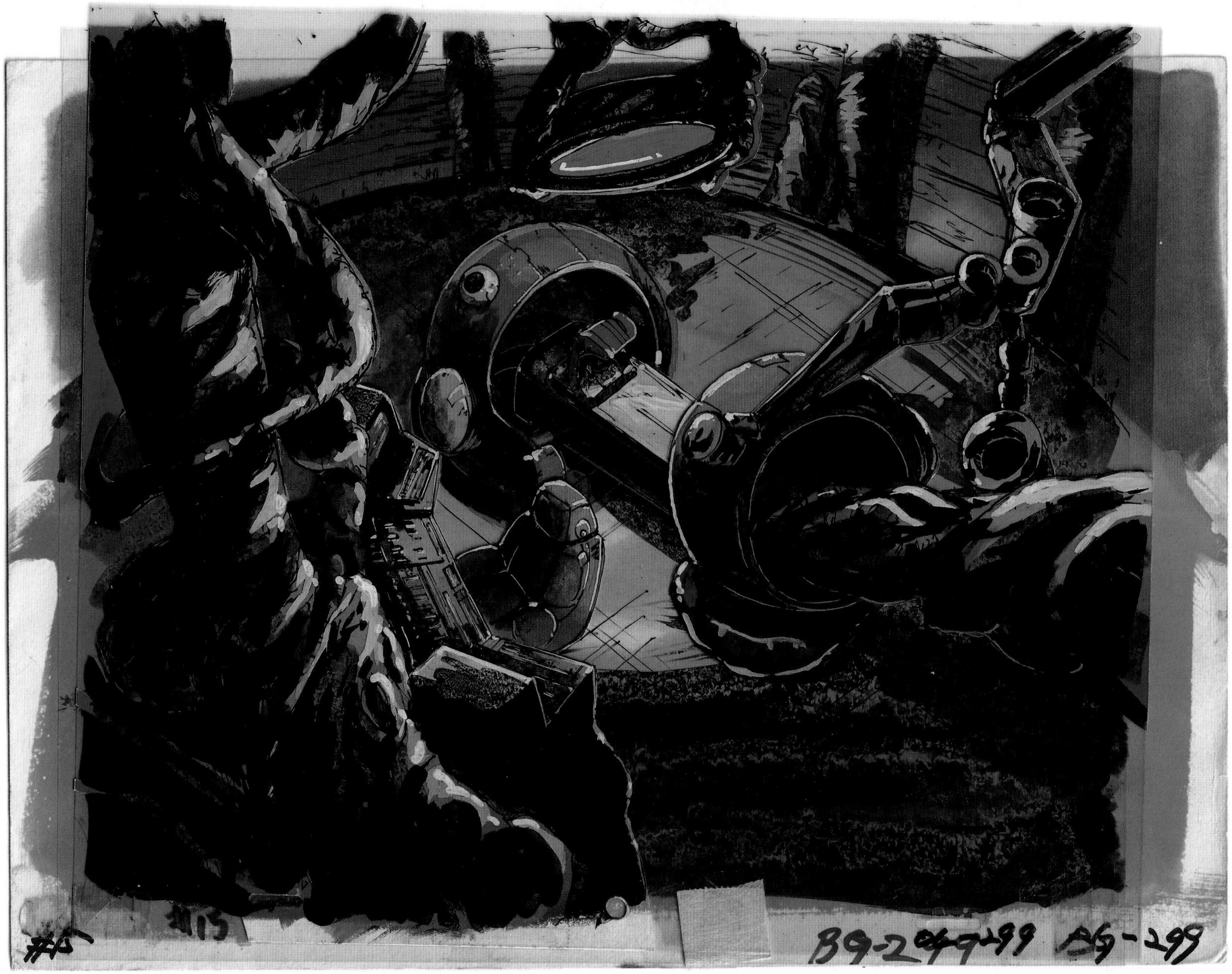

06

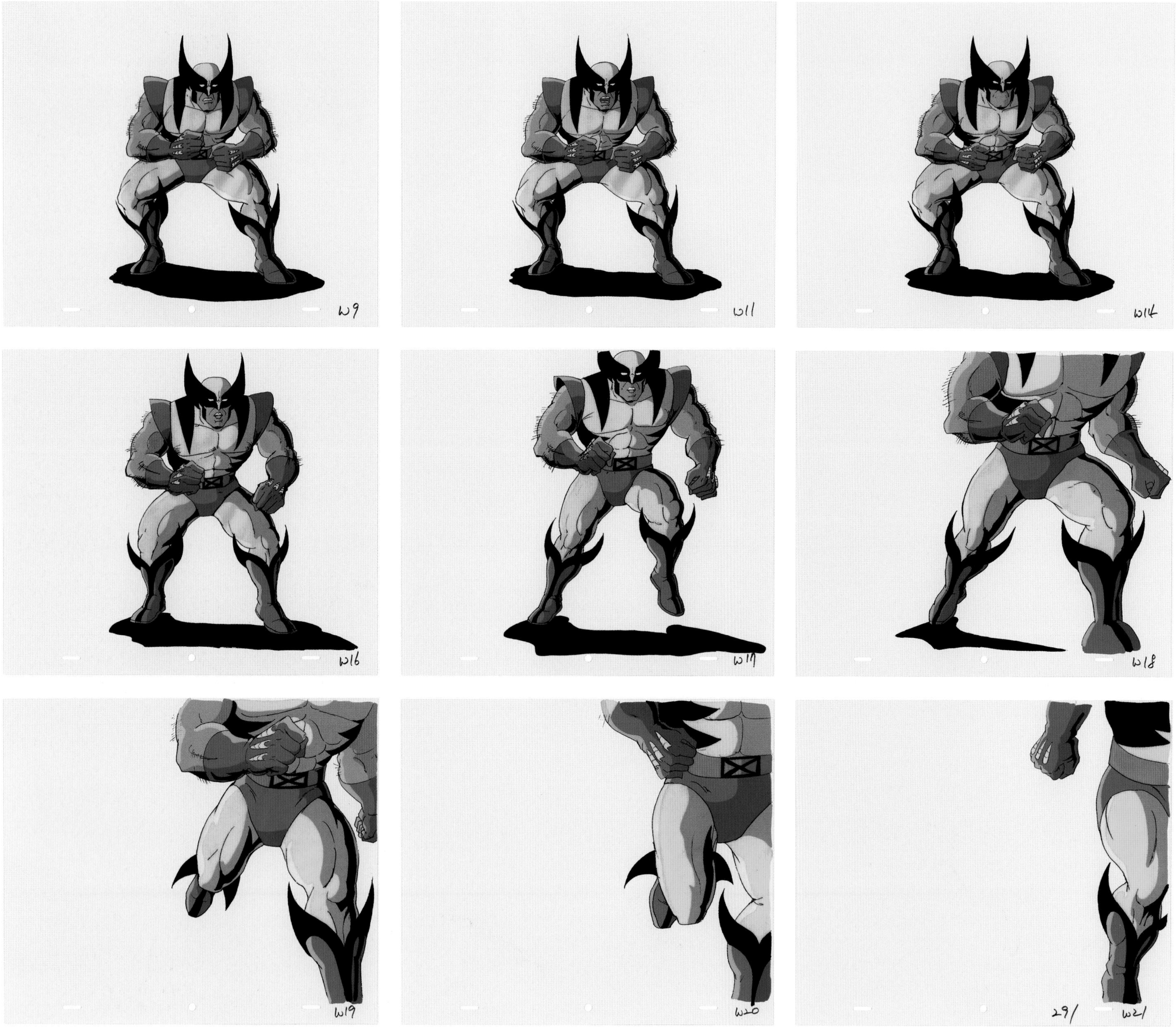
w9
w11
w14
w16
w17
w18
w19
w20
29/
w21

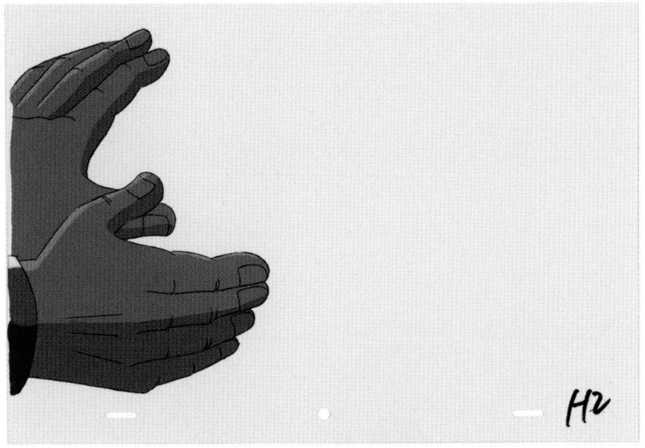
H2
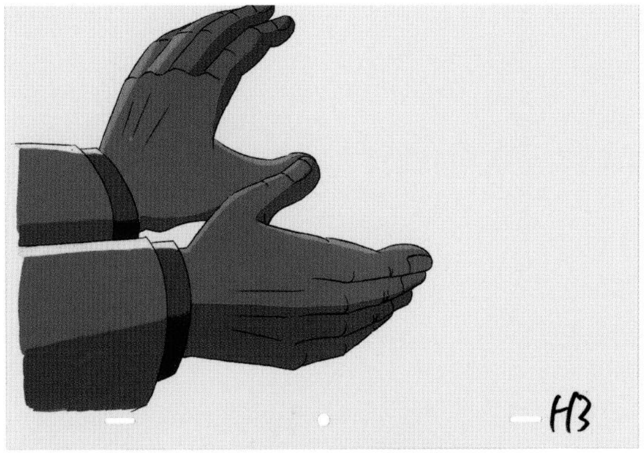
H3
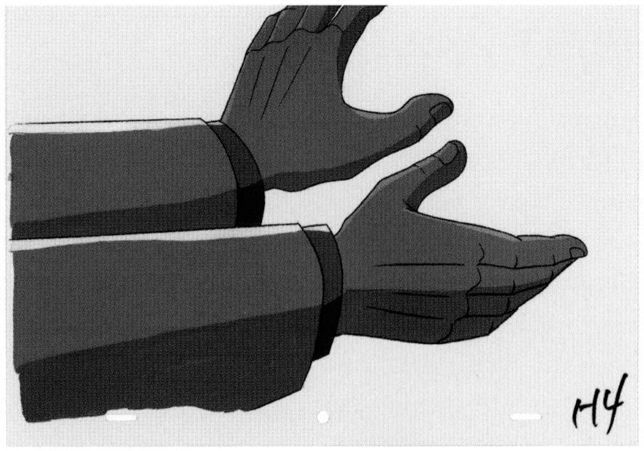
H4
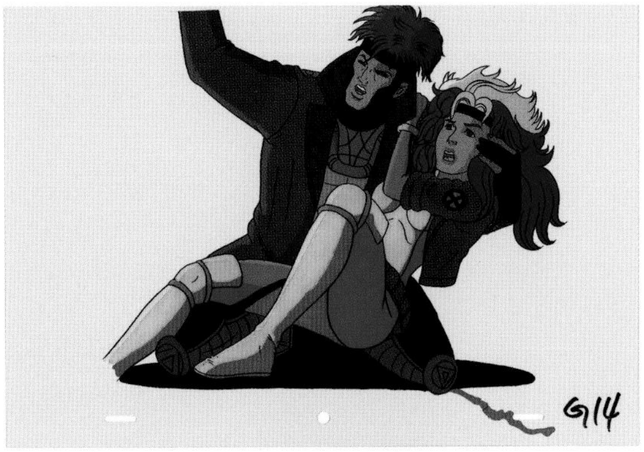
G14
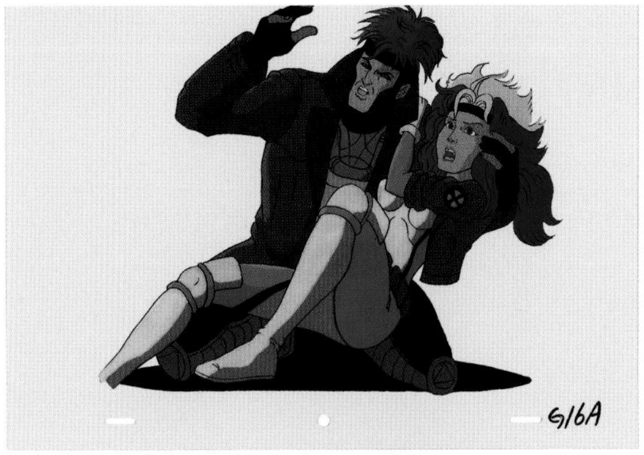
G16A
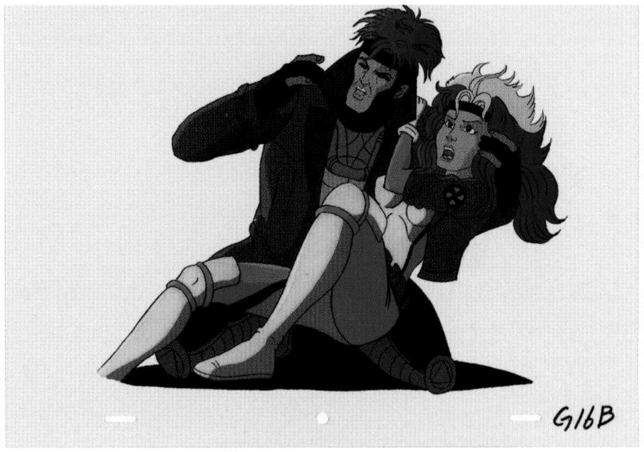
G16B
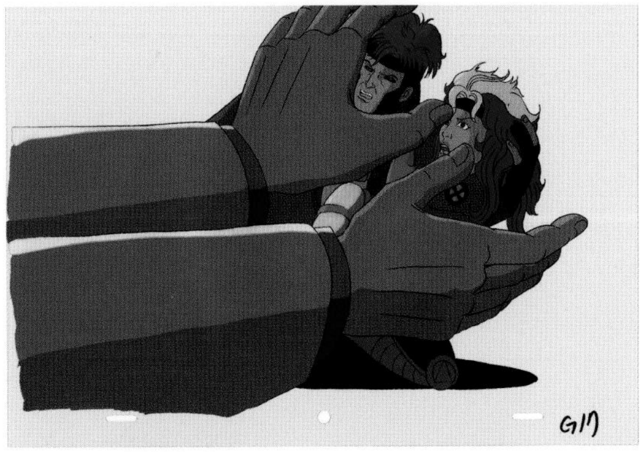
G17
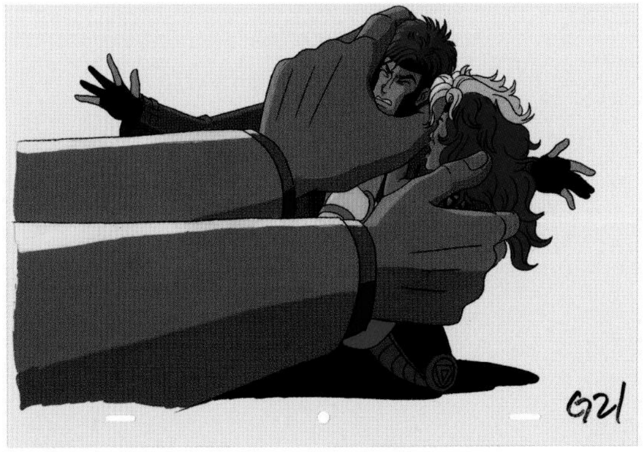
G21
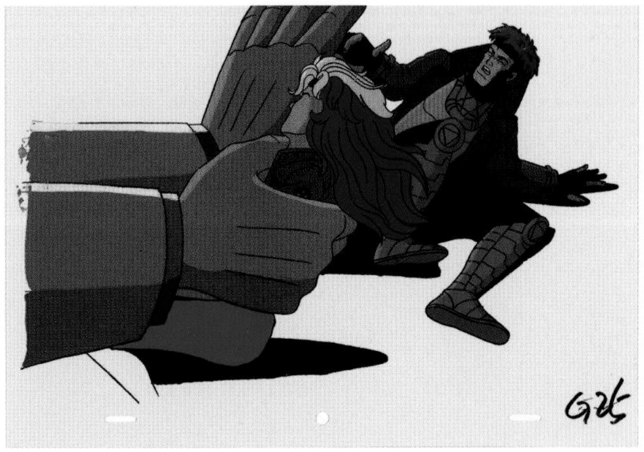
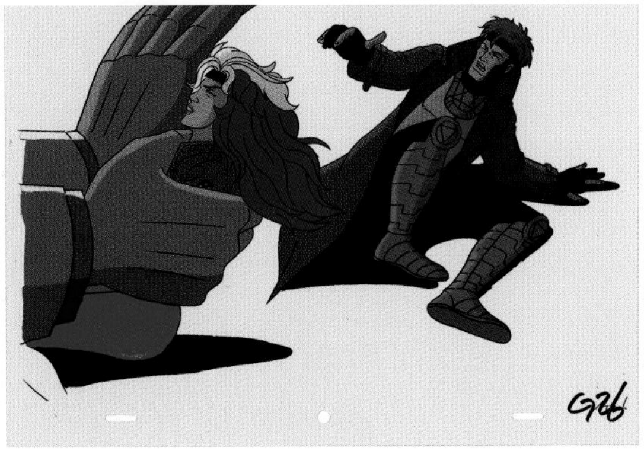
G26
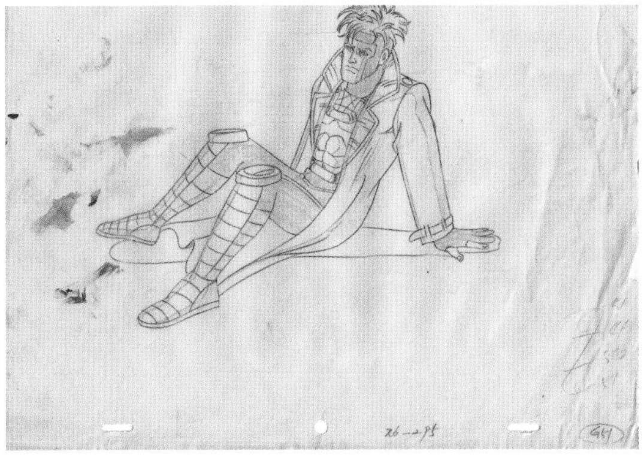

OPPOSITE Series of production cels showing Wolverine running out of frame. **THIS PAGE** Series of cels and drawings showing Gorgeous George reaching into frame, grabbing Rogue, and rebuffing Gambit the moment after Gambit declares his love to Rogue and they kiss ("Reunion, Part 2").

POST-PRODUCTION

ROUGH VERSIONS of the animated episodes would be sent from AKOM back to Los Angeles, where Saban Entertainment's post-production crew—led by producer Scott Thomas and video editor Sharon Janis—would fix smaller problems, tighten pacing, and call for animation "retakes" on issues that were beyond fixing in LA. Dana Booton would get all the feedback and get the details back to Cam Drysdale, in Korea. Dana would help Scott and Sharon try to make everything right, while Haim Saban, their boss, would push back, trying to minimize their efforts and the costs associated with them.

Dana: "Saban's people were there to push it through as quickly as they could, so it was a constant battle of trying to keep us on schedule and on budget."

Sharon: "When we received the rough footage from AKOM, I got each take [animated shot] separately, each with a label—12-A, 12-B, 12-C, whatever—the episode number and the letter of what part of the episode it was. Then I would do an assembly just as it was. I'd check the running time and start to trim. We did a lot of work on the fight scenes, but really it was a lot of intercutting [back and forth within the scene] to make the rhythm right.

"I would have a script and the voices. The voices gave me a nice backbone to work from. Most were written long. The show had to be to time, so tightening pauses and overlapping dialogue helped keep it moving. While someone's talking, you're cutting to someone sneaking into something in the background. I remember when they did the *Spider-Man: TAS* pilot, someone had edited it traditionally. Margaret [Loesch] was not happy because it didn't have 'the *X-Men* thing,' the pace, the energy. She hired me for a weekend to re-edit the pilot. She, as head of the network, came and worked with me on it. That was cool!"

Producer Scott Thomas—who had post-production experience on prime-time TV series like *Battlestar Galactica* and *Knight Rider*—arrived just as the first *X-Men: TAS* episodes were being cut together.

Scott says, "If things weren't quite working in a scene, a lot of times I'd re-create. I don't know if Sharon mentioned this. I would take bits and pieces, maybe from another episode, and adjust the scene to make the rhythm work better. It was fun, working with Larry [Houston], who had done the boards."

Scott was philosophical about dealing with time pressure and animation retakes: "There were always characters that came back [from being animated in Korea] looking like a flounder, two eyes on the same side of the face.

AKOM
AKOM PRODUCTION CO.
TEL:556-8974/5 FAX:556-8960
DATE:
INITIALS
LAYOUT
ANIMATOR
ANI-CHECKING
ASST' ANI.
VIDEO-TEST
ASST' CH
XEROX
INKING
PAINTING
EFX.
FINAL CH.
STOCK #
S/A.MAT.
OL-UL
PROD.
SC.
B.G.
CELS
FOOTAGE
TO-TAL
X34
the lay-out pose is correct
NOT THIS
X/M
93-100-26
4.06
179
79

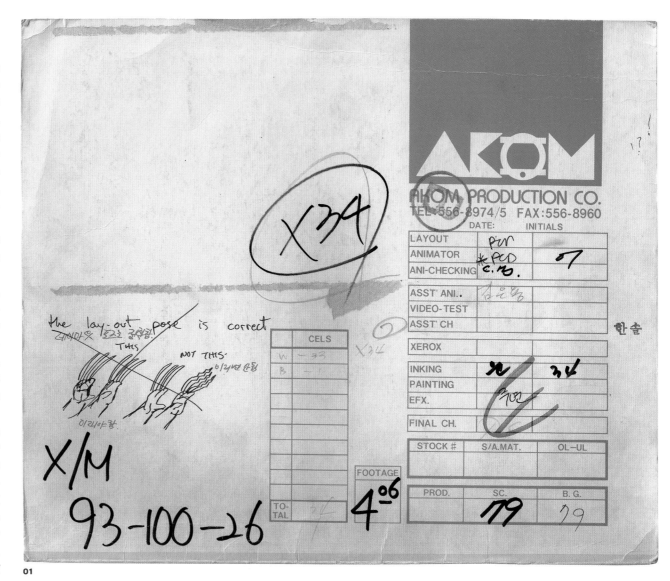

01

"But for the most part, story-wise, it always worked, and occasionally if the fixes, if the retakes you ordered, didn't come back in time, you'd just have to cheat it. Honestly, the toughest part was trying to fight Saban to get the quality—to get the time to get the music and sound and other elements right. It was always: 'Quicker, faster, cheaper.' I remember doing Foley [audio effects recording] for footsteps, because Saban didn't have footsteps in its audio library when I got there. They didn't want to bother with it, or other enriching details."

Larry Houston was also involved in asking for retakes to fix problems that perhaps only he could see in the animation.

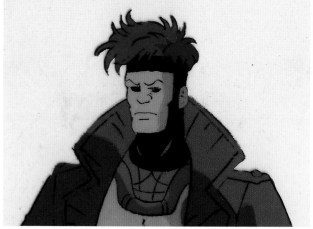

02

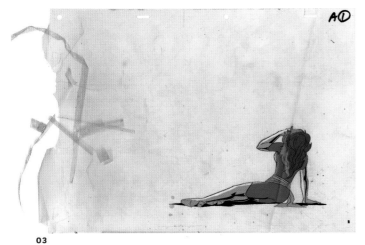

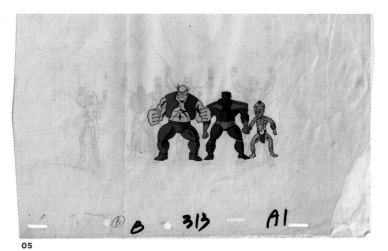

03

04

05

Larry: "You tried to get the retakes done in under two weeks, hopefully a week."

Dana: "If you wanted to have them do a retake, you would have to pull the reference materials, send them back to the overseas animators, and say, 'You did it wrong, this is how you're supposed to do it.' So our files of original creative elements were always being utilized."

Eric: "So the AKOM retake folders had notes on them about what was wrong and that they had addressed with new material. Wolverine had wavy claws, and they redid the claws. There was one where Rogue wasn't wearing a glove or *was* wearing a glove."

Dana: "There were all different types of errors that you would get, and because it was film and it was cels, there would be things "popping" all the time—light or glare getting into the photos. So you'd get something called a platen [lid] flash, because they'd be moving copies so fast and that they were getting extra light on them. Color correcting was much harder in the '90s, so any of that stuff would have to go back and be reshot."

Dana explained that *X-Men: TAS* generally had time and money for one quick set of limited retakes. Bigger-budget shows—at Warner Bros., Disney—would have many rounds of them, more even after an episode had aired. If something was unfixable on *X-Men*, and there was no time or money to do a retake, Larry, Sharon, and Scott would "get creative."

Larry explains, "You'd also have to figure out a Plan B so that if we didn't get the retakes, we'd have a way to fix it. If we had a mouth that's talking and goes over here, comes over here, or pink flashes, how could we fix it? Could we grab an image from another episode and cover it?"

"Then once you assembled the show, to time, they called it 'locked picture.' You couldn't make the show any shorter or

longer. You sent that out to do sound effects, sync the voices, and lay down the music. There were blanks or 'held' scenes, and you'd tell them, 'In this shot you're gonna have a helicopter. You can't see it, because we're waiting for a retake, but please drop in helicopter sound effects here. In this shot, he's going to be yelling over a cannon, so crank up the audio for the voice talent.'

"When you went to the final audio mix, that's where everything had to be decided, visually, because they were mixing the sound elements for good. 'Okay, let's bring the voices up here, bring your music down here.' You mixed on giant, really good speakers because the detail was great—usually took a full day. Then you watched the same show on little crappy speakers that people would have on their regular 1990s TV sets to see if it played. Then it would go in for color correction. After that, they would make copies of the film or video to send out, physically, to the client TV stations. Later on, it became, if you finished really late, you had to upload it via satellite."

AFTER FIVE YEARS of nonstop work from hundreds of artists, where are the hundreds of thousands of pieces of *X-Men: TAS* art today?

Gone. Almost all gone.

Julia: "At the end of the season what would happen with these massive packets of creative material? Would they just end up in file cabinets?"

Dana: "At Saban, we actually started to archive some other shows with Acme Archives [storage facilities]. But I don't think Marvel did. Acme was a storage facility for animation cels—in climate-controlled facilities, so that the materials would stay fresh. I don't know if they're still around. With nearly everything lost, I guess we should be thankful for what has been saved."

Cels were never created to be permanent art, and they are easily damaged. The acetate sheets bend, crease, or crack over time. Adhesive tape degrades.

The delicate painted images adhere to paper used to separate the sheets and become permanently stuck. Efforts to separate the sheets can lead to further damage. The paint itself is vulnerable to chipping, cracking, and flaking. Water seeps onto painted backgrounds and causes stains.

Today, studios are saving what they now understand to be precious work. With *X-Men: TAS*, a few producers and artists grabbed some boxes of items as offices were cleaned out to make way for "the next job." Larry Houston and some others have kept pieces in their own filing cabinets and in personal storage units.

More recently, collectors and galleries like Van Eaton have purchased cels and artwork when they learn of a cache of material that might otherwise be discarded. Unfortunately the informal archival work done by these artists, collectors, and galleries has led to production cels and backgrounds becoming mismatched—but better mismatched than destroyed entirely. Thanks to galleries like Van Eaton, series artists like Larry Houston, Mark Lewis, Frank Squillace, and Dan Veesenmeyer, and collectors like animation producer Tom Tataranowicz, a bit of this artistic legacy remains.

01 Primary animation studio AKOM's production folder, used for materials needed for re-takes of images—note the hand-drawn notation regarding Wolverine's claws. **02** Production cel of Gambit (off-model). **03** Damaged cel: broken, cracked, decaying adhesive tape. **04** Damaged cel: reverse, paper stuck to the paint—see page 86. **05** Damaged cel: drawing stuck to the paint.

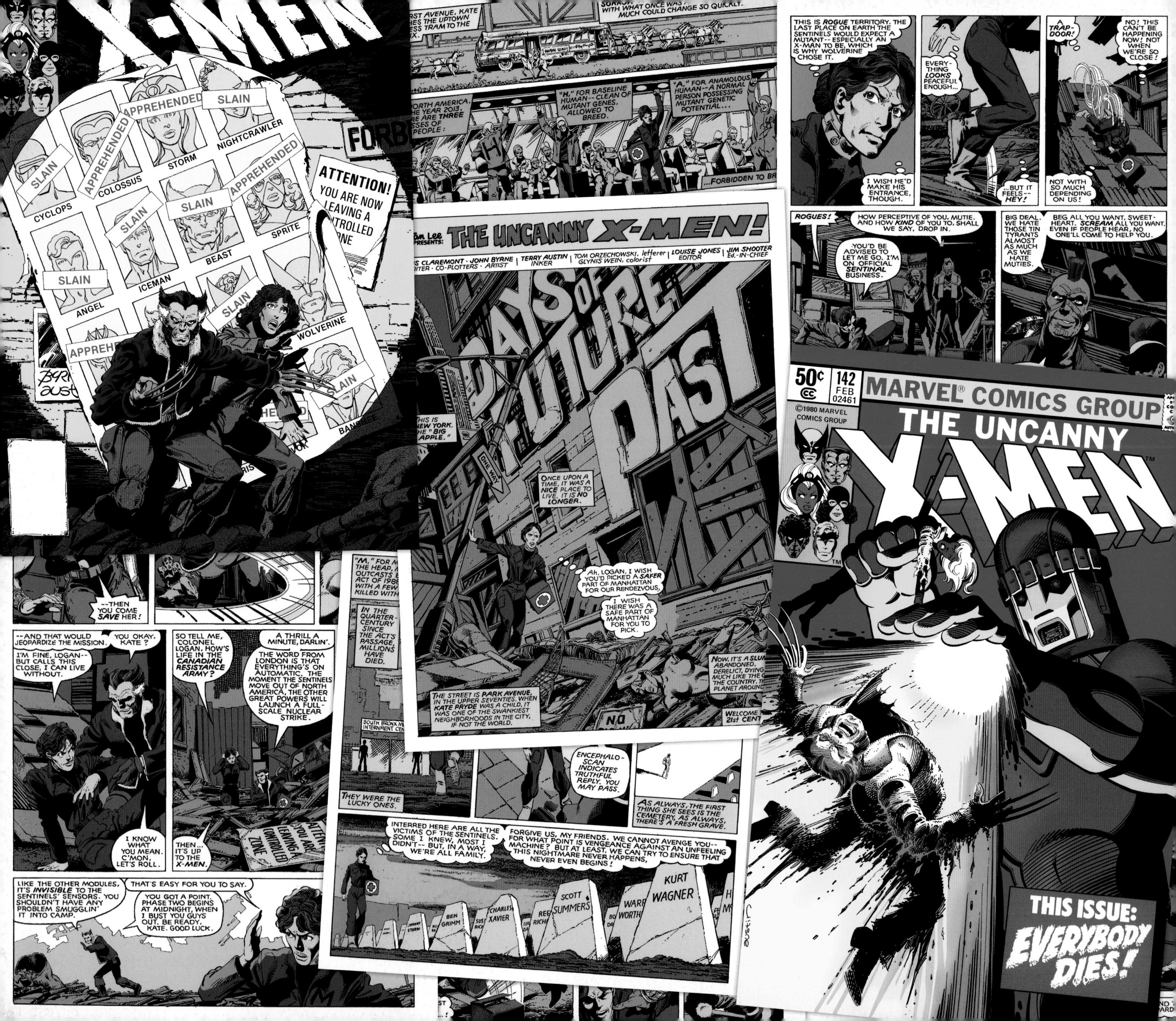

X-MEN
APPREHENDED
SLAIN
NIGHTCRAWLER
STORM
COLOSSUS
CYCLOPS
SPRITE
BEAST
ICEMAN
ANGEL
WOLVERINE
BANSHEE
ATTENTION!
YOU ARE NOW LEAVING A
WITH WHAT ONCE WAS? MUCH COULD CHANGE SO QUICKLY.
"H," FOR BASELINE HUMAN-- CLEAN OF MUTANT GENES, ALLOWED TO BREED.
"A," FOR ANAMOLOUS HUMAN-- A NORMAL PERSON POSSESSING MUTANT GENETIC POTENTIAL...
...FORBIDDEN TO BR
THIS IS ROGUE TERRITORY, THE LAST PLACE ON EARTH THE SENTINELS WOULD EXPECT A MUTANT-- ESPECIALLY AN X-MAN TO BE, WHICH IS WHY WOLVERINE CHOSE IT.
I WISH HE'D MAKE HIS ENTRANCE, THOUGH.
EVERYTHING LOOKS PEACEFUL ENOUGH...
...BUT IT FEELS-- HEY!
A TRAP-DOOR!
NO! THIS CAN'T BE HAPPENING NOW! NOT WHEN WE'RE SO CLOSE!
NOT WITH SO MUCH DEPENDING ON US!
ROGUES!
HOW PERCEPTIVE OF YOU, MUTIE. AND HOW KIND OF YOU TO, SHALL WE SAY, DROP IN.
YOU'D BE ADVISED TO LET ME GO. I'M ON OFFICIAL SENTINEL BUSINESS.
BIG DEAL. WE HATE THOSE TIN TYRANTS ALMOST AS MUCH AS WE HATE MUTIES.
BEG ALL YOU WANT, SWEET-HEART. SCREAM ALL YOU WANT. EVEN IF PEOPLE HEAR, NO ONE'LL COME TO HELP YOU.
THE UNCANNY X-MEN!
TERRY AUSTIN INKER
TOM ORZECHOWSKI, letterer GLYNIS WEIN, colorist
LOUISE JONES EDITOR
JIM SHOOTER Ed.-IN-CHIEF
DAYS OF FUTURE PAST
THIS IS NEW YORK, THE "BIG APPLE."
ONE WAY
ONCE UPON A TIME, IT WAS A NICE PLACE TO LIVE. IT IS NO LONGER.
Ah, LOGAN, I WISH YOU'D PICKED A SAFER PART OF MANHATTAN FOR OUR RENDEZVOUS.
I WISH THERE WAS A SAFE PART OF MANHATTAN FOR YOU TO PICK.
THE STREET IS PARK AVENUE. WHEN IN THE UPPER SEVENTIES. WHEN KATE PRYDE WAS A CHILD, IT WAS ONE OF THE SWANKIEST NEIGHBORHOODS IN THE CITY, IF NOT THE WORLD.
50¢
142 FEB 02461
MARVEL® COMICS GROUP
©1980 MARVEL COMICS GROUP
THE UNCANNY X-MEN
THIS ISSUE: EVERYBODY DIES!
--THEN YOU COME SAVE HER!
--AND THAT WOULD JEOPARDIZE THE MISSION.
YOU OKAY, KATE?
I'M FINE, LOGAN-- BUT CALL THIS CLOSE, I CAN LIVE WITHOUT.
SO TELL ME, COLONEL LOGAN, HOW'S LIFE IN THE CANADIAN RESISTANCE ARMY?
A THRILL A MINUTE, DARLIN'.
THE WORD FROM LONDON IS THAT EVERYTHING'S ON AUTOMATIC. THE MOMENT THE SENTINELS MOVE OUT OF NORTH AMERICA, THE OTHER GREAT POWERS WILL LAUNCH A FULL-SCALE NUCLEAR STRIKE.
I KNOW WHAT YOU MEAN. C'MON, LET'S ROLL.
THEN... IT'S UP TO THE X-MEN.
LIKE THE OTHER MODULES, IT'S INVISIBLE TO THE SENTINELS' SENSORS. YOU SHOULDN'T HAVE ANY PROBLEM SMUGGLIN' IT INTO CAMP.
THAT'S EASY FOR YOU TO SAY.
YOU GOT A POINT. PHASE TWO BEGINS AT MIDNIGHT, WHEN I BUST YOU GUYS OUT. BE READY, KATE. GOOD LUCK.
IN THE QUARTER-CENTURY SINCE THE ACT'S PASSAGE, MILLIONS HAVE DIED.
SOUTH BRONX MUTANT INTERNMENT CEN
THEY WERE THE LUCKY ONES.
ENCEPHALO-SCAN INDICATES TRUTHFUL REPLY. YOU MAY PASS.
AS ALWAYS, THE FIRST THING SHE SEES IS THE CEMETERY. AS ALWAYS, THERE'S A FRESH GRAVE.
INTERRED HERE ARE ALL THE VICTIMS OF THE SENTINELS. SOME I KNEW, MOST I DIDN'T-- BUT, IN A WAY, WE'RE ALL FAMILY.
FORGIVE US, MY FRIENDS. WE CANNOT AVENGE YOU-- FOR WHAT POINT IS VENGEANCE AGAINST AN UNFEELING MACHINE? BUT AT LEAST, WE CAN TRY TO ENSURE THAT THIS NIGHTMARE NEVER HAPPENS, NEVER EVEN BEGINS!
KURT WAGNER
SCOTT SUMMERS
CHARLES XAVIER
BEN GRIMM
WARREN WORTHINGTON

Days of Future Past

While many elements of the first ten episodes were taken from or inspired by the books, none were direct adaptations of specific comics issues. Mark and Eric were focused on introducing a world, not presenting individual comics stories in this new medium. This changed when someone (Larry? Will?) asked if Eric thought the writers could integrate Claremont and Byrne's seminal 1981 "Days of Future Past" into the ongoing Sentinel-threat story arc. Eric grabbed a reprint, and he and Mark immediately understood how its tough, grim tone fit right in with our other stories. There would have to be some casting changes to fit our team, but yes, we could make it fit. Bob Harras at Marvel Comics loved the idea and got the okay from Marvel. It would be a two-part episode. Eric picked Julia to write the first half and Bob Skir and Marty Isenberg to write the second. Will and Larry were so excited to get this story for our show that, despite their massive workload, they decided to draw most of the storyboard themselves.

There needed to be some changes to fit our 1992 story continuity—primarily substituting our Jubilee for the Kitty Pryde of the two-issue story (*Uncanny X-Men* volume 1, #141–42). We also decided that having Jubilee's "spirit" travel back in time wouldn't be as clear for our audience as sending a physical character back from the future would be. Bishop was chosen. This gave us an advantage of having fresh eyes looking at the X-Men as the mystery of a world-changing political assassination unfolded.

To show an interesting progression, here is the "teaser" for the episode—the short opening segment that "teases" you to watch the rest of the episode after the commercial—in five forms: premise, outline, script, storyboard, and actual frames from the episode. (Note that the working episode title "Future Tense" was used before we were sure we were being properly faithful to the original.)

First, the teaser from the two-page story premise:

"FUTURE TENSE – PT 1"
(premise)

TEASER

1. EXT. NEW YORK CITY – TWILIGHT - 2055

Sentinels rule harshly over humanity. They track down a band of mutants, who in turn destroy them. BISHOP, helping the sentinels, then takes out most of the mutants with his plasma rifle. When he returns to prison with the only remaining mutant, Old Wolverine, Bishop turns on his Sentinel masters. He helps a geriatric Wolverine (looking around 70) escape, introducing himself to Wolverine as humanity's and mutantkind's last and only hope.

Notice that, in our story's first incarnation, Bishop's character is *helpful* to Wolverine from the outset. In the outline, he becomes a merciless hunter who only helps the mutants after the Sentinels betray him.

Then from the eleven-page outline:

X-MEN: Episode Eleven
"Future Tense, Part One"
(outline)

TEASER

1.EXT. - NEW YORK/FUTURE - NIGHT

NEW YORK CITY, 2055: THREE REBEL MUTANTS dodge through the shadows of the burned-out cityscape. We don't see them clearly, but they're on a mission. Suddenly, TWO SENTINELS rise from the rubble, while a THIRD descends from the skies. The mutants quickly take the offensive, and attack with a fury.

It's a hard battle, but the mutants prevail. In the glow of a burning Sentinel, we see the three mutants for the first time: two we're not familiar with, then the third. He steps up to the fire and smiles wearily as he re-sheathes his claws—it's an impossibly old WOLVERINE. "Used ta take those tin cans out in half the time. Must be gettin' rusty."

"I'll say," says a FOURTH MUTANT from the shadows, who fires a disrupter rifle point blank into the other mutants. "Tracker!" cries one of the mutants as she falls. The other mutant and Wolverine crumble to the ground as BISHOP steps into the light and lowers his rifle. He surveys his stunned (but living) quarry. "Man, some days I really hate this gig."

2.EXT. - CITY/MUTANT CAMP - MOMENTS LATER

BISHOP pushes a hover-barrow cage through the streets. The THREE MUTANTS are heaped inside. WOLVERINE comes to and struggles briefly under the electric net covering him. Bishop is surprised, impressed with the old mutant's regenerative powers. Wolverine asides that it's been known to come in handy. Bishop says sure, except that it's just going to take Wolverine that much longer for the Sentinels to terminate him back at mutant base camp prison.

They near the base camp, a large ugly place with towering walls and sophisticated defenses. Wolverine argues with Bishop that the Sentinels want to kill all mutants. Bishop shoots back, "Just you rebels, old man," as he waits his turn in line for camp re-entry. Bishop then presents his three "recoveries" to the SENTINEL JAILER. The jailer runs Bishop's recovery card (think bank ATM) through a scanner, then pauses. Bishop impatiently demands, "So where are my credits?"

The jailer "fries" Bishop's recovery card and turns on him. "Recovery quota reached." A SECOND SENTINEL grabs a startled Bishop as the first one orders, "Terminate them all."

Then from the forty-page script:

X-MEN: Episode Eleven
"FUTURE TENSE - Part One"
(teleplay)
TEASER

FADE IN:

EXT. - NEW YORK/GRIM FUTURE/2055 – NIGHT

ESTAB. - PAN across a grim, burned-out cityscape (GRIM MUSIC STING). At the BOTTOM OF FRAME flashes the title: NEW YORK CITY, 2055. We're in the future, and it doesn't look pretty. PAN STOPS ON the end of a distant alleyway, where, through the wreckage, WE SEE THREE SHADOWY FIGURES hurry, picking their way through the rubble, into the alley.

OPPOSITE Collage of covers from *Uncanny X-Men* (vol. 1) #141 and 142—the original *Days of Future Past* storyline—along with the first four pages of #141. Covers by John Byrne and Terry Austin (#141) and Austin and Danny Crespi (#142); co-written by Chris Claremont and Byrne; pencils by Byrne; inks by Austin; colors by Glynis Wein; letters by Tom Orzechowski.

IN ALLEYWAY - ON TOWERING BRICK WALL - As the three figures hurry THROUGH SHOT in FG, TWO SENTINELS (updated, but recognizable) burst through the brick wall and look after the fleeing figures.

                    SENTINEL
              Halt, mutants!

TRACK WITH THE THREE MUTANTS - We still don't see them clearly as they hurry away, glancing over their shoulders as they run. Then suddenly they AND TRACK STOP, and they look up.

                MALE FUTURE MUTANT
              Another one!

CAMERA PANS to reveal a THIRD SENTINEL descending from the sky (THREE MUTANTS STILL IN FG). The mutants start to turn back...

ON FEMALE FUTURE MUTANT (female). A FIREBALL appears in her hand. She throws it like a softball as:

                FEMALE FUTURE MUTANT
              Back the other way!

TRACK WITH THE FIREBALL — It hits exposed WOODEN BEAMS near the approaching Sentinel. THE BEAMS EXPLODE in flames, and a big piece of wall falls onto the Sentinel, engulfing him, making him stagger back a bit.

ON MALE FUTURE MUTANT - Through the SMOKE, WE SEE that he's changing shape, his arms becoming HUGE AND METALLIC.

                MALE FUTURE MUTANT
              Gotta clear some trash.

Male Future Mutant lunges, OS, toward the burning Sentinel.

ON SENTINEL - As it struggles with the fire all over it, Male Future Mutant speeds INTO FRAME and SLAMS his out-stretched arms into him, sending the Sentinel over backwards.

ON SECOND SENTINEL - As it turns to fire a ray from its palm —

                    SENTINEL
              Surrender, or be —

— the first Sentinel CRASHES into him, and they tumble OS.

CLOSE UPSHOT ON THE TWO FUTURE MUTANTS - as they watch the OS sentinels tumble. Male Future Mutant's arms TRANSFORM to normal.

                MALE FUTURE MUTANT
              What a shame — now we can't surrender.

Then PULL BACK SLIGHTLY as, behind them, a third Sentinel steps, looming large, through the smoke, hand extended to blast them.

                    SENTINEL
              Halt!

The two mutants (FG) look up at the sentinel and freeze.

                FEMALE FUTURE MUTANT
              No!

Suddenly the third Sentinel looks confused. He shakes and shivers a bit, starts to take a step, then topples forward, AT CAMERA, forcing the mutants to leap away.

TIGHT - FROM SIDE - As the Sentinel's head and shoulders SLAM to the ground, a third mutant leaps off of his back and tucks and rolls, OS, to safety. SPARKS fly from the Sentinel's head.

ON TWO BURNING SENTINELS - The Future Mutants step to the fire.

                FEMALE FUTURE MUTANT
              That was close.

ON TWO FUTURE MUTANTS - FIRE IN FG - As they watch the burning sentinels, the Third Mutant steps up between them. It's an impossibly old WOLVERINE! (He looks 80, is 150).

                OLD WOLVERINE
              Used to take those tin cans out in *half* the time.

Wolverine re-sheathes his CLAWS.

                OLD WOLVERINE (CONT)
              Must be gettin' rusty.

                SHADOWY VOICE (OS/BISHOP)
              I'll say.

ON THE THREE MUTANTS — Their heads snap to the source of the sound (toward camera).

MUTANTS' POV - A fourth mutant, BISHOP, steps from the shadows. The fire casts an eerie light on him. BISHOP raises a DISRUPTOR RIFLE and quickly fires THREE SHOCK WAVES (BOARD NOTE: Please make anything to do with the future different and special.)

ON THE THREE MUTANTS - The waves hit them, knocking them flying:

                FEMALE FUTURE MUTANT
              Tracker!!

LOW ANGLE - ON THREE MUTANTS - WOLVERINE'S HEAD IN FG - Bishop steps up to the fallen mutants, towering over them.

                    BISHOP
              Scratch three rebels...

                    WOLVERINE
              (WEAK GROAN.)

Wolverine's head rolls over, TOWARD CAMERA, as his eyes close in close up, and we...

fade to black:

EXT. - CITY/MUTANT CAMP - MOMENTS LATER

LOW ANGLE - CLOSE UP ON WOLVERINE - His eyes open to reveal an ELECTRIC NET covering his face.

                    BISHOP (OS)
              Awake already, Sleeping Beauty?

TRACK WITH BISHOP AND HOVERBARROW - He rides a HOVERBARROW (hovercraft/wheelbarrow) through the crumbling war-torn streets.

The three mutants are heaped under the NET. WOLVERINE is the only one awake. He struggles against the NET and is ZAPPED.

                    WOLVERINE
              (EXERTION — CRY!)

TRACK - TIGHT ON BISHOP - He nods down toward the old MUTANT.

                    BISHOP
              You heal up pretty fast, for an old guy.

ON WOLVERINE - He shifts under the NET, frustrated, angry.

WOLVERINE
Thanks a lot!
(frowns, looks at Bishop)
Hey... Don't I know you from somewhere?

WIDE ON CAMP - The hover-barrow nears the CAMP, a large ugly place with towering walls and sophisticated defenses. The hover-barrow enters the camp through a huge gate, which has a guard house on one side, and a GUARD SENTINEL on either side.

BISHOP
Good try, rebel. But you're headin' to a mutant termination center, and the Sentinels there don't care who ya know.
(shakes his head)
Why can't you rebels stop attackin' those bucket-heads? All it gets ya is termination.

LOW ANGLE - UPSHOT ON WOLVERINE AND BISHOP -

WOLVERINE
Wake up, Rookie! The Sentinels want to kill all mutants!

BISHOP
Just you rebels, old man. They treat the rest of us just fine.

ON GUARD HOUSE AT GATE - Bishop pauses the hover-barrow in front of one of the Sentinel guards and offers him an ATM-LIKE CARD.

BISHOP
(to the Sentinel)
ID tracker, Bishop. Three recoveries.

The sentinel takes the card and runs it through a SCANNER, which BEEPS. The sentinel pauses a beat over the scanner.

ON BISHOP - He grows impatient.

BISHOP
So where's my money?

ON THE SENTINEL - It "fries" the CARD with a jolt of electricity, then turns to the other Sentinel guard.

ON GATE - The two Sentinel guards look at each other as Bishop and the captured mutants hover between them.

SENTINEL
Tracker Bishop no longer needed.

UPSHOT ON 1ST SENTINEL GUARD - OTS BISHOP - Bishop turns to him:

BISHOP
Whadaya mean?!

SENTINEL
Terminate them all.

CLOSE UP ON BISHOP - he takes in shock as we: fade out...

END TEASER

Will Meugniot's storyboard (he drew the first third) never stops moving; the horror of the future is established in three minutes. Bishop, having trusted the Sentinels, is betrayed. So he joins a last-ditch effort by the mutants to send someone back to "the present" (1993) and stop the major historical event, an assassination that precipitates the mutant-human civil war that has brought the future world to this ragged state. His mission is set. And the X-Men are his target.

Selections from Will's three-hundred-page storyboard appear below.

BELOW The storyboards for "Days of Future Past" begins. Note that this episode was titled "Future Tense" until we felt sure we were doing a properly faithful adaptation of *Days*.

GRAZ Entertainment
DO SC 1 ON VISTA FLD FOR EFFECTIVE TB...
Page 1
DX CLOUDS IN SKY ON DEAD SLOW PAN
SC.
BG.
FUTURE TENSE PART ONE ACT ONE TEASE
FI
SC. 1
BG.
TB
(TINY WHITE DOT)
(STARTS TO DROP)
NOTE: STATUE IS MISSING ITS RIGHT CHEEK
ACTION EXT. NIGHT - OPEN ON ECU OF WEATHER BEATEN EYE OF STATUE OF LIBERTY... WHITE OXIDATION MAKES EYE LOOK AS IF IT'S BEEN CRYING...
DIAL
SLG
TRANS
SC. CONT
BG.
ACTION AS TB CONTINUES WE SEE ALL OF STATUE'S FACE. "DOT" UNFOLDS WINGS - REVEALING ITSELF TO BE PIGEON AS IT FLIES...
DIAL
DISSOLVE 2^08
MAKE TB'S IN SC'S 1+2 CONTINUOUS THRU X-DISS
SLG
TRANS

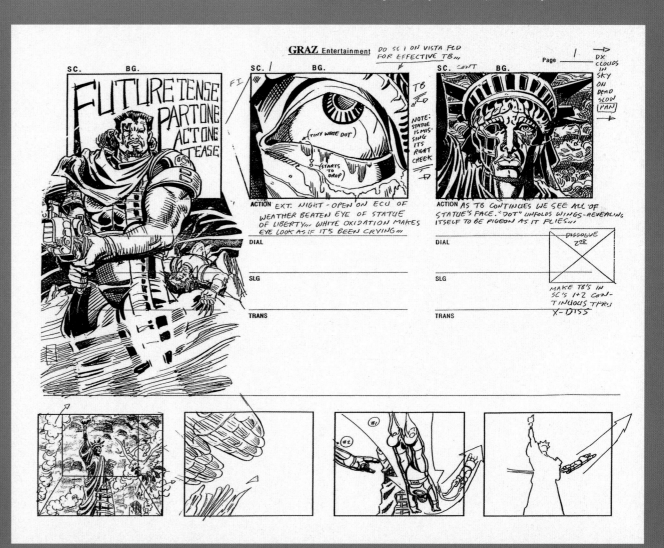

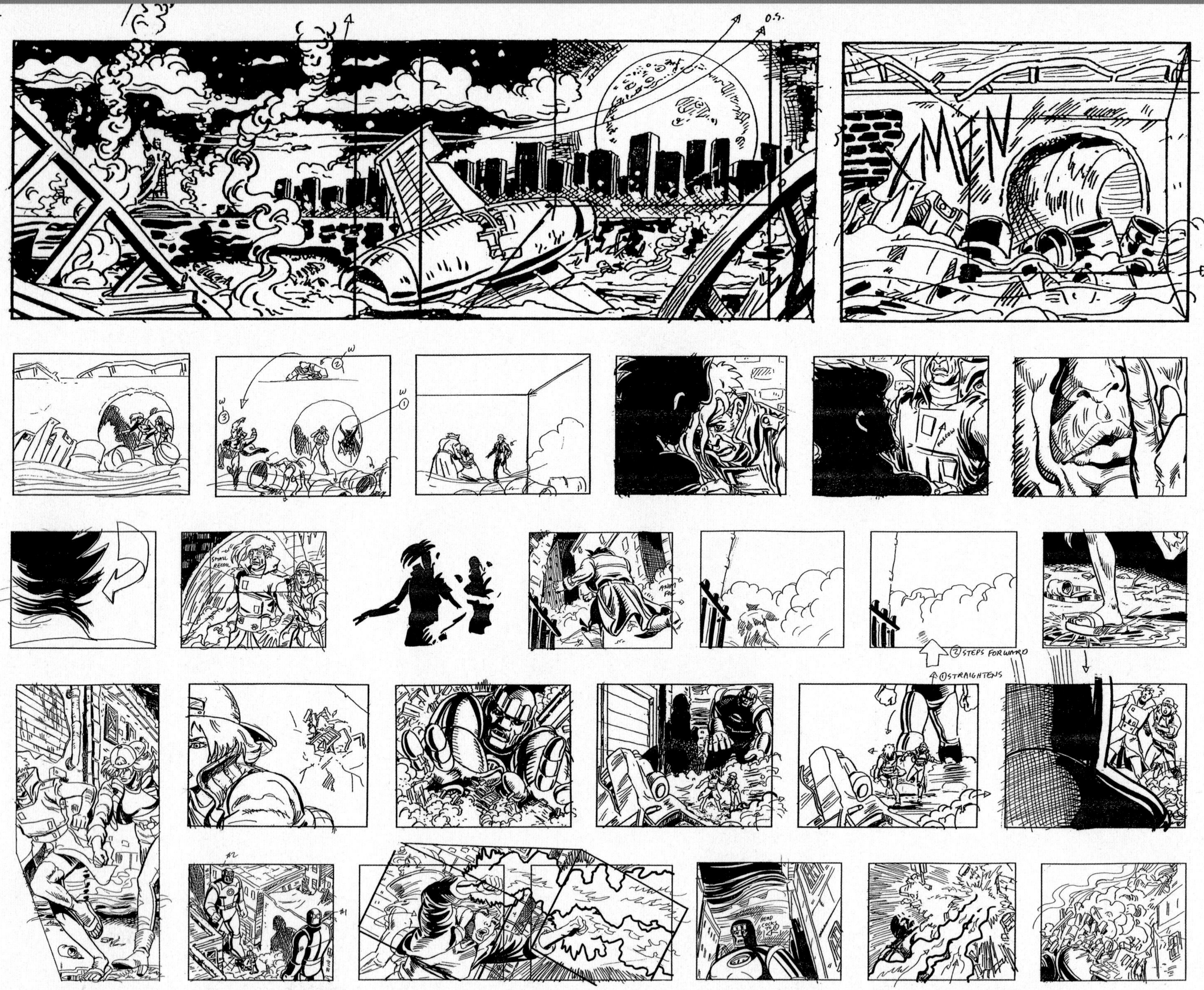
O.S.
X-MEN
①STRAIGHTENS
②STEPS FORWARD

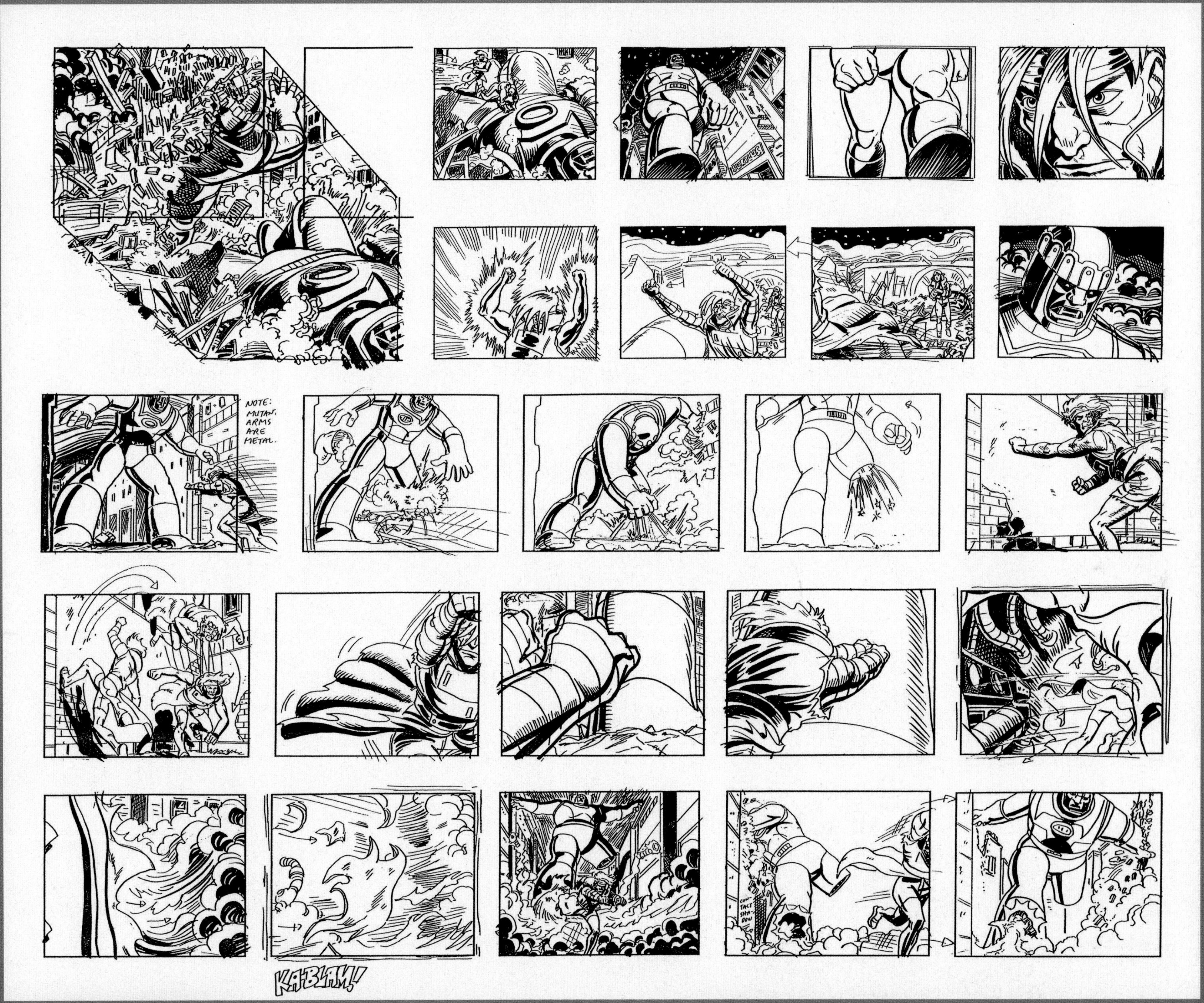
NOTE: MUTAN. ARMS ARE METAL.
CON-TACT SHA-DOW
KA-BLAM!

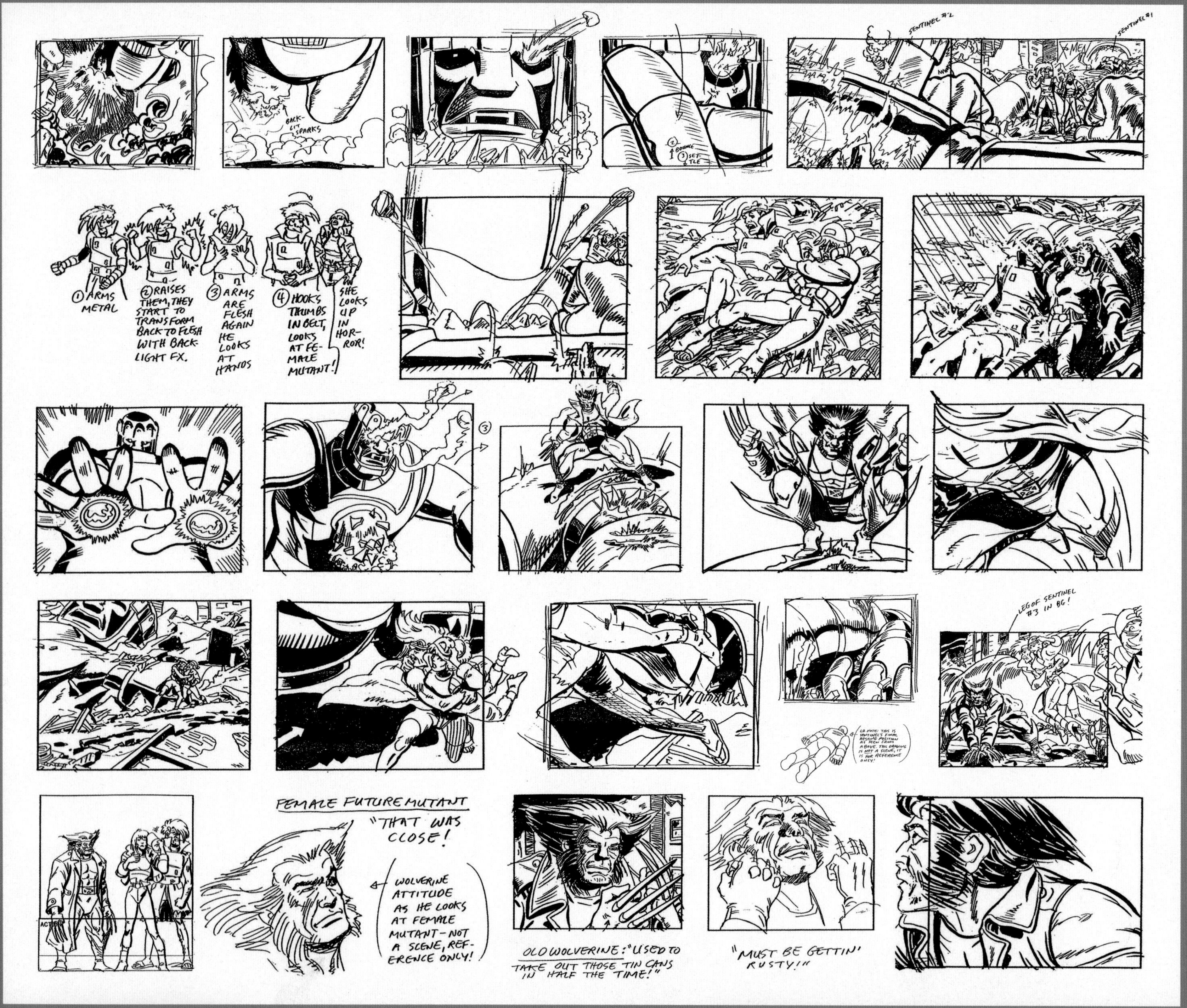

BACK-LIT SPARKS
SENTINEL #2
SENTINEL #1
X-MEN
① ARMS METAL
② RAISES THEM, THEY START TO TRANSFORM BACK TO FLESH WITH BACK-LIGHT FX.
③ ARMS ARE FLESH AGAIN HE LOOKS AT HANDS
④ HOOKS THUMBS IN BELT, LOOKS AT FEMALE MUTANT!
SHE LOOKS UP IN HORROR!
LEG OF SENTINEL #3 IN BG!
LO NOTE: THIS IS SENTINEL'S FINAL RESTING POSITION AS SEEN FROM ABOVE. THIS DRAWING IS NOT A SCENE, IT IS FOR REFERENCE ONLY!
FEMALE FUTURE MUTANT
"THAT WAS CLOSE!"
WOLVERINE ATTITUDE AS HE LOOKS AT FEMALE MUTANT—NOT A SCENE, REFERENCE ONLY!
OLD WOLVERINE: "USED TO TAKE OUT THOSE TIN CANS IN HALF THE TIME!"
"MUST BE GETTIN' RUSTY!"

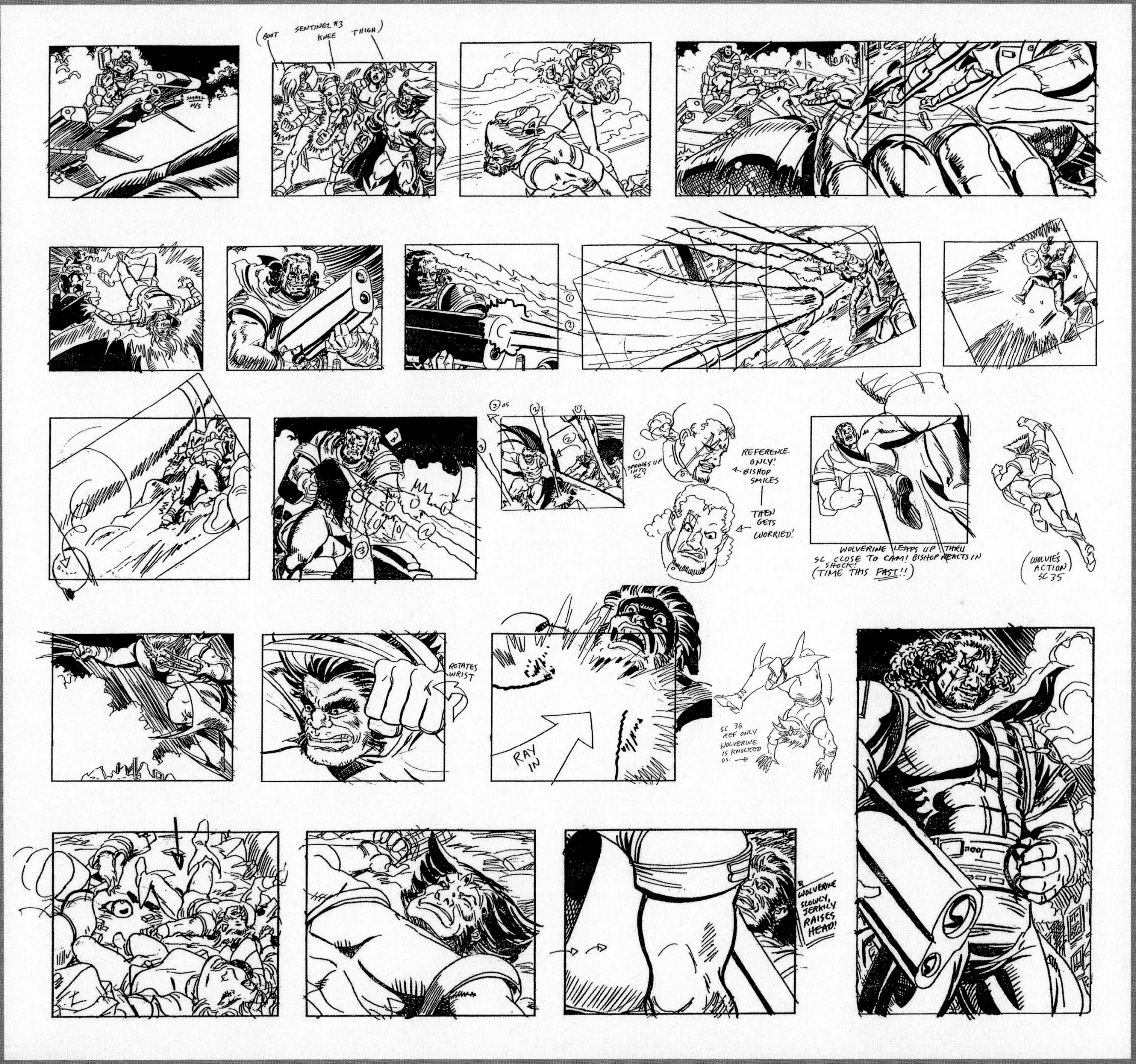
(BOOT SENTINEL #3 KNEE THIGH)
REFERENCE ONLY! BISHOP SMILES
THEN GETS WORRIED!
WOLVERINE LEAPS UP THRU SC CLOSE TO CAM! BISHOP REACTS IN SHOCK!
(TIME THIS FAST!!)
(WOLVIE'S ACTION SC 35)
ROTATES WRIST
RAY IN
SC 36 REF ONLY WOLVERINE IS KNOCKED OS.
WOLVERINE SLOWLY, JERKILY RAISES HEAD!

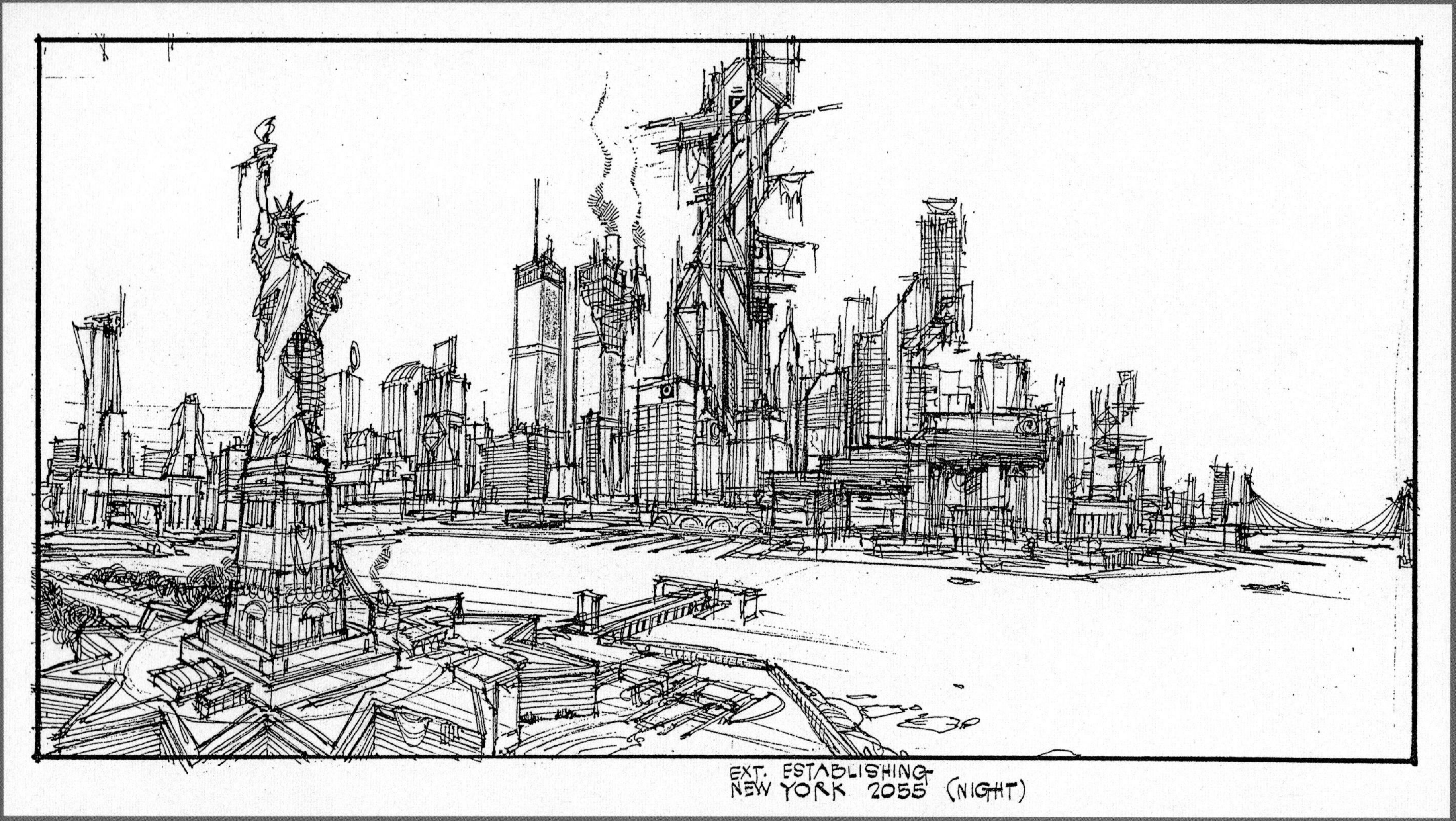
EXT. ESTABLISHING
NEW YORK 2055 (NIGHT)

01

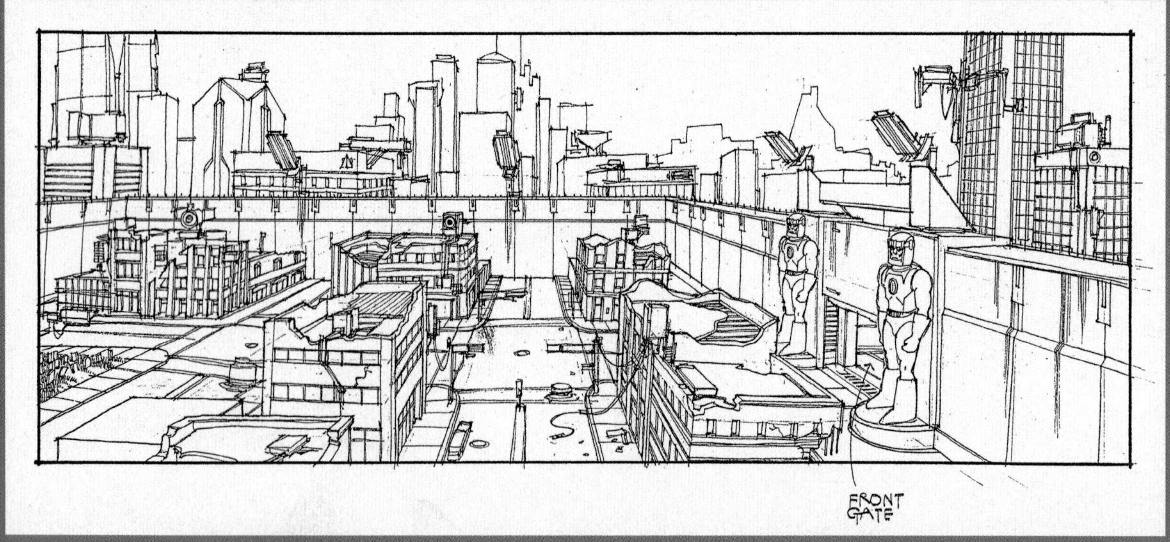
FRONT
GATE

02

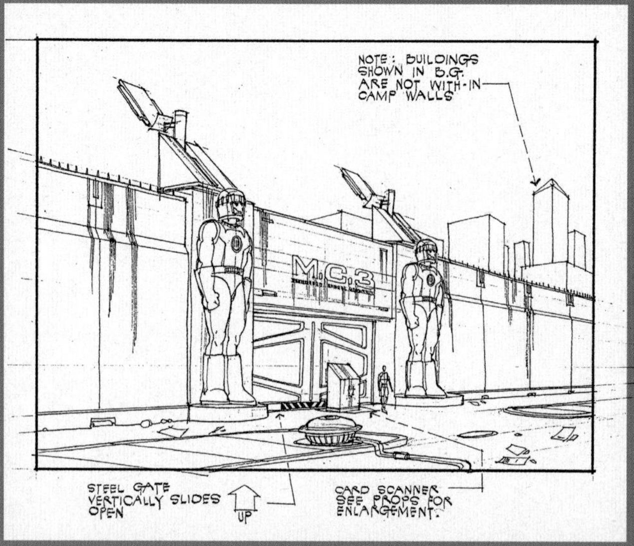
NOTE: BUILDINGS
SHOWN IN B.G.
ARE NOT WITH-IN
CAMP WALLS
M.C.3
STEEL GATE
VERTICALLY SLIDES
OPEN
UP
CARD SCANNER
SEE PROPS FOR
ENLARGEMENT.

03

01 Establishing-shot layout of New York City, 2055, with Statue of Liberty. **02** Exterior, Sentinel Detention Center entrance for "Rebel Mutants." **03** Exterior, Sentinel Detention Center front gate. Note the size comparison of the Sentinels with a human figure for reference; see note regarding the card scanner and see page 104 for a prop-list image of the scanner. **04** Exterior, Sentinel Detention Center interior grounds. Note the "Termination Center"; compare "Cemetery for Mutants" with page 94. **05** Exterior, Sentinel Detention Center, another angle. **06** Interior, Sentinel Detention Center, prison cells. **07** Interior, Forge's makeshift laboratory. **08** Exterior, decaying New York City alleyway; all layouts by Steve Olds.

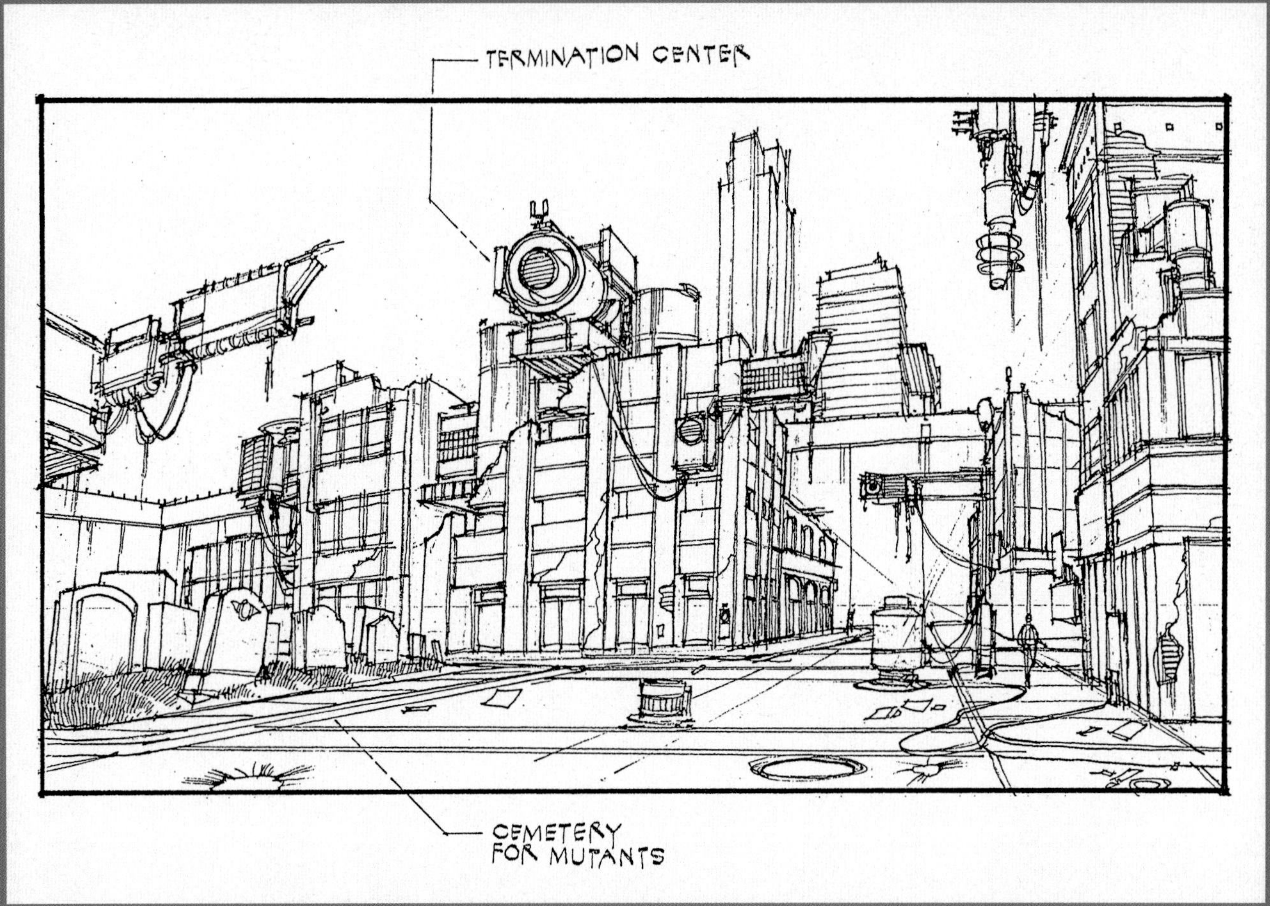
TERMINATION CENTER
CEMETERY
FOR MUTANTS

04

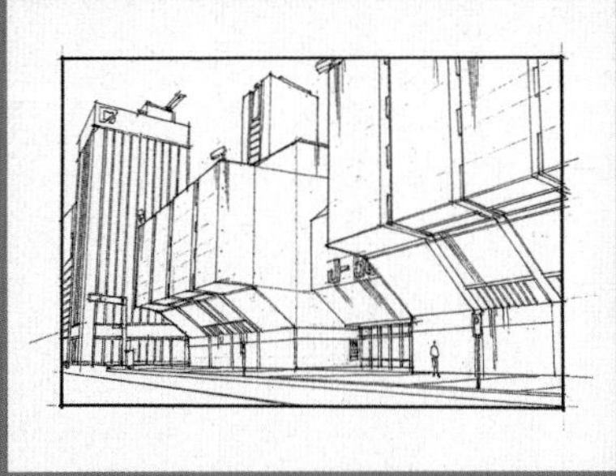

05

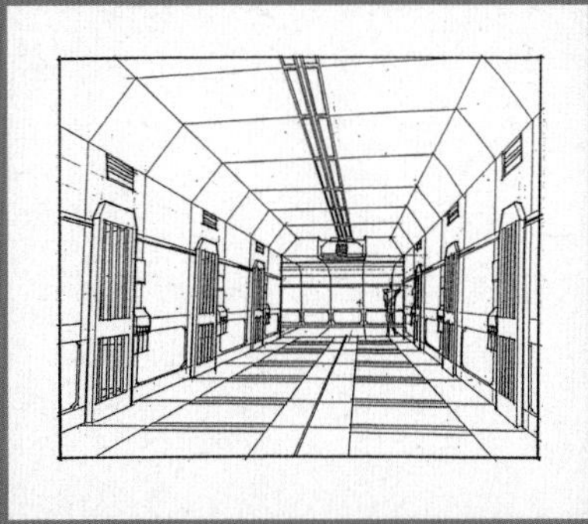

06

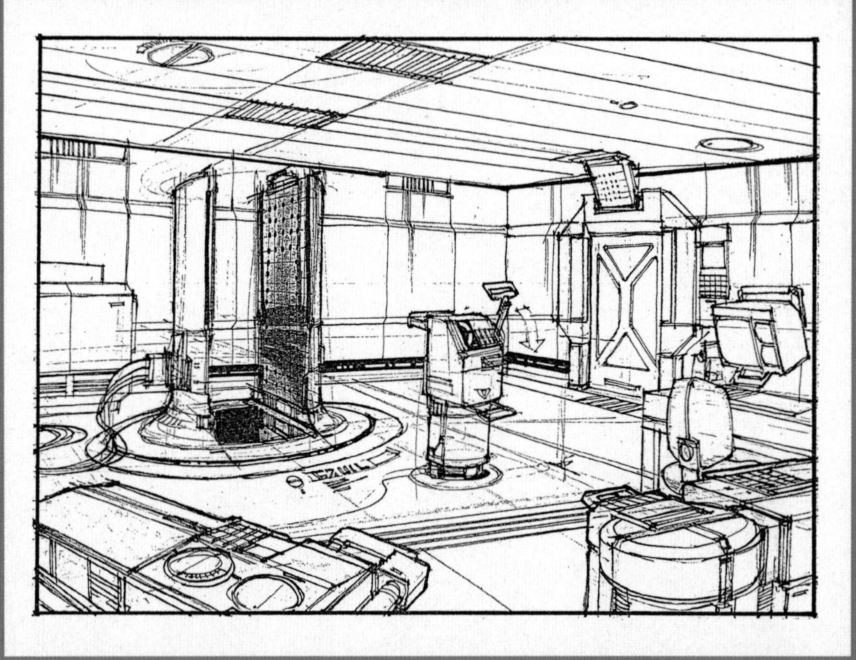

07

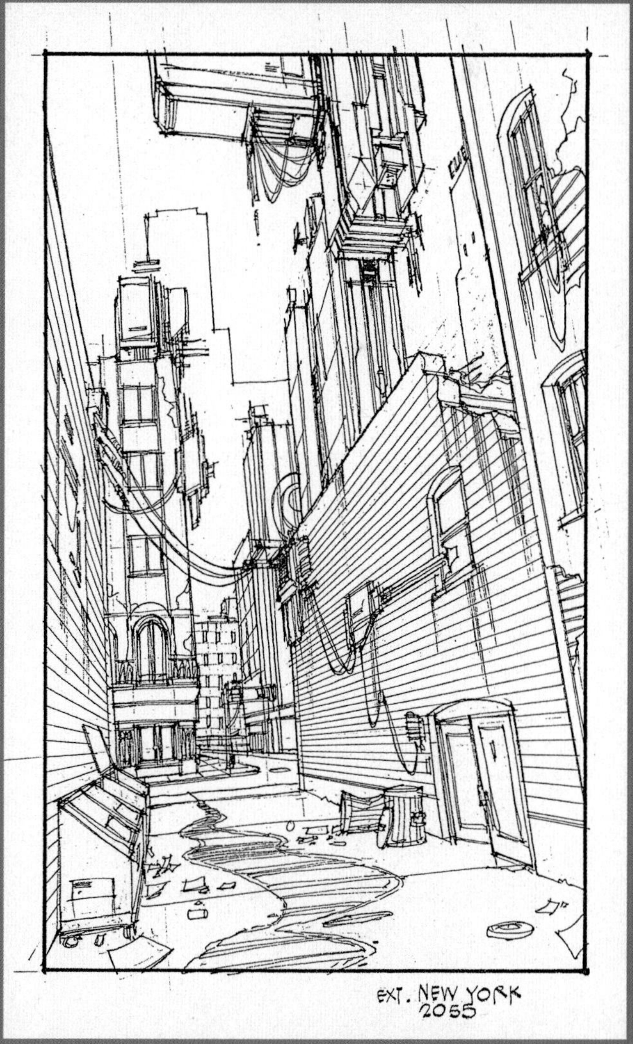
EXT. NEW YORK
2055

08

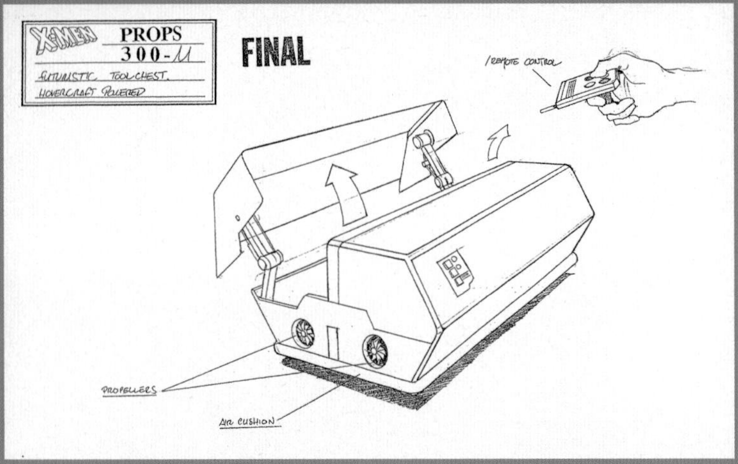
X-MEN PROPS 300-11
FUTURISTIC TOOLCHEST. HOVERCRAFT POWERED
FINAL
REMOTE CONTROL
PROPELLERS
AIR CUSHION

01

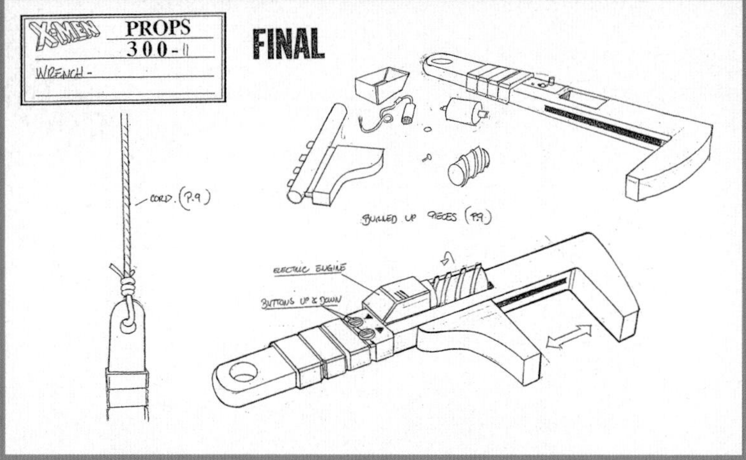
X-MEN PROPS 300-11
WRENCH -
FINAL
CORD. (P.9)
BUCKLED UP PIECES (P.9)
ELECTRIC ENGINE
BUTTONS UP & DOWN

02

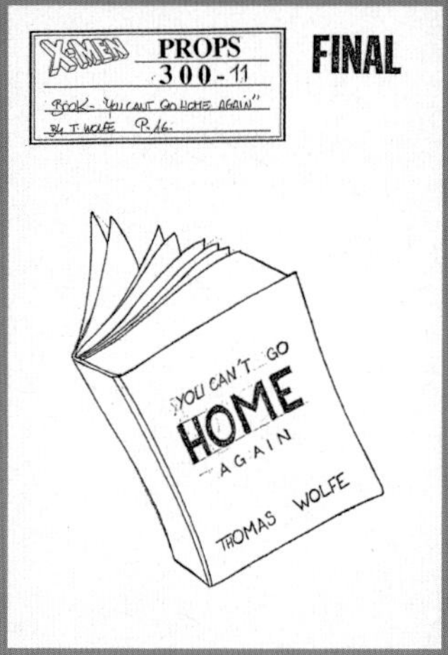
X-MEN PROPS 300-11
FINAL
YOU CAN'T GO
HOME
AGAIN
THOMAS WOLFE

03

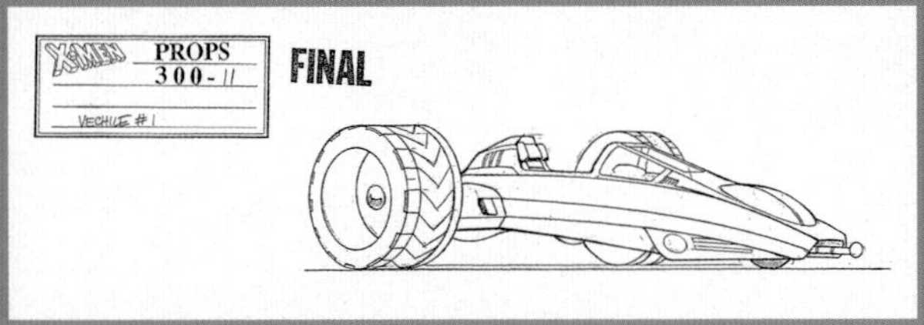
X-MEN PROPS 300-11
FINAL

04

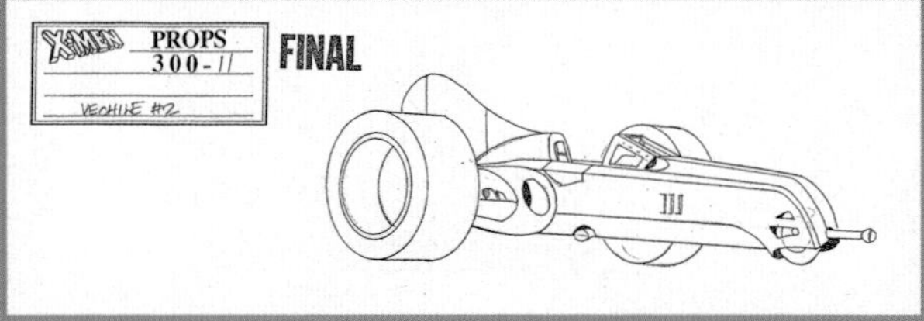
X-MEN PROPS 300-11
FINAL

05

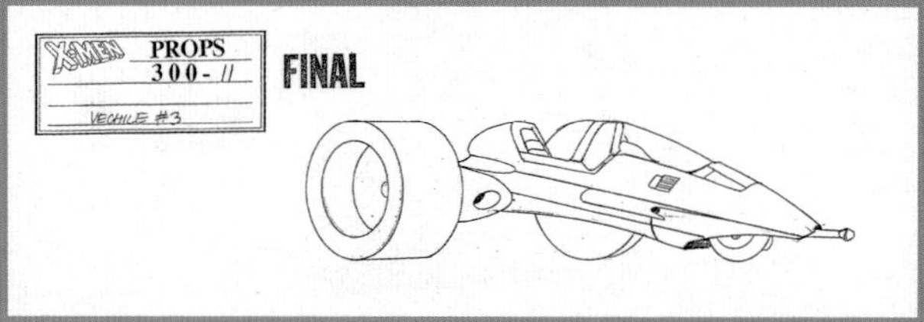
X-MEN PROPS 300-11
FINAL

06

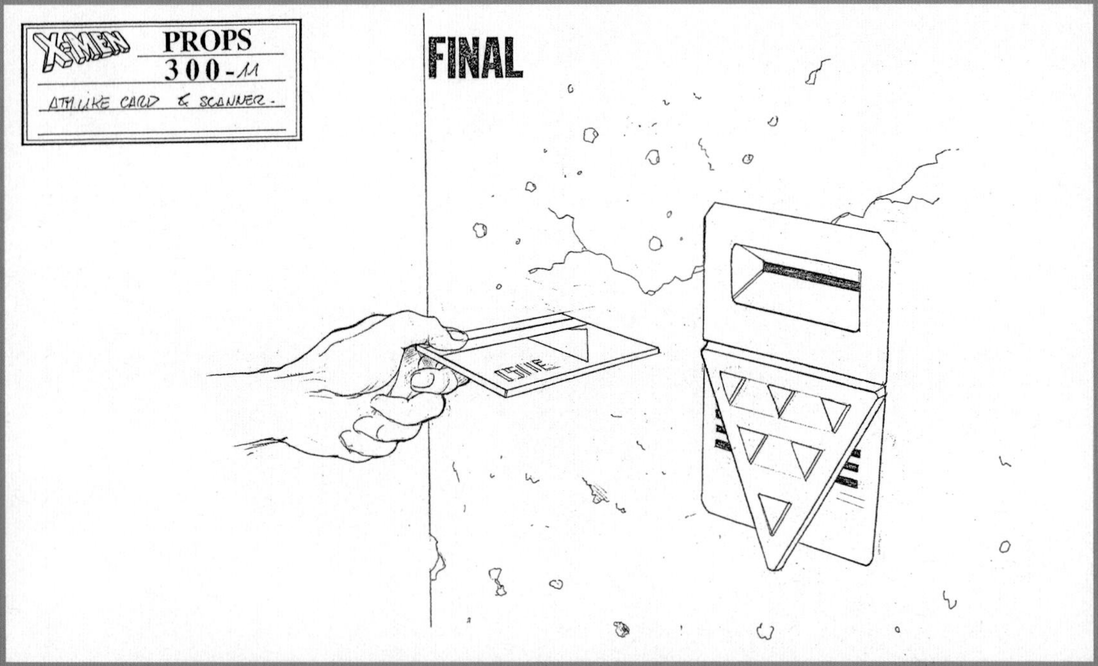
X-MEN PROPS 300-11
ATM LIKE CARD & SCANNER.
FINAL

07

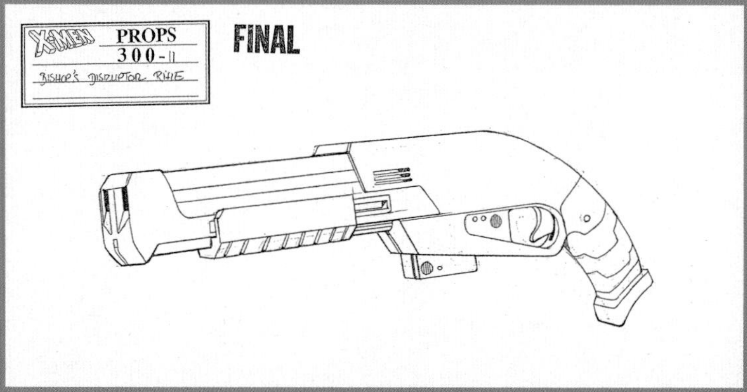
X-MEN PROPS 300-11
FINAL

08

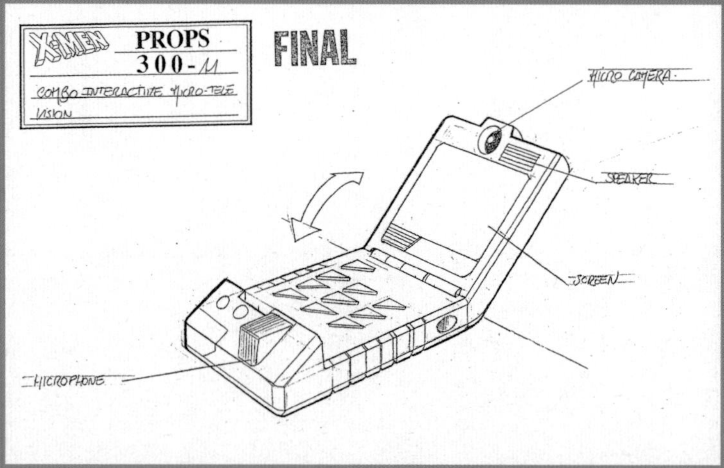
X-MEN PROPS 300-11
COMBO INTERACTIVE MICRO-TELEVISION
FINAL
MICRO CAMERA.
SPEAKER
SCREEN
MICROPHONE

09

01 Future tool chest. **02** Future wrench. **03** Surviving book: *You Can't Go Home Again* by Thomas Wolfe. **04–06** Future vehicles 1–3. **07** ATM-like card and scanner; see page 102 for card scanner in layout of Sentinel Detention Center front gate. **08** Bishop's Disruptor rifle. **09** Combo interactive micro-television; details read clockwise from lower left "microphone"; "micro camera"; "speaker"; "screen"; all props by Steve Olds. **OPPOSITE** Still-frames from "Days" teaser.

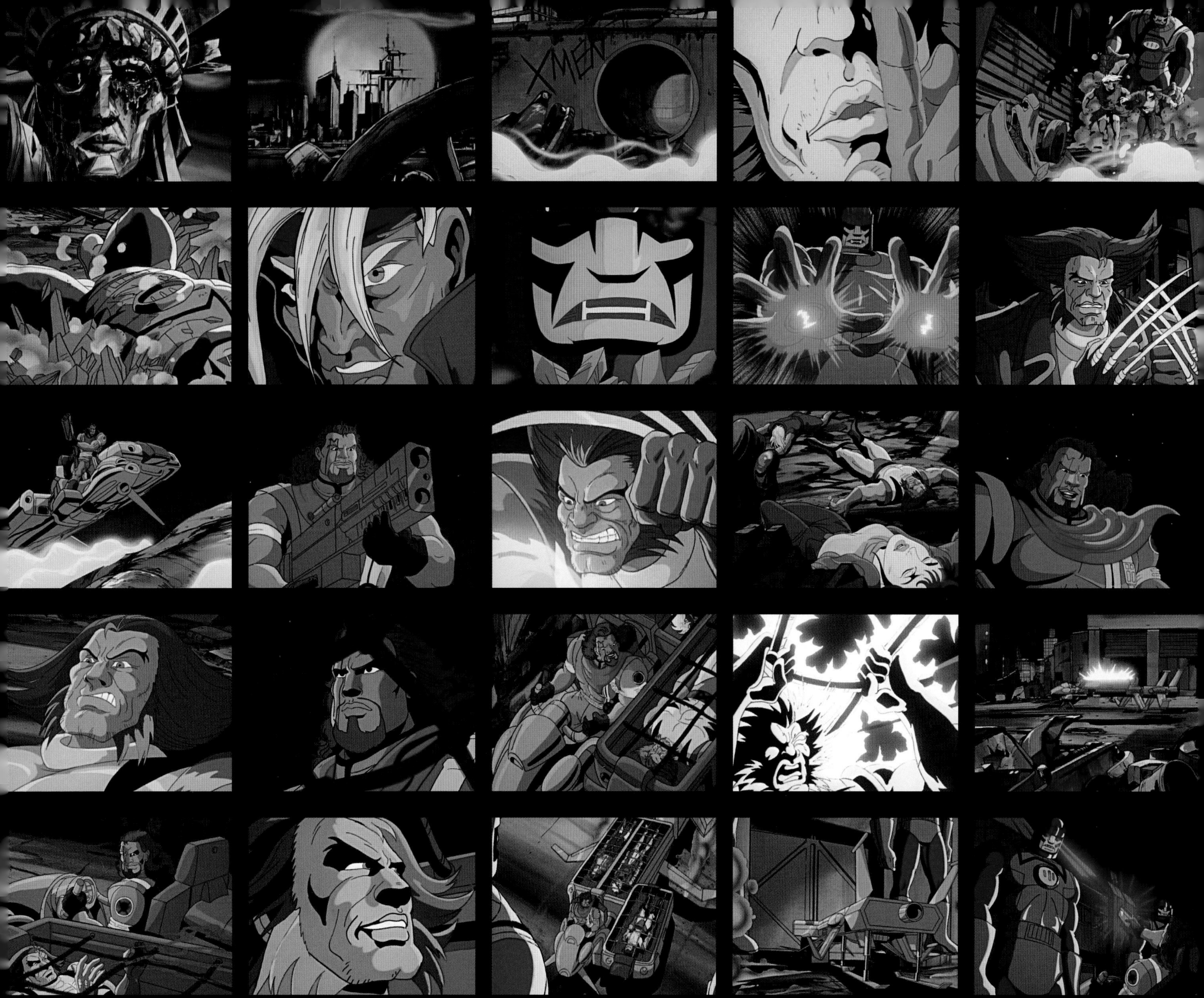

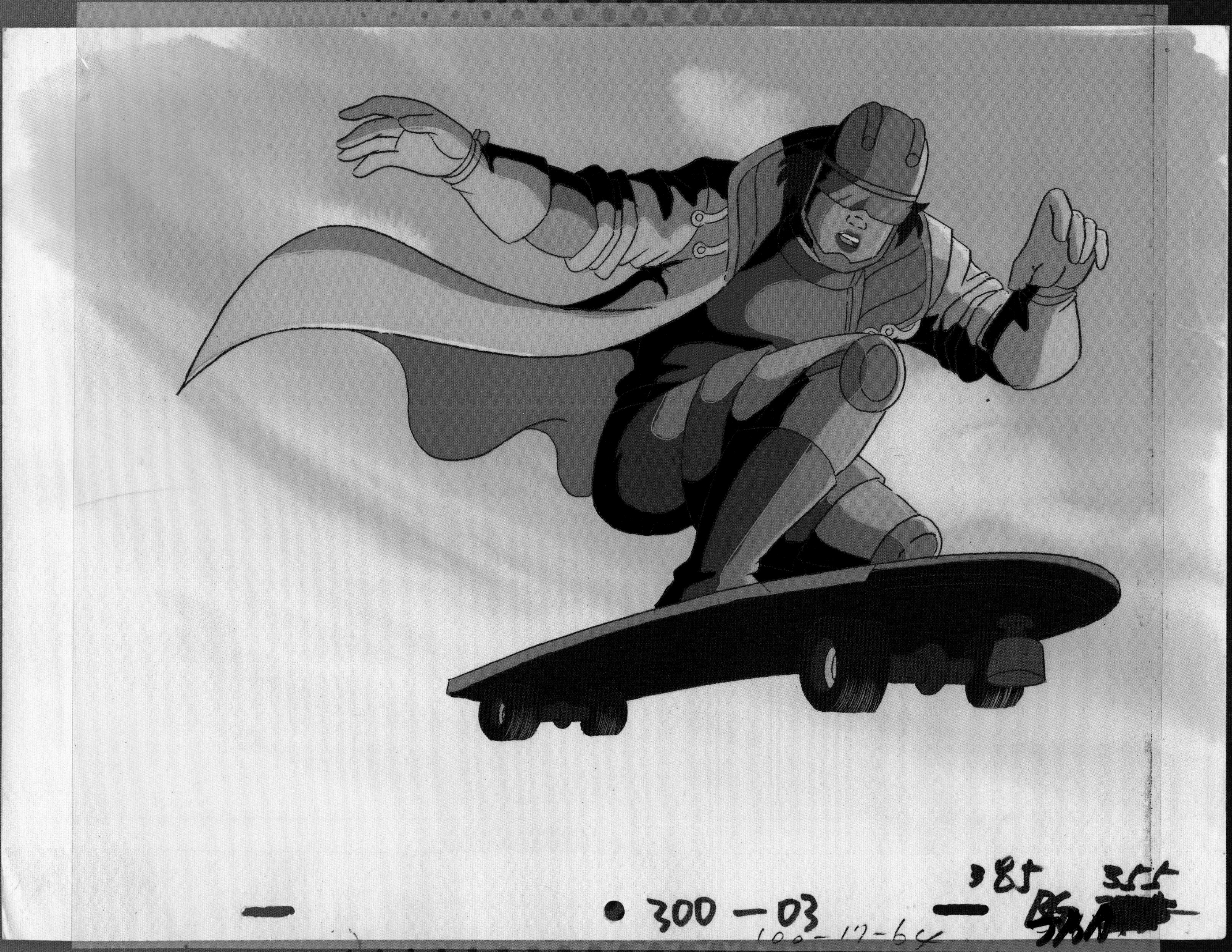
300 — 03
385
355

CHAPTER THREE

BUILDING ON SUCCESS!

SEASON TWO, EPISODES 14–26

PRODUCING SEASON TWO was a totally different experience. *X-Men: TAS* was the talk of Hollywood! The show had a ripple effect on the entire Fox network, and, in turn, on all of television. The fledgling Fox Kids Network had started 1993 in distant fourth place, with perhaps 10 percent of the nation's viewers, far behind the "Big Three," the half-century-old networks of ABC, CBS, and NBC. Six weeks into 1993, Fox Kids, based on the explosion of interest in *X-Men: TAS,* had streaked to number one in the entire Saturday-morning ratings—based on how many millions of households were watching—where they would reign for a decade. There soon were mornings when not just kids were watching, but when *more than half of America's TVs* were tuned in to *X-Men: TAS.*

As might be expected, all of the creative second-guessing and pushback that the writers and artists fought throughout the previous year vanished. Problems? What problems? Now they would be allowed to write and draw as they pleased. Of course, with great power comes great responsibility. As Eric instructed the writers:

NOTES ON YEAR TWO:
THE ANIMATED "X-MEN" LEGACY

We have a daunting legacy of quality to uphold in this second season of X-MEN. The first season has been an extraordinary popular and critical success—much to the credit, it should be mentioned, of the creative people who wrote, drew, designed, produced, directed, and shepherded a complicated, demanding project from start to finish. Most television shows of all kinds flounder and fail. "X-Men" was not allowed to.

Last year we were creating something new, with only a sense of obligation to the respected tradition of the comic book as a creative responsibility. There were no special expectations about the show's quality. This year we will be quite rightly expected to improve upon the hottest show in children's television. The character drama will have to be heightened, the opening teasers more compelling, the action more explosive, the problems more intractable, the decisions more difficult, the "answers" less reassuring. The fact that the "X-Men" audience has grown every week indicates that, beyond any demographic luck or marketing wizardry, our audience knows and loves our show and is hungry to see more. They are paying close attention. They won't take it lightly if we let them down.

It won't be easy but upholding the Animated X-Men legacy is just the sort of challenge our heroes would appreciate.

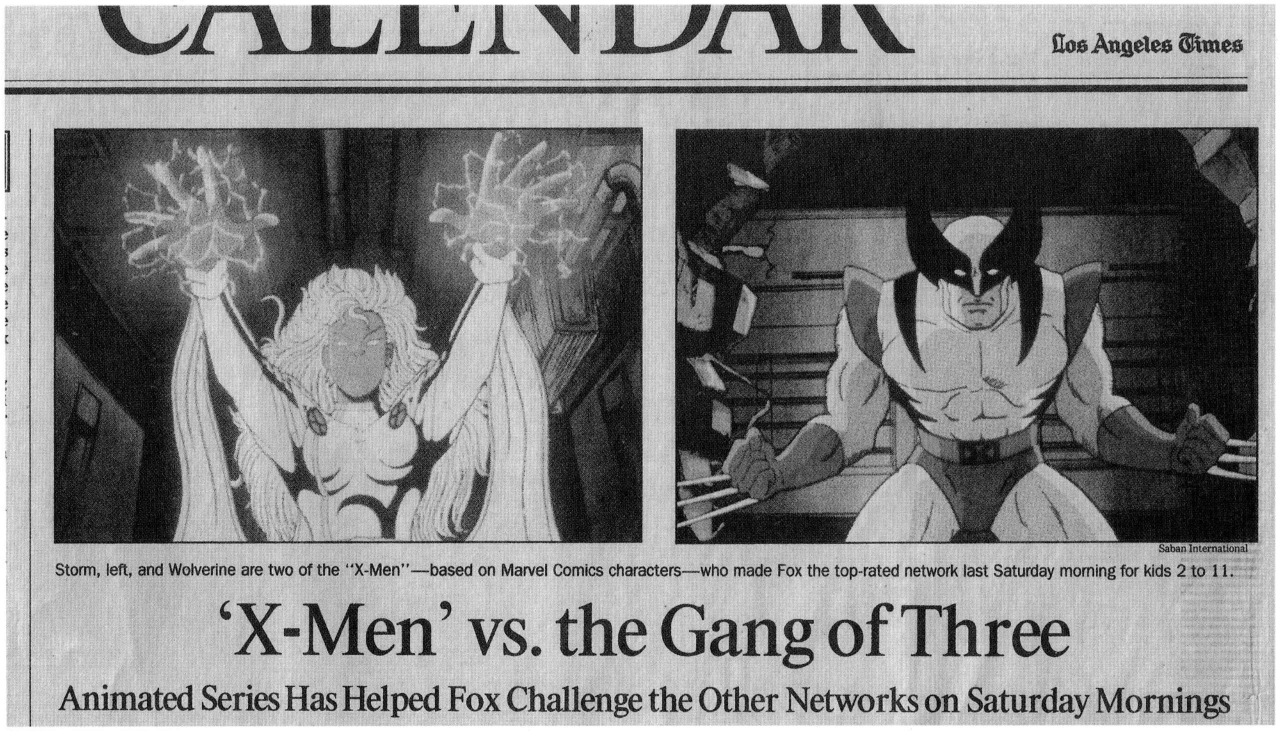
CALENDAR

Los Angeles Times

Saban International

Storm, left, and Wolverine are two of the "X-Men"—based on Marvel Comics characters—who made Fox the top-rated network last Saturday morning for kids 2 to 11.

'X-Men' vs. the Gang of Three

Animated Series Has Helped Fox Challenge the Other Networks on Saturday Mornings

OPPOSITE Production cel of Jubilee skateboarding, from "Red Dawn."
LEFT Major *Los Angeles Times* feature article (2/20/93) indicating that a cartoon show had, in just over a month, vaulted the tiny, new Fox network past the reigning US networks (ABC, NBC, CBS) that had been established for fifty years.

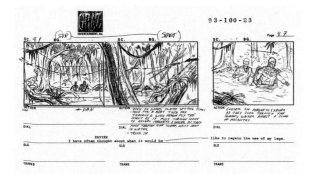

93-100-23
ENTERTAINMENT, Inc.
Page 47
SC. 81 BG.
STOP
START
SC. BG.
SC. BG.
IN
ACTION
← PAN
ACTION -OPEN ON DISMAL SWAMP SETTING START -HOLD FOR A BEAT THEN PAN TRACKING WITH DRAGON FLY TYPE INSECT AS IT FLYS THROUGH SCENE TO REVEAL MAGNETO & XAVIER AS THEY MOVE THROUGH THE SWAMP, WAIST DEEP IN WATER -TRUCK IN
ACTION CLOSER ON MAGNETO & XAVIER AS THEY SLOG THROUGH THE SWAMPY WATER AMIDST A CLOUD OF MOSQUITOS.
DIAL
XAVIER
I have often thought about what it would be
like to regain the use of my legs.
SLG
TRANS

01

93-100-23
ENTERTAINMENT, Inc.
Page 230
SC. 379 BG.
VERT BG PAN
SC. CONT BG.
PAN STOP
SC. BG.
THE END
ACTION
ON THE BACK OF BEAST - as he walks off into the night, under a full moon, alone.
DIAL
SLG
TRANS

02

ENTERTAINMENT, Inc.

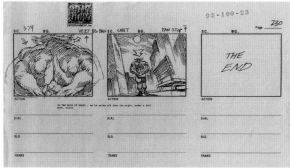

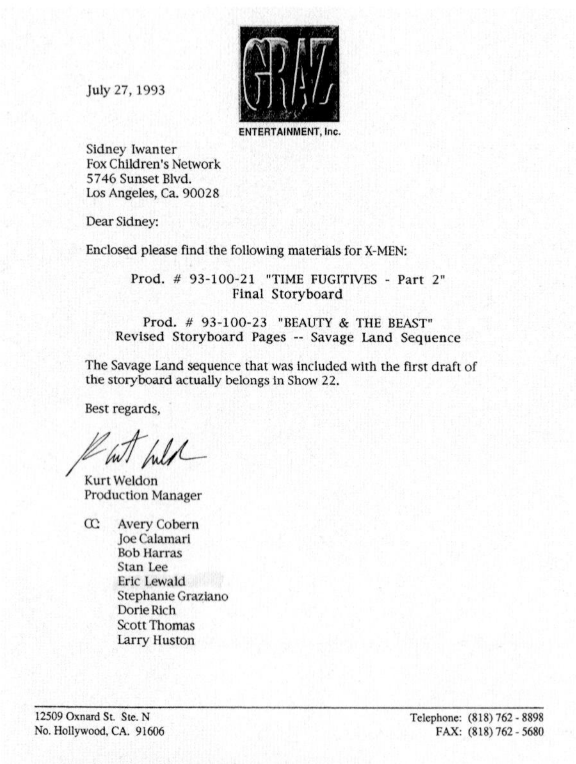

July 27, 1993

Sidney Iwanter
Fox Children's Network
5746 Sunset Blvd.
Los Angeles, Ca. 90028

Dear Sidney:

Enclosed please find the following materials for X-MEN:

Prod. # 93-100-21 "TIME FUGITIVES - Part 2"
Final Storyboard

Prod. # 93-100-23 "BEAUTY & THE BEAST"
Revised Storyboard Pages -- Savage Land Sequence

The Savage Land sequence that was included with the first draft of the storyboard actually belongs in Show 22.

Best regards,

Kurt Weldon
Production Manager

CC: Avery Cobern
Joe Calamari
Bob Harras
Stan Lee
Eric Lewald
Stephanie Graziano
Dorie Rich
Scott Thomas
Larry Huston

12509 Oxnard St. Ste. N
No. Hollywood, CA. 91606

Telephone: (818) 762 - 8898
FAX: (818) 762 - 5680

03

IN SEASON ONE, the staff had set up the X-Men's world and introduced the characters. In season two, the writers were determined to dig deeper into the lives of each of the team members, while the artists were eager to draw new Marvel characters—villains, mostly—and new locations.

Two decisions helped focus season two. First was the fact that Fox, burned by the animation delays of season one, said that the series could no longer be "serialized": Each episode must stand alone. That way, if an episode was delayed by production problems, another could be shown in its place without disturbing the story continuity. Two-part episodes, yes; thirteen-story seasonal arcs, no. This was a blow to many of the creative team who had fought for the comic-book-like feel of continuing stories.

To get around this restriction, Eric and Mark designed a "background continuity"—a secondary story that played out over the entire season, but only in small bits per episode, perhaps ninety seconds each—then resolved in a full episode at the end. This could all be designed and animated first and the small pieces kept in order. If the main part of, say, the season's fifth episode were delayed, for example, that stand-alone story could be shifted to a later slot. But the small bit of the continuing "background" story could stay in position, tacked into a different main fifth episode.

The ongoing background, or "B," story took Professor Xavier and his nemesis and oldest friend, Magneto, to the Savage Land, a spectacular, hidden, primitive world full of new characters and new challenges for the artists. This mysterious place also restored the use of Xavier's legs (don't ask). He got to walk for twelve episodes! And the professor's absence allowed the writers to explore how the X-Men team would work without its powerful leader.

The other creative adjustment involved Morph, the fun-loving X-Man who had died heroically for his friends. TV networks, it turns out, shouldn't be allowed to talk to young children. They herd them together in "focus groups" to elicit their opinions on various shows. On our show, one such group proclaimed that Morph was the younger viewers' favorite character during the first season—and we'd killed him off early in episode two!

Networks are nothing if not responsive to their viewers (and the money that flows from them). Fox's Sidney Iwanter called Eric about Morph: "Could we *please* bring him back?" No one on the production side of the series was happy about this—except, perhaps, Morph's voice actor—but they all understood that the "business" side of show business demanded it.

Eric and Mark decided to take the opportunity to do something different with Morph. Now he would be "damaged Morph," bitter at being left behind to die, so he has been led to believe, by the X-Men. Since he knew them so well and was a shape-shifter, he became, for a time, the team's most dangerous adversary.

And since we wanted someone truly evil to be manipulating Morph into this new, vengeful attitude, we introduced the first of the second season's major new villains, Mister Sinister.

We even went to the effort to *pre*-introduce him: When we decided that Sinister would be the force behind Morph's turn to evil, we went back and added a hint to the final moments of the final episode of season one, which had ended with Scott and Jean kissing on the beach as Jean accepted Scott's proposal of marriage.

Larry had the animators overlay a TV-screen matte over the happy couple, indicating that someone was watching them. And then we added Sinister's voice, teasing the audience that all was not as wonderful as it seemed.

We never would have thought to do this (now a fan-favorite moment) if we hadn't been told we had to bring Morph back from the dead.

From the artists' point of view, introducing Mister Sinister brought some obvious problems. After all of Will and Larry and Frank's work to draw our characters as simply as possible, here comes a character whose outfit is an animator's nightmare.

Larry says, "With Sinister, he had this rooster-tail cape; it wasn't one piece like Superman . . . it had all these fringe strips. He had a ribbed costume, and believe me, if you take that guy and want him to make a simple body-turn, you're going to kill the animators. The thing I kept doing when I went through the boards: I would edit out him making turns. The result was that when you saw him, he was, with only a few exceptions, already posed. If he needed to turn, I'd cut away to something else, then cut back to him already in the new pose. I tried not to turn him, so that the animators could draw him with all the detail, all the lines, all the color. If he had to turn, I tried to just do a head shot, a head-shoulder shot, so that the animators wouldn't blow the budget turning him."

An unintended but great result of our inability to afford to animate this character properly was that Sinister was suddenly creepy—different from other characters in an indefinable way. Like Bela Lugosi's Dracula, he would ease in and out of shadows, or seem to simply appear, still and menacing.

And then there were his teeth. Larry recalls: "One thing I remember about Sinister was that when we first designed

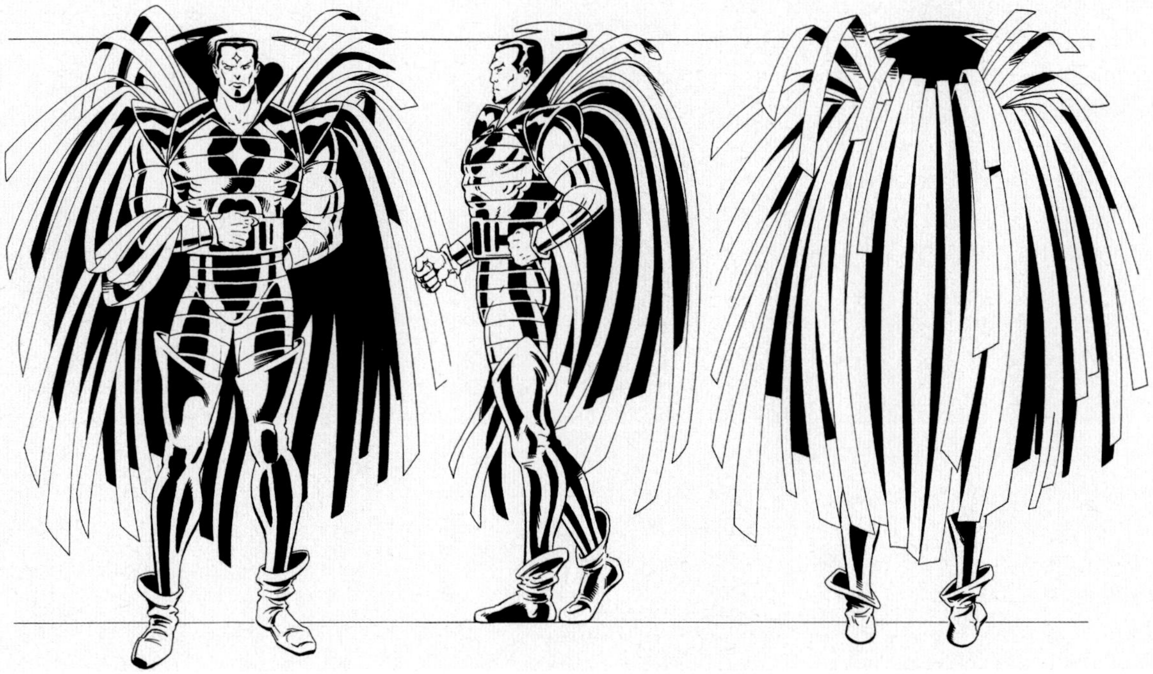

04

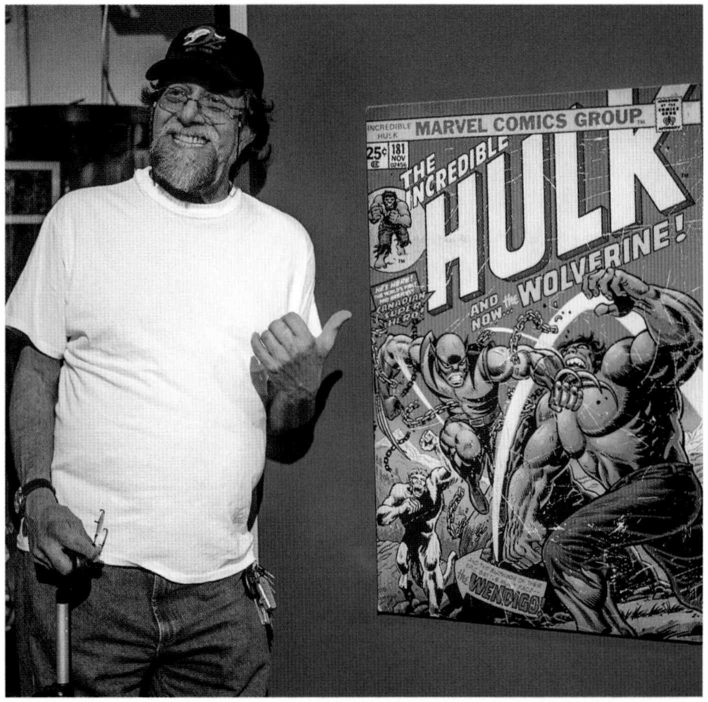
MARVEL COMICS GROUP
THE INCREDIBLE
HULK
AND NOW THE WOLVERINE!

05

him, I went to the very first issue that he was drawn [*Uncanny X-Men* vol. 1, no. 221]. I think Marc Silvestri drew it, and he was drawn with all those sharp teeth. Every issue after that he had normal teeth. I asked Bob [Harras, at Marvel]: 'Why did you guys change it?' I don't recall him having a good answer, but he said, 'We draw him with regular teeth now.' He hung up the phone, and I looked at Sinister and thought: 'This Dracula version looks so different.' I told the guys: 'Let's do this one.' It's still accurate, it's what they drew, but it's the very first version. From that point forward he had the Dracula teeth, and I think it made him look unique."

Then Storm's past, in Northern and Central Africa, was explored as the Shadow King villain was introduced. Storm and Rogue travel to the African village where Storm had been worshipped as a "goddess" and where she had left a godson, Mjnari, whose life was imperiled. On an inside note, Larry had Frank Brunner draw Mjnari to look like Larry's son Adrian, and Julia, having just birthed our second son, Alec, wrote the script with a great deal of maternal protectiveness.

Team friend (and frequent X-Man in the books) Colossus was visited in his Russian homeland, while major villain Omega Red was introduced. This "Cold War" story was of great interest to Eric, whose father had been a World War II refugee. In 1993, the story was topical—the Soviet Union had just collapsed, freeing a dozen sovereign nations from Russian control. The huge Soviet empire was in chaos. Colossus's peasant family were just the sort of people who can get trampled by such tectonic shifts in history. And Omega Red—whose tentacles made him an especially creepy, effective villain in animation—was a perfect incarnation of the deadly oppression of an "evil empire."

Wolverine's difficult past, in Canada, was delved into in "Repo Man," the first of four episodes to be written for us by his co-creator Len Wein. Who better to tell the origin story of our most popular character than the writer who came up with him? The story was structured so that those who were there when Wolverine was "weaponized"—when his struggle-filled future was forced upon him—are there now, working out the mystery of those days as they fight against the shadowy government agency that had been lying to them all these years. Logan's old Alpha Flight teammates and a caring couple who took Logan in are featured.

A hint of Gambit's mysterious past in the Louisiana bayou was revealed, featuring his family, his vengeful former fiancée, Bella Donna, and the most fantastical creature we had yet introduced, the X-Ternal. While it's clear that Gambit wanted nothing more to do with the three-hundred-year-old blood feud that was his legacy, he had to return to it to save his brother Bobby. Rogue and Logan help Gambit free himself of these struggles and find a place with his new "family," the X-Men.

After reusing major players Cable, Bishop, and Apocalypse in a sequel to "Days of Future Past," a story was crafted that detailed Rogue's past and introduced Carol Danvers, aka Ms. Marvel, as the source of much of Rogue's power and internal struggle, as well as the shape-shifter Mystique as a complicating influence in Rogue's life.

Then we gave easygoing Beast a tortured love story. "Beauty and the Beast" was inspired by Charlie Chaplin's 1931 classic *City Lights*. Julia suggested the idea, and Eric immediately saw how it would show a side of our beloved Beast that we wouldn't otherwise have seen. Our Beast had been a thoughtful,

01 Storyboard page of ongoing, second-season "B" story of Xavier and Magneto trapped in the Savage Land; this section was inserted in "Beauty and the Beast." **02** Storyboard page of intended ending for "Beauty and the Beast." It was trimmed during post-production for time and to end with a closer shot of Beast watching Carly go. Drawn by Diego Francisco. **03** Memo from production manager Kurt Weldon indicating the switching of a short Savage Land sequence (drawn separately) from one episode to another. **04** Mister Sinister turnaround. Art by Frank Brunner, inked by Mark Lewis. **05** Comics and animation writer Len Wein, pointing to the cover of *Incredible Hulk* (vol. 1) #181: the first appearance of Wolverine, one of the many X-Men characters Len co-created with Dave Cockrum.

even-tempered, brave scientist, not given to the rages and anxieties of his more volatile friends. Even though Dr. Henry McCoy was by far the most alien, most animalistic-looking X-Man, he was at peace with his mutant nature in a way few mutants were. Perhaps because he *couldn't* pass as normal and had to deal with the ridicule for years, he had learned to rise above it.

So when, through his medical work, a relationship grows with a young blind woman, Carly Anne Crocker, he is caught off guard when she is about to gain her sight: Feelings of being different well up inside him. While he feels great relief that she is not put off by his appearance, Beast can't help but see the storm of hate and trouble swirling around them. His clinic is firebombed and he is fired. Carly's bigoted father doesn't want Hank in the same room with her. Beast, self-conscious about his difference for the first time in years (a nice look back through a family photo album shows his gradual changes), wonders if he and Carly can in fact be together as they both want.

Finally, the bigoted antimutant hate group Friends of Humanity kidnaps Carly. Beast and other X-Men save her. But the fear and the guilt he feels for endangering her convince him of the sacrifice he must make. He tells her that in a world like this, they can't be together. Before Hank walks off alone, we see a small redemption in his great personal loss: Carly's formerly mutant-hating father sincerely thanks Beast for saving his daughter. It's a small thing, but it's real.

An entire new world—a "parallel dimension"—was designed for crazed villain and mega-showman Mojo. The "Mojovision" episode is wildly different in tone and focus from others from the first two seasons. It's more from the character Mojo's point of view—the audience doesn't even see the X-Men in the teaser. Mojo, while a ruthless, deadly villain, was over-the-top, high-speed funny! While *X-Men: TAS* always looked for moments of comic relief, the show was an adventure drama. Suddenly, there was an episode, with Mojo's comic energy at its center, that was entirely "other." While fans are split about him, Marvel was obviously pleased. When a third season was discussed, adding another Mojo episode was high on their list of suggestions.

Finally, the season wrapped up with the X-Men joining Xavier and Magneto in the Savage Land, where, together with locals like Ka-Zar, they defeated Sinister and his season-long conspiracy to use the X-Men in his genetic experiments. Professor Xavier, lost at the end of the season's opening two-part story—then stranded, feared dead, for nine episodes—is reunited with his X-Men family in the season-ending two-parter, "Reunion." The team also proved themselves to PTSD-damaged

Morph and were able to take him home to help him heal. After a full season stranded together, sworn-adversaries-yet-beloved-friends Charles Xavier and Magento are able to say heartfelt goodbyes. In classic villain fashion, Mister Sinister—when he believes he has won—gets to articulate his villainous ambition in a triumphant pronouncement.

A final bonus to the Savage Land, for us, was that since it suppressed mutant powers, not only was Xavier able to walk—again, we fail to recall our logic here—but Rogue and Gambit were, after two long seasons, able to passionately kiss without her putting him into a coma.

WHILE IT SEEMS THAT SEASON TWO—compared to the struggles, crises, delays, and anxious doubts surrounding season one—was a piece of cake, it had its challenges. During the lay-off break between seasons, *X-Men: TAS* lost Will Meugniot to Universal Studios's animated action series *Exosquad*. Mark and Michael Edens, and Eric, had helped Will develop the first season of *Exosquad*, and had done almost all of its first-season writing while all four of them were waiting the four months of *X-Men: TAS* downtime to see if it would be renewed for a second season. Animation work used to be seasonal—eight months on, four months off. The *Exosquad* opportunity during the usual "break" was a godsend.

When *X-Men: TAS* was renewed, Eric was able to leave *Exosquad* and return. Mark and Michael were able to find time to work on both shows, but less on ours than we would have liked. Will, as the former supervising producer, would not be able to return to us until his *Exosquad* work was complete about a year later, and then in a lesser capacity. Will had been the face and voice of the *X-Men* series, fighting our creative battles with Marvel, Fox, Saban, merchandisers—anyone who threatened what the staff saw as the best interests of the show. He had been responsible for much of the show's design. Luckily, all of the big battles had been fought, and Will had left his mark on the series. The team of artists Will left us, headed by Larry Houston, was ready and able to take *X-Men: TAS* to the next level. Post-production specialist Scott Thomas stepped in for Will, and the production never missed a beat.

While Eric was fighting to keep our best freelance writers as other projects tempted them away, Haim Saban decided to *cut* their script fees by five hundred dollars.

Instead of getting a bonus, a reward for their work in creating a number one show, they were told that "*X-Men* is a hit. Everyone wants to write for it. So we're offering less, and you'll take it."

Sadly, Saban was right: the writers took the pay cut. Julia remembers that Eric personally covered the difference that year out of a sense of anger at the injustice. But with hit status came creative freedom, respect, and support, all often more valuable than money. The writing staff's answer—now that the basics of the X-Men's world had been established in season one—was to write deeper, more personal stories. This was in part as competition with our only perceived rival, *Batman: TAS*. Sidney Iwanter was responsible for overseeing both series, the two animated shows that everybody in town wanted to write for.

Sidney Iwanter: "You know there was always a kind of competition between the *Batman: TAS* and *X-Men: TAS* people. My favorite show of the two was *X-Men*, because it was always the wayward child. The kind of financial support that *Batman* was given far outweighed *X-Men*'s, but I found the *X-Men* characters far more compelling than those in *Batman*. The *Batman* writing was great, there was nothing wrong; it was a stellar, superb, spectacular show. I just preferred the X-Men, because they were like a family, a street gang."

Eric Lewald: "My memory of your describing the difference between them was that *Batman* was cool jazz, and *X-Men* was a garage band. So we were cranked up to 11 and bumping heads and going as fast as we could, jamming two stories' worth of character conflict and drama into every episode—versus *Batman* smoothly, beautifully easing through."

Sidney: "It was Jerry Lee Lewis versus Miles Davis."

During the expansive second season, the artists wore themselves out designing personal worlds for half a dozen lead characters—and the entire Savage Land, the Shadow King's Astral Plain, and Mojo's parallel dimension. AKOM's animators were hitting their stride. Merchandise for our specific team of X-Men—one day to be referred to as "X-Men '92"—was flying off the shelves, a rarity for then-struggling Marvel. New Marvel partner Avi Arad, owner of ToyBiz, was suddenly seeing waves of new toy profits. Audiences were growing.

What could possibly be left for season three?

OPPOSITE Production cel of Wolverine, in the Danger Room, ferociously destroying a Sentinel robot that looked like Cyclops—who at that moment is marrying Jean Grey. Wolverine is formally dressed to go to the wedding, but his despair at losing Jean to Scott keeps him away.

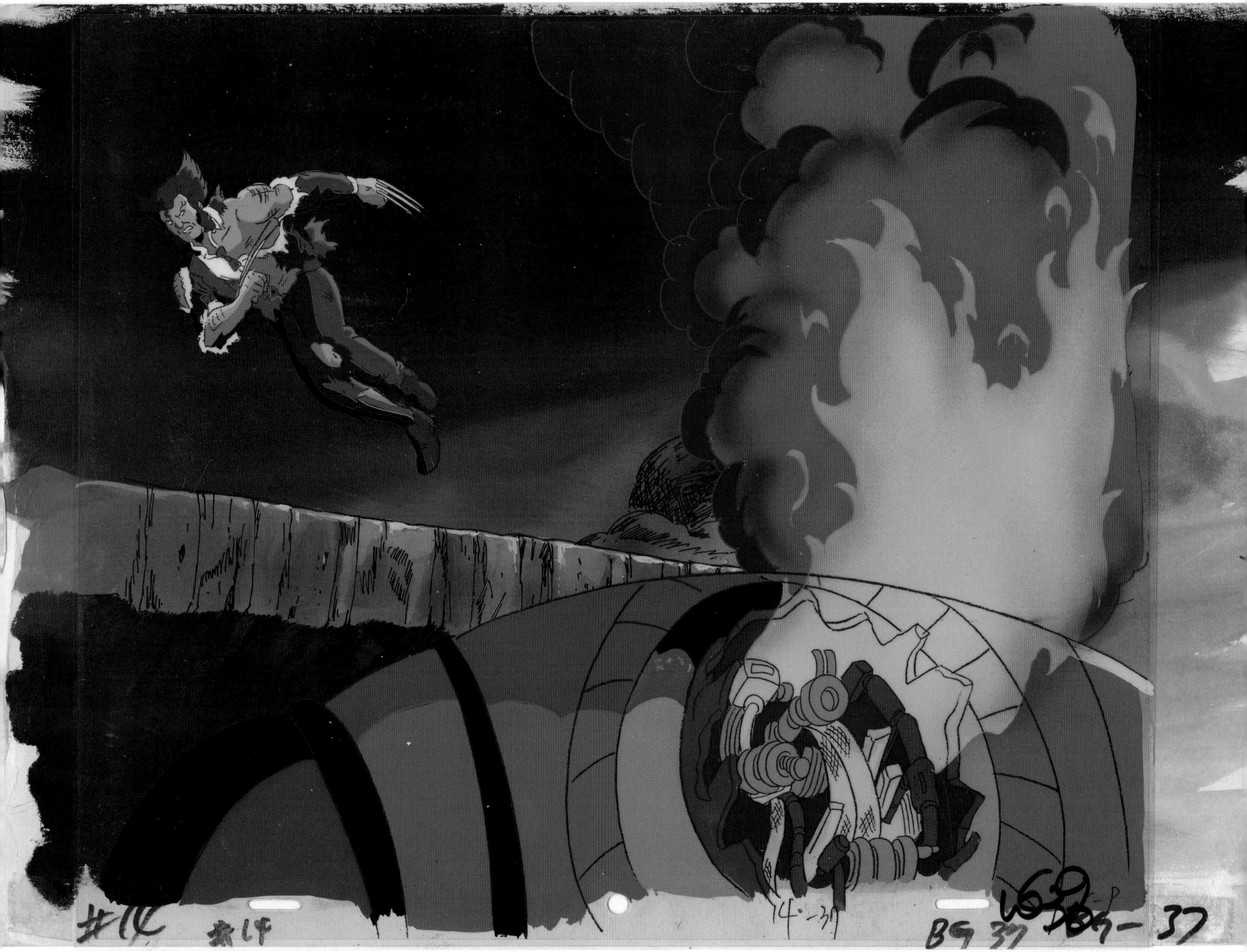
BG 37

01   02   03   04   05

PROF. X HAS A LONG-SLEEVE BLACK "T-SHIRT" ON UNDER THE JUMP SUIT.

01–02 Character models of Scott and Jean dressed for their wedding, by Frank Brunner. **03–04** Two wedding guest cameos for Marvel superfans, drawn to look like Marvel Universe characters J. Jonah Jameson and Doctor Strange, both by Frank Squillace. **05** Character model of Charles Xavier (standing, walking), to be used in Savage Land scenes during nine of the second season's episodes (#15–19 and #23–26). Revised by Mark Lewis. **06** Model of the robotic head of the Cyclops Sentinel that Wolverine chose to fight instead of going to Cyclops's and Jean's wedding. Drawn by Lewis from Brunner's full robot model. **07** Morph, presumed dead, makes a surprise reappearance—now suffering from PTSD and vowing revenge on the X-Men, whom he has been told had left him to die. By Brunner and Lewis. **08** Character model of Graydon Creed, evil leader of the anti-mutant militia The Friends of Humanity, by Brunner. **09** The Friends of Humanity logo, with echoes of Nazi insignia, designed and cleaned by Squillace. **10** Production cel of Morph having gone "bad" under the influence of Mister Sinister. **11** Storyboard of sleeping Rogue at her most stunning. Gambit is about to enter the room and wake her with a kiss. Penciled by Larry Houston.

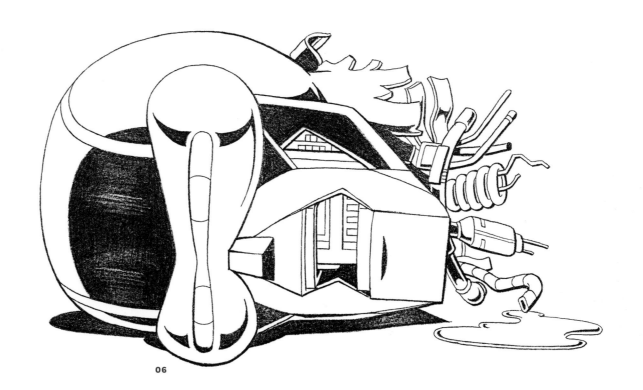

06

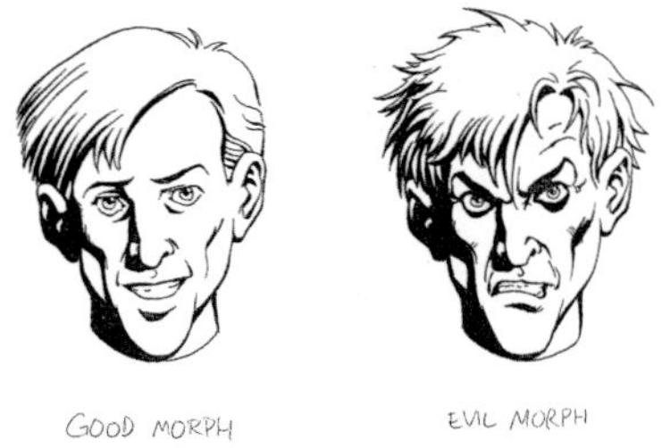
GOOD MORPH
EVIL MORPH

07

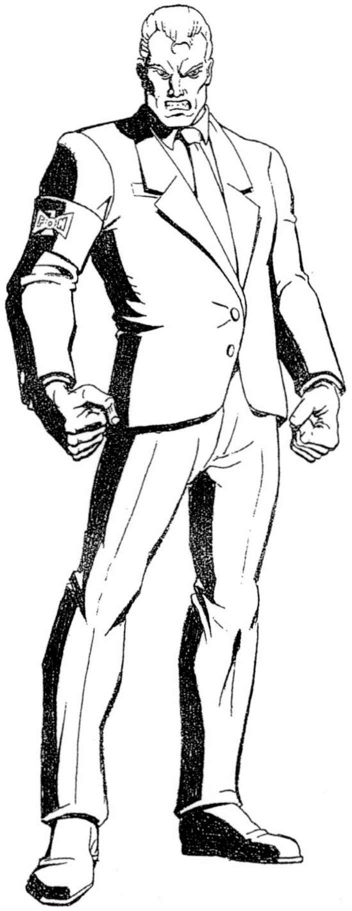

08

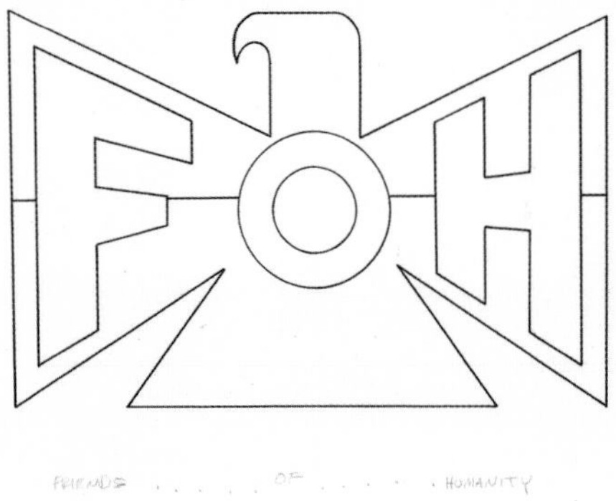
FOH
FRIENDS OF HUMANITY

09

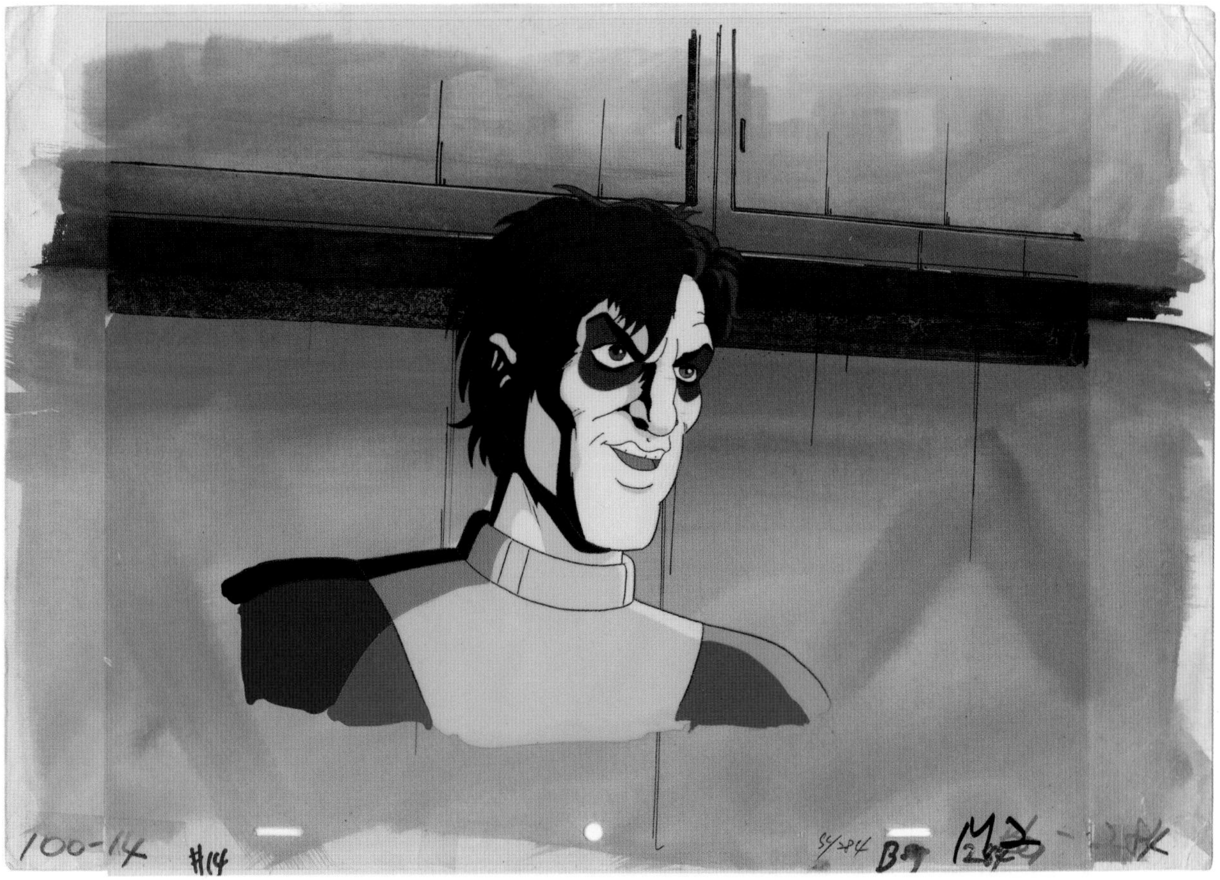
100-14
#14

10

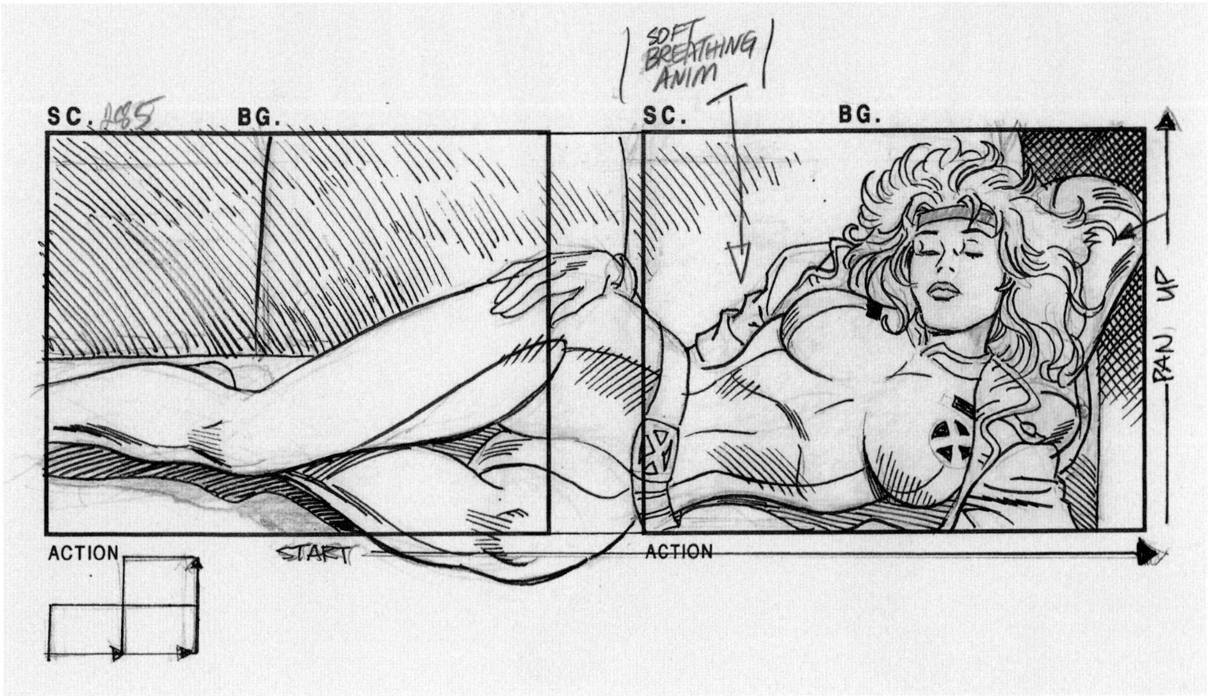
SOFT BREATHING ANIM
SC.
BG.
SC.
BG.
PAN UP
ACTION
START
ACTION

11

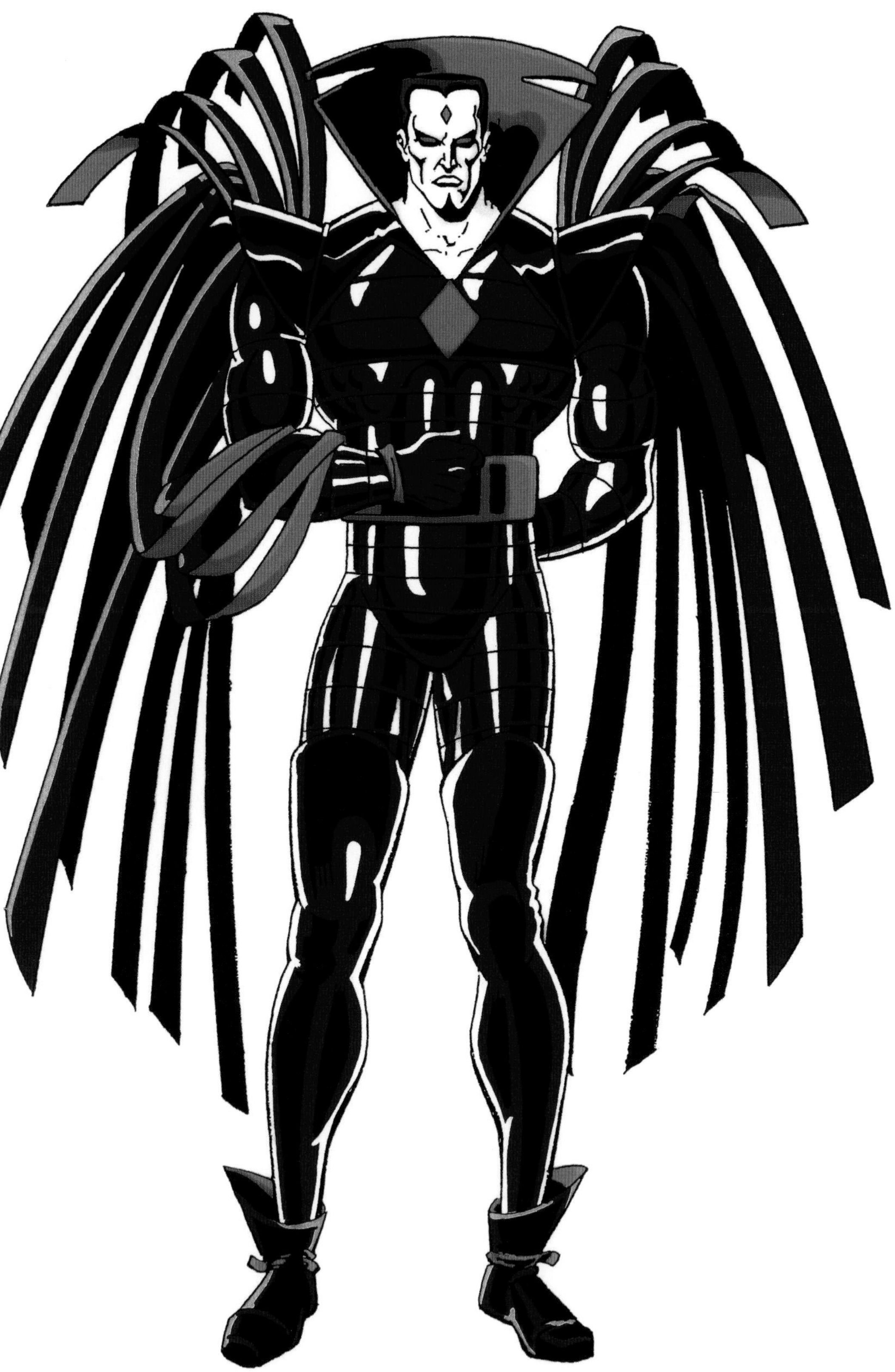

01

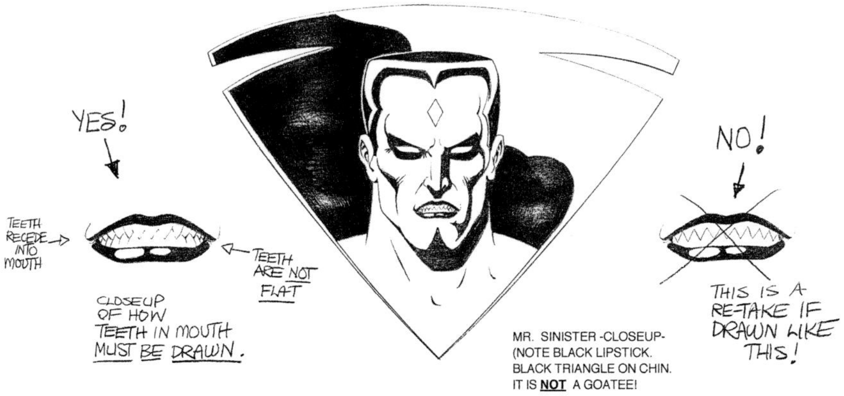
YES!
TEETH RECEDE INTO MOUTH
TEETH ARE NOT FLAT
CLOSEUP OF HOW TEETH IN MOUTH MUST BE DRAWN.
MR. SINISTER -CLOSEUP-
(NOTE BLACK LIPSTICK.
BLACK TRIANGLE ON CHIN.
IT IS **NOT** A GOATEE!
NO!
THIS IS A RE-TAKE IF DRAWN LIKE THIS!

02

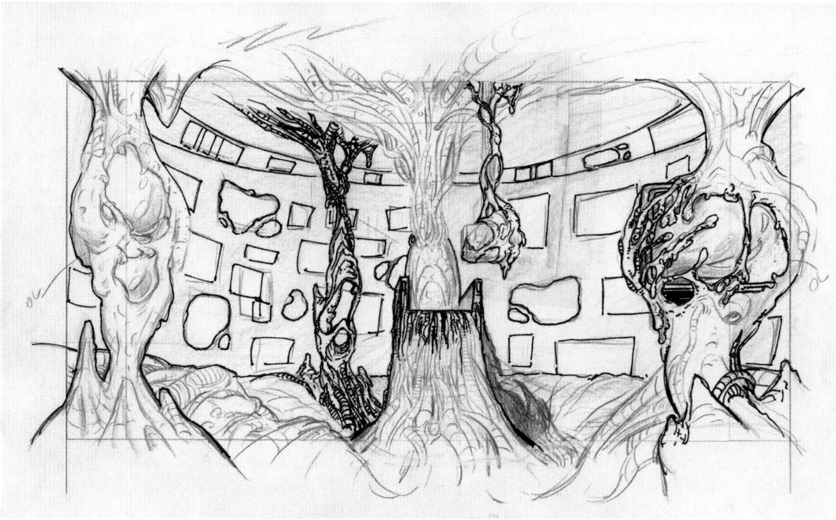
OL
OL

03

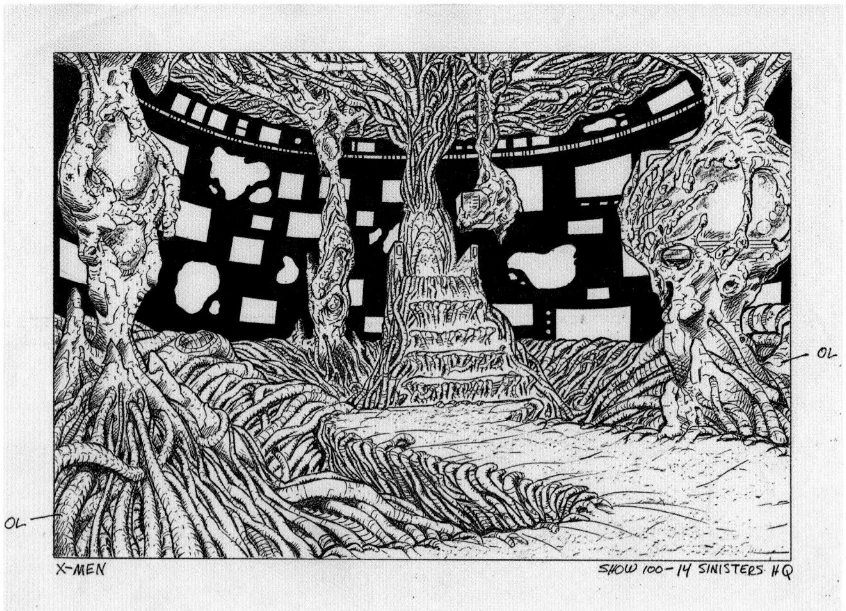
OL
OL
X-MEN
SHOW 100-14 SINISTERS HQ

04

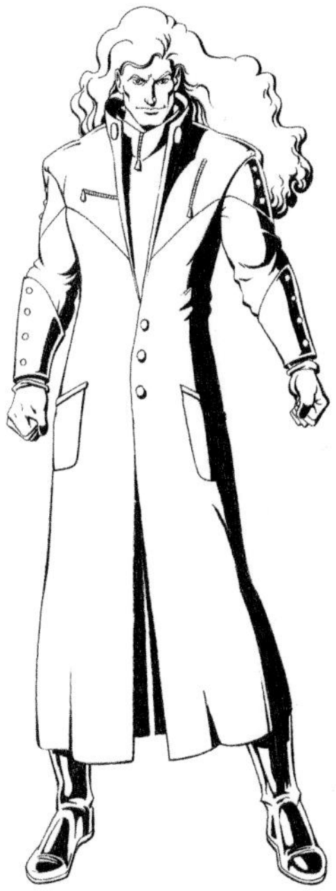

05

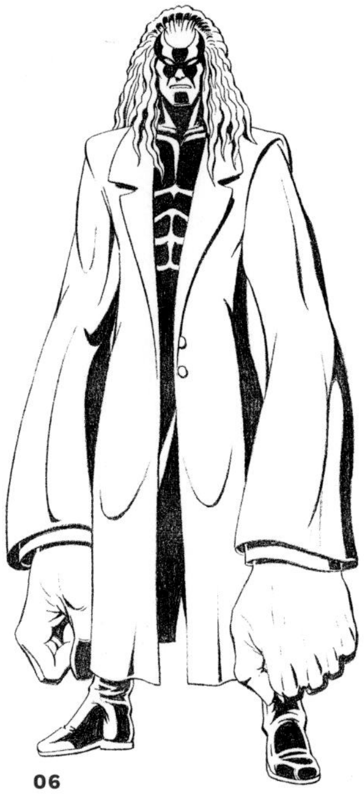

06

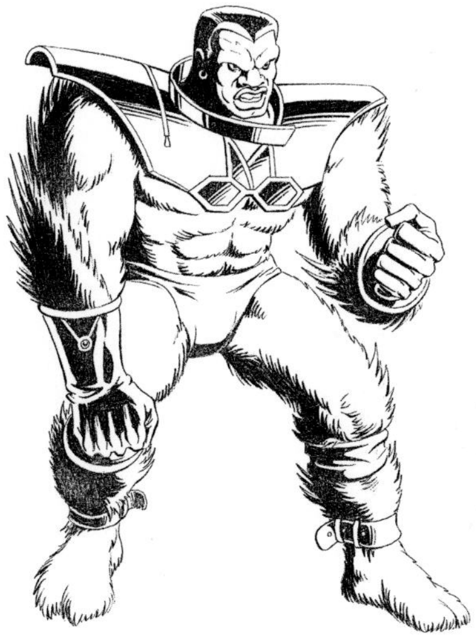

07

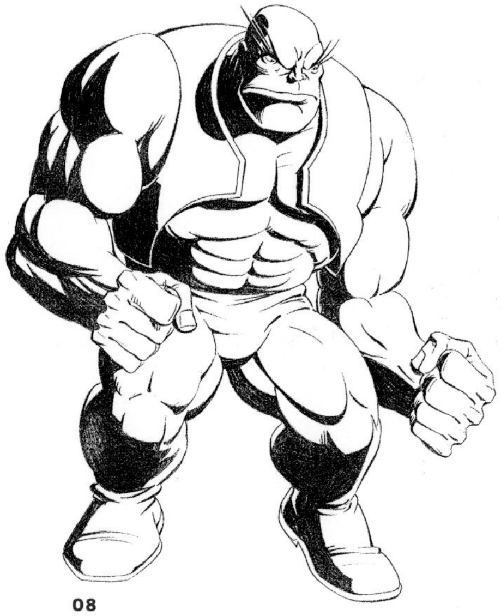

08

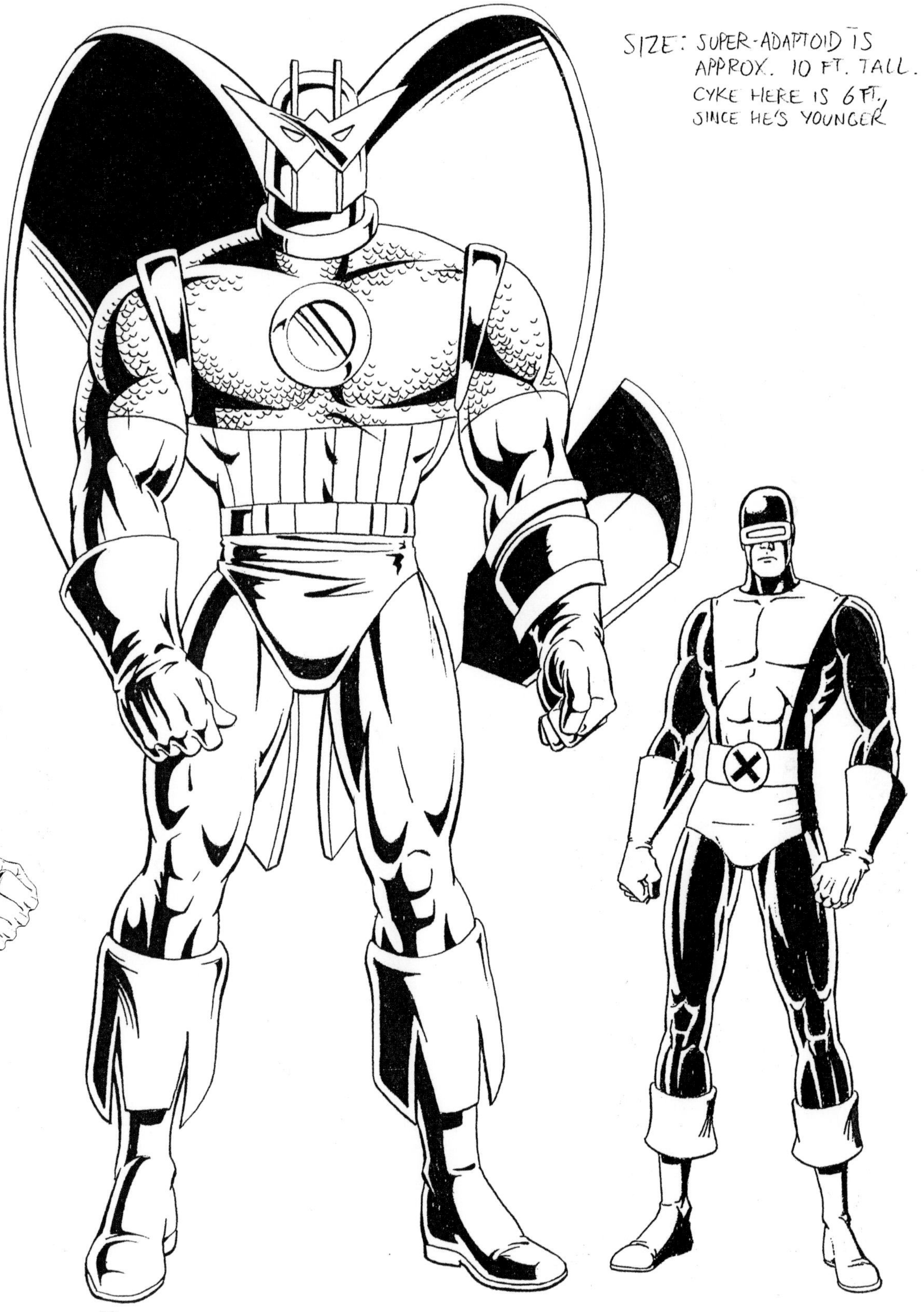
SIZE: SUPER-ADAPTOID IS APPROX. 10 FT. TALL. CYKE HERE IS 6 FT, SINCE HE'S YOUNGER

09

01 Color character model of Mister Sinister, complete with way-too-expensive-to-animate costume; penciled by Frank Brunner, inked by Mark Lewis. **02** Detailed artist's instructions for the design of Sinister's unique teeth—note to artists drawn by Larry Houston. **03–04** Early background sketches of Sinister's lair, the first with detailing in non-copy blue, the second in finer detail and depth of field, both by Frank Squillace. **05–09** Character models of Sinister's henchmen, including an old design of Cyclops to give a sense of scale to the oversized "Super-Adaptoid" (09). Henchmen by Brunner, Super-Adaptoid by Squillace, and old-school Cyclops by Lewis.

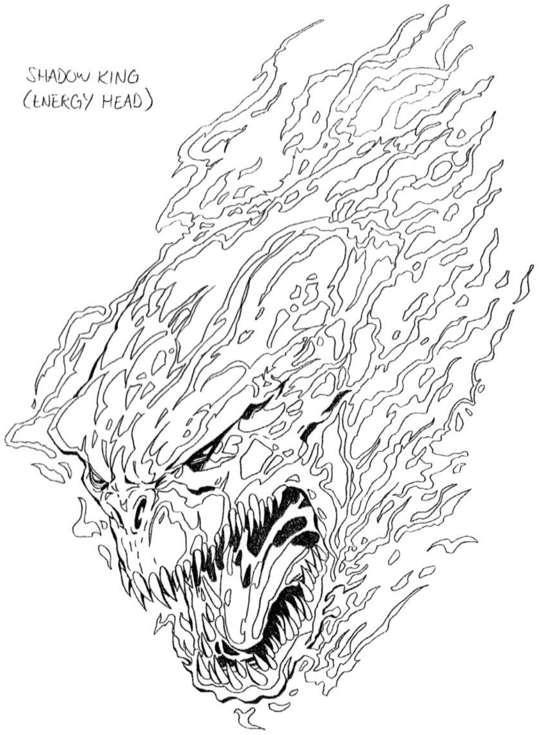
SHADOW KING
(ENERGY HEAD)

01

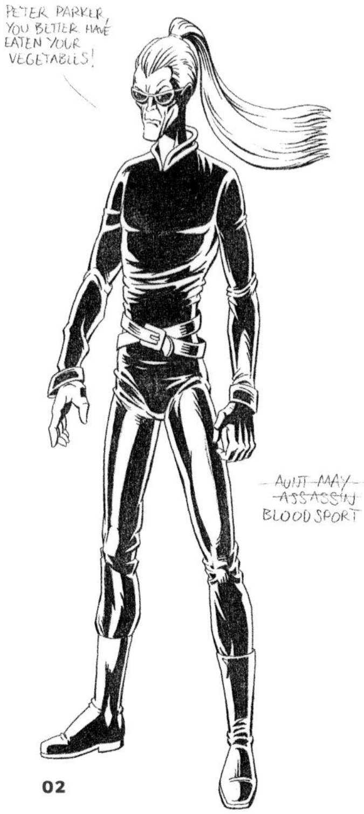
PETER PARKER, YOU BETTER HAVE EATEN YOUR VEGETABLES!
~~AUNT MAY ASSASSIN~~
BLOOD SPORT

02

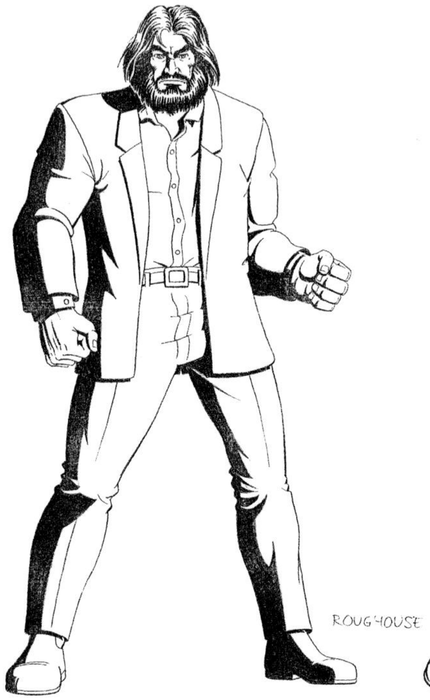
ROUGHOUSE

03

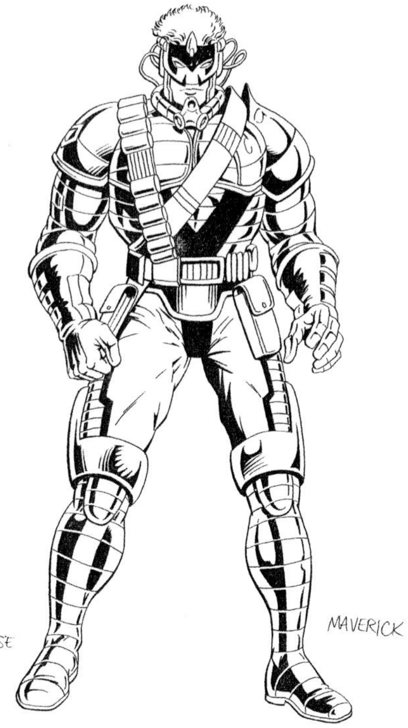
MAVERICK

04

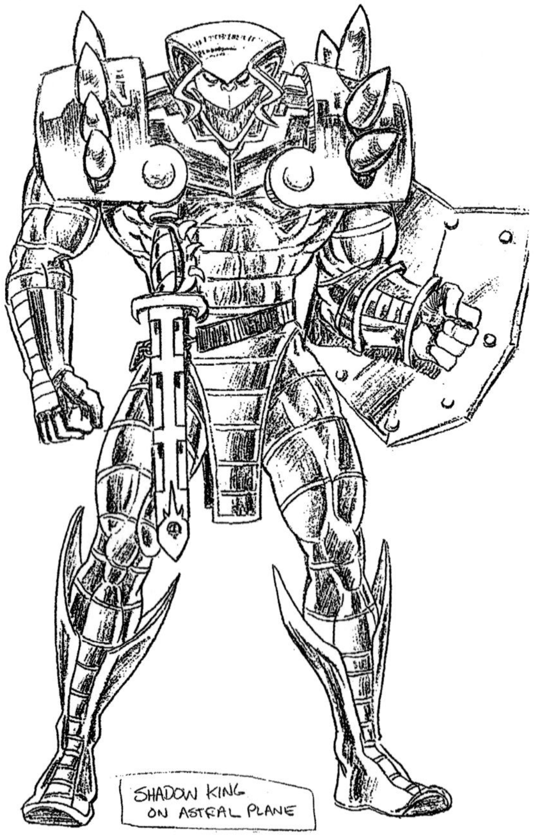
SHADOW KING
ON ASTRAL PLANE

05

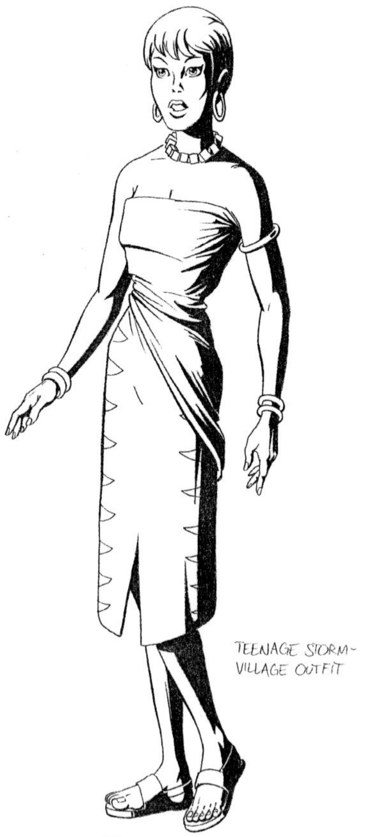
TEENAGE STORM-
VILLAGE OUTFIT

06

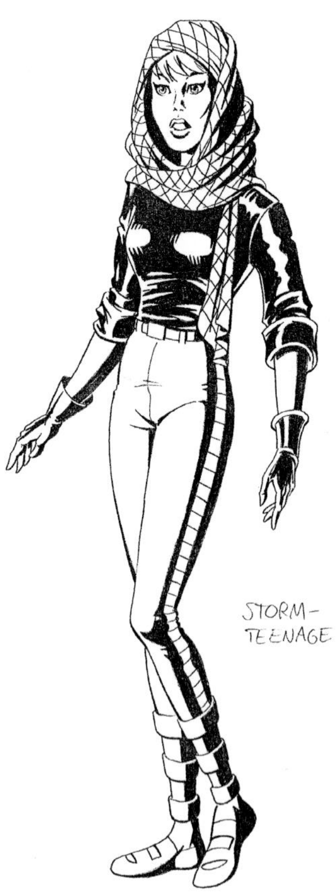
STORM-
TEENAGE

07

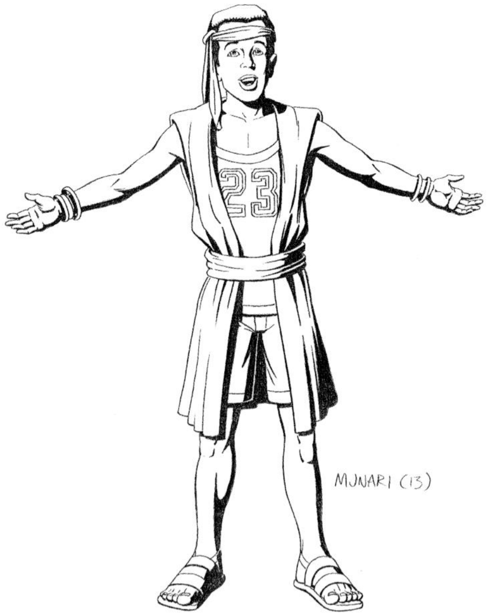
MJNARI (13)

08

01–08 Character models for "Whatever It Takes," including the Shadow King in two of his forms (01, 05); a teenage Storm from a flashback (06, 07); and Storm's godson Mjnari (08, modeled on Larry Houston's son, Adrian). All by Frank Brunner; humorous annotations by Mark Lewis. **OPPOSITE** Production cel of Rogue catching Storm after a confrontation with the Shadow King.

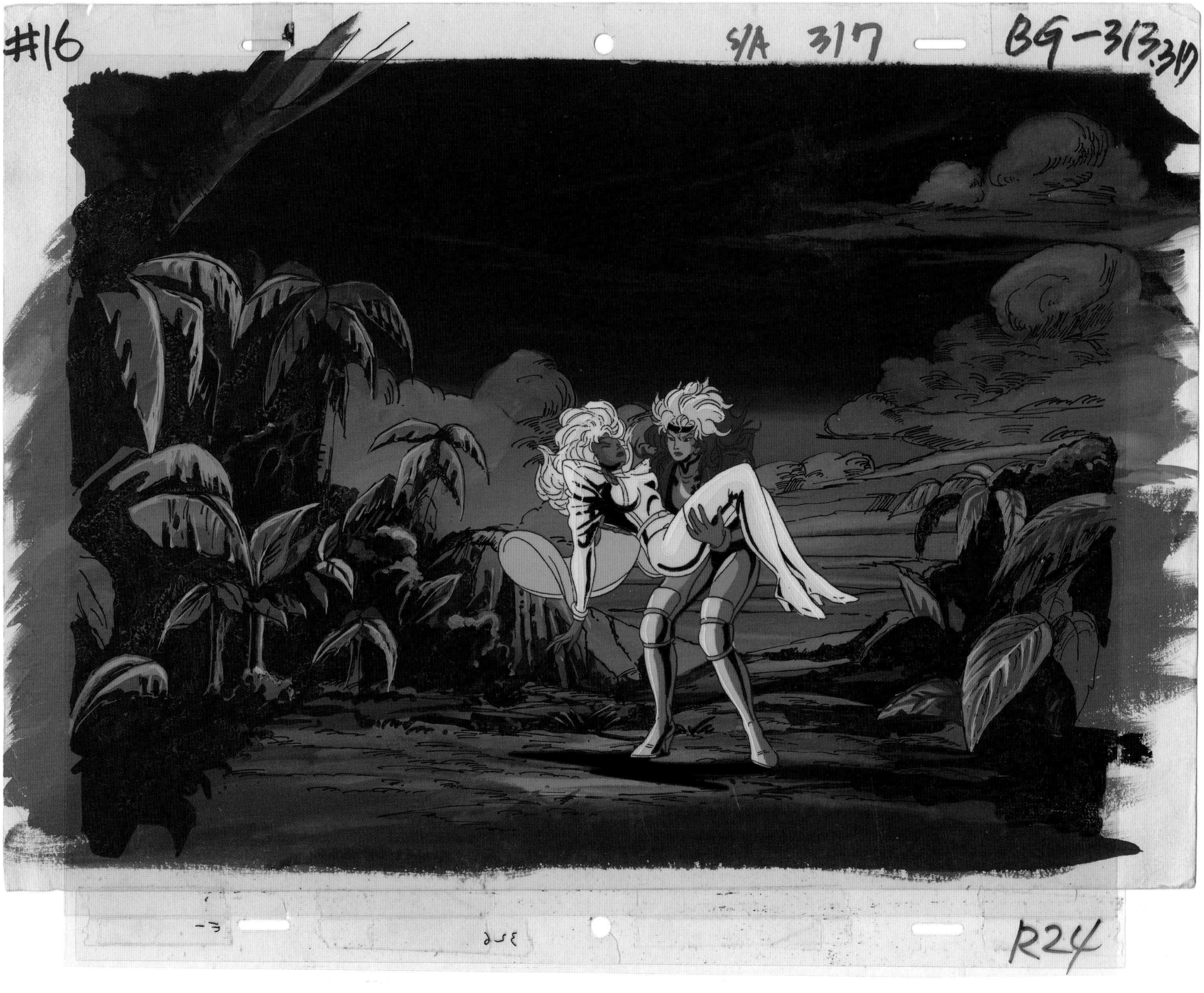
#16
S/A 317
BG-313,317
R24

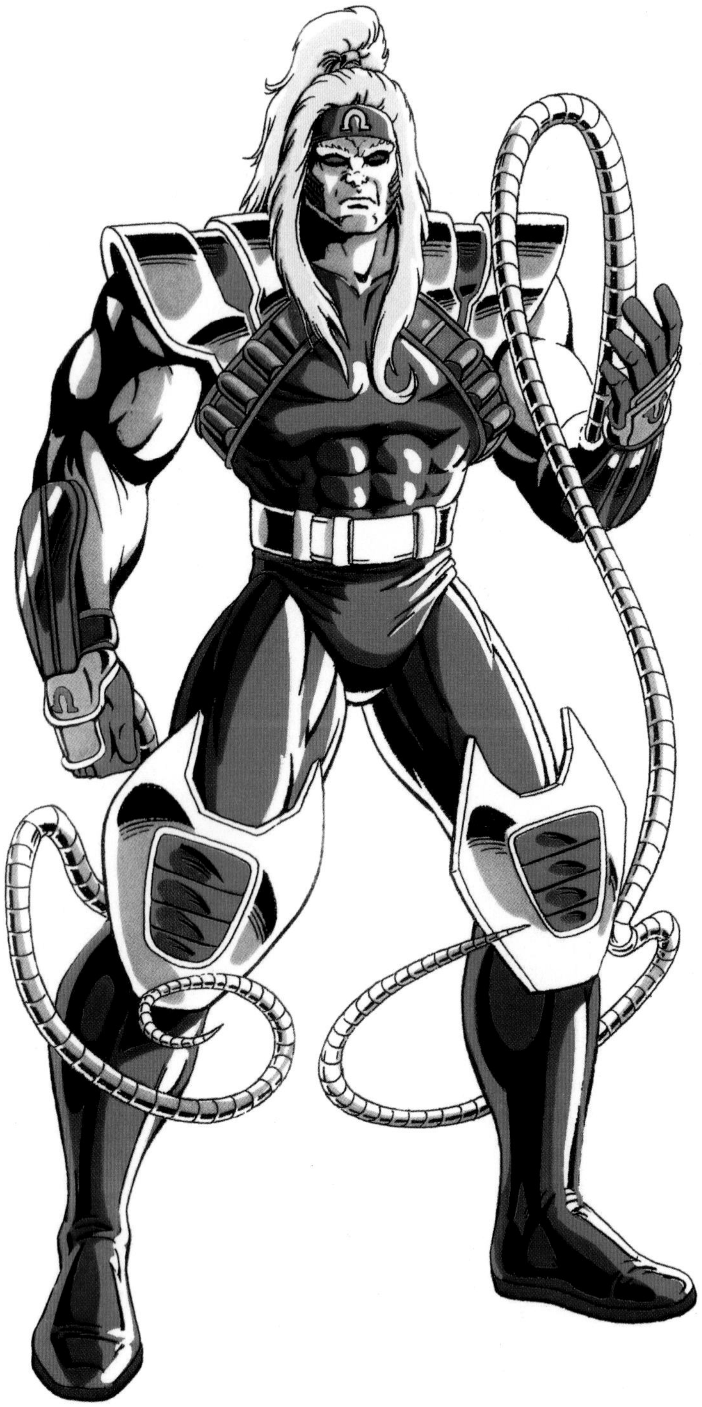

01

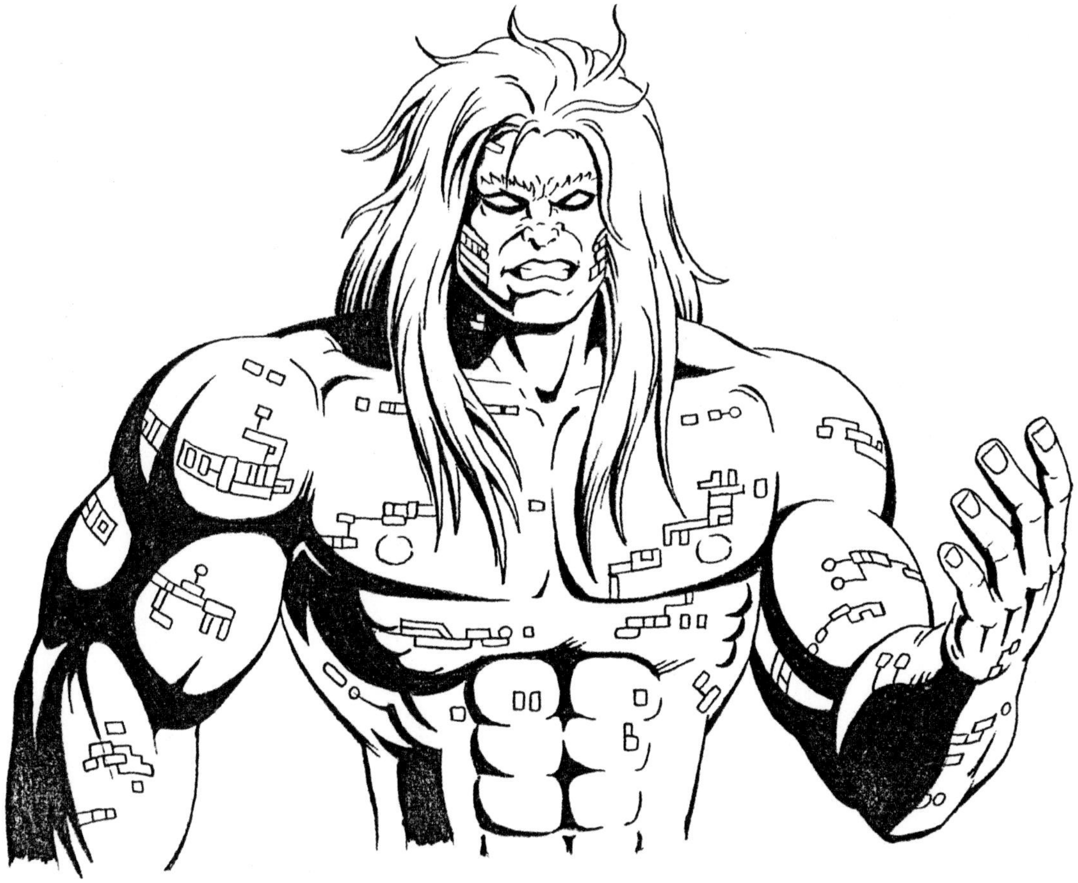

02

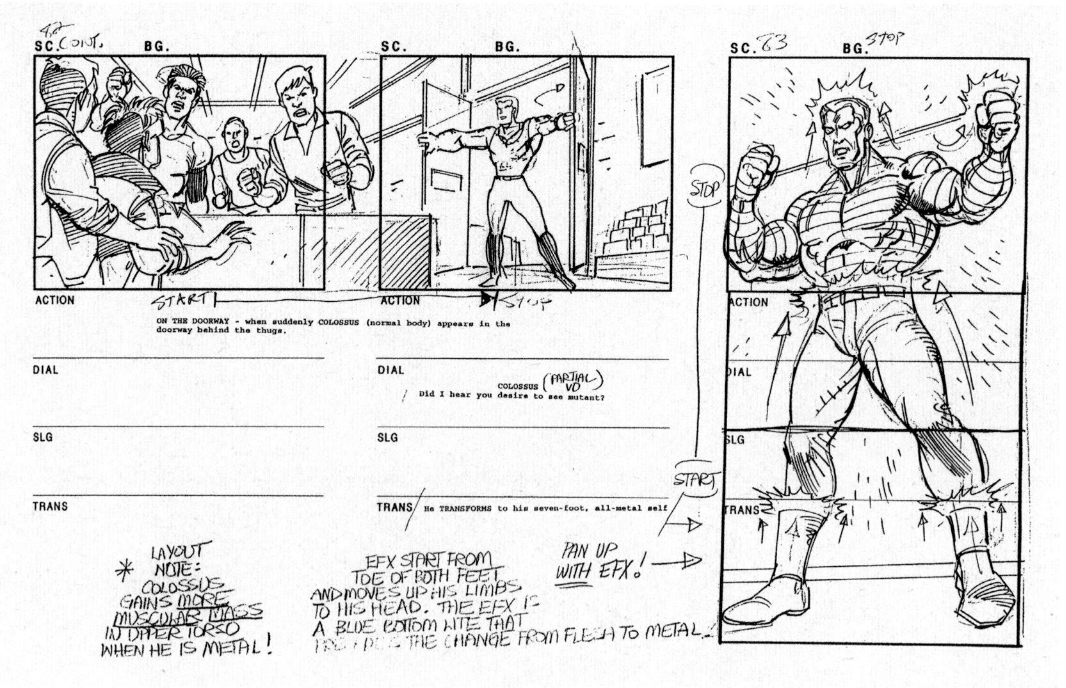

SC. CONT.
BG.
SC.
BG.
SC. 63
BG. STOP
START
STOP
STOP
START
ACTION
ON THE DOORWAY - when suddenly COLOSSUS (normal body) appears in the doorway behind the thugs.
DIAL
SLG
TRANS
ACTION
DIAL
COLOSSUS (PARTIAL VO)
Did I hear you desire to see mutant?
SLG
TRANS
He TRANSFORMS to his seven-foot, all-metal self
ACTION
DIAL
SLG
TRANS
* LAYOUT NOTE: COLOSSUS GAINS MORE MUSCULAR MASS IN UPPER TORSO WHEN HE IS METAL!
EFX START FROM TOE OF BOTH FEET AND MOVES UP HIS LIMBS TO HIS HEAD. THE EFX IS A BLUE BOTTOM LITE THAT
THE CHANGE FROM FLESH TO METAL
PAN UP WITH EFX!

03

01 Color character model of Omega Red, by Frank Brunner. **02** Out-of-uniform, flashback character model of Omega Red as he is turned into a living weapon, also by Brunner. **03** Storyboard page of Colossus bursting in to help Jubilee, then transforming from flesh to steel. **OPPOSITE** Series of four production cels showing Colossus's shift from steel to flesh.

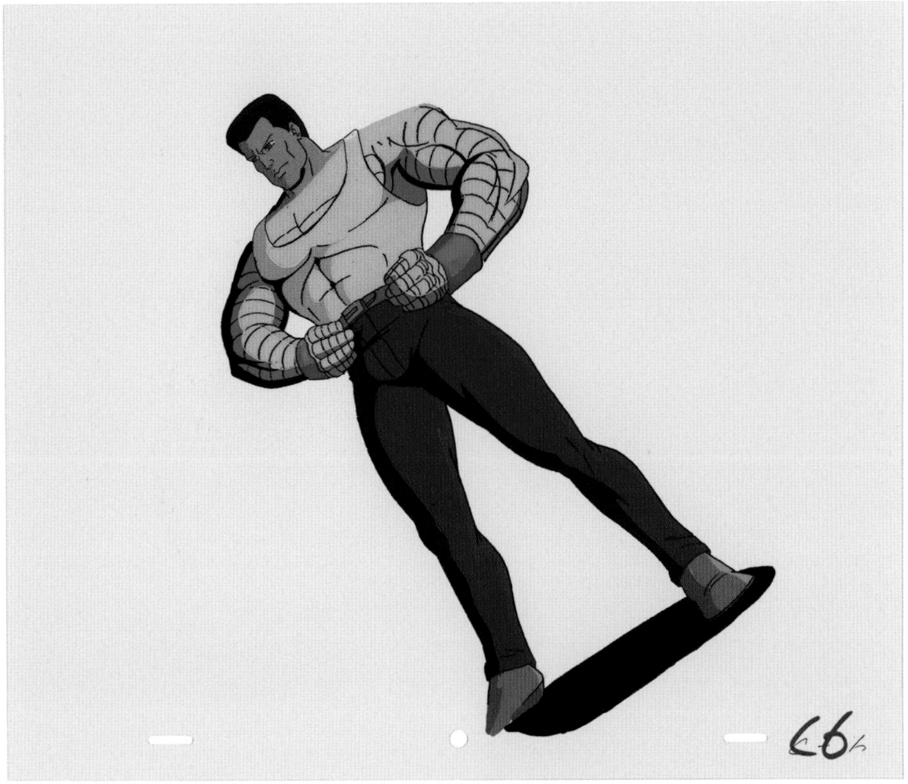
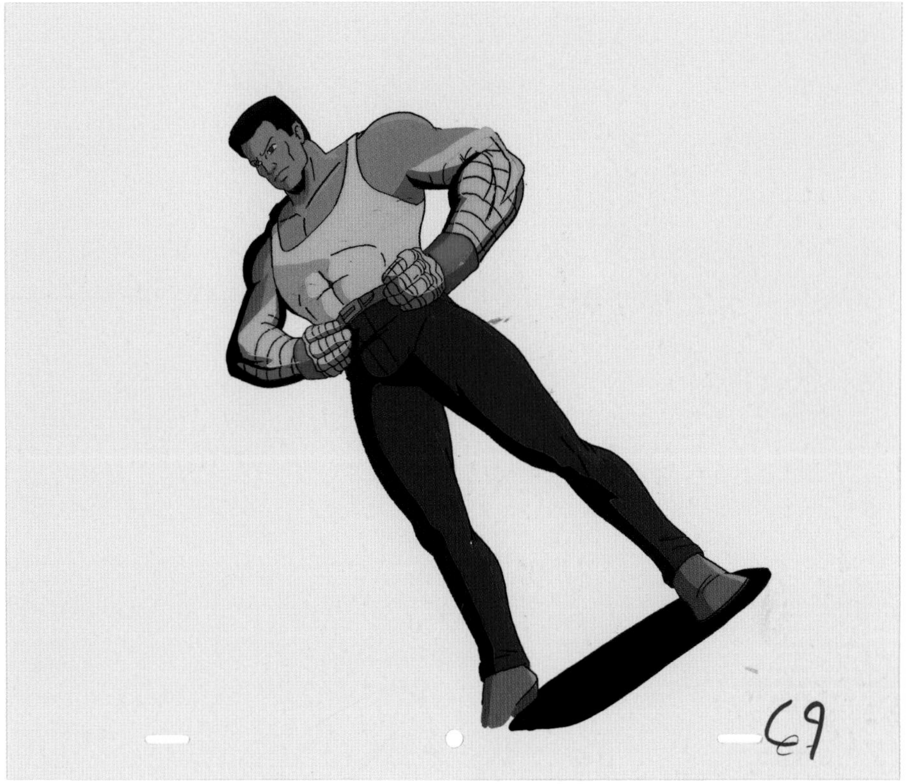
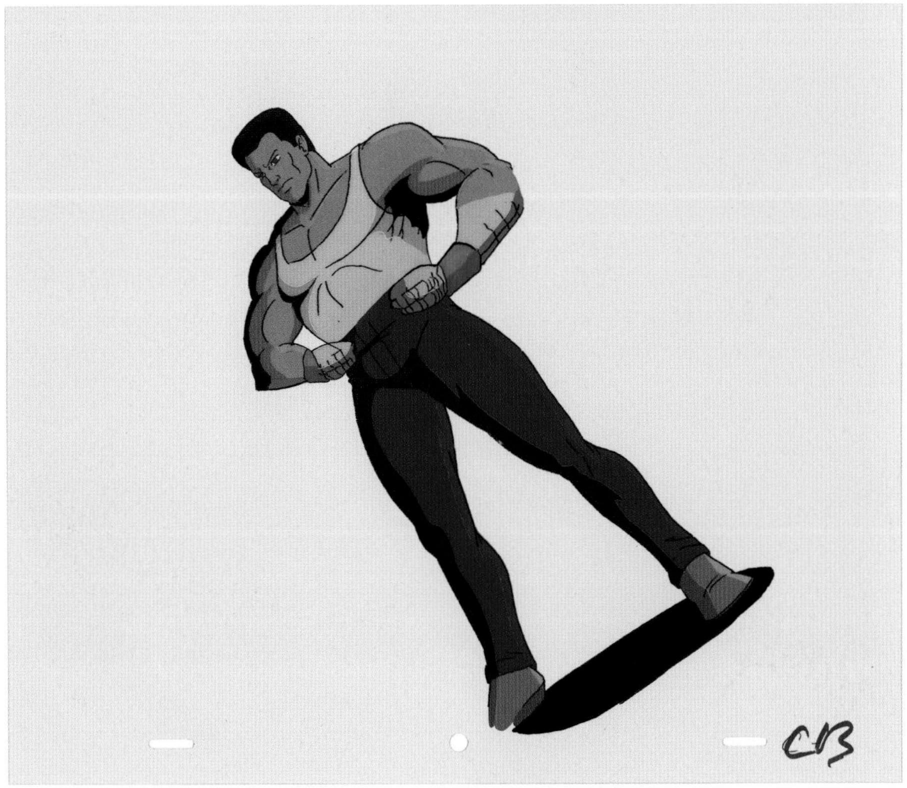
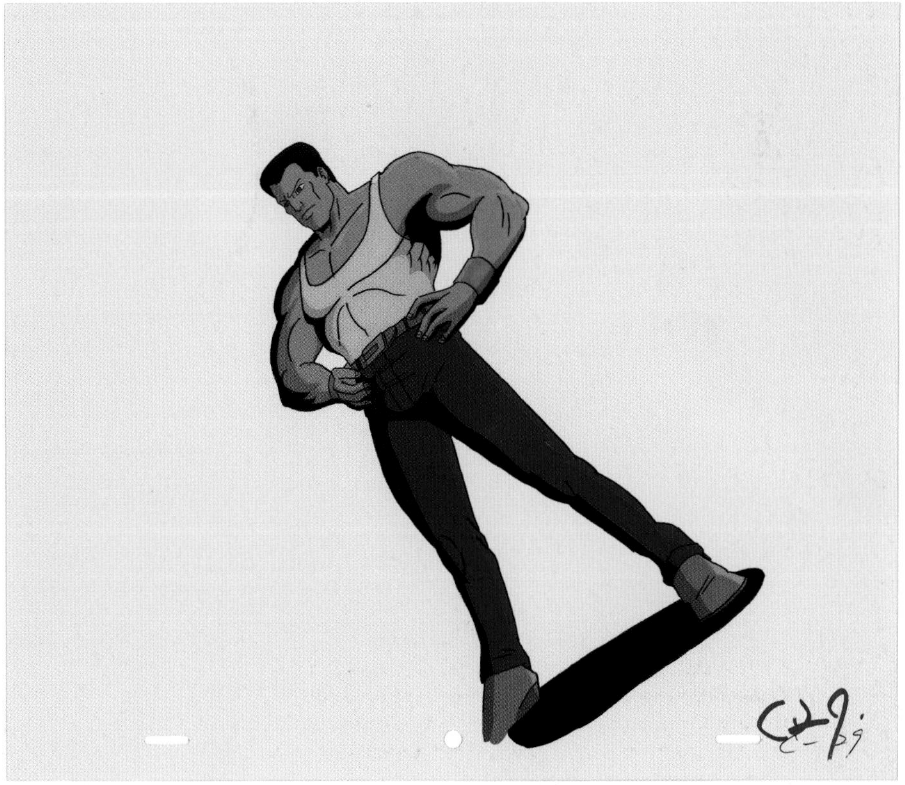

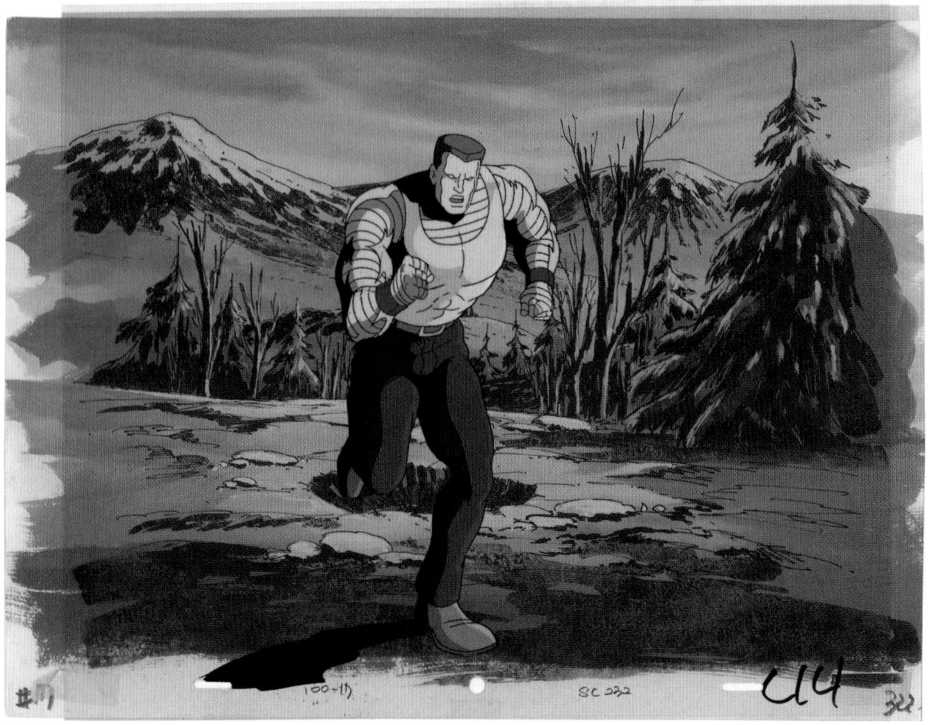

01

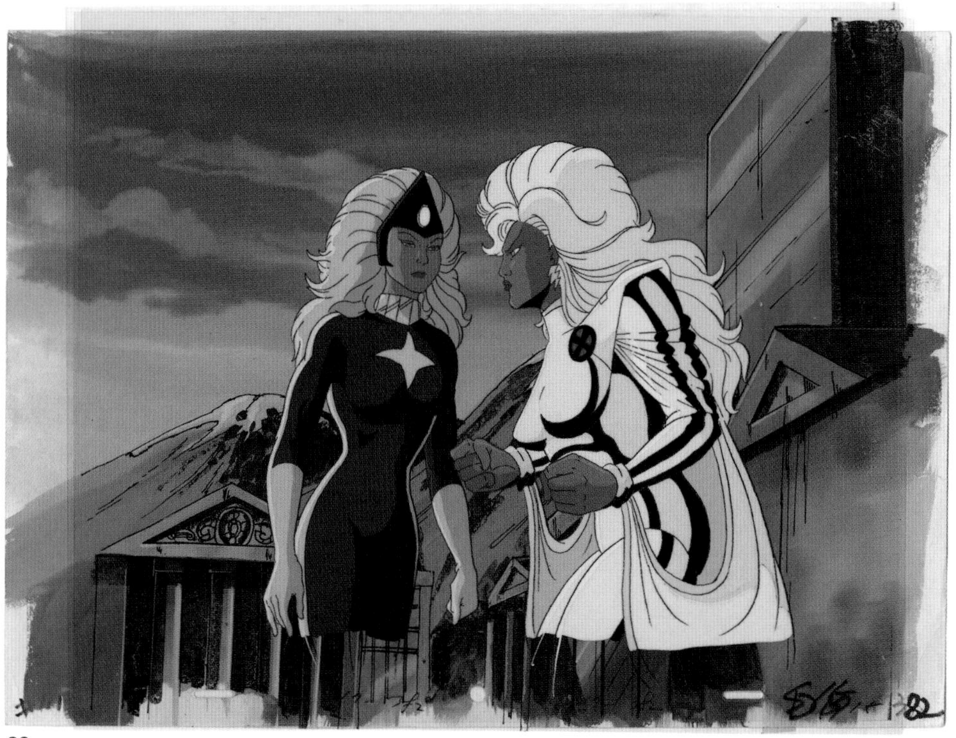

02

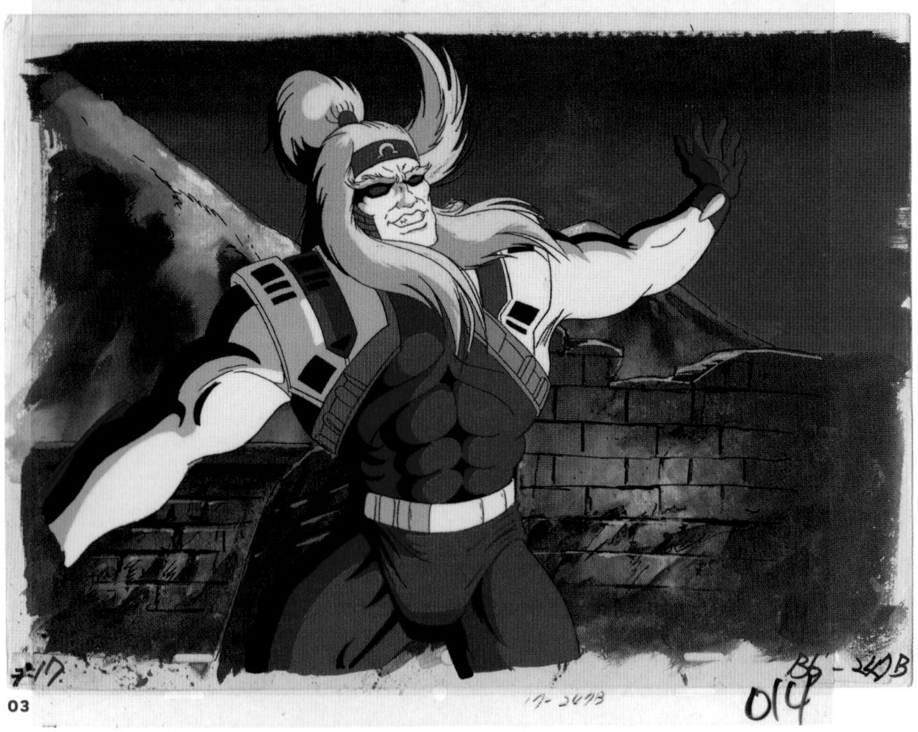

03

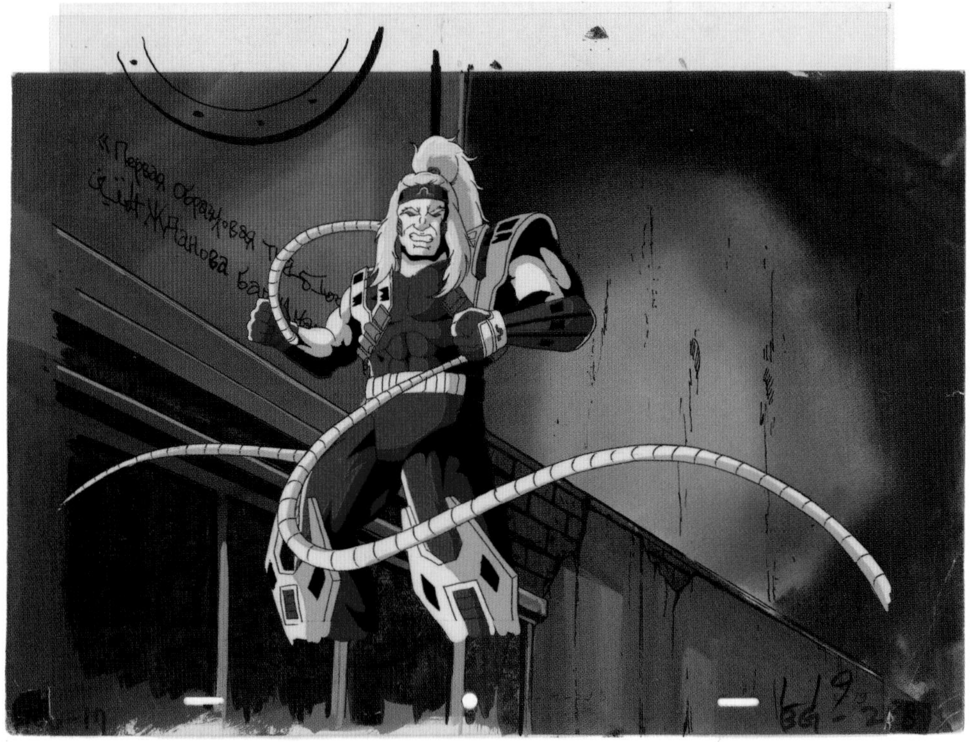

04

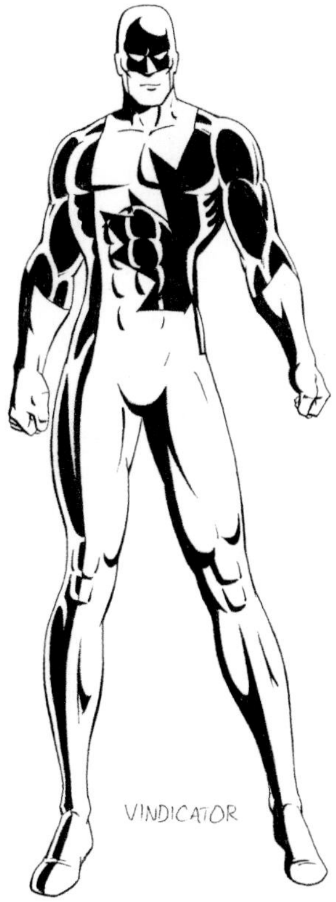
VINDICATOR

05

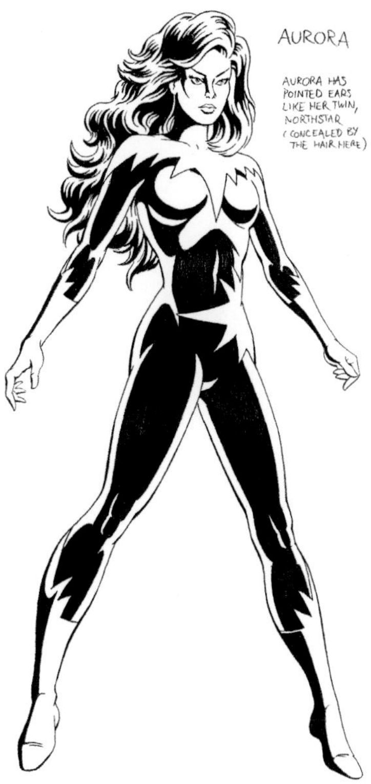
AURORA
AURORA HAS POINTED EARS LIKE HER TWIN, NORTHSTAR (CONCEALED BY THE HAIR HERE)

06

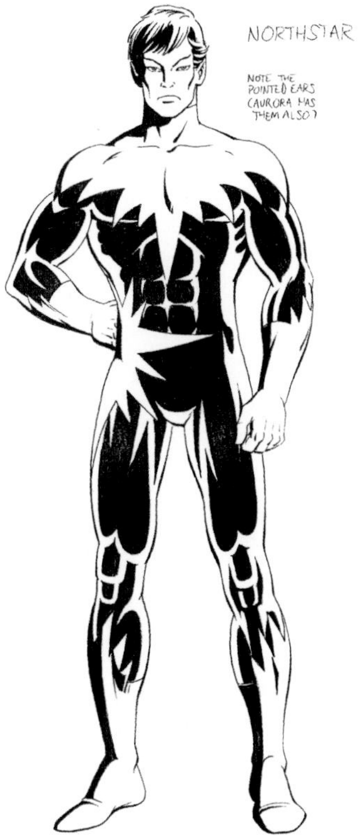
NORTHSTAR
NOTE THE POINTED EARS (AURORA HAS THEM ALSO)

07

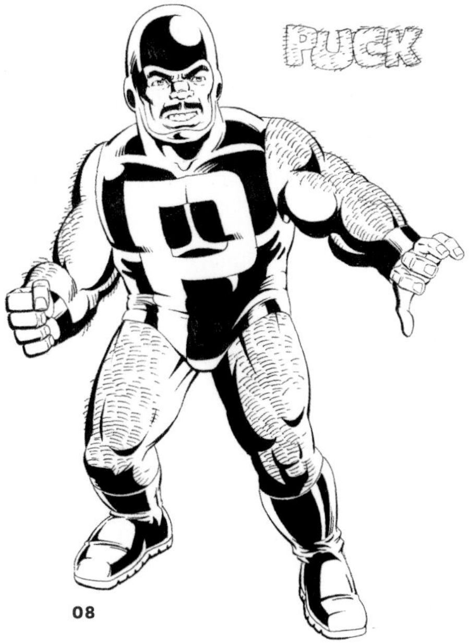
PUCK

08

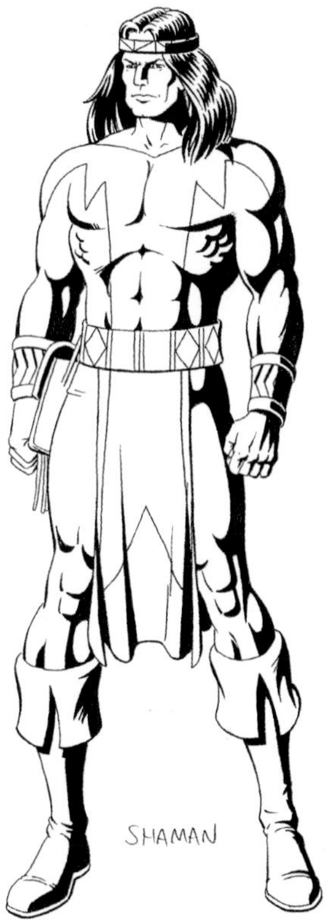
SHAMAN

09

01 Production cel of metal-form Colossus, in rural Russia, rushing to stop Omega Red. **02** Production cel of Russian mutant Darkstar helping Storm stop Omega Red. **03–04** Production cels of Omega Red, the first one missing an overlay of his tentacles. **05–11** Character models of Alpha Flight, a Canadian mutant team with whom Wolverine once worked. Snowbird (10) was not in the script (there was a tight budget limit on speaking parts), but Larry Houston added action with her to make sure the full team was represented. All by Frank Brunner, inked by Mark Lewis. **12** Character model of Heather Hudson, an old friend of Wolverine's. Rough design by Brunner; Lewis didn't get to ink this one.

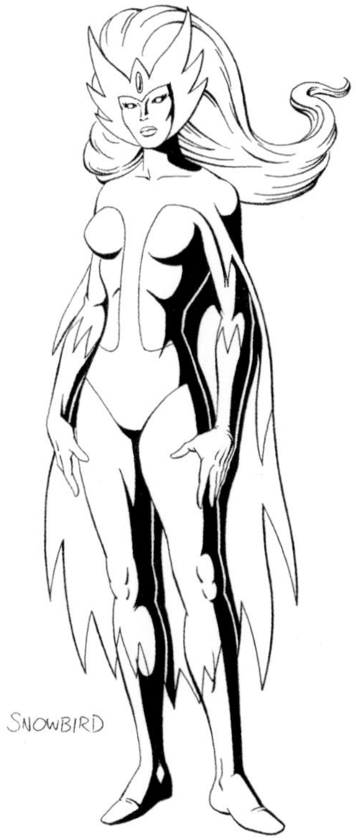
SNOWBIRD

10

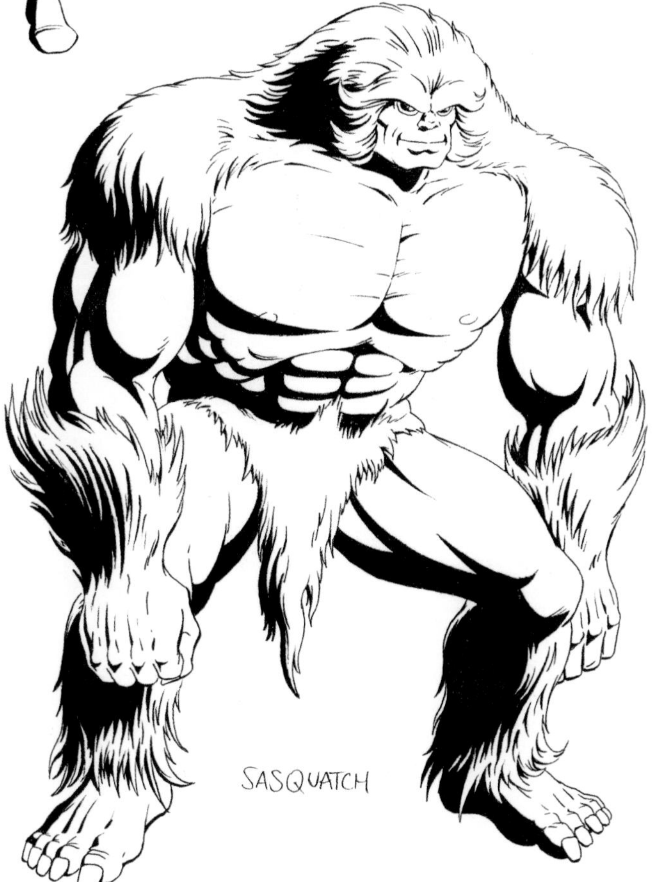
SASQUATCH

11

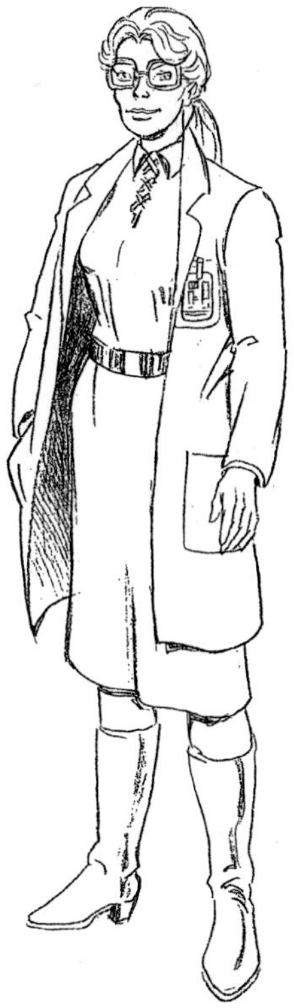

12

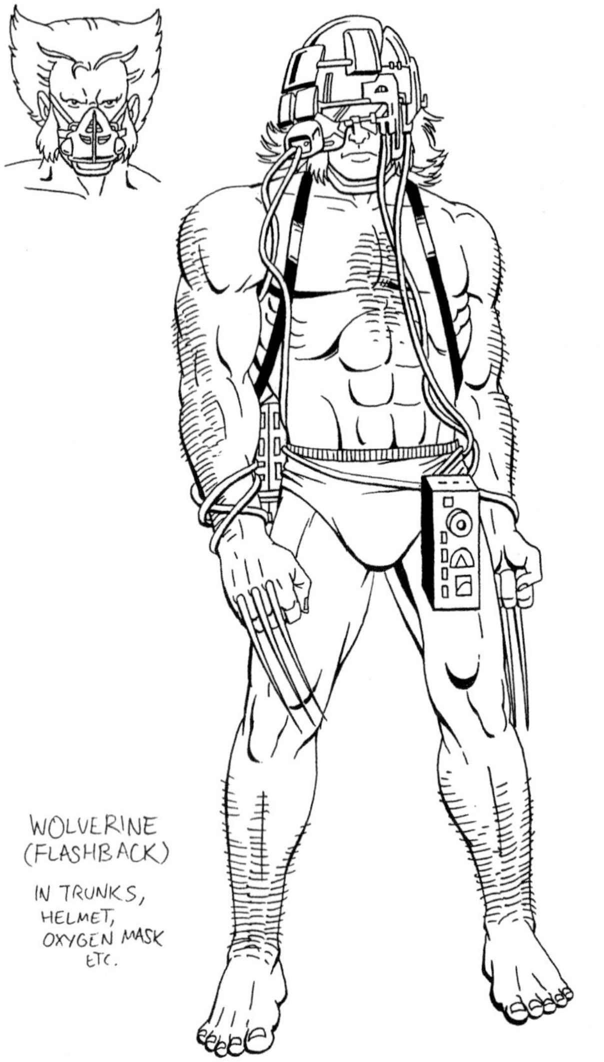
WOLVERINE
(FLASHBACK)
IN TRUNKS,
HELMET,
OXYGEN MASK
ETC.

01

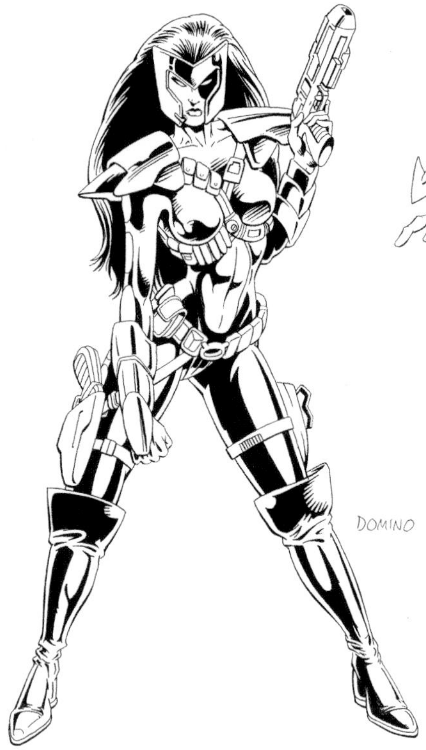
DOMINO

02

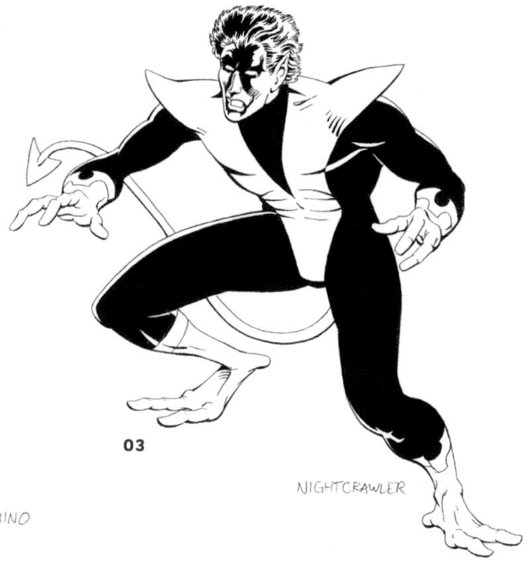
NIGHTCRAWLER

03

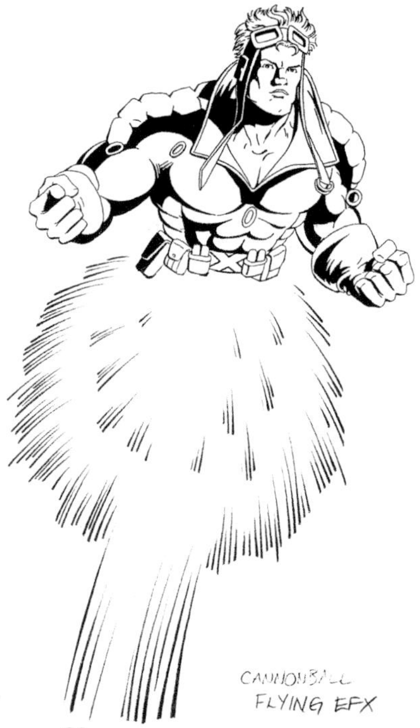
THIS IS AN ANIMATED
JET ROCKET EXHAUST EFX!
CANNONBALL
FLYING EFX

04

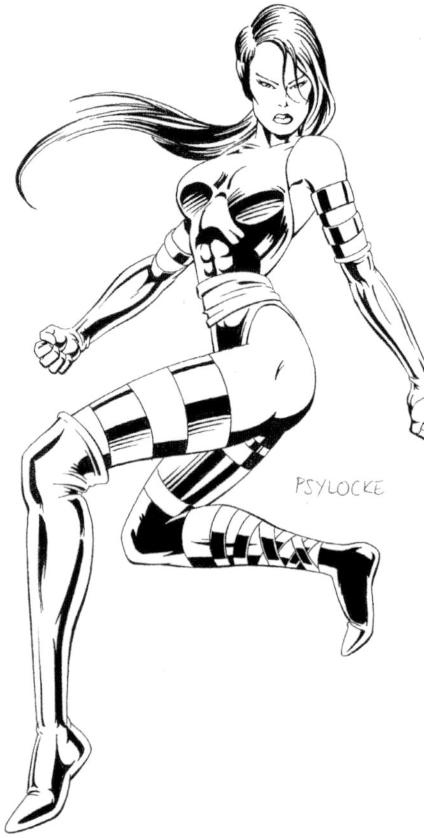
PSYLOCKE

05

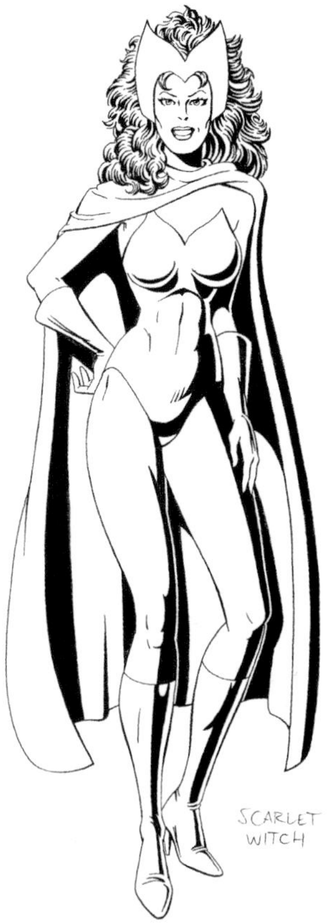
SCARLET
WITCH

06

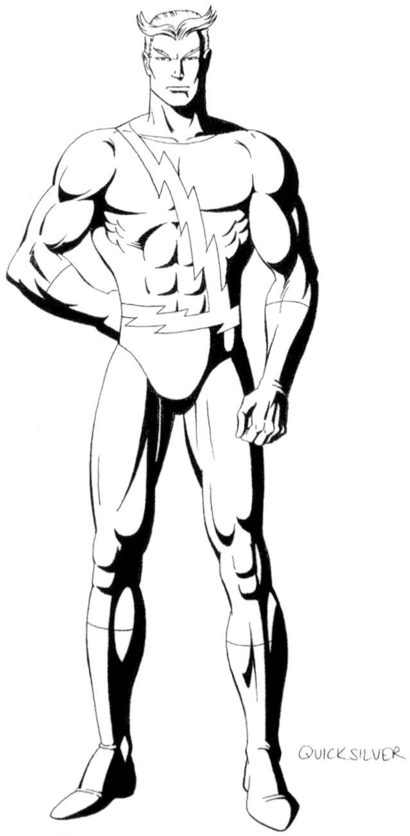
QUICKSILVER

07

01 Character model of flashback of Logan (pre-Wolverine), prepared for the tank where he is turned into a living weapon by fusing Adamantium with his claws-added skeleton, by Frank Brunner. **02–07** As Jean Grey uses Cerebro to allow her mind to search the world for the missing Professor X, these six mutants—major players in the X-Men universe, not yet introduced in our show—flash through her consciousness. By Brunner. **08** Character model of Lava Monster who attacks Cyclops in a Danger Room drill. Nothing is held back here by Brunner. **09** Colored storyboard panel of Omega Red's tentacle attacking Cyclops in an out-of-control Danger Room drill. **10–13** Character models of important people from Gambit's Bayou past. Included here among the Brunner drawings is the only completely original model that Larry Houston designed for the show—the supernatural being known as The External (12). Marvel didn't have a design for her in the comics by the time production began, so Houston improvised. He drew her as a Creole woman.

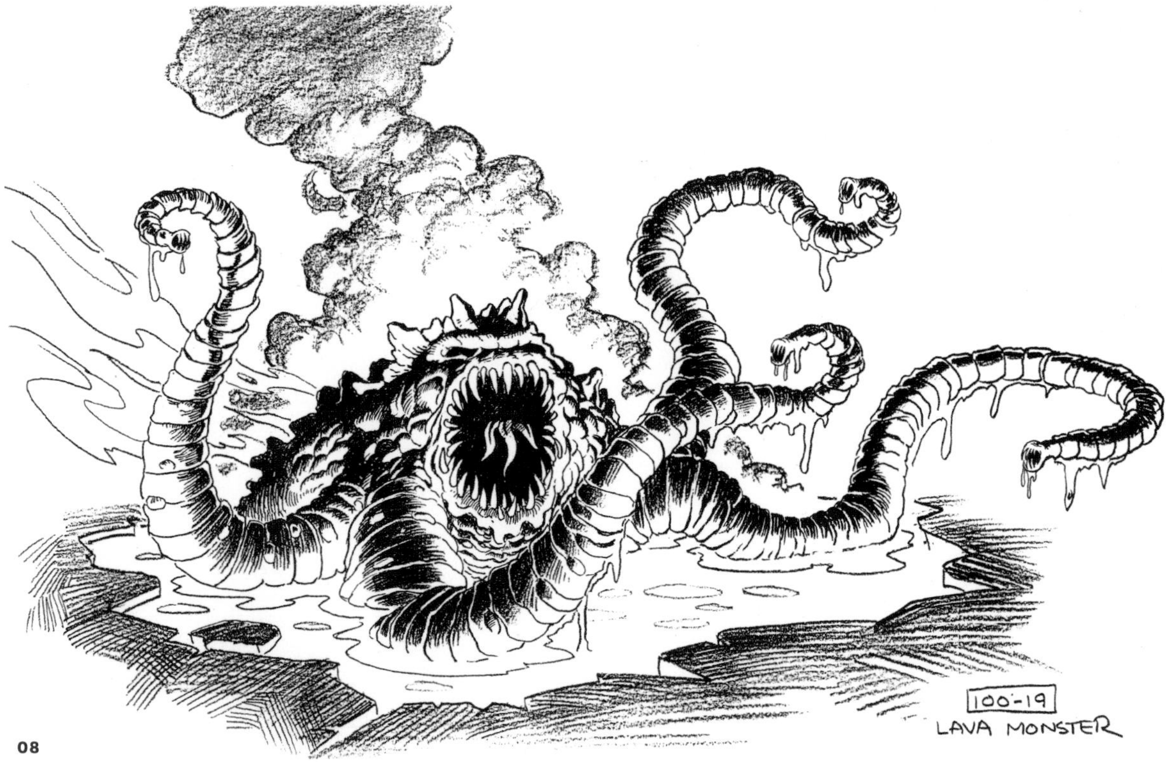
100-19
LAVA MONSTER

08

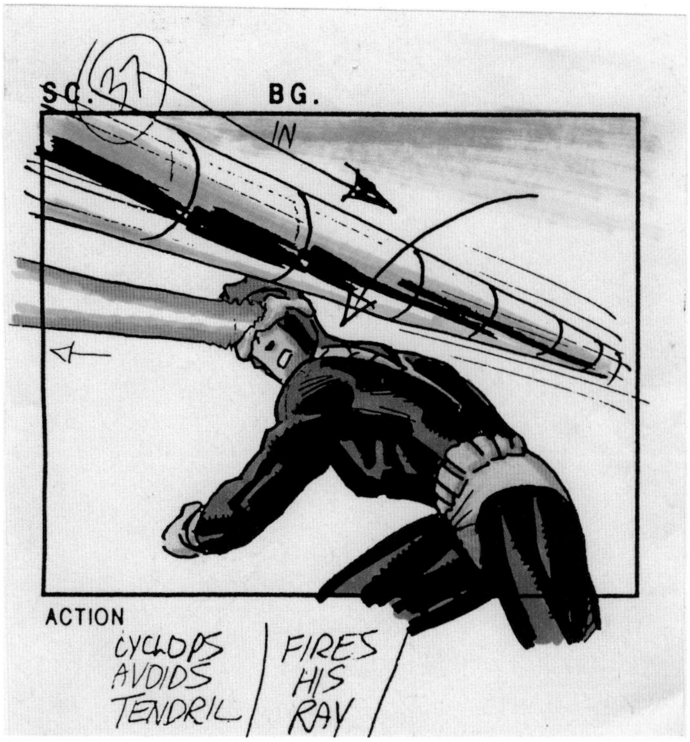
SC. 37
BG.
IN
ACTION
CYCLOPS AVOIDS TENDRIL
FIRES HIS RAY

09

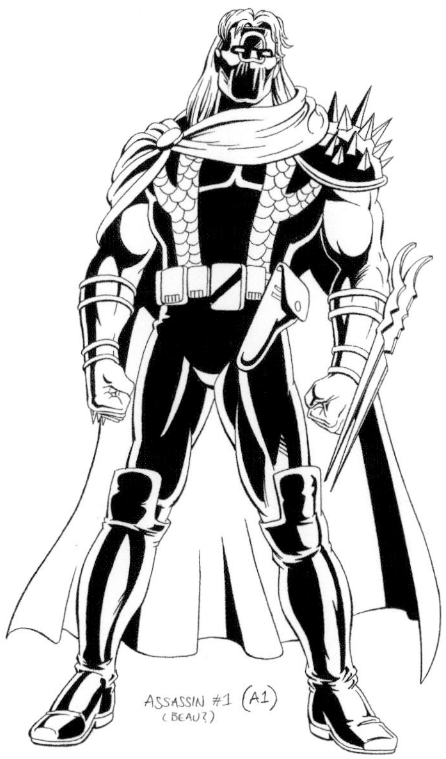
ASSASSIN #1 (A1)
(BEAU?)

10

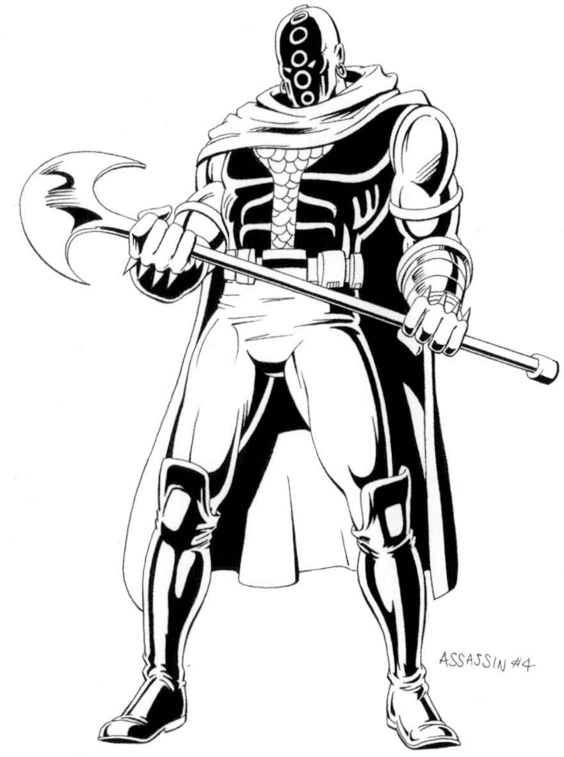
ASSASSIN #4

11

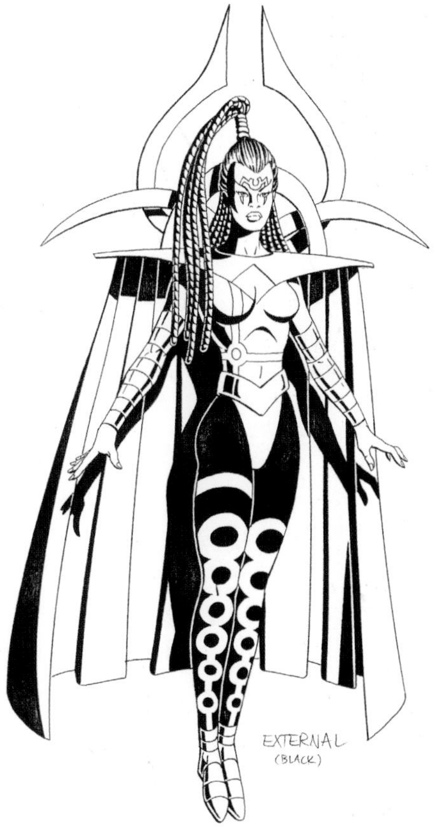
EXTERNAL
(BLACK)

12

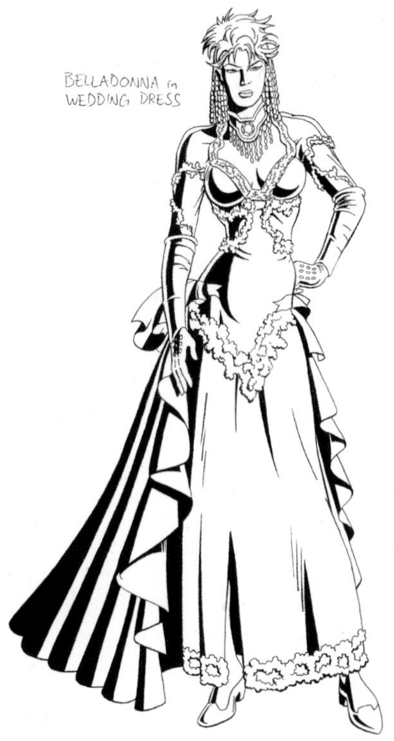
BELLADONNA in WEDDING DRESS

13

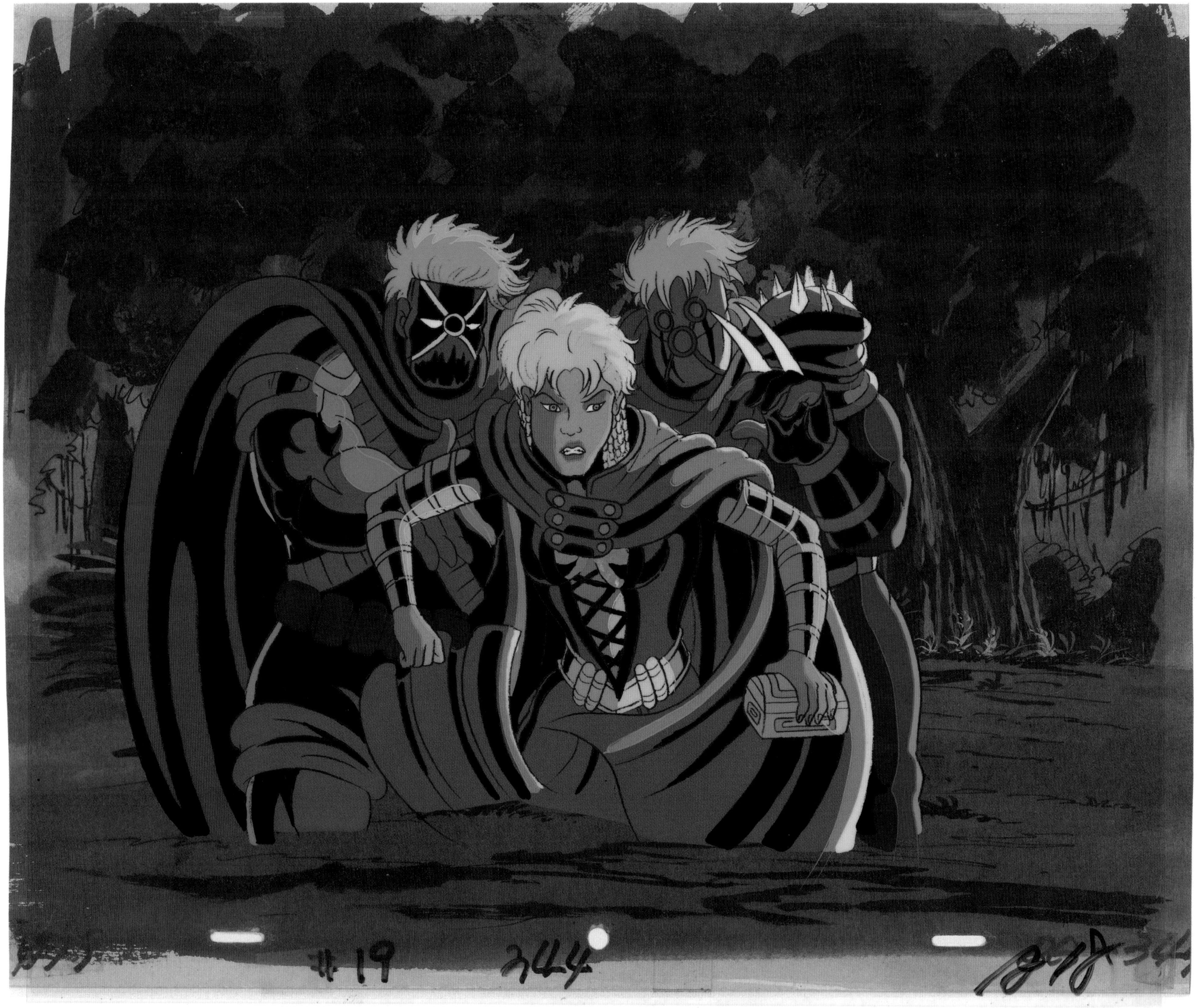

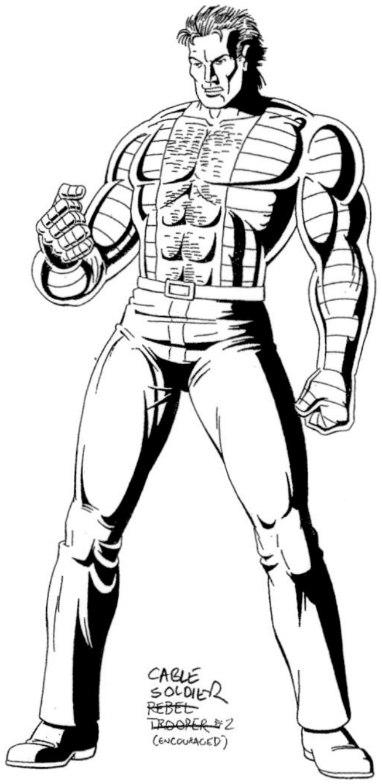
CABLE
SOLDIER
REBEL
TROOPER #2
(ENCOURAGED)

01

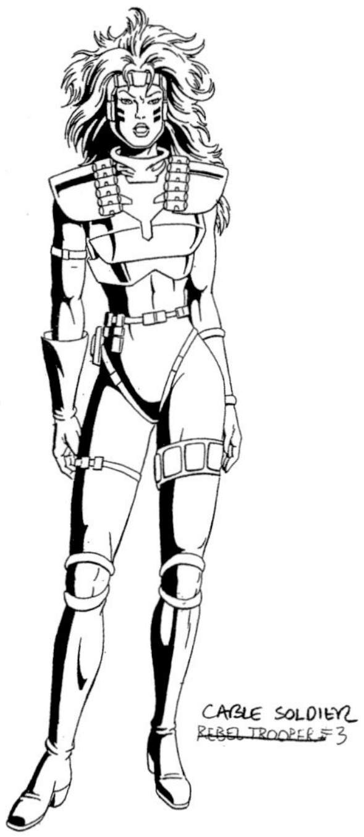
CABLE SOLDIER
REBEL TROOPER #3

02

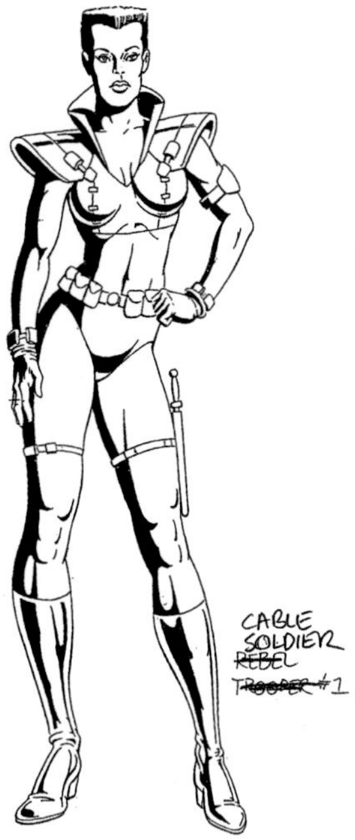
CABLE
SOLDIER
REBEL
TROOPER #1

03

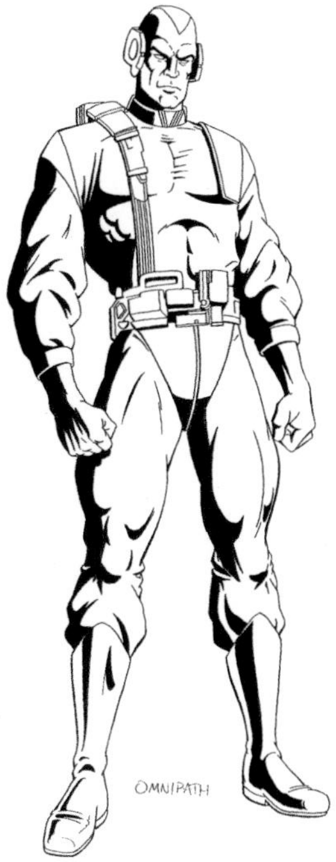
OMNIPATH

04

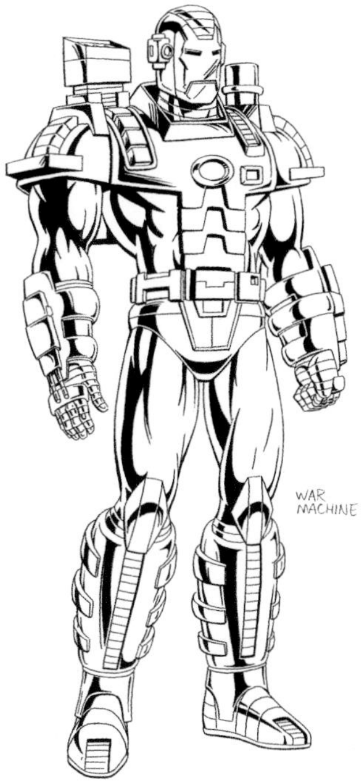
WAR
MACHINE

05

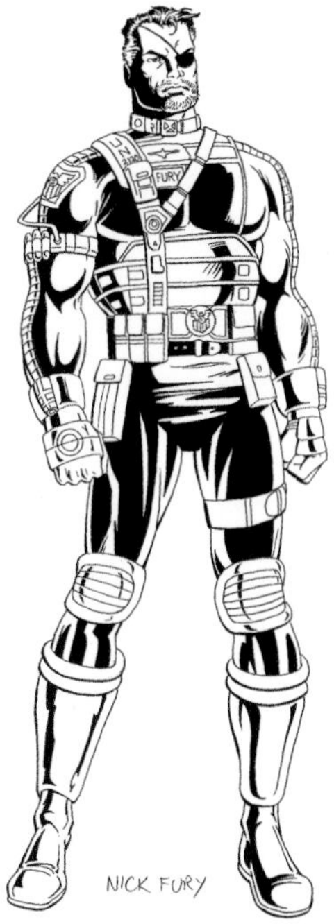
NICK FURY

06

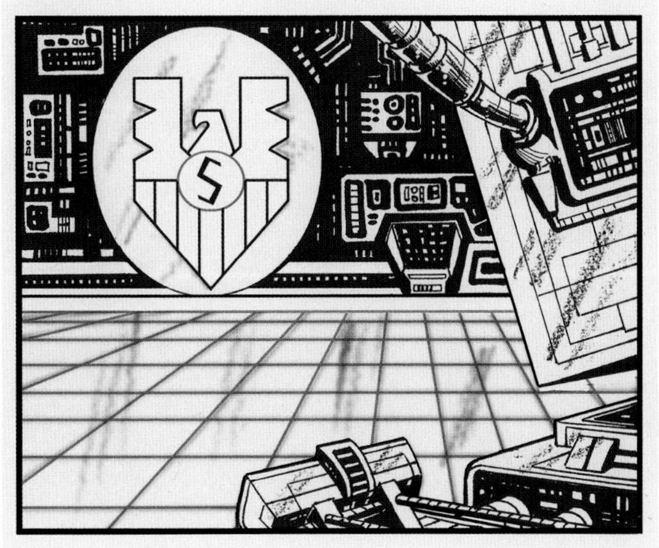

07

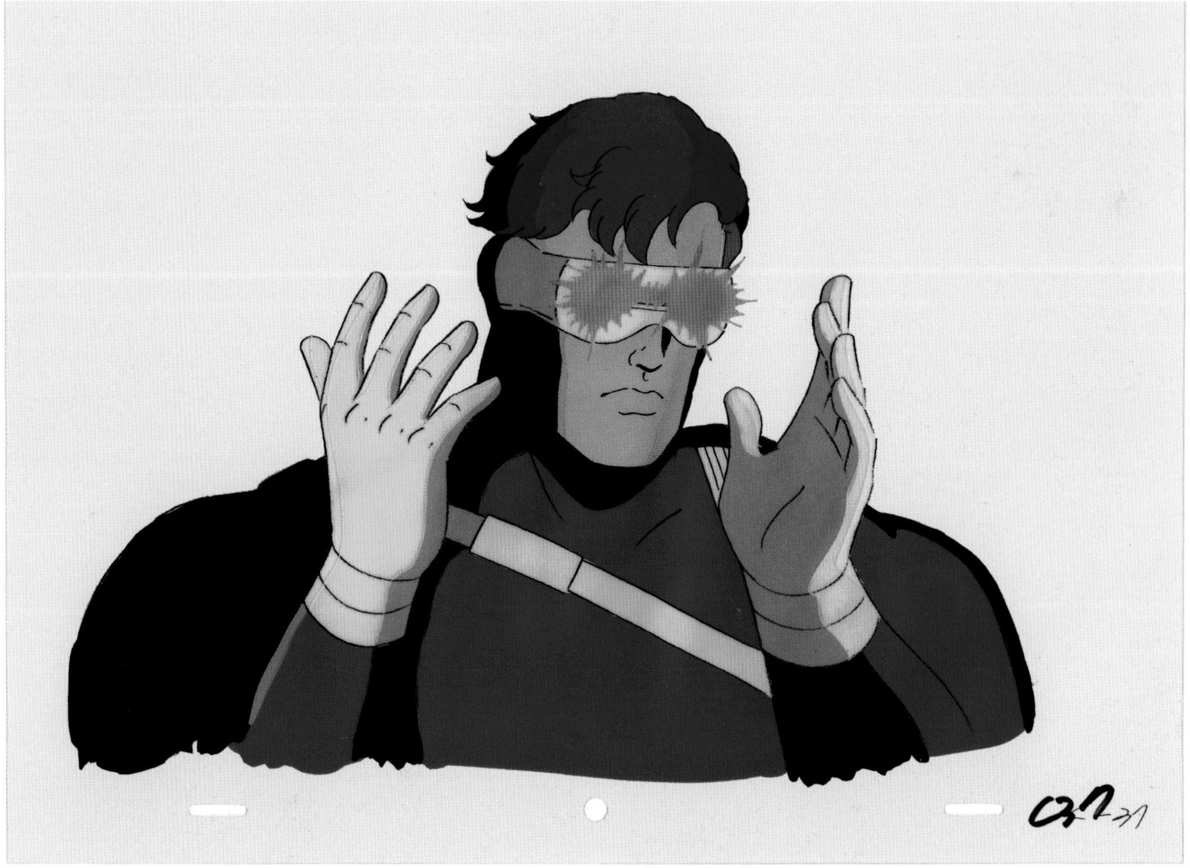

08

OPPOSITE Production cel of Assassins restraining former Gambit fiancée Bella Donna. **01–03** Character models of followers of Cable in the dystopian future by Frank Brunner. **04** Character model of Omnipath by Frank Squillace, cleaned by Mark Lewis. **05** Character model of War Machine by Frank Brunner, inked by Mark Lewis. **06** Character model of Nick Fury, designed and cleaned by Squillace. **07** Misc. interior background of Fury's S.H.I.E.L.D. headquarters, designed and cleaned by Squillace. **08** Production cel of Cyclops powering up his eye beam before blowing a tunnel into the ground below a building.

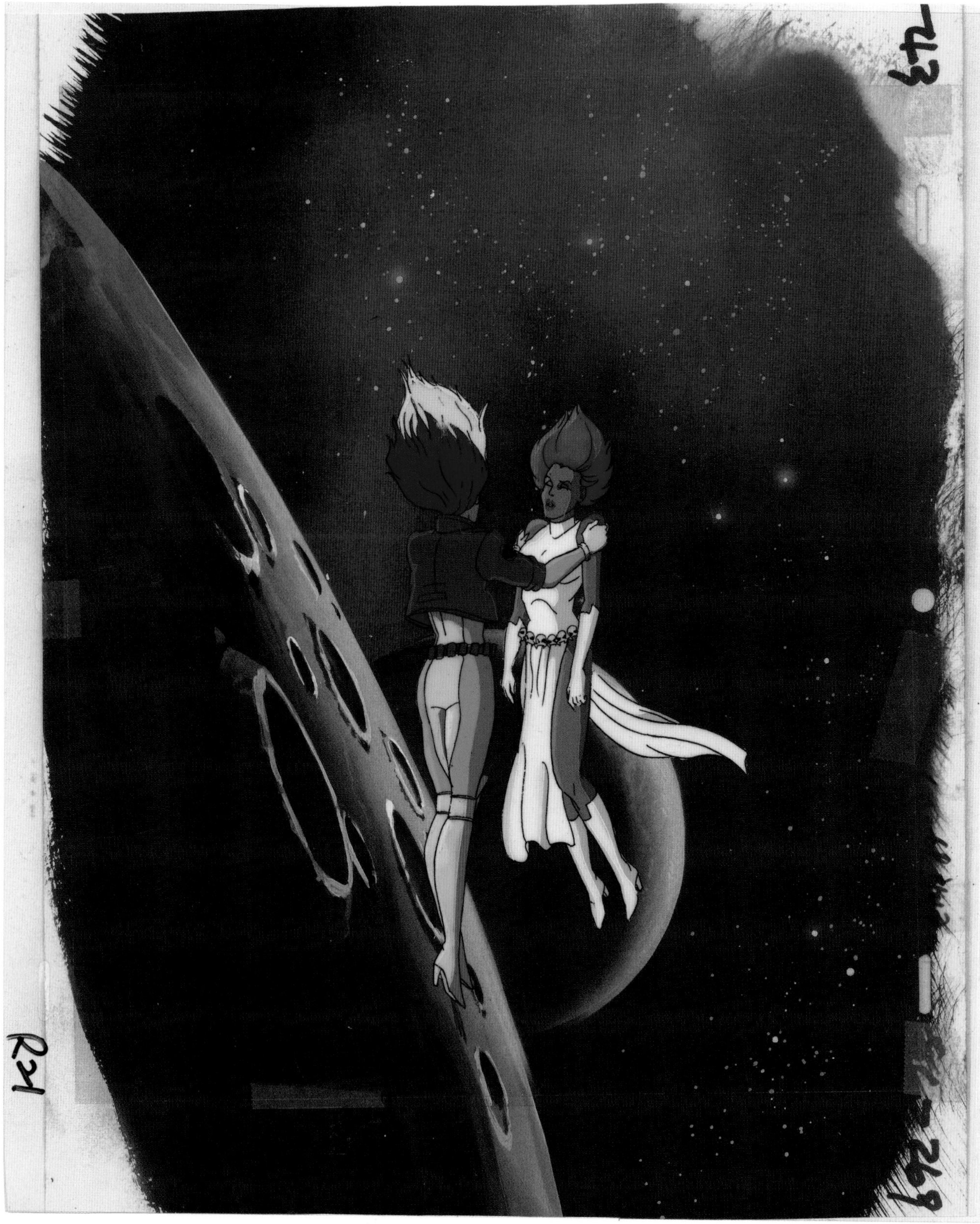

01

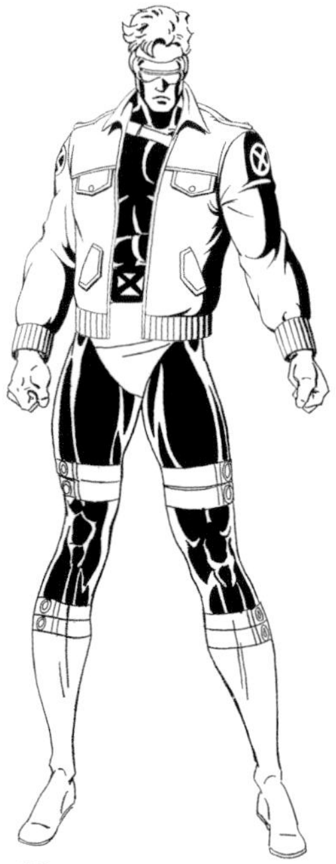

02

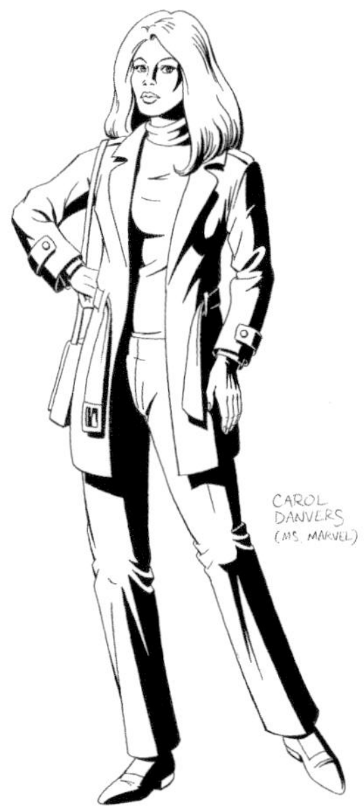
CAROL
DANVERS
(MS. MARVEL)

03

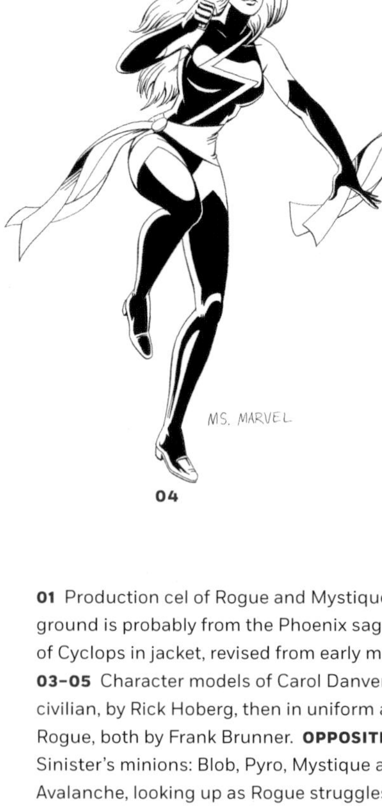
MS. MARVEL

04

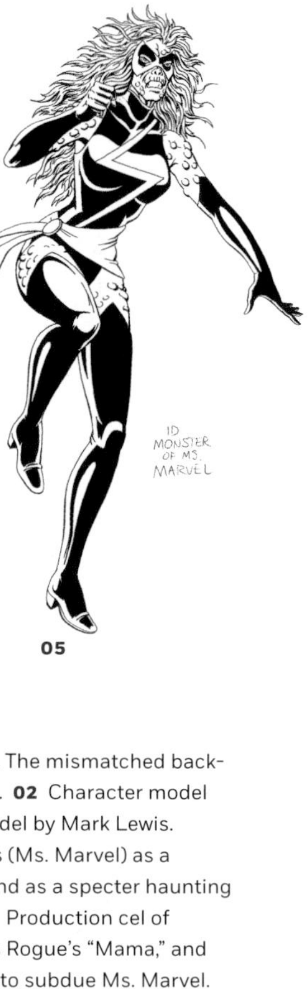
ID
MONSTER
OF MS.
MARVEL

05

01 Production cel of Rogue and Mystique. The mismatched background is probably from the Phoenix saga. **02** Character model of Cyclops in jacket, revised from early model by Mark Lewis. **03–05** Character models of Carol Danvers (Ms. Marvel) as a civilian, by Rick Hoberg, then in uniform and as a specter haunting Rogue, both by Frank Brunner. **OPPOSITE** Production cel of Sinister's minions: Blob, Pyro, Mystique as Rogue's "Mama," and Avalanche, looking up as Rogue struggles to subdue Ms. Marvel.

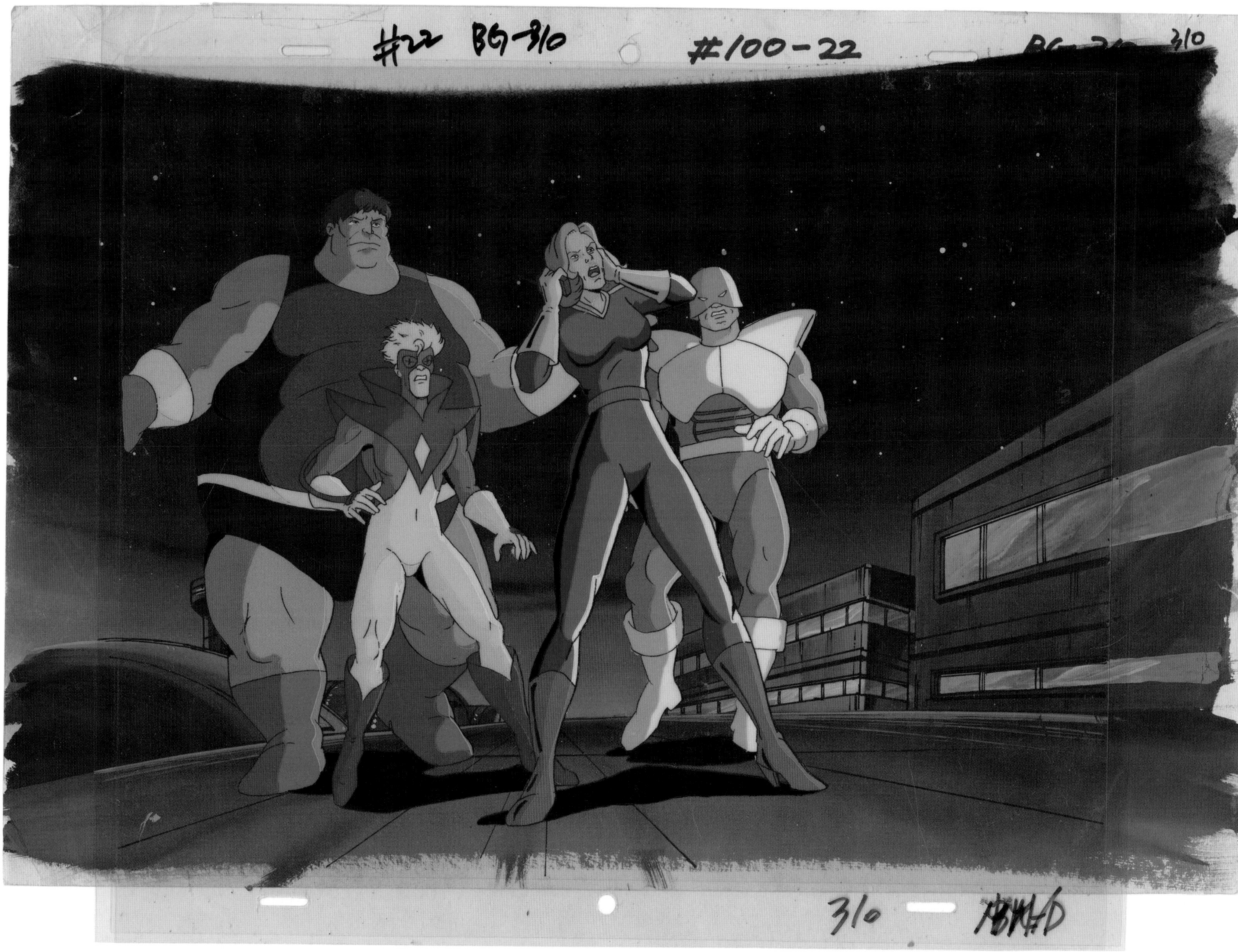

#22 BG-310
#100-22
310
310

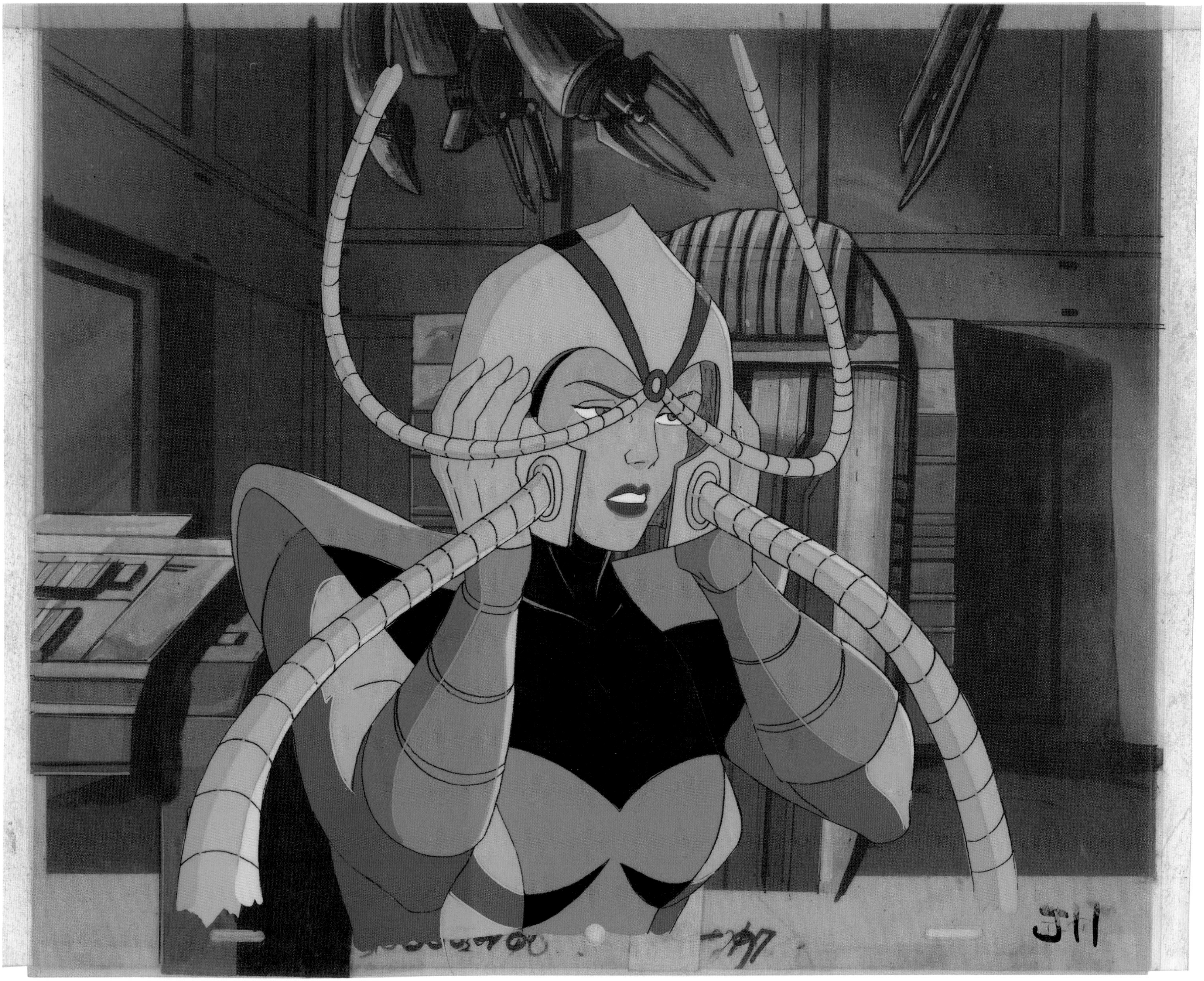

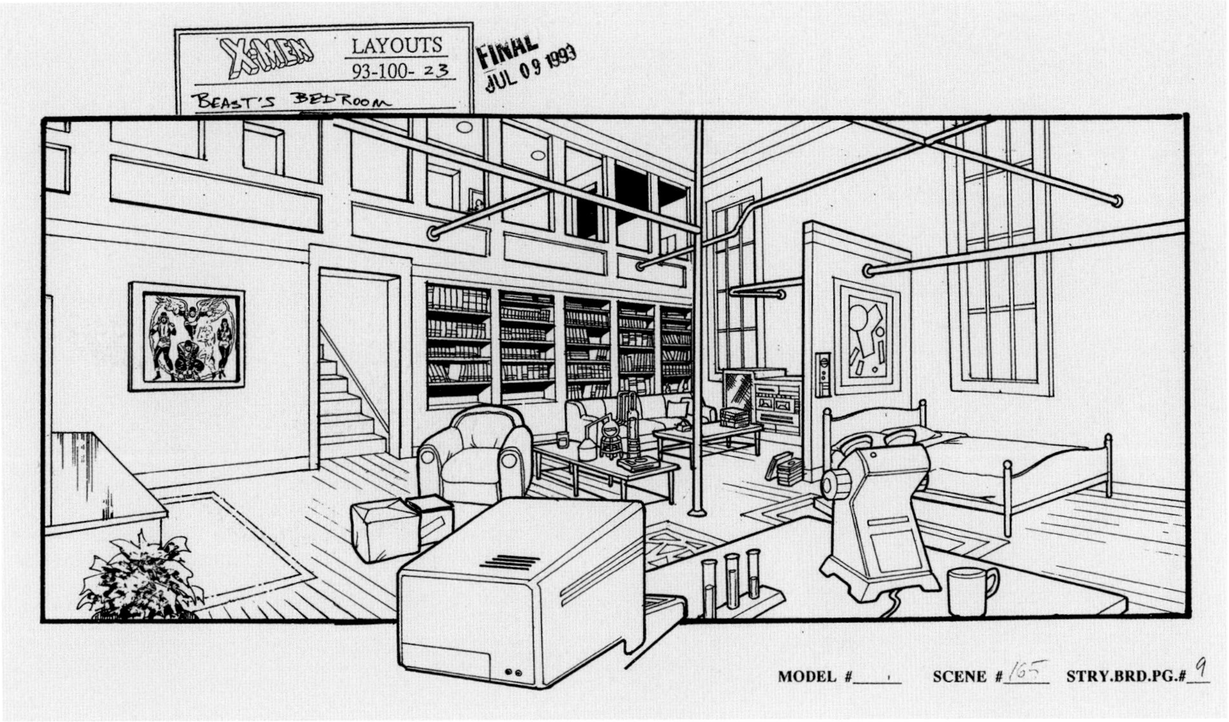

X-MEN
LAYOUTS
93-100- 23
BEAST'S BEDROOM
FINAL
JUL 09 1993
MODEL #
SCENE # 165
STRY.BRD.PG.# 9

01

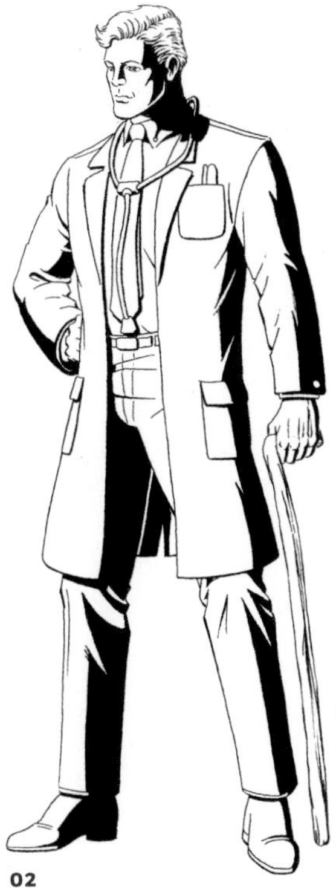

DOCTOR BOHLSON

02

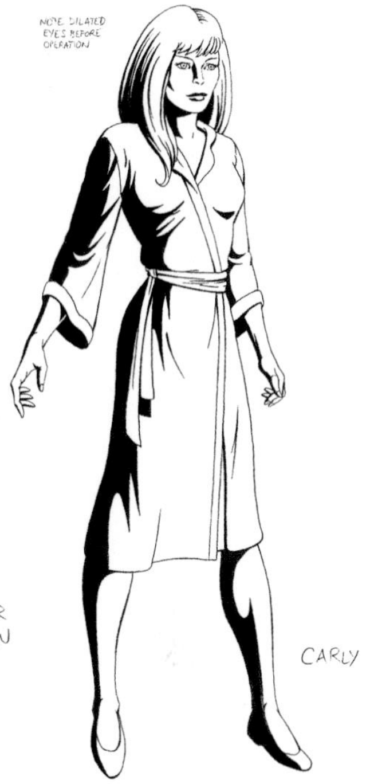

NOTE DILATED EYES BEFORE OPERATION
CARLY

03

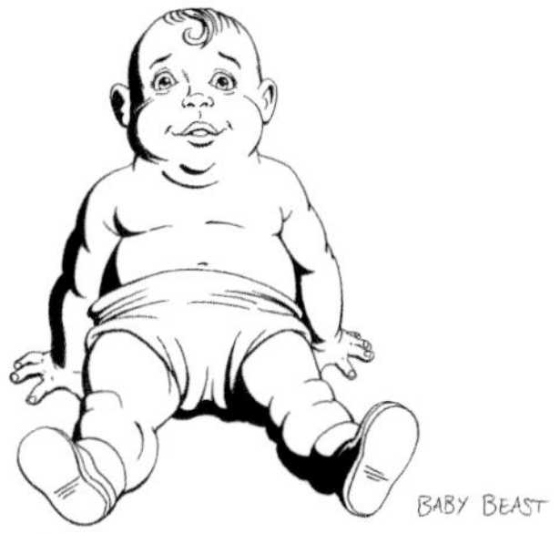

BABY BEAST

04

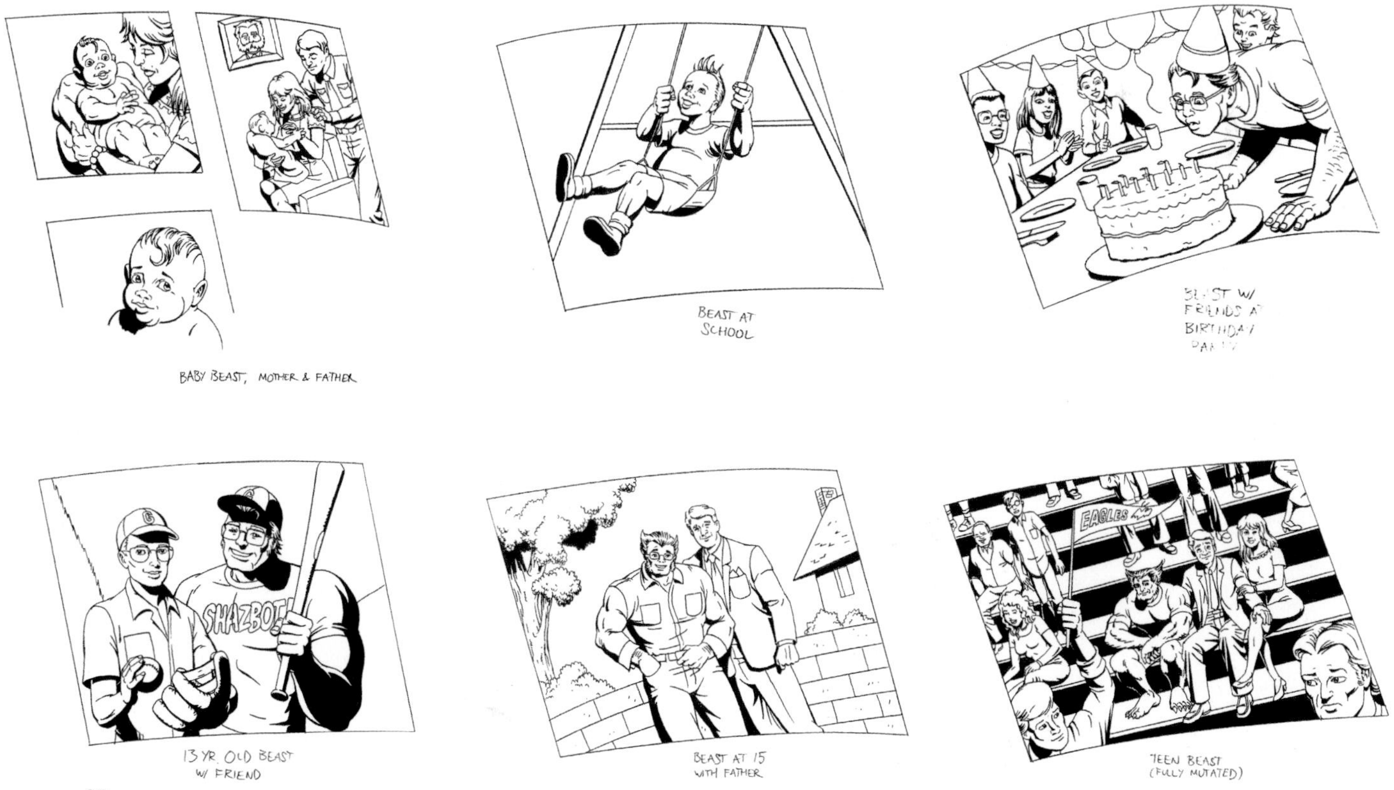

BABY BEAST, MOTHER & FATHER
BEAST AT SCHOOL
SHAZBOT!
13 YR. OLD BEAST W/ FRIEND
BEAST AT 15 WITH FATHER
EAGLES
TEEN BEAST (FULLY MUTATED)

05

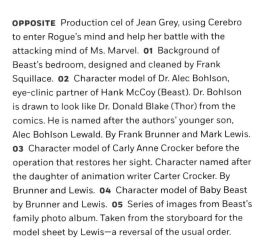

OPPOSITE Production cel of Jean Grey, using Cerebro to enter Rogue's mind and help her battle with the attacking mind of Ms. Marvel. **01** Background of Beast's bedroom, designed and cleaned by Frank Squillace. **02** Character model of Dr. Alec Bohlson, eye-clinic partner of Hank McCoy (Beast). Dr. Bohlson is drawn to look like Dr. Donald Blake (Thor) from the comics. He is named after the authors' younger son, Alec Bohlson Lewald. By Frank Brunner and Mark Lewis. **03** Character model of Carly Anne Crocker before the operation that restores her sight. Character named after the daughter of animation writer Carter Crocker. By Brunner and Lewis. **04** Character model of Baby Beast by Brunner and Lewis. **05** Series of images from Beast's family photo album. Taken from the storyboard for the model sheet by Lewis—a reversal of the usual order.

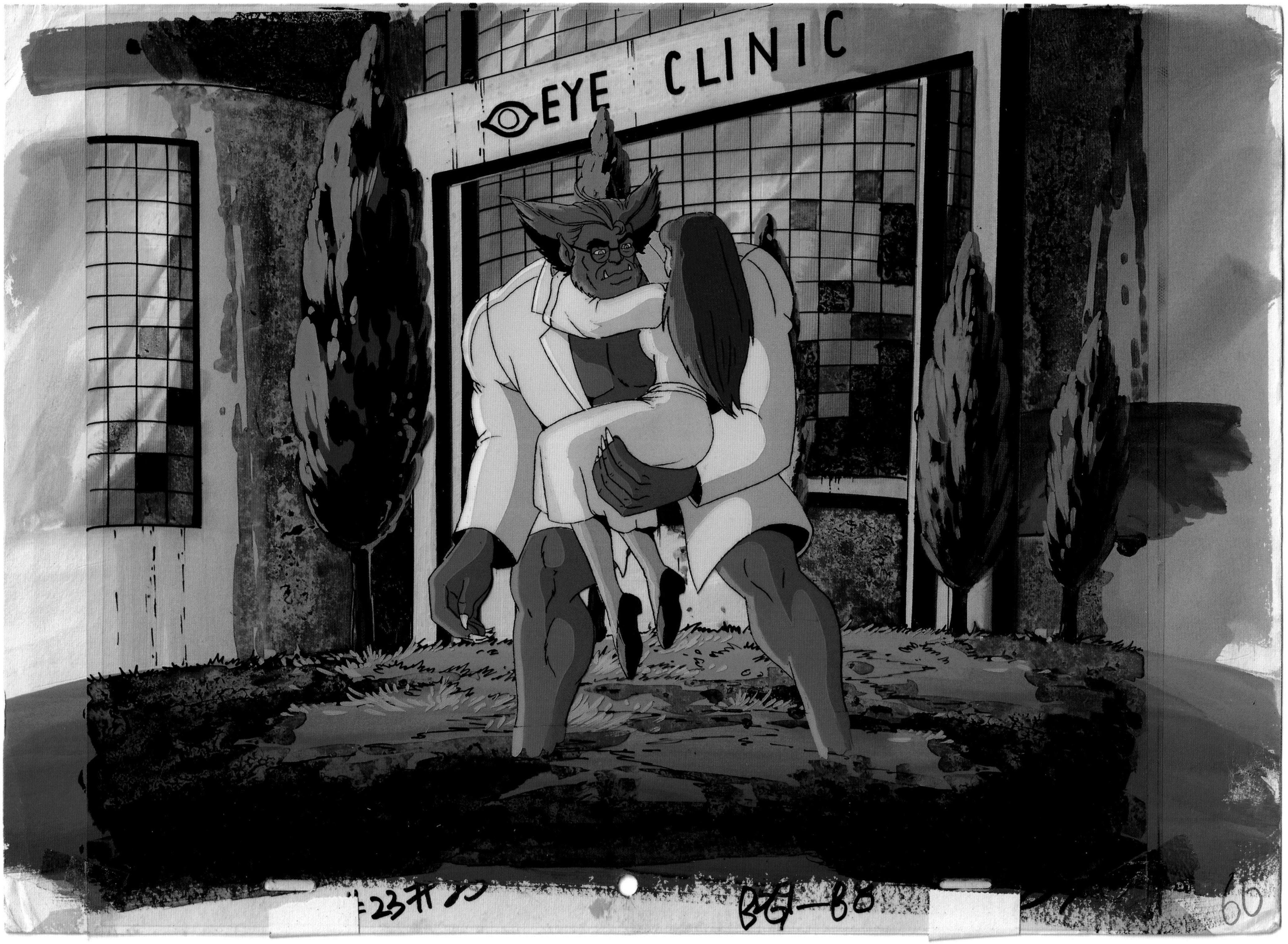
EYE CLINIC
#23 #
BG-68
60

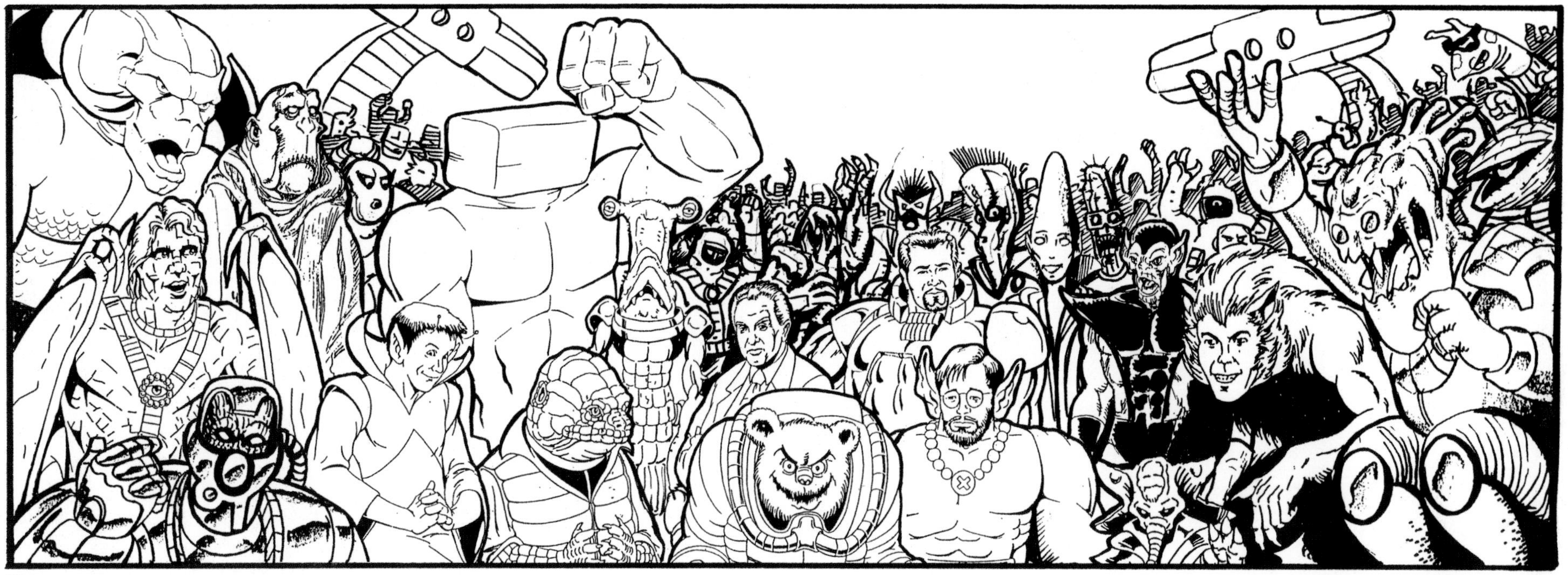

01

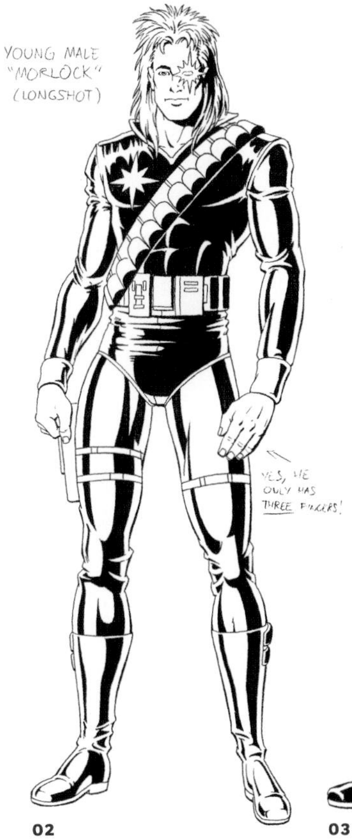
YOUNG MALE "MORLOCK" (LONGSHOT)
YES, HE ONLY HAS THREE FINGERS!

02

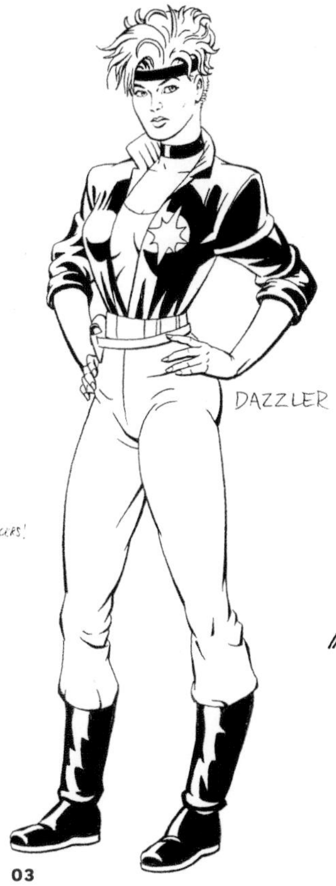
DAZZLER

03

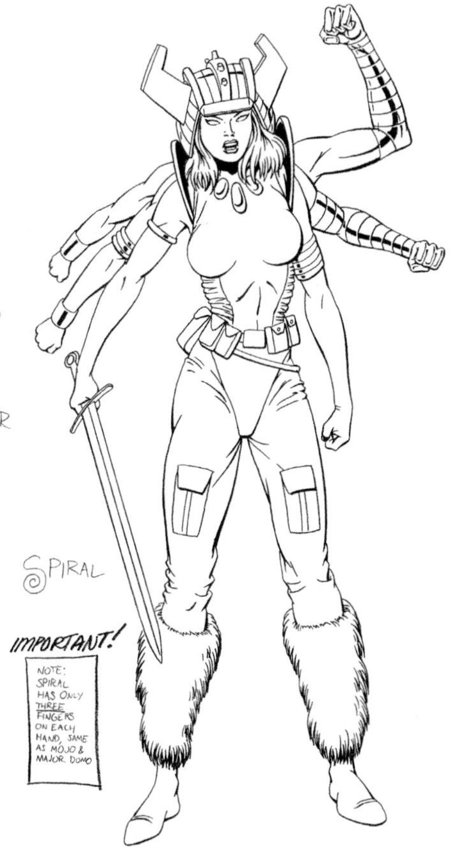
SPIRAL
IMPORTANT!
NOTE: SPIRAL HAS ONLY THREE FINGERS ON EACH HAND, SAME AS MOJO & MAJOR DOMO

04

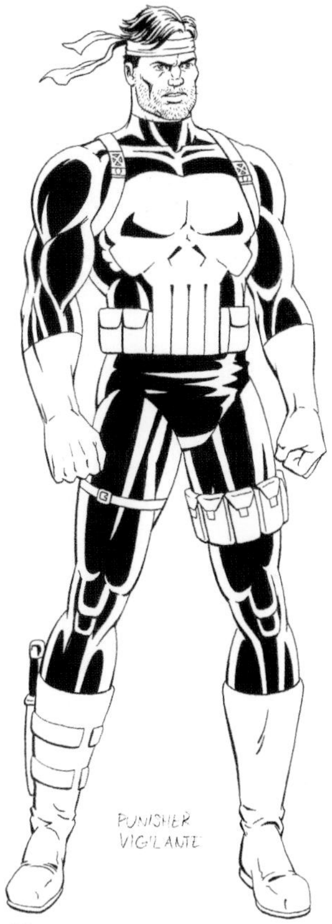
PUNISHER VIGILANTE

05

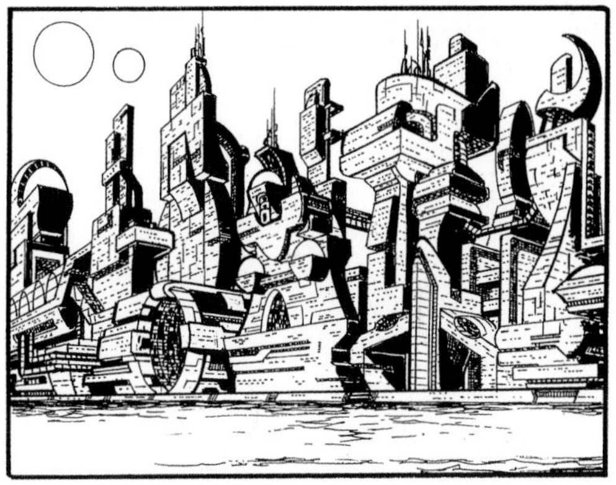

06

OPPOSITE Beast saving Carly Anne from the Friends of Humanity attack on his eye clinic. **01** Alien crowd in Mojo's world is populated with many creatures bearing the faces of *X-Men: TAS* staff: Frank Brunner, Frank Squillace, Mark Lewis, Scott Thomas, and Kurt Weldon. It is the work of many artists, assembled by Squillace. A center cameo appearance is of the immortal Jack Kirby; sadly, this episode first aired the week Kirby died. **02–05** Character models from Mojo's planet. It's odd that Dazzler (04) was used in Mojo World (no dialogue), when she then was used later on Earth, with no explanation given, in our Dark Phoenix saga. This was probably an "artist cameo addition," not called for in the script. All penciled by Brunner, with cleanup on the Longshot (03) model and inks by Lewis. **06** Background layout of twin-sunned Mojo world, designed and cleaned by Squillace.

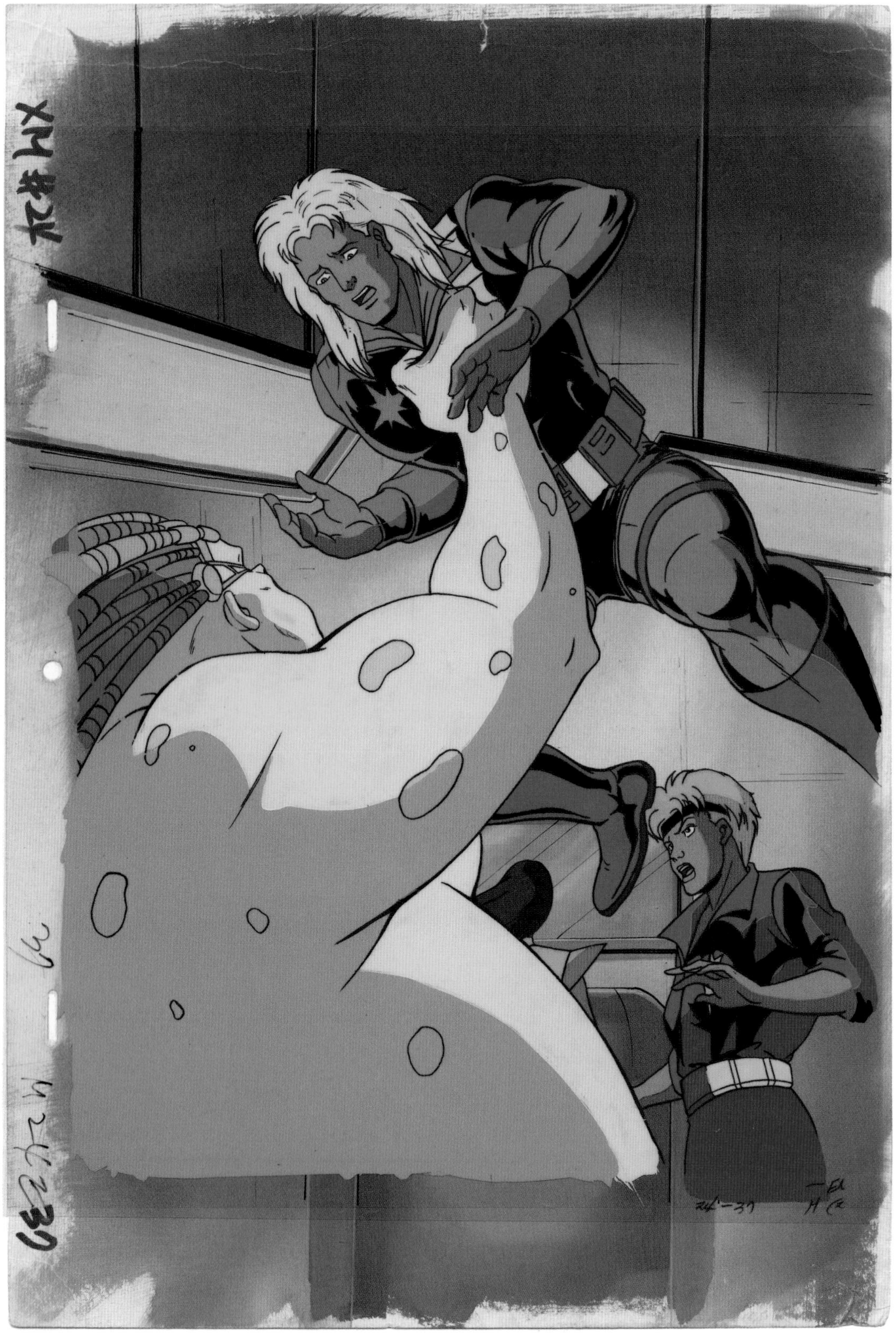

01

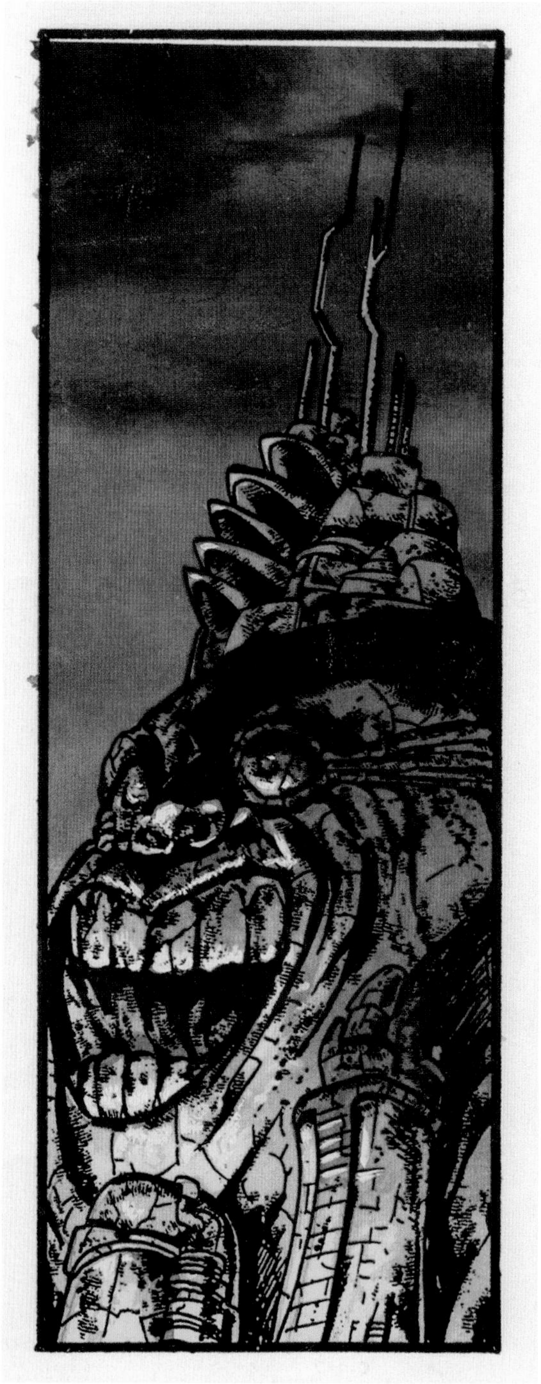

02

01 Production cel of Mojo abusing Longshot in front of Dazzler. **02** Production cel of the outer walls of Mojo city (aka "Mojo tower"), designed and cleaned by Frank Squillace, colored by Dennis Venizelos. **OPPOSITE** Production cel of Beast lecturing Mojo on the dangers of absolute power.

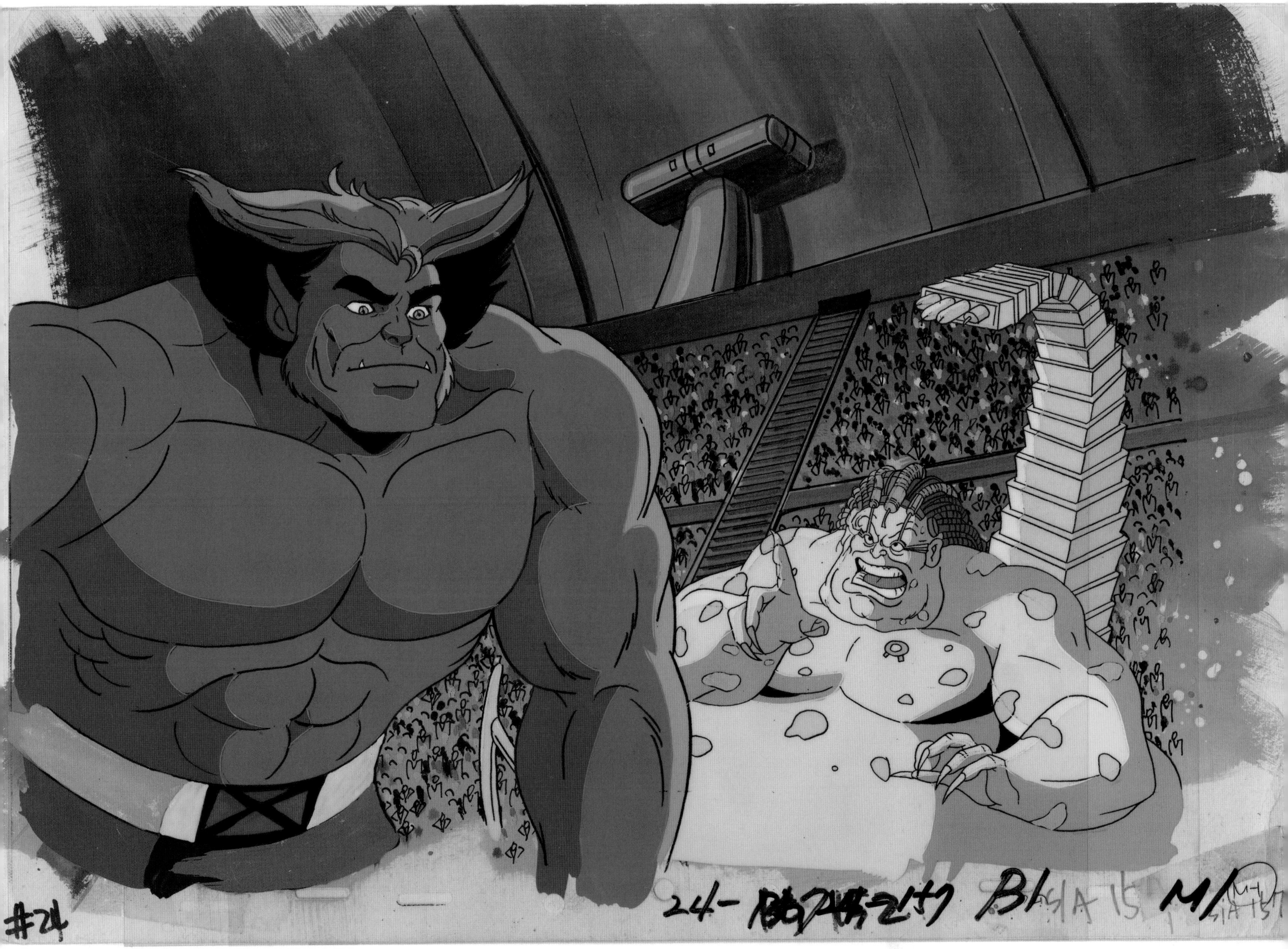
#24

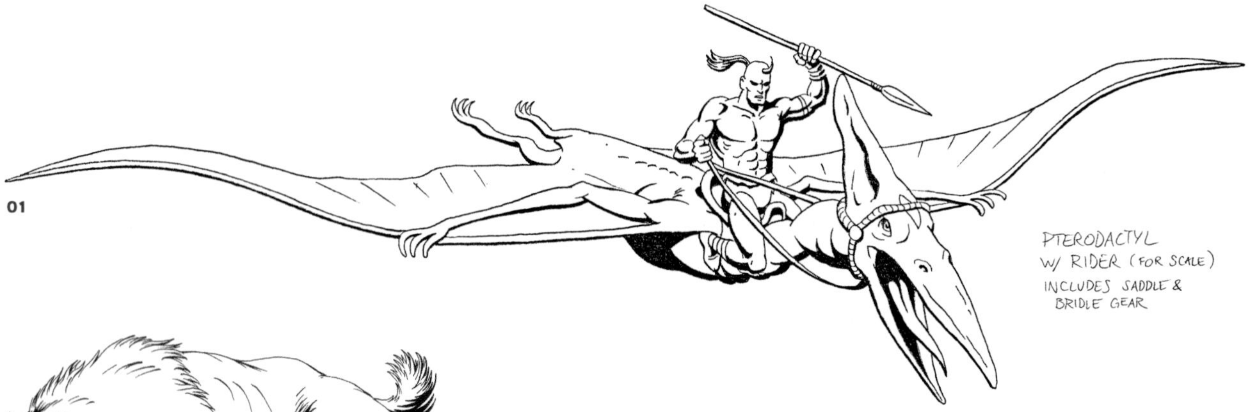
PTERODACTYL
W/ RIDER (FOR SCALE)
INCLUDES SADDLE & BRIDLE GEAR

01

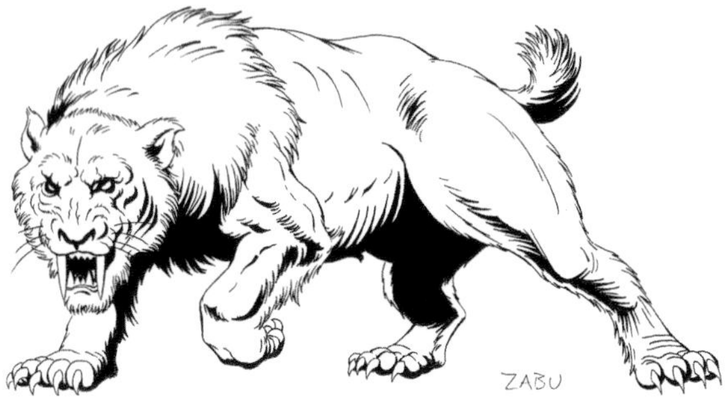
ZABU

02

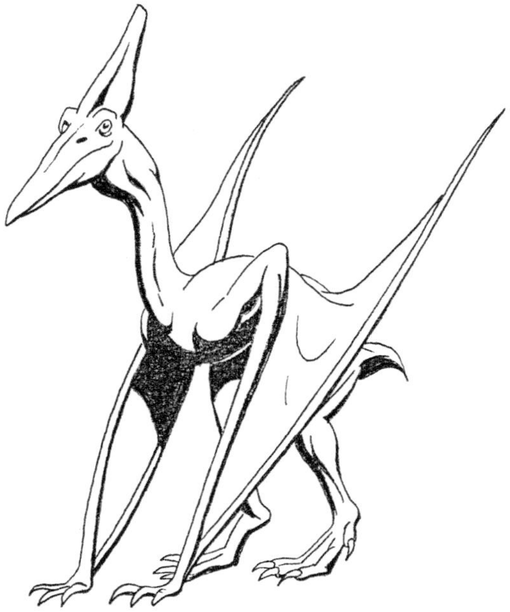

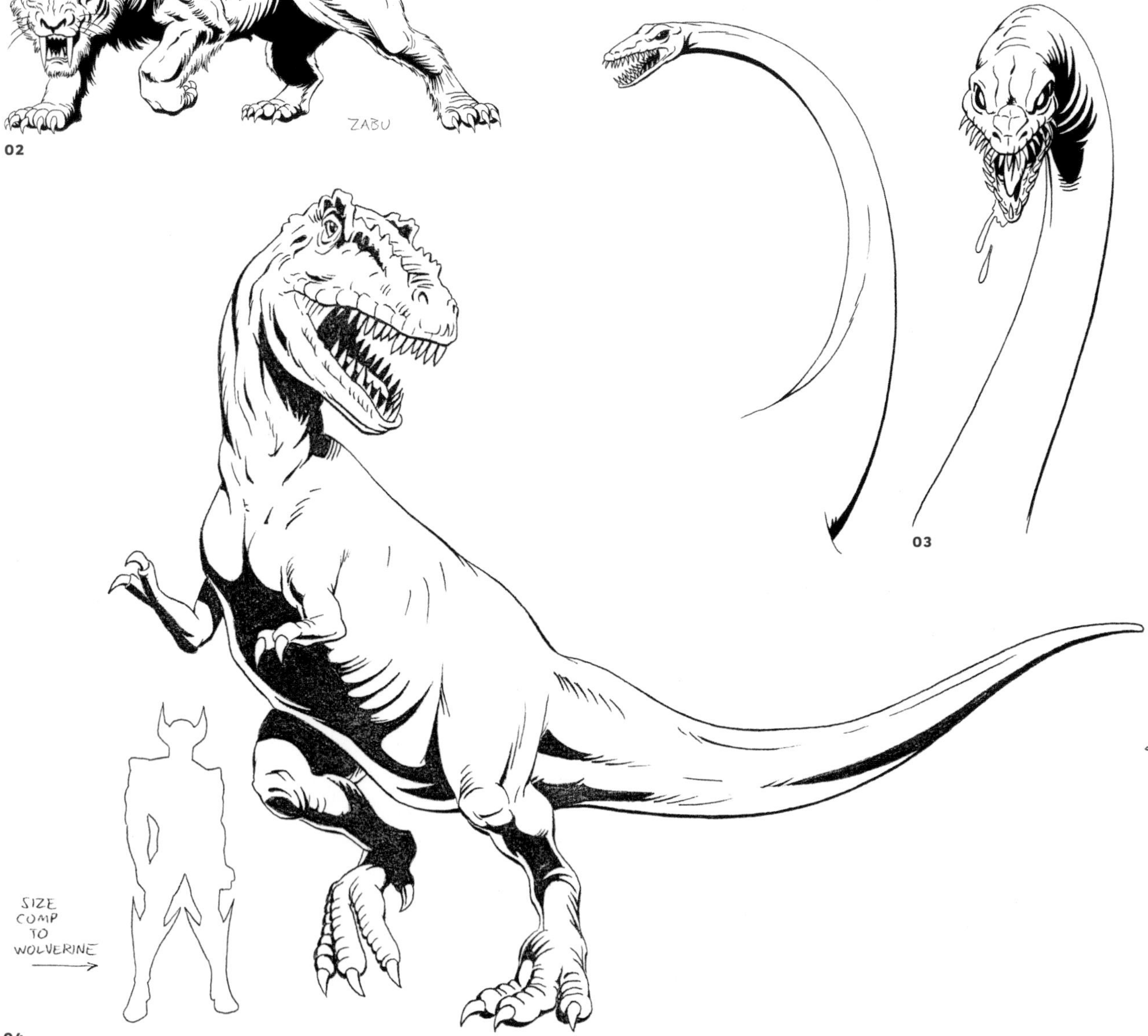
SIZE COMP TO WOLVERINE

03

04

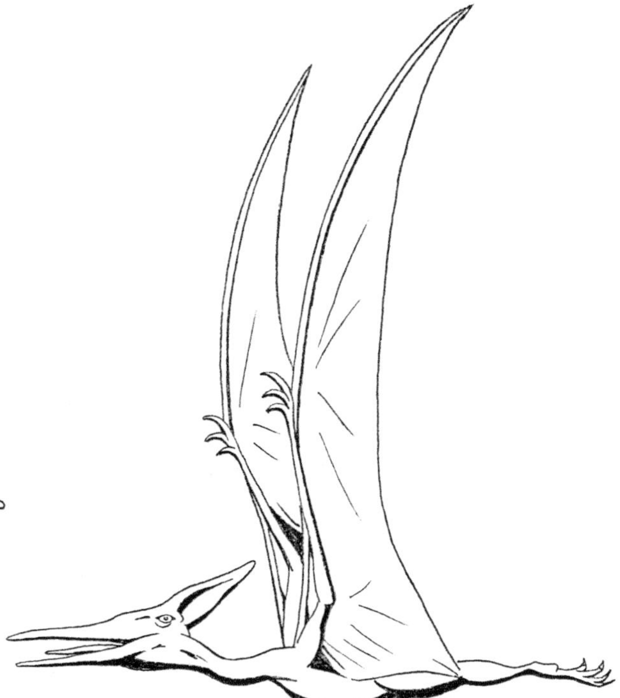

05

01–12 Character models of people and animals of the Savage Land, whose "B" story bits connected the end of "Till Death Us Do Part" through to their resolution in the season finale, "Reunion." All are penciled by Frank Brunner; those that are inked are by Mark Lewis.

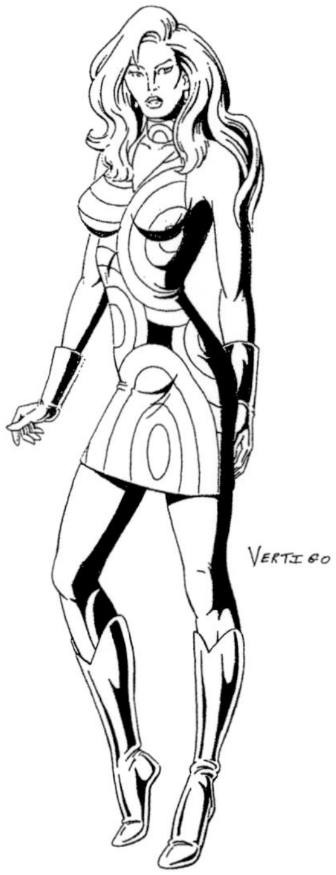
VERTIGO

06

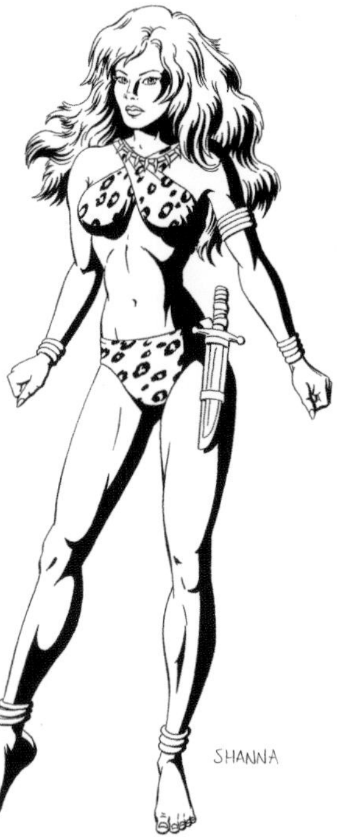
SHANNA

07

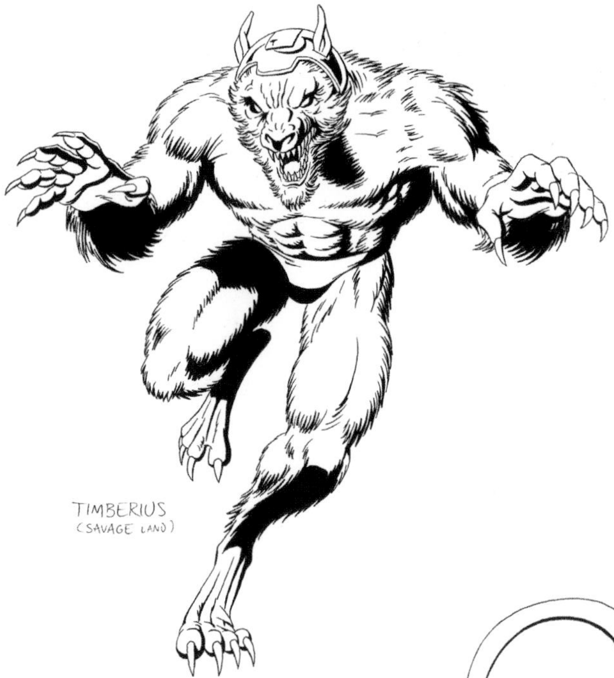
TIMBERIUS
(SAVAGE LAND)

08

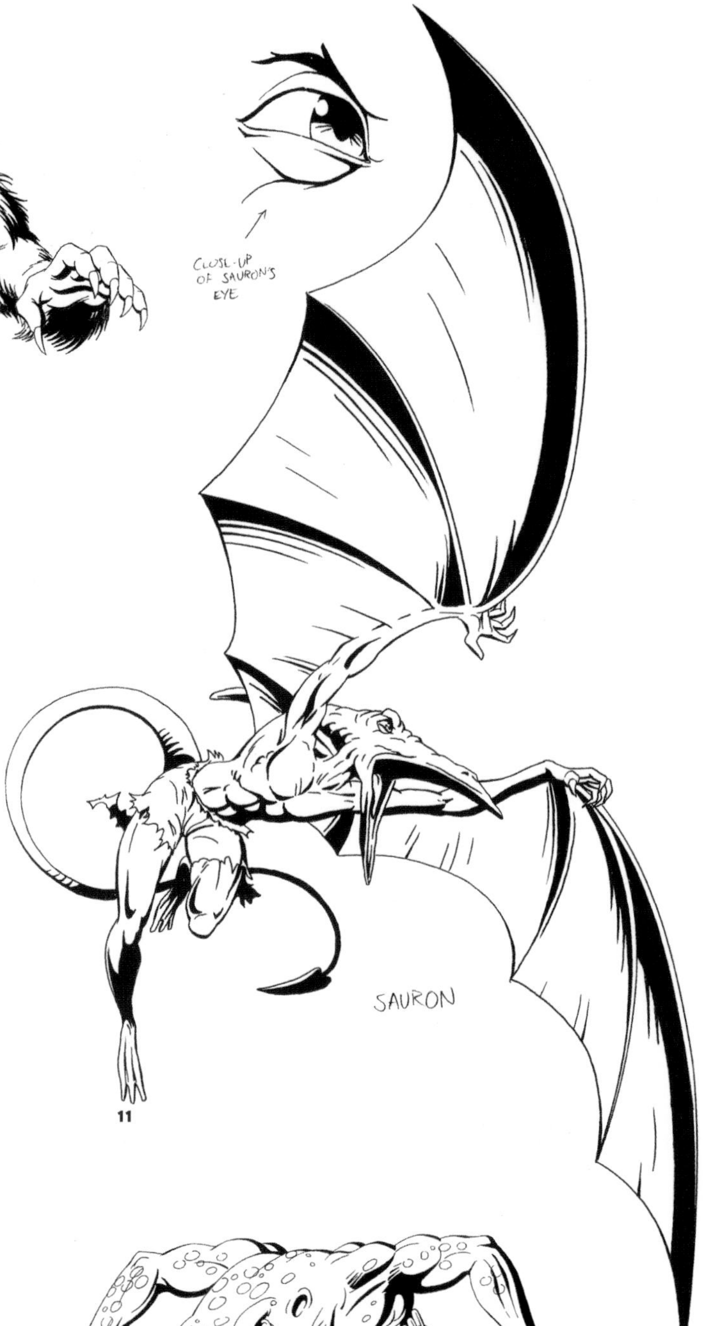
CLOSE-UP
OF SAURON'S
EYE
SAURON

11

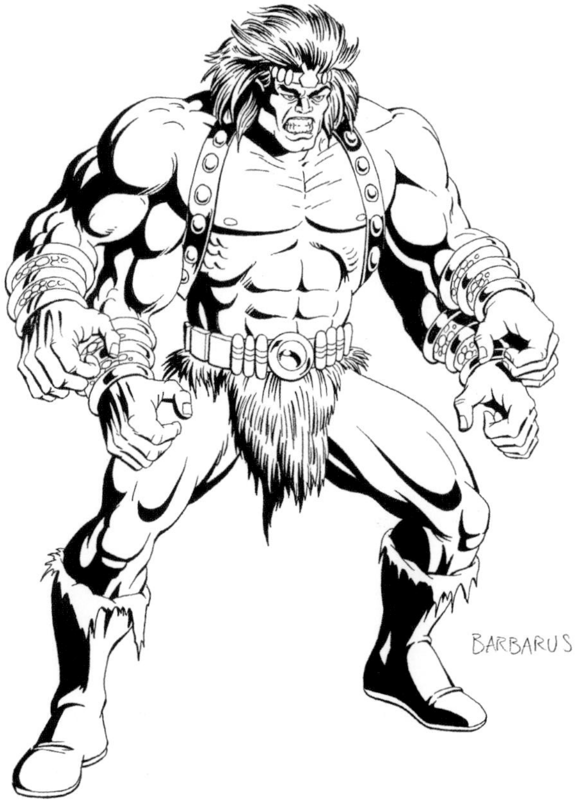
BARBARUS

09

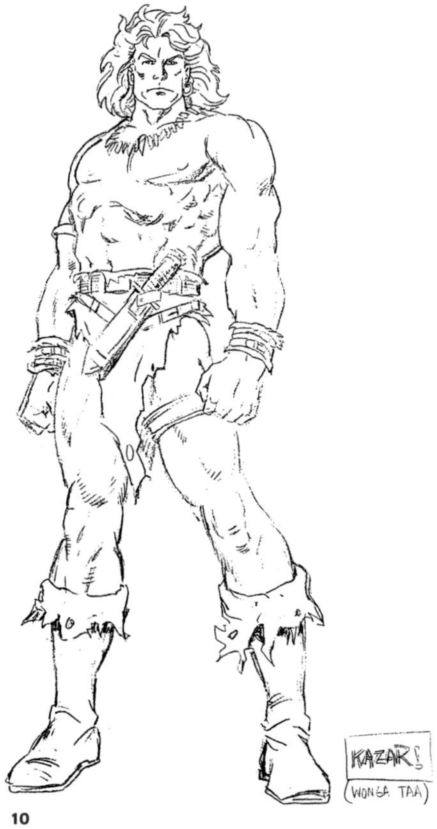
KAZAR!
(WONGA TAA)

10

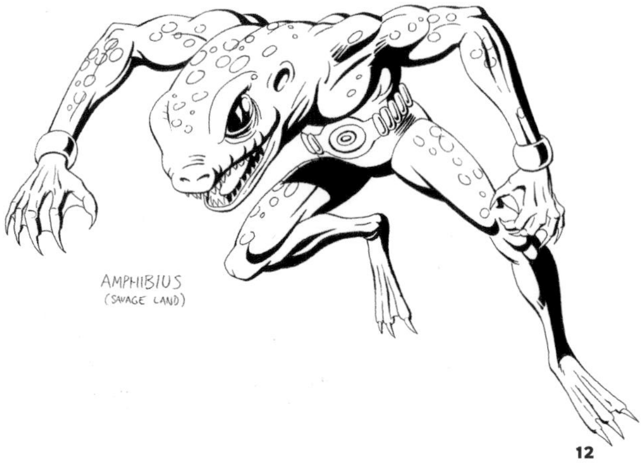
AMPHIBIUS
(SAVAGE LAND)

12

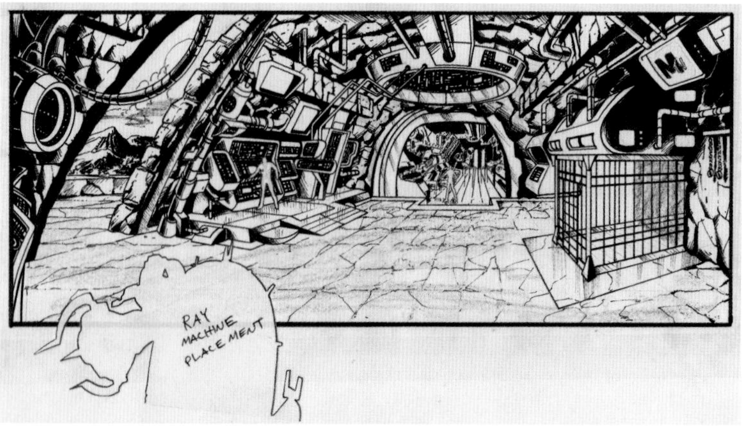
RAY
MACHINE
PLACEMENT

01

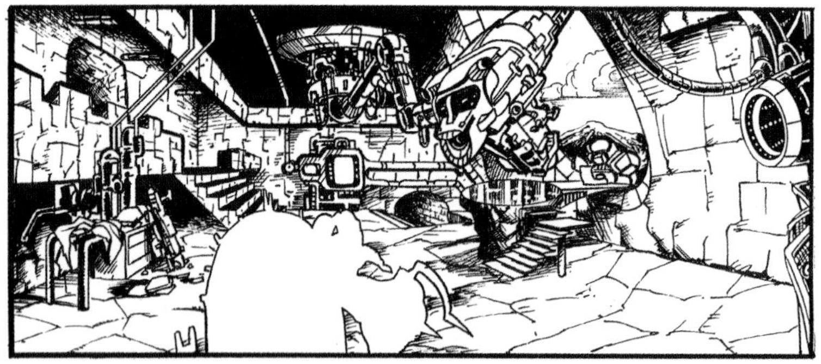

02

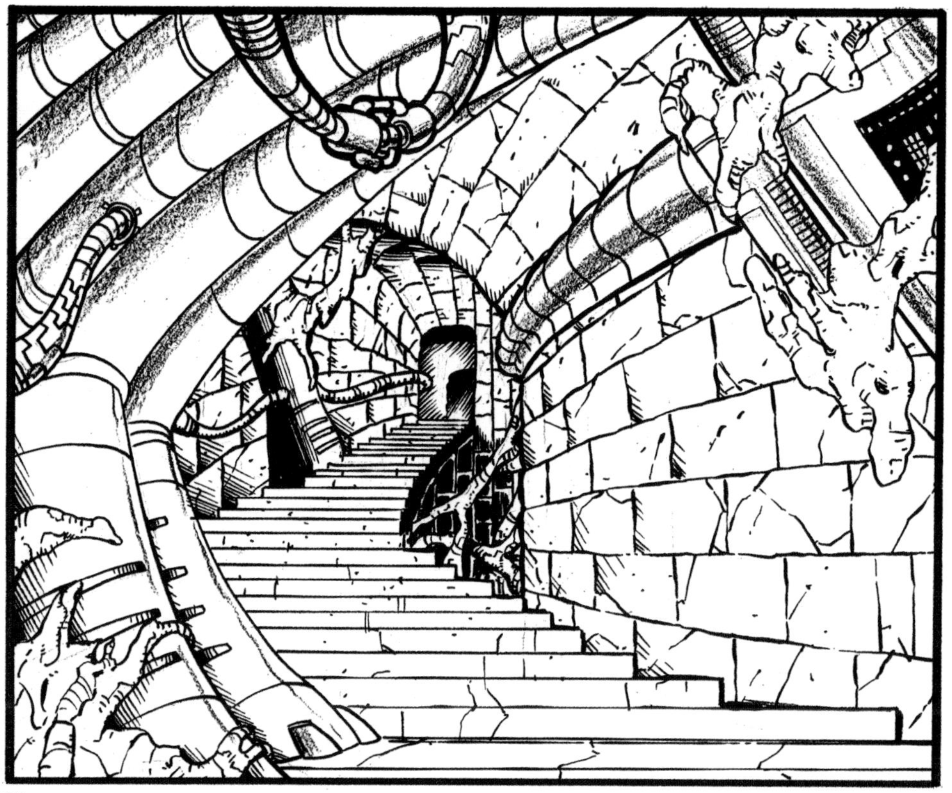

03

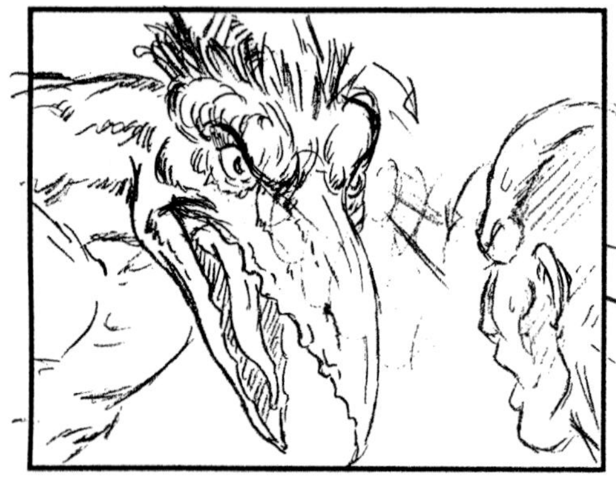

04

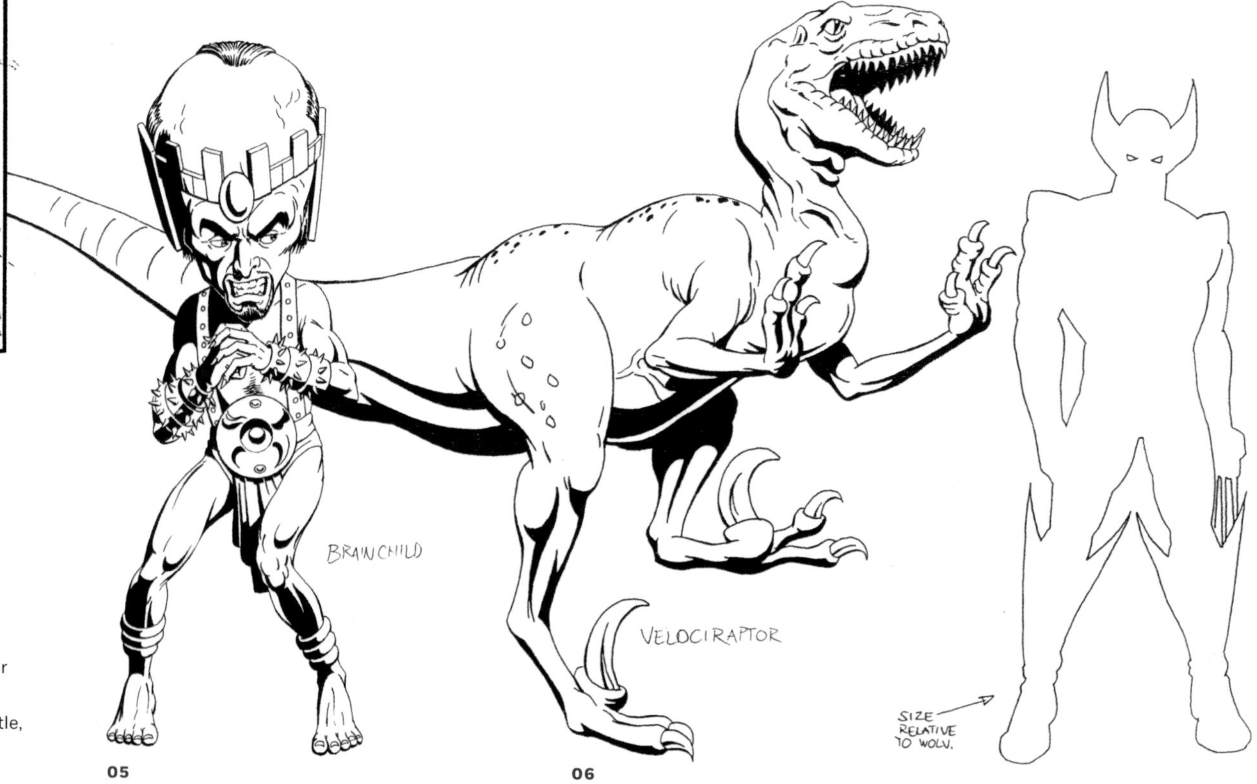
BRAINCHILD
VELOCIRAPTOR
SIZE RELATIVE TO WOLV.

05

06

01–03 Background layouts within Sinister's castle in the Savage Land, all designed and cleaned by Frank Squillace. **04** Storyboard panel of Sauron attempting to hypnotize Charles Xavier, who resists, drawn by Patrick Archibald. **05–06** Character model of Sinister minion Brainchild and model of velociraptor to scale, both by Frank Brunner and Mark Lewis. **OPPOSITE** Production cel of Mister Sinister in his castle, with the powerless X-Men and Magneto as prisoners.

#26   N BG-4DC   15/12

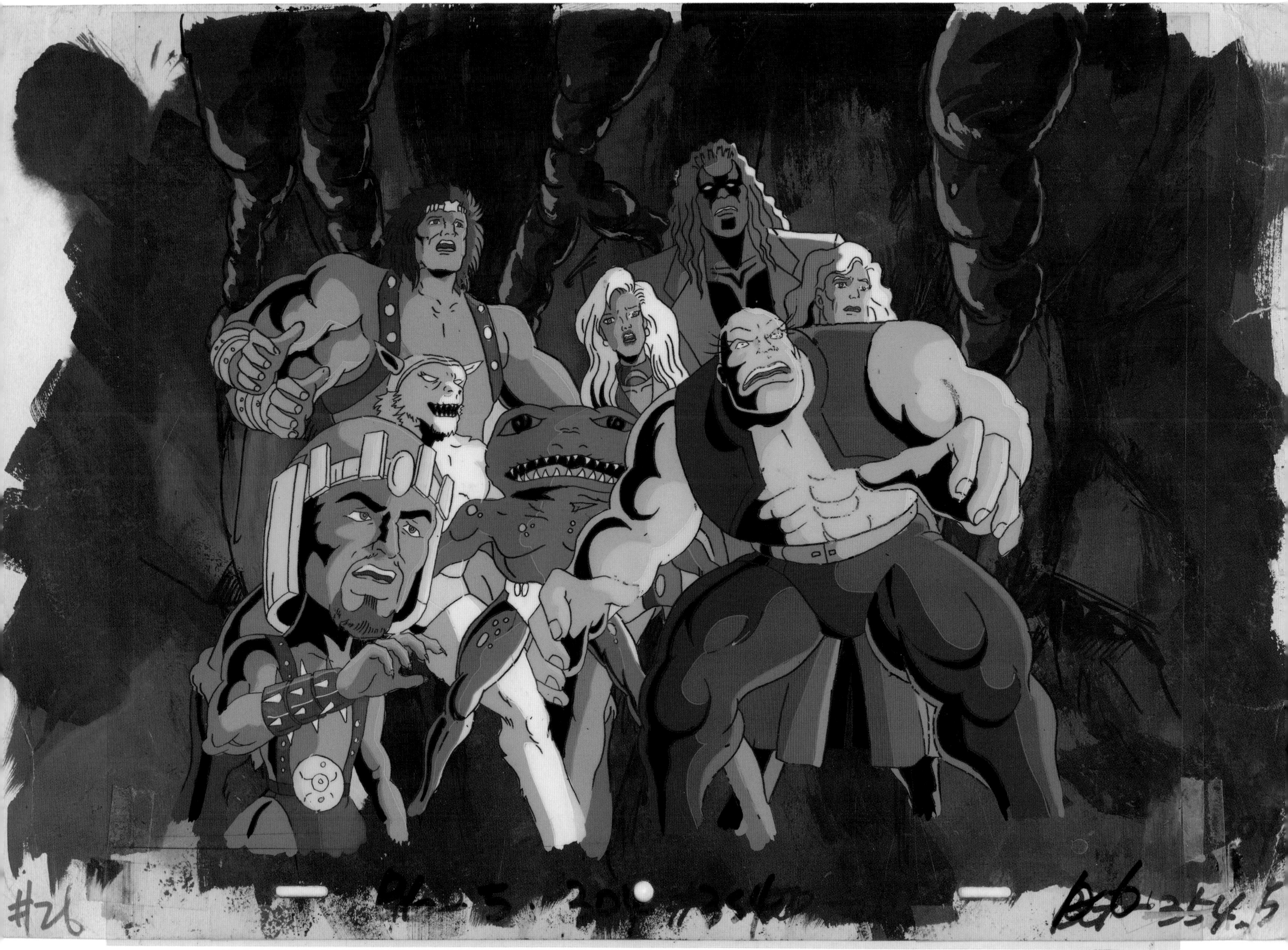
#26

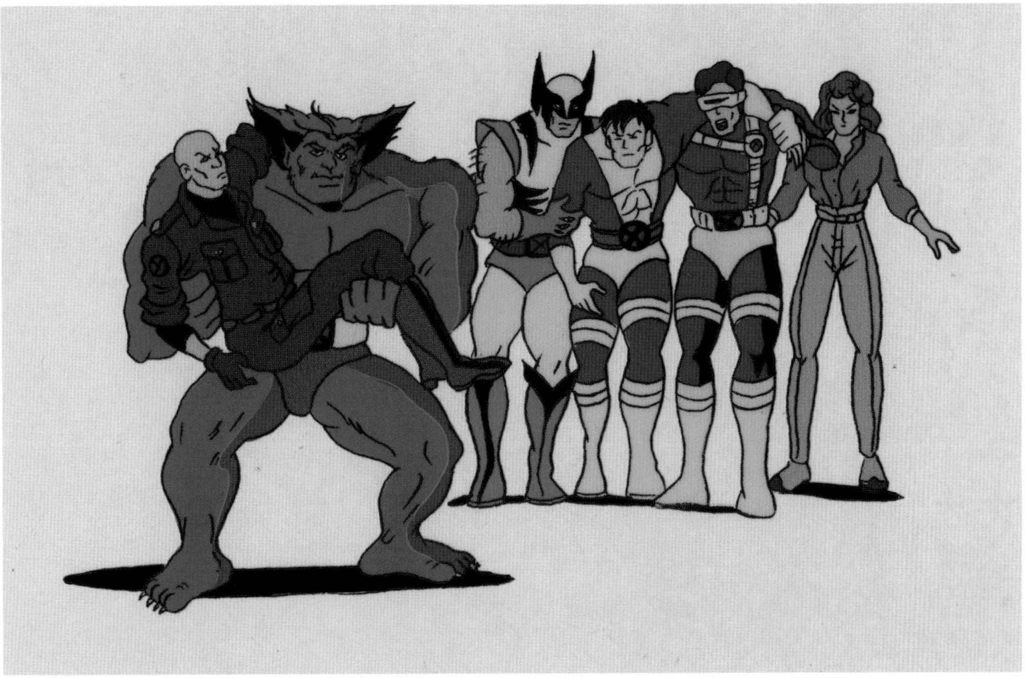

01

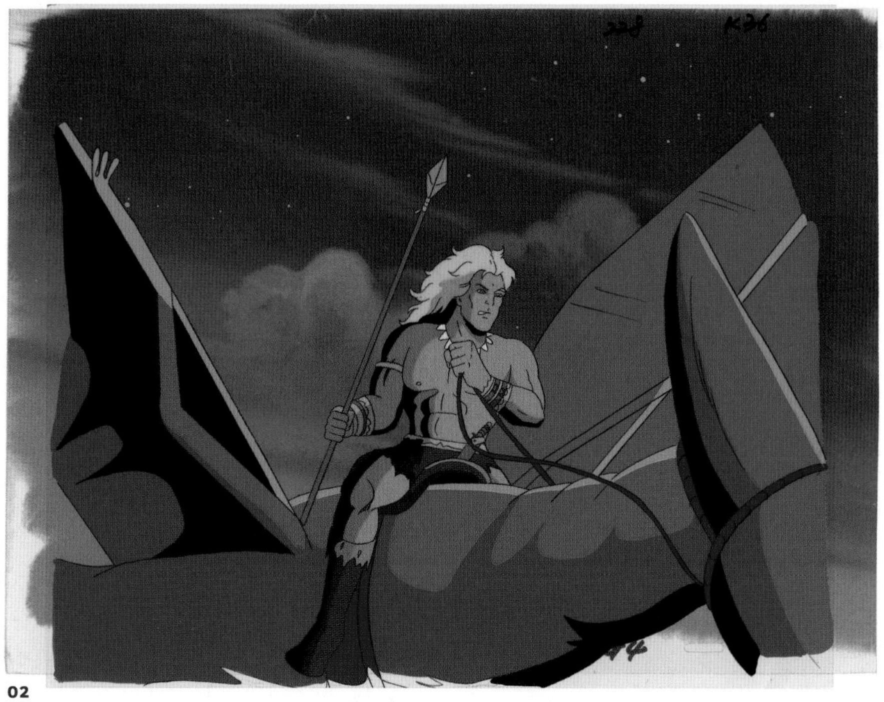

02

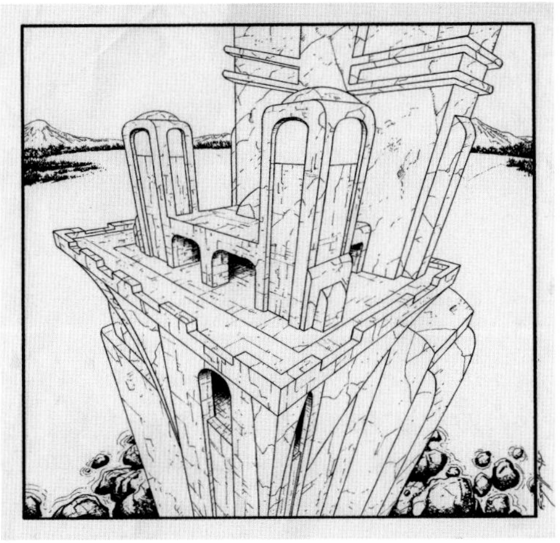

03

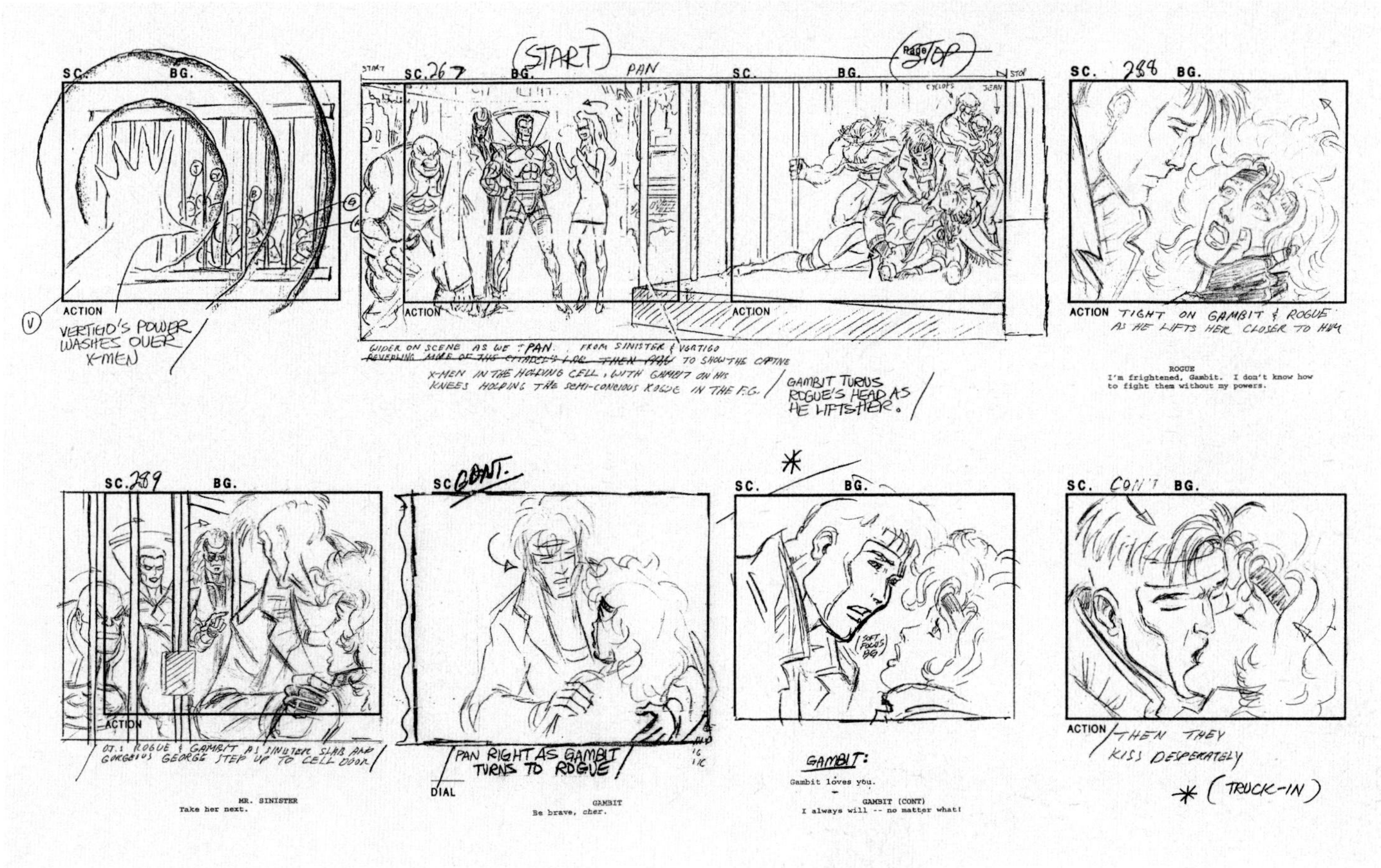

ACTION
VERTIGO'S POWER WASHES OVER X-MEN
SC. 267 BG.
(START)
PAN
(STOP)
ACTION
ACTION
WIDER ON SCENE AS WE PAN. FROM SINISTER & VERTIGO TO SHOW THE CAPTIVE X-MEN IN THE HOLDING CELL, WITH GAMBIT ON HIS KNEES HOLDING THE SEMI-CONCIOUS ROGUE IN THE F.G.
GAMBIT TURNS ROGUE'S HEAD AS HE LIFTS HER.
SC. 288 BG.
ACTION TIGHT ON GAMBIT & ROGUE AS HE LIFTS HER CLOSER TO HIM
ROGUE
I'm frightened, Gambit. I don't know how to fight them without my powers.
SC. 289 BG.
ACTION
ROGUE & GAMBIT AS SINISTER SLAB AND GORGEOUS GEORGE STEP UP TO CELL DOOR.
MR. SINISTER
Take her next.
SC CONT.
PAN RIGHT AS GAMBIT TURNS TO ROGUE
DIAL
GAMBIT
Be brave, cher.
SC. BG.
SOFT FOCUS BG
GAMBIT:
Gambit loves you.
GAMBIT (CONT)
I always will -- no matter what!
SC. CON'T BG.
ACTION THEN THEY KISS DESPERATELY
* (TRUCK-IN)

04

OPPOSITE Production cel of Sinister's minions.
01 Production cel of Beast carrying Xavier.
02 Production cel of Ka-Zar flying a pterodactyl.
03 Exterior layout of Sinister's castle, designed and cleaned by Frank Squillace. **04** Storyboard panels at the end of the struggle in the Savage Land, where, because none of them has their powers, Gambit can profess his love to Rogue and give her a passionate kiss. A mix of work from Patrick Archibald and Larry Houston.

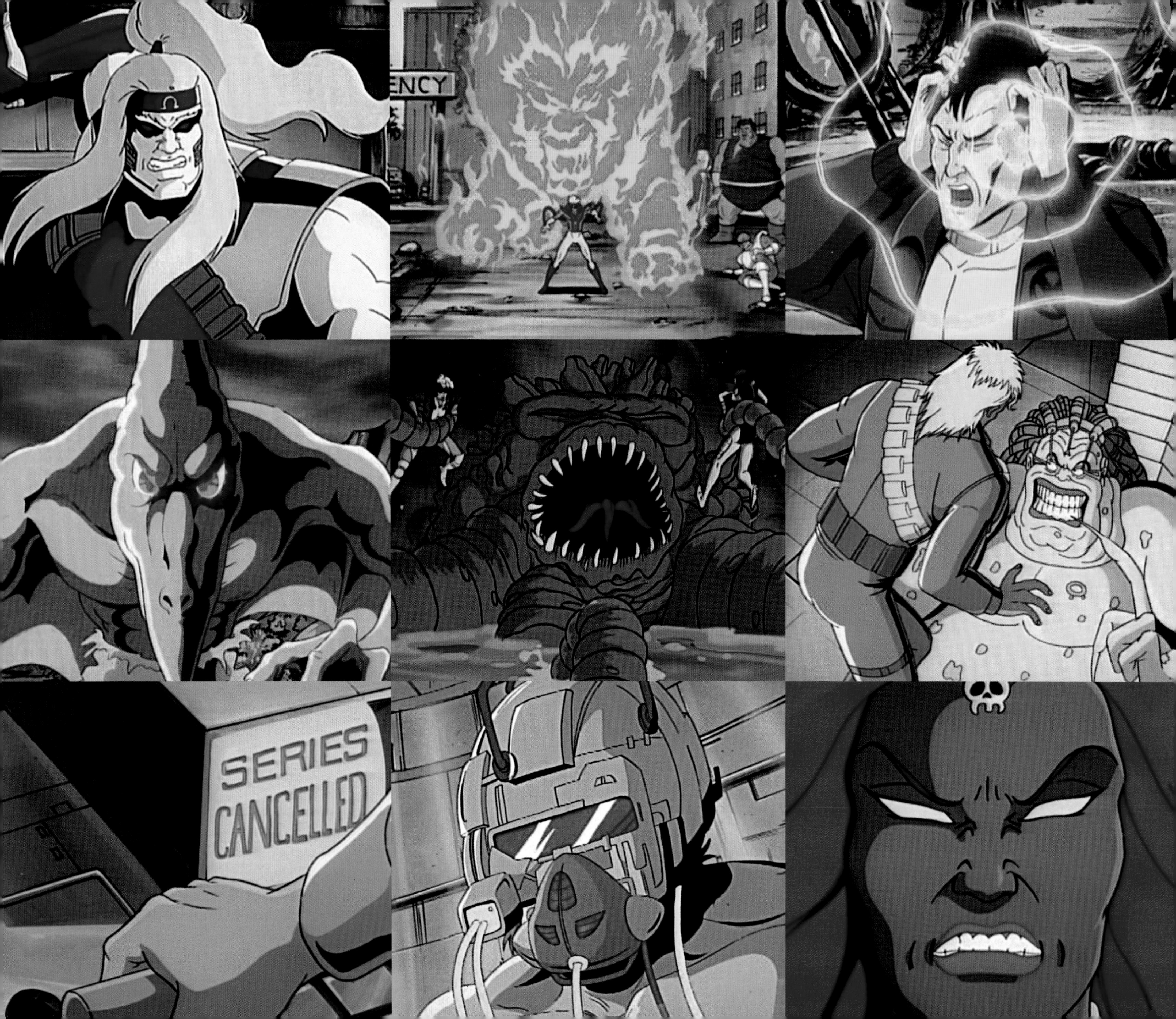
ENCY
SERIES
CANCELLED

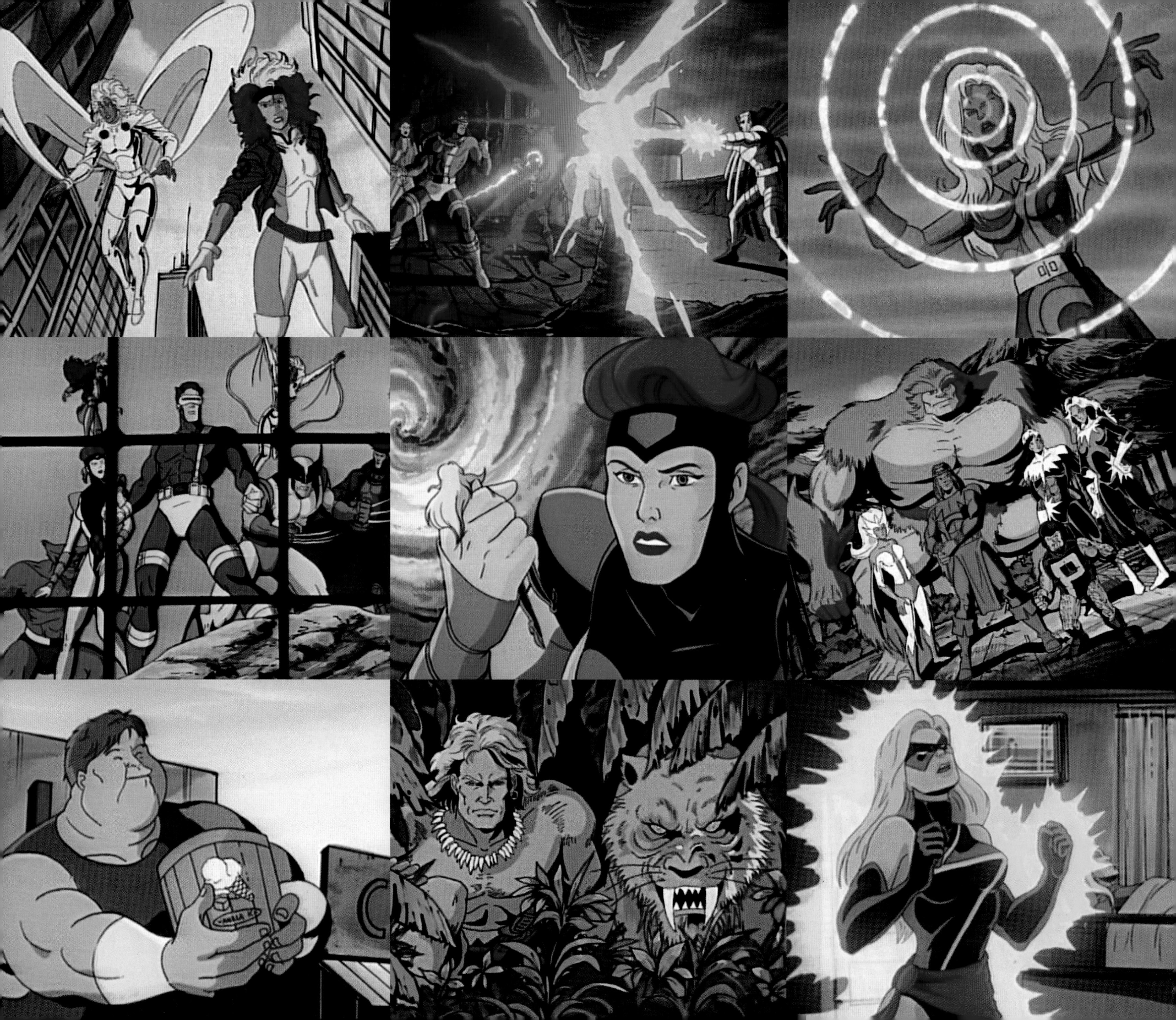

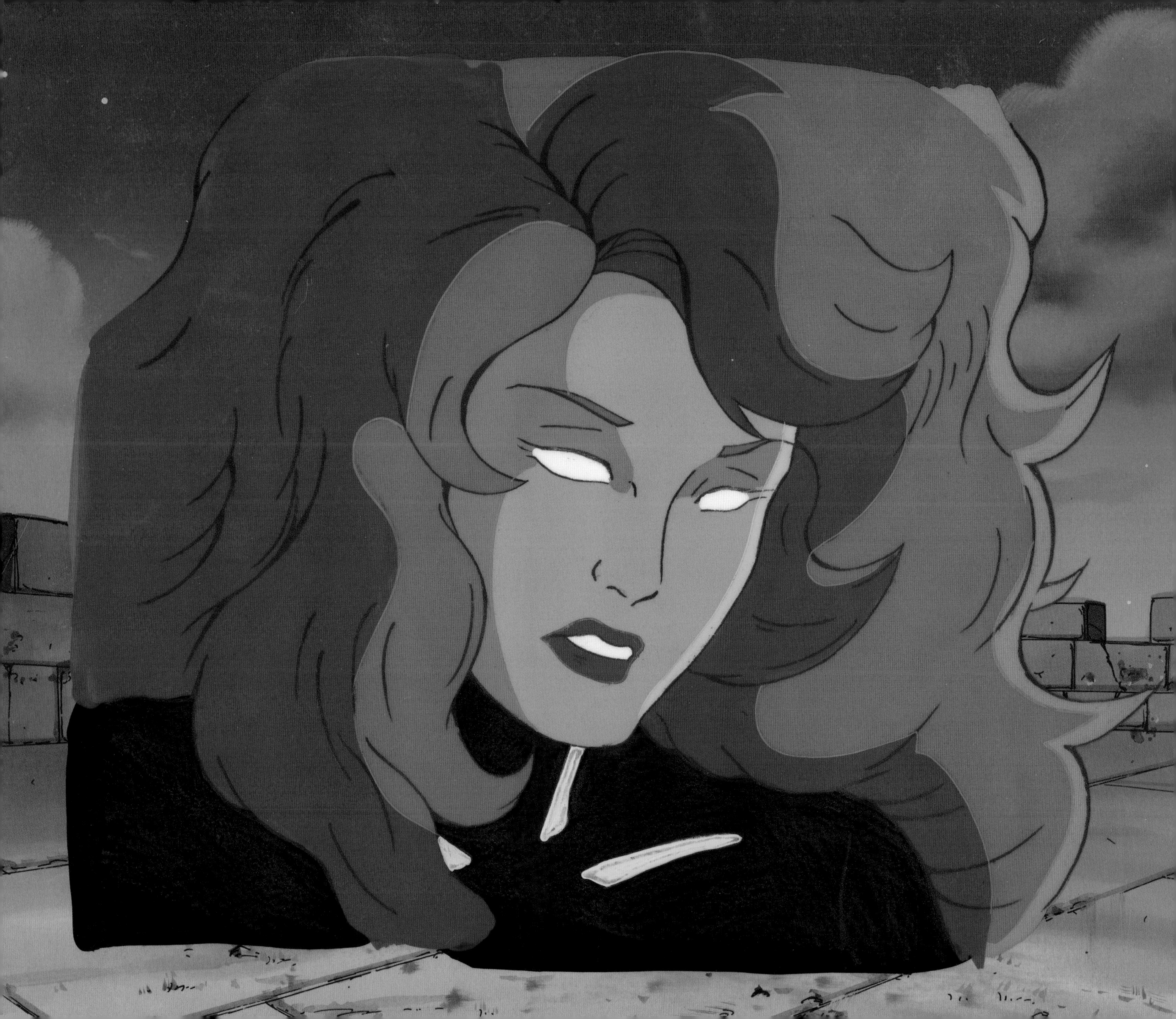

CHAPTER FOUR

THE DELUGE

SEASONS THREE AND FOUR, EPISODES 27–66

THE SHOW WAS DOING SO WELL in its first season, in the early summer of 1993, that, while we were just finishing the writing of season two, before we'd seen a foot of animation, a triple order (thirty-nine episodes) of new shows was made by Fox TV. There would be no downtime between seasons. This also meant wonderful job security for many writers and artists—a rarity in our business.

In August, Eric, producer/director Larry Houston, Fox executive Sidney Iwanter, and producer Scott Thomas all traveled to the Marvel Comics offices in New York City to brainstorm with Bob Harras and Joe Calamari about where the next thirty-nine episodes would go. Though it still was "Fox's show," Marvel now had a merchandise-powering international hit on their hands, and they were ready to become more involved.

As Eric's notes from the Manhattan meetings recorded:

X-MEN
THIRD SEASON
August 1993
Meetings, New York

1. STRIP COMMITMENT - The concluding thirty-nine episodes (#s 27-65) were committed to, to be finalled one every ten days, beginning September 10, 1993. This will allow the series to be "stripped" five days a week.

2. MAY TWO-PARTER - A two-part episode, starring Wolverine, Sabretooth, Callisto and The Morlocks, and Lady Deathstrike, will be delivered in time for the May 1994 Sweeps (TV ratings period). This will be the highest priority, numbered Episodes 27 & 28. Be sure to have an Xavier nightmare in it, foreshadowing "Phoenix" 5-parter.

3. EPIC FIVE-PARTER (PHOENIX) - The Fall 1994, season will be kicked off by a five-part epic story, based primarily on elements from the PHOENIX saga (Uncanny #94-110). Elements of this saga include:

A) the death/rebirth of Jean
B) Juggernaut & Black Tom (with Banshee in Ireland)
C) Princess Lilandra, the Shi'ar and their advanced space technology, and Xavier's love for her
D) Corsair (Cyclops's father) and the Starjammers
E) Moira MacTaggert; Xavier haunted by paralyzing nightmares; Magneto attack;
F) Firelord
G) Eric the Red
H) New X-Men vs Old X-Men Team
I) Jean's parents!
J) Professor X's frenzied dreams
K) Professor X's evil doppelganger
L) Jahf, little travel gate guardian
M) Gladiator, Praetor of the Imperial Guard

4. MISC. MEETING NOTES:

A) Father of Cyclops & Havoc is imprisoned, destroying family, Scott "never had a brother"
B) Use Nightcrawler (swashbuckler)
C) Use Proteus - Moira's son, she founded Muir Island to cure him, reality shifter, imprisoned by mother for own good, resentful, breaks out, drunk on power; baby Proteus, arriving while Xavier away at war, caused Moira/Xavier break-up (they were engaged); Proteus can absorb bodies/shapes; blow up island (make into two; include Banshee?
D) Guest star Forge??
E) Show Havoc and Wolverine's relationship
F) Show Rogue's attraction to Magneto (nobility), and the conflict this causes for Gambit
G) Use Exodus - He replaces Magneto as the most powerful adversary; use Quicksilver (Magneto's son); Exodus gathers Magneto's followers (the Acolytes), proclaiming he is Magneto's "True Son!"
H) Major Gambit Story W/Brood around New Orleans??
I) Storm/Forge Romance??
J) New Villain: GamesMaster
K) Look into the Wolverine-in-Japan story (Sunfire)
L) Juggernaut/Black Tom pairing, vs. Banshee (from "Deadpool" series)
M) Do another Mojo story
N) Magneto once used Volcanic bases - usable?
O) Put in Cable every ten episodes or so
P) Sabretooth and Gambit may have a history
Q) Use the Acolytes - young radical mutants (IRA, PLO)
R) Check Uncanny #303 for Jubilee story
S) Use Lady Deathstrike
T) Use the Brood
U) Do a Wolverine (alone) in the Savage land Story (Wolverine comics #70-72)
V) Archangel vs Apocalypse - vengeance story
W) Genosha rebuilt
X) "Bio-Sentinels" - Cameron Hodge and humanoid robots
Y) Gambit/Storm history story
Z) Remember to team Wolverine and Jubilee
AA) The Hellfire Club/Dark Phoenix - for later
BB) Build on space elements of the 5-parter: the Kree, the Skrull, the Shi'ar - travel through worm hole by the sun
CC) Big space fights endanger the Earth by endangering the sun - X-Men know, but must fight alone

Fans of the series will note that, while most of the plans made in those Marvel-hosted meetings made their way into production, many didn't. Over a run of thirty-nine episodes, stories evolved or proved untenable. As Eric instructed the writers:

OPPOSITE Production cel of Jean Grey as Phoenix from "The Phoenix Saga, Part 3: Cry of the Banshee."

NOTES ON THE THIRD SEASON

WELCOME TO "X-MEN."

By the late fall of 1994, we plan to have created thirty-nine more X-Men scripts to go with the twenty-six already completed. We hope you will be part of this rather overwhelming challenge.

Most of what you need to know to write for "X-Men" is contained in the rough series bible from the first season and the supplement from the second. Please read them. The attached premises will give you an idea of the kind of story ideas we are looking for. And above all, of course, watch the show. Get to know the characters and their voices. They are the key to all of our best episodes.

We have learned a great deal about writing this series during the past 18-months, and I will try to give you the benefit of that knowledge in the next few pages. There have also been discussions on the future direction of the series. Please take these all as helpful guidelines, not absolute requirements. While we definitely know what we want, we are open to the occasional surprise.

BUILDING ON THE FIRST TWO SEASONS

The first season (Episodes 1-13) introduced the characters and set up the X-Men's world. During the second season (14-26), we spent less time on exposition and more on the personal histories of our characters. "Origin stories" were popular. In these 39, we will be "opening up" their world a bit. As they did in the comics, for example, the X-Men will have some space-based adventures. We will be meeting new mutants, both good and bad, from the Marvel Universe. If you don't know the characters well yet, I suggest either getting a set of "X-Men" trading cards from your local comic shop, and/or picking up a copy of a "Wizard" magazine, just out, which celebrates 30 years of the X-Men. Also, video tapes of most of the first season's episodes are newly available at video stores.

ACTION ADVENTURE VS. SCI-FI/FANTASY OR SATURDAY MORNING

There is a very specific tone to our show that you must understand to write for it. The closest example I can give is an action-adventure movie or television hour drama. "X-Men" is not primarily interested in the speculative whimsy of Fantasy writing or the futurist/hardware obsession of some Science Fiction. Also, above all, for all of us who have written so much for Saturday morning, there is little concession to the "writing soft" or "writing young" that has been required so often in the past. The action and danger must seem real. While comedy is important to the show, it must only rarely be allowed to undercut the serious nature of our characters' jeopardy. The primary tone of the show is, for the lack of a better term, EMOTIONAL INTENSITY. The characters care desperately about their mission, their friends, and their place in the world. To succeed, we must take these characters seriously. Except for Jubilee, the X-Men and their antagonists are all adults. Imagine yourself in their place, with their personal struggles, with their heavy sense of responsibility. Make our comic book superhero mutants real, adult people.

FORMAT

"X-Men" premises should be a page or two, with a one sentence summary at the head, with a notation of whose story it is. This sense of dramatic POV is crucial. It affects all of the story-telling decisions.

The outlines should be no more than ten pages. Only use dialogue when it really adds something special. Perhaps because of the large cast, "X-Men" stories have tended to become overlong and too complex. We have had to struggle to keep them simple. Much better to be focused and concise here than to have to have your favorite scenes cut out of the overlong storyboard.

The scripts should be 32-35 pages, absolutely no more. Again, shorter is better. Our board people are among the best, and, as at Disney, they like to "play out" important moments, especially the big action scenes that we like to write for them. There is a Teaser (3-5 pages) then two acts of similar length. We definitely need a cliffhanger at both commercial breaks, and Sidney (FOX) has a distinct weakness for BIG ACTION/JEOPARDY TEASERS to draw audiences in. Margins are 1" top, .8" on the sides and bottom.

I will always need both a hard copy and a diskette of outlines and scripts. I use Microsoft Word 5.0 (soon 6.0), with the Scriptor or Beetlescr Style sheets, but can convert almost any IBM-compatible document (Wordperfect, ASCII, etc.). If you use an unusual style sheet, please include it on the diskette. Mac diskettes need to be converted to IBM before delivery.

PLEASE FOLLOW THE SAMPLE SCRIPT FORMAT EXACTLY! There are a dozen ways to set up an animation script. Some of our idiosyncrasies are to capitalize sound effects and to capitalize the names of characters only the first time they are seen and use transitions only between major locations. When in doubt, call me.

GETTING ASSIGNMENTS

Now the important part. The first two seasons, we created premises in house and handed them out. There was no way for you to "pitch" your way into extra work. This year far less has been developed. So, aside from a two-part and five-part episode already in the works, your ideas and pitches may help you get some of the other 32 assignments. We will continue to develop ideas and full premises and assign them, but the practical truth is that some of your story ideas will be used. We may give some of you ideas to work on toward the creation of approved premises. As always, the writers who do good work for us and fit the show will be given multiple opportunities. Pitches will be written and sent or faxed to me. Although I am not interested in verbal pitches, it makes sense for you to call and ask me about the suitability of storylines before you put in the hard work developing them.

We contacted the best people we could find to work on this project. We look forward to working with you.

Eric

ON THE ART SIDE, the series had two major animation-studio adventures, each born out of trying to find either more production capacity for our growing series (AKOM only had so many strong crews) or cost savings—or both.

The *good* adventure involved a Philippine animation house called Philippine Animation Studio, Inc. (PASI). They were assigned the first crucial story from the Marvel list, the "May Two-Parter" guest-starring Lady Deathstrike, now known as "Out of the Past." TV series used to be rated for audience size during three "Sweeps" weeks: February, May, and November. So having a special *X-Men: TAS* double episode set for May 1994 (rather than waiting for September) could be a ratings/financial boost. In the end, these two premiered in July/August as a tease for the upcoming season. Either way, they had to be good.

PASI wanted to earn *X-Men: TAS*'s business, so they bent over backward to produce beautiful animation.

Larry and the others were thrilled, except for one thing: Lady Deathstrike's cleavage. Her costume, in the models sent to PASI, was a vest, on top of uncovered skin, cut down to her navel.

This was not an issue in a static model, especially since word came down from the network to make her flat-chested ("This is a kids' show!"), which is the way her model was drawn. Well, the enthusiastic artists at PASI gave her a fuller figure and nicely animated movement, and a grave issue arrived for this "kid's show": conspicuous breasts. There wasn't time or money to reanimate every frame of a main character over two full episodes. When Eric and Julia spoke with production manager Dana Booton, who had to pack and ship everything involved with this fix, a story emerged.

Eric Lewald: "Larry's story was that we sent over Lady Deathstrike's model with a flat chest and no shirt, and we get animated footage back from these enthusiastic Philippine artists where she's got cleavage and she's bigger and she's far too well animated. Larry's version of the fix was, 'Since we can't do thirty minutes of retakes, let's paint a shirt front.' Were the people overseas able to just quickly slap some white paint on, shoot it again and send it back, rather than having to reanimate something?" [see page 151].

Dana Booton: "I was so involved with that—my god, that was a nightmare. We were able to get them to do a lot of actual retakes, because I think if you look at that show, she's not as busty in half of the scenes. So I think we redid key, closer scenes where we insisted that they redraw and flatten the chest. And because something like a hundred and fifty scenes had to be redone, Larry did come up with the idea of just painting that area, and overseas had to go back in and repaint that, just to be sure."

Eric: "So they both flattened her chest from what you received on the first pass and drew in the shirt."

Dana: "Right. Any scenes where it was a close-up of her, we still felt she's way too busty, that BS&P [Broadcast Standards and Practices] is not going to let us put that on the air."

The *bad* adventure had to do with two episodes—"No Mutant Is an Island" and "Longshot"—that were sent to another studio, believed, actually, to have subcontracted its work to yet another studio in China (at the time a primitive but upcoming market). Haim Saban was always looking to find a way to cut the budget and save money, and evidently an early outreach to China was one that he tried. The results were so terrible that these two episodes (written as numbers thirty-four and thirty-six) ended up premiering two years late (as numbers sixty-six and sixty-seven)! They had to be completely redone, and the fight over who would do it and who would pay for the reanimating stretched on that long.

This made no difference to "Longshot," the stand-alone story of a return to Mojo's world that was requested at the Marvel meeting in August. But the delay on "No Mutant Is an Island" was devastating to those of us who cared about the show. At the end of the five-part story just before it ("The Phoenix Saga,"

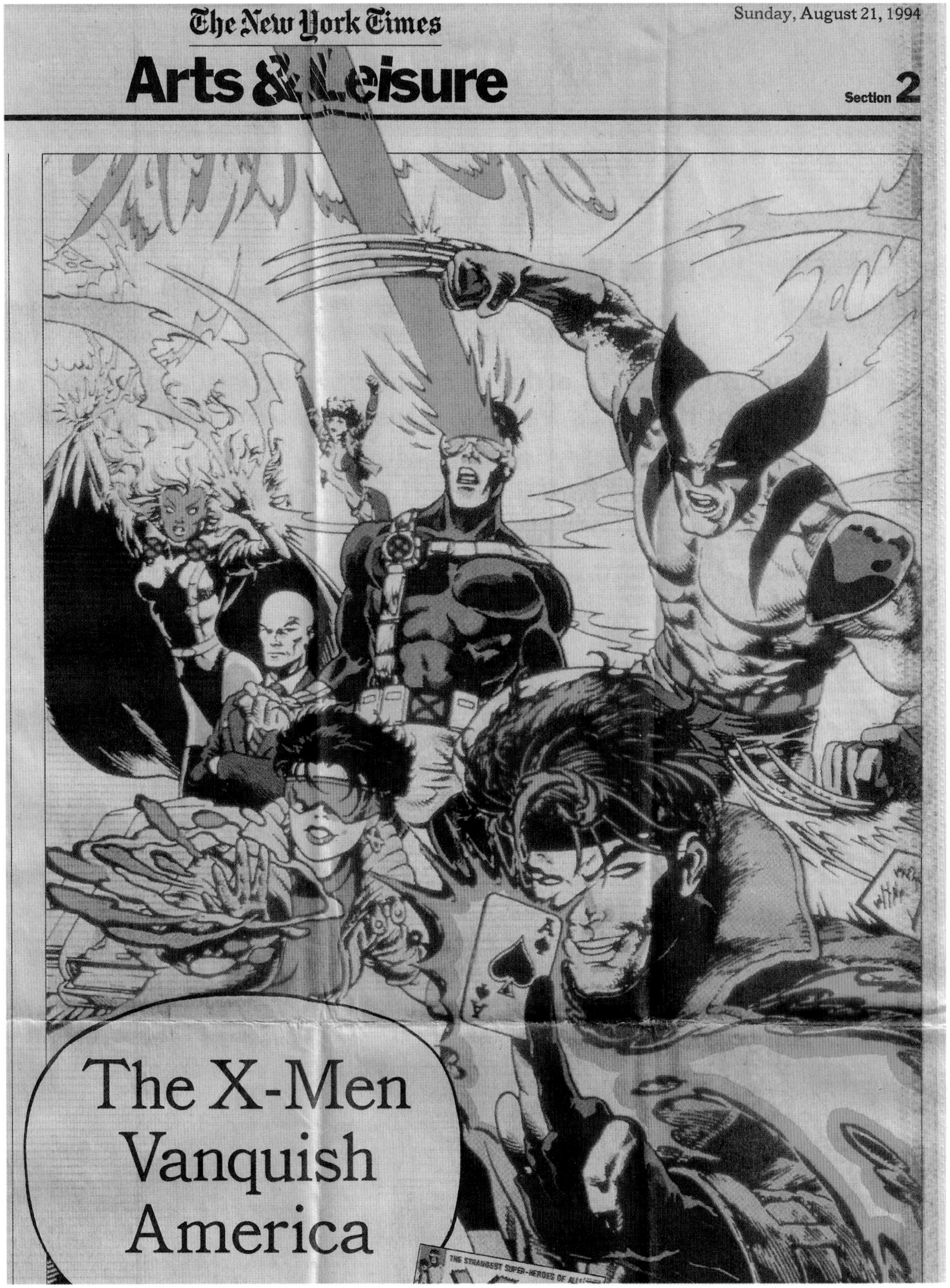
The New York Times
Sunday, August 21, 1994
Arts & Leisure
Section 2
The X-Men Vanquish America

RIGHT *New York Times* cover article for their Arts & Leisure section (8/21/94): "The X-Men Vanquish America"—after *X-Men: TAS* had dominated children's animated television for twenty months.

episodes twenty-nine through thirty-three), Jean Grey flies the Phoenix into the sun, seeming to sacrifice her life for the good of the planet.

"No Mutant" is supposed to follow, starting with a memorial to Jean's life. It proceeds with Scott, in his grief, leaving the X-Men, and ends with a flicker of hope that Jean might in fact be alive.

But in 1994, that story wasn't seen. Instead, after Jean has sacrificed her life, flying into the sun, boom, there she is in the next episodes—"Obsession," "Cold Comfort"—no worse for wear, and with no explanation for her miraculous return. Oh well. . . . The fans seemed to take it in stride.

SPEAKING OF "THE PHOENIX SAGA": This two-hundred-page script, fifteen-hundred-panel storyboard, 110-minute, five-part episode was arguably the peak of the *X-Men: TAS* production. Fox TV made it an event that was shown over five consecutive weekdays running up to the first Saturday of the 1994 season. It was the show's first major foray into space, and it was the second time Marvel entrusted the series, after "Days of Future Past," with one of their "gems"—story lines beloved for more than a decade by their most fervent X-Men fans. Eric was able to work closely on his adaptation of the spectacular but, for our needs, overly complex Chris Claremont story with Marvel's Bob Harras. And since the big order had given the team extra lead time, Eric was also able to persuade Fox TV to allow him to use only his former writing partners Mark and Michael Edens to write it with him—rather than immediately handing out the episodes to five different writers to hit short deadlines as was usual.

Sadly, this would be some of the last work the Edens could do on our show, as they went on to run their own series. Eric reviewed the "Phoenix" comics and sent the Edens the following memo as preparation for their first meeting on the massive five-part story:

BACKGROUND ON "PHOENIX 5-PARTER"

First, Sidney doesn't know what he wants yet. The good news is that we can make most of the creative decisions ourselves. The bad is that he may learn what he wants along the way, requiring a change of direction. All he has said is that this miniseries will "set up" a lot of the material to follow in the remaining 32 episodes — by which he means, I suppose, introducing a lot of new characters, locations, and conflicts that we will use again.

As it stands, over 16 comic books, there are too many armies of characters rushing every which way, and almost no human story concerning either the X-Men or the new allies and antagonists. I assume we will pare down the characters a bit and find a focus. Look it over. Cyclops would seem a natural POV choice since all of this Phoenix stuff is happening to his fiancée. The second major story involves Xavier falling for Shi'ar Princess Lilandra.

The leisurely schedule, which would be nice to beat, is:

	Outline In	1st Draft In
PART ONE:	Tues, 9/7	Mon, 9/27
PART TWO:	Thurs, 9/16	Thurs, 10/7
PART THREE:	Mon, 9/27	Mon, 10/18
PART FOUR:	Thurs, 10/7	Thurs, 10/28
PART FIVE:	Mon, 10/18	Mon, 11/8

It would be good to get me your outlines at least a day before the deadline, and the scripts at least two. Story notes from the comics follow:

STORY NOTES ON "PHOENIX 5-PARTER" COMICS AND THE NYC MEETING

MASTERWORKS #11 (comics #94-100)

* Don't bother with 94 & 95
* The Phoenix-creating villain (DR. STEVEN LANG) is set up on p. 86
* The Professor starts having a recurring nightmare premonition - important.
* You can use Banshee or not, as you prefer (might be easier not to since so many others are introduced)
* Been told we'd like to use Nightcrawler, but not here if you don't want to - I'm sure he'd need a major introduction.
* Dump the grave demons.
* Havoc & Lorna Dane can be dropped.
* They want to try to keep voices per episode down (right . . .)
* The New-X-men-vs.-Old-X-Men doesn't work — but some sort of robot impersonators (slashable) might.

MASTERWORKS #12 (comics 101-110)

* We can play up Jean's heroism, then Scott's grieving.
* Perhaps delay her resurrection, stretch out her near-death.
* The Irish Castle/Juggernaut/Black Tom stuff needs to be dropped or made much more integral to Phoenix problems.
* Marvel wants to showcase Corsair and the Starjammers. He is Cyclops' renegade father, but Cyclops doesn't know it.

* Perhaps we can expand this section — allowing Cyclops to confront the father who abandoned him.
* All the space fighting is fine spectacle — Imperial Guards, Guardians of the Crystal, etc., as long as we tie them in even better with Lilandra and Phoenix
* It would be good to let things get bad enough for Phoenix to "Go Birdlike", in her solar-system melting form.
* It would be good to build the Lilandra-Xavier romance so that, when they must part, Lilandra to lead her people, Xavier to lead his, that the drama is high.
* Perhaps Phoenix should drift off into space or be lost some other way (as a result of her fighting the good fight), so Scott can mourn her at the end.
* So have a look at #96-109, extract what you can, decide what you want to do, call me, and we'll get a short, 5-part premise to those who must be obeyed. We will want the outlines shorter (7-10 pages), and also the scripts (33-35).

AFTER "PHOENIX" and the delayed episodes, in "Cold Comfort" we introduced one of the original 1960s X-Men: Iceman, aka Bobby Drake. We made an issue of his having walked away from the X-Men—friction with Xavier and Cyclops—and with characters like Jubilee and Wolverine having not met him. This made for a lot of drama, with Beast, an original team member, as would-be peacemaker. The X-Men Universe team of X-Factor was introduced as well.

AFTER A RETURN TO THE SAVAGE LAND—and a newly discovered sympathy for a villainous character, Sauron—two favorite X-Men characters, Archangel and Apocalypse, faced off, with the X-Men getting in the way of Archangel's Ahab-like obsession of taking down the creature that had wronged him (fittingly, this episode would be titled "Obsession").

THEN—as in the comics by the endlessly inventive Chris Claremont—Jean Grey's extraordinary experience of being possessed by Phoenix, "an entity from somewhere deep across the galaxy"—had to be properly resolved. We did it in a four-part, eighty-eight-minute teleplay, based on a series of the books that came to be known to comics readers as "The Dark Phoenix Saga." Again, this space-based struggle not only provided some of the most spectacular visuals in the series run, but it also focused on the depth of emotion felt by the rest of the team toward Jean Grey, whose life and sanity seemed constantly in the balance. For Jean's beloved Scott Summers especially, these were trying times.

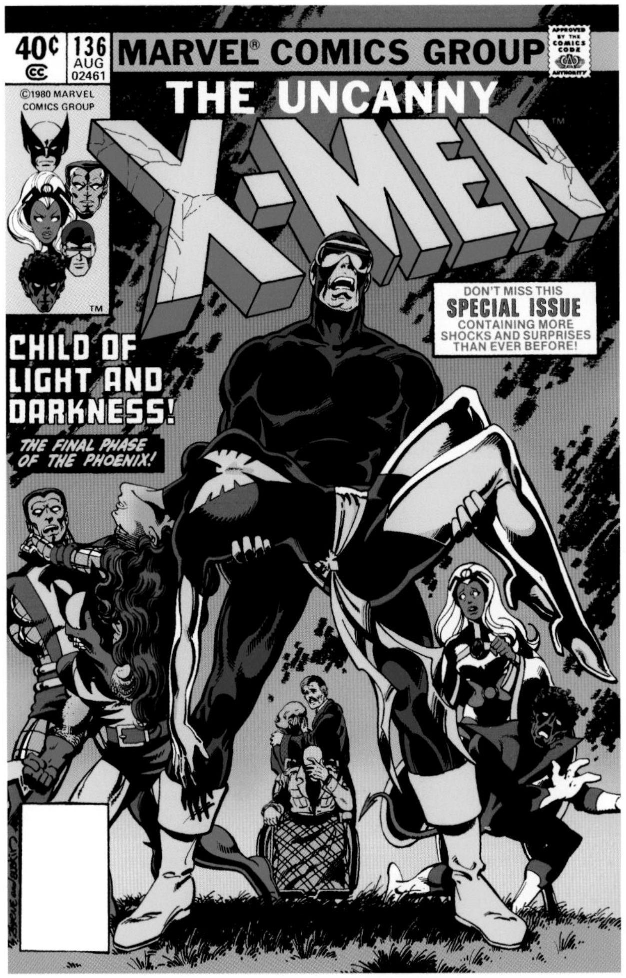
40¢
136
AUG
02461
MARVEL® COMICS GROUP
©1980 MARVEL COMICS GROUP
THE UNCANNY
X-MEN
DON'T MISS THIS
SPECIAL ISSUE
CONTAINING MORE SHOCKS AND SURPRISES THAN EVER BEFORE!
CHILD OF LIGHT AND DARKNESS!
THE FINAL PHASE OF THE PHOENIX!

Eric's one regret was that Jean was not allowed to die a hero's death, something that the story surely built to. But, as in the comics, Jean would be needed for more stories, so a compromise "partial, communal sacrifice" was made.

IN "ORPHAN'S END," Scott was allowed to confront Corsair, the father who abandoned him and his brother when they were small children. A further connection is made to the Shi'ar people, who end up playing such a central role in Professor Xavier's life.

"LOVE IN VAIN" was a treat for the artists. This nasty, sci-fi-feeling episode guest-starred parasitic aliens who took over human bodies. When they did, the infected person gradually started changing in appearance. Mark Lewis and the other model designers had a great time distorting and mutating our lead characters. For Rogue, it was a chance to have a few private moments with her first young love—the kiss that made her realize she was a mutant.

ABOVE Cover of *Uncanny X-Men* (vol. 1) #136, part of *The Dark Phoenix Saga*. Art by John Byrne, Terry Austin, and Jim Novak.

WE LEARN MORE about Professor Xavier's stepbrother, Cain Marko aka Juggernaut, and why he has grown to hate Xavier. At the same time, the Juggernaut's power and size are transferred to a nerdy guy, Eugene Torbet Wiederspahn—named after friends and family—and more than our usual amount of humor is enjoyed.

THEN THERE WAS A COMPLETELY WRITTEN EPISODE—"Bring Me Charles Xavier"—that never was produced (but remains tucked away in our filing cabinet). This was the one case of the back-and-forth notes-giving process failing to catch major story problems early. That, and Eric stubbornly pushing a story he liked against early worries from everyone else involved. Eric's penance was having to write, over a short weekend, a whole new forty-page script— "Deal with the Devil"—to replace the discarded one.

AFTER THE BIG "PHOENIX" STORIES, we realized we needed to have a grand return to our number one villain, Magneto. Of all of the Magneto tales in in the books, the Asteroid M stories seemed to us to provide the most spectacle and, at the same time, a great visual manifestation of Erik "Magnus" Lehnsherr's philosophy of mutant separatism. Asteroid M provided Magneto with his utopia, his "Sanctuary." But utopias never last, and Magneto's was no different.

AMID ALL OF THIS BROADENING of the X-Men's universe, it finally occurred to us that we were neglecting Morph, who, though "damaged," had started a healing reconciliation with his teammates in episode twenty-six. His next appearance, in "Courage," comes a couple of seasons later and focuses on Morph's attempt to return to the X-Men. It reminds the audience about his PTSD, allows him to struggle, to fail, and then to redeem himself against the creatures that traumatized him and nearly killed him.

ANOTHER CORE X-MAN from the post-1975 books that we needed to introduce was Nightcrawler. Kurt Wagner was one of the comics series's best-realized characters: a gentle, devout Christian who looked like a demon and was therefore shunned from an early age.

Eric decided to center the episode on Nightcrawler's faith—unique within the X-Men universe—and placed the story in a medieval Bavarian village to give it a visual sense of old-world religious persecution. He picked Wolverine, struggling with his own faith, as a "way in" to get to know Nightcrawler. As Eric wrote to Bob Harras at the time:

> Dear Bob,
>
> Thanks for the notes on "Nightcrawler" and "Weapon X." . . . Much to your credit, we were already discussing and implementing a number of your suggestions. I think we're close on most of them. I especially appreciate the detailed "Weapon X" notes, setting us straight on the history.
>
> PLEASE tell Joe that Wolverine is spiritual. He doesn't know this. My instinct about the bible verse at the end also was that it was too much, but I thought I'd let people see it. My original intention was simply that Rogue saw Wolverine praying in church, that that image/moment was powerful enough.
>
> I'm sorry, I know you HATE the X-Men being on vacation and stumbling into an adventure. While we are tightening up a lot of the other questions you have, this one we have all discussed and we REALLY like it better this way. First, it's a change. After 52 episodes where the X-Men almost always rush out to deal with a detected crisis or presence, this provides us variety. Second, the coincidence doesn't bug us. There could be hundreds of different adventures to stumble into around the globe at any one time. The just happens to be the one unfolding in Bavaria. It's normal story-telling. I wish I could help you on this, but with all of the struggling we've been having lately making the stories work, I have a hard time throwing out a sequence that all of us out here like.
>
> The Wolverine/Nightcrawler religious discussions point is fascinating—and tough. I'm going to have to walk a tightrope on this. The intention was to show that Wolverine is a troubled, searching person—as opposed to a casual heathen like Gambit. For him to be struggling—and then affected by Nightcrawler's faith, the whole point of the story—he has to have doubts and questions. Rogue's doubts and questions are okay, but less important. We must have Wolverine wrestling with religious questions—angry, wondering, questioning—or we have no emotional story. Yes, Wolverine is intensely, seriously searching for peace. But the Wolverine I have come to know hasn't come close to achieving it.

CEREBRO: We've been using it as a "mental amplifier," when worn (thus its use in this scene in #61), not simply as a mutant detector. Did we screw up??

I hope you aren't even more overworked than usual—though it's been 100 degrees here for a week, so I'm going to be short on sympathy.

Talk to you soon,
Eric

Finally, on the art side, staff artist Frank Squillace, a big fan of the Nightcrawler character, campaigned to be able to draw the first section of storyboard. As Larry Houston said: "Frank [who drew the opening of this board], like every artist, will tell a story his own way. If it worked for the story, I usually never touched it. I wouldn't necessarily draw it that way, but I let it go, let everybody have their expression about how to tell the story. Frank did an excellent job on the opening of "Nightcrawler"; I didn't touch it.

Frank Squillace: "I started off as Larry Houston's creative assistant. I did everything from freelance storyboarding, mouth charts, character design, props, backgrounds, colorings—everything he needed done quickly. A few years later, after episode sixty-five, Larry left the show, and through the good graces of Stephanie Graziano, Will Meugniot, and Larry, I got promoted to be the producer/director of the show."

Eric: "Do you remember any breakthroughs for you personally?"

Frank: "The very first Nightcrawler episode. I boarded the teaser. I loved the mood of it."

ERIC'S FAVORITE OF ALL THE X-MEN STORIES—and the one chosen to start the official fourth season of the series—was the two-parter "One Man's Worth." Eric felt that his idea of showing what the world would turn out to be if the X-Men had never existed was the clearest way the writers had ever presented the answer to the question: "Why do the X-Men exist?" And the sacrifice made by the one properly-and-happily married X-Men couple ever shown on the series—alternate-future Storm and Wolverine—was as heartfelt as any that we wrote. Of course, we all owe the classic movie *It's a Wonderful Life* for making the basic idea so affecting.

CHARLES XAVIER was again at the center of an emotional story in "Proteus," where he travels to Scotland to help former love Moira MacTaggert with her out-of-control mutant son. Proteus was as sympathetic an "adversary" as the X-Men ever dealt with: a troubled teen. Yet he was so powerful that he actually reduced Wolverine to tears. We hinted that Proteus could have been Charles and Moira's child, adding another level of emotion for Xavier.

IN FLESHING OUT THE X-MEN'S UNIVERSE as the season wound down, we met Scarlet Witch, Quicksilver, and Silver Samurai, and discovered more about Nightcrawler's and Wolverine's pasts. We even, at Fox's insistence, tried a Christmas episode—not necessarily a fan favorite.

AS WE REACHED THE END of our sixty-five-episode order, Fox TV's Sidney Iwanter mandated that the series should "go out with a bang!" We were to set up a story as big as the Phoenix multiparters that not only included most of the major characters from throughout the many seasons but also *ended with a new X-Men team*! This moment felt well earned, that it would be satisfying for loyal fans.

Eric was able to lure Mark Edens back from other work, and the two of them laid out a four-part, eighty-eight-minute story—"Beyond Good and Evil," in a nod to Friedrich Nietzsche—that did all of that and more. The hundred-and-sixty-page script appropriately had time itself at stake, and five of the X-Men ended up leaving, making way for four new ones. As you can see by the end of the fourth premise:

As Apocalypse tries to stop them, Xavier, the other psychic beings, and the X-Men pass through the time portal. Magneto volunteers to stay behind to fight a rear-guard action against Apocalypse and his minions until the portal is closed. But Magneto, Mister Sinister, and Mystique are drawn through the portal in the "backwash" of the others.

In a dazzling display of energy, Apocalypse reassembles himself and tries to follow the X-Men and the others through the portal. But Xavier and the other psychics close it before he reaches it. Apocalypse is trapped forever.

The X-Mansion. Archangel and Psylocke ask to join the X-Men permanently. Shard and Bishop realize that they're stranded in the 20th Century: with the portal closed, time travel is now impossible. They'll never see the bright future made possible by the defeat of Apocalypse. "You'll see the future as we all do," says Xavier: "One day at a time." He invites Bishop and Shard to join the X-Men.

Cyclops and Jean decide to take an extended leave of absence, to lead "normal" lives—and start a family. Xavier says that he'll be devoting most of his time to instructing Generation X and offers command of the X-Men to Storm. But Storm has her own plans: she too intends to work with young people, on her own in her native Africa, to help them choose the right side in the eternal battle between good and evil.

Xavier tells the X-Men—Wolverine, Beast, Gambit, Rogue, Archangel, Psylocke, Shard, and Bishop—that they must choose their own leader. "Choose wisely," he tells them.

END OF THE FOUR-PART MINI-SERIES

BUT THERE WAS A SMALL PROBLEM. As a dozen artists were leaping into the four nine-hundred-image storyboards, word came down from Fox TV: There suddenly needed to be five *more* episodes produced for another season, *with the original X-Men team still in place* (six additional episodes were added soon thereafter).

And so all of the painstaking writing that set up five X-Men with reasons for leaving, and four new ones having reasons to join, all had to be undone. Bishop and Shard would not be stranded in our time after all, and Psylocke and Archangel, whose sympathies for the X-Men had grown, simply went back to their own lives. Xavier, Storm, Jubilee, Scott, and Jean all lost their yearning to go off and start afresh.

"But keep the basic story," Eric was told, since there was no time to rethink four entire half-hour episodes, whose spectacular backgrounds and characters and props had mostly been drawn. It wasn't a pleasant compromise for our storytellers to have to make, but sometimes to be a professional means making the best of a tough situation.

01-05 Characters models of various Reavers, penciled by Frank Brunner with cleanup by Mark Lewis. **06** Character model of Lady Deathstrike. Note the vest with no shirt over the chest area. By Brunner with cleanup by Lewis. **07** Character model of Lady Deathstrike, arms extended for combat, by Brunner and Lewis.

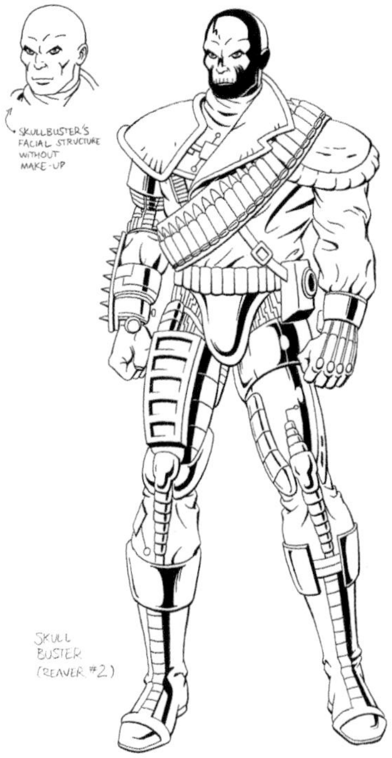
SKULLBUSTER'S
FACIAL STRUCTURE
WITHOUT
MAKE-UP
SKULL
BUSTER
(REAVER #2)

01

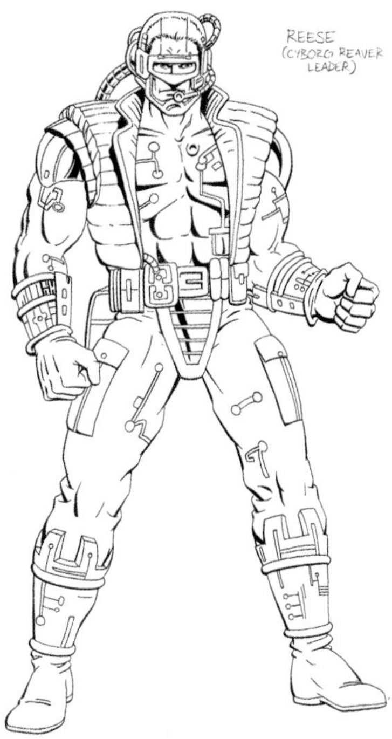
REESE
(CYBORG REAVER
LEADER)

02

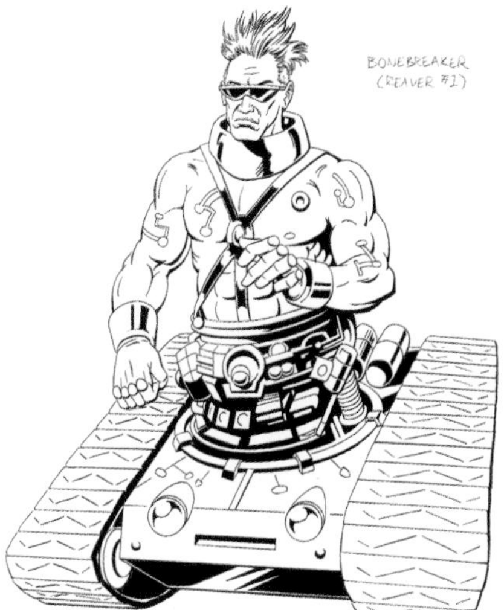
BONEBREAKER
(REAVER #1)

03

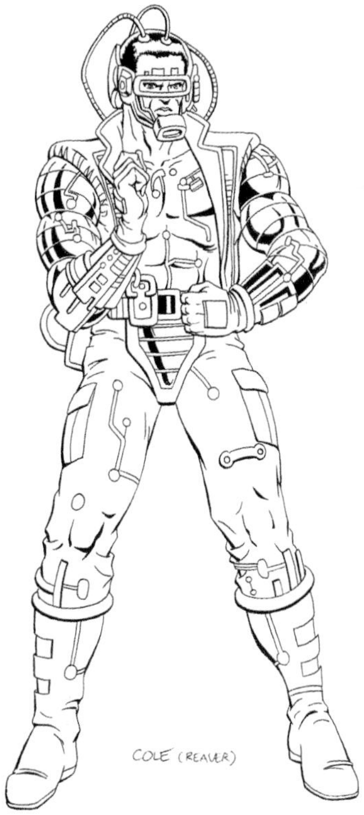
COLE (REAVER)

04

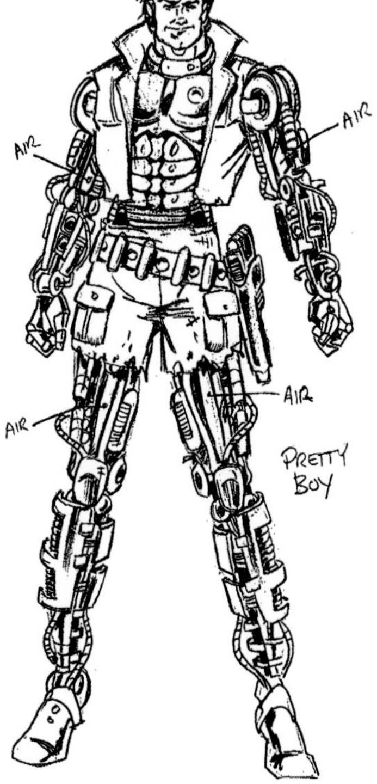
AIR
AIR
AIR
AIR
PRETTY
BOY

05

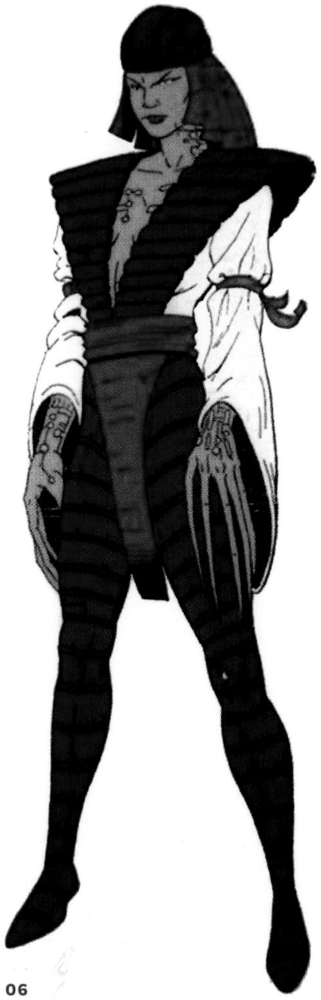

06

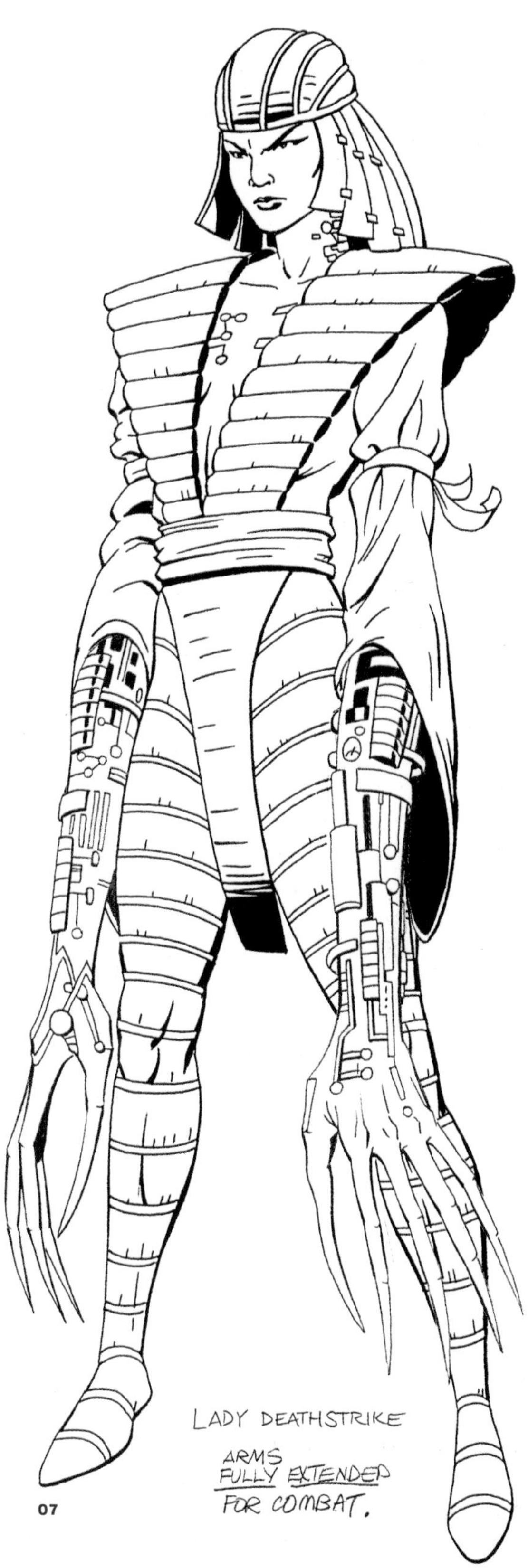
LADY DEATHSTRIKE
ARMS
FULLY EXTENDED
FOR COMBAT.

07

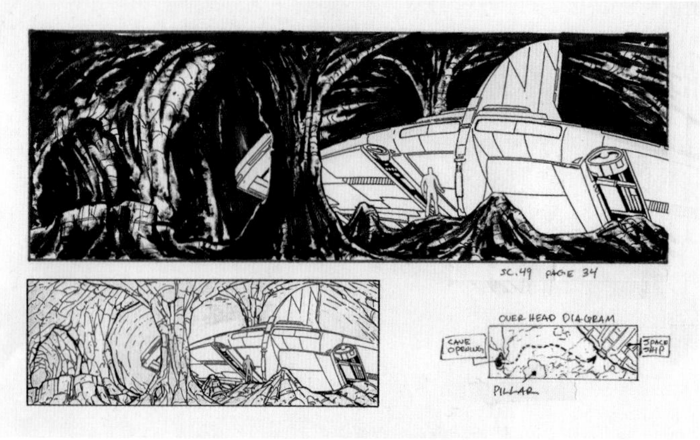
SC. 49 PAGE 34
OVER HEAD DIAGRAM
CAVE OPENING
SPACE SHIP
PILLAR

01

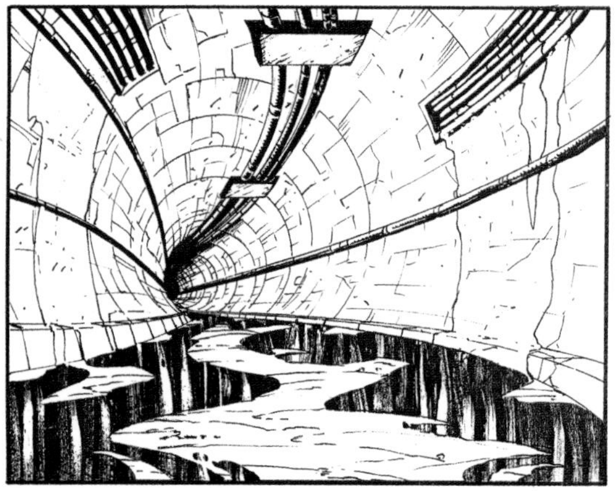

02

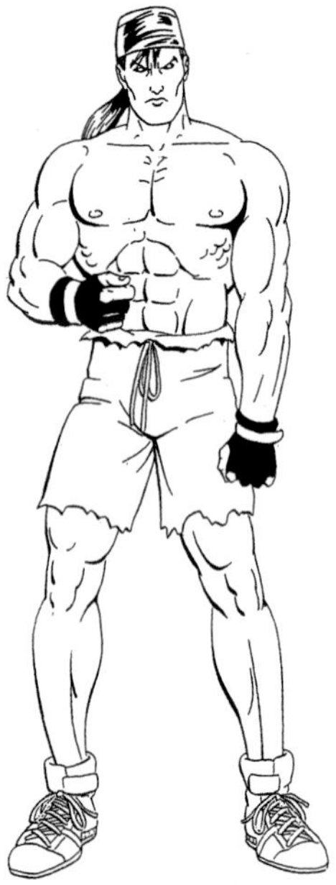

03

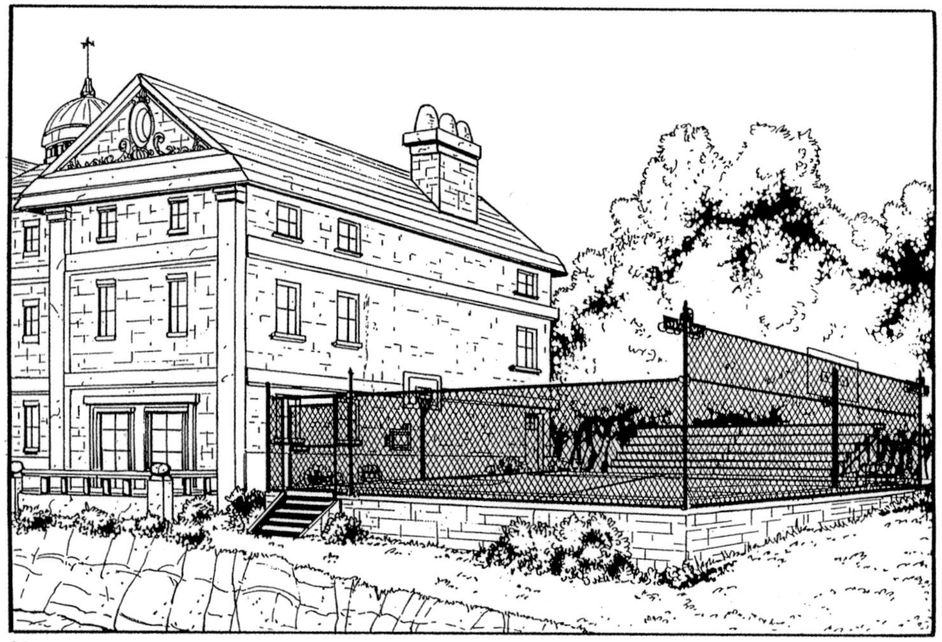

04

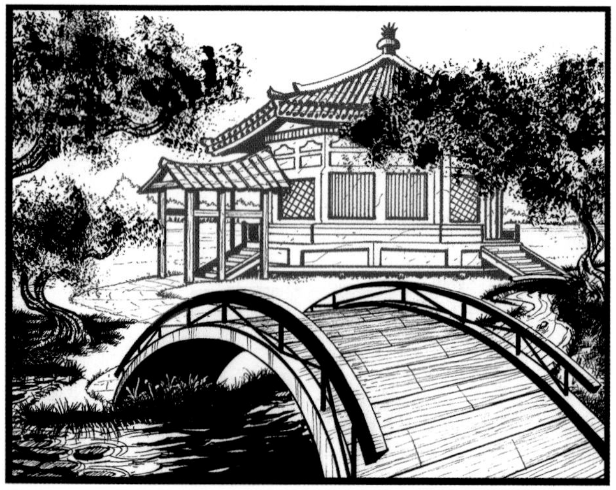

05

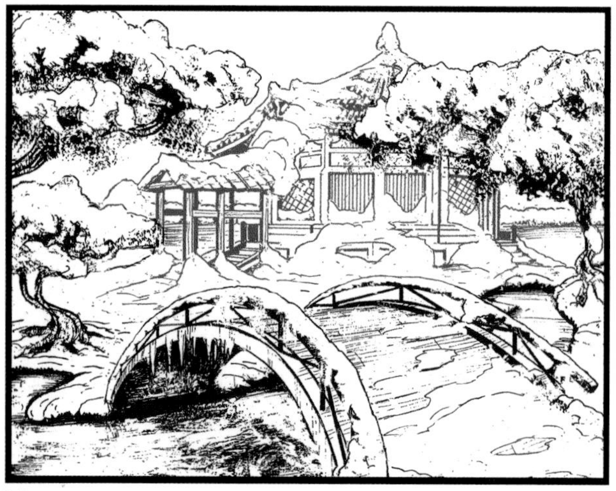

06

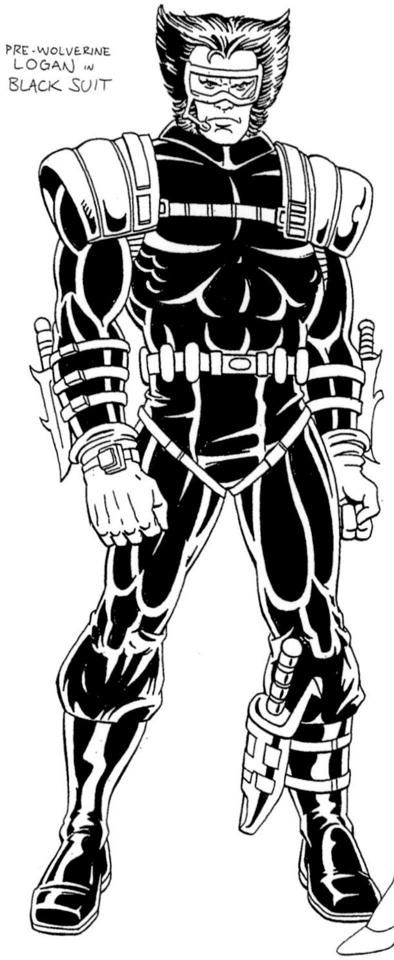
PRE-WOLVERINE
LOGAN IN
BLACK SUIT

07

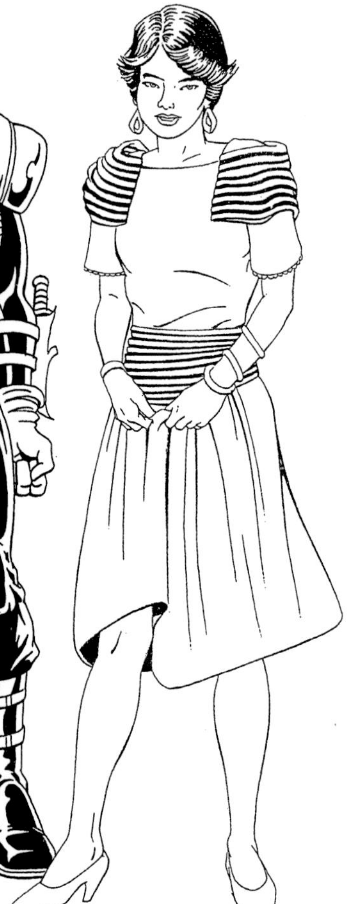

08

01 Layout interior of underground crash site of an alien ship that Lady Deathstrike is determined to open—but it will unintentionally release an imprisoned alien "spirit drinker." Designed and cleaned by Frank Squillace. **02** Layout of interior underground subway tunnel leading to crash site, designed and cleaned by Squillace. **03** Character model of Gambit dressed for basketball, by Mark Lewis. **04** Layout of exterior of Xavier's School, fenced basketball court with bleachers, where Gambit, Wolverine, and Jubilee play, designed and cleaned by Squillace. **05** Layout of Japanese bridge in the spring, where Logan tells Yuriko he has to leave her but promises he will come back to her, designed and cleaned by Squillace. **06** Layout of same Japanese bridge in the winter, designed and cleaned by Squillace. **07** Character models of pre-Wolverine Logan in black suit, pencils by Frank Brunner with cleanup by Lewis. **08** Yuriko, Wolverine's old love, before becoming Lady Deathstrike, pencils by Brunner with cleanup by Lewis.

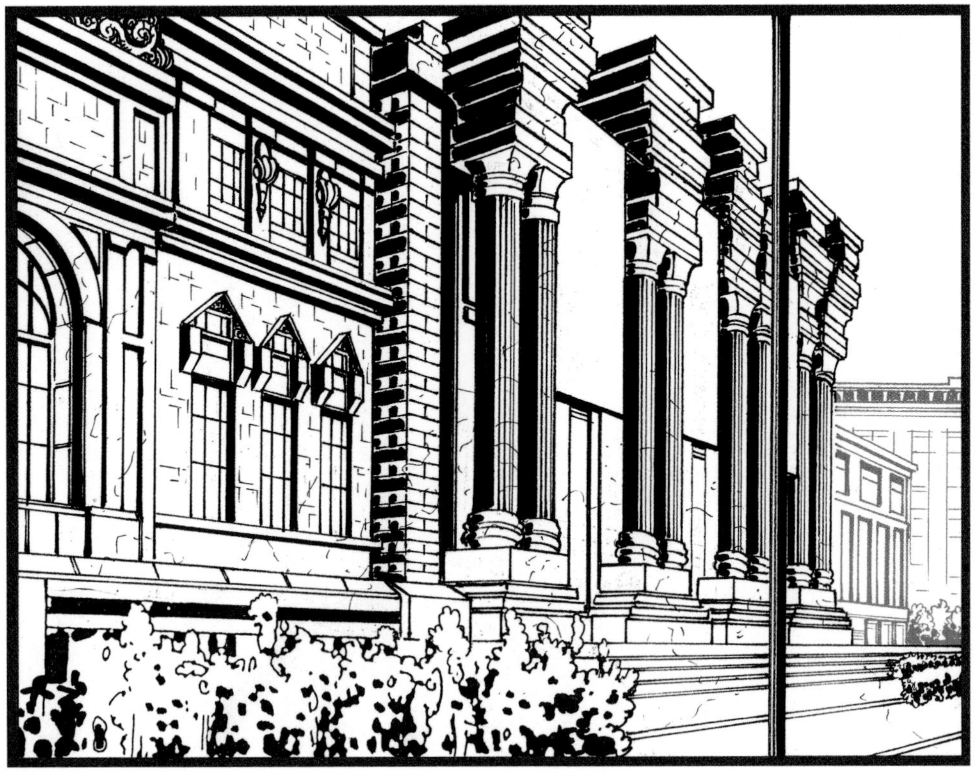

09

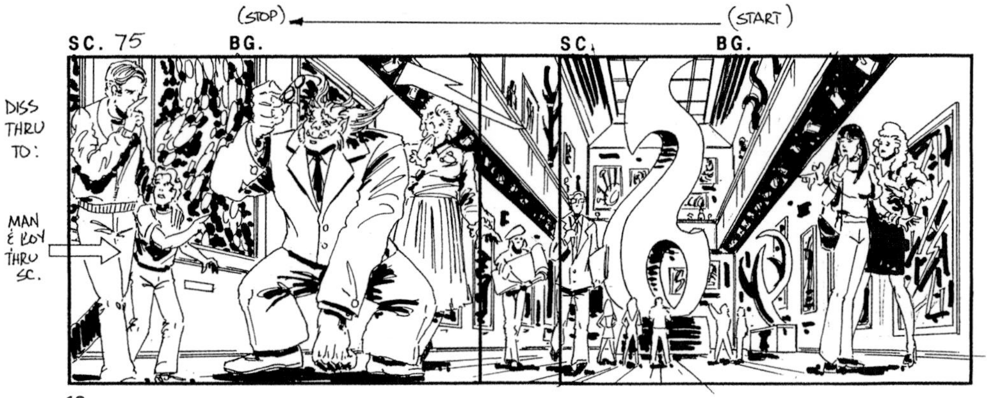
(STOP)
(START)
SC. 75
BG.
SC.
BG.
DISS THRU TO:
MAN & BOY THRU SC.

10

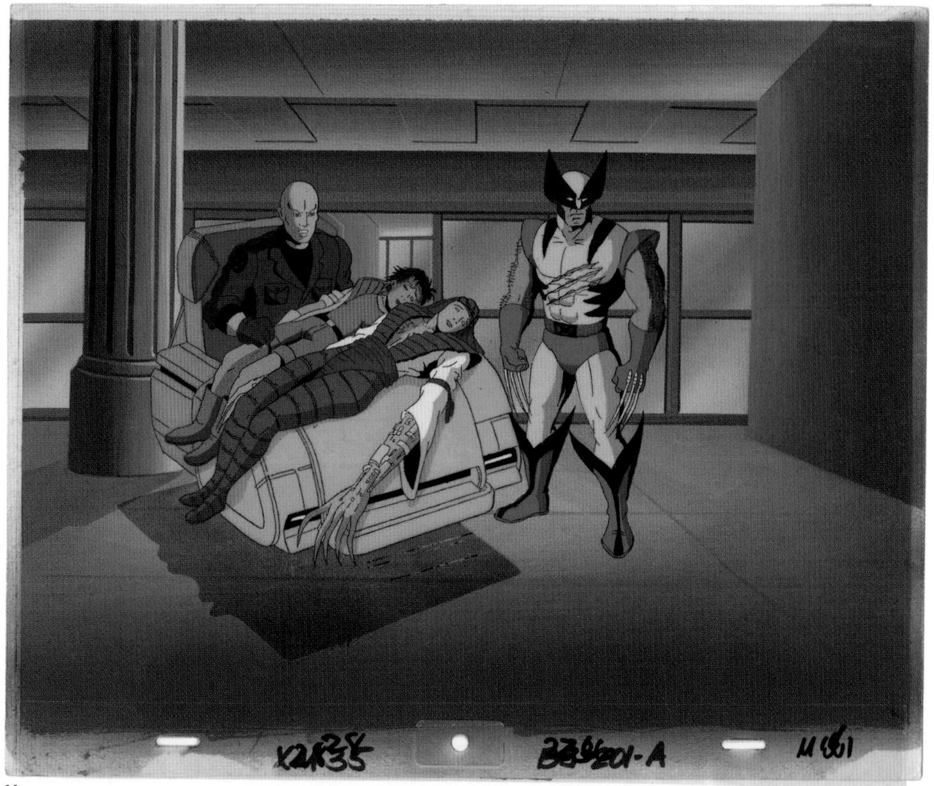

11

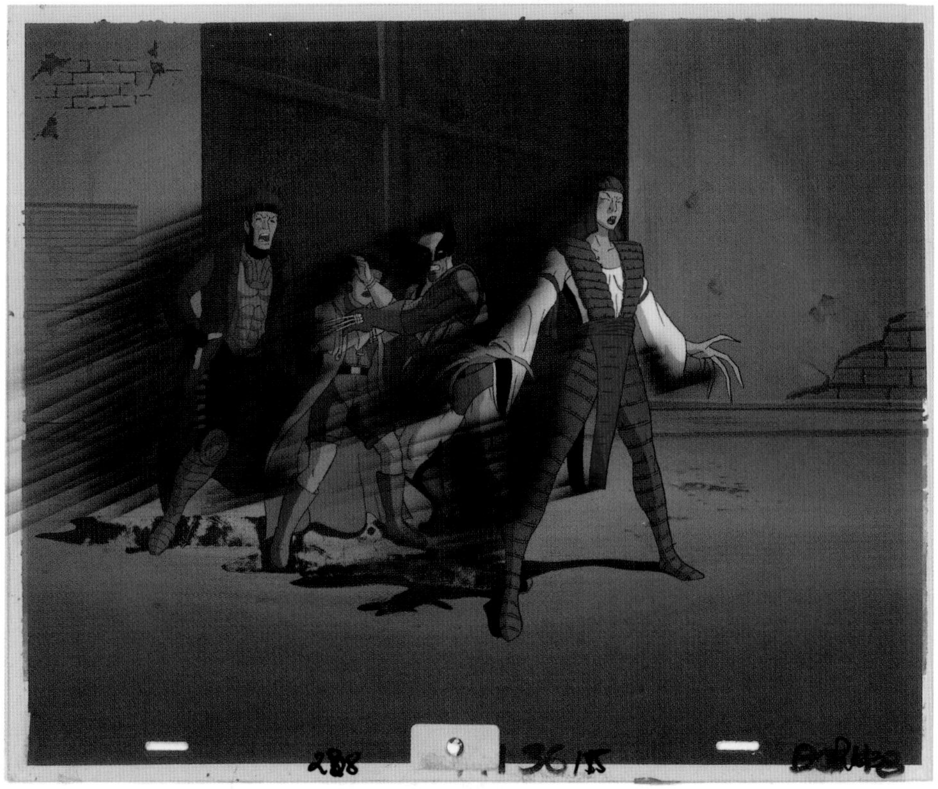

12

09 Layout of exterior of art museum, New York, designed and cleaned by Squillace. **10** Storyboard page, interior of art museum, where Beast enjoys a moment to himself and engages other patrons before being recalled to the X-Mansion by Professor Xavier. **11** Production cel with Professor Xavier, Wolverine, and unconscious Jubilee and Lady Deathstrike. Note that Lady Deathstrike wears a vest with no shirt over her chest area. **12** Production cel with Gambit, Jubilee, Wolverine, and Lady Deathstrike confronting the off-screen spirit drinker. Lady Deathstrike now has a white shirt painted over her chest.

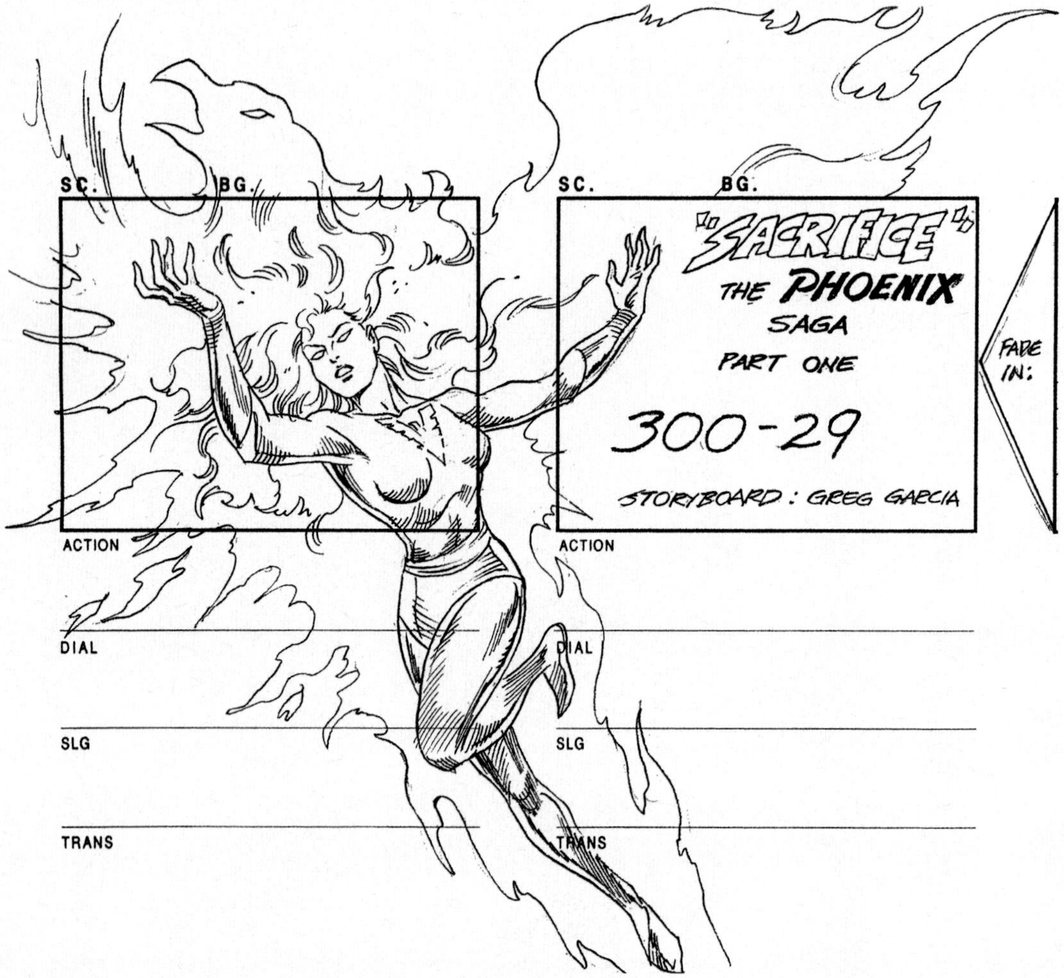
SC.
BG.
ACTION
DIAL
SLG
TRANS
SC.
BG.
"SACRIFICE"
THE PHOENIX
SAGA
PART ONE
300-29
STORYBOARD : GREG GARCIA
ACTION
DIAL
SLG
TRANS
FADE IN:

01

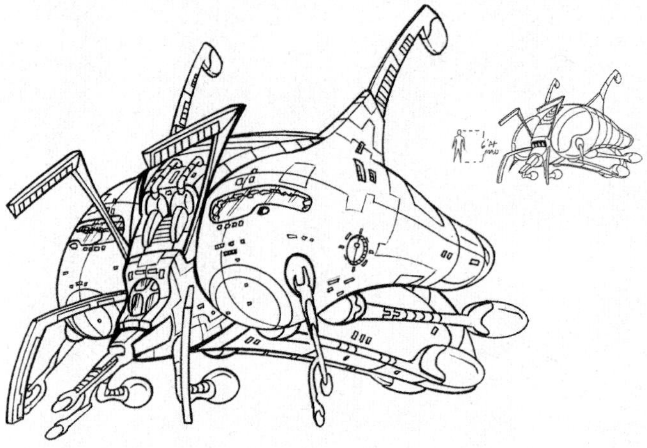

02

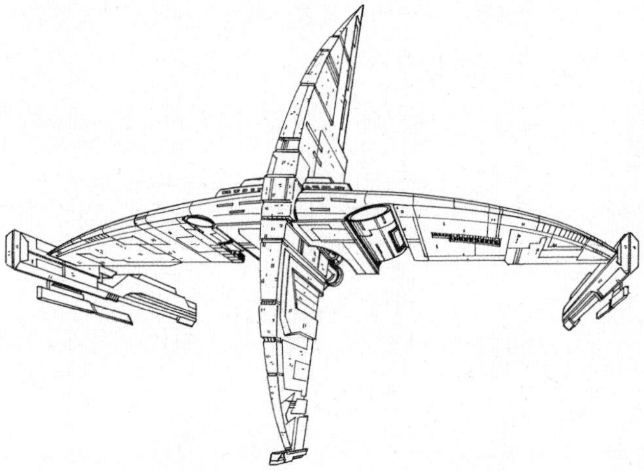

03

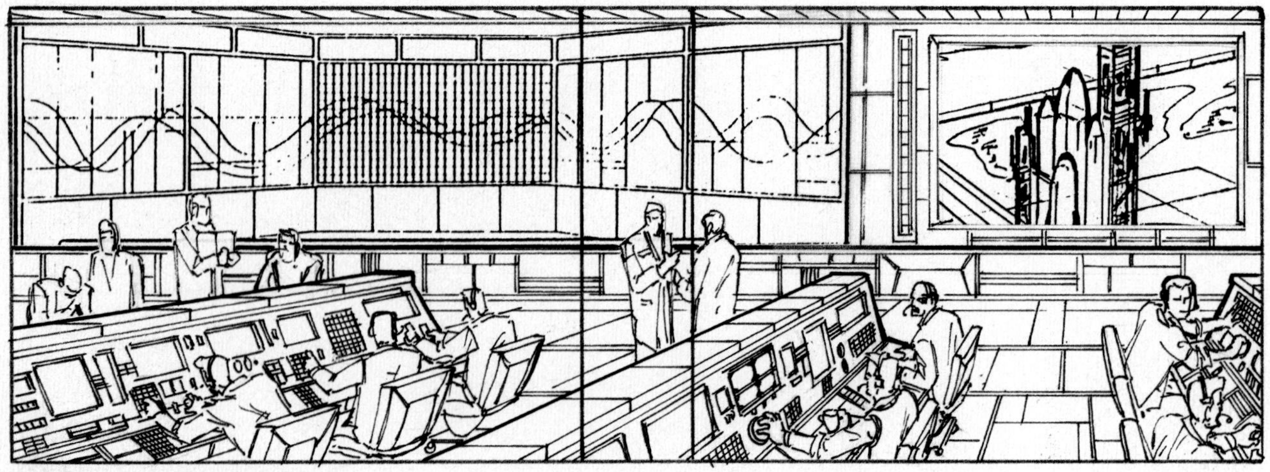

04

01 Page one storyboard of "Phoenix Saga, Part 1: Sacrifice." First act drawn by Greg Garcia. **02** Prop models of Rebel Princess Lilandra Neramani's renegade star cruiser space vehicle, by Marcos Borregales. Designed and cleaned by Frank Squillace, based on Dave Cockrum's original comic-book designs. **03** Three-quarter view of Shi'ar Intergalactic Patrol spaceship, by Borregales. Designed and cleaned by Squillace, based on Cockrum's original comic-book designs. **04** Layout of space shuttle mission control, interior, for Space Shuttle Star Corps. Designed and cleaned by Squillace. **OPPOSITE** Production cel with Wolverine and Beast in space suits.

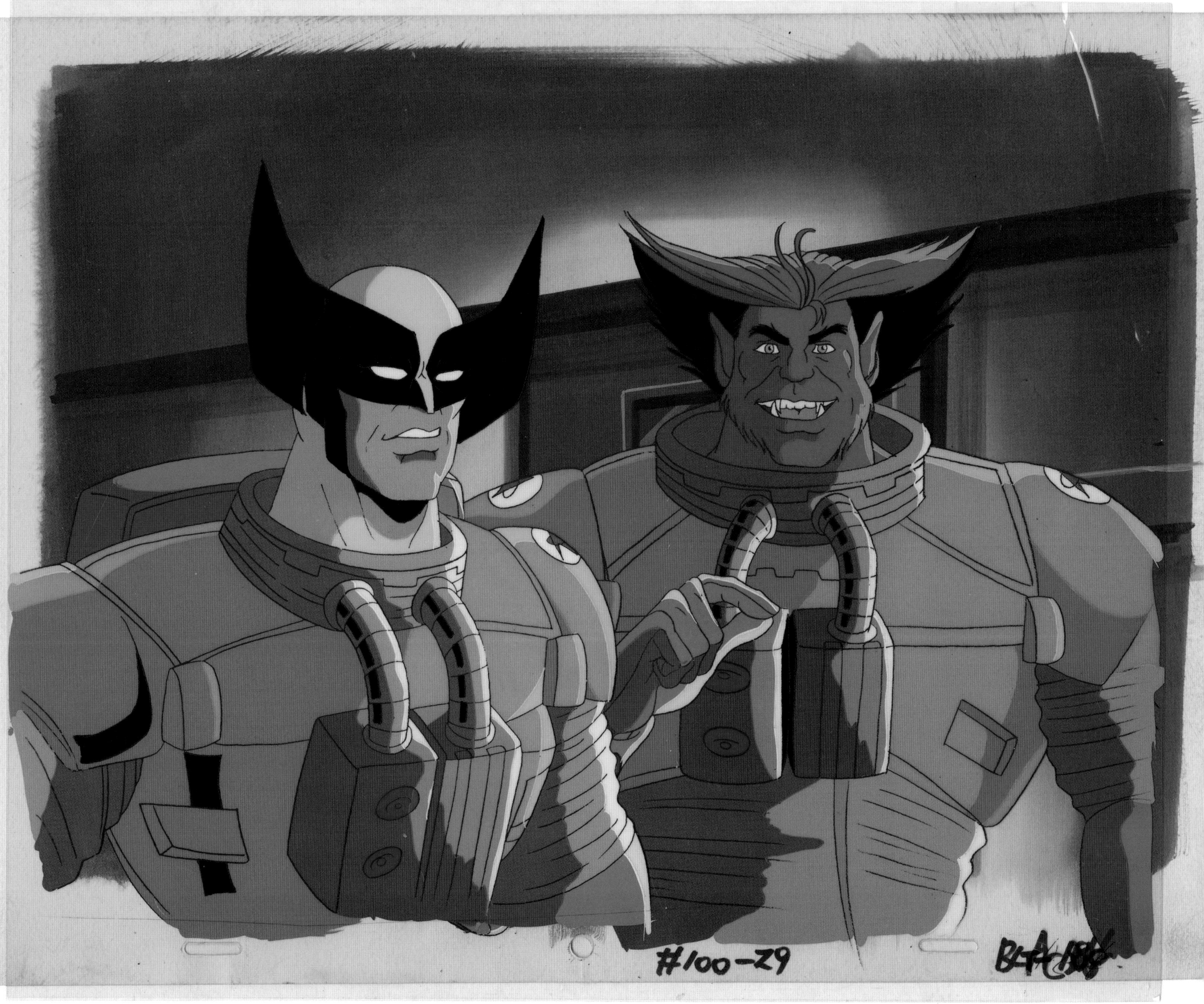
#100-29

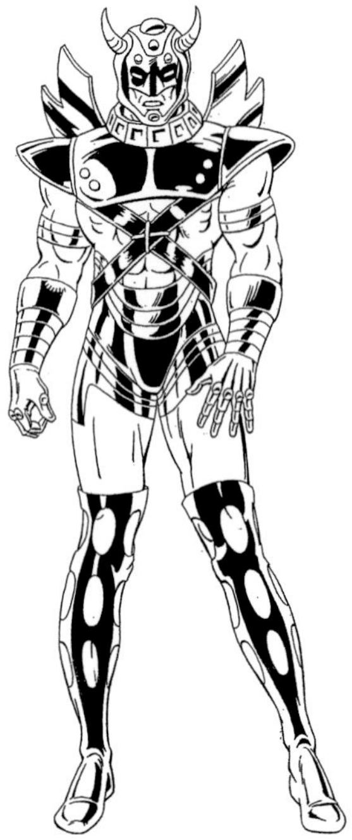

01

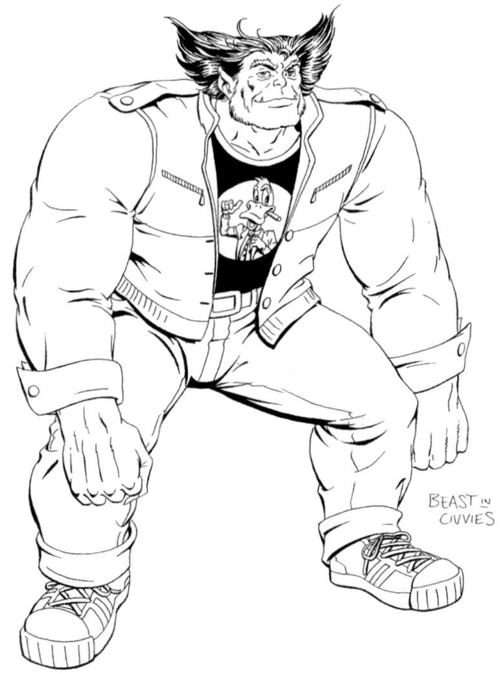
BEAST IN CIVVIES

02

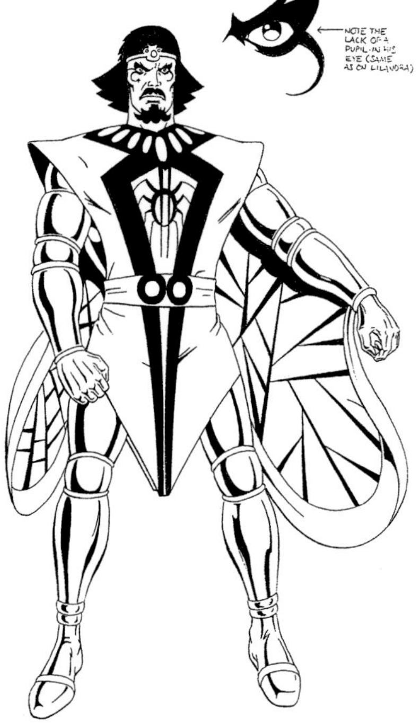
NOTE THE LACK OF A PUPIL IN HIS EYE (SAME AS ON LILANDRA)

03

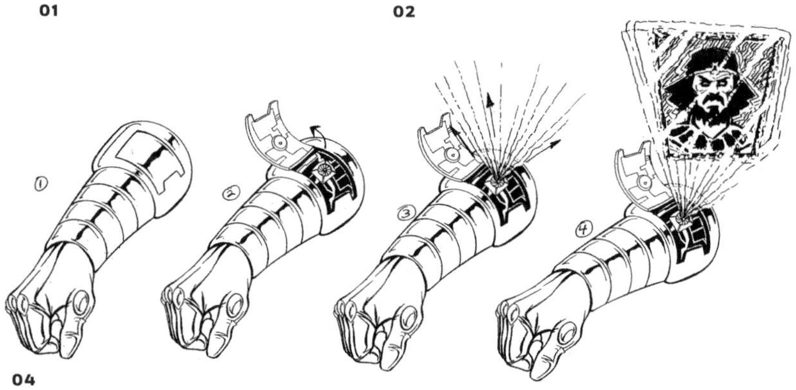
①
②
③
④

04

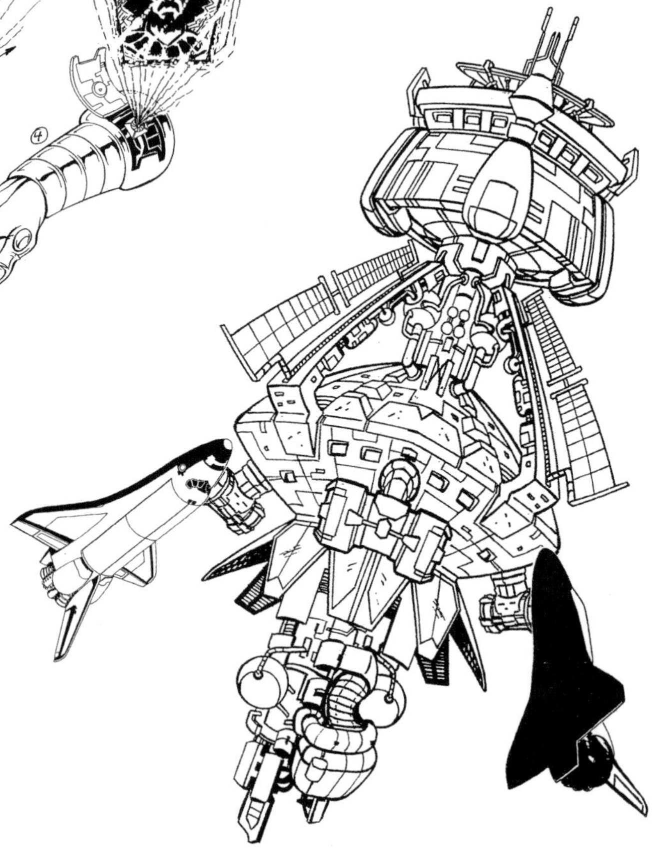

05

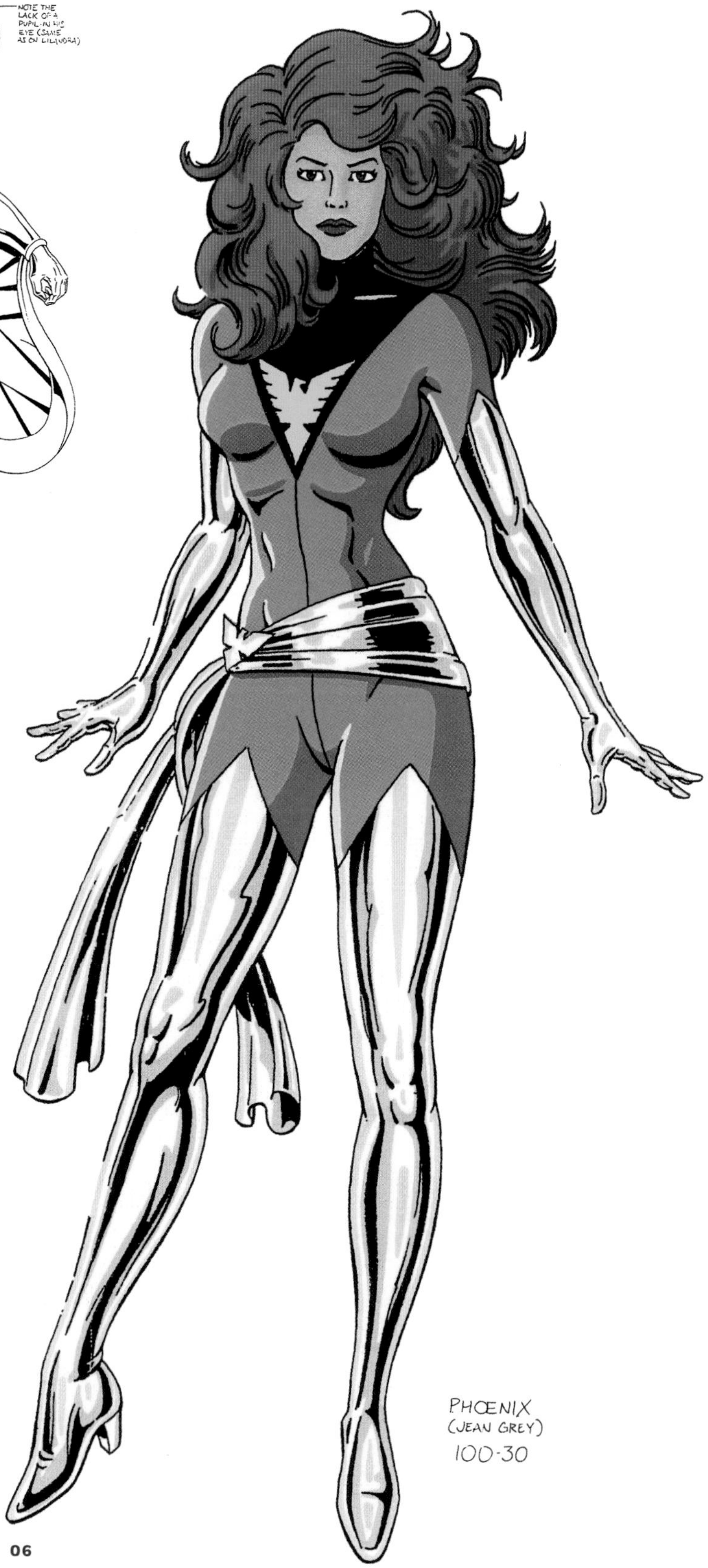
PHŒNIX
(JEAN GREY)
100-30

06

01 Character model of Eric the Red, by Frank Brunner and Mark Lewis. **02** Character model of Beast in civvies, by Brunner and Lewis. Brunner worked on the *Howard the Duck* comic, and Beast's T-shirt design is his homage. **03** Character model of Shi'ar Emperor D'Ken; detail reads "note lack of pupil in his eye (same as Lilandra)." Pencils by Brunner, inks by Lewis. **04** Eric the Red's arm amulet with broadcasting device for communication in its four stages of use, designed and cleaned by Frank Squillace. **05** Layout of the exterior of the *Eagle 1* Space Station, designed and cleaned by Squillace. **06** Color character model of Jean Grey as Phoenix, by Brunner and Lewis. **07** Production cel with a haunted Professor Xavier defying his off-screen X-Men. **08** Storyboards for the second full-body appearance of Deadpool; he previously made cameo appearances in "Deadly Reunions" (as a floating head) and "Whatever It Takes" (when Morph briefly takes his form to taunt Wolverine).

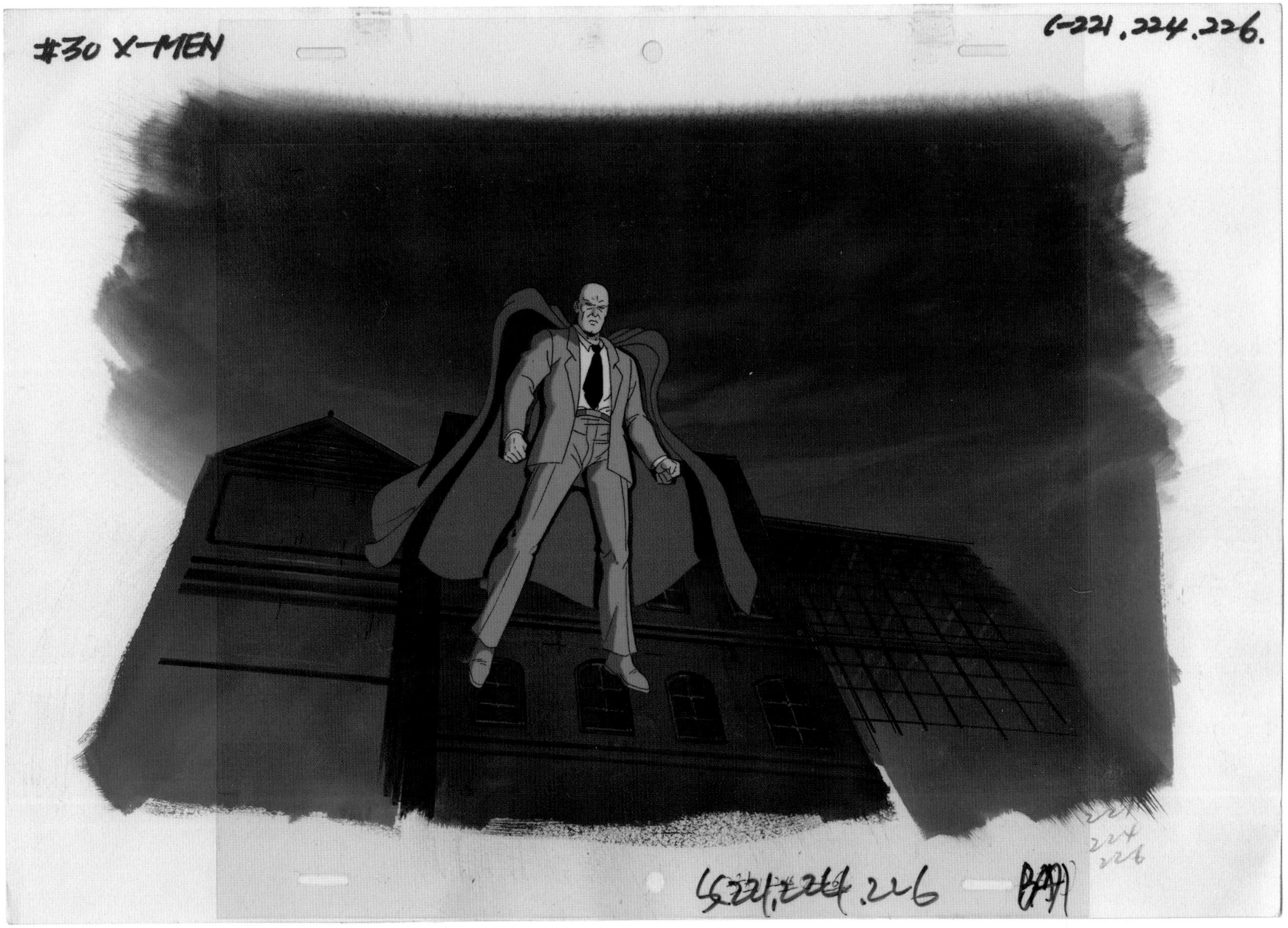
#30 X-MEN
6-221, 224, 226.
6-221, 224, 226

07

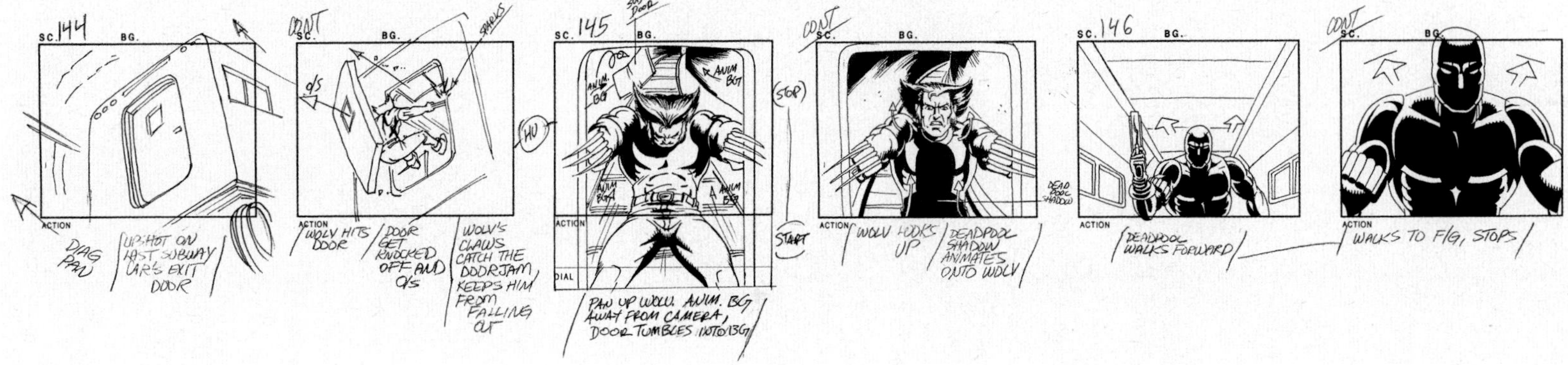
SC. 144
BG.
ACTION
DIAG PAN
UP SHOT ON 1ST SUBWAY CAR'S EXIT DOOR
CONT
O/S
WOLV HITS DOOR
DOOR GET KNOCKED OFF AND O/S
WOLV'S CLAWS CATCH THE DOORJAM, KEEPS HIM FROM FALLING OUT
SC. 145
ANIM BG
ACTION
DIAL
PAN UP WOLV. ANIM. BG AWAY FROM CAMERA, DOOR TUMBLES INTO BG
STOP
START
CONT
WOLV LOOKS UP
DEADPOOL SHADOW ANIMATES ONTO WOLV
SC. 146
DEADPOOL WALKS FORWARD
CONT
WALKS TO F/G, STOPS

08

01

02

03

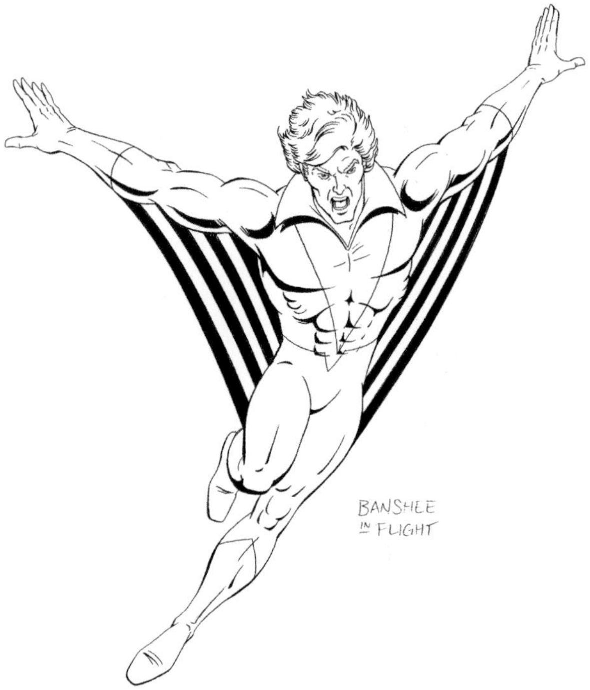
BANSHEE
IN FLIGHT

04

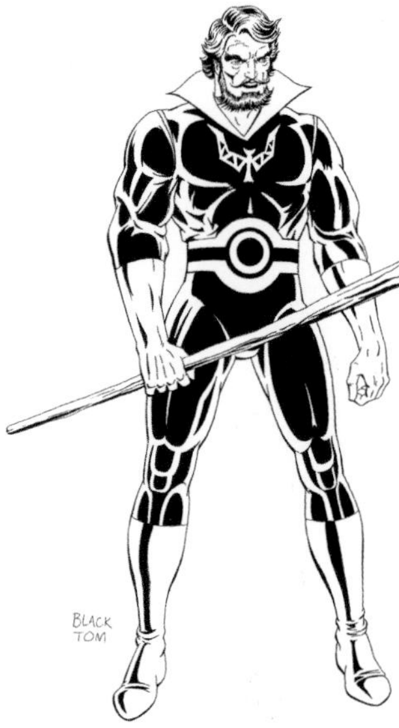
BLACK
TOM

05

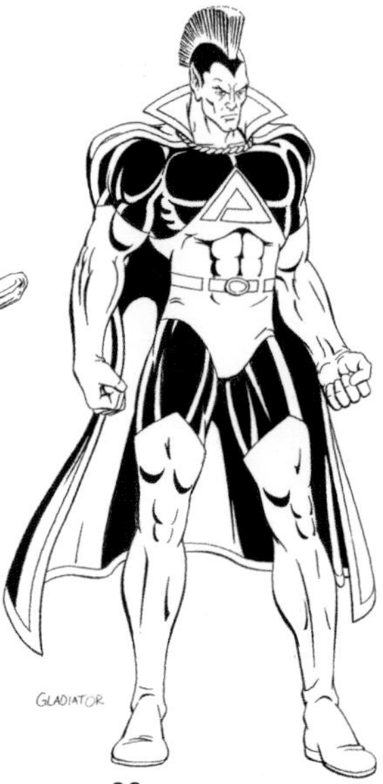
GLADIATOR

06

01 Production cel with Professor Xavier, Juggernaut, and Shi'ar Princess Lilandra, on Muir Island. **02** Production cel of Eric the Red on the roof of Cassidy Keep, Muir Island. **03** Production cel of Banshee inside Cassidy Keep. **04** Character model of Banshee in flight, by Frank Brunner and Mark Lewis. **05–06** Character models of Black Tom and Gladiator, by Brunner and Lewis. **07** Production overlay cel of Phoenix clutching the M'Krann crystal, with Phoenix special-effect paint.

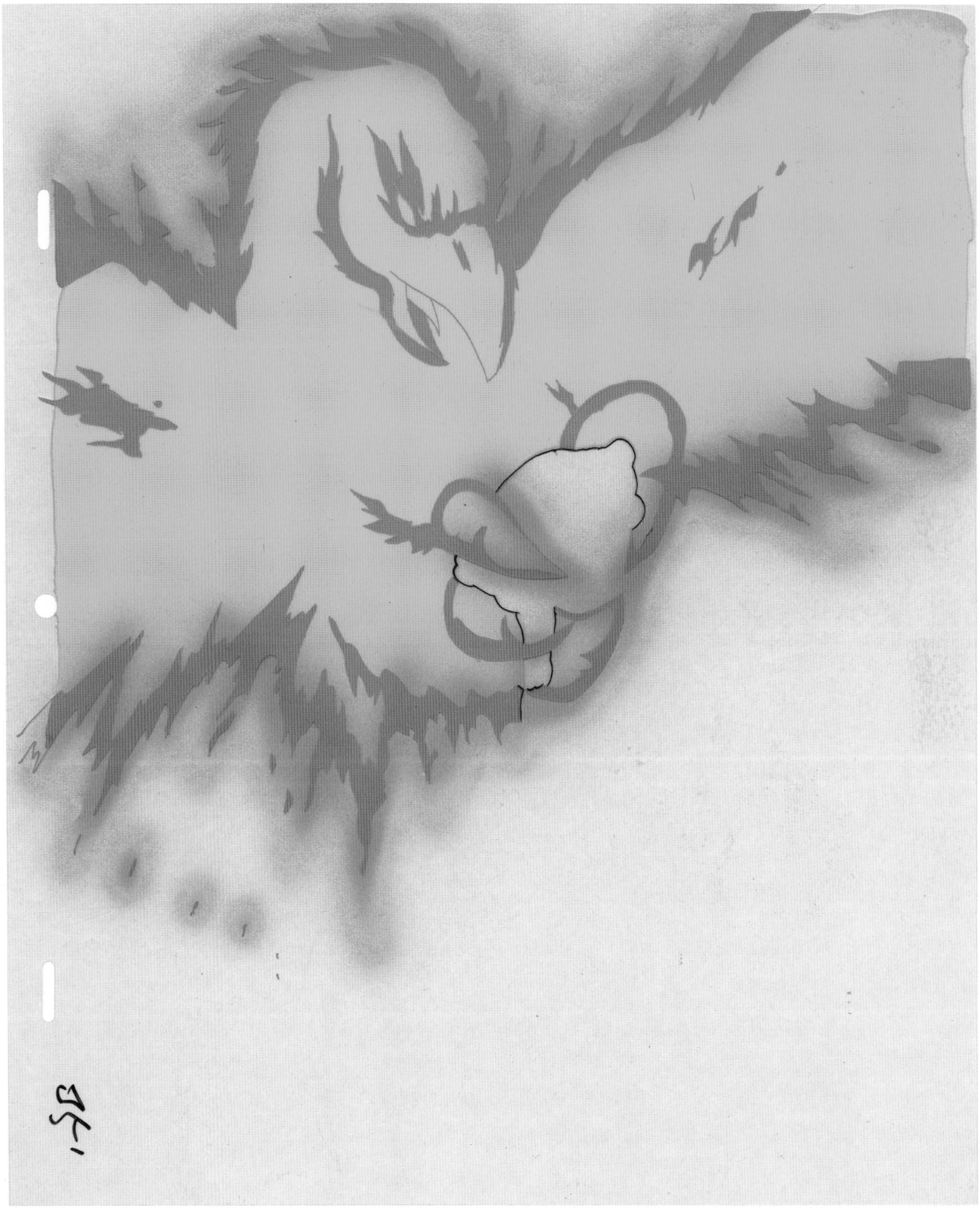

07

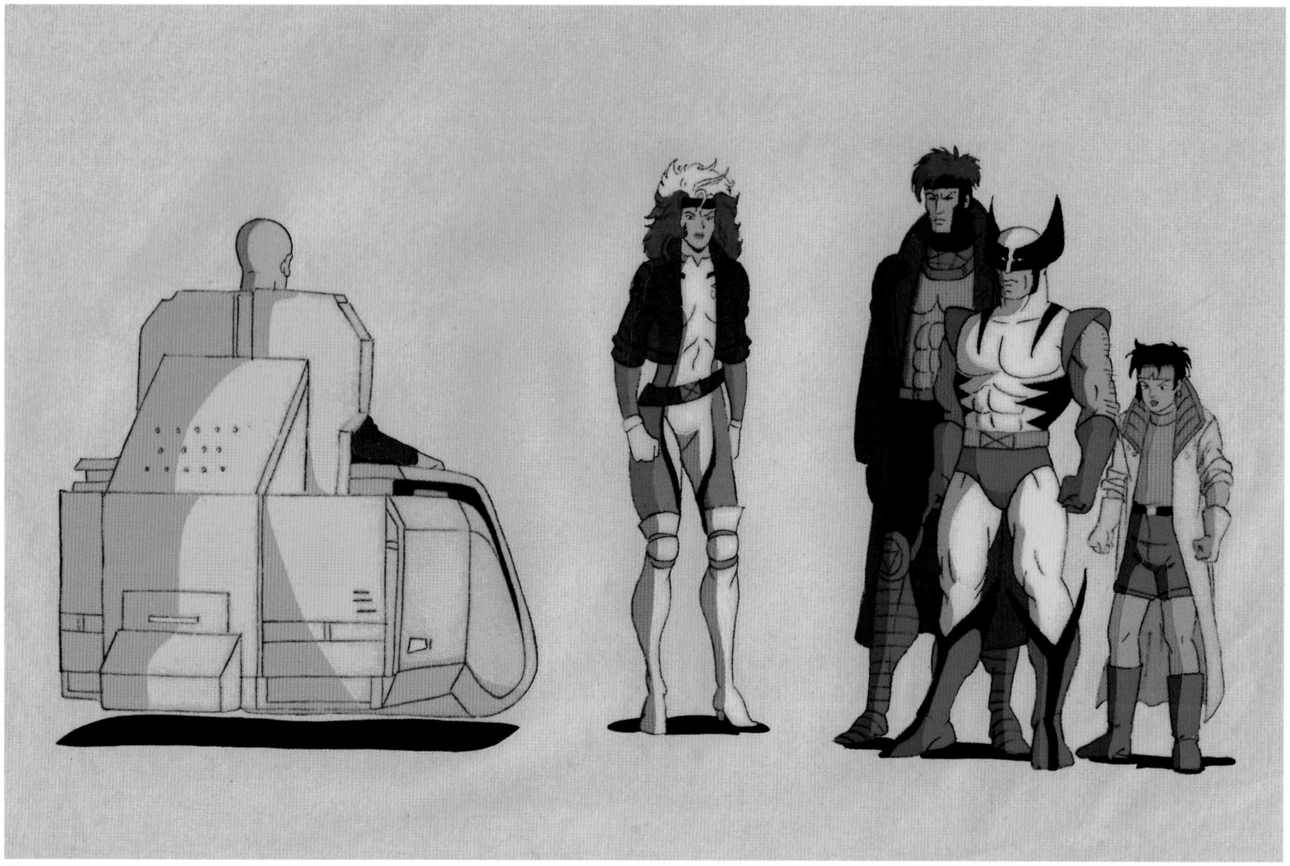

01

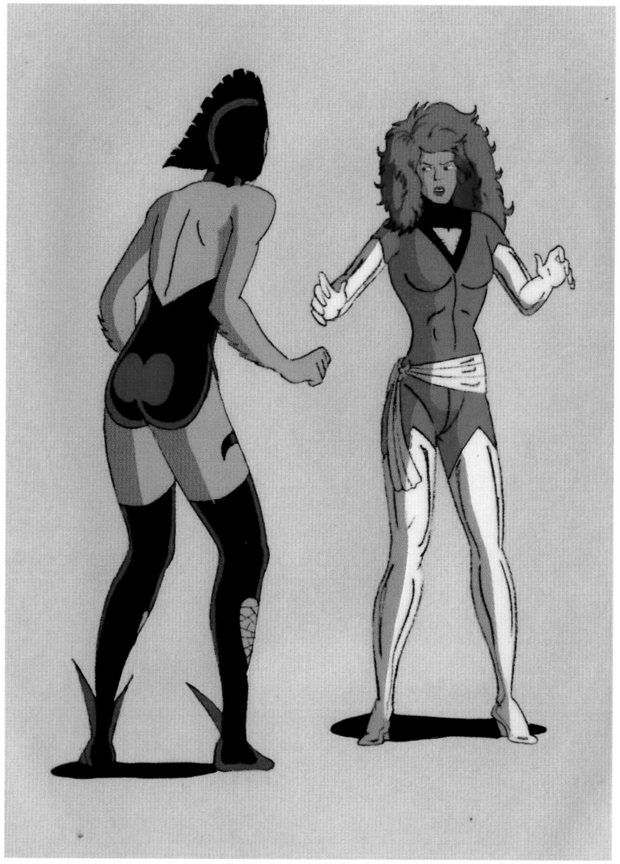

02

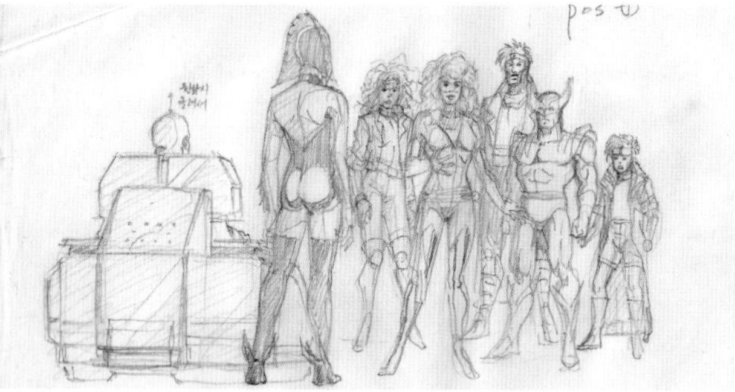

03

01 Cel layer with Professor Xavier, Rogue, Gambit, Wolverine, and Jubilee. **02** Cel layer with Lilandra and Jean Grey as Phoenix; note how the two cels combine to form the grouping seen in the sketch (03). **03** Animator's drawing of Professor Xavier, Lilandra, Rogue, Jean Grey as Phoenix, Gambit, Wolverine, and Jubilee. **04–11** Character models of: Captain Britain, Imperial Guard Oracle, Lilandra's Crewperson 1, Lilandra's Crewperson 2, Starjammer Corsair 3/4 front, Starjammer Ch'od, Starjammer Mam'selle Hepzibah, Starjammer Raza—all penciled by Frank Brunner and cleaned up by Mark Lewis. **12** Page one storyboard of "The Phoenix Saga, Part 5: Child of Light"; storyboard by Dan Veesenmeyer.

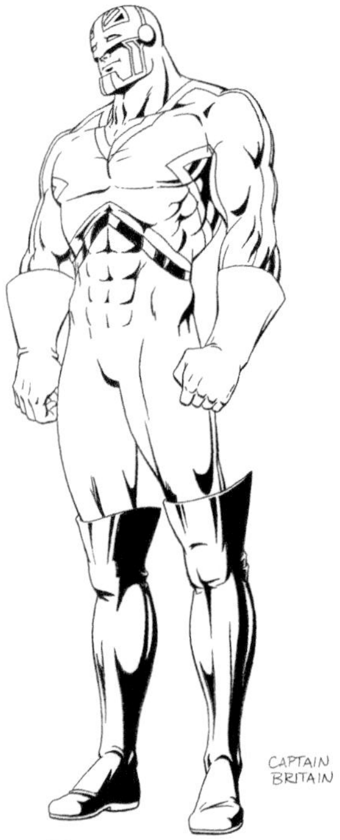
CAPTAIN BRITAIN

04

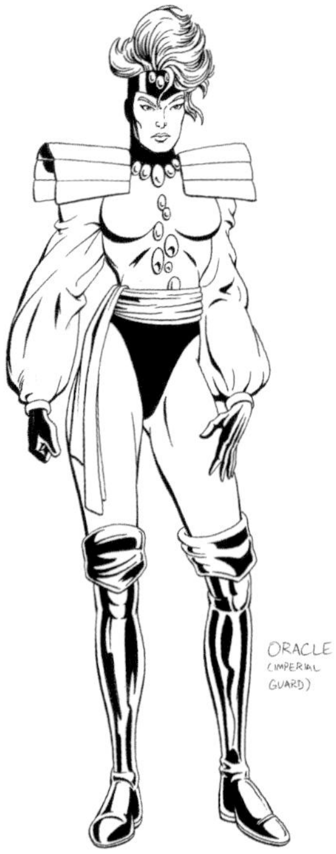
ORACLE (IMPERIAL GUARD)

05

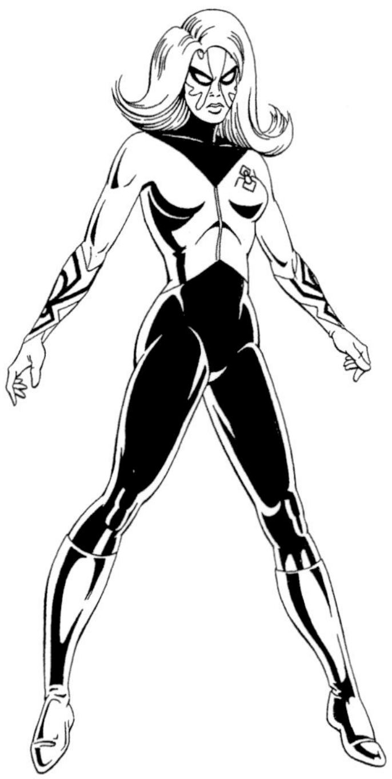

06

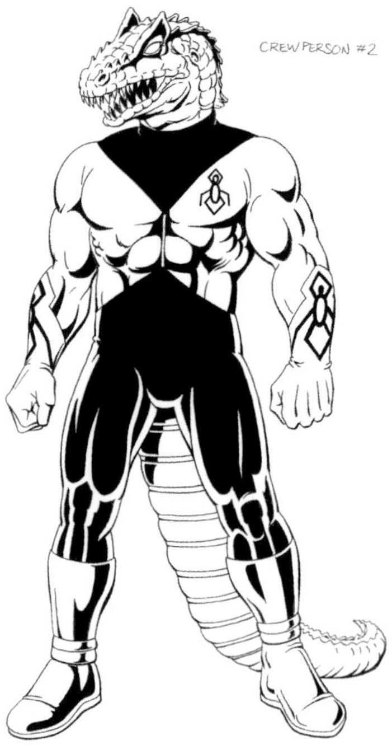
CREW PERSON #2

07

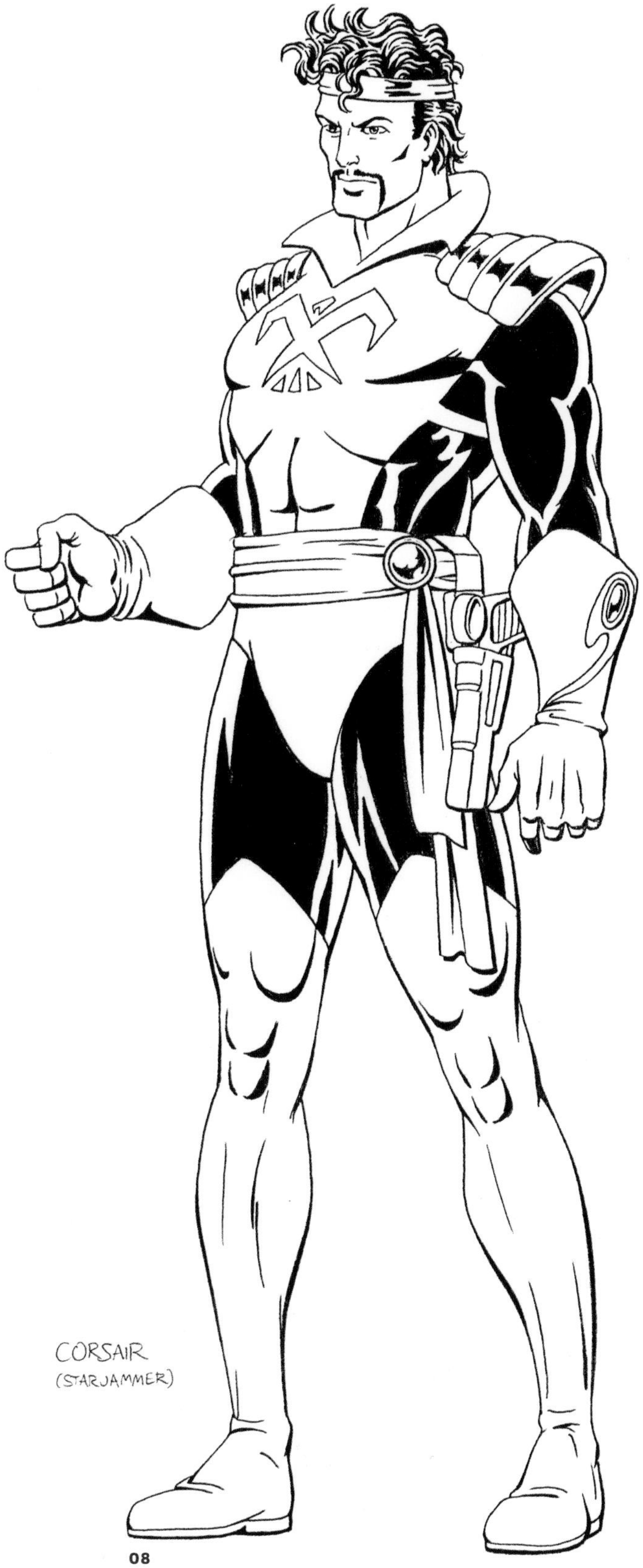
CORSAIR
(STARJAMMER)

08

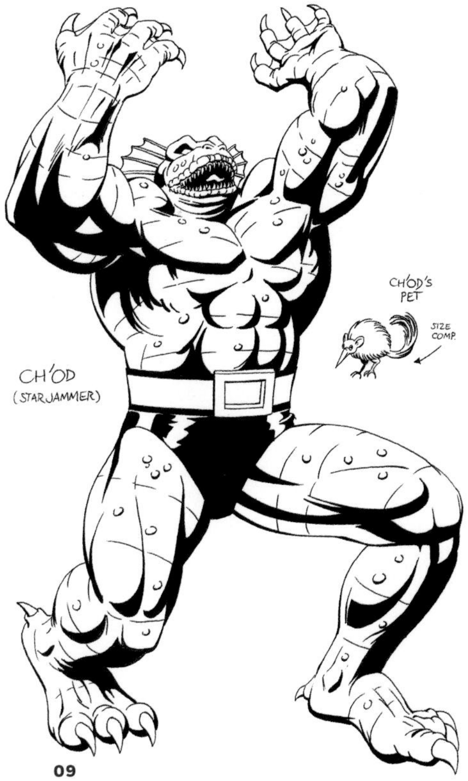
CH'OD
(STARJAMMER)
CH'OD'S PET
SIZE COMP.

09

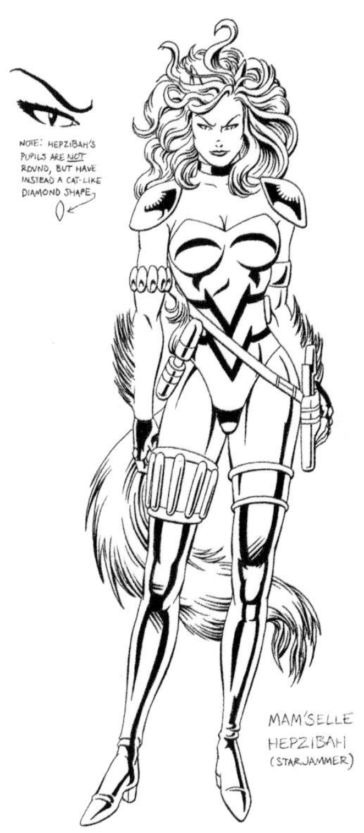
NOTE: HEPZIBAH'S PUPILS ARE NOT ROUND, BUT HAVE INSTEAD A CAT-LIKE DIAMOND SHAPE.
MAM'SELLE HEPZIBAH
(STARJAMMER)

10

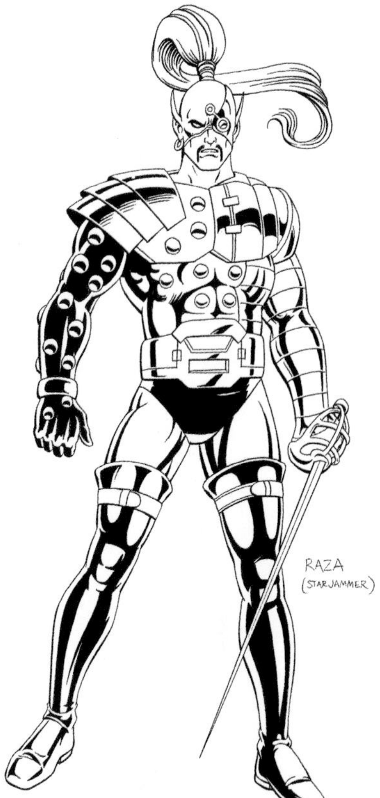
RAZA
(STARJAMMER)

11

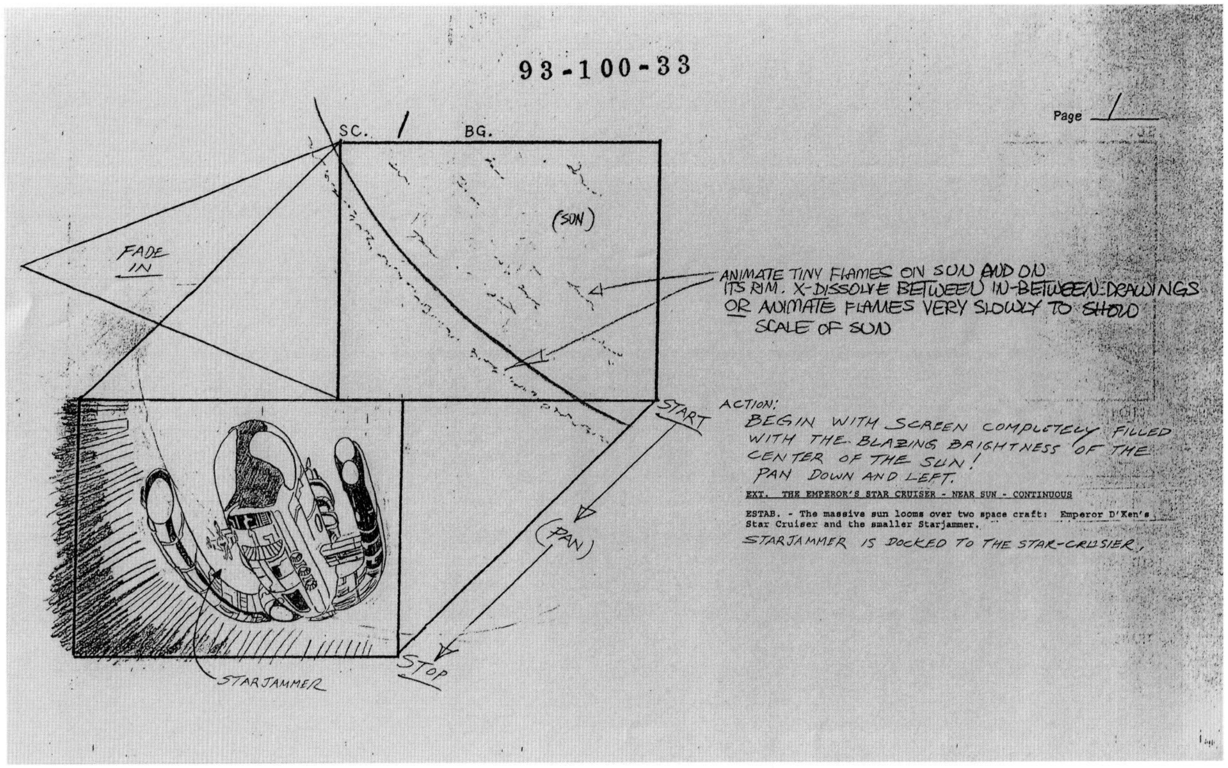
93-100-33
Page 1
SC. 1 BG.
(SUN)
FADE IN
ANIMATE TINY FLAMES ON SUN AND ON ITS RIM. X-DISSOLVE BETWEEN IN-BETWEEN DRAWINGS OR ANIMATE FLAMES VERY SLOWLY TO SHOW SCALE OF SUN
START
(PAN)
STOP
STARJAMMER
ACTION:
BEGIN WITH SCREEN COMPLETELY FILLED WITH THE BLAZING BRIGHTNESS OF THE CENTER OF THE SUN!
PAN DOWN AND LEFT.
EXT. THE EMPEROR'S STAR CRUISER - NEAR SUN - CONTINUOUS
ESTAB. - The massive sun looms over two space craft: Emperor D'Ken's Star Cruiser and the smaller Starjammer.
STARJAMMER IS DOCKED TO THE STAR-CRUSIER,

12

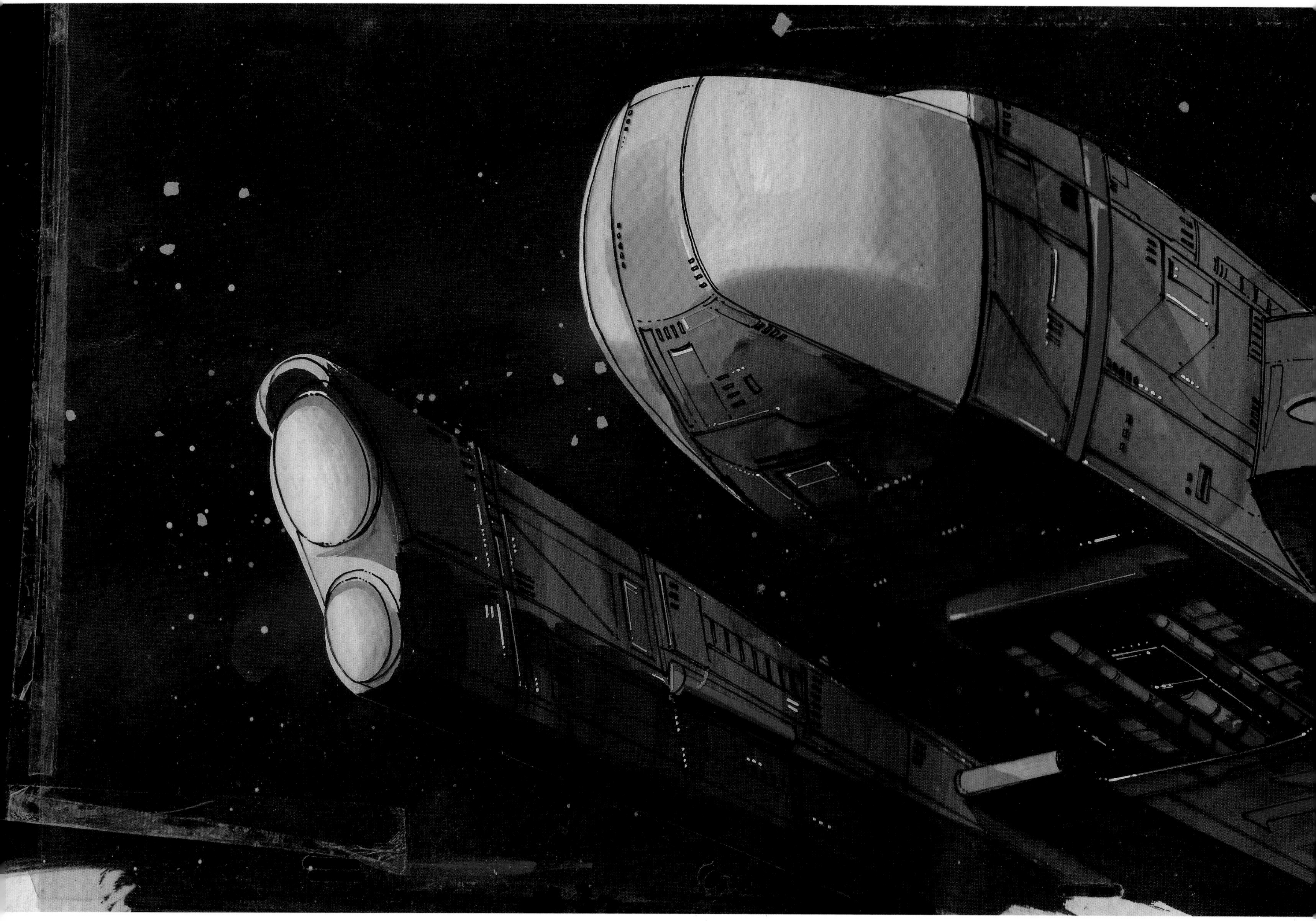

ABOVE Production cel, three-panel painted background, with Emperor D'Ken's Star Cruiser from "The Phoenix Saga, Part 4: The Fate of the Phoenix." Drawn from the storyboard by Dan Veesenmeyer.

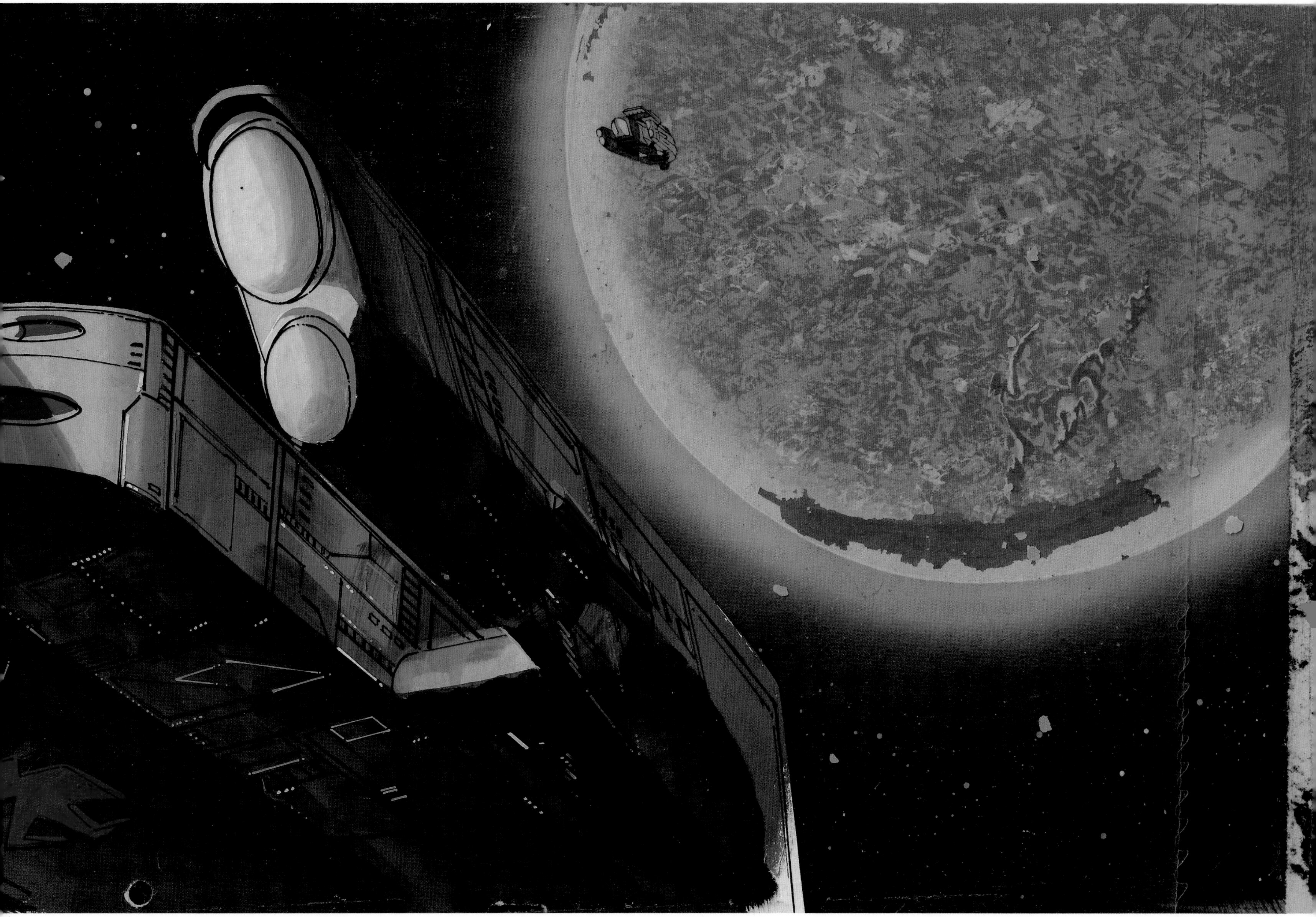

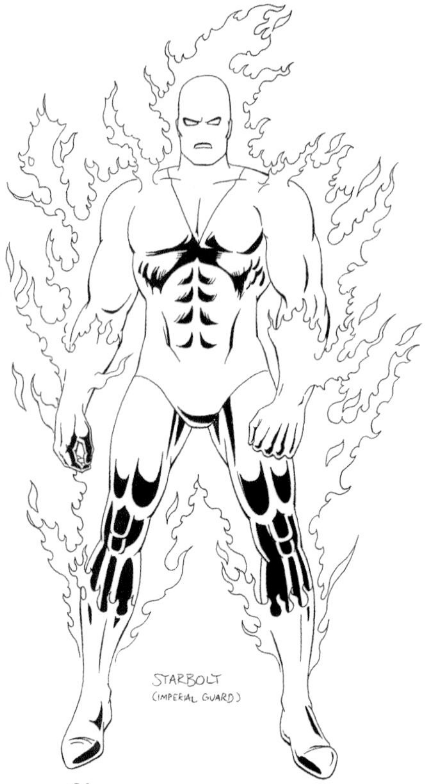
STARBOLT
(IMPERIAL GUARD)

01

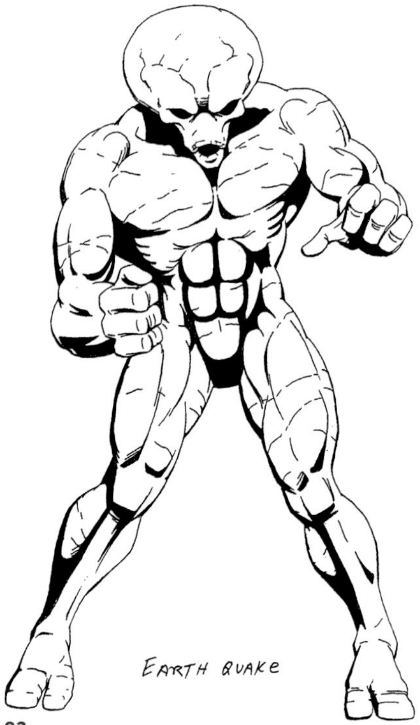
EARTH QUAKE

02

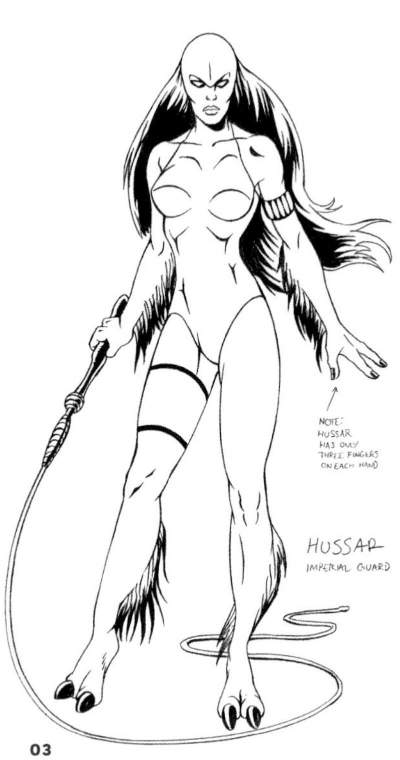
NOTE:
HUSSAR
HAS ONLY
THREE FINGERS
ON EACH HAND
HUSSAR
IMPERIAL GUARD

03

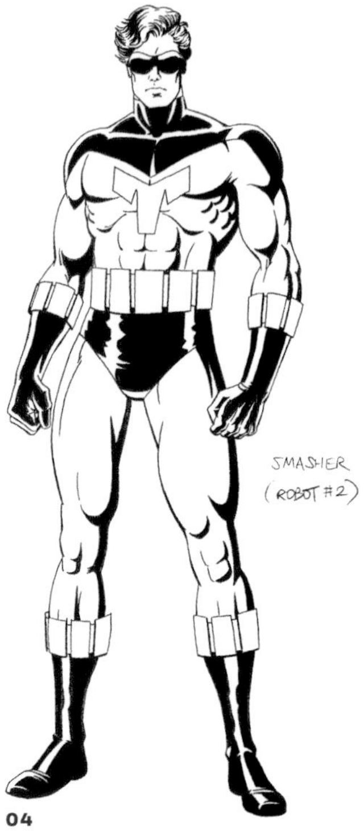
SMASHER
(ROBOT #2)

04

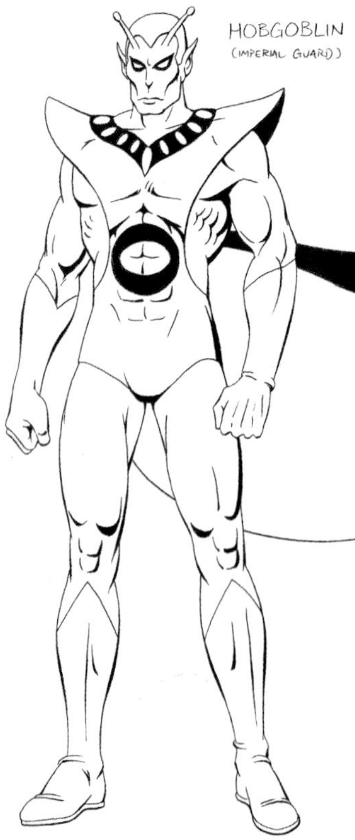
HOBGOBLIN
(IMPERIAL GUARD)

05

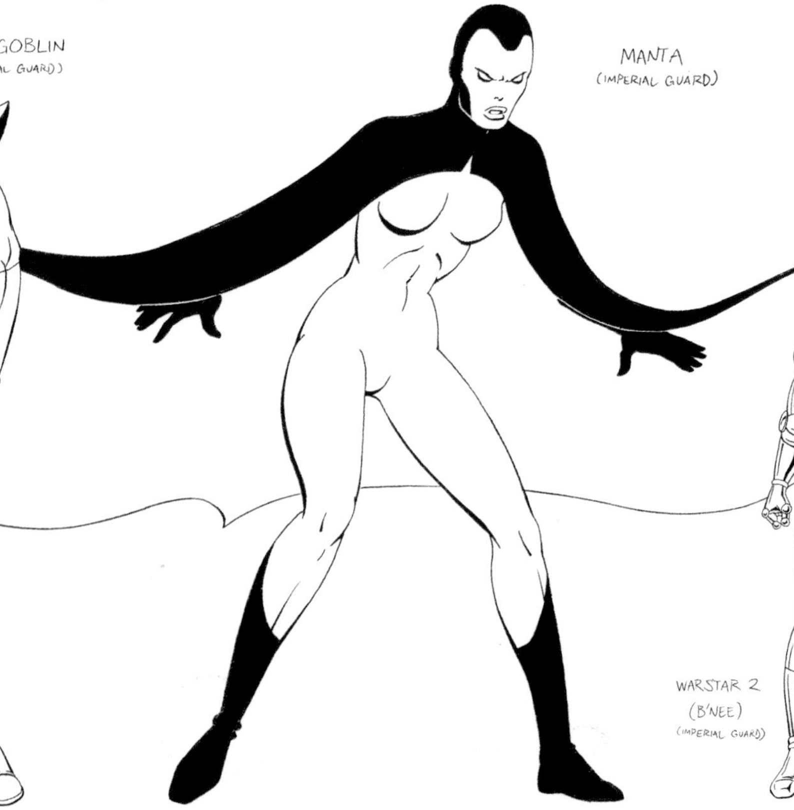
MANTA
(IMPERIAL GUARD)

06

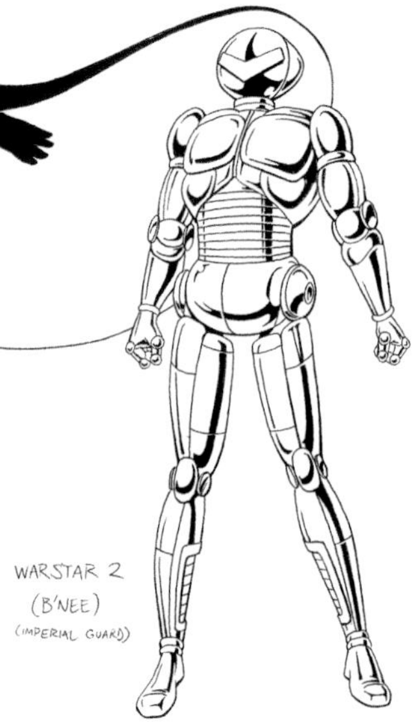
WARSTAR 2
(B'NEE)
(IMPERIAL GUARD)

07

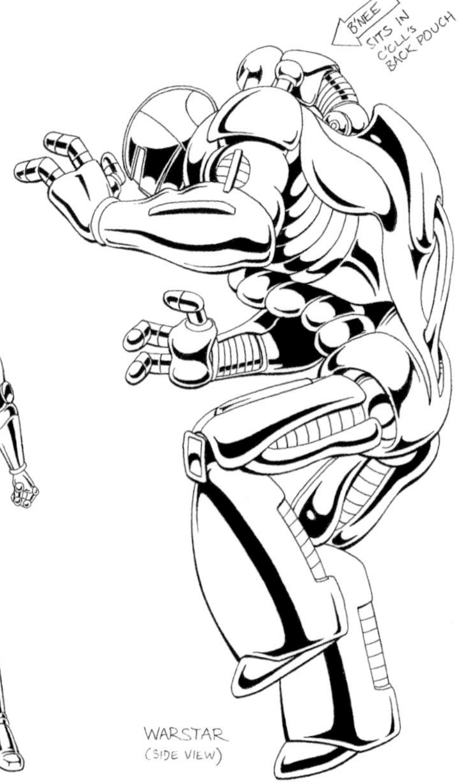
B'NEE
SITS IN
C'CLL'S
BACK POUCH
WARSTAR
(SIDE VIEW)

08

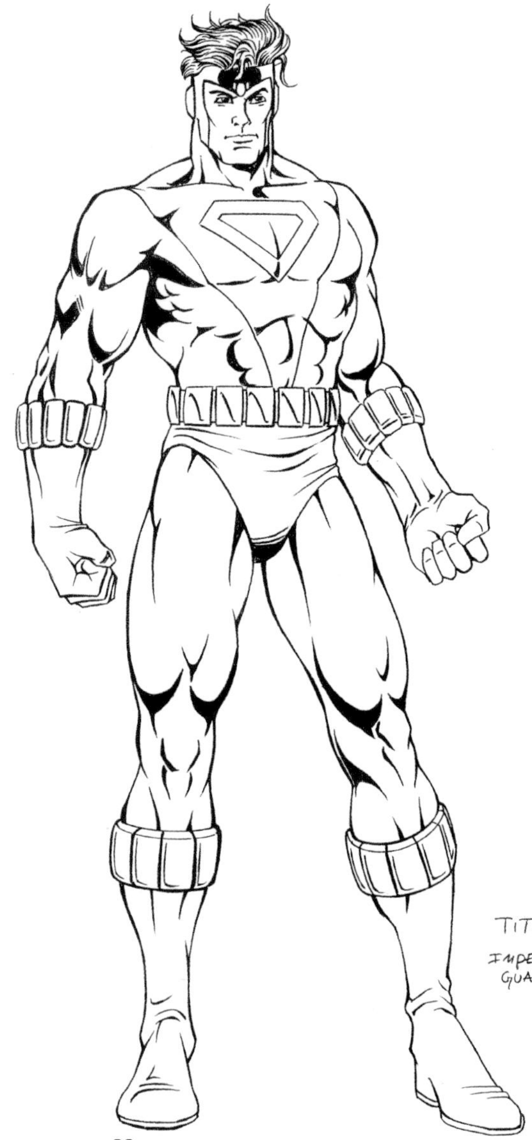
TITAN
IMPERIAL GUARD

09

01 Imperial Guard Starbolt; penciled by Frank Brunner, cleanup by Mark Lewis. **02** Character model of Earthquake; penciled by Brunner, cleanup by Lewis. **03** Character model of Imperial Guard Hussar; penciled by Brunner with cleanup by Lewis. **04** Character model of Smasher; penciled by Brunner with cleanup by Lewis **05** Imperial Guard Hobgoblin, by Brunner and Lewis. **06** Character model of Imperial Guard Manta, by Brunner with cleanup by Lewis. **07–08** Character model of B'nee (07), who climbs into the back of C'cll to form Imperial Guard Warstar (08)—all penciled by Brunner with cleanup by Lewis. **09** Character model of Imperial Guard Titan, designed Frank Squillace and cleaned by Lewis, based on Dave Cockrum's original comic-book designs. **10** Production cel of D'Ken holding the all-powerful M'Krann crystal, with painted background of space.

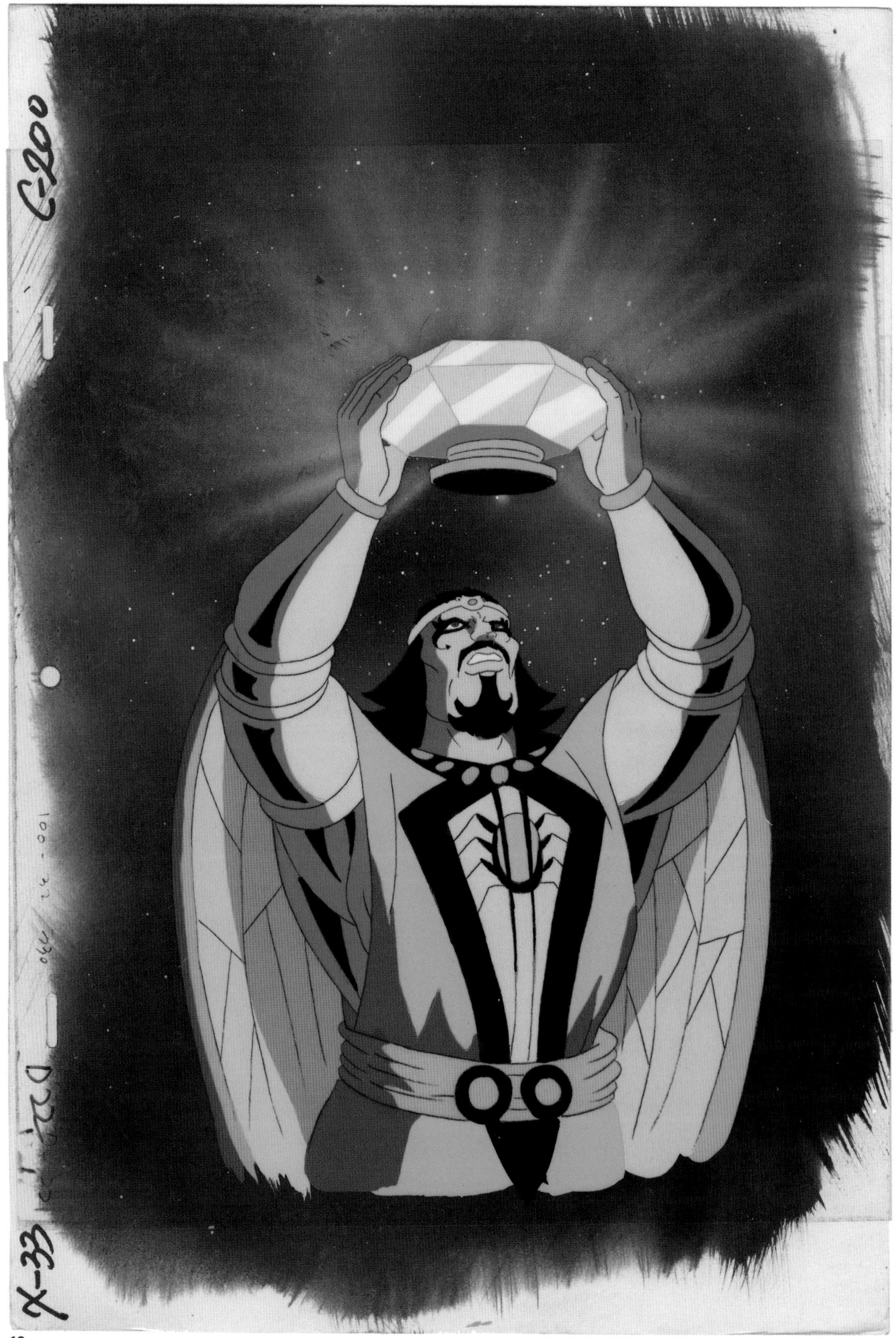
C-200
X-33

10

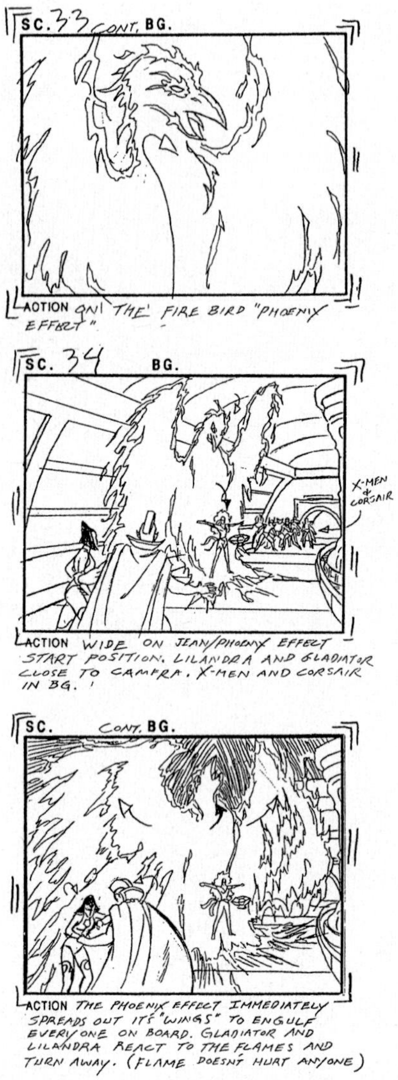
SC. 33 CONT. BG.
ACTION ON THE FIRE BIRD "PHOENIX EFFECT".
SC. 34 BG.
X-MEN & CORSAIR
ACTION WIDE ON JEAN/PHOENIX EFFECT START POSITION. LILANDRA AND GLADIATOR CLOSE TO CAMERA. X-MEN AND CORSAIR IN BG.
SC. CONT. BG.
ACTION THE PHOENIX EFFECT IMMEDIATELY SPREADS OUT IT'S "WINGS" TO ENGULF EVERYONE ON BOARD. GLADIATOR AND LILANDRA REACT TO THE FLAMES AND TURN AWAY. (FLAME DOESN'T HURT ANYONE)

01

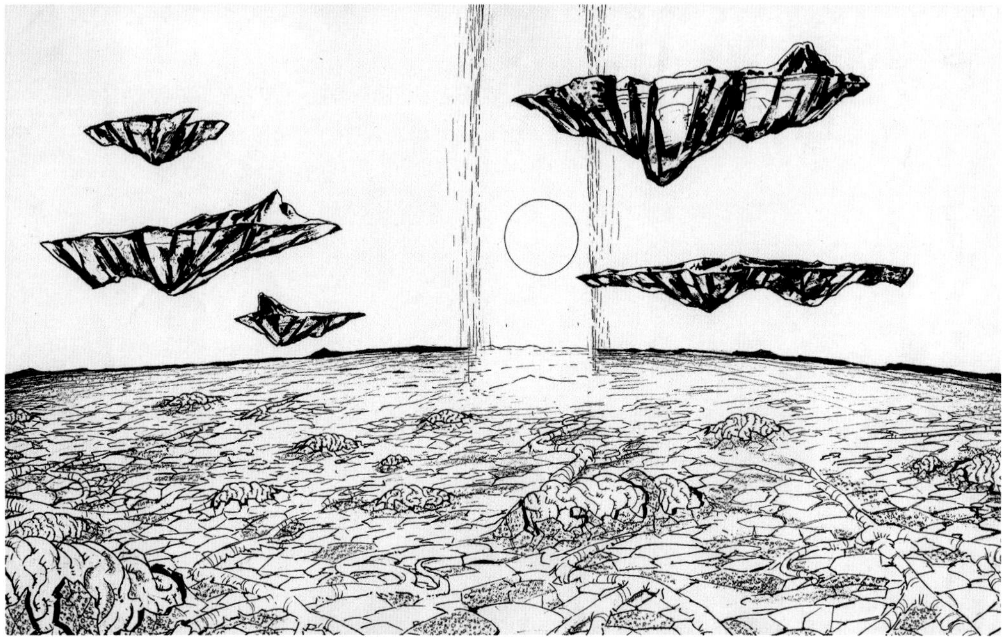

02

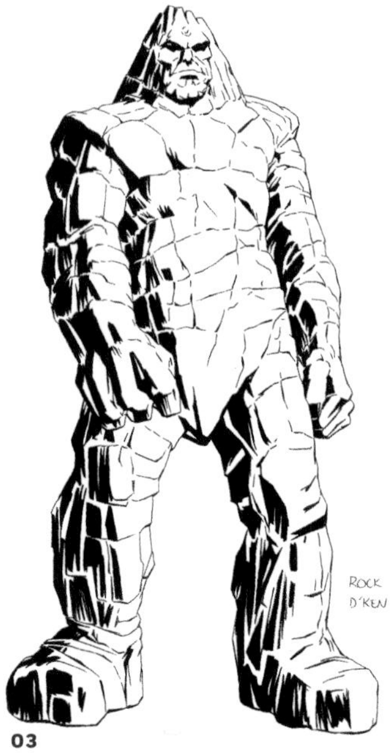
ROCK D'KEN

03

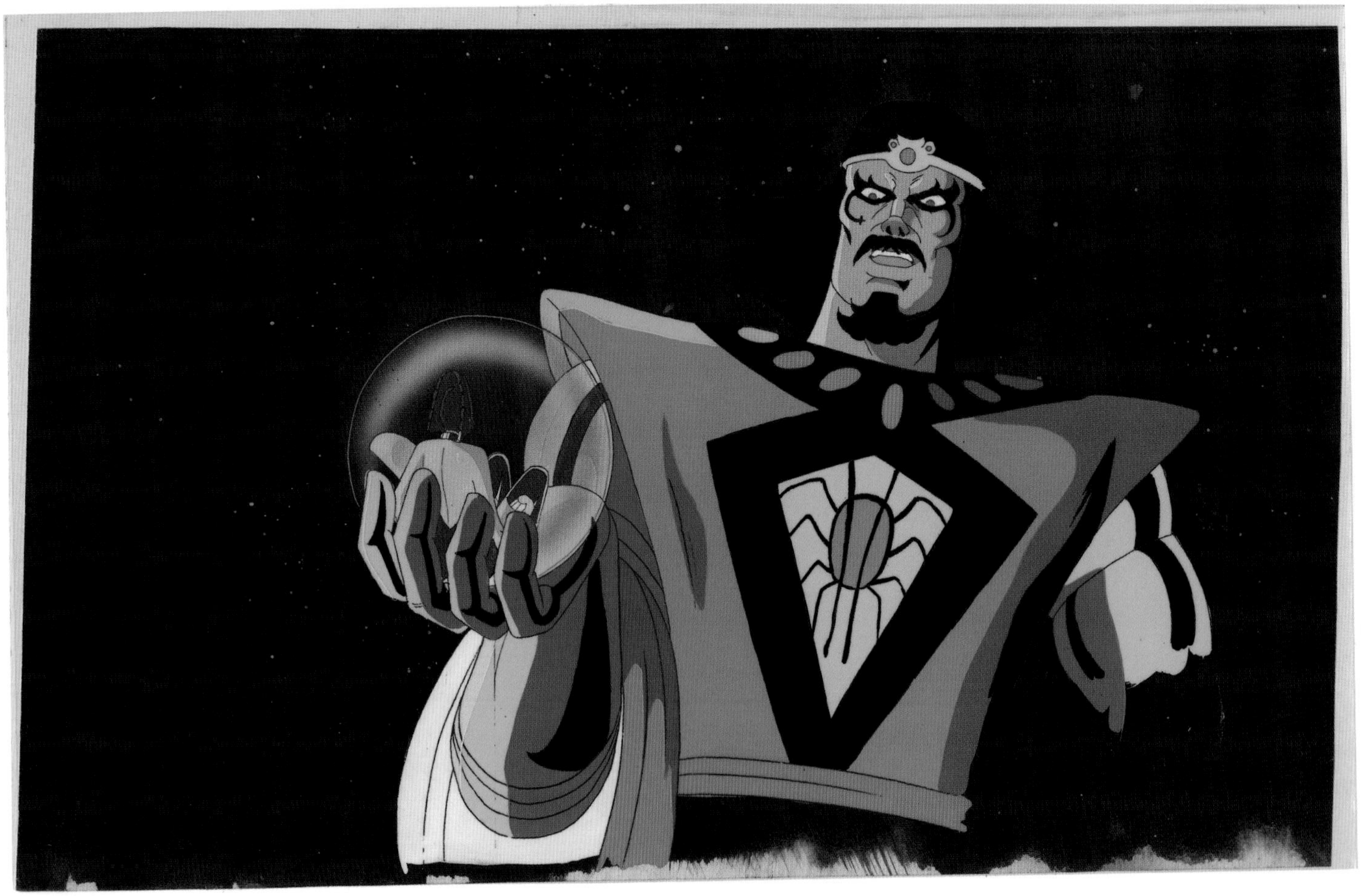

04

01 Page sixteen storyboard of "The Phoenix Saga, Part 5: Child of Light." Storyboard by Dan Veesenmeyer. **02** Layout of vista of D'Ken's own universe, inside the M'Krann crystal, designed and cleaned by Frank Squillace. **03** Character Model of Rock D'Ken; penciled by Frank Brunner with cleanup by Mark Lewis. **04** Production cel of D'Ken holding an imprisoned Lilandra, with painted background of space. **05** Production cel of Jean Grey as Phoenix with Cyclops, with painted background and special-effect fire overlay. **06** Storyboards from "The Phoenix Saga, Part 5: Child of Light," with the Phoenix flying into the sun and Cyclops mourning her back at Muir Island, on the roof of Cassidy Keep.

05

93-100-33
GRAZ ENTERTAINMENT, Inc.
SC. 368 BG. DIAG PAN SETUP (SEE NEXT PAGE)
EXT. SPACE NEAR THE SUN
WIDE ON LILANDRA'S STAR CRUISER AND PHOENIX - near one another in space.
PHOENIX (JEAN)
The crystal shall be buried forever!
SC. CONT BG.
THE crystal now forms the "heart" of the fiery energy creature
the Phoenix spreads its wings. turning away from Lilandra's ship
SC. CONT. BG. START PAN Page 207
ACTION TURNS UP TOWARD CAM

06

93-100-33
GRAZ ENTERTAINMENT, Inc.
SC. CONT. 369 BG. STOP PAN
The Phoenix soars, UP PAST CAM, AWAY TOWARD THE SUN
FOLLOW PHOENIX
START
SC. 369 BG. PAN BG Page 208
ACTION PHOENIX FLIES TOWARD CAM (MULTIPLANE) (SHIP IN FOCUS)

07

93-100-33
GRAZ ENTERTAINMENT, Inc.
SC. 398 CONT. BG.
ACTION. XAVIER TURNS HIS CHAIR, LOOKS BACK AT CYCLOPS
XAVIER (CONT)
(gently)
Please. think about it, Cyclops.
SC. CONT. BG.
O.S.
ACTION PROF. EXITS PAST CAM CYCLOPS LOOKS DOWN.
SC. 399 BG. TRUCK IN Page 232
ACTION DOWNSHOT ON TOWER PROF. EXITS TRUCK IN ON CYCLOPS.
93-100-33
SC. 400 BG. STOP PAN
SUN IS ALMOST GONE DOWN
PAN
START PAN ON PARAPET, MOVE UP, REFLECTION ON WATER, TO SUNSET
START PAN
SC. 401 BG.
CLOSE ON CYCLOPS - HIS LIPS PURSED
SC. CONT. BG. Page 233
ACTION HE LOOKS UP AT HORIZON. (O.S.)
The SUN REFLECTED IN HIS VISOR.
SC. CONT. 401 BG. TRUCK IN
FADE OUT
ACTION TRUCK IN AS THE SUN SETS, THE LIGHT IN THE REFLECTION DISAPPEARS.
A single tear trickles out from beneath his visor.
CYCLOPS
(quietly heart-broken)
Jean.

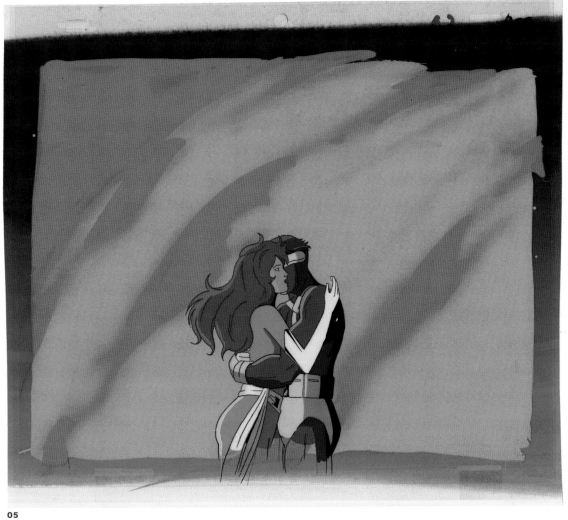

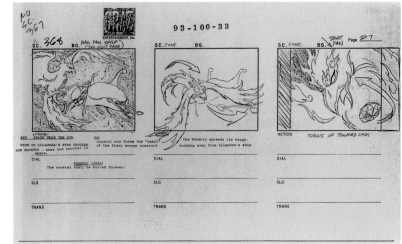

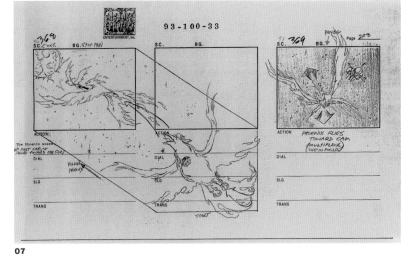

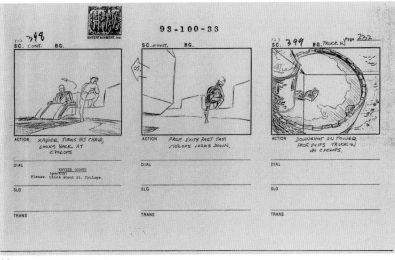

08

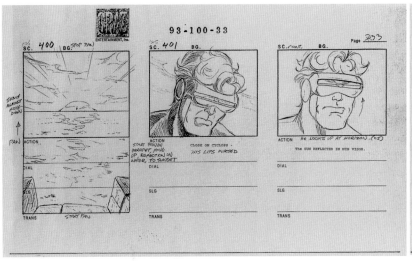

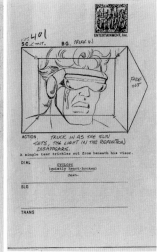

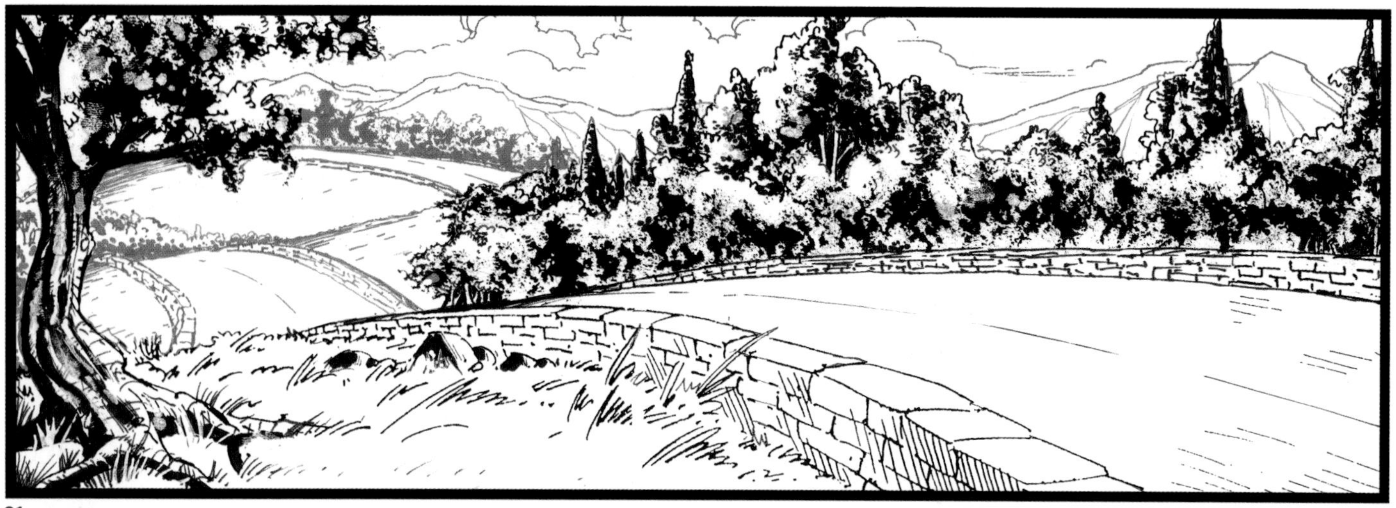

01

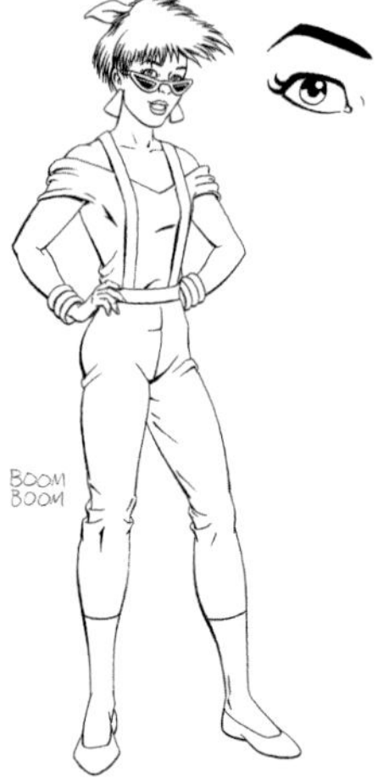
BOOM
BOOM

02

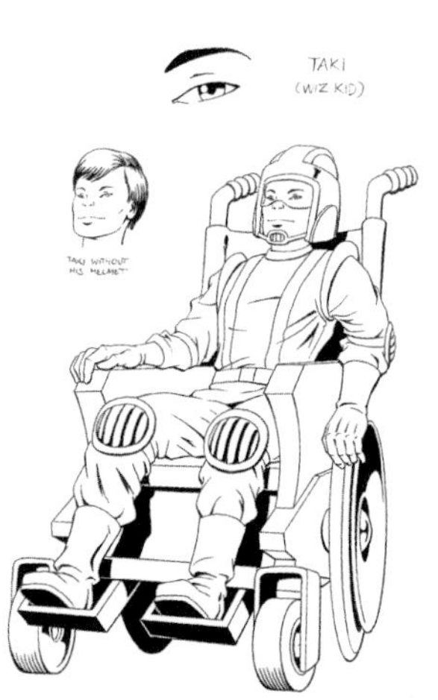
TAKI
(WIZ KID)

03

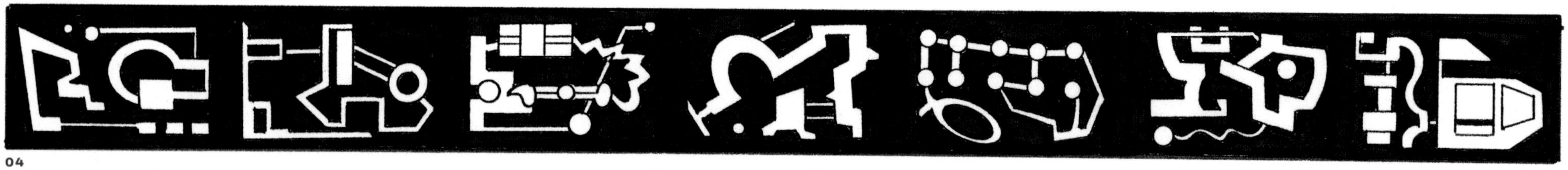

04

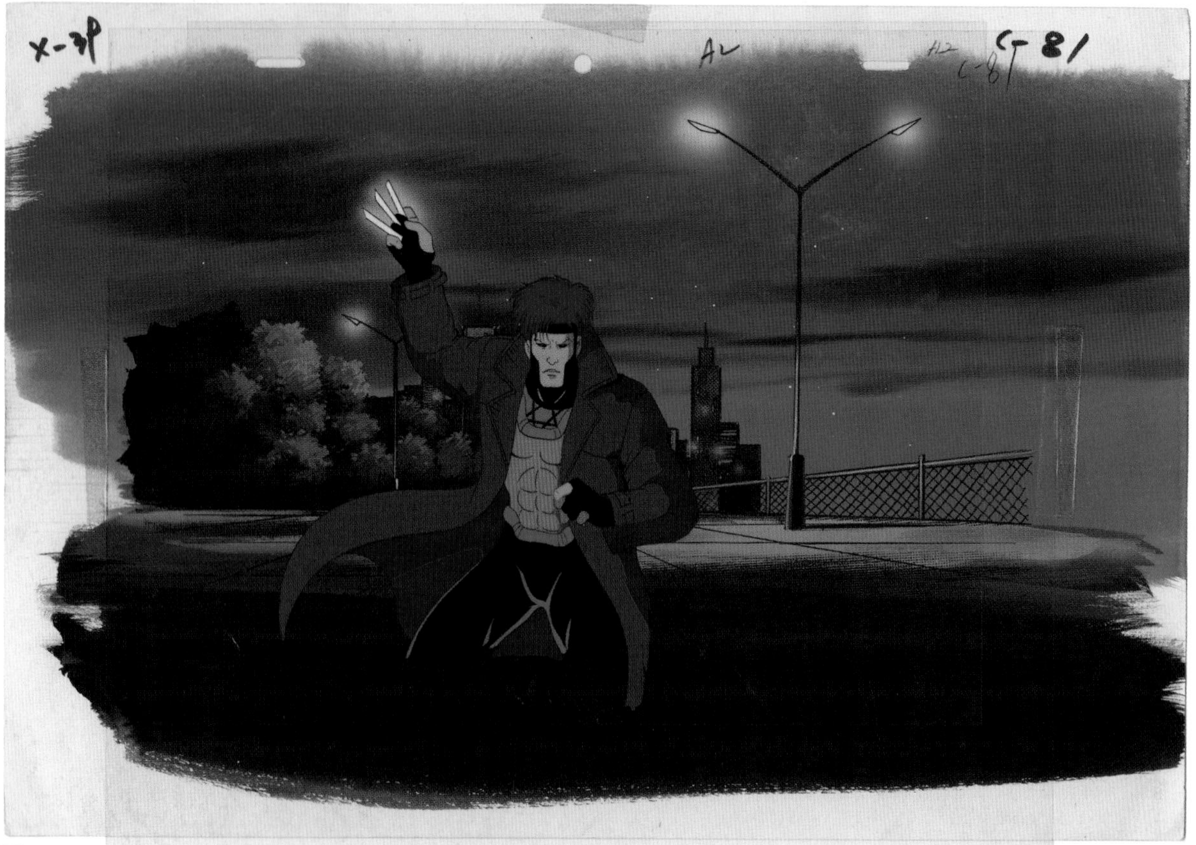
X-3P
C-81

05

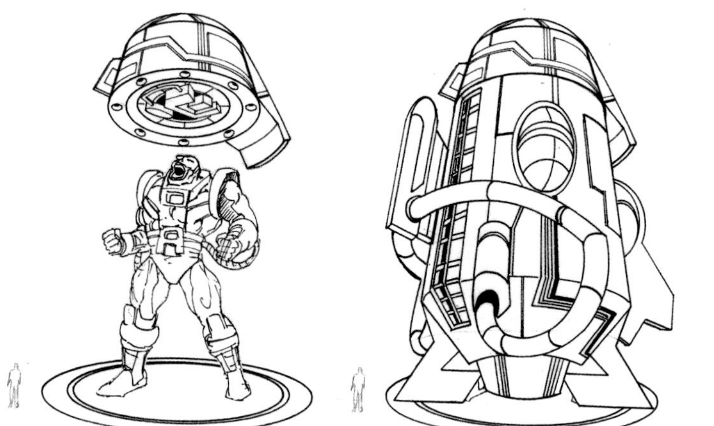

06

01 Layout of the road for Cyclops's journey by bus after he leaves the X-Men out of his grief over the loss of Jean Grey in "No Mutant Is an Island." Designed and cleaned by Frank Squillace. **02–03** Character models of Boom Boom and Wiz Kid Taki, penciled by Frank Brunner with cleanup by Mark Lewis. **04** Prop model of computer panel with alien glyphs of sentient ship from "Obsession"—a loving homage to Jack Kirby's original "Celestial Tech" from the comics. Designed and cleaned by Squillace. **05** Production cel of Gambit with special-effect lights. **06** Models of Apocalypse standing in capsule/cell-ship on sentient ship; note human figure for size comparison. Designed and cleaned by Squillace. **OPPOSITE** Production cel of Gambit, Beast, Cyclops, and Rogue in the X-Mansion War Room.

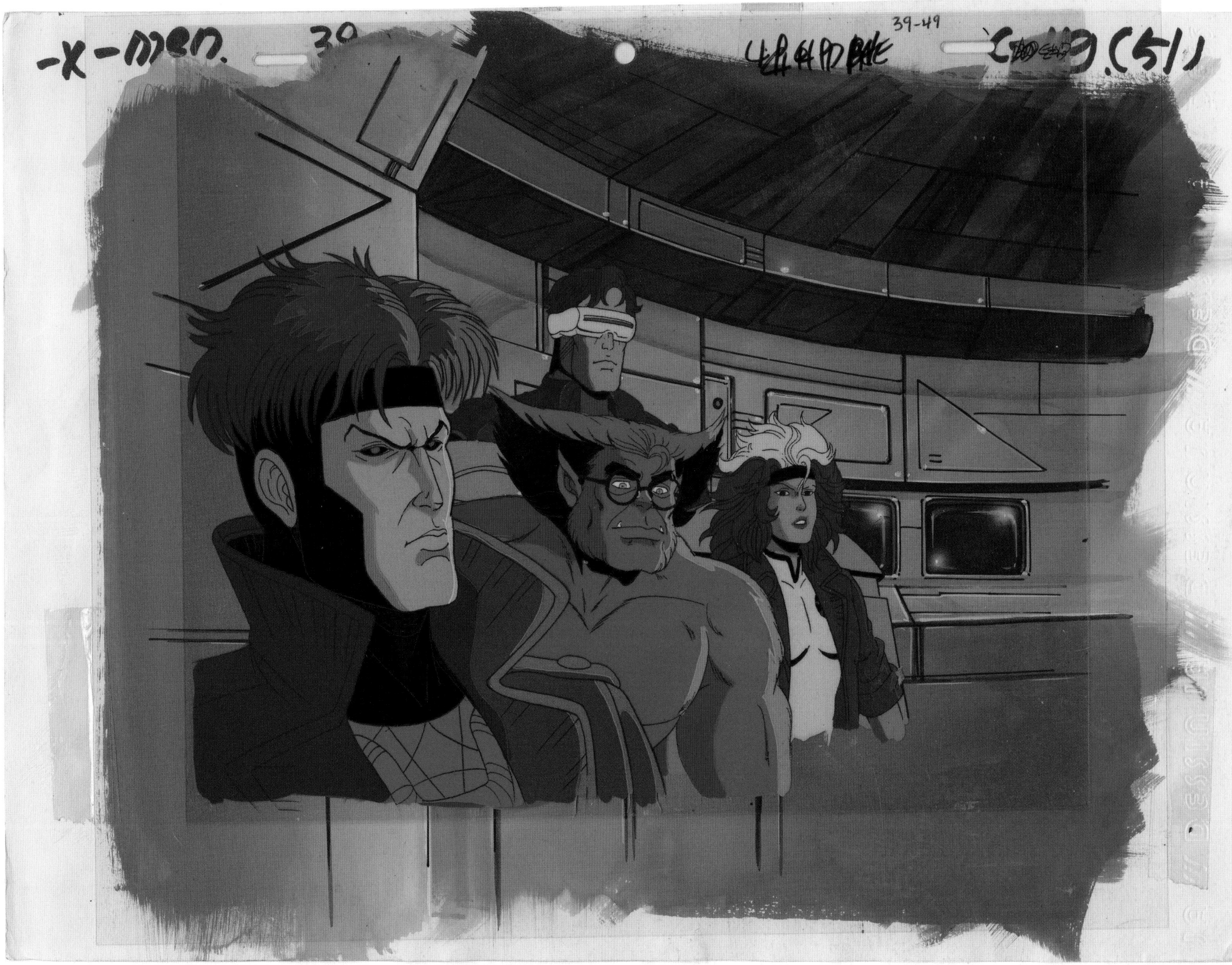

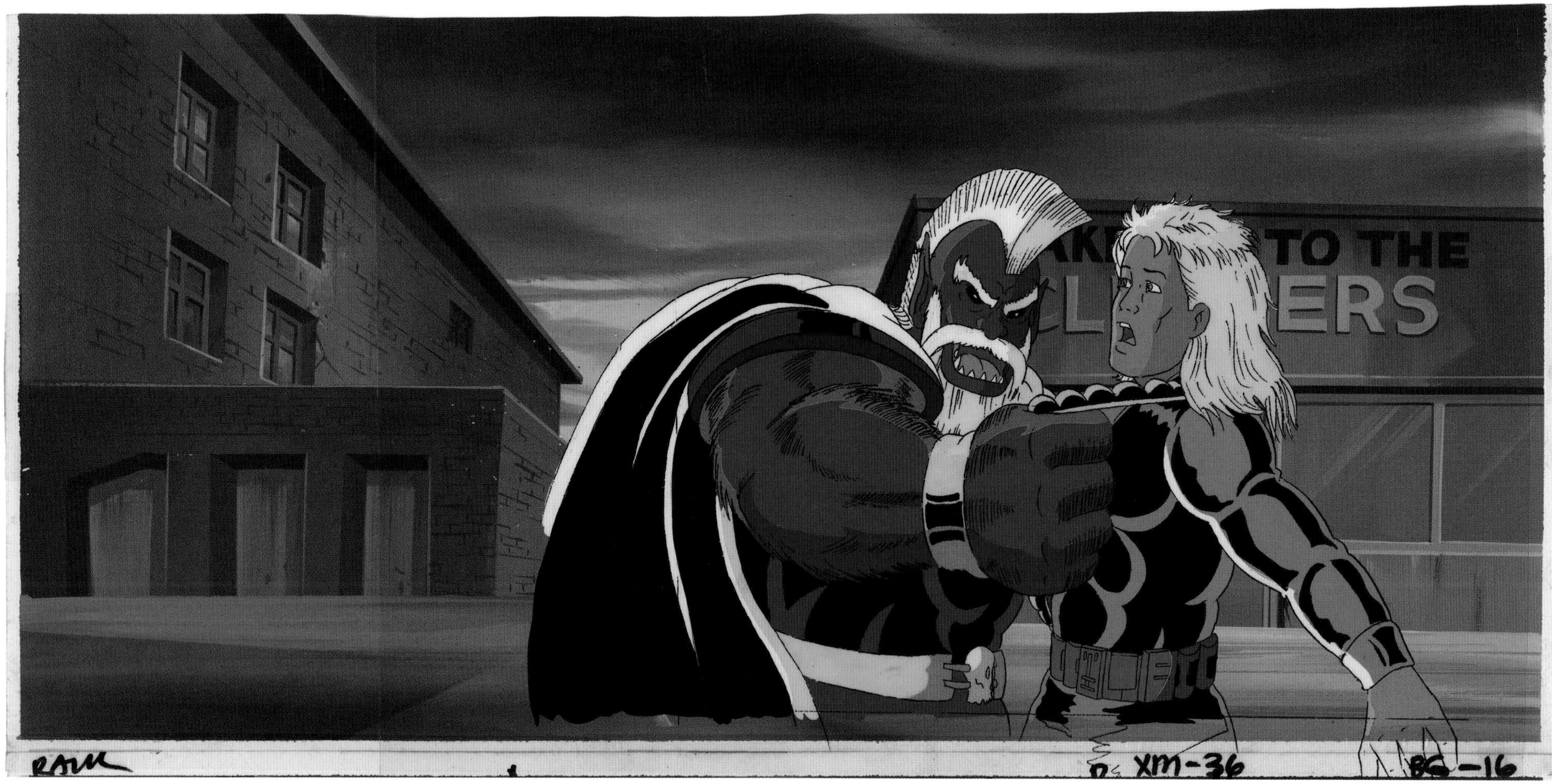
TO THE
ERS
XM-36

01

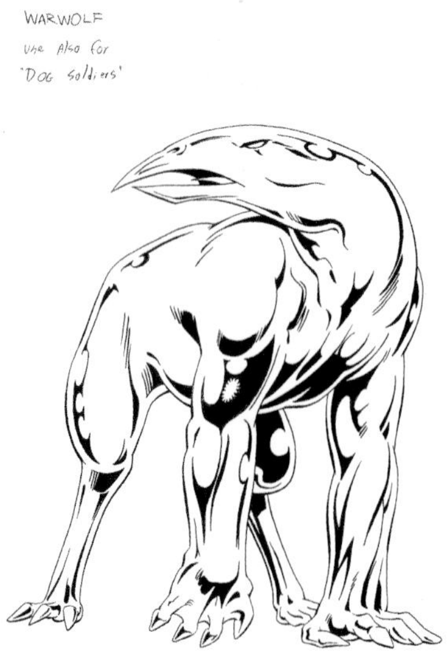
WARWOLF
Use Also for
'Dog Soldiers'

02

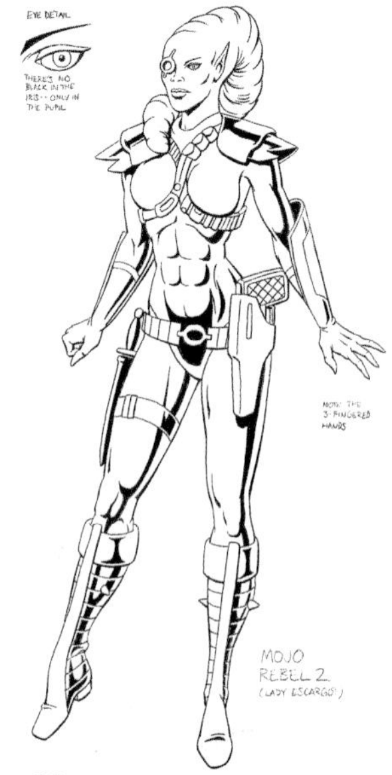
EYE DETAIL
THERE'S NO BLACK IN THE IRIS -- ONLY IN THE PUPIL
MOJO
REBEL 2
(LADY ESCARGO)

03

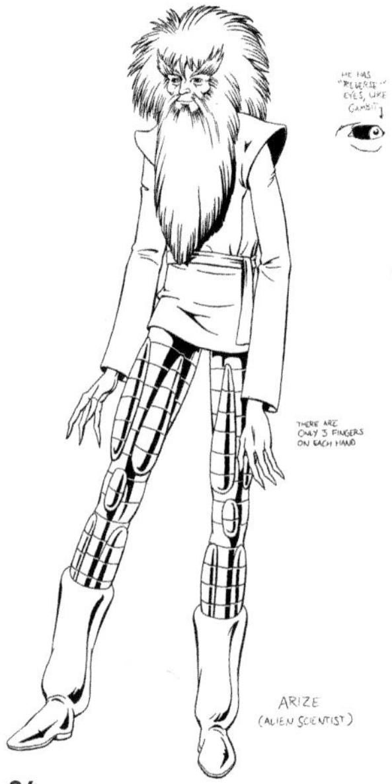
THERE ARE ONLY 3 FINGERS ON EACH HAND
ARIZE
(ALIEN SCIENTIST)

04

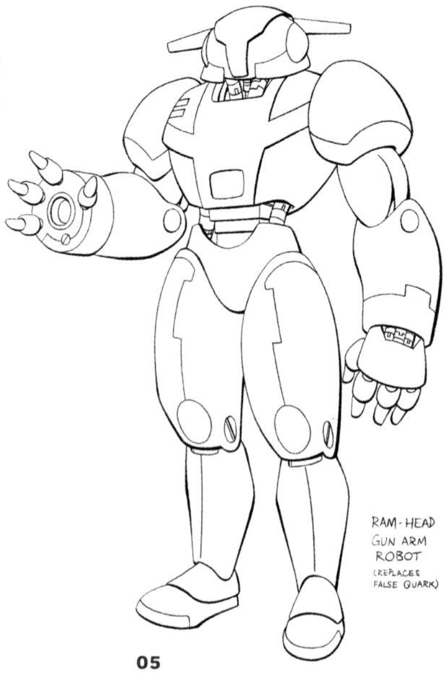
RAM-HEAD
GUN ARM
ROBOT
(REPLACES
FALSE QUARK)

05

01 Production cel of Gog capturing Longshot on Earth. **02–04** Character models of Warwolf, Mojo Rebel 2 Lady Escargo, and Arize Alien Scientist; penciled by Frank Brunner with cleanup by Mark Lewis. **05** Character model of Ram-Head gun-arm robot, by Lewis. **06** Character model of Quark; penciled by Brunner with cleanup by Lewis. **07** Model Marvel Girl Robot 2nd version; by Lewis, retrofitted from existing model. **08** Production cel of Mojo. **09** Production cel of Quark, early Cyclops robot, early Archangel robot, early Beast robot, early Marvel Girl robot, and early Ms. Marvel robot, in action for Mojo. "Longshot" was heavily redone over two years so several drawings, paintings, and cels exist for characters and scenes that do not appear in the final episode.

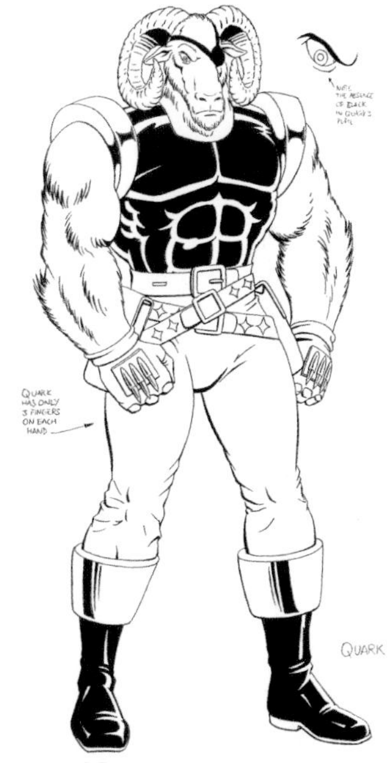
QUARK HAS ONLY 3 FINGERS ON EACH HAND
QUARK

06

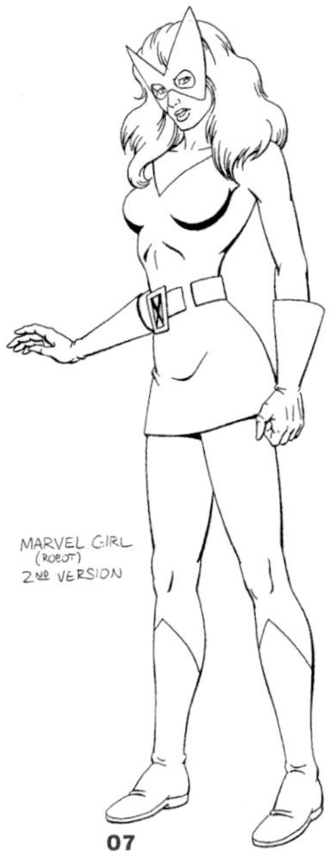
MARVEL GIRL (ROBOT) 2ND VERSION

07

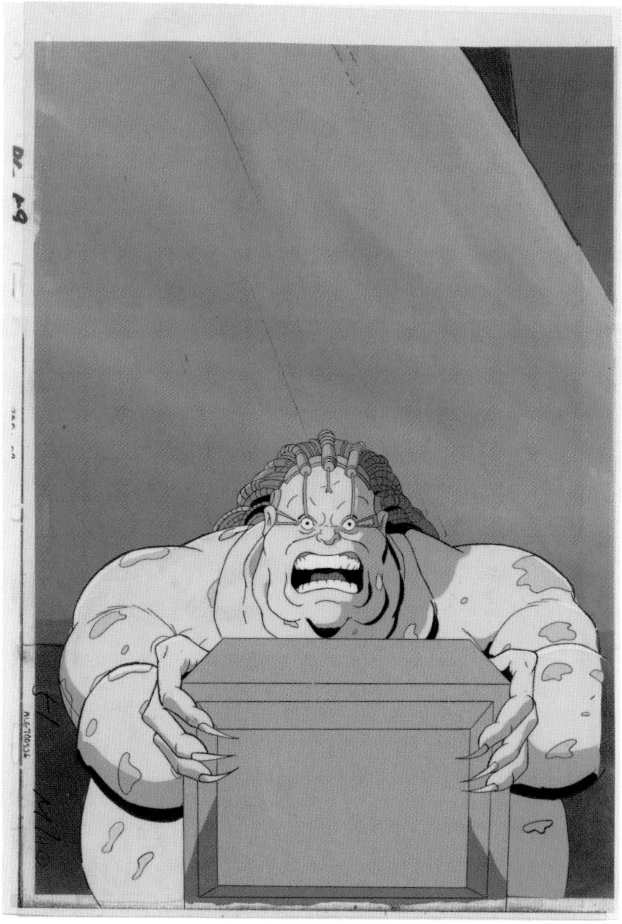

08

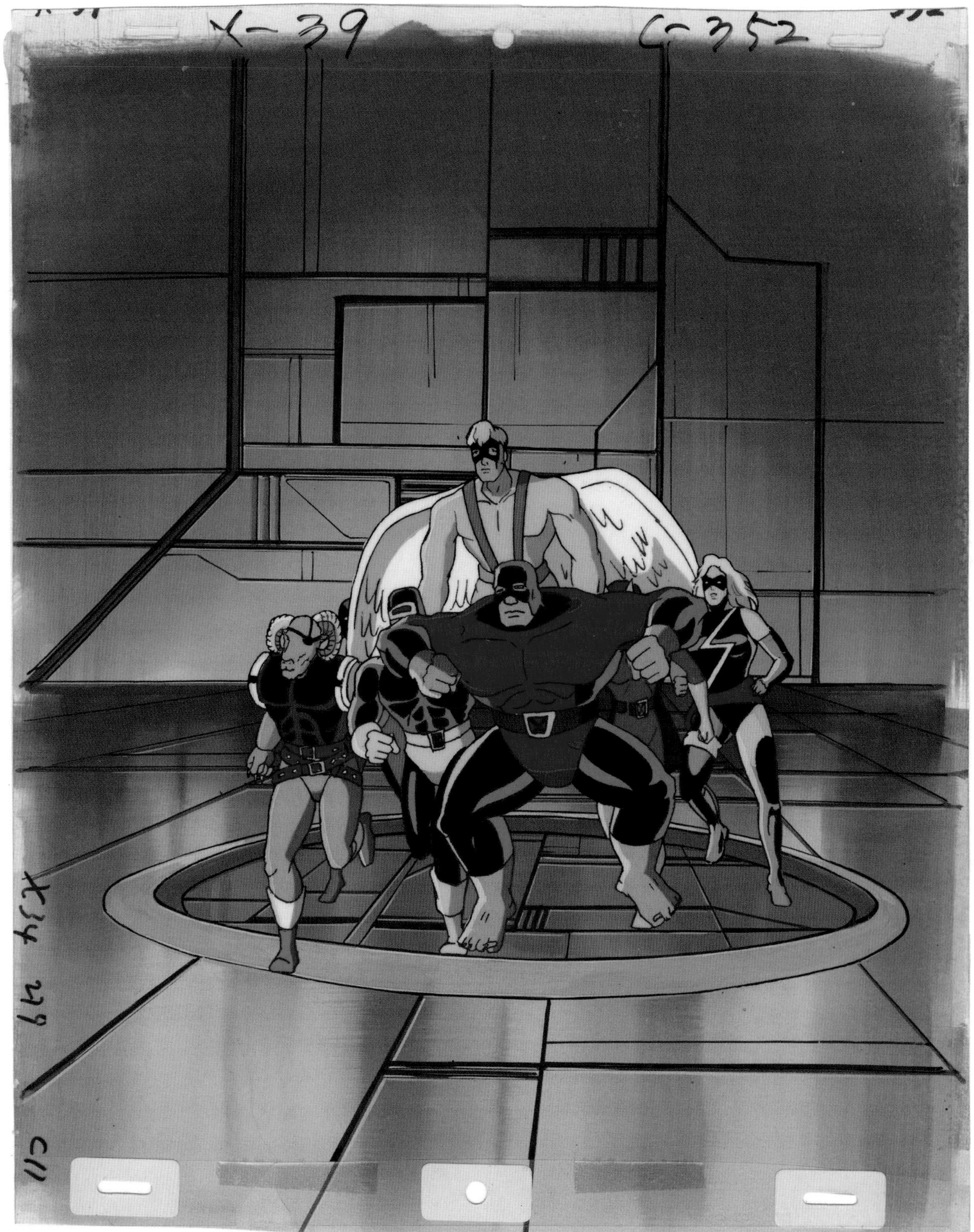
X-39
C-352

09

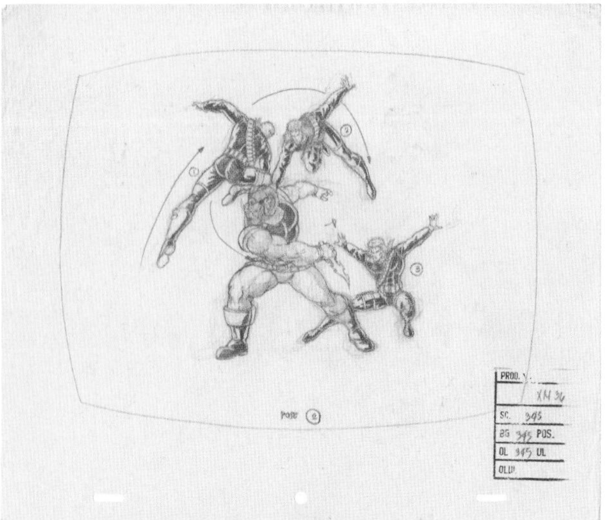

01

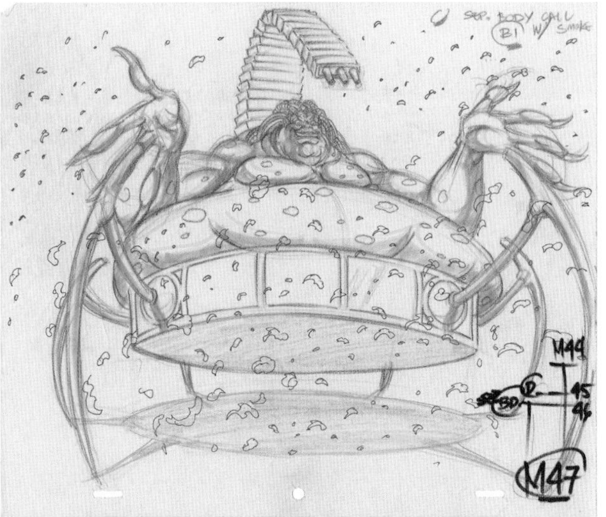

02

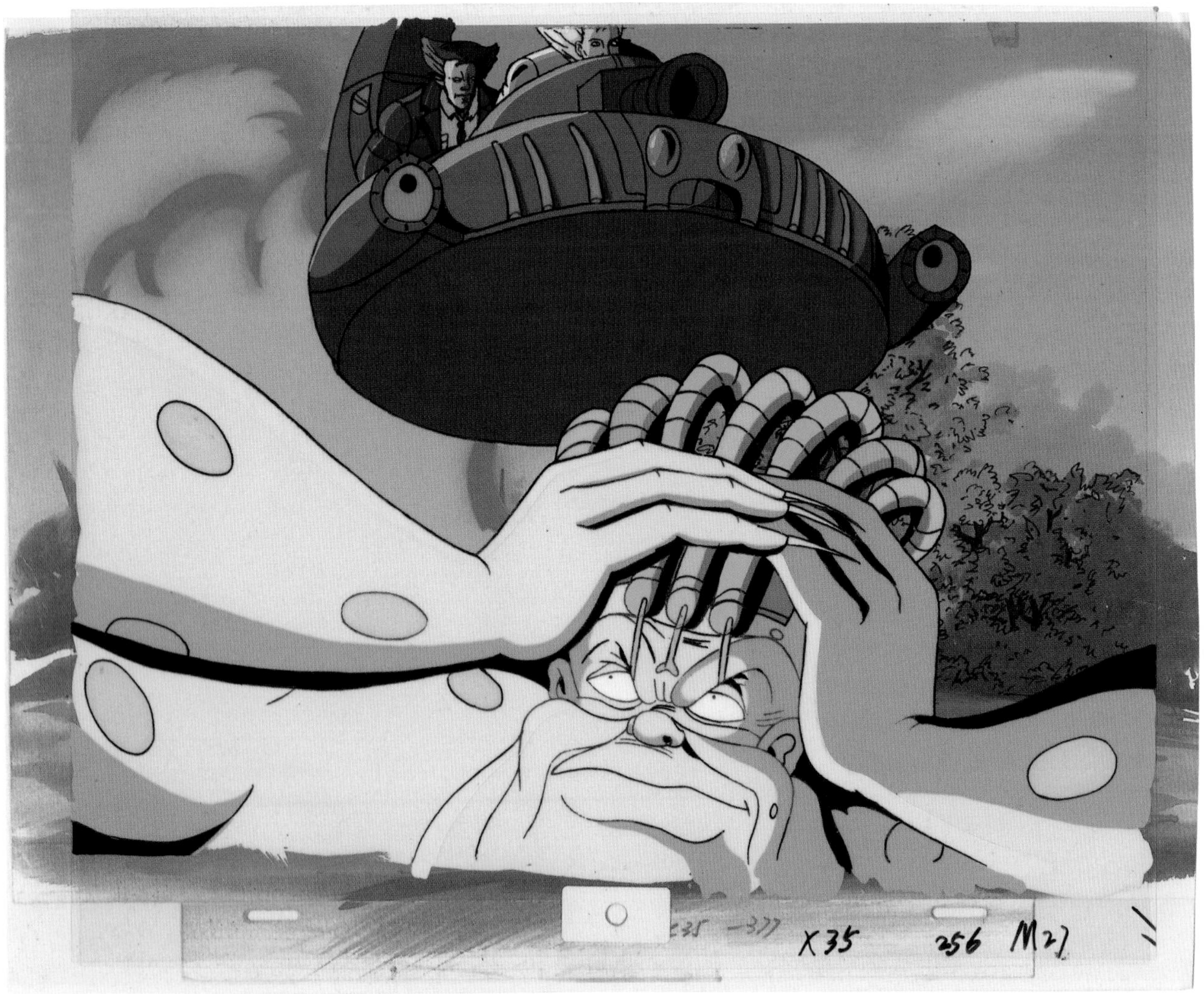

03

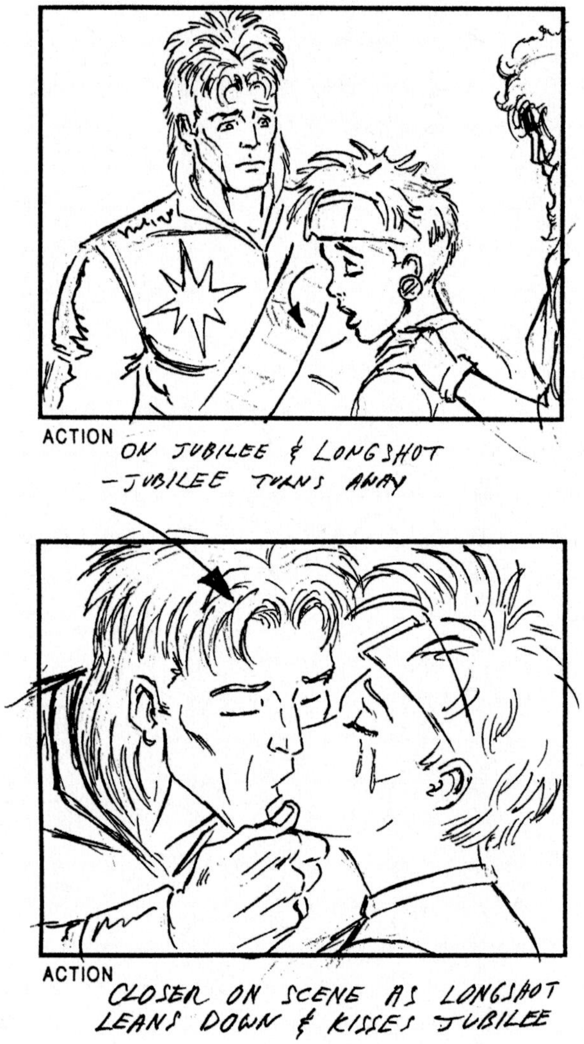
ACTION
ON JUBILEE & LONGSHOT
-JUBILEE TURNS AWAY
ACTION
CLOSER ON SCENE AS LONGSHOT
LEANS DOWN & KISSES JUBILEE

04

01 Production sketch of Longshot fighting Quark. **02** Production sketch of Mojo in motion. **03** Production cel with Mojo, Wolverine, and Longshot. A slightly different look from what aired after the troubled episode was reshot. **04** Storyboard with Longshot and Jubilee. He kisses her on the lips here, but in the aired episode he kisses her on the forehead—broadcast standards prevailed. **05-07** Character models of Polaris (Lorna Dane) in old costume, Polaris, and Strong Guy; all by Frank Brunner and Mark Lewis. **08** A different take on Strong Guy, sketch in motion, by Frank Squillace. **09** Character model of Multiple Man (Jamie Madrox); by Brunner and Lewis. **10-14** Character models of Forge, Havok, Wolfsbane (Rahne Sinclair human form), Wolfsbane (Rahne Sinclair transitory state), and Wolfsbane (Rahne Sinclair full wolf, stage 3); all penciled by Brunner with cleanup by Lewis.

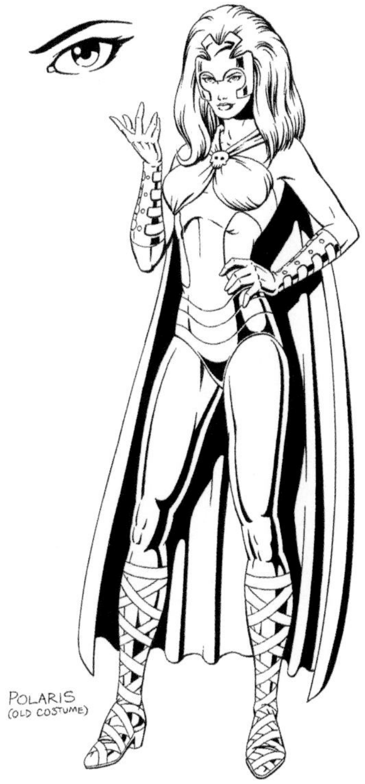
POLARIS
(OLD COSTUME)

05

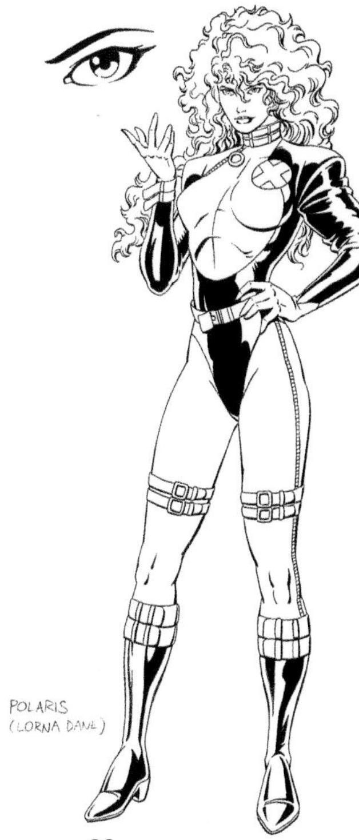
POLARIS
(LORNA DANE)

06

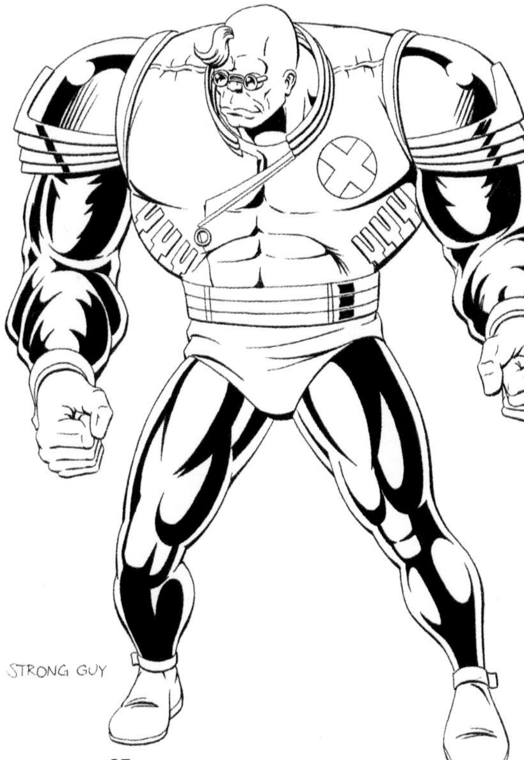
STRONG GUY

07

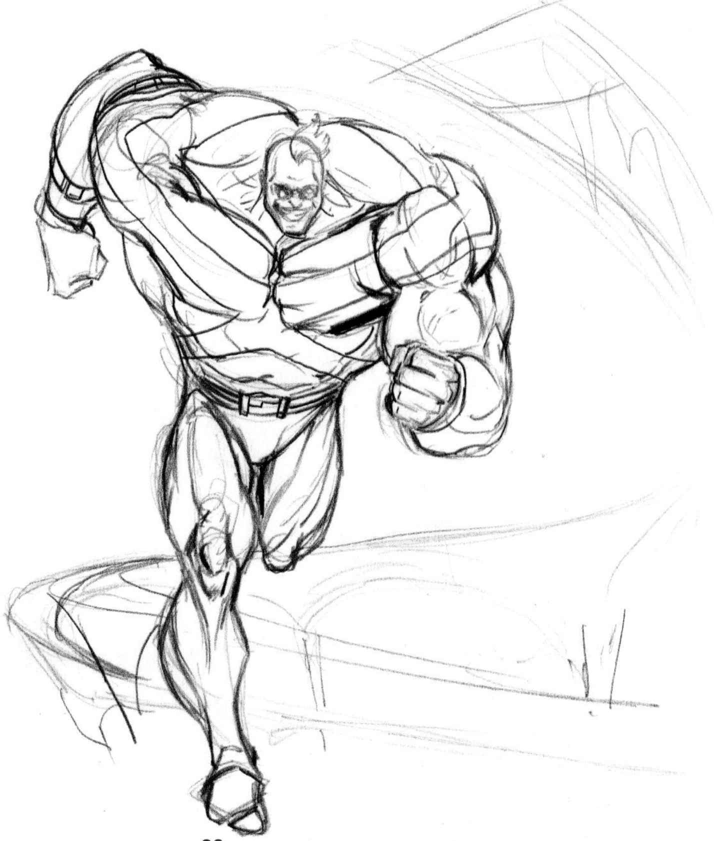

08

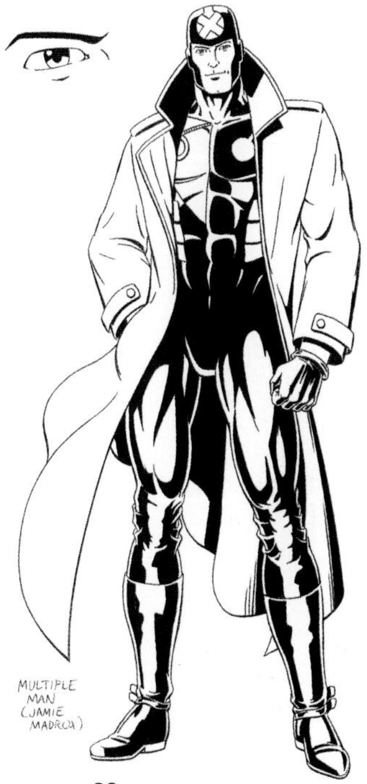
MULTIPLE
MAN
(JAMIE
MADROX)

09

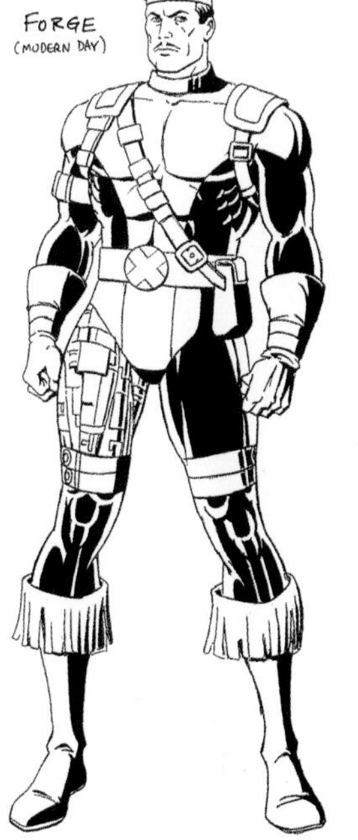
FORGE
(MODERN DAY)

10

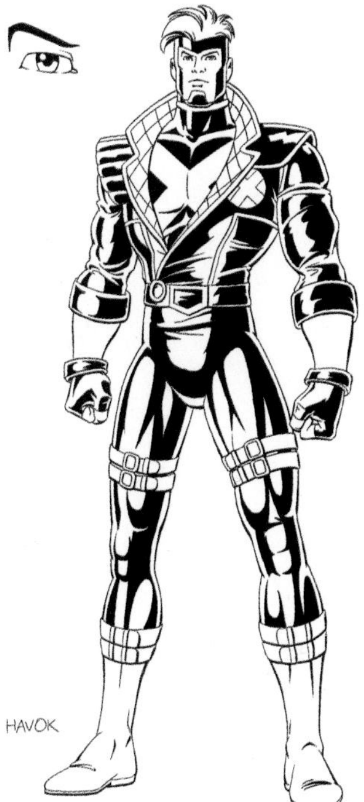
HAVOK

11

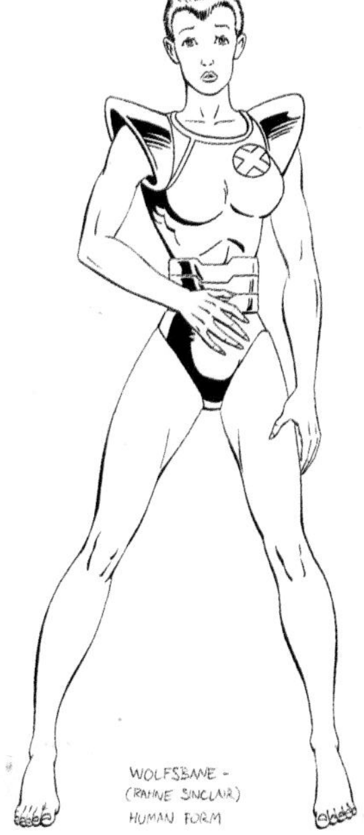
WOLFSBANE -
(RAHNE SINCLAIR)
HUMAN FORM

12

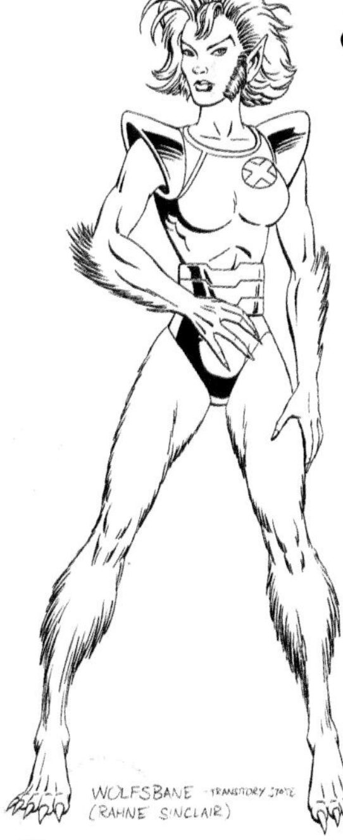
WOLFSBANE - TRANSITORY STATE
(RAHNE SINCLAIR)

13

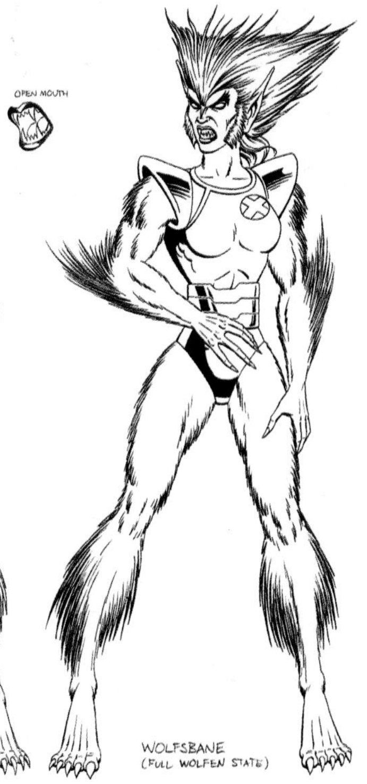
OPEN MOUTH
WOLFSBANE
(FULL WOLFEN STATE)

14

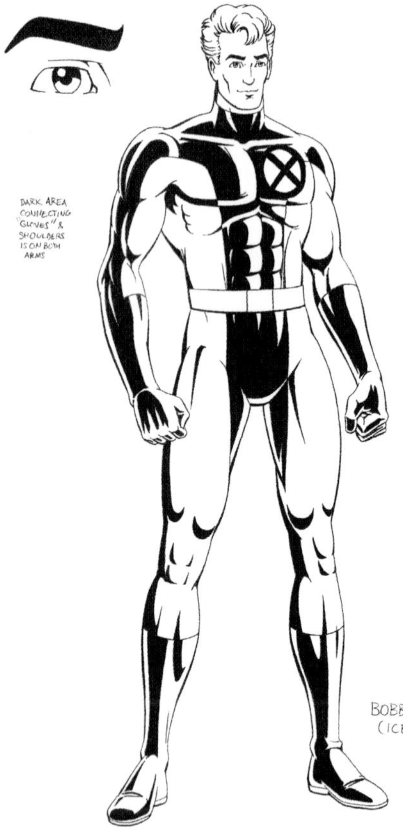
DARK AREA CONNECTING "GLOVES" & SHOULDERS IS ON BOTH ARMS
BOBBY DRAKE (ICEMAN)

01

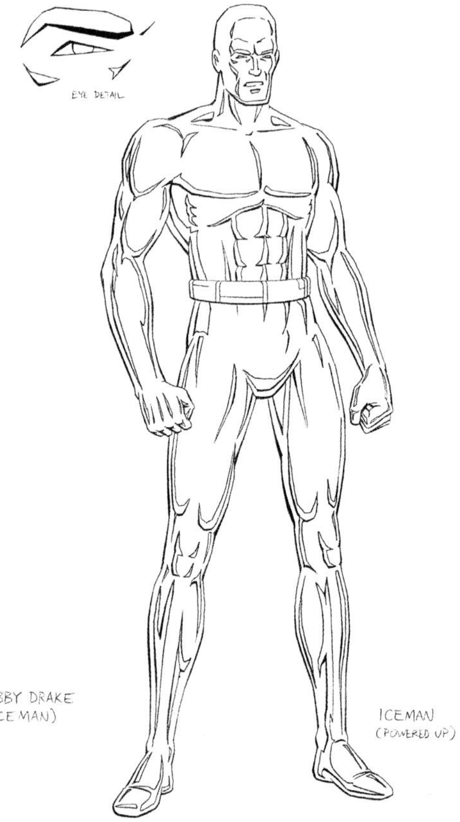
EYE DETAIL
ICEMAN (POWERED UP)

02

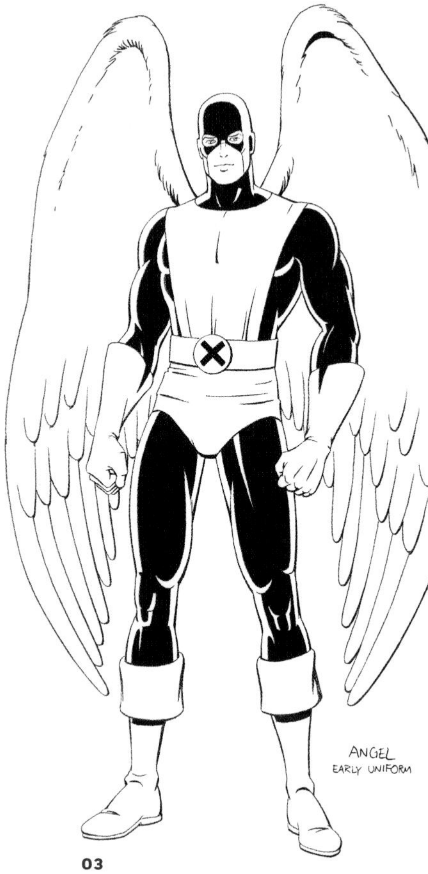
ANGEL
EARLY UNIFORM

03

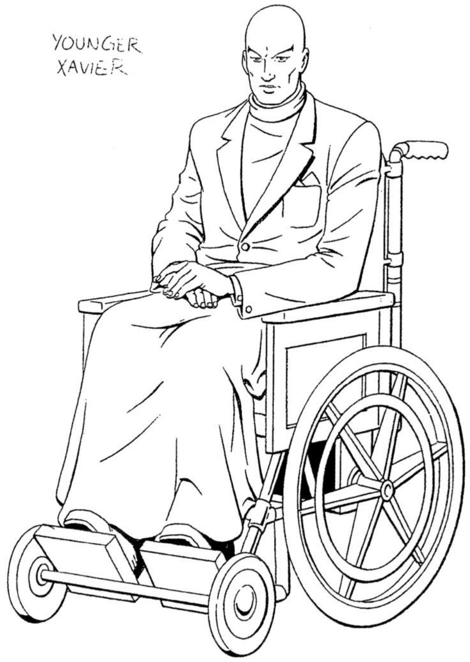
YOUNGER XAVIER

04

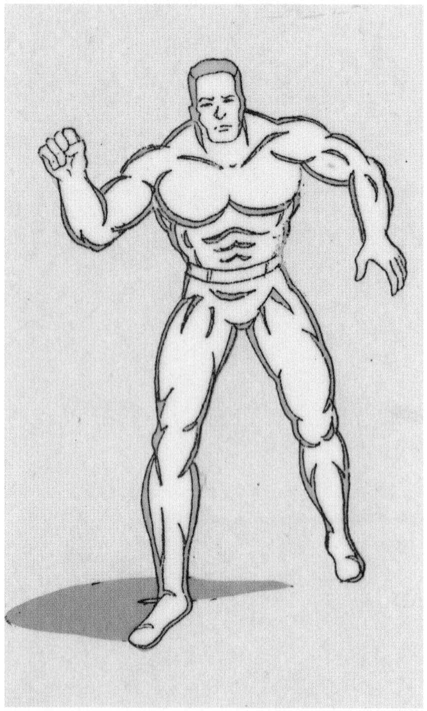

05

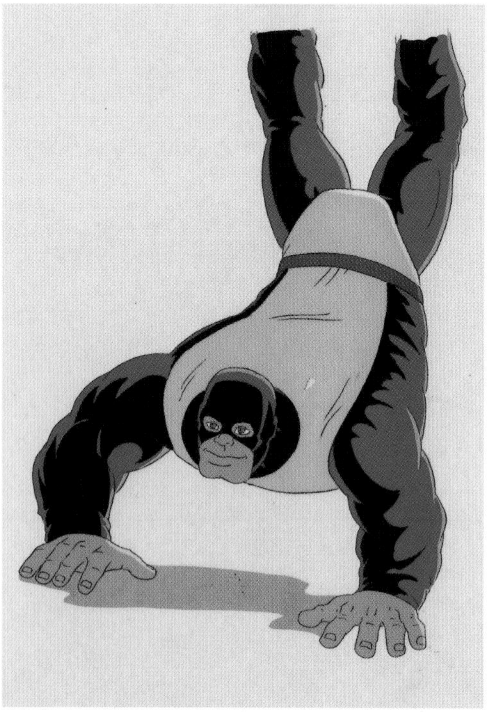

06

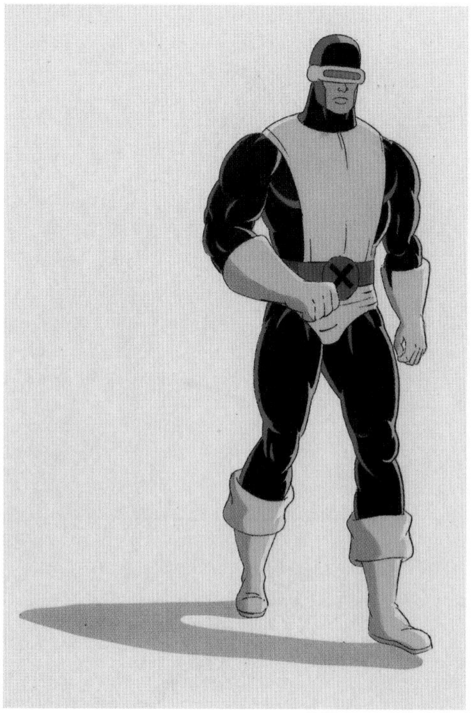

07

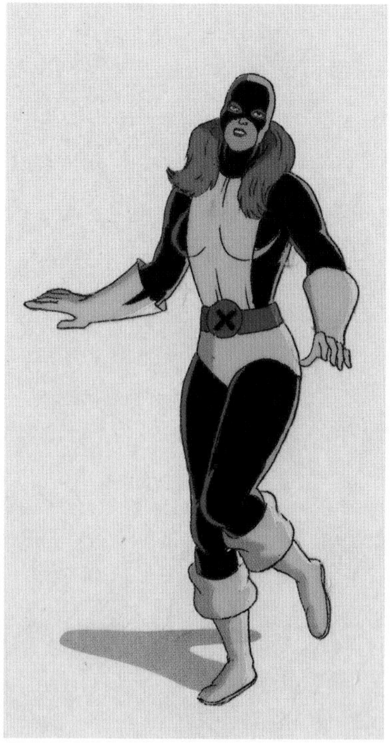

08

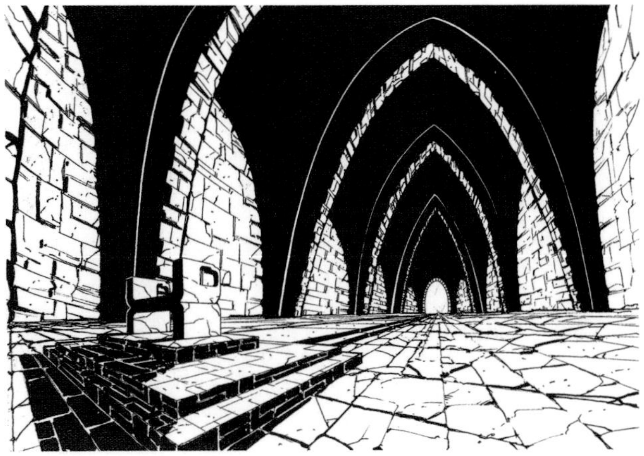

09

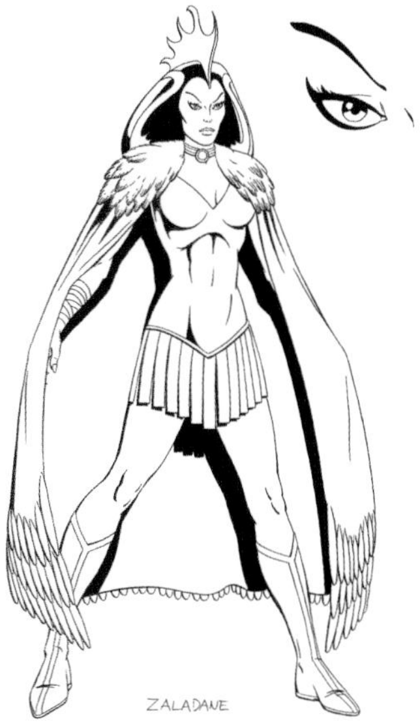
ZALADANE

10

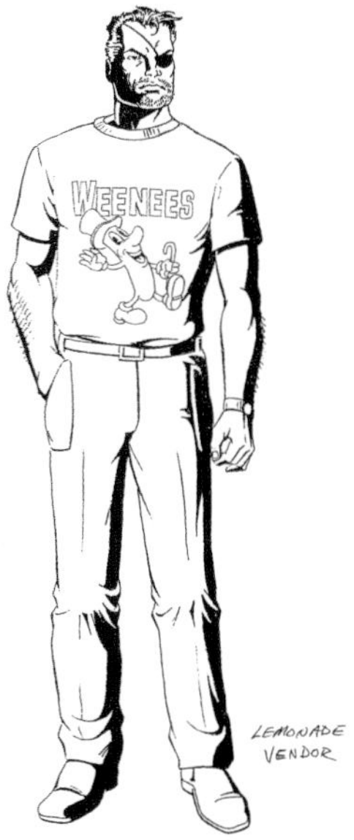
WEENEES
LEMONADE VENDOR

11

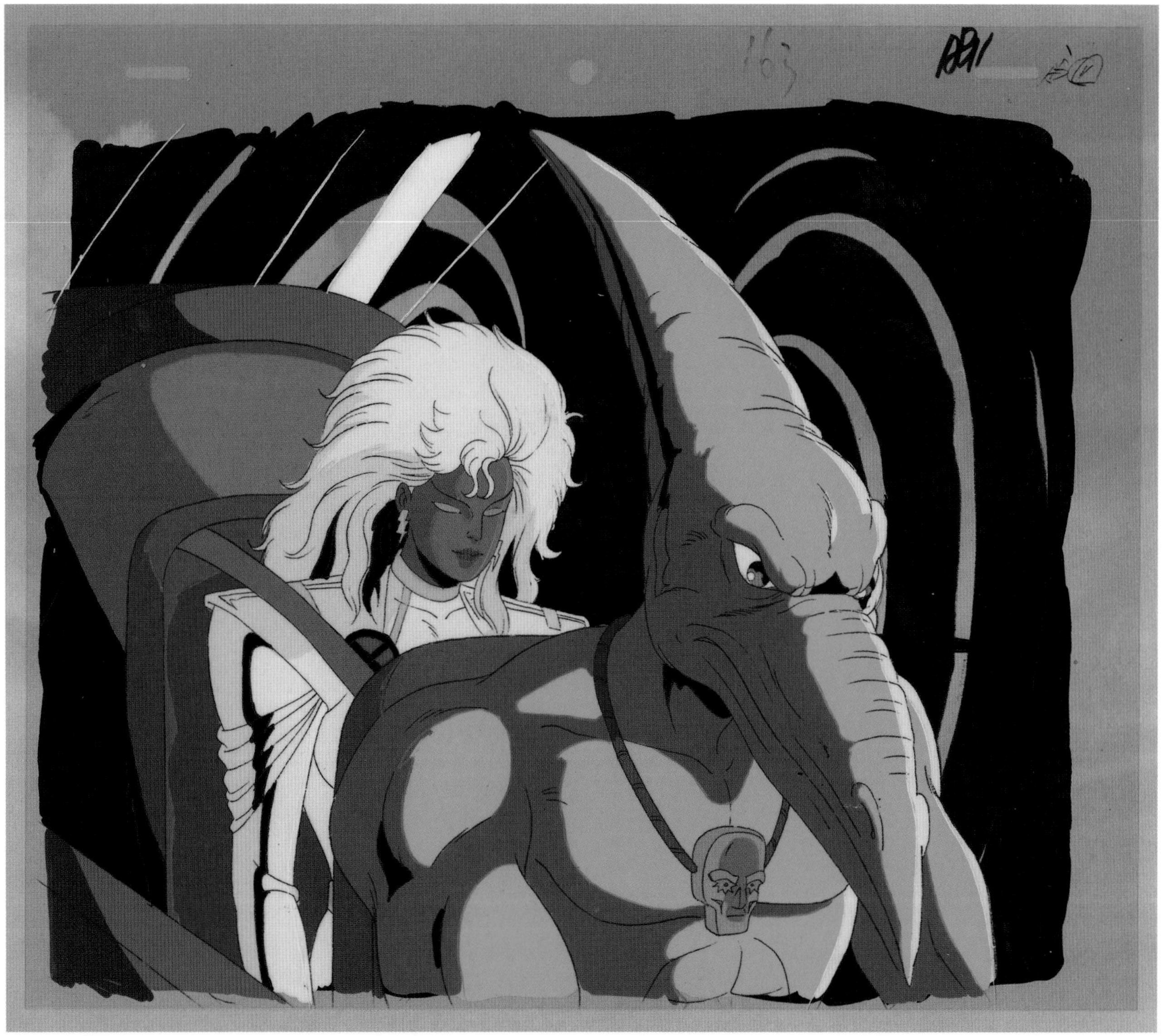

12

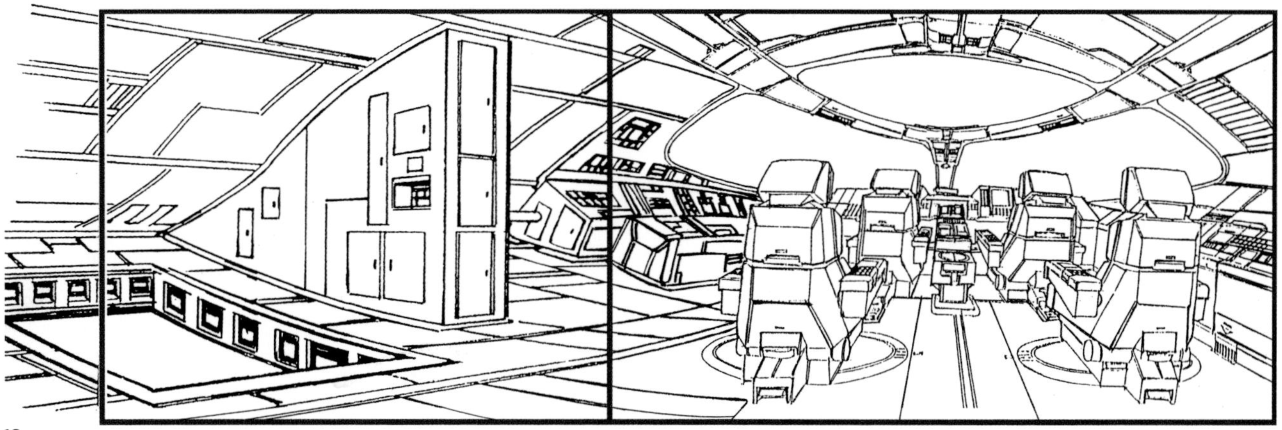

13

01–04 Character models of Bobby Drake in uniform, then as Iceman, Angel early uniform, Xavier. All penciled by Frank Brunner (reworking existing models) with cleanup by Mark Lewis. **05–08** Production cels of Iceman, early Beast, early Cyclops, early Jean Grey, from a flashback to their original look as "exceptional young people." **09** Layout of the interior of Sauron's fortress, designed and cleaned by Frank Squillace. **10** Character model of Zaladane, by Brunner and Lewis. **11** Character model of Nick Fury as a hot dog vendor, an in-house inside-joke (with Nick Fury used again as a cameo with War Machine in "Sanctuary"), by Brunner and Lewis. Note the fanciful "weenees" T-shirt. **12** Production cel of Storm and Sauron. **13** Layout of the interior of the X-Men's *Blackbird* jet. Left side of background pan (interior Blackbird) open hatch designed and cleaned by Squillace. Right side from stock series background design.

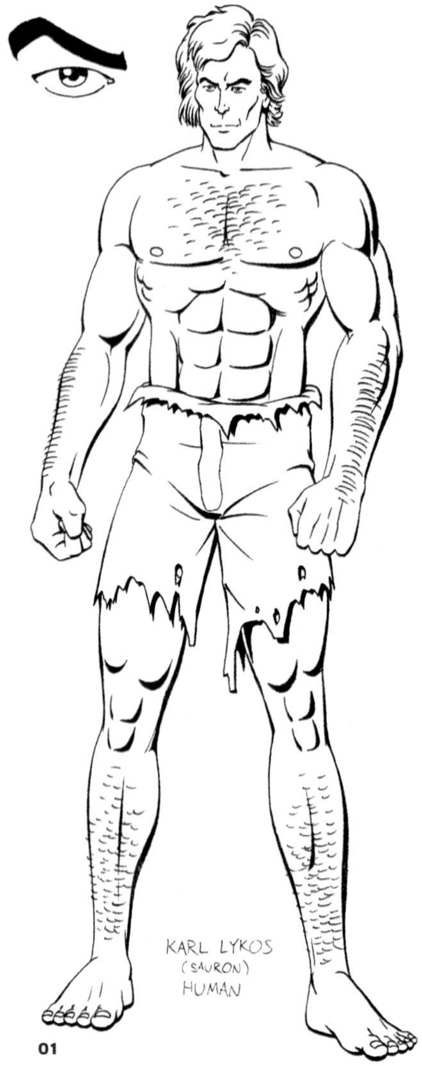
KARL LYKOS
(SAURON)
HUMAN

01

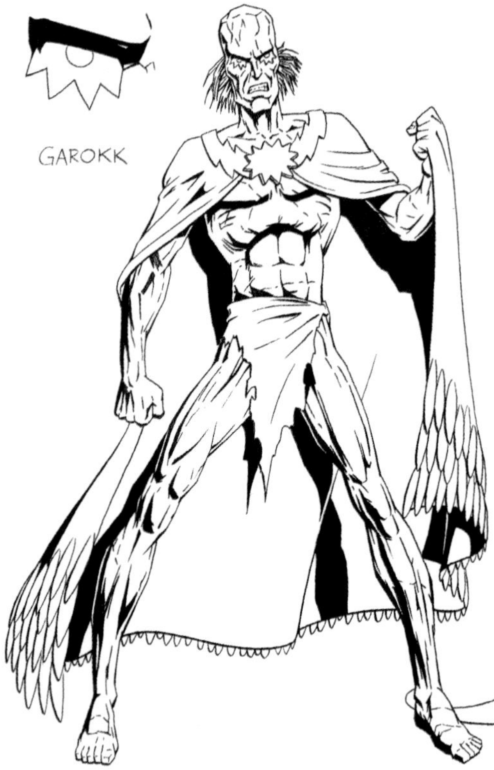
GAROKK

02

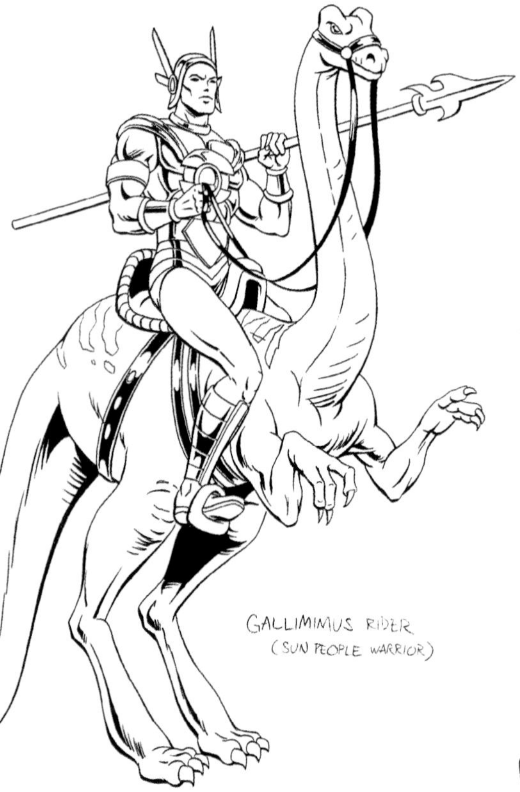
GALLIMIMUS RIDER
(SUN PEOPLE WARRIOR)

03

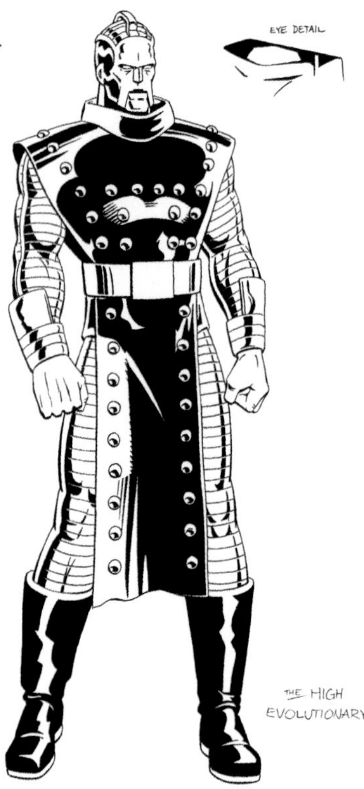
EYE DETAIL
THE HIGH
EVOLUTIONARY

04

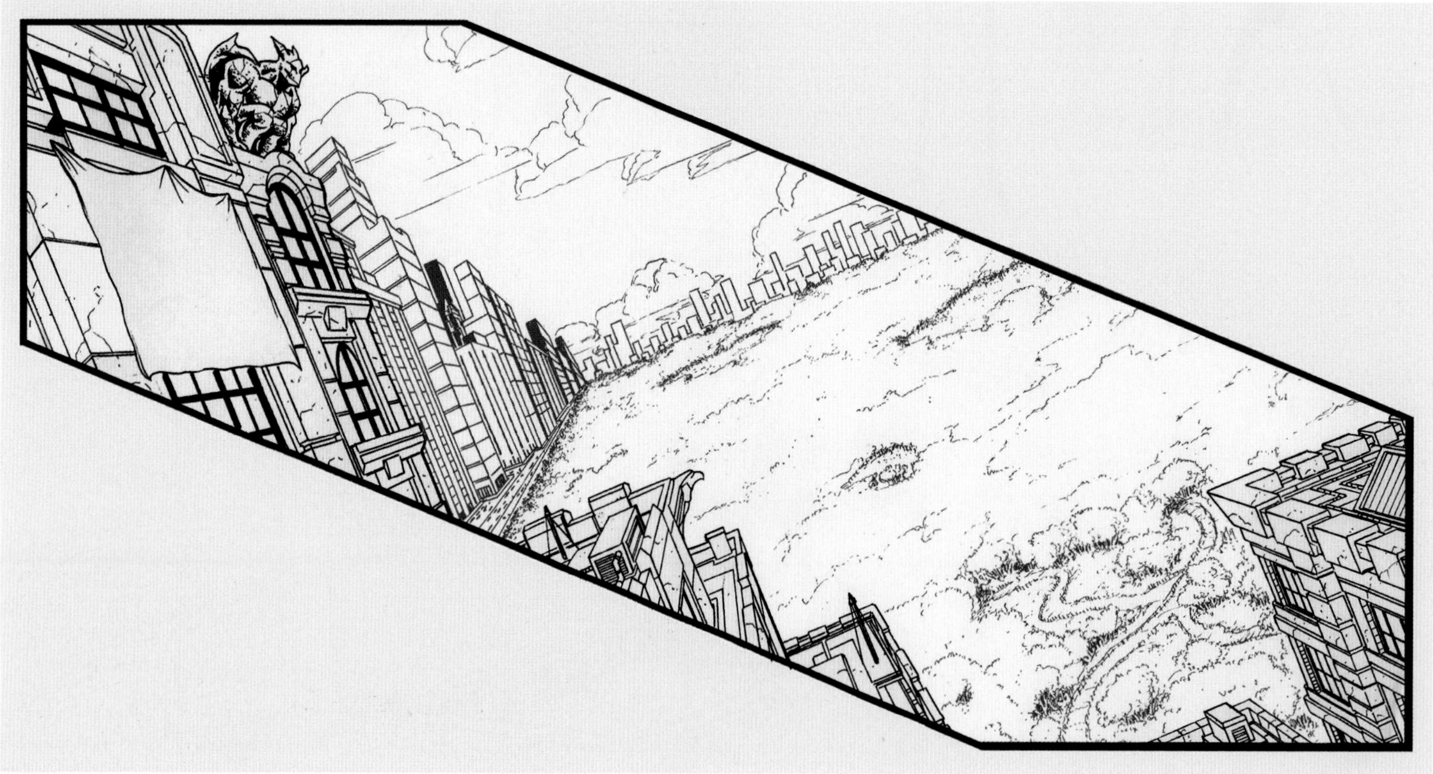

05

01 Character model of Karl Lykos (Sauron in human form), by Frank Brunner and Mark Lewis. **02–04** Character models of Garokk, Gallimimus Rider (Sun People Warrior), The High Evolutionary; all penciled by Brunner with cleanup by Lewis. **05** Layout of New York City Central Park, designed and cleaned by Frank Squillace. **06–15** Character models of Donald Pierce with torn sleeve (robot arm), Sebastian Shaw, Harry Leland, Jason Wyngarde, The White Queen, Liveried Guard 1, Cyclops in eighteenth-century garb, Jean Grey in eighteenth-century costume, Jean Grey in cloak, Jean Grey as the Black Queen; all penciled by Brunner with cleanup by Lewis.

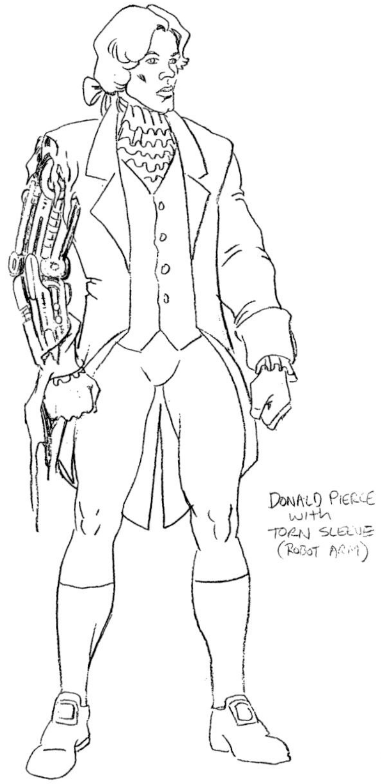
DONALD PIERCE
with
TORN SLEEVE
(ROBOT ARM)

06

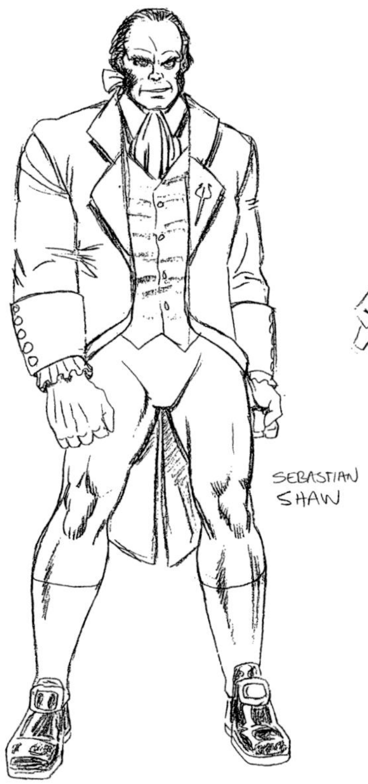
SEBASTIAN
SHAW

07

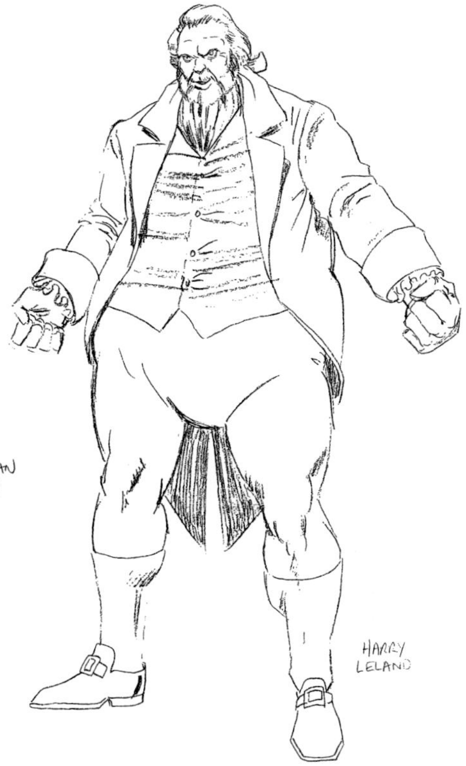
HARRY
LELAND

08

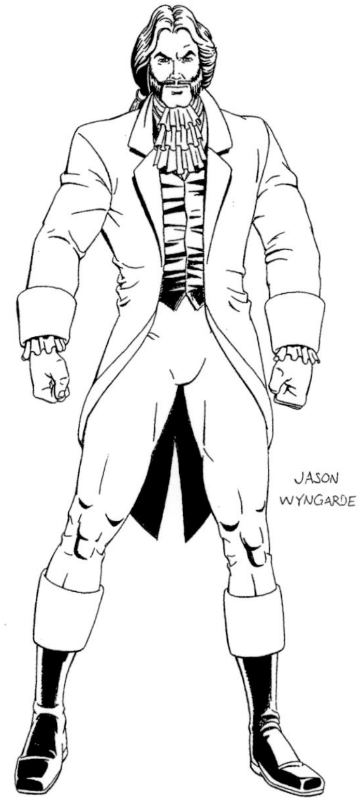
JASON
WYNGARDE

09

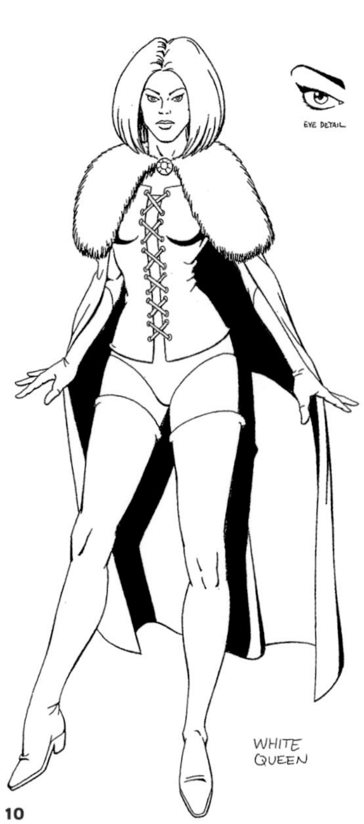
EYE DETAIL
WHITE
QUEEN

10

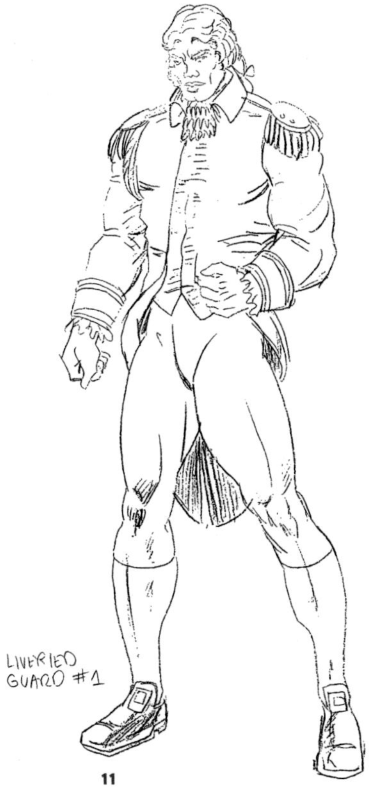
LIVERIED
GUARD #1

11

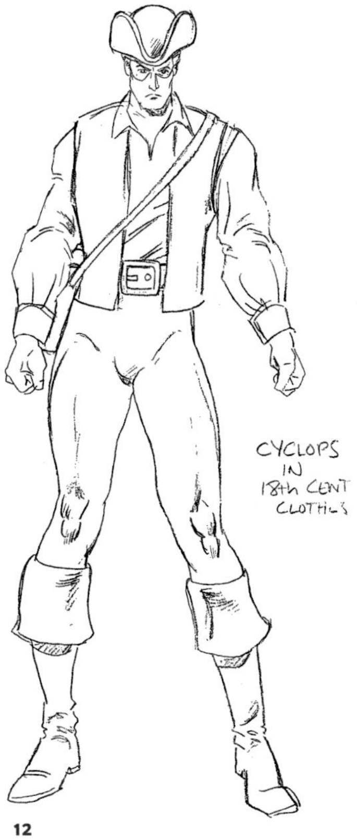
CYCLOPS
IN
18th CENT
CLOTHES

12

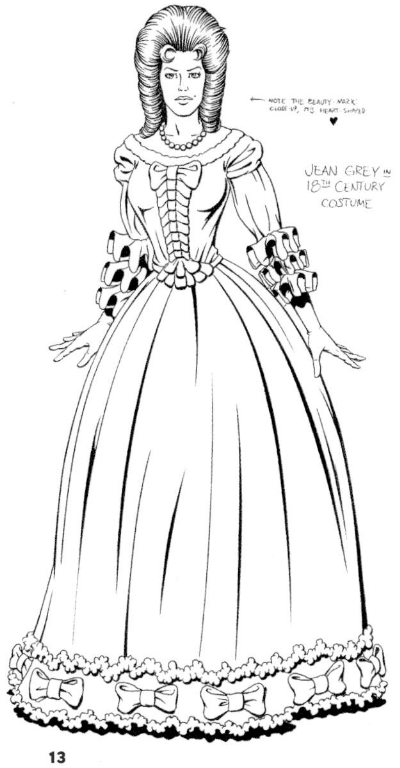
NOTE THE BEAUTY-MARK:
CLOSE-UP, IT'S HEART-SHAPED
JEAN GREY IN
18TH CENTURY
COSTUME

13

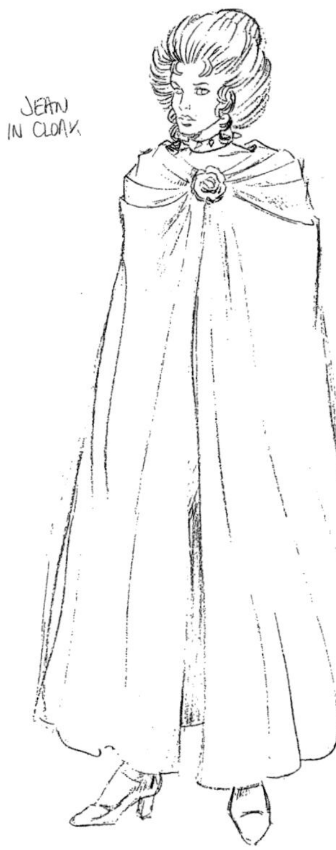
JEAN
IN CLOAK

14

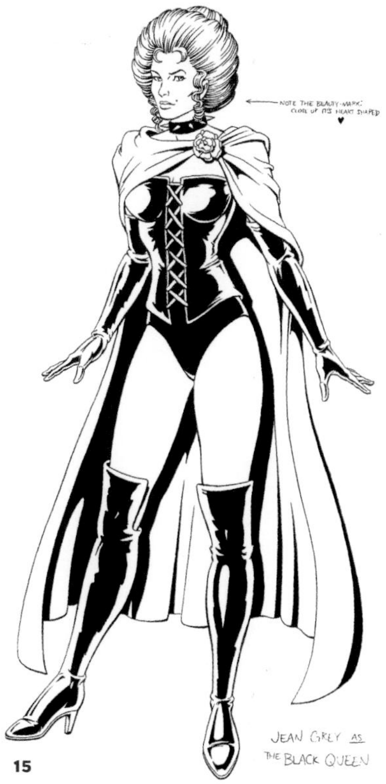
NOTE THE BEAUTY-MARK:
CLOSE UP IT'S HEART SHAPED
JEAN GREY AS
THE BLACK QUEEN

15

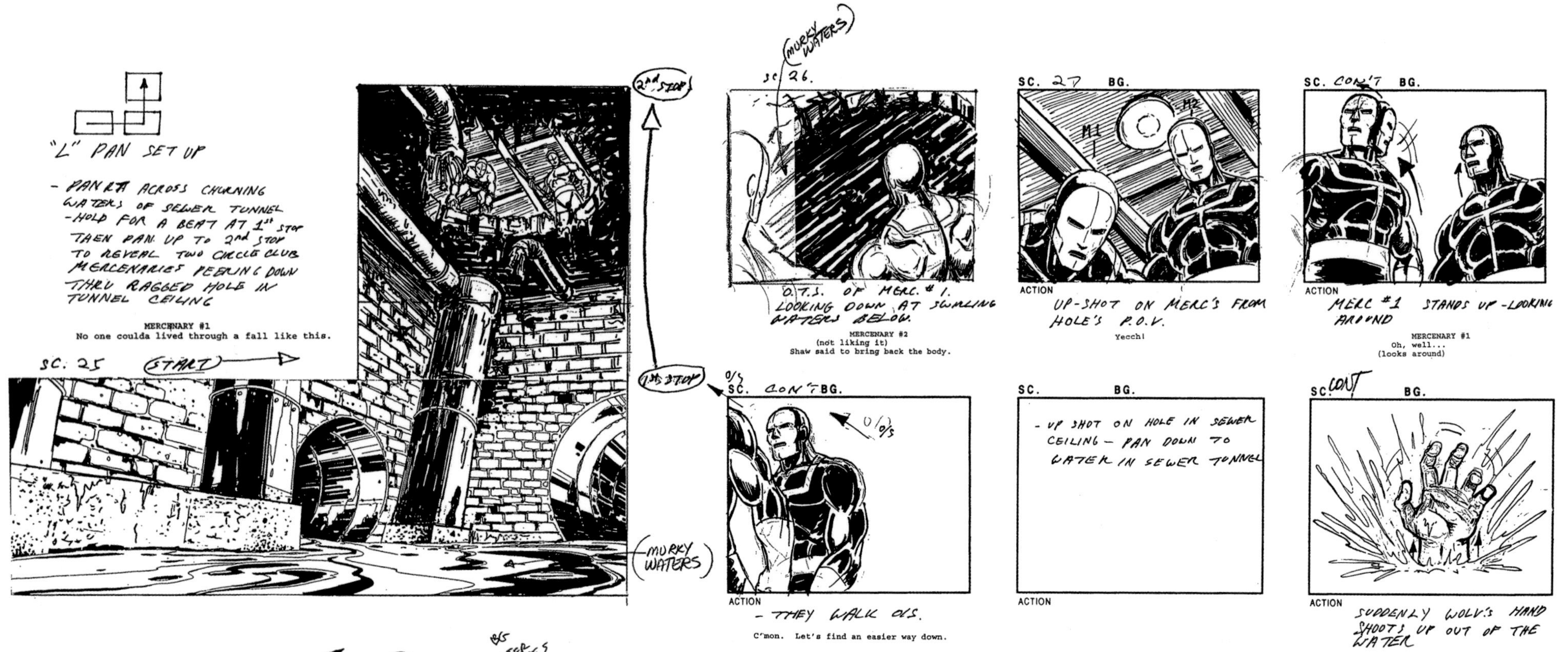
"L" PAN SET UP
- PAN R/L ACROSS CHURNING WATERS OF SEWER TUNNEL
- HOLD FOR A BEAT AT 1st STOP THEN PAN UP TO 2nd STOP TO REVEAL TWO CIRCLE CLUB MERCENARIES PEERING DOWN THRU RAGGEO HOLE IN TUNNEL CEILING
MERCENARY #1
No one coulda lived through a fall like this.
SC. 25
START
2nd STOP
1st STOP
MURKY WATERS
MURKY WATERS
SC. 26.
O.T.S. OF MERC. #1. LOOKING DOWN AT SWIRLING WATERS BELOW.
MERCENARY #2
(not liking it)
Shaw said to bring back the body.
SC. 27 BG.
ACTION
UP-SHOT ON MERC'S FROM HOLE'S P.O.V.
Yecch!
SC. CON'T BG.
ACTION
MERC #1 STANDS UP - LOOKING AROUND
MERCENARY #1
Oh, well...
(looks around)
O/S SC. CON'T BG.
O/S
ACTION
- THEY WALK O/S.
C'mon. Let's find an easier way down.
SC. BG.
- UP SHOT ON HOLE IN SEWER CEILING - PAN DOWN TO WATER IN SEWER TUNNEL
ACTION
SC. CONT BG.
ACTION
SUDDENLY WOLV'S HAND SHOOTS UP OUT OF THE WATER

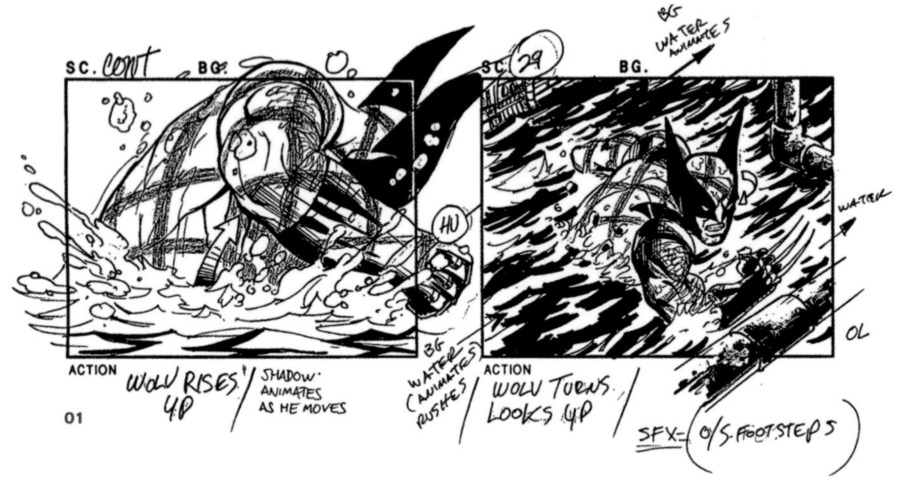
SC. CONT BG.
HU
ACTION
WOLV RISES UP
SHADOW ANIMATES AS HE MOVES
SC. 29 BG.
BG WATER ANIMATES
WATER
OL
BG WATER (ANIMATES) RUSHES
ACTION
WOLV TURNS. LOOKS UP
SFX - O/S FOOTSTEPS

01

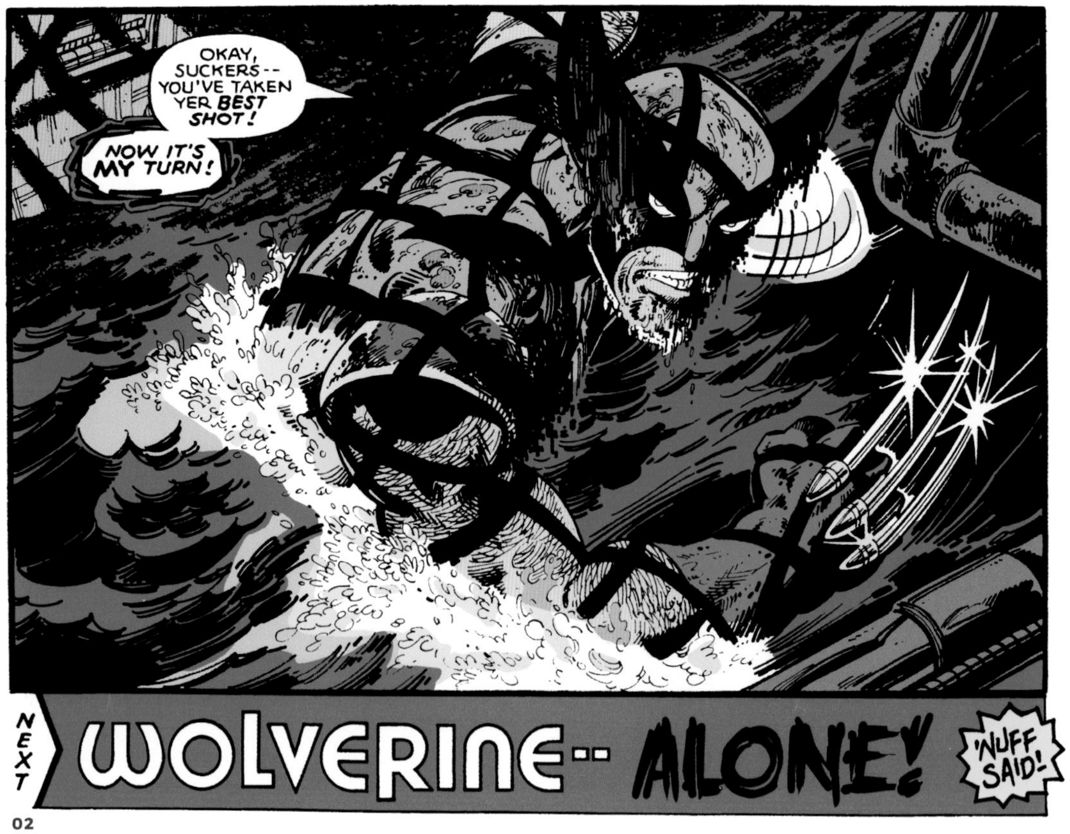
OKAY, SUCKERS-- YOU'VE TAKEN YER BEST SHOT!
NOW IT'S MY TURN!
NEXT
WOLVERINE-- ALONE!
'NUFF SAID!

02

01 Storyboard of underground system beneath the Circle Club, after Harry Leland drops Wolverine from three stories up. Two Circle Club mercenaries give up their search for him when Wolverine suddenly shoots up from the water. By Larry Houston. **02** Panel from *Uncanny X-Men* (vol. 1) #132. Co-written by Chris Claremont and John Byrne, with pencils by Byrne, inks by Terry Austin, colors by Glynis Wein, and letters by Tom Orzechowski. Note the adjacent storyboard panel's reflection of the comic-book art. To quote Houston: "I tried to include and animate favorite panels from the X-Men comic books, those rare times it was possible." **OPPOSITE** Storyboard pages of Jean Grey's transformation into the Phoenix and her command over a shattered Jason Wyngarde as he turns back into Mastermind.

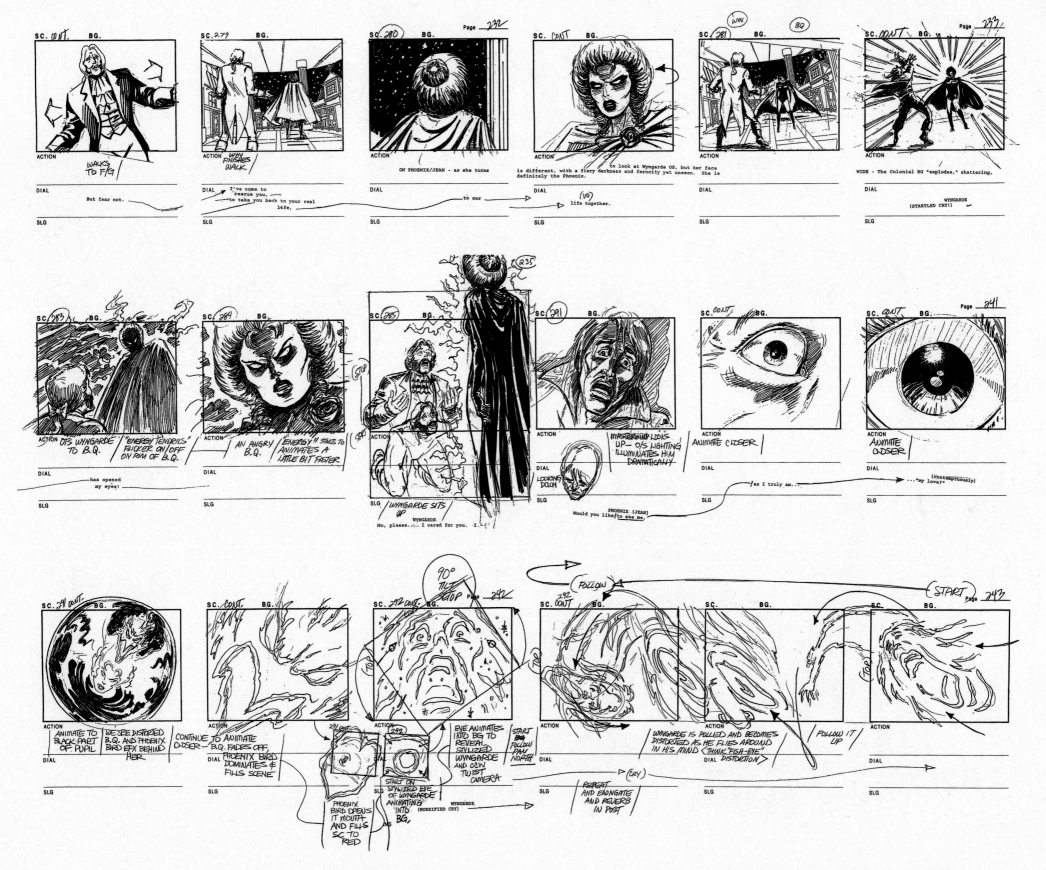

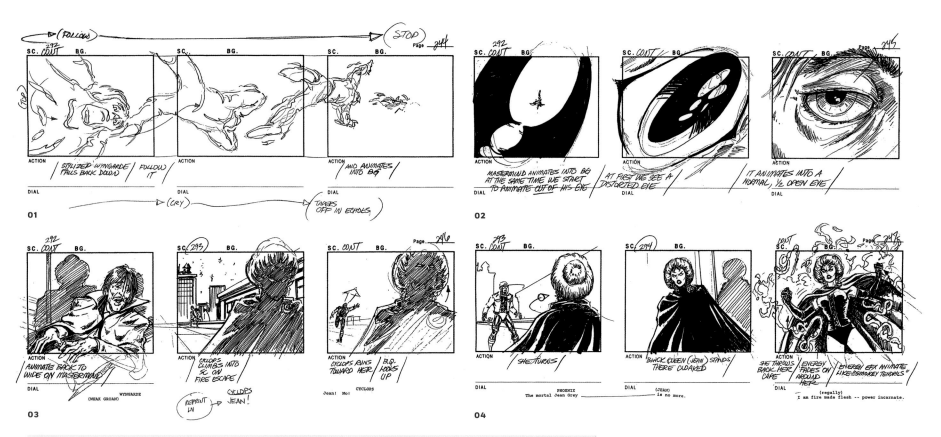

01
STYLIZED WYNGARDE | FOLLOW
FALLS BACK DOWN | IT
AND ANIMATES INTO BG
(CRY) | TAPERS OFF IN ECHOES.)

02
MASTERMIND ANIMATES INTO BG AT THE SAME TIME WE START TO ANIMATE OUT OF HIS EYE | AT FIRST WE SEE A DISTORTED EYE | IT ANIMATES INTO A NORMAL, ½ OPEN EYE

03
ANIMATE BACK TO WIDE ON MASTERMIND | CYCLOPS CLIMBS INTO SC ON FIRE ESCAPE | CYCLOPS RUNS TOWARD HER | B.Q. LOOKS UP

WYNGARDE
(WEAK GROAN) | REPRINT LN | CYCLOPS Jean! | Jean! No! CYCLOPS

04
SHE TURNS | BLACK QUEEN (JEAN) STANDS THERE CLOAKED | SHE THROWS BACK HER CAPE | ENERGY FADES ON AROUND HER | ENERGY EFX ANIMATE LIKE "SMOKEY TENDRILS"

PHOENIX
The mortal Jean Grey | (JEAN) is no more. | (regally) I am fire made flesh -- power incarnate.

05

01–04 Storyboards of the spectral images Jean Grey as Phoenix projects into Mastermind, Mastermind's eye refocusing, Cyclops on the roof rushing toward Jean Grey, The Phoenix announcing that Jean Grey is no more. **05** Production cel of Jean Grey as the Black Queen, drawn from the adjacent board panel. **OPPOSITE** Storyboard pages of Jean Grey bursting into flame, revealing her new Dark Phoenix costume; a distraught Cyclops as the Dark Phoenix expands; the horrified X-Men down below, observing the Dark Phoenix transformation in the sky; Beast, Storm, and Wolverine reacting; the Dark Phoenix burst of light as it animates over stunned Cyclops's visor.

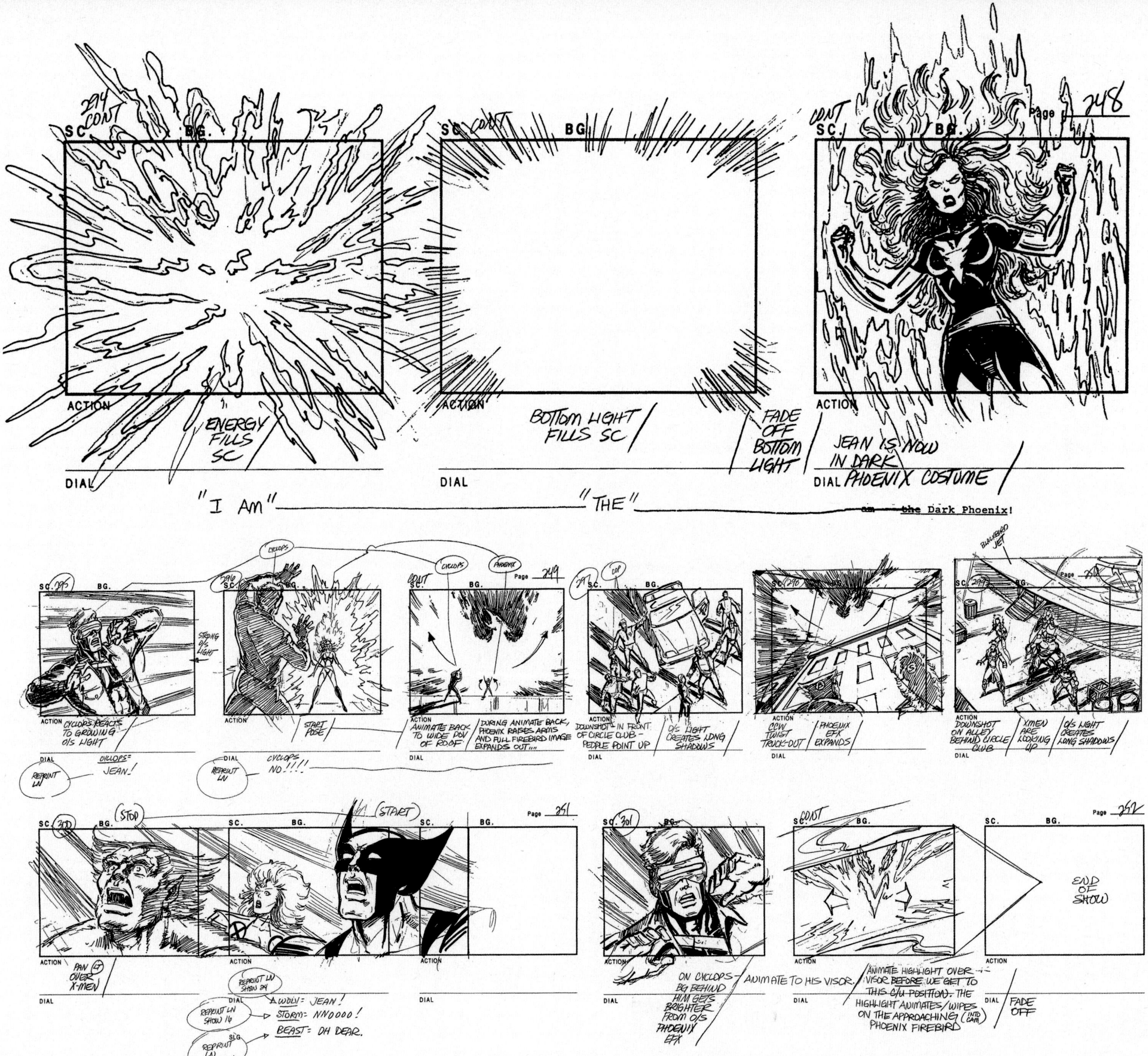

294 CONT
ENERGY FILLS SC
CONT
BOTTOM LIGHT FILLS SC
FADE OFF BOTTOM LIGHT
CONT
Page 248
JEAN IS NOW IN DARK PHOENIX COSTUME
"I AM" "THE"
am the Dark Phoenix!
295
CYCLOPS REACTS TO GROWING O/S LIGHT
STRONG O/S LIGHT
CYCLOPS= JEAN!
REPRINT LN
296
CYCLOPS
START POSE
CYCLOPS NO!!!!
REPRINT LN
CONT
CYCLOPS
PHOENIX
Page 249
ANIMATE BACK TO WIDE POV OF ROOF
DURING ANIMATE BACK, PHOENIX RAISES ARMS AND FULL FIREBIRD IMAGE EXPANDS OUT....
297
COP
DOWNSHOT - IN FRONT OF CIRCLE CLUB - PEOPLE POINT UP
O/S LIGHT CREATES LONG SHADOWS
298
CCW TWIST TRUCK-OUT
PHOENIX EFX EXPANDS
BLACKBIRD JET
299
Page 250
DOWNSHOT ON ALLEY BEHIND CIRCLE CLUB
XMEN ARE LOOKING UP
O/S LIGHT CREATES LONG SHADOWS
300
(STOP)
(START)
Page 251
PAN (LT) OVER X-MEN
REPRINT LN SHOW 24
WOLV= JEAN!
REPRINT LN SHOW 16
STORM= NNOOOO!
SLG
REPRINT LN SHOW 14
BEAST= OH DEAR.
301
ON CYCLOPS - BG BEHIND HIM GETS BRIGHTER FROM O/S PHOENIX EFX
ANIMATE TO HIS VISOR.
CONT
ANIMATE HIGHLIGHT OVER VISOR BEFORE WE GET TO THIS C/U POSITION. THE HIGHLIGHT ANIMATES/WIPES ON THE APPROACHING (INTO CAM) PHOENIX FIREBIRD
Page 252
END OF SHOW
FADE OFF

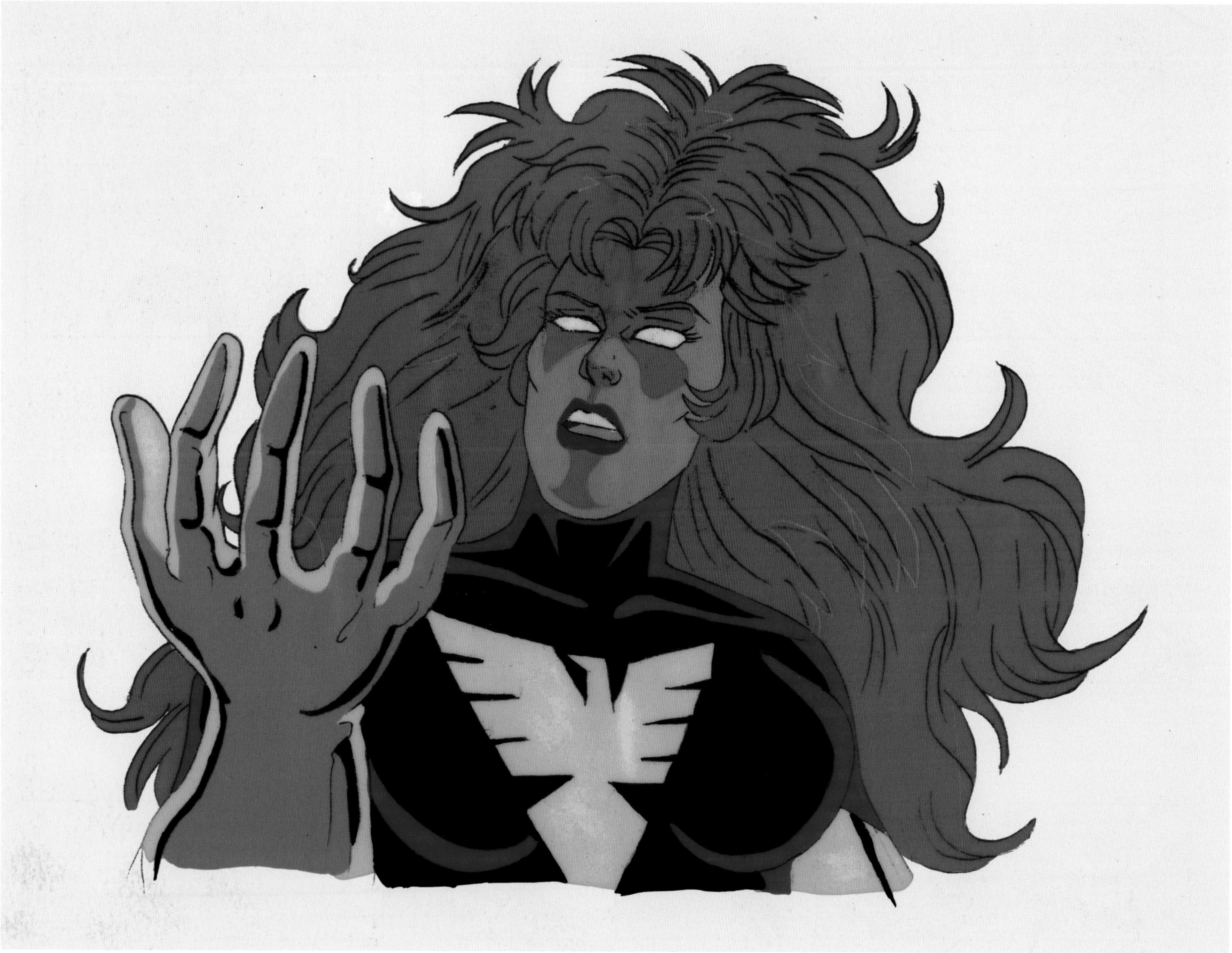

ABOVE Production cel of Jean Grey transformed into the Dark Phoenix, minus its line-detailing overlay.
OPPOSITE Production cel of Rogue, Beast, Wolverine, Storm, Cyclops, and Gambit blasted off of the roof of the Inner Circle's headquarters by the Dark Phoenix.

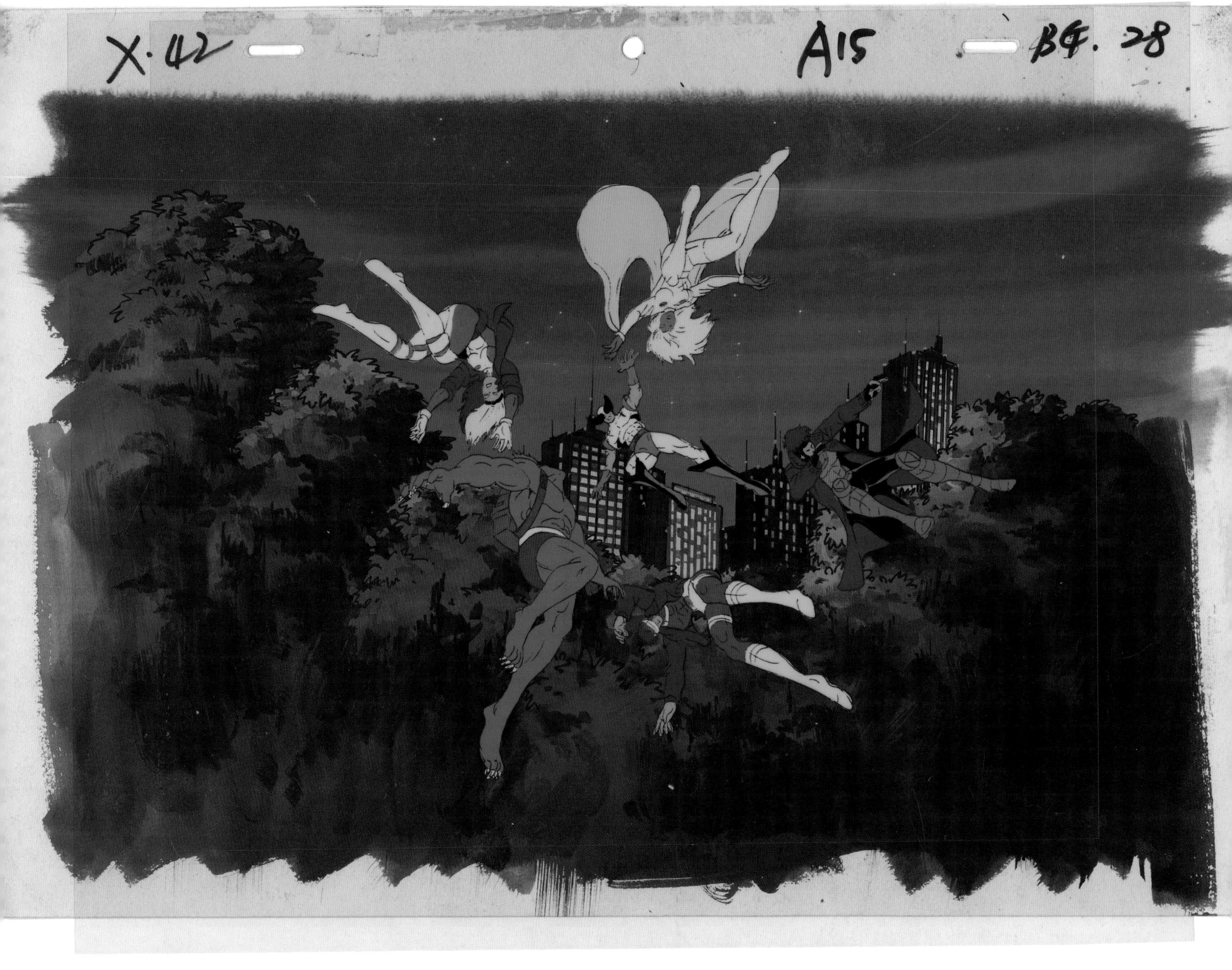
X·42
A15
BG. 28

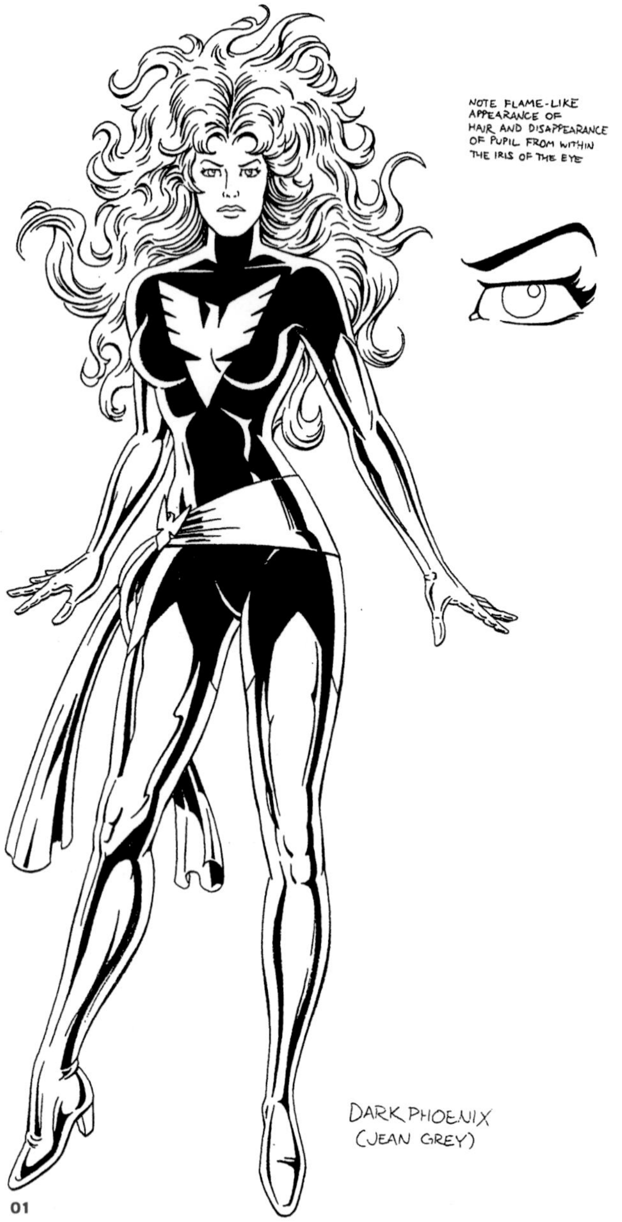
NOTE FLAME-LIKE APPEARANCE OF HAIR AND DISAPPEARANCE OF PUPIL FROM WITHIN THE IRIS OF THE EYE
DARK PHOENIX (JEAN GREY)

01

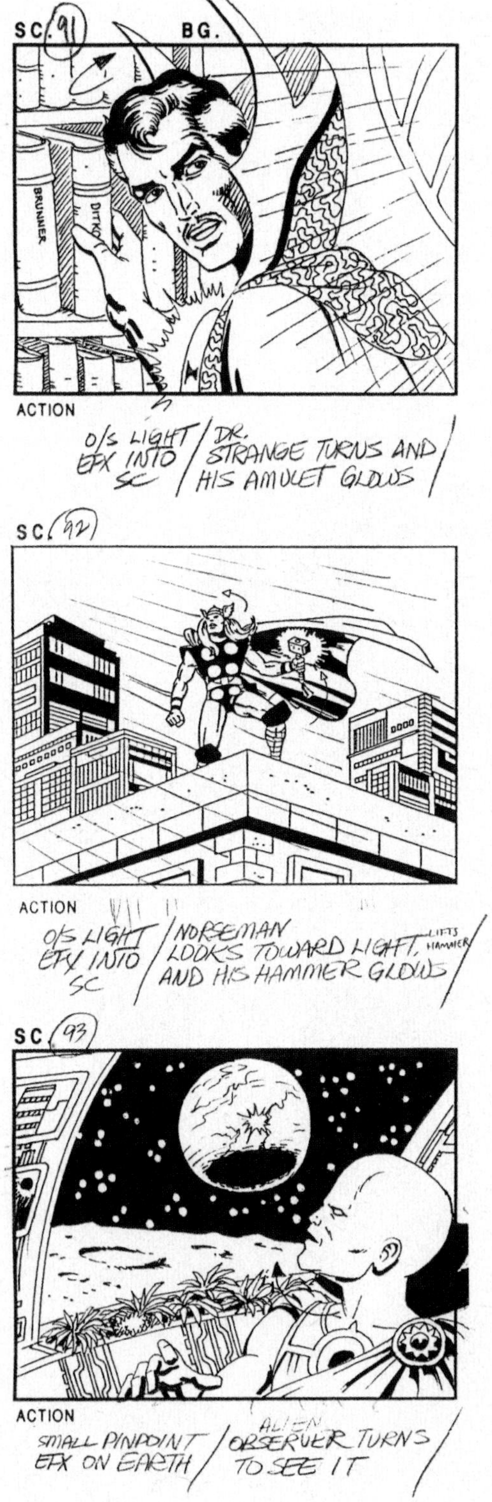
SC. 91
BG.
ACTION
O/S LIGHT EFX INTO SC
DR. STRANGE TURNS AND HIS AMULET GLOWS
SC. 92
ACTION
O/S LIGHT EFX INTO SC
NORSEMAN LOOKS TOWARD LIGHT, LIFTS HAMMER AND HIS HAMMER GLOWS
SC. 93
ACTION
SMALL PINPOINT EFX ON EARTH
ALIEN OBSERVER TURNS TO SEE IT

02

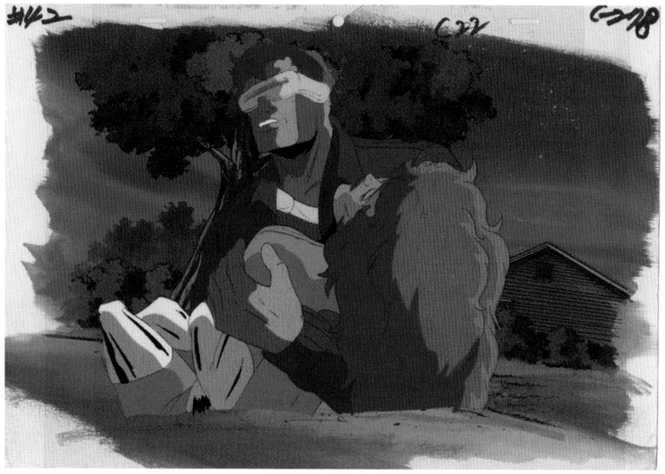

03

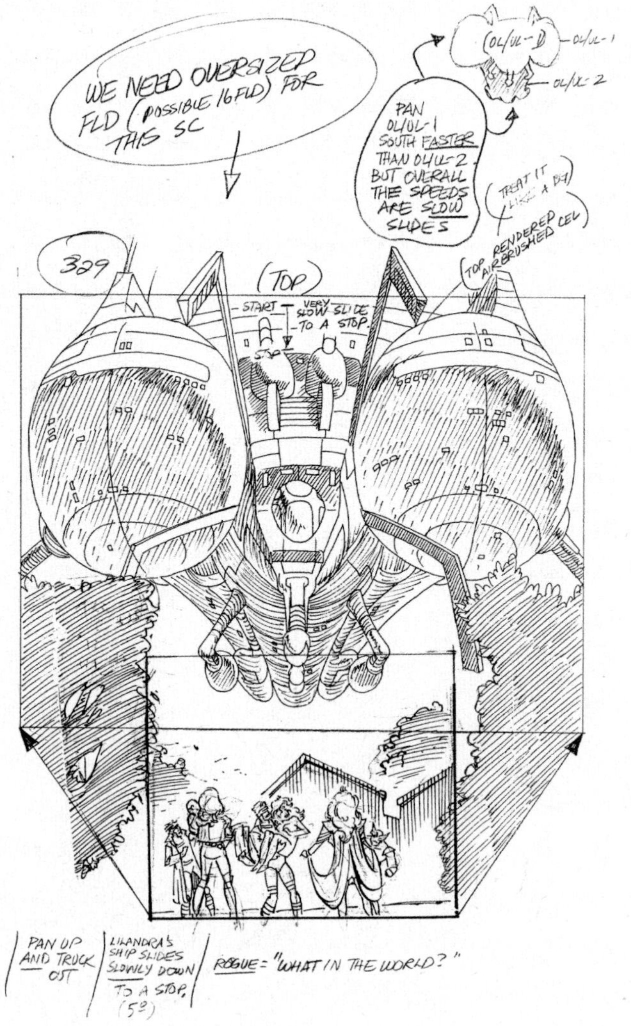
WE NEED OVERSIZED FLD (POSSIBLE 16FLD) FOR THIS SC
PAN OL/UL-1 SOUTH FASTER THAN OL/UL-2 BUT OVERALL THE SPEEDS ARE SLOW SLIDES
OL/UL-1
OL/UL-2
(TREAT IT LIKE A BG)
(TOP RENDERED AIRBRUSHED CEL)
329
(TOP)
START
VERY SLOW SLIDE TO A STOP.
PAN UP AND TRUCK OST
LILANDRA'S SHIP SLIDES SLOWLY DOWN TO A STOP. (5º)
ROGUE = "WHAT IN THE WORLD?"

04

01 Character model of Dark Phoenix Jean Grey, by Frank Brunner and Mark Lewis. **02** Storyboard page of Dark Phoenix–blast reactions, including Doctor Strange, Thor (called "Norseman"), and the Watcher (called "Alien Observer"). See page 261 for an explanation of these "Easter eggs." Storyboard page by Larry Houston. **03** Production cel of Cyclops carrying Dark Phoenix Jean Grey. **04** Storyboard for reveal of Lilandra's spaceship. **05–06** Character models of Alien Audience 1 (The Watcher) and Alien Entity 2 (Eternity), both by Brunner and Lewis. **07** Background layout of Shi'ar homeworld with docking ring, by Frank Squillace with cleanup by Lewis. **08** Production cel of Lilandra in battle suit.

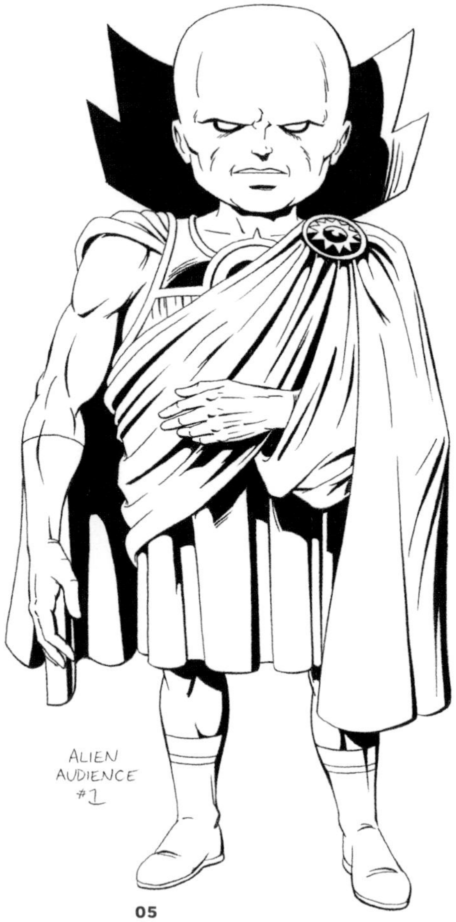
ALIEN
AUDIENCE
#1

05

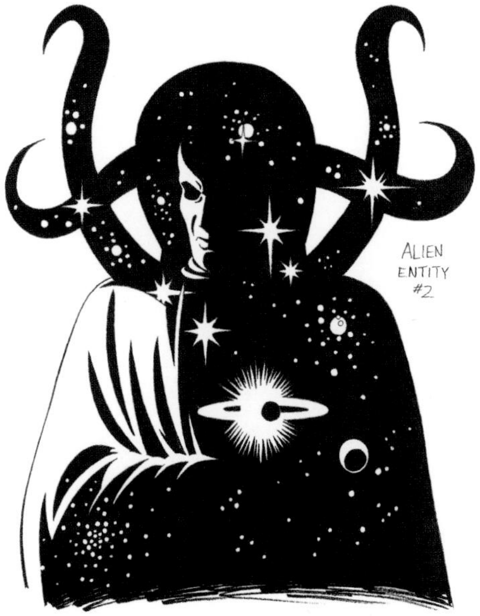
ALIEN
ENTITY
#2

06

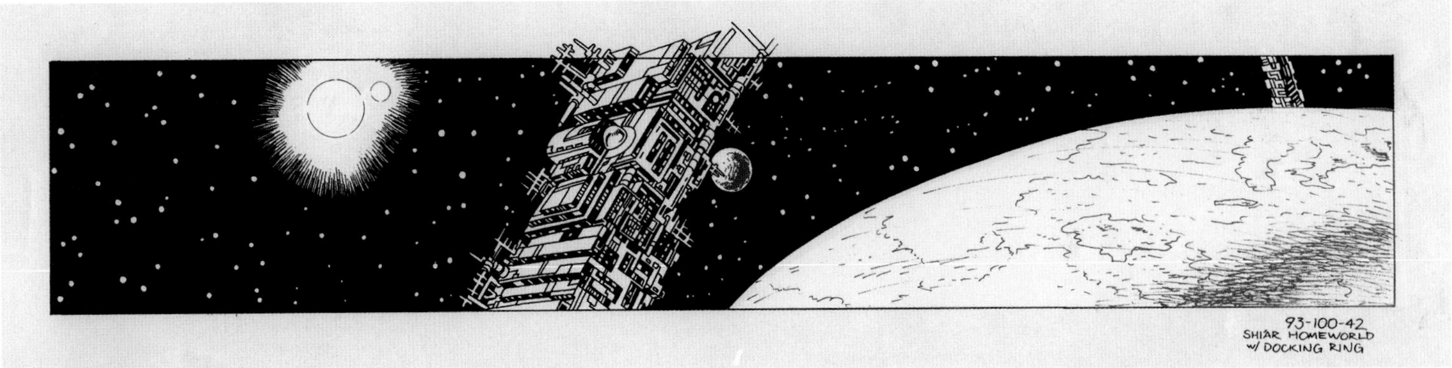
93-100-42
SHIAR HOMEWORLD
w/ DOCKING RING

07

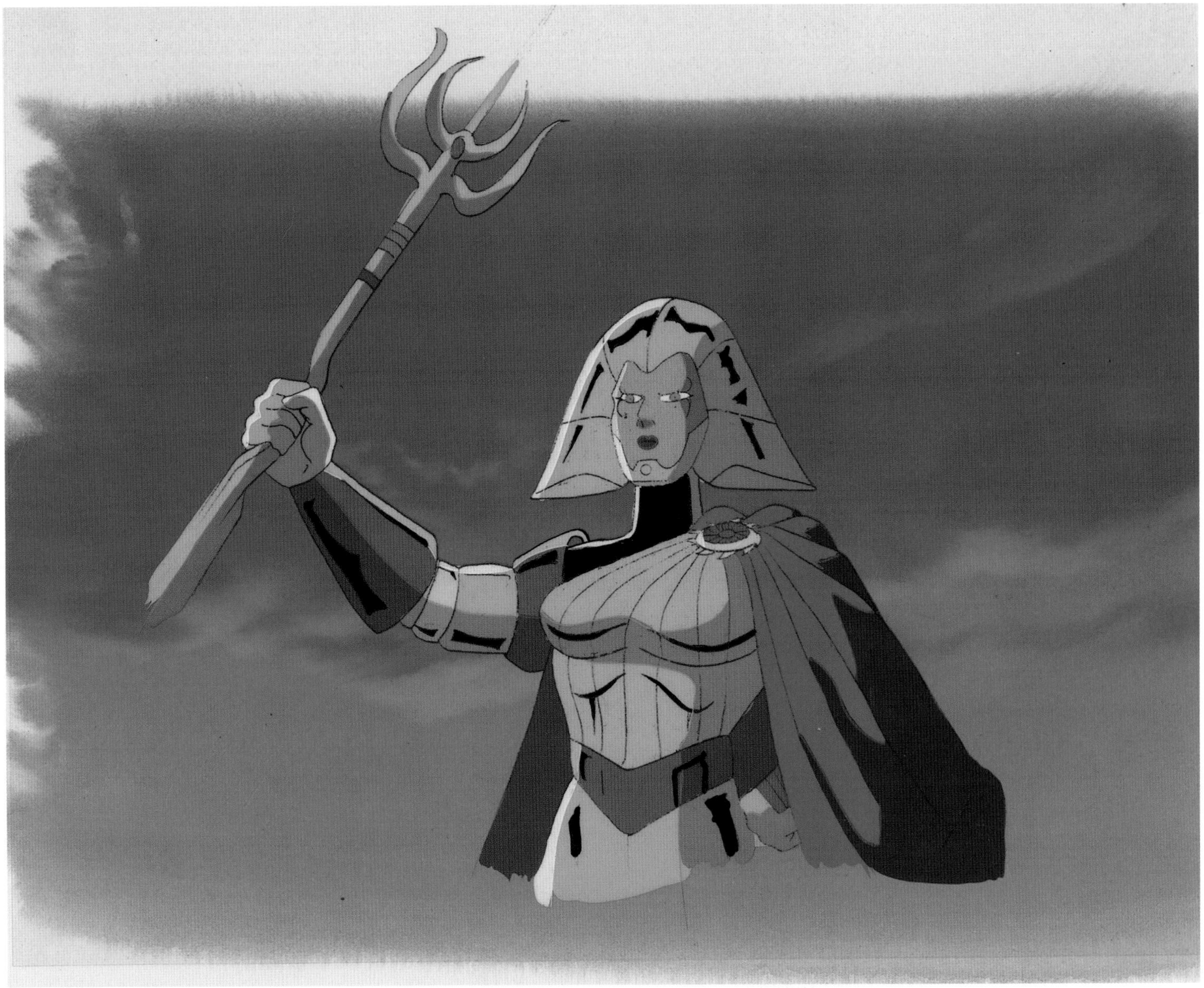

08

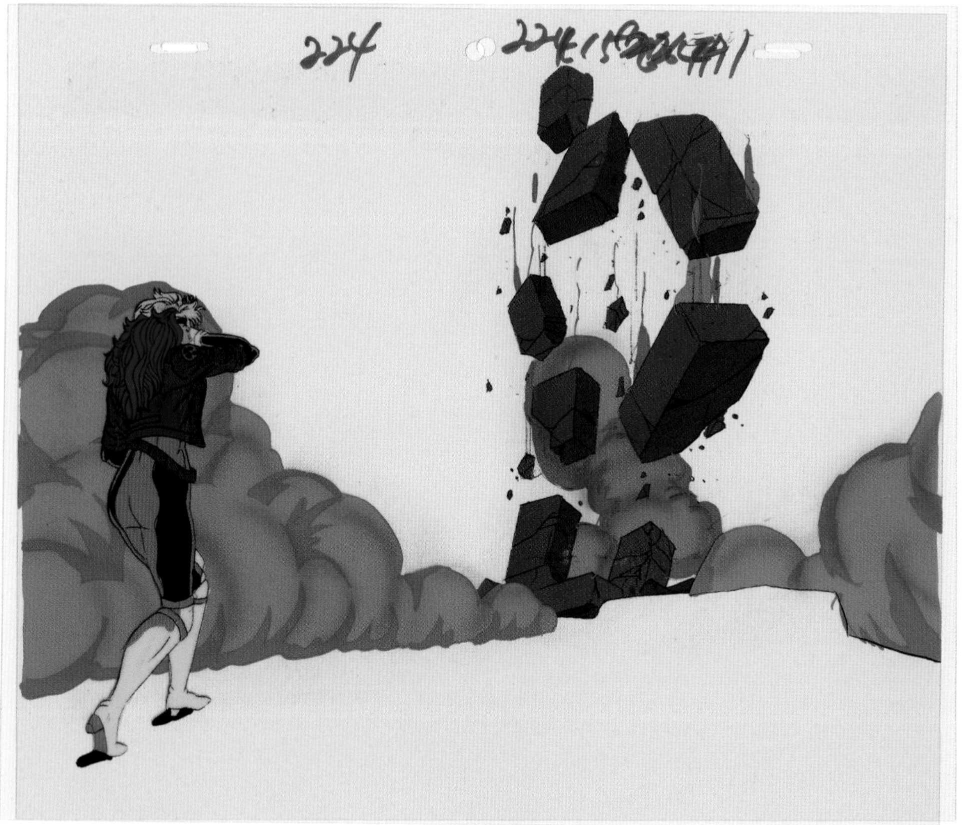
224

01

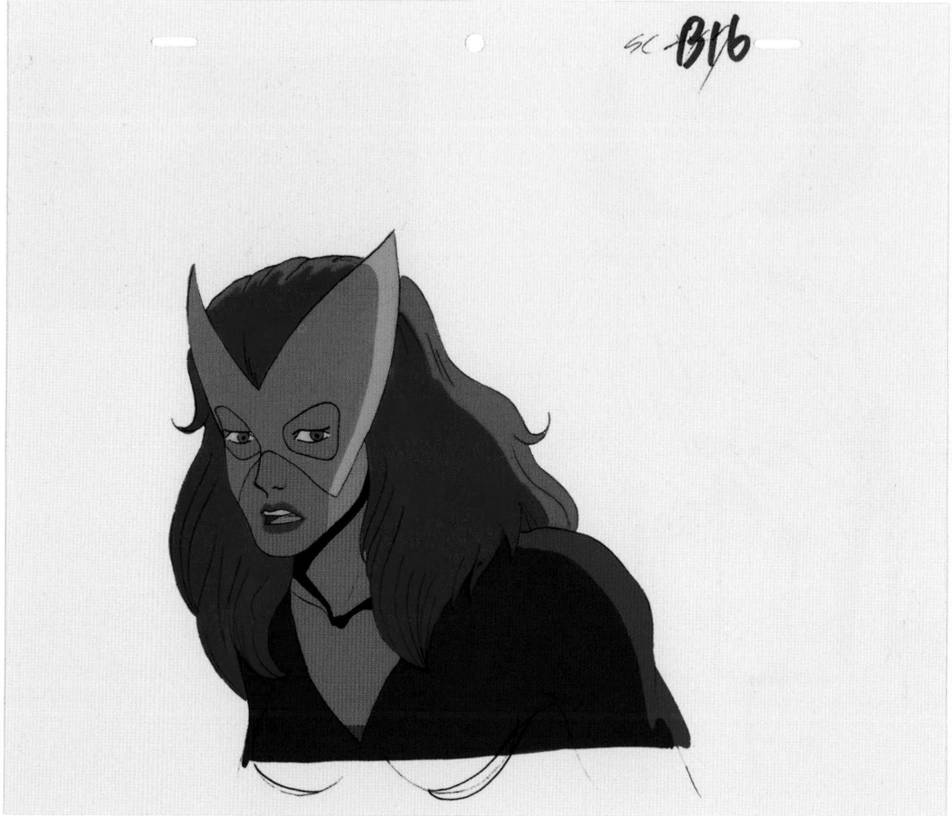

02

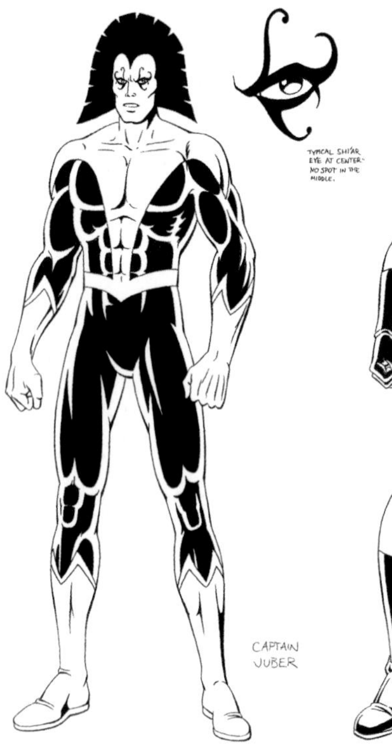
TYPICAL SHI'AR EYE AT CENTER- NO SPOT IN THE MIDDLE.
CAPTAIN JUBER

03

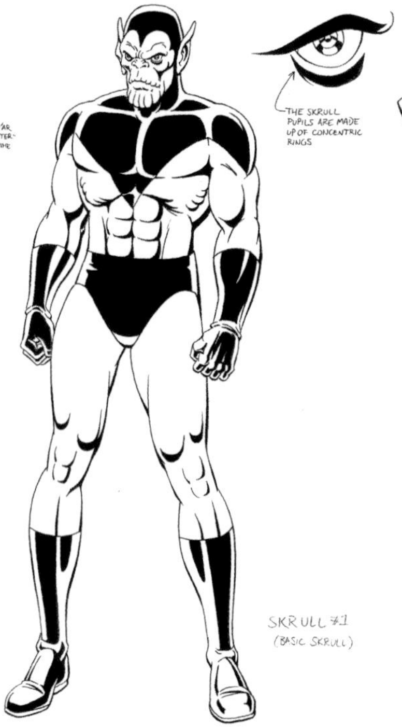
THE SKRULL PUPILS ARE MADE UP OF CONCENTRIC RINGS
SKRULL #1
(BASIC SKRULL)

04

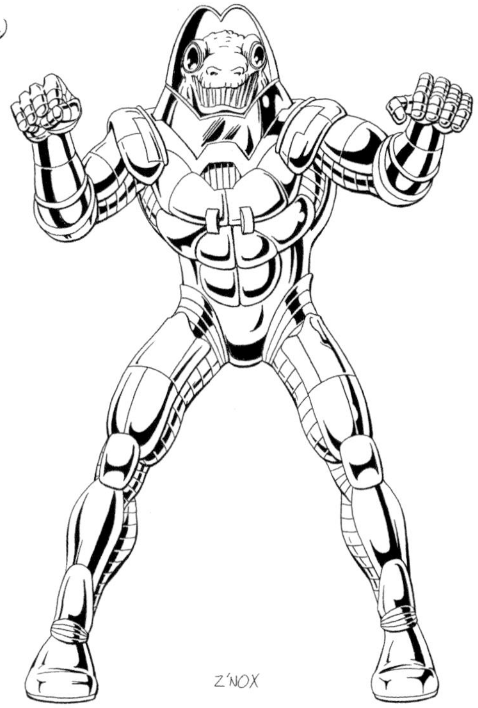
Z'NOX

05

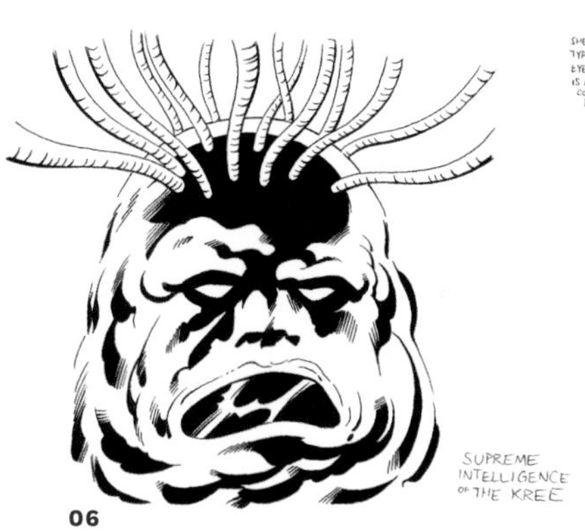
SUPREME INTELLIGENCE OF THE KREE

06

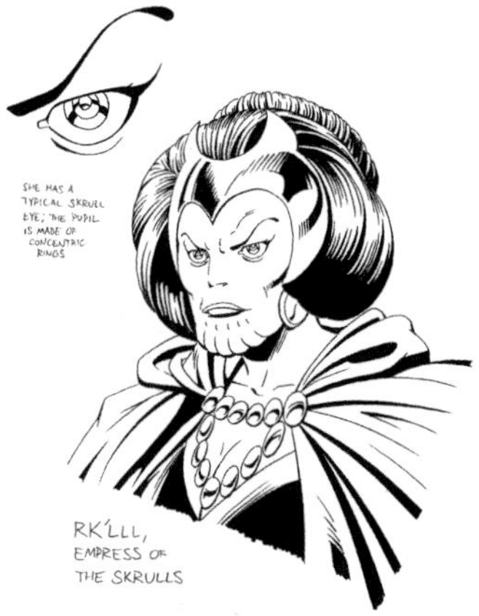
SHE HAS A TYPICAL SKRULL EYE; THE PUPIL IS MADE OF CONCENTRIC RINGS
RK'LLL, EMPRESS OF THE SKRULLS

07

01–02 Production cels of Rogue burying Gladiator under rubble and Jean Grey as Marvel Girl. **03** Character model of Commander Rakner, by Frank Brunner and Mark Lewis. **04–07** Character Models of Skrull 1; Z'Nox; Supreme Intelligence of the Kree; and RK'LII, empress of the Skrulls—all penciled by Frank Brunner with cleanup by Mark Lewis. **OPPOSITE** Color drawing of the Monorail below the X-Mansion, where Cyclops confronts his father, Corsair, on their way to the minijet. Designed and cleaned by Frank Squillace; colored by Dennis Venizelos.

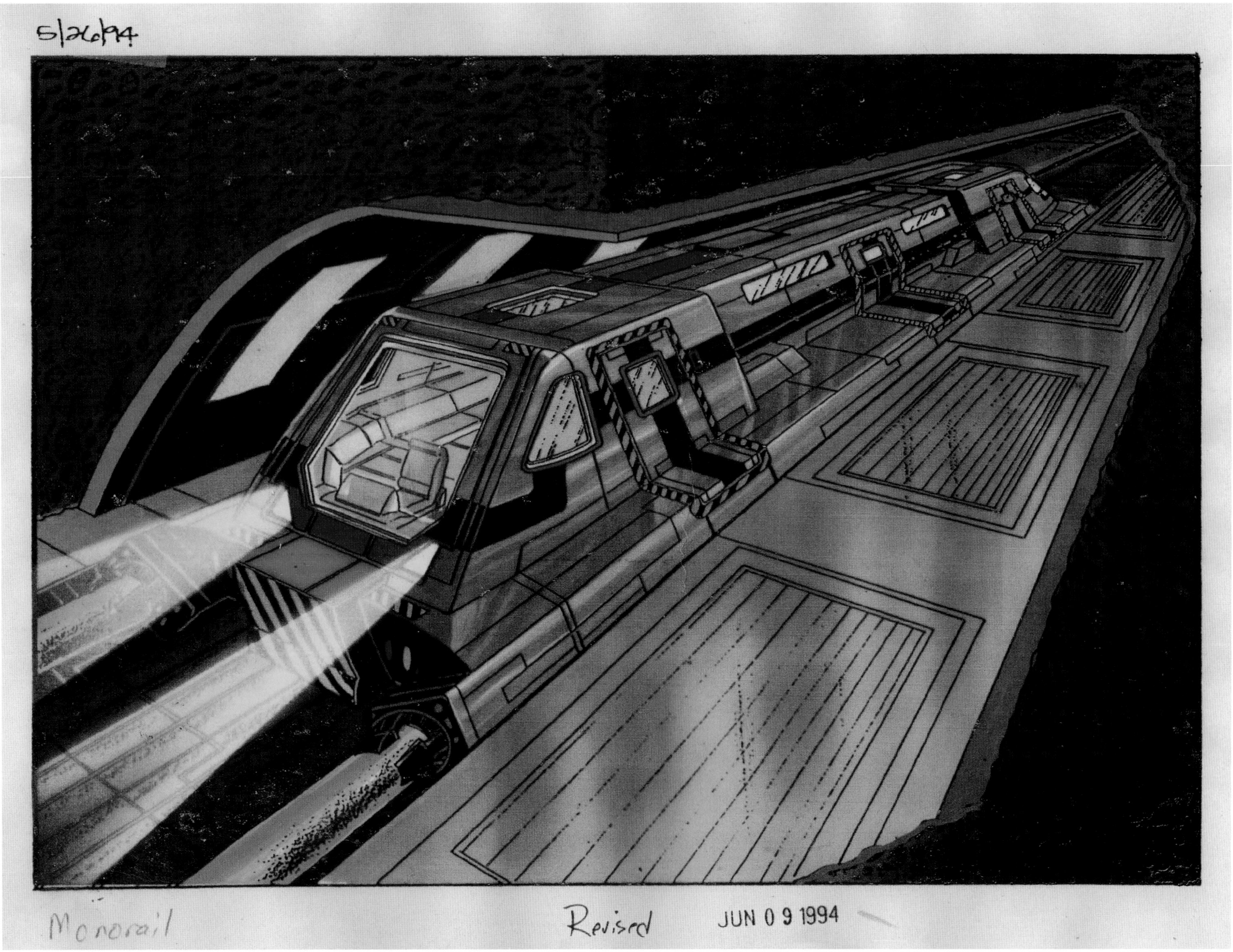
5/26/94
Monorail
Revised
JUN 0 9 1994

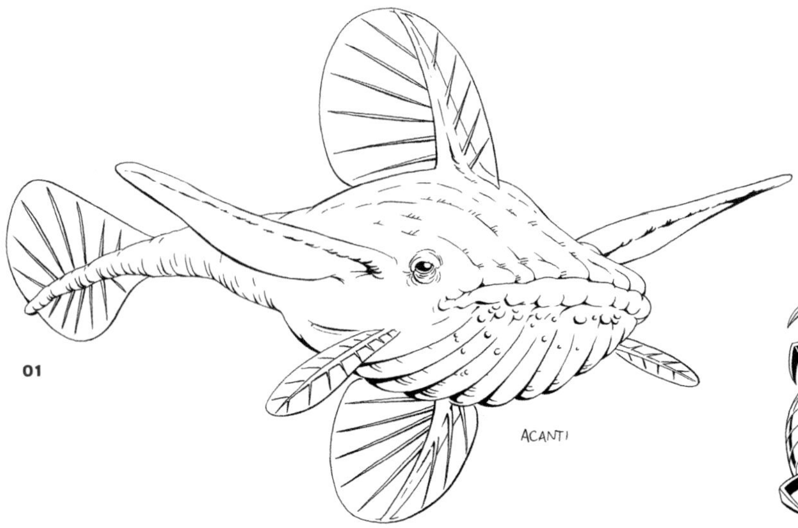
ACANTI

01

01–04 Character models of Acanti organic spaceship, Colony Alien, Colony Queen, and Wolverine semi-transformed, all by Frank Brunner and Mark Lewis. 05 Storyboard of Cody, who has transformed into a Colony Alien, seizing Rogue. 06 Production sketch of Rogue, semi-transformed. **OPPOSITE** Production cel of Professor Xavier, overwhelmed by using Cerebro.

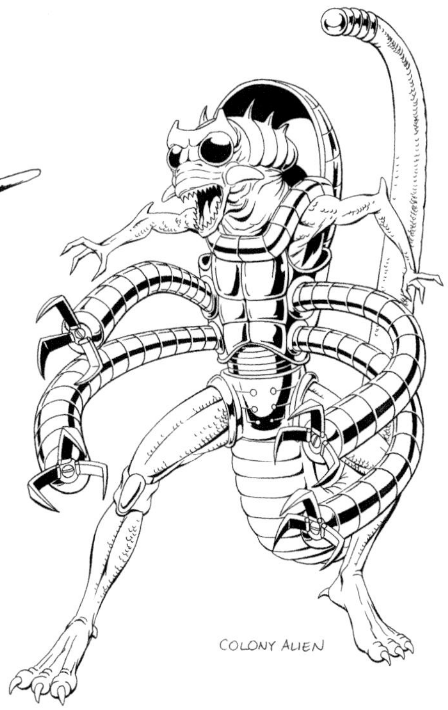
COLONY ALIEN

02

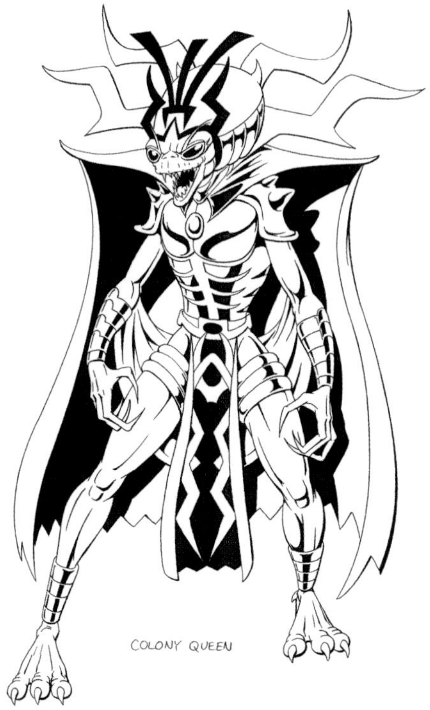
COLONY QUEEN

03

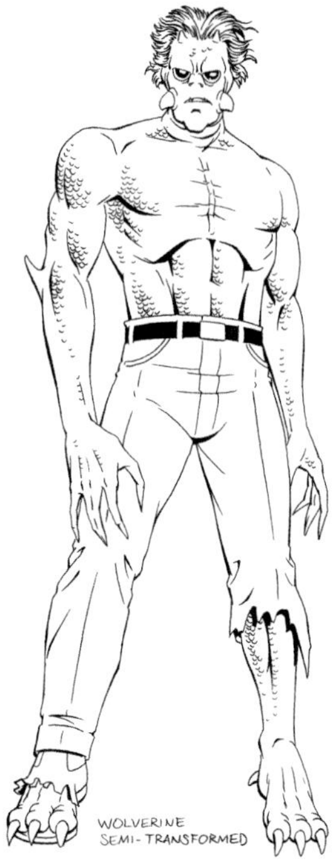
WOLVERINE
SEMI-TRANSFORMED

04

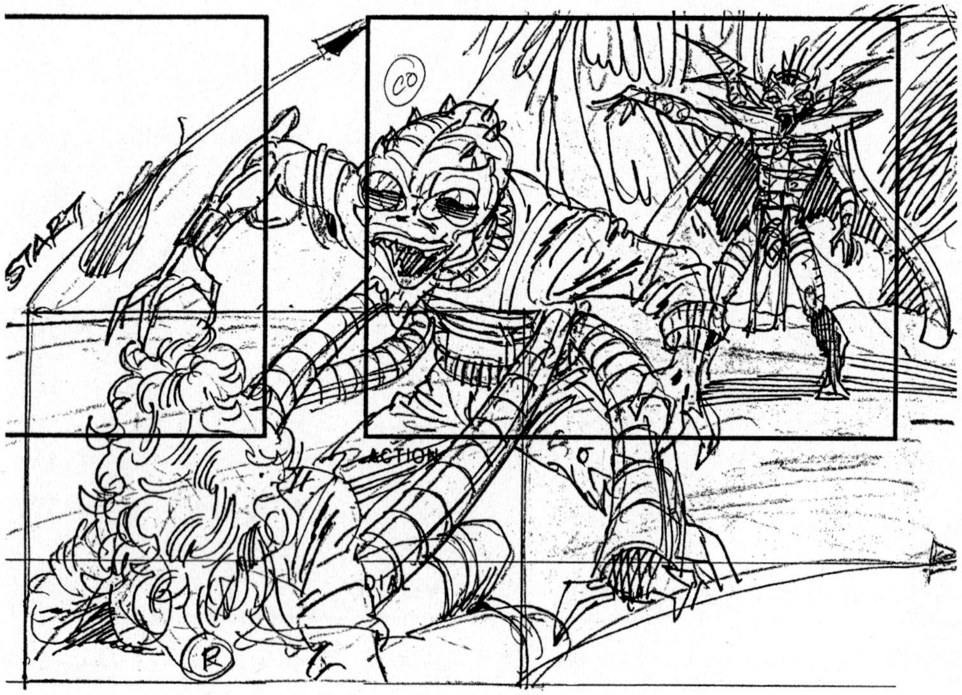
START
ACTION

05

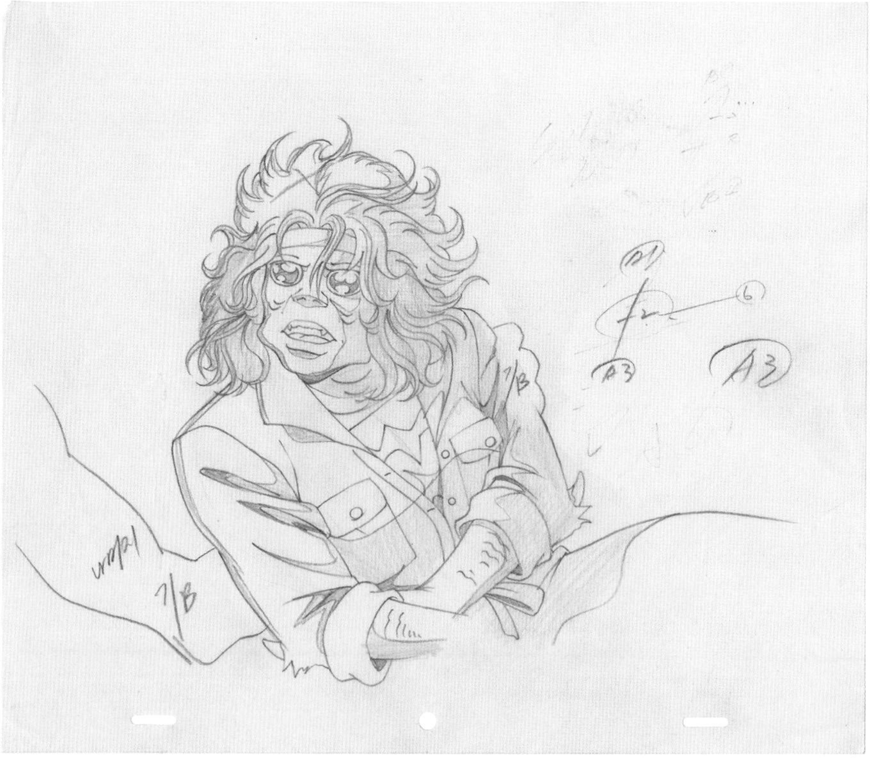
7/B
A3

06

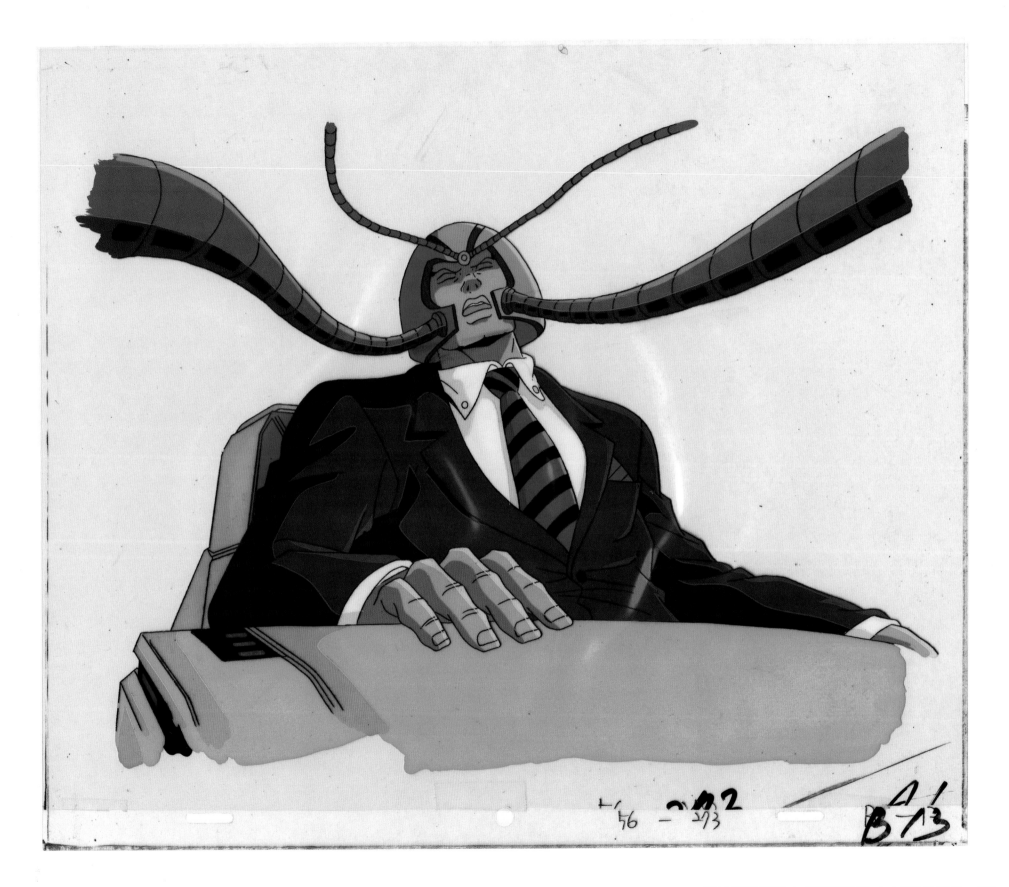

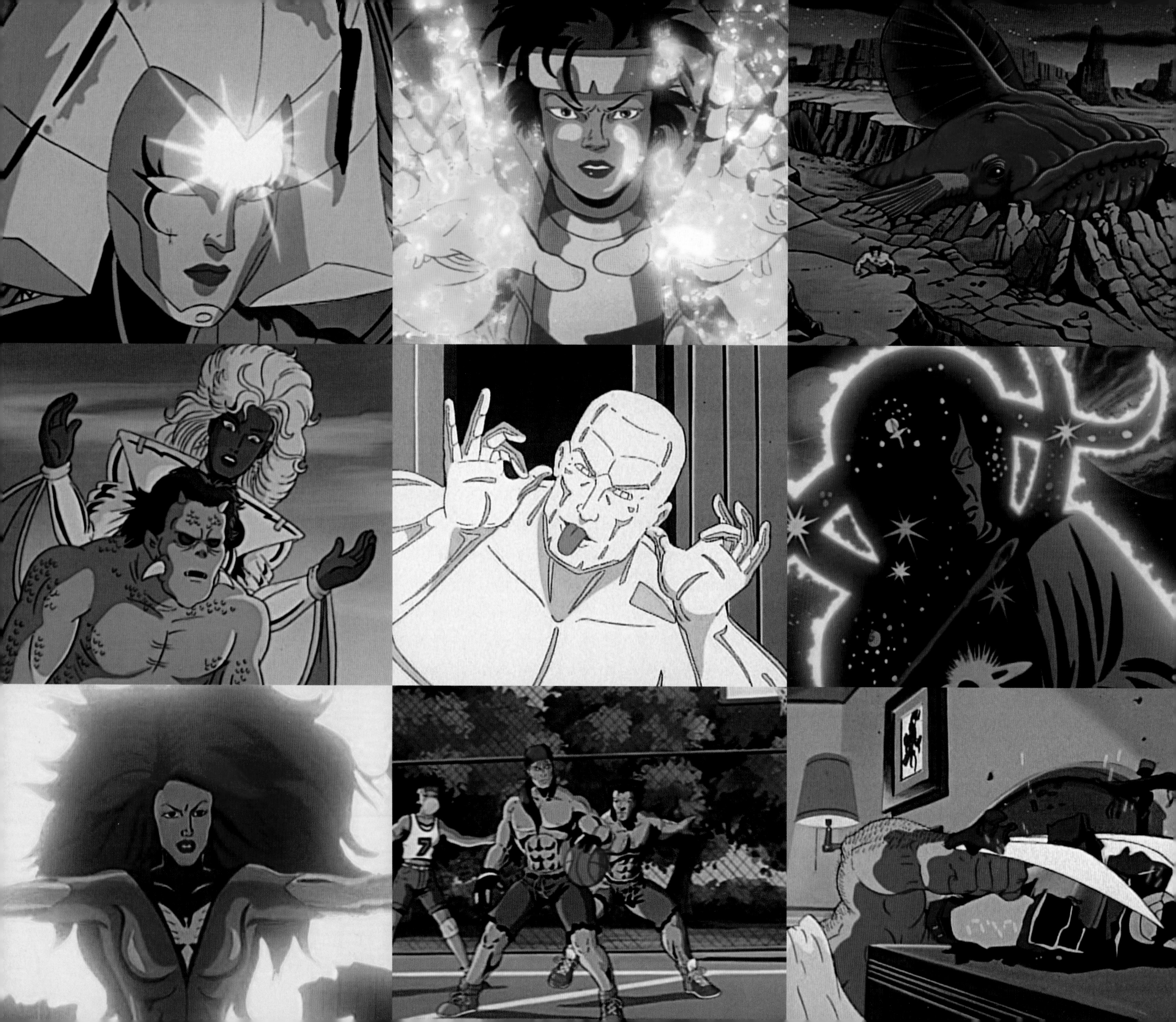

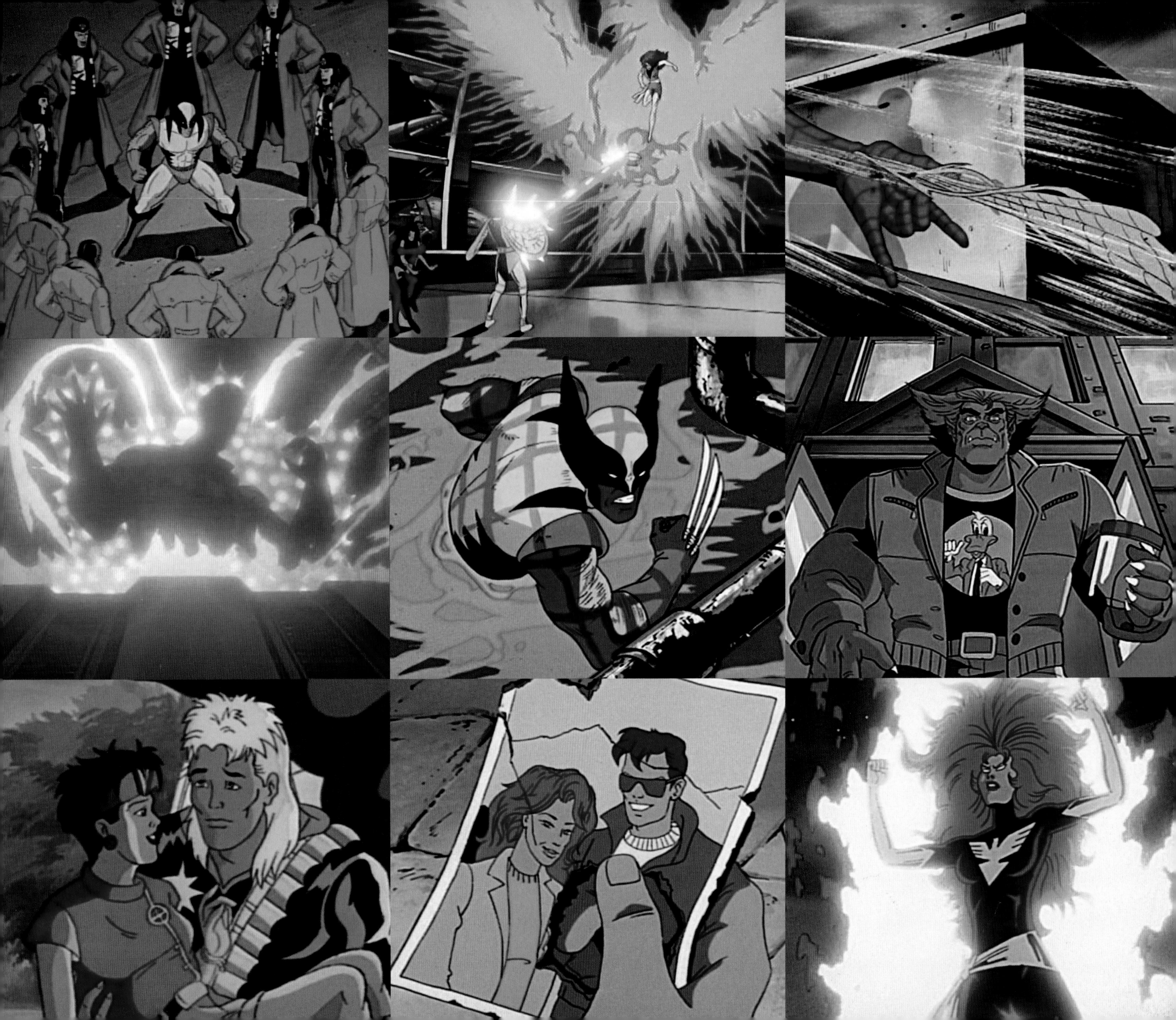

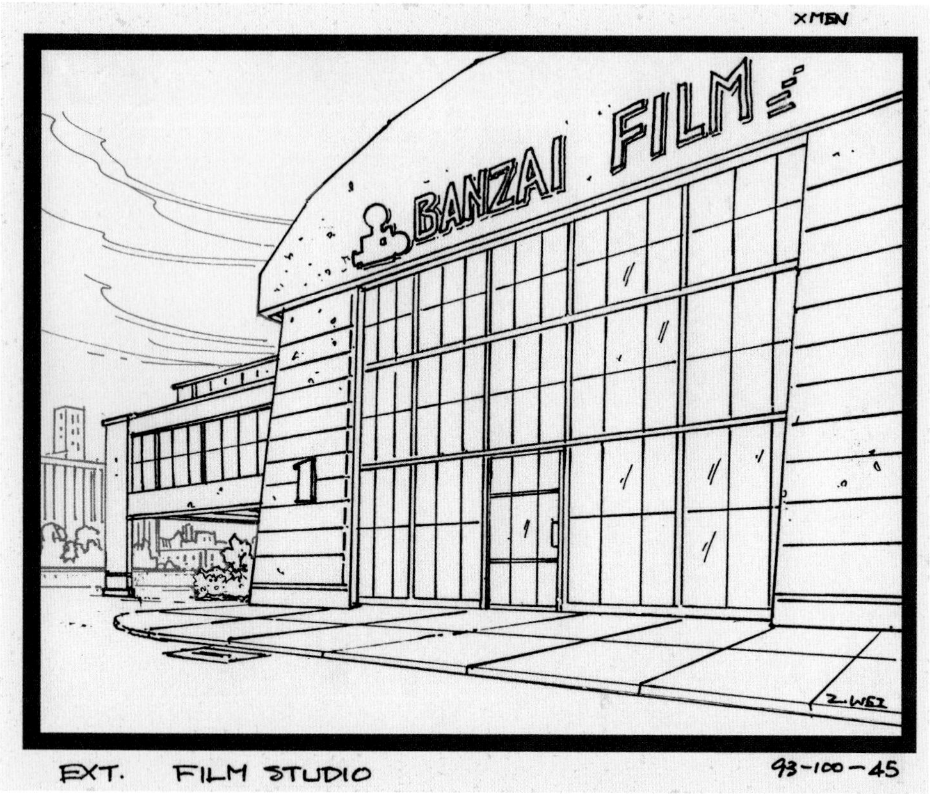
XMEN
BANZAI FILM
EXT. FILM STUDIO
93-100-45

01

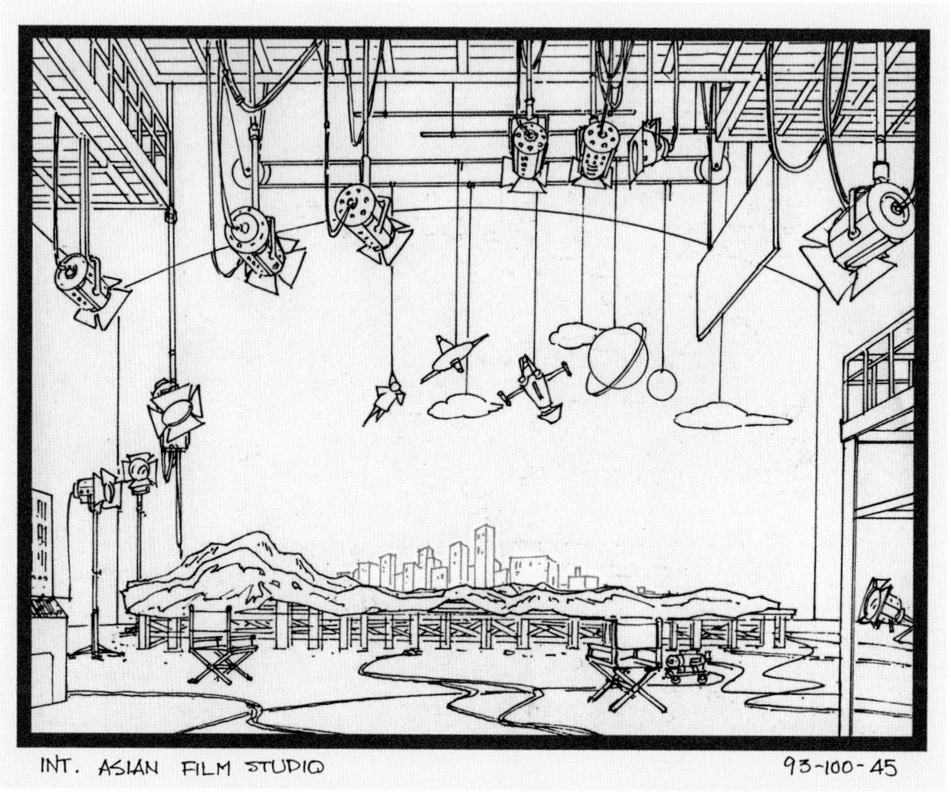
INT. ASIAN FILM STUDIO
93-100-45

02

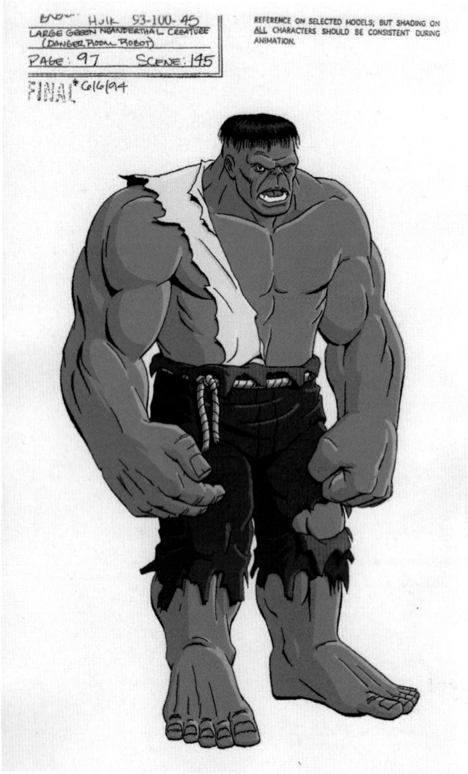
HULK 93-100-45
LARGE GREEN NEANDERTHAL CREATURE
(DANGER ROOM ROBOT)
PAGE: 97 SCENE: 145
FINAL *6/6/94
REFERENCE ON SELECTED MODELS; BUT SHADING ON ALL CHARACTERS SHOULD BE CONSISTENT DURING ANIMATION.

03

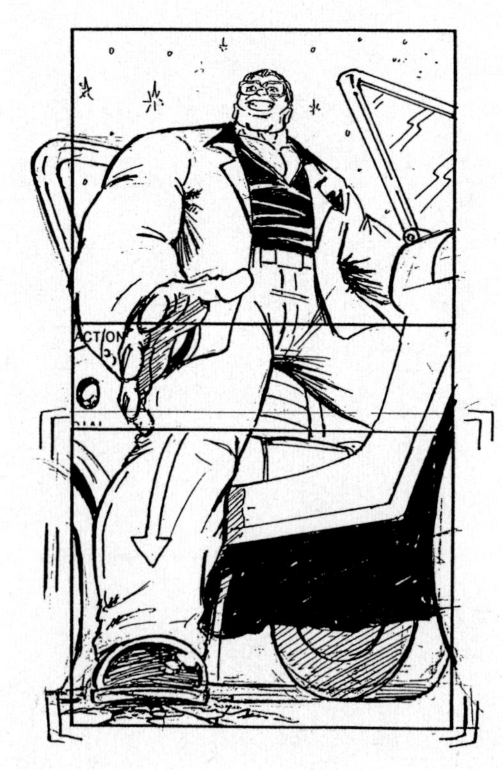

04

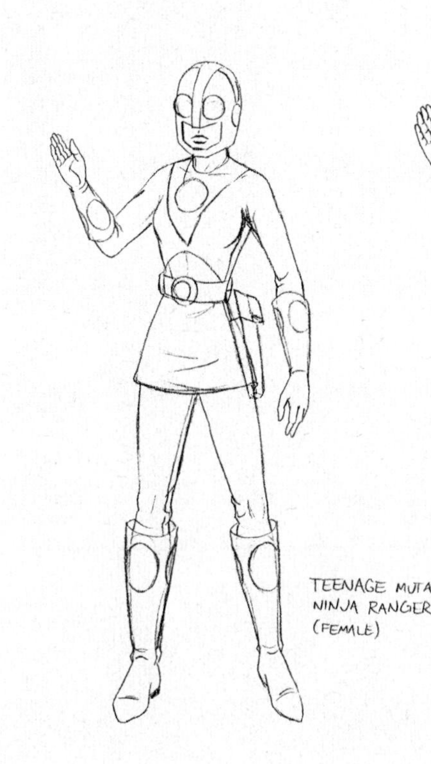
TEENAGE MUTANT
NINJA RANGER
(FEMALE)

05

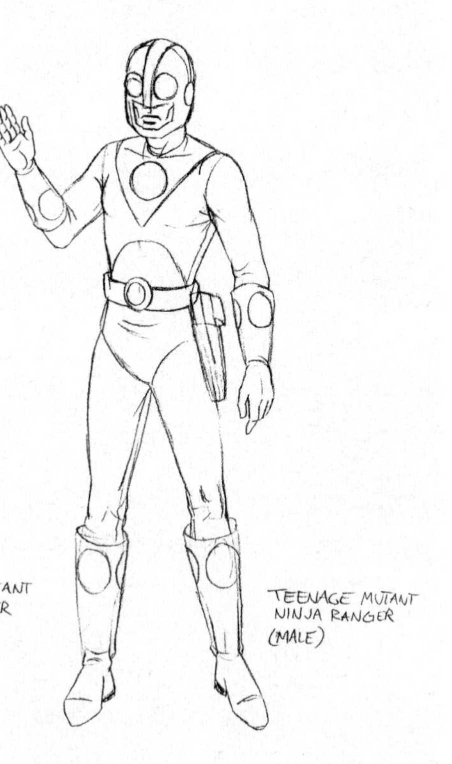
TEENAGE MUTANT
NINJA RANGER
(MALE)

06

01-02 Background layouts of film studio exterior and interior, fallen into by the "Wiederspahn Juggernaut" during a chase. Designed by Frank Squillace and cleaned by Zhaoping Wei. 03 Colored character model of "Large Green Neanderthal Creature Danger Room Robot" (aka the Hulk), by Squillace with cleanup by Mark Lewis. 04 Storyboard panel of Eugene Torbet Wiederspahn transformed with Juggernaut's powers—Wiederspahn was named after two family members and a friend of the authors; storyboard by Patrick Archibald. 05-06 Character models of Teenage Mutant Ninja Ranger female and male, by Mark Lewis. 07 Cast list from script of never-produced episode (it would have been episode 47): "Bring Me Charles Xavier." 08 Storyboard of Omega Red from "A Deal with the Devil," written by Eric over a weekend to substitute for the tossed-out "Bring Me Charles Xavier."

X-MEN

Cast List : "Bring Me Charles Xavier" (Prod # 300-47)

X-MEN -   5 Speaking Parts

GAMBIT
XAVIER
JUBILEE
ROGUE
WOLVERINE

===

Major Recurring -   4 Speaking Parts

COLOSSUS - Good-natured Russian metallic mutant

ILLYANA - Colossus' 14 Year old, pony tailed sister.

OMEGA RED - The three hundred pound, man-made, tentacle-slashing, Russian "Super Weapon".

*DARKSTAR - beautiful female Russian mutant (see EP. 17), who projects "dark energy", she hates Omega Red

COLOSSUS' FATHER - Cries and one line
*COLOSSUS' MOTHER - Cries only

===

OTHERS -   3 Speaking Parts

DIMITRI - Burly, bearded, Russian mountain climber
IVANOVITCH - Slightly thinner Bearded Russian mountain climber
*LARA SMIRNOVA - Third climber, female, athletic - Wallah only.
*SOLDIERS - Neo-nationalist skin-heads, dressed in black
          uniforms, reminiscent of storm troopers - Wallah only.
*PRISONERS - men, stripped to the waist, working in slave labor
          munitions factory - Wallah only.
COMPUTER VOICE - two lines - female, monotone

TOTAL -   12 Speaking Parts

ACTION

OMEGA RED LOOKS UP

DIAL

          OMEGA RED
      (smiles)
   I like dealing with serious people. Your
   terms are satisfactory --

07

08

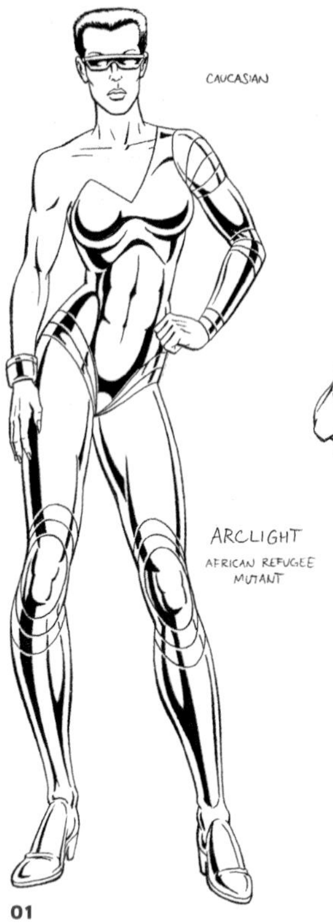
CAUCASIAN
ARCLIGHT
AFRICAN REFUGEE MUTANT

01

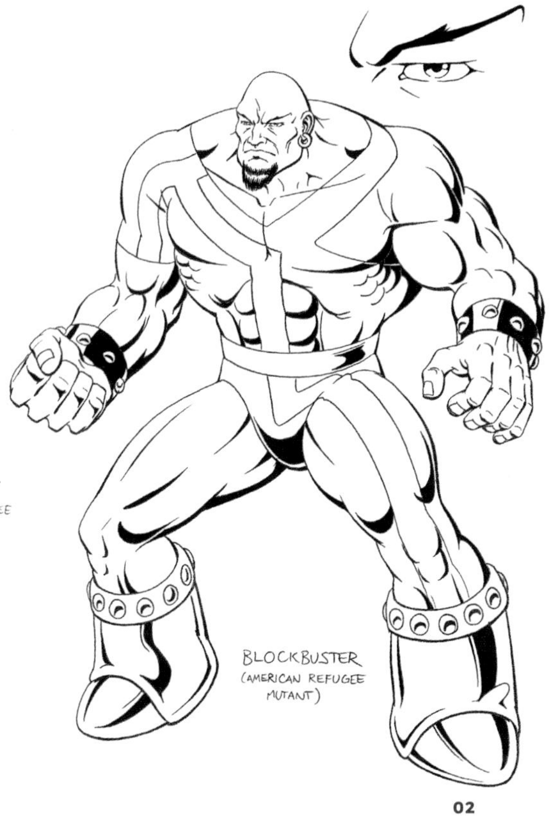
BLOCKBUSTER
(AMERICAN REFUGEE MUTANT)

02

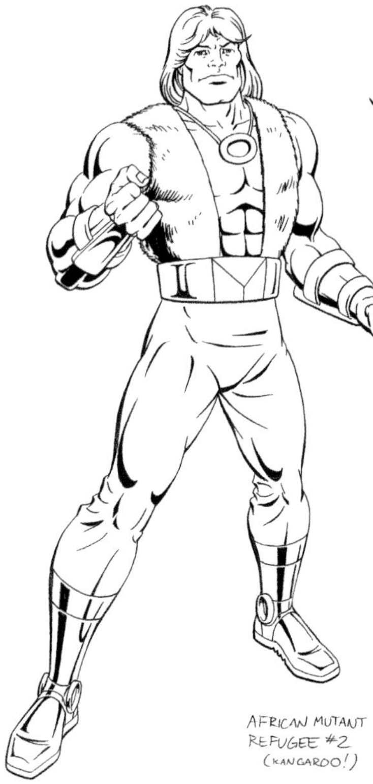
AFRICAN MUTANT REFUGEE #2
(KANGAROO!)

03

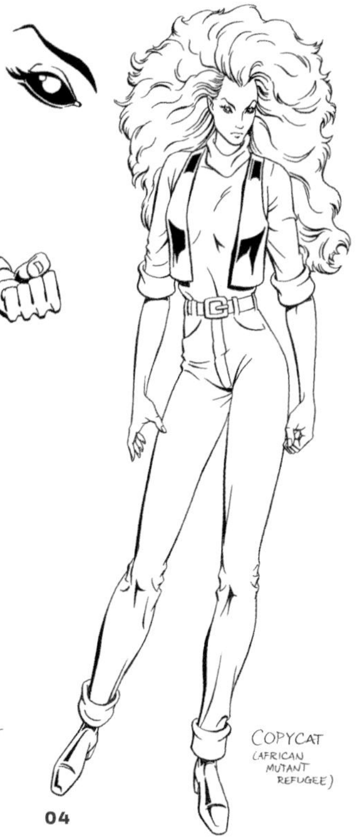
COPYCAT
(AFRICAN MUTANT REFUGEE)

04

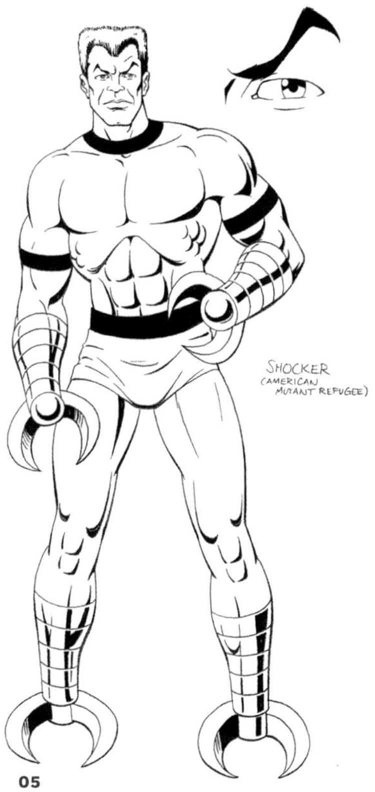
SHOCKER
(AMERICAN MUTANT REFUGEE)

05

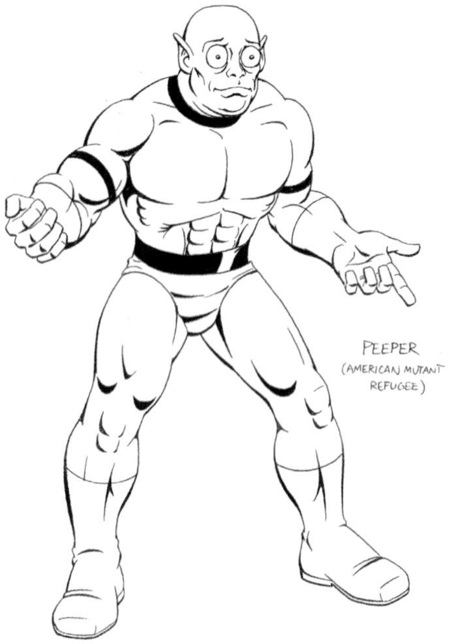
PEEPER
(AMERICAN MUTANT REFUGEE)

06

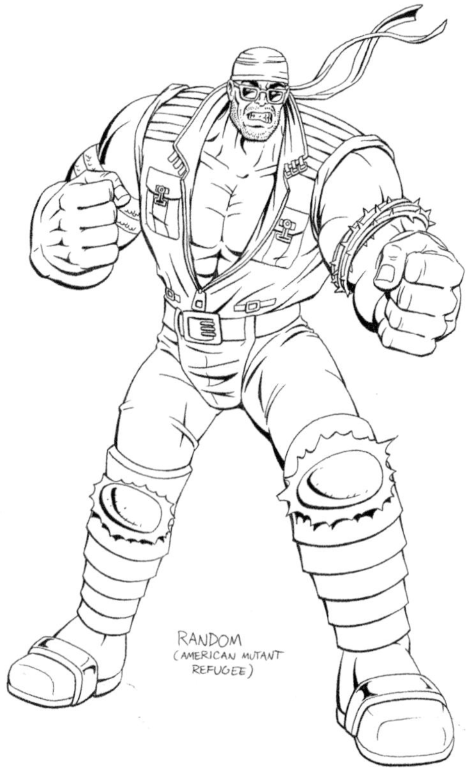
RANDOM
(AMERICAN MUTANT REFUGEE)

07

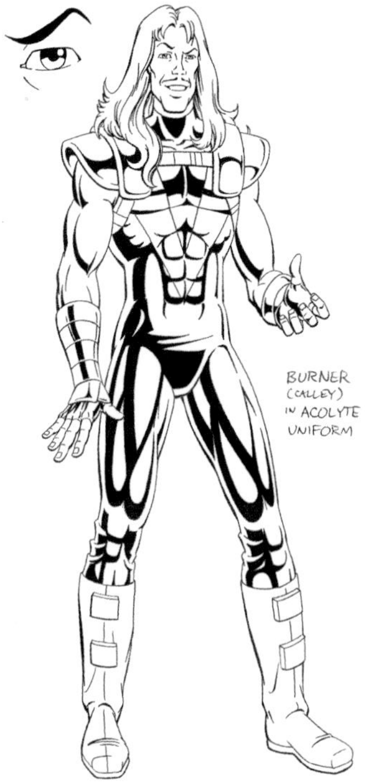
BURNER
(CALLEY)
IN ACOLYTE UNIFORM

08

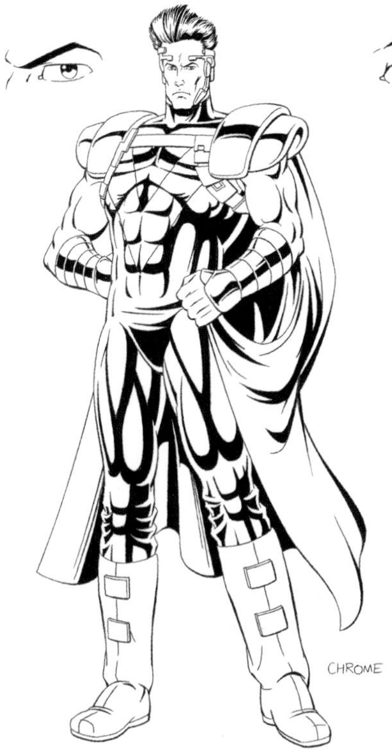
CHROME

09

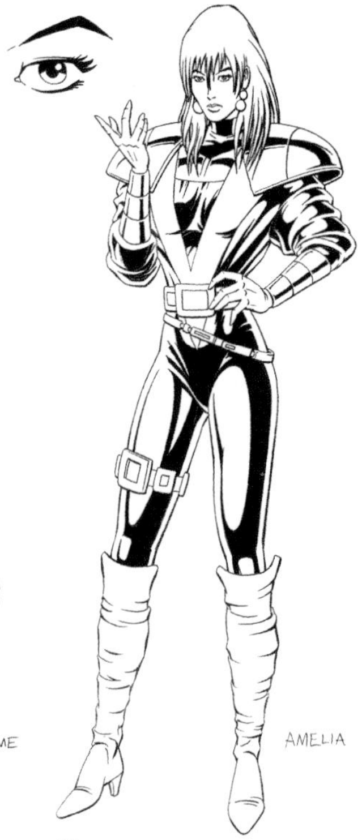
AMELIA

10

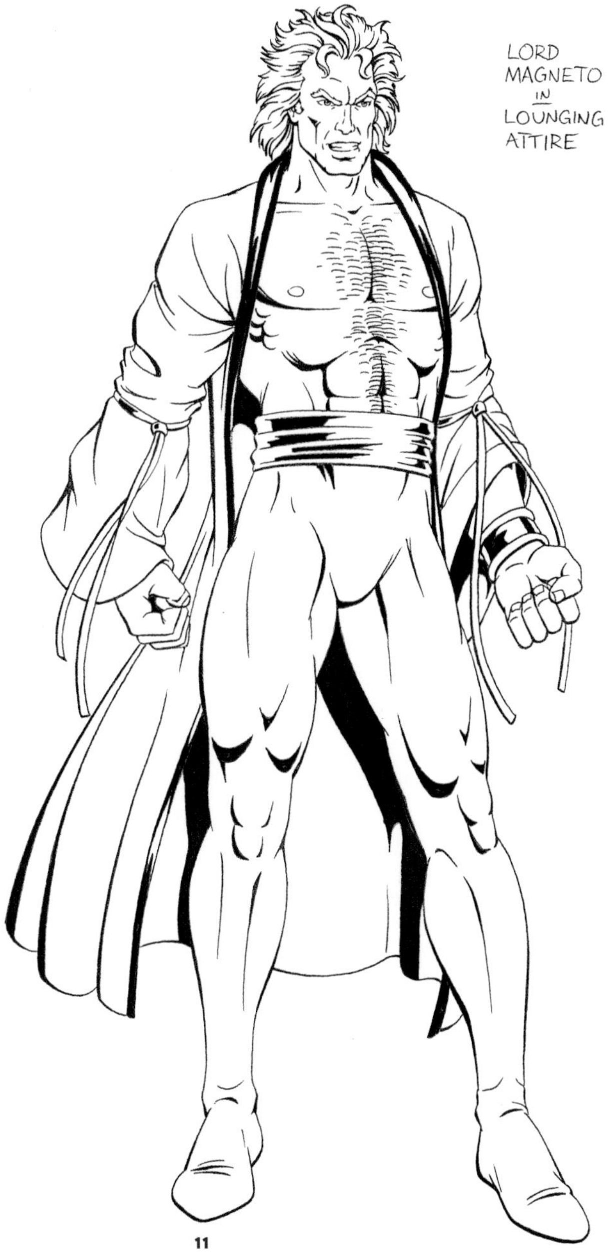
LORD
MAGNETO
IN
LOUNGING
ATTIRE

11

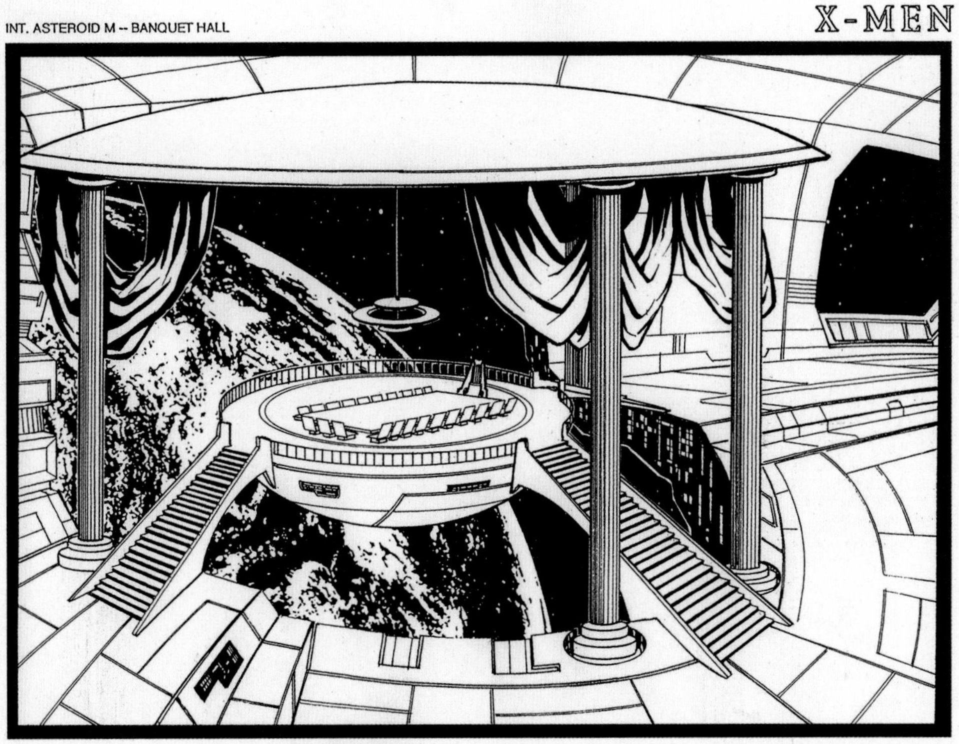
INT. ASTEROID M -- BANQUET HALL
X-MEN

12

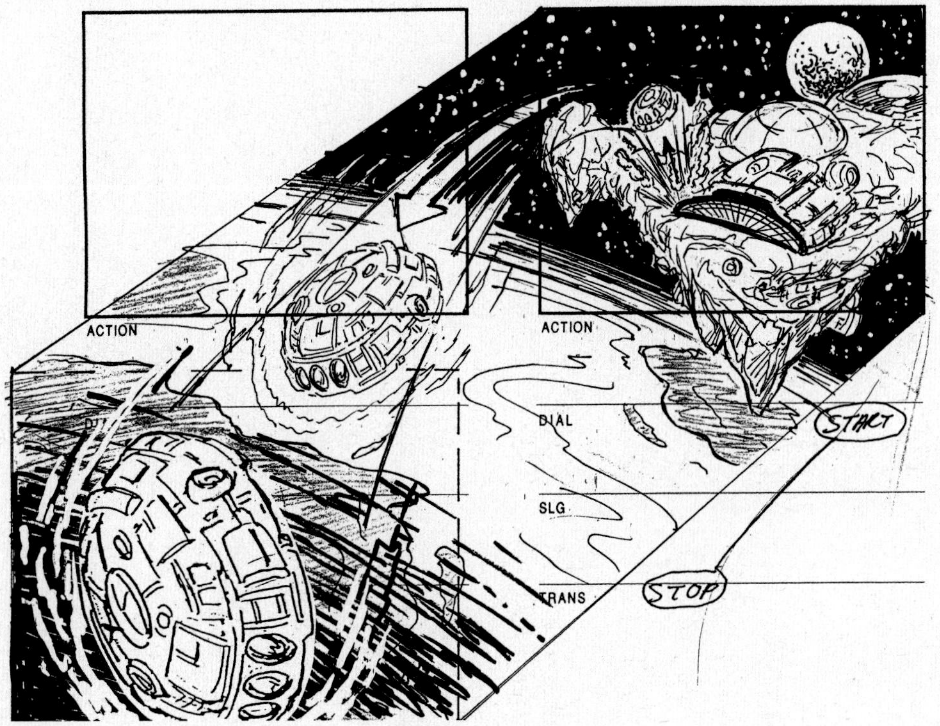
ACTION
ACTION
DIAL
START
SLG
TRANS
STOP

13

01–10 Character models of Arclight African Refugee Mutant, Blockbuster African Refugee Mutant, African Mutant Refugee Kangaroo, African Mutant Refugee Copycat, Shocker American Mutant Refugee, Peeper American Mutant Refugee, Random American Mutant Refugee, Burner Calley in Acolyte Uniform, Chrome, and Amelia—all penciled by Frank Brunner with cleanup by Mark Lewis.
11 Character model of a remarkably robust Lord Magneto in lounging attire.
12 Layout of interior of Asteroid M banquet room, on Magneto's proposed "utopian" sanctuary for mutants, designed and cleaned by Frank Squillace.
13 Storyboard page of damaged Magneto's prison chamber jettisoned off Asteroid M by traitor Fabian Cortez.

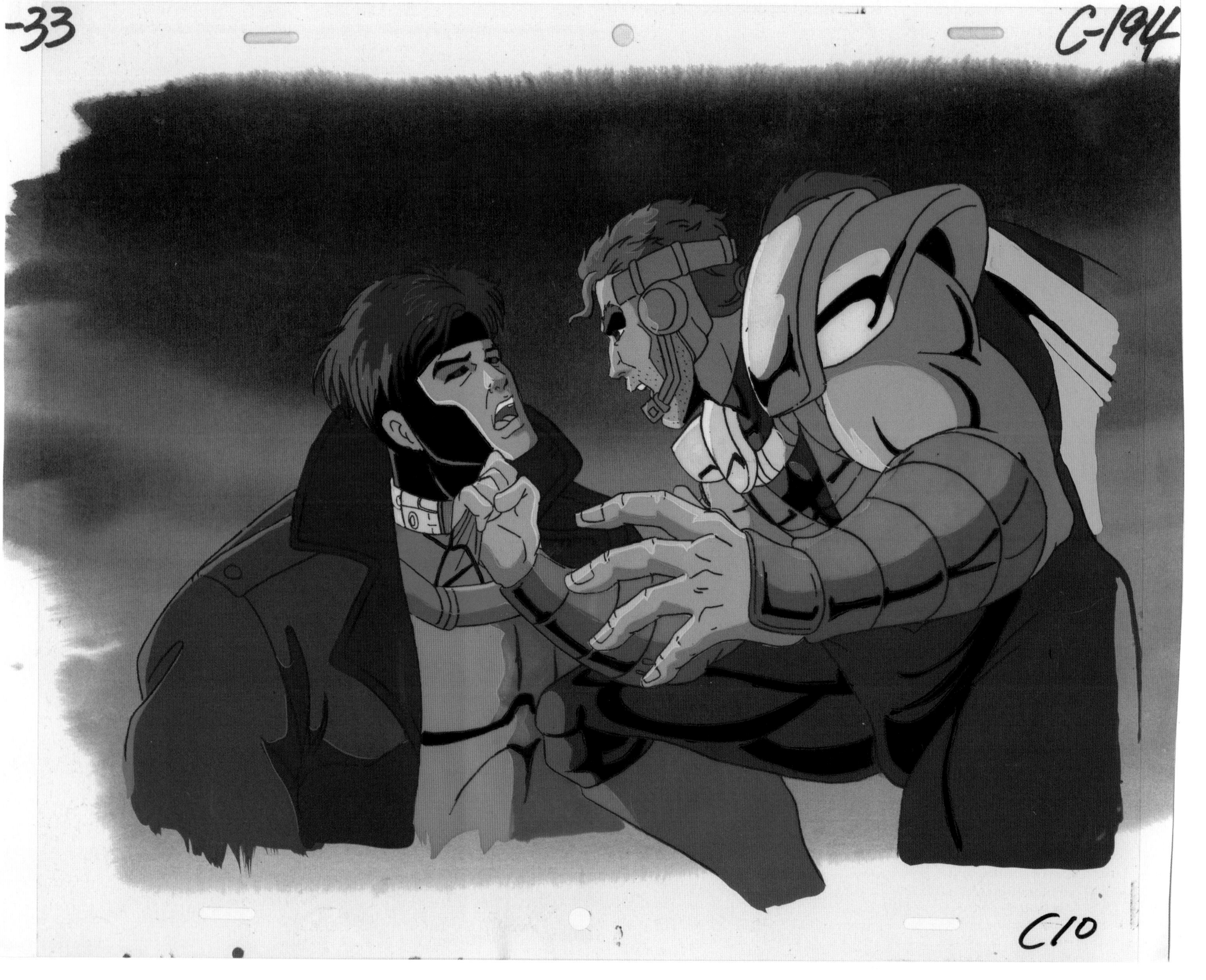
-33
C-194
C10

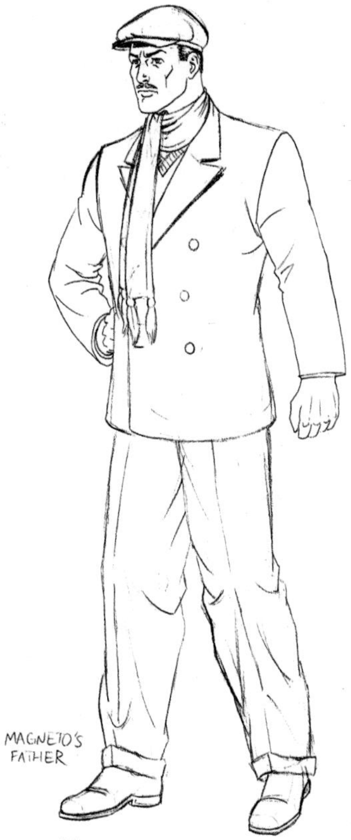
MAGNETO'S FATHER

01

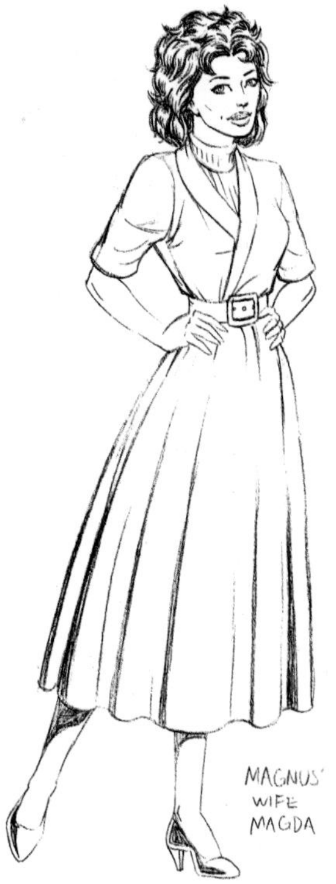
MAGNUS' WIFE MAGDA

02

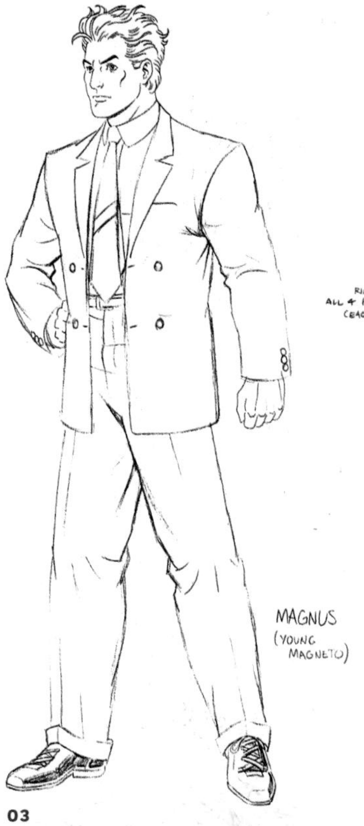
MAGNUS (YOUNG MAGNETO)

03

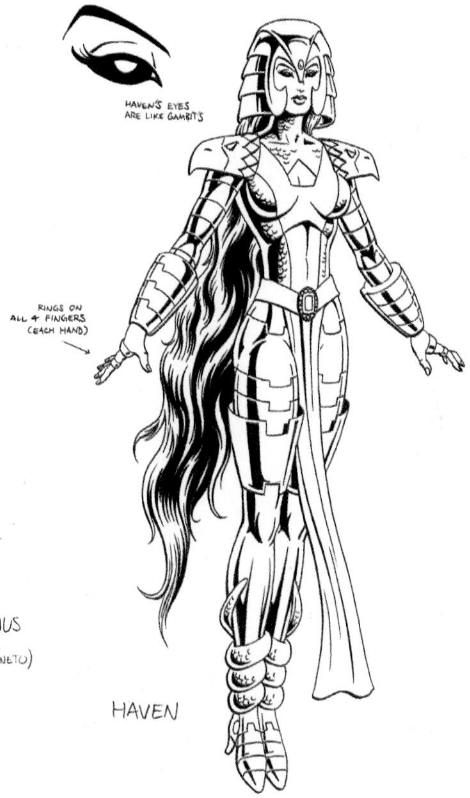
HAVEN'S EYES ARE LIKE GAMBIT'S
RINGS ON ALL 4 FINGERS (EACH HAND)
HAVEN

04

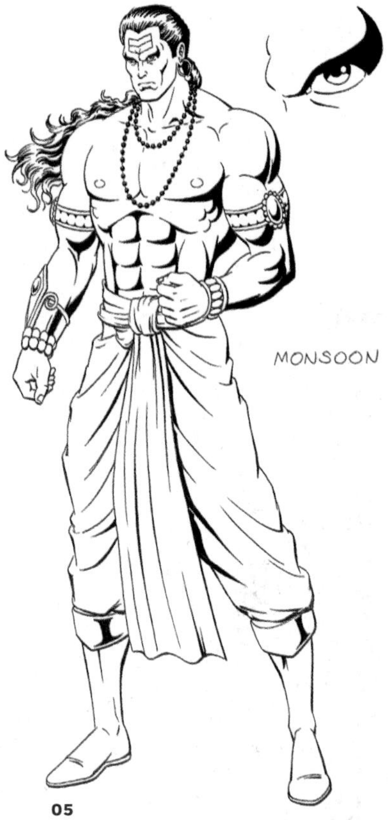
MONSOON

05

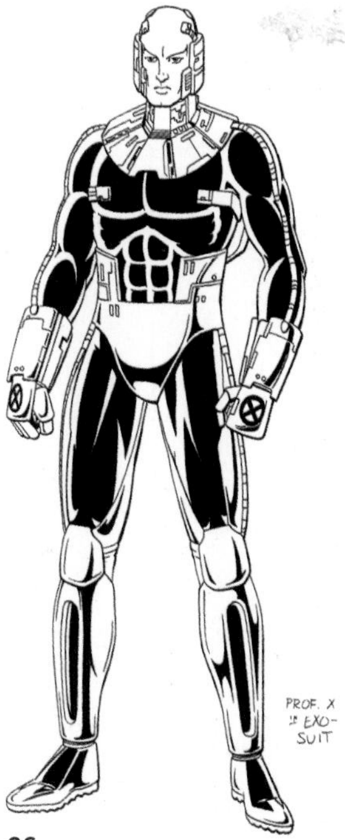
PROF. X # EXO-SUIT

06

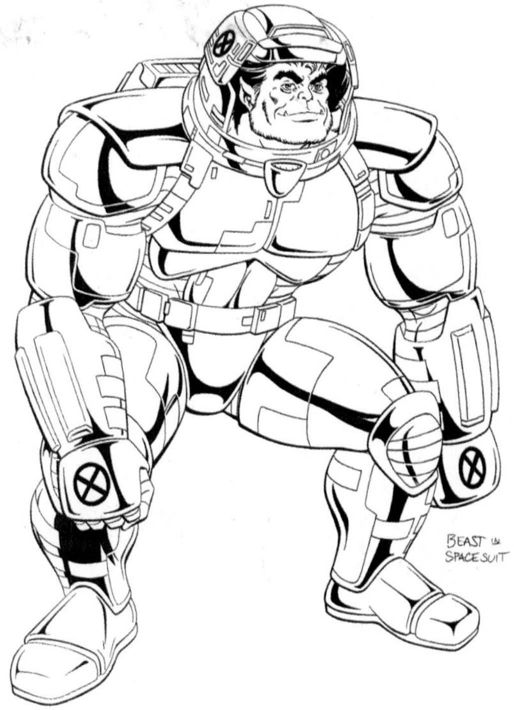
BEAST IN SPACESUIT

07

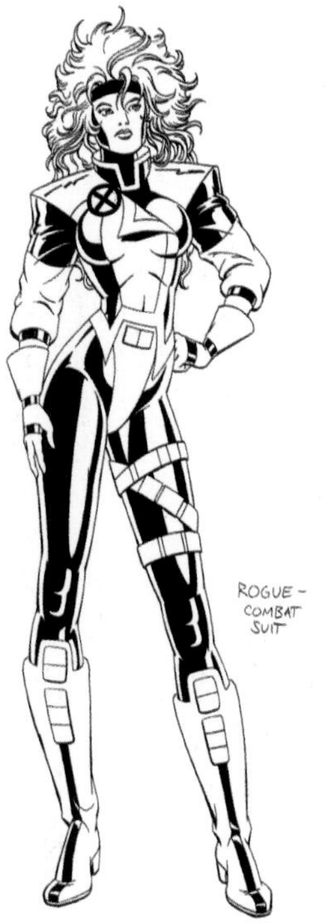
ROGUE - COMBAT SUIT

08

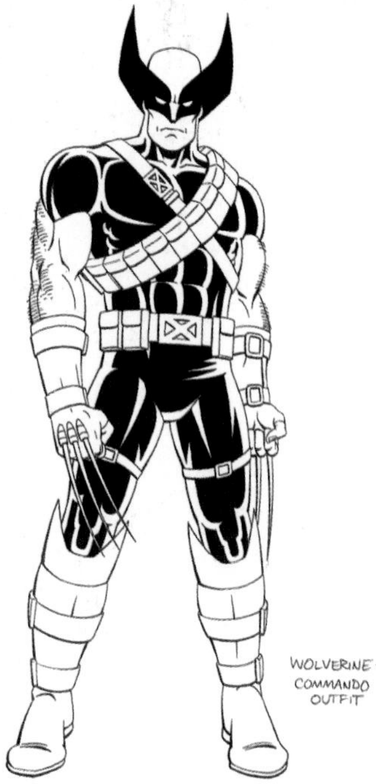
WOLVERINE - COMMANDO OUTFIT

09

OPPOSITE Production cel of Gambit threatened by Fabian Cortez. **01–03** Character Models of Magnus/Magneto's Father, Magnus's wife Magda, and Young Magnus—all by Mark Lewis. **04** Character model of Haven, by Lewis. **05** Character model of Monsoon; penciled by Frank Brunner with cleanup by Lewis. **06** Character model of Professor Xavier in Exo-Suit; penciled by Frank Squillace with cleanup by Lewis. **07** Character model of Beast in space suit, by Lewis. **08** Character model of Rogue in combat suit; penciled by Frank Squillace with cleanup by Lewis. **09** Character model of Wolverine in commando outfit, penciled by Squillace with cleanup by Lewis.

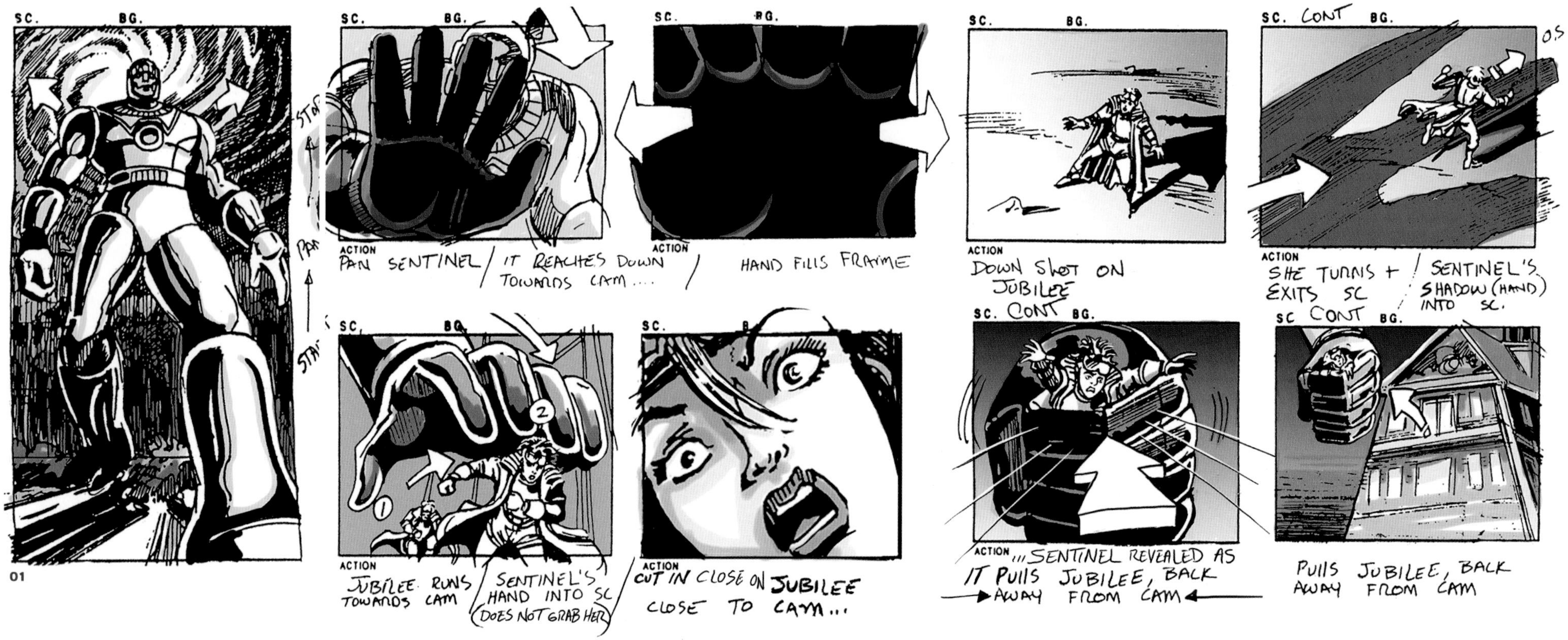
PAN SENTINEL / IT REACHES DOWN TOWARDS CAM....
HAND FILLS FRAME
DOWN SHOT ON JUBILEE
SHE TURNS + EXITS SC
SENTINEL'S SHADOW (HAND) INTO SC.
JUBILEE RUNS TOWARDS CAM
SENTINEL'S HAND INTO SC (DOES NOT GRAB HER)
CUT IN CLOSE ON JUBILEE CLOSE TO CAM...
...SENTINEL REVEALED AS IT PULLS JUBILEE, BACK AWAY FROM CAM
PULLS JUBILEE, BACK AWAY FROM CAM

01

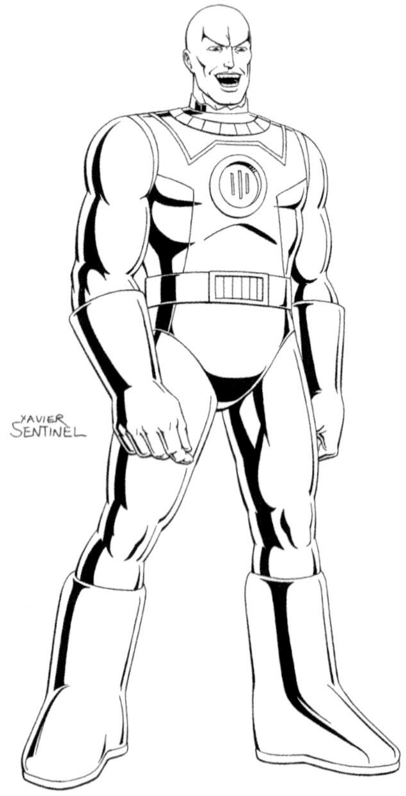
XAVIER SENTINEL

02

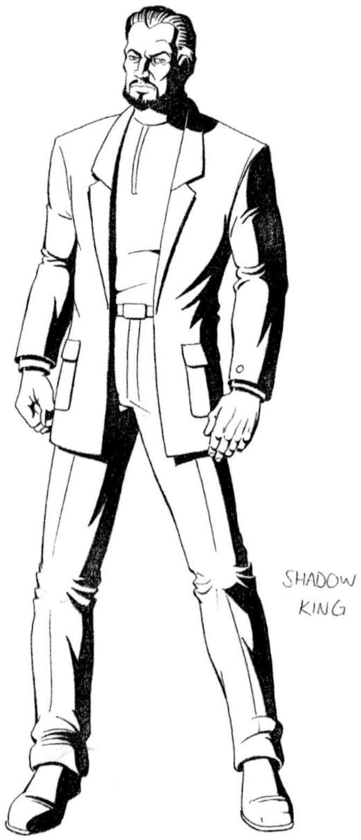
SHADOW KING

03

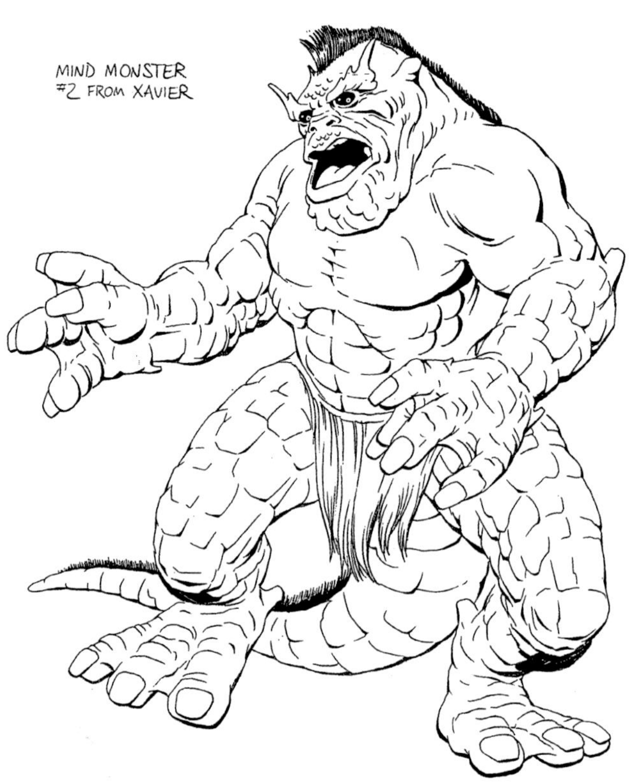
MIND MONSTER
#2 FROM XAVIER

04

01 Storyboard pages by Keith Tucker, digitally shaded. **02** Character model of Xavier Sentinel; penciled by Frank Brunner with cleanup by Mark Lewis. **03** Character model of Shadow King (a re-use from episode 16); penciled by Brunner with cleanup by Lewis. **04** Character model of "Mind Monster 2", a version of the Shadow King that Xavier fights on the Astral Plane; penciled by Brunner with cleanup by Lewis. **OPPOSITE** X-Men and friends; from a board panel blown up by Lewis at the request of Larry Houston, to see the characters more clearly and call out IDs.

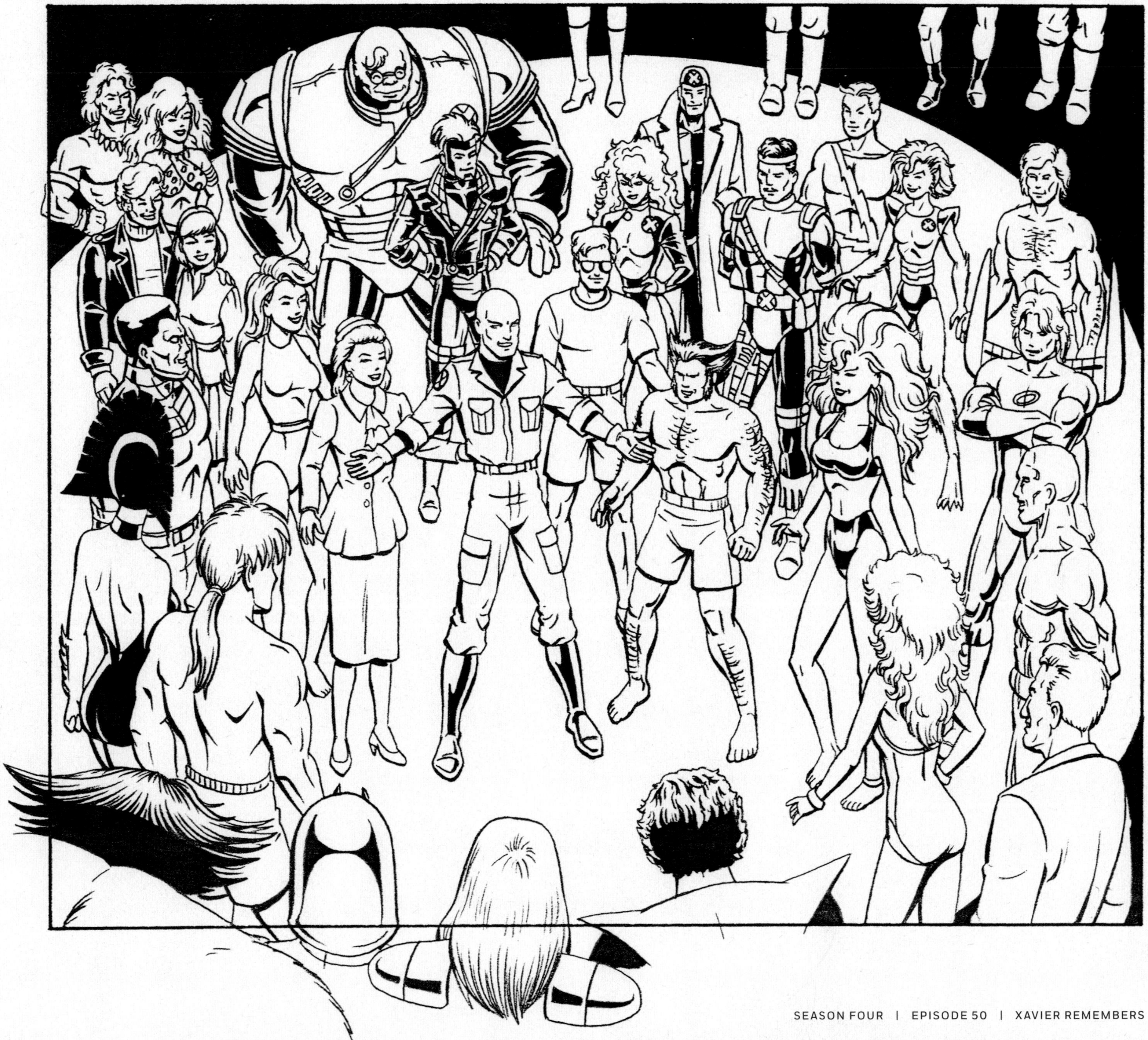

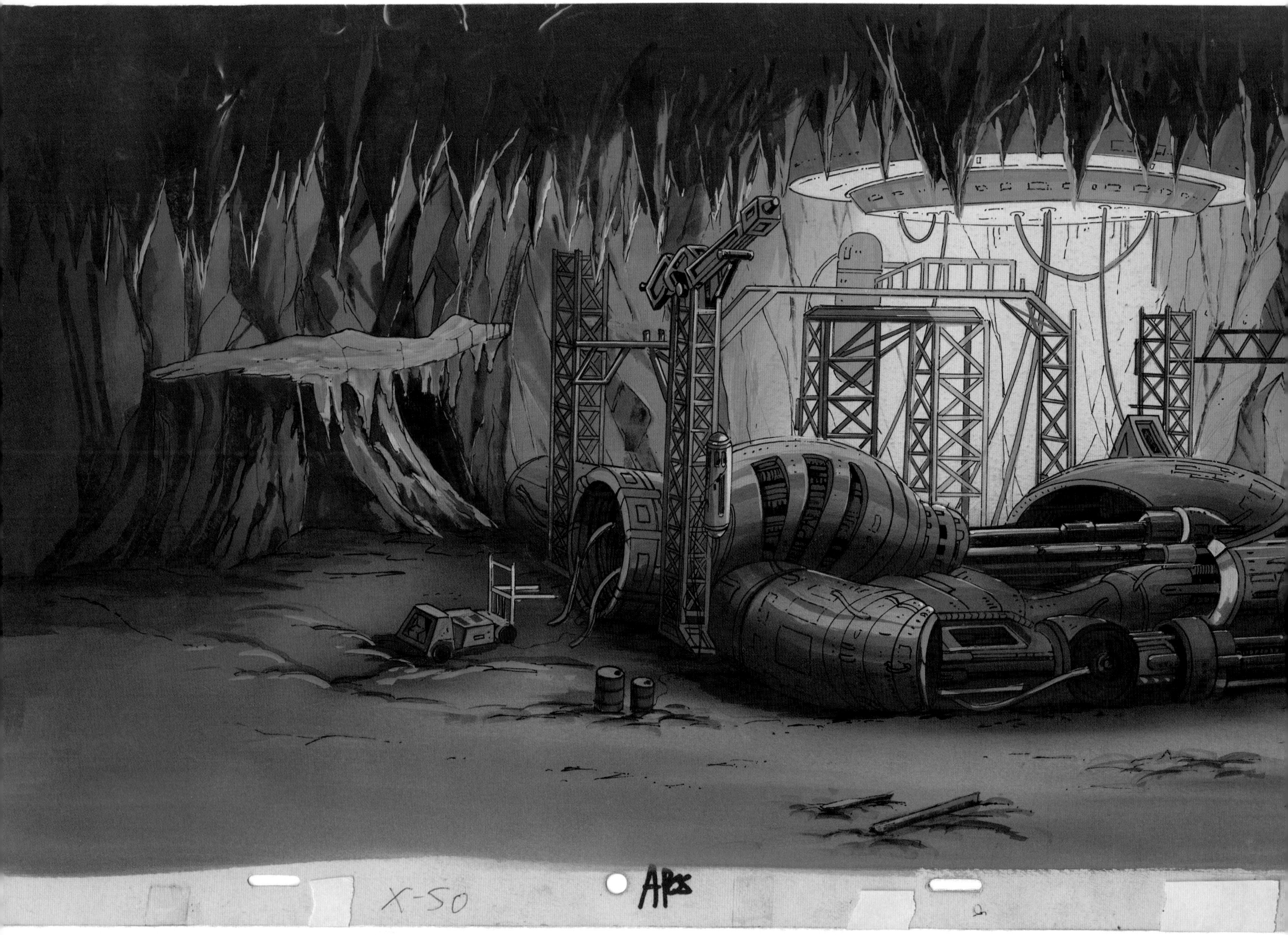
X-50

ABOVE Master layout background production cels of Master Mold's underground construction lair, where he plots to re-build his body.

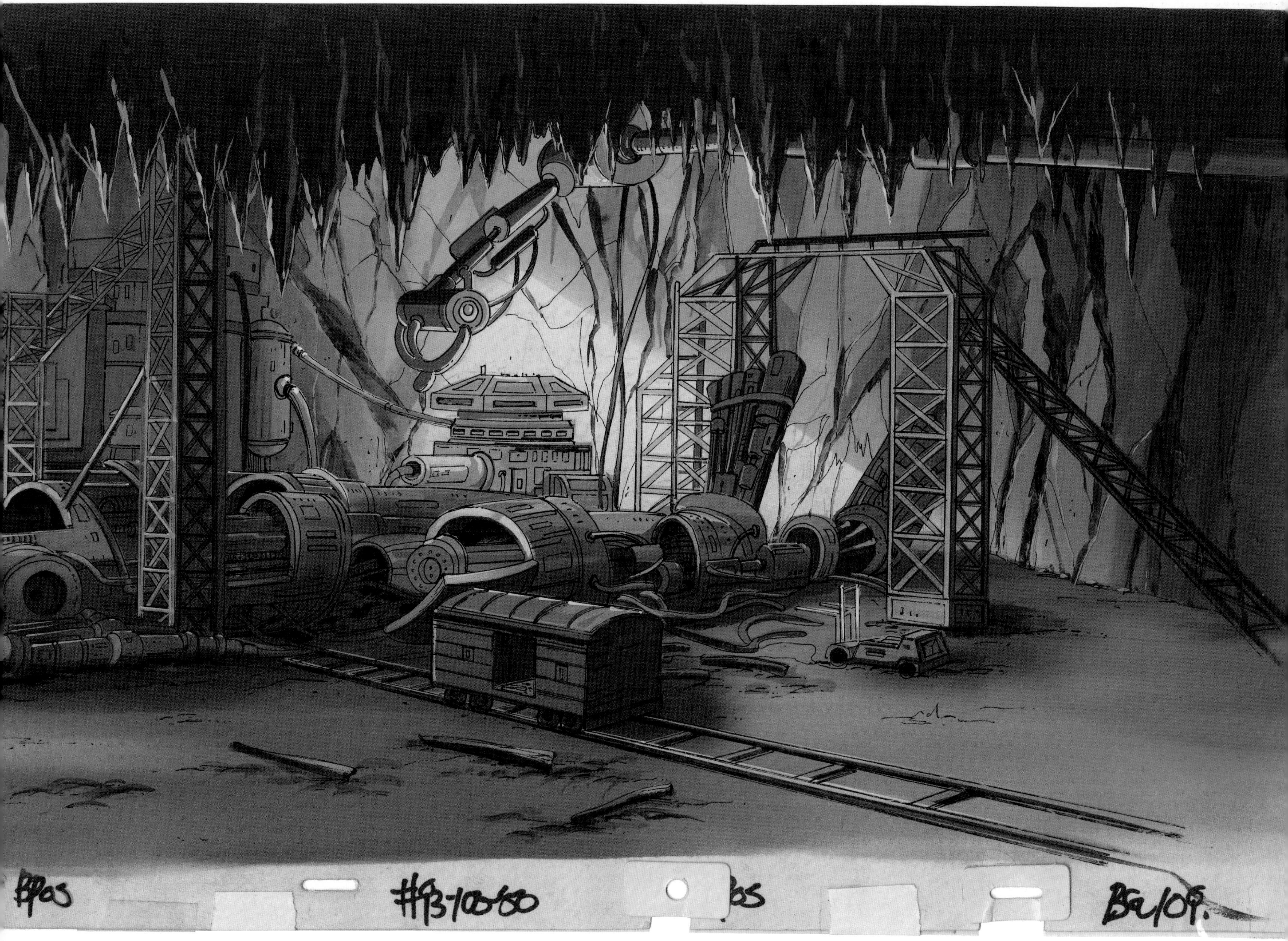

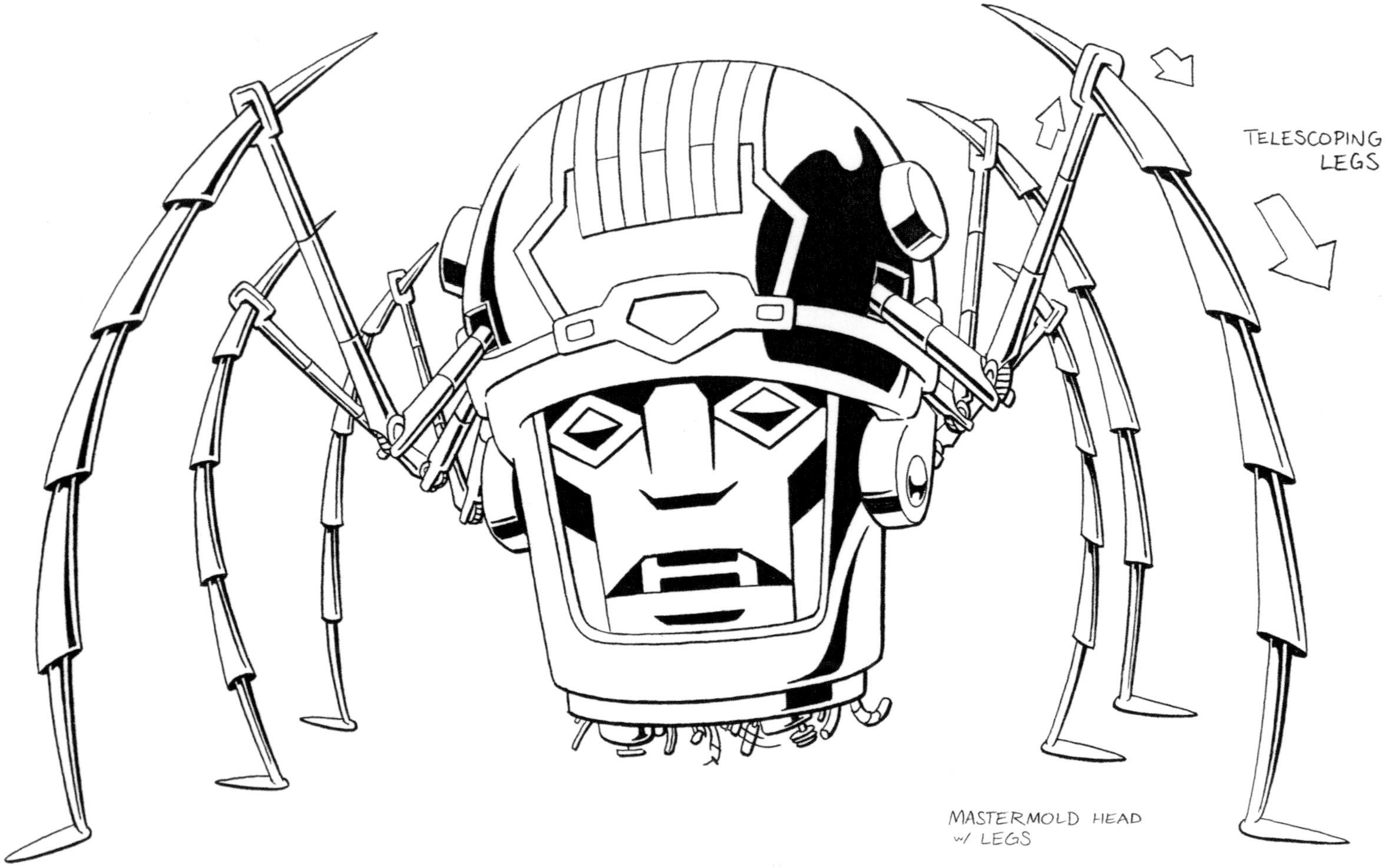
TELESCOPING LEGS
MASTERMOLD HEAD w/ LEGS

01

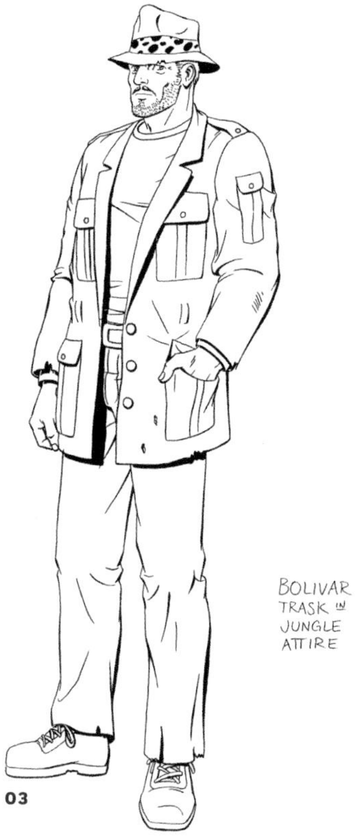
BOLIVAR TRASK IN JUNGLE ATTIRE

03

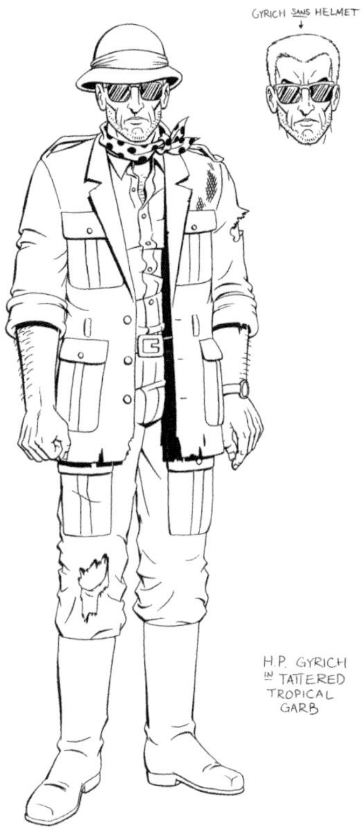
GYRICH SANS HELMET
H.P. GYRICH IN TATTERED TROPICAL GARB

04

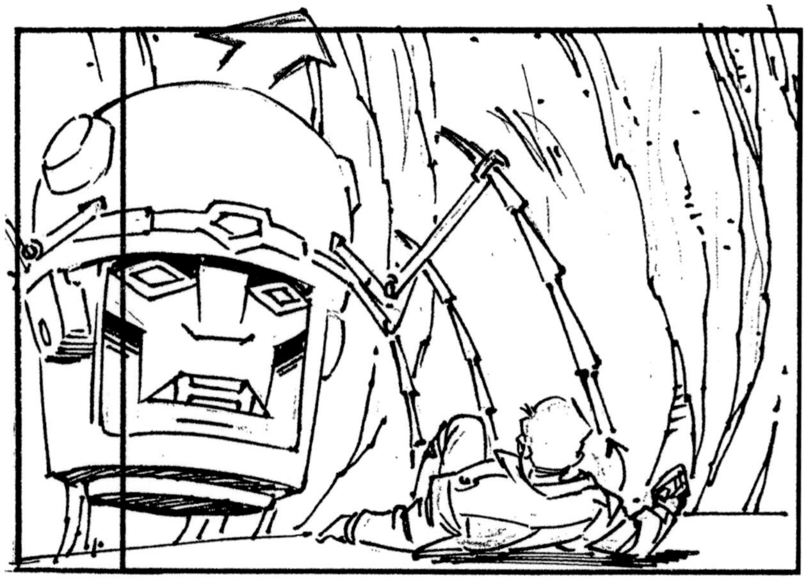

02

01 Character model of Master Mold Head with legs, by Mark Lewis. **02** Storyboard panel of Master Mold Head with Morph, by Romeo Francisco. **03–04** Character models of Bolivar Trask in Jungle Attire and H. P. Gyrich in Tattered Tropical Garb; penciled by Frank Brunner, cleanup by Lewis. **05–09** Character models of Watchdog, Tusk, Solarr (Bill Braddock), Good Mutant Forearm, and Toad—all penciled by Brunner, cleanup by Lewis. **11–13** Character models of Bad Mutant Strobe, Bad Mutant Reaper, and Bad Mutant Senyaka—all by Lewis.

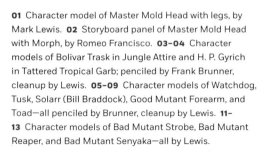

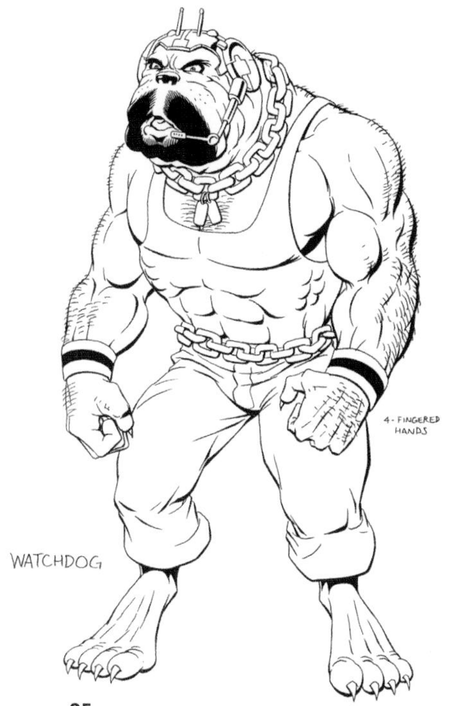
4-FINGERED HANDS
WATCHDOG

05

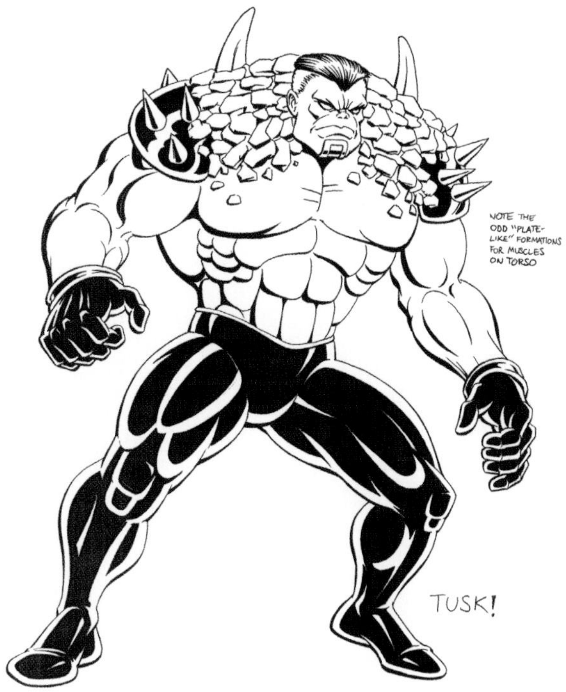
NOTE THE ODD "PLATE-LIKE" FORMATIONS FOR MUSCLES ON TORSO
TUSK!

06

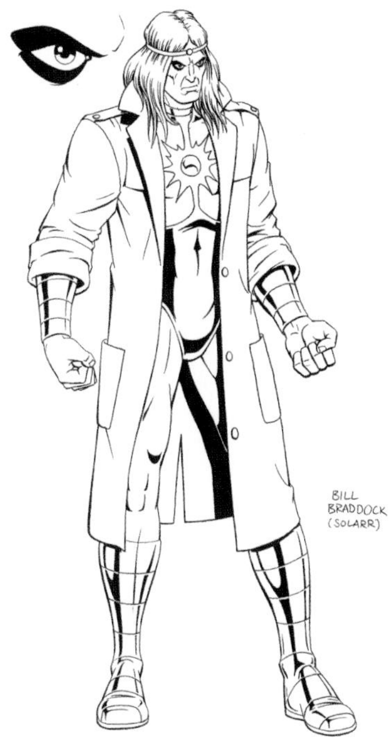
BILL BRADDOCK (SOLARR)

07

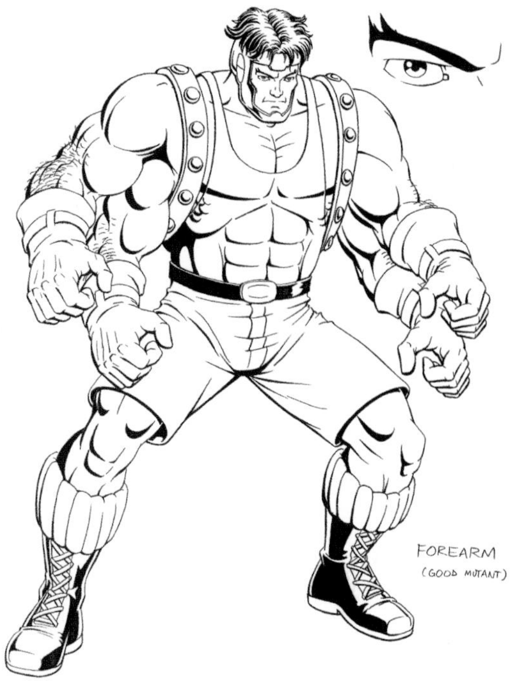
FOREARM
(GOOD MUTANT)

08

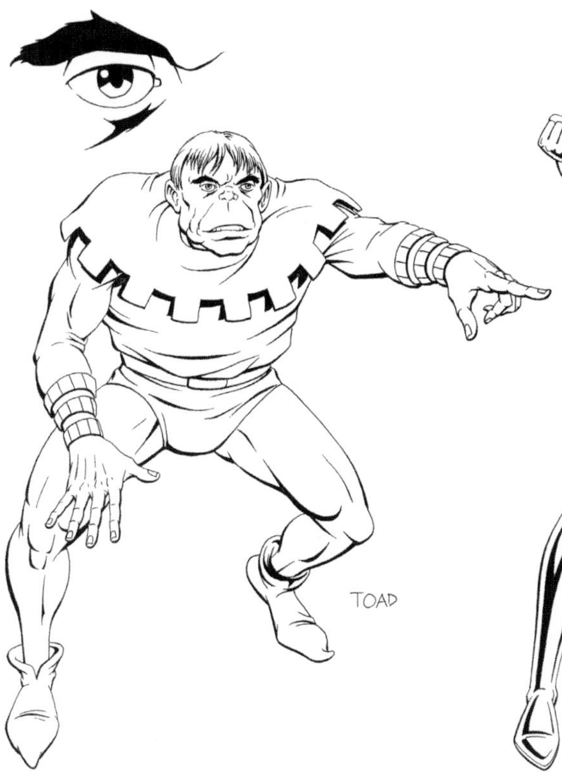
TOAD

09

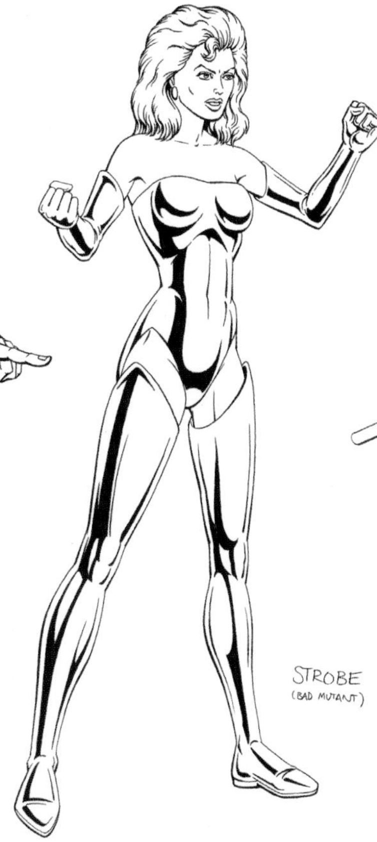
STROBE
(BAD MUTANT)

10

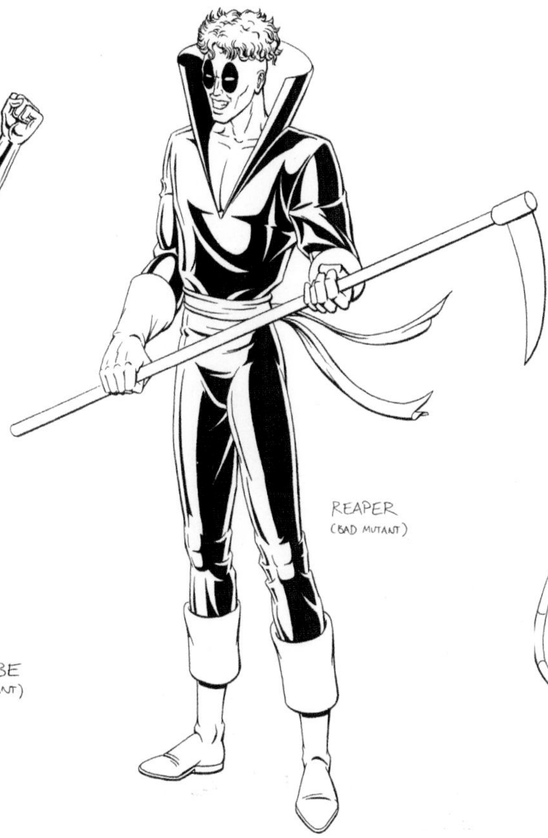
REAPER
(BAD MUTANT)

11

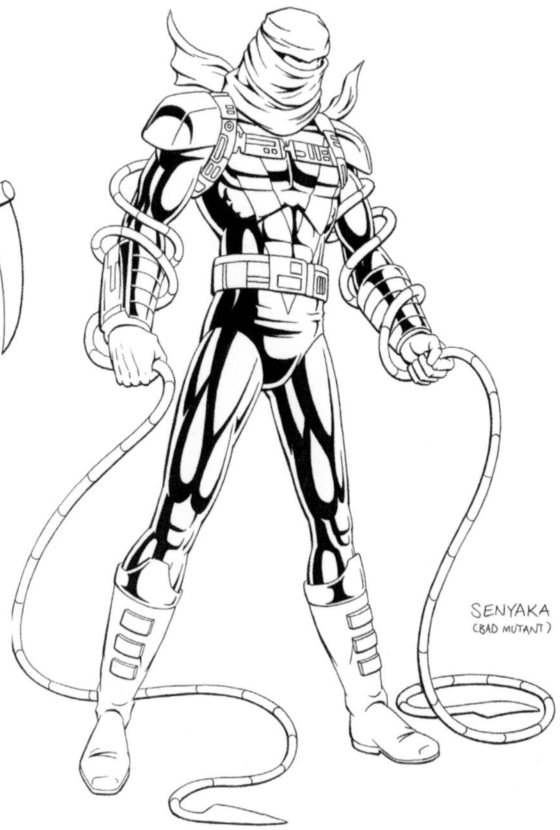
SENYAKA
(BAD MUTANT)

12

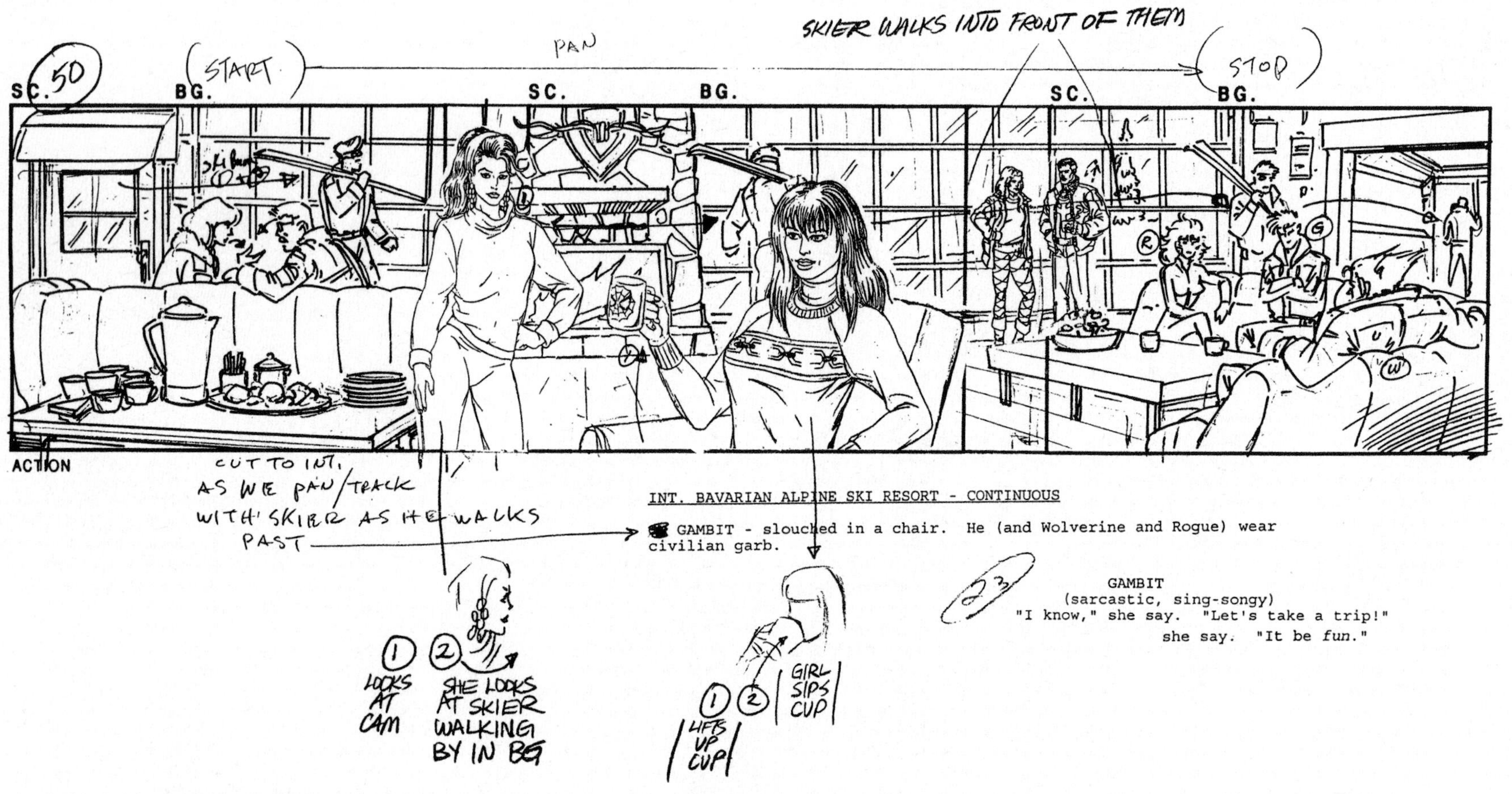
SKIER WALKS INTO FRONT OF THEM
PAN
SC. 50
BG. (START)
SC.
BG.
SC.
BG. (STOP)
ACTION
CUT TO INT, AS WE PAN/TRACK WITH SKIER AS HE WALKS PAST
INT. BAVARIAN ALPINE SKI RESORT - CONTINUOUS
GAMBIT - slouched in a chair. He (and Wolverine and Rogue) wear civilian garb.
GAMBIT
(sarcastic, sing-songy)
"I know," she say. "Let's take a trip!" she say. "It be *fun*."
① LOOKS AT CAM
② SHE LOOKS AT SKIER WALKING BY IN BG
① LIFTS UP CUP
② GIRL SIPS CUP

01

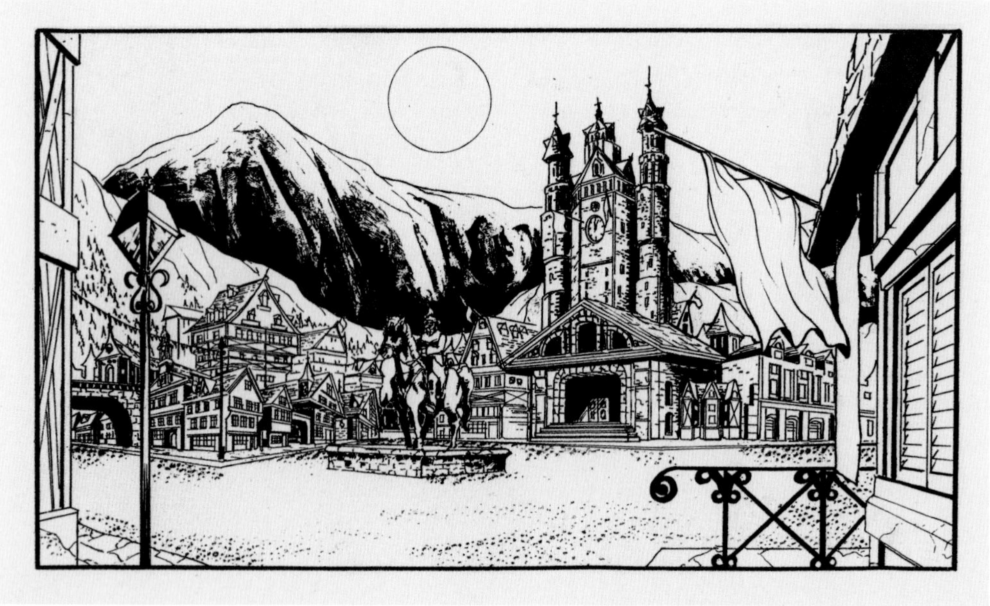

02

01 Storyboard of interior of ski lodge with Rogue, Gambit, and Wolverine. Note the appearance of Mary Jane Watson, complete with spider-mug and spider-sweater, as well as Doctor Strange's protégé, Cleo, with Doctor Strange himself in the background by the windows. By Frank Squillace. Cleaned by Pat Agnasin. Mary Jane model by Mark Lewis. **02** Layout of an exterior of an Alpine village, designed and cleaned by Squillace. **03–05** Character models of Brother Reinhard, Rogue in monk robes, and Brother Johann, all by Frank Brunner and Lewis. **06** Character model of Jimaine, Nightcrawler's stepsister, by Lewis. **07** Character model of Mother Mystique; penciled by Brunner, cleanup by Lewis. **08** Character model of Nightcrawler's Foster Mother, by Lewis. **09** Character model of Mystique "re-cleaned 6/29/94" by Lewis; "first season model would fit better with the current look of the show." **10–11** Character models of Baby Kurt and Nightcrawler in Monk Robes hood down, both penciled by Brunner with cleanup by Lewis.

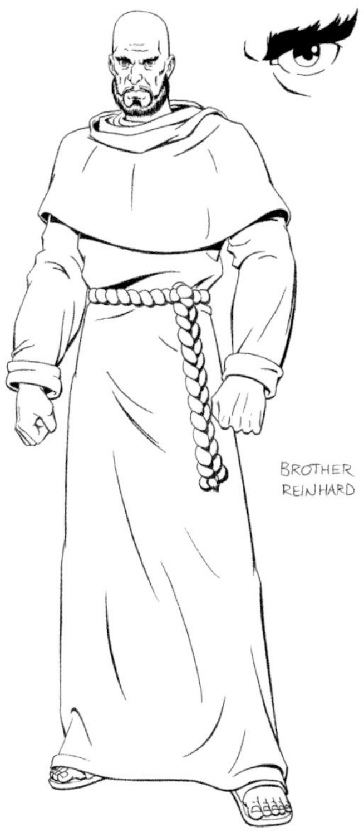
BROTHER REINHARD

03

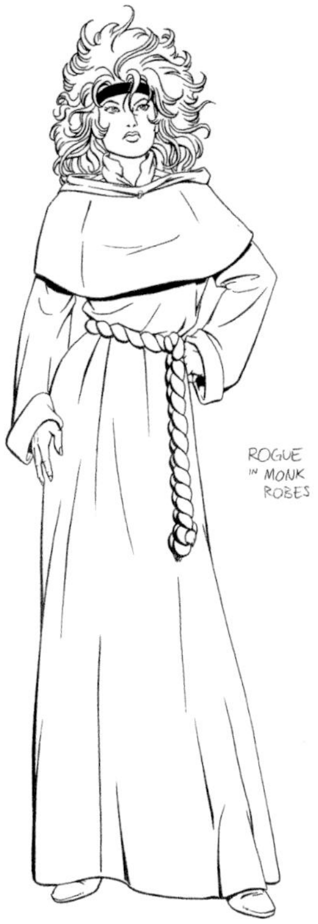
ROGUE IN MONK ROBES

04

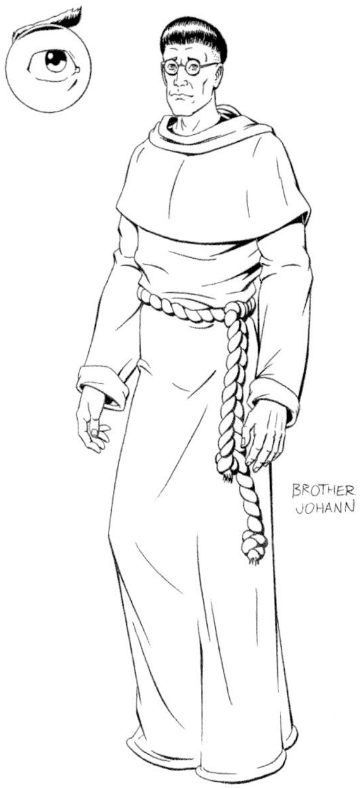
BROTHER JOHANN

05

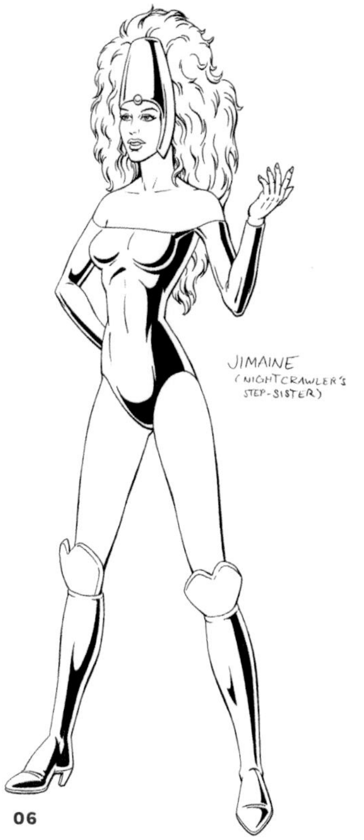
JIMAINE
(NIGHTCRAWLER'S STEP-SISTER)

06

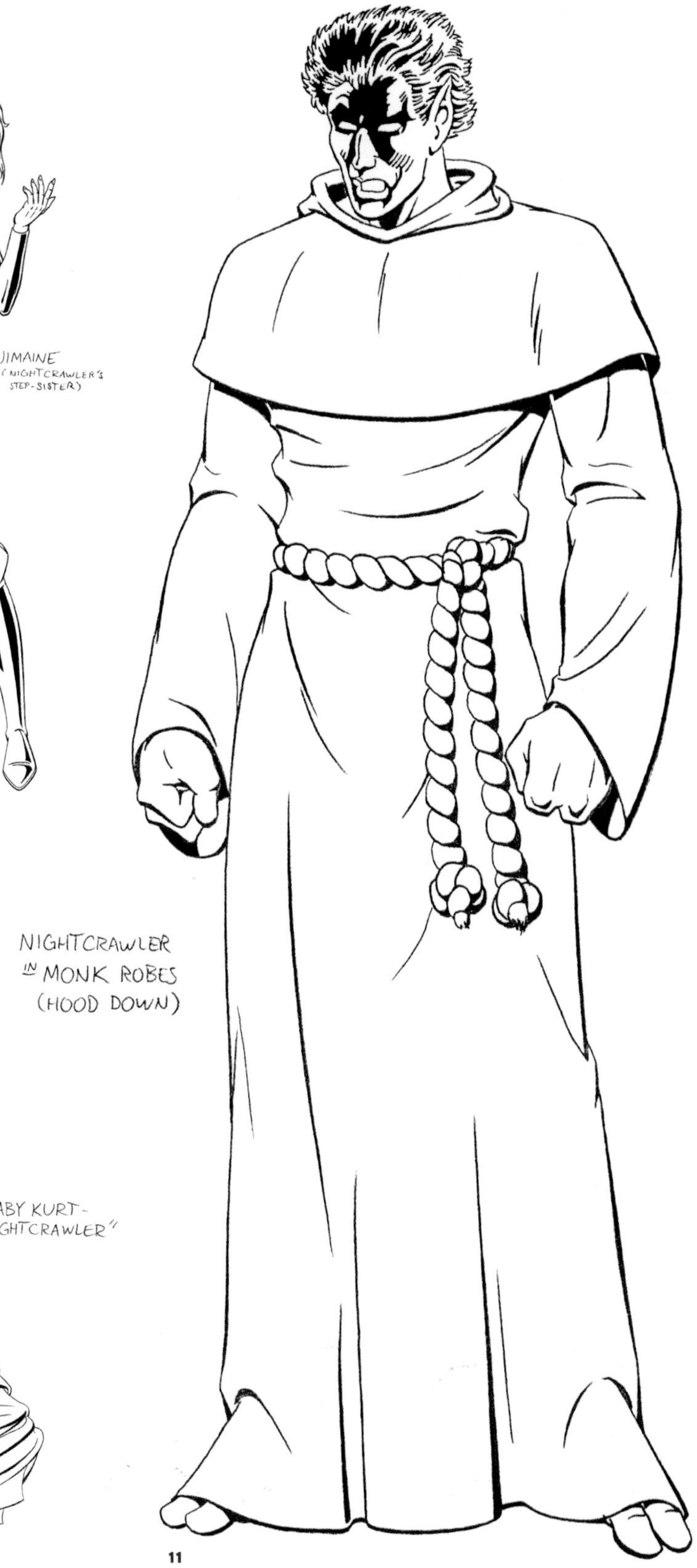
NIGHTCRAWLER IN MONK ROBES (HOOD DOWN)

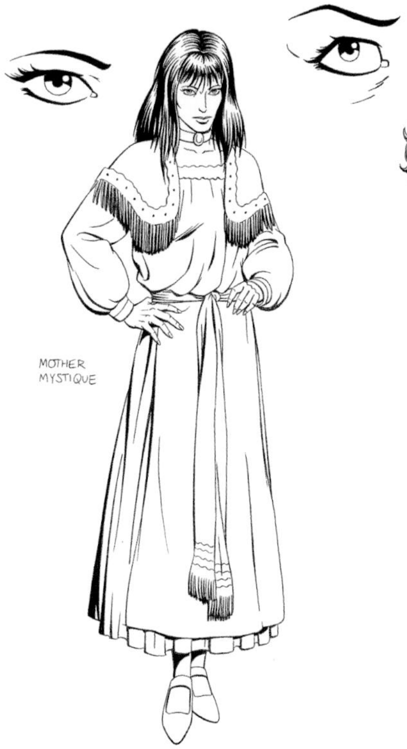
MOTHER MYSTIQUE

07

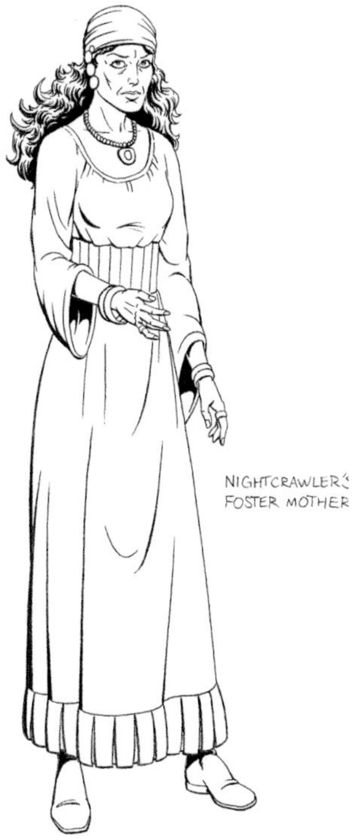
NIGHTCRAWLER'S FOSTER MOTHER

08

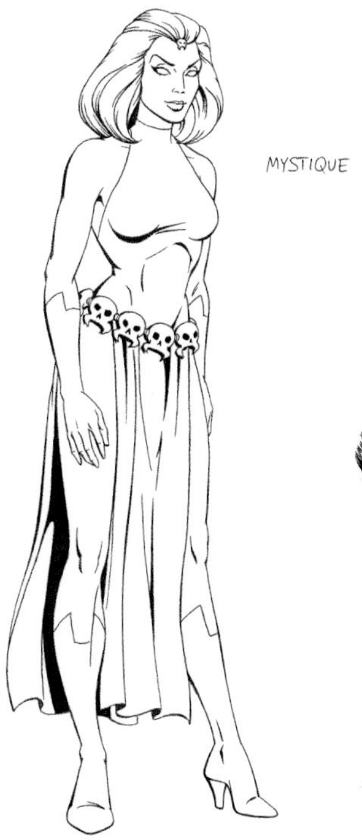
MYSTIQUE

09

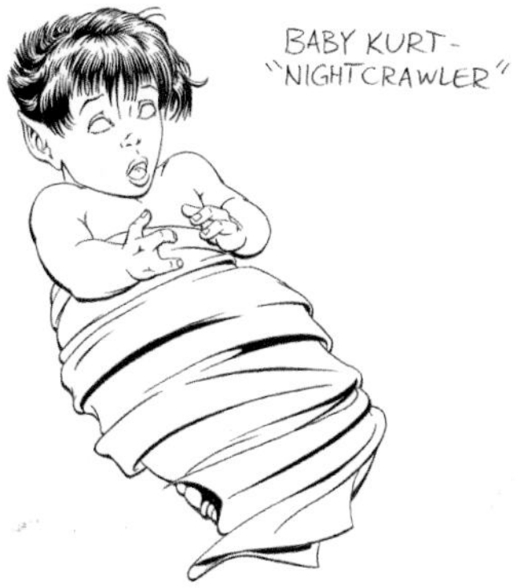
BABY KURT-
"NIGHTCRAWLER"

10

11

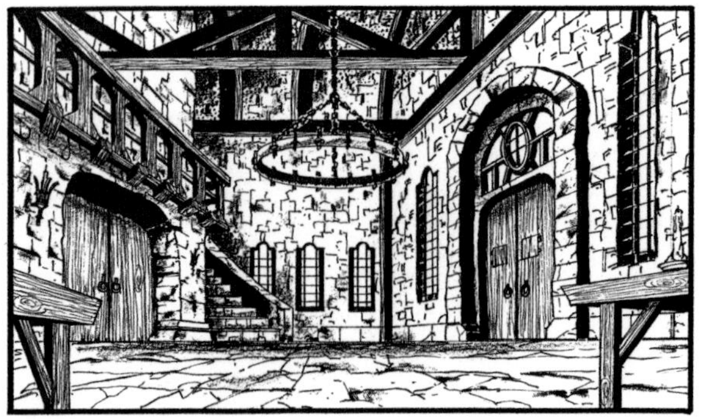

01

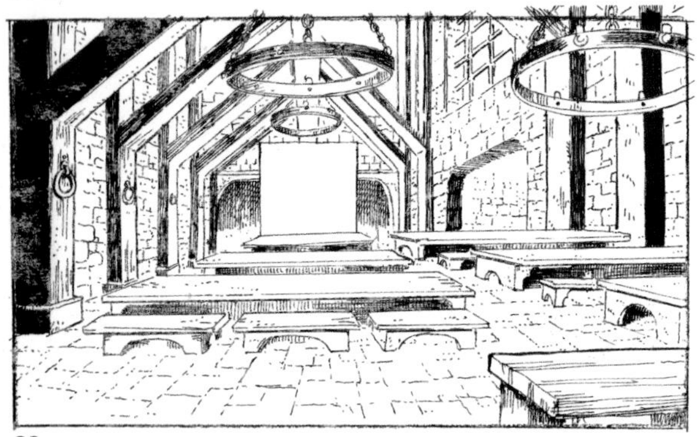

02

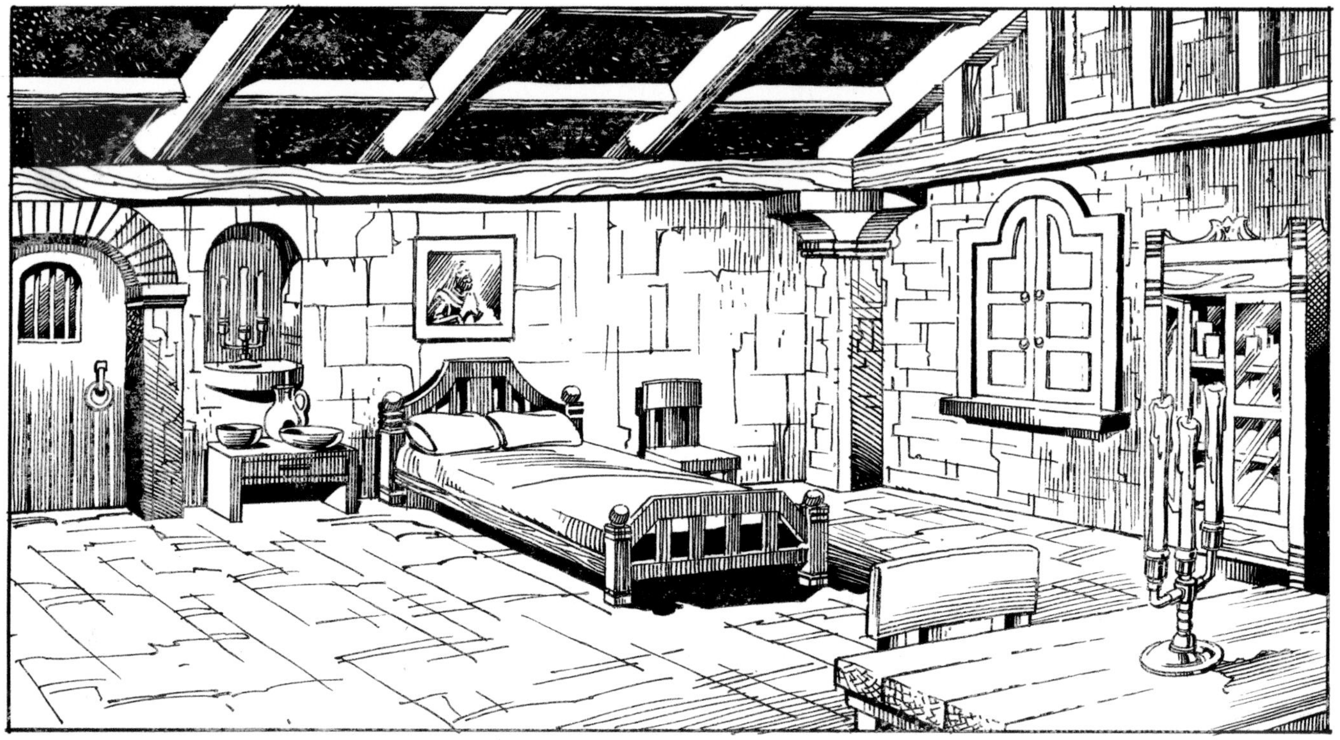
INTERIOR / MONASTARY INFIRMIRY

03

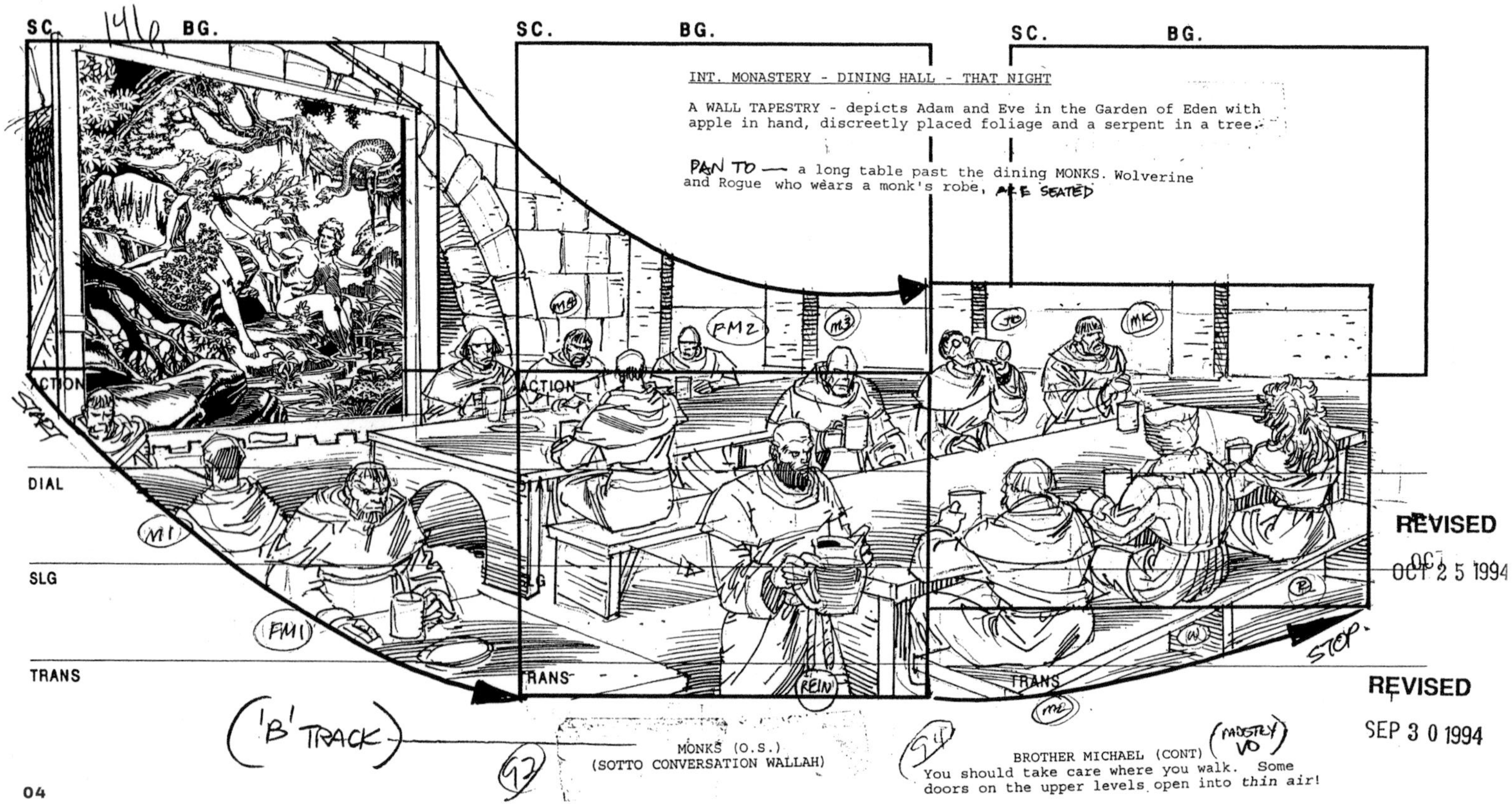
SC. 141 BG.
SC. BG.
SC. BG.
INT. MONASTERY - DINING HALL - THAT NIGHT
A WALL TAPESTRY - depicts Adam and Eve in the Garden of Eden with apple in hand, discreetly placed foliage and a serpent in a tree.
PAN TO — a long table past the dining MONKS. Wolverine and Rogue who wears a monk's robe, ARE SEATED
ACTION
START
DIAL
SLG
TRANS
STOP
REVISED
OCT 2 5 1994
REVISED
SEP 3 0 1994
'B' TRACK
MONKS (O.S.)
(SOTTO CONVERSATION WALLAH)
BROTHER MICHAEL (CONT) (MOSTLY VO)
You should take care where you walk. Some doors on the upper levels open into thin air!

04

01 Layout of the interior of the monastery that is home to Nightcrawler, designed and cleaned by Frank Squillace. **02–03** Layouts of monastery dining hall and monastery bedroom, designed by Squillace with cleanup by Pat Agnasin. **04** Storyboard page of Wolverine and Rogue with the monks in the dining hall, by Romeo Francisco with cleanup by Agnasin. **05–06** Layouts of monastery chapel and monastery library, designed by Squillace with cleanup by Agnasin. **07** Storyboards of flashback of younger Nightcrawler with a traveling circus: on a trapeze, as an acrobat, and performing his "volcano" finale, all by Larry Houston.

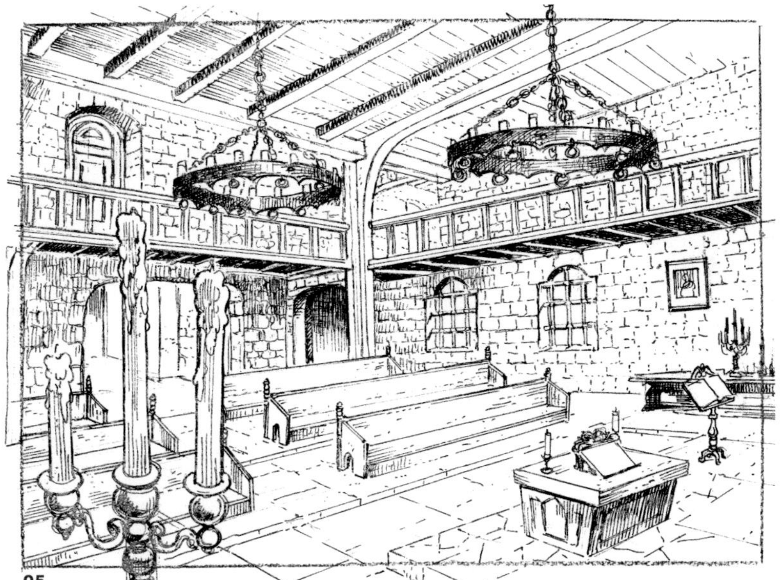

05

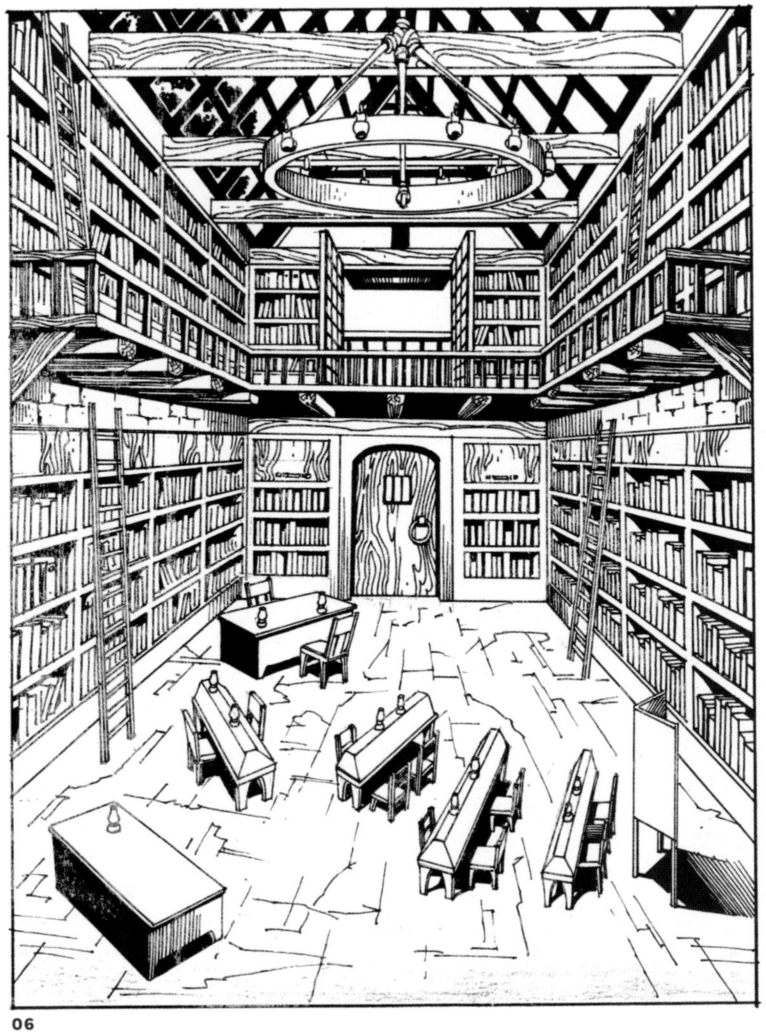

06

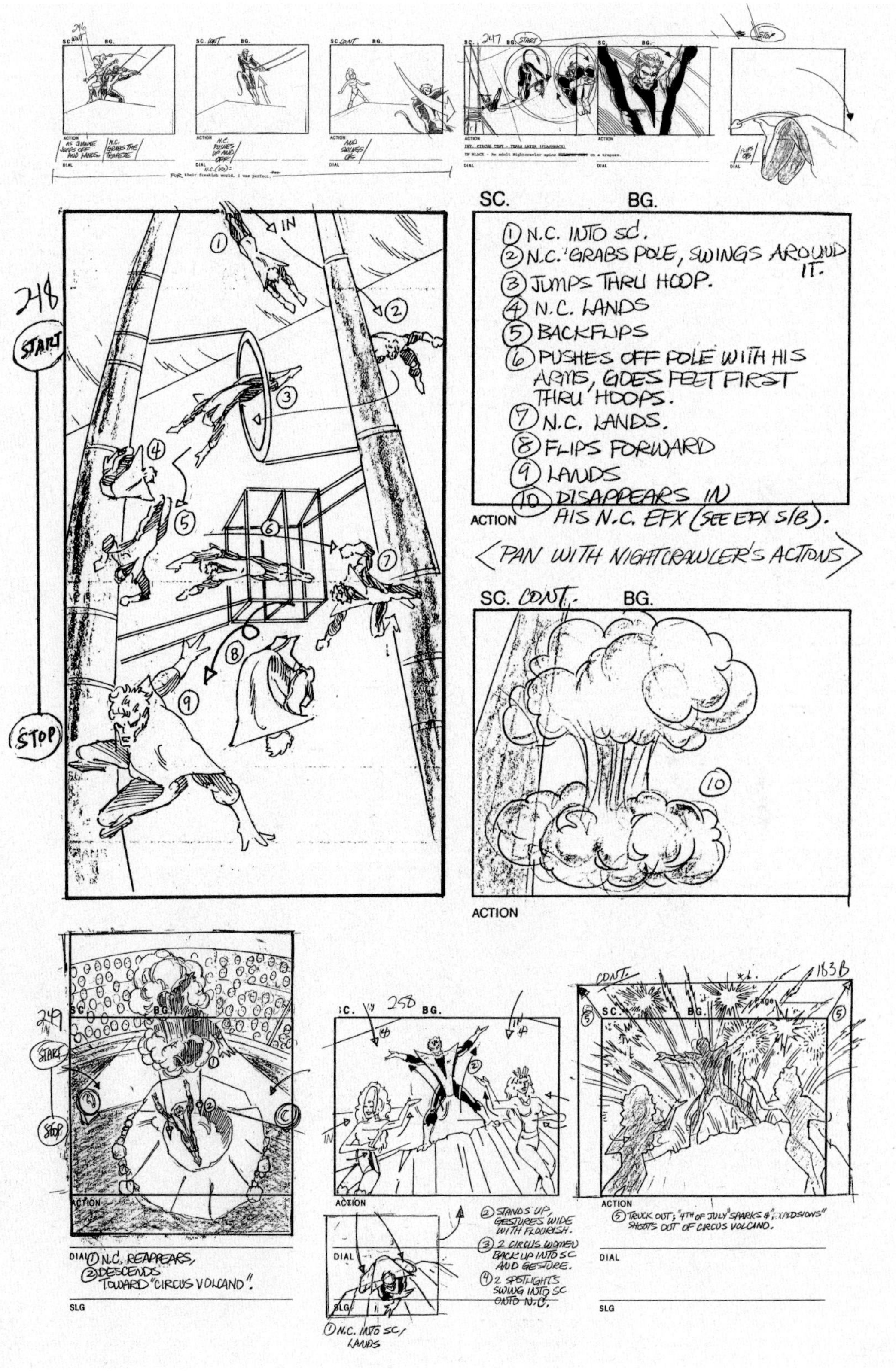
248
START
STOP
SC.
BG.
① N.C. INTO sc.
② N.C. GRABS POLE, SWINGS AROUND IT.
③ JUMPS THRU HOOP.
④ N.C. LANDS
⑤ BACKFLIPS
⑥ PUSHES OFF POLE WITH HIS ARMS, GOES FEET FIRST THRU HOOPS.
⑦ N.C. LANDS.
⑧ FLIPS FORWARD
⑨ LANDS
⑩ DISAPPEARS IN HIS N.C. EFX (SEE EFX S/B).
ACTION
<PAN WITH NIGHTCRAWLER'S ACTIONS>
SC. CONT.
BG.
ACTION
START
STOP
ACTION
DIAL ① N.C. REAPPEARS, ② DESCENDS TOWARD "CIRCUS VOLCANO".
SLG
BG.
ACTION
② STANDS UP, GESTURES WIDE WITH FLOURISH.
③ 2 CIRCUS WOMEN BACK UP INTO SC AND GESTURE.
④ 2 SPOTLIGHTS SWING INTO SC ONTO N.C.
DIAL
SLG
① N.C. INTO SC/ LANDS
CONT.
SC.
ACTION
⑤ TRUCK OUT; "4TH OF JULY" SPARKS & "EXPLOSIONS" SHOOTS OUT OF CIRCUS VOLCANO.
DIAL
SLG

07

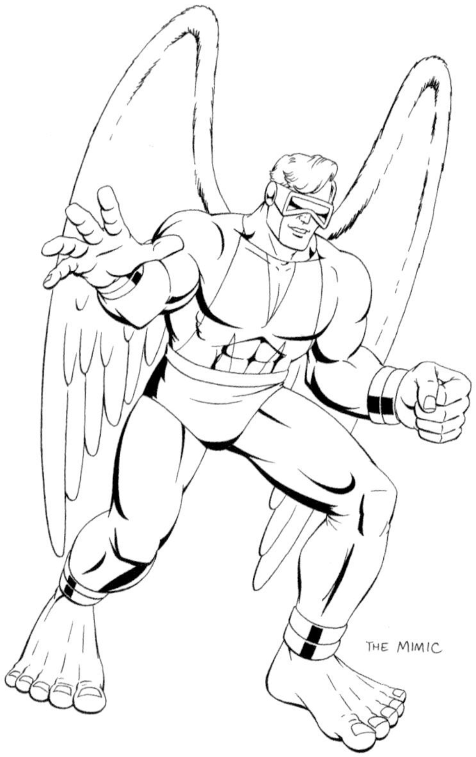
THE MIMIC

01

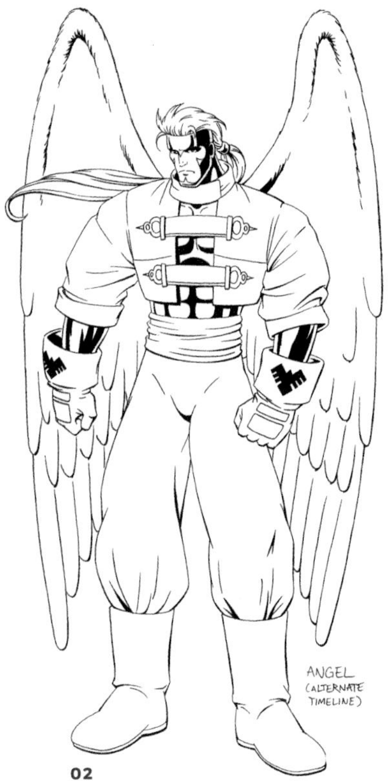
ANGEL
(ALTERNATE
TIMELINE)

02

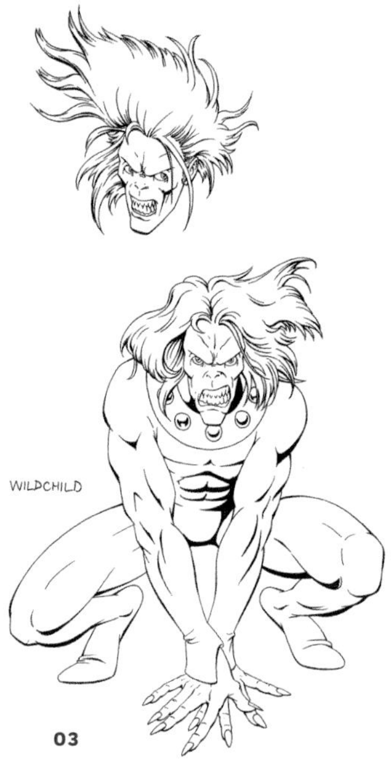
WILDCHILD

03

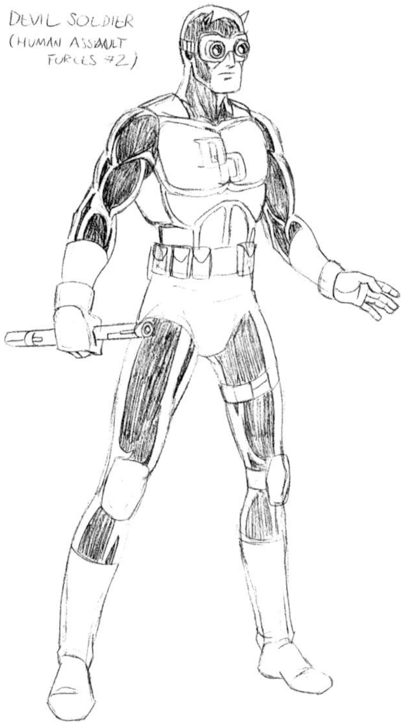
DEVIL SOLDIER
(HUMAN ASSAULT
FORCES #2)

04

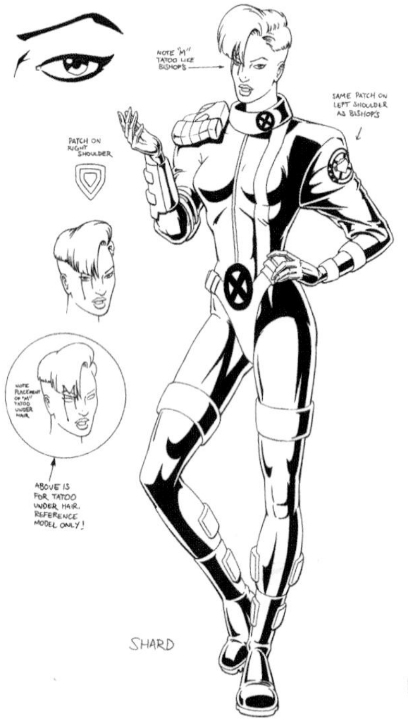
NOTE "M" TATOO LIKE BISHOP'S
SAME PATCH ON LEFT SHOULDER AS BISHOP'S
PATCH ON RIGHT SHOULDER
NOTE PLACEMENT OF "M" TATOO UNDER HAIR
ABOVE IS FOR TATOO UNDER HAIR. REFERENCE MODEL ONLY!
SHARD

05

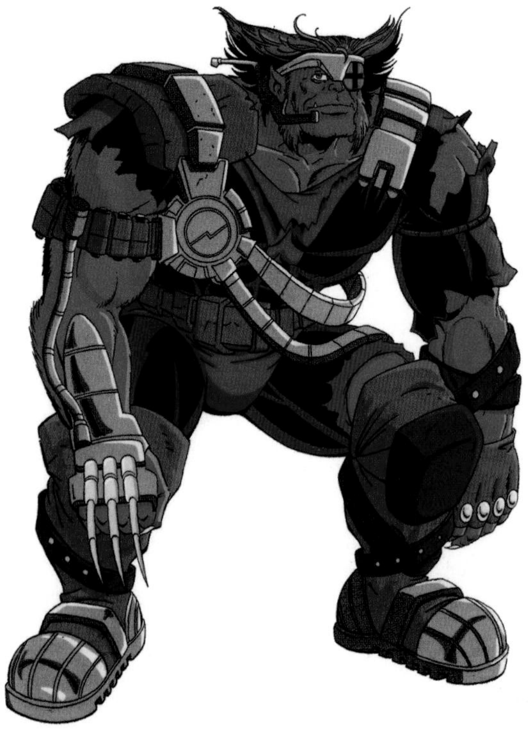

06

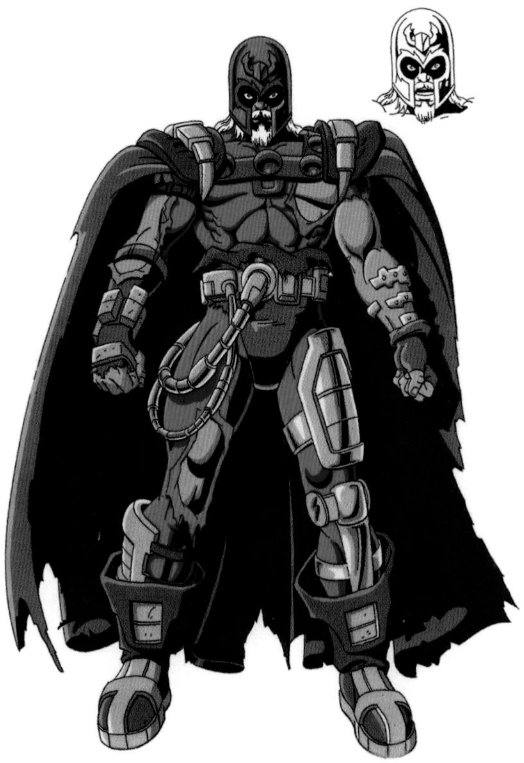

07

01 Character model: of The Mimic (alternate timeline, 2055) by Mark Lewis. **02** Character model of Angel (2055), penciled by Frank Squillace with cleanup by Lewis. **03** Character model of Wildchild (2055), penciled by Frank Brunner with cleanup by Lewis. **04** Devil Soldier (human assault forces 2, 2055, based on Daredevil) by Lewis. **05** Character model with details of Shard (2055), penciled by Brunner with cleanup by Lewis. **06–07** Colored character models of Beast (combat, 2055) and Magneto (2055); designed by Squillace with cleanup and finishes by Lewis. **OPPOSITE** Production cel of enraged, alternate-timeline Magneto (2055).

300-04   EP5-83

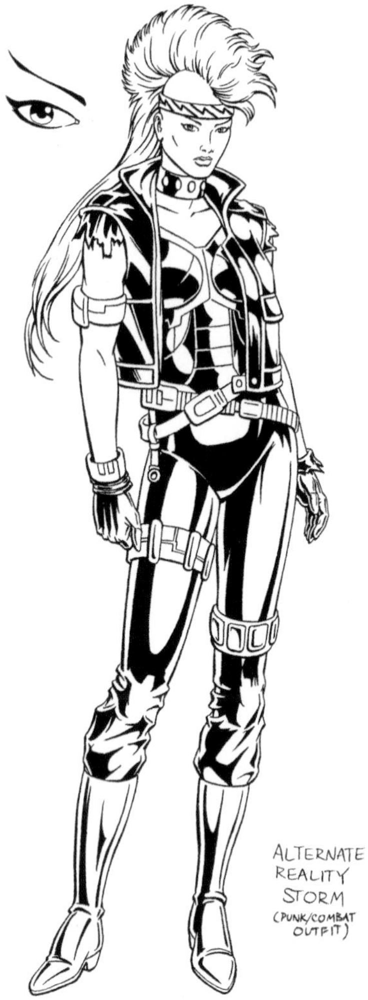
ALTERNATE REALITY STORM
(PUNK/COMBAT OUTFIT)

01

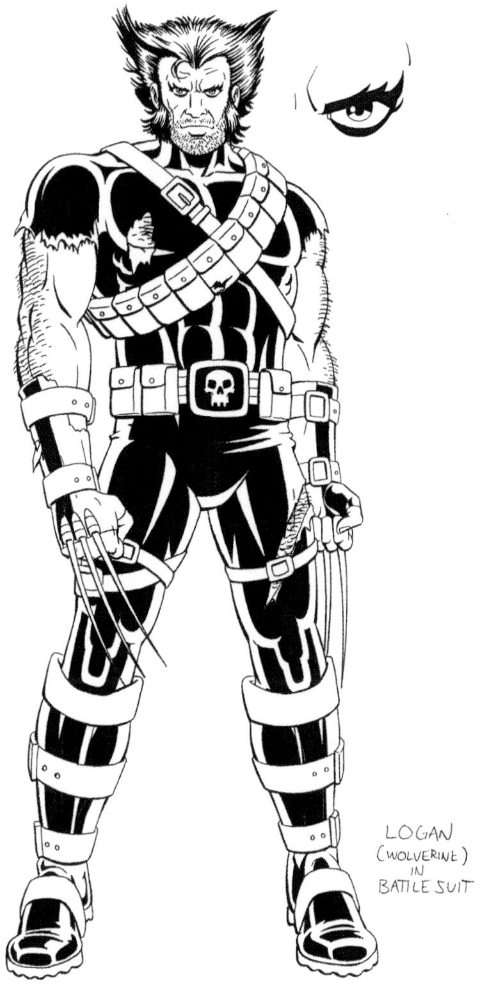
LOGAN (WOLVERINE) IN BATTLE SUIT

02

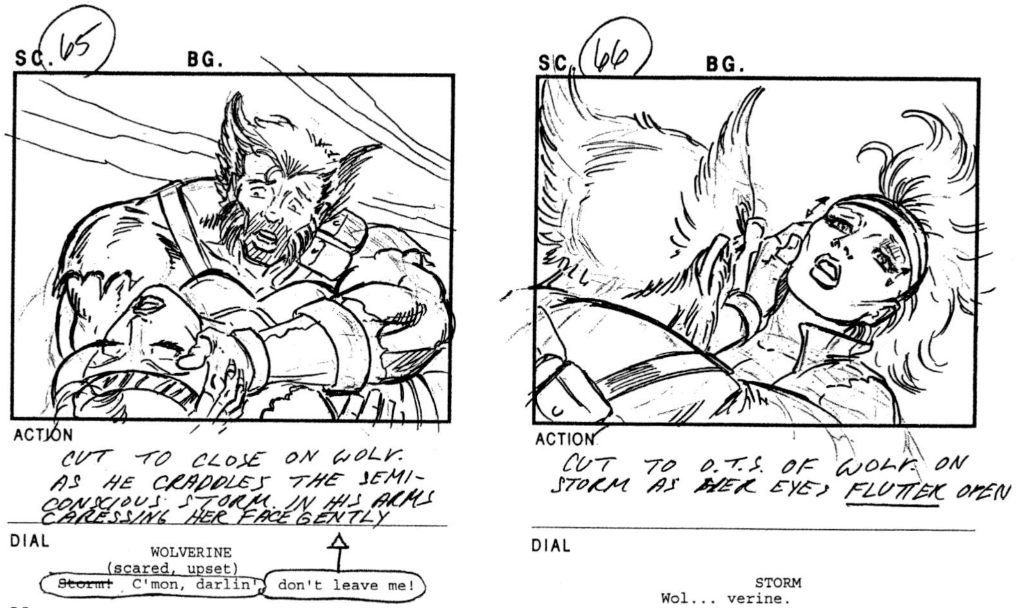
SC. 65
BG.
ACTION
CUT TO CLOSE ON WOLV. AS HE CRADDLES THE SEMI-CONSCIOUS STORM IN HIS ARMS CARESSING HER FACE GENTLY
DIAL
WOLVERINE
(scared, upset)
Storm! C'mon, darlin' don't leave me!
SC. 66
BG.
ACTION
CUT TO O.T.S. OF WOLV. ON STORM AS HER EYES FLUTTER OPEN
DIAL
STORM
Wol... verine.

03

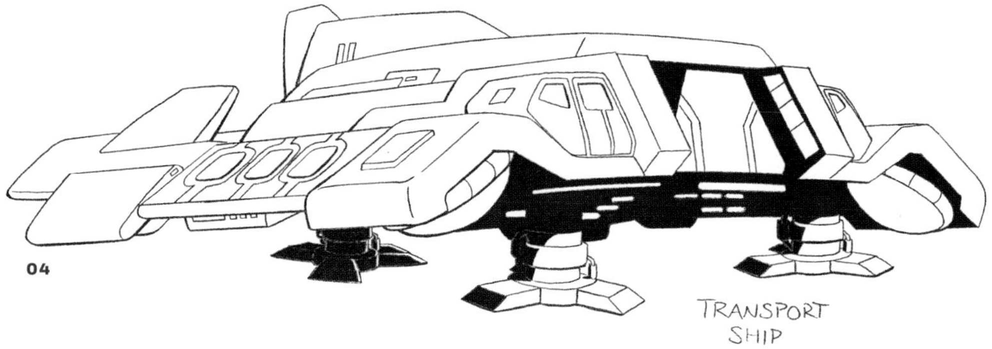
TRANSPORT SHIP

04

01–02 Character models of alternate-timeline Storm (combat, 2055) and Logan (battle suit, 2055); penciled by Frank Squillace with cleanup by Mark Lewis. **03** Storyboard of alternate-timeline Wolverine cradling Storm; they are married to each other, and wear wedding rings (2055); by Patrick Archibald. **04** Prop model of Transport Ship (2055), designed and cleaned by Squillace. **05** Layout of exterior battlefield near hall of the master sentinel (2055). Designed by Squillace with cleanup by Zhaoping Wei. **06** Character model of Sabretooth (2055), penciled by Frank Brunner with cleanup by Lewis. **07–13** Character models of Colossus (2055), Nightcrawler (2055), Holocaust (2055), Morph (2055), Human Assault Forces 1, 3, and 4 (2055), all by Mark Lewis, revising over the existing models, except Goliath (#11), designed by Squillace with cleanup by Lewis. **14** Human Assault Forces 5 (2055)—aka Captain America; designed by Squillace with cleanup by Lewis.

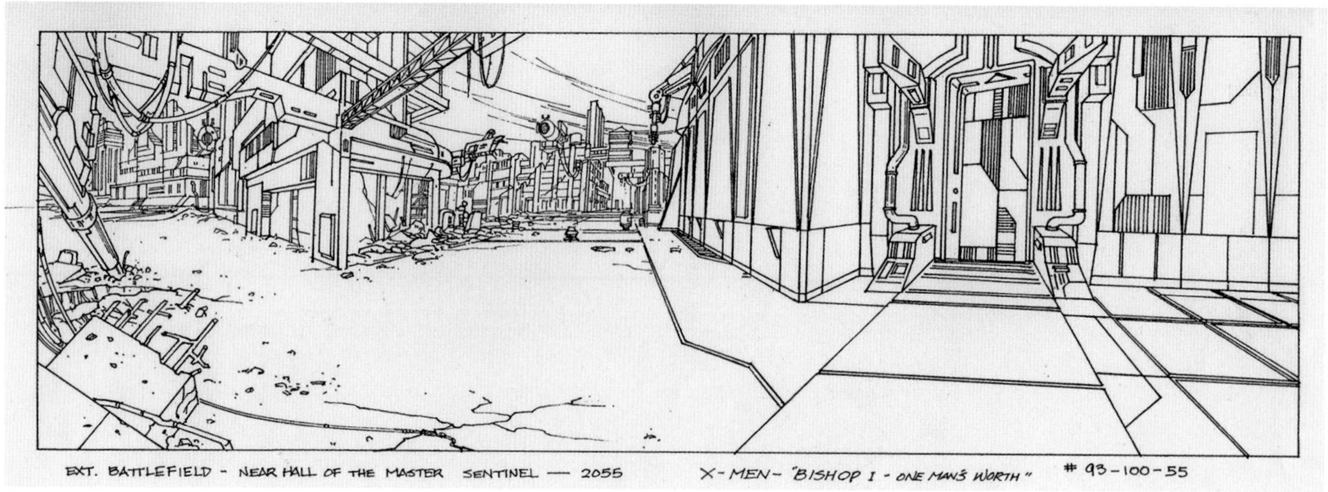
EXT. BATTLEFIELD - NEAR HALL OF THE MASTER SENTINEL — 2055
X-MEN- "BISHOP I - ONE MAN'S WORTH"
93-100-55

05

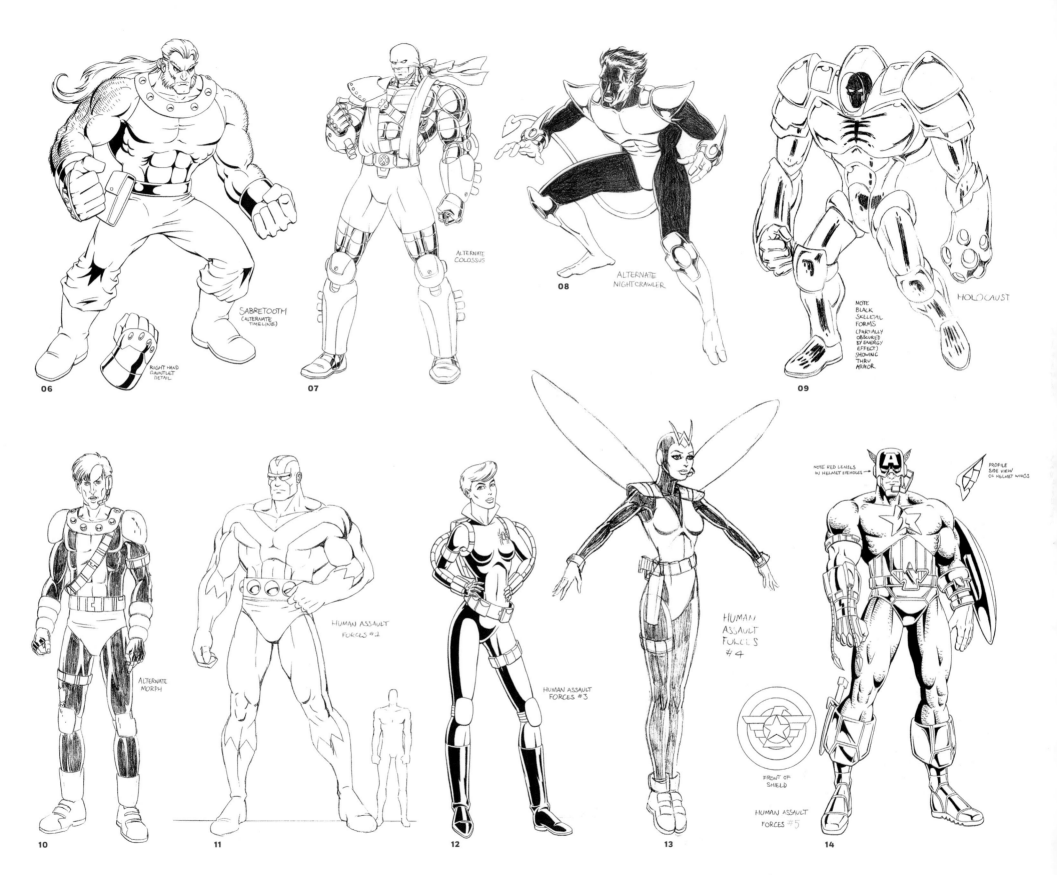

SABRETOOTH
(ALTERNATE
TIMELINE)

RIGHT HAND
GAUNTLET
DETAIL

06

ALTERNATE
COLOSSUS

07

08
ALTERNATE
NIGHTCRAWLER

NOTE
BLACK
SKELETAL
FORMS
(PARTIALLY
OBSCURED
BY ENERGY
EFFECT)
SHOWING
THRU
ARMOR

HOLOCAUST

09

ALTERNATE
MORPH

10

HUMAN ASSAULT
FORCES #1

11

HUMAN ASSAULT
FORCES #3

12

HUMAN
ASSAULT
FORCES
#4

13

NOTE RED LENSES
IN HELMET EYEHOLES

PROFILE
SIDE VIEW
OF HELMET WINGS

FRONT OF
SHIELD

HUMAN ASSAULT
FORCES #5

14

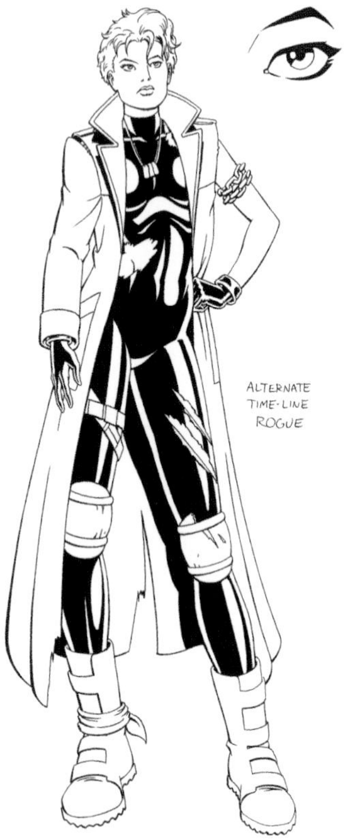
ALTERNATE
TIME-LINE
ROGUE

01

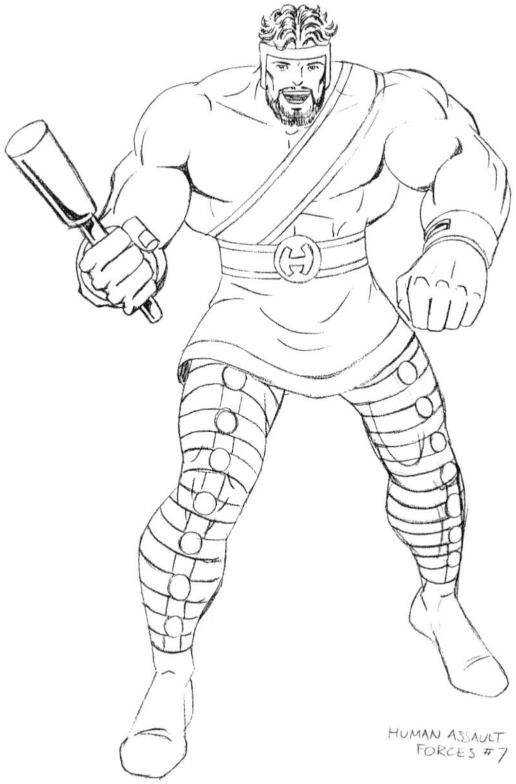
HUMAN ASSAULT
FORCES #7

02

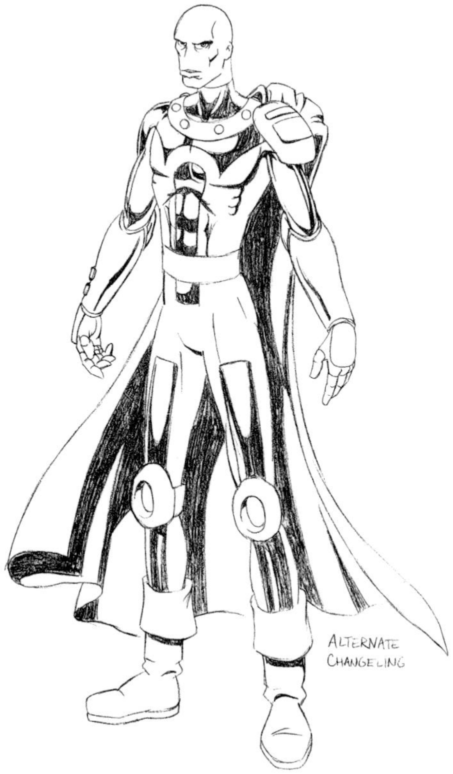
ALTERNATE
CHANGELING

03

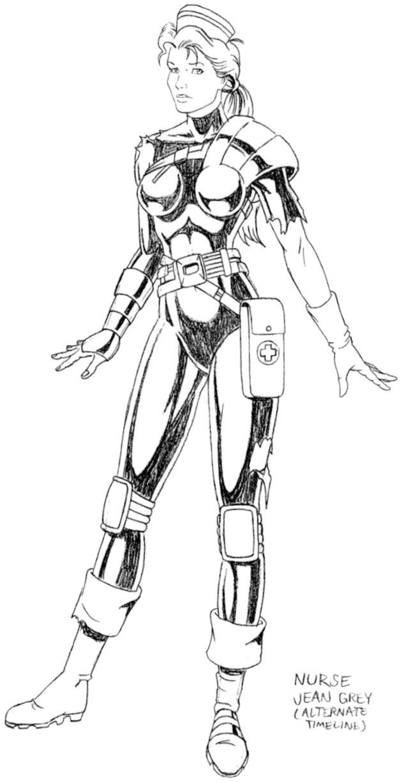
NURSE
JEAN GREY
(ALTERNATE
TIMELINE)

04

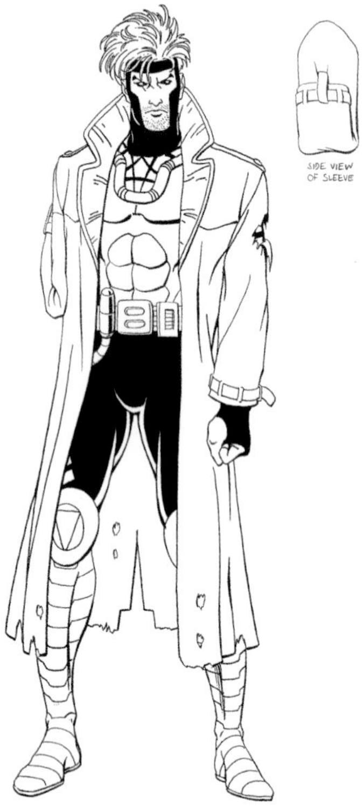
SIDE VIEW
OF SLEEVE

05

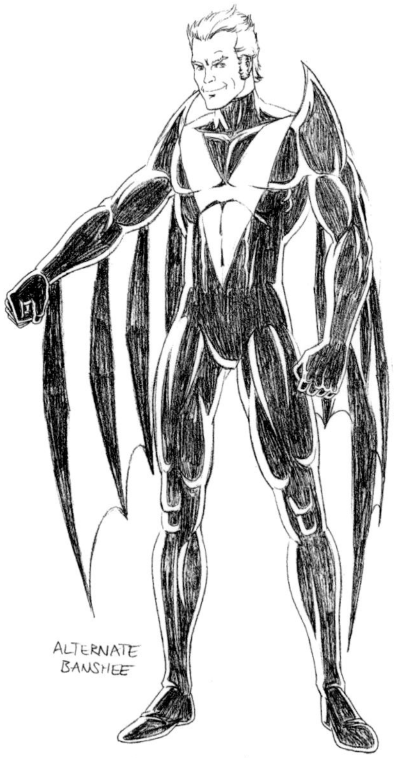
ALTERNATE
BANSHEE

06

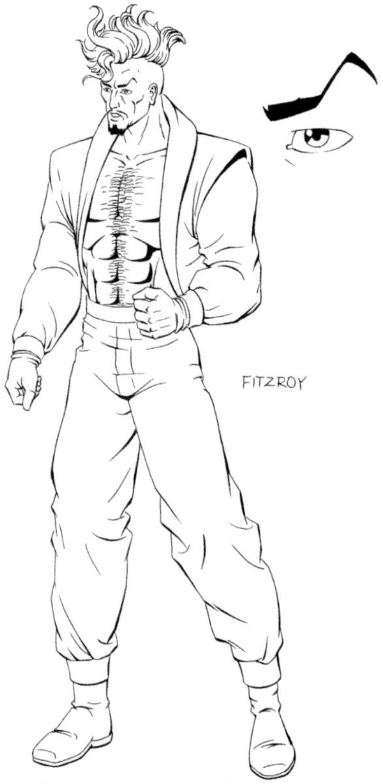
FITZROY

07

01 Character models of alternate-timeline Rogue (2055); pencils by Frank Squillace with cleanup by Mark Lewis. **02–04** Character models of Human Assault Forces 7 (Hercules, 2055), Changeling (2055), Nurse Jean Grey (2055), all by Mark Lewis—except Hercules (02); designed by Squillace with cleanup by Lewis. **05** Character model of Gambit (2055), missing right arm, by Frank Brunner and Lewis. **06** Character model of Banshee (2055) by Lewis. **07** Character model of Fitzroy (2055) by Brunner and Lewis. **08–12** Character models of alternate-timeline Sunfire (2055), Giant Mutant (2055), Havok (2055), Human Assault Forces 9 (2055)—aka Scarlet Spider—and Quicksilver (2055); all by Lewis, retrofitting the existing models. **13** Character model Cyclops Mutant Forces (2055); idea by Squillace, implementation and cleanup by Lewis. **14–15** Character model Shadowcat (2055), expandable claws, and Blink (2055), by Brunner and Lewis. **16** Character model Forge (2055), part-cyborg by Lewis. **17** Character model Human Assault Forces 6 (2055)—aka Iron Man 2020; designed by Squillace with cleanup by Lewis.

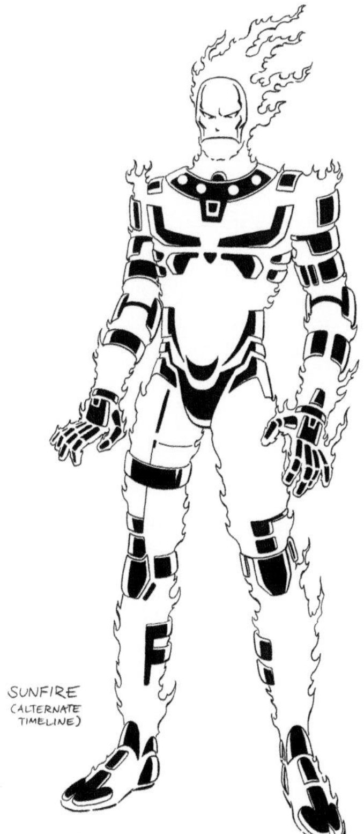
SUNFIRE
(ALTERNATE
TIMELINE)

08

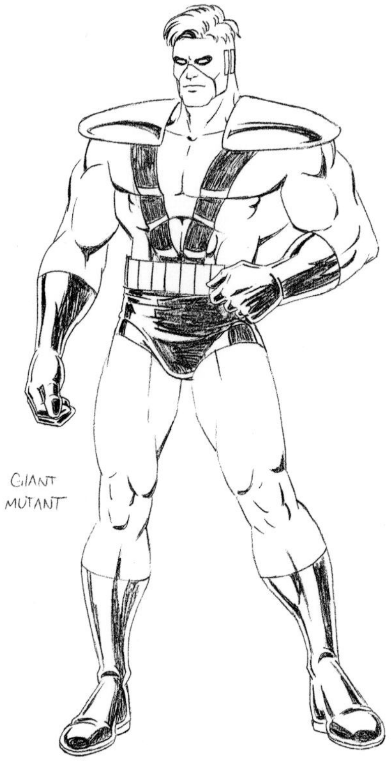
GIANT
MUTANT

09

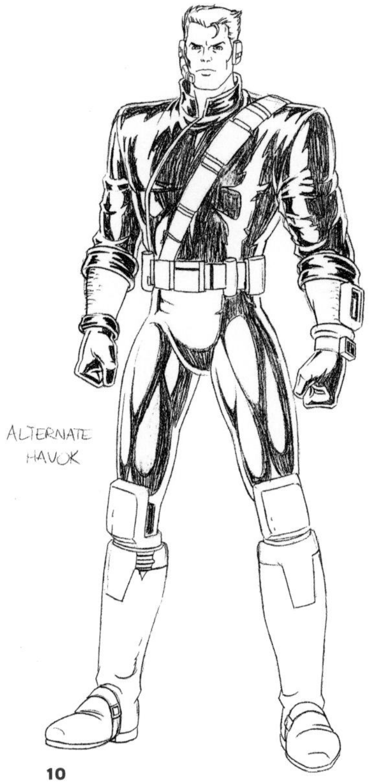
ALTERNATE
HAVOK

10

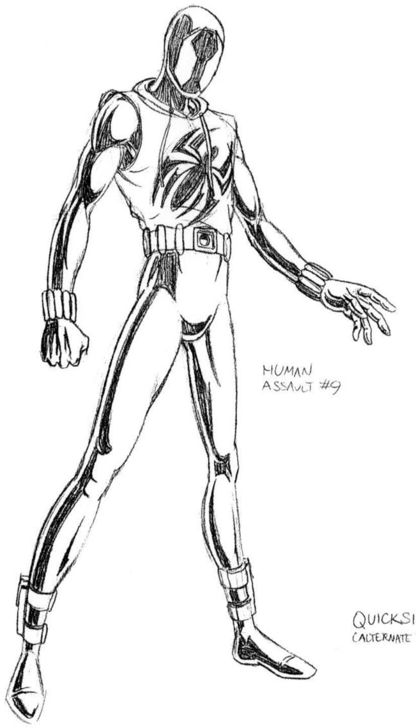
HUMAN
ASSAULT #9

11

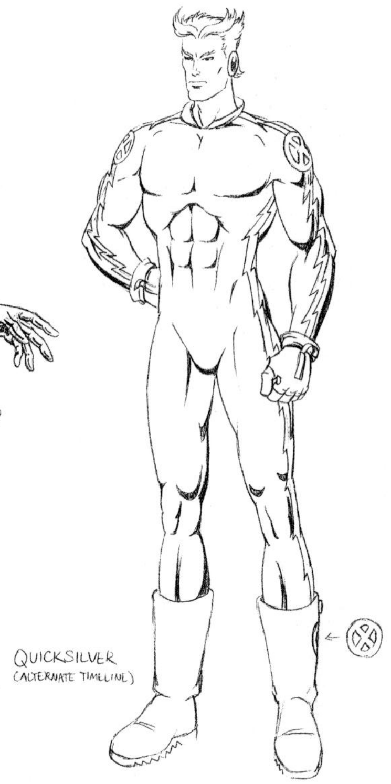
QUICKSILVER
(ALTERNATE TIMELINE)

12

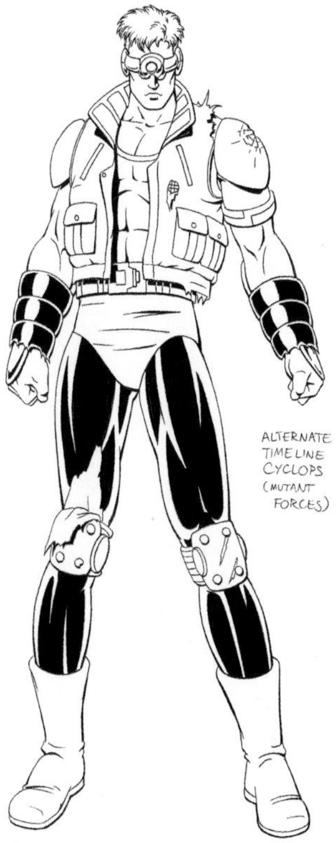
ALTERNATE
TIMELINE
CYCLOPS
(MUTANT
FORCES)

13

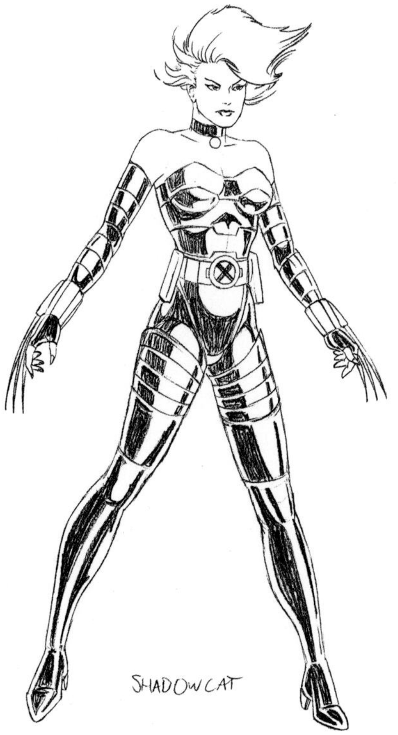
SHADOWCAT

14

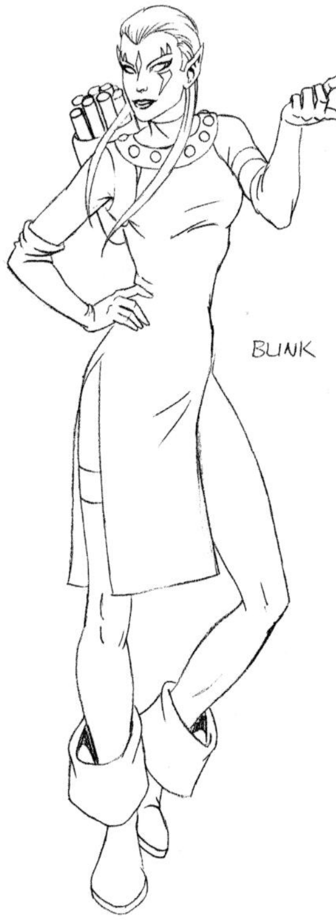
BLINK

15

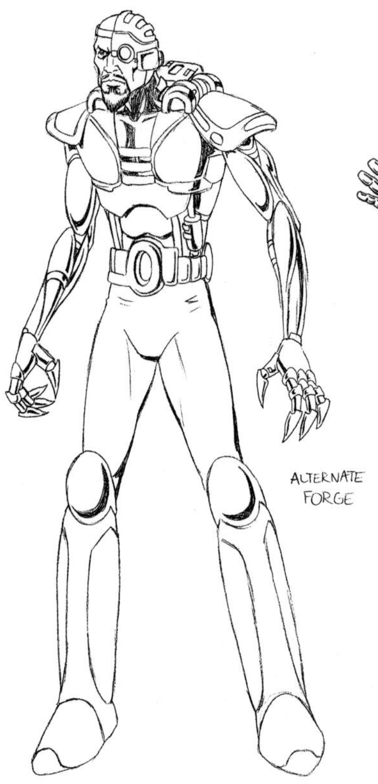
ALTERNATE
FORGE

16

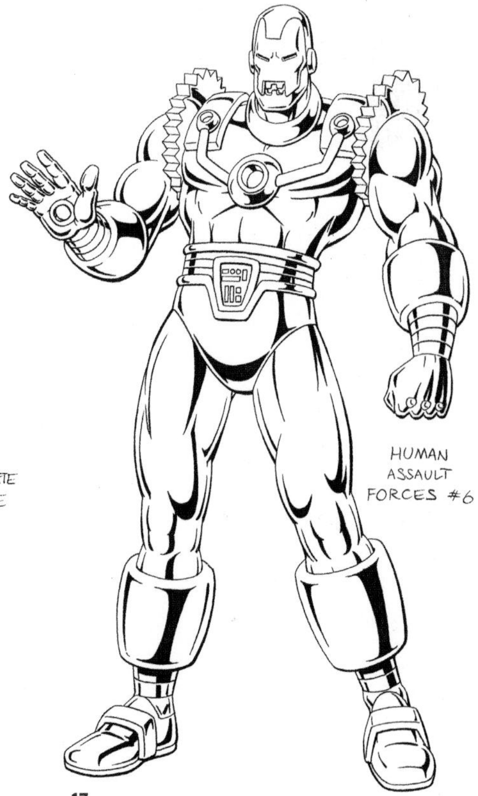
HUMAN
ASSAULT
FORCES #6

17

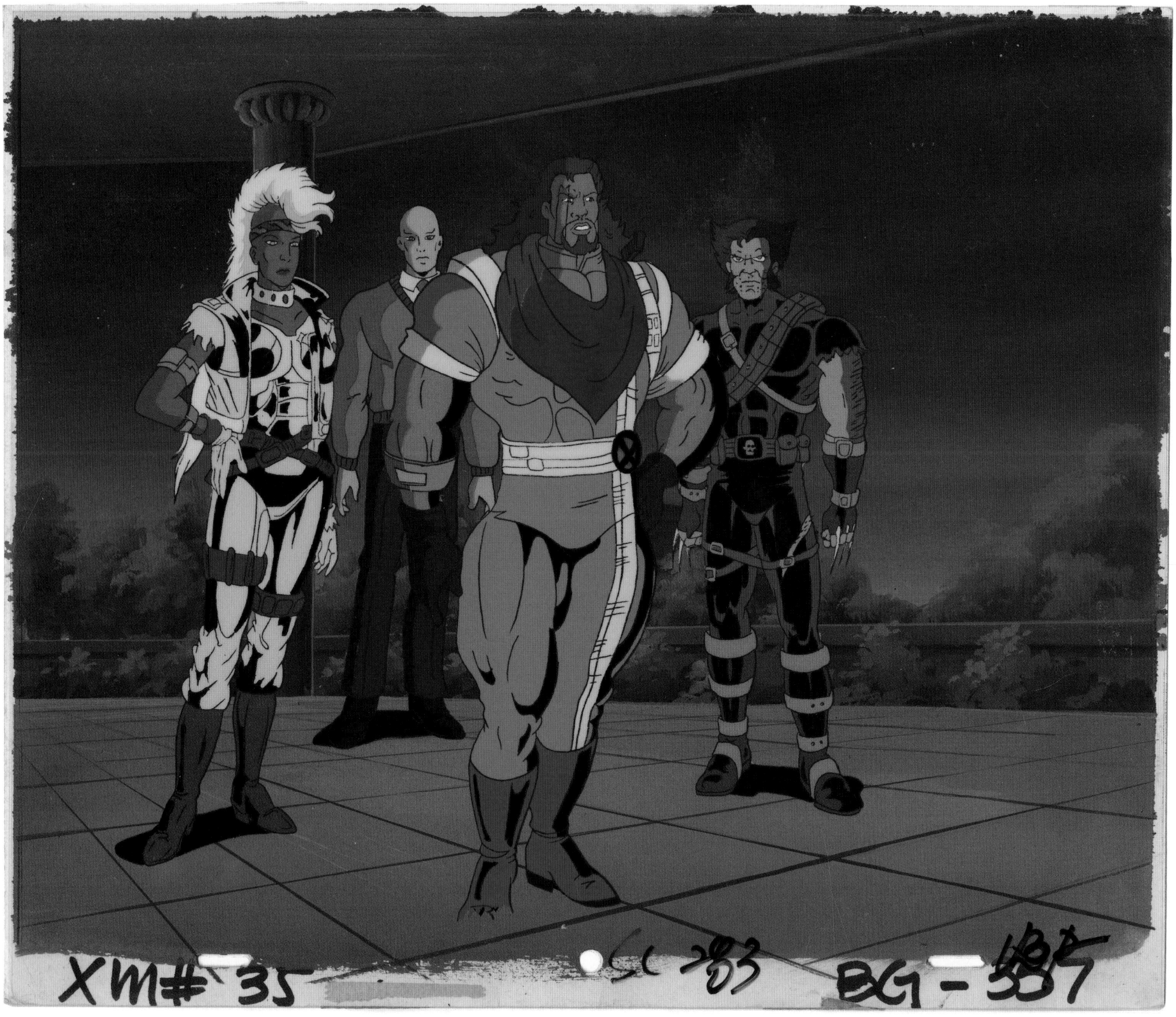
XM# 35
SC 283

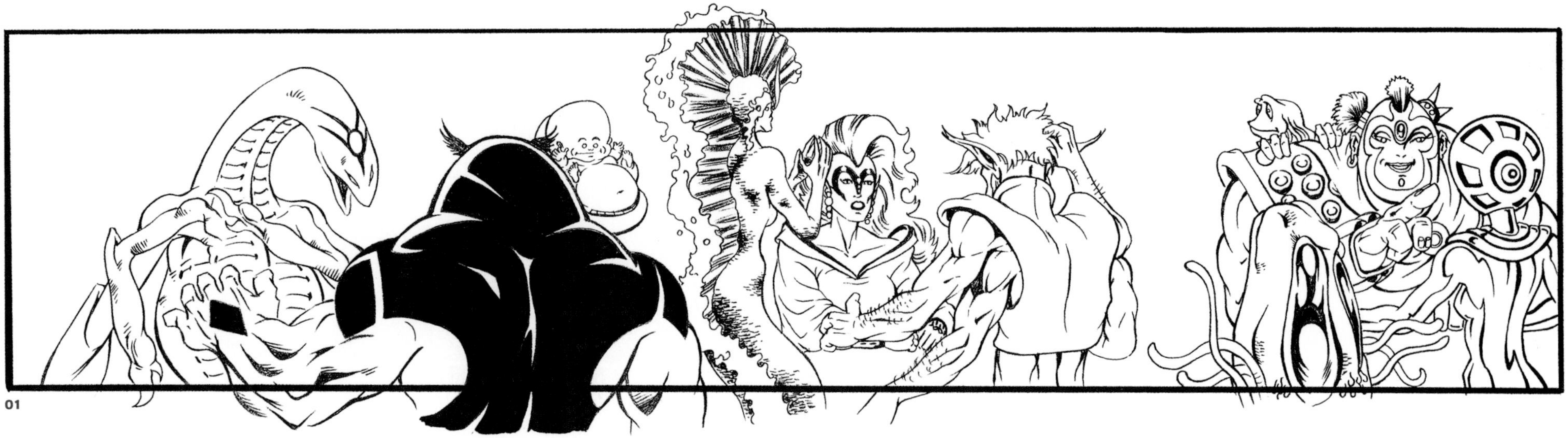

01

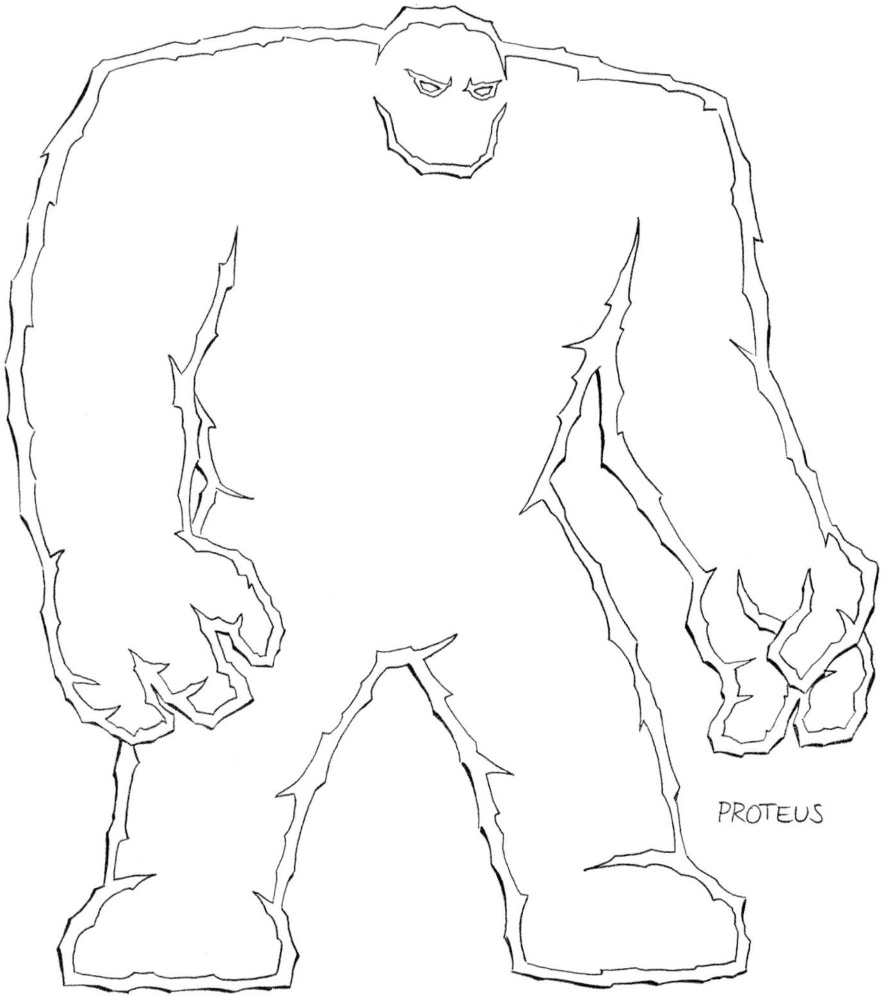
PROTEUS

02

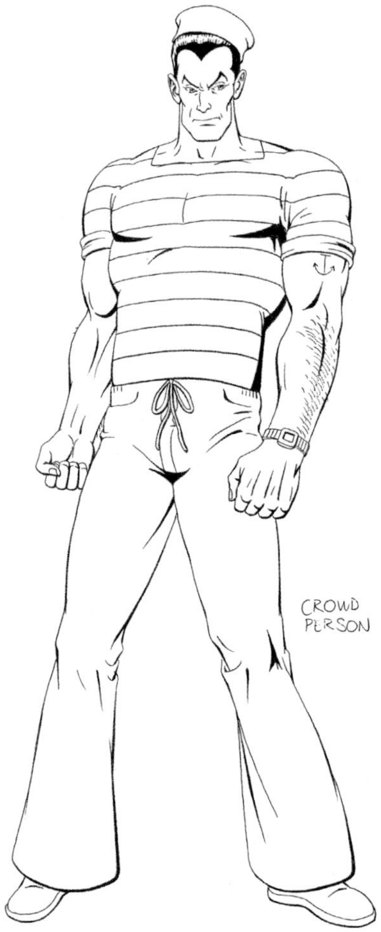
CROWD PERSON

03

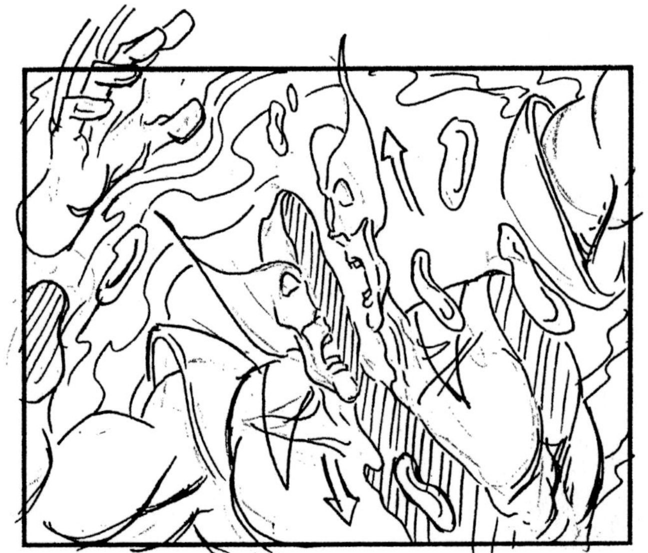
ACTION
-HE SPLITS DOWN THE MIDDLE (B.S.&P. NOTE - JUST FLAT COSTUME COLORS NO BLOOD, BONE ETC.

04

OPPOSITE Production cel with alternate-timeline Storm (2055), Young Professor Xavier, Bishop, and alternate-timeline Wolverine (2055). **01** Drawing of fantastical patrons in seaside dive bar, designed and cleaned by Frank Squillace. **02** Character model of Transformed Proteus, designed by Squillace with cleanup by Mark Lewis. **03** Character model of Crowd Person (Namor; note the in-house, inside joke—he's dressed as a certain spinach-eating sailor man), by Frank Brunner and Lewis. **04** Storyboard panel of Proteus making Wolverine believe he is "splitting down the middle." By Patrick Archibald.

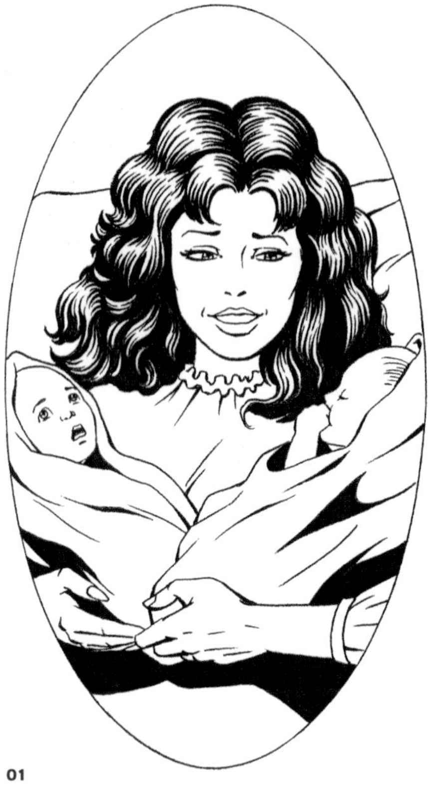

01

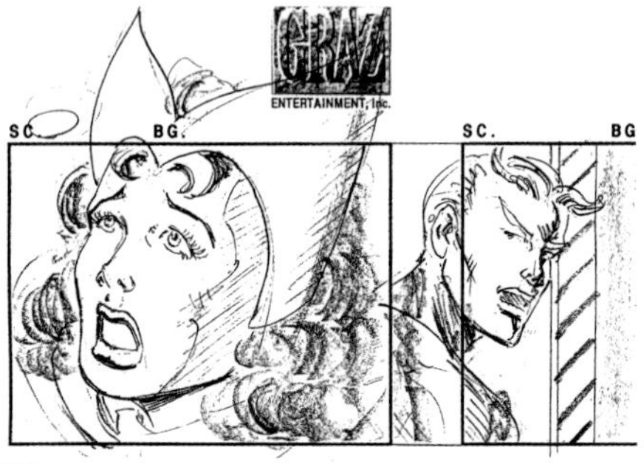
ENTERTAINMENT, Inc.
SC.
BG.
SC.
BG

02

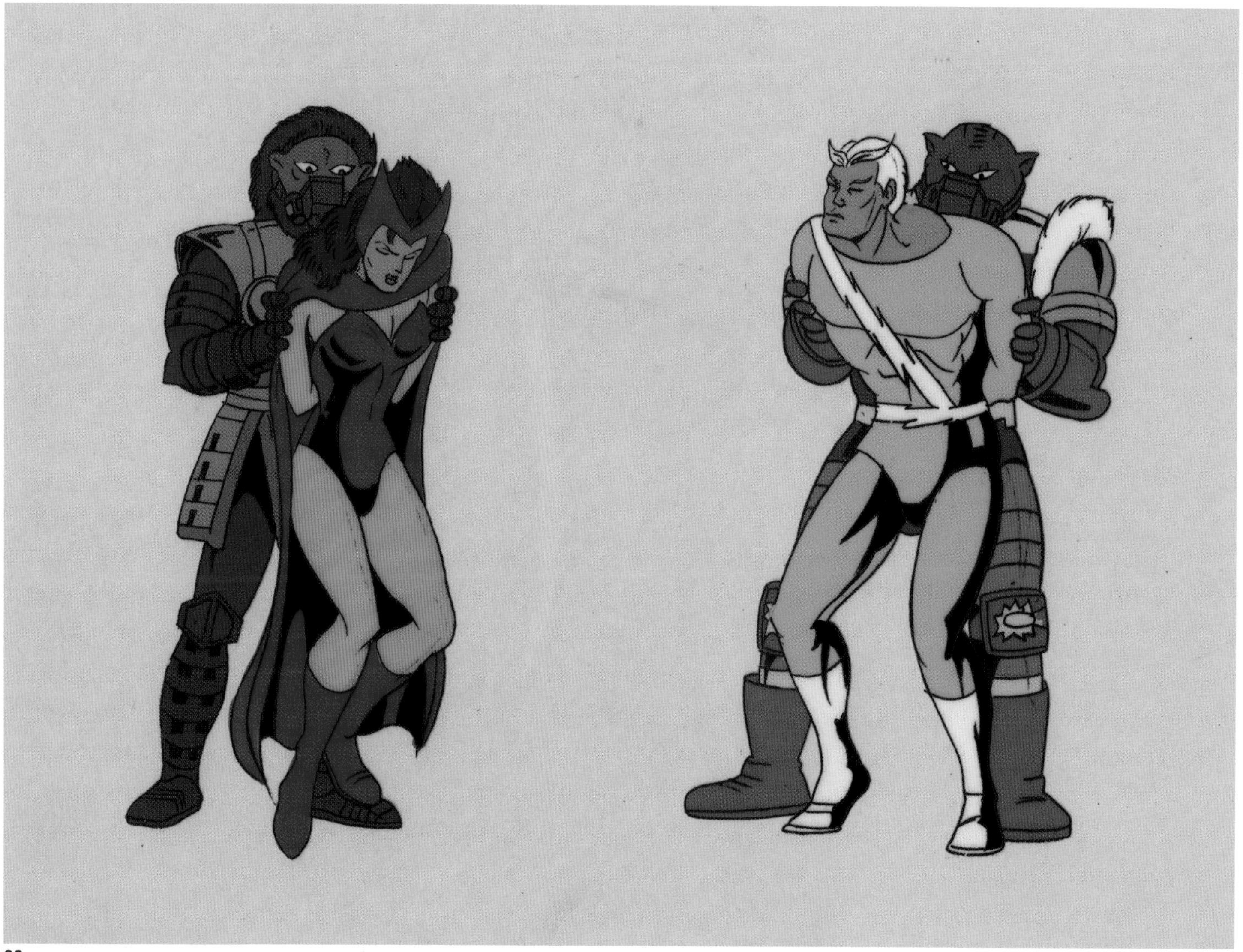

03

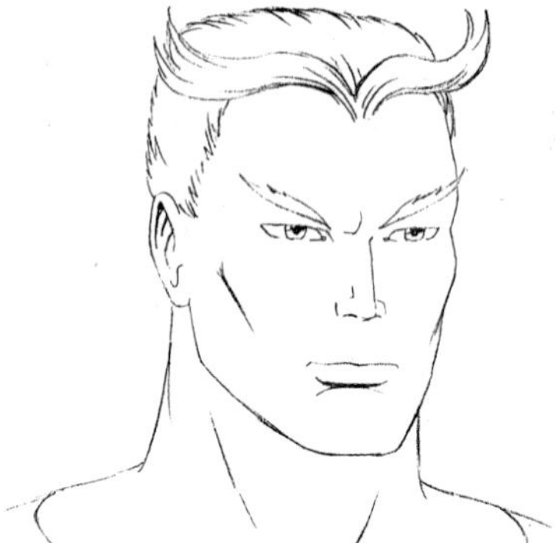

04

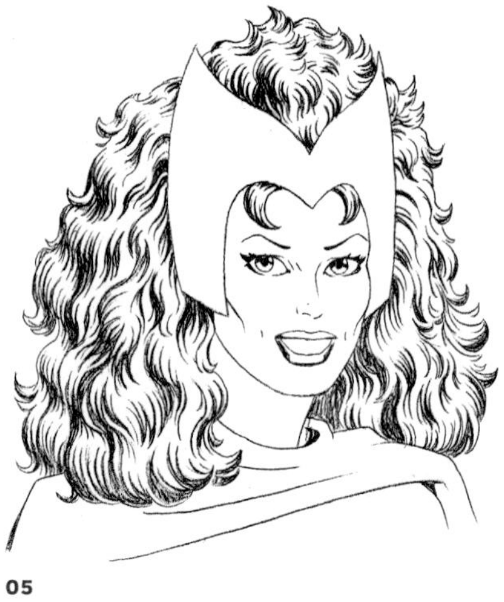

05

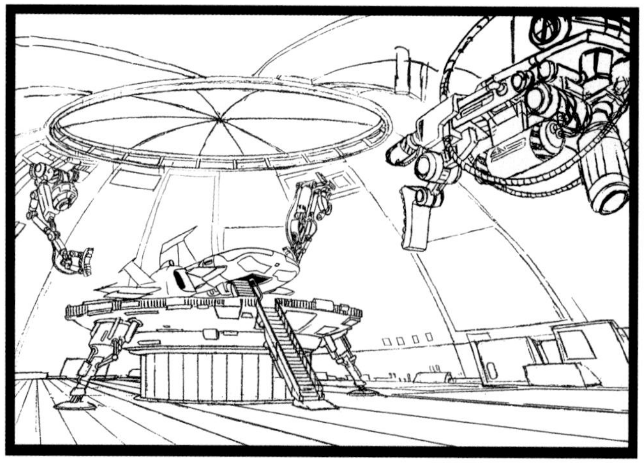

06

01 Character models of young mother Magda and twin babies Scarlet Witch and Quicksilver, by Frank Brunner and Mark Lewis. **02** Partial storyboard page with Scarlet Witch and Quicksilver, by Jerry Acerno. **03** Production cel of Scarlet Witch held by Sir Liyan and Quicksilver held by Sir Ossilot. **04–05** Quicksilver and Scarlet Witch head turns, by Lewis. **06** Background layout of X-Factor HQ hangar with Hummingbird craft, by Frank Squillace. **07–14** Character models of Bova, Sir Liyan, Sir Chita, Sir Lepard, Sir Rhyneaux, Sir Karabu, Sir Woolf, and Sir Ossilot—all by Brunner and Lewis.

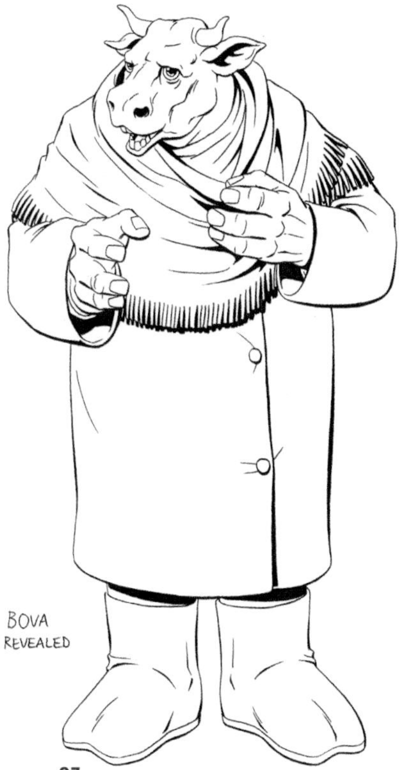
BOVA
REVEALED

07

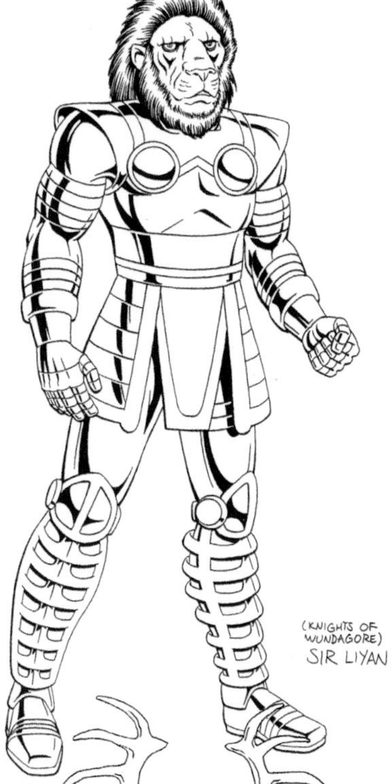
(KNIGHTS OF
WUNDAGORE)
SIR LIYAN

08

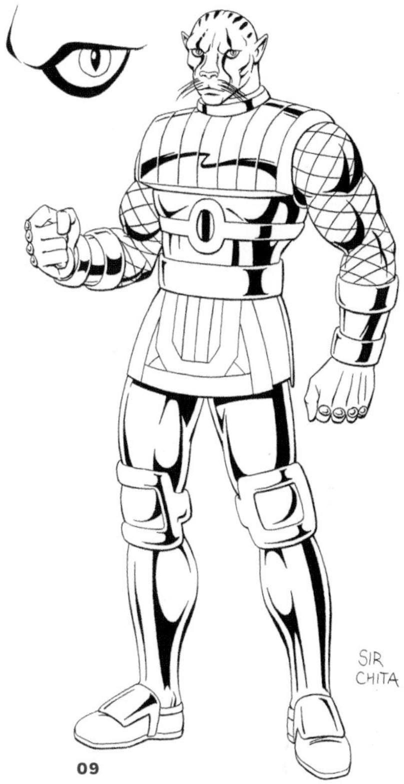
SIR
CHITA

09

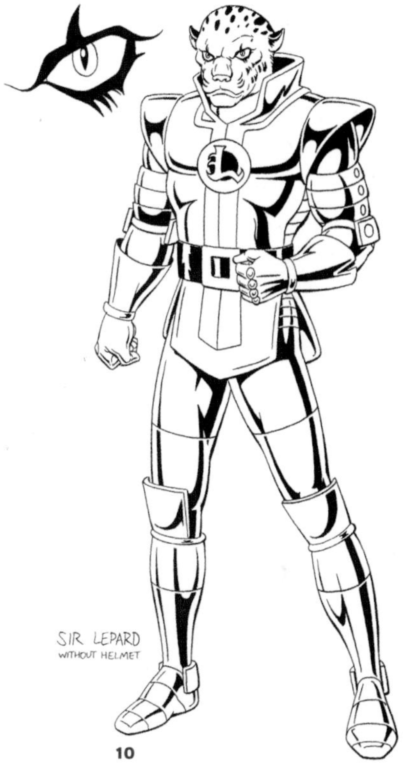
SIR LEPARD
WITHOUT HELMET

10

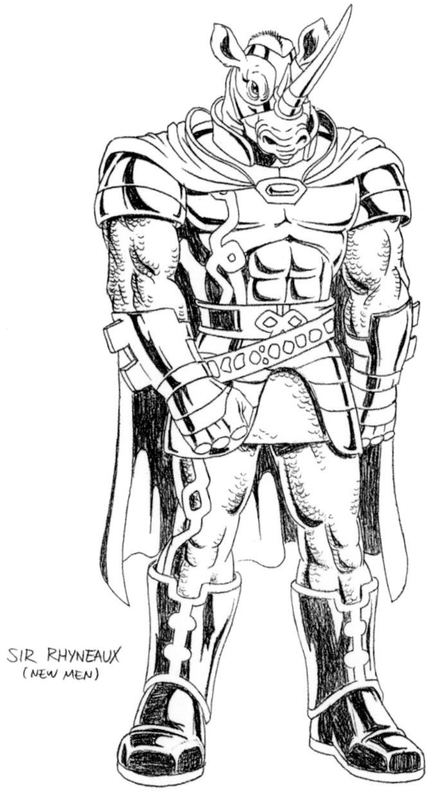
SIR RHYNEAUX
(NEW MEN)

11

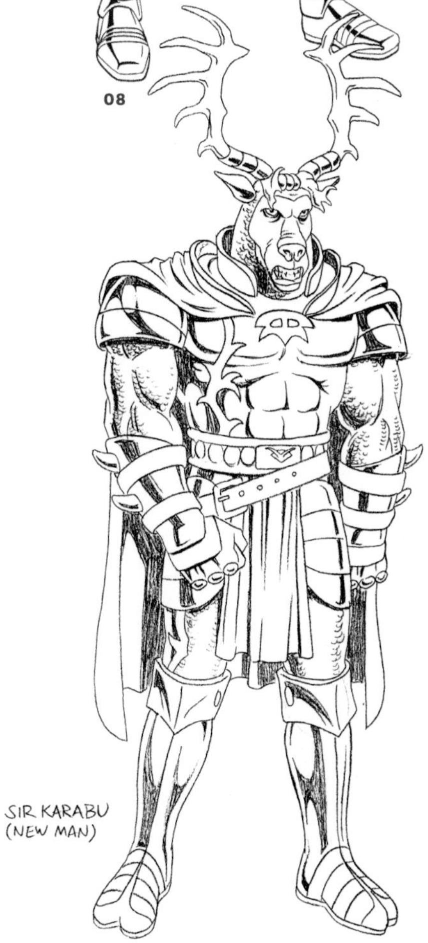
SIR KARABU
(NEW MAN)

12

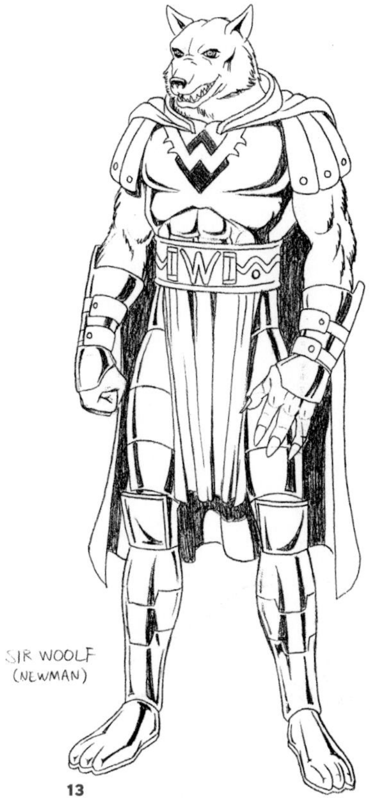
SIR WOOLF
(NEWMAN)

13

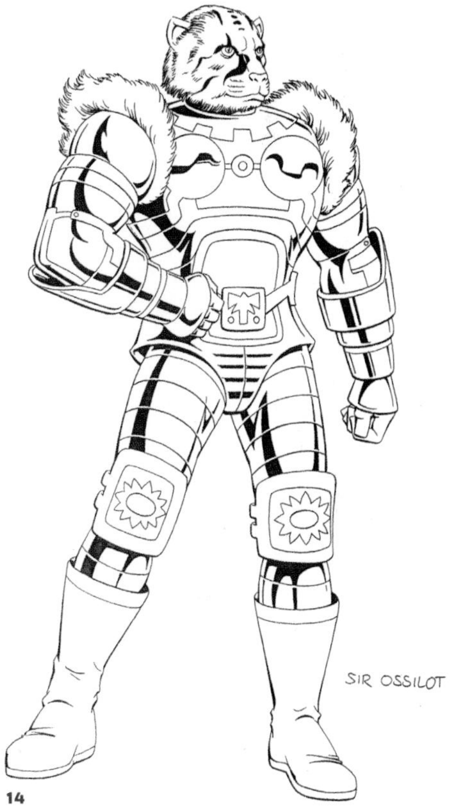
SIR OSSILOT

14

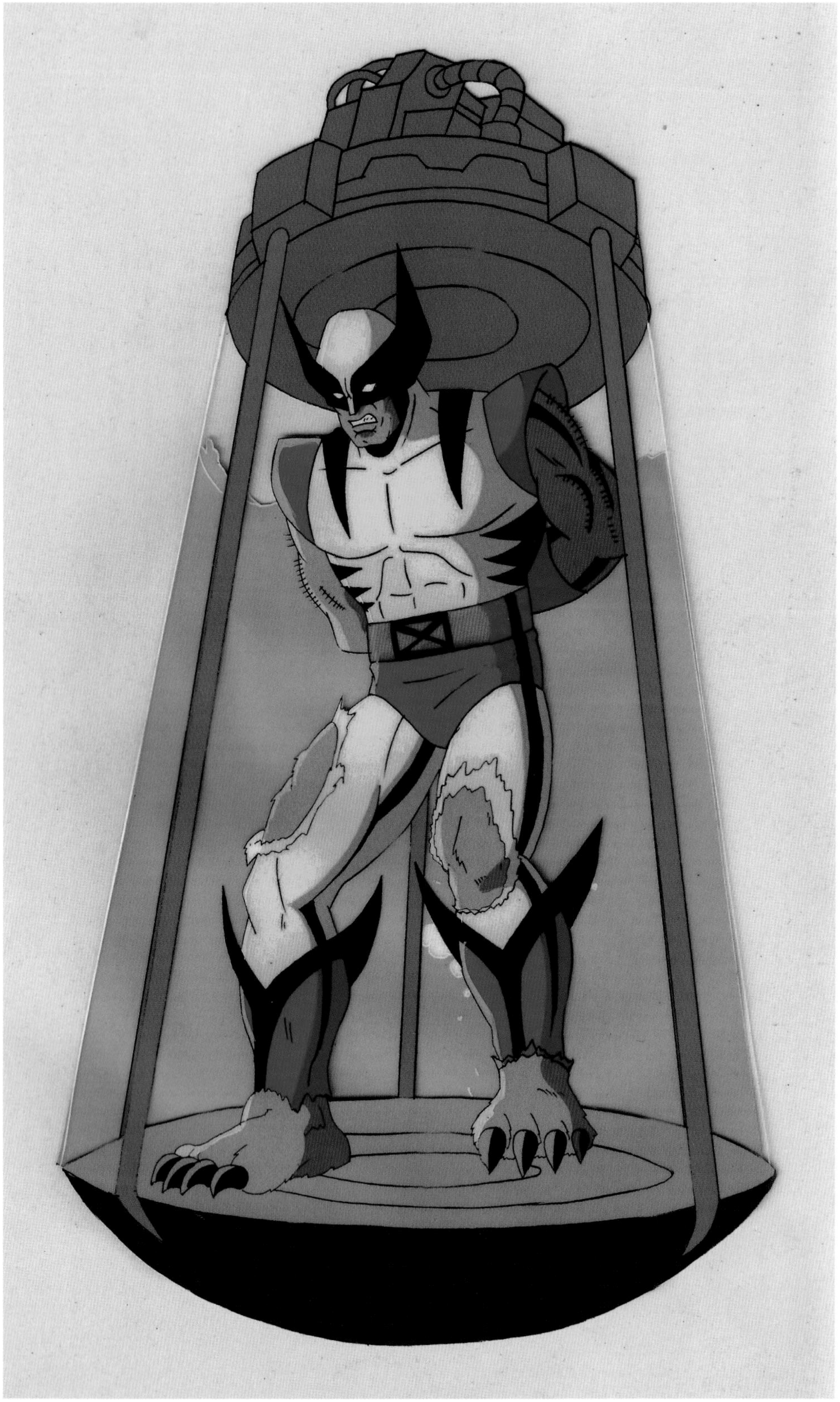

01

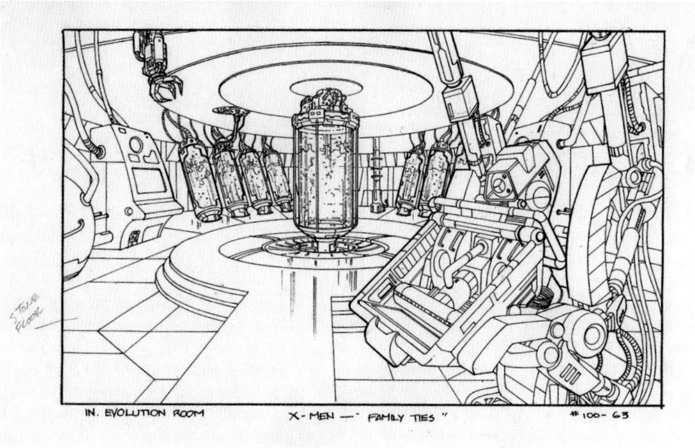
IN. EVOLUTION ROOM
X-MEN — "FAMILY TIES"
#100-63

02

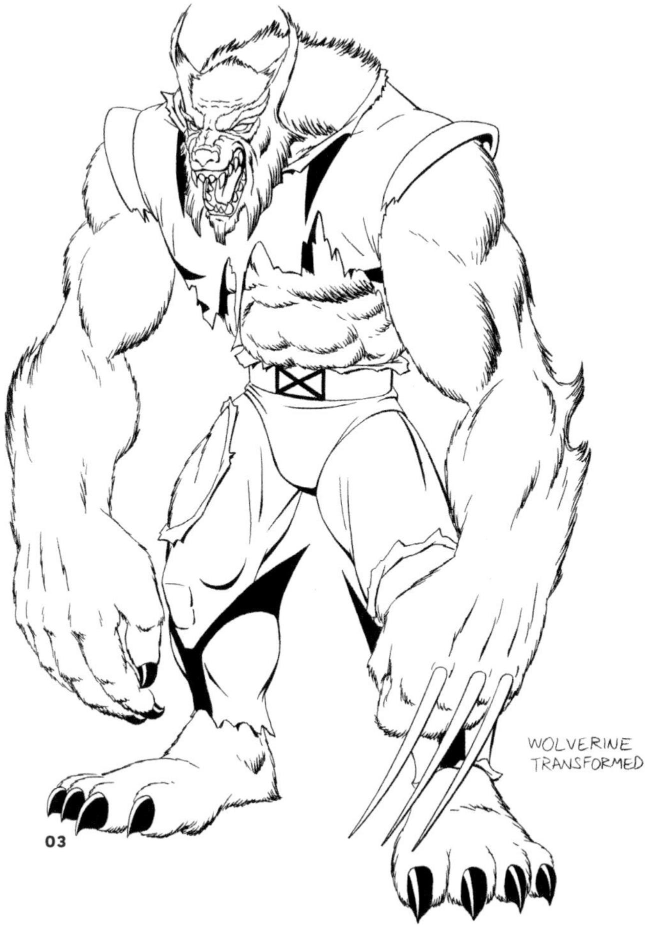
WOLVERINE
TRANSFORMED

03

01 Production cel of Wolverine trapped in a transformation tube. Missing translucent cel of more green fluid covering Wolverine. **02** Layout of interior Evolution Room; rough design by Frank Squillace with cleanup by Zhaoping Wei. **03** Character model of Wolverine transformed into a wolf-like creature by the High Evolutionary. **OPPOSITE** Production cel of Beast forced to fight with a transformed Wolverine.

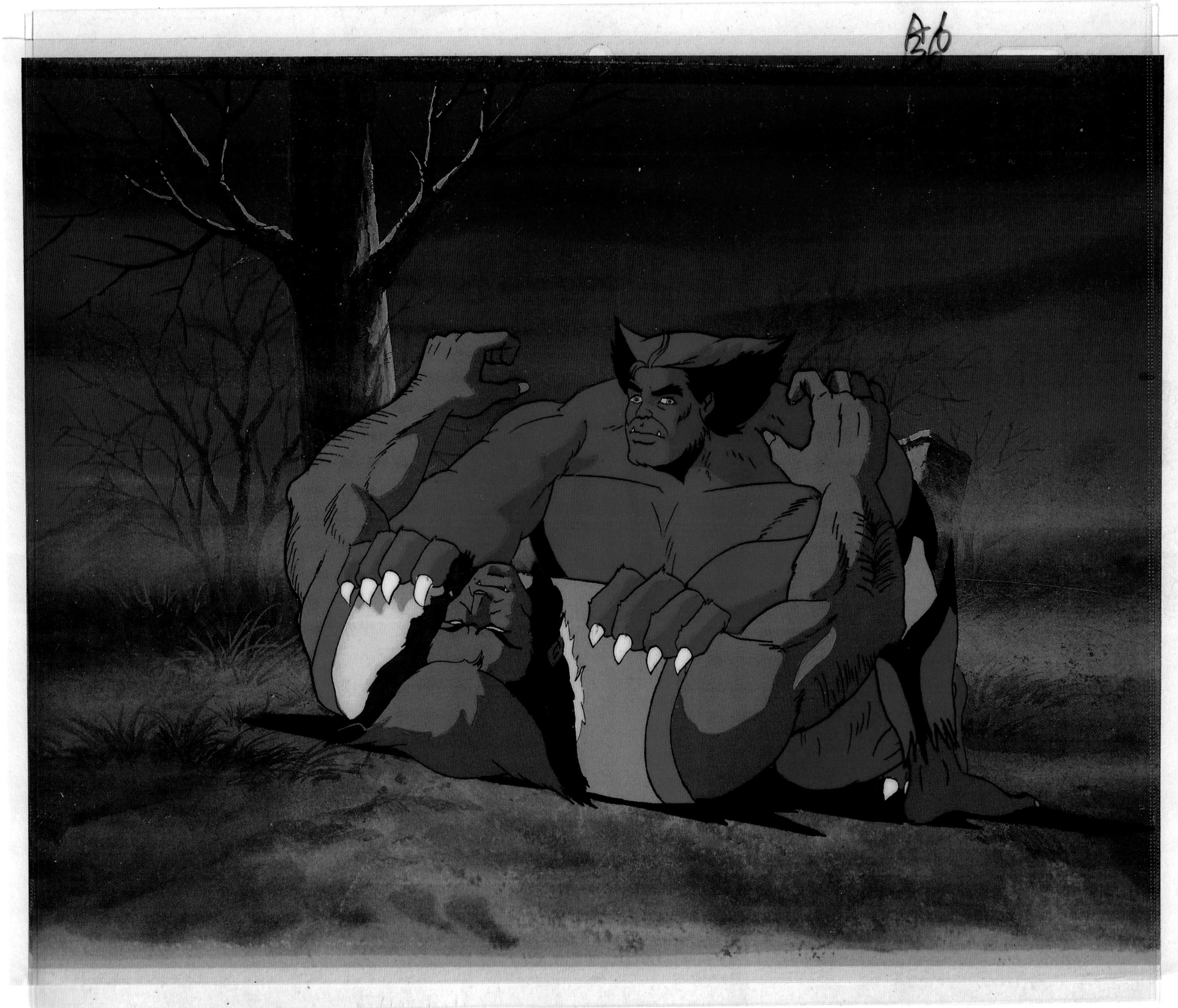

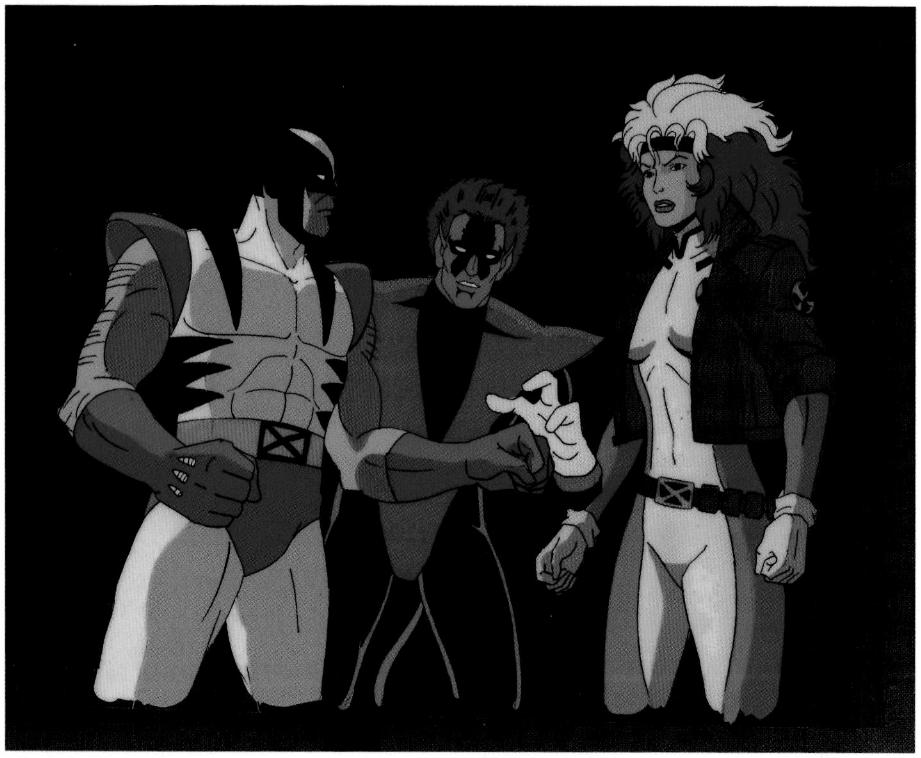

01

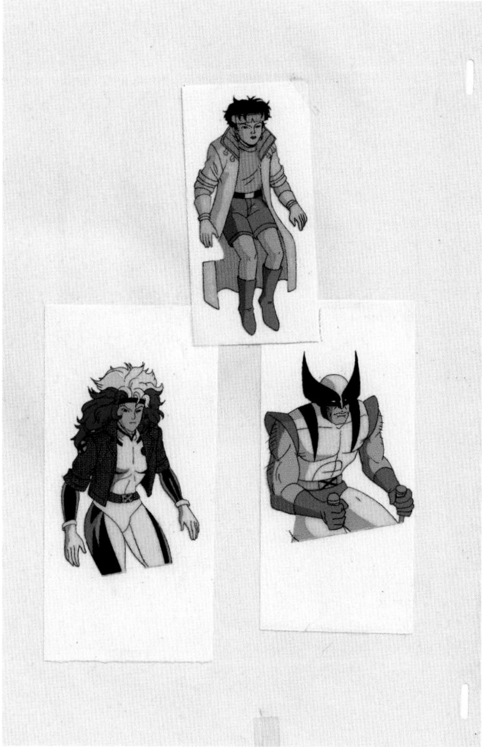

02

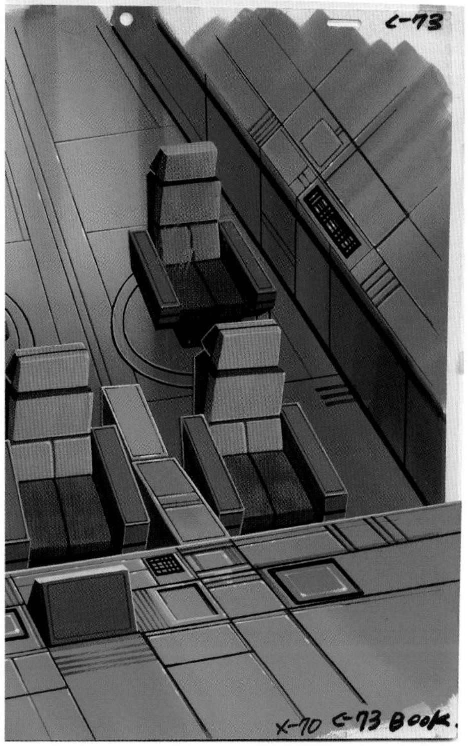
C-73
X-70 C-73 Book.

03

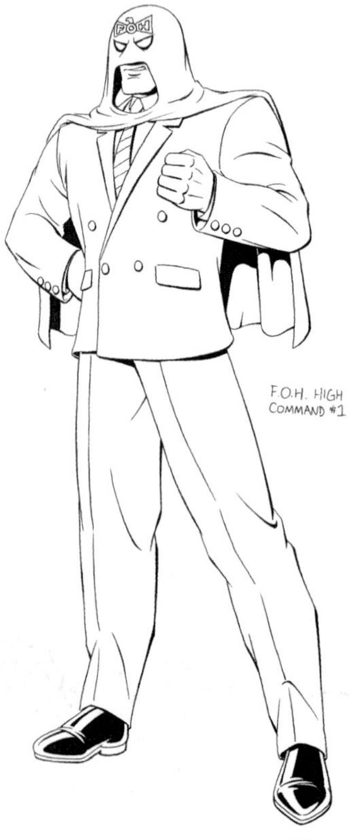
F.O.H. HIGH
COMMAND #1

04

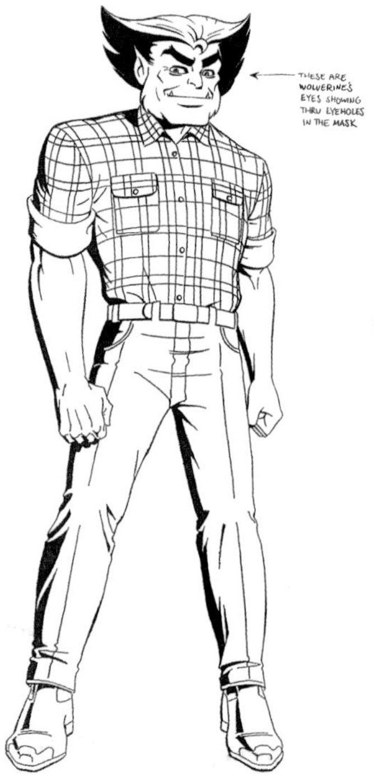
THESE ARE
WOLVERINES
EYES SHOWING
THRU EYEHOLES
IN THE MASK

05

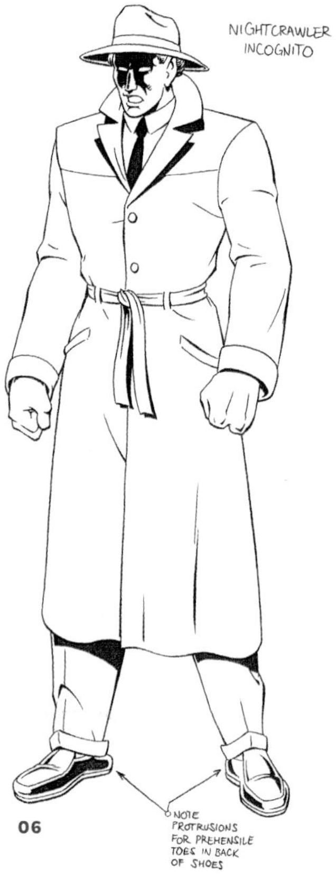
NIGHTCRAWLER
INCOGNITO
NOTE
PROTRUSIONS
FOR PREHENSILE
TOES IN BACK
OF SHOES

06

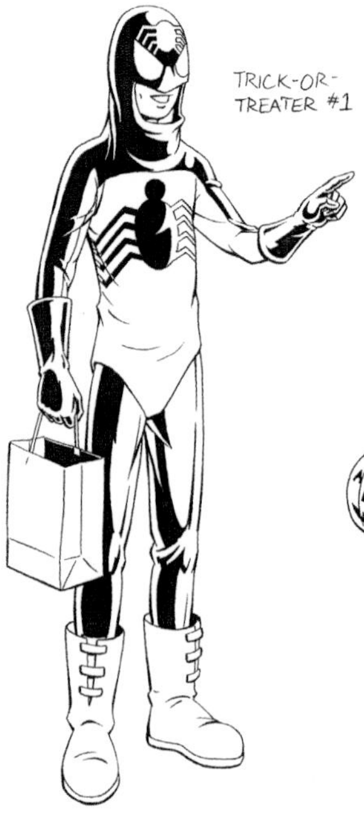
TRICK-OR-
TREATER #1

07

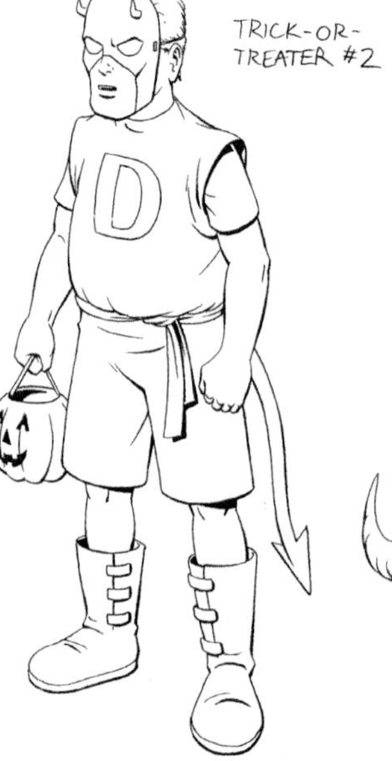
TRICK-OR-
TREATER #2

08

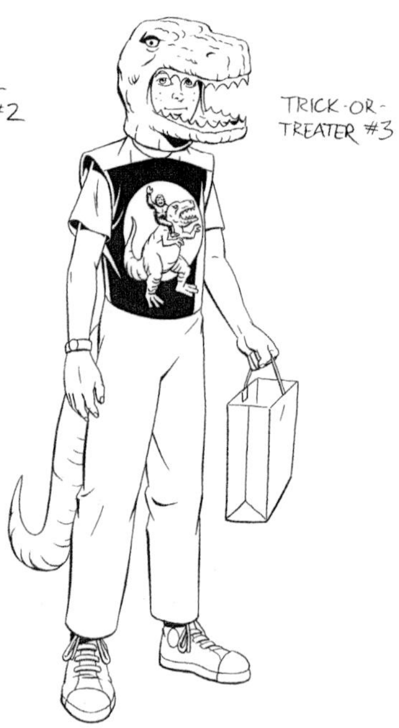
TRICK-OR-
TREATER #3

09

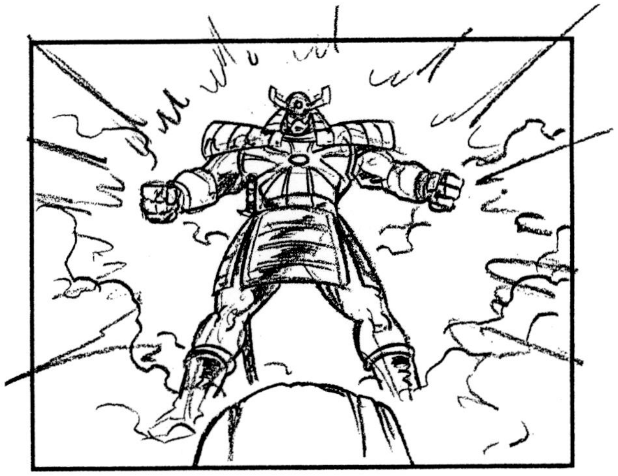

10

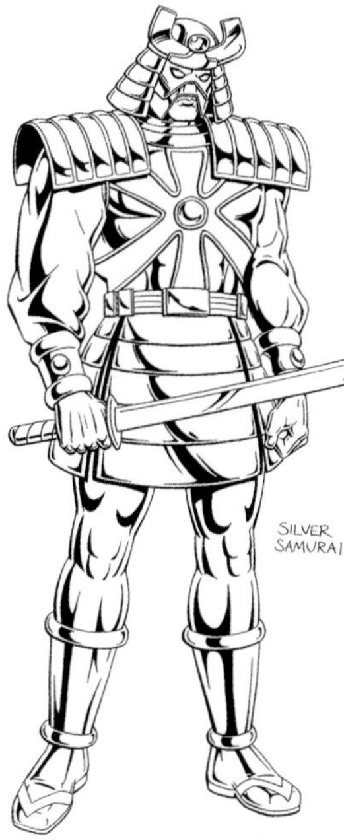
SILVER SAMURAI

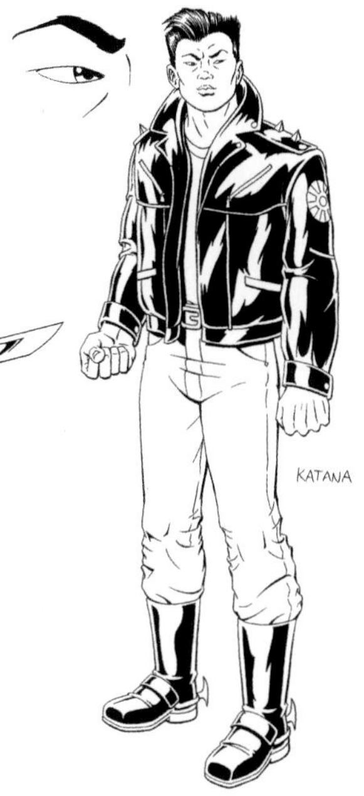
KATANA

11 12

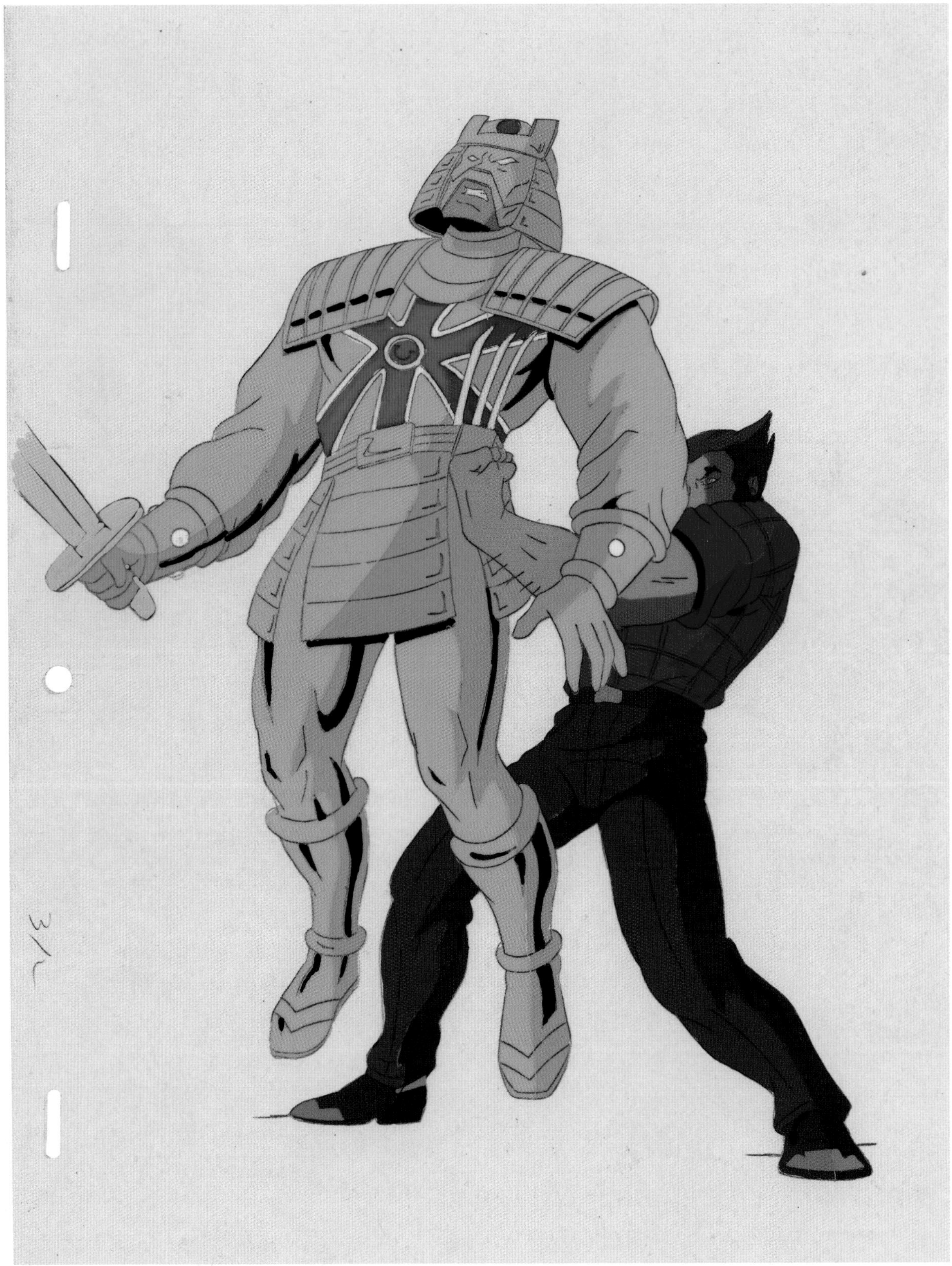

13

01 Production cel of Wolverine, Nightcrawler, and Rogue. **02** Production cels of Jubilee, Rogue, and Wolverine when seated in the Blackbird jet. **03** Production cel with the background of the interior of the Blackbird jet where Jubilee, Rogue, and Wolverine sit. **04** Character model of F.O.H. (Friends of Humanity terrorist group) High Command 1, by Mark Lewis. **05–09** Wolverine in civvies wearing Beast Halloween mask, Nightcrawler incognito, Trick-or-treater 1 (aka Spider-Man), Trick-or-treater 2 (aka Daredevil), Trick-or-treater 3 (aka Devil Dinosaur)—all by Mark Lewis. **10** Storyboard panel of the Silver Samurai. **11–12** Character models of Silver Samurai and Katana, by Frank Brunner and Lewis. **13** Production cel of Silver Samurai hoisted by Wolverine's claws. Note that because of kids' TV limits, the claws do not pierce the Silver Samurai, only his costume.

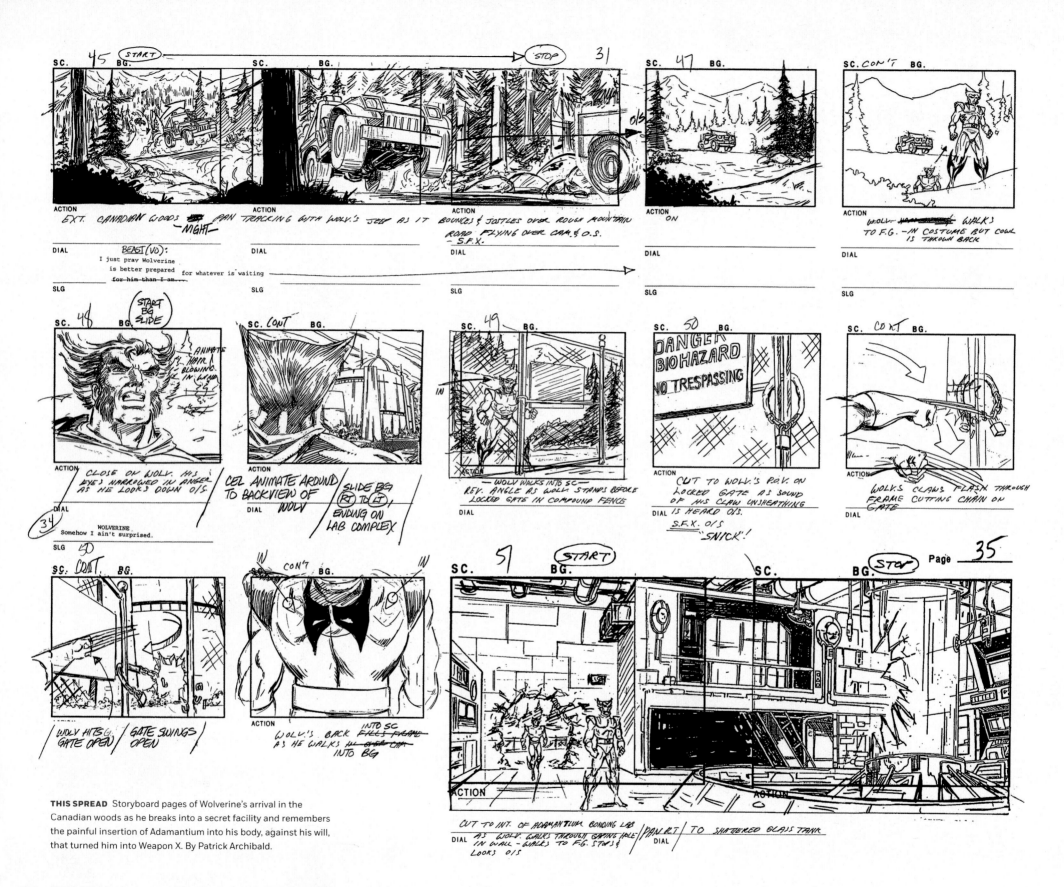

SC. 45 START ➞ STOP 31

SC. BG.

SC. BG.

SC. 47 BG.

SC. CON'T BG.

ACTION
EXT. CANADIAN WOODS ~~SC~~ PAN TRACKING WITH WOLV.'S JEEP AS IT BOUNCES & JOSTLES OVER ROUGH MOUNTAIN —NIGHT— ROAD FLYING OVER CAM. & O.S. —S.F.X.

ACTION
ON

ACTION
WOLV. ~~HAND~~ WALKS TO F.G. —IN COSTUME BUT COWL IS THROWN BACK

DIAL
BEAST (VO):
I just pray Wolverine is better prepared for whatever is waiting for him than I am...

DIAL

DIAL

DIAL

SLG

SLG

SLG

SLG

SLG

SC. 48 BG. START BG SLIDE

SC. CONT BG.

SC. 49 BG.

SC. 50 BG.

SC. CONT BG.

ACTION
CLOSE ON WOLV. HIS EYES NARROWED IN ANGER AS HE LOOKS DOWN O/S.
ANIMATE HAIR BLOWING IN WIND

ACTION
CEL ANIMATE AROUND TO BACKVIEW OF WOLV
SLIDE BG (RT) TO (LT) ENDING ON LAB COMPLEX

ACTION
—WOLV WALKS INTO SC—
REV. ANGLE AS WOLV. STANDS BEFORE LOCKED GATE IN COMPOUND FENCE

ACTION
CUT TO WOLV.'S P.O.V. ON LOCKED GATE AS SOUND OF HIS CLAW UNSHEATHING IS HEARD O/S.
S.F.X. O/S "SNICK"!

ACTION
WOLV.'S CLAWS FLASH THROUGH FRAME CUTTING CHAIN ON GATE

DIAL
34
WOLVERINE
Somehow I ain't surprised.

DIAL

DIAL

DIAL

SLG 50

SC. CONT BG.

SC. CONT BG.

SC. 51 BG. START

SC. BG. STOP   Page 35

ACTION
WOLV HITS & GATE OPEN / GATE SWINGS OPEN /

ACTION
WOLV.'S BACK FILLS FRAME AS HE WALKS ~~ALL OVER THAT~~ INTO SC INTO BG

ACTION
CUT TO INT. OF ADAMANTIUM BONDING LAB AS WOLV. WALKS THROUGH GAPING HOLE IN WALL - WALKS TO F.G. STOPS & LOOKS O/S
PAN RT / TO SHATTERED GLASS TANK

DIAL

DIAL

THIS SPREAD Storyboard pages of Wolverine's arrival in the Canadian woods as he breaks into a secret facility and remembers the painful insertion of Adamantium into his body, against his will, that turned him into Weapon X. By Patrick Archibald.

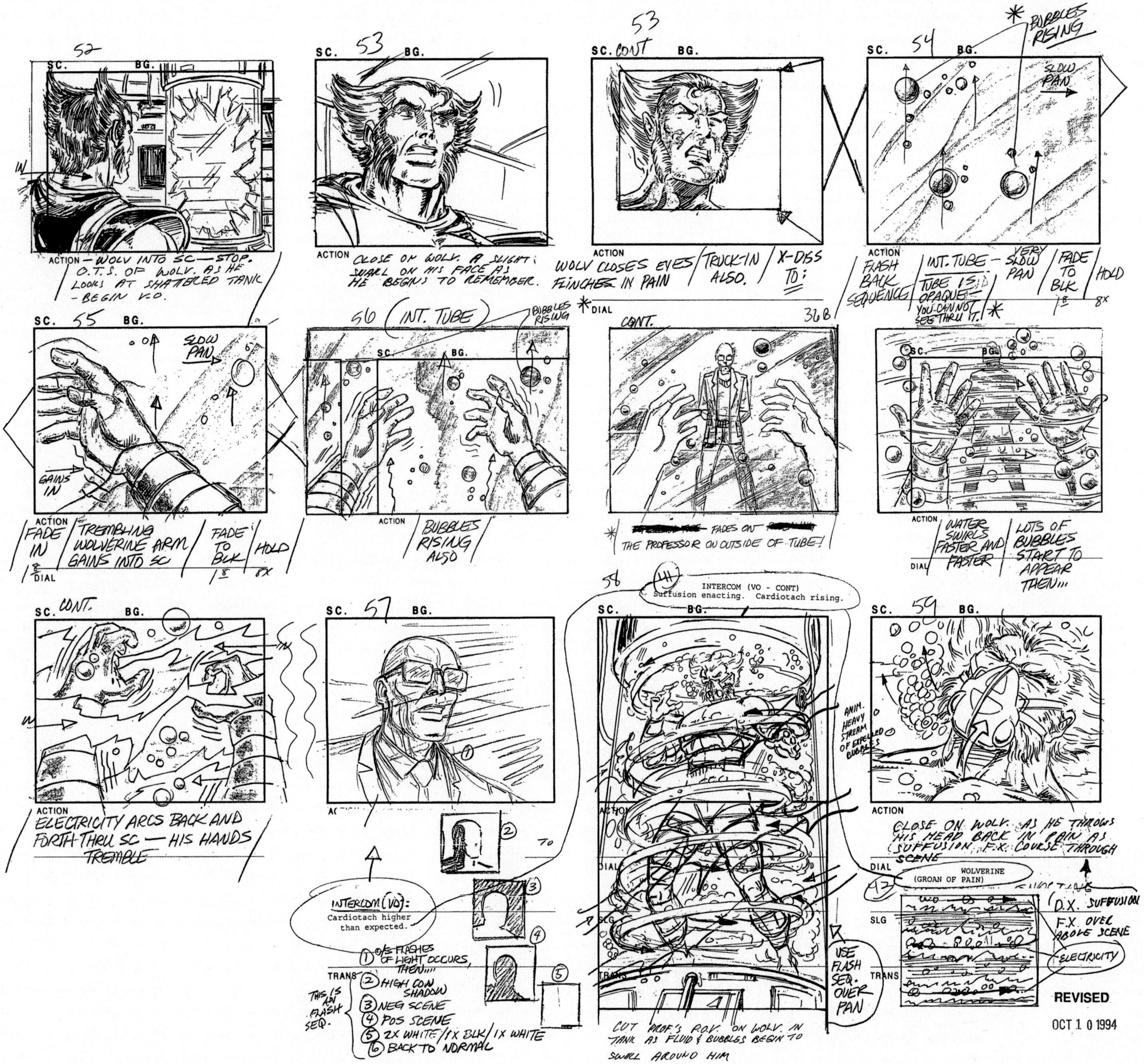
52
IN
WOLV INTO SC — STOP. O.T.S. OF WOLV. AS HE LOOKS AT SHATTERED TANK — BEGIN V.O.
53
CLOSE ON WOLV. A SLIGHT SWIRL ON HIS FACE AS HE BEGINS TO REMEMBER.
53 CONT
WOLV CLOSES EYES FLINCHES IN PAIN
TRUCK-IN ALSO.
X-DISS TO:
54
BUBBLES RISING
SLOW PAN
FLASH BACK SEQUENCE
INT. TUBE — TUBE IS OPAQUE — YOU CANNOT SEE THRU IT.
VERY SLOW PAN
FADE TO BLK
HOLD
55
SLOW PAN
GAINS IN
FADE IN
TREMBLING WOLVERINE ARM GAINS INTO SC
FADE TO BLK
HOLD
56 (INT. TUBE)
BUBBLES RISING
BUBBLES RISING ALSO
CONT.
36B
FADES ON
THE PROFESSOR ON OUTSIDE OF TUBE!
WATER SWIRLS FASTER AND FASTER
LOTS OF BUBBLES START TO APPEAR THEN...
CONT.
IN
ELECTRICITY ARCS BACK AND FORTH THRU SC — HIS HANDS TREMBLE
57
INTERCOM (VO):
Cardiotach higher than expected.
1 O/S FLASHES OF LIGHT OCCURS, THEN...
2 HIGH CON SHADOW
3 NEG SCENE
4 POS SCENE
5 2X WHITE / 1X BLK / 1X WHITE
6 BACK TO NORMAL
THIS IS AN FLASH SEQ.
58
INTERCOM (VO - CONT)
Suffusion enacting. Cardiotach rising.
ANIM. HEAVY STREAM OF EXPELLED BUBBLES
USE FLASH SEQ. OVER PAN
CUT PROF'S P.O.V. ON WOLV. IN TANK AS FLUID & BUBBLES BEGIN TO SWIRL AROUND HIM
59
CLOSE ON WOLV. AS HE THROWS HIS HEAD BACK IN PAIN AS SUFFUSION F.X. COURSE THROUGH SCENE
WOLVERINE
(GROAN OF PAIN)
ELECTRICITY
REVISED
OCT 1 0 1994

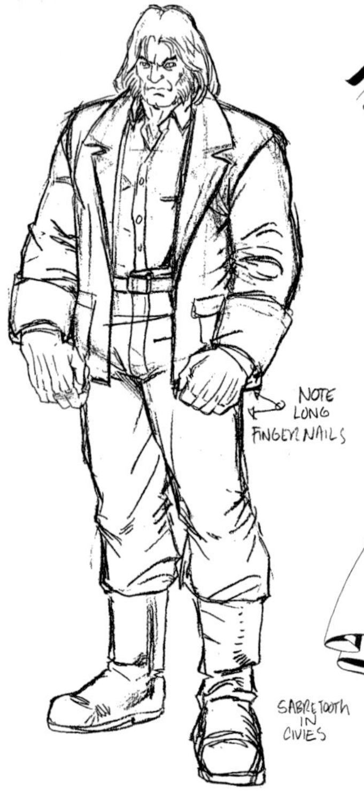
NOTE
LONG
FINGERNAILS
SABRETOOTH
IN
CIVIES

01

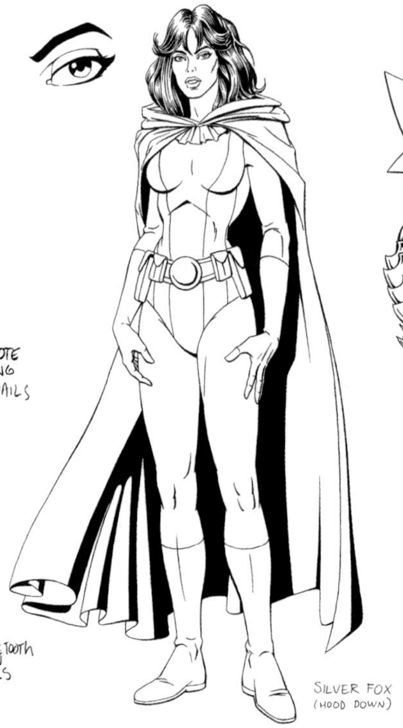
SILVER FOX
(HOOD DOWN)

02

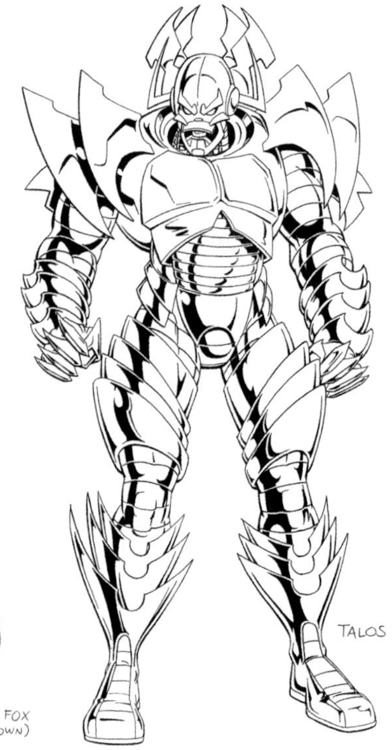
TALOS

03

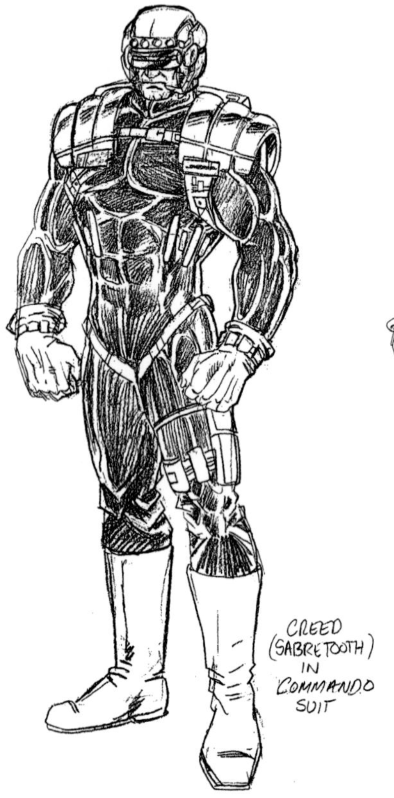
CREED
(SABRETOOTH)
IN
COMMANDO
SUIT

04

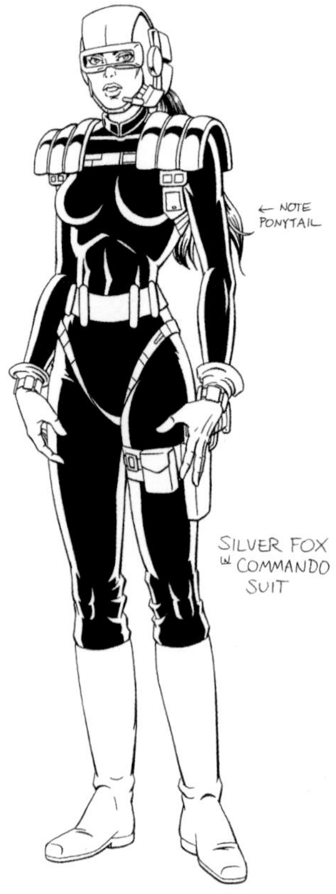
NOTE
PONYTAIL
SILVER FOX
IN COMMANDO
SUIT

05

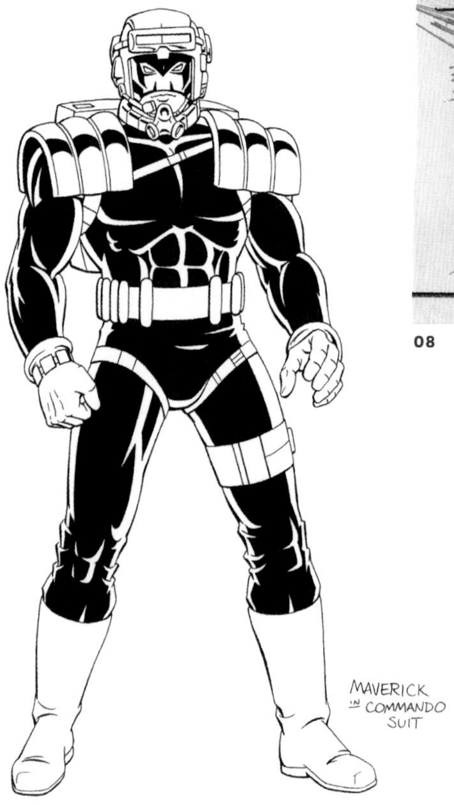
MAVERICK
IN COMMANDO
SUIT

06

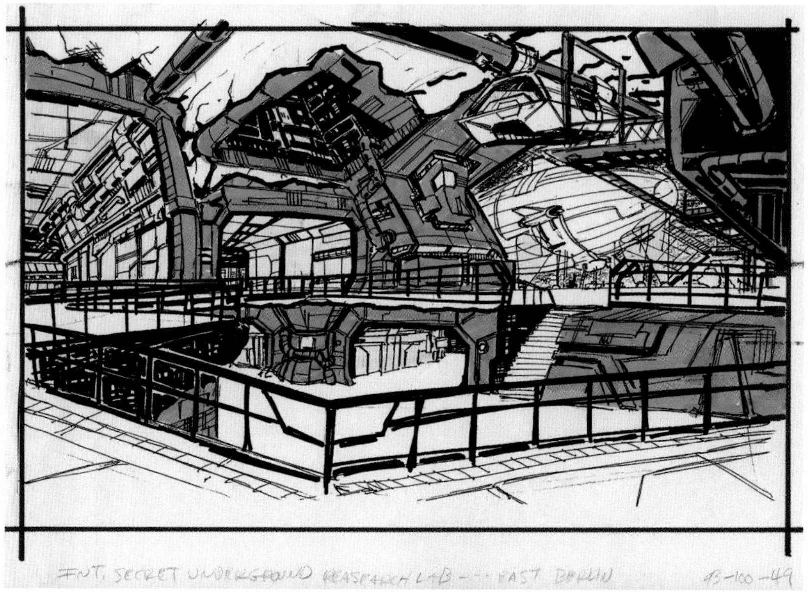

07

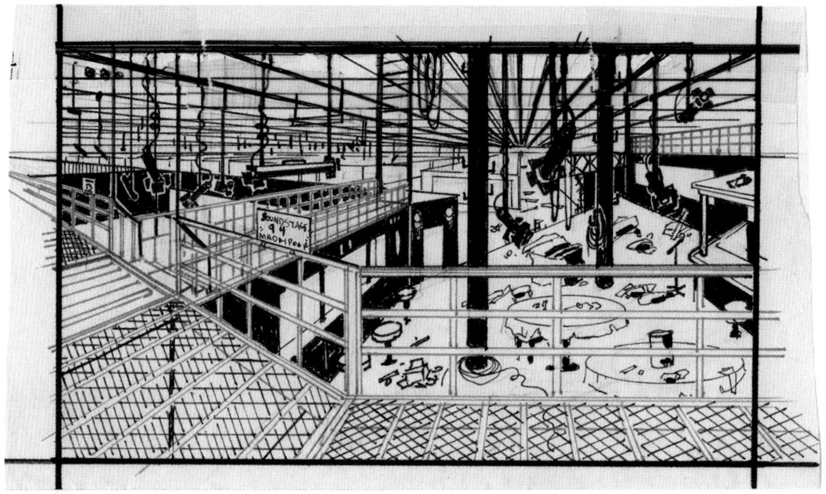
SOUNDSTAGE
94

08

01 Character models of Sabretooth in civvies, by Frank Brunner. **02–03** Character models of Silver Fox (hood down) and Talos by Brunner and Mark Lewis. **04** Character model of Creed (Sabretooth) in commando suit by Brunner. **05–06** Character models of Silver Fox and Maverick in commando suits by Brunner and Lewis. **07–08** Layouts of interior secret underground research and studio area by Frank Squillace. **09–12** Production cels of Beast with Wolverine; Wolverine struggling with memories in front of the set for Dan's Diner; Talos; and a tree with a carving of a heart with the names "Logan and Silver Fox"—proof that Wolverine's feelings for her had been authentic.

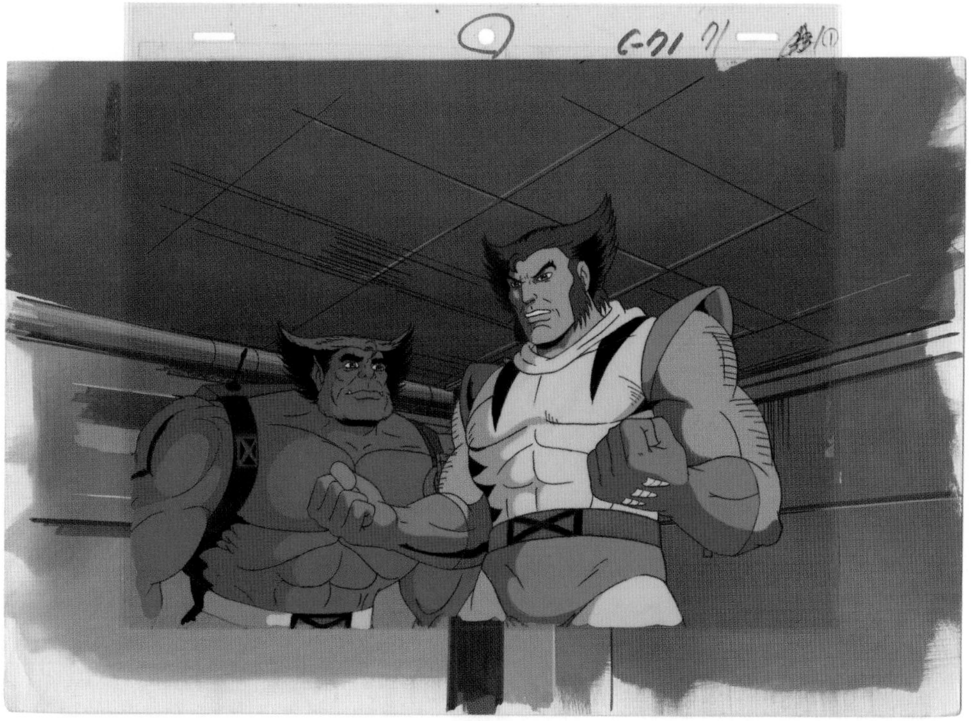

09

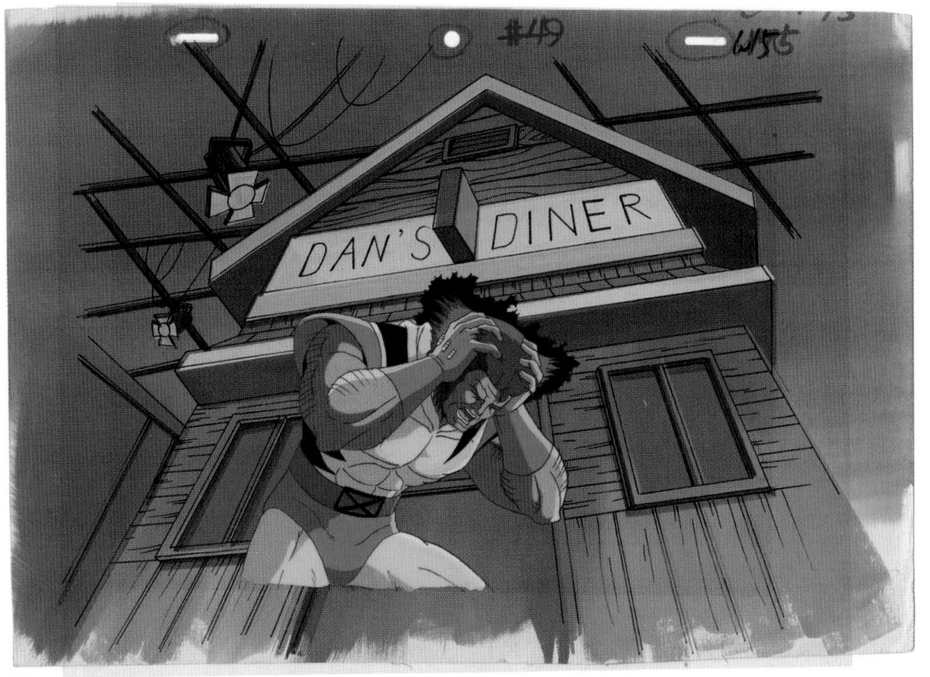
DAN'S DINER

10

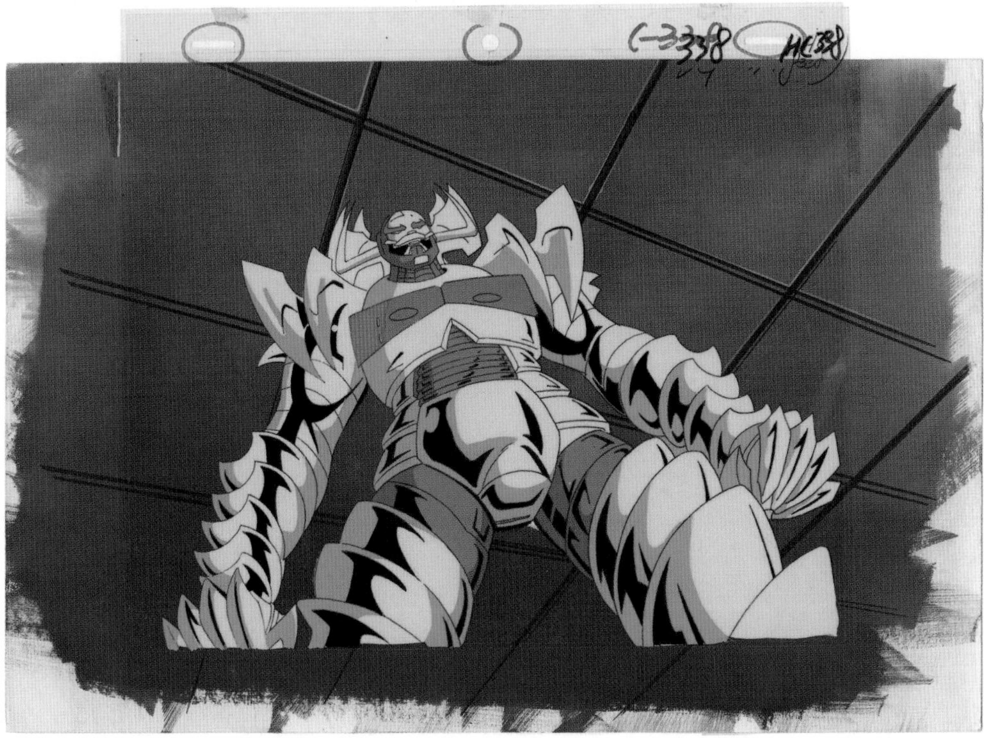

11

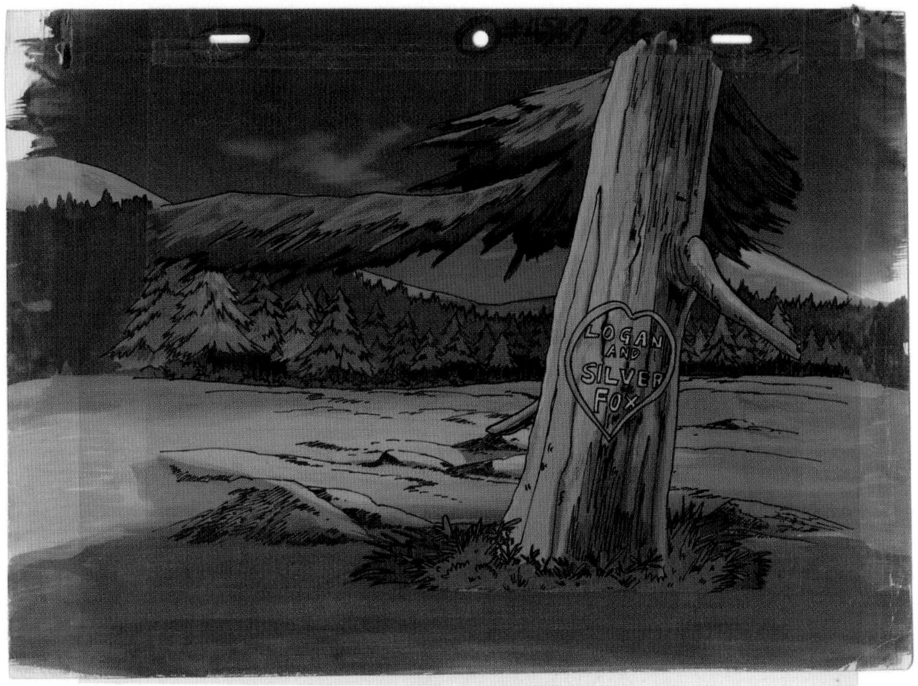
LOGAN AND SILVER FOX

12

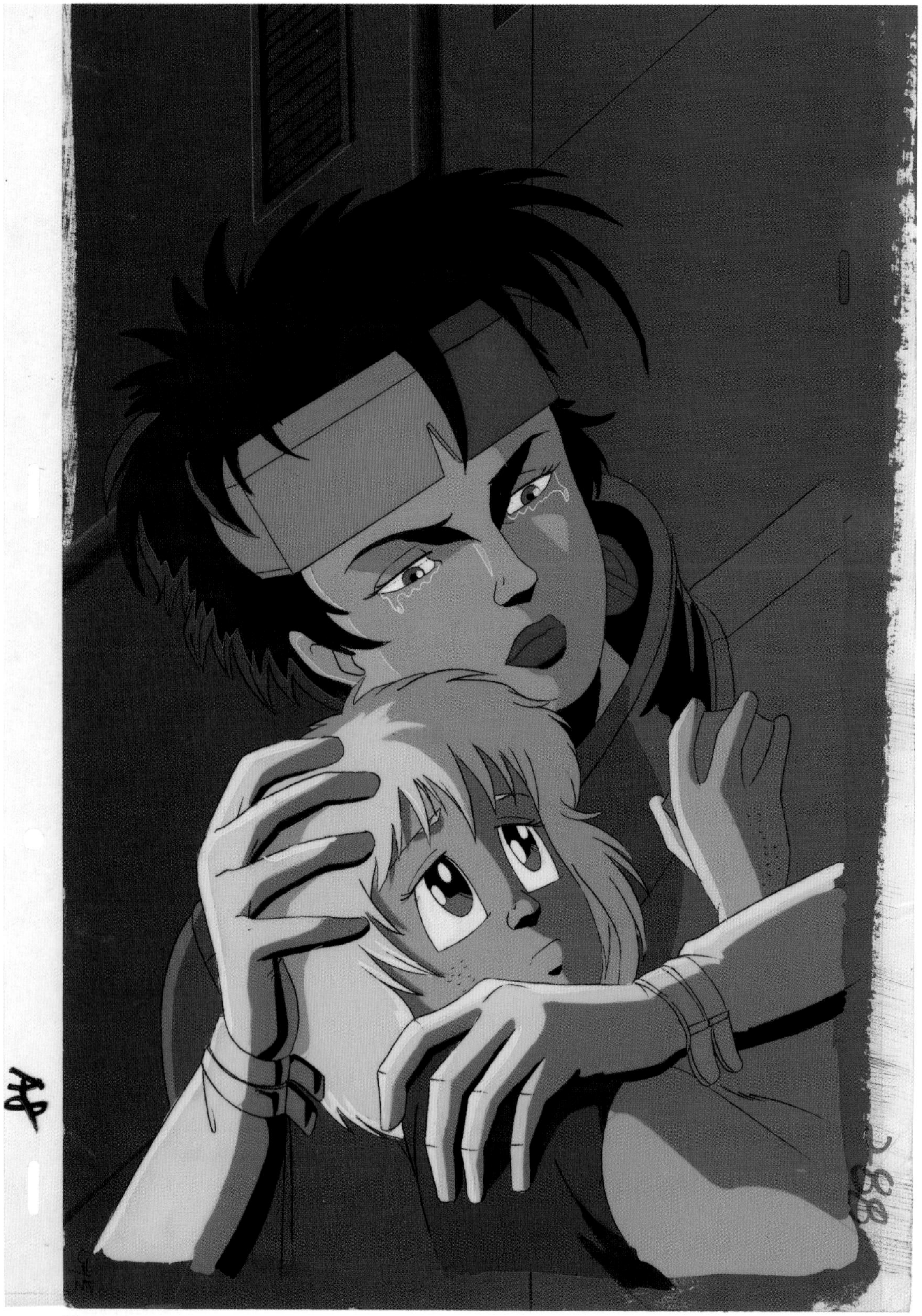

01

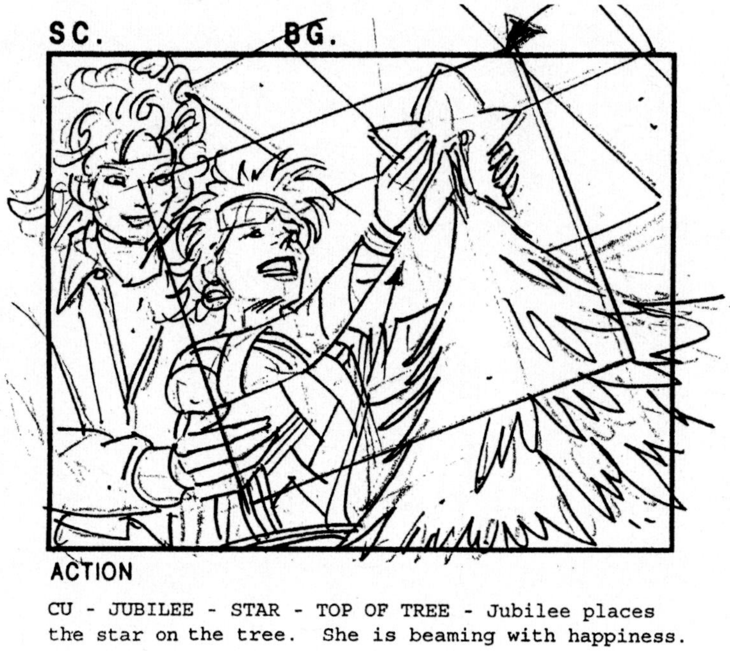
SC.
BG.
ACTION
CU - JUBILEE - STAR - TOP OF TREE - Jubilee places the star on the tree. She is beaming with happiness.

02

01 Production cel of Jubilee comforting a Morlock child.
02 Storyboard panel of Rogue holding up Jubilee so she can place the star on top of the Christmas tree at the X-Mansion, by Romeo Francisco.
03-04 Background concept and Apocalypse altar by Frank Squillace.
05 Layout of exterior ancient Egyptian pyramid by Zhaoping Wei.
06-07 Character models of Bender by Frank Brunner and Mark Lewis.
08 Character model of Rogue in bridesmaid's dress by Brunner and Lewis.
09 Character model of Psylocke—note "eye detail"—by Lewis.

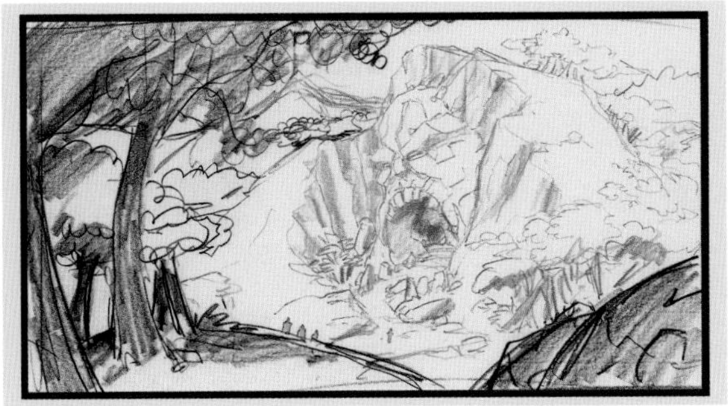

03

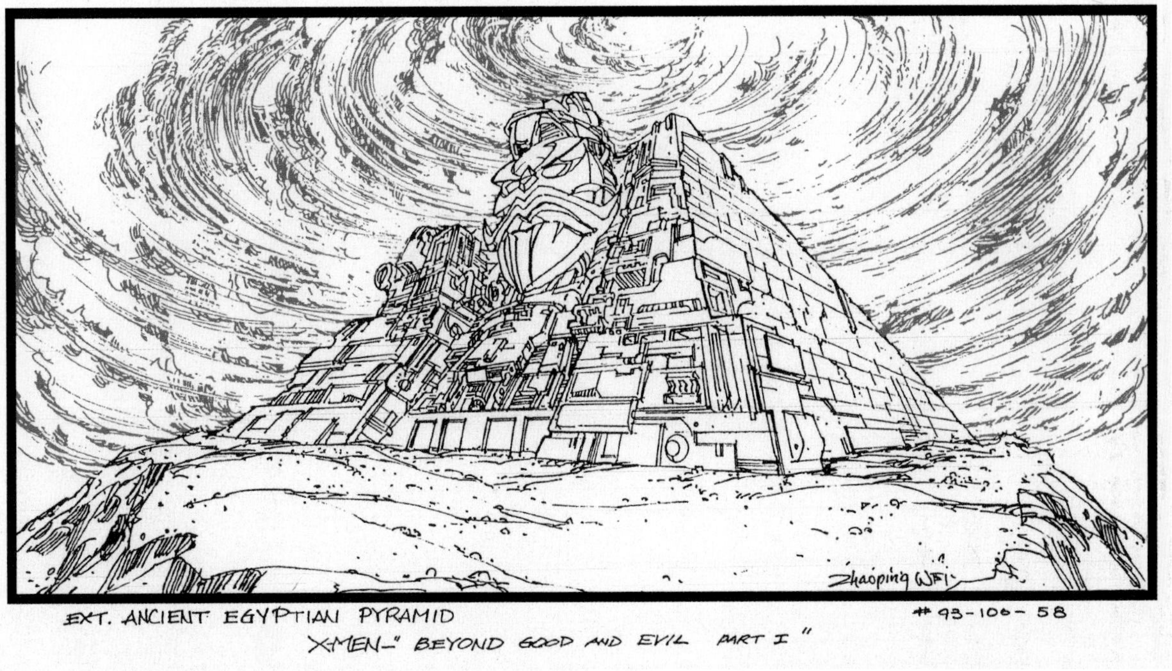
Zhaoping Wei
EXT. ANCIENT EGYPTIAN PYRAMID
#93-106-58
X-MEN-" BEYOND GOOD AND EVIL PART I"

05

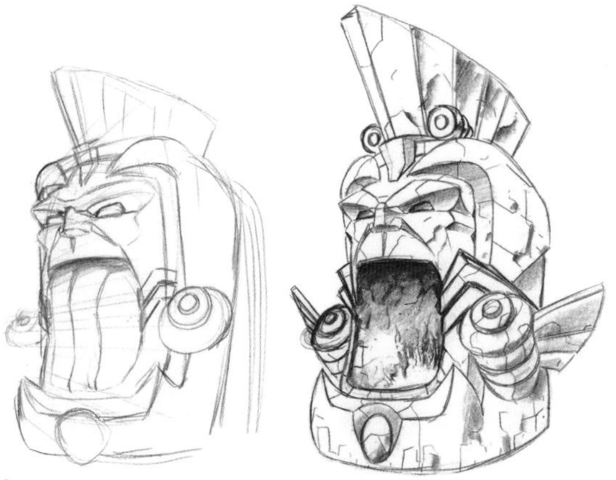

04

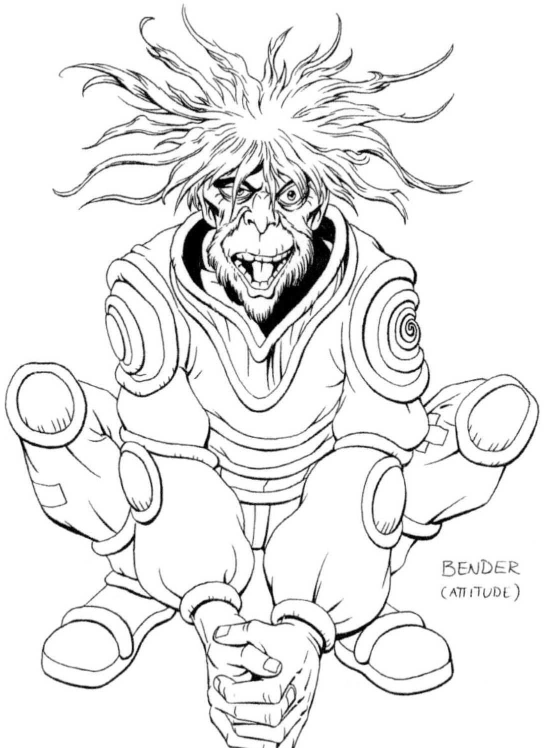
BENDER
(ATTITUDE)

06

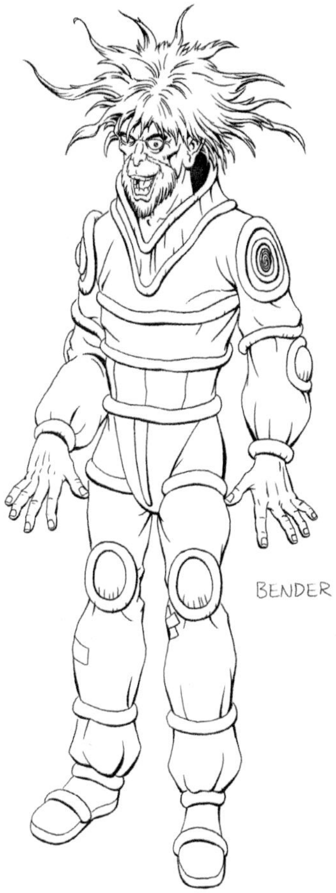
BENDER

07

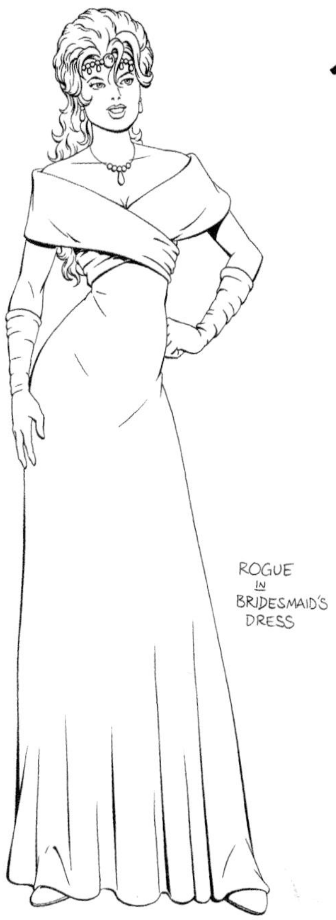
ROGUE
IN
BRIDESMAID'S
DRESS

08

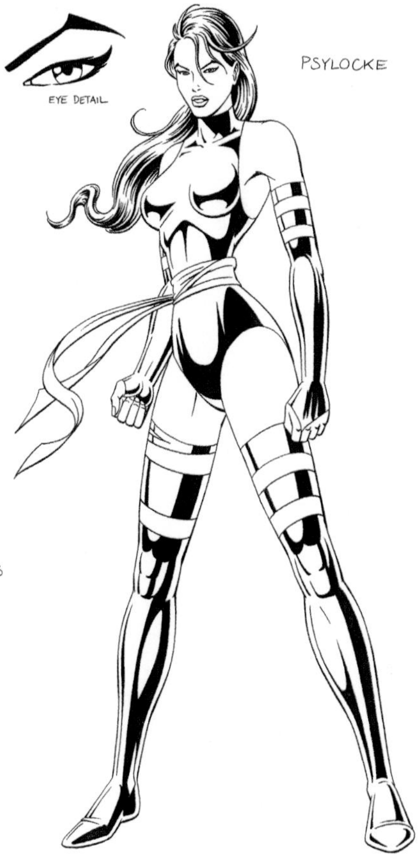
EYE DETAIL
PSYLOCKE

09

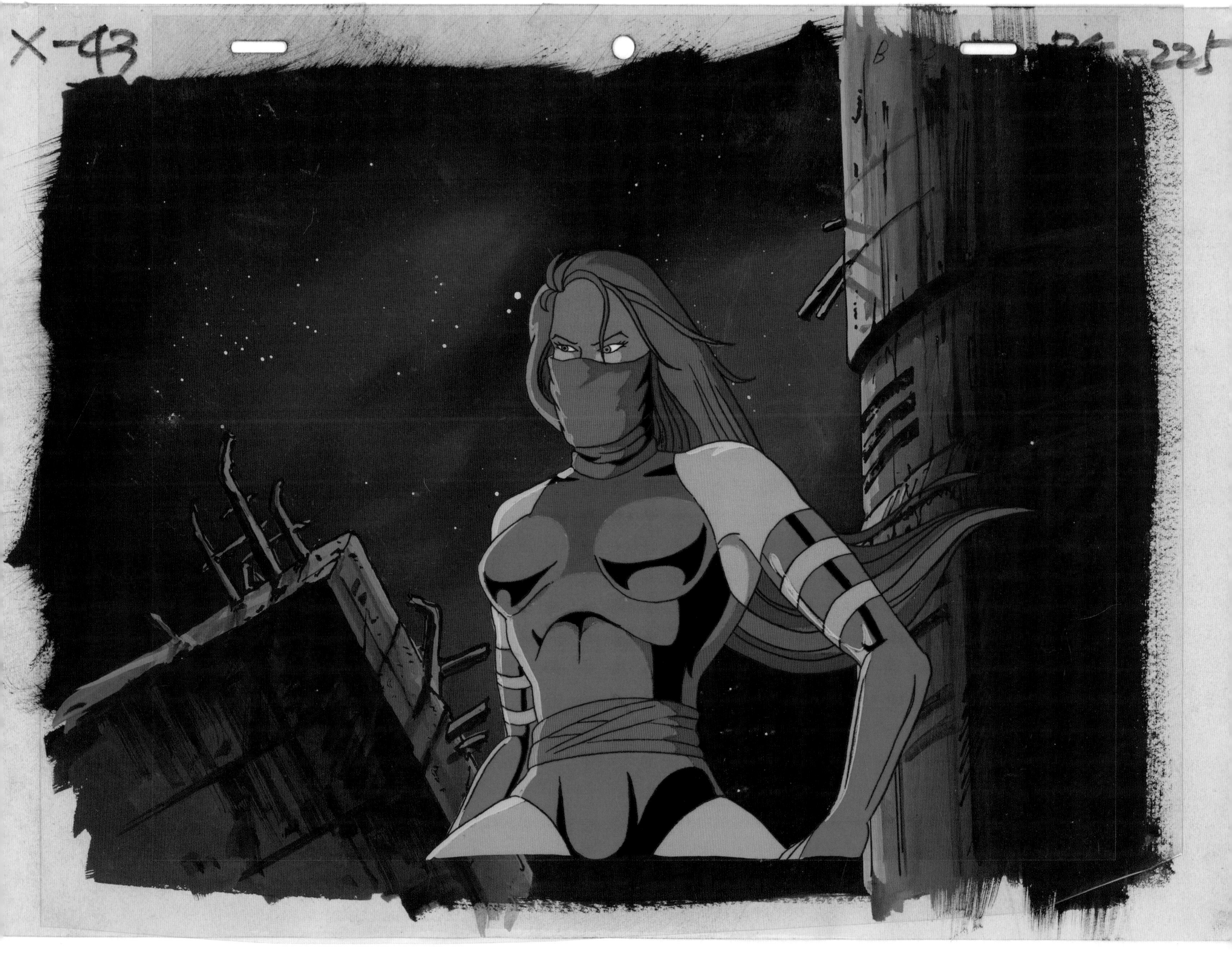
X-43

OPPOSITE Production cel of Psylocke. **01** Character model of Archangel, pencil rough by Frank Brunner and Mark Lewis pasted to an old drawing of the wings. **02** Production cel of Apocalypse brooding. **02** Layout of interior of the Graymalkin Monorail Bay by Zhaoping Wei. **04** Character model of Robot Guard by Frank Brunner.

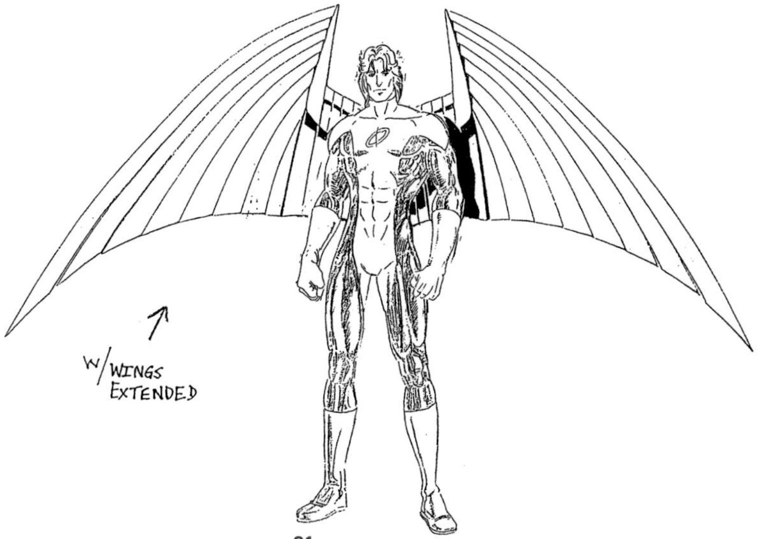
W/WINGS
EXTENDED

01

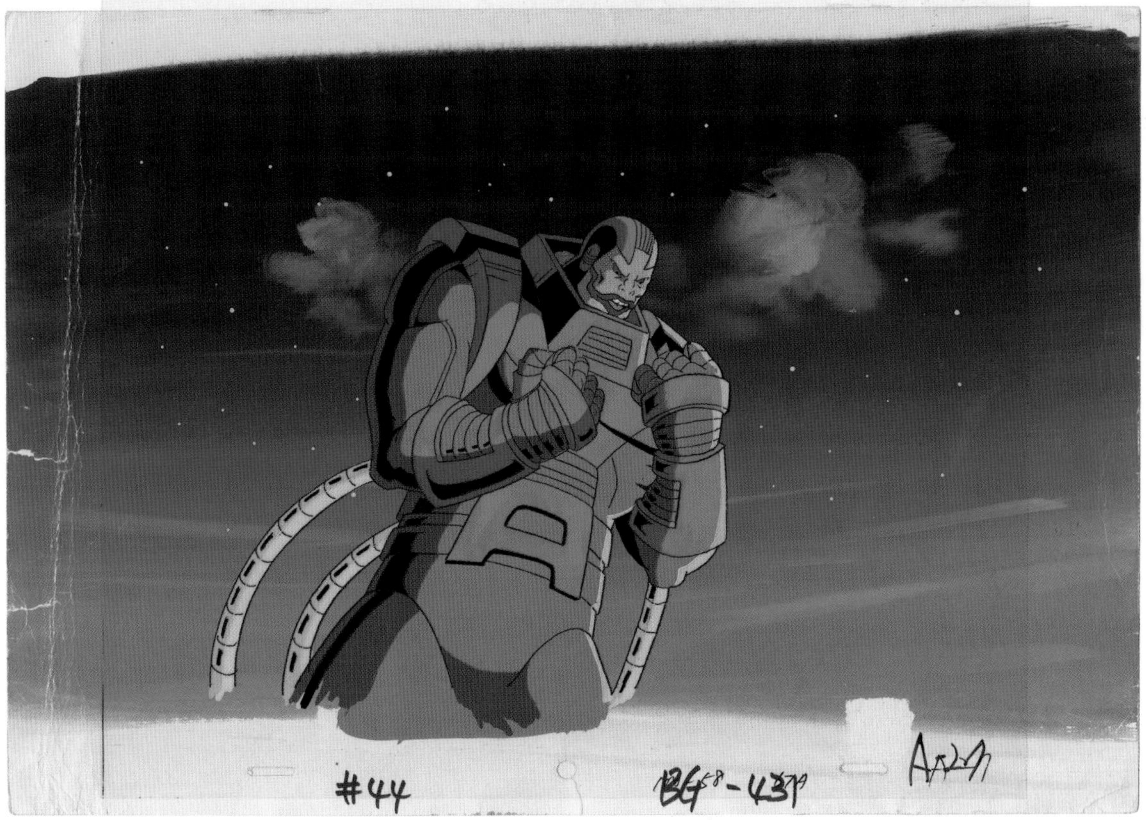
#44

02

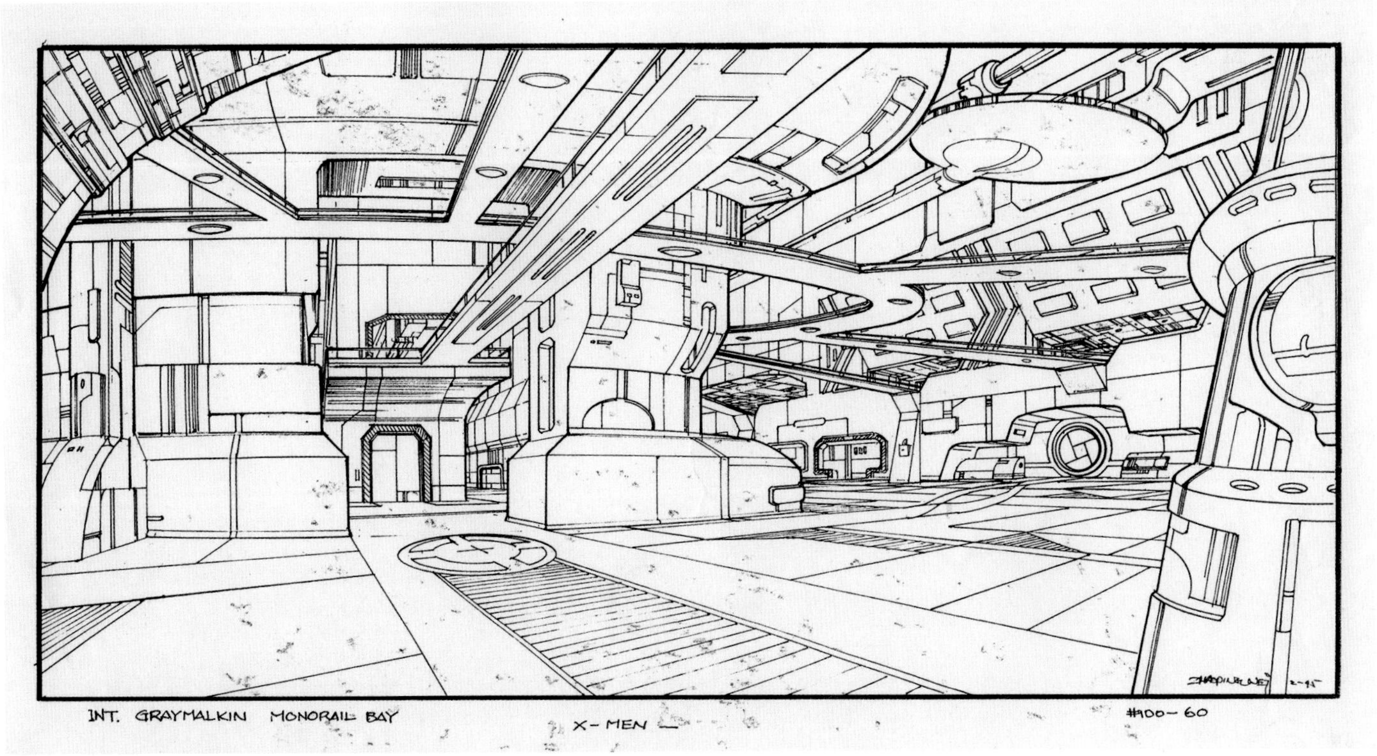
INT. GRAYMALKIN MONORAIL BAY
X-MEN
#400-60

03

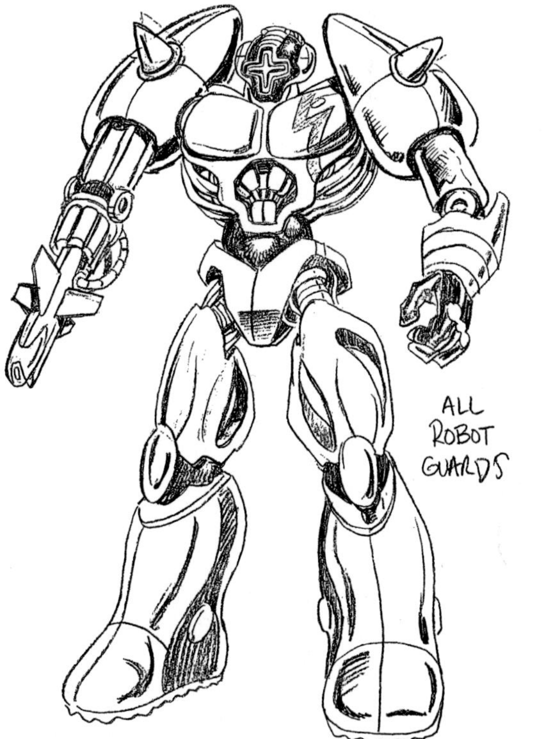
ALL
ROBOT
GUARDS

04

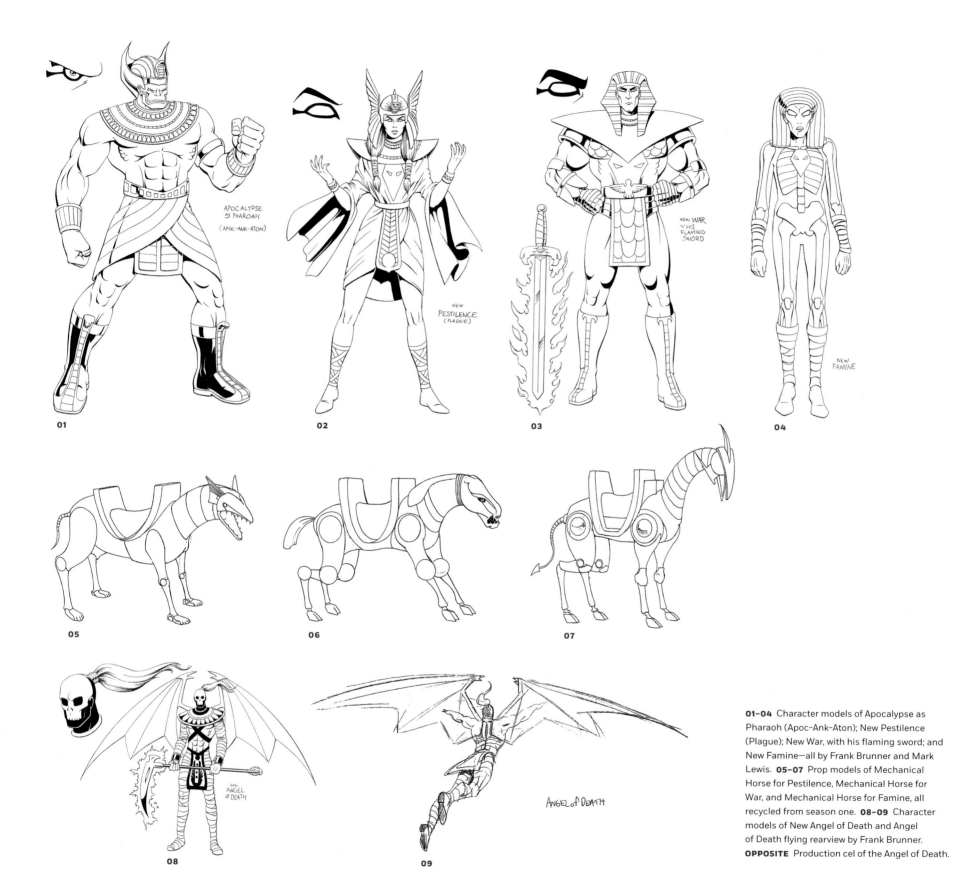

01 APOCALYPSE AS PHAROAH (APOC·ANK·ATON)

02 NEW PESTILENCE (PLAGUE)

03 NEW WAR W/ HIS FLAMING SWORD

04 NEW FAMINE

08 NEW ANGEL OF DEATH

09 ANGEL OF DEATH

01-04 Character models of Apocalypse as Pharaoh (Apoc-Ank-Aton); New Pestilence (Plague); New War, with his flaming sword; and New Famine—all by Frank Brunner and Mark Lewis. 05-07 Prop models of Mechanical Horse for Pestilence, Mechanical Horse for War, and Mechanical Horse for Famine, all recycled from season one. 08-09 Character models of New Angel of Death and Angel of Death flying rearview by Frank Brunner. OPPOSITE Production cel of the Angel of Death.

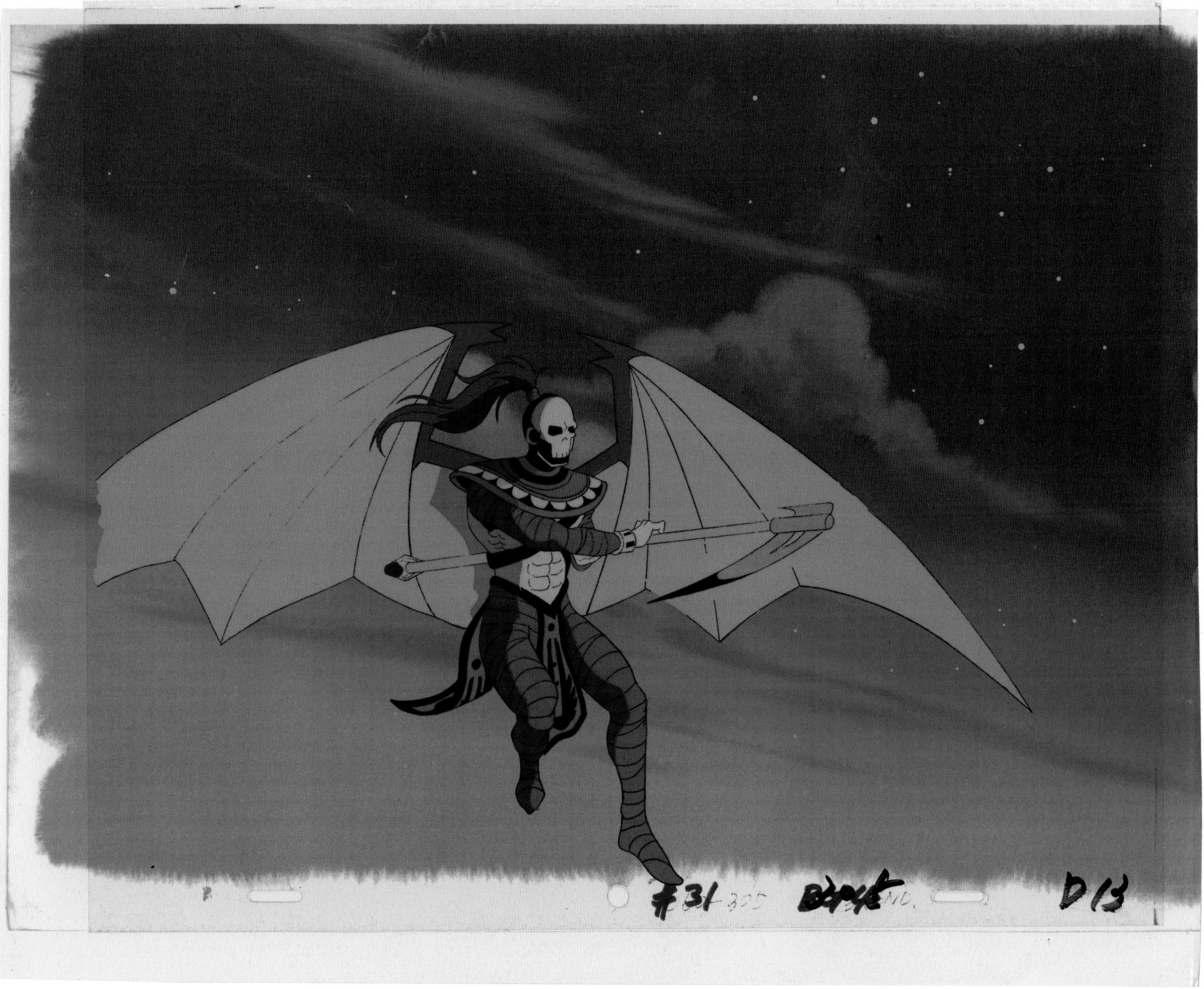
#31
D13

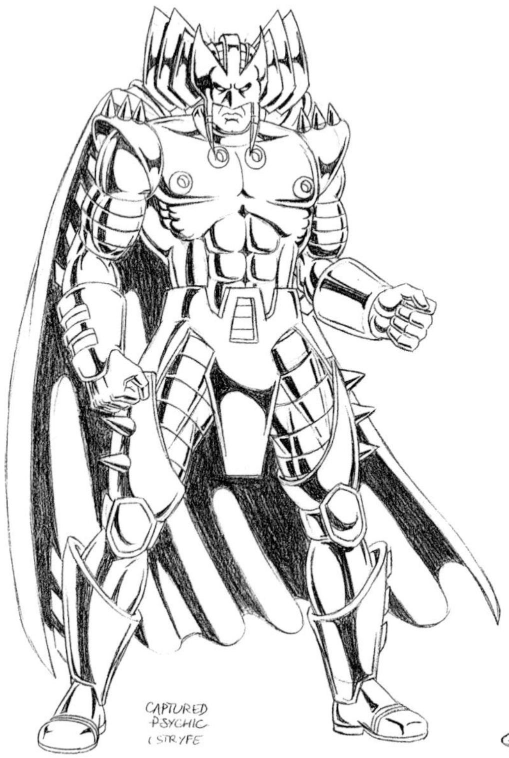
CAPTURED PSYCHIC (STRYFE

01

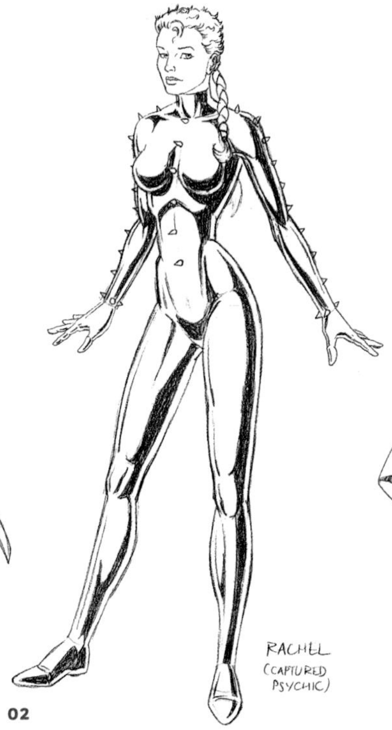
RACHEL (CAPTURED PSYCHIC)

02

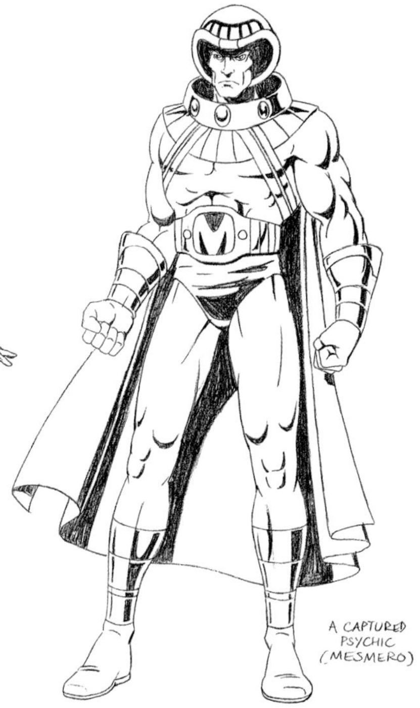
A CAPTURED PSYCHIC (MESMERO)

03

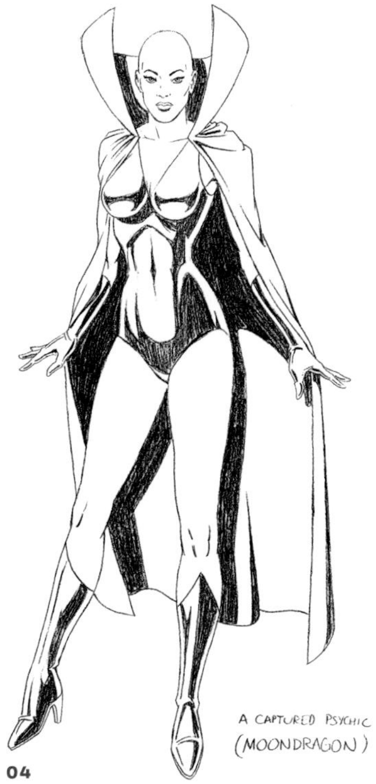
A CAPTURED PSYCHIC (MOONDRAGON)

04

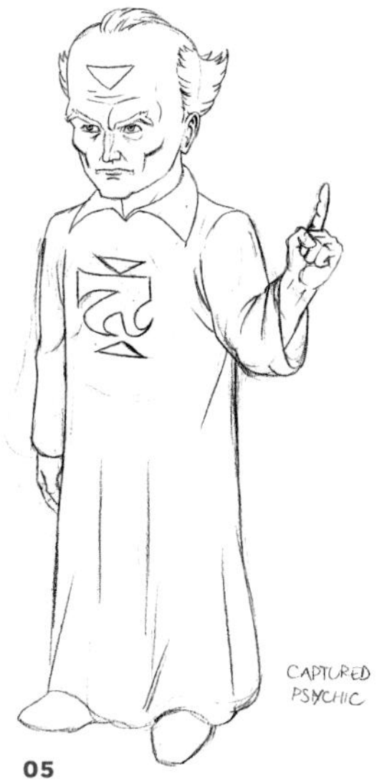
CAPTURED PSYCHIC

05

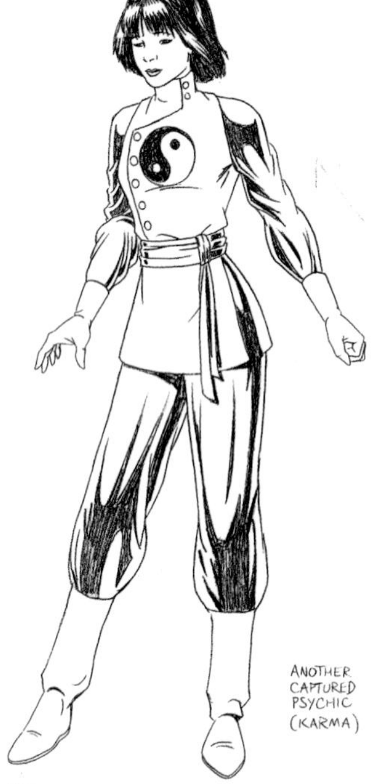
ANOTHER CAPTURED PSYCHIC (KARMA)

06

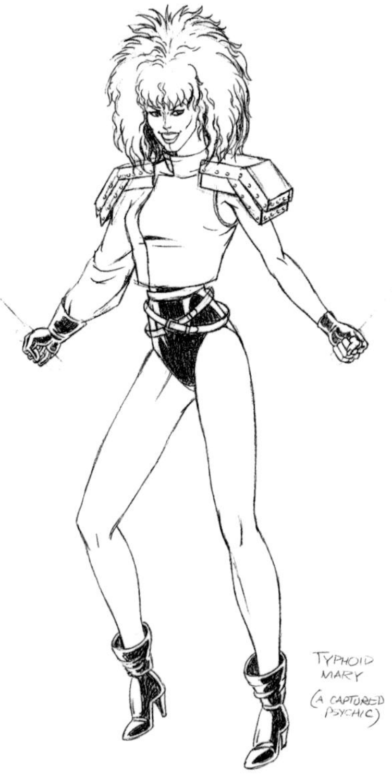
TYPHOID MARY
(A CAPTURED PSYCHIC)

07

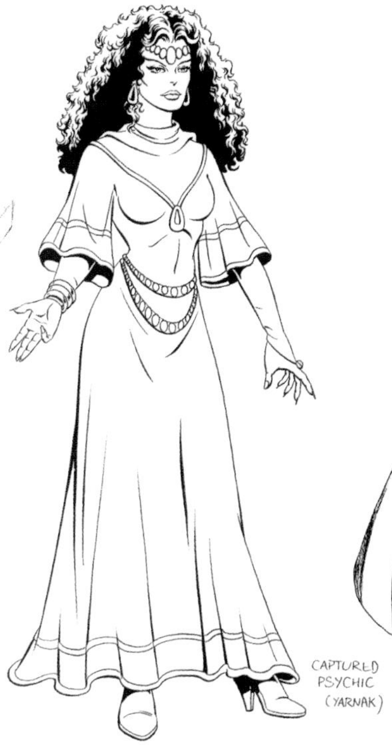
CAPTURED PSYCHIC (YARNAK)

08

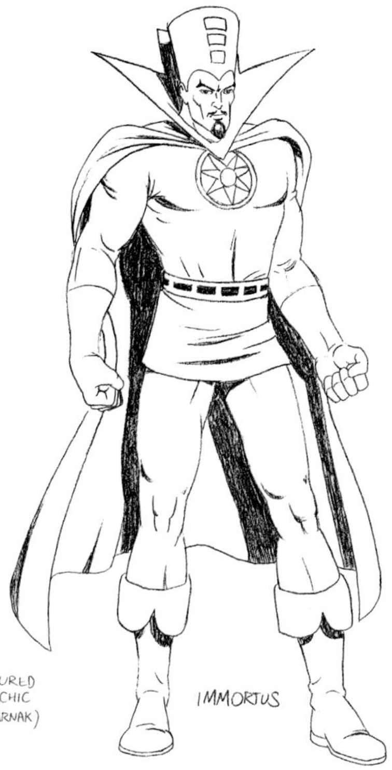
IMMORTUS

09

01–02 Character models of Captured Psychic (aka Stryfe) and Captured Physic (aka Rachel Summers), both by Frank Brunner and Mark Lewis. **03** Character model of Captured Psychic (aka Mesmero) by Lewis. **04** Character model of Captured Psychic (aka Moondragon) by Brunner and Lewis. **05** Character model of Captured Psychic, by Lewis. **06** Character model of Captured Psychic (aka Karma) by Lewis. **07** Character model of Captured Psychic (aka Typhoid Mary), by Lewis. **08** Character model of Captured Psychic (aka Yarnak) by Lewis. **09** Character model of Immortus by Brunner and Lewis. **10** Production cel of Mister Sinister. **11** Layout of interior X-Mansion holding cell where Wolverine confronts Sabretooth. Frank Squillace designed and cleaned the left side (the hallway leading to an open door). **12** Artist's Post-it note of Sabretooth with production details, by Squillace. **13** Storyboard panel showing the Axis of Time as it explodes, by Squillace.

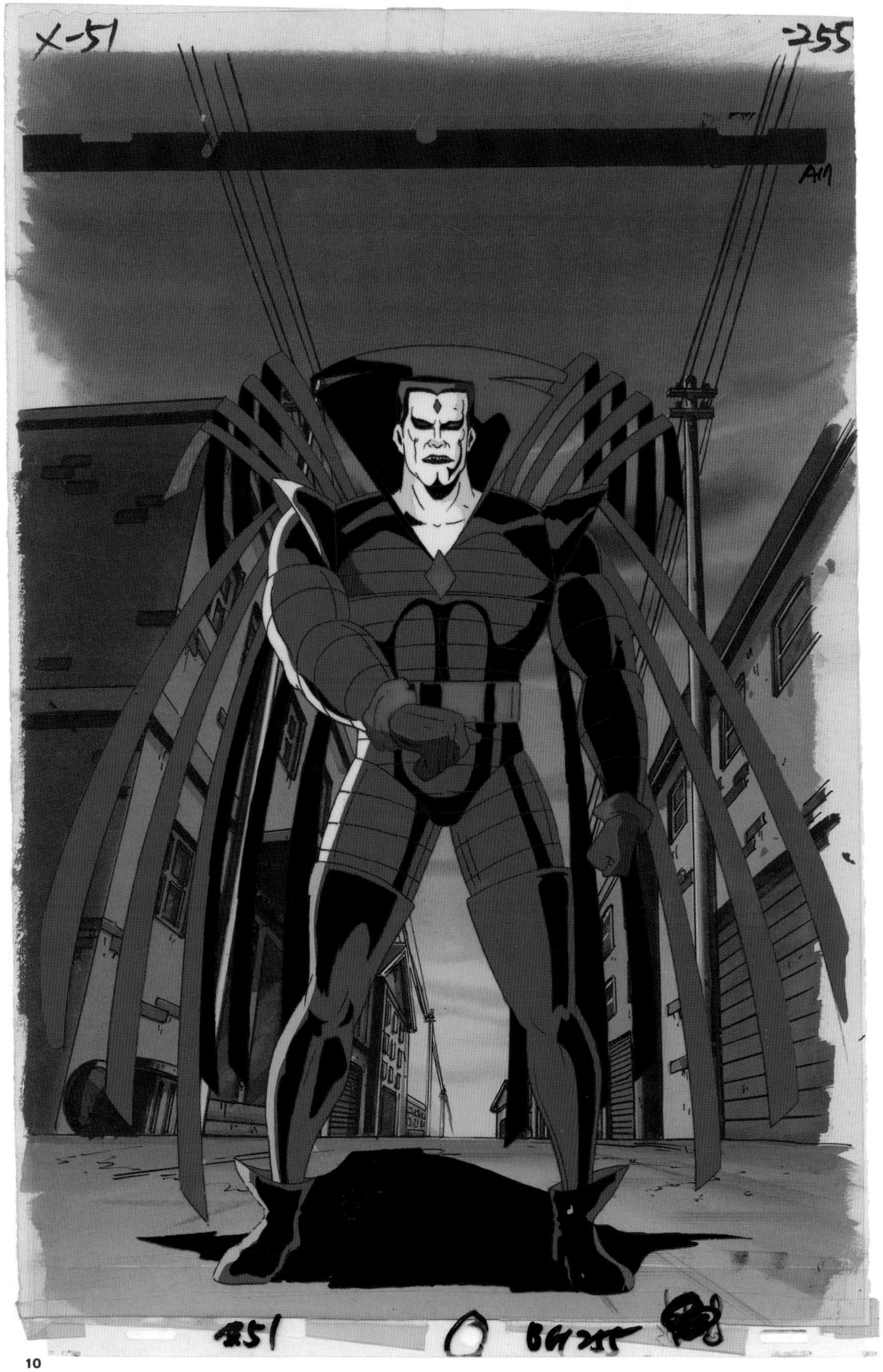
X-51
255
10

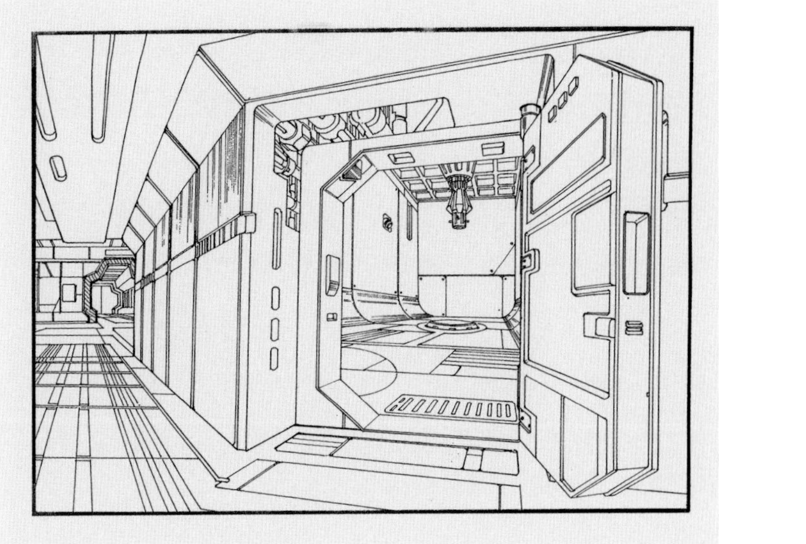
11

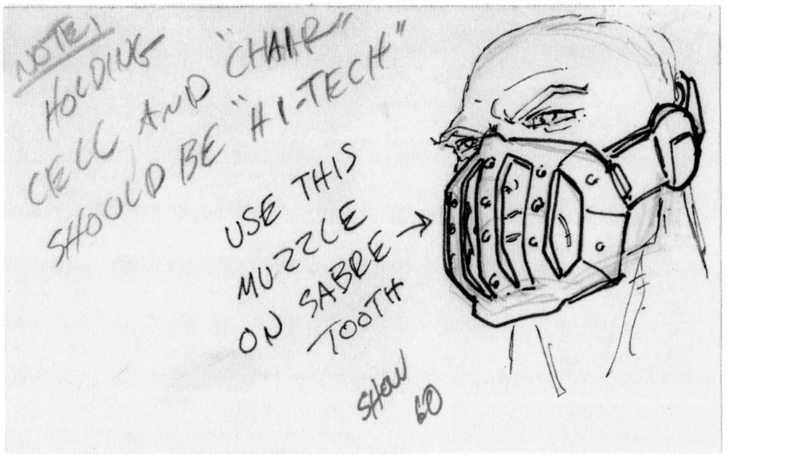
NOTE!
HOLDING CELL AND "CHAIR" SHOULD BE "HI-TECH"
USE THIS MUZZLE ON SABRE TOOTH →
SHOW 60
12

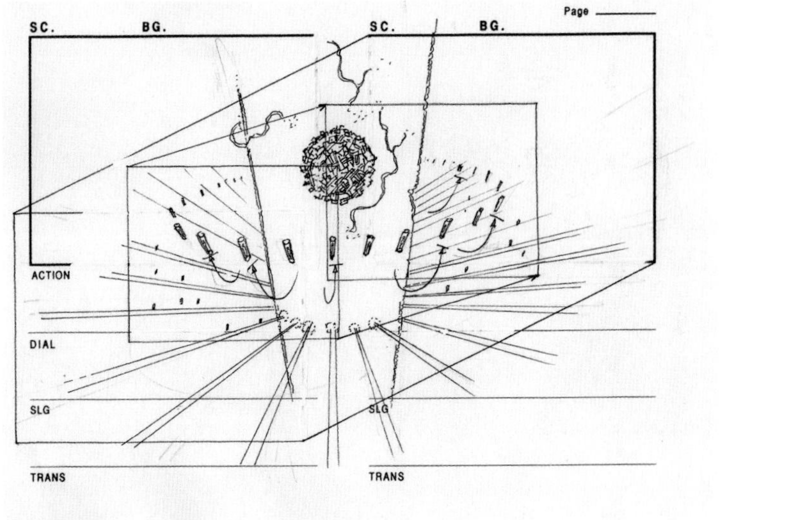
Page
SC.
BG.
SC.
BG.
ACTION
DIAL
SLG
TRANS
SLG
TRANS
13

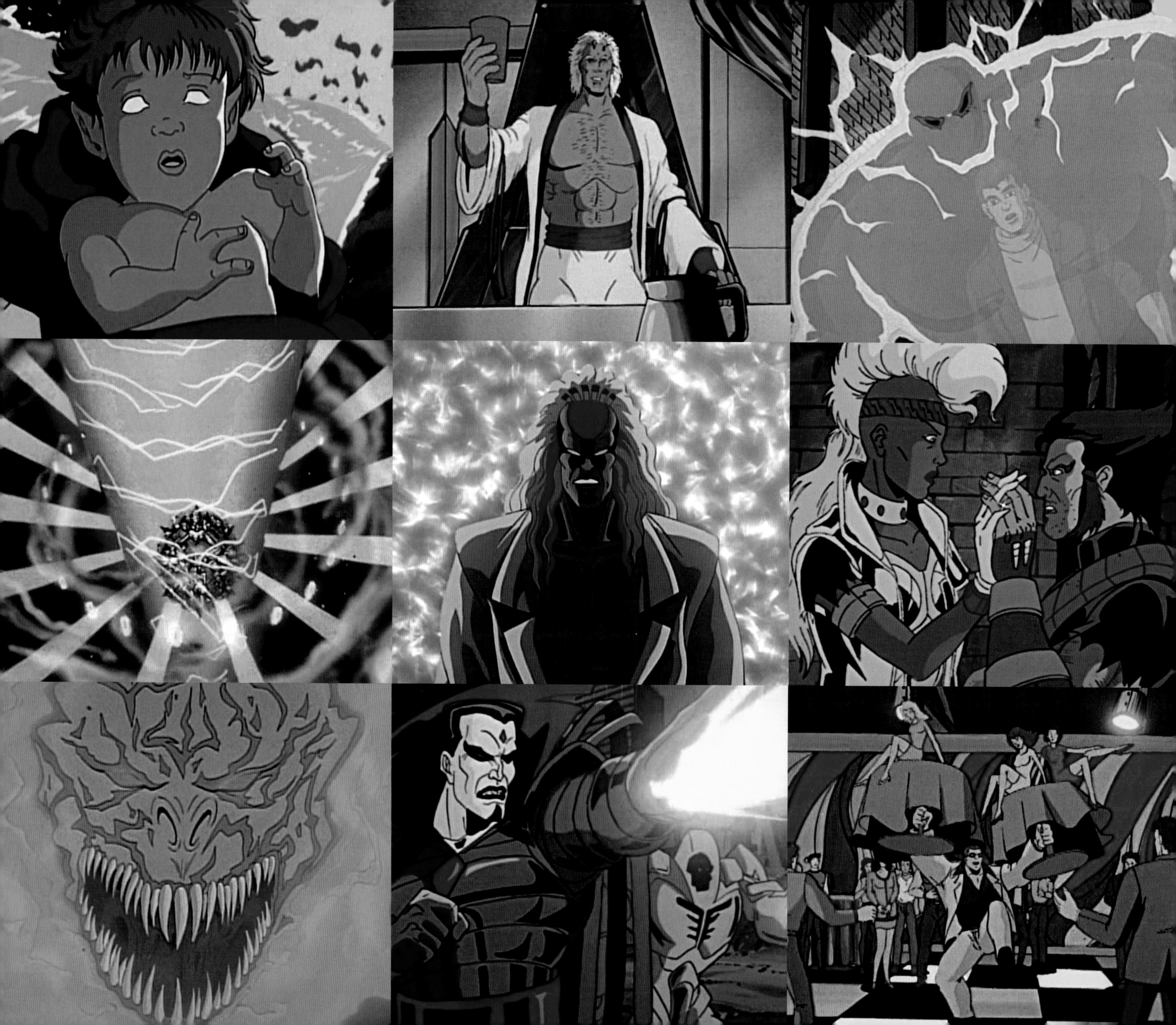

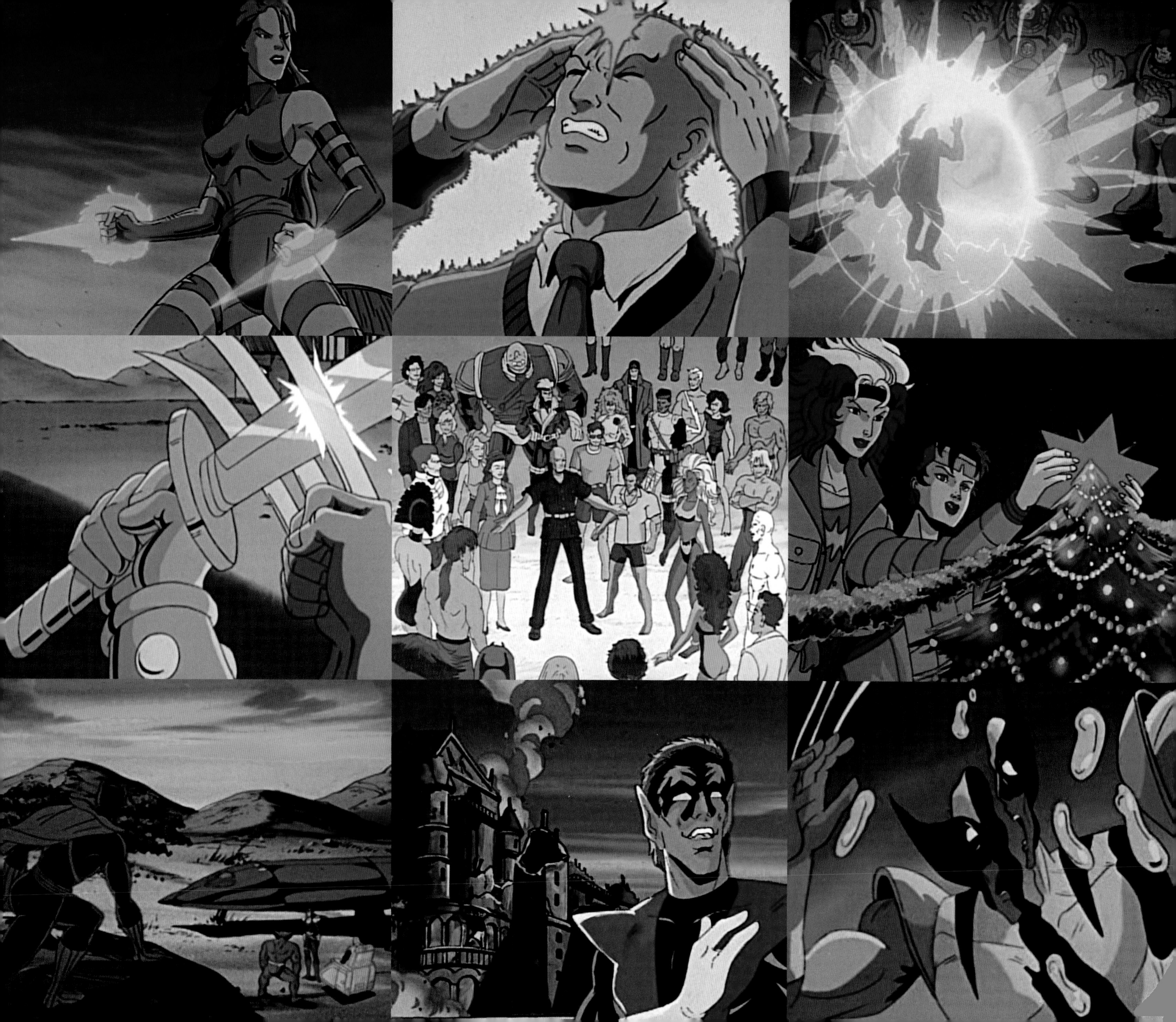

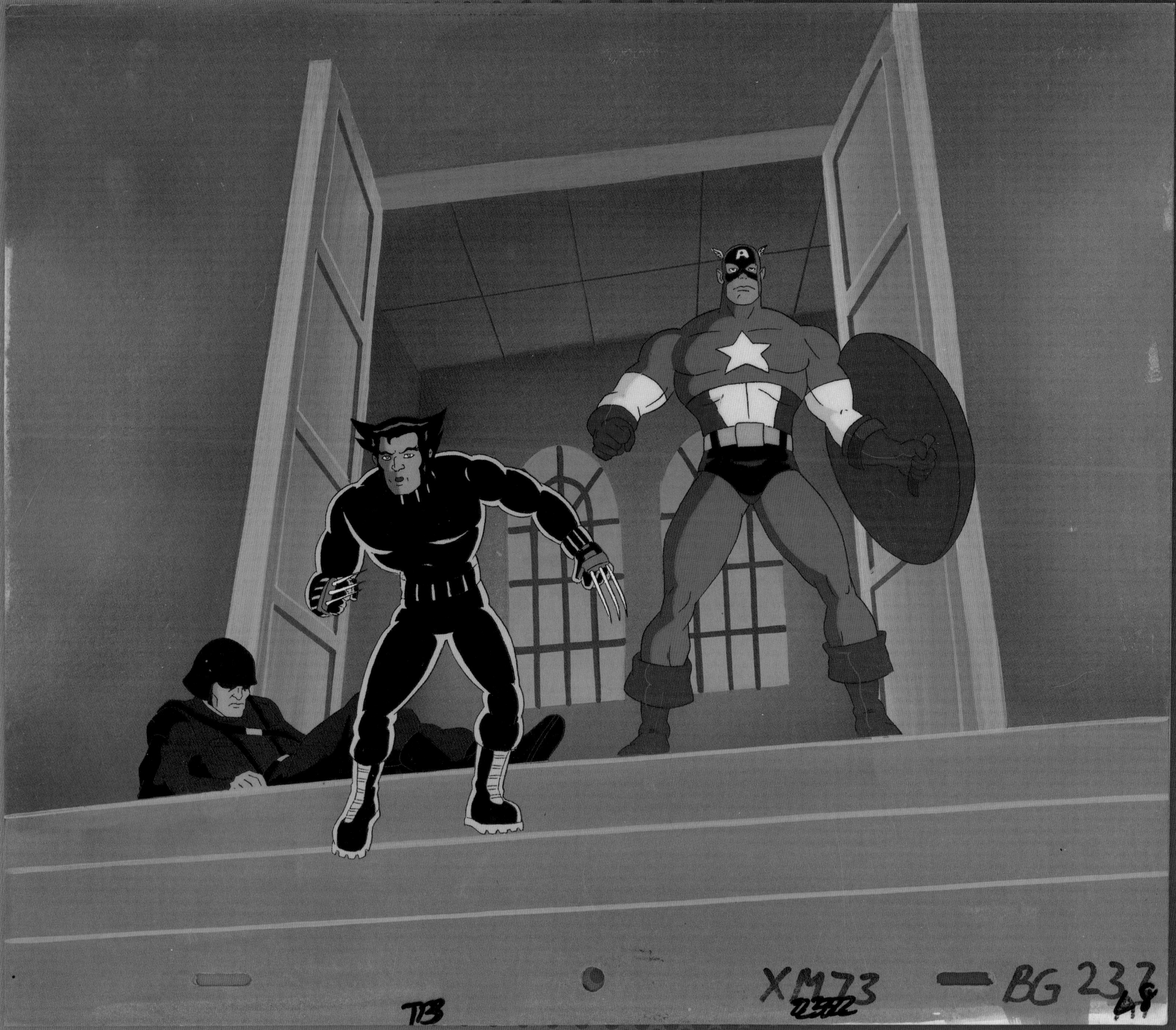
XM73
BG 237

CHAPTER FIVE

THE LAST SEASON

SEASON FIVE, EPISODES 67–76

MUCH CHANGED for these last eleven episodes; they were an afterthought. We had written and drawn the huge, four-part story "Beyond Good and Evil" as a slam-bang series finale. Now, nothing was final, and more stories were needed.

Larry Houston had committed to leave after the art for the first sixty-five episodes was delivered so he could head on to a new *Fantastic Four* series. Mark and Michael Edens had new commitments, as did Will Meugniot. We had started considering other offers.

Then the orders came down: first five more episodes, then, soon after, six more. We were never to find out why for sure. A home-video deal? Merchandise tie-in?

While the artists at Graz Entertainment finished the storyboards on the first five of these final eleven episodes, the company then shut down, as Jim and Stephanie were hired away to head TV animation production at the recently founded DreamWorks studio. Saban took over the last of the art pre-production. The models and storyboards came out quicker and simpler, with less detailing—less of Stephanie Graziano's prized "pencil mileage" to the drawing. (Compare Graz model designs on pages 32–33 with Saban's on page 236.)

Fans noticed this change in the quality and look of the *X-Men: TAS* design and animation in the last eleven episodes. Mark Lewis explained that part of this was a well-intended hope on the part of the remaining designers, including Frank Squillace, that if they helped simplify the designs, the lower animation budget would be easier for the overseas animators to deal with. It may have helped a little, but the animation still suffered with the limited design.

OPPOSITE Production cel of Logan and Captain America in 1944, defeating Nazi followers of Red Skull. Note the last-season, budget-cut, Saban-simplified design—both in characters and backgrounds.

There was less sound work done. Saban stopped doing the "Previously on X-Men" recaps. The video editing staff lost their leader, Sharon Janis, and the pacing seemed to suffer. Larry Houston was gone.

As Mark Lewis recalls, "At some point before Graz closed, it was explained to us that *X-Men* pre-production was going to be absorbed into Saban, and that some of us would be going with it. We got over there and found that Saban wasn't used to actual production. They seemed to think production was just dubbing things into English. We found it frustrating. A number of us didn't like the situation and had had enough by the end of our first week. Three of us (myself, prop designer Marcos Borregales, and backgrounds designer Zhaoping Wei) gave our two weeks' notice that first Friday at Saban. Frank Squillace (now in charge) understood why we couldn't stay. I tried to generate as much work as I could for him before my last day."

Saban switched some production from AKOM to lower-cost overseas animation studios. We could never be sure what our characters or their backgrounds would end up looking like—their facial expressions, movements, etc. And without Larry or Margaret or Stephanie demanding costly retakes, mistakes and awkward images were not fixed.

There were some bright spots to the final season. Eric got to work one more time on an X-Men story with the legendary Len Wein, co-creator of so many of the new X-Men characters.

Asked what it would take to bring him back, Len said: "A Captain America story with Logan (pre-claws Wolverine) in World War II." This was a challenge because Marvel Comics was at the time very stingy with their characters, and Cap was not licensed to Fox TV for use in *X-Men: TAS*. But Len Wein was Len Wein, and a couple of weeks of phone calls and lawyering got us our Captain America story, "Old Soldiers."

TOWARD THE END, we somehow got the okay to do an X-Men story *without the X-Men*! "Descent" was an 1890s London story about the earliest origins of mutants. A young Mister Sinister stars along with Professor Xavier's grandfather. How the series creative team got away with this—and the cost of designing even small bits of 1890s London—is a happy mystery.

DESPITE THE BUDGET and personnel cutbacks, one of the best stories of the final season—and most interesting visuals and most distinctive dilemmas—was a Borg-like entity that was absorbing characters, good and evil alike: "The Phalanx Covenant" came close to wiping out the team and imperiling Earth. At one point, only Beast and his empathetic new friend Warlock stood in the way of total annihilation. A great relationship and a tight, fast-paced story made this a highlight of our weakest season.

FINALLY, WE HAD TO SAY GOODBYE to this amazing world we had started five years earlier. Our finale, "Graduation Day," was designed to bring all of the major players together. Professor X is shot by Henry Peter Gyrich with a "psychic energy disrupter" and is dying. The team, including long-absent Morph, along with lifelong friend Magneto and space-voyager lover Lilandra, struggle to save Charles. While it is discovered that technology on Lilandra's planet can keep Charles alive, he must go with her to her distant world and say farewell to everyone he cares for. As Xavier's loved ones surround his sick bed, he bids each a personal goodbye. Then, as Charles leaves with Lilandra, the "family" that he created, the X-Men, watch, skyward, as if they were witnessing their beloved Professor's ascent to Heaven.

Ending a television series is difficult. Many excellent series "don't stick the landing." We feel that *X-Men: TAS*'s goodbye worked. "Graduation Day" remains an emotional episode for fans who did not want to say goodbye to this beloved family.

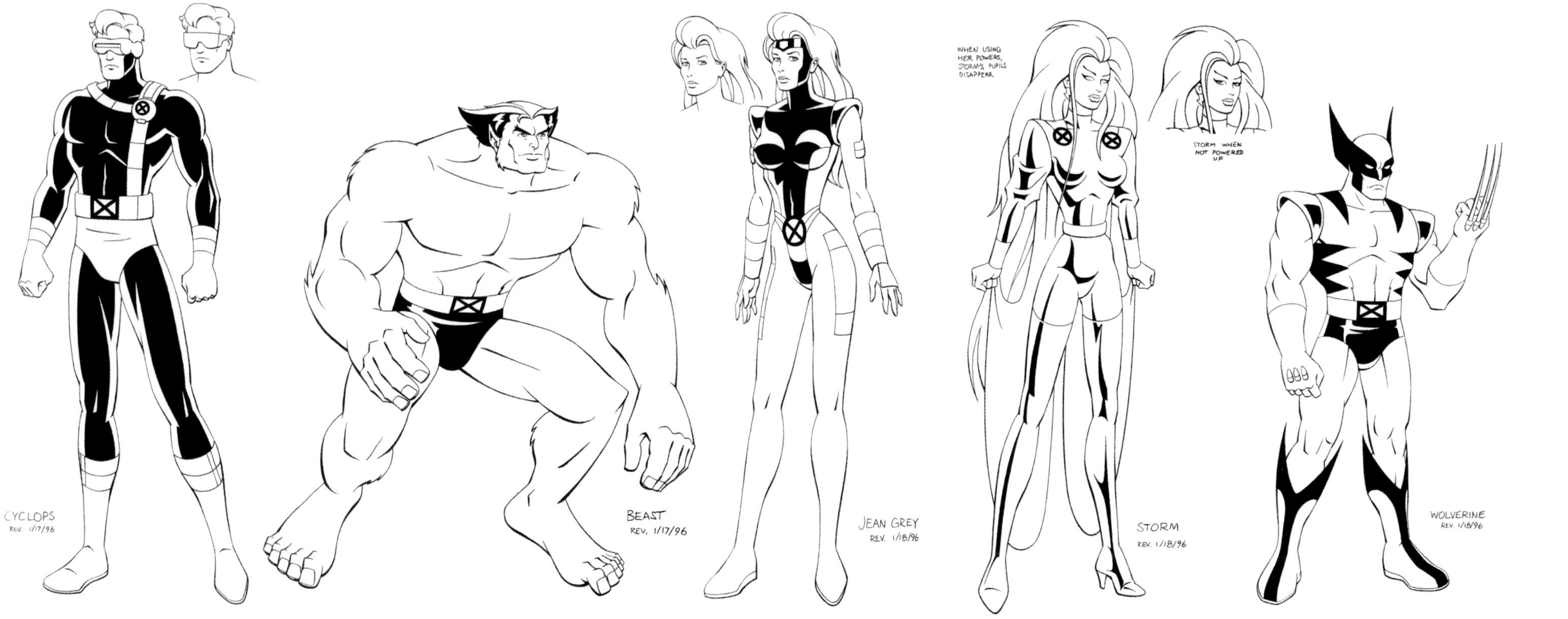
CYCLOPS
REV. 1/17/96
BEAST
REV. 1/17/96
JEAN GREY
REV. 1/18/96
WHEN USING HER POWERS, STORM'S PUPILS DISAPPEAR
STORM WHEN NOT POWERED UP
STORM
REV. 1/18/96
WOLVERINE
REV. 1/18/96

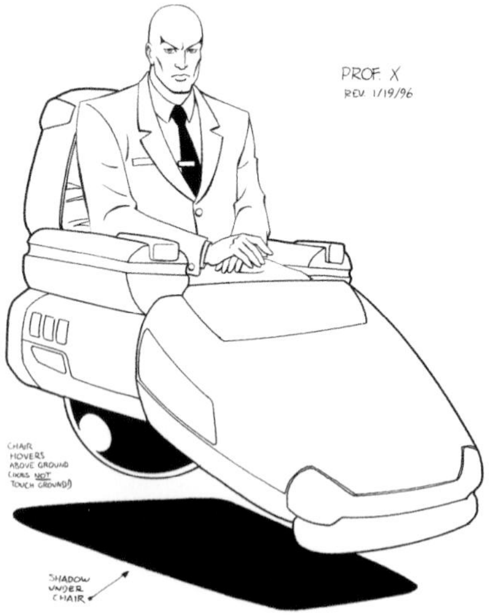
PROF. X
REV. 1/19/96
CHAIR HOVERS ABOVE GROUND (DOES NOT TOUCH GROUND!)
SHADOW UNDER CHAIR

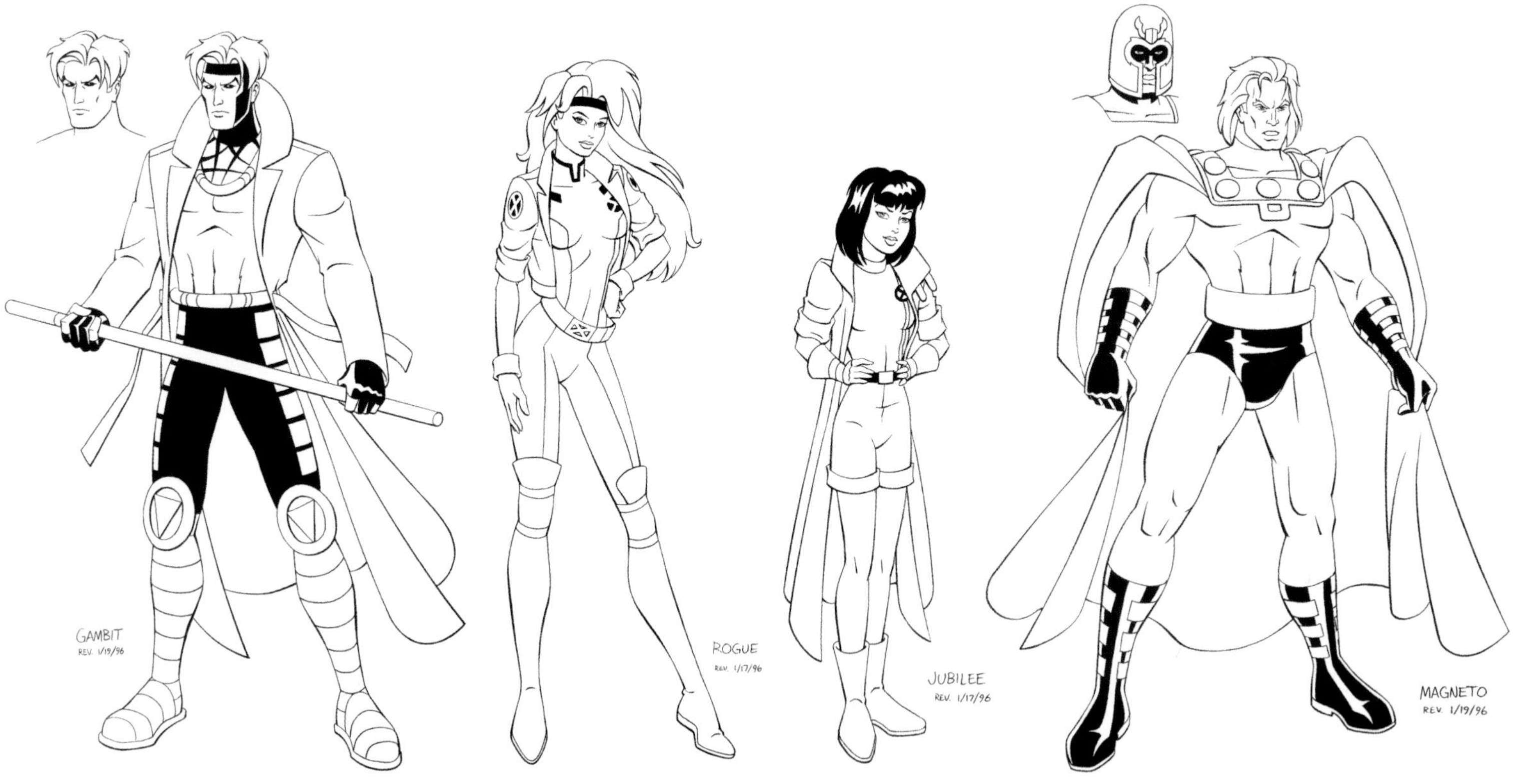
GAMBIT
REV. 1/19/96
ROGUE
REV. 1/17/96
JUBILEE
REV. 1/17/96
MAGNETO
REV. 1/19/96

THIS PAGE Newly simplified-design, lead-cast character models. Compare to examples from first seasons in chapter one (pages 25-31). By Frank Squillace and Mark Lewis. **OPPOSITE** Production cel of Beast ("Friend Hank") and Warlock fighting the Phalanx.

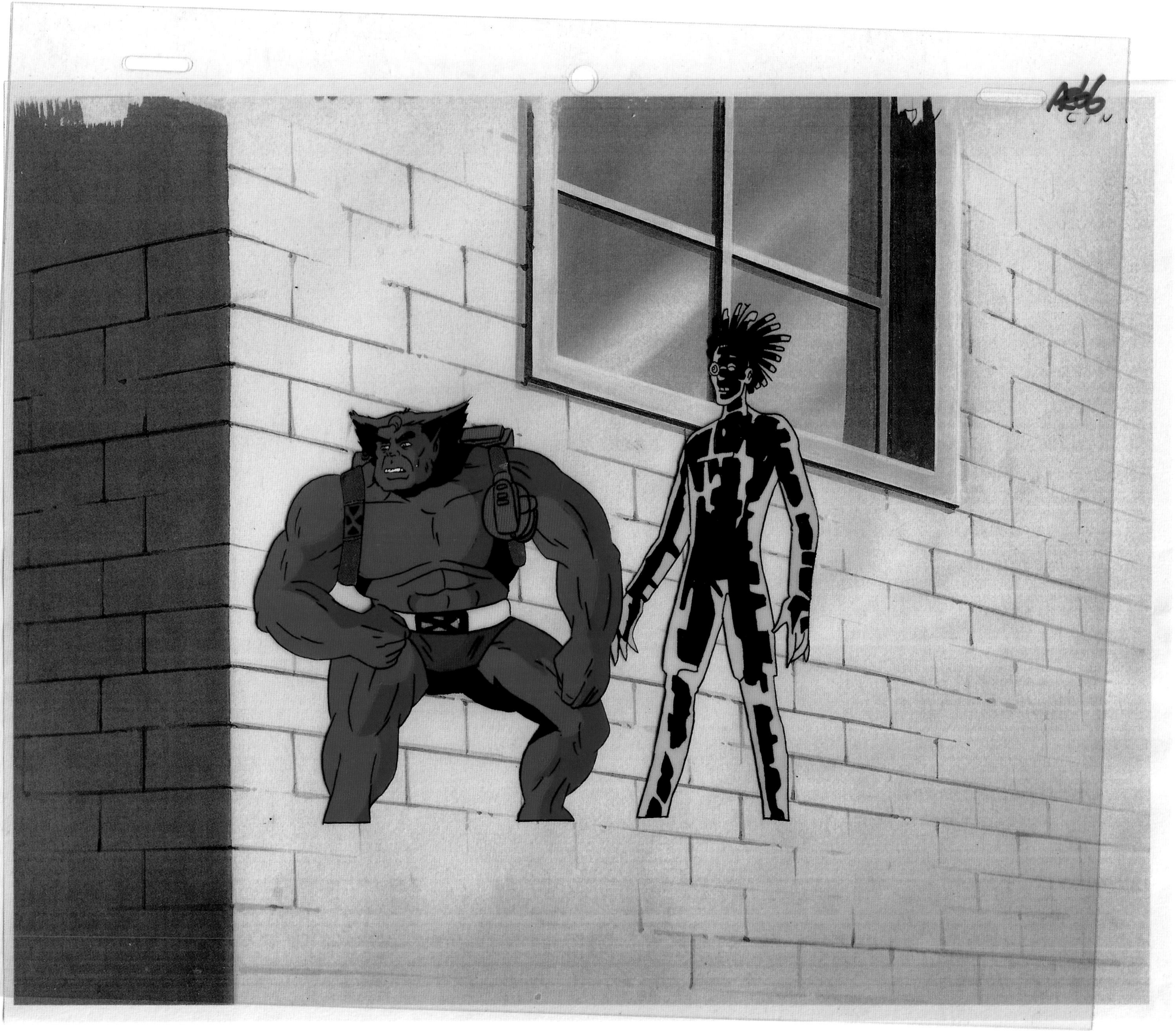

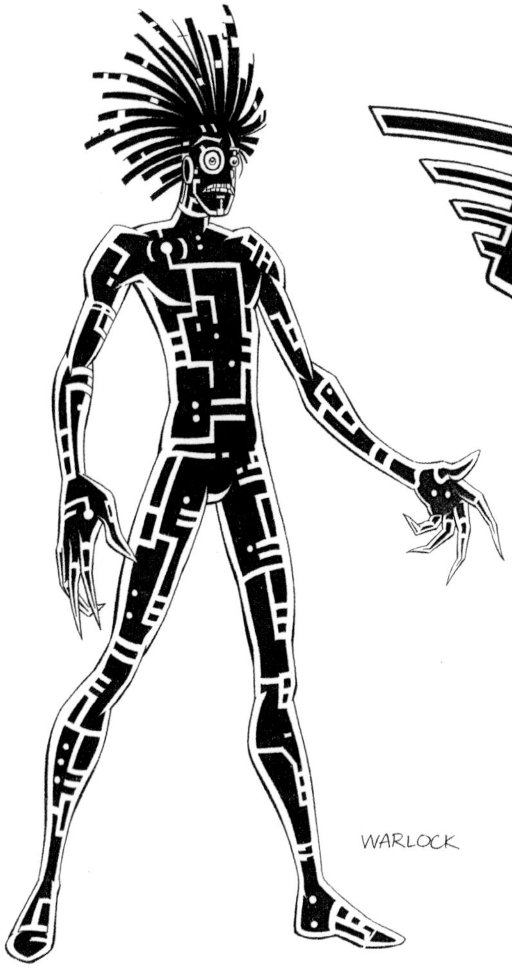
WARLOCK

01

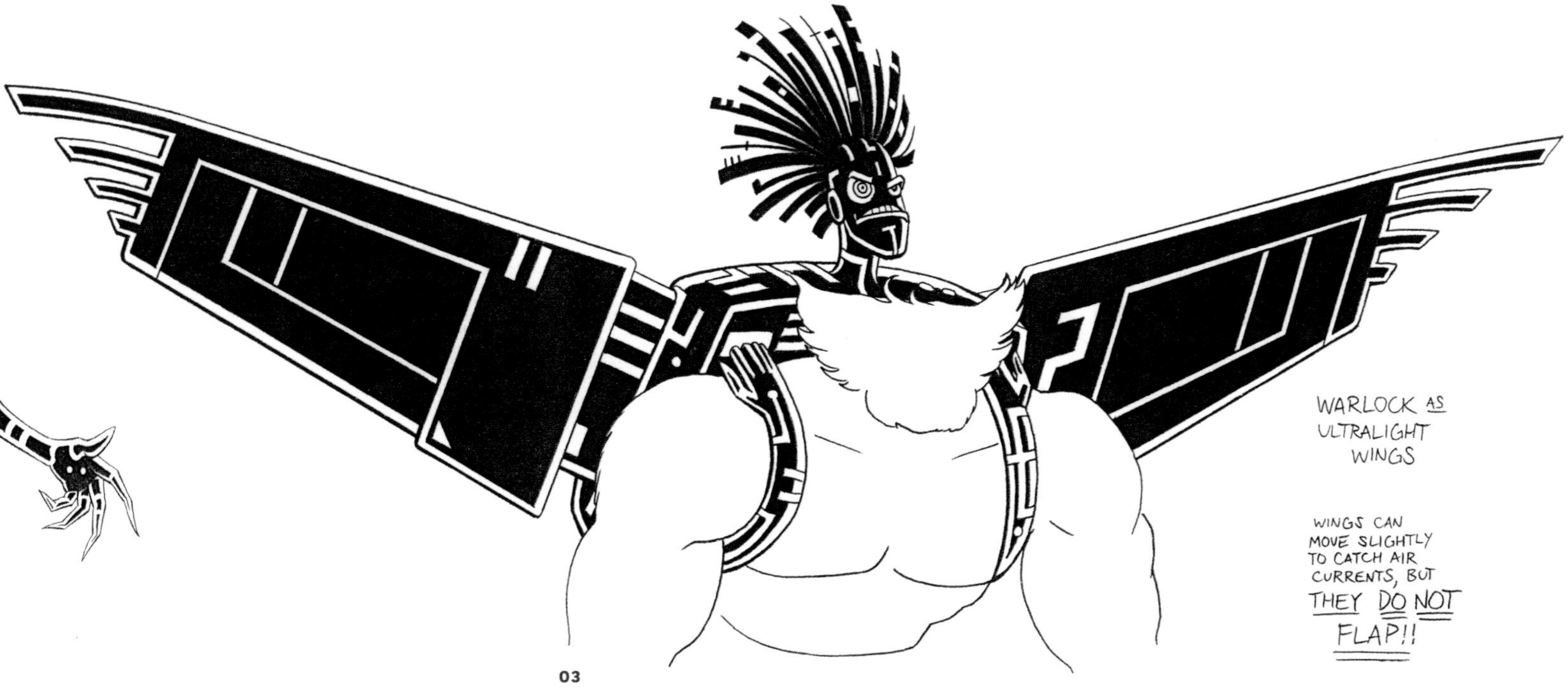
WARLOCK AS
ULTRALIGHT
WINGS
WINGS CAN
MOVE SLIGHTLY
TO CATCH AIR
CURRENTS, BUT
THEY DO NOT
FLAP!!

03

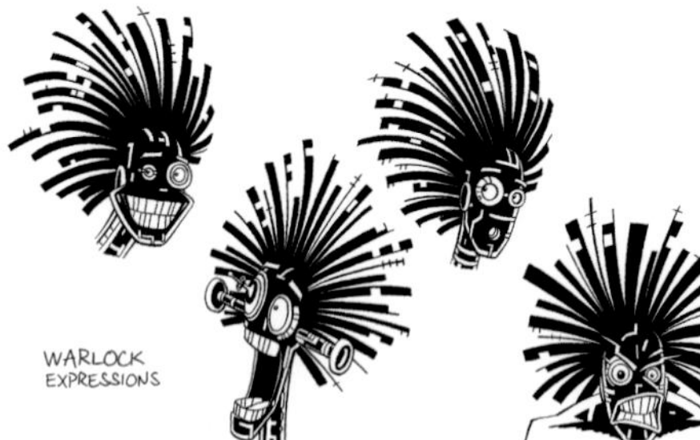
WARLOCK
EXPRESSIONS

02

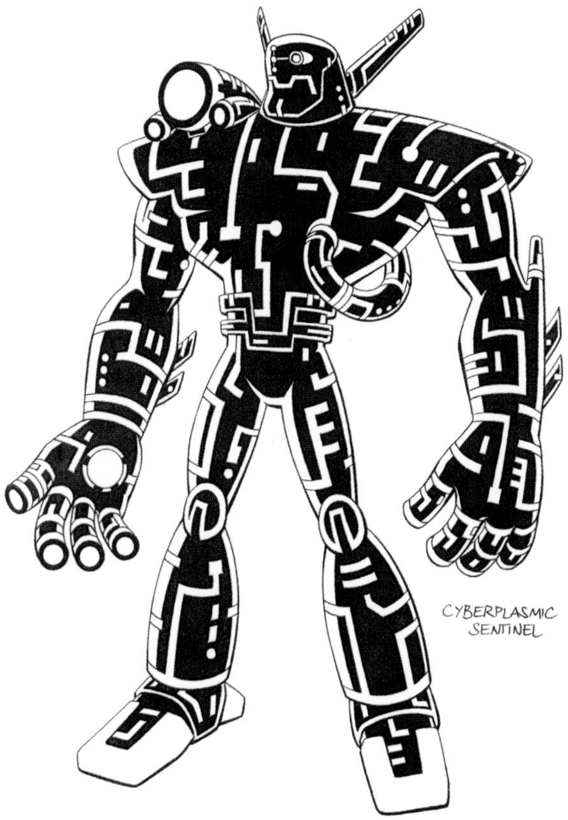
CYBERPLASMIC
SENTINEL

04

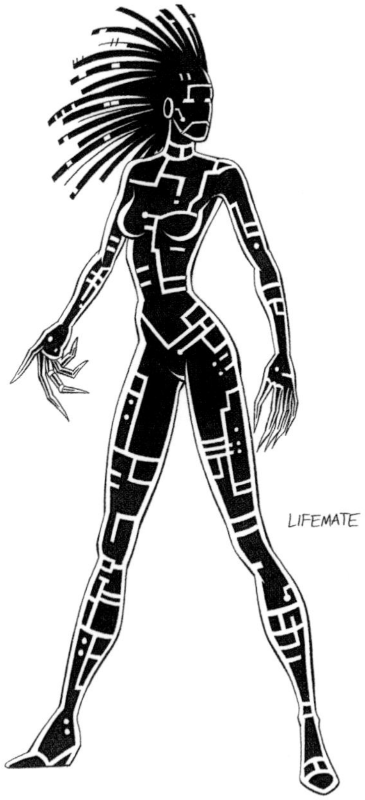
LIFEMATE

05

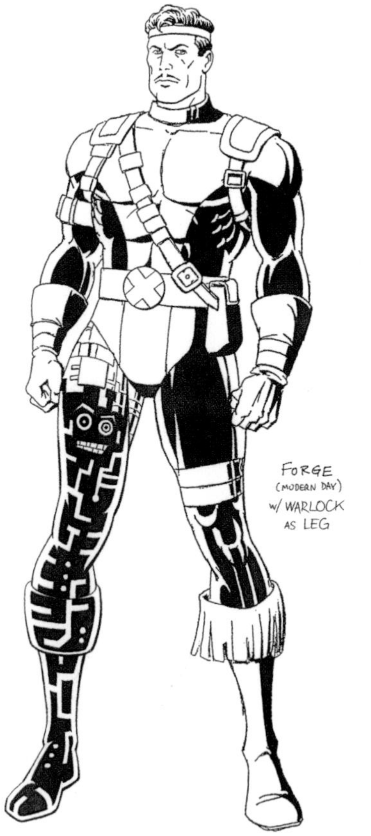
FORGE
(MODERN DAY)
W/ WARLOCK
AS LEG

06

01–15 Character models from "The Phalanx Covenant," including versions of characters corrupted by the Phalanx. The original penciling and concepts for Warlock, the Cyberplasmic Sentinel, Lifemate, and Cameron Hodge (01, 04, 05, 11) by Frank Squillace; the Phalanx Nucleus (11) penciled by Frank Brunner; cleanup on all models by Mark Lewis.

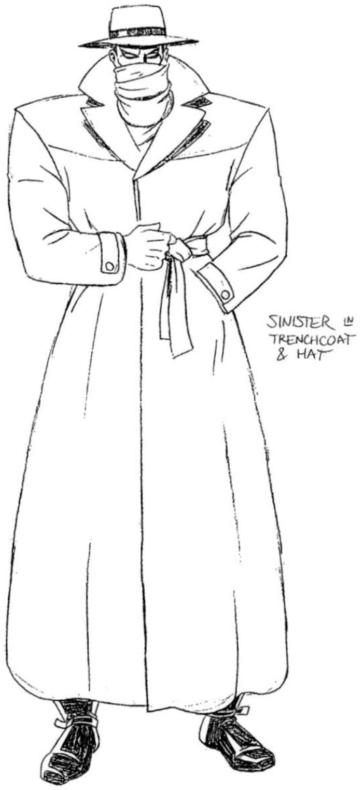
SINISTER in TRENCHCOAT & HAT

07

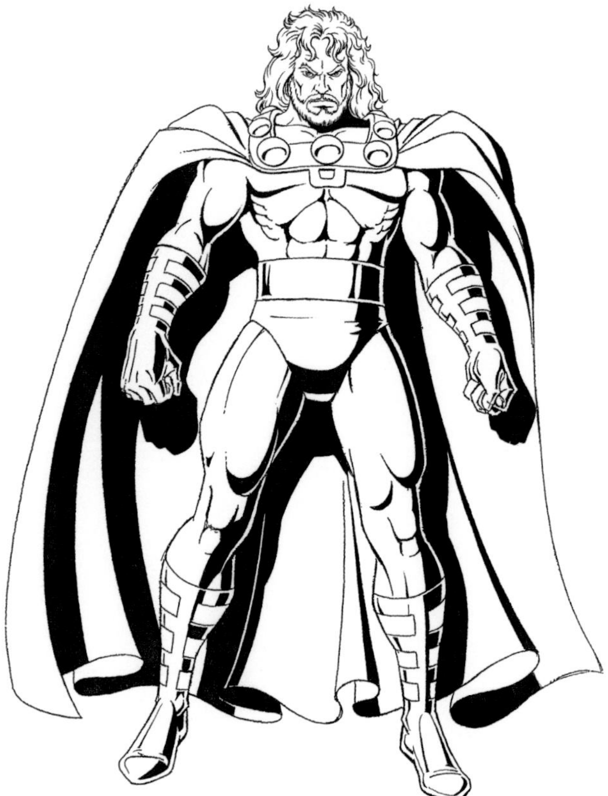

08

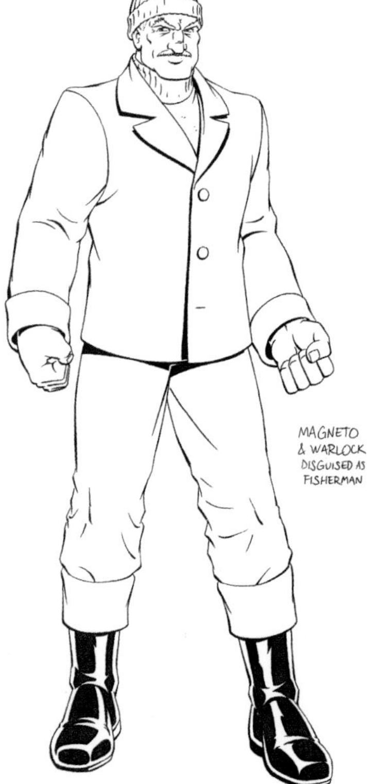
MAGNETO & WARLOCK DISGUISED AS FISHERMAN

09

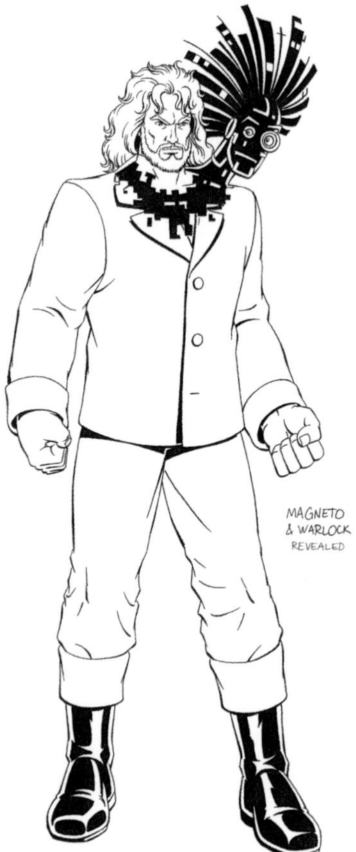
MAGNETO & WARLOCK REVEALED

10

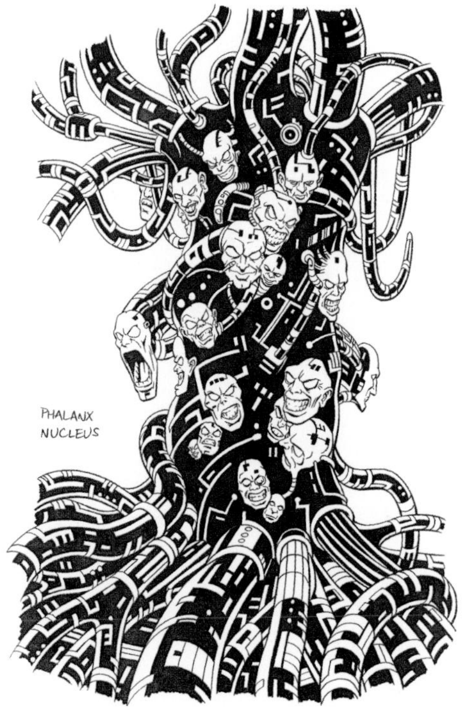
PHALANX NUCLEUS

11

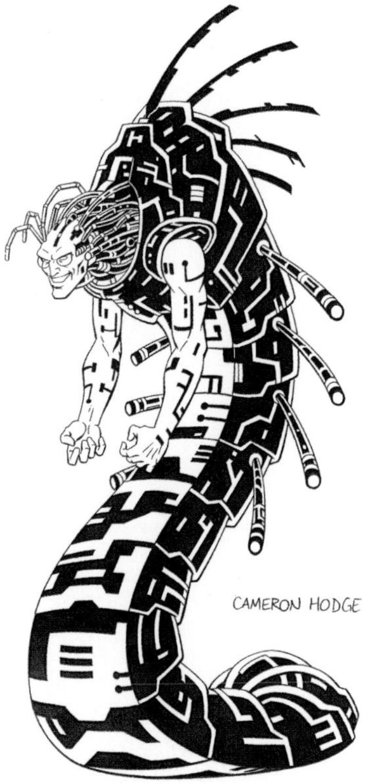
CAMERON HODGE

12

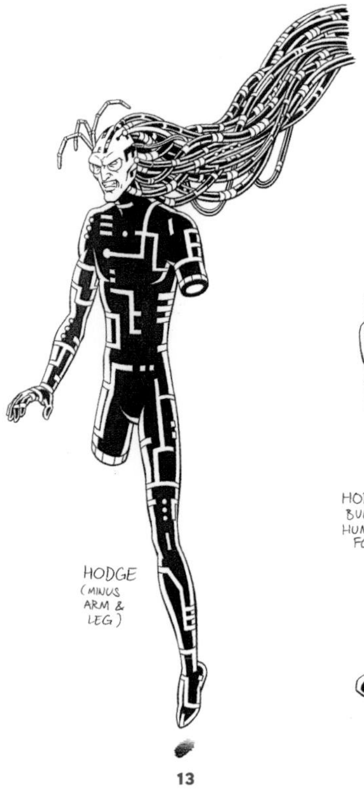
HODGE (MINUS ARM & LEG)

13

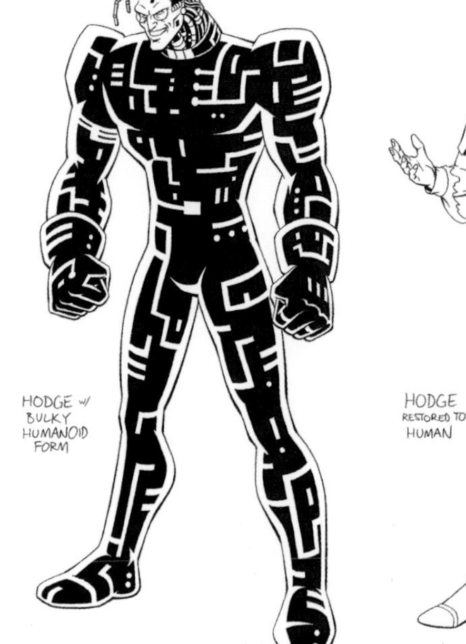
HODGE w/ BULKY HUMANOID FORM

14

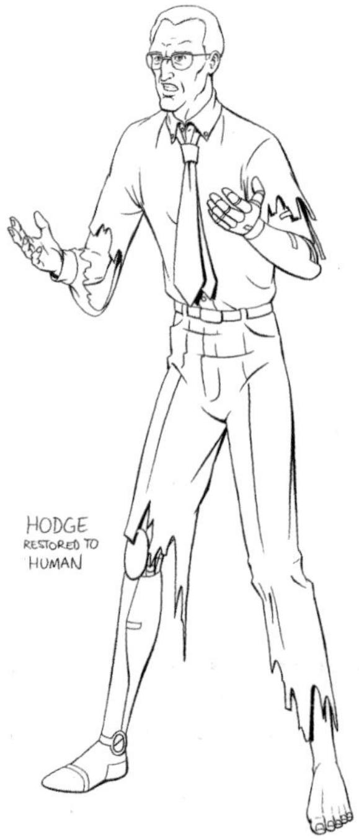
HODGE RESTORED TO HUMAN

15

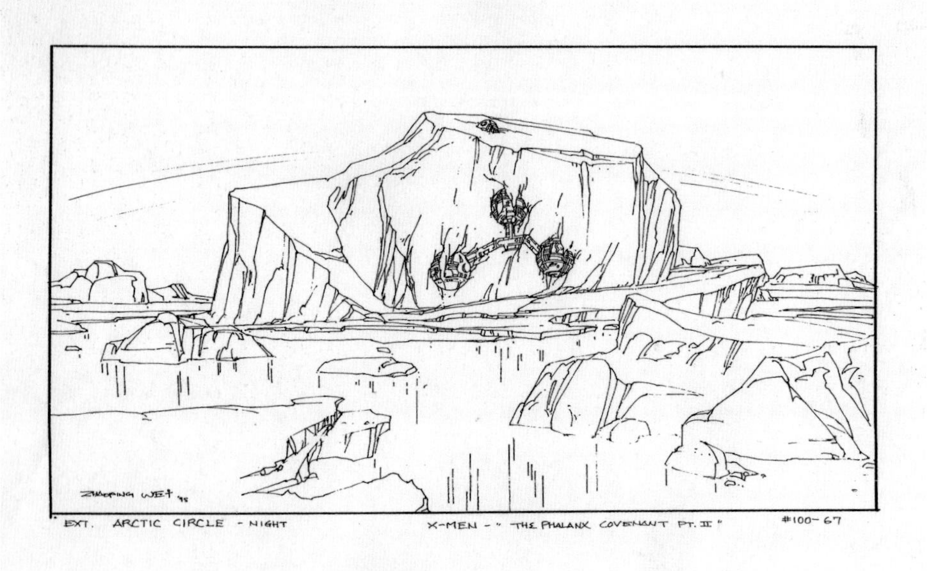
EXT. ARCTIC CIRCLE - NIGHT
X-MEN - "THE PHALANX COVENANT PT. II"
#100-67

01

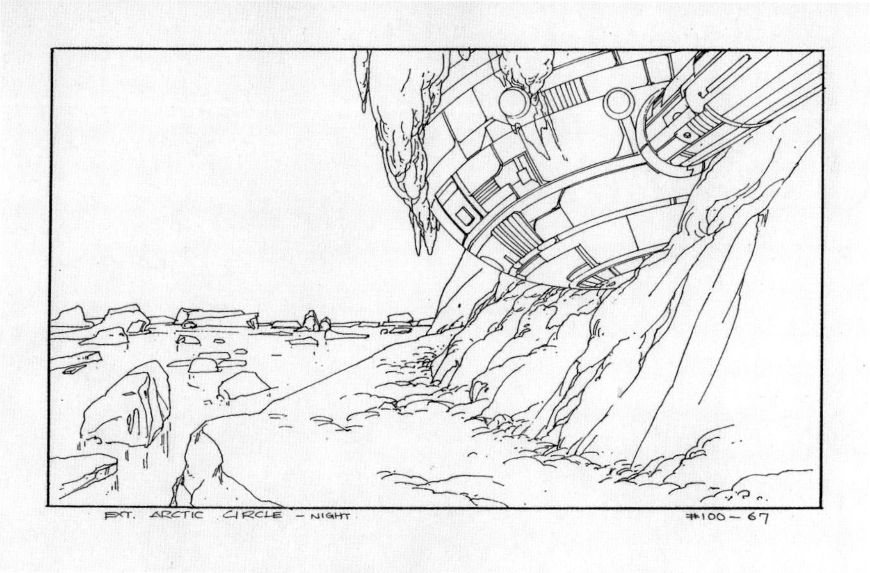
EXT. ARCTIC CIRCLE - NIGHT
#100-67

02

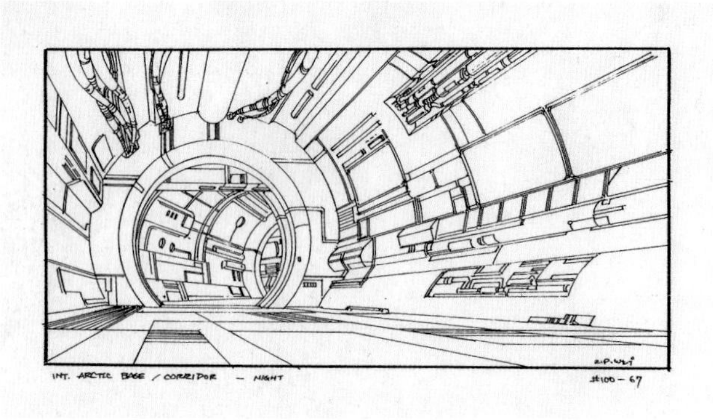
INT. ARCTIC BASE / CORRIDOR - NIGHT
#100-67

03

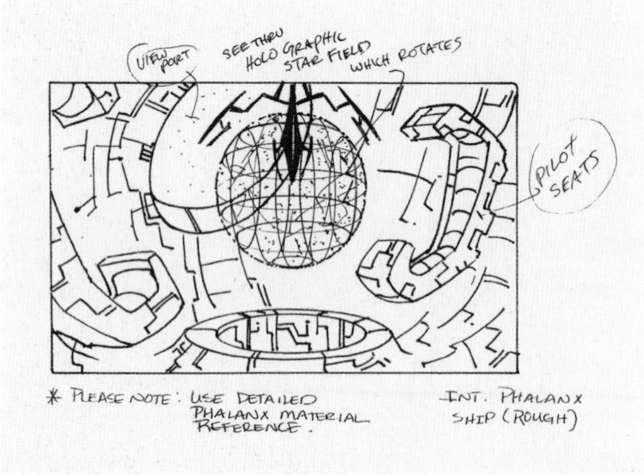
VIEW PORT
SEE THRU HOLO GRAPHIC STAR FIELD WHICH ROTATES
PILOT SEATS
* PLEASE NOTE: USE DETAILED PHALANX MATERIAL REFERENCE.
INT. PHALANX SHIP (ROUGH)

04

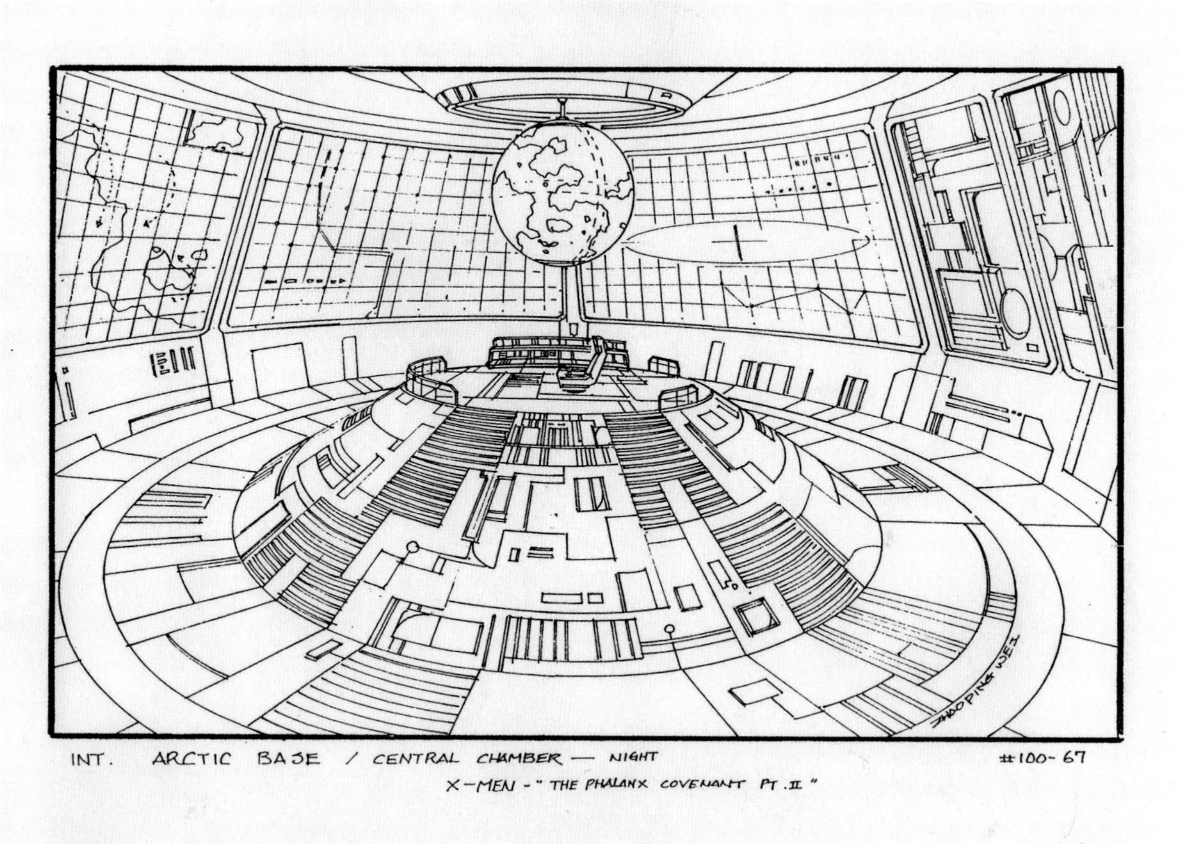
ZHAOPING WEI
INT. ARCTIC BASE / CENTRAL CHAMBER — NIGHT
#100-67
X-MEN - "THE PHALANX COVENANT PT. II"

05

01-05 Background layouts for "The Phalanx Covenant." The rough background of the Phalanx ship interior (04) by Frank Squillace. The rest were designed by Squillace with cleanup by Zhaoping Wei.
06 Production cel of Sinister and Magneto (note the new, simpler designs).

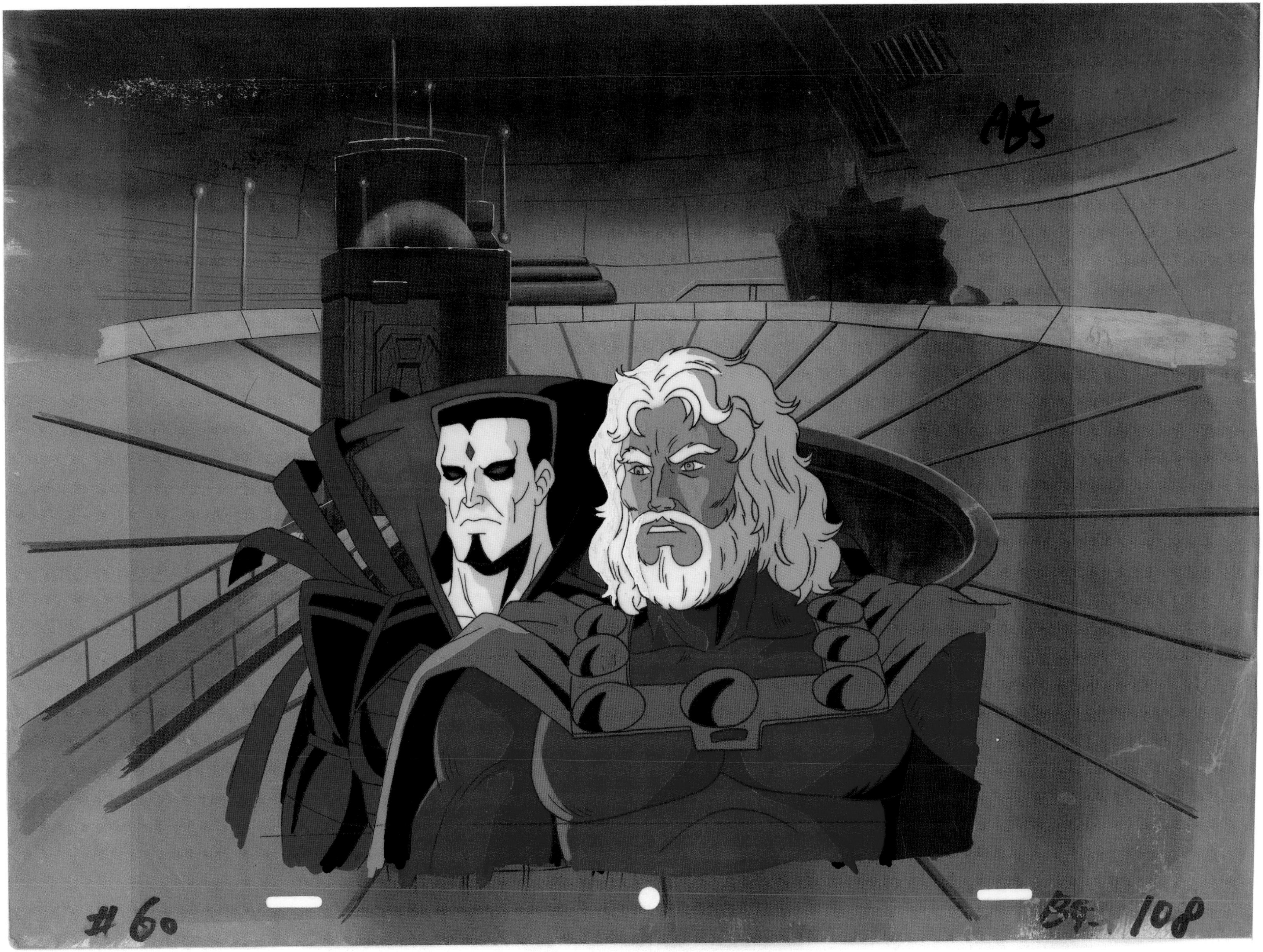
#60
BG-108

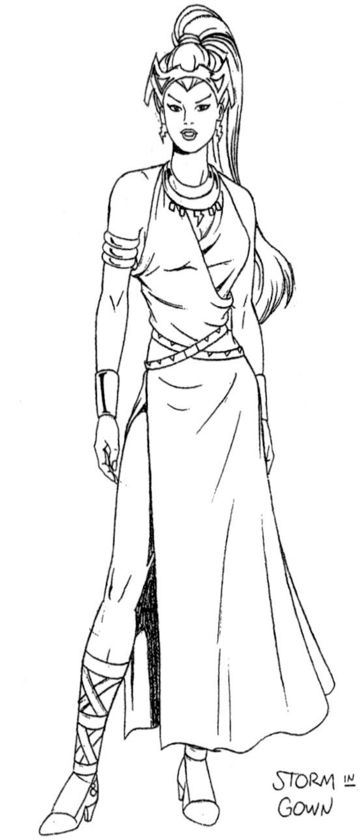
STORM IN
GOWN

01

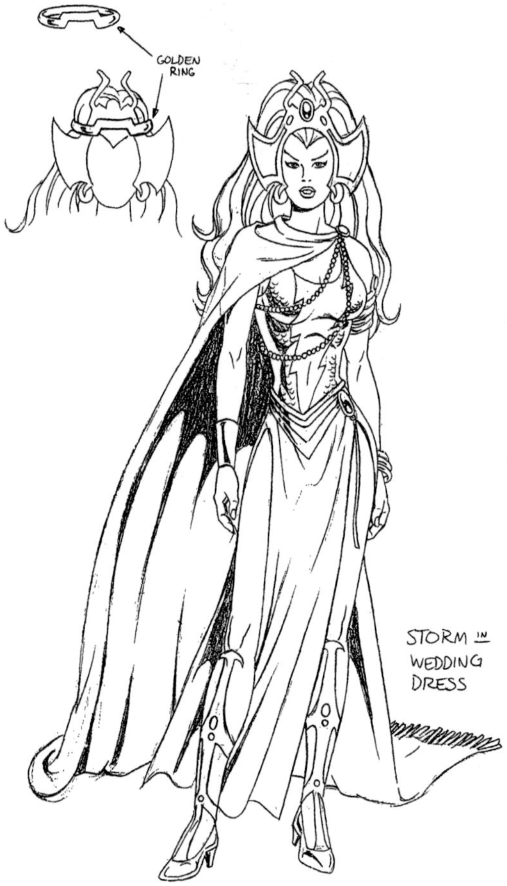
GOLDEN RING
STORM IN
WEDDING
DRESS

02

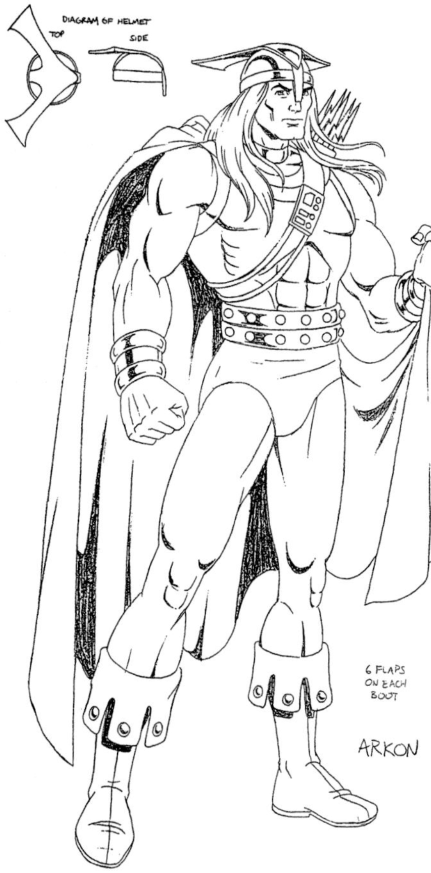
DIAGRAM OF HELMET
TOP
SIDE
6 FLAPS ON EACH BOOT
ARKON

03

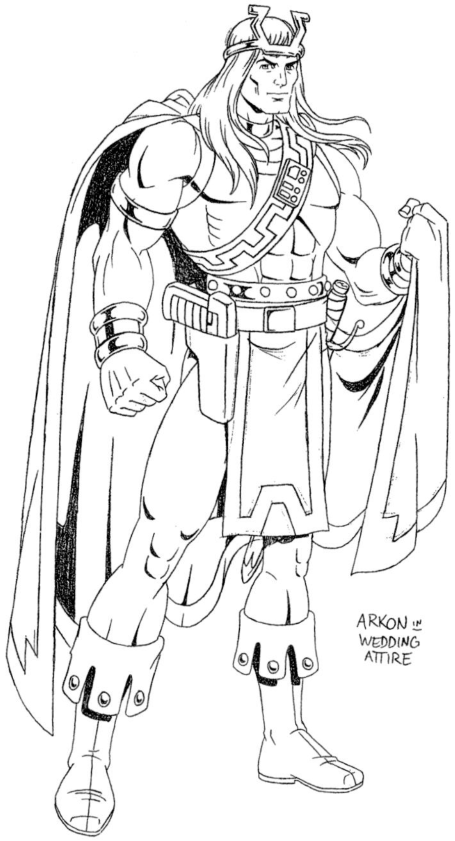
ARKON IN
WEDDING
ATTIRE

04

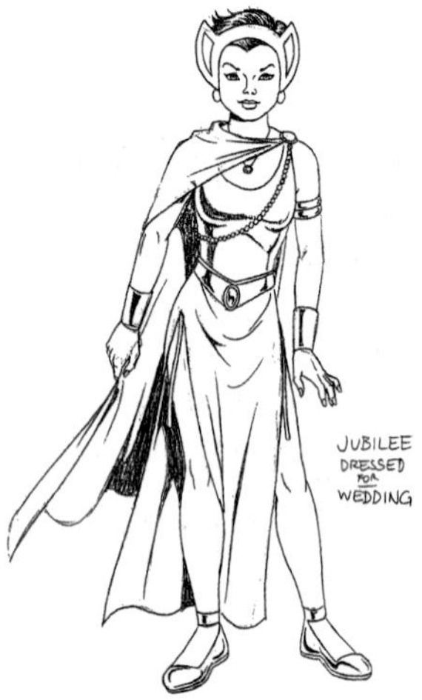
JUBILEE
DRESSED
FOR
WEDDING

05

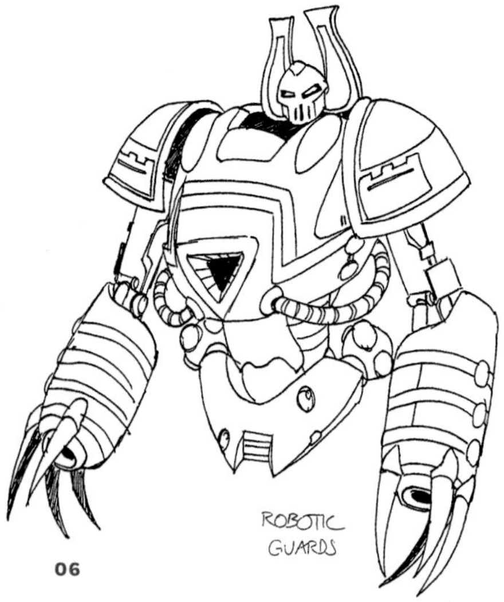
ROBOTIC
GUARDS

06

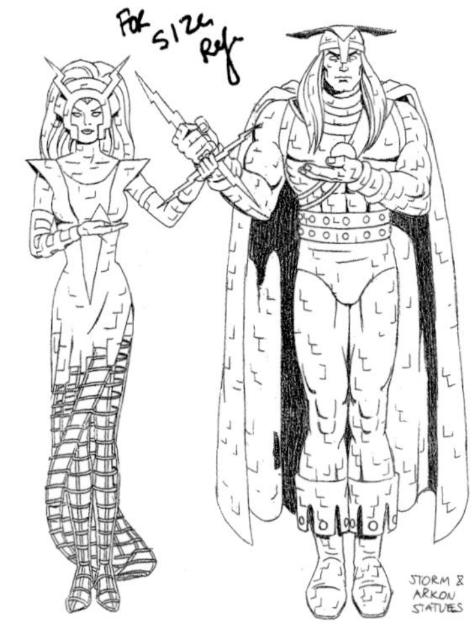
For size Ref
STORM & ARKON STATUES

07

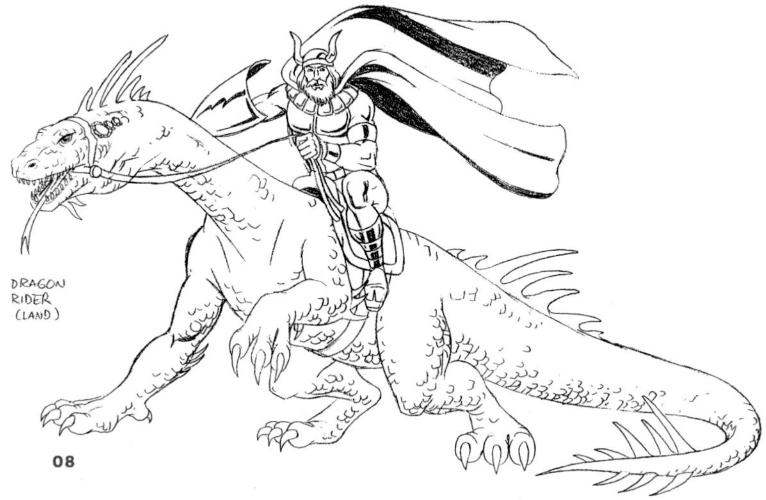
DRAGON
RIDER
(LAND)

08

01–05 Character models, in various outfits, for "Storm Front." **06** Character model of robotic guard by Marco Borregales. **07** Model of massive statues of Storm and her royal fiancé Arkon; designed by Frank Squillace with cleanup by Mark Lewis. **08** Dragon design by Squillace, with cleanup by Lewis.

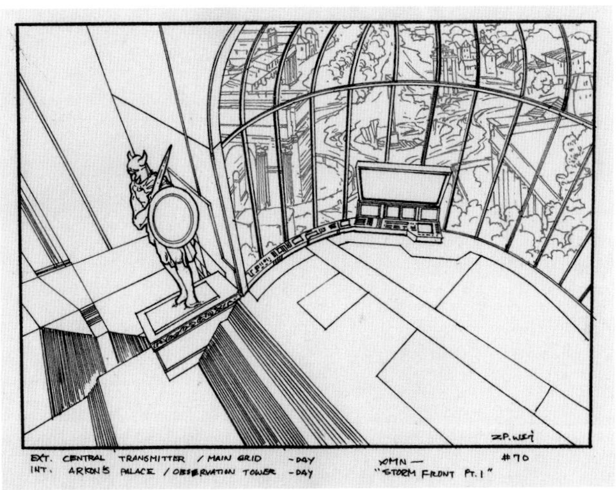
EXT. CENTRAL TRANSMITTER / MAIN GRID -DAY
INT. ARKON'S PALACE / OBSERVATION TOWER -DAY
XMN —
"STORM FRONT PT. I"
#70

09

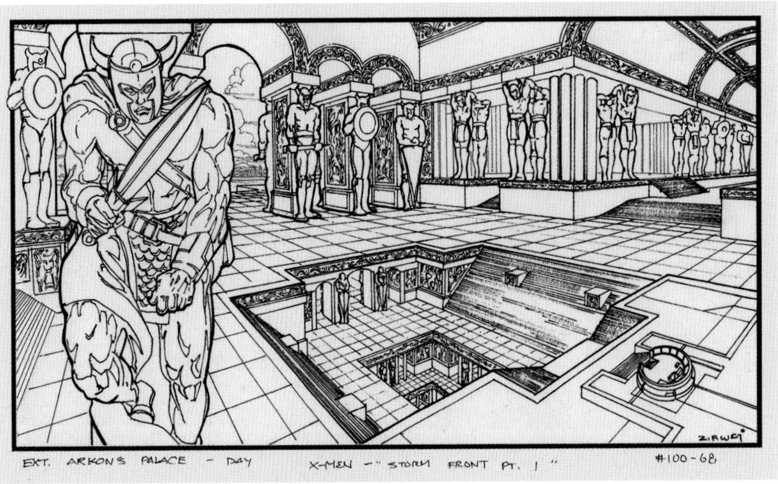
EXT. ARKON'S PALACE - DAY
X-MEN — "STORM FRONT PT. I"
#100-68

10

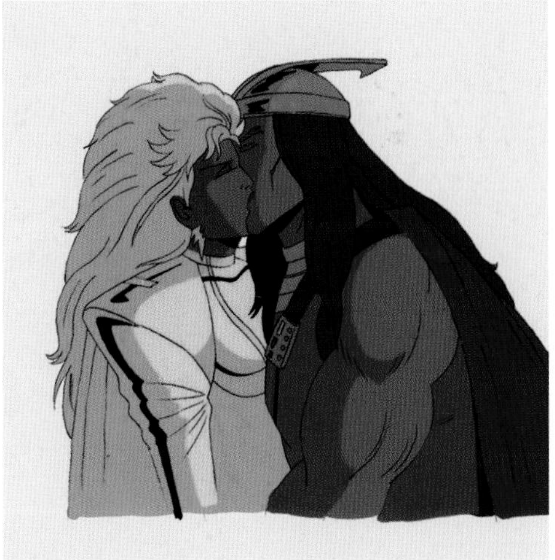

11

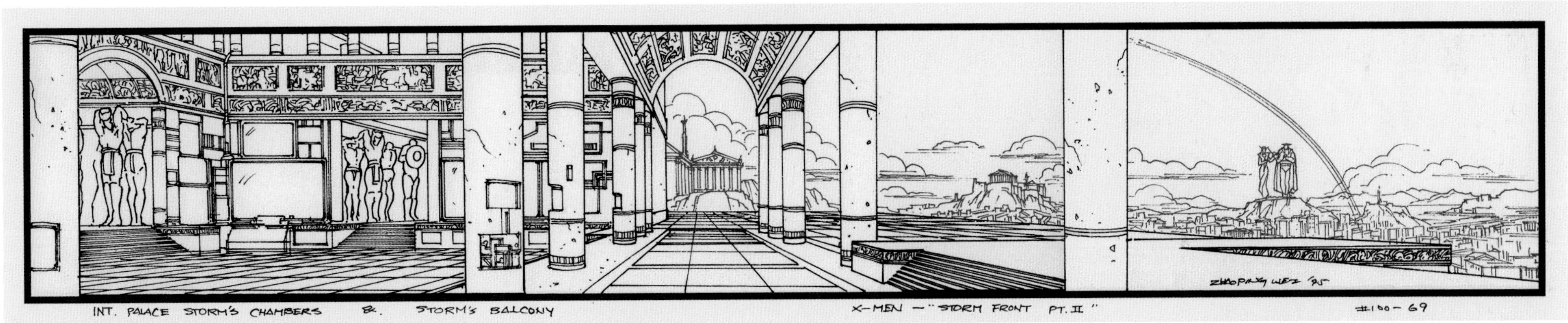
INT. PALACE STORM'S CHAMBERS & STORM'S BALCONY
X-MEN — "STORM FRONT PT. II"
#100-69

12

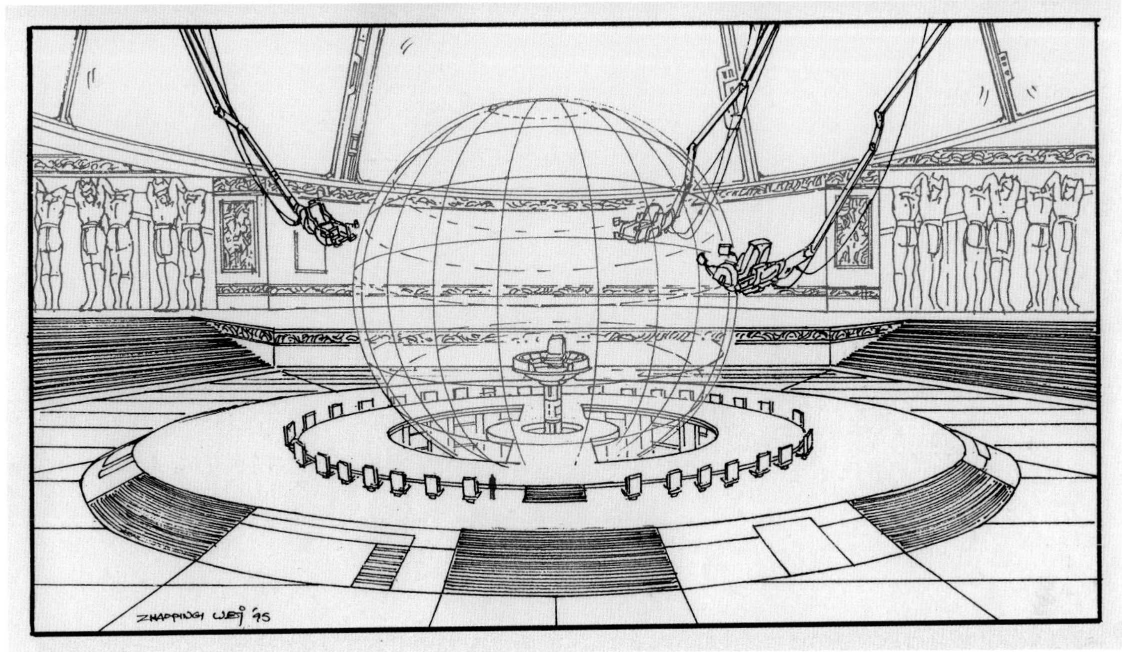

13

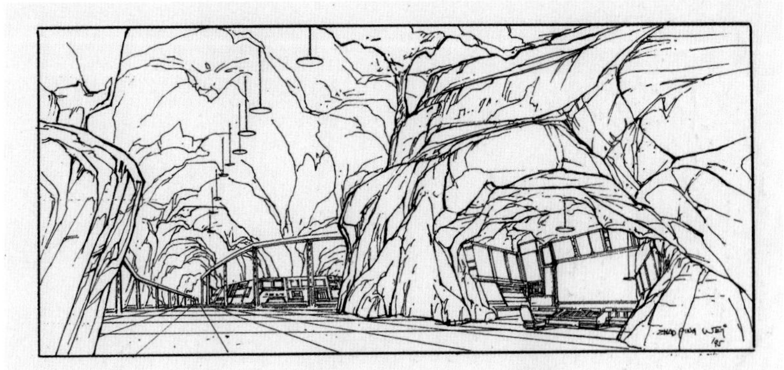

14

09–10 Backgrounds of two areas of the vast palace of King Arkon, designed by Squillace with cleanup by Zhaoping Wei. **11** Production cel of Arkon and Storm kissing. **12** Background layout key of Storm's balcony in Arkon's palace, looking out over the city. Designed by Squillace with cleanup by Wei. **13** Background of meeting room in Arkon's palace. Designed by Squillace with cleanup by Wei. **14** Background of organized resistance tunnel headquarters. Designed by Squillace with cleanup by Wei.

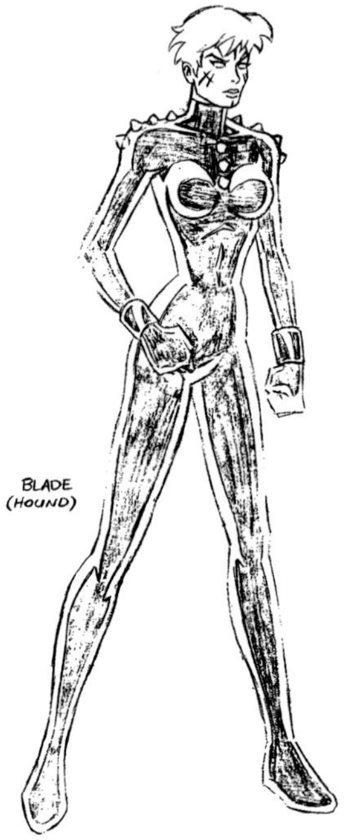
BLADE
(HOUND)

01

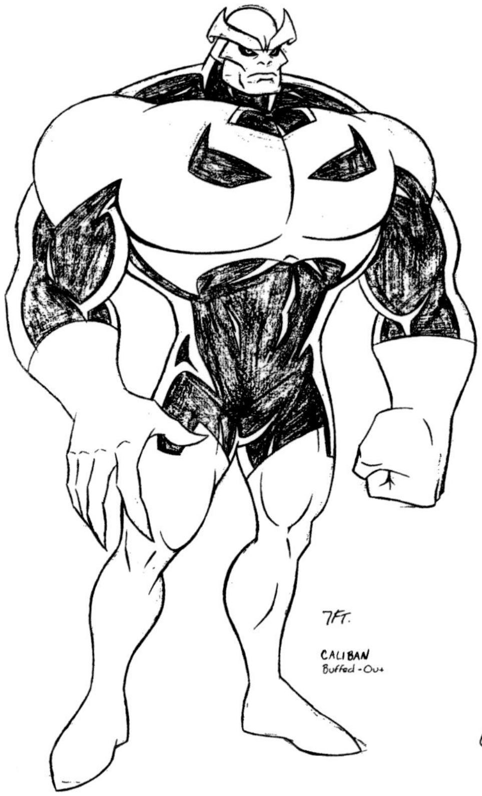
7FT.
CALIBAN
Buffed-Out

02

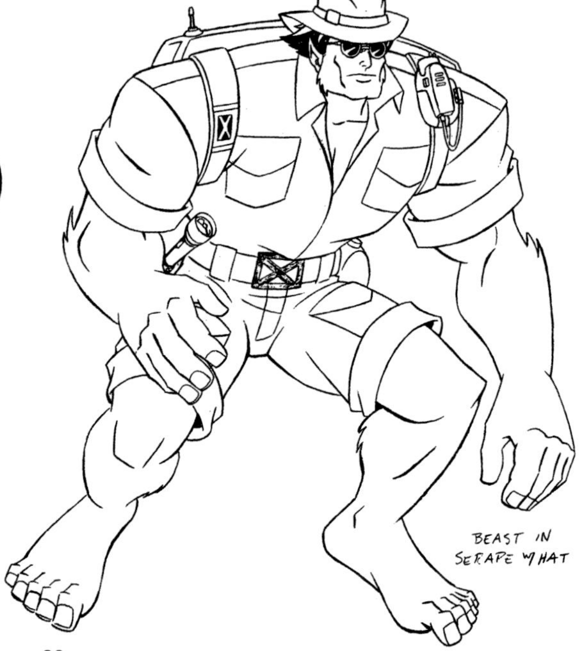
BEAST IN
SERAPE W/HAT

03

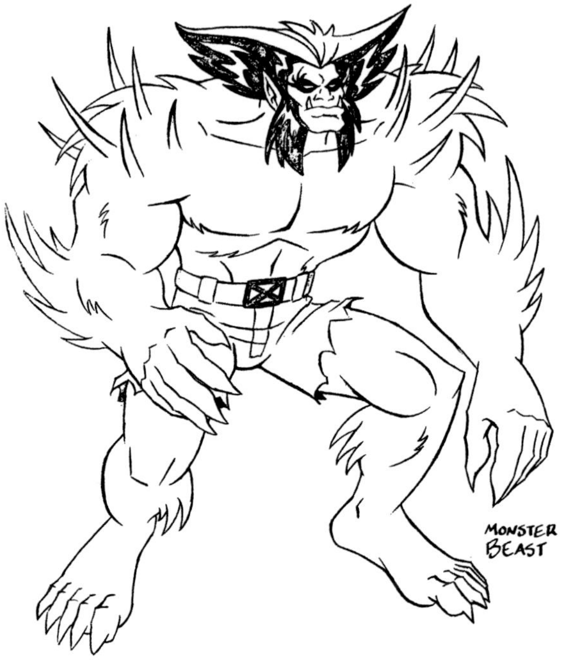
MONSTER
BEAST

04

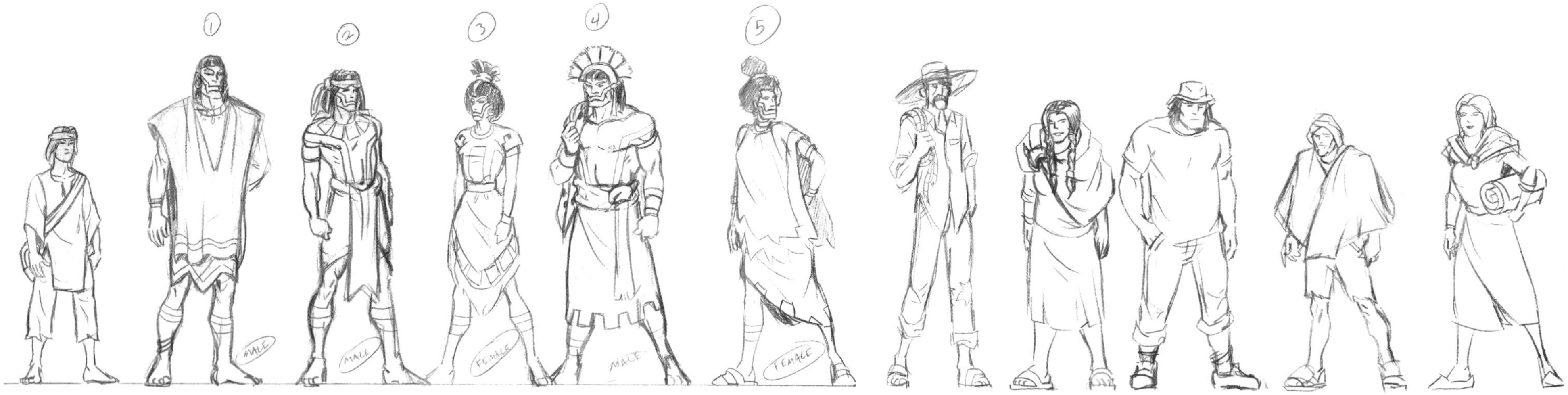
1
2
3
4
5
MALE
MALE
FEMALE
MALE
FEMALE

05

01–04 Character models of transformed Hound and Caliban; normal civilian Beast; and Transformed Beast (simplified Saban look). Penciled by Roy Burdine. **05** Early roughs (in non-copy blue) of South American Indians and villagers, by Frank Squillace. **06–10** Character models of Fabian Cortez, Jubilee, and Apocalypse (simplified Saban look). Penciled by Roy Burdine. Apocalypse redesign by Squillace. **11** Rough sketch of Apocalypse. **12** Rough of Cortez being knocked back by a pyrotechnic energy blast from Jubilee.

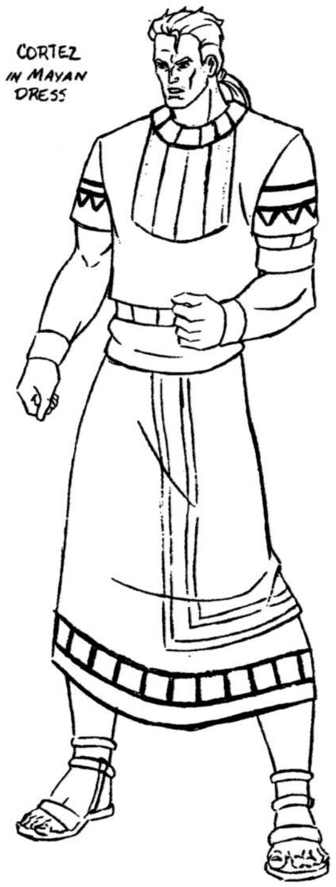
CORTEZ
IN MAYAN
DRESS

06

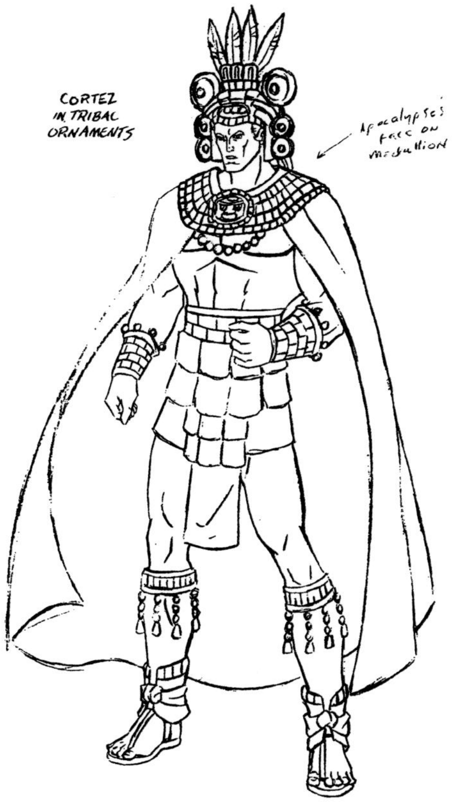
CORTEZ
IN TRIBAL
ORNAMENTS
Apocalypse's
face on
medallion

07

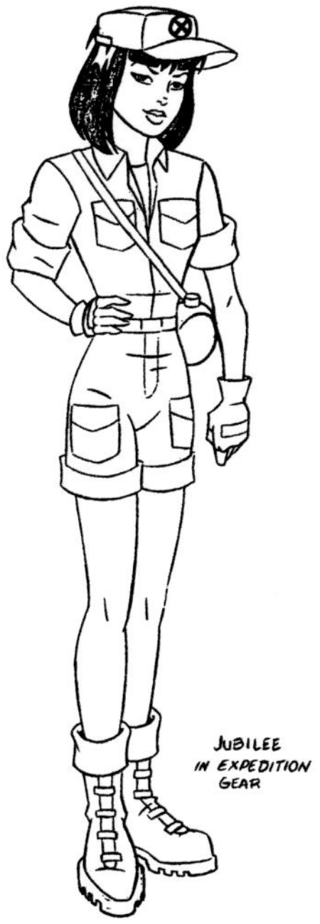
JUBILEE
IN EXPEDITION
GEAR

08

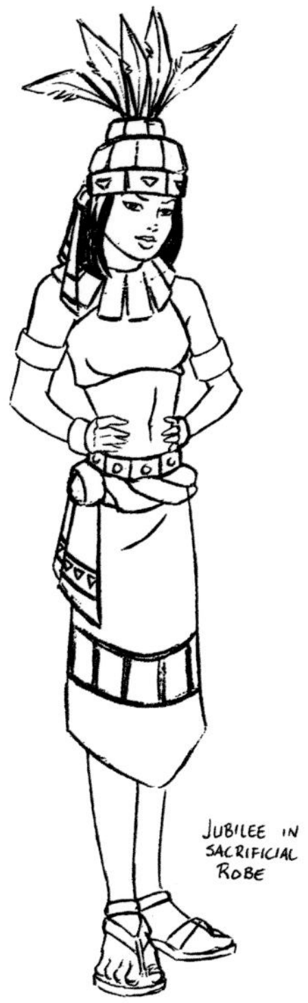
JUBILEE IN
SACRIFICIAL
ROBE

09

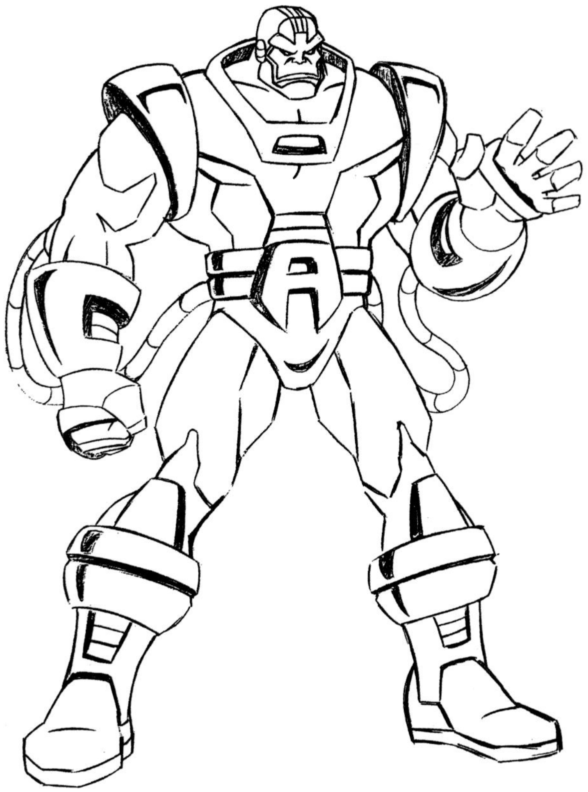

10

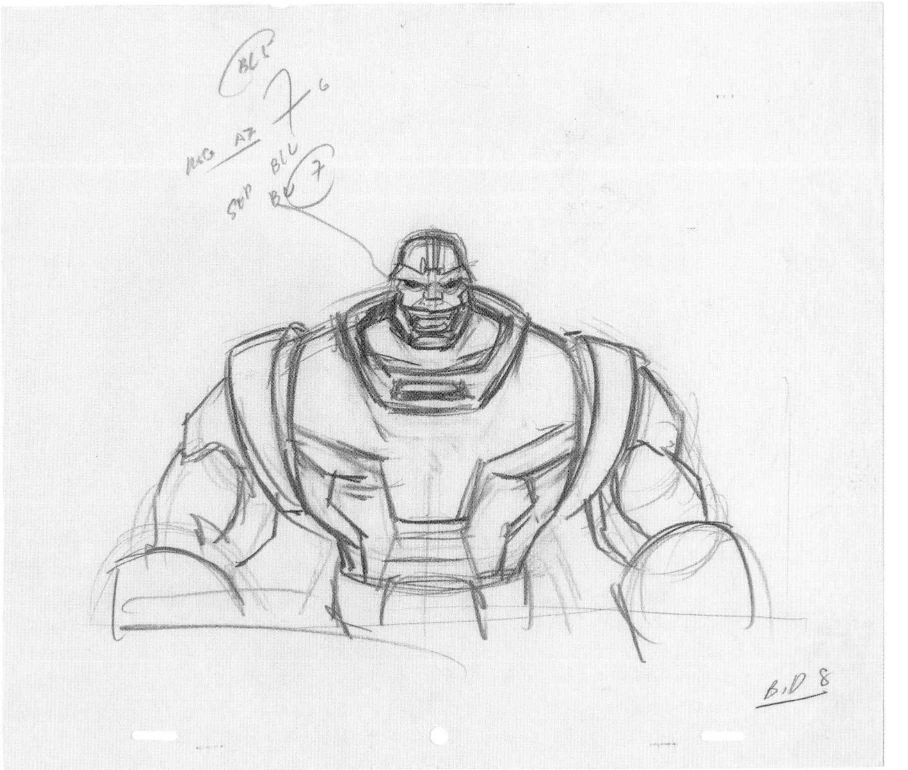

11

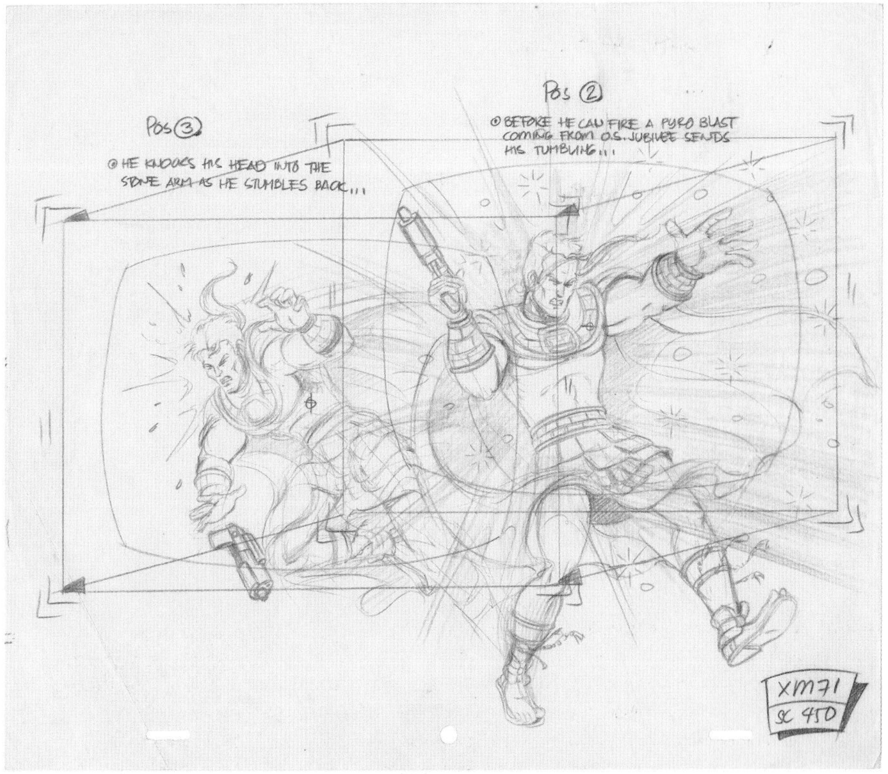
Pos ③
HE KNOCKS HIS HEAD INTO THE
STONE ARM AS HE STUMBLES BACK...
Pos ②
BEFORE HE CAN FIRE A PYRO BLAST
COMING FROM O.S. JUBILEE SENDS
HIS TUMBLING...
XM71
SC 450

12

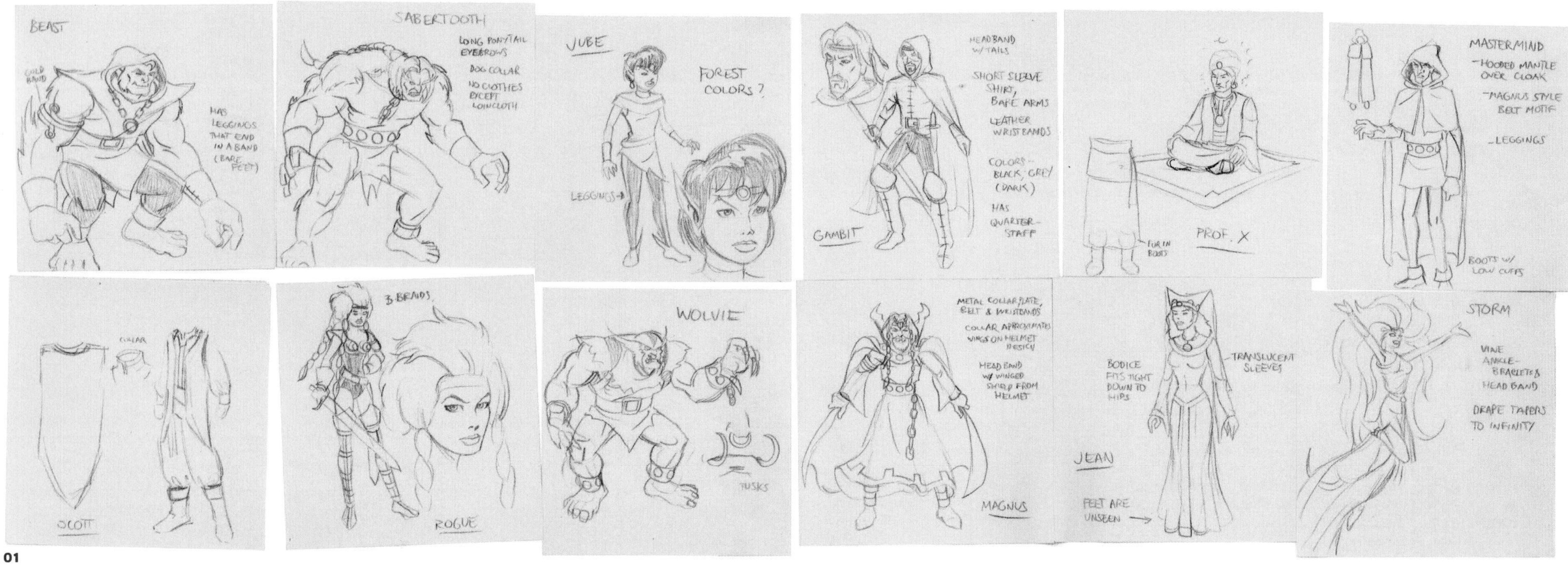
BEAST
SABERTOOTH
JUBE
FOREST COLORS ?
GAMBIT
PROF. X
MASTERMIND
SCOTT
ROGUE
WOLVIE
TUSKS
MAGNUS
JEAN
STORM

01

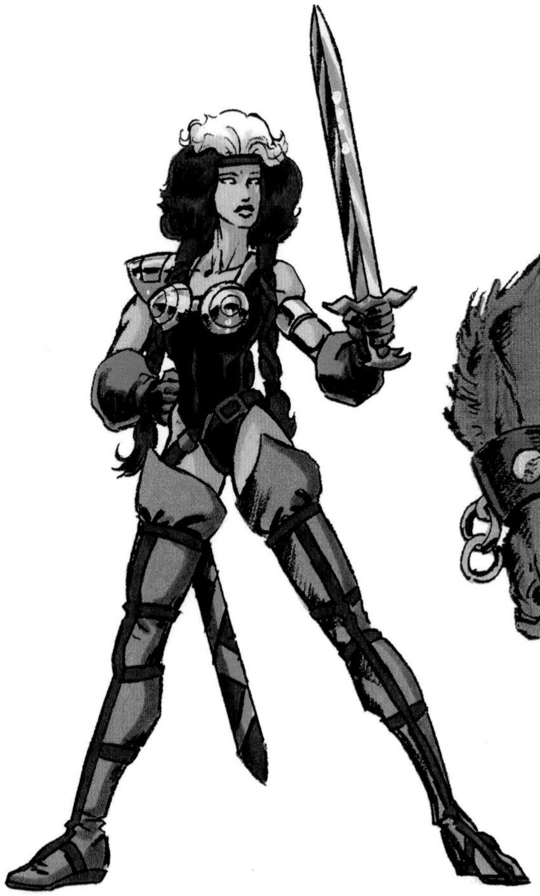

02

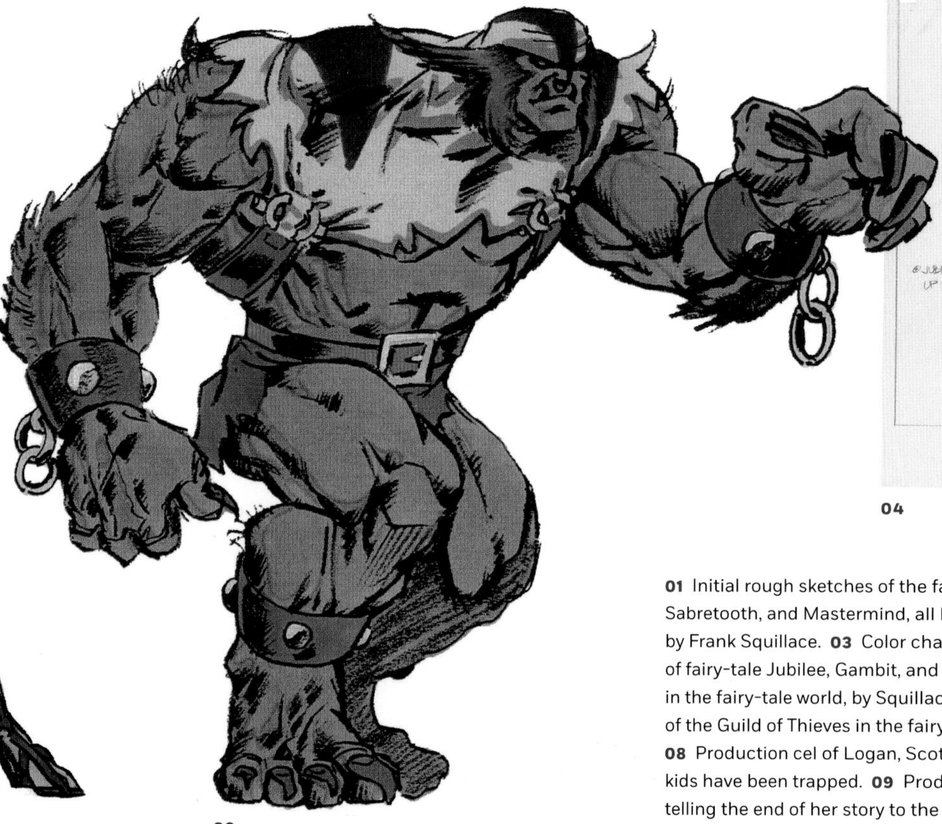

03

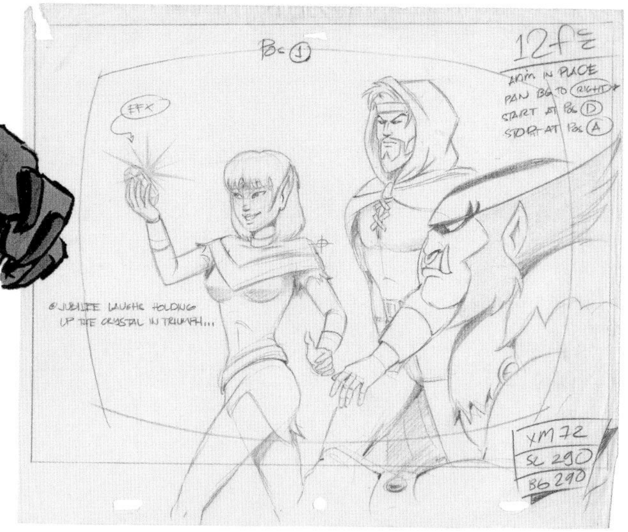
XM 72
SC 290
BG 290

04

01 Initial rough sketches of the fairy-tale versions of nine X-Men, Magento (Magnus), Sabretooth, and Mastermind, all by Mark Lewis. **02** Color character model of fairy-tale Rogue, by Frank Squillace. **03** Color character model of fairy-tale Wolverine, by Squillace. **04** Rough of fairy-tale Jubilee, Gambit, and Wolverine. **05–06** Sketches outside the Cavern of the Lost in the fairy-tale world, by Squillace. **07** Sketch for background layout of the Secret Stronghold of the Guild of Thieves in the fairy-tale world, by Squillace with tighter clean by Pat Agnasin. **08** Production cel of Logan, Scott, and Remy, as they find the cave where Jubilee and the school kids have been trapped. **09** Production cel of Jubilee sitting on the steps of Xavier's mansion, telling the end of her story to the school kids (missing cel layers) as Xavier and Jean Grey listen.

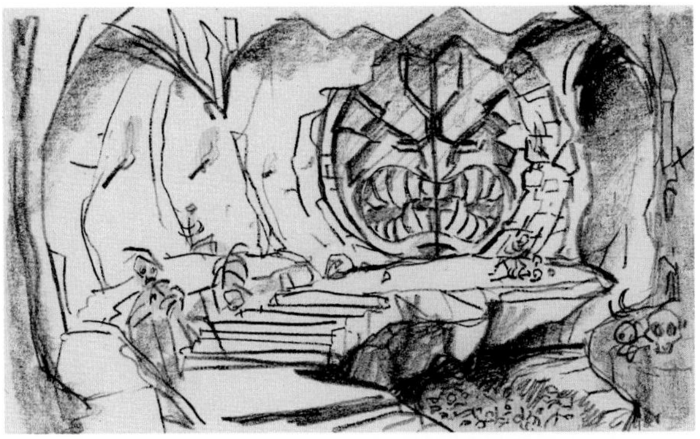
05

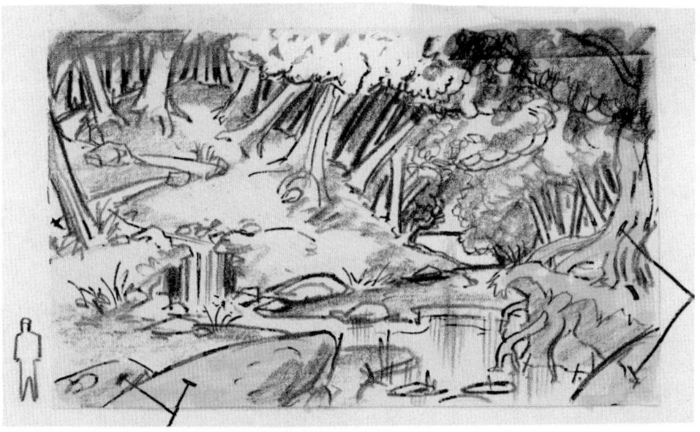
06

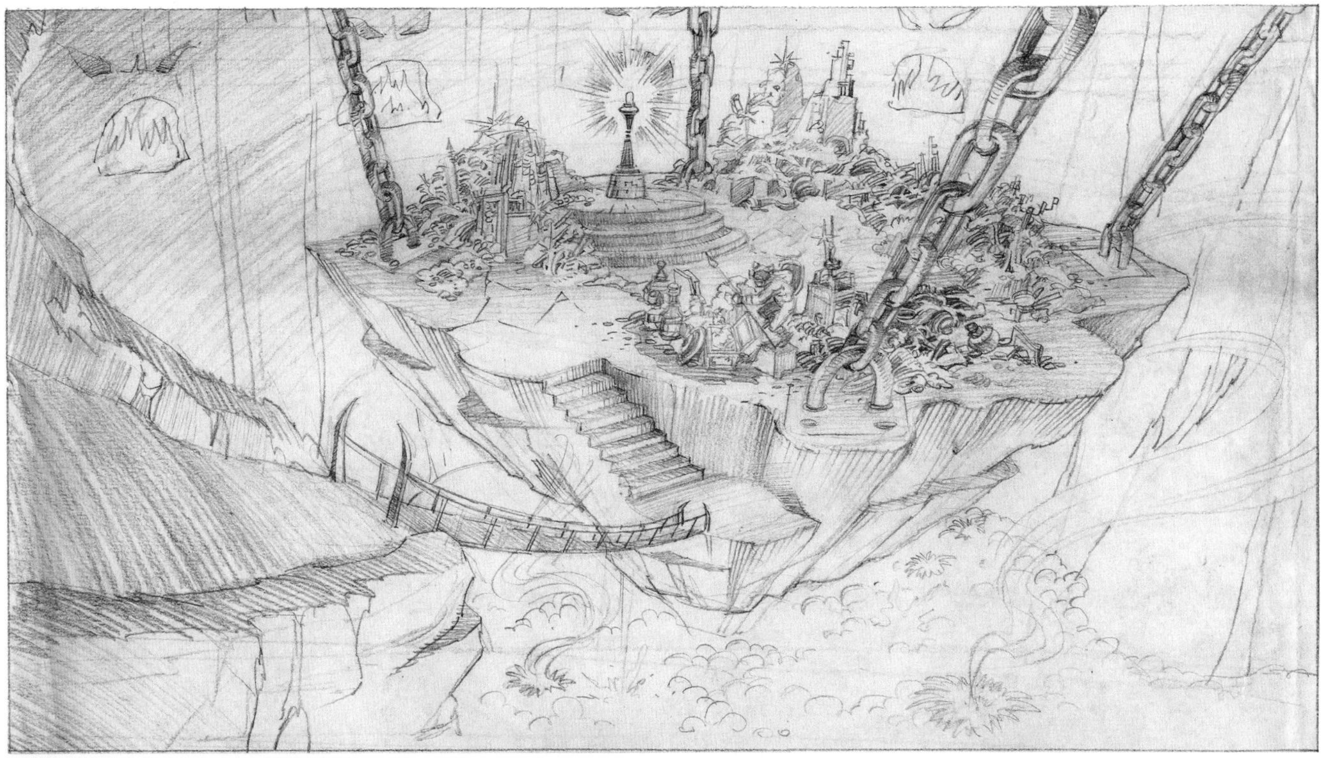
07

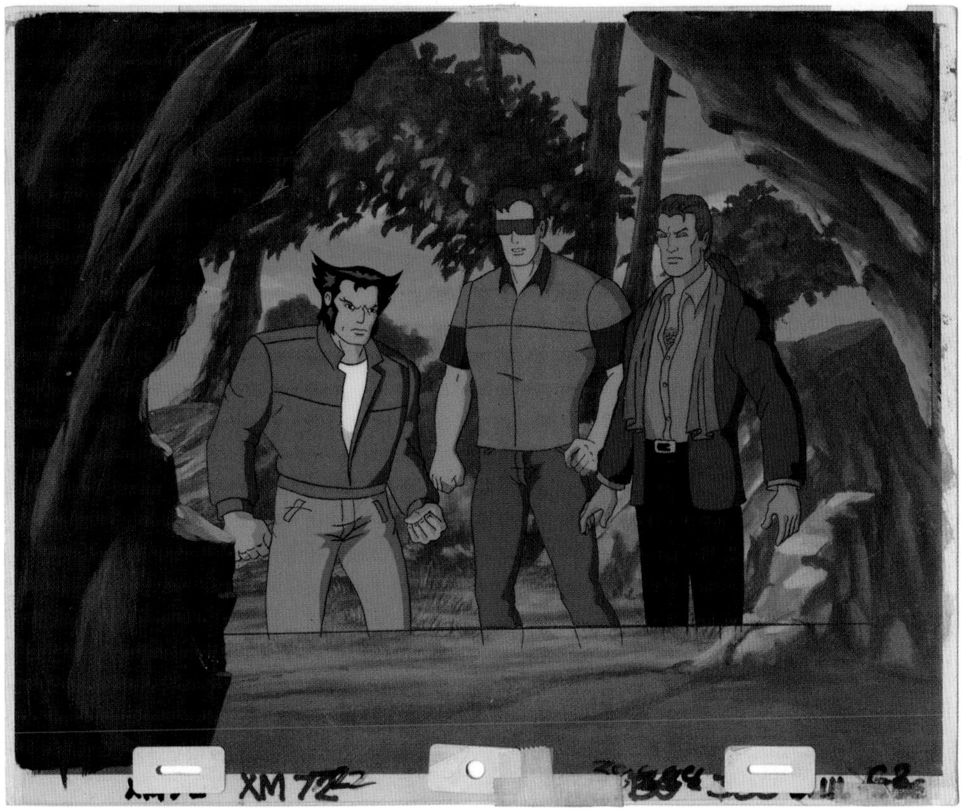
XM72
08

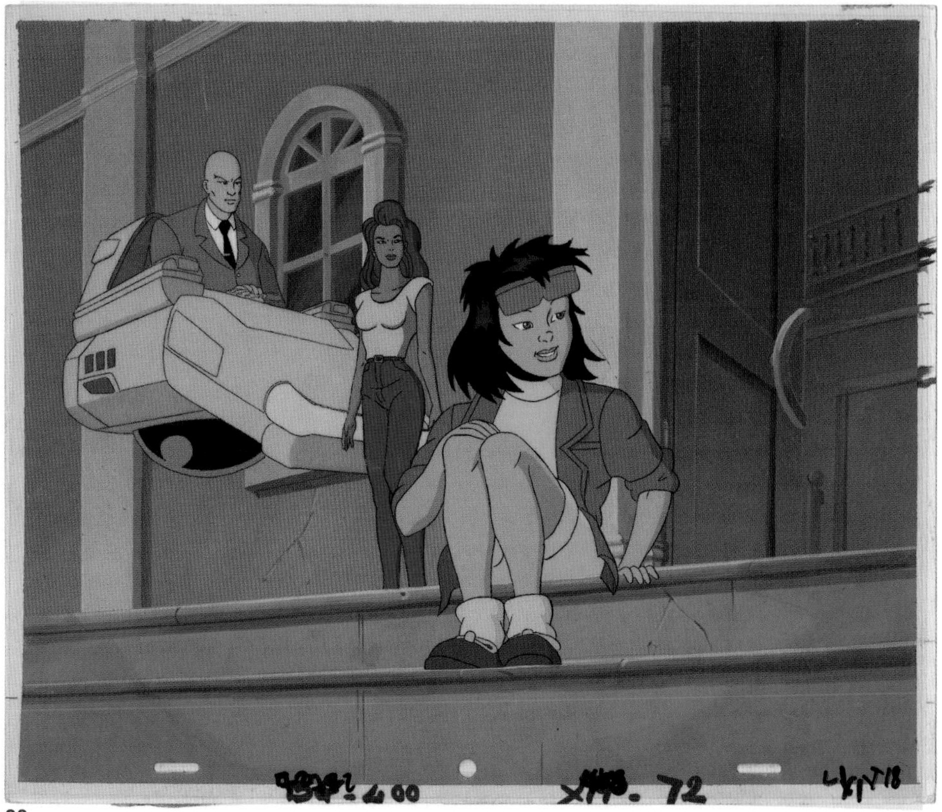
09

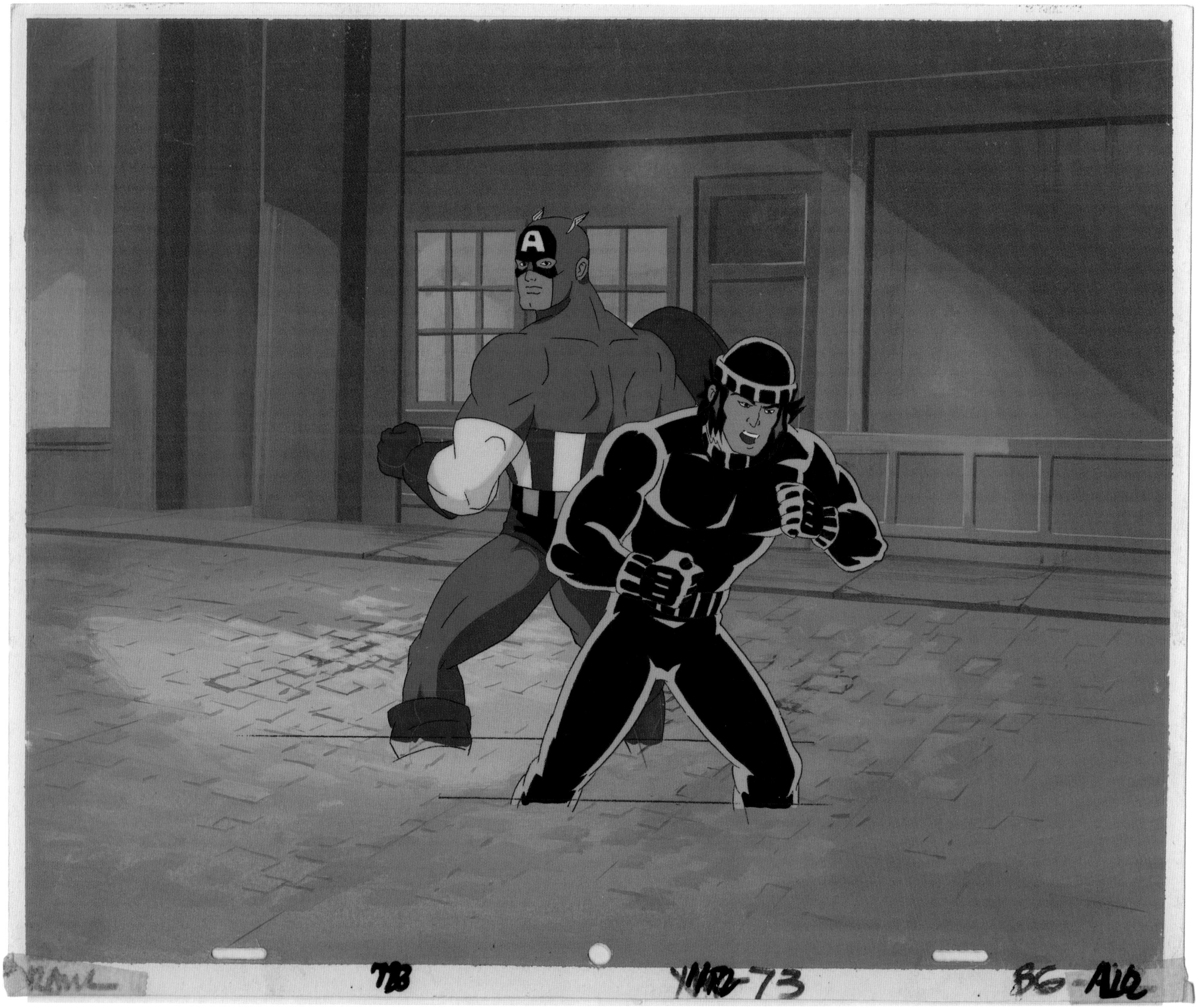

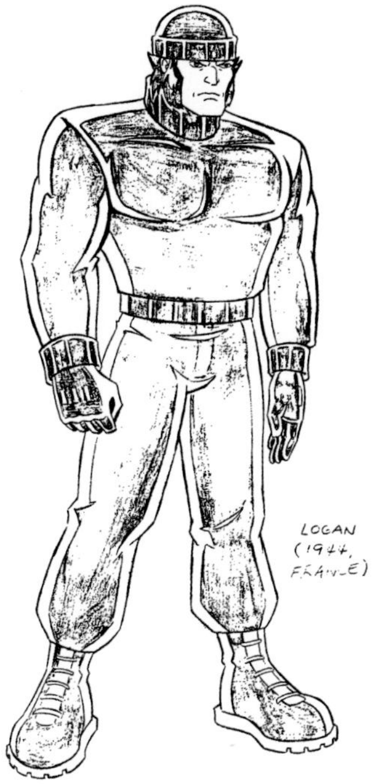
LOGAN
(1944,

01

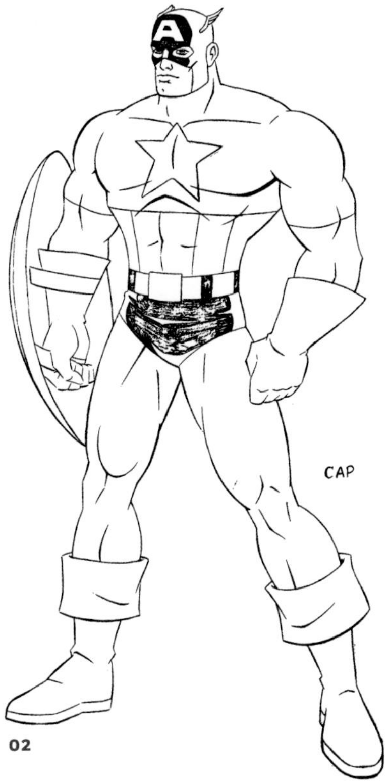
CAP

02

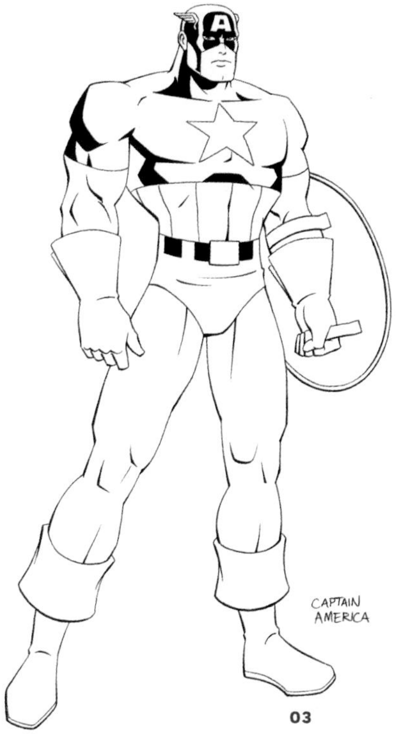
CAPTAIN AMERICA

03

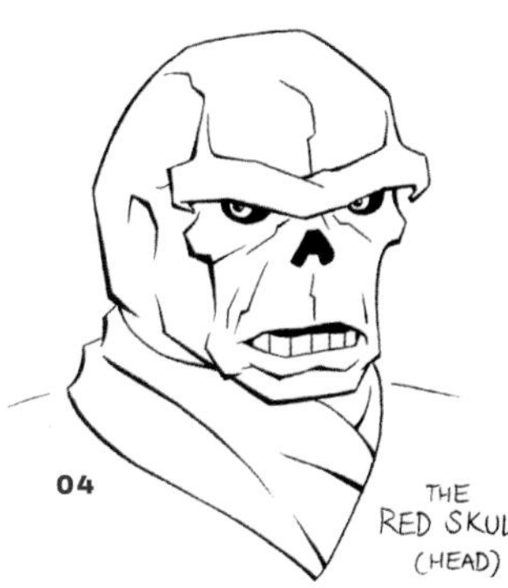
THE RED SKULL (HEAD)

04

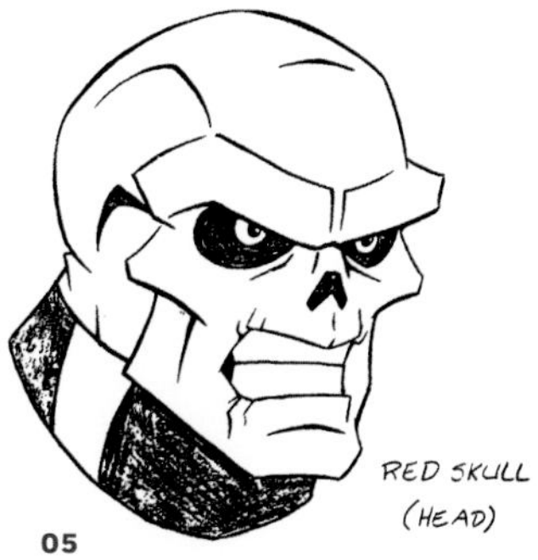
RED SKULL (HEAD)

05

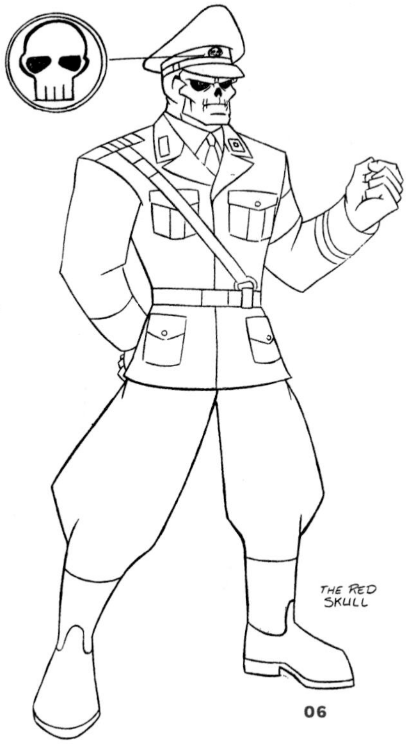
THE RED SKULL

06

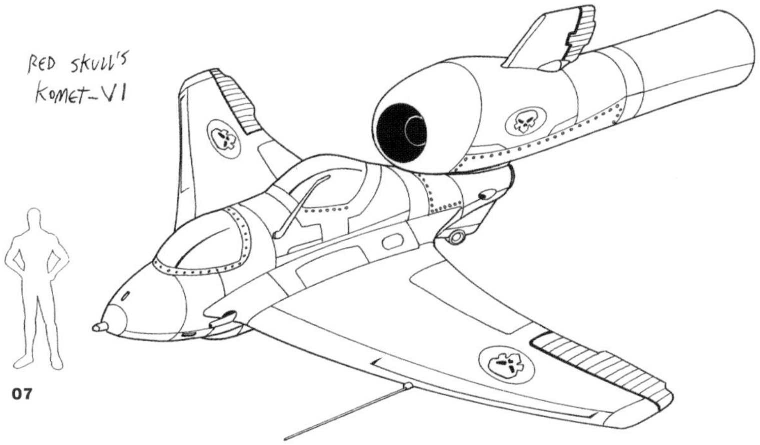
RED SKULL'S Komet-VI

07

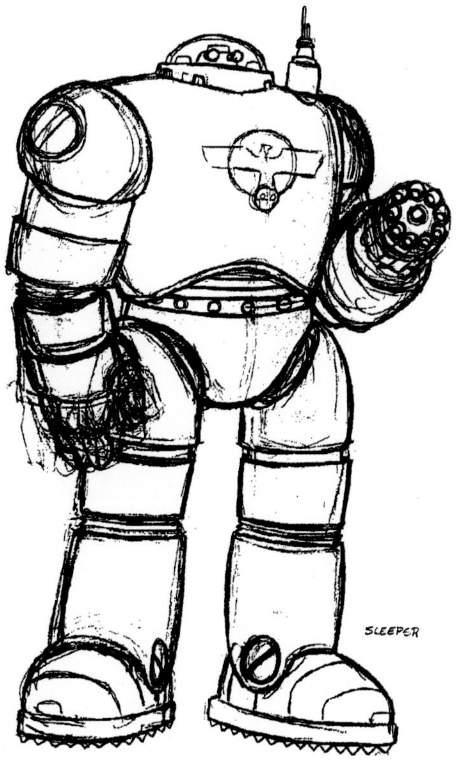
SLEEPER

08

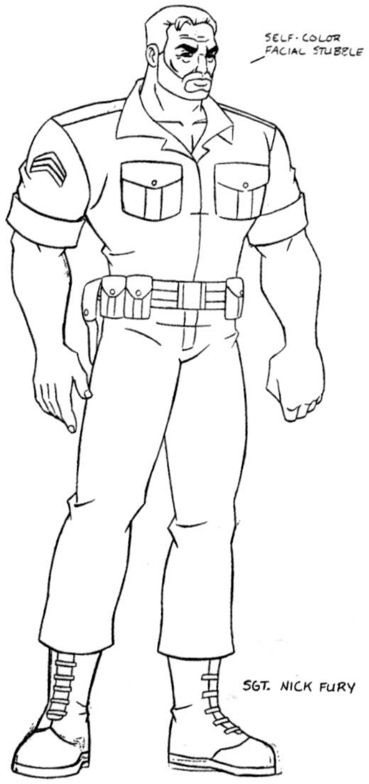
SELF-COLOR FACIAL STUBBLE
SGT. NICK FURY

09

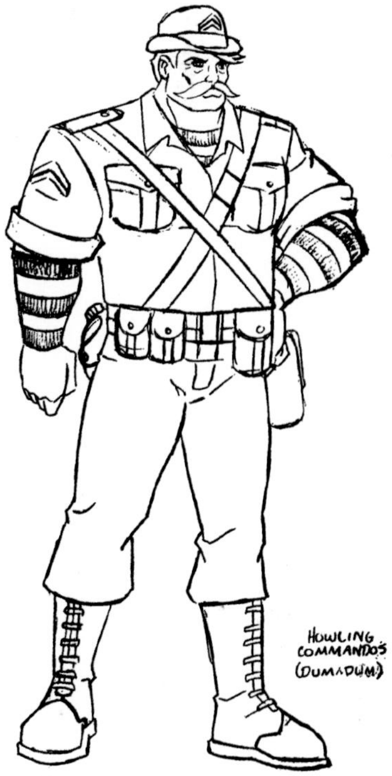
HOWLING COMMANDOS

10

OPPOSITE Production cel of Logan and Captain America in 1944 Paris, about to fight some Nazi goons. Wolverine co-creator Len Wein, who wrote the script, helped us get permission to use Captain America in *X-Men: TAS*. He loved the resulting episode but had one regret: "Cap does not have red trunks!" **01–10** Character and prop models for Logan's flashback-to-1944 episode. Except for the model of the Komet-VI plane ([07] designed by Frank Squillace and cleaned by Marcos Borregales and Mark Lewis) and the Sleeper robot ([08] designed by Squillace and cleaned by Lewis), all character models are by Roy Burdine and Lewis.

01–02 Initial sketches of 1944 Logan "trying on his first set of claws," climbing aids. Contrary to current canon, Wolverine co-creator Len Wein insisted that Logan was born only with his mutant healing powers, and that the claws, along with his Adamantium skeleton, were imposed upon him much later ("Logan was a healer who was turned into a weapon"). Thus the need for climbing aids here. **03** Initial sketches for Logan and Cap's fight with Nazi soldiers in Red Skull's castle base. **04** Sketches of "Unit One," an experimented-upon mutant deployed by a secret, fake-government, anti-mutant group, with color key notes. **05** Background of a high-tech lab where the secret anti-mutant group captured and experimented on mutants; designed and cleaned by Frank Squillace. **06** Animation production sketch for "Descent," of Dr. Nathaniel Essex (to become Mister Sinister) rushing through a London night in 1888, scaring a horse. **07** Animation production sketch of Charles Xavier's great-grandfather.

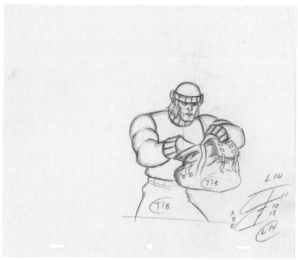

01

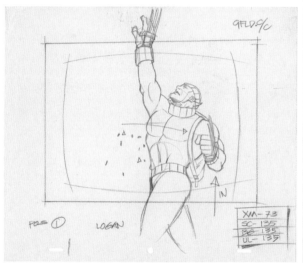

02

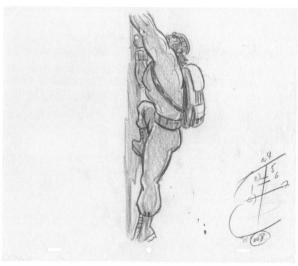

03

05

-INT. HI-TECH MEDICAL LAB-

04

06

07

01 New vehicle model for Blackbird and mini-jet, by Marco Borregales. **02** Rough of various mutant extras, including Sunfire, Feral, and Toad, as they react to Magneto's rallying cry. **03–04** Fifteen of the last pages of the storyboard (simplified style) of the X-Men and Magneto at Charles Xavier's bedside, paying their last respects as he lies dying. Lilandra appears. A heavy emotional scene, drawn by Dan Veesenmeyer.

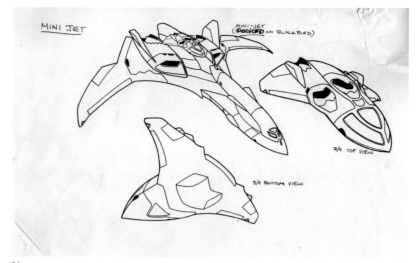

MINI JET

MINI-JET (DOCKED ON BLACKBIRD)

3/4 TOP VIEW

3/4 BOTTOM VIEW

01

XM-76

02

SC.   BG.   SC.   BG.   SC.   BG.

ACTION   ACTION   ACTION

START   (PAN)   STOP

XAVIER LOOKS TOWARDS THE END OF HIS BED, WEAK. SLOW PAN ACROSS ROOM TO SHOW THE X-MEN STANDING NEARBY, STARING BACK AT HIM IN LOVE AND RESPECT.

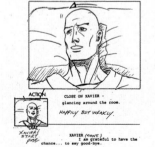

CLOSE ON XAVIER -
glancing around the room.

HAPPILY BUT WEAKLY.

XAVIER (CONT.)
I am grateful to have the
chance... to say good-bye.

ACTION
He looks forward towards
Morph, OS. Raises his head
a bit.

XAVIER (CONT.)
Morph... it is nice to see you home.

ACTION
ON MORPH - He's obviously choked up.

HE SMILES BACK AT XAVIER BUT
TEARS BEGIN TO WELL UP IN HIS
EYES.

XAVIER (OS)
... in facing your fears... you have proven
yourself truly... an X-Man. Gambit.

ACTION
ON GAMBIT -

LOOKING BACK SADLY.

XAVIER (OS)
... how often must... "the scoundrel" prove
himself a hero

ACTION
looking away, uncomfortable.

XAVIER (CONT. OS)
... before he believes it
himself? Jubilee...

ACTION
ON JUBILEE - Tears are streaming down her face.

XAVIER (OS)
... you are the future... when I look at
your face.

ACTION
JUBILEE BREAKS DOWN AND
BURIES HER FACE IN HER HANDS

XAVIER (CONT. OS)
I see hope... Storm...

03

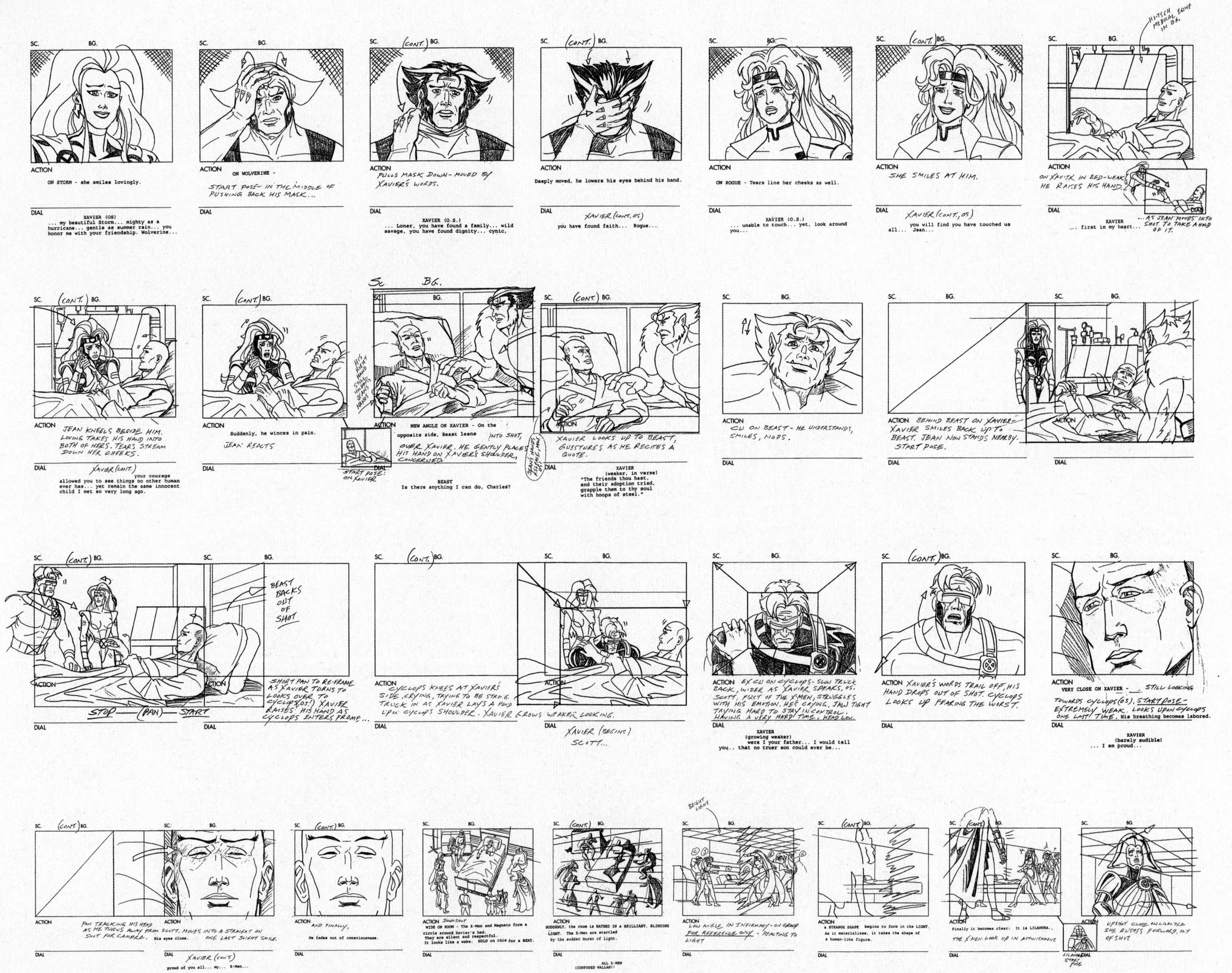
ON STORM - she smiles lovingly.
XAVIER (OS)
... my beautiful Storm... mighty as a hurricane... gentle as summer rain... you honor me with your friendship. Wolverine...
ON WOLVERINE - START POSE- IN THE MIDDLE OF PUSHING BACK HIS MASK...
PULLS MASK DOWN- MOVED BY XAVIER'S WORDS.
XAVIER (O.S.)
... Loner, you have found a family... wild savage, you have found dignity... cynic,
Deeply moved, he lowers his eyes behind his hand.
XAVIER (CONT, OS)
you have found faith... Rogue...
ON ROGUE - Tears line her cheeks as well.
XAVIER (O.S.)
... unable to touch... yet, look around you...
SHE SMILES AT HIM.
XAVIER (CONT, OS)
you will find you have touched us all... Jean...
HI-TECH MEDICAL EQUIP IN BG.
ON XAVIER IN BED- WEAK HE RAISES HIS HAND...
XAVIER
... first in my heart...
...AS JEAN MOVES INTO SHOT TO TAKE A HOLD OF IT.
JEAN KNEELS BESIDE HIM. LOVING TAKES HIS HAND INTO BOTH OF HERS. TEARS STREAM DOWN HER CHEEKS.
XAVIER (CONT.)
your courage allowed you to see things no other human ever has... yet remain the same innocent child I met so very long ago.
Suddenly, he winces in pain.
JEAN REACTS
HIS RIGHT HAND STILL HOLDING JEAN'S HANDS
START POSE: ON XAVIER
NEW ANGLE ON XAVIER - On the opposite side, Beast leans INTO SHOT, OVER XAVIER. HE GENTLY PLACES HIS HAND ON XAVIER'S SHOULDER, CONCERNED.
BEAST
Is there anything I can do, Charles?
XAVIER LOOKS UP TO BEAST, GUESTURES AS HE RECITES A QUOTE.
XAVIER
(weaker, in verse)
"The friends thou hast, and their adoption tried, grapple them to thy soul with hoops of steel."
CU ON BEAST - HE UNDERSTANDS, SMILES, NODS.
BEHIND BEAST ON XAVIER- XAVIER SMILES BACK UP TO BEAST. JEAN NOW STANDS NEARBY. START POSE.
BEAST BACKS OUT OF SHOT
STOP (PAN) START
SHORT PAN TO RE-FRAME AS XAVIER TURNS TO LOOKS OVER TO CYCLOPS(OS!) XAVIER RAISES HIS HAND AS CYCLOPS ENTERS FRAME...
CYCLOPS KNEES AT XAVIER'S SIDE, CRYING, TRYING TO BE STRONG. TRUCK IN AS XAVIER LAYS A HAND UPON CYCLOPS SHOULDER. XAVIER GROWS WEAKER LOOKING.
XAVIER (BEGINS)
SCOTT...
EX CU ON CYCLOPS- SLOW TRUCK BACK, WIDER AS XAVIER SPEAKS, OS. SCOTT, FIRST OF THE X-MEN, STRUGGLES WITH HIS EMOTION. HE'S CRYING. JAW TIGHT TRYING HARD TO STAY IN CONTROL. HAVING A VERY HARD TIME. HEAD LOW.
XAVIER
(growing weaker)
were I your father... I would tell you.. that no truer son could ever be...
XAVIER'S WORDS TRAIL OFF, HIS HAND DROPS OUT OF SHOT. CYCLOPS LOOKS UP FEARING THE WORST.
VERY CLOSE ON XAVIER - STILL LOOKING TOWARDS CYCLOPS(OS), START POSE- EXTREMELY WEAK. LOOKS UPON CYCLOPS ONE LAST TIME. His breathing becomes labored.
XAVIER
(barely audible)
... I am proud...
PAN TRACKING HIS HEAD AS HE TURNS AWAY FROM SCOTT. MOVES INTO A STRAIGHT ON SHOT FOR CAMERA. His eyes close. ONE LAST SLIGHT SMILE.
XAVIER (CONT)
proud of you all... my... X-Men...
AND FINALLY, He fades out of consciousness.
DOWNSHOT WIDE ON ROOM - The X-Men and Magneto form a circle around Xavier's bed. They are silent and respectful. It looks like a wake. HOLD on this for a BEAT.
SUDDENLY, the room is BATHED IN A BRILLIANT, BLINDING LIGHT. The X-Men are startled by the sudden burst of light.
ALL X-MEN
(CONFUSED WALLAH!)
BRIGHT LIGHT
LOW ANGLE IN INFIRMARY- ON GROUP FOR REFERENCE ONLY - REACTING TO LIGHT
a STRANGE SHAPE begins to form in the LIGHT. As it materializes, it takes the shape of a human-like figure.
Finally it becomes clear: It is LILANDRA.
THE X-MEN LOOK UP IN ASTONISHMENT.
LILANDRA START POSE
UPSHOT CLOSE ON LILANDRA SHE RUSHES FORWARD, OUT OF SHOT.

04

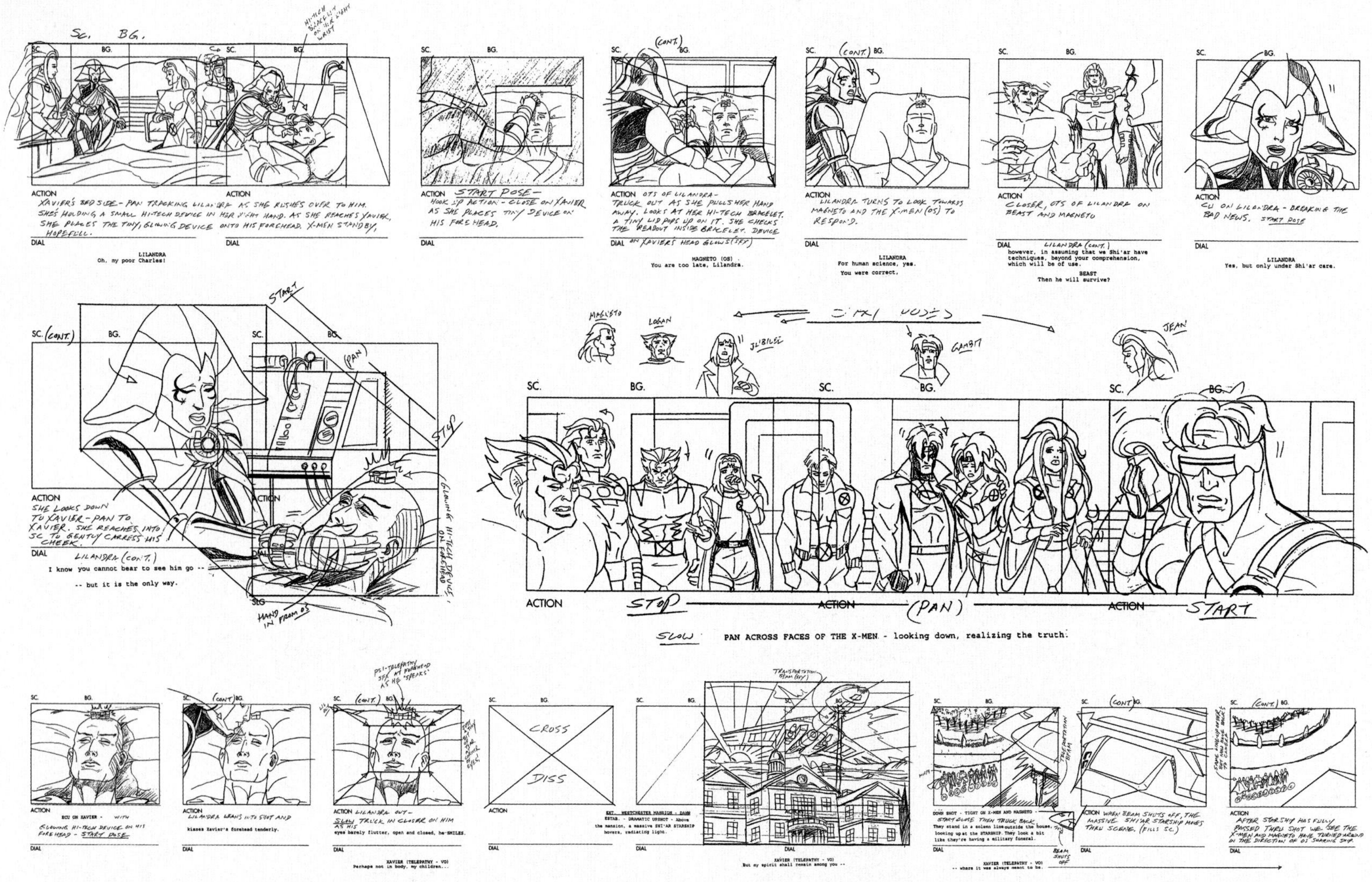

LILANDRA
Oh, my poor Charles!
MAGNETO (OS)
You are too late, Lilandra.
LILANDRA
For human science, yes.
You were correct.
LILANDRA (CONT.)
however, in assuming that we Shi'ar have techniques, beyond your comprehension, which will be of use.
BEAST
Then he will survive?
LILANDRA
Yes, but only under Shi'ar care.
I know you cannot bear to see him go --
-- but it is the only way.
PAN ACROSS FACES OF THE X-MEN. - looking down, realizing the truth.
STOP
(PAN)
START
CROSS
DISS
XAVIER (TELEPATHY - VO)
Perhaps not in body, my children...
XAVIER (TELEPATHY - VO)
But my spirit shall remain among you --
XAVIER (TELEPATHY - VO)
-- where it was always meant to be.

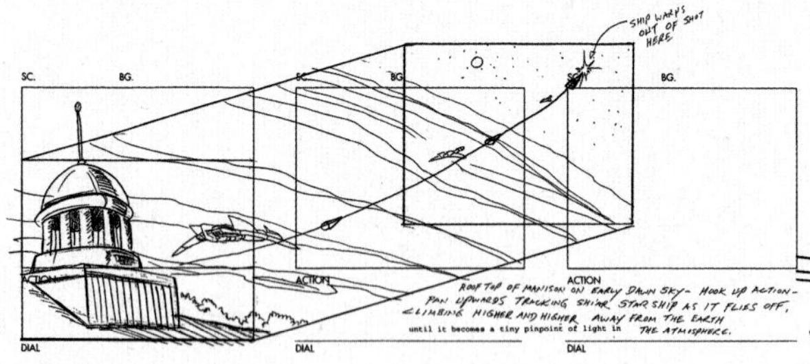

until it becomes a tiny pinpoint of light in

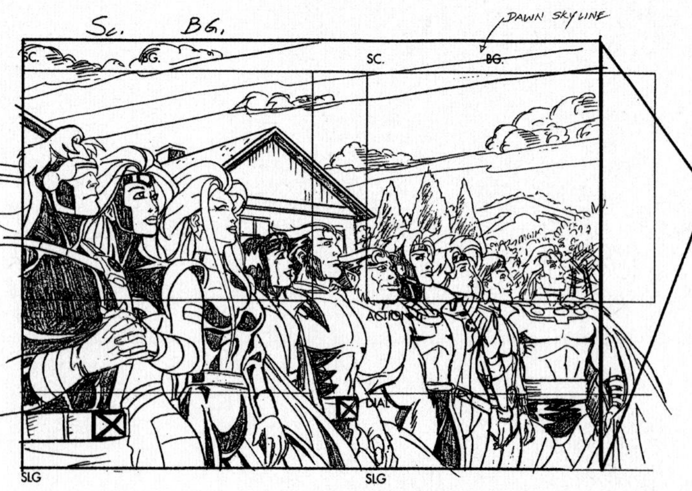

DAWN SKYLINE

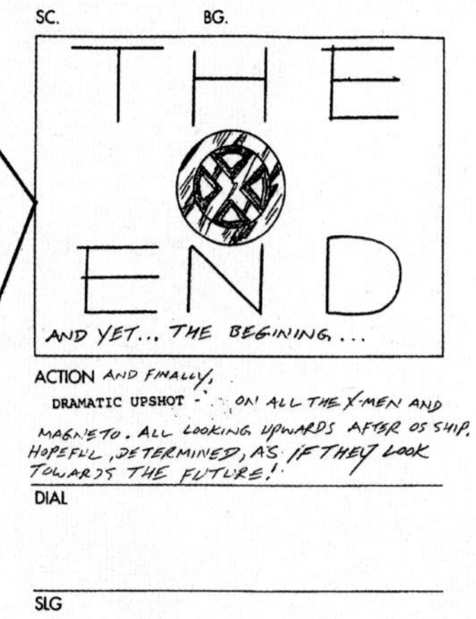

THE
END
AND YET... THE BEGINING...
DRAMATIC UPSHOT

THIS PAGE The final nine pages of the storyboard (continued) for the last scene of the series. By Dan Veesenmeyer. **OPPOSITE** Animation production sketch of the final group of Xavier's loved ones watching him being carried away in Lilandra's ship.

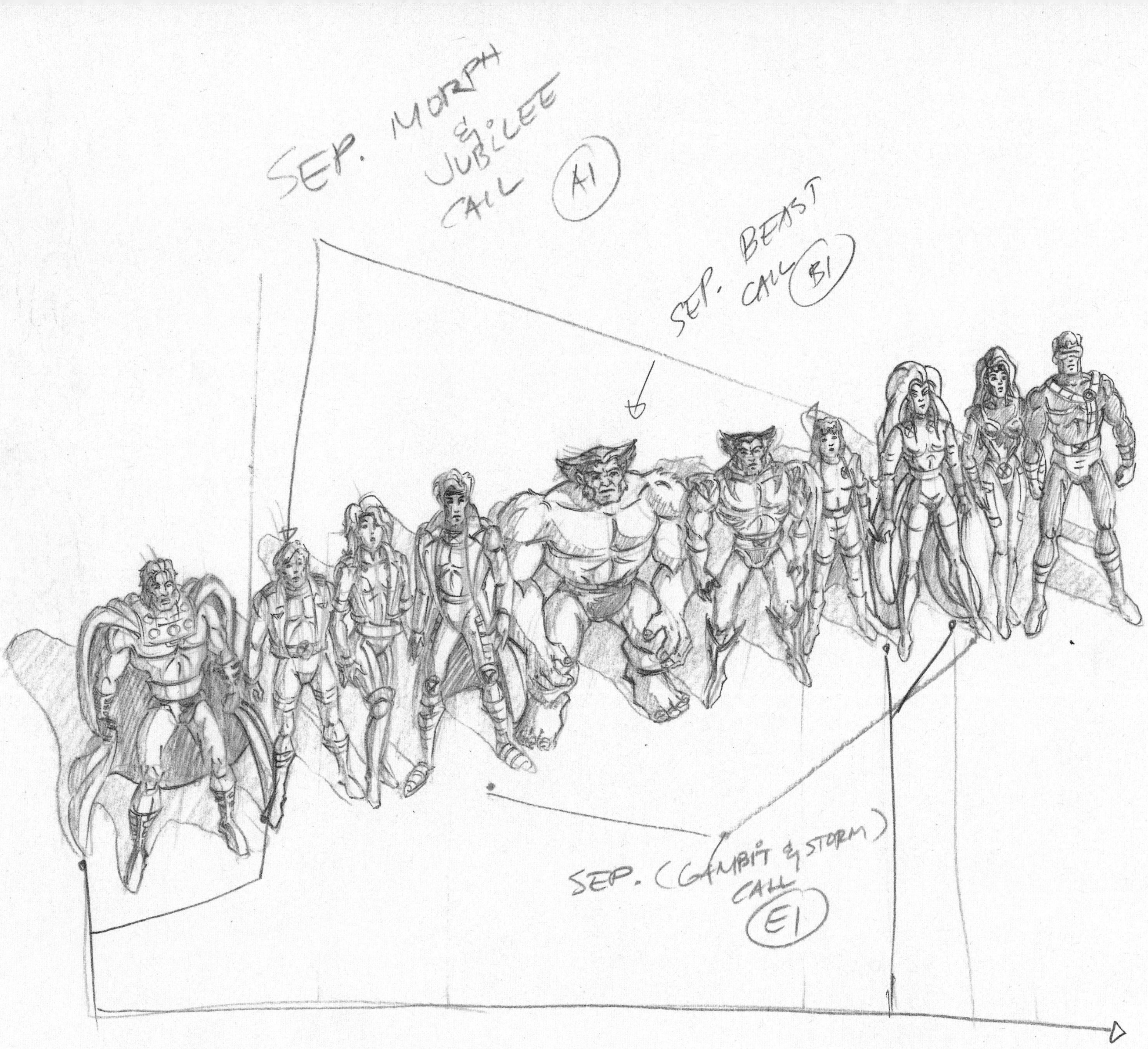
SEP. MORPH & JUBILEE CALL (A1)
SEP. BEAST CALL (B1)
SEP. (GAMBIT & STORM) CALL (E1)

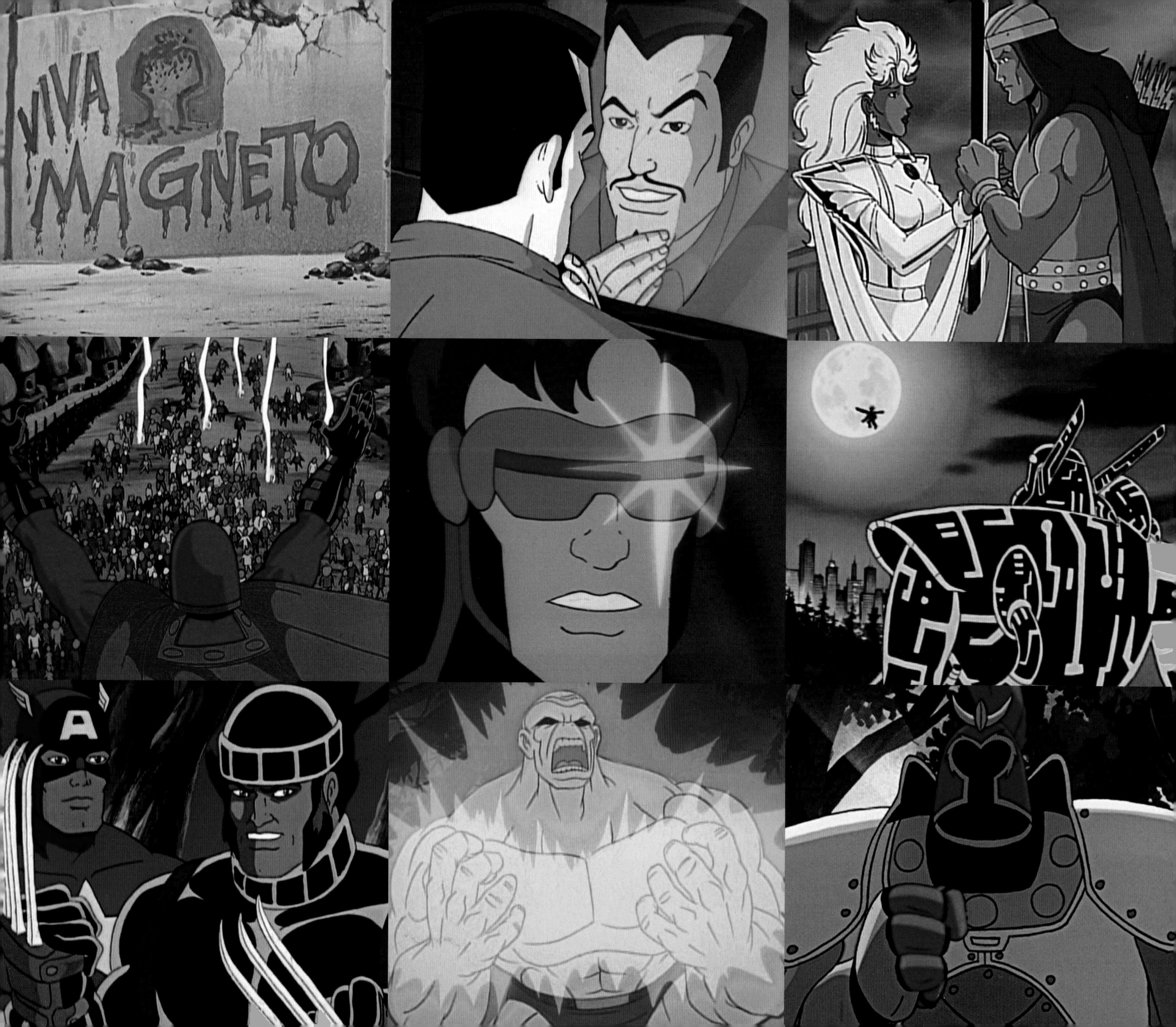
VIVA
MAGNETO

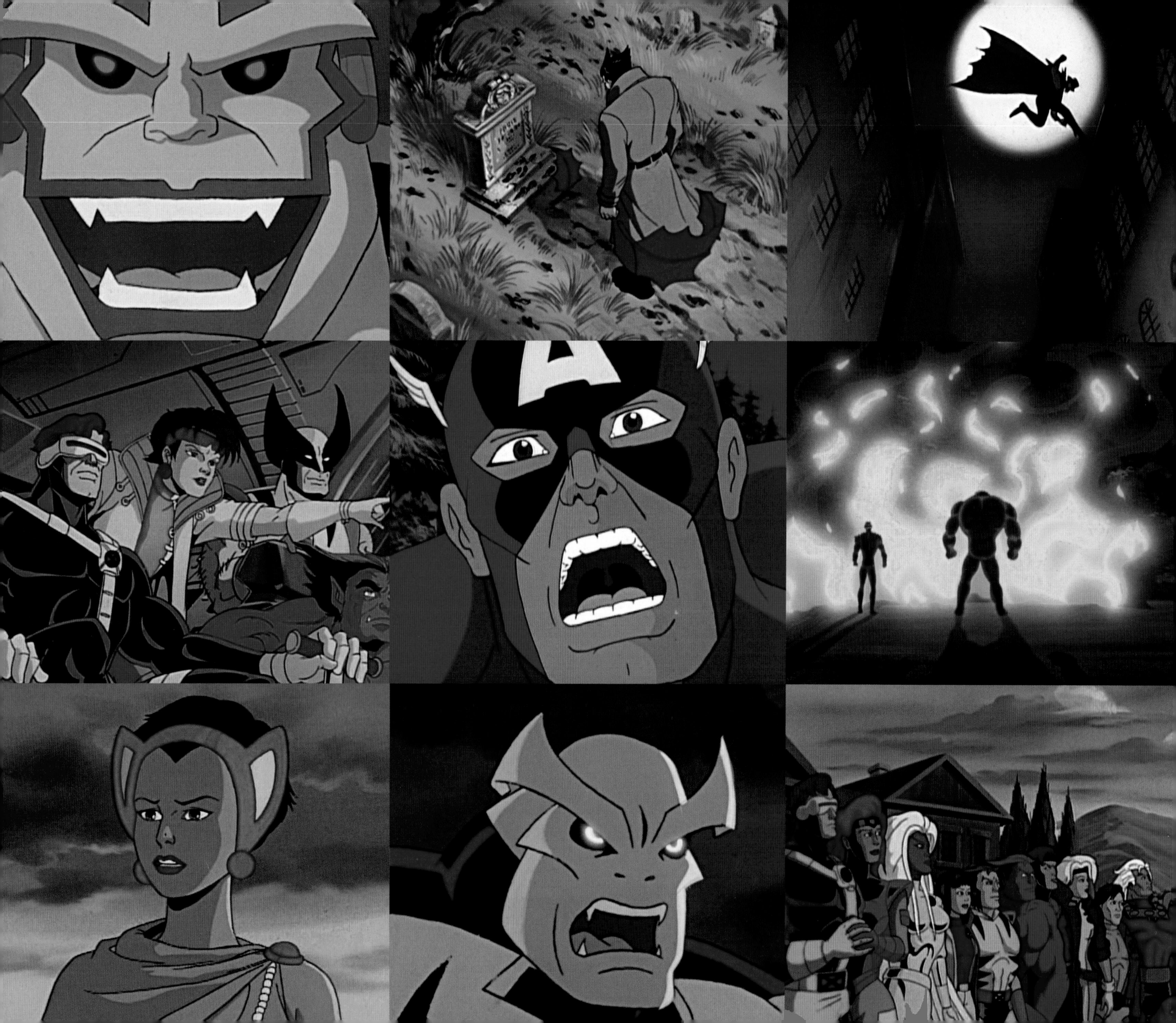

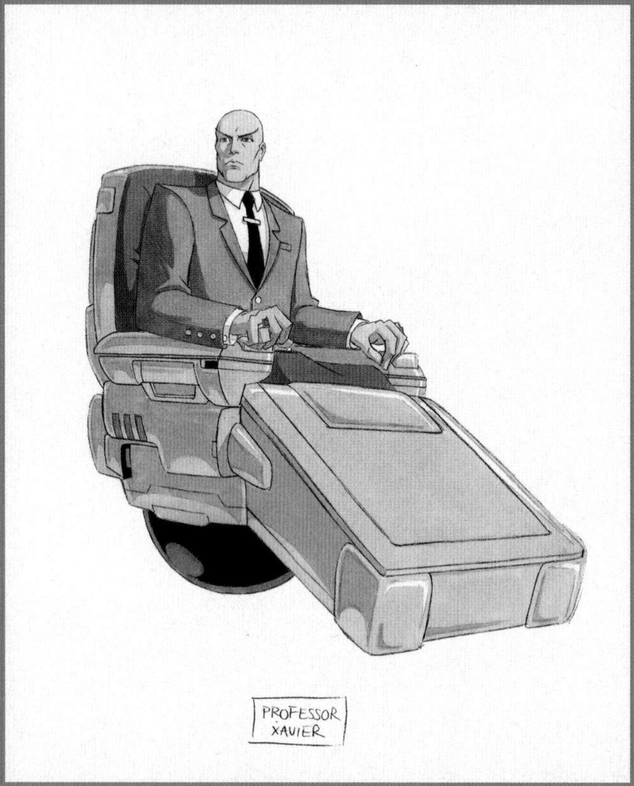
PROFESSOR XAVIER

01

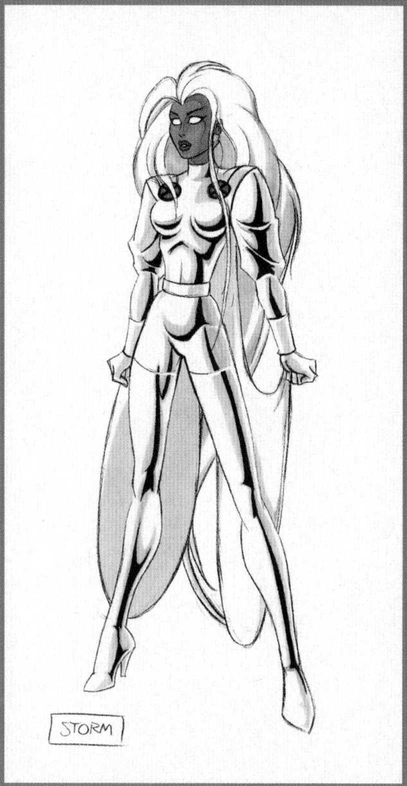
STORM

02

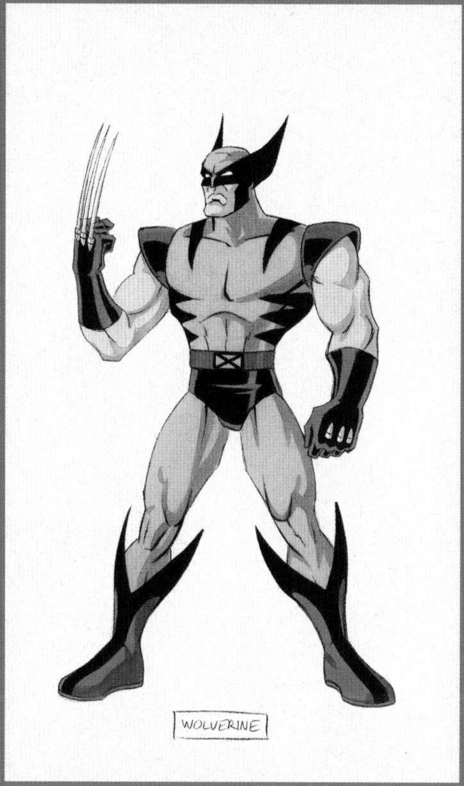
WOLVERINE

03

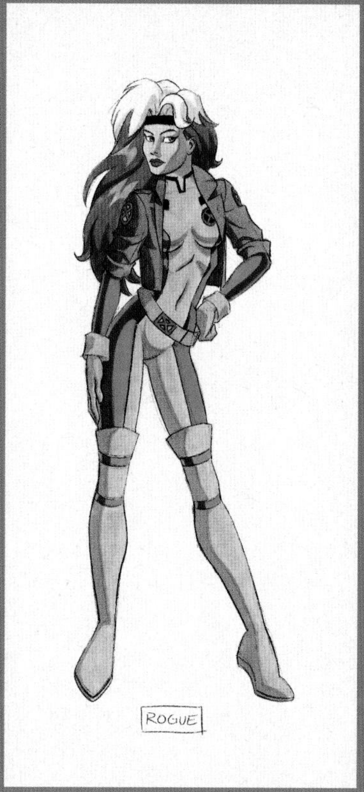
ROGUE

04

Artists at Play

During the final, afterthought season of eleven episodes, the new design team, led by series veterans Frank Squillace and Mark Lewis, came up with a fun idea amid all the cutbacks: a fresh look for the entire cast. Longer, leaner, even more anime-influenced, these character models were proposed by our dedicated artists at exactly the wrong time. When budgets were being slashed, the last thing the production supervisors needed was the added expense of redesigning the characters (that in fact had just been severely "simplified" to save money).

The "no" was quick and firm.

However, thanks to model designer Mark Lewis, this potential "new look" for the X-Men team has been preserved and is presented here for the first time.

01–15 Artists Frank Squillace and Mark Lewis offer a more anime-inspired look to the cast. Squillace designed models 03, 06, 07, 09, 10, 11, 14, and 15. Lewis designed models 01, 02, 04, 05, 08, 12, and 13. All models were consolidated with a pencil-tightening pass by Lewis for consistency, and Squillace and Lewis split the coloring work.

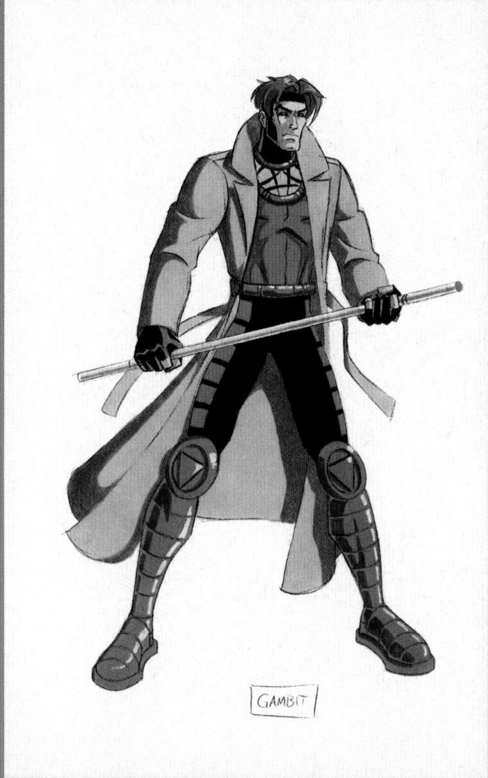
GAMBIT

05

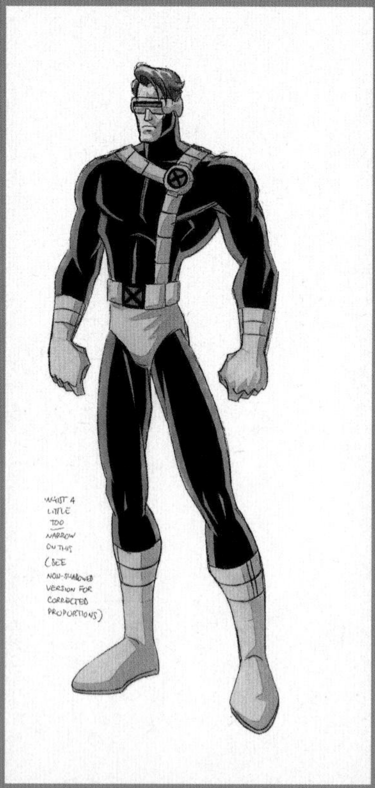
WAIST A LITTLE TOO NARROW ON THIS (SEE NON-SHADOWED VERSION FOR CORRECTED PROPORTIONS)

06

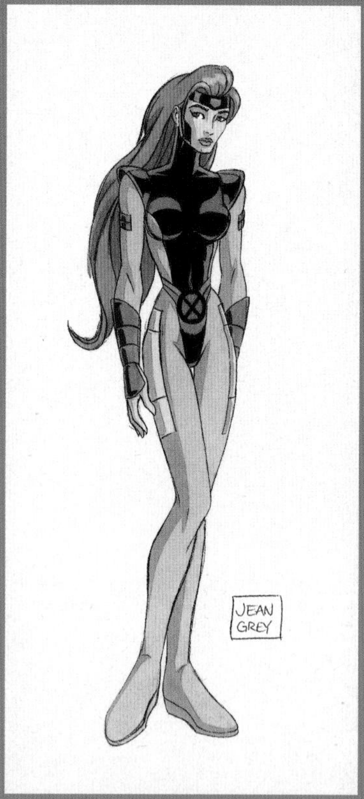
JEAN GREY

07

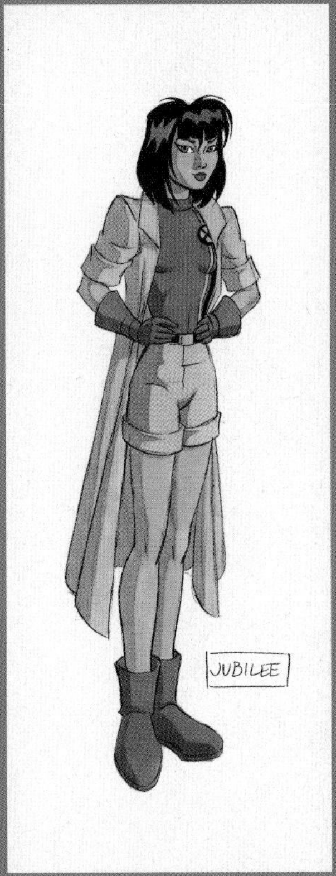
JUBILEE
08

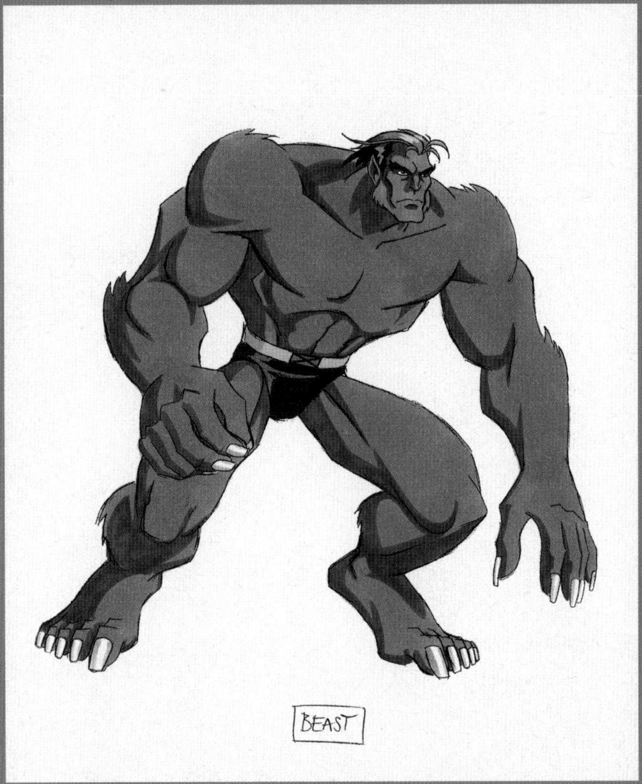
BEAST
09

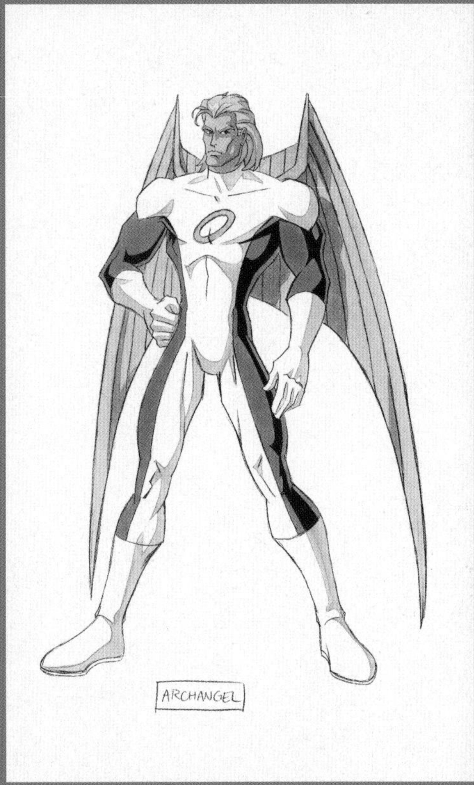
ARCHANGEL
10

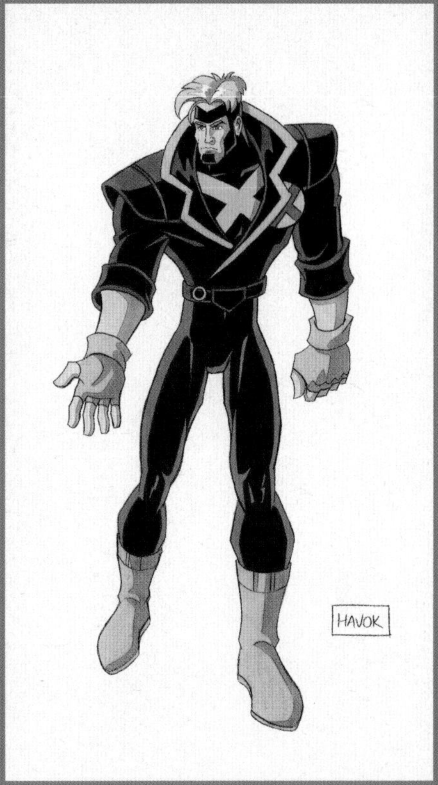
HAVOK
11

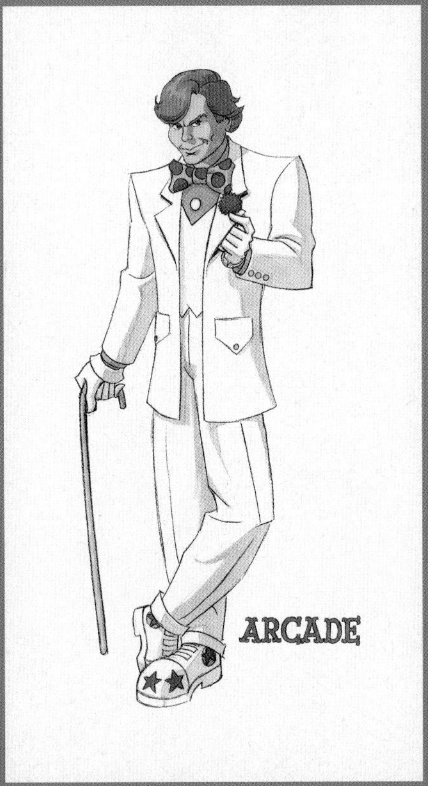
ARCADE
12

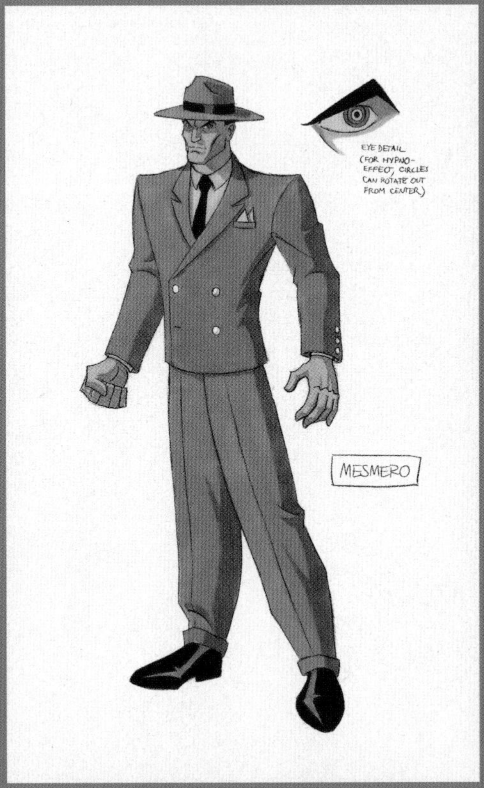
EYE DETAIL
(FOR HYPNO-EFFECT, CIRCLES CAN ROTATE OUT FROM CENTER)
MESMERO
13

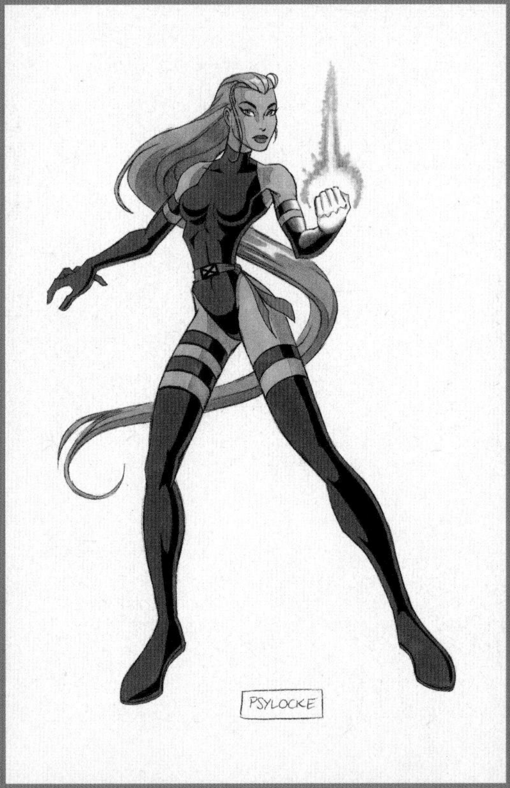
PSYLOCKE
14

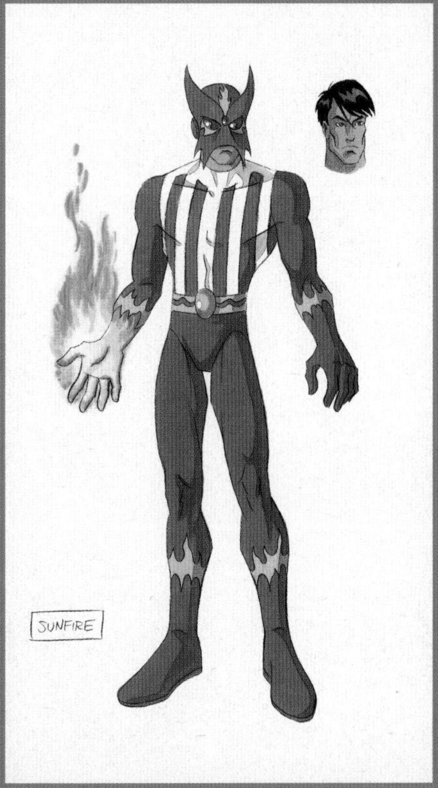
SUNFIRE
15

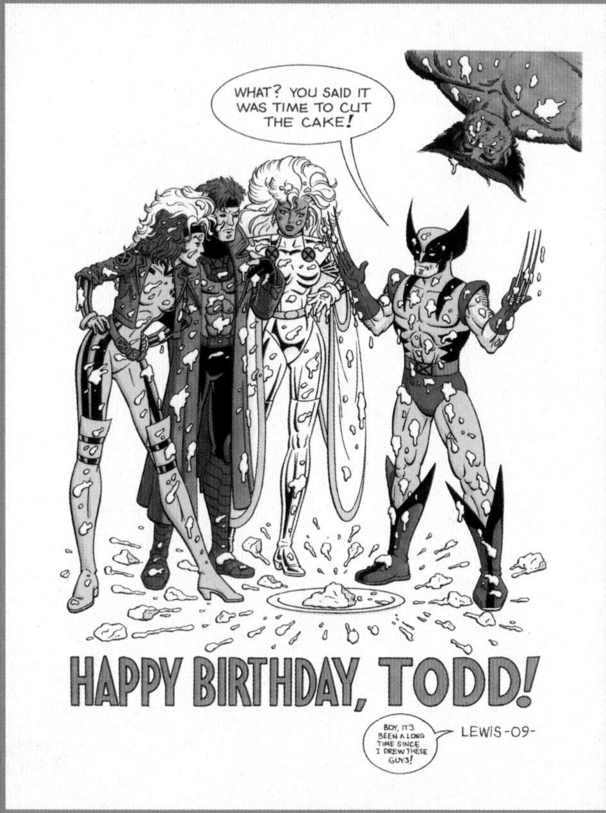
WHAT? YOU SAID IT WAS TIME TO CUT THE CAKE!
HAPPY BIRTHDAY, TODD!
BOY, IT'S BEEN A LONG TIME SINCE I DREW THESE GUYS!
LEWIS -09-

01

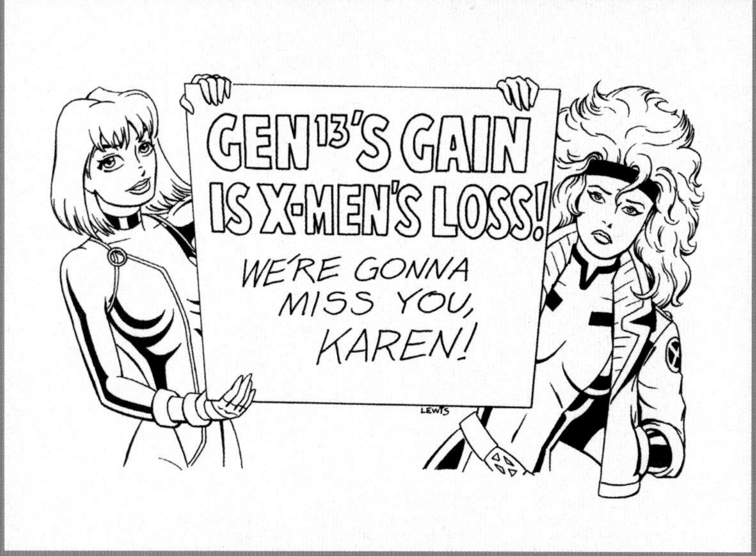
GEN13'S GAIN IS X-MEN'S LOSS!
WE'RE GONNA MISS YOU, KAREN!
LEWIS

02

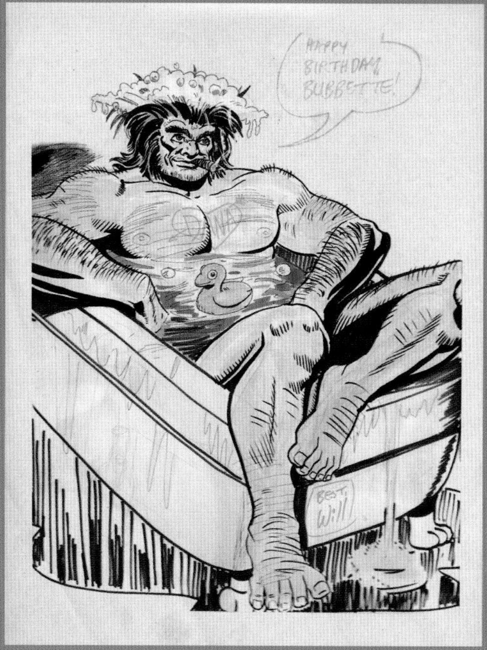
HAPPY BIRTHDAY, BUBBETTE!
BEST, WILL

03

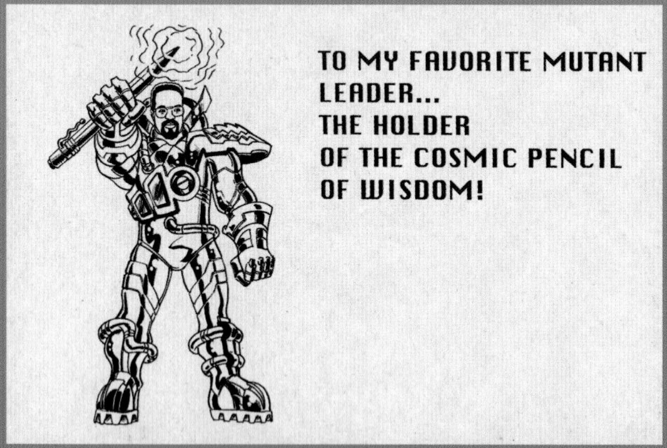
TO MY FAVORITE MUTANT LEADER...
THE HOLDER OF THE COSMIC PENCIL OF WISDOM!

04

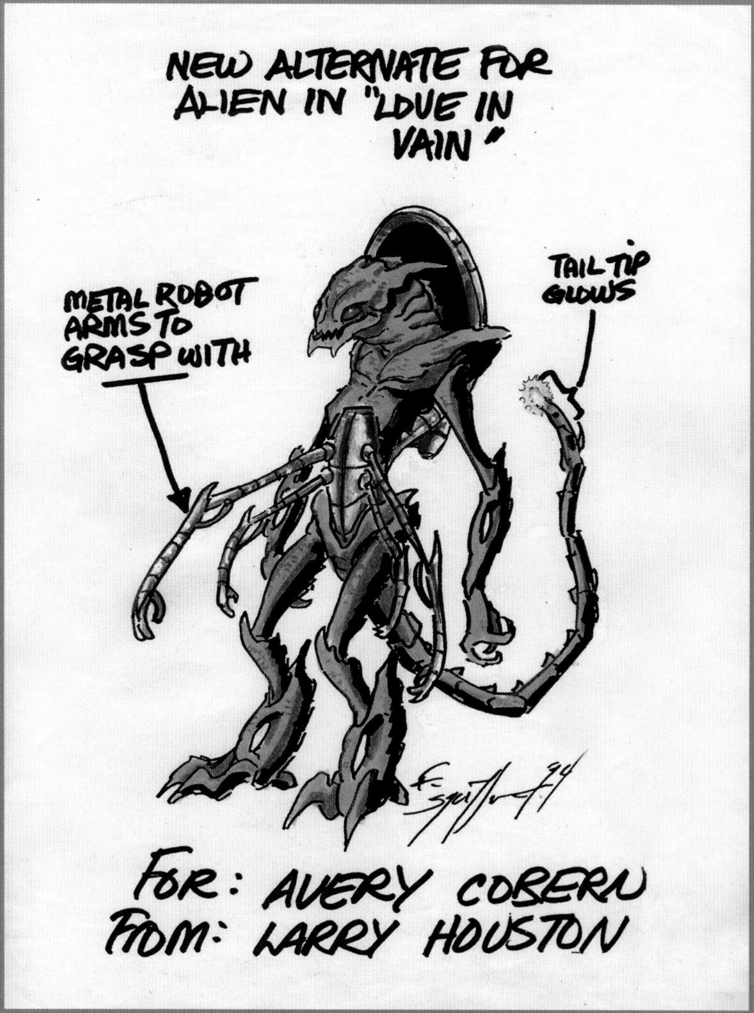
NEW ALTERNATE FOR ALIEN IN "LOVE IN VAIN"
METAL ROBOT ARMS TO GRASP WITH
TAIL TIP GLOWS
FOR: AVERY COBERN
FROM: LARRY HOUSTON

05

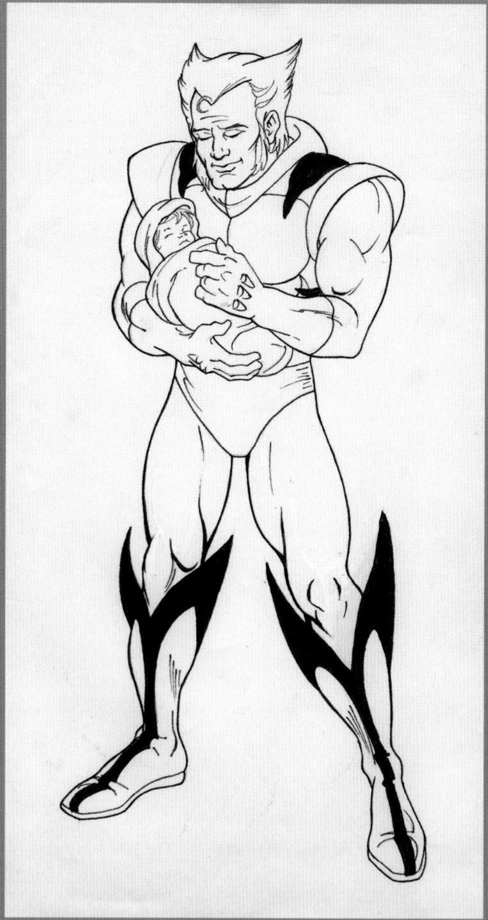

06

01 Model designer Mark Lewis hasn't lost his touch. **02** A farewell card to a departing crew member, Karen Kollis, by Lewis. **03** Will Meugniot rewards our hard-working production manager (Dana) with a tub full of Logan. **04** A salute to the art staff's fearless leader, Larry Houston, by Frank Squillace. **05** What appears to be a gift, even a Valentine, from producer/director Houston to our network censor Avery Cobern, is in fact a re-submission of creature design (by Squillace) for the alien who attacks Rogue in "Love in Vain." **06** A loving Logan drawn for a staff-member parent, unknown, designed by Squillace.

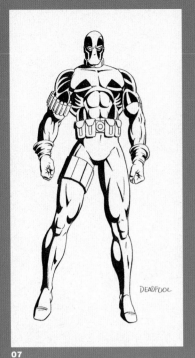

DEADPOOL

07

AFRICAN
MUTANT
REFUGEE #3

08

(START)
(STOP)
SC.
BG.
SC.
BG.
SC.
AURORA
BOOM BOOM
RICTOR
LASERS
FERAL
BLOB
ACTION
ACTION
ACTION
DIAL
RANDOM LASERS ZIP BY!
NORTHSTAR AND AURORA TAKE OFF INTO SKY
BOOM-BOOM THROWS 2 ENERGY TIME BOMBS
RICTOR SHOOTS OUT SEISMIC EARTHQUAKE WAVES OF ENERGY
FERAL RUNS FORWARD FAST! CAT-LIKE!
BLOB KIND-OF STOMPS FORWARD. HE'S NOT VERY FAST

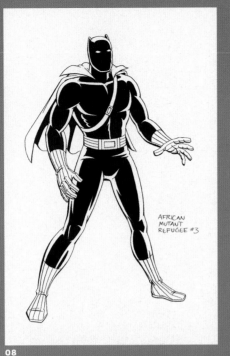

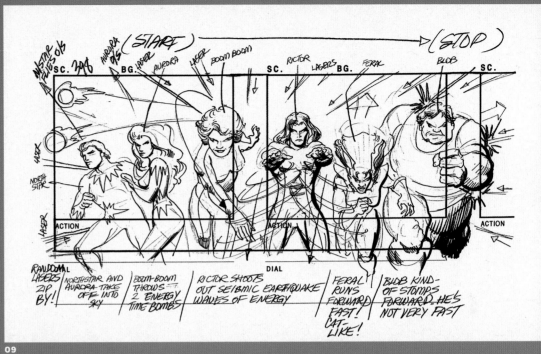

09

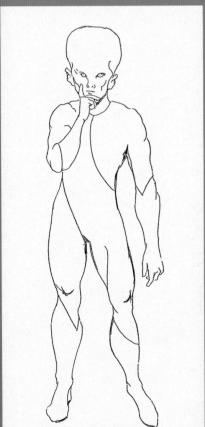

10

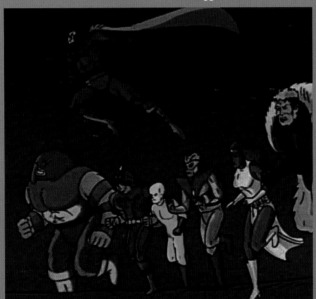

11

07–08 Character models of cameo-appearing Deadpool, by Frank Brunner and Mark Lewis, and Black Panther, by Lewis (for the first TV or film appearance of Black Panther). **09** Dynamic, annotated storyboard page of six attacking villains. **10** Character model of mystery villain from the opening-credit sequence—now known to be Gremlin. **11** Gremlin in action, in the opening-title sequence.

ALL OF THE ARTISTS WERE FANS of the Marvel Universe. So, rather than make up characters for background or cameo bits, they populated the screen with Marvel characters that they loved and wanted to celebrate. It started at the top with Larry Houston; in fact, the first televised images of Deadpool and Black Panther appeared on our series, courtesy of Larry.

Larry explains, "It clicked with the audience by making the incidental characters somebody that they already knew. I then brought in my collection of *X-Men* books and so did the other guys, and we would give them to the model designers, Frank Brunner and Mark Lewis, and we'd just make background mutants look like characters from the books. I think that really helped the first season because people started seeing what they would now call Easter eggs."

Much to our delight, we discovered later that fans noticed these small indulgences and enjoyed keeping track of them. In the early '90s, there was no real Internet over which to share information, but fans managed. From school playgrounds to college common rooms, from early message boards to office water coolers, word got around. Fans loved these extra touches.

For the eagle-eyed fan, in the opening credits the pink-and-green mutant running next to Warpath has always been a mystery. At long last, Larry Houston supplies the definitive answer: "At first I thought it was a [coloring] mistake and wanted AKOM to correct the animation." But then Larry remembered there was an obscure mutant called Gremlin, son of Gargoyle. Gremlin had been added without Larry's prior approval by another artist. By the time it was all straightened out, it was too late to change the animation, and Gremlin remained.

It just goes to show that effective television creation is not all hard work and rational decisions but can benefit from the fun and joy that the creators take in the doing of it.

WHEN ARTISTS ARE THROWN TOGETHER on a long, demanding, repetitive job, inevitably they look for ways to play. The *X-Men: TAS* crew was no different. Crew members were constantly drawing themselves and their colleagues into episodes. Fox Executive Sidney Iwanter was a favorite target.

Video editor Sharon Janis, responsible for the "Previously on X-Men" recaps on top of her other editing duties, appeared in the episode "Nightcrawler."

Frank Squillace, Scott Thomas, Joe Calamari, production manager Kurt Weldon, and Mark Lewis were also represented in various episodes.

Larry Houston may hold the honors for most appearances, from a senator to a copilot to assault force member, among others.

Behind-the-scenes staffers Linda De La Rosa and Leanne Moreau appeared as a captured psychic and a waitress. Overseas supervisor Cam Drysdale's name showed up on a personalized license plate.

In the episode "Beauty and the Beast," our youngest son, Alec Bohlson Lewald, lent his first and middle names to Beast's fellow researcher, while Carly's name came from the daughter of our good friends Carter and LuAnne Crocker.

In the third part of the "Dark Phoenix" saga, a touching call-back occurs when we see that Beast has taped a photograph of his beloved Carly to his computer monitor.

Larry Houston's sons Andrew and Adrian were used as models, as were Frank Brunner's wife, Kisara, and daughter, Nicole.

In the "Time Fugitives" saga, a list of the "plague-infected" was filled with the names of production people.

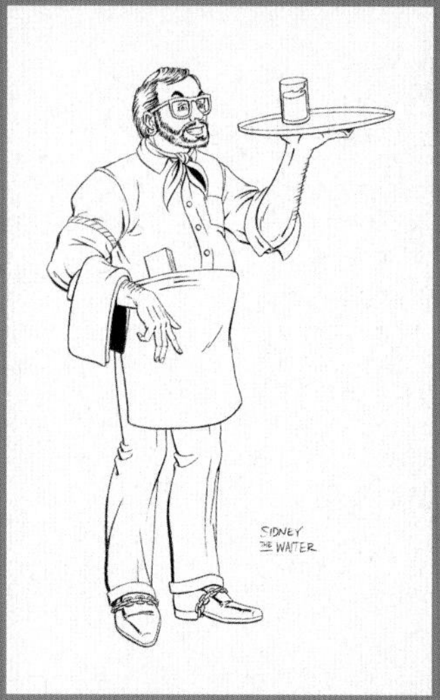
SIDNEY THE WAITER
01

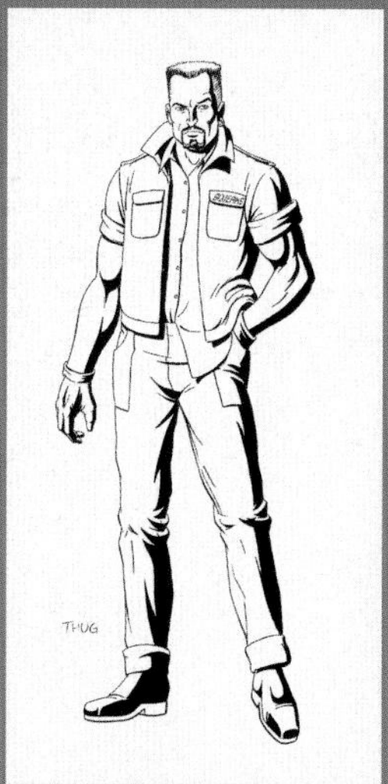
THUG
02

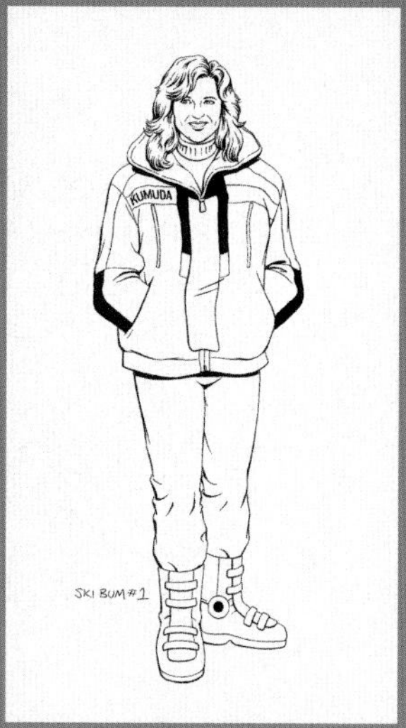
SKI BUM #1
03

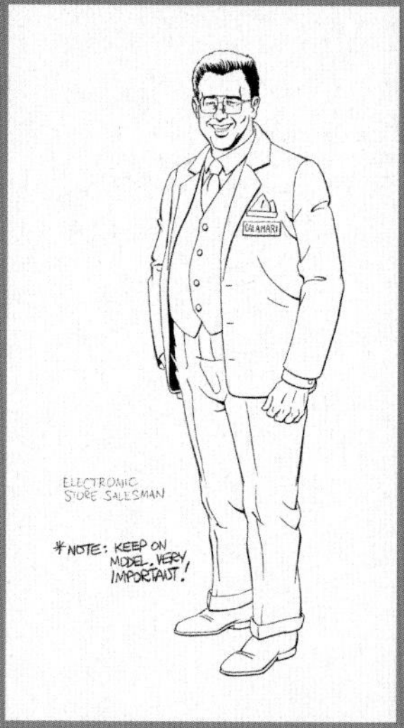
ELECTRONIC STORE SALESMAN
*NOTE: KEEP ON MODEL. VERY IMPORTANT!
04

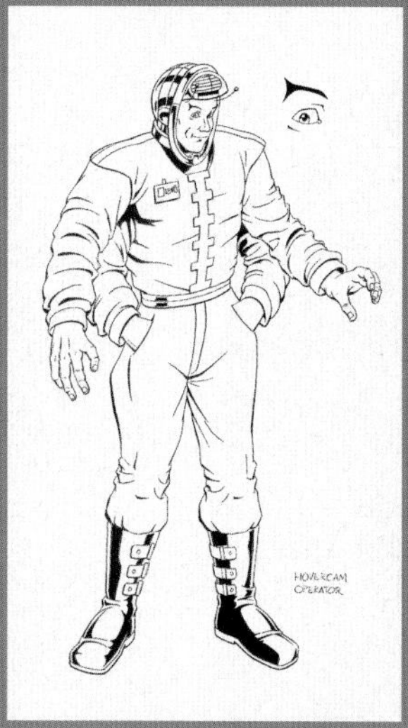
HOVERCAM OPERATOR
05

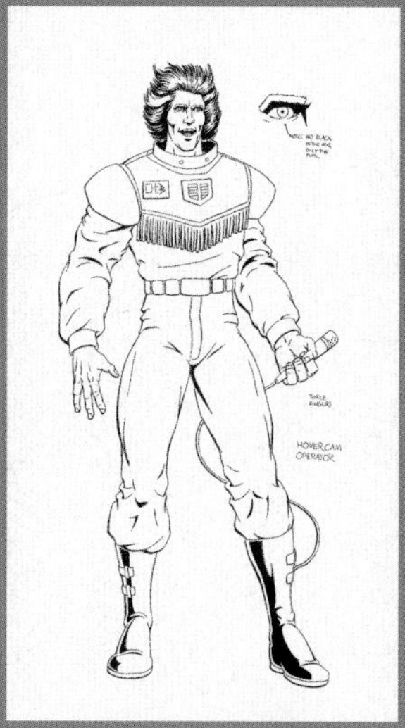
HOVERCAM OPERATOR
06

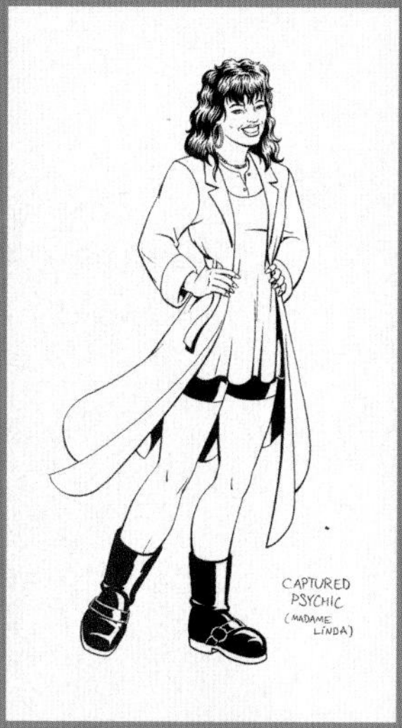
CAPTURED PSYCHIC
(MADAME LINDA)
07

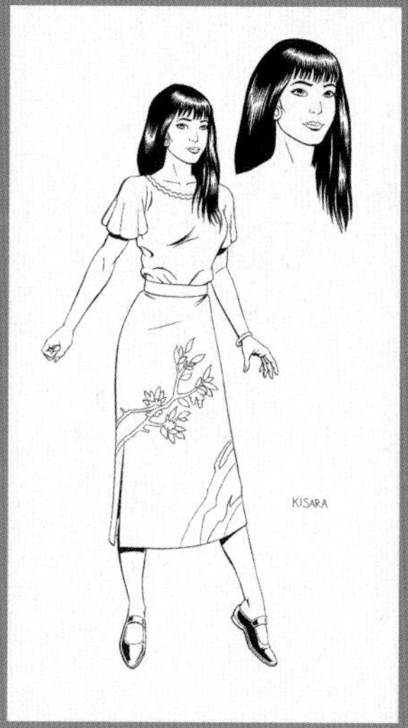
KISARA
08

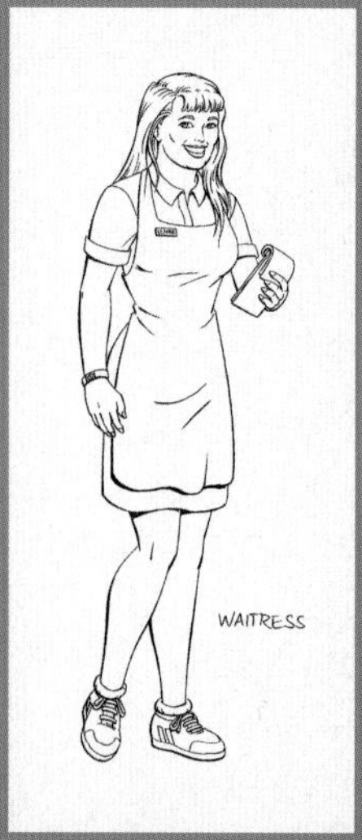
WAITRESS
09

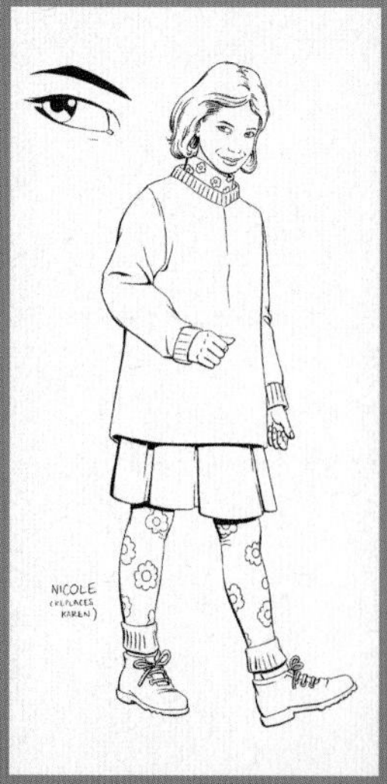
NICOLE
10

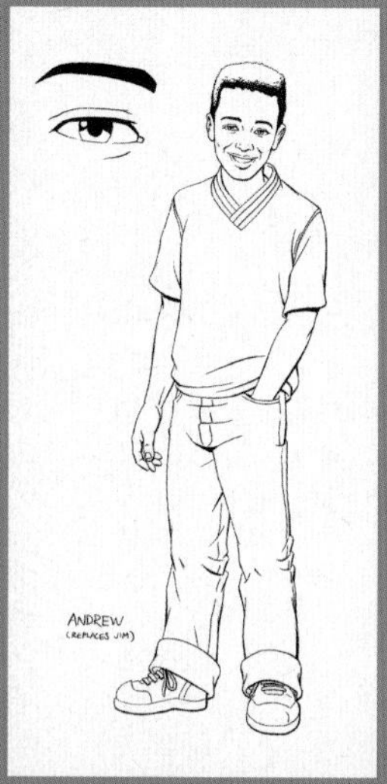
ANDREW
11

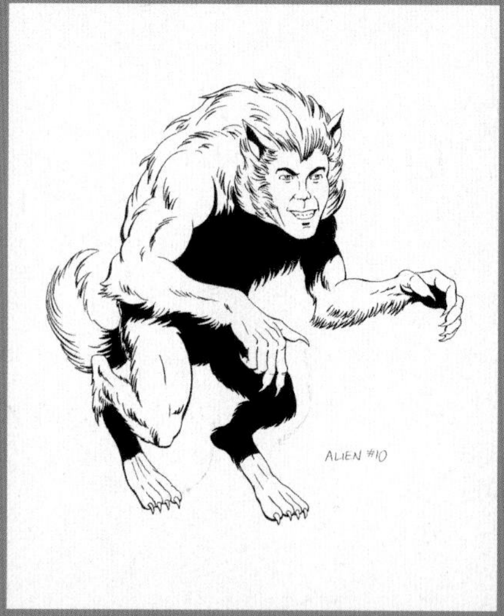
ALIEN #10
12

01–12 Character models all based on staff, friends, and family. Sidney Iwanter, Frank Squillace, Sharon Janis, Joe Calamari, Mark Lewis, Frank Brunner, Linda De La Rosa Peterson, Kisara Brunner, Leanne Moreau, Nicole Brunner, Andrew Houston, and Scott Thomas—all by Frank Brunner and/or Mark Lewis. **13** *X-Men* animation artists Larry Houston and Frank Squillace guest-starring, at work, amid a Sauron/Storm scene. Squillace boarded this scene, and then Houston reused it in the '90s *Fantastic Four* animated series. **14** Production art showing the "CAM-D" license plate in "Till Death Us Do Part, Part 1," a nod to Cam Drysdale. **15** Still-frame of a call-back, twenty episodes and two seasons later, to Beast's one brush with love in our series: Carly Anne Crocker of "Beauty and the Beast." **16** Still-frame of a list of *X-Men: TAS* staff, family, and friends, masquerading as a list of medical patients.

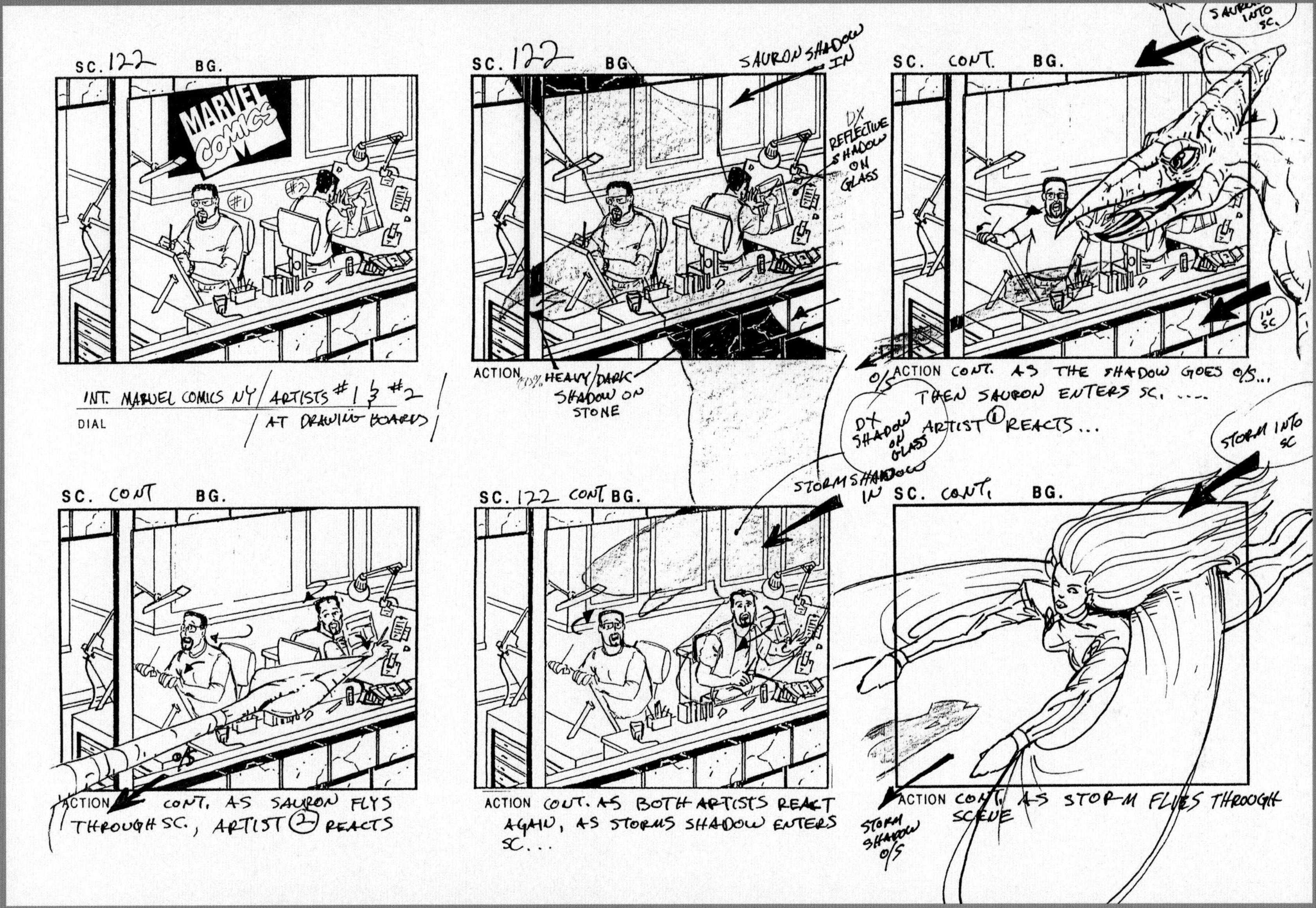
SC. 122 BG.
MARVEL COMICS
#1
#2
INT. MARVEL COMICS NY / ARTISTS #1 & #2 / AT DRAWING BOARDS
DIAL
SC. 122 BG
SAURON SHADOW IN
DX REFLECTIVE SHADOW ON GLASS
ACTION
HEAVY DARK SHADOW ON STONE
SC. CONT. BG.
SAURON INTO SC.
IN SC
O/S
ACTION CONT. AS THE SHADOW GOES O/S... THEN SAURON ENTERS SC. ....
DX SHADOW ON GLASS
ARTIST ① REACTS...
SC. CONT BG.
ACTION CONT. AS SAURON FLYS THROUGH SC., ARTIST ② REACTS
O/S
SC. 122 CONT. BG.
STORM SHADOW IN
ACTION CONT. AS BOTH ARTISTS REACT AGAIN, AS STORMS SHADOW ENTERS SC...
SC. CONT. BG.
STORM INTO SC
ACTION CONT. AS STORM FLYS THROUGH SCENE
STORM SHADOW O/S

13

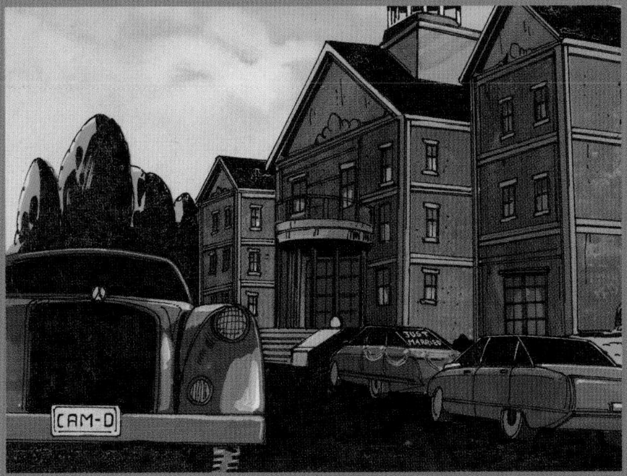
CAM-D

14

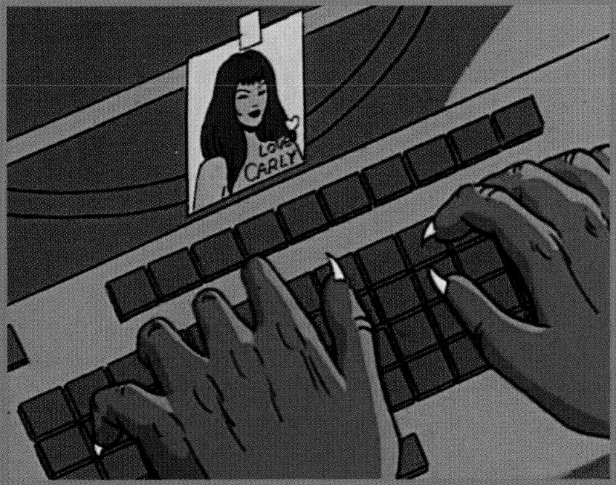
LOVE CARLY

15

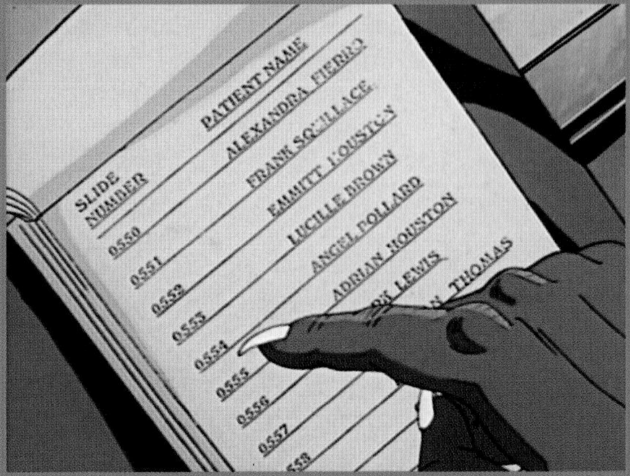
SLIDE NUMBER
PATIENT NAME
0550
0551
0552
0553
0554
0555
0556
0557
ALEXANDRA FIERRO
FRANK SQUILLACE
EMMITT HOUSTON
LUCILLE BROWN
ANGEL POLLARD
ADRIAN HOUSTON

16

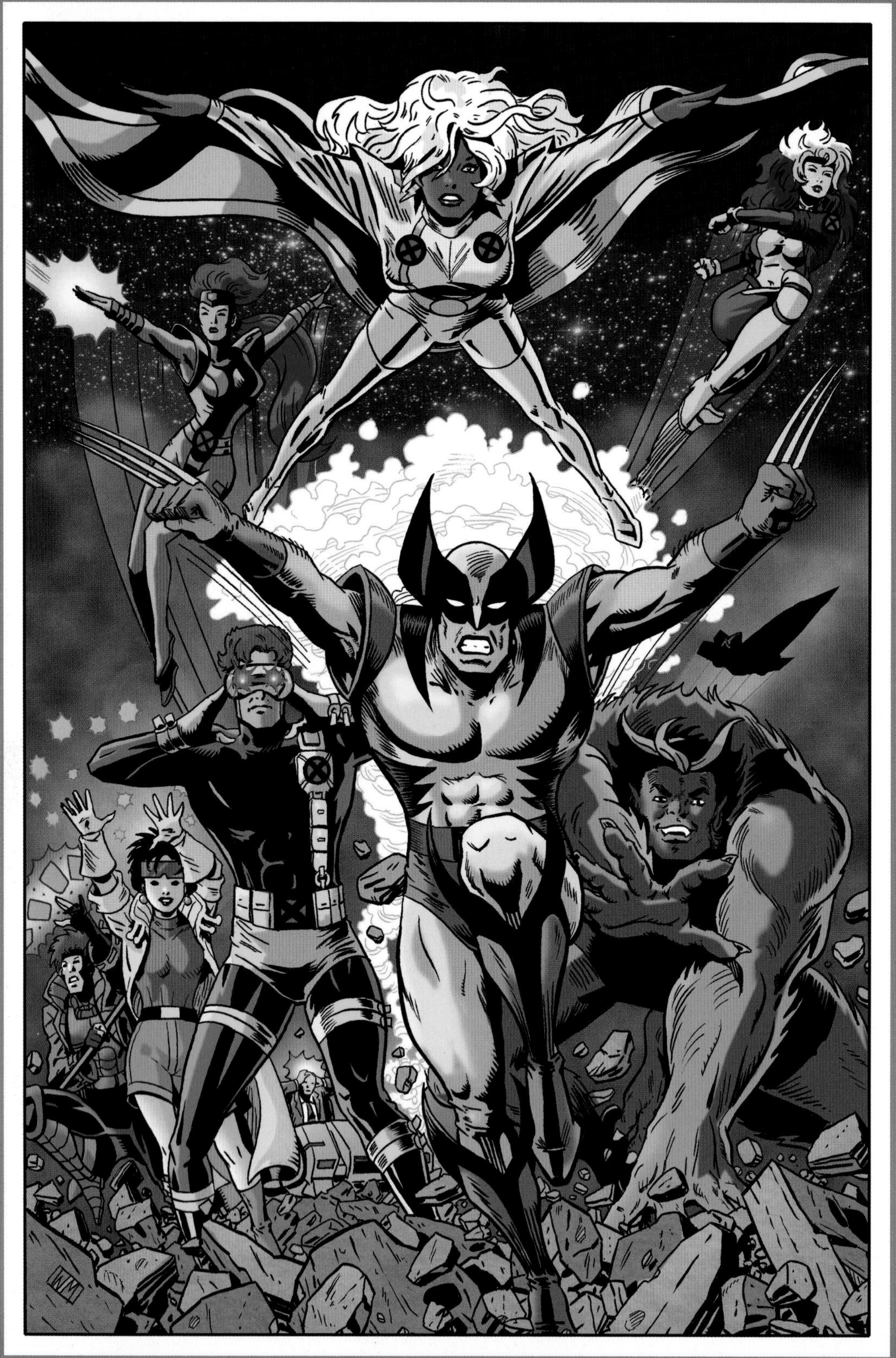

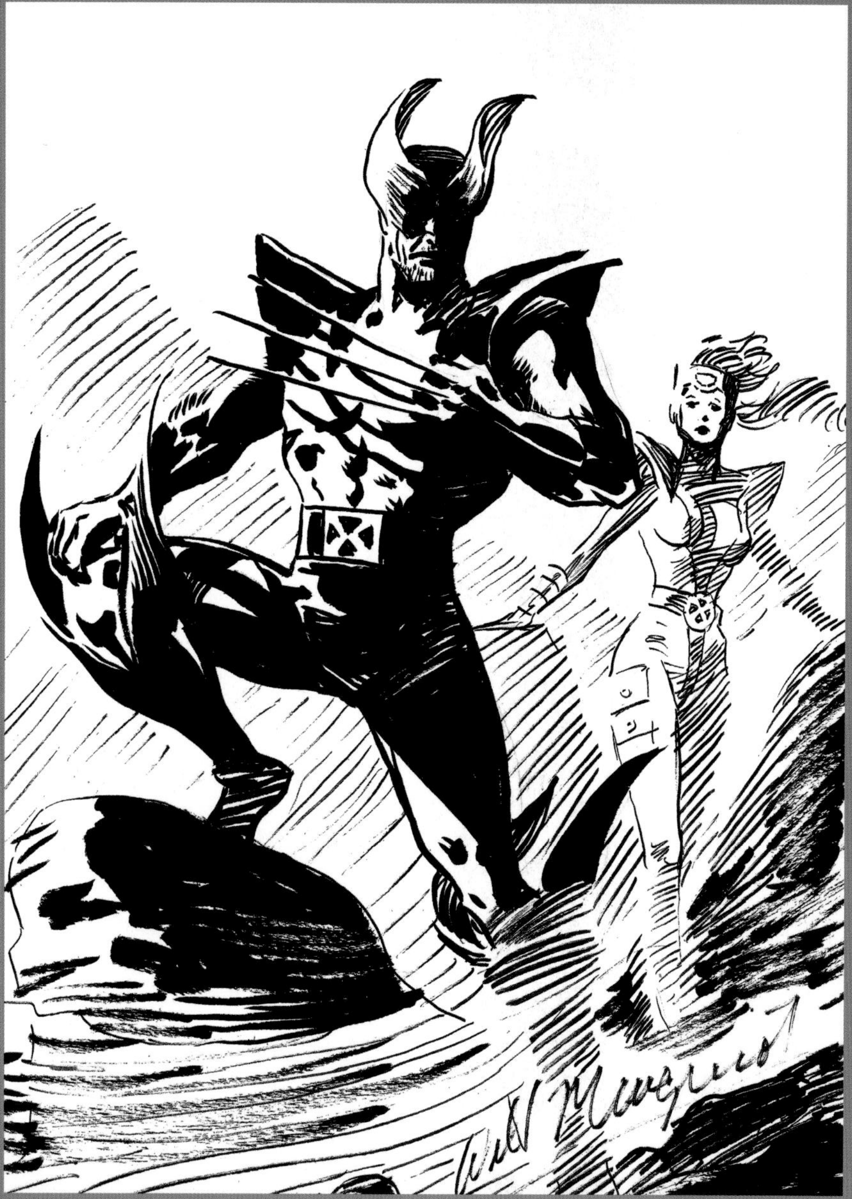

THIS SPREAD Supervising Producer Will Meugniot was in charge of our design team. Will had a hundred responsibilities that first year, so even though his vision for the series pervades it, artists like Frank Brunner and Rick Hoberg ended up doing much of the actual drawing that built our world of memorable characters. But Will loves drawing our X-Men, even in retirement. Here are five examples of his work. While the individual character pieces are contemporary to the making of our show, the team picture (left) was newly commissioned for this book.

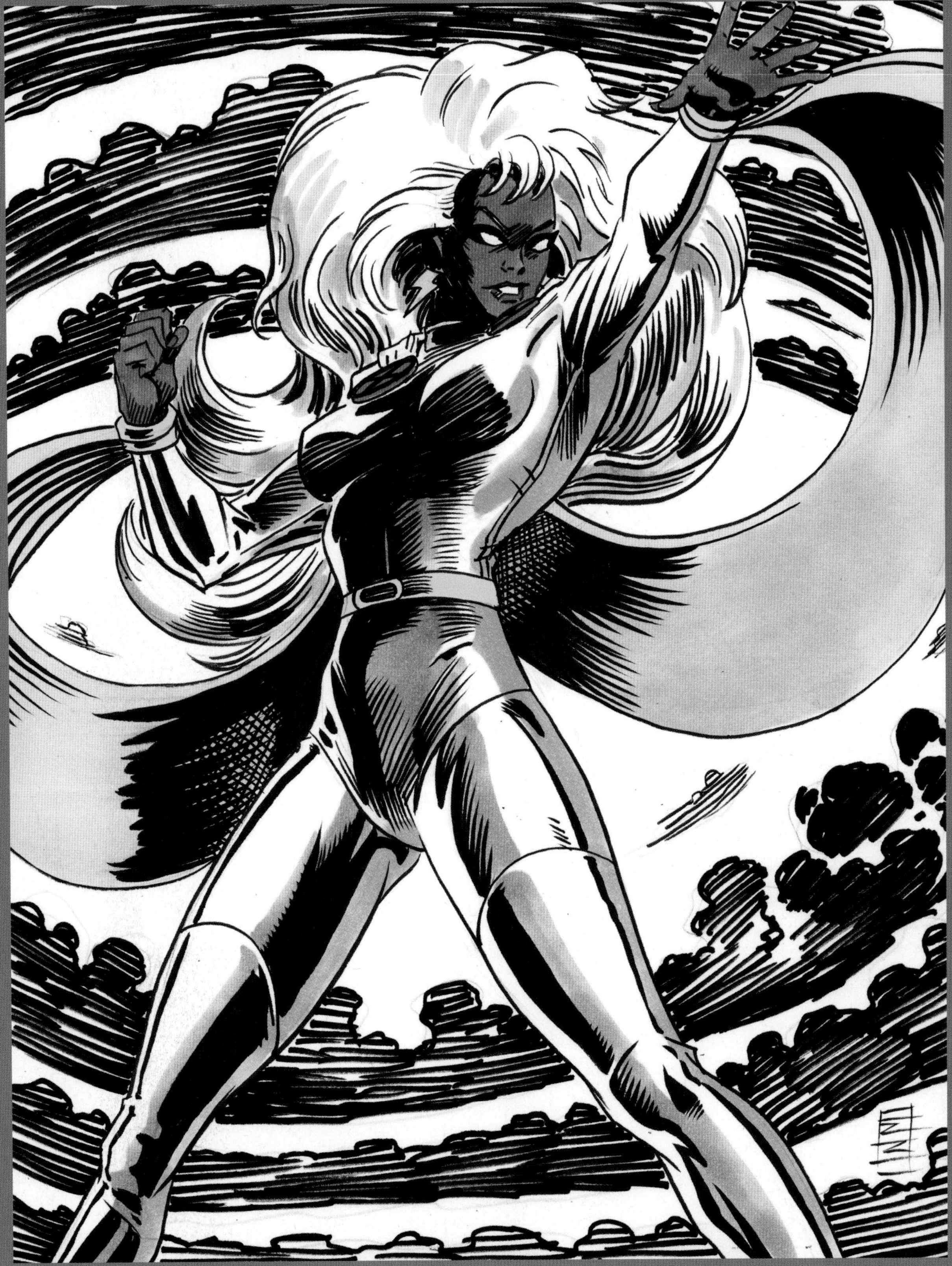

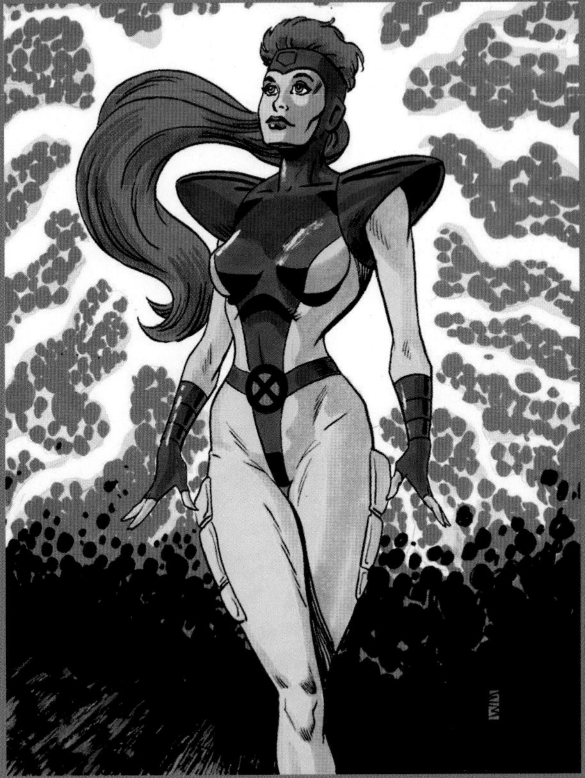

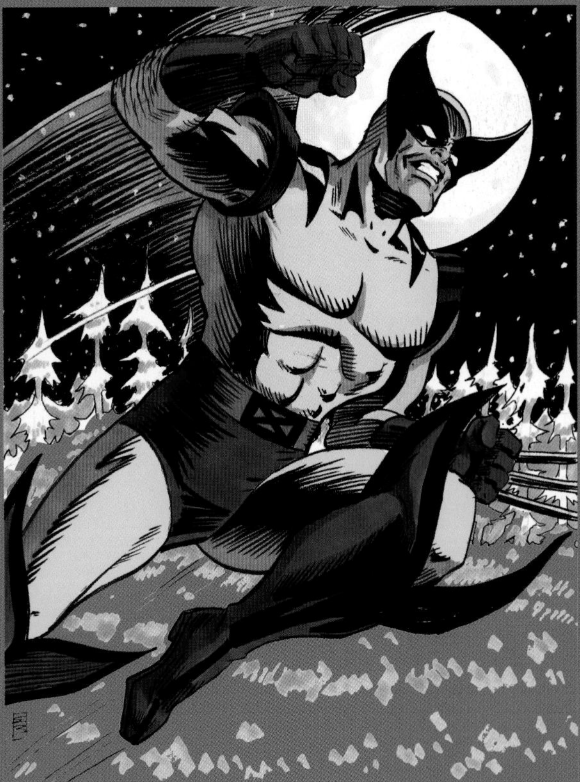

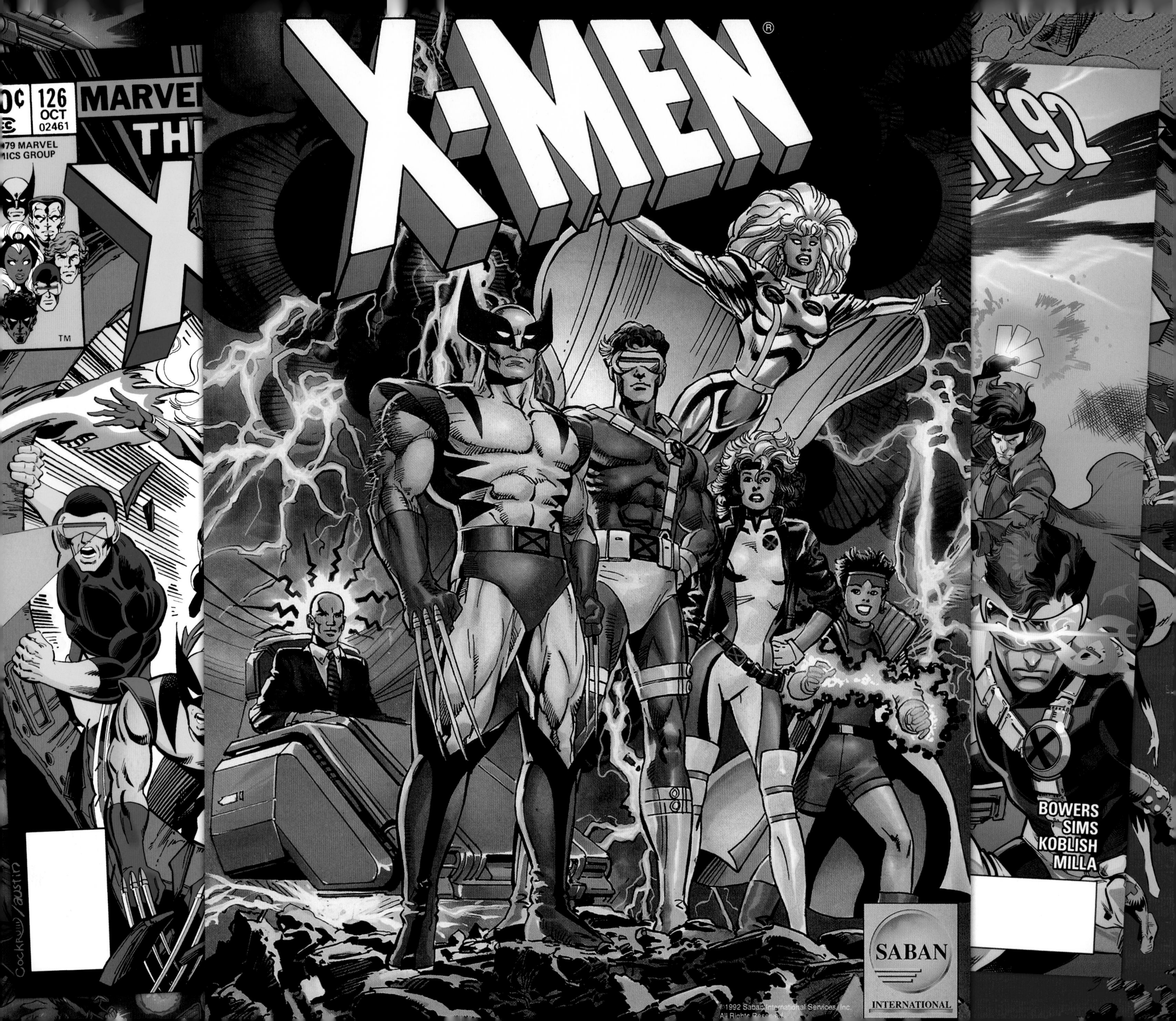

126
OCT
02461
MARVEL
THE
79 MARVEL
MICS GROUP
TM
X-MEN®
'92
BOWERS
SIMS
KOBLISH
MILLA
SABAN
INTERNATIONAL
©1992 Saban International Services, Inc.

CHAPTER SIX

LEGACY

1963–2020, AND BEYOND . . .

THE X-MEN HAVE HAD A STUNNING RIDE through popular culture: starting as a brilliant idea, only partly realized; faltering; then resurrecting, first taking over the world of comics, then animated television, and then the movies as the characters spread their story of tolerance and heroic sacrifice to hundreds of millions of viewers in every corner of the globe.

The X-Men were born in 1963. They were young, white, and very American. They wisecracked with the street-smart slang of "The Greatest Generation," voiced and drawn by Americans who had survived the Great Depression and World War II.

The team died in 1970 and were then reborn in 1975—older, more diverse, harder-edged, more world-weary. A new generation of writers and artists, post–Vietnam War, post-Watergate, post-moonwalk, brought a new look at heroes and villains and the place of "the other" in our society.

The X-Men were born again in 1992, voiced and animated, and brought into the homes of hundreds of millions. Since then, through the miracle of television and the Internet, they've conquered the world of popular culture.

We and others mentioned in this book are but a few out of the thousands who have worked to bring *X-Men: TAS* to audiences. Over the decades, the series has proved to be a lasting legacy. Every kind of merchandise imaginable was created, from the frivolous to the fantastic, indicating just how much people wanted these characters to become part of their lives.

AND THEN CAME THE MOVIES. Fox Studios, having been shown that X-Men stories could be a hit on television, were then gradually persuaded—by the team's tireless champion, Margaret Loesch—to try to replicate that success at the movie theater. David Hayter, writer of the first two *X-Men* films, told us, "The director, Bryan Singer, never picked up a comic book. We all just watched your animated show." With, by then, nearly forty years of X-Men characters and stories to pick from, the feature film folks basically chose the *X-Men: TAS* world to work with. As Hal Rudnick told us on *The ScreenJunkies Show*: "Your show stands as a true precursor, and it seeded the clouds for the [comics-based] films that we have today."

WHEN MARVEL LEGEND STAN LEE passed on November 12, 2018, there were hundreds of ways that Hollywood's premiere newspaper could have remembered him. So many of his creations had touched so many people across the world, in so many forms, for more than half a century. The *Los Angeles Times* chose for a feature story about Stan the defining image of *X-Men: TAS*—the original 1992 Saban promotional pose of the team, drawn by Neal Adams (opposite, right).

The article's author, Tracy Brown, described how our series changed her life. "[*X-Men: TAS*] led me into a brand-new world of superheroes that changed my understanding of being different in America. . . . It helped me then. It helps me now." It is a message we have heard a thousand times over. It is just as gratifying and humbling every time.

As the "new century" progresses, there is now a full-fledged superhero genre of movies and television, where before there were only rare, random attempts to tell these stories on screen. The "Fox Kids revolution of the nineties," lead by *X-Men: TAS*, *Batman: TAS*, *Spider-Man: TAS*, and others—Margaret's vision and Sidney's obsession—has changed the face of Hollywood storytelling. *X-Men: TAS* made the biggest splash. It grabbed and maintained the biggest audience and sparked the first series of successful Marvel-based movies. And now, with its availability on Disney+ streaming service, the show can thrill and delight new generations of fans.

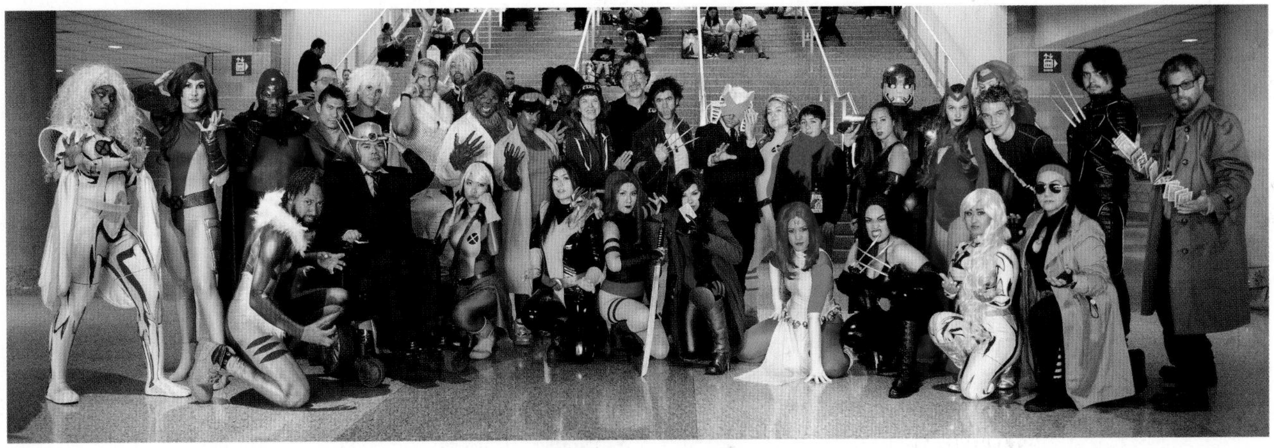

01

OPPOSITE, LEFT Dave Cockrum, Terry Austin, and Danny Crespi's cover art for *Uncanny X-Men* (vol. 1) #126 (October 1979). **OPPOSITE, CENTER** The first promotional poster for the series, courtesy of comics legend Neal Adams. Note the lack of Beast, Jean Grey, Gambit, or Morph. This was drawn early on, before we had finalized who would be our leads. **OPPOSITE, RIGHT** Pepe Larraz and Jim Charalampidis's cover art for *X-Men '92* (vol. 1) #1 (March 2016). **01** The authors (center) with a few of the many X-Men cosplayers from the 2019 Los Angeles Comic Con.

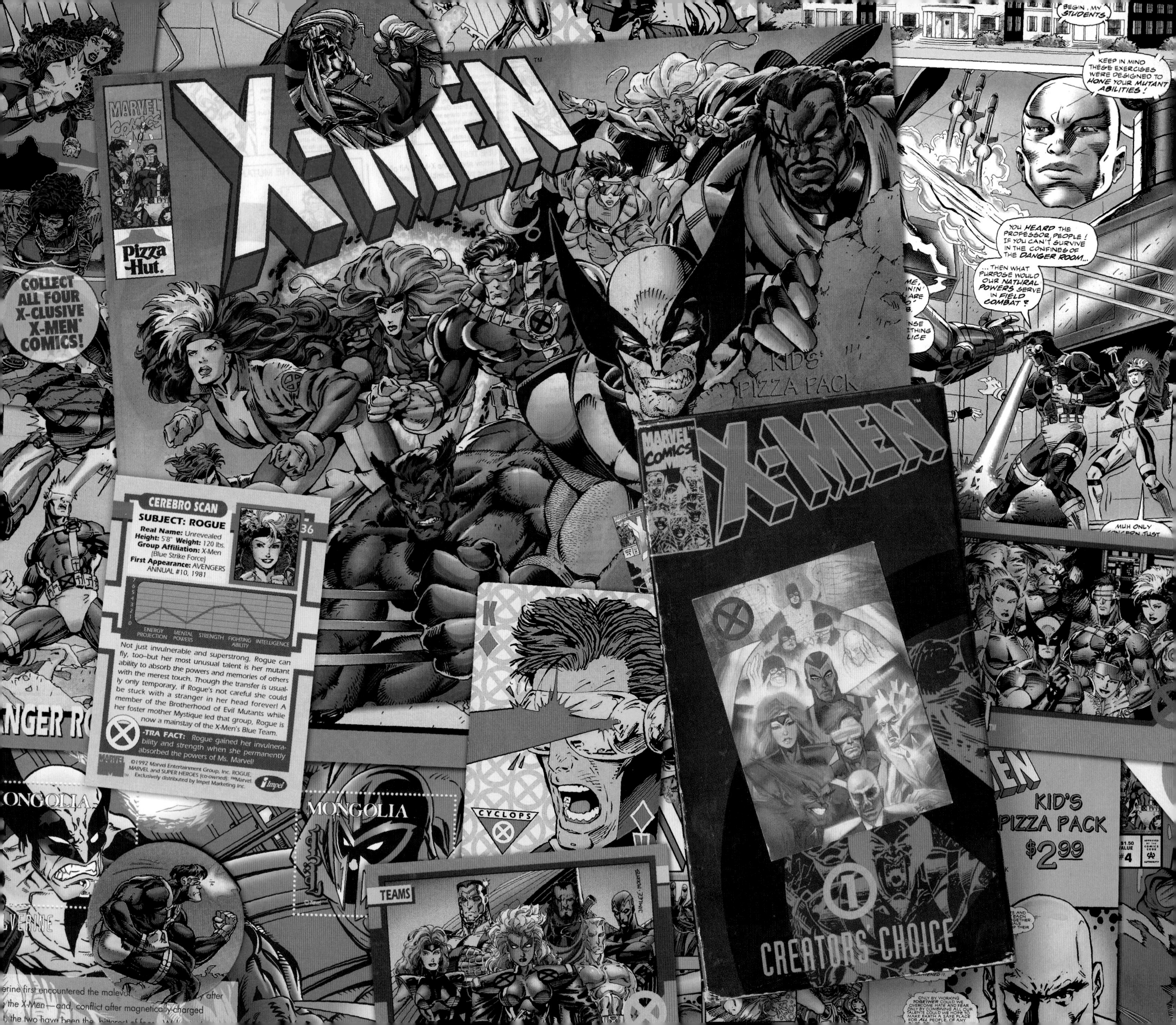

X-MEN
MARVEL COMICS
Pizza Hut
COLLECT ALL FOUR X-CLUSIVE X-MEN COMICS!
KIDS' PIZZA PACK
BEGIN, MY STUDENTS.
KEEP IN MIND THESE EXERCISES WERE DESIGNED TO HONE YOUR MUTANT ABILITIES!
YOU HEARD THE PROFESSOR, PEOPLE! IF YOU CAN'T SURVIVE IN THE CONFINES OF THE DANGER ROOM...
...THEN WHAT PURPOSE WOULD OUR NATURAL POWERS SERVE IN FIELD COMBAT?
X-MEN
MARVEL COMICS
CEREBRO SCAN
SUBJECT: ROGUE
36
Real Name: Unrevealed
Height: 5'8" Weight: 120 lbs.
Group Affiliation: X-Men (Blue Strike Force)
First Appearance: AVENGERS ANNUAL #10, 1981
ENERGY PROJECTION
MENTAL POWERS
STRENGTH
FIGHTING ABILITY
INTELLIGENCE
Not just invulnerable and superstrong, Rogue can fly, too–but her most unusual talent is her mutant ability to absorb the powers and memories of others with the merest touch. Though the transfer is usually only temporary, if Rogue's not careful she could be stuck with a stranger in her head forever! A member of the Brotherhood of Evil Mutants while her foster mother Mystique led that group, Rogue is now a mainstay of the X-Men's Blue Team.
-TRA FACT: Rogue gained her invulnerability and strength when she permanently absorbed the powers of Ms. Marvel!
©1992 Marvel Entertainment Group, Inc. ROGUE, MARVEL and SUPER HEROES (co-owned): TMMarvel. Exclusively distributed by Impel Marketing Inc.
Impel
NGER RO
MONGOLIA
MONGOLIA
CYCLOPS
TEAMS
CREATORS' CHOICE
KID'S PIZZA PACK
$2.99
#4
MUH ONLY

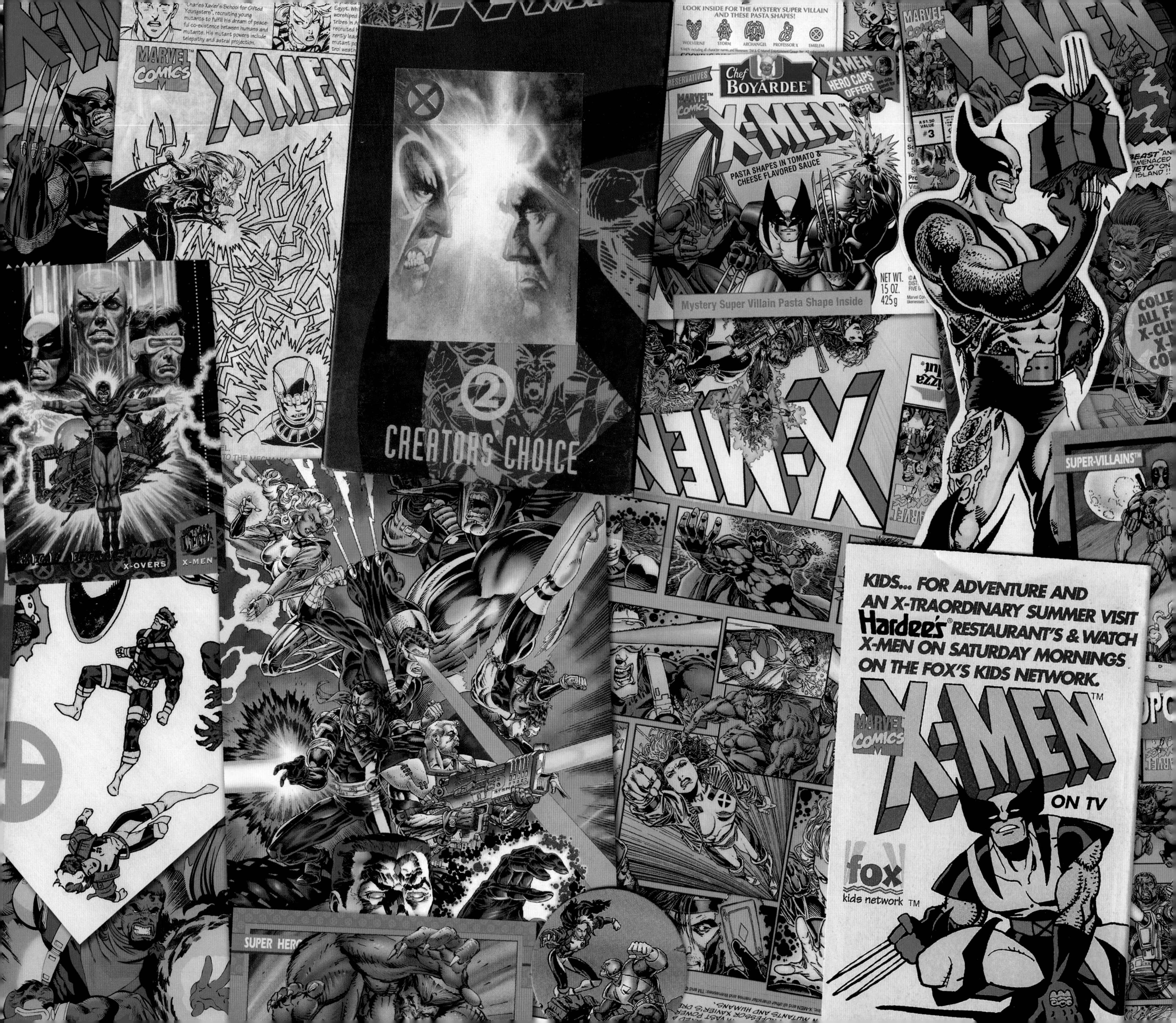
"Charles Xavier's School for Gifted Youngsters", recruiting young mutants to fulfill his dream of peaceful co-existence between humans and mutants. His mutant powers include telepathy and astral projection.
MARVEL COMICS
X-MEN
CREATORS' CHOICE
X-OVERS
X-MEN
LOOK INSIDE FOR THE MYSTERY SUPER VILLAIN AND THESE PASTA SHAPES!
WOLVERINE STORM ARCHANGEL PROFESSOR X EMBLEM
Chef BOYARDEE
X-MEN HERO CAPS OFFER!
MARVEL COMICS
X-MEN
PASTA SHAPES IN TOMATO & CHEESE FLAVORED SAUCE
NET WT. 15 OZ. 425 g
Mystery Super Villain Pasta Shape Inside
X-MEN
SUPER-VILLAINS™
KIDS... FOR ADVENTURE AND AN X-TRAORDINARY SUMMER VISIT Hardee's® RESTAURANT'S & WATCH X-MEN ON SATURDAY MORNINGS ON THE FOX'S KIDS NETWORK.
MARVEL COMICS
X-MEN™
ON TV
fox kids network TM
SUPER HERO

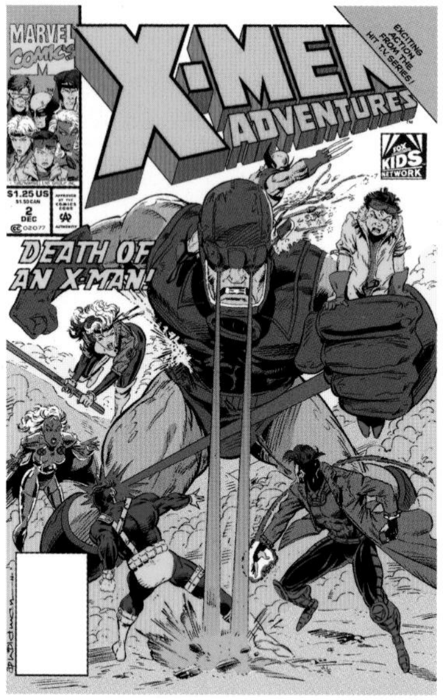
MARVEL COMICS
X-MEN ADVENTURES
FOX KIDS NETWORK
$1.25 US
2
DEC
DEATH OF AN X-MAN!

01

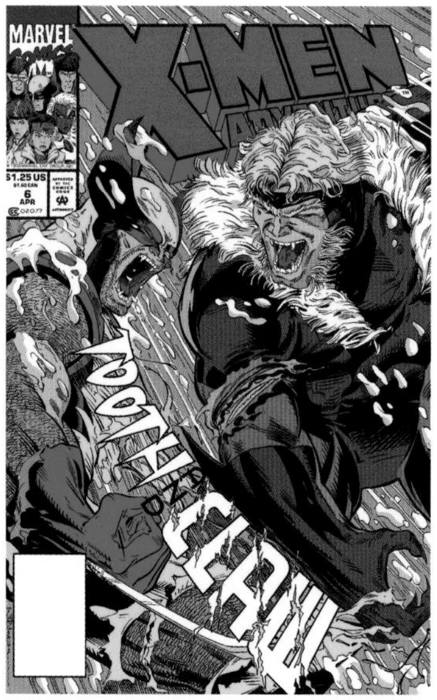
MARVEL COMICS
X-MEN ADVENTURES
$1.25 US
6
APR
TOOTH AND CLAW!

02

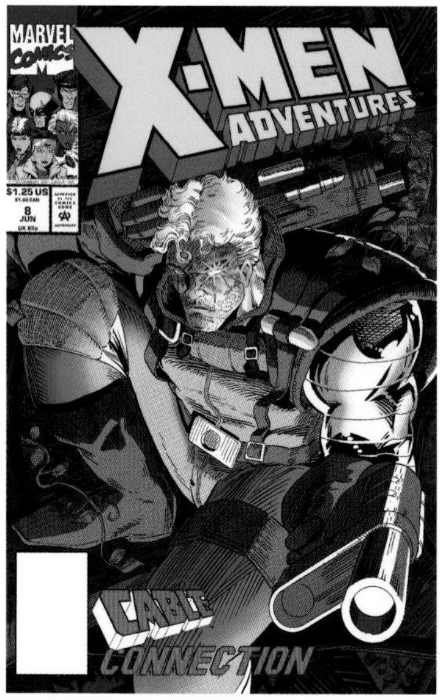
MARVEL COMICS
X-MEN ADVENTURES
$1.25 US
8
JUN
CABLE CONNECTION

03

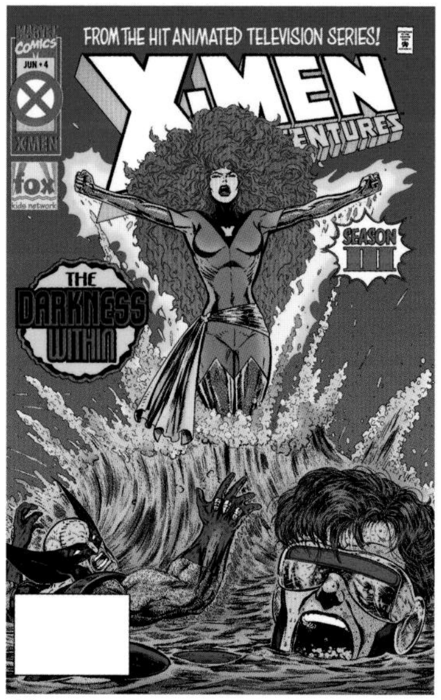
FROM THE HIT ANIMATED TELEVISION SERIES!
MARVEL COMICS
JUN 4
X-MEN
X-MEN ADVENTURES
fox
SEASON III
THE DARKNESS WITHIN

04

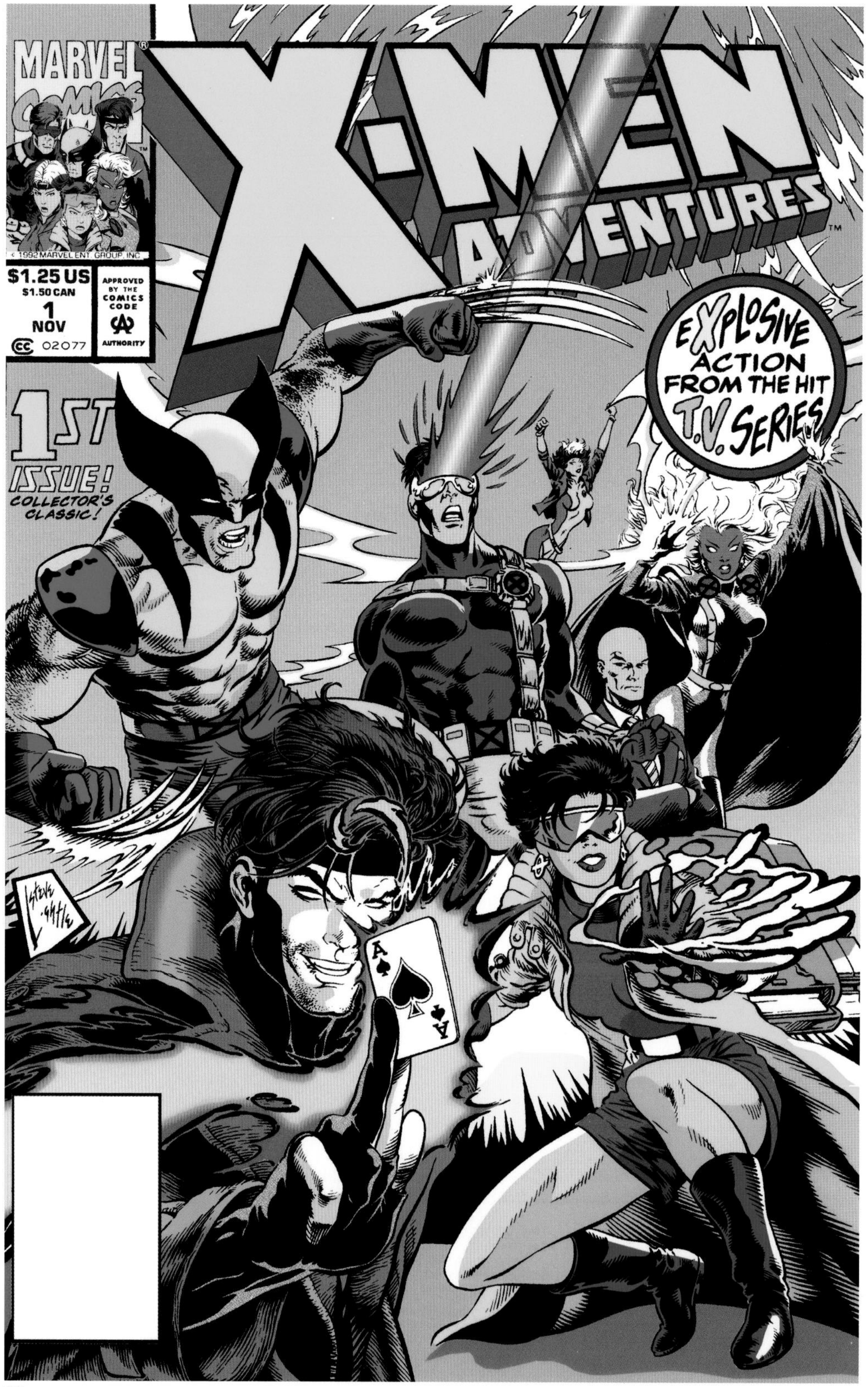
MARVEL COMICS
X-MEN ADVENTURES
© 1992 MARVEL ENT. GROUP, INC.
$1.25 US
$1.50 CAN
1
NOV
02077
APPROVED BY THE COMICS CODE AUTHORITY
EXPLOSIVE ACTION FROM THE HIT T.V. SERIES
1ST ISSUE! COLLECTOR'S CLASSIC!

05

BEYOND SIMPLE MERCHANDISING, one of the more interesting creations to be prompted by the show was a new comic-book series known as *X-Men Adventures*. In an unusual reversal, these were comics based on our animated teleplay episodes—which were, of course, based on elements and characters mostly taken from previous comic books. Others need to judge how successfully the comics-to-TV-to-comics storytelling came out. They are different media, as we who struggled to make the animated teleplays work all knew. But there is no doubt that some top Marvel artists did work on the series. Here are some highlights:

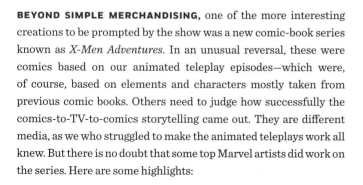

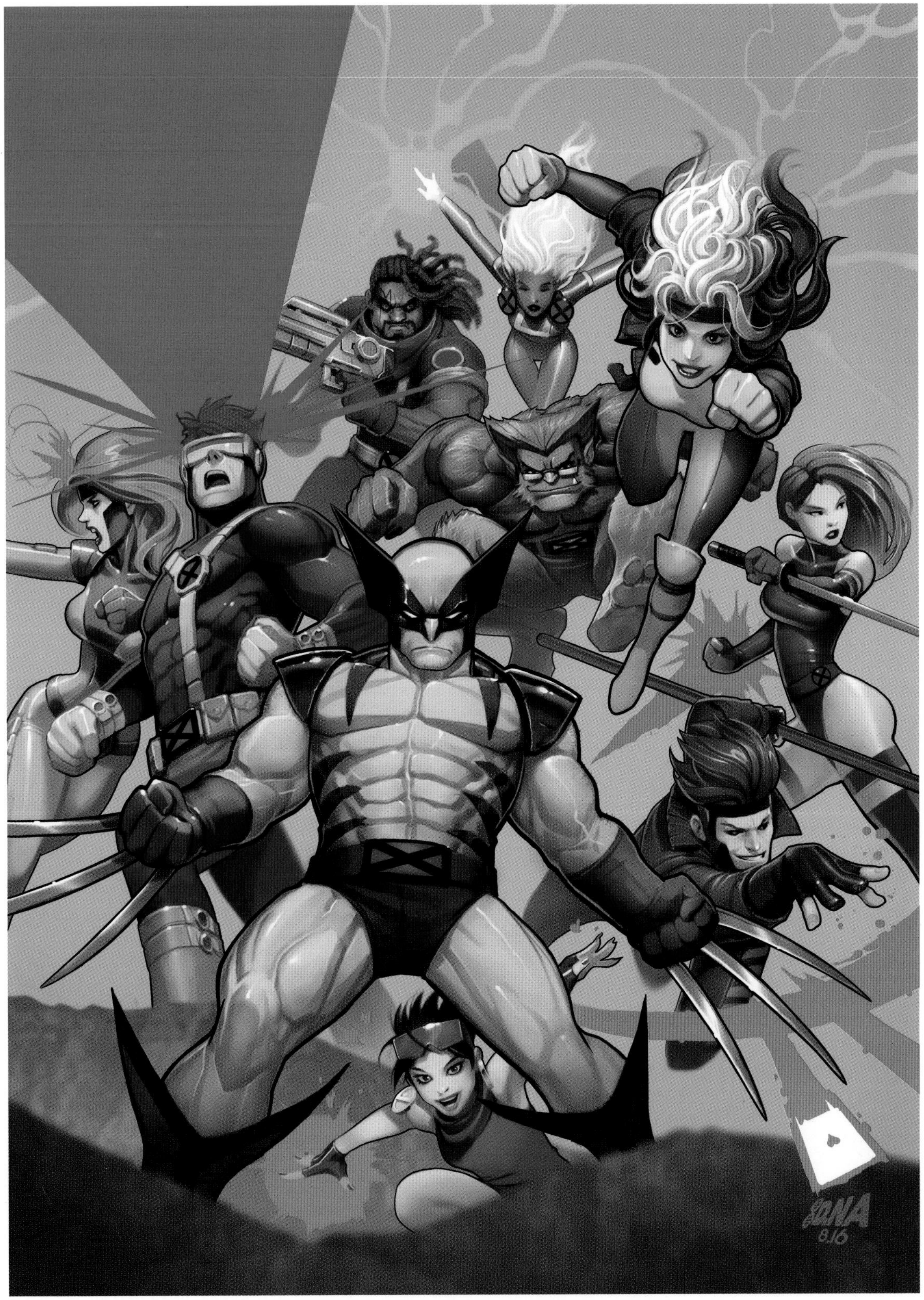

06

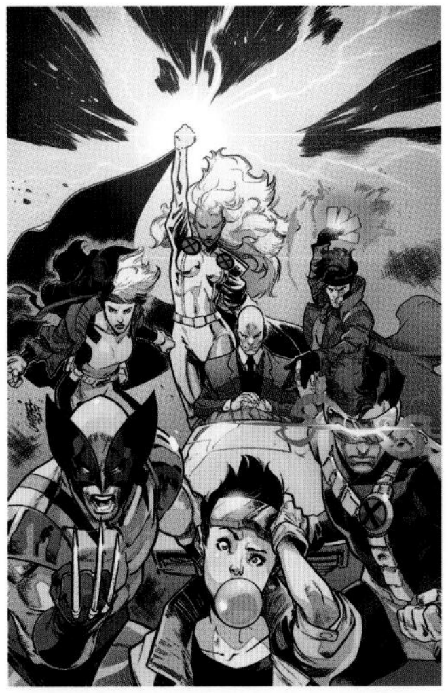

07

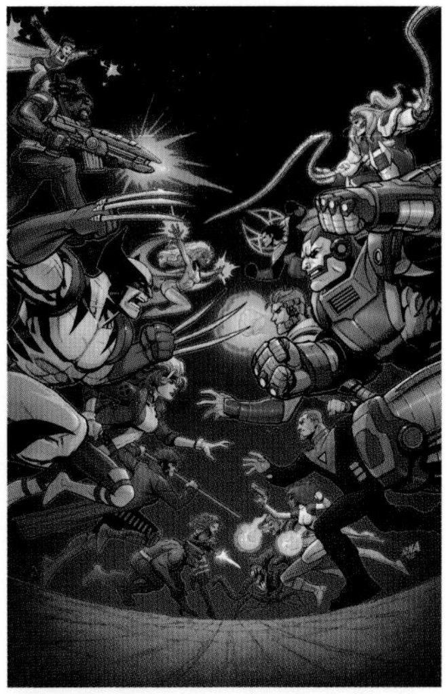

08

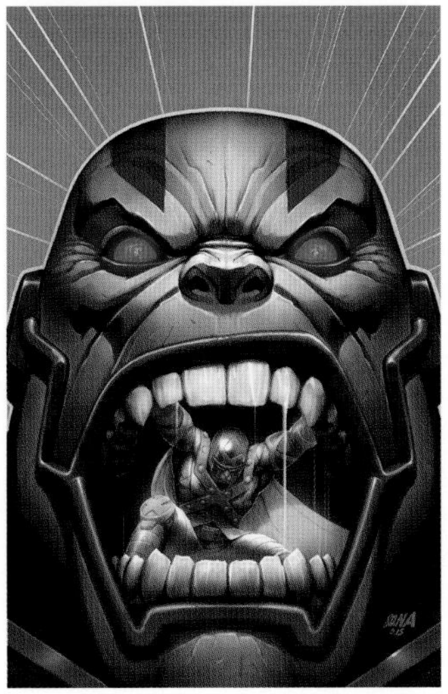

09

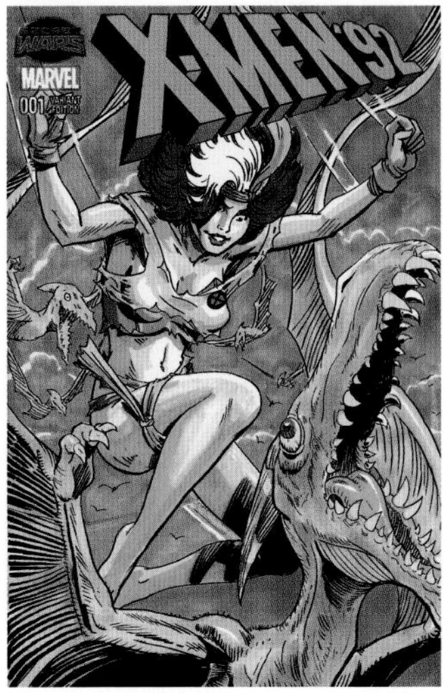
X-MEN '92
MARVEL

10

PREVIOUS SPREAD Pizza Hut's 1993 Kid's Pizza Pack promotional comics, poster/placemat, personal pan pizza box, and the seminal Creators' Choice video tapes featuring "Night of the Sentinels," alongside the title page of the 1992 *X-Men: TAS* preview comic from *Totally Kids* magazine; miscellaneous 1992 Impel and 1994 Fleer Ultra X-Men trading cards; Hardee's 1995 X-Men hero caps, tattoos, and *X-Men: TAS* ad; 1995 postage stamps from the country of Mongolia; Chef Boyardee's 1994 promotional poster and 1995 X-Men pasta shapes label; a Wolverine Christmas cardboard standee; and other assorted X-Men bits and bobs from the era. **01–05** Covers of *X-Men Adventures* (vol. 1) #1, 2, 6, and 8, as well as (vol. 3) #4—comics based on stories from a show based on comics. Art by Steve Lightle (01); Andrew Wildman (02, 04, 05); and John Hebert (04). **06–10** More recently, the idea of "X-Men '92" has sprung up within Marvel and among X-Men merchandisers. Shown here is art for and published covers of the *X-Men '92* series of comics published in 2015 and 2016, using characters, designs, and history from the show. Art by Pepe Larraz and Jim Charalampidis (vol. 1, #1 [07]); Will Meugniot (vol. 1, #1 [sketch variant, 10]); and David Nakayama (vol. 2, #1, 9, and 10 [08, 09, and 06, respectively]).

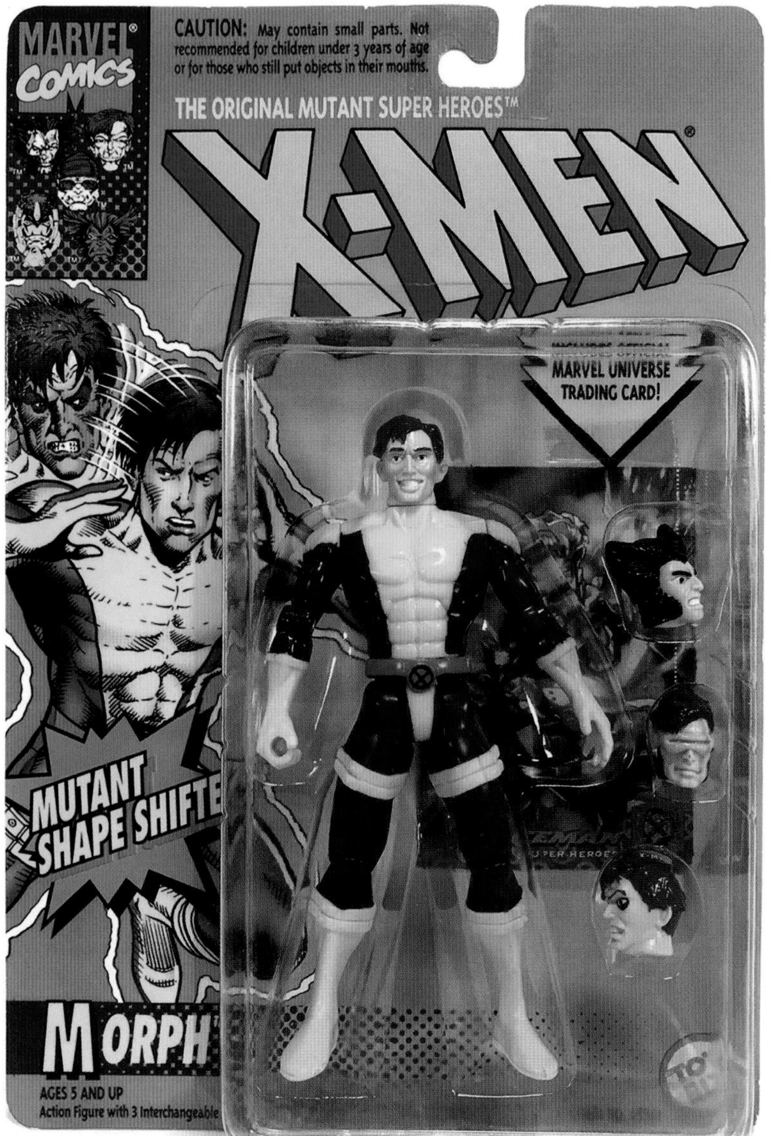
MARVEL
COMICS
CAUTION: May contain small parts. Not recommended for children under 3 years of age or for those who still put objects in their mouths.
THE ORIGINAL MUTANT SUPER HEROES™
X-MEN
MARVEL UNIVERSE TRADING CARD!
MUTANT SHAPE SHIFTE
MORPH
AGES 5 AND UP
Action Figure with 3 Interchangeable

01

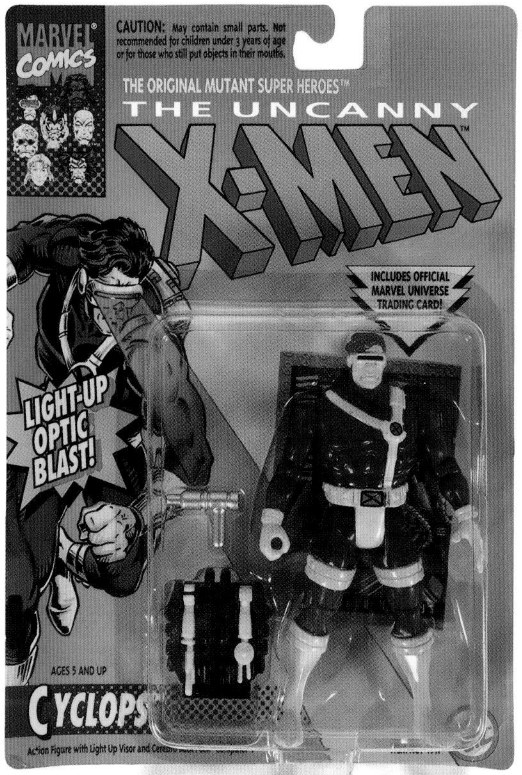
MARVEL
COMICS
CAUTION: May contain small parts. Not recommended for children under 3 years of age or for those who still put objects in their mouths.
THE ORIGINAL MUTANT SUPER HEROES™
THE UNCANNY
X-MEN
INCLUDES OFFICIAL MARVEL UNIVERSE TRADING CARD!
LIGHT-UP OPTIC BLAST!
AGES 5 AND UP
CYCLOPS

02

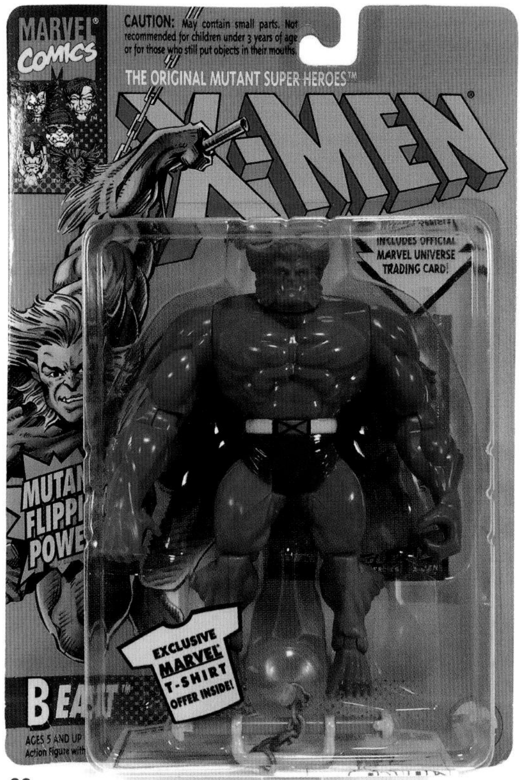
MARVEL
COMICS
THE ORIGINAL MUTANT SUPER HEROES™
X-MEN
INCLUDES OFFICIAL MARVEL UNIVERSE TRADING CARD!
EXCLUSIVE MARVEL T-SHIRT OFFER INSIDE!

03

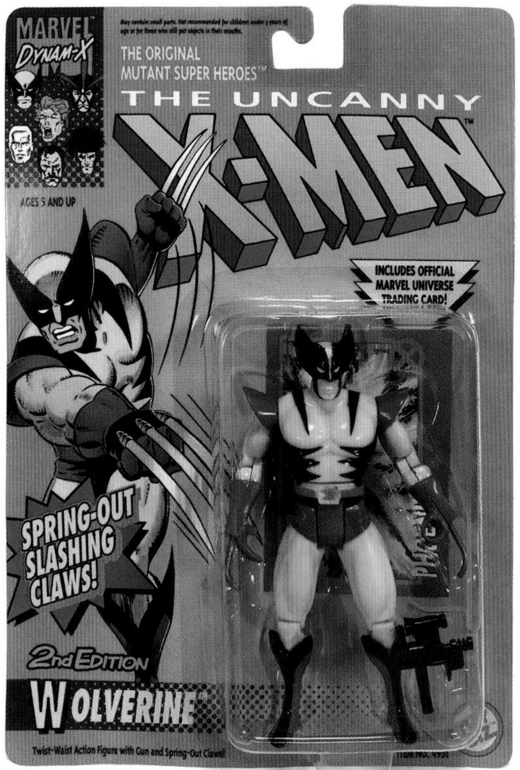
MARVEL
DYNAM-X
THE ORIGINAL MUTANT SUPER HEROES™
THE UNCANNY
X-MEN
AGES 5 AND UP
INCLUDES OFFICIAL MARVEL UNIVERSE TRADING CARD!
SPRING-OUT SLASHING CLAWS!
2nd EDITION
WOLVERINE
Twist-Waist Action Figure with Gun and Spring-Out Claws!

04

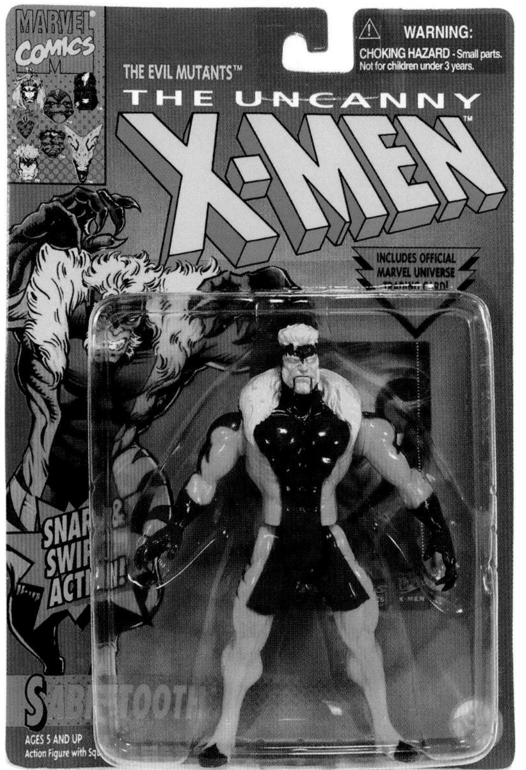
MARVEL
COMICS
WARNING:
CHOKING HAZARD - Small parts. Not for children under 3 years.
THE EVIL MUTANTS™
THE UNCANNY
X-MEN
INCLUDES OFFICIAL MARVEL UNIVERSE
AGES 5 AND UP

05

01–05 X-Men merchandizing exploded worldwide after *X-Men: TAS* arrived, in no small part courtesy of ToyBiz. The ToyBiz line debuted, independent of our work on *TAS*, to modest sales in 1991, but quickly synergized with *TAS* designs and characters, and rapidly proliferated before it ended a seven-year run in 1998. The line drew inspiration liberally from a wide variety of comics and *TAS* sources, but the provenance for the Morph figure (01) is as unambiguous as it gets. **06–09** While waves of *X-Men: TAS*–inspired toys have found their way into kids' and collectors' bedrooms over the past three decades, more recently, the collector-focused toy and hobby manufacturer Kotobukiya has created a stunning line of ARTFX+ statues celebrating the series.

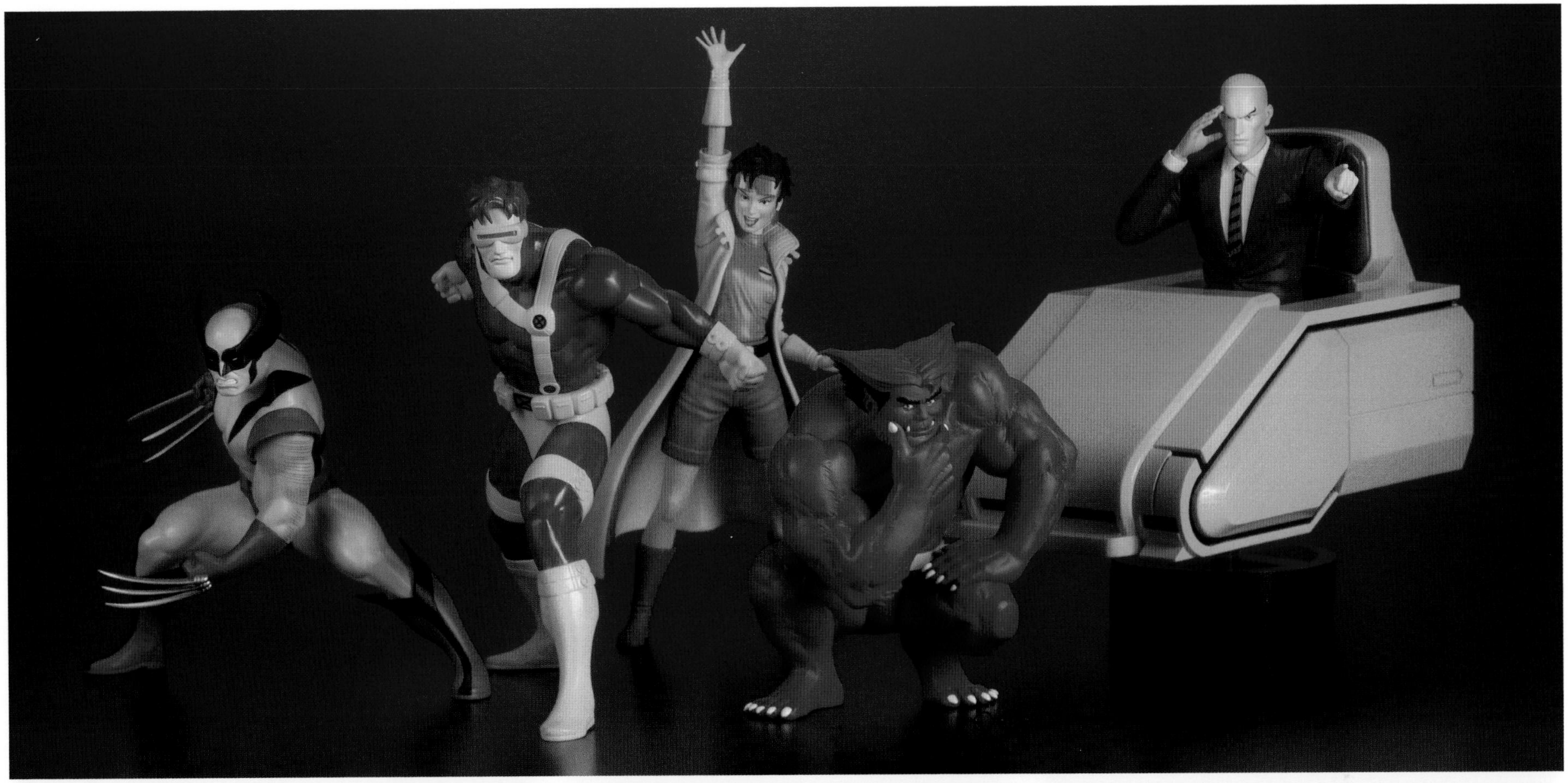

06

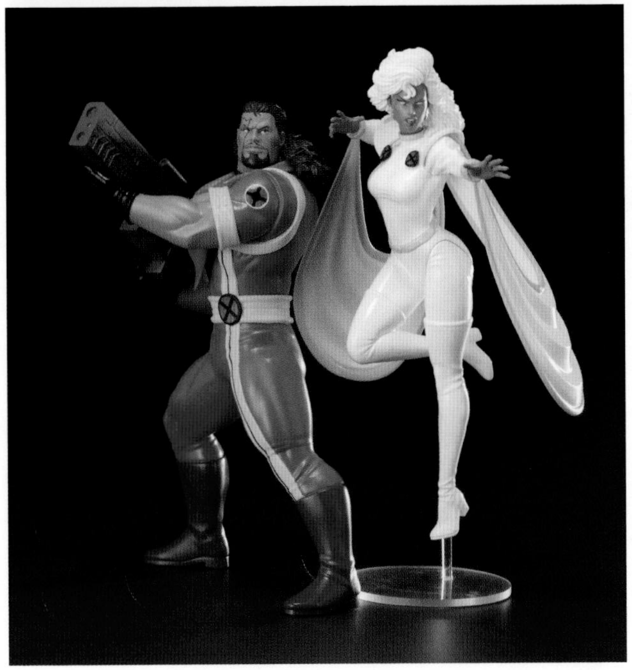

07

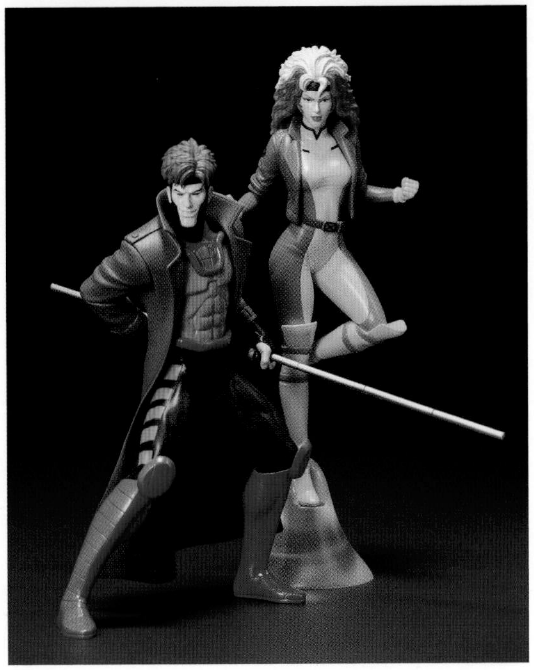

08

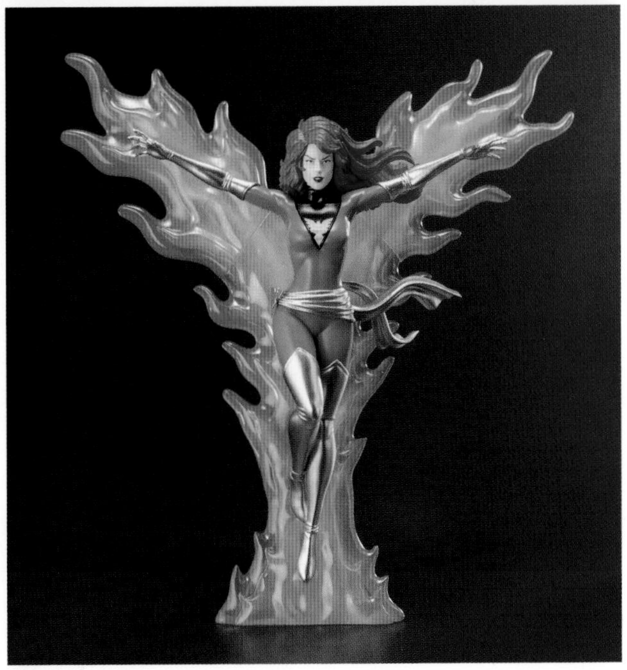

09

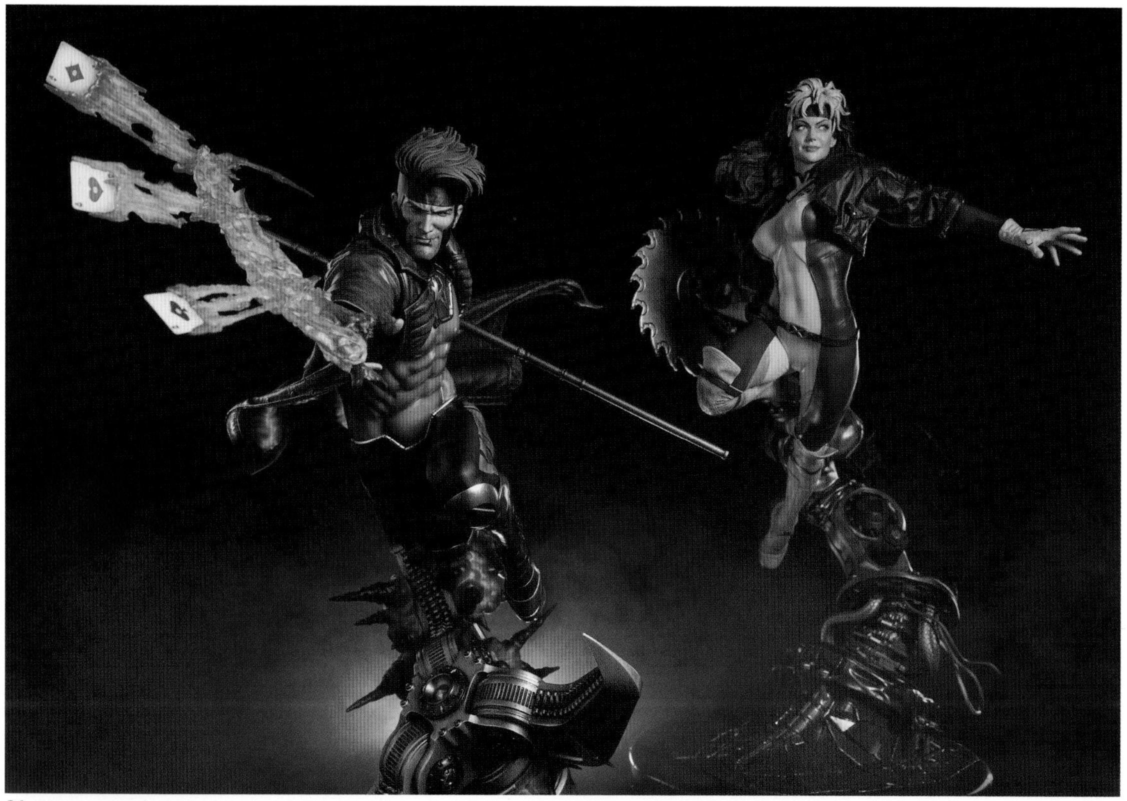

01

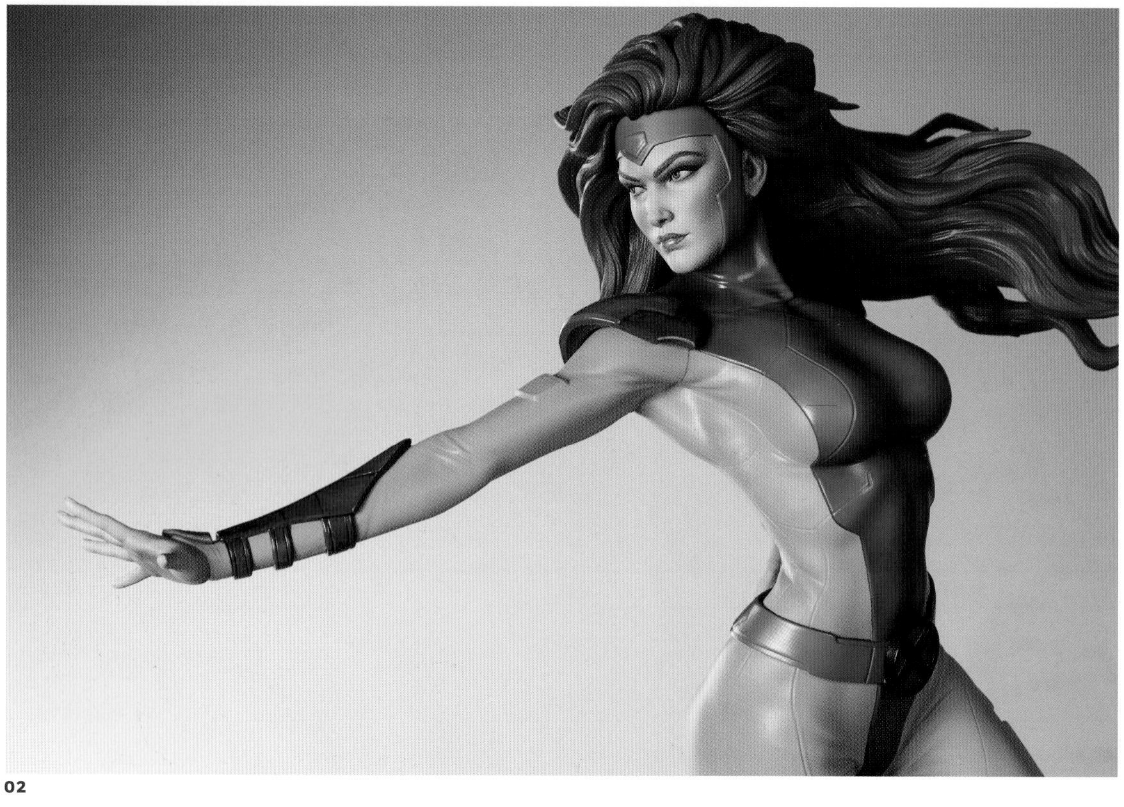

02

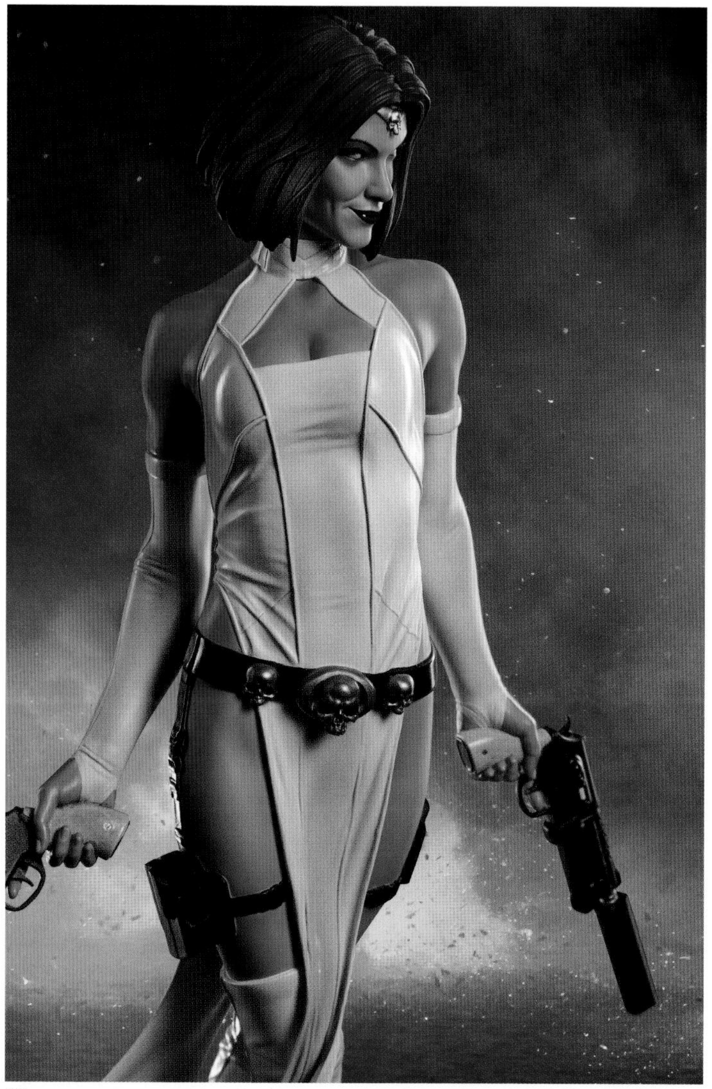

03

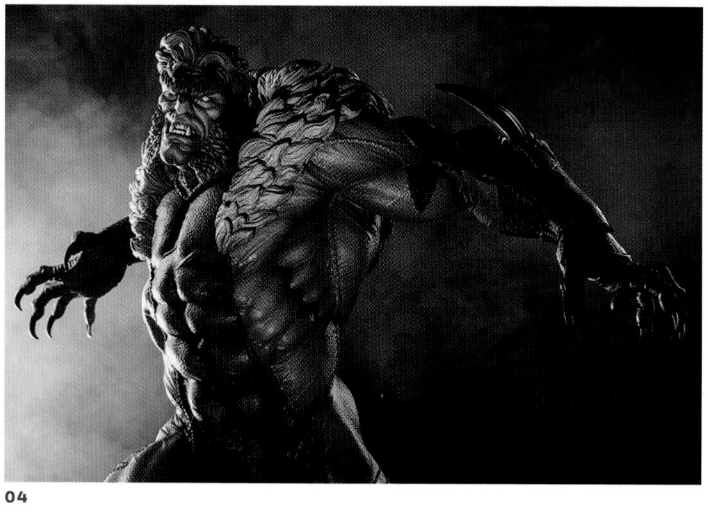

04

05

COMIC-BOOK CONVENTIONS ("cons") have exploded across the globe. There are hundreds every year, and nearly all have art and cosplay representing the series. This has provided a new community gathering place for those millions around the world who feel that *X-Men: TAS* is an important part of their lives. Since the 2017 release of Eric's *Previously on X-Men* book, Eric, Julia, Larry, cast members, writers, and artists have been invited to speak on panels and host tables.

The very first con that featured *X-Men: TAS* creators was the world-renowned San Diego Comic Con (SDCC) in late summer 1993, six months after the series premiered. Soon thereafter, in February 1994, a more modest con in Los Angeles hosted Eric, Larry Houston, and Frank Brunner as their head-liners. Twenty-four years later, the same LA con asked Eric and Larry back again.

To our delight, the next-gen fans are often named "Logan," "Xavier," "Scott," "Jean," "Remy," or "Remi" (girls).

Included in that group is the prime minister of Canada, Justin Trudeau, who, as his country's biggest *X-Men: TAS* fan, received the first copy of Eric's *Previously on X-Men*—hand-delivered by Jubilee (Alyson Court) and Wolverine (Cal Dodd).

More than twenty-five years after we wrote and drew and voiced these stories, new audiences are finding them just as satisfying as their parents and older friends did. Few things could be more gratifying.

01-04 The peak of X-Men–inspired collectibles are the rare, hand-crafted sculptures by Sideshow. 05 At SDCC 2018 with Katherine "Louie" DeMetre, Alec Lewald, Reveille Wiederspahn, Taylor Faust, authors Julia Lewald and Eric Lewald, Carter Lewald, and Andy Snodgress. 06 Our second comic-convention appearance, during the middle of season two. 07 Frank Brunner, Eric Lewald, and Larry Houston attempt to answer fan questions in 1994. 08 *X-Men: TAS* actor Cal Dodd (Wolverine) crushes the hand of Canadian Prime Minister Justin Trudeau after presenting him with the very first copy of *Previously on X-Men*. Cal, like the rest of the cast, is Canadian. The PM is a huge X-Men fan. He named his first-born son Xavier. Coincidence? We like to think not.

LOS ANGELES
COMIC BOOK AND SCIENCE FICTION CONVENTION

A SPECIAL SHORT FEATURETTE ON THE UPCOMING MOVIE *"THE SHADOW"* WILL BE SCREENED AT 1:45 P.M.
"THE SHADOW" MOVIE BUTTON WILL BE GIVEN AWAY *FREE* (WHILE SUPPLIES LAST) TURN FLYER OVER ▶

| SHRINE AUDITORIUM EXPO CENTER 700 WEST 32ND STREET LOS ANGELES, CALIF. | FEBRUARY 13, 1994 10:00 A.M. - 5:00 P.M. | ADMISSION FOR THIS SPECIAL SHOW IS $5.00 |

MARVEL COMICS X-MEN™ & © 1994 MARVEL ENTERTAINMENT GROUP, INC. ALL RIGHTS RESERVED

MEET THE CREATIVE PEOPLE BEHIND ONE OF T.V.'S HOTTEST ANIMATED SHOWS ON STAGE AT 2:00 P.M.

GO BEHIND THE SCENES AND FIND OUT HOW THE "X-MEN" CARTOON SERIES IS CREATED.

FIND OUT WHAT IS HAPPENING TO YOUR FAVORITE CHARACTERS ON UPCOMING EPISODES.

"X-MEN" CARTOONS WILL BE SHOWN ON A LARGE SCREEN STARTING AT 11:00 A.M.

X-MEN
CARTOON DAY
APPEARING IN PERSON!

| LARRY HOUSTON PRODUCER | ERIC LEWALD STORY EDITOR |

FRANK BRUNNER
CHIEF MODEL DESIGNER
(FRANK HAS ALSO DRAWN "HOWARD THE DUCK," "MAN-THING" AND "DR. STRANGE" FOR MARVEL COMICS.)

| SPECIAL GUEST APPEARANCE 1:00 P.M. - 3:00 P.M. | WOLVERINE IN PERSON | IN FULL COSTUME BRING YOUR CAMERA AND POSE WITH WOLVERINE |

06

07

08

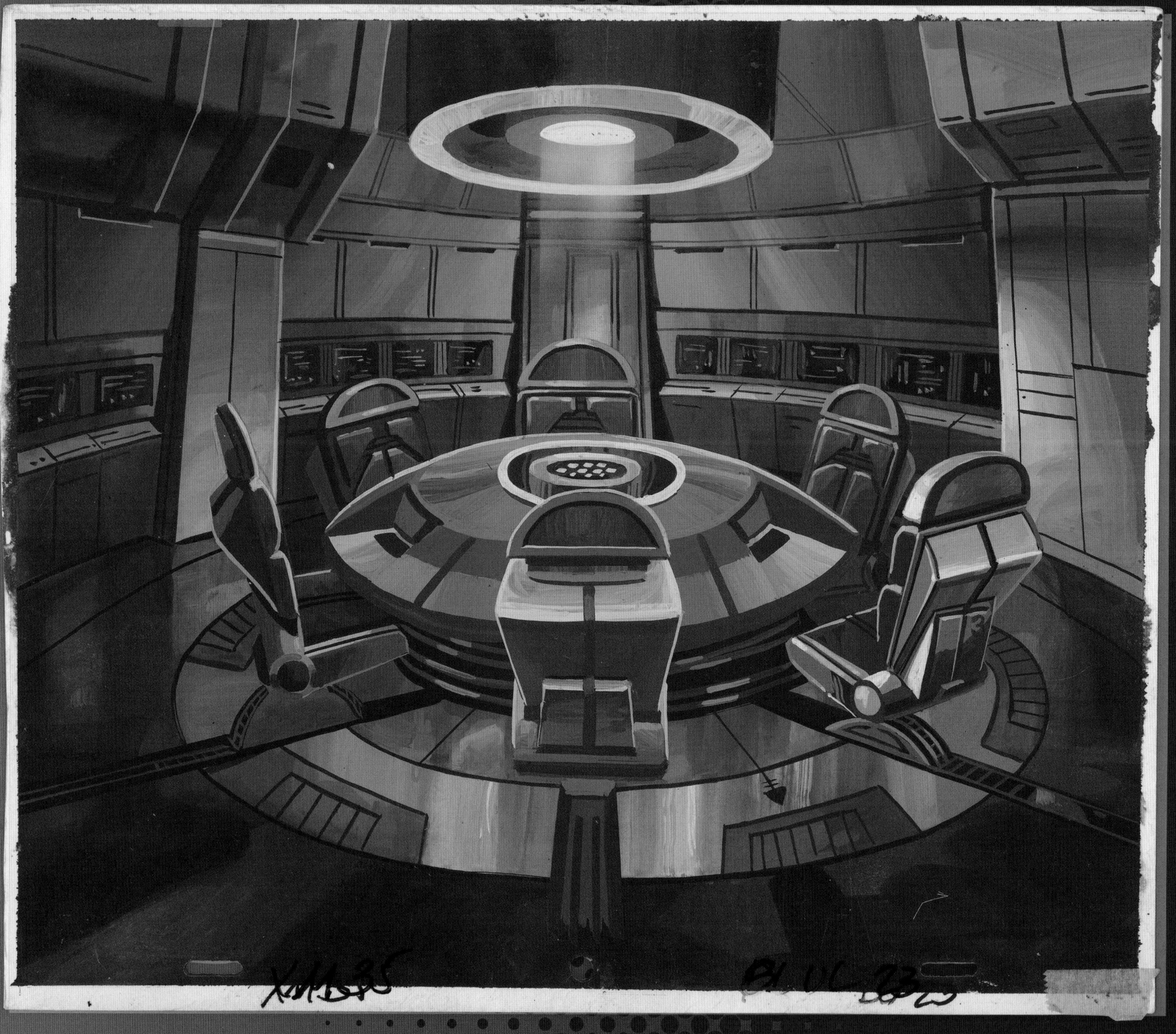

AFTERWORD

WHAT *X-MEN: TAS* HAS MEANT TO US

AFTER FAMILY AND FRIENDS, *X-Men: TAS* has had more impact on our lives than anything else. What started, in 1992, as simply "the next job" became a defining highlight of our long and varied careers. Lifelong friendships began with colleagues that shared the challenges and triumphs of the struggle to create a television show, a cartoon, that meant something to us and to our audience.

Modern popular culture is an amazing thing. The mutant world of the X-Men that started, in 1963, as a struggling comic book, has become a place known and loved by hundreds of millions of people. We can't wear a "Previously on X-Men" hat or jacket in public without someone stopping us and asking: "The animated series? From the nineties?" Recently, in the luggage line at the Singapore airport, a Malaysian security agent eagerly called her colleagues over for a picture with us, proclaiming: "We all love the show. Storm is so strong!"

X-Men: TAS even affected the lives of its three primary writers—Eric, Mark Edens, and Michael Edens—when the three found themselves celebrated by the University of Tennessee early in 2018. After a panel and book signing, the three received "Accomplished Alumni" awards and were featured in the university's quarterly magazine, *Torchbearer*, for their work on *X-Men: TAS*. Forty years after the three college buddies started writing together, our "little cartoon show" brought us back together where we first met for a night of celebration.

WHILE WE CAN'T EXPLAIN THE MAGIC that this series captured, when fans gush, "You gave us our childhood," we understand. We both have had TV series, movies, books, and music that has changed us forever, and that fifty years later evoke the same emotions of excitement and joy. Somehow, we two were

lucky enough to find a way to be part of something that gave that feeling to millions of people. We've asked others, like the artists whose work we are celebrating with this book, if they can explain that magic; they have no simple answers, either. Time and money were tight; this may or may not represent every creative contributor's absolute best work. But there was a passion there, all the same. As Margaret Loesch said: "More than any show I've worked on, this show had a zealous group of believers [among the creative staff]. Believers that were ready to fight."

But why were we all such believers, even those of us who hadn't grown up as X-Men fans? What about this show provoked such dedication in the people who wrote and drew it? Perhaps it was the same thing that compelled the show's fans to never miss an episode—and then, a generation later, to make sure to watch it all again with their children: the characters. Characters who were given a unique depth of humanity by the artists who drew them.

The X-Men were mostly outcasts, from broken homes, feared and reviled for a perceived "difference" that they were born with, brought together to form a new family where they could express their humanity and be better understood. Their struggles mirrored our struggles. Their yearning to be part of a family echoed our own.

We've certainly learned to appreciate the skill of the people who have created the very American art form of the comic book, the inspiration for so much of what became *X-Men: TAS*. No one contributed more to the creation of this world than writer Chris Claremont, artist John Byrne, and inker Terry Austin, whose work was at the heart of the kind of X-Men story we chose to tell and draw.

OUR OWN FAMILY has enjoyed being part of the huge community that continues to celebrate the series. Our sons and niece grew up on the show, sharing it with their friends. Now in their twenties, together with current friends, they help us with con panels and appearances, with our web presence, and even with this book.

AND WHILE THIS EXTENDED FAMILY has taken great joy in celebrating the enduring legacy of *X-Men: TAS*, there is one image that sums up how special these characters and their world have become for us.

Think about it. On Halloween, 1994, our national holiday of aspiration and personal expression—when we can choose to *be* anyone, real or imagined, throughout history—our three-year-old son, Carter, chose to dress up as a member of the X-Men. He wanted to be part of the family that we helped create for five years, whose characters we helped mold, whose lives we helped design. *X-Men: TAS* gave us the opportunity to be part of this continuing, special world, and for that we will be forever grateful.

OPPOSITE Production cel of the empty War Room from "The Phalanx Covenant, Part 1." **01** Larry Houston, Chris Claremont, Julia Lewald, and Eric Lewald pose at Eric and Julia's table at the 2019 New Mexico Comic Con, in Albuquerque. This was the first time Larry, Eric, and Julia met the man who was responsible for so many of the best X-Men stories that inspired them and provided the foundation for their work. **02** Carter Lewald, Halloween 1994, living out his parents' stories—and ready to snag some candy with his claws.

01

02

EPISODE LOG LINES

NOTE: From season three onward, the television air-date order, the DVD-release order, and the Disney+ streaming order for the overall series have all been presented without regard to the order of episodes as originally scripted, which is as follows (and is adhered to throughout this book).

SEASON 1

1. NIGHT OF THE SENTINELS, PART 1

When her foster parents register her with a new government program to "help" mutants, adolescent Jubilee is attacked by giant robotic Sentinels that enforce the program. She meets the X-Men as they rescue her and take her to their base: Xavier's School for the Gifted. Jubilee, concerned about her foster family, sneaks off to check on them but is captured by the Sentinels.

2. NIGHT OF THE SENTINELS, PART 2

In the fight to rescue Jubilee, the X-Men learn more about the Mutant Control Agency. One of the X-Men is arrested, and the others are left to mourn a shocking loss. Heartbroken teammates manage to free Jubilee from the Sentinels' HQ and return home to grieve. Jubilee decides to join Xavier's school.

3. ENTER MAGNETO

Cyclops brings a wounded Sabretooth to the X-Mansion for medical aid, following a botched attempt by Magneto to free Beast from prison. Wolverine, who considers Sabretooth to be a dangerous enemy, is not pleased. Magneto, Xavier's closest friend and oldest enemy, advocates for the violent overthrow of human oppressors, which gives antimutant Senator Kelly a reason to rant.

4. DEADLY REUNIONS

Professor X, a staunch, empathetic advocate for mutant-human peaceful coexistence, psychically melds with Sabretooth to heal him, which rankles Wolverine. Magneto attacks a chemical plant to draw out Professor X and the X-Men team.

5. CAPTIVE HEARTS

Storm faces her claustrophobia when she confronts the underground-dwelling Morlocks and their leader, Callisto. They've taken Cyclops hostage, and Wolverine is forced to face his own feelings for Jean Grey as he helps to save Scott.

6. COLD VENGEANCE

Wolverine, nursing his unresolved feelings for Jean, leaves for parts unknown in Northern Canada. He finds solace in a peaceful Inuit village, but Sabretooth tracks him there. Storm, Jubilee, and Gambit head to island of Genosha, a presumed paradise of mutant-human tolerance.

7. SLAVE ISLAND

Jubilee, Storm, and Gambit are put to work as slaves alongside other duped mutants to complete a dam to power Sentinel creator Master Mold. A mysterious mutant from a bleak future arrives and helps the X-Men, though his allegiances are unclear.

8. THE UNSTOPPABLE JUGGERNAUT

When the X-Mansion is destroyed, newly arrived Russian mutant Colossus is the prime suspect. The X-Men learn that the real culprit is closer to home.

9. THE CURE

Rogue travels to Muir Island on the chance that an experimental treatment available there could "cure" her mutation and allow her to touch others.

10. COME THE APOCALYPSE

Apocalypse, the world's first and most powerful mutant, enslaves four unsuspecting mutants, turning them into his Four Horsemen and attacks the Paris World Peace conference. Rogue and the X-Men must fight them.

11. DAYS OF FUTURE PAST, PART 1

Bishop, a mutant from a bleak future, travels back in time to the present day to prevent a political assassination, which will touch off a never-ending human-mutant war. Bishop believes one of the X-Men is the assassin.

12. DAYS OF FUTURE PAST, PART 2

When Bishop identifies Gambit as the would-be assassin, the team races to Washington to thwart the assassination of Senator Kelly.

13. THE FINAL DECISION

Master Mold, breeder of the Sentinels, unleashes a mass of Sentinels to wipe out humans and mutants alike. The X-Men find themselves working together with adversary Magneto to defeat the menace.

SEASON 2

14. TILL DEATH US DO PART, PART 1

Cyclops and Jean wed, but the false officiant is in truth a dangerous imposter, now aligned with manipulative Mister Sinister. A new raging militant antimutant group called the Friends of Humanity rises.

15. TILL DEATH US DO PART, PART 2

Cyclops and Jean are captured by Mister Sinister and his Nasty Boys to extract their DNA for Sinister's genetic experimentation. The remaining X-Men find themselves battling their new nemesis at the X-Mansion as Professor X and Magneto find themselves trapped, without their powers, in the strange, hidden world of the Savage Land.

16. WHATEVER IT TAKES

The Shadow King escapes imprisonment in the Astral Plane, emerging near an African village that once revered X-Men's Storm as a goddess. The Shadow King possesses her godson. Storm and Rogue head to Africa.

17. RED DAWN

In the wake of the collapse of the Soviet Union, uncontrollably dangerous mutant Omega Red is freed to "restore the glory of the lost empire." When Colossus's village is imperiled, he reaches out to the X-Men.

18. REPO MAN

Wolverine is lured back to Canada and captured by the evil Canadian government personnel responsible for the insertion of his Adamantium skeleton. In his struggle to escape, he encounters important people from his past.

19. X-TERNALLY YOURS

Gambit reluctantly returns to his Cajun home, as required by an old blood feud, to save his brother Bobby from Gambit's old flame Bella Donna, who wants Gambit back.

20. TIME FUGITIVES, PART 1

In the year 3999, Cable learns that the plague destroying his world was caused by Bishop's time-travel trip to the X-Men during "Days of Future Past." Cable must now time-travel himself to try to set things right.

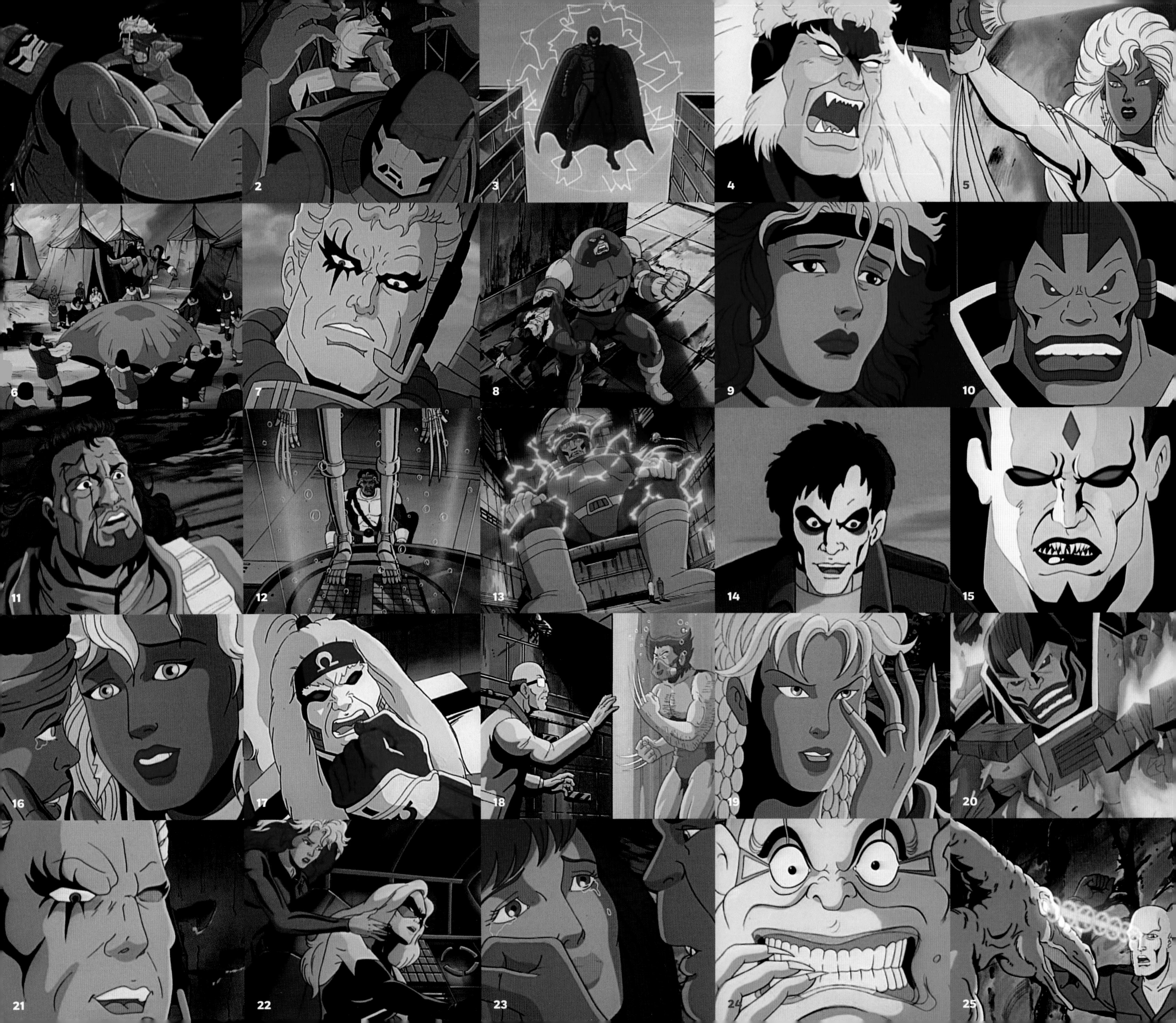
1
2
3
4
5
6
7
8
9
10
11
12
13
14
15
16
17
18
19
20
21
22
23
24
25

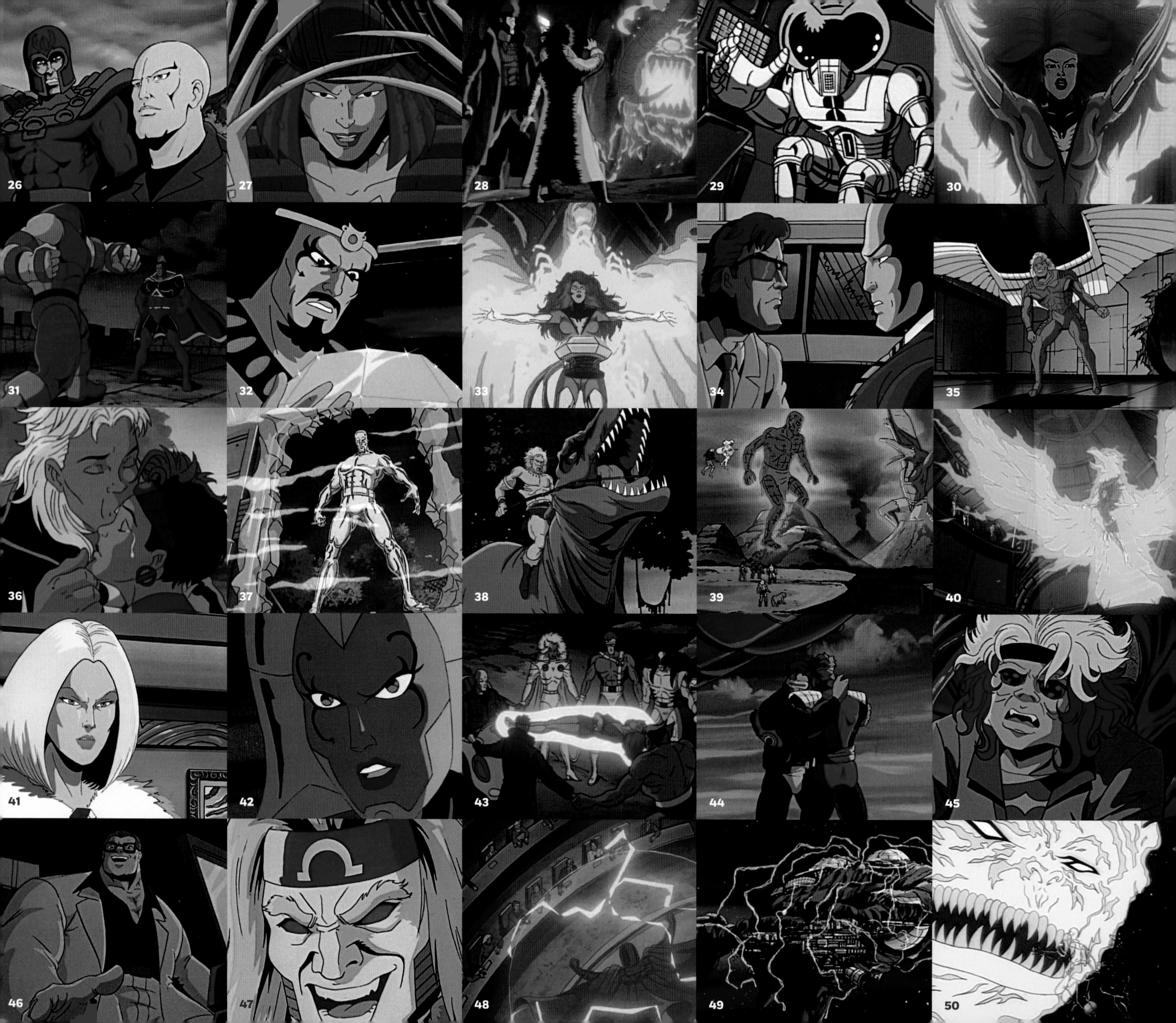
26
27
28
29
30
31
32
33
34
35
36
37
38
39
40
41
42
43
44
45
46
47
48
49
50

21. TIME FUGUTIVES, PART 2

Wolverine's unique healing abilities may prove key to securing both Bishop's and Cable's future timelines.

22. A ROGUE'S TALE

With Professor X still missing, Mystique interferes with the mental suppression mechanism that allows Rogue to forget the disturbing way she obtained her powers. Now Rogue is forced to confront the darkest moments of her past.

23. BEAUTY AND THE BEAST

To his amazement, Beast falls in love with a blind patient of his and she with him. His experimental treatment restores her vision, but her father is a militant mutant-hater.

24. MOJOVISION

Mojo, a super showman from another dimension, grabs the X-Men and forces them to participate in his intergalactic hit entertainment spectacle.

25. REUNION, PART 1

Mister Sinister lures the X-Men to the Savage Land—using Professor X and Magneto as bait—where all their powers are neutralized and Sinister plans to use them in his genetic experiments.

26. REUNION, PART 2

The Nasty Boys and Mutates capture all the X-Men, except for Wolverine, as part of Mister Sinister's plot to grab mutant DNA for his experiments.

SEASON 3

27. OUT OF THE PAST, PART 1

Yuriko, aka Lady Deathstrike, a Japanese woman from Wolverine's past, induces him to come to the Morlocks' deep tunnel network, where she has found an alien spaceship that only Wolverine's claws can open.

28. OUT OF THE PAST, PART 2

The alien craft, a Shi'ar vessel, is actually a prison ship. Wolverine's opening of it unleashes something truly monstrous. Wolverine and Gambit struggle to keep it from escaping to the surface as the other X-Men join the fight to save their friends.

29. THE PHOENIX SAGA, PART 1: DAZZLED

The Earth-orbiting Space Station and its astronauts are attacked and overcome by alien Shi'ar warrior Erik the Red. Professor X experiences powerful visions of the crisis and sends the X-Men, in a space shuttle, to attempt a rescue.

30. THE PHOENIX SAGA, PART 2: THE DARK SHROUD

The other X-Men are stunned to witness a transformation in Jean. Professor X's dark side emerges in an astral projection caused by his psychic connection to an alien life-form. Something is trying to get to him.

31. THE PHOENIX SAGA, PART 3: CRY OF THE BANSHEE

Alien Shi'ar royalty Lilandra is rescued from Juggernaut by the X-Men and Banshee. She is desperate to protect the powerful M'Kraan crystal from her crazed brother D'Kenn.

32. THE PHOENIX SAGA, PART 4: STARJAMMERS

The M'Kraan crystal is secreted on Lilandra's ship, where Phoenix takes the X-Men. The Starjammers, space pirates, attack and grab the crystal. Lead Starjammer Corsair dupes Cyclops into aiding in his plans to assassinate D'Kenn.

33. THE PHOENIX SAGA, PART 5: CHILD OF LIGHT

D'Kenn is transported inside the crystal and becomes increasingly unstable. The X-Men must team up with the Shi'ar Imperial Guard to stop him, but it will take a sacrifice from Phoenix to win the battle and save existence.

34. NO MUTANT IS AN ISLAND

Bitter Cyclops quits the X-Men and returns to the orphanage where he was raised. There he confronts local criminal Zebediah Kilgrave. Appears on DVDs as episode 66.

35. OBSESSION

Archangel's obsessive desire to strike at Apocalypse sends the X-Men into a Shi'ar spacecraft, itself an actual sentient life-form. Appears on DVDs as episode 36.

36. LONGSHOT

Jubilee gets her first kiss from Longshot, a handsome young man from another dimension, as the X-Men return to Mojo's wild world of gladiatorial entertainment. Appears on DVDs as episode 67.

37. COLD COMFORT

Iceman Bobby Drake, an original X-Man, returns to his former home to ask for help in finding his missing beloved, Lorna Dane. Appears on DVDs as episode 41.

38. SAVAGE LAND STRANGE HEART, PART 1

Storm is lured by prehistoric beast Sauron back to the Savage Land, where Sauron plans to free his evil master.

39. SAVAGE LAND STRANGE HEART, PART 2

Garokk, trapped in the land and the rock, needs Storm to unleash all her powers to free him. The other X-Men struggle to save her.

40. DARK PHOENIX, PART 1: DAZZLED

The Inner Circle (aka The Hellfire Club) wants to possess the incredible power of the Phoenix, which continues to inhabit Jean's body.

41. DARK PHOENIX, PART 2: INNER CIRCLE

The Phoenix, inside Jean's body, develops a hunger for human sensations and starts going "dark" as Professor X and Emma Frost fight for psychic control over her.

42. DARK PHOENIX, PART 3: DARK PHOENIX

The Dark Phoenix takes complete control of Jean.

43. DARK PHOENIX, PART 4: THE FATE OF THE PHOENIX

The Shi'ar court condemns the Dark Phoenix to death after it destroys the D'Bari solar system.

44. ORPHAN'S END

Cyclops discovers that space pirate Corsair is his long-lost father, who he remembers as having abandoned him when Cyclops was a child. Appears on DVDs as episode 42.

45. LOVE IN VAIN

Rogue's first sweetheart, human Cody, shows up, but when she kisses him, he no longer falls into a coma. That's because he's the pawn of grotesque aliens who need the X-Men—and Earth—to complete a terrifying mission. Appears on DVDs as episode 59.

SEASON 4

46. JUGGERNAUT RETURNS

Professor X's bitter stepbrother Cain Marko loses the jewel that gives him the powers to be Juggernaut, and that sustains his life. Appears on DVDs as episode 43.

47. A DEAL WITH THE DEVIL

A sunken but functioning Soviet nuclear submarine needs help from Omega Red to be recovered, but he'll only cooperate if Storm and Wolverine accompany him. Appears on DVDs as episode 65.

48. SANCTUARY, PART 1

Mutant separatist Magneto sets up a mutant-only sanctuary on an artificial, orbiting asteroid (Asteroid M), but a betrayal may be in the works. Appears on DVDs as episode 51.

49. SANCTUARY, PART 2

An injured Magneto, with the X-Men's help, halts a vicious attack. Appears on DVDs as episode 52.

50. XAVIER REMEMBERS

Professor X suffers head trauma, and, as he finds himself near death, he discovers himself fighting the Shadow King in the Astral Plane. Appears on DVDs as episode 61.

51. COURAGE

After a long absence, Morph tries to return to the X-Men, but his old traumas may overwhelm him. Appears on DVDs as episode 48.

52. SECRETS, NOT LONG BURIED

On a trip to a small Western town to visit an old friend, Cyclops discovers the town has been overtaken by a radical pro-mutant hate group called the Children of the Shadow. Appears on DVDs as episode 60.

53. NIGHTCRAWLER

In Germany, Gambit, Rogue, and Wolverine encounter mutant Nightcrawler, who looks like a demon but is peaceful and deeply devout. Local villagers, terrified by his appearance, attack the monastery where Nightcrawler had found solace. Appears on DVDs as episode 44.

54. ONE MAN'S WORTH, PART 1

Master Mold has sent assassins back in time to kill college-age Professor X in 1959—so there would be no X-Men to thwart him. The current timeline, created by this killing, is a dystopian hellscape. Appears on DVDs as episode 46.

55. ONE MAN'S WORTH, PART 2

Storm and Wolverine must make a wrenching sacrifice to stop young Xavier's death, a journey that requires them to go forward in time before they can go back to Xavier's college days if they are to save him. Appears on DVDs as episode 47.

56. PROTEUS, PART 1

Moira MacTaggert reaches out to the X-Men when her powerful, unbalanced adolescent son, Kevin—aka Proteus—escapes their island lab and goes off in search of his absentee father. Appears on DVDs as episode 49.

57. PROTEUS, PART 2

The prominent "family values" politician who abandoned his son Proteus is uncovered as a fraud, but when confronted by Proteus continues to reject his mutant son. Appears on DVDs as episode 50.

58. FAMILY TIES

Mutant twins Scarlet Witch and Quicksilver go in search of the father they never knew. Magneto requests the X-Men's assistance searching for his late wife, now rumored to be alive. Appears on DVDs as episode 62.

59. BLOODLINES

Nightcrawler enlists the X-Men when he receives a mysterious message, perhaps from the mother who abandoned him at birth. Appears on DVDs as episode 68.

60. LOTUS AND THE STEEL

Wolverine goes into a self-imposed exile in a Japanese fishing village he once knew. The village is then attacked by the Silver Samurai. Appears on DVDs as episode 58.

61. WEAPON X, LIES AND VIDEOTAPE

Beast goes with a troubled Wolverine in search of the top secret Weapon-X facility where the Adamantium was added to Wolverine's bones. Appears on DVDs as episode 45.

62. HAVE YOURSELF A MORLOCK LITTLE CHRISTMAS

The holiday spirit is strong with Jubilee, a foster child who hasn't really celebrated much before joining the X-Men. While out shopping, they cross paths with Morlock Leech, in desperate need of their help. Appears on DVDs as episode 57.

63. BEYOND GOOD AND EVIL, PART 1: THE END OF TIME

Cable and Apocalypse fight in the year 3999. Apocalypse traps Bishop. Appears on DVDs as episode 53.

64. BEYOND GOOD AND EVIL, PART 2: PROMISE OF APOCALYPSE

Professor X determines that psychic mutants are being kidnapped. Wolverine, together with Shard in search of her brother Bishop, heads out to protect the psychic Psylocke. Appears on DVDs as episode 54.

65. BEYOND GOOD AND EVIL, PART 3: THE LAZARUS CHAMBER

Apocalypse disrupts Cable's time-travel. After agreeing to destroy the Lazarus Chamber—which maintains Apocalypse's life—the X-Men head to ancient Cairo. Appears on DVDs as episode 55.

66. BEYOND GOOD AND EVIL, PART 4: END AND BEGINNING

X-Men and Cable find their way to Professor X. Magneto feels betrayed by the kidnapped psychics who were part of Apocalypse's plan to destroy all time and create a new universe-kingdom for him. Appears on DVDs as episode 56.

SEASON 5

67. THE PHALANX COVENANT, PART 1

The Phalanx techno-organic creatures attack Earth, absorbing every living thing in their path. Appears on DVDs as episode 63.

68. THE PHALANX COVENANT, PART 2

Magneto is happy to watch humanity perish until he learns his son Quicksilver has been captured by the Phalanx. Appears on DVDs as episode 64.

69. STORM FRONT, PART 1

Alien Arkon goes to Earth in desperate need of Storm's powers to save his planet from destruction. She goes, saves Arkon's planet, then is startled by an unexpected proposal.

70. STORM FRONT, PART 2

Preparations begin for the royal wedding in Arkon's world, but the X-Men discover that Storm's fiancé is not who he seems to be.

71. THE FIFTH HORSEMAN

Jubilee is kidnapped by Fabian Cortez to serve as a host body for Apocalypse when a celestial conjunction frees Apocalypse from his imprisonment in the Astral Plane.

72. JUBILEE'S FAIRY TALE THEATER

Jubilee is trapped by a cave-in under the X-Mansion with several children. To ease their panic, she tells them fairy tales featuring familiar X-Men.

73. OLD SOLDIERS

Fifty years after World War II, Wolverine visits the grave of a scientist he feels betrayed him. Wolverine remembers when he and Captain America fought together in the war.

74. HIDDEN AGENDAS

Rogue goes to the South and meets Cannonball, a mutant with all the love and support she never had. A dark army operation attempts to use the unwitting young mutant. Appears on DVDs as episode 75.

75. DESCENT

In the 1800s London of Charles Darwin, the origin of Mister Sinister and his interest in genetics is revealed. Appears on DVDs as episode 74.

76. GRADUATION DAY

Professor X is gravely wounded and must leave Earth with Lilandra and the Shi'ar if he is to have a chance to survive.

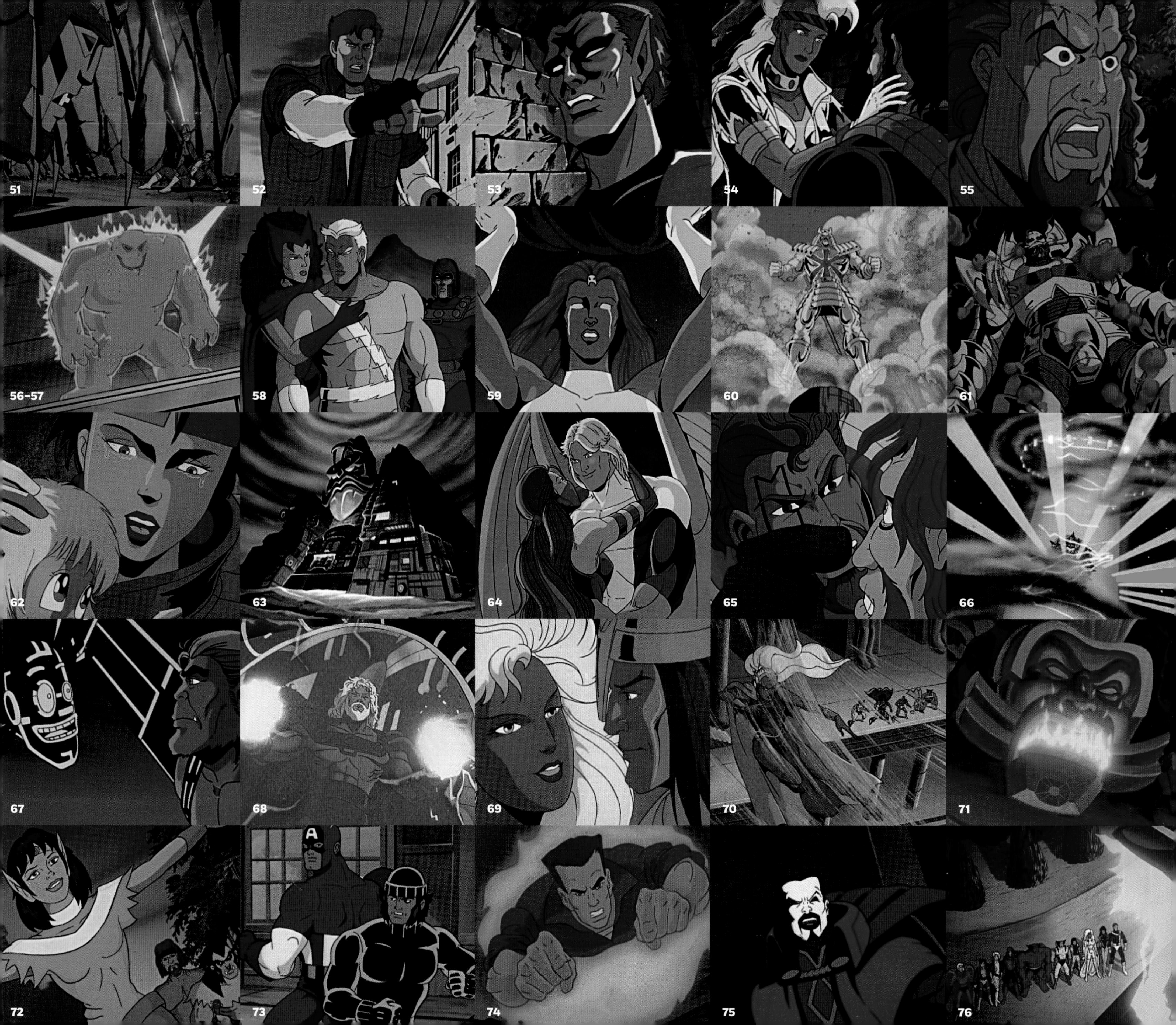

51 52 53 54 55

56–57 58 59 60 61

62 63 64 65 66

67 68 69 70 71

72 73 74 75 76

KEY CREATIVE AND SCREEN CREDITS

KEY CREATIVE

WILL MEUGNIOT

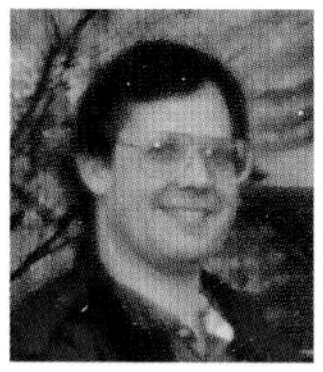

Will was ten years old when *Fantastic Four* #1 went on sale; he became an avid Marvel fan. While in high school, Will decided to try writing and drawing comics, hoping one day to work for Marvel. In 1975, he made his first sale to them. In 1978, Will started his animation career at Hanna-Barbera, where he worked for animation greats Doug Wildey, Tex Avery, Alex Lovy, and Don Jurwich. Besides *X-Men: TAS*, Meugniot was supervising producer and director on much-loved series such as *Exosquad*, *The Real Ghostbusters*, *Captain Planet*, *Conan the Adventurer*, *G.I. Joe*, *Street Fighter*, and *Spider-Man Unlimited*. Will fought all the major creative battles to keep *X-Men: TAS* on track to be the show we all enjoy. Now retired, Will lives in Southern California with his wife of forty-nine years, comic-book colorist Jo Meugniot.

ERIC LEWALD

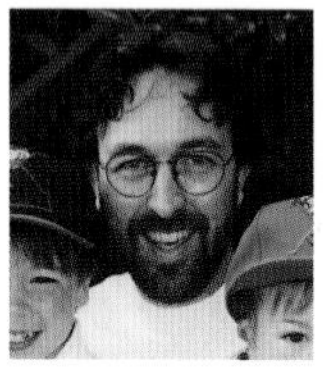

Eric did not come to the project as an "X-pert." He simply loved stories and storytelling. Movies, books, TV shows, comics, old song lyrics: He has succumbed to them all. His European father used to read him bloody Greek and Norse myths at bedtime, mixed in with Lewis Carroll. During high school, he memorized the original *Star Trek* series over TV-tray suppers. Eric programmed films at the University of Tennessee (with *X-Men: TAS* writers Mark and Michael Edens). Hollywood beckoned: Where else do they pay you to tell stories? And that's how—after seven years writing for Hanna-Barbera, TMS Entertainment, and Disney—he found himself getting "the phone call" offering him a job working on a show about mutants.

LARRY HOUSTON

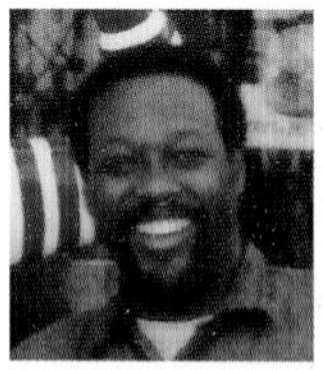

Larry Houston, a veteran of more than eighty animated TV series, was the first African American storyboard artist ever hired for Saturday-morning television. Larry has been nominated for an Emmy, won a Golden Reel, and received an Inkpot Award from the San Diego Comic-Con for lifetime achievement. Larry was the senior, hands-on producer/director of *X-Men: TAS* for the first four of our five seasons. He has loved the X-Men all his life. Larry worked as an artist on *Teenage Mutant Ninja Turtles*, *The Real Ghostbusters*, *Batman: TAS*, *Static Shock*, *Buzz Lightyear*, *TaleSpin*, *G.I. Joe*, *Transformers*, and *Spawn*. Stan Lee hired Larry as creative director of his Internet company, Stan Lee Media, and Larry has worked on a dozen projects as producer/director, including *RoboCop: Alpha Commando* and *Captain Planet*. Larry was the main force behind our beloved *X-Men: TAS* title sequence. Larry lives with his wife of many years, Alexandra, in Southern California.

SIDNEY IWANTER

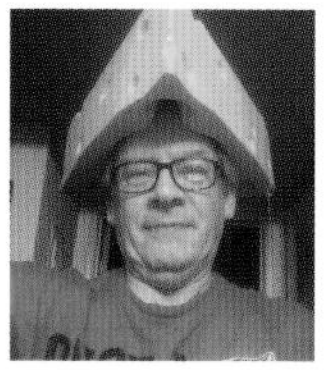

Sidney was the most hands-on creative executive in the history of children's network programming and certainly the most memorable. The dyed-in-the-wool Wisconsin Badger oversaw every word written, every line spoken, every image crafted for *X-Men: TAS* while doing the same for *Batman: TAS*, *The Tick*, *Spider-Man: TAS*, and, over his short network tenure, a dozen more Fox TV hits. Sidney insisted on serious, challenging storytelling in Saturday-morning animated television despite an industry tradition that often didn't. Margaret Loesch gave us this once-in-a-lifetime chance. Sidney made sure we gave it our best.

JOE CALAMARI

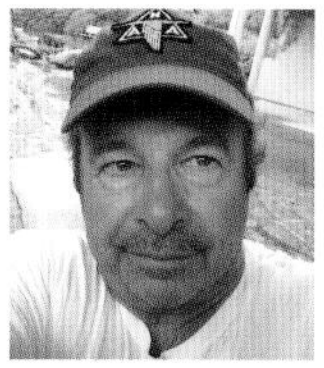

Joe was Marvel's TV/movie guy from way back. He was a Marvel lifer, an attorney who probably knows more about the business history of the company than any living soul. Joe was a central figure in Marvel's late-nineties takeover fight, but the *X-Men: TAS* cast, writers, artists, and executives knew him as the watchful eye of Marvel Comics, as the company's voice at the table. "Joey the Squid" is now happily retired and living in New Jersey.

MARK AND MICHAEL EDENS

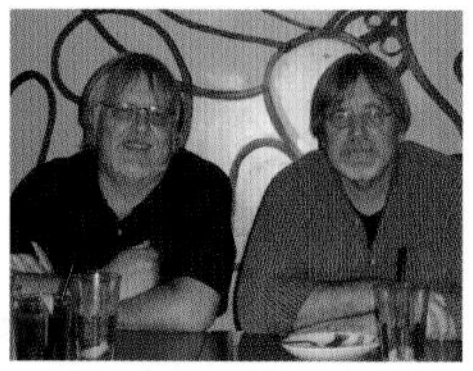

One or both of these sons of a middle-Tennessee farm family had a hand in the majority of the stories we told. Both are historians for whom the extraordinary world of the X-Men surely holds no awe. Mark and Michael brought heart and conviction to heroic action writing in a way that helped *X-Men: TAS* distinguish itself from the animated television that had come before it. Each had a long, successful run in Hollywood, then chose to return home. Michael and his wife, Cindy, enjoy a peaceful stretch of family farmland near Bowling Green, Kentucky. Mark and his wife, Amy, command a mountaintop outside Sewanee, Tennessee.

SCOTT THOMAS

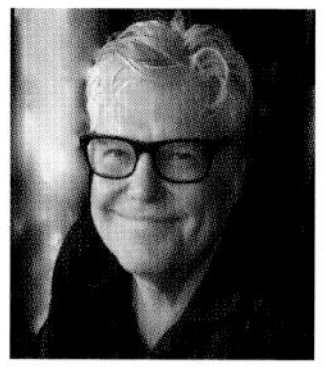

Producer/director Scott Thomas has more than forty years' experience in planning, development, and production of filmed entertainment. Besides *X-Men: TAS*, he produced the animated television series *Gargoyles: The Goliath Chronicles* and *Ultraforce*. Thomas wrote, directed, and produced the live-action feature film *Flight of the Living Dead*, which has won numerous awards and has become a cult favorite. He has also won awards for his original feature film *Deranged*.

SHARON JANIS

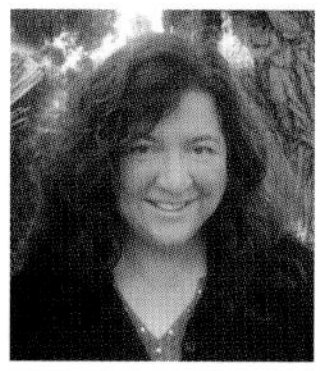

Before moving to Hollywood, video editor Sharon Janis had spent nearly a decade living a monastic ashram life, going by the Sanskrit name Komuda, and producing videos about spiritual wisdom. Her award-winning Hollywood career included video editing *X-Men: TAS* and *Mighty Morphin Power Rangers* at the same time, when they were the top two children's shows in the world. Janis eventually moved to a more peaceful life by the sea, producing documentary films and writing books, including *Spirituality for Dummies* and *Secrets of Spiritual Happiness*.

AVERY COBERN

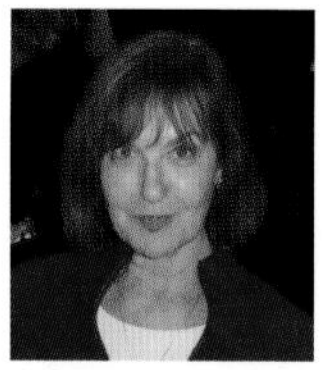

We may be the only series in history to list our censor (Broadcast Standards and Practices) as a key creative partner. But she was. Avery had total control over every word uttered and every act committed by our characters. Not just many, but most shows "made for kids" are limited, hobbled, even ruined by well-meaning BS&P executives who have no feeling for the characters or for the needs of storytelling. Avery respected the X-Men; she allowed us to kill Morph and for Wolverine to struggle to find a connection to God. Her trust in us allowed *X-Men: TAS* to become the series that it needed to be.

RICK HOBERG

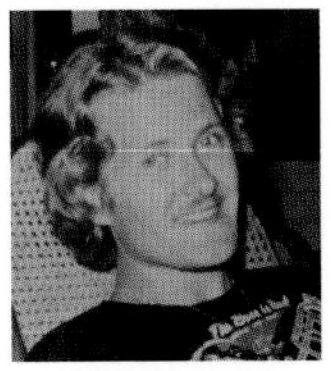

Rick has hundreds and hundreds of produced credits on seventy-six different animated projects over his long, continuing career in animation. There probably isn't a Marvel character he hasn't drawn for television. Rick pushed as hard as anyone to "get X-Men right!" While the rest of us seem to be easing toward retirement, Rick's work continues to be in demand. He has left the Southern California rat race for the pleasures of Washington State.

FRANK BRUNNER

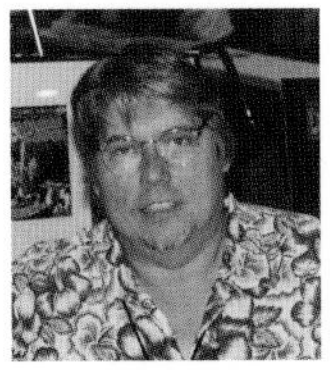

Frank entered the comics profession as a horror writer-artist for the black-and-white comics magazines *Web of Horror*, *Creepy*, *Eerie*, and *Vampirella*. Brunner's best-known color-comics work is his Marvel Comics collaboration with writer Steve Engelhart on the supernatural hero Doctor Strange in *Marvel Premiere* numbers 9–14 (July 1973–March 1974) and in *Doctor Strange: Master of the Mystic Arts* numbers 1–2 and 4–5 (June–August 1974 and October–December 1974). Brunner moved to Hollywood and began a career in movie and television animation, working on projects for Hanna-Barbera (*Jonny Quest*), Walt Disney Imagineering (Euro Disneyland Resort's *Tomorrowland* movie), Warner Bros. (pre-production *Batman* design) and DreamWorks (*Invasion USA*). Frank was the head of character design for *X-Men: TAS*. His sure hand allowed us to create empathetic, believable characters within a spectacular world. He made our mutants human.

FRANK SQUILLACE

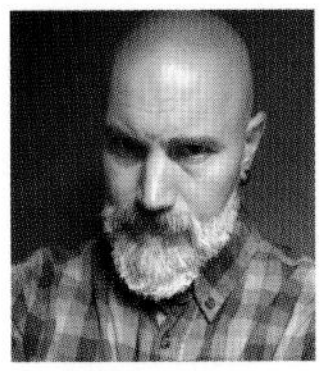

Frank started his animation career working for Will Meugniot on *Captain Planet*. He joined the *X-Men: TAS* crew during its second season as Larry Houston's creative assistant, what Frank calls Larry's "Swiss Army knife"—handling anything and everything that came along. When Larry was lost for the last season, Frank was a natural to step up and take over. He now lives and works in Arizona.

MARK LEWIS

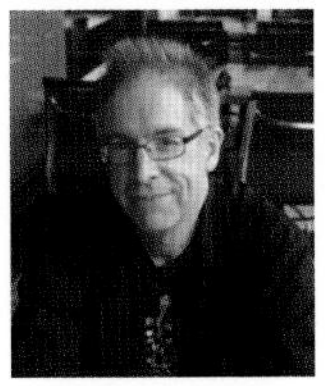

Sometimes it seems like Mark had a hand in almost every *X-Men: TAS* image that made it to the screen. As our principal cleanup artist, his obsessive nature helped make sure that characters, props, and vehicles were consistent in the smallest detail and looked their best. The designers would craft something solid, then Mark would enhance and polish it into its final form. Mark's fierce attention to detail was also crucial to the creation of this book. Like a completist scholar, he has kept memories and files about everything he touched. While *X-Men: TAS* was Mark's first major assignment, nearly thirty years later, after dozens of other projects, the Southern California resident remains active in the animation industry.

STEPHANIE GRAZIANO & JIM GRAZIANO

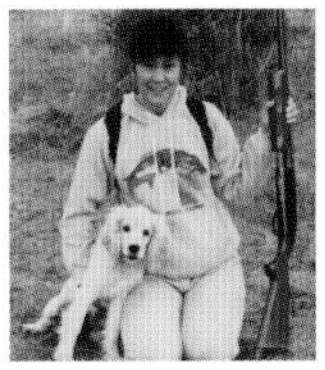

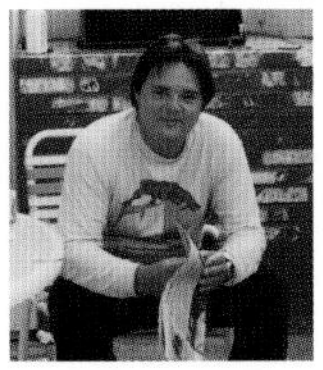

Stephanie would always say that everyone else—writers, artists, actors—was "the creative staff." But the company that she and Jim, her husband, put together, and fought to keep together those many long seasons, made the creative contributions of the rest of us possible. Her endless hours of dedication to *X-Men: TAS* allowed our under-resourced "little show" to thrive and become something special.

SCREEN CREDITS

DEVELOPED FOR TELEVISION BY

Eric Lewald

DIRECTED BY

Larry Houston
Fred Miller
Richard Bowman
Frank Squillace

EXECUTIVE STORY EDITOR

Eric Lewald

SERIES WRITING CREDITS

Mark Edward Edens
Michael Edens
David McDermott
Steven Melching
Marty Isenberg
Robert N. Skir
Len Wein
Eric Lewald
Brooks Wachtel
Julianne Klemm
Dean Stefan (writing as Sandy Scesney)
Len Uhley
Julia Lewald
Francis Moss
Ted Pedersen
Stephanie Mathison
Larry Parr
Jan Strnad
Jim Carlson
Terrence McDonnell
Donald F. Glut
Elliot S. Maggin
Adam Gilad
Steven Levy
Doug Booth
Steve Cuden
Gary Greenfield
Matthew Malach
Richard Mueller
Jeff Saylor
Bruce Reid Schaefer
Carter Crocker (writing as LuAnne Crocker)
Marley Clark
Mirith J. Colao
Martha Moran
Mark Onspaugh
James Krieg

SERIES CAST

Cathal J. Dodd
George Buza
Norm Spencer
Cedric Smith
Lenore Zann
Catherine Disher
Chris Potter
Alyson Court
Alison Sealy-Smith
Lawrence Bayne
Ron Rubin
John Colicos
David Hemblen
Don Francks
Jennifer Dale
Paul Haddad
Stephen Ouimette
Philip Akin
Lally Cadeau
Jeremy Ratchford
Stuart Stone
Barry Flatman
David Fox
Rick Bennett
Iona Morris
Brett Halsey
Adrian Egan
George Merner
Rod Coneybeare
Graham Haley
Randall Carpenter
Judy Marshak
James Millington
Ross Petty
Kay Tremblay
Chris Britton
Robert Calt
Marc Strange
Len Carlson
John Stocker
Dan Hennessey
Susan Roman
Camilla Scott
Rod Wilson
Catherine Gallant
Tara Strong
Tony Daniels
Robert Cait
David Corban
Robert Bockstael
James Blendick
Len Doncheff
Melissa Sue Anderson
Rene Lemieux
Peter Wildman
Nigel Bennett
John Blackwood
Jane Luk
Megan Smith-Harris
Denis Akiyama
Adrian Hough
Rick Bonnell
Terri Hawkes
Harvey Atkin
Rebecca Jenkins
Marc Muirhead
Elizabeth Rukavina
Maurice Dean Wint
Richard Epcar
Roscoe Handford
Peter McCowatt
Cynthia Belliveau
Janusz Bukowski
Tomasz Marzecki
Brian Taylor
Ho Chow

SERIES PRODUCED BY

Will Meugniot
Larry Houston
Scott Thomas
Joseph Calamari
Frank Squillace
Sharon Janis
Eric S. Rollman
Winston Richard
Stan Lee
Avi Arad

SERIES MUSIC BY

Ron Wasserman
Shuki Levy
Haim Saban

SERIES FILM EDITING BY

Sharon Janis
John C. Walts

SERIES CASTING BY

Karen Goora

SERIES PRODUCTION DESIGN BY

John Petrovitz
Shannon Denton

SERIES PRODUCTION-MANAGEMENT

EXECUTIVES IN CHARGE OF PRODUCTION

Dana C. Booton
Stephanie Graziano
Jim Graziano

PRODUCTION MANAGER

Dana C. Booton
Karen Kollis
Kurt Weldon
Leanne Moreau
Kathleen Thorpe
Beth Gunn
Dorie Rich

ASSISTANT PRODUCTION MANAGER

Clark B. Weaver

UNIT PRODUCTION MANAGER

Jim Graziano

EXECUTIVE IN CHARGE OF POST-PRODUCTION

Eric S. Rollman

POST-PRODUCTION SUPERVISORS

Dan LaBorico
John Bryant

SERIES ART DEPARTMENT

STORYBOARD ARTIST

Pat Agnasin
Romeo Francisco
Greg Garcia
Patrick Archibald
Frank Squillace
Daniel Veesenmeyer
Michael Swanigan
Larry Houston
Armando Carrillo
Francis Barrios
Rick Hoberg
Tom Nesbitt
Adrian Gonzales
Del Barras
Tenny Henson
Keith Tucker
Jim Janes
Doug Murphy
Curt Geda
Gerry Acerno
Troy Adomitis
Dave Simons
Mike Sosnowski
Douglas P. Battle
Dan Fausett
Victor Dal Chele
John Fox
Don Manuel
Lewis Williams
John Ahern
Clint Taylor
Will Meugniot

STORYBOARD CLEANUP

Pat Agnasin
Romeo Francisco
Abel Laxamana
Romeo Lopez
Mark Lewis
Tec Manalac
Andres Nieves
Del Barras
Tenny Henson
Cesar Magsombol
Rudy Messina
Steve Simone
Phil Stapleton
Marcos Borregales
Gerald Forton
Ernie Guanlao
Mike Sosnowski
Fred Carrillo
Alan Gibson
Patrico Aganasin

PROP DESIGNER

Steve Olds
Frank Squillace
Darrel Bowen
Mark Lewis

Andres Nieves
Russell G. Chong
Marcos Borregales
Claude Denis
Warren Greenwood
Shayne Poindexter
Thibault Descamps

PROPS

Steve Olds
Thibault Descamps

PROP DESIGN

Mark Lewis

LAYOUT SUPERVISOR: OVERSEAS PRODUCTION

Armand Serrano

BACKGROUND DESIGNER

Dennis Venizelos

SERIES SOUND DEPARTMENT

POST-PRODUCTION AUDIO COORDINATOR

Xavier Garcia

SOUND OPERATIONS MANAGER

Xavier Garcia

EXECUTIVE IN CHARGE OF SOUND OPERATIONS

Clive H. Mizumoto

RERECORDING MIXER

Clive H. Mizumoto
Mark Ettel

SOUND SUPERVISOR

Clive H. Mizumoto

RERECORDING ENGINEER

Clive H. Mizumoto

SOUND EFFECTS EDITOR

Ron Salaises
Martin Flores

John Valentino
Scott Page-Pagter

SOUND EFFECTS DESIGN

Ron Salaises

SUPERVISING SOUND EDITOR

Ron Salaises

SOUND EFFECTS DESIGNER

Ron Salaises

ASSISTANT ENGINEER

Don Sexton
Steve Garelick
Mike Garcia
Kevin Newson
Karl Warme

AUDIO ASSISTANT

Don Sexton
David W. Barr
Brian Densmore
Andrew Kines

ASSISTANT SOUND ENGINEER

Don Sexton
Steve Garelick
Kevin Newson
Karl Warme

RECORDING ENGINEER

Paul Shubat
Rick Pacholko
Colin Caddies

SOUND RECORDING ENGINEER

Paul Shubat
Colin Caddies

DIALOGUE EDITOR

Jamie Simone
Mike Garcia
Laurie Wetzler
Denny Densmore

FOLEY ARTIST

Taryn Simone
Kalea Morton

Kalea L. Morton
Gregg Barbanell

ADDITIONAL SOUND EFFECTS EDITOR

John Valentino
Scott Page-Pagter

TRACK READING

Laurie Wetzler
Tom Anderson
Joe Trueba

ASSISTANT ENGINEER DIALOGUE

Colin Caddies

ASSISTANT RECORDING ENGINEER

Colin Caddies

PRE-PRODUCTION DIALOGUE EDITOR

Mike Trueba
Jay Bixsen
Arthur J. Codron

SERIES VISUAL EFFECTS BY

MODEL DESIGNER

Frank Brunner
Mark Lewis
Kathi Castillo
Rick Hoberg
Lewis Williams

SERIES ANIMATION DEPARTMENT

ANIMATION LIP SYNC

Erik Jan Peterson
Jeffrey Peterson

TIMING DIRECTORS

Erik Jan Peterson
Dora Case
Marlene Robinson May
Richard Bowman
Erin Gurn
Gabor Karpatty

Jang Gil Kim
Richard Collado
Rudy Cataldi
Milton Gray
Margaret Nichols
Maxwell Becraft
Brett Hisey
Ron Myrick
Bob Tyler

SHEET TIMERS

Erik Jan Peterson
Dora Case
Erin Gurn
Gabor Karpatty
Jang Gil Kim
Richard Collado
Rudy Cataldi
Milton Gray
Margaret Nichols
M. Kay Anderson
Carla Breene
Jim Simon

LAYOUT DESIGNERS

Frank Squillace
Cesar Magsombol
Zhaoping Wei
Wayne Schulz
Claude Denis
Pat Agnasin
Tenny Henson
Alfredo Alcala
Ted Blackman
Richie Chavez
Andrew Gentle
Charles Payne
Ric Quiroz
Tim Soman
Steve Olds

PRODUCER/DIRECTOR

Frank Squillace

CLEANUP ARTIST

Mark Lewis

CHARACTER DESIGNER

Mark Lewis

MODEL DESIGNERS

Frank Brunner
Mark Lewis

ANIMATION DIRECTORS

Sue Peters
J. K. Kim
Graham Morris
Karen Peterson

SLUGGING

Sue Peters

COLOR BACKGROUNDS

Dennis Venizelos
Phillip Kim
Sung Woo Hong
Laura Rasey Miller

BACKGROUND DESIGNERS

Dennis Venizelos
Zhaoping Wei
Jeff Richards

FINAL CHECKER

Fred Miller

INK AND PAINT ARTIST

Helga van den Berge

COLOR KEY ARTIST

Patricia Mendelson

KEY ANIMATORS

Ulysses Esguerra
Tito Romero

SERIES EDITORIAL DEPARTMENT

COLOR KEYS

Patricia Mendelson
Flavia Mitman
Allyn Conley
Tania Francisco

TELECINE COLORISTS

Lee Anne Went
Paul Bronkar

EXECUTIVE IN CHARGE OF POST-PRODUCTION
Eric S. Rollman

ON-LINE EDITORS
John C. Walts
Michael Hutchinson
Scott Reynolds
Patty Gannon

OFF-LINE EDITORS
John C. Walts
Terry Marlin

POST-PRODUCTION ASSISTANTS
John C. Walts
Wendi McNeese
Karl Warme

VIDEOTAPE COORDINATORS
Jerry Buettner
Dan LaBorico
Mike Garcia

SUPERVISING EDITOR
Ron Salaises

POST-PRODUCTION COORDINATORS
Dan LaBorico
Rob Philipp
Francesca Urbini
Peter Bruno
Dana C. Booton

POST-PRODUCTION ASSOCIATE
Wendi McNeese

AVID EDITOR
Sharon Janis

SERIES MUSIC DEPARTMENT

COMPOSER: THEME MUSIC
Ron Wasserman

MUSIC PRODUCERS
Ron Wasserman
Noam Kaniel
David Hillenbrand
Amotz Plessner
Christopher Rife

MUSIC ENGINEERS
Ron Wasserman
Barron Abramovitch

MUSIC EDITORS
Barron Abramovitch
Mark Ryan

EXECUTIVE IN CHARGE OF MUSIC
Ron Kenan

MUSIC SUPERVISORS
Mark Ryan
Lloyd Michael Cook II

MUSIC COORDINATOR
David Hillenbrand

MUSIC ASSISTANT
Jeremy Sweet

COMPOSER: TITLE THEME
Michael Kamen

SONGS
Rick Hromadka

SERIES OTHER CREW

STORY CONSULTANT
Bob Harras

VOICE DIRECTOR
Dan Hennessey

ASSISTANT TO STAN LEE
Pamela Dovale

OVERSEAS SUPERVISOR
Cam Drysdale

VOICE TALENT COORDINATOR
Elaine Justein

ASSISTANT TO JOSEPH CALAMARI
Rita Adelstein

TRACK READING
Tom Anderson
Joe Trueba

PRODUCTION ASSISTANTS
Leanne Moreau
Linda De La Rosa

PRODUCTION COORDINATORS
Fred Miller
Kathleen Clark

VIDEOTAPE COORDINATORS
Dan LaBorico
Jerry Buettner
Mike Garcia

VIDEOTAPE SUPERVISOR
Dan LaBorico

SLUGGER
Sue Peters

PUBLICIST
Brad Stephens

ACKNOWLEDGMENTS

FIRST, WE WOULD LIKE TO THANK all of the comic-book artists, starting with Jack Kirby, who have envisioned and created the visual world of the X-Men. We are indebted to all the Graz Entertainment artists who then magically made these characters come alive onscreen—Will, Larry, Frank, Rick, Frank, and Dan among them. We honor the executives, producers, and staff who made the show possible, starting with Margaret, Sidney, Avery, Stephanie, Scott, and Dana.

Gabriel Cobb and Van Eaton Galleries were generous with their time and their unparalleled collection. Also invaluable were Jeremy Cushner's wise counsel, Tom Tataranowicz's and Larry Houston's dusty storerooms, and the superheroic memory of Mark Lewis, *X-Men: TAS* artist and archivist supreme. The book would not exist without the hard work of our support staff: Reveille Wiederspahn, Carter Lewald, Alec Lewald, Taylor Faust, Katherine "Louie" DeMetre, and Amanda Burke-Hernandez.

Finally, we want to express thanks for the exacting but thoughtful supervision of our tireless editor, Eric Klopfer, the uncanny eye of designer Liam Flanagan, and the faith of Marvel's Sven Larsen, who first proposed that we all do this book together.

ERIC LEWALD & JULIA LEWALD, GLENDALE, CA, MARCH 2020

IMAGE CREDITS

COURTESY OF AUTHORS pp. 1; 11 (9); 12 (3); 13 (4, 5); 16; 17 (1); 44 (2); 46 (2); 51 (2); 52 (3); 53 (5-7); 59 (13); 60 (4-5); 62 (1); 66; 67 (1, 2); 78; 79; 97 – 101; 107; 108 (1-3); 113 (11); 118 (3); 130; 136 (4); 136 (4); 139 (4); 145; 149 (6); 151 (10); 152 (1); 159 (12); 164 (1); 165 (6-8); 170 (4); 176 (1); 177; 178 (1-4); 179; 182 (2); 186 (5); 190 (4); 191 (7, 8); 193 (13); 200 (2); 204 (4); 205 (7); 208 (3); 213 (4); 214 (2); 216 (1); 217; 219 (10); 220; 221; 224 (2); 237; 261 (9); 268-9; 275 (5); 277 (1, 2). **COURTESY OF VAN EATON GALLERIES (VEGALLERIES.COM)** pp. 2; 3; 4; 49; 50; 54 (6); 55; 57; 59 (10); 61; 63; 70; 84; 106; 111; 113 (10); 117; 119; 120 (1-4); 124; 126 (1); 127; 128; 132 (1); 133; 137; 138; 139 (1, 2); 142; 151 (11, 12); 153; 155 (7); 156 (1-3); 157 (7); 163; 164 (4); 165 (5); 166 (5); 167; 168 (1); 169 (8, 9); 170 (1-3); 172 (5-8); 173 (12); 178 (5); 180; 181; 182 (3); 183 (8); 186 (6); 187; 194; 198-9; 207; 212; 214 (3); 219 (13); 223 (9-12); 224 (1); 226; 227 (2); 229; 231 (10); 234; 241; 243 (11); 245 (11-12); 246 (4); 247 (8, 9); 248; 250 (1-3); 251 (4, 6, 7); 252 (2); 263 (14); 276. **COURTESY OF MARK LEWIS** pp. 65 (11); 73 (3); 109 (4); 112 (1-6); 113 (7); 114 (2); 115 (5-9); 116 (1-8); 118 (2); 121 (5-12); 122 (1-7); 123 (8, 10-13); 125 (4-6); 126 (2-5); 129 (2-5); 131 (2-5); 134 (1-5); 135 (7, 8, 9, 11, 12); 136 (5, 6); 149 (1-4, 7); 154 (2); 155 (8); 157 (4-6); 158 (4, 5, 7); 159 (8-11); 162 (1, 3-8); 163 (9); 164 (3); 166 (2, 3); 168 (2-5); 169 (6); 171 (5-7, 9-14); 172 (1-3); 173 (10, 11, 12); 174 (1-4); 175 (13, 15); 182 (4); 183 (5-7); 184 (3-7); 186 (1-4); 190 (5, 6); 192 (1-10); 193 (11); 195 (1-9); 196 (2, 3); 197; 200 (1, 3, 4); 201 (5-12); 203 (3-11); 206 (1-5); 208 (1, 2); 209 (6-14); 210 (1-7); 211 (8-17); 213 (2, 3); 214 (1, 4, 5); 215 (7-14); 216 (3); 218 (4-9); 219 (11, 12); 222 (2, 3, 5, 6); 225 (6-9); 228 (1-4, 8); 230 (1-9); 236; 238 (1-6); 239 (8-15); 242 (7); 243 (1); 246 (1); 249 (3-5); 258 (1-7); 259 (8-15); 260 (1, 2); 261 (7, 8); 262 (1–12). **COURTESY OF DAN VEESENMEYER** pp. 26 (1, 3, 4); 27 (6-8); 28 (1, 3, 4); 30 (2); 32 (3); 33; 41; 42; 43; 44 (1); 52 (1, 2, 4); 54 (1-5); 56 (1-10); 58 (1-9); 59 (11, 12); 60 (1-3); 62 (2-6); 64 (1, 2, 4, 5); 65 (6, 8, 9, 10); 73 (2); 113 (8); 125 (1-3); 135 (6, 10); 149 (5); 150 (3, 7, 8); 154 (1, 3); 158 (6); 162 (2); 172 (4); 182 (1); 196 (4); 222 (1, 4); 227 (1, 4); 228 (5, 6, 7, 9); 239 (7); 242 (1-6); 244 (1-4); 245 (6-10); 249 (1, 2, 6, 8, 9, 10); 252 (3); 253; 254; 255; 275 (6); 288. **COURTESY OF FRANK SQUILLACE** pp. 6; 7; 88 (1); 113 (9); 114 (3, 4); 123 (9); 125 (7); 129 (1); 131 (1, 6); 132 (2); 136 (1, 2, 3); 139 (3); 150 (1, 2, 4, 5, 6); 151 (9); 152 (2, 3, 4); 154 (4, 5); 164 (2); 166 (1, 4, 6); 171 (8); 173 (9, 13); 174 (5); 185; 190 (1, 2, 3); 193 (12); 202 (2); 204 (1, 2, 3); 205 (5, 6); 206 (6, 7); 208 (4, 5); 213 (1); 214 (6); 216 (2); 222 (7, 8); 225 (3, 4, 5); 227 (3); 231 (11, 12, 13); 240 (1, 2, 3, 4, 5); 242 (8); 243 (9, 10, 12, 13, 14); 244 (5); 246 (2, 3); 247 (5, 6, 7); 249 (7); 251 (5); 252 (1); 260 (4, 5, 6). **COURTESY OF TOM TATARANOWICZ** pp. 11 (8); 14; 64 (3); 65 (7); 74 (1); 80 (1); 81 (3); 82; 83; 85 (3); 86 (1); 87 (2, 3, 4); 89 (2, 3, 4, 5, 6); 90; 91; 92 (1, 2); 93 (3-5); 125 (8); 158 (1, 2, 3); 184 (1, 2); 160; 161; 184 (1, 2). **COURTESY OF LARRY HOUSTON** pp. 11 (4, 5); 12 (2); 25 (1, 2); 26 (2); 27 (5); 28 (2); 29 (5, 6); 30 (1); 31 (3, 4); 35-40; 75 (2, 3); 76 (1, 2); 77 (3, 4); 80 (2); 85 (2); 102 (1-3); 103 (4-8); 104 (1-9); 114 (1); 118 (1); 154 (6); 202 (1); 263 (13). **COURTESY OF DANA BOOTON** p. 62 (7); 72 (1); 80 (1); 81 (3); 218 (1, 2, 3); 260 (3). **COURTESY CORY LAFFIN** p. 267 (1). **COURTESY BLAEDE COURT-SUZUKI** p. 275 (7). **COURTESY OF CHRISTINE VALADA** p. 109 (5). **COURTESY OF TOM BREVOORT** p. 11 (6, 7). **COURTESY OF KEITH TUCKER** p. 196 (1). **COURTESY OF JEREMY CUSHNER** p. 8. **COURTESY OF WILL MEUGNIOT** pp. 12 (1); 24; 264; 265. **COURTESY OF JIM KRIEG** p. 255. **COURTESY OF RICK HOBERG** pp. 10 (2-3); 32 (1). **COURTESY OF FRANK BRUNNER** pp. 32 (2); 275 (6). **COURTESY OF SIDESHOW COLLECTIBLES** p. 274. **COURTESY OF KOTOBUKIYA** p. 273.

DARK BACKGROUND WITH SHAFT OF LIGHT SHINNING DOWN ON FIGURE

X-MEN SYMBOL ON COMPUTER GENERATED GRAPHIC "BLOCKS"

ROGUE FIGURE SEEMS TO 'HOVER' IN CASUAL POSE

LEFT Sketch of Rogue by major *X-Men: TAS* storyboard artist Dan Veesenmeyer. The pose is for an image of her character, produced in early 3-D CGI, turning in place, with a sentence about her and her powers showing beneath her. This was done for each member of the main team, and a sequence of each character model, one after the other, aired alongside the closing credits, as a way to remind viewers about our lead characters and, of all things, to satisfy a request that the series integrate some CGI material—at the time extremely expensive and time-consuming. After seven or eight episodes, word came down from network attorneys that these end-credits animations looked too much like toy advertising, and they were discontinued.

Editor: Eric Klopfer
Designer: Liam Flanagan
Production Manager: Larry Pekarek

Library of Congress Control Number: 2020931025

ISBN: 978-1-4197-4468-6
eISBN: 978-1-6833-5917-3

© 2020 MARVEL

Case credits
Pencil roughs by Larry Houston
Finishes and inks by Rick Hoberg
Colors by Laura Martin

Printed and bound in China
10 9 8 7 6 5 4 3 2 1

Abrams books are available at special discounts when purchased in quantity for premiums and promotions as well as fundraising or educational use. Special editions can also be created to specification. For details, contact specialsales@abramsbooks.com or the address below.

Abrams® is a registered trademark of Harry N. Abrams, Inc.

ABRAMS The Art of Books
195 Broadway, New York, NY 10007
abramsbooks.com

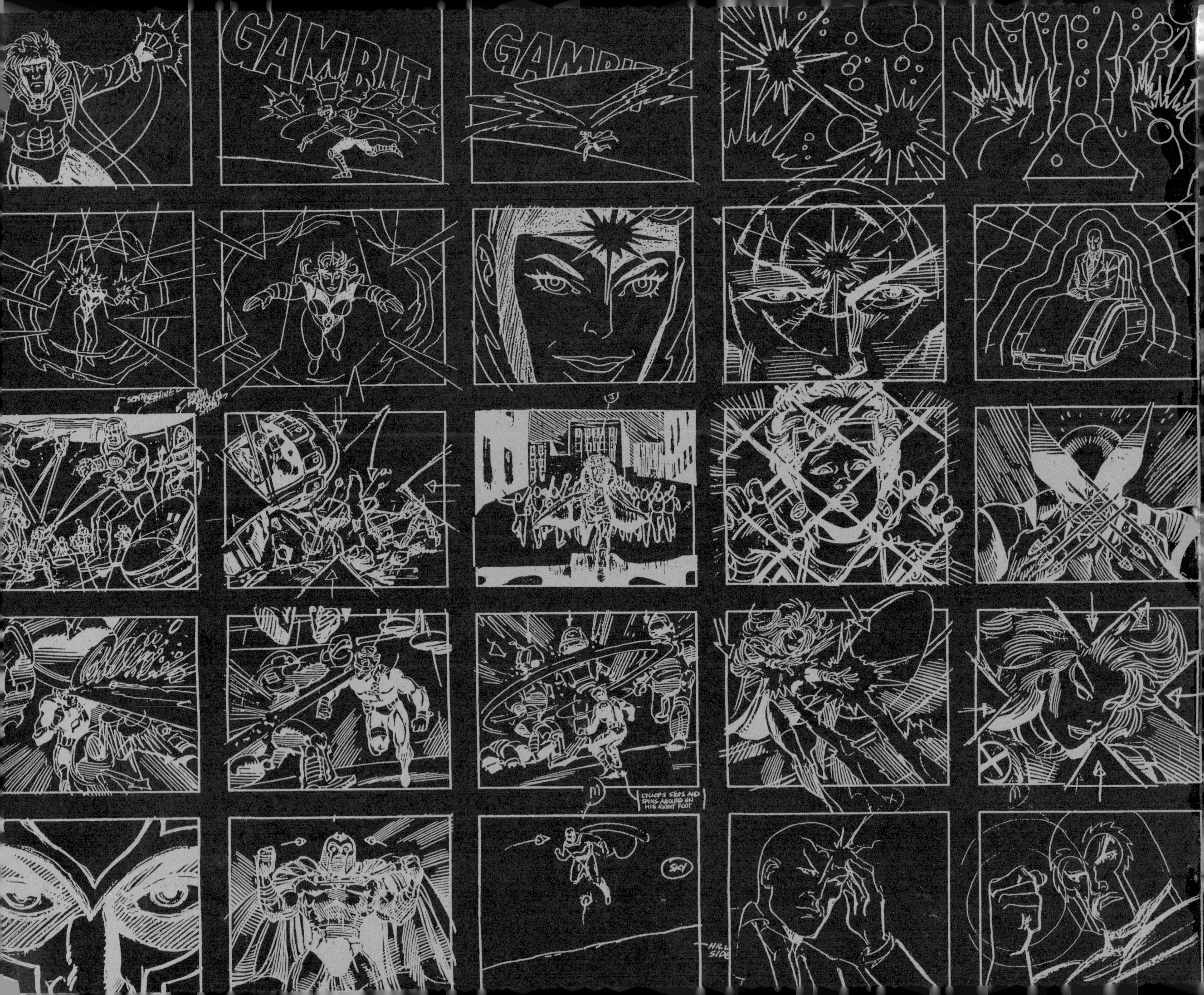
GAMBIT
CYCLOPS STOPS AND SPINS AROUND ON HIS RIGHT FOOT
SKY